International Marketing

FOURTH EDITION

International Marketing

FOURTH EDITION

Michael R. Czinkota
Georgetown University

Ilkka A. Ronkainen
Georgetown University

THE DRYDEN PRESS
Harcourt Brace College Publishers

Fort Worth   Philadelphia   San Diego   New York   Orlando   Austin   San Antonio
Toronto   Montreal   London   Sydney   Tokyo

Executive Editor   *Lyn Keeney Hastert*
Developmental Editor   *R. Paul Stewart*
Production Manager   *Kelly Cordes*
Cover Designer   *Melinda Huff*
Publisher   *Elizabeth Widdicombe*
Project Management and Text Design   *Elm Street Publishing Services, Inc.*
Compositor   *G&S Typesetters, Inc.*
Text Type   *10/12 Clearface*
Cover Illustration   *Linda Ryan St. Clair*

Address for Editorial Correspondence
The Dryden Press, 301 Commerce Street, Suite 3700, Fort Worth, TX 76102

Address for Orders
The Dryden Press, 6277 Sea Harbor Drive, Orlando, FL 32887
1-800-782-4479, or 1-800-433-0001 (in Florida)

ISBN: 0-03-098342-8
Library of Congress Catalog Number: 94–77209

Printed in the United States of America
4 5 6 7 8 9 0 1 2 3   032   10 9 8 7 6 5 4 3 2 1

THE DRYDEN PRESS
Harcourt Brace College Publishers

To Ilona   MRC

To Susan and Sanna   IAR

THE DRYDEN PRESS SERIES IN MARKETING

ASSAEL
Marketing: Principles and Strategy
Second Edition

BATESON
Managing Services Marketing: Text and Readings
Third Edition

BLACKWELL, BLACKWELL, AND TALARZYK
Contemporary Cases in Consumer Behavior
Fourth Edition

BOONE AND KURTZ
Contemporary Marketing^{Plus}
Eighth Edition

CHURCHILL
Basic Marketing Research
Second Edition

CHURCHILL
Marketing Research: Methodological Foundations
Sixth Edition

CZINKOTA AND RONKAINEN
International Marketing
Fourth Edition

CZINKOTA AND RONKAINEN
International Marketing Strategy: Environmental
  Assessment and Entry Strategies

DICKSON
Marketing Management

ENGEL, BLACKWELL, AND MINIARD
Consumer Behavior
Eighth Edition

FUTRELL
Sales Management
Fourth Edition

GHOSH
Retail Management
Second Edition

GROVER
Market Orientation Simulation

HASSAN AND BLACKWELL
Global Marketing: Managerial Dimensions and Cases

HUTT AND SPEH
Business Marketing Management: A Strategic View
  of Industrial and Organizational Markets
Fifth Edition

INGRAM AND LAFORGE
Sales Management: Analysis and Decision Making
Third Edition

KRUGMAN, REID, DUNN, AND BARBAN
Advertising: Its Role in Modern Marketing
Eighth Edition

MURPHY AND CUNNINGHAM
Advertising and Marketing Communications Management:
  Cases and Applications

OBERHAUS, RATLIFFE, AND STAUBLE
Professional Selling: A Relationship Process
Second Edition

RACHMAN
Marketing Today
Third Edition

ROSENBLOOM
Marketing Channels: A Management View
Fifth Edition

SCHELLINCK AND MADDOX
Marketing Research: A Computer-Assisted Approach

SCHNAARS
MICROSIM
Marketing simulation available for IBM PC and Apple

SHIMP
Promotion Management and Marketing Communications
Third Edition

SISODIA AND MENTZER
Marketing Decision Systems: Transformation through
  Information Technology

TALARZYK
Cases and Exercises in Marketing

TERPSTRA AND SARATHY
International Marketing
Sixth Edition

TOOTELIAN AND GAEDEKE
Cases and Classics in Marketing Management

WEITZ AND WENSLEY
Readings in Strategic Marketing Analysis, Planning,
  and Implementation

ZIKMUND
Exploring Marketing Research
Fifth Edition

Harcourt Brace College Outline Series

PETERSON
Principles of Marketing

PREFACE

Practicing international marketing and writing a text on the subject have some things in common: It is a lot of work, the competition is tough, and it's fun to succeed. It is therefore with great pleasure that we present this fourth edition of *International Marketing*. Given the resounding market acceptance of the earlier editions, we felt an obligation to further strengthen our lead by developing an even better book. Our goal continues to be excellence in content, combined with user friendliness for both the student and the professor.

This book is special for many reasons.

- The text reflects the realities of educational and marketplace needs.
- It goes far beyond a discussion of the glamorous operations of the multinational corporations by adding a specific focus on the activities of small and medium-sized firms.
- It covers the entire range of international marketing, beginning with start-up operations, continuing with new market entry considerations, and concluding with the international issues confronting giant global marketers, therefore exposing the reader to the full spectrum of international marketing.
- This book examines international marketing from a truly global perspective rather than just from the U.S. point of view in order to communicate the need for awareness, sensitivity, and adaptation.
- The reality of the interchange between business and government is specifically addressed by analyzing international marketing issues from both the business and the policy perspective.
- This text also offers an integration of the important societal dimensions of diversity, environmental concern, ethics, and economic transformation.
- Finally, it presents many up-to-date, market-based examples, in-depth research information, and the best writing that we can deliver.

ORGANIZATION

This text is designed primarily for the advanced undergraduate student with prior exposure to the marketing field. Because of its in-depth development of topical coverage, however, it also presents an excellent challenge for graduate instruction and executive education.

The text is divided into three parts. First, the basic concepts of international marketing are outlined, and the environmental forces that the international marketer has to consider are discussed. The second part focuses on the various activities necessary for international marketing planning and concentrates on the beginning of international marketing activities. Export and import operations are covered here, together with elements of the marketing mix that tend to be most important for firms at an initial level of international experience. The third part discusses marketing management and strategy issues most relevant for the multinational corporation.

Both the instructor and the student can work with this text in two ways. One alternative is to cover the material sequentially, progressing from the initial international effort to multinational activities. In this way, marketing dimensions such as distribution, promotion, and pricing are covered in the order in which they are most relevant for the particular level of expertise within the firm. Another approach is to use the text in a parallel manner, by pairing comparable chapters from Parts Two and Three. In this way, the primary emphasis can be placed on the functional approach to international marketing.

CHANGES IN THE FOURTH EDITION

The highly dynamic nature of the international marketplace is reflected in the number of new features in this fourth edition. It was our objective to enhance the text's up-to-date information, practical nature, and reader-friendliness with both the student and the instructor in mind. Chapter content reflects the newest advances in both research and practice. All tables and figures were updated to present the latest available data. The International Marketplace boxes are virtually all new to reflect the most recent market developments. More than one half of the cases are either new or revised. The number of video cases has been doubled in order to make the tasks of teaching easier and learning more efficient and fun.

The chapters in Part One, which deals with the international environment, have a better global and policy perspective. Given economic shifts, more emphasis has been placed on integrating Asia's role in the world economy. Extensive discussions are devoted to changes in international institutions, agreements, and approaches. The new GATT agreement, the NAFTA implementation, the progress of the European Union, the abolishment of the CoCom export control regime, and the evolution of more activist government approaches are presented and analyzed as to their meaning for the international marketer's decision framework. In addition, the global emergence of environmental and ethical concerns is addressed through analysis and corporate examples. In order to broaden the understanding of diversity, increased emphasis is also placed on comparing international approaches to issues such as antitrust legislation and tax policy. Also highlighted is a contrast between legal systems, including theocracy, and legal applications.

Beginning international marketing activities in Part Two are now placed more in the context of market expansion strategy with a focus both on management commitment and on the role of and interaction between profit and risk in the international initiation phase. Greatly expanded has been the role of intellectual property rights and their protection, as well as the influence of environmental concerns on market strategy. The effects of new technologies and new marketing capabilities on international corporate tactics are now also presented.

Advanced international marketing topics in Part Three are now presented with more strategy and policy orientation. The foreign direct investment process is linked to the competitive positioning of the firm. Also analyzed are the FDI economic impact, decision criteria, and the decision process. Services marketing is presented much earlier in this edition and is linked closely to the globalization process. Systemic and institutional service issues have been added. They include a comparison of service marketing in different market environments and the benefits and shortcomings for marketers resulting from the new General Agreement for Trade in Services (GATS). Every chapter now has a section addressing global functional management and coordination. An analysis of different approaches to market liberalization and their impact on corporate activities has been added, together with a new section on international career management and government-sponsored exchange and training programs.

SPECIAL FEATURES

Contemporary Realism

Each chapter offers several current International Marketplace boxes. Virtually all of them are new in this edition. They focus on real marketing situations and are intended to help students understand and absorb the presented materials. The instructor can highlight the boxes to exemplify theory or use them as mini-cases for class discussion.

Research Emphasis

A special effort has been made to provide current research information and data. Chapter notes are augmented by lists of relevant recommended readings incorporating the latest research findings. In addition, a wide variety of sources and organizations that provide international information are listed in the text. These materials enable the instructor and the student to go beyond the text whenever time permits.

Maps

In order to improve students' geography literacy, several full-color maps are furnished in this text, covering the social, economic, and political features of the world. In addition, several chapters have maps particularly designed for this book, which integrate the materials discussed in the text and reflect a truly "global" perspective. These maps enable the instructor to visually demonstrate concepts such as political blocs and socio-economic variables. They also highlight distributive issues such as the spread of franchising around the world.

Cases

Following each of the three parts of the text are a variety of cases, half of them new and most written especially for this book, that present students with real business situations. In addition, the number of video cases has been doubled to further assist in enlivening classroom activity. Challenging questions accompany each case, permitting in-depth discussion of the materials covered in the chapters.

Instructor's Materials

The text is accompanied by an in-depth *Instructor's Manual,* devised to provide major assistance to the professor. The material in the manual includes the following:

Teaching Plans Alternative teaching plans and syllabi are presented to accommodate the instructor's preferred course structure and varying time constraints. Time plans are developed for the course to be taught in a semester format, on a quarter basis, or as an executive seminar.

Discussion Guidelines For each chapter, specific teaching objectives and guidelines are developed to help stimulate classroom discussion.

End-of-Chapter Questions   Each question is fully developed in the manual to accommodate different scenarios and experience horizons. Where appropriate, the relevant text section is referenced.

Cases   A detailed case-chapter matrix is supplied that delineates which cases are most appropriate for each area of the international marketing field. In addition, detailed case discussion alternatives are provided, outlining discussion strategies and solution alternatives.

Video and Film References   An extensive listing of video and film materials available from educational institutions, companies, and government agencies is provided. Materials are briefly discussed, possible usage patterns are outlined, and ordering/availability information is supplied. In addition, each adopter of this text can receive the free video cases in international marketing, which contain still images from the text and a selection of CBS news stories relevant to issues in international marketing.

Test Bank   The manual includes a greatly expanded test bank, consisting of more than 1,000 short essay questions, true/false questions, and multiple choice questions. This test bank is also computerized and available to adopters on IBM computer diskettes.

Transparency Masters   The manual contains a substantial number of transparency masters, including some materials from the text, but also drawing heavily on non-text materials such as advertisements, graphs, and figures, which can be used to further enliven classroom interaction and to develop particular topics in more depth.

ACKNOWLEDGMENTS

We are deeply grateful to the professors, students, and professionals using this book. Your interest demonstrates the need for more knowledge about international marketing. As our market, you are telling us that our product adds value to your lives. As a result, you add value to ours. Thank you!

We also thank the many reviewers for their constructive and imaginative comments and criticisms, which were instrumental in making this edition even better.

We remain indebted to the reviewers of this and earlier editions of this text:

Sanjeev Agarwal
Iowa State University
Lyn S. Amine
St. Louis University
Jessica M. Bailey
The American University
Warren Bilkey
University of Wisconsin
S. Tamer Cavusgil
Michigan State University
Alex Christofides
Ohio State University
John Dyer
University of Miami

Donna Goehle
Michigan State University
Neelima Gogumala
Kansas State University
Paul Groke
Northern Illinois University
Andrew Gross
Cleveland State University
Braxton Hinchey
University of Lowell
Basil Janavaras
Mankato State University
Denise Johnson
University of Louisville

Sudhir Kale
Arizona State University
Hertha Krotkoff
Towson State University
Kathleen La Francis
Central Michigan University
Trina Larsen
Drexel University
Bertil Liander
University of Massachusetts
Mushtaq Luqmani
Western Michigan University
James Maskulka
Lehigh University
Fred Miller
Murray State University

Henry Munn
California State University, Northridge
Jacob Naor
University of Maine, Orono
John Ryans
Kent State University
Tyzoon T. Tyebjee
Santa Clara University
Robert Underwood
Virginia Polytechnic Institute and State University
Nittaya Wongtada
Thunderbird
Van R. Wood
Texas Tech University

Many thanks to all the faculty members and students who have helped us sharpen our thinking by cheerfully providing challenging comments and questions. In particular, we thank Bernard LaLonde, The Ohio State University; Lyn Amine, St. Louis University; Tamer Cavusgil, Michigan State University; and James Wills, University of Hawaii.

Many colleagues, friends, and business associates graciously gave their time and knowledge to clarify concepts; provide us with ideas, comments, and suggestions; and deepen our understanding of issues. Without the direct links to business and policy that you have provided, this book could not offer its refreshing realism. In particular, we are grateful to Secretaries Malcolm Baldrige, C. William Verity, Clayton Yeutter, and William Brock for the opportunity to gain international business policy experience and to William Morris, Paul Freedenberg, H. P. Goldfield, and J. Michael Farrell for enabling its implementation. We also thank William Casselman of Stairs Dillenbeck Kelly Merle and Finley, Robert Conkling of Conkling Associates, Lew Cramer of US WEST, Mark Dowd of IBM, Joseph Lynch of ADI, Veikko Jaaskelainen and Reijo Luostarinen of HSE, and Mike Wukitsch of The American Marketing Association.

Valuable research assistance was provided by Peter Fitzmaurice as well as Michelle Le Blanc of Georgetown University. LuAnn Hartley assisted in the preparation of the manuscript. We appreciate all of your work!

A very special word of thanks to the people at The Dryden Press. Lyn Hastert and Paul Stewart made the lengthy process of writing a text bearable with their enthusiasm, creativity, and constructive feedback. Major assistance was also provided by the friendliness, expertise, and help of Michele Heinz, Barb Lange, and Abby Westapher of Elm Street Publishing Services.

Last, but foremost, we are grateful to our families, who have truly participated in the writing of this book. Only the patience, understanding, and love of Ilona, Ursula, Michael, and Thomas Czinkota and Susan and Sanna Ronkainen enabled us to have the energy, stamina, and inspiration to write this book.

Michael R. Czinkota
Ilkka A. Ronkainen
Washington, D.C.
October 1994

ABOUT THE AUTHORS

MICHAEL R. CZINKOTA

Michael R. Czinkota is on the faculty of marketing and international business of the Graduate School and the School of Business at Georgetown University. From 1981 to 1986 he was the Chairman of the National Center for Export-Import Studies at the university.

From 1986 to 1989 Dr. Czinkota served in the U.S. government as Deputy Assistant Secretary of Commerce. He was responsible for macro trade analysis, departmental support of international trade negotiations and retaliatory actions, and policy coordination for international finance, investment, and monetary affairs. He also served as Head of the U.S. Delegation to the OECD Industry Committee in Paris and as Senior Trade Advisor for Export Administration and Controls.

Dr. Czinkota's background includes eight years of private sector business experience as a partner in an export-import firm and in an advertising agency and fifteen years of research and teaching in the academic world. He has been the recipient of research grants from the National Science Foundation, the National Commission of Jobs and Small Business, and the Organization of American States. He was listed as one of the three most prolific contributors to international business research in the *Journal of International Business Studies* and has written several books including *International Business, The Global Market Imperative,* and *Unlocking Japan's Market.*

Dr. Czinkota served on the Board of Directors of the American Marketing Association and is currently on the Board of Governors of the Academy of Marketing Science and the editorial boards of the *Journal of International Business Studies, Journal of International Marketing* and *Asian Journal of Marketing.* In 1991, he was named a Distinguished Fellow of the Academy of Marketing Science.

Dr. Czinkota has served as advisor to a wide range of individuals and institutions in the United States and abroad. He has worked with corporations such as AT&T, IBM, GE, and Nestlé and has assisted organizations such as the National Economic Council and the General Accounting Office in the structuring of effective trade promotion policies.

Dr. Czinkota was born and raised in Germany and educated in Austria, Scotland, Spain, and the United States. He studied law and business administration at the University of Erlangen-Nürnberg and was awarded a two-year Fulbright Scholarship. He holds an MBA in international business and a Ph.D. in marketing from The Ohio State University. He and his wife, Ilona, live in Luray, located in Virginia's Shenandoah Valley.

ILKKA A. RONKAINEN

Ilkka A. Ronkainen is a member of the faculty of marketing and international business at the School of Business at Georgetown University. From 1981 to 1986 he served as Associate Director and from 1986 to 1987 as Chairman of the National Center for Export-Import Studies. Currently, he directs Georgetown University's Hong Kong Program.

Dr. Ronkainen serves as docent of international marketing at the Helsinki School of Economics. He was visiting professor at HSE during the 1987–1988 and 1991–1992 academic years and continues to teach in its Executive MBA, International MBA, and International BBA programs.

Dr. Ronkainen holds a Ph.D. and a master's degree from the University of South Carolina as well as an M.S. (Economics) degree from the Helsinki School of Economics.

Dr. Ronkainen has published extensively in academic journals and the trade press. He is a co-author of *International Business* and *The Global Market Imperative.* He serves on the review boards of the *Journal of Business Research, International Marketing Review,* and *Journal of Travel Research* and has reviewed for the *Journal of Advertising* and the *Journal of International Business Studies.* He served as the North American coordinator for the European Marketing Academy 1984–1990. He was a member of the board of the Washington International Trade Association from 1981 to 1986 and started the association's newsletter, *Trade Trends.*

Dr. Ronkainen has served as a consultant to a wide range of U.S. and international institutions. He has worked with entities such as IBM, the Rank Organization, and the Organization of American States. He maintains close relations with a number of Finnish companies and their internationalization and educational efforts.

BRIEF CONTENTS

CONTENTS

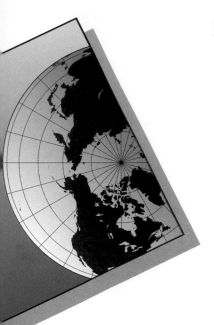

13   Licensing, Franchising, and Export Intermediaries   372

PART THREE
Advanced International Marketing Activities   436

International Marketing

FOURTH EDITION

PART ONE

The International Environment

art One introduces the international trade framework and environment. It highlights the need for international marketing activities and explains why the international market is an entirely new arena for a firm and its managers. The chapters devoted to macroenvironmental factors explain the many forces to which a firm is exposed. The marketer must adapt to these foreign environments and adeptly resolve conflicts between political, cultural, and legal forces in order to be successful.

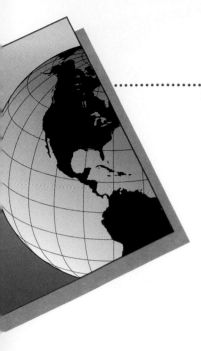

CHAPTER 1

The International Marketing Imperative

THE INTERNATIONAL MARKETPLACE

Global Opportunities Abound

After just two weeks in China, a salesman for Ohio-based banking equipment maker Diebold Corporation returned with orders for 93,000 bank safety deposit boxes—more than the company can produce in a year. Diebold has now gone beyond exporting by joining Chinese partners to make automated teller machines (ATMs) in a new Shanghai factory. A few thousand have already been sold to banks and corporations to accommodate the growing number of Chinese companies that deposit workers' wages directly into banks. The Chinese government is upgrading 100,000 bank branches, and Diebold estimates each branch will need a $30,000 ATM, a $12,000 vault door, and safe deposit boxes. What will this vast market mean for Diebold's future sales? According to Chairman Robert W. Mahoney, "I hate to even contemplate it in strategy meetings, it gets me so excited; it's a staggering figure."

If U.S. businesses want to compete internationally, they will have to play catch-up with Japanese and European competitors who have been far more aggressive in the global marketplace. In addition, local problems always exist, making it difficult and risky to do business abroad. Nevertheless, nations and consumers around the globe have big "wish lists," such as heavy machinery, aerospace, agricultural, and industrial equipment, power plants, consumer goods, and telecommunications gear.

General Electric Company estimates that electricity demand in Asia will grow at twice the world rate, accounting for 35 percent of global power-generation orders. In 1992, GE recorded $1.7 billion in Asian orders. New joint ventures are popping up everywhere, including three in India in 1993 alone.

PPG Industries, a Pittsburgh glass maker, recently commissioned its fourth factory in China. "We're focusing more of our non-U.S. expansion toward the

Asia-Pacific than in the 1980s, when we were concentrating more on Europe," explains a company spokesman.

Colgate-Palmolive Company has added a toothbrush factory in Colombia, a toothpaste plant in Brazil, and a facility to make mouth rinse in Chile. Colgate's Latin American sales increased 22 percent in 1992.

With international business activity expanding well beyond traditional foreign markets, the importance of international marketing is ever-increasing. Rising incomes, economic liberalization, and increasingly stable governments will only encourage future marketing activity around the globe.

Source: Valerie Reitman, "U.S. Firms Turn to the Developing World," *The Wall Street Journal,* August 4, 1993.

You are about to begin an exciting, important, and necessary task: the exploration of international marketing. International marketing is exciting because it combines the science and the art of business with many other disciplines. Economics, anthropology, cultural studies, geography, history, languages, jurisprudence, statistics, demographics, and many other fields combine to help you explore the global market. Environmental differences will stimulate your intellectual curiosity, which will enable you to absorb and understand new phenomena. International marketing has been compared by many who have been active in the field to the task of mountain climbing: challenging, arduous, and exhilarating.

International marketing is important because the world has become globalized. Figure 1.1 shows one large corporation's perspective of its global business activities. International marketing takes place all around us every day, has a major effect on our lives, and is crucial to the survival and success of firms, as The International Marketplace 1.1 shows. After reading through this book, and observing international marketing phenomena, you will see what happens, understand what happens, and at some time in your future, perhaps even make it happen. All of this is much better than to stand by and wonder what happened.

International marketing is necessary because, from a national standpoint, economic isolationism has become impossible. Failure to participate in the global marketplace assures a nation of declining economic influence and its citizens of a decrease in the standard of living. Successful international marketing, however, holds the promise of an improved quality of life, a better society, and as some have stated, even a more peaceful world.

This chapter is designed to increase your awareness of what international marketing is all about. It describes the current levels of world trade activities, projects future developments, and discusses the resulting repercussion on countries, institutions, and individuals worldwide. Both the opportunities and the threats that emanate from the global marketplace are highlighted, and the need for an international "marketing" approach on the part of individuals and institutions is emphasized.

This chapter text ends with an explanation of the major organizational thrust of this book, which is a differentiation between the beginning internationalist and the multinational corporation. This theme, which carries through the entire book, takes into account that the concerns, capabilities, and goals of firms will differ widely based on their level of international expertise, resources, and involvement. The stepwise approach to international marketing taken here will therefore permit you to understand the entire range of international activities and allow a useful and early transfer of the acquired knowledge into practice.

FIGURE 1.1   A Global Perspective

You might think our global perspective is
an unusual response to local problems. But on a planet
as small as this one has become, there's simply
no room for borders. Between nations or even between ideas.

Difficulties may remain, but we're bringing the Socratic
method to pressing issues. Asking the right
questions and encouraging new thinking.

And coming up with the answers that you would
expect from a citizen of the world.

C.P.O. BOX 595, TOKYO 100-91, JAPAN

Source: *Tokyo Business*, September 1993, p. 4. Reprinted courtesy of Marubeni Corporation.

WHAT INTERNATIONAL MARKETING IS

In brief, **international marketing** is concerned with planning and conducting transactions across national borders to satisfy the objectives of individuals and organizations. International marketing has forms ranging from export-import trade to licensing, joint ventures, wholly owned subsidiaries, turnkey operations, and management contracts.

As this definition indicates, international marketing very much retains the basic marketing tenet of "satisfaction." International marketing is the tool used to obtain the goal of improvement of one's present position. The fact that a transaction takes place "across national borders" highlights the difference between domestic and international marketing. The international marketer is subject to a new set of macroenvironmental factors, to different constraints, and to quite frequent conflicts resulting from different laws, cultures, and societies. The basic principles of marketing still apply, but their applications, complexity, and intensity may vary substantially. It is in the international marketing field where one can observe most closely the role of marketing as a key agent of societal change and as a key instrument for the development of societally responsive business strategy. When one looks, for example, at the newly emerging market economies of Central Europe, one can see the many new challenges that international marketing is confronted with. How does the marketing concept fit into these societies? How can marketing contribute to economic development and the betterment of society? How should distribution systems be organized? How can one get the price mechanism to work? What role should advertising play? These are just a few of the issues that the international marketer needs to address. The capability to successfully master these challenges affords the international marketer the potential for new opportunities and high rewards.

The definition also focuses on international transactions. The use of the term recognizes that marketing internationally is an activity, which needs to be pursued, often aggressively. Those who do not participate in the transactions are only exposed to international marketing and subject to its changing influences. The international marketer is part of the exchange, recognizes the changing nature of transactions, and adjusts to a constantly moving target subject to environmental shifts. This need for adjustment, for comprehending change and, in spite of it all, successfully carrying out transactions, highlights the fact that international marketing is as much art as science.

To achieve success in the art of international marketing, it is necessary to be firmly grounded in the scientific aspects. Only then will individual consumers, policymakers, and business executives be able to incorporate international marketing considerations into their thinking and planning. Only then will they be able to consider international issues and repercussions and make decisions based on the answers to such questions as these:

- How will my idea, product, or service fit into the international market?
- What adjustments are or will be necessary?
- What threats from global competition should I expect?
- How can I work with these threats to turn them into opportunities?
- What are my strategic global alternatives?

If all of these issues are integrated into each decision made by individuals and by firms, international markets can become a source of growth, profit, needs satisfaction, and quality of life that would not have existed had they limited themselves to domestic activities. To aid in this decision process is the purpose of this book.

THE IMPORTANCE OF WORLD TRADE

World trade has assumed an importance heretofore unknown to the global community. In past centuries, trade was conducted internationally but not at the level or with the impact on nations, firms, and individuals that it has recently achieved. In the past two decades, world trade has expanded from $200 billion to more than $4 trillion. Countries that had never been considered major participants in world trade have suddenly emerged as major economic powers.

The Iron Curtain has disintegrated, offering a vast array of new marketing opportunities—albeit amid uncertainty. Firms invest on a global scale, with the result that entire industries shift their locations. International specialization and cross-sourcing has made production much more efficient while at the same time consumers, union leaders, policymakers, and sometimes even the firms themselves are finding it increasingly difficult to define where a particular product has been made. New trading blocs are emerging with the European Union in Europe, with Canada, the United States, and Mexico in North America, and maybe in the not-too-distant future, with a Japanese-led group of countries in Asia. Firms increasingly believe that to remain viable, they need to be active in all parts of the economic triad: the United States, Europe, and Japan.

Individuals and firms have come to recognize that they are competing not only domestically but in a global marketplace. World trade has given rise to global linkages of markets, technology, and living standards that were previously unknown and unanticipated. At the same time, it has deeply affected domestic policy-making and has often resulted in the emergence of totally new opportunities and threats to firms and individuals.

Global Linkages

World trade has forged a network of **global linkages** that bind us all—countries, institutions, and individuals—much closer than ever before. These linkages were first widely recognized during the worldwide oil shock of 1970. But they continue to increase. A drought in Brazil and its effects on coffee production are felt around the world. The global crash of 1987 reverberated in financial quarters all around the globe.

World trade has also brought about a global reorientation in production strategies. As an example, only a few decades ago, it would have been thought impossible to produce parts for a car in more than one country, assemble the car in yet another country, and sell it in still other nations. Yet such global investment strategies, coupled with production and distribution sharing, are occurring with increasing frequency.

The level of global investment is at an unprecedented high. The United States, after having been a net creditor to the world for many decades, has now become a **world debtor.** This means that the United States owes more to foreign institutions and individuals than they owe to U.S. entities. The shifts in financial flows have had major effects. They resulted in the buildup of international debt by the U.S. government, affected the international value of the dollar, provided foreign capital for U.S. firms, and triggered major foreign direct-investment activities. Currently, well over one-third of the workers in the U.S. chemical industry toil for foreign owners. Many of the office buildings we work in are held by foreign landlords. The opening of plants abroad and in the United States increasingly takes the place of trade. All these developments make us more and more dependent on one another.

This interdependence, however, is not stable. On virtually a daily basis, realignments taking place on both micro and macro levels make past orientations at least partially obsolete. For example, for the first 200 years of its history, the United States looked to Europe for markets and sources of supply. However, despite the maintenance of this orientation by many individuals, firms, and policymakers, the reality of trade relationships is gradually changing. U.S. two-way trade with Asia totaled $348 billion in 1993, $111 billion more than U.S. trade with Europe.[1] This gap will continue to grow because the newly industrializing countries in Asia average a 7 percent annual growth, whereas the

---

[1] U.S. Department of Commerce, *Survey of Current Business* (Washington, D.C.: Government Printing Office, March 1994).

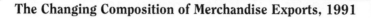

The Changing Composition of Merchandise Exports, 1991 **FIGURE 1.2**

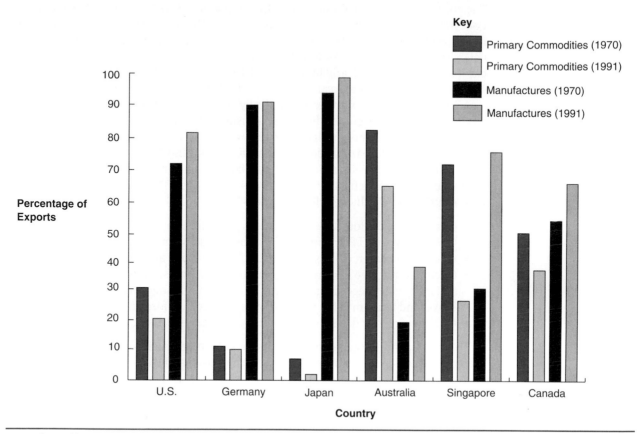

Key
- Primary Commodities (1970)
- Primary Commodities (1991)
- Manufactures (1970)
- Manufactures (1991)

Source: The World Bank, *World Development Report 1993* (1993).

nations of the European Union struggle for nominal increases in their domestic economic growth.[2]

Not only is the environment changing, but the pace of change grows faster. "A boy who saw the Wright brothers fly for a few seconds at Kitty Hawk in 1903 could have watched Apollo II land on the moon in 1969. The first electronic computer was built in 1946; today, the world rushes from the mechanical into the electronic age. The double helix was first unveiled in 1953; today, biotechnology threatens to remake mankind."[3]

These changes and the speed with which they come about significantly affect countries, corporations and individuals. One change is the role participants play. For example, the United States accounted for nearly 25 percent of world exports in the 1950s, but by 1993, this share had declined to 12 percent. Also, the way countries participate in world trade is shifting. Figure 1.2 demonstrates how the composition of merchandise exports has changed in two decades for some countries. In all instances, the role of primary commodities has dropped precipitously, while the importance of manufactured goods has increased.

[2] The World Bank, *World Development Report 1993* (1993).

[3] Arthur M. Schlesinger, Jr., *The Cycles of American History* (Boston: Houghton Mifflin, 1986), xi.

Domestic Policy Repercussions

The effects of closer global linkages on the economies of countries have been dramatic. Policymakers have increasingly come to recognize that it is very difficult to isolate domestic economic activity from international market events. Again and again, domestic policy measures are vetoed or counteracted by the activities of global market forces. Decisions that once were clearly in the domestic purview have now become subject to revision by influences from abroad.

A lowering of interest rates domestically may make consumers happy or may be politically wise, but it quickly becomes unsustainable if it results in a major outflow of funds to countries that offer higher interest rates. Agricultural and farm policies, which historically have been strictly domestic issues, are suddenly thrust into the international realm. Any policy consideration must now be seen in light of international repercussions due to influences from global trade and investment. The following examples highlight some of these influences in the United States:

- One out of every four U.S. farm acres is producing for export.
- One of every six U.S. manufacturing jobs produces for export.
- One of every seven dollars of U.S. sales is to someone abroad.
- One of every three cars, nine of every ten television sets, two of every three suits, and every video recorder sold in the United States is imported.
- Travel and tourism is the number one source of U.S. foreign exchange.
- One of every four dollars of U.S. bonds and notes is issued to foreigners.[4]

To some extent, the economic world as we knew it has been turned upside down. For example, trade flows used to determine currency flows and therefore the level of the exchange rate. In the more recent past, **currency flows** took on a life of their own and have, independent of trade, set the value of relations of currencies to each other, that is, of exchange rates. These **exchange rates** in turn have now begun to determine the level of trade. Governments that wish to counteract these developments with monetary policies find that currency flows outnumber trade flows by 100 to 1. Also, private-sector financial flows vastly outnumber the financial flows that can be marshaled by governments, even when acting in concert. Similarly, constant rapid technological change and vast advances in communication permit firms and countries to quickly emulate innovation and counteract carefully designed plans. As a result, governments are often powerless to implement effective policy measures, even when they know what to do.

Policymakers therefore find themselves with increasing responsibilities yet with fewer and less-effective tools to carry out these responsibilities. At the same time that more parts of a domestic economy are vulnerable to international shifts and changes, these parts are becoming less controllable. To regain some of their power to influence events and to reassert their national sovereignty, policymakers have sought to restrict the impact of global trade and financial flows by erecting barriers, charging tariffs, designing quotas, and implementing other import regulations. However, these measures too have been restrained by international agreements that regulate trade restrictions. World trade has therefore changed many previously held notions about nation-state sovereignty and extraterritoriality. The same interdependence that has made us more affluent has also left us more vulnerable. Because this vulnerability is spread out over all major trading nations, however, some have credited international marketing with being a pillar

[4] Raymond J. Waldmann, *Managed Trade: The Competition between Nations* (Cambridge, MA: Ballinger, 1986), 6; *Ward's Automotive Report,* January 9, 1989; and John Naisbitt, *Global Paradox* (New York: Morrow and Co., 1994), 105.

THE INTERNATIONAL MARKETPLACE 1.2

Does International Marketing Create Peace?

One really big surprise of the postwar era has been that historic enemies, such as Germany and France, or Japan and the United States, have not had the remotest threat of war since 1945. Why should they? Anything Japan has that we want we can buy, and on very easy credit terms, so why fight for it? Why should the Japanese fight the United States and lose all those profitable markets? France and Germany, linked intimately through marketing and the European Union, are now each other's largest trading partners. Closed systems build huge armies and waste their substance on guns and troops; open countries spend their money on new machine tools to crank out Barbie dolls or some such trivia. Their bright young people figure out how to tool the machines, not how to fire the latest missile. For some reason, they not only get rich fast but also lose interest in military adventures. Japan, that peculiar superpower without superguns, confounds everyone simply because no one has ever seen a major world power that got that way by selling you to death, not shooting you to death. In short, if you trade a lot with someone, why fight? The logical answer—you don't—is perhaps the best news mankind has had in millennia.

Source: Adapted from Richard N. Farmer, "Would You Want Your Granddaughter to Marry a Taiwanese Marketing Man?" *Journal of Marketing* 51 (October 1987): 114–115.

of international peace, as The International Marketplace 1.2 shows. Clearly, closer economic relations can result in many positive effects. At the same time, however, interdependence brings with it risks, such as dislocations of people and economic resources and a decrease in a nation's capability to do things its own way. Given the ease—and sometimes desirability—of blaming a foreign rather than a domestic culprit for economic failure, it may well also be a key task for the international marketer to stimulate societal thinking about the long-term benefits of interdependence.

OPPORTUNITIES AND CHALLENGES IN INTERNATIONAL MARKETING

To prosper in a world of abrupt changes and discontinuities, of newly emerging forces and dangers, of unforeseen influences from abroad, firms need to prepare themselves and develop active responses. New strategies need to be envisioned, new plans need to be made, and our way of doing business needs to be changed. The way to obtain and retain leadership, economically, politically, or morally, is—as the examples of Rome, Constantinople, and London have amply demonstrated—not through passivity but rather through innovation and a continuous, alert adaptation to the changing world environment. To stay on top, firms need to aggressively participate in the changes that take place and respond with innovation and creativity.

The growth of global business activities offers increased opportunities. International activities can be crucial to a firm's survival and growth. By transferring knowledge around the globe, an international firm can build and strengthen its competitive position. The International Marketplace 1.3 shows how Whirlpool Corporation has been able

1.3

THE INTERNATIONAL MARKETPLACE

Whirlpool Succeeds Abroad

Holding the top market position in North America, the number 3 position in Europe, and a leading presence in South America, Whirlpool Corporation is, according to a market analyst, "the best-positioned appliance company for the 1990s." U.S. rival companies such as Maytag Corp. have struggled with global strategies, but Whirlpool is making its aggressive expansion work. By moving into Europe and developing nations, the firm aims to tap growth areas to complement its mature, slow-growth business in North America.

After acquiring the European appliance business of Philips Electronics NV, Whirlpool is posting higher profits and bigger market share in Europe, despite the recession and very slow recovery there. Whirlpool executives say their European appliance business will contribute to record corporate operating earnings.

In 1993, European shipments rose about 5 percent, even as the overall European appliance business was flat or declining. This marked the fifth consecutive year of increased market share for Whirlpool, leading to its current 10 to 15 percent market share. Further increases are likely over the next few years. Currently, Europe has a collection of 200 appliance brand names, many of them popular in just one country. Whirlpool's strategy is to stand out with strong pan-European brands. President of Whirlpool Europe NV, Hank Bowman, explains that "Research tells that the trends, preferences and biases of consumers, country to country, are reducing as opposed to increasing." Although regional preferences will remain, the company sees a chance to take advantage of the move toward a less-fractured Europe.

When Whirlpool first entered Europe, it used a dual Philips/Whirlpool brand to introduce consumers to its flagship Whirlpool brand. It is now going it alone, silencing skeptics who thought Europeans would not buy the new American name. According to Andrew Haskins, electronics analyst at London's James Capel and Co., the Whirlpool name connotes quality to consumers: "Philips had a strong brand name, and Whirlpool has been able to build on that quite considerably."

Source: Robert L. Rose, "Whirlpool Is Expanding in Europe Despite the Slump," *The Wall Street Journal*, January 27, 1994, B4.

to position itself in the world. Firms that heavily depend on long production runs can expand their activities far beyond their domestic markets and benefit from reaching many more customers. Market saturation can be avoided by lengthening or rejuvenating product life cycles in other countries. Production policies that once were inflexible suddenly become variable when plants can be shifted from one country to another and suppliers can be found on every continent. Cooperative agreements can be formed that enable all parties to bring their major strengths to the table and emerge with better products, services, and ideas than they could produce on their own. In addition, research has found that multinational corporations face a lower probability of insolvency and less average risk than do domestic companies.[5] At the same time, international marketing enables

---

[5] Israel Shaked, "Are Multinational Corporations Safer?" *Journal of International Business Studies* 17 (Spring 1986): 100.

THE INTERNATIONAL MARKETPLACE   **1.4**

Affluence through Global Marketing

Consumers in advanced nations are learning how to be affluent. Consider this example of an affluent person living in Asia: He wears Ferragamo-designed shirts and Hermes ties, sports a Rolex or Cartier watch, has a Louis Vuitton attaché case, signs his signature with a Montblanc pen, goes to work in his flashy BMW, endlessly talks on a mobile Motorola cellular phone, puts all his charges on an American Express card, and travels Singapore Airlines. He uses Giorgio Armani aftershave and buys Poison perfume for his girlfriend. As a career woman, the girlfriend's wardrobe is filled with Christian Dior and Nina Ricci clothes, her dressing table is congested with makeup and skin-care products from Guerlain, YSL, and Estée Lauder, her shoes are from Bruno Magli, and she wears Chanel No. 5 and jewelry from Tiffany. They both listen to Beethoven's Ninth Symphony on their Sony compact disc player in her Mazda sports car.

Adapted from John Naisbitt, *Global Paradox* (New York: Morrow and Co., 1994), 31.

consumers all over the world to find greater varieties of products at lower prices and to improve their life-styles and comfort. The International Marketplace 1.4 shows how global marketers can make life more comfortable, enjoyable, and affluent.

Realization of Opportunities

All of these opportunities require careful exploration. What is needed is an awareness of global developments, an understanding of their meaning, and a development of capabilities to adjust to change. Furthermore, firms must adapt to the international market.

One key facet of the marketing concept is adaptation to the environment. The validity of this concept was recognized some time ago, and it has been implemented domestically to such an extent that the United States has been called a marketing society. The transference of the concept to the international realm, however, has not occurred with equal speed. International marketing is a field of underdeveloped knowledge, one that is only now beginning to attract attention and to be considered worthwhile to teach and learn in an academic setting.

Academic concern with international marketing has been much greater abroad. For example, at the turn of this century, Emperor Franz Joseph of Austria founded the Export-akademie in Vienna; it is now the Vienna University of Economic Sciences. In the United States, it was not until the late 1970s that the American Assembly of Collegiate Schools of Business (AACSB) began to require the incorporation of international dimensions into the business school curriculum. International marketing has therefore only recently begun the tortuous process of becoming an academic discipline in the United States. Initial exploratory research is now used to gradually identify relevant building blocks for a general foundation of the field. As these building blocks are put into place, it becomes possible to carry out research with a general focus based on this foundation. Currently, we are in the midst of building a framework of knowledge that can be called international marketing and of disseminating this knowledge to improve the way society functions.

This development is necessary and long overdue because business firms have been aware for some time that many of the key difficulties encountered in doing business

TABLE 1.1

The World's 50 Largest Non-Financial Multinationals, 1992 (Ranked by Foreign Assets)

Rank	Industry	Country	Foreign Assets (billions of dollars)	Total Assets (billions of dollars)	Foreign Sales (billions of dollars)	Percent of Total Sales
1. Royal Dutch/Shell	Oil	Britain/Holland	n.a.	106.3	56.0†	49
2. Ford Motor	Cars and trucks	United States	55.2	173.7	47.3	48
3. General Motors	Cars and trucks	United States	52.6	180.2	37.3	31
4. Exxon	Oil	United States	51.6	87.7	90.5	86
5. IBM	Computers	United States	45.7	87.6	41.9	61
6. British Petroleum	Oil	Britain	39.7	59.3	46.6	79
7. Nestlé	Food	Switzerland	n.a.	27.9	33.0	98
8. Unilever	Food	Britain/Holland	n.a.	24.8	16.7†	42
9. Asea Brown Boveri	Electrical	Switzerland/Sweden	n.a.	30.2	22.7‡	85
10. Philips Electronics	Electronics	Holland	n.a.	30.6	28.6‡	93
11. Alcatel Alsthom	Telecoms	France	n.a.	38.2	17.7	67
12. Mobil	Oil	United States	22.3	41.7	44.3	77
13. Fiat	Cars and trucks	Italy	19.5	66.3	15.8	33
14. Siemens	Electrical	Germany	n.a.	50.1	15.1‡	40
15. Hanson	Diversified	Britain	n.a.	27.7	5.6	46
16. Volkswagen	Cars and trucks	Germany	n.a.	41.9	27.5‡	65
17. Elf Aquitaine	Oil	France	17.0	42.6	12.2	38
18. Mitsubishi	Trading	Japan	16.7	73.8	41.2	32
19. General Electric	Diversified	United States	16.5	153.9	8.3	14
20. Mitsui	Trading	Japan	15.0	60.8	43.6	32
21. Matsushita Electric Industrial	Electronics	Japan	n.a.	59.1	16.6	40
22. News Corp.	Publishing	Australia	14.6	20.7	5.3	78
23. Ferruzzi/Montedison	Diversified	Italy	13.5	30.8	9.1	59
24. Bayer	Chemicals	Germany	n.a.	25.4	21.8	84
25. Roche Holding	Drugs	Switzerland	n.a.	17.9	6.8‡	96
26. Toyota Motor	Cars and trucks	Japan	n.a.	55.5	26.3‡	42
27. Daimler-Benz	Cars and trucks	Germany	n.a.	48.8	32.7‡	61
28. Pechiney	Metals	France	n.a.	14.3	9.2	65
29. Philip Morris	Food	United States	12.5	46.6	15.2	3
30. Rhône-Poulenc	Chemicals	France	12.2	21.4	10.4	72
31. E.I. Du Pont de Nemours	Chemicals	United States	11.9	38.1	17.4	43
32. Hoechst	Chemicals	Germany	n.a.	23.8	14.1‡	50
33. Michelin	Tires	France	n.a.	14.9	9.1	79
34. Dow Chemical	Chemicals	United States	10.9	24.0	10.3	52
35. Total	Oil	France	n.a.	20.8	18.2	77
36. Thomson	Electronics	France	n.a.	20.7	10.4‡	75
37. Amoco	Oil	United States	10.6	32.2	8.5	30
38. Saint-Gobain	Construction	France	9.9	17.6	8.3	65
39. ENI	Chemicals	Italy	n.a.	60.5	7.9	19
40. Electrolux	Electrical	Sweden	n.a.	11.7	12.5‡	89
41. Petrofina	Oil	Belgium	n.a.	12.3	5.7	33
42. Générale des Eaux	Miscellaneous	France	n.a.	27.9	5.9	29
43. Hitachi	Electronics	Japan	n.a.	49.3	10.5‡	21
44. Chevron	Oil	United States	8.4	35.1	9.8	25
45. Sandoz	Chemicals	Switzerland	n.a.	10.1	6.3‡	70
46. C. Itoh	Trading	Japan	n.a.	47.8	19.1	13
47. Toshiba	Electronics	Japan	n.a.	32.7	8.5	29
48. Xerox	Office machinery	United States	8.0	31.5	7.5	42
49. Stora	Paper	Sweden	n.a.	15.0	8.9‡	84
50. Texaco	Oil	United States	7.8	26.0	18.0	44

Where not available, foreign assets have been estimated for ranking.

†Outside Europe

‡Including export sales

Source: *The Economist* (March 27, 1993): 6–7. Copyright © 1993, The Economist, Ltd. Distributed by the New York Times Special Features.

internationally are marketing problems. Judging by corporate needs, a background in international marketing for business students seeking employment is highly desirable, not only for today but also for long-term career plans.[6]

Many firms do not participate in the global market. Often, managers believe that international marketing should only be carried out by large multinational corporations. It is true that there are some very large players from many countries active in the world market, as Table 1.1 shows. But smaller firms are major players, too. For example, 50 percent of German exports are created by firms with 19 or fewer employees.[7]

Those firms and industries that are not participating in the world market are beginning to recognize that in today's trade environment, isolation has become impossible. Willing or unwilling, firms are becoming participants in global business affairs. Even if not by choice, most firms and individuals are affected directly or indirectly by economic and political developments that occur in the international marketplace. Those firms that refuse to participate are relegated to reacting to the global marketplace, and therefore expose themselves to harsh competition from abroad because they are unprepared.

Some industries have recognized the need for international adjustments. Farmers understand the need for high productivity in light of stiff international competition. Car producers, computer makers, and firms in other technologically advanced industries have learned to forge global relationships to stay in the race. Firms in the steel, textile, or leather sectors have shifted production, and perhaps even adjusted their core business, in response to overwhelming onslaughts from abroad. Other industries in some countries have been caught unawares and have been unable to adjust. The result is some extinct industries or firms such as VCRs in the United States and coal mining and steel smelting in some other countries.

THE GOALS OF THIS BOOK

This book aims to make the reader a better, more successful participant in the international marketplace by providing information about what is going on in international markets and by helping to translate knowledge into successful business transactions. By learning about both theory and practice, the reader can obtain a good conceptual understanding of the field of international marketing as well as become firmly grounded in the realities of the global marketplace. Therefore, this book approaches international marketing in the way the manager of a firm does, reflecting different levels of international involvement and the importance of business-government relations.

Firms differ widely in their international activities and needs, depending on their level of experience, resources, and capabilities. For the firm that is just beginning to enter the global market, the level of knowledge about international complexities is low, the demand on time is high, expectations about success are uncertain, and the international environment is often inflexible. Conversely, for a multinational firm that is globally oriented and employs thousands of people on each continent, much more leeway exists in terms of resource availability, experience, and information. In addition, the multinational firm has the option of responding creatively to the environment by shifting resources or even shaping the environment itself. For example, the heads of large corporations have access to government ministers to plead their case for a change in policy, an alternative that is rarely afforded to smaller firms.

---

[6] Theodor Kohers, "Corporate Employment Needs and Their Implications for an International Business Curriculum: A Survey of Firms Located in the Southeastern United States," *Issues in International Business* 2 (Summer–Fall 1985): 33–37.

[7] *Cognetics,* Cambridge, MA: 1993

To become a large, international corporation, however, a firm usually has to start out small. Similarly, to direct far-flung global operations, managers first have to learn the basics. The structure of this text reflects this reality by presenting initially a perspective of the business environment, which covers national and global marketing and policy issues and their economic, political, legal, cultural, and financial dimensions.

Subsequently, the book discusses in detail the beginning internationalization of the firm. The emphasis is on the needs of those who are starting out and the operational questions that are crucial to success. Some quite basic yet essential issues addressed are: What is the difference between domestic and international marketing? Does the applicability of marketing principles change when they are transferred to the global environment? How do marketers find out whether there is a market for a product abroad without spending a fortune in time and money on research? How can the firm promote its products in foreign markets? How do marketers find and evaluate a foreign distributor, and how do they make sure that the firm gets paid? How can marketers minimize government red tape yet take advantage of any governmental programs that are of use to them?

These questions are addressed both conceptually and empirically, with a strong focus on export and import operations. The reader will see how the international commitment is developed and strengthened within the firm.

Once these important dimensions are covered, the transition is made to the multinational corporation. The focus is now on the transnational allocation of resources, the coordination of multinational marketing activities, and the attainment of global synergism. Finally, emerging issues of challenge to both policymakers and multinational firms, such as countertrade, marketing to economies in transition, and the future outlook of the global market, are discussed.

All of the marketing issues are considered in relation to national policies so as to apprise the reader of the divergent forces at play in the global market. Increased awareness of and involvement with international marketing on the part of governments requires managers to be aware of the role of governments and also to be able to work with them in order to attain marketing goals. Therefore, the continued references in the text to business-government interaction represent a vital link in the development of international marketing strategy.

We expect that this gradual approach to international marketing will permit the reader not only to master another academic subject, but also to become well versed in both the operational and the strategic aspects of the field. The result should be a better understanding of how the global market works and the capability to participate in the international marketing imperative.

SUMMARY

In the past two decades, world trade has expanded from $200 billion to more than $4 trillion. As a result, nations are much more affected by international business than in the past. Global linkages have made possible investment strategies and marketing alternatives that offer tremendous opportunities. Yet these changes and the speed of change also can represent threats to nations and firms.

On the policy front, decision makers have come to realize that it is very difficult to isolate domestic economic activity from international market events. Factors such as currency exchange rates, financial flows, and foreign economic actions increasingly render the policymaker powerless to implement a domestic agenda. International interdependence, which has contributed to greater affluence, has also increased our vulnerability.

Both firms and individuals are also greatly affected by international trade. Whether willing or not, they are participating in global business affairs. Entire industries have been threatened in their survival as a result of international trade flows and have either adjusted to new market realities or left the market. Individuals have experienced the loss of their workplace and reduced salaries. At the same time, global business changes have increased the opportunities available. Firms can now reach many more customers, product life cycles have been lengthened, sourcing policies have become variable, new jobs have been created, and consumers all over the world can find greater varieties of products at lower prices.

To benefit from the opportunities and deal with the adversities of international trade, business needs to adopt the international marketing concept. The new set of macroenvironmental factors has to be understood and responded to in order to let international markets become a source of growth, profit, and needs satisfaction.

Questions for Discussion

1. Will expansion of world trade in the future be similar to that in the past?
2. Discuss reasons for the shift in the U.S. share of the world market.
3. Does increased world trade mean increased risk?
4. Discuss specific effects of world trade on domestic economic policy-making.
5. Is it beneficial for nations to become dependent on one another?
6. With foreign wages at one-tenth of U.S. wages, how can America compete?
7. Compare and contrast domestic and international marketing.
8. Why do more firms in other countries enter international markets than do U.S. firms?
9. Can you think of examples of international marketing contributing to world peace?

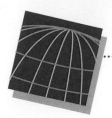

APPENDIX A

Basics of Marketing

This appendix provides a summary of the basic concepts in marketing for the reader who wishes to review them before applying them to international marketing.

A new definition of marketing that reflects the wide range of activities and entities covered by marketing was approved in 1985 by the American Marketing Association.[1] *Marketing* is defined as "the process of planning and executing the conception, pricing, promotion, and distribution of ideas, goods, and services to create exchanges that satisfy individual and organizational objectives." The concepts of satisfaction and exchange are at the core of marketing. For an exchange to take place, two or more parties must come together physically, through the mails, or through technology, and they must communicate and deliver things of perceived value. Potential customers should be perceived as information seekers who evaluate marketers' efforts in terms of their own drives and needs. When the offering is consistent with their needs, they tend to choose the product; if it is not, other alternatives are chosen. A key task of the marketer is to recognize the ever-changing nature of needs and wants. Increasingly, the task of marketing has been expanded from sensing, serving, and satisfying individual customers to taking into consideration the long-term interests of society.

Marketing is not limited to business entities but involves governmental and nonbusiness units as well. Marketing techniques are applied not only to goods but also to ideas (for example, the "Made in the U.S.A." campaign) and to services (for example, international advertising agencies). The term *business marketing* is used for activities directed at other businesses, governmental entities, and various types of institutions. Business marketing composes well over 50 percent of all marketing activities.

STRATEGIC MARKETING

The marketing manager's task is to plan and execute programs that will ensure a long-term competitive advantage for the company. This task has two integral parts: (1) the determining of specific target markets and (2) marketing management, which consists of manipulating marketing mix elements to best satisfy the needs of individual target markets.

Target Market Selection

Characteristics of intended target markets are of critical importance to the marketer. These characteristics can be summarized by eight Os: occupants, objects, occasions, objectives, outlets, organization, operations, and opposition.[2]

Occupants are targets of the marketing effort. The marketer must determine which customers to approach and also define them along numerous dimensions, such as demographics (age, sex, and nationality, for example), geography (country or region), psy-

---

[1] "AMA Board Approves New Marketing Definition," *Marketing News,* March 1, 1985, 1.

[2] Philip Kotler presents the eight Os in the sixth edition of *Marketing Management: Analysis, Planning, and Control* (Englewood Cliffs, NJ: Prentice-Hall, 1988), 174–175.

chographics (attitudes, interests, and opinions), or product-related variables (usage rate and brand loyalty, for example). Included in this analysis must be the major influences on the occupants during their buying processes.

Objects are what is being bought at present to satisfy a particular need. Included in this concept are physical objects, services, ideas, organizations, places, and persons.

Occasions are when members of the target market buy the product or service. This characteristic is important to the marketer because a product's consumption may be tied to a particular time period—for example, imported beer and a festival.

Objectives are the motivations behind the purchase or adoption of the marketed concept. A computer manufacturer does not market hardware but, instead, solutions to problems. Additionally, many customers look for hidden value in the product they purchase, which may be expressed, for example, through national origin of the product or through brand name.

Outlets are where customers expect to be able to procure a product or to be exposed to messages about it. This includes not only the entities themselves but also location within a particular outlet. Although aseptic packaging made it possible to shelve milk outside the refrigerated area in supermarkets, customers' acceptance of the arrangement was not automatic: the product was not where it was supposed to be. In the area of services, outlet involves (1) making a particular service available and communicating its availability and (2) the particular types of facilitators (such as brokers) who bring the parties together.

Organization describes how the buying or acceptance of a (new) idea takes place. Organization expands the analysis beyond the individual consumer to the decision-making unit (DMU). The DMU varies in terms of its size and its nature from relatively small and informal groups to large groups (more than ten people) to quite formal buying committees. Compare, for example, the differences in the processes between a family buying a new home-entertainment center and the governing board at a university deciding which architectural firm to use. In either case, to develop proper products and services, the marketer should know as much as possible about the decision-making processes and the roles of various individuals.

Operations represents the behavior of the organization that is buying products and services. Increasingly, industrial organizations are concentrating their purchases to fewer suppliers and making longer-term commitments. Supermarkets may make available only the leading brands in a product category, thereby complicating the marketer's attempts to place new products in these outlets.

Opposition refers to the competition to be faced in the marketplace. The nature of competition will vary from direct product-type competition to products that satisfy the same need. For example, Prince tennis rackets face a threat not only from other racket manufacturers but also from any company that provides a product or service for leisure-time use. Competitive situations will vary from one market and from one segment to the next. Gillette is number one in the U.S. market for disposable razors, with Bic a distant runner-up; however, elsewhere, particularly in Europe, the roles are reversed. In the long term, threats may come from outside the industry in which the marketer operates. As an example, digital watches originated in the electronics industry rather than the watch industry.

Analyzing the eight Os, and keeping in mind other uncontrollable environments (cultural, political, legal, technological, societal, and economic), the marketer must select the markets to which efforts will be targeted. In the short term, the marketer has to adjust to these environmental forces; in the long term, they can be manipulated to some extent by judicious marketing activity. Consumerism, one of the major forces shaping marketing activities, is concerned with protecting the consumer whenever an exchange relationship exists with any type of organization. Manifestations of the impact of consumerism on marketing exist in labeling, product specifications, promotional campaigns, recycling expectations, and demands for environmentally friendly products.

Because every marketer operates in a corporate environment of scarcity and comparative strengths, the target market decision is a crucial one. In some cases, the marketer may select only one segment of the market (for example, motorcycles of +1,000 cc) or multiple segments (for example, all types of motorized, two-wheeled vehicles) or may opt for an undifferentiated product that is to be mass marketed (for example, unbranded commodities or products that satisfy the same need worldwide, such as Coca-Cola).

Marketing Management

The marketing manager, having analyzed the characteristics of the target market(s), is in a position to specify the mix of marketing variables that will best serve each target market. The elements the marketing manager controls are known as the elements of the marketing mix, or the four Ps: product, price, place, and promotion.[3] Each consists of a submix of variables, and policy decisions must be made on each.

Product policy is concerned with all of the elements that make up the product, service, or idea that is offered by the marketer. Included are all possible tangible characteristics (such as the core product and packaging) and intangible characteristics (such as branding and warranties). Many products are a combination of a concrete product and the accompanying service; for example, in buying an Otis elevator, the purchaser buys not only the product but an extensive service contract as well.

Pricing policy determines the cost of the product to the customer—a point somewhere between the floor created by the costs to the firm and the ceiling created by the strength of demand. An important consideration of pricing policy is pricing within the channel of distribution; margins to be made by the middlemen who assist in the marketing effort must be taken into account. Discounts to middlemen include functional, quantity, seasonal, and cash discounts, as well as promotional allowances. An important point to remember is that price is the only revenue-generating element of the marketing mix.

Distribution policy covers the *place* variable of the marketing mix and has two components: channel management and logistics management. Channel management is concerned with the entire process of setting up and operating the contractual organization, consisting of various types of middlemen (such as wholesalers, agents, retailers, and facilitators). Logistics management is focused on providing product availability at appropriate times and places in the marketing channel.[4] Place is the most long term of all the marketing mix elements; it is the most difficult to change in the short term.

Communications policy uses *promotion* tools to interact with customers, middlemen, and the public at large. The communications element consists of these tools: advertising, sales promotion, personal selling, and publicity. Because the purpose of all communications is to persuade, this is the most visible and sensitive of the marketing mix elements.

Blending the various elements into a coherent program requires trade-offs based on the type of product or service being offered (for example, detergents versus fighter aircraft), the stage of the product's life cycle (a new product versus one that is being revived), and resources available for the marketing effort (money and manpower), as well as the type of customer to whom the marketing efforts are directed.

[3] The four Ps were popularized by E. Jerome McCarthy. See E. Jerome McCarthy and William Perreault, *Basic Marketing: A Managerial Approach,* 9th ed. (Homewood, IL: Irwin, 1987).

[4] Bert Rosenbloom, *Marketing Channels: A Management View,* 3d ed. (Hinsdale, IL: Dryden, 1987), 8–9.

THE MARKETING PROCESS

The actual process of marketing consists of four stages: analysis, planning, implementation, and control.

Analysis begins with collecting data on the eight Os, using various quantitative and qualitative techniques of marketing research. Data sources will vary from secondary to primary, internal to external (to the company), and informal to formal. The data are used to determine company opportunities by screening a plethora of environmental opportunities. The company opportunities must then be checked against the company's resources to judge their viability. The key criterion is competitive advantage.

Planning refers to the blueprint generated to react to and exploit the opportunities in the marketplace. The planning stage involves both long-term strategies and short-term tactics. A marketing plan developed for a particular market includes a situation analysis, objectives and goals to be met, strategies and tactics, and cost and profit estimates. Included in the activity is the formation of new organizational structure or adjustments in the existing one to prepare for the execution of the plan.

Implementation is the actual carrying out of the planned activity. If the plans drawn reflect market conditions, and if they are based on realistic assessments of the company's fit into the market, the implementation process will be a success. Plans must take into account unforeseeable changes within the company and the environmental forces and allow for corresponding changes to occur in implementing the plans.

For this reason, concurrently with implementation, control mechanisms must be put into effect. The marketplace is ever dynamic and requires the monitoring of environmental forces, competitors, channel participants, and customer receptiveness. Short-term control tools include annual plan control (such as comparing actual sales to quota), profitability control, and efficiency control. Long-term control is achieved through comprehensive or functional audits to make sure that marketing not only is doing things right but is doing the right things. The results of the control effort provide valuable input for subsequent planning efforts.

These marketing basics do not vary, regardless of the type of market one is planning to enter or to continue to operate within. They have been called the technical universals of marketing.[5] The different environments in which the marketing manager must operate will give varying emphases to the variables and will cause the values of the variables to change more drastically.

[5] Robert Bartels, "Are Domestic and International Marketing Dissimilar?" *Journal of Marketing* 36 (July 1968): 56–61.

CHAPTER 2

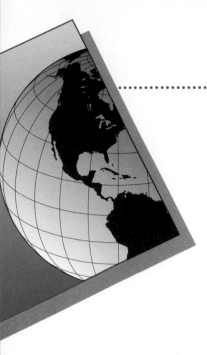

International Trade
and the United States

2.1

THE INTERNATIONAL MARKETPLACE

America's Future in World Trade

The coincidence of widespread layoffs and slow income growth, coupled with large trade deficits and burgeoning foreign debt, has led many Americans to question whether the United States will enjoy a more prosperous future. Alarm about the current and impending decline of the U.S. international position has become widespread, even fashionable.

Implicit in the rhetoric of decline is the notion that things were far "better," "stronger," or "larger" in the past than at present and than they will be in the future. The idea is clear enough, but the facts don't support it.

For example, if one compares the U.S. economy's share of the global product from 1938 or from the mid-1960s to today, it has remained almost unchanged. Yes, the economies of Japan and the Pacific Rim countries have grown more rapidly than the U.S. economy. But the U.S. GNP still has grown more rapidly than that of Western or Central Europe and much of the so-called developing world. Similarly, if one looks at the impact and power of U.S. ideas, one can see that never before has the world so readily accepted the values we have held dear: the role of market forces, economic incentives, price competition, and the privatization of economic activity.

As far as trade is concerned, the key policy question is not one of survival but rather one of the adjustment process: Which countries will have reduced trade surpluses, and how will the reductions occur? Will the adjustment process be smooth or fraught with political friction?

We need to recognize that change is inevitable and that it is the key to growth and a better future. The United States must meet head on the challenge of increased competition in the global economy. America should welcome the competition. Competition is what prods us all to do better.

Sources: C. Michael Aho, "Looking at the Options," *Journal of Japanese Trade and Industry* 4 (July/August 1988):14; Charles Wolf, Jr., *Linking Economic Policy and Foreign Policy* (New Brunswick, NJ: Transaction Publishers, 1991), 7.

The international environment is changing rapidly. Firms, individuals, and policy-makers are affected by these changes. Yet, as The International Marketplace 2.1 shows, these changes are not a sign of weakness but rather of opportunity. Although major economic and security shifts will have a profound impact on the United States and the world, coping with them successfully through imagination, investment, and perseverance can produce a new, better world order and an improved quality of life.

This chapter begins by highlighting the importance of trade to humankind. Selected historical developments that were mainly triggered or influenced by international trade are delineated. Subsequently, more recent trade developments are presented, together with the international institutions that have emerged to regulate and facilitate trade.

The chapter will analyze and discuss the position of the United States in the world trade environment and explain the impact of trade on the United States. Various efforts undertaken by governments to manage trade by restricting or promoting exports, imports, technology transfer, and investments will be described. Finally, the chapter will present a strategic outlook for future developments in trade.

THE HISTORICAL DIMENSION

Many peoples have gained preeminence in the world through their trade activities. Among them are the Etruscans, Phoenicians, Egyptians, Chinese, Spaniards, and Portuguese. To underscore the role of trade, we will take a closer look at some selected examples.

One of the major world powers in ancient history was the Roman Empire. Its impact on thought, knowledge, and development can still be felt today. Even while expanding their territories through armed conflicts, the Romans placed primary emphasis on encouraging international business activities. The principal approaches used to implement this emphasis were the **Pax Romana,** or the Roman Peace, and the common coinage. The Pax Romana ensured that merchants were able to travel safely on roads that were built, maintained, and protected by the Roman legions and their affiliated troops. The common coinage, in turn, ensured that business transactions could be carried out easily throughout the empire. In addition, Rome developed a systematic law, central market locations through the founding of cities, and an excellent communication system that resembled an early version of the Pony Express; all of these measures contributed to the functioning of the international marketplace and to the reduction of business uncertainty. As a result, economic well-being within and outside the empire started to differ sharply.

Soon, city-nations and tribes that were not part of the empire wanted to share in the benefits of belonging. They joined the empire as allies and agreed to pay tribute and taxes. Thus, the immense growth of the Roman Empire occurred through the linkages of business rather than through the marching of its legions and warfare. Of course, the Romans had to engage in substantial efforts to facilitate business in order to make it worthwhile for others to belong. For example, when pirates threatened the seaways, Rome, under Pompeius, sent out a large fleet to subdue them. The cost of international distribution, and therefore the cost of international marketing, was substantially reduced because fewer goods were lost to pirates. As a result, goods could be made available at lower prices, which, in turn, translated into larger demand.

The fact that international business was one of the primary factors holding the empire together can also be seen in its decay. When "barbaric" tribes overran the empire, it was not mainly through war and prolonged battles that Rome lost ground. The outside tribes were actually attacking an empire that was already substantially weakened, because it could no longer offer the benefits of affiliation. Former allies no longer saw any advantage in being associated with the Romans and, rather than face prolonged battles, willingly cooperated with the invaders.

In a similar fashion, one could interpret the evolution of European feudalism to be a function of trade and marketing. Because farmers were frequently deprived of their harvests as a result of incursions by other (foreign) tribes, or even individuals, they decided to band together and provide for their own protection. By delivering a certain portion of their "earnings" to a protector, they could be assured of retaining most of their gains. Although this system initially worked quite well in reducing the cost of production and the cost of marketing, it did ultimately result in the emergence of the feudal system, which, perhaps, was not what the initiators had intended it to be.

Interestingly, the feudal system encouraged the development of a closed-state economy that was inwardly focused and ultimately conceived for self-sufficiency and security. This static system resulted in a dearth of local commerce. However, medieval commerce still thrived and developed through export trade. In Italy, the Low Countries, and the German Hanse towns, the impetus for commerce was provided by East-West trade. Profits from the spice trade through the Middle East created the wealth of Venice and other Mediterranean ports. Europe also imported rice, oranges, dyes, cotton, and silk. Western European merchants in turn exported timber, arms, and woolen clothing in exchange for these luxury goods. A remaining legacy of this trade are the many English and French words of Arabic origin, such as divan, bazaar, artichoke, orange, jar, and tariff.[1]

The importance of trade has not always persisted, however. For example, in 1896, the Empress Dowager Tz'u-hsi, in order to finance the renovation of the summer palace, impounded government funds that had been designated for Chinese shipping and its navy. As a result, China's participation in world trade almost ground to a halt. In the subsequent decades, China operated in almost total isolation, without any transfer of knowledge from the outside, without major inflow of goods, and without the innovation and productivity increases that result from exposure to international trade.

More recently, the effect of turning away from international trade was highlighted during the 1930s. The Smoot-Hawley Act raised duties to reduce the volume of imports into the United States, in the hopes that this would restore domestic employment. The result, however, was a raising of duties and other barriers to imports by most other trading nations as well. These measures were contributing factors in the subsequent worldwide depression and the collapse of the world financial system, which in turn set the scene for World War II.

International marketing and international trade have also long been seen as valuable tools for foreign policy purposes. The use of economic coercion—for example, by nations or groups of nations—can be traced back as far as the time of the Greek city-states and the Peloponnesian War or, in more recent times, to the Napoleonic wars. Combatants used blockades to achieve their goal of "bringing about commercial ruin and shortage of food by dislocating trade."[2] Similarly, during the Civil War in the United States,

---

[1] Henri Pirenne, *Economic and Social History of Medieval Europe* (New York: Harcourt, Brace, and World, 1933), 142–146.

[2] Margaret P. Doxey, *Economic Sanctions and International Enforcement* (New York: Oxford University Press, 1980), 10.

the North consistently pursued a strategy of denying international trade opportunities to the South and thus deprived it of export revenue needed to import necessary products. In the 1990s, the Iraqi invasion of Kuwait resulted in a trade embargo of Iraq by the United Nations, with the goal of reversing the aggression. Although such deprivations of trade are not always successful in bringing about policy change, they certainly have a profound impact on the standard of living of a nation's citizens.

The Emergence of Global Division

After 1945, the world was sharply split ideologically into West and East, a division that had major implications for trade relations. The Soviet Union, as the leader of the Eastern bloc, developed the Council for Mutual Economic Assistance (CMEA or COMECON), which focused on developing strong linkages among the members of the Soviet bloc and discouraged relations with the West. The United States, in turn, was the leading proponent of creating a "Pax Americana" for the Western world, driven by the belief that international trade was a key to worldwide prosperity. Many months of international negotiations in London, Geneva, and Lake Success (New York) culminated on March 24, 1948, in Havana, Cuba, with the signing of the charter for an International Trade Organization (ITO).

This charter, a series of agreements between 53 countries, was designed to cover international commercial policies, restrictive business practices, commodity agreements, employment and reconstruction, economic development and international investment, and a constitution for a new United Nations agency to administer the whole.[3] In addition, a General Agreement on Tariffs and Trade was initiated, with the purpose of reducing tariffs among countries, and international institutions such as the World Bank and the International Monetary Fund were negotiated.

Even though the International Trade Organization incorporated many farsighted notions, most nations refused to ratify it, fearing its power, its bureaucratic size, and its threats to national sovereignty. As a result, the most forward-looking approach to international trade never came about. However, other organizations conceived at the time are still in existence and have made major contributions toward improving international trade.

TRANSNATIONAL INSTITUTIONS AFFECTING WORLD TRADE

General Agreement on Tariffs and Trade (GATT)

The General Agreement on Tariffs and Trade (GATT) has been called "a remarkable success story of a postwar international organization that was never intended to become one."[4] It began in 1947 as a set of rules for nondiscrimination, transparent procedures, and settlement of disputes in international trade. Gradually it evolved into an institution that sponsored successive rounds of international trade negotiations.

Early in its existence, the GATT achieved the liberalization of trade in 50,000 products, amounting to two-thirds of the value of the trade among its participants.[5] In subsequent years, special GATT negotiations such as the Kennedy Round and the Tokyo Round further reduced trade barriers and developed improved dispute-settlement mechanisms, better provisions dealing with subsidies, and a more explicit definition of rules for import controls.

---

[3] Edwin L. Barber III, "The Investment-Trade Nexus," in *U.S. International Economic Policy*, 1981, ed. Gary Clyde Hufbauer (Washington: International Law Institute, 1982), 9–4.

[4] Thomas R. Graham, "Global Trade: War and Peace," *Foreign Policy* (Spring 1983): 124–137.

[5] Barber, "Investment-Trade Nexus," 9–5.

In spite of, or perhaps because of, these impressive gains, GATT has become less effective today. Duties have already been drastically reduced—for example, the average U.S. tariff rate fell from 26 percent in 1946 to 5 percent in 1987[6]—and further reductions are unlikely to have a major impact on world trade. Concurrently, many nations have developed new tools for managing and distorting trade flows, tools that are not covered under GATT rules. Examples are "voluntary agreements" to restrain trade, bilateral or multilateral special trade agreements such as the multifiber accord that restricts trade in textiles and apparel, and nontariff barriers. Also, GATT, which was founded by 24 like-minded governments, is designed to operate by consensus. With a current membership of 110, this consensus rule often leads to a stalemate of many GATT activities.

In order to restore its importance, GATT commenced a new set of negotiations, called the Uruguay Round, in 1987. The discussions in this round still addressed the issue of tariffs. However, since tariffs had already been reduced greatly in earlier negotiations, any further reduction would do little to encourage trade. Therefore, the main thrust of the Uruguay Round was to sharpen the use of existing rules by strengthening the dispute-settlement procedures and to integrate into the treaty the trade areas that were outside of the GATT. Several key areas emerged: nontariff barriers were to be reduced or eliminated; trade areas such as textiles, agriculture, and services were to become subject to GATT rules; intellectual property rights rules were to be developed to protect patents and trademarks; and trade-related investment measures were to be agreed upon to avoid rules that would distort trade flows.

In December 1993, a GATT accord was finally reached, and major progress had been achieved in several areas. In the agricultural sector, subsidies will be gradually reduced and nontariff barriers will be converted into more transparent tariff barriers. The textile and clothing industry, governed for decades by the Multifibre Agreement, will eventually be brought under the GATT regime with reduced subsidies and market restrictions. An entire set of rules was designed to govern the services area, and new rules to encourage international investment flows were agreed to. Important progress was achieved in safeguarding intellectual property rights and streamlining the settlement of disputes. One key aspect was the formation of the World Trade Organization (WTO) which will supervise and adjudicate GATT agreements and encourage future negotiations. In concept, the WTO starkly resembles the International Trade Organization envisioned, but never ratified, in 1948.

The GATT accords have addressed many issues important to world trade. Even though some tariff cuts were agreed upon, the key focus was on other issues much more important to the future of the world economy. Many countries have made concessions in areas that for decades have been considered "sacred cows." Undoubtedly, the implementation of many provisions is likely to cause adjustment pain. Yet such adjustments are necessary if the new realities of the world economy are to be accepted. Whether all parties sign on to the agreement remains to be seen in light of domestic difficulties and fears for national sovereignty. If ratified by the member countries, the new GATT provisions will take effect in January 1995. Yet even agreement among most members is sufficient to achieve much progress.

International Monetary Fund (IMF)

The International Monetary Fund (IMF), conceived in 1944 at Bretton Woods in New Hampshire, was designed to provide stability for the international monetary framework. It obtained funding from its members, who subscribed to a quota based on expected trade patterns and paid 25 percent of the quota in gold or dollars and the rest in their local

---

[6] Graham, "Global Trade," 127.

currencies. These funds were to be used to provide countries with protection against temporary fluctuations in the value of their currency. Therefore, it was the original goal of the IMF to provide for fixed exchange rates between countries.

The perhaps not so unintended result of using the U.S. dollar as the main world currency was a glut of dollar supplies in the 1960s. This forced the United States to abandon the gold standard and devalue the dollar and resulted in flexible or floating exchange rates in 1971. However, even though this major change occurred, the IMF as an institution has clearly contributed toward providing international liquidity and to facilitating international trade.

Although the system has functioned well so far, it is currently under severe pressure. In the 1980s, some of this pressure was triggered by the substantial debts incurred by less-developed countries as a result of overextended development credits and changes in the cost of energy. In the 1990s, major additional pressure has resulted from the financial requirements of the former socialist countries, which search for help to improve their economies. For example, on April 27, 1992, 12 former Soviet republics joined the IMF. As a result of all these global financial needs, the future role of the IMF may be very different. If the institution can mobilize its members to provide the financial means for an active role, its past accomplishments may pale in view of the new opportunities.

At the same time, however, the newness in orientation also will require a rethinking of the rules under which the IMF operates. For example, it is quite unclear whether stringent economic rules and performance measures are equally applicable to all countries seeking IMF assistance. New economic conditions that have not been experienced to date, such as the privatization of formerly centrally planned economies, may require different types of approaches. Also, perhaps the link between economic and political stability requires more and different considerations, therefore magnifying but also changing the mission of the IMF.

World Bank

The World Bank, whose official name is the International Bank for Reconstruction and Development, has had similar success. It was initially formed in 1944 to aid countries suffering from the destruction of war. After completing this process most successfully, it has since taken on the task of aiding world development. With more and more new nations emerging from the colonial fold of the world powers of the early twentieth century, the bank has played a major role in assisting fledgling economies to participate in a modern economic trade framework. More recently, the bank has begun to participate actively with the IMF to resolve the debt problems of the developing world and may also play a major role in bringing a market economy to the former members of the Eastern bloc.

Regional Institutions

GATT, IMF, and the World Bank operate on a global level. Regional changes have also taken place, based on the notion that trade between countries needs to be encouraged. Of particular importance was the formation of **economic blocs** that integrated the economic and political activities of nations.

The concept of regional integration was used more than 100 years ago when Germany developed the Zollverein. Its modern-day development began in 1952 with the establishment of the European Coal and Steel Community, which was designed to create a common market among six countries in coal, steel, and iron. Gradually, these nations developed a Customs Union and created common external tariffs. The ultimate goal envisioned was the completely free movement of capital, services, and people across national borders and the joint development of common international policies. Over time, parts of the goal have been attained. The European Union (EU) now represents a formidable market size internally and market power externally. Even though not all restrictions have been dropped as envisioned, the well-being of all EU members has increased substantially since the bloc's formation.

Similar market agreements have been formed by other groups of nations. Examples are the North American Free Trade Agreement (NAFTA) and the Gulf Cooperation Council (GCC). These unions were formed for different reasons and operate with different degrees of cohesiveness as appropriate for the specific environment. They focus on issues such as forming a customs union, a common market, an economic union, or a political union. They demonstrate that the joining of forces internationally permits better, more successful international marketing activities, results in an improved standard of living, and provides an effective counterbalance to other large economic blocs. Just as in politics, trade has refuted the old postulate of "the strong is most powerful alone." Nations have come to recognize that trade activities are of substantial importance to their economic well-being. A nation or a group of nations has to generate sufficient outflow activities to compensate for the inflow activities taking place. In the medium and long run, the balance of payments has to be maintained. In the short run, "an external deficit can be financed by drawing down previously accumulated assets or by accumulating debts to other countries. In time, however, an adjustment process must set in to eliminate the deficit."[7]

The urgency of the adjustment will vary according to the country in question. Some countries find it very hard to obtain acceptance for an increasing number of IOUs. Others, like the United States, can run deficits of hundreds of billions of dollars and still be a preferred borrower because of political stability and perceived economic security. Yet, over the long term, it is the outward orientation of international business activities that is the key to the facilitation of inward flows.

As a result of this understanding, much of the ideological trade separation of the world has been swept aside. Today, virtually all nations wish to take part in international trade and make efforts to participate in as much of it as possible.

THE CURRENT U.S. INTERNATIONAL TRADE POSITION

Over the years, the U.S. international trade position has eroded substantially when measured in terms of world market share. In the 1950s, U.S. exports composed 25 percent of total world exports. This share has declined precipitously. It is not that U.S. exports have actually dropped during that time. The history of the U.S. decline in world market share began with the fact that the U.S. economy was not destroyed by the war. Because other countries had little to export and a great need for imports, the U.S. export position was powerful. Over time, however, as other trade partners entered the picture and aggressively obtained a larger world market share for themselves, U.S. export growth was not able to keep pace with total world export growth. Figure 2.1 shows the world share of exports and imports of key trading countries. Notable is the degree to which U.S. imports exceed exports and Japanese exports exceed imports.

In spite of the decline in world market share, U.S. exports as a share of the GNP have grown substantially in recent years. However, this increase pales when compared with the international trade performance of other nations. Germany, for example, has consistently maintained an export share of well over 20 percent of GNP. Japan, in turn, which

[7] Mordechai E. Kreinin, *International Economics: A Policy Approach*, 5th ed. (New York: Harcourt Brace Jovanovich, 1987), 12.

Merchandise Exports and Imports as a Percentage of World Total FIGURE 2.1

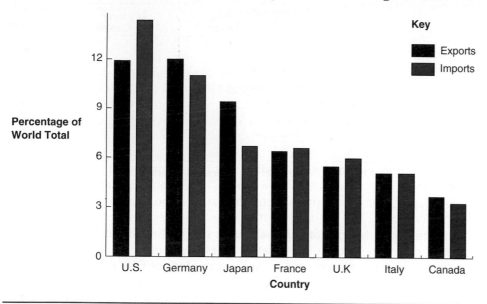

Source: The World Bank, *World Development Report, 1993* (Washington, D.C., 1993).

is so often maligned as the export problem child in the international trade arena, exports less than 10 percent of its GNP. Comparative developments of exports across countries in terms of percentage of GNP can be seen in Table 2.1.

Clearly, as an economy, the United States is not as internationally oriented as are many other nations. At the same time, the numbers themselves must be interpreted

Merchandise Exports as a Percentage of Gross National Product[a] TABLE 2.1

Period	United States	France	Germany[b]	Italy	Nether-lands	United Kingdom	Japan	Canada
1980	8.1	17.5	23.6	17.1	43.7	20.5	12.2	24.6
1981	7.7	18.2	25.7	18.4	48.5	19.8	13.0	23.5
1982	6.7	17.5	26.8	18.2	48.0	20.0	12.8	22.6
1983	5.9	18.0	25.7	17.5	48.3	19.9	12.4	22.3
1984	5.8	19.5	27.6	17.7	52.4	21.6	13.5	27.1
1985	5.3	19.3	29.1	18.4	53.7	22.0	13.2	26.5
1986	5.1	17.2	27.1	16.1	45.4	18.8	10.7	25.7
1987	5.4	16.8	26.3	15.4	43.7	18.8	9.5	24.3
1988	6.6	17.4	26.9	15.3	45.6	17.3	9.1	24.5
1989	7.0	18.6	28.6	16.3	48.0	18.2	9.5	22.7
1990	7.2	18.2	27.2	15.8	47.0	18.8	9.7	22.8
1991	7.4	18.1	23.6	14.7	45.6	18.3	9.3	21.5
1992	7.4	17.8	22.2	14.5	43.7	18.2	9.2	23.6
1993	7.2	16.4	19.9	16.4	n.a.	19.4	8.6	25.9

Note: 1993 data are nine months at annual rate, except for Germany and Italy, which are six months at annual rate.

[a]Gross domestic product for France and Italy.

[b]Data are from the former West Germany up to 1990. From 1991 on, data are for unified Germany.

n.a.—Not available.

Sources: Various 1994 editions of OECD Main Economic Indicators, January 1994; Deutsche Bundesbank; Wirtschaft und Statistik; Informations Rapides; U.S. Bureau of the Census; and London Telegram.

TABLE 2.2

Exports and Imports per Capita for Selected Countries, 1993

Country	Exports per Capita	Imports per Capita
United States	$1,816	$2,270
Canada	4,898	4,710
France	4,111	4,177
Germany	5,334	5,067
Netherlands	9,220	8,815
United Kingdom	3,284	3,830
Japan	2,734	1,876
Italy	3,083	3,261

Sources: U.S. Department of Commerce, *FT 900*, 1994; IMF *International Financial Statistics*, January 1994; Deutsche Bundesbank, 1993.

with caution, since they do not reflect the large size of the U.S. internal market. For example, if one considered the European Union as one market, the exclusion of intra-EU trade would drastically reduce the export percentage of GNP for the EU member nations.

The impact of international trade and marketing on individuals is highlighted when trade is scrutinized from a per-capita perspective. Table 2.2 presents this information on a comparative basis. Among the major industrialized nations, the United States has the lowest exports per capita, amounting to about one-third of Germany's figure and less than one-fifth of the per-person exports of the Netherlands. Even though imports per capita are also relatively low, they substantially exceed the level of export activity, thus producing major trade deficits for the United States.

A Diagnosis of the U.S. Trade Position

The developments just enumerated foster the question: Why did these shifts occur? We should not attribute changes in U.S. trade performance merely to temporary factors such as the value of the dollar, the subsidization of exports from abroad, or the high price of oil. We need to search further to determine the root causes for the decline in U.S. international competitiveness.

Since World War II, it had been ingrained in the minds of American policymakers that the United States is the leading country in world power and world trade. Together with this opinion came the feeling that the United States should assist other countries with their trade performance because without American help, they would never be able to play a meaningful role in the world economy. At the same time, there was admiration for "Yankee ingenuity"—for the idea that U.S. firms were the most aggressive in the world. Therefore, the U.S. private sector appeared not to need any help in its international trade efforts.

The result of this overall philosophy was a continuing effort to aid countries abroad in their economic development. At the same time, no particular attention was paid to U.S. domestic firms. This policy was well conceived and well intentioned and resulted in spectacular successes. Books written in the late 1940s describe the overwhelming economic power of the United States and the apparently impossible task of resurrecting foreign economies. Comparing those texts with the economic performance of countries such as Japan and Germany today demonstrates that the policies of helping to stimulate foreign economies were indeed crowned by success.

These policies were so successful that no one wished to tamper with them. The United States continued to encourage trade abroad and not to aid domestic firms throughout the 1960s and the 1970s. Although the policies were well conceived, the environment to which they were applied was changing. In the 1950s and early 1960s, the United States successfully encouraged other nations again to become full partners in world trade. However, U.S. firms were placed at a distinct disadvantage when these policies continued into the late 1970s.

U.S. firms were assured that "because of its size and the diversity of its resources, the American economy can satisfy consumer wants and national needs with a minimum of reliance on foreign trade."[8] The availability of a large U.S. domestic market and the relative distance to foreign markets resulted in U.S. manufacturers simply not feeling a compelling need to seek business beyond national borders. Subsequently, the perception emerged within the private sector that exporting and international marketing was "too risky, complicated, and [therefore] not worth it."[9]

This perception also resulted in increasing gaps in international marketing knowledge between managers in the United States and those abroad. Whereas business executives abroad were forced, by the small size of their markets, to look very quickly to foreign markets and to learn about cultural sensitivity and market differences, most U.S. managers remained blissfully ignorant of foreign markets. Similarly, U.S. education, until recently, did not make knowledge about the global environment, foreign languages, and cultures an area of major priority.

Given such lack of global interest, inadequacy of information, ignorance of where and how to market internationally, unfamiliarity with foreign market conditions, and complicated trade regulations, the private sector became fearful of conducting international business activities.

Beginning in early 1993, the Clinton Administration advocated a more active role for government in international trade. Government offices were encouraged to work more closely with business and to represent U.S. business interests abroad. By intervening directly into purchase negotiations, government was able to procure several large-scale orders for U.S. firms. For example, in February 1994, Saudi Arabia announced that it would source its commercial aircraft from the United States, resulting in an inflow of $6 billion of new orders. While the immediate effects of such government involvement are beneficial, some are concerned about the long-term international repercussions of this approach. One possible outcome could be increased involvement by governments around the globe, with the determining factor for a sale becoming government pressure rather than commercial competitiveness.

THE IMPACT OF TRADE AND INVESTMENT ON THE UNITED STATES

If complacency with the status quo and fear of change exist with regard to foreign market activities, why should we not simply let U.S. business managers worry about the domestic market and get on with it? Why should we be bothered that the largest portion of U.S. exports are carried out by only 2,500 companies? Why should we be concerned that the Department of Commerce estimates that thousands of U.S. firms are believed to be capable of exporting but do not do so?

---

[8] Kreinin, *International Economics*, 6.

[9] House Subcommittee of the Committee on Government Operations, *Commerce and State Department's Export Promotion Programs*, 95th Cong., 1st sess., 1977, 66.

The Effect of Trade

Exports are important in a macroeconomic sense, in terms of balancing the trade account. Exports are special because they can affect currency values and the fiscal and monetary policies of governments, shape public perception of competitiveness, and determine the level of imports a country can afford. The steady erosion of the American share of total world exports that took place in the 1960s and 1970s has had more than purely optical repercussions. It has also resulted in a merchandise **trade deficit,** which since 1975 has been continuous. In 1987, the United States posted a record trade deficit with imports of products exceeding exports by more than $171 billion. Since then, due to increases in exports, there has been a gradual decline, with a 1993 trade deficit of $115 billion. Yet even such lower levels are unsustainable in the longer run.

These trade deficits have a major impact on the United States and its citizens. They indicate that a country, in its international activities, is consuming more than it is producing. Trade deficits also affect the domestic employment picture, since increased imports often affect levels of local production. One key way to reduce trade deficits is to increase exports. Such an approach is highly beneficial for various reasons.

One billion dollars worth of exports creates, on average, 22,800 jobs.[10] Increases in exports can become a major contributor to economic growth. This fact became particularly evident during the economic slowdown of the early 1990s, when export growth accounted for most of the domestic economic growth rate and produced most new employment.

Equally important, through exporting, firms can achieve **economies of scale.** By broadening its market reach and serving customers abroad, a firm can produce more and do so more efficiently. As a result, the firm may achieve lower costs and higher profits both at home and abroad. Through exporting, the firm also benefits from market diversification. It can take advantage of different growth rates in different markets and gain stability by not being overly dependent on any particular market. Exporting also lets the firm learn from the competition, makes it sensitive to different demand structures and cultural dimensions, and proves its ability to survive in a less-familiar environment in spite of higher transaction costs. All these lessons can make the firm a stronger competitor at home.[11]

The Effect of International Investment

International marketing activities consist not only of trade but of a spectrum of involvement, much of which results in international direct-investment activities. As the International Marketplace 2.2 shows, such investment activities can be crucial to a firm's success in new and growing markets.

For decades, the United States was the leading foreign direct investor in the world. U.S. multinationals and subsidiaries sprouted everywhere. Of late, however, because of the low value of the dollar, which has made acquisitions in the United States

---

[10] Lester A. Davis, *Contribution of Exports to U.S. Employment: 1980–87* (Washington, D.C.: Government Printing Office, 1989).

[11] Michael R. Czinkota, "A National Export Development Strategy for New and Growing Businesses," Remarks delivered to the National Economic Council, Washington, D.C., August 6, 1993.

THE INTERNATIONAL MARKETPLACE

Hewlett-Packard Invests Abroad

The Asia-Pacific region has long been seen as a supplier of cheap, diligent labor but with little potential for anything else. When Hewlett-Packard, a producer of computers, printers, and other electronic equipment, first entered the region via Singapore in 1970, it paid 62 employees to string tiny magnetic rings on strands of wire for use in computers. Today, the company maintains a work force of 13,000 throughout Asia.

This overwhelming growth has been largely driven by Asia's emergence as one of the world's major markets. No longer is the focus just on cheap labor and producing the products, it is now largely on marketing them! Hewlett-Packard now expects Asian sales to grow to one-fifth of its corporate total by the end of the decade.

These accomplishments portray the increasing importance of the region to America's economic future. Asia's burgeoning economies represent a giant opportunity for U.S. industry, especially the most advanced companies. According to Alan Bickell, Hewlett-Packard's senior vice president for geographic operations, "The potential for growth is far greater in [the] Asia-Pacific [region] than in any other part of the world." The United States exports more to the Asia-Pacific region than to Western Europe, Canada, or Mexico. These U.S. sales support an estimated 2.5 million jobs.

Despite barriers to trade and investment, Hewlett-Packard's commitment to Asia is unflagging because the market has become too big and too vital to ignore. Hewlett-Packard executives in Asia state, "If you're not investing in the competition's home market, they'll be able to build economies of scale that enable them to become much tougher competitors worldwide." Although Japan overtook the United States as the area's top foreign investor in the late 1980s, the massive wave of Japanese investment has benefited Hewlett-Packard by fueling the economic boom and contributing to an annual 30 percent increase in sales.

Investments in local operations earn returns not only in additional sales, but provide the company with skills and expertise that it lacks in the United States. As its Asian customers become more prosperous and critical to the company's fortunes, Hewlett-Packard finds itself drawn to expand and upgrade its operations in the region. States Alex Chan, managing director of Hewlett-Packard Singapore: "In Asia especially, we have to be close to the customer. It's very important for American companies to be here, to maximize their reach and their competitiveness."

Source: Paul Blustein, "Finding a Home Among the Tigers," *The Washington Post*, November 19, 1993, A1.

cheap, and because of fears of being excluded from trade by means of governmental action, foreign firms increasingly invest in the United States. At the same time, investment continues to expand around the globe, following attractive factor conditions and entering new markets. The International Marketplace 2.3 reports on an Asian example.

2.3

THE INTERNATIONAL MARKETPLACE

Foreign Investment Expands

With low wages and productive workers, South Korea snatched up the global athletic shoe market during the 1980s. The Kukje Corporation's factory in Pusan, South Korea, ran 24 lines and employed 20,000 workers at its peak, making it the largest shoe factory in the world. Korean conglomerate HS Corporation's shoe factory employed 9,000 people by the late 1980s and made hundreds of thousands of shoes for such giants as Nike Inc. and Reebok International Ltd. The "Made in Korea" label on athletic shoes being sold around the world helped create the image of South Korea as a new industrial power.

An interesting thing has happened to the industry since reaching the top. Both of these huge shoe factories are now closed and are waiting to be converted into apartments. Factories like these are shutting down all over Korea, as well as economically similar Taiwan. The reason? As Taiwan and Korea, once low-wage countries themselves, open up trade and investment links with China, hundreds of thousands of jobs have vanished over the past three years in the shoe industry and many others, including apparel and toys. Rising wages have simply priced the products out of much of the world market.

At first, one might hear the "giant sucking sound" created by low-wage labor. But a closer look offers a much different lesson. The South Korean and Taiwanese economies are being transformed into more advanced industrial nations, spurred in part by a surge in exports to China. The economic benefits of expanded investment and trade relations with China clearly outweigh the costs for these two "Little Dragons." The explosive growth of the Chinese economy is stimulating demand for Korean and Taiwanese products that involve high technology and heavy industry. These growing industries include steel, machinery, petrochemicals, and autos. For example, the Chinese have been buying up 20 percent of South Korea's auto exports. Consider the continuing advances made by Taiwanese and Korean electronics companies in areas such as memory chips and notebook computers and the resulting major spur to job creation. This example illustrates how free trade can help speed economic development and raise overall living standards.

"This is the free market at work," proclaims a Hong Kong economist. "Labor is being released from low-wage, low-productivity industries . . . and it's moving into higher value-added, higher-productivity industries and into services." This transition is occurring so fast that those jobs lost in such industries as shoes barely show up in the unemployment statistics. The jobless rates are 2.6 percent in South Korea and 1.4 percent in Taiwan. "People are moving from dirty-hand work to skilled-hand work—this is what drives the region's growth," explains Nicholas Kwan, senior economist at Merrill Lynch Asia Pacific Ltd. in Hong Kong.

Another example is Seoul-based SunStar Sewing Machine Co., whose exports have soared to places like Indonesia and China, where huge garment-manufacturing industries have developed, and the employment rate has more than doubled in the past seven years. While SunStar has lost domestic sales, its overall market has increased. The region needs more sewing machines than ever, because as China and Indonesia develop their economies, more of their people can afford to buy more clothing. China has become South Korea's third largest trading partner just 20 months after Seoul and Beijing signed an agreement ending their Cold War freeze on relations.

While demand from China is presently helping to fuel economic advancement, the two countries know that Chinese industrial companies will become competitors in the future. According to a Korean official, "In the long run, we foresee fierce competition between Korea and China; the only solution is to produce better goods and services at better prices."

Sources: Paul Blustein, "Asia's Dragons Accept Trade's Pains and Gains," *The Washington Post*, November 7, 1993, H1; and Steve Glain, "Korea Is Overthrown as Sneaker Champ," *The Wall Street Journal*, October 7, 1993, A14.

The extent of **foreign direct investment** in different U.S. manufacturing industries is shown in Table 2.3. Foreign affiliates account for almost one-fifth of total U.S. manufacturing assets. However, the foreign ownership is not equally distributed across all manufacturing sectors. Foreign direct investment tends to be concentrated in specific industries where the foreign investors believe they are able to contribute the best and benefit the most from their investment. For example, in the U.S. chemical industry, more than 40 percent of all assets are held by foreign entities. By contrast, less than 8 percent of assets in the U.S. transportation equipment industry are held by owners from abroad. As a result of such concentration, some individuals and policymakers may grow concerned about dependency on foreign owners, even though firm proof for the validity of such concern has been difficult to establish.

Many of these investments are carried out by the largest trading partners of the United States. Although the United Kingdom still leads all foreign countries in terms of the value of direct investment, Japan is rapidly catching up. As Table 2.4 shows, Japanese

TABLE 2.3

Total Assets of U.S. Affiliates of Foreign Corporations and of All U.S. Businesses in Manufacturing, 1991

Products	Affiliates (millions of dollars)	All Businesses (millions of dollars)	Affiliates (as a % of all businesses)
Stone, clay, and glass products	25,835	59,174	43.7
Chemicals and allied products	144,412	357,665	40.4
Primary metal industries	33,210	105,558	31.5
Rubber and plastics products	17,818	61,884	28.8
Electric and electronic equipment	44,331	211,567	21.0
Petroleum and coal products	68,080	327,961	20.8
Fabricated metal products	17,721	94,936	18.7
Printing and publishing	25,422	159,752	15.9
Food and kindred products	(D)	319,782	(D)
Instruments and related products	15,917	117,939	13.5
Machinery, except electrical	35,096	268,912	13.1
Textile mill products	3,827	40,744	9.4
Paper and allied products	10,245	130,748	7.8
Transportation equipment	16,443	337,038	4.9
Other	(D)	94,761	(D)
Total Manufacturing	516,671	2,688,422	19.2

DData are suppressed to avoid disclosure of data of individual companies.

Source: U.S. Department of Commerce, *Survey of Current Business*, May 1993.

TABLE 2.4   Japan-Related Firms in the 50 States

	Total Firms 1990	Total Factories 1990	Total Employment 1990
Alabama	31	20	5,800+
Alaska	14	13	n.a.
Arizona	n.a.	n.a.	n.a.
Arkansas	14	13	4,000*
California	2,000**	650+**	65,000**
Colorado	36	4	2,708
Connecticut	43	11	2,000
Delaware	5	3	225
Florida	92	19	4,878
Georgia	276	68	16,014
Hawaii	1,000*	20	n.a.
Idaho	1	1	100
Illinois	592	74	29,800
Indiana	90	58	10,000*
Iowa	n.a.	n.a.	n.a.
Kansas	21	8	900
Kentucky	74	64	19,192
Louisiana	20	4	1,650
Maine	2	1	40–200
Maryland	51	13*	3,400
Massachusetts	103	12	7,200*
Michigan	300*	90	30,000*
Minnesota	35	3	2,257
Mississippi	12	10	2,600*
Missouri	48	18	2,000*
Montana	5	0	60
Nebraska	11	10	1,707
Nevada	24	13	3,717
New Hampshire	7*	6+*	1,550+*
New Jersey	300*	180*	12,000*
New Mexico	1	1	250
New York	900*	35	48,000
North Carolina	76	51	7,400
North Dakota	1	1	3
Ohio	200*	100*	25,000
Oklahoma	19	18	n.a.
Oregon	n.a.	n.a.	n.a.
Pennsylvania	100	67	n.a.
Rhode Island	6	3	822
South Carolina	31	29	8,748
South Dakota	2	2	120*
Tennessee	90	56	17,500
Texas	313*	62*	7,000*
Utah	16	7	400
Vermont	3	3	359
Virginia	57	23	6,000
West Virginia	3	2	180
Washington	72	34	10,158*
Wisconsin	11	5	250*
Wyoming	1	0	n.a.
Totals	7,109	1,885	360,088–361,148

*Estimate/approximation

**Changed compilation methods

Source: *Economic World,* November 1990, 49.

corporations alone operated more than 1,800 factories in the United States in 1990. It should also be recognized that these factories employed more than 360,000 individuals in the country.

To some extent, these foreign direct investments substitute for trade activities. As a result, firms operating only in the domestic market may be surprised by the onslaught of foreign competition and, by being unprepared to respond quickly, may lose their domestic market share. However, the substitution for trade is far from complete. In many instances, foreign affiliates themselves are major participants in trade. They may import raw materials or components and export some of their output.

Even though the United States has an open investment policy that welcomes foreign corporations to U.S. shores, some degree of unease exists about the rapid growth of such investment. Increasingly, major foreign investments are reviewed by a specially created U.S. government interagency committee called the Committee for Foreign Investments in the United States (CFIUS). This committee primarily scrutinizes foreign investment activities from the standpoint of their impact on U.S. national security.

A general restriction of foreign investments aimed to help U.S. firms might well be contrary to the general good of U.S. citizens. Industries may be preserved, but only at great peril to the free flow of capital and at substantial cost to consumers. A restriction of investments may permit more domestic control over industries, yet it also denies access to foreign capital and often innovation. This in turn can result in a tightening up of credit markets, higher interest rates, and a decrease in willingness to adapt to changing world market conditions.

To avoid these negative repercussions, the United States as a nation and its citizens must encourage more involvement in the international market by U.S. firms. Greater participation in international trade can be achieved by exporting more and by investing, licensing, or franchising abroad. For all these activities, however, the key issue will be the maintenance of high levels of U.S. international competitiveness in order to retain and regain domestic and international market share.

U.S. AND FOREIGN POLICY RESPONSES TO TRADE PROBLEMS

The word *policy* implies that there is a coordinated set of continuous activities in the legislative and executive branches of government that attempts to deal with U.S. international trade. Unfortunately, such concerted efforts only rarely come about. Policy responses have consisted mainly of political ad hoc reactions, which over the years have changed from deploration to protectionism. Whereas in the mid-1970s most lawmakers and administration officials simply regretted the lack of U.S. performance in international markets, more recently industry pressures have forced increasing action.

Restrictions of Imports

In light of persistent trade deficits, growing foreign direct investment, and the tendency by some firms and industries to seek legislative redress for failures in the marketplace, the U.S. Congress in the past two decades has increasingly been ready to provide the president with more powers to restrict trade. Many resolutions have also been passed and legislation enacted admonishing the president to pay closer attention to trade. However, most of these admonitions provided only for an increasing threat against foreign importers, not for better conditions for U.S. exporters. The power of the executive to improve international trade opportunities for U.S. firms through international negotiations and a relaxation of rules, regulations, and laws has become increasingly restricted over time.

A tendency has also existed to disregard the achievements of past international negotiations. For example, in the 98th Congress, an amendment was attached to protectionistic legislation, stipulating that U.S. international trade legislation should not take effect if it is not in conformity with internationally negotiated rules. The amendment was voted down by an overwhelming majority, demonstrating a legislative lack of concern for such international trade agreements. There has also been a growing tendency to seek short-term political favor domestically in lieu of long-term international solutions. Trade legislation has become increasingly oriented to specific trading partners and specific industries. The United States often attempts to transfer trade laws abroad, in areas such as antitrust or export controls, resulting in bilateral conflicts. During international trade negotiations, U.S. expectations regarding production costs, social structure, and cultural patterns are often expected to be adopted in full abroad.

Yet, in spite of all these developments, the United States is still a strong advocate of free trade. Although this advocacy is shared, at least officially, by nations around the world, governments have become very creative in designing and implementing trade barriers, examples of which are listed in Table 2.5.

One typical method consists of "voluntary" import restraints that are applied selectively against trading partners. Because they are "voluntary," they do not fall under the purview of previously negotiated international agreements. Such measures have been used mainly in areas such as textiles, automobiles, and steel. Voluntary restrictions, which are, of course, implemented with the assistance of severe threats against trading partners, are intended to aid domestic industries to reorganize, restructure, and recapture their trade prominence of years past. They fail to take into account that foreign importers may not have caused the economic decline of the domestic industry.

TABLE 2.5   Types of Trade Barriers

- Tariff and other import charges (for example, high tariffs, surtaxes, and other import duties)
- Quantitative restrictions (for example, quotas or embargoes on imports)
- Import licensing (for example, restrictive licensing practices)
- Customs barriers (for example, uplift of invoice value for duty assessment purposes and certain practices related to rules of origin)
- Standards, testing, labeling, and certification (for example, use of regional rather than international product standards, unnecessarily restrictive application of phytosanitary standards, and refusal to accept importing manufacturers' self-certification of conformance to foreign product standards)
- Government procurement (for example, "buy national" policies and closed bidding)
- Export subsidies (for example, export financing on preferential terms and agricultural export subsidies that displace exports in third-country markets)
- Lack of intellectual property protection (for example, piracy of copyrighted works, inadequate patent protection, and counterfeiting of trademarks)
- Countertrade and offsets (for example, foreign-government-mandated barter agreements that displace exports in third-country markets and government requirements for company exports as a condition for allowing imports)
- Services barriers (for example, prohibitions on imports, screen time quotas for foreign films, and requirements that imports be carried by national flag vessels)
- Investment barriers (for example, limitations on foreign equity participation, local content and export performance requirements, and restrictions on transferring earnings and capital)

Source: Office of the United States Trade Representative, *Foreign Trade Barriers* (Washington, D.C.: U.S. Government Printing Office, 1988), 2; (1994), 1–2.

The steel industry provides a good example. World steel production capacity and supply clearly exceed world demand. This is the result both of overly ambitious industrial development projects motivated by nationalistic aspirations and of technological innovation. However, a closer look at the steel industries of developed nations shows that demand for steel has also been reduced. In the automobile industry, for example, fewer automobiles are being produced, and they are being produced differently from ten years ago. Automobiles are more compact, lighter, and much more fuel efficient as a result of different consumer tastes and higher oil prices. The average automobile in the 1990s weighs more than 700 pounds less than in the 1970s. Accordingly, less steel is needed for its production. In addition, many components formerly made of steel are now being replaced by components made from other materials such as plastic. Even if imports of steel were to be excluded totally from the markets of industrialized nations, the steel industries could not regain the sales lost from a substantial change in the automotive industry.

If countries do not resort to the subtle mechanism of voluntary agreements, they often resort to old-fashioned quotas and tariffs. For example, Japanese heavy motorcycles imported into the United States were assessed a duty of 49.4 percent. This regulation kept the last U.S. producer of motorcycles, the Harley-Davidson Company, in business. Even though these tariffs have since been removed—and one year early at that—and the firm keeps on producing heavy motorcycles, one can rightfully question whether the cost imposed on U.S. consumers who preferred foreign products during the four years of tariff imposition was justified. Similarly, quotas have been proposed on imports of tuna fish packed in water. U.S. producers have complained that Japanese processors are taking away their market share in this field. However, from a historical perspective, it was U.S. processors who encouraged Japanese concentration in water-packed tuna by preventing them in the early 1970s from entering the U.S. market with tuna fish packed in oil. At that time, the vast majority of canned tuna sold in the United States was packed in oil; only 7 percent was packed in water. Today, the situation has reversed itself; most canned tuna purchased is now packed in water. The Japanese, having had to concentrate since the 1970s on this small market niche, have grown quite successful in penetrating it and have become even more successful since it became a larger market niche. The market share situation changed not because of Japanese ingenuity but because of changing consumer tastes, to which the Japanese were ready to respond while many U.S. manufacturers were not.

A third major method by which trade has been restricted is through **nontariff barriers.** Typically, these barriers are much more subtle than tariffs. Compared with tariffs or even subsidies, which are visible and at least force products to compete for market acceptance on dimensions other than price, such nontariff barriers are much more difficult to detect, prove, and quantify. For example, these barriers may be government or private-sector "buy domestic" campaigns, which affect importers and sometimes even foreign direct investors. Other nontariff barriers consist of providing preferential treatment to domestic bidders over foreign bidders, using national standards that are not comparable to international standards, placing emphasis on design rather than performance, and providing for general difficulties in the market entry of foreign products. Most famous in this regard are probably the measures implemented by France. To stop or at least to reduce the importation of foreign video recorders, France ruled in 1983 that all of them had to be sent through the customs station at Poitiers. This customshouse is located in the middle of the country, was woefully understaffed, and was open only a few days each week. In addition, the few customs agents at Poitiers insisted on opening each package separately in order to inspect the merchandise. Within a few weeks, imports of video recorders in France came to a halt. The French government, however, was able to point to

TABLE 2.6   Back-to-School Bill

Item	Free Market Price[a]	Price with Current Trade Restraints
1 boy's sweater	$20	$25
1 pair cotton blue jeans	$14.50	$18
1 book-bag knapsack	$12	$16
1 vinyl handbag	$10	$12
1 leather handbag	$40	$44
1 clock radio	$30	$32
1 Walkman-style radio	$18.70	$20
1 tuna sandwich	$ 1.80	$ 2
1 peanut butter sandwich	$ 1	$ 1.50
1 candy bar	$ 0.15	$ 0.30

[a]Prices calculated based on G. Hufbauer, Diane T. Berliner, and Kimberly Ann Elliott, *Trade Protection in the United States* (Washington, D.C.: Institute for International Economics, 1986), and 1986 tariff rates quoted by the U.S. International Trade Commission and the U.S. Commerce Department.

international agreements and to the fact that officially all measures were in full conformance with the law.

In 1994, the Clinton Administration attempted a new approach to trade policy negotiations. Major efforts were made to introduce new import quotas, this time not to keep imports out but to increase exports. The focus of U.S.-Japanese trade negotiations rested on committing the Japanese government to agree to quantitative import goals for U.S. products. Basically, the idea was to ensure more U.S. exports to Japan, not through the negotiation of reduced import barriers, but through agreements that would guarantee specific market penetration outcomes for U.S. industries. While the Japanese government disagreed with the approach, it was widely hailed in the United States as a new strategy in trade policy. Yet at the same time, cautious voices argued that this approach encouraged government planning and control of the private economy, an approach that had proven unsuccessful with the demise of the centrally planned Soviet Union.[12]

The primary result of all of these trade restrictions is that many actions are taken that are contrary to what we know is good for the world and its citizens. Industries are preserved, but only at great peril to the continued existence of the world trade framework and at a substantial cost to consumers. The direct costs of these actions are hidden and do not evoke much public complaint because they are spread out over a multitude of individuals. Yet, as Table 2.6 shows, these costs are real and burdensome and directly affect the standard of living of individuals and the competitiveness of firms. It has been estimated that in 1990, the total cost to U.S. consumers alone due to import restraints amounted to $70 billion. For example, abolishing import barriers in the apparel industry would let U.S. consumers gain more than $21 billion. Consumer gains would be $3.2 billion in the textile industry; $1.3 billion for sugar; $1.2 billion for dairy products; and $54 million for peanuts.[13] Even though each trade restriction may not be very significant in its impact on individuals, it should be remembered that over time and across products these costs accumulate and prevent consumers from spending their hard-earned money on other products of their choice.

---

[12] Michael R. Czinkota, "U.S. and Japan Must Find a New Common Ground," *The Asian Wall Street Journal Weekly*, February 28, 1994.

[13] Gary Clyde Hufbauer and Kimberly Ann Elliott, *Measuring the Costs of Protection in the United States* (Washington, D.C.: Institute for International Economics, 1994).

Restrictions of Exports

In addition to imposing restraints on imports, nations also control their exports. The United States, for example, places a major emphasis on export controls because it regards trade as a privilege rather than a right or a necessity. U.S. export-controls legislation focuses on national security controls—that is, the controls of exports that might adversely affect the safety of the nation in areas such as weapons exports or high-technology exports. In addition, exports are controlled for the purposes of foreign policy and short supply. These controls restrict the international marketing activities of firms if an administration feels that such a restriction would or could send a necessary foreign policy message to another country. This is done regardless of whether the message will have any impact or whether similar products can easily be obtained from companies in other nations. Although perhaps valuable as a tool of international relations, such policies give U.S. firms the reputation of being unreliable suppliers and may divert sales to firms in other countries.

Countries also often establish and implement domestic regulations without regard for their international trade effects. In the United States, for example, the breakup of AT&T and the subsequent changes in the purchasing practices of this organization were never considered in light of the potential impact they might have on foreign sourcing. The same holds true for the deregulation of the airline industry in the United States. All over the world, countries pass legislation that has a profound impact on the ability of firms to compete abroad. The "side effects" of such laws on the international marketplace are often ignored because countries view the setting of domestic policies as their sovereign right. Yet, given the linkages among economies, this view is unwarranted and often very dangerous. It places firms at a competitive disadvantage in the international marketplace and makes easier the competition of foreign firms in the domestic market.

Export Promotion Efforts in the United States

Many countries provide export promotion assistance to their firms. Key reasons for such assistance are the national need to earn foreign currency, the encouragement of domestic employment, and the increase in domestic economic activity. Many forms of export promotion can also be seen as government distortion of trade, since government support simply results in a subsidization of profitability or reduction of risk. The International Marketplace 2.4 gives an example of such a situation. Yet, there are instances where such intervention may be justified. Government support can be appropriate if it annuls unfair foreign practices, increases market transparency and therefore contributes to the better functioning of markets,[14] or helps overcome, in the interest of long-term national competitiveness, the short-term orientation of firms.[15]

U.S. policymakers have taken several steps to improve the international trade performance of U.S. firms. The Department of Commerce has added new information services that provide U.S. companies with data on foreign trade and marketing developments. Also, the Foreign Commercial Service, which formerly was part of the Department of State, has been reformed and now falls under the aegis of the U.S. Department of

---

[14] *Die Aussenwirtschaftsförderung der wichtigsten Konkurrenzländer der Bundesrepublik Deutschland—Ein Internationaler Vergleich* (The export promotion of the most important countries competing with the Federal Republic of Germany—An international comparison)(Berlin: Deutsches Institut für Wirtschaftsforschung, June 1991).

[15] Masaaki Kotabe and Michael R. Czinkota, "State Government Promotion of Manufacturing Exports: A Gap Analysis," *Journal of International Business Studies* (Winter 1992): 637–658.

Need Help Advertising? Tax Dollars Will Pay!

In 69 countries on 6 continents, Dole Food Company sells more than 100 different products. It is the world's single largest supplier of fresh fruit and vegetables. The corporate motto is "The sun never sets on a Dole farm or a Dole ship." Dole is proud, but not too proud, or too big, to win a government subsidy of its advertising costs. Since 1986, the company has received almost $15 million in federal funds for supermarket promotions in Japan and magazine ads in Europe. All the while, Dole doubled its revenue and posted $570 million in profits.

"It's a great deal if you can get it," says agricultural economist Gordon Rausser. The deal is the U.S. Department of Agriculture's (USDA) Market Promotion Program (MPP), which has paid out $400 million since 1986 to individual companies to spend, basically as they please, on advertising their products. An additional $600 million has gone to generic ads of U.S. products. This great deal does not stop at U.S. shores—foreign firms with U.S. suppliers have collected $78 million. Gunze, one of Japan's largest underwear manufacturers, received $1.6 million and a Turkish cigarette factory received $650,000.

"This is an outrageous program . . . an especially egregious program" states former Pennsylvania Congressman Peter H. Kostmayer, who had made attempts to restrict the funding. The former legislator and others like him attack the program because they say many of the companies would spend the money anyway. Former USDA Chief Economist Daniel Sumner has a similar view: "The question is not, do these funds help us sell more. The question is, why are you and I paying for it instead of the industries?" A case in point: The government's $785,000 subsidy to M&M/Mars in 1992 was minuscule for a company with an annual advertising budget of $272.4 million. When asked why Mars would even bother applying for federal funds, the company spokesman said, "The analogy is to a mortgage deduction; if it's available, you would certainly take advantage of it." A USDA study showed that $1 of program funds generates $2 to $7 worth of exports. But the issue remains: Are taxpayers simply reimbursing companies for money they would have spent anyway?

The Department of Agriculture does not focus on whether huge, profitable corporations need this help or whether they would have spent their own money regardless. Officials simply tout the increases in agricultural exports, especially of "high-value" foods like Dole's, and the help they bring to the trade deficit. Emphasis is placed on the fact that 60 percent of the funds go to generic ads which convey the virtues of buying American products. Program officials say the department helps guarantee that individual firms will spend their checks wisely by requiring them to put up matching funds. No graduation date, however, is given to the recipient companies—two-thirds of those receiving at least $1 million have benefited from the program for at least five years.

When Congress created the MPP (now referred to by some as "More Perks Please") in 1986, agricultural exports had greatly fallen in the previous five years. Congress enacted the Export Enhancement Program for such goods as wheat, barley, and rice. This program begat MPP, MPP begat SOAP (sunflower seed oil program), and SOAP begat COAP (cotton seed oil program). In the end, nonagricultural goods, which account for 90 percent of U.S. exports, received only 10 percent of federal export promotion funds.

Source: Sharon LaFraniere, "U.S. Helps Pay for Food Ads Abroad," *The Washington Post*, May 16, 1993, A1.

Commerce. Many new professionals were hired to provide an inward and outward link for U.S. business in terms of information flow and market assistance. In addition, new programs were implemented at the State Department and the Foreign Service Institute aimed at providing some training in international business to embassy staff serving abroad. Even ambassadors are now briefed on how to encourage and support U.S. business interests at their posts.

In terms of comparative efforts, however, U.S. export promotion activities still lag far behind the support provided by other major industrial nations. The United States ranks rather low in both financial expenditures and manpower, as Figure 2.2 shows. Moreover, the numbers reflect only official—that is, public-sector—export promotion support. Many countries also provide substantial levels of private-sector support, which exists to

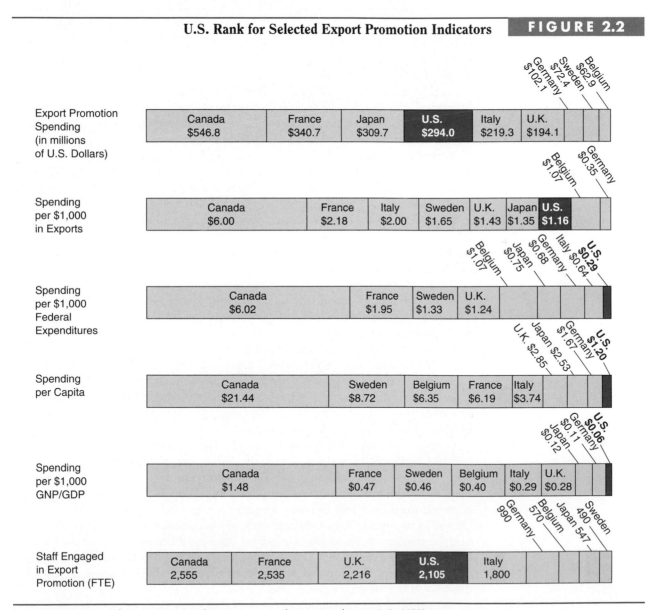

U.S. Rank for Selected Export Promotion Indicators — FIGURE 2.2

Source: U.S. Department of Commerce, U.S. and Foreign Commercial Service (Washington, D.C., 1988).

2.5

THE INTERNATIONAL MARKETPLACE

The Mittelstand: A Role Model for U.S. Exporters

Looking for an export model? A small but growing number of American executives are starting to view Germany's small to mid-sized companies as a more appropriate model for U.S. exporters than the often praised Japanese model. This group of German companies, commonly called the Mittelstand, has more than 300,000 members and collectively generates 30 percent of the country's yearly exports. With fewer than 500 employees apiece, the Mittelstand companies produce two-thirds of Germany's gross national product, train nine out of every ten apprentices, and employ four of every five workers.

Mittelstand companies manufacture all kinds of products. Generally, they have grown large by targeting small but highly profitable niches in global markets. Pumping large portions of revenue into research and development, these companies routinely beat larger firms to market with new products. For example, the Dortmund-based Geers Company brought the world's smallest hearing aid from the drawing board to shop floors in just nine months. In contrast, Siemens Company, Geers's large and powerful rival, took almost three years to get a micro hearing aid to market. Geers's new hearing aid now generates 30 percent of the company's $34 million in annual sales.

In another example, the 65-person Ludwigsburg-based G. W. Barth Company, a manufacturer of cocoa bean roasting machinery, risked almost $2 million on complex new equipment. Developed in the early 1980s, the technologically advanced machinery offers customers like Ghiradelli Chocolate Company and Hershey Foods Corporation added control over the taste of their chocolate products. Although G. W. Barth remains the smallest company in the industry based on the number of employees, it now holds more than 70 percent of the international market, an increase from 25 percent a decade ago.

An additional reason for the Mittelstand success is a superior export infrastructure that greatly assists smaller companies. Staffed by diplomats, bankers, and trade-association officials, the government-sponsored export network helps spot, process, and finance export orders. The network, consisting of local/national agencies, universities, chambers of commerce, and industry associations, has helped to drive Germany's exporting success. Although this system is similar to the one being set up in the United States, it has one major advantage: Because Germany started the export drive in the 1950s, it has had several decades to work out the kinks. The United States, on the other hand, is just beginning to build an export assistance network.

Principal benefits of the German export network for small business are financial and technical assistance. Small companies are eligible for up to $6 million in inexpensive funding from the government and are also eligible to receive substantial research grants. Industry associations provide standard contracts translated into different languages and offer legal assistance at no charge to members. A centralized embassy information network provides export information at the touch of a button. And local banks go out of their way to help the Mittelstand. For example, Deutsche Bank gave G. W. Barth use of an office and a secretary while the machinery manufacturer prospected for business in Indonesia, Nigeria, and Russia.

The result of this assistance network is that even companies competing at a global labor cost disadvantage are able to excel. Take the Wilhem Zuleeg company, an 85-person, $18-million textile manufacturer. Pressured by low-cost Asian rivals, Zuleeg still churns out high-fashion fabrics for designers such as Anne Klein, Cerruti, and Georges Resch. Boasting the most modern machinery available, the company has increased exports from zero three years ago to 20 percent today. Indeed, Zuleeg, along with hundreds of similar Mittelstand companies, has led Germany to a position as the world's number one textile exporter, with combined sales of more than $11 billion a year.

Sources: Gail E. Shares, John Templeman, Robert Neff, and Stanley Reed, "Think Small: Export Lessons to Be Learned from Germany's Mid-size Companies," *Business Week*, November, 4, 1991, 58–65; William J. Holstein, "Why Johann Can Export but Johnny Can't," *Business Week*, November 4, 1991, 64.

a much lesser degree in the United States. The International Marketplace 2.5 provides an example.

A new focus has come about in the area of export financing. Although many efforts were made in the past to reduce the activities of the Export-Import Bank of the United States, policymakers have increasingly recognized that U.S. business may be placed at a disadvantage if it cannot meet the subsidized financing rates of foreign suppliers. The bank, charged with the new mission of aggressively meeting foreign export-financing conditions, has in recent years even resorted to offering mixed aid credits. These take the form of loans composed partially of commercial interest rates and partially of highly subsidized developmental aid interest rates. In addition, the bank also collaborates more with U.S. commercial banks to be more accessible to firms, and has decided to accept larger commitments, such as the $6 billion Boeing/McDonnell Douglas sale to Saudi Arabia. The long-term effect of these actions will be difficult to predict, particularly since some of the repayment terms stretch over a substantial length of time. In the short term, more financing and guarantees by the Export-Import Bank will certainly increase international sales.

Tax legislation that inhibited the employment of Americans by U.S. firms abroad has also been altered to be more favorable to U.S. firms. In the past, U.S. nationals living abroad were, with some minor exclusion, fully subject to federal taxation. Because the cost of living abroad can often be quite high—rent for a small apartment can approach the range of $2,000-plus per month—this tax structure often imposed a significant burden on U.S. firms and citizens abroad. Therefore, companies frequently were not able to send U.S. employees abroad. However, as the result of a tax code revision that allows a substantial amount of income (up to $70,000) to remain tax free, more Americans can now be posted abroad. In their work they may specify the use of American products and thus enhance the competitive opportunities of U.S. firms.

One other export promotion development was the passage of the Export Trading Company Act of 1982. Intended to be the American response to Japanese sogoshoshas, this legislation permits firms to work together to form **export consortia.** The basic idea was to provide the foreign buyer with a one-stop shopping center in which a group of U.S. firms could offer a variety of complementary and competitive products. By exempting U.S. firms from current antitrust statutes, and by permitting banks to cooperate in the formation of these ventures through direct capital participation and the financing of trading activities, the government hoped that more firms could participate in the international marketplace. Although this legislation was originally hailed as a masterstroke and a key measure in turning around the decline in U.S. competitiveness abroad, it has not attracted a large number of successful firms. It appears that the legislation may not have provided sufficient incentive for banks, export service firms, or exporters to participate. Banks simply may find domestic profit margins to be more attractive and safe; export service firms may be too small; and exporters themselves may be too independent to participate in such consortia.

A STRATEGIC OUTLOOK

Even though the United States currently may not appear to have an international trade policy, men and women in responsible positions have recognized the crucial importance of international trade to the national well-being. The U.S. national economy has simply become too intertwined with world trade to be considered independent from it.

Critical in the years to come will be the development of a trade policy in a positive fashion rather than in a reactive way that aims only at reducing imports. Protectionistic legislation can be helpful if it is not enacted. Proposals in Congress can be quite useful as bargaining chips in international negotiations. However, if passed, signed into law, and implemented, protectionistic legislation can result in the destruction of the international trade framework.

The mid-1990s are also witnessing a new perspective on government-business relations. In previous decades, government and business stayed at arm's length, and it was seen as inappropriate to involve the government in private-sector activities. Now, however, closer government-business collaboration is seen as one key to enhanced competitiveness. More mutual listening to each other and joint consideration of the long-term domestic and international repercussions of policy actions and business strategy can indeed pay off. Perhaps it will make both business and government more responsive to each other's needs. At least it will reduce the failures that can result from a lack of collaboration and insufficient understanding of linkages, as described in the International Marketplace 2.6.

2.6

THE INTERNATIONAL MARKETPLACE

A Marketing Approach to Trade

U.S. trade negotiations with Japan in the wood-products industry and subsequent results provide an excellent example of American industry's difficulties in understanding and responding to foreign demand. The U.S. General Accounting Office reports that for more than a decade, the United States has negotiated with the Japanese government to allow more U.S. solid wood products to enter the Japanese market, particularly in the construction field. High-level meetings, ongoing negotiations, government financial support, and industry demonstration projects were to achieve that goal.

After all of these efforts, much has been accomplished. Japanese building codes which, due to fire-code provisions had prohibited construction of multistory wooden buildings, were changed. Product certification was made less costly and less complicated. Certification authority, previously the exclusive purview of the Ministry of Construction, was delegated to foreign testing organizations such as the American Plywood Association in the United States. Japan's tariffs were lowered for processed solid wood products—for softwood plywood to 10 percent from 16 percent, for glue-laminated beams to 4 percent from 15 percent. To top it all off, the Foreign Agricultural Service spent close to $18 million to promote U.S. wood-product sales in Japan.

Considering these successes, one would expect U.S. leadership in the market for solid wood products in Japan and rapid employment growth back home. Instead, the market leadership belongs to Canada, and job increases in the United States have been marginal.

There are several reasons for this situation. First, Canadian firms were much quicker than U.S. companies to take advantage of the changes. Canadian firms obtained certification much faster and were more aggressive in their marketing. They understand the different specifications and grades of wood products used in Japan, they pay attention to product quality and appearance, and they demonstrate more commitment to market and after-sales service requirements such as the development of manuals in Japanese. By contrast, U.S. firms tend to provide their information in English, tend to be less reliable as long-range suppliers, show little interest in after-sales service, and do not meet Japanese quality and appearance standards.

Second, and of even greater importance, is the U.S. disregard of the Japanese market. American companies try to sell what they produce to the Japanese, rather than producing what the Japanese want to buy. The largest portion of Japan's market for solid wood products is in post and beam construction, not in timber frames. Only 7 percent of new wooden homes are built with U.S. two-by-four products. Most other wooden housing construction uses four-by-four posts and boards for framing and is based on a three-by-six-foot module that fits the standard-sized tatami mats that cover Japanese floors. In other words, U.S. companies have focused all of their energies on increasing their penetration of the smallest part of the market, and have done so with only limited success.

Third, those U.S. firms that do attempt to adjust their products to Japanese market requirements encounter major problems in financing the new equipment and longer export payment terms. They also run into human resource problems when trying to meet Japanese quality standards or searching for international business expertise.

What do U.S. companies need to do differently? As Washington becomes more involved in trade, it should do so in a market-oriented way. The key considerations for U.S. trade policy need to be:

- A focus on market opportunities that make a difference;
- Identification of the needs and desires of foreign customers;
- Industry commitment to government market-opening approaches; and
- A link between trade policy and domestic assistance to firms planning to go abroad.

Washington needs to explicitly recognize that the times when the United States opened foreign markets simply for the well-being of the world are over. Funds should only be expended if the market is large enough to warrant attention and government actions are fully supported and followed up by industry. American trade policy needs to be focused on those issues that make a meaningful difference in terms of jobs and economic activity. After all, that is what funds government operations, provides taxes, reduces adjustment expenditures, and pays for health care.

Source: Michael Czinkota, "Washington Needs a Marketing Approach to Trade," *The Asian Wall Street Journal Weekly*, June 28, 1993, 12.

Very important is also the consideration of the **locus of control of trade policy.** A variety of regulatory agencies could become involved in administering U.S. trade policy. Although such agencies would be useful from the standpoint of addressing narrowly defined grievances, they carry the danger that commercial policy will be determined by a new chorus of discordant voices. This seems even more threatening when one considers that many regulatory agencies see themselves mainly responsible to Congress or to specific constituencies rather than to the administration. By shifting the power of setting trade policy from the administration to agencies or even to states, the term *new federalism* could be given a quite unexpected meaning and might cause progress at the international negotiation level to grind to a halt. No U.S. negotiator can expect to retain the goodwill of foreign counterparts if he or she cannot place on the table issues that can be negotiated without constantly having to check back with different authorities.

Trade policy can also take either a multilateral or a bilateral approach. In a **bilateral approach,** negotiations are carried out mainly between two nations, whereas in a **multilateral approach,** negotiations are carried out among a wide variety of nations. The approach can also be broad, covering a wide variety of products and services, or it can be narrow, focusing on specific sectoral problems.

As a quick and temporary measure, bilateral approaches and a **sectoral focus** seem quite appealing. Very specific problems can be discussed and can be resolved expediently. Yet, even though negotiators may be well intentioned, **sectoral negotiation** outcomes may, on occasion, produce some quite unexpected results. For example, when the United States negotiated a reduction of Japanese market barriers to citrus fruits and juice imports, the expectation was that mainly U.S. firms would benefit. Yet, in reality, it was Brazilian orange juice producers that were the primary beneficiaries. Their products were lower priced and most of them are owned by Japanese investors.

Bilateral approaches in turn may seem quite appealing, particularly in an era in which there appears to be an emergence of new trading blocs in both Europe and the Western Hemisphere. The growth in bilateral legislation and the increasingly country-specific orientation of trade negotiators bear witness to the appeal. However, every time bilateral negotiations take place, their very nature excludes a multitude of other interested parties. To be successful, negotiations need to produce winners. If a constant set of winners and losers is produced, then negotiations have no chance for long-term success because no one wants to take the position of the loser. This points in the direction of multilateral negotiation approaches on a broad scale. Here concessions can be traded off, thus making it possible for all nations to emerge and declare themselves as winners. The difficulty lies in devising enough incentives to bring the appropriate and desirable partners to the bargaining table.

SUMMARY

International trade has often played a major role in world history. The rise and fall of the Roman Empire and the emergence of feudalism can be attributed to trade. Since 1945, the Western nations have made concerted efforts to improve the trade environment and expand trade activities. In order for them to do so, various multinational organizations, such as the GATT, the IMF, and the World Bank, were founded. In addition, several economic blocs like the EU, NAFTA, and the GCC were formed. Many of these organizations have been very successful in their mission, yet new realities of the trade environment demand new types of action.

Over the years, the U.S. international trade position has eroded substantially, and the U.S. share of world exports has declined precipitously from 25 percent in the 1950s. This has occurred mainly because other countries have expanded their trade activities. U.S. firms have been too complacent and disinterested in foreign markets to keep up the pace. As a result, the great majority of U.S. exports are carried out by only 2,500 companies.

Successful foreign competitiveness in international trade has resulted in major trade deficits for the United States. Since each billion dollars worth of exports creates, directly and indirectly, almost 23,000 jobs, it is important for U.S. firms to concentrate on the opportunities the international market has to offer.

Some policymakers have responded to the poor U.S. trade performance by threatening the world with increasing protectionism. The danger of such a policy lies in the fact that world trade would shrink and standards of living would decline. Protectionism cannot, in the long run, prevent adjustment or increase productivity and competitiveness. It is therefore important to improve the capability of firms to compete internationally and to provide an international trade framework that facilitates international marketing activities.

Questions for Discussion

1. Why is international trade important to a nation?
2. Give examples of the effects of the "Pax Americana."
3. Discuss the role of "voluntary" import restraints in international marketing.
4. What is meant by multilateral negotiations?
5. How have consumer demands changed international trade?
6. Discuss the impact of import restrictions on consumers.
7. Discuss the effect of foreign direct investment on trade.

Recommended Readings

Baldassari, Mario, John McCallum, and Robert Mundell, eds. *Global Disequilibrium in the World Economy.* New York: St. Martin's Press, 1992.

Czinkota, Michael R., ed. *Improving U.S. Competitiveness.* Washington, D.C.: Government Printing Office, 1988.

Guide to the Evaluation of Trade Promotion Programmes. Geneva: International Trade Centre, UNCTAD/GATT, 1987.

Howell, Thomas R., ed. *Conflict among Nations: Trade Policies in the 1990s.* Boulder, CO: Westview Press, 1992.

Hufbauer, Gary Clyde, and Kimberly Ann Elliott. *Measuring the Costs of Protection in the United States.* Washington, D.C.: Institute for International Economics, 1994.

McKibbin, Warwick J., and Jeffrey D. Sachs. *Global Linkages: Macroeconomic Interdependence and Cooperation in the World Economy.* Washington, D.C.: Brookings Institution, 1991.

Porter, Michael E. *The Competitive Advantage of Nations.* New York: Free Press, 1990.

Stern, Robert M., ed. *The Multilateral Trading System: Analysis and Options for Change.* Ann Arbor: University of Michigan Press, 1993.

Waldmann, Raymond J. *Managed Trade.* Cambridge, MA: Ballinger, 1986.

Wolf, Charles, Jr. *Linking Economic Policy and Foreign Policy.* New Brunswick, NJ: Transaction Publishers, 1991.

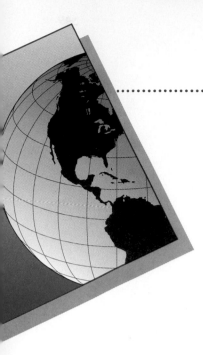

CHAPTER 3

The International Economic Environment

3.1

THE INTERNATIONAL MARKETPLACE

Finding A Home Amongst The Tigers

Sometime early in the next century, Asia will eclipse North America as the world's most powerful region. The region outpaced the growth of the world's 24 leading industrial economies by more than six times in 1993, having grown at least four times as fast each year in the 1990s. How can Asia grow at an average 7 percent (with some economies growing even faster, such as China at 12 percent) when Europe, Japan, and the United States are growing at an average of only 2 percent? The answer lies in a blend of ingredients that includes the region's traditional prowess at exporting, its rapid emergence as a market unto itself, and its resulting attraction to foreign investors.

A conservative assumption is that fully one billion Asians—not much less than the entire populations of North America, South America, and Europe—will be living in households with some consumer-spending power (meaning that they can buy at least basic goods such as color televisions, refrigerators and motorbikes). Perhaps 400 million of these consumers will have disposable incomes, at least equal to the rich-world average in 1993, to spend on houses, cars, computers, holidays, health care, and education. And if all of this consumer spending is to take place, immense investments will be needed to make it possible: power plants, roads, and airports among other things. Japan's Long-Term Credit Bank puts these investment needs at $1 trillion over the next decade.

Many marketers have had to adjust their thinking about Asia. Not long ago, companies such as Hewlett-Packard viewed Asia as a region with a large supply of labor but little potential for anything else. Today, Hewlett-Packard maintains a work force of 13,000 throughout Asia and had sales of $2 billion in 1992—about one-eighth of the corporate total.

As Asian customers have become more prosperous and more critical of the company's fortunes, Hewlett-Packard has expanded and upgraded its operations in the region. The company opened a laboratory in Japan in 1991, new manufacturing facilities in Japan and Malaysia in 1992, and beefed up its project management and design capacity in Singapore. Such investments in local operations have earned returns not only in additional sales, but also by providing the company with skills and expertise that it lacks in the United States.

"A company like ours has to be selling and competing out here," says Lee Ting, the Hong Kong–based chief of Hewlett-Packard's Asia-Pacific operations.

Sources: "A Growing Presence," *The Washington Post,* November 19, 1993, G1-G4; "A Survey of Asia," *The Economist,* October 30, 1993; "That Hum You Hear Is Asia Growing," *The Wall Street Journal,* October 18, 1993; and "Belief in an Imminent Asian Century Is Gaining Sway," *The Wall Street Journal,* May 17, 1993, A12.

The assessment of a foreign-market environment should start with the evaluation of economic variables relating to the size and nature of the markets. Because of the large number of worthwhile alternatives, initial screening of markets should be done efficiently yet effectively enough, with a wide array of economic criteria, to establish a preliminary estimate of market potential. One of the most basic characterizations of the world economy is provided in Figure 3.1, which incorporates many of the economic variables pertinent to marketers.

The Group of Five—listed in Figure 3.1 as the United States, Britain, France, Germany, and Japan—consists of the major industrialized countries of the world. This group is sometimes expanded to the **Group of Seven** (by adding Italy and Canada) and to the **Group of Ten** (by adding Sweden, the Netherlands, and Belgium). It may also be expanded to encompass the members of the Organization for Economic Cooperation and Development, OECD (which consists of 24 countries: Western Europe, the United States, Canada, Japan, Australia, and New Zealand).

Important among the middle-income developing countries are the newly industrialized countries (NICs), which include Singapore, Taiwan, Korea, Hong Kong, Brazil, and Mexico (some propose adding Malaysia and the Philippines to the list as well). Some of these NICs will earn a new acronym, RIC (rapidly industrializing countries); for example, by the end of the 1990s, South Korea expects to claim 7 percent of the global electronics market.[1] And, as seen in The International Marketplace 3.1, many of these countries will become important markets as well.

The major oil-exporting countries, in particular members of the Organization of Petroleum Exporting Countries (OPEC) and countries such as Nigeria, Venezuela, and Indonesia, are dependent on the price of oil for their world-market participation. Few analysts expect the dollar price per barrel to climb much higher than the mid-20s by 1995, which will not work in these countries' favor.

Many of the less-developed countries will depend on the success of their industrialization efforts in the years to come, even in the case of resource-rich countries that may find commodity prices being driven down by man-made substitutes. China, one of the major less-developed countries, became the second-largest exporter of textiles to the United States after it began increasing production in the 1980s. Despite an image of hopeless poverty, India has over 75 million middle-class consumers, more

---

[1] Richard I. Kirkland, "We're All in This Together," *Fortune,* February 2, 1987, 26–29.

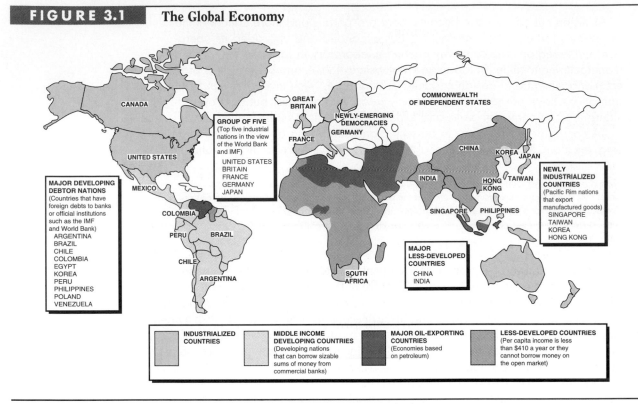

FIGURE 3.1   The Global Economy

Source: Adapted from "The Global Economy," *Washington Post*, January 19. 1986, H1. Reprinted with permission.

than Germany. A special group in this category consists of the countries saddled with a major debt burden, such as Egypt and Peru. The degree and form of their participation in the world market will largely depend on how the debt issue is solved with the governments of the major industrialized countries and the multilateral and commercial banks.

In the former centrally planned economies, dramatic changes are under way. A hefty capital inflow will be key to modernizing both the newly emerging democracies of Central Europe and the nations of the Commonwealth of Independent States. They are crippled by $60 billion in foreign debt and decades of Communist misrule. Desperately needed will be Western technology, management, and marketing know-how to provide better jobs and put more locally made and imported consumer goods in the shops. Within the groups, prospects vary: The future for countries such as Hungary, the Czech Republic, and Poland looks far better than it does for Romania, Bulgaria, the Baltics, and Russia.[2]

Classifications of markets will vary by originator and intended use. Marketers will combine economic variables to fit their planning purposes by using those that relate directly to the product and/or service the company markets, such as the market's ability to buy. For example, Table 3.1 provides a summary of an economic classification system used by the General Electric Company. This approach has countries divided into four basic categories, with the centrally planned economies given separate consideration because of their unique characteristics of strict governmental control and centralized

[2] "Pain of Reform," *Time*, February 17, 1992, 8–10; "Eastward, Ho!" *Business Week*, April 15, 1991, 51–53.

	TABLE 3.1
Economic Development Variable in Countries' Use of Electricity and Electrical Goods	

Less developed: These countries have primarily agrarian and/or extractive economies. High birthrates, along with limited infrastructures, account for the low per-capita income and usage of electricity. Electrification is limited to the main population centers. Generally, basic electrical equipment is imported.

Early developing: These countries have begun initial development of an infrastructure and have infant industries, especially mining and selected cottage manufactures. Target economic sectors may enjoy high growth rates even though per-capita income and electricity consumption are still modest. Progressively more sophisticated electrical equipment is imported, frequently to achieve forward integration of extractive industries.

Semideveloped: These countries have started an accelerated expansion of infrastructure and wide industrial diversification. Thus, per-capita income and electricity consumption are growing rapidly. Increased discretionary income and electrification allow greater ownership of autos and electrical appliances among the expanding middle class. Larger quantities of high-technology equipment are imported.

Developed: These countries enjoy well-developed infrastructures, high per-capita income and electricity consumption, and large-scale industrial diversification. They are also characterized by low rates of population and economic growth, as well as shifts in emphasis from manufacturing to service industries—notably transportation, communication, and information systems.

Centrally planned: The separate listing for these countries does not imply that they represent either a higher or a lower stage of economic development. They could have been distributed among each of the above four categories.

Source: V. Yorio, *Adapting Products for Export* (New York: Conference Board, 1983), 11.

procurement. This format takes into account both general country considerations—such as population, GNP, geography, manufacturing as a percentage of national product, infrastructure, and per-capita income—and narrower industry-specific considerations of interest to the company and its marketing efforts, such as extent of use of the product, total imports, and U.S. share of these imports.

The discussion that follows is designed to summarize a set of criteria that helps identify foreign markets and screen the most opportune ones for future entry or change of entry mode. Discussed are variables on which information is readily available from secondary sources such as international organizations, individual governments, and private organizations or associations.

The Statistical Yearbook of the United Nations, World Bank publications, and individual countries' *Statistical Abstracts* provide the starting point for market investigations. The more developed the market, the more data are available. Data are available on past developments as well as on projections of broader categories such as population and income. *Business International,* for example, annually compiles market-size indicators for 116 countries that account for more than 90 percent of the world's output in goods and services. The most recent summary, provided in the Appendix to Chapter 3, will be used throughout the discussion.

MARKET CHARACTERISTICS

The main dimensions of a market can be captured by considering variables such as those relating to the population and its various characteristics, infrastructure, geographical features of the environment, and foreign involvement in the economy.

TABLE 3.2	World Population Distribution, 1991 (in millions)			
	Western Europe	419.5	Middle East	192.2
	Eastern Europe	410.0	Latin America	416.3
	North America	279.7	Caribbean	35.4
	Asia	2,964.0	Africa	503.2
	Oceania	20.7		

Source: Indicators of Market Size, *Crossborder Monitor*, 1993.

Population

The total world population exceeded five billion people in 1990. The number of people in a particular market provides one of the most basic indicators of market size and is, in itself, indicative of the potential demand for certain staple items that have universal appeal and are generally affordable. As indicated by the data in Table 3.2, population is not evenly divided among the major regions of the world; Asia holds over half of the world's population.

These population figures can be analyzed in terms of marketing implications by noting that countries belonging to the European Union (EU) constitute 79 percent of the Western European population, and with the expansion of the EU in 1995, the percentage will rise to 85. The two largest entities in Asia, China and India, constitute nearly 70 percent of Asia's population. The greatest population densities are also to be found in Europe, providing the international marketer with a strategically located center of operation and ready access to the major markets of the world.

Population figures themselves must be broken down into meaningful categories in order for the marketer to take better advantage of them. Because market entry decisions may lie in the future, it is worthwhile to analyze population projections in the areas of interest and focus on their possible implications. Table 3.3 includes United Nations projections that point to a population explosion, but mainly in the developing countries. Northern Europe will show nearly zero population growth for the next 30 years, whereas the population of Africa will triple. Even in the low- or zero-growth markets, the news is not necessarily bad for the international marketer. Those in the 25-to-45 age group, whose numbers will be increasing between now and 1995, are among the most affluent consumers of all, having formed family units and started to consume household goods in large quantities as they reach the peak of their personal earnings potential. By the year 2000, they are expected to start spending more on leisure goods and health care and related services.[3]

To influence population growth patterns, governments will have to undertake, with the help of private enterprise, quite different social marketing tasks. These will range from promoting and providing incentives for larger families (in Scandinavia, for example) to increased family planning efforts (in Thailand, for example). Regardless of the outcome of such government programs, current trends will further accelerate the division of world markets into the "haves" and the "have-nots." More adjustment capability will be required on the part of companies that want to market in the developing countries because of lower purchasing power of individuals and increasing government participation in the marketing of basic products.

Depending on the marketer's interest, population figures can be classified to show specific characteristics of their respective markets. Age distribution and life expectancy

---

[3] *Consumer Europe* (London: Euromonitor, 1988), 24.

Population Projections by Region and Countries, 1990 to 2025

TABLE 3.3

Region and Country	1990	1995	2000	2025
World, total	5,248.5	5,679.3	6,127.1	8,177.1
More developed[a]	1,208.8	1,242.8	1,275.7	1,396.7
Less developed[a]	4,039.7	4,436.4	4,851.5	6,780.4
Africa	645.3	753.2	877.4	1,642.9
Eastern Africa[b]	189.7	224.7	266.2	531.4
Burundi	5.3	6.1	7.0	11.0
Kenya	25.4	31.4	38.5	82.9
Madagascar	11.6	13.4	15.6	29.7
Mozambique	16.2	18.8	21.8	39.7
Somalia	5.9	6.2	7.1	13.2
Tanzania	27.0	32.5	39.1	83.8
Uganda	18.8	22.5	26.8	52.3
Zimbabwe	10.5	12.6	16.1	32.7
Middle Africa[b]	71.9	83.0	96.1	183.5
Angola	10.0	11.5	13.2	24.5
Cameroon	11.1	12.6	14.4	25.2
Zaire	38.4	44.8	52.4	104.4
Northern Africa[b]	143.8	164.3	185.7	295.0
Algeria	26.0	30.5	35.2	57.3
Egypt	52.7	58.9	65.2	97.4
Morocco	27.6	31.9	36.3	59.9
Tunisia	8.1	8.9	9.7	13.6
Southern Africa[b]	42.3	48.1	54.5	90.7
South Africa	36.8	41.6	46.9	76.3
Western Africa[b]	197.6	233.1	275.0	542.4
Ghana	15.9	18.7	21.9	37.7
Guinea	6.1	7.0	7.9	13.9
Ivory Coast	11.5	13.4	15.6	28.1
Mali	9.3	10.7	12.4	21.4
Nigeria	113.3	135.5	161.9	338.1
Senegal	7.5	8.7	10.0	18.9
Latin America	453.2	501.3	550.0	786.6
Caribbean[b]	34.6	37.7	40.8	57.7
Cuba	10.5	11.2	11.7	13.6
Dominican Republic	7.0	7.7	8.4	12.2
Haiti	7.5	8.6	9.9	18.3
Middle America[b]	119.7	134.4	149.6	222.6
El Salvador	6.5	7.5	8.7	15.0
Guatemala	9.7	11.1	12.7	21.7
Mexico	89.0	99.2	109.2	154.1
Nicaragua	3.9	4.5	5.3	9.2
Temperate South America[b]	49.1	52.3	55.5	70.1
Argentina	32.9	35.1	37.2	47.4
Chile	13.1	14.0	14.9	18.8
Uruguay	3.1	3.2	3.4	3.9
Tropical South America[b]	249.8	276.9	304.1	436.3
Bolivia	7.3	8.4	9.7	18.3
Brazil	150.4	165.1	179.5	245.8
Colombia	31.8	34.9	38.0	51.7
Ecuador	10.9	12.7	14.6	25.7
Paraguay	4.2	4.8	5.4	8.6
Peru	22.3	25.1	28.0	41.0
Venezuela	21.3	24.2	27.2	42.8
Northern America[b]	275.2	286.8	297.7	347.3
Canada	27.1	28.3	29.4	34.4
United States	248.0	258.3	268.1	312.7
East Asia[b]	1,317.2	1,390.4	1,470.0	1,696.1
China: Mainland	1,119.6	1,184.2	1,255.7	1,460.1
Hong Kong	6.1	6.6	6.9	7.9

continued

TABLE 3.3   *Continued*

Region and Country	1990	1995	2000	2025
Japan	122.7	125.1	127.7	127.6
North Korea	22.4	24.9	27.3	37.6
South Korea	43.8	46.8	49.5	58.6
South Asia	1,740.2	1,909.4	2,073.7	2,770.6
Eastern South Asia[b]	440.4	480.8	519.7	684.7
Indonesia	178.4	191.9	204.5	255.3
Malaysia	17.3	19.1	20.6	26.9
Philippines	61.4	68.3	74.8	102.3
Singapore	2.7	2.9	3.0	3.2
Thailand	56.2	61.1	66.1	88.3
Vietnam	55.4	71.7	78.1	105.1
Middle South Asia[b]	1,189.9	1,279.9	1,386.7	1,815.9
Afghanistan	19.3	21.7	24.2	35.9
Bangladesh	115.2	130.3	145.8	219.4
India	831.9	899.1	961.5	1,188.5
Iran	51.8	58.7	65.5	96.2
Pakistan	113.3	128.0	142.6	212.8
Western South Asia[b]	129.9	148.7	168.3	270.0
Iraq	18.5	21.6	24.9	42.7
Israel	4.7	5.0	5.4	7.0
Lebanon	3.0	3.3	3.6	5.2
Saudi Arabia	13.5	16.1	18.9	33.5
Turkey	56.0	62.4	68.5	99.3
Europe (excluding former nations of the Soviet Union)	499.5	506.5	513.1	526.9
Central Europe	115.7	118.2	121.0	131.2
Bulgaria	9.4	9.6	9.7	10.2
Czechoslovakia	16.0	16.3	16.8	18.8
Hungary	10.8	10.8	10.9	10.9
Poland	39.0	40.2	41.4	45.9
Romania	23.9	24.8	25.6	29.2
Northern Europe[b]	82.6	83.0	83.4	83.6
Denmark	5.2	5.1	5.1	4.8
Finland	4.9	5.0	5.0	4.8
Ireland	3.8	4.0	4.2	5.2
Norway	4.2	4.2	4.2	4.3
Sweden	8.2	8.2	8.1	7.5
United Kingdom	55.8	56.0	56.2	56.4
Southern Europe[b]	146.4	150.0	153.1	162.8
Greece	10.2	10.5	10.7	11.8
Italy	57.4	57.9	58.2	56.9
Portugal	10.4	10.7	11.0	11.9
Spain	40.5	42.0	43.4	49.2
Western Europe[b]	154.8	155.3	155.6	149.3
Austria	7.5	7.5	7.5	7.3
Belgium	9.9	9.9	9.9	9.8
France	55.4	56.3	57.1	58.5
Netherlands	14.7	14.9	15.0	14.6
Switzerland	6.2	6.0	5.9	4.9
Germany	77.3	76.8	76.4	75.9
Former nations of the Soviet Union	291.3	303.1	314.8	367.1
Oceania[b]	26.7	28.5	30.4	39.5
Australia	16.7	17.7	18.7	23.5
New Zealand	3.4	3.6	3.7	4.2

[a] Regions

[b] Includes countries not shown separately

Source: Bureau of the Census, *Statistical Abstract of the United States, 1991* (Washington, D.C.: Government Printing Office, 1992), 830–832.

correlate heavily with the level of development of the market. Industrialized countries, with their increasing median age and a larger share of the population above 65, will open unique opportunities for international marketers with new products and services. A number of companies in the United States, for example, are marketing an adult diaper.

As the life expectancy in a market extends and new target markets become available, international marketers may be able to extend their products' life cycles by marketing them abroad. Interpretation of demographics will require some degree of experiential knowledge. As an example, which age categories of females should be included in an estimate of market potential for a new contraceptive? This would vary from the very early teens in the developing countries to higher age categories in Northern countries, where the maturing process is later.

An important variable for the international marketer is the size of the household. A **household** describes all the persons, both related and unrelated, who occupy a housing unit.[4] Within the EU, the average household size has shrunk from 2.9 to 2.7 persons since 1977 and is expected to decline further.[5] One factor behind the overall growth in households, and the subsequent decline in the average size, has been the increase in the numbers of divorced and sole-survivor households. One-person households are most common in Norway and Germany. This compares strikingly with countries such as Colombia, where the average household size is 6. With economic development usually bringing about more, but smaller-sized, households, international marketers of food products, appliances, and household goods have to adjust to patterns of demand; for example, they may offer single-serving portions of frozen foods and smaller appliances.

The increased urbanization of many markets has distinctly changed consumption patterns. Urban populations as a percentage of the total will vary from a low of 6 percent in Burundi to a high of 97 percent in Belgium.[6] The degree of urbanization often dictates the nature of the marketing task the company faces, not only in terms of distribution but also in terms of market potential and buying habits. Urban areas provide larger groups of consumers who may be more receptive to marketing efforts because of their exposure to other consumers (the demonstration effect) and to communication media. In markets where urbanization is recent and taking place rapidly, the marketer faces additional responsibility as a change agent, especially when incomes may be low and the conditions for the proper use of the products may not be adequate. This is especially true in countries where rapid industrialization is taking place, such as Greece, Spain, and Portugal.

When using international data sources, the international marketer must recognize that definitions of a construct may vary among the many secondary sources. The concept of **urbanization,** for example, has different meanings depending on where one operates. In the United States, an urban area is defined as a place of 2,500 or more inhabitants; in Sweden, it is a built-up area with at least 200 inhabitants with no more than 200 meters between houses; in Mauritius, it is a town with proclaimed legal limits. Comparability, therefore, is concerned with the ends and not the means (or the definition).

Income Markets require not only people but also purchasing power, which is a function of income, prices, savings, and credit availability.

Apart from basic staple items, for which population figures provide an estimate, income is most indicative of the market potential for most consumer and industrial

---

[4] James F. Engel, Roger D. Blackwell, and Paul W. Miniard, *Consumer Behavior* (Hinsdale, IL: Dryden, 1991), 270.

[5] *European Marketing Data and Statistics 1994* (London: Euromonitor, 1994), 391.

[6] The World Bank, *World Development Report 1993* (New York: Oxford University Press, 1993), 298–299.

TABLE 3.4	Gross National Product by Country										
	Current Dollars (billions)				**Constant (1989) Dollars (billions)**				**Per Capita (dollars)**		
Country	**1980**	**1985**	**1988**	**1989**	**1980**	**1985**	**1988**	**1989**	**1980**	**1985**	**1989**
United States	2,732.0	4,015.0	4,881.0	5,201.0	3,865.0	4,389.0	4,881.0	5,201.0	16,970	18,340	20,910
Afghanistan	2.9	3.1[1]	3.1[1]	(NA)	4.1	3.4[1]	3.1[1]	(NA)	276	246	(NA)
Algeria	30.2	49.0	52.3	45.3	42.8	53.5	52.3	45.3	2,270	2,427	1,831
Argentina	76.3	84.4	97.3	54.1	108.0	92.2	97.3	54.1	3,824	3,038	1,694
Austria	78.0	108.9	123.7	125.2	110.3	119.0	123.7	125.2	14,620	15,750	16,430
Bangladesh	10.1	15.6	19.0	20.0	14.3	17.1	19.0	20.0	162	168	180
Belgium	95.4	128.0	149.3	154.6	135.0	140.0	149.3	154.6	13,710	14,200	15,620
Brazil	217.8	300.9	372.6	462.3	308.2	328.9	372.6	462.3	2,502	2,349	3,090
Bulgaria	34.9	47.0	53.8	49.6	49.3	51.4	53.8	49.6	5,576	5,743	5,530
Burma	6.1	9.9	11.0	16.3	8.6	10.9	11.0	16.3	255	291	404
Canada	260.6	384.8	471.8	531.0	368.7	420.6	471.8	531.0	15,320	16,570	20,240
Chile	12.7	15.3	20.3	23.3	17.9	16.8	20.3	23.3	1,613	1,389	1,809
China:											
Mainland[1]	180.6	377.1	545.6	603.5	255.5	412.2	545.6	603.5	260	394	547
Taiwan	46.0	81.7	119.4	150.2	65.1	89.3	119.4	150.2	3,659	4,632	7,390
Colombia	21.0	29.4	36.6	36.9	29.7	32.2	36.6	36.9	1,119	1,094	1,139
Czechoslovakia	87.7	120.5	138.4	123.2	124.0	131.7	138.4	123.2	8,129	8,494	7,876
East Germany	115.0	163.5	186.5	159.4	162.7	178.7	186.5	159.4	9,720	10,740	9,669
Egypt	35.6	61.8	77.6	69.8	50.4	67.6	77.6	69.8	1,193	1,376	1,342
Ethiopia	3.4	4.2	5.5	6.0	4.7	4.6	5.5	6.0	123	106	120
France	573.5	790.8	920.0	954.1	811.4	864.4	920.0	954.1	15,060	15,670	17,000
Ghana	3.1	3.9	5.0	5.1	4.4	4.3	5.0	5.1	407	330	350
Greece	34.5	46.3	52.3	52.9	48.8	50.6	52.3	52.9	5,064	5,089	5,286
Hungary	46.7	62.5	71.8	64.7	66.1	68.3	71.8	64.7	6,174	6,417	6,119
India	122.2	208.3	268.7	267.4	173.0	227.7	268.7	267.4	251	297	321
Indonesia	38.4	62.4	76.2	89.4	54.4	68.2	76.2	89.4	351	394	479
Iran	221.1	311.8	318.4[1]	77.5	312.9[1]	340.9[1]	318.4[1]	77.5	7,988	7,252	1,440
Iraq[1]	88.1	61.7	65.8	(NA)	124.6	67.4	65.8	(NA)	9,441	4,267	(NA)
Italy	479.6	669.4	796.5	860.0	678.5	731.7	796.5	860.0	12,020	12,810	14,940
Japan	1,470.0	2,314.0	2,856.0	2,820.0	2,080.0	2,530.0	2,856.0	2,820.0	17,810	20,950	22,900
Kenya	4.2	6.3	8.3	7.9	6.0	6.9	8.3	7.9	358	336	338
Madagascar	1.3	1.5	1.7	2.3	1.9	1.7	1.7	2.3	217	168	205
Malaysia	16.1	25.7	32.3	36.0	22.8	28.1	32.3	36.0	1,659	1,825	2,099

products and services. For the marketer to make use of information on gross national products of various nations, such as that summarized in Table 3.4, further knowledge is needed on distribution of income. Per-capita GNP is often used as a primary indicator for evaluating purchasing power. This figure shows great variation between countries, as indicated by Switzerland's $27,510 and Bangladesh's $180. The wide use of GNP figures can be explained by their easy availability, but they should nevertheless be used with caution. In industrialized countries, the richest 10 percent of the population consume 20 percent of all goods and services whereas the respective figure for the developing countries may be as high as 47 percent.[7] In some markets, income distribution produces wide gaps between population groups. The more developed the economy, the more income distribution tends to converge toward the middle class.

---

[7] The World Bank, *World Development Report 1993* (New York: Oxford University Press, 1993), 296.

Country	Current Dollars (billions)				Constant (1989) Dollars (billions)				Per Capita (dollars)		
	1980	1985	1988	1989	1980	1985	1988	1989	1980	1985	1989
Mexico	112.2	157.5	173.4	186.7	158.7	172.2	173.4	186.7	2,264	2,191	2,170
Morocco	10.0	14.4	18.8	21.7	14.1	15.8	18.8	21.7	687	680	866
Mozambique	1.0	1.0	1.0	1.1	1.4	1.1	1.0	1.1	117	77	78
Nepal	1.5	2.5	3.2	2.8	2.1	2.7	3.2	2.8	143	162	150
Netherlands	142.5	194.1	225.5	222.5	201.5	212.2	225.5	222.5	14,250	14,640	14,980
Nigeria	21.4	25.4	28.7	27.5	30.2	27.7	28.7	27.5	335	270	239
North Korea[1]	21.9	26.3	29.2	30.0	31.0	28.8	29.2	30.0	1,732	1,410	1,427
Pakistan	15.6	27.8	36.4	36.8	22.0	30.4	36.4	36.8	258	307	330
Peru	26.5	33.1	39.3	40.8	37.5	36.2	39.3	40.8	2,168	1,836	1,903
Philippines	26.1	32.1	40.4	44.0	37.0	35.1	40.4	44.0	727	602	697
Poland	120.2	160.5	179.7	174.7	170.1	175.5	179.7	174.7	4,780	4,716	4,625
Portugal	24.0	31.8	40.6	44.6	34.0	34.7	40.6	44.6	3,474	3,419	4,323
Romania	75.8	102.9	117.7	113.4	107.3	112.5	117.7	113.4	4,832	4,949	4,896
South Africa	50.2	71.3	84.1	86.8	71.0	78.0	84.1	86.8	2,437	2,379	2,253
South Korea	58.9	111.1	168.0	210.1	83.3	121.4	168.9	210.1	2,184	2,958	4,920
Soviet Union	1,532.0	2,145.0	2,526.0	2,664.0	2,167.0	2,345.0	2,526.0	2,664.0	8,136	8,408	9,226
Spain	193.2	266.8	330.1	370.7	273.3	291.7	330.1	370.7	7,291	7,555	9,471
Sri Lanka	3.5	5.8	6.9	6.9	5.0	6.4	6.9	6.9	335	399	409
Sudan	5.5	6.4	7.4	15.6	7.8	7.0	7.4	15.6	412	310	608
Sweden	107.5	149.3	175.3	185.8	152.1	163.2	175.3	185.8	18,300	19,540	21,900
Switzerland	115.7	163.1	188.9	184.3	163.7	178.3	188.9	184.3	25,640	27,300	27,510
Syria	9.3	13.6	14.8	19.3	13.1	14.9	14.8	19.3	1,512	1,435	1,608
Tanzania	1.8	2.4	2.9	2.6	2.6	2.7	2.9	2.6	137	120	105
Thailand	24.3	41.0	56.3	68.8	34.3	44.8	56.3	68.8	731	866	1,246
Turkey	32.2	52.3	68.4	77.3	45.5	57.2	68.4	77.3	1,008	1,128	1,380
Uganda	2.6	4.0	4.5	4.0	3.7	4.3	4.5	4.0	291	294	233
United Kingdom	459.1	657.3	801.6	834.4	649.5	718.5	801.6	834.4	11,530	12,690	14,580
Venezuela	40.8	47.7	60.0	41.5	57.7	52.1	60.0	41.5	3,837	3,007	2,158
West Germany	748.0	1,029.0	1,213.0	1,207.0	1,058.0	1,124.0	1,213.0	1,207.0	17,190	18,430	19,520
Yugoslavia	42.2	55.4	61.2	58.6	59.8	60.6	61.2	58.6	2,679	2,621	2,474
Zaire	3.8	4.9	5.9	9.2	5.4	5.3	5.9	9.2	202	174	258

[1] Estimated

Source: Bureau of the Census, *Statistical Abstract of the United States, 1993* (Washington, D.C.: Government Printing Office, 1994), 852.

The international marketer can use the following classification as a planning guide:

1. Very low family incomes. Subsistence economies tend to be characterized by rural populations in which consumption relies on personal output or barter. Some urban centers may provide markets. Example: Cameroon.
2. Mostly low family incomes. Economies that are industrializing along Marxist lines sacrifice personal income to allow as much industrial capital formation as possible. Most goods are produced domestically by state-owned enterprises or enter into the market as a result of bilateral trade agreements. Example: China.
3. Very low, very high family incomes. Some countries exhibit strongly bimodal income distributions. The majority of the population may live barely above the subsistence level, but there is a strong market for imported (luxury) items. The affluent are truly affluent and will consume accordingly. Examples: India, Mexico.

4. Low, medium, high family incomes. Industrialization produces an emerging middle class with increasing disposable income. The very low and very high income classes tend to remain for traditional reasons of social class barriers. Example: Portugal.
5. Mostly medium family incomes. The advanced industrial nations tend to develop institutions and policies that reduce extremes in income distribution, resulting in a large and comfortable middle class able to purchase a wide array of both domestic and imported products and services. Example: Denmark.[8]

Although the national income figures provide a general indication of a market's potential, they suffer from various distortions. Figures available from secondary sources are often in U.S. dollars. The per-capita income figures may not be a true reflection of purchasing power if the currencies involved are distorted in some way. For example, fluctuations in the value of the U.S. dollar may distort real-income and standard-of-living figures. The goods and services in different countries have to be valued consistently if the differences are to reflect real differences in the volumes of goods produced. The use of **purchasing power parities** (**PPP**) instead of exchange rates is intended to achieve this objective. PPPs show how many units of currency are needed in one country to buy the amount of goods and services that one unit of currency will buy in another country. Table 3.5 provides an example of such data.

Second, using a monetary measure may not be a proper and all-inclusive measure of income. For example, in developing economies where most of the consumption is either self-produced or bartered, reliance on financial data alone would seriously understate the standard of living. Further, several of the service-related items (for example, protective services and travel), characteristic of the industrialized countries' national income figures, do not exist for markets at lower levels of development. Moreover, the costs of products and services must be considered because they vary dramatically among nations. As an example, despite the country's wealth, the Japanese do not enjoy the same type of life-style that average families in other industrialized democracies appear able to afford. By the Japanese Construction Ministry's own standards, 11.4 percent of Japanese families live in substandard housing (less than a 50-square-meter house or apartment with a kitchen and three rooms for a family of four or a 29-square-meter dwelling for a couple). In many respects, Japanese living standards have been subjugated to the goals of an export-led economy.[9]

In general, income figures are useful in the initial screening of markets. However, in product-specific cases, income may not play a major role, and startling scenarios may emerge. Some products, such as motorcycles and television sets in China, are in demand regardless of their high price in relation to wages because of their high-prestige value. Some products are in demand because of their foreign origin. As an example, European luxury cars have lucrative markets in countries where per-capita income figures may be low but there are wealthy consumers who are able and willing to buy them. Further, the lack of income in a market may preclude the marketing of a standardized product but, at the same time, provide an opportunity for an adjusted product. A packaged-goods company, confronted with considerable disparity in income levels within the same country, adapted a deodorant product to fit two separate target income groups—the regular

[8] Philip Kotler, *Marketing Management* (Englewood Cliffs, NJ: Prentice-Hall, 1991), 405.
[9] "The Rabbit-Hutch Image—Embarrassing, But True," *Far Eastern Economic Review*, June 13, 1985, 91–92.

Gross Domestic Product/Purchasing Power Parities										TABLE 3.5
	Gross Domestic Product (billions)					**Gross Domestic Product per Capita (dollars)**				
Country	1970	1975	1980	1985	1990	1970	1975	1980	1985	1990
United States	1,009.2	1,583.9	2,688.5	3,967.5	5,392.0	4,922	7,334	11,804	16,581	21,449
OECD Europe	1,041.7	1,700.5	2,859.0	3,980.2	5,871.0	2,825	4,440	7,266	9,857	14,070
Belgium	28.5	47.4	79.7	106.1	164.0	2,952	4,844	8,094	10,768	16,405
Denmark	16.9	26.3	43.0	62.8	86.0	3,439	5,188	8,389	12,279	16,765
France	166.2	277.1	467.8	646.6	984.0	3,274	5,259	8,683	11,720	17,431
Germany	205.0	319.1	544.1	738.7	1,157.0	3,380	5,161	8,838	12,105	18,291
Greece	13.5	24.3	43.6	59.7	75.0	1,540	2,690	4,522	6,010	7,349
Ireland	5.2	9.4	16.9	24.4	37.0	1,777	2,947	4,977	6,901	10,659
Italy	152.8	246.3	449.8	624.2	924.0	2,848	4,443	7,973	10,927	16,021
Luxembourg	1.2	2.0	3.3	4.8	7.0	3,676	5,645	9,012	13,003	19,340
Netherlands	45.1	74.1	122.0	164.3	236.0	3,456	5,424	8,624	11,339	15,766
Portugal	12.3	21.4	39.7	53.2	82.0	1,458	2,451	4,277	5,516	8,389
Spain	74.6	135.1	213.2	292.5	459.0	2,203	3,803	5,702	7,597	11,792
United Kingdom	180.1	279.1	442.2	624.0	903.0	3,236	4,964	7,852	11,020	15,720
Austria	20.4	34.8	59.4	81.2	128.0	2,735	4,591	7,865	10,748	16,620
Finland	13.2	22.6	37.9	56.1	82.0	2,861	4,802	7,938	11,447	16,453
Iceland	0.6	1.1	2.3	3.2	4.0	2,894	5,192	9,892	13,101	15,851
Norway	11.9	20.9	38.4	58.0	68.0	3,063	5,227	9,390	13,963	15,921
Sweden	30.5	48.7	75.8	106.3	144.0	3,794	5,947	9,115	12,727	16,867
Switzerland	29.9	43.7	68.8	94.3	143.0	4,772	6,832	10,778	14,440	20,997
Turkey	33.6	66.9	111.0	179.7	190.0	945	1,658	2,482	3,547	3,316
Australia	43.4	73.9	123.5	184.4	273.0	3,389	5,319	8,402	11,682	15,951
Canada	82.7	149.9	262.9	388.8	509.0	3,880	6,596	10,924	15,440	19,120
Japan	286.8	498.0	918.0	1,425.4	2,179.0	2,765	4,466	7,859	11,805	17,634
New Zealand	9.3	16.1	22.6	33.1	45.0	3,303	5,216	7,180	10,126	13,258

Source: Adapted from Bureau of the Census, *Statistical Abstract of the United States, 1993* (Washington, D.C.: Government Printing Office, 1994), 854.

product version in an aerosol can and the less expensive one in a plastic squeeze bottle. By substituting cheaper parts and materials, successful international marketers can make both consumer and industrial products more affordable in less affluent markets and therefore reach a wider target audience.[10]

A forecast of the impact of the change in consumer demographics around the world is provided in The International Marketplace 3.2.

Consumption Patterns   Depending on the sophistication of a country's data-collection systems, economic data on consumption patterns can be obtained and analyzed. The share of income spent on necessities will provide an indication of the market's development level as well as an approximation of how much money the consumer has left for other purchases. Engel's laws provide some generalizations about consumers' spending patterns and are useful generalizations when precise data are not available. They state that as a family's income increases, the percentage spent on food will decrease, the percentage spent on housing and household operations will be roughly constant, and the amount saved or spent on other purchases will increase. Private expenditure comparisons

[10] V. Yorio, *Adapting Products for Export* (New York: Conference Board, 1983), 29–39.

3.2

THE INTERNATIONAL MARKETPLACE

Consumers in the 1990s: Emerging Differences

The industrialized world will age dramatically in the 1990s, resulting in markets very different from those that exist today. As the baby-boom generation settles into middle age throughout the industrialized world, the market for consumer products will expand, not only in size but also in purchasing power. In the United States, the greatest population increase during the 1990s will occur in the 40–59 age group, but there will also be a sharp growth spurt among those 80 and over. Japan, whose baby-boom ended in 1950, well before that of the United States (1964), will see its 30–40 age bracket actually shrink, while its 50–59 bracket will soar. In the European Union (EU), where the postwar baby boom came later and was less distinct, the growth trend is moderate. The sharpest growth will be registered among Europeans aged 70 to 74, whereas the number of people in their 20s will decline significantly.

The newly industrialized countries (NICs), such as Taiwan, South Korea, and Singapore, are also beginning to age. As health standards improve and economic development alters traditional social behavior, birth rates are tumbling and the population distribution is beginning to resemble that of developed countries. (Poor nations have traditionally been demographically young because of short life spans, high infant mortality, and compensating high birthrates.)

For example, the population segment that will grow fastest in Korea and Singapore in the 1990s will be the 40–44 category, while the population below age 25 (in Korea) and below 35 (in Singapore) will decline substantially. By the year 2000, both nations should be at optimal productive capacity, since much of their populations will be in the 15–64 working age group (71 percent in Korea, 72 percent in Singapore).

The NICs, therefore, should emerge as strong markets for products traditionally consumed by working-age people—items they are increasingly making themselves. Only 69 percent of Taiwan's population had TV sets in 1980, for instance, but by 1986 the figure had risen to 88 percent, and by 1994 it had reached 99 percent. Sales of other consumer goods can be expected to follow this trend in the NICs.

In most developing countries, the population is expected to continue to rise for all age groups, but even here a gradual aging is taking place. In Malaysia, for example, the greatest growth in the 1990s will be among people 45–59. And Nigeria will experience rapid population growth across the board—but the fastest increase will occur in the 70–74 segment.

Few statistics serve as better indicators of future economic prospects or consumer demand than working-age population. These people are not only the workers but also providers for children and the elderly. Advanced economies inevitably have a high percentage of working-age people, whereas poor countries have a low one.

A key factor in consumer markets has always been the number of women entering the work force. The reason is that women who work outside the home create a demand for labor-saving devices, packaged and prepared foods, and other products. Working women also typically have smaller households and greater disposable income than their stay-at-home counterparts.

In most countries, the percentage of women in the work force will grow between now and 2000. Nowhere is this more true than in the Arab countries, where the number of working women is currently very low.

Another notable population trend is the world's continuing urbanization. As a general rule, in countries whose population is growing, the urban population increases faster than the rest, whereas in countries with decreasing populations (such as Germany), the urban population declines more slowly than the rest. Thus, companies must plan to supply urban-oriented products and services.

Accompanying the aging of the world's population, particularly in the industrialized countries, will be a shift in the distribution of wealth. On the one hand, wealth and purchasing power will continue to move away from North America toward Germany, Italy (now the fourth-largest economy in the world), Japan, and the NICs. On the other hand, wealth within national borders will shift to older people. The rapid growth of the 60-and-over age group will dramatically increase the demand for health care, convenience items, and premium products.

Other clues to future demand for consumer products are found by examining countries' relative infrastructure development as well as current product sales. For example, the huge installed base of personal computers in the United States, compared with a much smaller number in Japan, suggests that the United States will remain a much larger market for software, while Japan should become a major market for computers. Some countries show longer-term promise: While China still has only one computer for every 6,000 people (the U.S. figure is one for every four), sales are expected to grow 22.4 percent per year for the rest of the decade. Similarly, the United States leads the world in TVs in use (81 per 100 people), but the greatest sales growth for television sets is in less saturated markets, such as Spain, Malaysia, and Brazil. Ownership of sets should continue to rise globally at 5 percent (and at twice that rate in Asia) until at least 2000. When sales of color TVs are compared with sales of VCRs, the patterns are fairly similar, although the former represents an older technology and the latter a newer one. Per-capita sales in the EU, however, significantly lag those in the United States and Japan, perhaps reflecting state dominance of broadcasting and a narrower choice of programs.

All told, companies can look forward to more consumers, in absolute terms, in the future, with more money to spend. And although the mature economies are aging and offer vast sales and profits to firms catering to older people, makers of products for the young and middle-aged will find plenty of market potential in the emerging industrial economies.

Sources: "A Survey of Television," *The Economist*, February 12, 1994; "What Country Has a Computer for Every 6,000 People?" *Business Week*, September 13, 1993, 50; and "Consumers in the 1990s: Older, Richer, and More Numerous," *Business International*, April 1, 1991, 113–116.

reveal that the percentage spent on food in 1992 varied from 16 percent in the United States to 54 percent in China (see Table 3.6).

In Western Europe, expenditures on clothing typically account for 5 to 9 percent of all spending, but in poorer countries the proportion may be lower. In some low-wage areas, a significant proportion of clothing is homemade or locally made at low cost, making comparisons not entirely accurate. Eastern European households spend an

TABLE 3.6	Consumer Spending by Category, as Percent of Total, 1992

	Food, Beverages, Tobacco	Clothing, Foot- wear, Textiles	House- hold Fuels	House- hold Goods	Housing	Health	Leisure and Education	Transport and Communi- cations	Other
Argentina	39.6	4.5	6.3	5.1	11.5	4.2	4.8	5.5	18.5
Australia	28.1	7.2	3.0	5.5	16.8	5.1	13.9	17.9	2.5
Brazil	29.6	5.0	6.1	5.0	28.3	5.2	5.0	9.1	6.9
Canada	17.6	5.0	3.5	6.7	19.9	4.4	7.6	10.1	25.3
China	54.1	13.4	1.5	10.1	0.7	1.5	5.6	1.2	11.8
CIS[a]	43.3	19.2	3.8	8.0	3.2	2.7	8.3	2.9	8.0
Colombia[a]	48.2	6.1	1.7	6.0	9.1	5.4	5.5	14.5	3.6
Germany	17.5	7.8	3.6	7.1	15.3	14.3	10.0	16.0	8.5
India	46.4	9.8	n.a.	2.6	9.7	2.1	2.5	7.0	20.0
Indonesia	53.4	4.5	n.a.	8.0	15.2	n.a.	1.9	3.4	13.5
Israel	24.8	5.4	3.8	9.9	21.8	14.0	9.7	9.9	0.6
Japan	27.2	7.3	5.5	4.1	5.1	2.8	14.0	9.3	24.8
Mexico	33.7	10.0	n.a.	11.6	8.4	4.9	4.8	11.8	14.8
Singapore	24.0	8.6	0.0	10.5	11.1	5.3	18.9	16.3	5.3
South Korea	32.2	8.1	4.2	5.7	10.4	5.3	13.3	8.6	12.3
Thailand	32.1	13.8	2.0	2.0	7.5	9.4	14.0	10.6	8.7
United Kingdom	21.9	5.4	3.7	5.9	12.7	1.4	9.8	13.2	25.9
United States	15.9	5.4	2.9	7.6	14.8	14.8	5.9	11.4	21.2
Zimbabwe[a]	35.6	12.1	8.6	n.a.	7.4	1.9	7.5	7.4	19.5

n.a.—Not available.

[a]1990 data.

Sources: *International Marketing Data and Statistics 1993* (London: Euromonitor, 1993), 411; *European Marketing Data and Statistics 1994* (London: Euromonitor, 1994), 276–277.

inordinate proportion of their incomes on foodstuffs but quite a low proportion on housing. The remaining, less absolutely central areas of consumption (household goods, leisure, and transportation) are most vulnerable to short-term cancellation or postponement and thus serve as indicators for the strength of confidence in the market in general.

Data on product saturation or diffusion—information on the percentage of households in a market that own a particular product—allow a further evaluation of market potential. Table 3.7 presents the percentage of households that own certain appliances and indicates that saturation levels in the markets for which the data exist are quite high. This does not necessarily indicate lack of market potential; replacement markets or the demand for auxiliary products may offer attractive opportunities to the international marketer. Low rates of diffusion should be approached cautiously, because they can signal a market opportunity or lack thereof resulting from low income levels, use of a substitute product, or lack of acceptance. As an example of lack of acceptance, the time-saving feature of microwave ovens may not be as attractive in more tradition-bound societies as it is in the United States.

General consumption figures are valuable, but they must be viewed with caution because they may conceal critical product-form differences; for example, appliances in European households tend to be smaller than their U.S. counterparts. Information about existing product usage can nevertheless provide indirect help to international marketers. As an example, a large number of telephones, and their even distribution among the population or a target group, may allow market research via telephone interviewing.

Appliance	United States[1,2]	Bel-gium	Den-mark	France	Ger-many	Italy	Nether-lands	Spain	Sweden	Switzer-land	United Kingdom
Cassette recorder	n.a.	75	82	76	74	64	81	67	88	82	82
Clothes washer	76	88	76	88	88	96	91	87	72	78	78
Dishwasher	45	26	26	33	34	18	12	11	31	32	11
Food processor	n.a.	91	83	83	92	48	84	50	77	91	80
Freezer (separate)	n.a.	86	92	77	73	89	54	55	70	68	82
Home computer	n.a.	15	14	14	16	12	25	8	12	14	18
Microwave oven	79	21	14	25	36	6	22	9	37	15	48
Mobile phone	n.a.	1	3	n.a.	3	3	6	1	6	5	4
Radio	n.a.	90	98	98	84	92	99	95	93	99	90
Refrigerator[2]	86	94	84	97	91	88	98	94	96	96	93
Television set:											
color/mono	96	97	98	94	97	98	95	98	97	93	98
Tumbledrier	53	39	22	12	17	10	27	5	18	27	32
Vacuum cleaner	n.a.	92	96	89	96	56	98	29	97	93	98
Video recorder	n.a.	42	39	35	42	25	48	40	48	41	58

Percentage of Households Owning Selected Appliances, 1991 — **TABLE 3.7**

n.a.—Not available.

[1]Represents appliances possessed and generally used by the household (as of November).

[2]1988 data.

Sources: U.S. Energy Information Administration *Annual Energy Review,* 1993; *European Marketing Data and Statistics,* 1994 (London: Euromonitor, 1994), 392–395.

A problem for marketers in general is **inflation;** varying inflation rates complicate this problem in international markets. Many of the industrialized countries, such as the United States, Germany, and Japan, have recently been able to keep inflation rates at single-digit levels. At the same time, countries such as Bolivia, Argentina, and Israel have suffered from chronic inflation (see Table 3.8). Inflation affects the ability of both industrial customers and consumers to buy and also introduces uncertainty into both the marketer's planning process and consumers' buying habits. In high-inflation markets, the marketer may have to make changes in the product (more economical without compromising quality), promotion (more rational), and distribution (more customer involvement) to meet customer needs and maintain demand. In response to rapidly escalating prices, a government will often invoke price controls. The setting of maximum prices for products may cause the international marketer to face unacceptable profit situations, future investments may not be made, and production may even have to be stopped.[11]

Another challenge for international marketers is the **debt problem.** Many of the developing countries are saddled with a collective debt of $1.2 trillion (see Figure 3.2). Latin America calls the 1980s "the lost decade," but other countries have suffered indirectly. In 1980, the United States sold $6 billion more in goods and services to Latin America than it imported. The debt crisis crushed the region's purchasing power and forced up exports to meet interest payments. By 1987, the United States was running a $15-billion trade deficit with Latin America; the $21-billion swing accounted for nearly 10 percent of the record trade gap that year.[12] To continue growing, many companies

---

[11] Victor H. Frank, Jr., "Living with Price Control Abroad," *Harvard Business Review* 62 (March–April 1984): 137–142.

[12] "Fitting into a Global Economy," *U.S. News and World Report,* January 2, 1989, 80–82.

TABLE 3.8	Consumer Price Index					
Country	1986–1987	1987–1988	1988–1989	1989–1990	1990–1991	1991–1992
United States	3.7	4.0	4.8	5.4	4.2	3.0
Argentina	131.3	343.0	3,079.8	2,314.0	171.7	24.9
Australia	8.5	7.2	7.6	7.3	3.2	1.0
Austria	1.4	1.9	2.6	3.3	3.3	4.0
Bangladesh	9.5	9.3	10.0	8.1	7.2	n.a.
Belgium	1.6	1.2	3.1	3.4	3.2	2.4
Bolivia	14.6	16.0	15.0	17.3	21.0	n.a.
Brazil	229.7	682.3	1,287.0	2,937.8	440.8	n.a.
Canada	4.4	4.0	5.0	4.8	5.6	1.5
Chile	19.9	14.7	17.0	26.0	21.8	15.4
Colombia	23.3	28.1	25.8	29.1	30.4	27.0
Ecuador	29.5	58.2	75.6	48.5	48.7	54.6
Egypt	19.7	17.7	21.3	16.8	19.8	13.6
France	3.3	2.7	3.5	3.4	3.2	2.4
Germany	.2	1.3	2.8	2.7	3.5	4.0
Ghana	39.8	31.4	25.2	37.3	18.0	n.a.
Greece	16.4	13.5	13.7	20.4	19.5	15.8
Guatemala	12.3	10.8	11.4	41.2	33.2	10.0
India	8.8	9.4	6.2	9.0	13.9	11.8
Indonesia	9.2	8.0	6.4	7.5	9.2	7.5
Iran	28.6	28.7	22.3	7.6	17.1	22.9
Israel	19.8	16.3	20.2	17.2	19.0	11.9
Italy	4.7	5.1	6.3	6.5	6.4	n.a.
Japan	—	.7	2.3	3.1	3.3	1.7
Malaysia	.9	2.0	2.8	2.6	4.4	n.a.
Mexico	131.8	114.2	20.0	26.7	22.7	45.5
Netherlands	–.7	.7	1.1	2.5	4.0	n.a.
Norway	8.7	6.7	4.6	4.1	3.4	2.3
Pakistan	4.7	8.8	7.8	9.1	11.8	9.5
Peru	85.8	667.0	3,398.6	7,482.0	409.5	73.5
Philippines	3.8	8.8	10.6	12.7	18.7	8.9
Portugal	9.4	9.6	12.6	13.4	11.4	8.9
Romania	.5	2.9	.6	4.7	n.a.	n.a.
South Africa	16.1	12.8	14.7	14.3	15.3	13.9
South Korea	3.0	7.1	5.7	8.6	9.7	6.2
Spain	5.3	4.8	6.8	6.7	5.9	5.8
Sweden	4.2	5.8	6.4	10.5	9.3	2.3
Switzerland	1.4	1.9	3.2	5.4	5.8	4.0
Thailand	2.5	3.9	5.4	5.9	5.7	n.a.
Turkey	38.8	75.4	69.6	63.6	66.0	70.1
United Kingdom	4.1	4.9	7.8	9.5	5.9	3.7
Venezuela	28.1	29.5	84.2	40.8	34.2	31.4

n.a.—Not available.

Source: *International Financial Statistics* (Washington, D.C.: International Monetary Fund, monthly).

are looking at developing nations because of the potential they see 10 to 15 years ahead. U.S. companies typically face competition in these regions from Japanese companies, which are often aided by their government's aid grants, as well as by Europeans, who do business with the help of government export credits that have interest rates lower than those provided by U.S. entities. Access to these markets can be achieved by helping political leaders provide jobs and by increasing exports. Heinz, for example, operates in many developing countries through joint ventures in which Heinz holds 51 percent. To sell copiers and printers in Brazil, Xerox exports Brazilian steel to Europe and Brazilian

Nations in Debt: 1992 Debt Outstanding (billions of dollars) FIGURE 3.2

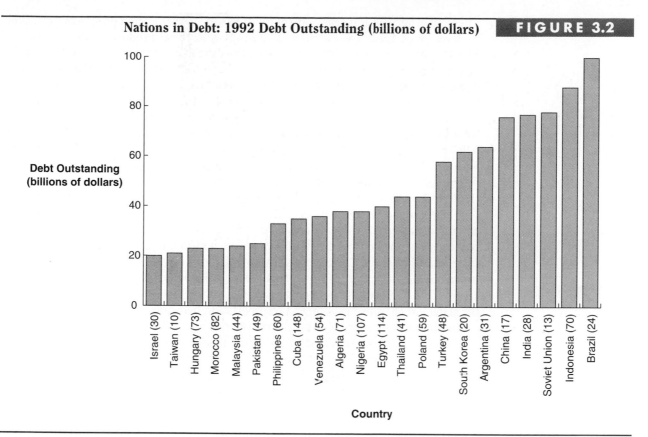

Numbers in parentheses indicate percentages of GDP. Source: "Emerging Market Indicators," *The Economist*, January 22, 1994, 114. Copyright © 1994, The Economist, Ltd. Distributed by the New York Times Special Features.

venetian blinds to the United States, among other products worth $100 million annually.[13] Many industrialized countries, such as Japan, France, and the United States, are seeking ways to ease the burden facing debtor nations.[14]

Infrastructure

The availability and quality of an infrastructure is critically important in evaluating marketing operations abroad. Each international marketer will rely heavily on services provided by the local market for transportation, communication, and energy as well as on organizations participating in the facilitating functions of marketing: marketing communications, distributing, information, and financing. Indicators such as steel consumption, cement production, and electricity production relate to the overall industrialization of the market and can be used effectively by suppliers of industrial products and services. As an example, energy consumption per capita may serve as an indicator of market potential for electrical markets, provided evenness of distribution exists over the market. Yet the marketer must make sure that the energy is affordable and compatible (in terms of current and voltage) with the products to be marketed.

The existence and expansion of basic infrastructure has contributed significantly to increased agricultural output in Asia and Latin America. The Philippines has allocated

[13] Louis Kraar, "How to Sell to Cashless Buyers," *Fortune*, November 7, 1988, 147–154.
[14] *World Development Report* (Washington, D.C.: World Bank, 1991), 124–127.

5 percent of agricultural development funds to rural electrification programs. On a similar level, basic roads are essential to moving agricultural products. In many parts of Africa, farmers are more than a day's walk from the nearest road. As a result, measures to improve production without commensurate improvements in transportation and communications are of little use because the crops cannot reach the market. In addition, the lack of infrastructure cuts the farmers off from new technology, inputs, and ideas.

Transportation networks by land, rail, waterway, or air are essential for physical distribution. The major world land and ocean transportation flows are summarized in the following color map insert. An analysis of rail traffic by freight tons per kilometer offers a possible way to begin an investigation of transportation capabilities; however, these figures may not always indicate the true state of the system. China's railway system carries five times as much freight as India's does, which is an amazing feat considering that only 20 percent of the network is doubletracked and that it is shared by an ever-growing amount of passenger traffic. In spite of its greater use, the international marketer has to rely on other methods of distribution. The tremendous logistics challenge makes national distribution in China only a dream and slows down expansion from the major urban population centers of Guangzhou, Shanghai, and Beijing.[15] With the same type of caution, the number of passenger cars as well as buses and trucks can be used to analyze the state of road transportation and transportation networks.

Communication is as important as transportation. The ability of a firm to communicate with entities both outside and within the market can be estimated by using indicators of the communications infrastructure: telephones, broadcast media, and print media in use. The countries of the former Eastern bloc possess some of the world's worst telephone systems. Western Europe has 49 main telephone lines per 100 people; while Russia has 12, Hungary has 9, and Poland has 8. Upgrading the telephone system will be expensive (estimated at $50 billion for Central Europe alone) but necessary for competing in the world market and attracting international investors.[16] Official figures may not reveal the quality of the services provided and their possible reach. For example, the telephone system in Egypt, especially in Cairo, is notorious for its frequent breakdowns and lack of capacity.

Data on the availability of commercial (marketing-related) infrastructure are often not readily available. Data on which to base an assessment may be provided by government sources, such as *Overseas Business Reports*, by trade associations, such as the Business Equipment Manufacturers' Association, and by trade publications, such as *Advertising Age*. The more extensive the firm's international involvement, the more it can rely on its already existing support network of banks, advertising agencies, and distributors to assess new markets.

Geography

The physical characteristics of individual markets in terms of distance, topography, climate, and natural resources will have an impact on the international marketer's decision to enter a market and the possible adjustments needed in the marketing mix.

In this context, **distance** relates to the physical separation of the marketer from potential customers. In many cases, physical distance is accompanied by psychological distance, which manifests itself in cultural differences. Physical distances between locations are often quite extensive and can affect marketers in many ways, not the least of which is pricing. The landed cost of Indonesian textiles on the West Coast of the United

---

[15] Paul Cheng, "Gateway to China," presentation made to the 36th CIES Annual Executive Congress, Sydney, Australia, April 22–24, 1993.

[16] "Finding Their Voice," *The Economist*, February 8, 1992, 74.

States can easily be two-and-a-half times their cost in Bali. Long distances may require the use of more expensive modes of transportation to secure availability and proper quality of the product. Air transportation, for example, must be used when marketing fresh flowers from Europe or the Caribbean in the United States.

For marketers, **topography** can mean complicating factors such as barriers formed by land and water. These barriers can signify separate target groups within a target market because of cultural differences. For example, people living in the highlands of a country may display behavioral characteristics very different from those in the valleys.

Certain markets that have few access points may be vulnerable to international incidents. For example, Iraq's oil flow to the West was severely hindered during the Iran-Iraq conflict because the Syrians did not allow use of a pipeline that runs through their territory. Finally, for some marketers, topography may be a major determinant in their product offering—the Club Med in its site location to attract tourists, for example.

Which products a company can market and how they may have to be adjusted for logistics or marketing purposes may be affected by **climate.** The market's climatic conditions, and the degree of their variation during the year, can have a direct effect on the consumption pattern of any market. The major caveat is stereotyping or making hasty decisions. As an example, windsurfing or sailing equipment may not, offhand, seem to have major markets in Northern Europe because of the shortness of the summer season. However, windsurfers have extended their season by using wetsuits. As a result of the five-month sailing season and the expense involved, sailing has a well-defined, quite affluent target market.

Products must be modified to withstand extremes in temperture, humidity, or altitude. Among the products that are usually modified are engines for altitude or emissions-control requirements, electric devices for humidity, oil-refining controls for insulation against Arctic cold and desert heat, and measuring and precision instruments for maintaining their accuracy under extreme temperatures. For example, Belarus tractors, when first marketed in the United States, had cabs fitted with heating devices designed for Russian winters, which naturally made them too warm for American conditions.

Climate may have an impact on distribution as well. Products must be protected (by extra coats of preservatives, for example) for long periods in transit as well as for the possibility of longer-than-normal shelf life in a foreign market.

Charting the **natural resources** of markets will provide the international marketer with an assessment of both marketing and procurement potential. The endowment of natural resources alone does not determine the level of economic development of a particular region because resources are required for their exploitation. If they are not on hand, they must be imported and access to supplies guaranteed. Some countries without natural resources (such as Japan) have obtained resources through the exchange processes and achieved success, whereas some countries with rich endowments (such as Angola) have not developed because internal strife has kept interested parties out. Increasingly, the issue of resources has focused on fossil fuels and strategic minerals. The capital-surplus oil-exporting countries—Kuwait, Oman, Qatar, Saudi Arabia, and United Arab Emirates—have been able to fuel their economic development through their resource base. Similarly, South Africa has done well with its minerals.

The possibility of exhausting these resource bases is of concern to industrialized countries, which remain the main users, with dwindling supplies of their own. Furthermore, the industrial marketer's decisions are affected by risks associated with production (capacity, labor disputes, and violent conflicts), transportation (disruptions in the flow of materials and derived products), and trade (collusive price agreements and embargoes).[17]

---

[17] D. Hargreaves and S. Fromson, *World Index of Strategic Minerals* (New York: Facts on File, 1983), 15–34.

| FIGURE 3.3 | Regulations Governing Foreign Direct Investment |

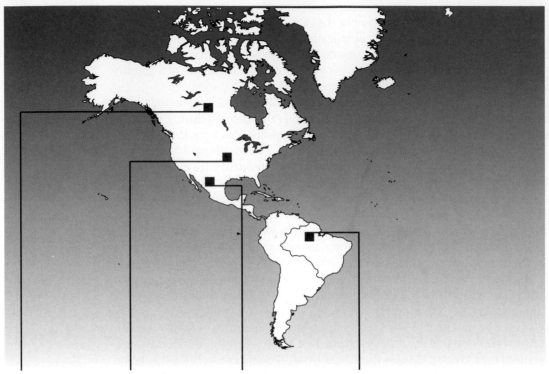

Canada
Canada took down its KEEP OUT sign with the Investment Canada Act of 1985. But the government is still reluctant to approve deals in film, publishing, and other areas that could compromise Canada's "cultural heritage or national identity."

United States
Come one, come all, unless you come from Cambodia, Cuba, Libya, Nicaragua, North Korea, or Vietnam. Buy anything, anywhere, but not more than 25% of a freshwater or coastal shipping enterprise, airline, or broadcast station. Expect heat from the government if you're eyeing a company that affects national security.

Mexico
The Law to Promote Mexican Investment and Regulate Foreign Investment is a bureaucratic migraine. Don't expect government clearance mañana. And save your breath if your business is oil, nuclear power, mining, electricity, railroads, or communications.

Brazil
Best bet: Buy some of Brazil's foreign debt and swap it for an equity stake in a local business. Like the rest of Latin America, Brazil is desperate to cut its debt burden.

A joint venture in an extractive industry, for example, may not be attractive in its own right, but as a means of securing long-term supply it may be invaluable. In the case of some minerals such as platinum and vanadium, U.S. supplies might be cut off in the event of adverse political developments—with major repercussions for manufacturers that need these materials. U.S. action against the South African government and apartheid resulted in threats by the Pretoria government to cut off exports of strategic minerals to the United States.

The international marketer has to make contingency plans for the eventuality of **shortages.** In cases of temporary shortages (lack of cocoa for chocolate or coffee affected by adverse weather, for example), companies prepare by stockpiling adequate reserves. For longer-term shortages, the company may reassess the use of certain raw materials and search for substitutes. Shortages and the price increases that usually result are problems for some companies, opportunities for others. For example, the Bandeirante, a

Continued   **FIGURE 3.3**

South Korea
Look elsewhere if you want to invest in publishing, flowers, electric power plants, bars, savings banks, transportation, communications, or gambling. What's left? High-tech industries. Approval is a snap and comes with a tax holiday.

Japan
The world's most frenetic shoppers don't want a reciprocal onslaught. Vague prohibitions against acquisitions that would harm national security or disturb the public order give the government ample room to trip up deals. That's one reason foreigners have only $8 billion invested in Japanese hard assets—3% of what foreigners own in the United States.

Taiwan
The Statute for Investment by Foreign Nationals and Overseas Chinese is essentially a toothless tiger. Capital-intensive and high-tech ventures get swift approval; textiles and other light manufacturing businesses do not.

Britain
Official stance: total congeniality. But the government can influence who buys what by exerting behind-the-scenes pressure. Scandinavian Airways found that out recently and dropped plans to bid for British Caledonian.

France, Germany, and Switzerland
France has loosened up considerably since 1984, and Germany is a breeze. Switzerland has no laws against foreign investment, but as in many European countries, tacit prohibitions abound. Smaller countries don't want their tiny industrial bases swelled by foreign buyers.

Saudi Arabia
Wanted: foreign investors willing to take in Saudi partners and teach them technical, managerial, and marketing skills. Not wanted: investments in legal services, cleaning, and businesses considered sensitive. A word to the wise businesswoman: Go elsewhere.

Hong Kong
A foreign investor's dream: Disclosure laws are nil and restrictions virtually nonexistent. But beware of 1997, when the island reverts to Chinese control.

12- to 18-passenger turboprop plane designed for markets in the developing countries by Embraer (a Brazilian mixed state-private enterprise), found a niche in industrialized countries for feeder routes as fuel prices rose.

Foreign Involvement in the Economy

For the international marketer interested in entering a foreign market, it is important to know the extent to which such entry is accepted by a country. An economy's overall acceptance of foreign involvement can be estimated by analyzing the degree of foreign direct investment by country and by industry in a given market as well as by the rules governing such investment.

A summary of the conditions for foreign direct investment in selected countries is provided in Figure 3.3. Restrictions exist mainly by industry type, but also by origin of investor. Many nations have established investment-screening agencies to assess foreign direct-investment proposals. For example, in the United States, major foreign direct investments must be reviewed by the Committee for Foreign Investments in the United States (CFIUS). Concerns have been raised mainly in terms of national security and origin of investors: in the 1970s, Arabs; in the late 1980s and early 1990s, the Japanese.

By 1990, the total number of multinational corporations—firms that own or control production or service facilities outside the country in which they are based—exceeded 35,000 with 150,000 affiliates around the world.[18] The global sales of foreign affiliates of multinationals are estimated to be $4.4 trillion, far greater than world exports of $2.5 trillion. The largest 600 multinationals are estimated to generate between one-fifth and one-fourth of the value added in global production of goods and services. Cross-border business has been driven by three main factors: falling regulatory barriers to overseas investment, smaller costs in telecommunications and transportation, and freer domestic and international capital markets in which companies can be bought.[19] The estimated total world stock of direct investment abroad reached $1.937 trillion in 1992.[20]

The favored investment regions of U.S. companies are Europe and Canada; for Japanese companies, North America and Asia; and for German companies, Europe and North America. In general, direct investments are growing in the Far East (for example, Singapore and Malaysia), whereas certain regions are witnessing decline (for example, South Africa for political reasons). Driving this investment are need for efficiency and to participate directly in the international market that cannot adequately be reached through exports and imports alone. Investing companies come from an ever-increasing number of countries. In the 1970s, half of all multinational corporations were U.S. or British; today, just less than half are from the United States, Japan, Germany, and Switzerland (with Britain coming in seventh).

The foreign investment activities of Japan are quite interesting. With its $232 billion in foreign direct investment, Japan is competing with Germany to be the third-largest foreign direct investor in the world after the United States and Great Britain. In 1992, U.S. total foreign direct investment abroad amounted to nearly $487 billion.[21] However, the rapid rise of Japan's foreign stakes in recent years, and the assured prospect of further high growth, are certain to result in increasing dominance of both Japanese products and financial influence. The areas in which Japanese investment has concentrated are provided in Figure 3.4. This development has been boosted both by countries competing for Japanese investment with incentives and by the Japanese Ministry of Finance offering loan programs. The United States remains a favorite destination, with 44 percent of regional foreign direct investment, but Europe's share has increased recently due to Japanese firms' desire to establish bases there. In the late 1980s, the low value of the dollar made U.S. assets particularly attractive for foreign buyers, and foreign direct investment totaled $420 billion in 1992.[22] European companies have been active as well. The Japanese are concentrating their efforts in North America and Europe because of their market size and advanced technology, whereas investment in Asia is driven by the desire to have a base for exports to third countries, re-exports to Japan, and production for foreign firms.

[18] United Nations, *World Investment Report: An Executive Summary* (New York: United Nations, 1993), 1.
[19] "A Survey of Multinationals," *The Economist,* March 27, 1993.
[20] U.S. Department of Commerce, Bureau of Economic Analysis, *Survey of Current Business,* August, 1993.
[21] Ibid.
[22] Ibid.

Japanese Foreign Direct Investment by Region, 1991   FIGURE 3.4

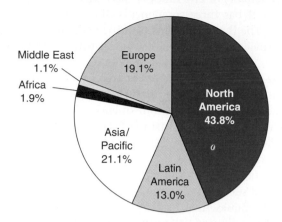

Source: "Japanese Investment Drops, Hitting U.S. the Hardest," *Business International*, July 22, 1991, 245–250. Courtesy of *Aviation Week & Space Technology*.

Foreign direct investment in Japan, however, is relatively modest. Foreign-affiliated companies accounted for only 1.5 percent of total sales and 2.8 percent in the manufacturing sector. (In the United States, the figure for the manufacturing sector is 15 percent; however, some sectors are higher, with chemicals 32 percent owned by foreigners.[23]) Japan ranks low among the investment priorities of U.S. and European companies. Reasons cited are active discouragement by Japan through rigorous case-by-case reviews of applications, favoritism toward licensing rather than joint manufacturing ventures between Japanese and foreign companies, high start-up costs (although eventual rewards may be considerable), difficulty in hiring, and the companies' own negative feelings toward joint ventures rather than wholly owned or controlled subsidiaries.

IMPACT OF THE ECONOMIC ENVIRONMENT ON SOCIAL DEVELOPMENT

Many of the characteristics discussed are important beyond the numbers. Economic success comes with a price tag. All the social traumas that were once believed endemic only to the West are now hitting other parts of the world as well. Many countries, including the nations of Southeast Asia, were able to achieve double-digit growth for decades while paying scant attention to problems that are now demanding treatment: infrastructure limits, labor shortages, demands for greater political freedom, environmental destruction, urban congestion, and even the spread of drug addiction.[24]

Because of the close relationship between economic and social development, many of the figures can be used as social indicators as well. Consider the following factors and their significance: share of urban population, life expectancy, number of physicians per capita, literacy rate, percentage of income received by the richest 5 percent of the population, and percentage of the population with access to electricity. In addition to these factors, several other variables can be used as cultural indicators: number of

---

[23] John J. Curran, "What Foreigners Will Buy Next," *Fortune*, February 13, 1989, 94–98.

[24] "Asia: The Next Era of Growth," *Business Week*, November 11, 1991, 17–22.

public libraries, registered borrowings, book titles published, and number of daily news-papers. The **Physical Quality of Life Index** (**PQLI**) is a composite measure of the level of welfare in a country. It has three components: life expectancy, infant mortality, and adult literacy rates.[25] The three components of the PQLI are among the few social indicators available to provide a comparison of progress through time in all of the countries of the world.

Differences in the degree of urbanization of target markets in lesser-developed countries influence international marketers' product strategies. If products are targeted only to urban areas, products need minimal adjustments, mainly to qualify them for market entry. However, when targeting national markets, firms may need to make extensive adaptations to match more closely the expectations and the more narrow consumption experiences of the rural population.[26]

In terms of infrastructure, improved access in rural areas brings with it an expansion of nonfarm enterprises such as shops, repair services, and grain mills. It also changes customs, attitudes, and values. As an example, a World Bank study on the impact of rural roads of Yucatan in Mexico found that roads offered an opportunity for enlarging women's role by introducing new ideas, education, medical care, and economic alternatives to maize cultivation.[27] In particular, women married later, had fewer children, and pursued more nondomestic activities. The same impact has been observed with increased access to radio and television. These changes can, if properly understood and utilized, offer major new opportunities to the international marketer.

The presence of multinational corporations, which by their very nature are change agents, will accelerate social change. If government control is weak, the multinational corporation bears the social responsibility for its actions. In some cases, governments restrict the freedom of multinational corporations if their actions may affect the environment. As an example, the Indonesian government places construction restrictions (such as building height) on hotels in Bali to avoid the overcrowding and ecological problems incurred in Hawaii when that state developed its tourism sector vigorously in the 1960s and 1970s.

REGIONAL ECONOMIC INTEGRATION

Economic integration has been one of the main economic developments affecting world markets since World War II. Countries have wanted to engage in economic cooperation to use their respective resources more effectively and to provide larger markets for member-country producers. Some integration efforts have had quite ambitious goals, such as political integration; some have failed as the result of perceptions of unequal benefits from the arrangement or parting of ways politically. Figure 3.5, a summary of the major forms of economic cooperation in regional markets, shows the varying degrees of formality with which integration can take place. These economic integration efforts are dividing the world into trading blocs, as seen in The International Marketplace 3.3.

[25] Ben Crow and Alan Thomas, *Third World Atlas* (Milton Keynes, England: Open University Press, 1984), 85.
[26] John S. Hill and Richard R. Still, "Effects of Urbanization on Multinational Product Planning: Markets in Lesser-Developed Countries," *Columbia Journal of World Business* 19 (Summer 1984): 62–67.
[27] The World Bank, *World Development Report 1982* (New York: Oxford University Press, 1982), 63.

Forms of Economic Integration in Regional Markets | FIGURE 3.5

Sources: Ilkka A. Ronkainen, "Trading Blocs: Opportunity or Demise for International Trade?" *Multinational Business Review* 1 (Spring 1993): 1–9; Paivi Vihma, "Gatt Kituu, Kauppablokit Nousevat," *Talouselama* 11, 1992, 42–43; and Joseph L. Brand, "The New World Order," *Vital Speeches of the Day* 58 (December 1991): 155–160.

Levels of Economic Integration

Free Trade Area The **free trade area** is the least restrictive and loosest form of economic integration among nations. In a free trade area, all barriers to trade among member countries are removed. Goods and services are freely traded among member countries. Each member country maintains its own trade barriers vis-à-vis nonmembers.

The European Free Trade Area (EFTA) was formed in 1960 with an agreement by eight European countries. Since that time, EFTA has lost much of its original significance due to its members joining the European Union (EU) (Denmark and the United Kingdom in 1973, Portugal in 1986, and Austria, Finland, Norway, and Sweden in 1995). All EFTA countries have cooperated with the EU through bilateral free trade agreements, and since 1994 through the European Economic Area (EEA) arrangement that allows for free movement of people, products, services, and capital within the combined area of the EU and EFTA. Of the EFTA countries, Iceland and Liechtenstein have decided not to apply for membership in the EU. Switzerland's decision to stay out of the EEA has stalled its negotiations with the EU.

After three failed tries during this century, the United States and Canada signed a free trade agreement that went into effect in 1989. The agreement created a single, $5-trillion continental economy—one that is 10 percent bigger than the United States' own and 15 percent larger than the EU's.[28] The two countries already had sectoral free trade arrangements; for example, one for automotive products had existed for 23 years. Duties

[28] "Summary of the U.S.-Canada Free Trade Agreement," *Export Today* 4 (November–December 1988): 57–61.

A World of Trading Blocs

Regional groupings based on economics will become increasingly important in the 1990s. Countries around the globe are making efforts to suppress national interests in favor of regional ones. A total of 32 such groupings is estimated to be in existence: three in Europe, four in the Middle East, five in Asia, and ten each in Africa and the Americas. Trade inside the three major blocs—North American, Western European, and Asian—has grown at a rapid pace, while trading between these blocs or with outsiders is either declining or growing far more moderately.

Some of these groupings around the world have the superstructure of nation states (such as the European Union) and some (e.g., ASEAN Free Trade Area) are multinational agreements that may be more political arrangements than cohesive trading blocs at present. Some arrangements are not trading blocs per se, but work to further them. The Enterprise for the Americas Initiative is a foreign policy initiative designed to further democracy in a region through incentives to capitalistic development and trade liberalization. The Andean Common Market and Mercosur both have indicated an intention to negotiate with the North American Free Trade Agreement (NAFTA) to create a hemispheric market. Regional economic integration in Asia has been driven more by market forces than by treaties and by a need to maintain balance in negotiations with Europe and North America. Broader formal agreements are in formative stages; for example, Malaysians have led a move to form the East Asian Economic Group (EAEG) of AFTA countries plus Hong Kong, Japan, South Korea, and Taiwan. The Asia Pacific Economic Cooperation (APEC) initiated in 1988 would bring together partners from multiple continents: AFTA members are joined by Australia, Canada, Hong Kong, Japan, New Zealand, South Korea, Taiwan, and the United States.

Regional groupings mean that companies will face ever-intensifying competition and trading difficulties for sales inside a bloc. In the long term, firms will come under pressure to globalize and source locally. Actions of these global companies may also allay fears that regional blocs are nothing but protectionism on a grander scale.

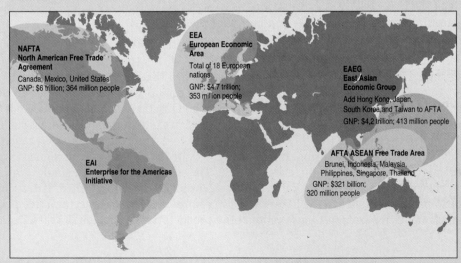

Sources: Ilkka A. Ronkainen, "Trading Blocs: Opportunity or Demise for International Trade?" *Multinational Business Review* 1 (Spring 1993): 1–9; Paivi Vihma, "Gatt Kituu, Kauppablokit Nousevat," *Talouselama* 11, 1992, 42–43; and Joseph L. Brand, "The New World Order," *Vital Speeches of the Day* 58 (December 1991): 155–160.

are eliminated in three stages over a ten-year period, with the sensitive sectors (such as textiles and steel) to be liberalized last. For both countries, the goal was to ensure enhanced global competitiveness, job creation, and enhanced growth. North American free trade expanded in 1994 by the inclusion of Mexico into the North American Free Trade Agreement (NAFTA). The NAFTA agreement will be discussed in detail later in the chapter.

Customs Union   The **customs union** is one step further along the spectrum of economic integration. As in the free trade area, members of the customs union dismantle barriers to trade in goods and services among members. In addition, however, the customs union establishes a common trade policy with respect to nonmembers. Typically, this takes the form of a common external tariff, whereby imports from nonmembers are subject to the same tariff when sold to any member country. The Benelux countries formed a customs union in 1921 that later became part of wider European economic integration.

Common Market   The **common market** amounts to a customs union covering the exchange of goods and services, the prohibition of duties in exports and imports between members, and the adoption of a common external tariff in respect to nonmembers. In addition, factors of production (labor, capital, and technology) are mobile among members. Restrictions on immigration and cross-border investment are abolished. The importance of **factor mobility** for economic growth cannot be overstated. When factors of production are mobile, then capital, labor, and technology may be employed in their most productive uses.

Despite the obvious benefits, members of a common market must be prepared to cooperate closely in monetary, fiscal, and employment policies. Furthermore, although a common market will enhance the productivity of members in the aggregate, it is by no means clear that individual member countries will always benefit. Because of these difficulties, the goals of common markets have proved to be elusive in many areas of the world, notably Central and South America and Asia. In the mid-1980s, the European Community (EC) embarked on an ambitious effort to remove the barriers between the 12 member countries to free the movement of goods, services, capital, and people. The process was ratified by the passing of the **Single European Act** in 1987 with the target date of December 31, 1992, to complete the internal market. In December 1991, the EC agreed in Maastricht that the so-called 1992 process would be a step toward cooperation beyond the economic dimension. While many of the directives aimed at opening borders and markets were completed on schedule, some sectors, such as automobiles, will take longer to open up.[29]

Economic Union   The creation of a true **economic union** requires integration of economic policies in addition to the free movement of goods, services, and factors of production across borders. Under an economic union, members will harmonize monetary policies, taxation, and government spending. In addition, a common currency is to be used by members. This could be accomplished, de facto, by a system of fixed exchange rates. Clearly, the formation of an economic union requires members to surrender a large measure of their national sovereignty to supranational authorities in community-wide institutions such as the European Parliament. The final step would be a **political union** calling for political unification. The ratification of the Maastricht Treaty in late

[29] Carla Rapoport, "Europe Looks Ahead to Hard Choices," *Fortune,* December 14, 1992, 144–149.

1993 by all of the 12 member countries of the EC created the **European Union,** effective January 1, 1994. The treaty calls for a commitment to economic and monetary union (EMU), with the ecu to become a common European currency by 1999. In addition, a move would be made toward political union with common foreign and security policy.[30]

European Integration

The most important implication of the freedom of movement for products, services, people, and capital within the EU and the EEA is the economic growth that is expected to result.[31] Several specific sources of increased growth have been identified. First, there will be gains from eliminating the transaction costs associated with border patrols, customs procedures, and so forth. Second, economic growth will be spurred by the economies of scale that will be achieved when production facilities become more concentrated. Third, there will be gains from more intense competition among European companies. Firms that were monopolists in one country will now be subject to competition from firms in other member countries. Economists have estimated that the reforms will cause an increase in European gross domestic product of about 5 percent over the medium term. In addition, perhaps two million new jobs will be created.

The integration has important implications for firms within and outside Europe because it poses both threats and opportunities, benefits and costs. There will be substantial benefits for those firms aleady operating in Europe. These firms will gain because their operations in one country can now be freely expanded into others and their products may be freely sold across borders. In a borderless Europe, firms will have access to approximately 380 million consumers. Substantial economies of scale in production and marketing will also result. The extent of these economies of scale will depend on the ability of the marketers to find pan-regional segments or to homogenize tastes across borders through promotional activity.

For firms from nonmember countries, there are various possibilities depending on the firm's position within the market.[32] Table 3.9 provides four different scenarios with proposed courses of action. Well-established U.S.-based multinational marketers such as H. J. Heinz and Colgate-Palmolive will be able to take advantage of the new economies of scale. For example, 3M plants earlier turned out different versions of the company's products for various markets. Now, the 3M plant in Wales, for example, makes videotapes and videocassettes for all of Europe.[33] Colgate-Palmolive has to watch out for competitors, like Germany's Henkel, in the brutally competitive detergent market. At the same time, large-scale retailers, such as France's Carrefour and Germany's Aldi group, are undertaking their own efforts to exploit the situation with hypermarkets supplied by central warehouses with computerized inventories. Their procurement policies have to be met by companies like Heinz. Many multinationals are developing pan-European strategies to exploit the emerging situation; that is, they are standardizing their products and processes to the greatest extent possible without compromising local input and implementation.

A company with a foothold in only one European market is faced with the danger of competitors who can use the strength of multiple markets. Furthermore, the elimination

---

[30] "The Maths of Post-Maastricht Europe," *The Economist,* October 16, 1993, 51–52.

[31] Rudiger Dornbusch, "Europe 1992: Macroeconomic Implications," *Brookings Papers on Economic Activity* 2 (1989): 341–362.

[32] John F. Magee, "1992: Moves Americans Must Make," *Harvard Business Review* 67 (May–June 1989): 72–84.

[33] Richard I. Kirkland, "Outsider's Guide to Europe in 1992," *Fortune,* October 24, 1988, 121–127.

Proposed Company Responses to European Integration   TABLE 3.9

Company Status	Challenges	Response
Established multinational market/multiple markets	Exploit opportunities from improved productivity Meet challenge of competitors Cater to customers/intermediaries doing same	Pan-European strategy
Firm with one European subsidiary	Competition Loss of niche	Expansion Strategic alliances Rationalization Divestment
Exporter to Europe	Competition Access	European branch Selective acquisition Strategic alliance
No interest	Competition at home Lost opportunity	Entry

Source: John F. Magee, "1992: Moves Americans Must Make," *Harvard Business Review* 67 (May–June 1989): 78–84.

of barriers may do away with the company's competitive advantage. For example, more than half of the 45 major European food companies are in just one or two of the individual European markets and seriously lag behind broader-based U.S. and Swiss firms. Similarly, automakers PSA and Fiat are nowhere close to the cross-manufacturing presence of Ford and GM. The courses of action include expansion through acquisitions or mergers, formation of strategic alliances (for example, AT&T's joint venture with Spain's Telefonica to produce state-of-the-art microchips), rationalization by concentrating only on business segments in which the company can be a pan-European leader, and finally, divestment.

Exporters will need to worry about maintaining their competitive position and continued access to the market. Companies with a physical presence may be in a better position to assess and to take advantage of the developments. Some firms, like Filament Fiber Technology Inc. of New Jersey, have established production units in Europe. Digital Microwave Corporation of California decided to defend its market share in Europe by joining two British communications companies and setting up a digital microwave radio and optical-fiber plant in Scotland.[34] In some industries, marketers do not see a reason either to be in Europe at all or to change from exporting to more involved modes of entry. Machinery and machine tools, for example, are in great demand in Europe, and marketers in these companies say they have little reason to manufacture there.

The term **Fortress Europe** has been used to describe the fears of many U.S. firms about a unified Europe. The concern is that while Europe dismantles internal barriers, it will raise external ones, making access to the European market difficult for U.S. and other non-EU firms. In a move designed to protect European farmers, for example, the EU has occasionally banned the import of certain agricultural goods from the United States. The EU has also called on members to limit the number of American television programs broadcast in Europe. Finally, many U.S. firms are concerned about the relatively strict domestic-content rules recently passed by the EU. These rules require certain products sold in Europe to be manufactured with European inputs. One effect of the perceived threat of Fortress Europe has been increased direct investment in Europe

[34] "Should Small U.S. Exporters Take the Plunge?" *Business Week*, November 14, 1988, 64–68.

by U.S. firms. Fears that the EU will erect barriers to U.S. exports and of the domestic-content rules governing many goods have led many U.S. firms to initiate or expand European direct investment.

North American Integration

Although the EU is undoubtedly the most successful and well-known integrative effort, North American integration efforts, although only a few years old, have gained momentum and attention. What started as a trading pact between two close and economically well-developed allies has already been expanded conceptually to include Mexico, and long-term plans call for further additions. However, North American integration is for purely economic reasons; there are no constituencies for political integration.

The ratification of NAFTA created the world's largest free market with 364 million consumers and a total output of $6 trillion, which is 25 percent larger than that of the EU.[35] The pact marked a bold departure: Never before have industrialized countries created such a massive free trade area with a developing-country neighbor.

Since Canada stands to gain very little from NAFTA (its trade with Mexico is 1 percent of its trade with the United States), much of the controversy has centered on the gains and losses for the United States and Mexico. Proponents argue that the agreement will give U.S. firms access to a huge pool of relatively low-cost Mexican labor at a time when demographic trends are resulting in labor shortages in many parts of the United States. At the same time, many new jobs are created in Mexico. The agreement will give firms in both countries access to millions of additional consumers, and the liberalized trade flows will result in higher economic growth in both countries. Overall, the corporate view toward NAFTA has been overwhelmingly positive: 81 percent of corporate executives favor the agreement.

Reforms have turned Mexico into an attractive market in its own right. Mexico's gross domestic product has been expanding by more than 3 percent every year since 1989, and exports to the United States have increased 72 percent since 1986. Inflation has dropped from 131 percent in 1987 to 22 percent in 1991. By institutionalizing the nation's turn to open its markets, the free trade agreement will likely attract considerable new foreign investment.[36] The United States has benefited from Mexico's success. The U.S. trade deficit with Mexico has shrunk from $4.9 billion in 1986 to $1.4 billion in 1991 due to a doubling of exports during that period. This has resulted in 264,000 jobs. Among the U.S. industries to benefit are computers, autos and auto parts, petrochemicals, and financial services. In 1990, Mexico opened its computer market by eliminating many burdensome licensing requirements and cutting the tariff from 50 to 20 percent. As a result, exports surged 23 percent in that year alone. IBM, which makes personal and mid-range computers in Mexico, anticipates sales growth to be about $1 billion from that country by the mid-1990s. By becoming a more advanced society, Mexican manufacturers of consumer goods will also stand to benefit. NAFTA has already had a major impact on the emergence of new retail chains, many of which were developed to handle new products from abroad.[37]

Free trade produces both winners and losers. Although opponents concede that the agreement is likely to spur economic growth, they point out that segments of the U.S.

[35] See *The Likely Impact on the United States of a Free Trade Agreement with Mexico* (Washington, D.C.: United States International Trade Commission, 1991).

[36] Ann Reilly Dowd, "Viva Free Trade with Mexico," *Fortune,* June 17, 1991, 97–100.

[37] "Mexico Retail Feels NAFTA Pinch," *Advertising Age,* January 17, 1994, 1–4.

economy will be harmed by the agreement. It is likely that wages and employment for unskilled workers in the United States will decrease because of Mexico's low-cost labor pool. U.S. companies have been moving operations to Mexico since the 1960s. The door was opened when Mexico liberalized export restrictions to allow for more so-called **maquiladoras,** plants that make goods and parts or process food for export to the United States. The supply of labor in the maquiladoras is plentiful, the pay and benefits are low, and the work regulations are lax by U.S. standards. The average maquiladora wage is $1.73 per hour, compared with $2.17 an hour for Mexican manufacturers.[38] U.S. labor leaders also charge that Mexico's inadequate environmental and worker protection laws will encourage U.S. companies to move there to evade tougher standards at home. In fact, Mexican laws are just as strict as U.S. regulations, but until recently nobody enforced them. A 1993 International Trade Commission assessment estimates that while NAFTA would create a net gain of 35,000 to 93,500 U.S. jobs by 1995, it would also cause U.S. companies to shed as many as 170,000 jobs.[39] The good news is that free trade will create higher-skilled and better-paying jobs in the United States as a result of growth in exports. Potential losers are going to be U.S. manufacturers of furniture and household glass; sugar, peanut, and citrus growers; and seafood and vegetable producers. In most cases, high Mexican shipping and inventory costs will continue to make it more efficient for many U.S. industries to serve their home market from U.S. plants.[40]

Countries dependent on trade with NAFTA countries are concerned that the agreement would divert trade and impose significant losses on their economies. Asia's continuing economic success depends largely on easy access to the North American markets, which account for more than 25 percent of annual export revenue for many Asian countries. Lower-cost producers in Asia are likely to lose some exports to the United States if they are subject to tariffs but Mexican firms are not.[41] Similarly, many in the Caribbean and Central America fear that the apparel industries of these regions will be threatened as would much-needed investments.[42]

NAFTA may be the first step toward a hemispheric bloc, although nobody expects it to happen any time soon. It took more than three years of tough bargaining to reach an agreement between the United States and Canada—two countries with parallel economic, industrial, and social systems.[43] The challenges of expanding free trade throughout Latin America will be significant. However, many of Latin America's groupings are making provisions to join in the 1990s.

Other Economic Alliances

Perhaps the world's developing countries have the most to gain from successful integrative efforts. Because many of these countries are also quite small, economic growth is difficult to generate internally. Many of these countries have adopted policies of **import substitution** to foster economic growth. An import substitution policy involves developing industries to produce goods that were formerly imported. Many of these industries, however, can be efficient producers only with a higher level of production than can be

[38] Jim Carlton, "The Lure of Cheap Labor," *The Wall Street Journal,* September 14, 1992, R16.

[39] "A Noose around NAFTA," *Business Week,* February 22, 1993, 37.

[40] Ann Reilly Dowd, "Let's Just Say Yes to NAFTA," *Fortune,* November 29, 1993, 108–109.

[41] Andrew Stoeckel, David Pearce, and Gary Banks, *Western Trade Blocks* (Canberra, Australia: Centre for International Economics, 1990).

[42] Jose De Cordoba, "Alarm Bells in the Caribbean," *The Wall Street Journal,* September 24, 1992, R8.

[43] "A Giant Step Closer to North America Inc.," *Business Week,* December 5, 1988, 44–45.

consumed by the domestic economy. Their success, therefore, depends on accessible export markets made possible by integrative efforts.

Integration in Latin America   Before the signing of the U.S.-Canada Free Trade Agreement, all of the major trading bloc activity had taken place elsewhere in the Americas. However, none of the activity in Latin America has been hemispheric; that is, Central America had its structures, the Caribbean nations had theirs, and South America had its own different forms. However, for political and economic reasons, these attempts have never reached set objectives. In a dramatic transformation, these nations are now looking for free trade as a salvation from stagnation, inflation, and debt.[44] Recent U.S. foreign policy has also responded to Latin American regionalism. The **Enterprise for the Americas Initiative (EAI)** was designed to further democracy in the region by providing incentives to capitalistic development and trade liberalization. Frameworks already have been signed under the EAI. In response to the recent developments, Brazil, Argentina, Uruguay, and Paraguay set up a common market, with completion by the end of 1994, called Mercosur.[45] Bolivia, Colombia, Ecuador, Peru, and Venezuela have formed the Andean Common Market (ANCOM). Many Latin nations are realizing that if they do not unite, they will become increasingly marginal in the global market. Some countries, such as Chile, have already indicated their interest in joining NAFTA.[46]

The ultimate goal is a free trade zone from Point Barrow, Alaska, to Patagonia. The argument is that free trade throughout the Americas would channel investment and technology to Latin nations and give U.S. firms a head start in those markets. If Latin America grows, as estimated, at an average of 4 percent annually during the 1990s under trade liberalization, imports will increase by $170 billion, 40 percent of which U.S. firms can capture. Integrative efforts thus far have already allowed international marketers to start talking about pan-Latin American marketing campaigns.[47]

Integration in Asia   Development in Asia has been quite different from that in Europe and in the Americas. While European and North American arrangements have been driven by political will, market forces may force more formal integration on Asian politicians. The fact that regional integration is increasing around the world may drive Asian interest in it for pragmatic reasons. First, European and American markets are significant for the Asian producers, and some type of organization or bloc may be needed to maintain leverage and balance against the two other blocs. Second, given that much of the Asian trade growth is from intraregional trade, having a common understanding and policies will become necessary. Future integration will most likely use the frame of the most established arrangement in the region, the Association of Southeast Asian Nations (ASEAN). Before late 1991, ASEAN had no real structures, and consensus was reached through informal consultations. In October 1991, ASEAN members announced the formation of a customs union called Asean Free Trade Area (AFTA). The Malaysians have pushed for the formation of the East Asia Economic Group (EAEG), which would add Hong Kong, Japan, South Korea, and Taiwan to the membership list. This proposal makes sense, because without Japan and the rapidly industrializing countries of the region, such as South Korea and Taiwan, the effect of the arrangement would be nominal.

[44] Thomas Kamm, "Latin Links," *The Wall Street Journal,* September 24, 1992, R6.

[45] "The World's Newest Trading Bloc," *Business Week,* May 4, 1992, 50–51.

[46] Stephen C. Messner, "Latin America after NAFTA," *Export Today* 10 (February–March 1994): 49–50.

[47] "Regional Commonalities Help Global Ad Campaigns Succeed in Latin America," *Business International,* February 17, 1992, 47–52.

Japan's reaction has been generally negative toward all types of regionalization efforts, mainly because it has the most to gain from free trade efforts. However, part of what has been driving regionalization has been Japan's reluctance to foster some of the elements that promote free trade, for example, reciprocity.[48] Should the other trading blocs turn against Japan, its only resort may be to work toward a more formal trade arrangement in the Asia-Pacific.

Another formal proposal for cooperation would start building bridges between two emerging trade blocs. Some individuals have publicly called for a U.S.-Japan common market. Given the differences on all fronts between the two countries, the proposal may be quite unrealistic at this time. Negotiated trade liberalization will not open Japanese markets because of major institutional differences, as seen in many rounds of successful negotiations but totally unsatisfactory results. The only solution, especially for the U.S. government, is to forge better cooperation between the government and the private sector to improve competitiveness.[49]

In 1988, Australia proposed the Asia Pacific Economic Cooperation (APEC) as an annual forum to maintain a balance in negotiations. The proposal calls for ASEAN members to be joined by Australia, New Zealand, Japan, South Korea, Canada, and the United States. The model for APEC would not be the EC, with its Brussels bureaucracy, but the Organization for Economic Cooperation and Development (OECD), which is a center for research and high-level discussion. Some experts recommend that APEC should establish an ultimate goal of achieving free trade in the area.

Integration in Africa and the Middle East Africa's economic groupings range from currency unions among European nations and their former colonies to customs unions between neighboring states. In 1975, sixteen West African nations attempted to create a megamarket large enough to interest investors from the industrialized world and reduce hardship through economic integration. The objective of the Economic Community of West African States (ECOWAS) was to form a customs union and eventually a common market. Although many of its objectives have not been reached, its combined population of 160 million represents the largest economic entity in sub-Saharan Africa. Many of the other blocs, however, have not been successful due to small memberships and lack of economic infrastructure to produce goods to be traded within the blocs.

Countries in the Arab world have made some progress in economic integration. Economically speaking, the Gulf Corporation Council (GCC) is one of the most powerful of any trade groups. The per-capita income of its six member states (Bahrain, Kuwait, Oman, Qatar, Saudi Arabia, and the United Arab Emirates) is $7,690. The GCC was formed in 1980 mainly as a defensive measure due to the perceived threat from the Iran-Iraq war. Its aim is to achieve free trade arrangements with the European nations.

A listing of the major regional trade agreements is provided in Table 3.10.

Economic Integration and the International Marketer

Regional economic integration creates opportunities and potential problems for the international marketer. It may have an impact on a company's entry mode by favoring direct investment because one of the basic rationales of integration is to generate

---

[48] Paul Krugman, "A Global Economy Is Not the Wave of the Future," *Financial Executive* 8 (March–April 1992): 10–13.

[49] Michael R. Czinkota and Masaaki Kotabe, "America's New World Trade Order," *Marketing Management* 1 (Summer 1992): 49–56.

TABLE 3.10	Major Regional Trade Associations
AFTA	**ASEAN Free Trade Area**
	Brunei, Indonesia, Malaysia, Philippines, Singapore, Thailand
ANCOM	**Andean Common Market**
	Bolivia, Colombia, Ecuador, Peru, Venezuela
APEC	**Asia Pacific Economic Cooperation**
	Australia, Brunei, Canada, China, Hong Kong, Indonesia, Japan, Malaysia, New Zealand, Philippines, Singapore, South Korea, Taiwan, Thailand, United States
CACM	**Central American Common Market**
	Costa Rica, El Salvador, Guatemala, Honduras, Nicaragua
CARICOM	**Caribbean Community**
	Anguilla, Antigua, Bahamas, Barbados, Belize, Dominica, Grenada, Guyana, Jamaica, Montserrat, St. Kitts-Nevis, St. Lucia, St. Vincent and the Grenadines, Trinidad-Tobago
ECOWAS	**Economic Community of West African States**
	Benin, Berkina Faso, Cape Verde, Gambia, Ghana, Guinea, Guinea-Bissau, Ivory Coast, Liberia, Mali, Mauritania, Niger, Nigeria, Senegal, Sierra Leone, Togo
EU	**European Union**
	Belgium, Denmark, France, Germany, Greece, Ireland, Italy, Luxembourg, Netherlands, Portugal, Spain, United Kingdom
EFTA	**European Free Trade Association**
	Austria, Finland, Iceland, Liechtenstein, Norway, Sweden, Switzerland
GCC	**Gulf Cooperation Council**
	Bahrain, Kuwait, Oman, Qatar, Saudi Arabia, United Arab Emirates
LAIA	**Latin American Integration Association**
	Argentina, Bolivia, Brazil, Chile, Colombia, Ecuador, Mexico, Paraguay, Peru, Uruguay, Venezuela
MERCOSUR	**Southern Common Market**
	Argentina, Brazil, Paraguay, Uruguay
NAFTA	**North American Free Trade Agreement**
	Canada, Mexico, United States

favorable conditions for local production and intraregional trade. By design, larger markets are created with potentially more opportunity. Because of harmonization efforts, regulations may be standardized, thus positively affecting the international marketer.

The international marketer must, however, make integration assessments and decisions from four points of view.[50] The first task is to envision the outcome of the change. Change in the competitive landscape can be dramatic if scale opportunities can be exploited in relatively homogeneous demand conditions. This could be the case, for example, for industrial goods, consumer durables, such as cameras and watches, as well as professional services. The international marketer will have to take into consideration varying degrees of change readiness within the markets themselves; that is, governments and other stakeholders, such as labor unions, may oppose the liberalization of competition in all market segments. For example, while plans have called for liberalization of air travel and automobile marketing in Europe, EU members have found loopholes to protect their own companies.

The international marketer will then have to develop a strategic response to the new environment to maintain a sustainable long-term competitive advantage. Those companies already present in an integrated market should fill in gaps in European product/market portfolios through acquisitions or alliances to create a balanced pan-regional

---

[50] Eric Friberg, Risto Perttunen, Christian Caspar, and Dan Pittard, "The Challenges of Europe 1992," *The McKinsey Quarterly* 21 no. 2 (1988): 3–15.

company. Those with a weak presence, or none at all, may have to create alliances with established firms.[51] For example, to take advantage of the new situation in Europe, James River Corporation from the United States, Nokia from Finland, and Cragnotti & Partners from Italy launched a pan-European papermaking joint venture called Jamont. Before 1992, papermaking was highly fragmented in Europe, but the joint venture partners saw the chance to develop a regional manufacturing and marketing strategy. A total of 13 companies in 10 countries were acquired and production was consolidated. For example, before the new strategy, each individual company made colored napkins; now all of Jamont's products come from one plant in Finland.[52] One additional option for the international marketer is to leave the market altogether if it cannot remain competitive because of new competitive conditions or the level of investment needed. For example, Bank of America sold its operations in Italy to Deutsche Bank after it discovered the high cost of becoming a pan-European player.

Whatever changes are made, they will require company reorganization.[53] Structurally, authority will have to become more centralized to execute regional programs. In staffing, focus will have to be on individuals who understand the subtleties of consumer behavior across markets and are therefore able to evaluate the similarities and differences between cultures and markets. In developing systems for the planning and implementation of regional programs, adjustments have to be made to incorporate views throughout the organization. If, for example, decisions on regional advertising campaigns are made at headquarters without consultation with country operations, resentment from the local marketing staff could lead to less-than-optimal execution. Companies may even move corporate or divisional headquarters from the domestic market to be closer to the customer; for example, AT&T estimates that several of its units in the future may have their headquarters abroad, especially in Europe.

Finally, economic integration will create its own powers and procedures similar to those of the EU commission and its directives. The international marketer is not powerless to influence both of them; as a matter of fact, a passive approach may result in competitors gaining an advantage or it may put the company at a disadvantage. For example, it was very important for the U.S. pharmaceutical industry to obtain tight patent protection as part of the NAFTA agreement; therefore, substantial time and money were spent on lobbying both the executive and legislative branches of the U.S. government. Often, policymakers rely heavily on the knowledge and experience of the private sector to carry out its own work. Influencing change will therefore mean providing industry information, such as test results, to the policymakers. Many marketers consider lobbying a public relations activity and therefore go beyond the traditional approaches, as seen in The International Marketplace 3.4. Lobbying will usually have to take place at multiple levels simultaneously; within the EU, this means the European Commission in Brussels, the European Parliament in Strasbourg, or the national governments within the EU. Marketers with substantial resources have established their own lobbying offices in Brussels, while smaller companies get their voices heard through joint offices or their industry associations. In terms of lobbying, U.S. firms have an advantage because of their experience in their home market; however, for many European firms, lobbying is a new, yet necessary, skill to be acquired.

---

[51] John A. Quelch, Robert D. Buzzell, and Eric R. Salama, *The Marketing Challenge of 1992* (Reading, MA: Addison-Wesley, 1990), Chapter 13.

[52] "A Joint-Venture Papermaker Casts Net across Europe," *The Wall Street Journal,* December 7, 1992, B4.

[53] Gianluigi Guido, "Implementing a Pan-European Marketing Strategy," *Long Range Planning,* 24 no. 5 (1991): 23–33.

Working the New Bloc

Boeing played a major role in hosting the meeting of the Asia Pacific Economic Conference (APEC) held in Seattle in November 1993, as the airplane maker pushed for liberalized Pacific Rim trade. Aerospace already constitutes the main export to the Pacific Rim and prospects are good for its increase.

Similar to other U.S. companies, Boeing donated $50,000 to defray APEC host committee expenses. A dozen Boeing employees were assigned to help organize and operate the conference. They included Dean Thornton, president of the commercial airplane group who served as chairman of the host committee, and Ray Waldman, director of federal affairs who was the committee's executive director. Boeing provided a fleet of vans and buses and a transportation coordinator to meet APEC conference needs. The company also agreed to host 1,000 journalists who traveled to Seattle to cover APEC events.

Aerospace orders announced during the week underscored the importance of Pacific Rim trade to the United States and to Boeing specifically. United Parcel Service added ten new Boeing 757s to its order book. The $600-million purchase, including spares, will help UPS accommodate the growing international demand for its small-package delivery services. Japan Air System specified United Technologies' Pratt & Whitney 4000-series engines for its new 777 transports.

Exports to APEC countries (see accompanying table) accounted for about 31 percent of Boeing sales in 1993 compared with 3 percent in 1988. Japan has traditionally been among the top three export markets, and China, with 100 Boeing transports on order, is rapidly rising in importance.

Boeing Orders in APEC Countries*

Country	Total Ordered	Total Delivered	Unfilled, Announced Orders
Australia	315	311	4
Brunei	6	6	0
Canada	201	193	8
China	167	105	62
Hong Kong	45	31	14
Indonesia	35	10	25
Japan	373	292	81
Malaysia	81	56	25
New Zealand	38	28	10
Philippines	6	4	2
Singapore	99	78	21
South Korea	88	40	48
Taiwan	43	36	7
Thailand	42	28	14
Total**	1,539	1,218	321

*Figures do not include leased aircraft, which are substantial in China and Philippines.

**Totals equal 18 percent of all Boeing transport orders, 16 percent of all deliveries, and 25 percent of all unfilled but announced orders, respectively.

Source: Boeing

Source: "Boeing Pushes Trade Issues at Asia-Pacific Conference," *Aviation Week & Space Technology* 139 (November 22, 1993): 39–40.

SUMMARY

Economic variables relating to the various markets' characteristics—population, income, consumption patterns, infrastructure, geography, and attitudes toward foreign involvement in the economy—form a starting point for assessment of market potential for the international marketer. These data are readily available but should be used in conjunction with other, more interpretive data because the marketer's plans often require a long-term approach. Data on the economic environment produce a snapshot of the past; in some cases, old data are used to make decisions affecting operations two years in the future. Even if the data are recent, they cannot themselves indicate the growth and the intensity of development. Some economies remain stagnant, plagued by natural calamities, internal problems, and lack of export markets, whereas some witness booming economic development.

Economic data provide a baseline from which other more market/product-specific and even experiential data can be collected. Understanding the composition and interrelationships between economic indicators is essential for the assessment of the other environments and their joint impact on market potential. The international marketer needs to understand the impact of the economic environment on social development.

The emergence of economic integration in the world economy poses unique opportunities and challenges to the international marketer. Eliminating barriers between member markets and erecting new ones vis-à-vis nonmembers will call for adjustments in past strategies to fully exploit the new situations. In the late 1980s, economic integration increased substantially. The signing of the North American Free Trade Agreement produced the largest trading bloc in the world, whereas the Europeans are moving in their cooperation beyond the pure trade dimension.

Questions for Discussion

1. Place these markets in the framework that follows.

   a. Indonesia g. Turkey m. Peru
   b. Mozambique h. Spain n. Jamaica
   c. India i. Singapore o. Poland
   d. Bangladesh j. Nigeria p. United Kingdom
   e. Niger k. Algeria q. Iraq
   f. Brazil l. Zambia r. Saudi Arabia

	Income Level		
Trade Structure	**Low**	**Middle**	**High**
Industrial			
Developing			
• Semi-Industrial			
• Oil-Exporting			
• Primary Producing			
• Populous South Asia			
• Least Developed			

2. Using the data in the Appendix to Chapter 3, assess the market potential for (a) power generators and (b) consumer appliances in (1) the Philippines, (2) Jordan, and (3) Portugal.

3. From the international marketer's point of view, what are the opportunities and problems caused by increased urbanization in developing countries?

4. Comment on this statement: "A low per-capita income will render the market useless."

5. Comment on this statement: "the economic straits of developing countries have cost the United States more than $60 billion in exports and 1.7 million jobs in the past five years."

6. Comment on this statement: "Regional trading blocs are nothing but the Berlin Walls of the 1990s."

7. Explain the difference between a free trade area and a common market. Speculate why negotiations were held for a North American Free Trade Agreement rather than for a North American Common Market.

8. What type of adjustments will U.S. firms make as a result of NAFTA?

Recommended Readings

Current issues of *Business International, Business Europe, Business East Europe, Business Asia, Business Latin America, Business China.*

Europe 1992: The Single Market. Brussels: Ernst and Whinney, 1988.

Farmer, Richard N., and Barry M. Richman. *Comparative Management and Economic Progress.* Homewood, IL: Irwin, 1965.

International Marketing Data and Statistics 1994. London: Euromonitor, 1994.

Rostow, Walt W. *The Stages of Economic Growth.* London: Cambridge University Press, 1960.

Ryans, John K., and Pradeep A. Rau. *Marketing Strategies for the New Europe: A North American Perspective on 1992.* Chicago, IL: American Marketing Association, 1990.

U.S. Department of Commerce. "Annual Survey of Foreign Direct Investment Activity." Washington, D.C.: U.S. Government Printing Office, 1984.

Vernon, Raymond, and Louis T. Wells. *Manager in the International Economy.* Englewood Cliffs, NJ: Prentice-Hall, 1981.

The Arthur Andersen North American Business Sourcebook. Chicago: Triumph Books, 1994.

World Development Report 1993. New York: Oxford University Press, 1993.

The NAFTA. Washington, D.C.: U.S. Government Printing Office, 1993.

The World in Figures. London: Economist Publications, 1994.

Yearbook of International Trade Statistics. New York: United Nations, 1994.

APPENDIX A

Indicators of Market Size for 116 Countries

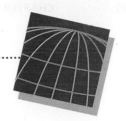

Some terms require a word of explanation in order to make country-by-country comparisons more meaningful.

Population figures are midyear UN estimates or Economist Intelligence Unit (EIU) estimates. Working age is defined as ages 15–64 inclusive.

Gross Domestic Product (GDP) is the total value in current market prices of all goods and services produced by residents of a country before deduction of depreciation charges on fixed capital. It is equal to the sum of (a) personal consumption expenditure; (b) gross domestic capital formation (investments), including inventory changes; (c) the net of exports minus imports of goods and services; and (d) government consumption expenditure. GDP differs from Gross National Product (GNP) by excluding net factor income received from abroad (an amount usually about 1 percent of GDP). GDP and GNP reports tend to run late and are subject to constant revision (the United States normally makes about six changes after its first estimate). Thus, some 1991 figures are provisional or are estimates made by EIU analysts. Sources: *International Financial Statistics* (International Monetary Fund—IMF), EIU.

National Income is the sum of the incomes of nationals of a country, resident or not, before deducting direct taxes. It can also be thought of as GNP minus consumption of fixed capital. The main components are wages and salaries, employee benefits, corporate earnings accruing to residents, income from business operations, net interest and royalties. Sources: *International Financial Statistics* (IMF), *Yearbook of National Accounts Statistics* (UN).

Average Wages in Manufacturing. Great care should be exercised in the use of this statistic because of inconsistencies in reporting and definitions of manufacturing, as well as differences in the workweek and treatment of overtime, benefits, and payments in kind. Sources: *Yearbook of Labor Statistics* (International Labor Organization), U.S. Department of Labor, Bureau of Labor Statistics.

Total Exports are presented fob (free on board) (approximately the seller's price before overseas transportation costs). Source: *Direction of Trade Statistics* (IMF).

Total Imports are presented cif (cost of goods plus insurance and freight). Exports are often compared with imports fob to obtain a country's balance of trade. However, the EIU believes imports cif better indicate the significance of imports to an economy. If imports cif is unavailable, then imports fob is used and indicated. Sources: *Direction of Trade Statistics* (IMF), central bank and government publications.

Source: "Indicators of Market Size for 116 Countries," *Crossborder Monitor,* August 4, 1993.

Sources used include: *Monthly Bulletin of Statistics* (UN); *OECD Economic Surveys: Direction of Trade Statistics* (IMF); *International Financial Statistics* (IMF); U.S. Department of Commerce; Agency for International Development; *World Automotive Market* (Johnston International Publishing Corp.); *The World's Telephones* (American Telephone and Telegraph); *World Radio-TV Handbook* (AT&T Communications); *Statistical Yearbook* (UN); *Yearbook of Labor Statistics* (ILO); *Yearbook of National Accounts Statistics* (UN); *Yearbook of Energy Statistics* (UN); *International Iron and Steel Institute; Key Indicators of Developing Member Countries of ADB* (Asian Development Bank); *Selected World Demographic Indicators by Countries, 1950–2000* (UN); central banks and government publications.

Private Consumption Expenditure is the value of final expenditure by households and private nonprofit institutions on current goods and services, less sales of similar goods. Sources: *International Financial Statistics* (IMF), *Country Reports* (EIU), *Euromonitor International and Euromonitor European Marketing Data and Statistics, Monthly Bulletin of Statistics* (UN), *Yearbook of National Accounts Statistics* (UN).

Passenger Cars in Use denotes motor vehicles seating fewer than eight passengers, including taxis, jeeps, and station wagons. Source: *World Automotive Report* (Johnston International Publishing Co).

Trucks and Buses in Use includes vans, lorries, buses, and tractor and semitrailer combinations (except trailers and farm tractors). Source: *World Automotive Market Report* (Johnston International Publishing Co).

Telephone Sets in Use comprises both public and private telephone sets in use, including those connected to a PBX. Source: *Yearbook of Common Carrier Telecommunications Statistics* (International Telecommunications Union).

Television Sets in Use is the total number of receiving sets in each country. Some figures are estimates. Source: *World Radio and TV Handbook* (Billboard Publications).

Personal Computers refers to the total installed base of personal computers, defined as programmable, microprocessor-based, single-user machines capable of supporting peripherals and typically costing less than $12,000. Source: International Data Corp.

Steel Consumption is apparent consumption of crude steel (i.e., production plus imports minus exports), disregarding inventory changes. Source: *Steel Statistical Yearbook* (International Iron and Steel Institute).

Cement Production includes all types of cement products. Sources: *Monthly Bulletin of Statistics* (UN), *UN Industrial Statistics Yearbook, European Annual Review* (Cembureau).

Electricity Production includes generation of electricity by utility firms for public use and production by companies for their own use. Sources: *Monthly Bulletin of Statistics* (UN), *Energy Statistics Yearbook* (UN).

Energy Consumption is denominated in per-capita oil equivalent. Coal equivalent can be calculated by dividing the oil equivalent figure by 0.687623. Total cumulative energy consumption increases are based on aggregate national energy consumption figures not displayed in the table. Source: *Energy Statistics Yearbook* (UN).

ADDITIONAL SOURCES

Economic Surveys (OECD); U.S. Department of Commerce; Agency for International Development; *Key Indicators of Developing Member Countries* (Asian Development Bank); *The World Factbook and Handbook of Economic Statistics* (CIA); *World Tables, Annual Report* (World Bank); *Economic and Social Progress in Latin America* (Inter-American Development Bank); *Main Economic Indicators* (OECD); and central bank and government publications; and EIU.

HOW TO USE THE STATISTICS

These indicators provide a ready source of data for general comparisons between countries and world regions. Since the emphasis is on comparison, the EIU has selected statistics that are available for many countries, which present a minimum of ambiguity. In the case of the most developed countries, this has entailed some sacrifice of timeliness.

It should be noted that countries frequently revise data or change the definitional basis for the statistics they report. In addition to the caveats accompanying the definition of terms, please be aware of the following:

Currency Conversion   For the presentation of GDP, private consumption expenditure and average hourly wages, the EIU has converted data in local currencies to U.S. dollars, using average exchange rates for the year from the IMF's *International Financial Statistics,* national publications, and in some cases, the UN's *Monthly Bulletin of Statistics.* In countries with multiple exchange rates, a choice was made based on EIU's best judgment.

Although conversion to a common currency is essential for comparisons between countries, a degree of distortion is inevitable. In countries with multiple exchange rates, the choice of one as opposed to another can mean a difference in GDP of 100 percent or more. Furthermore, exchange rates apply only to goods traded internationally. Countries vary in their degree of involvement in international trade. As a result, there is no perfect way to compare noninternationally traded goods among economies.

Yet another source of distortion is the tendency of floating currencies to overshoot in the process of adjusting to market forces. In some countries, inflation and managed currency rates are not necessarily in step. Therefore, a value in dollars may appear either high or low, compared with values for other countries in a given year or with a value for the same country from a previous year.

Variation in National Accounting   Most centrally planned economies (CPEs), with the notable exceptions of Hungary and Poland, use Net Material Product (NMP) instead of GDP as a measure of gross economic activity. This concept deliberately excludes government and other services and is thus, in local currency terms, roughly 20 to 30 percent lower than GDP. (In contrast, Gross Social Product [GSP], utilized by Yugoslavia for certain measures of economic performance, closely resembles GDP.) The absence of a good exchange rate in most CPEs, however, means the official rate must be used for conversion, resulting in exaggerated values for NMP in dollar terms. Some CPEs undergoing economic reform are in the process of revising their methods of accounting.

National accounts data in general must be regarded with special care since they are subject to frequent revision, and early estimates often underestimate the effect of inflation.

Cumulative Percent Change Figures   All figures for cumulative percent change (versus annual change) cover a five-year period. To determine simple annual percent change from five-year cumulative figures, divide the five-year figure by five. To obtain the more precise compound annual percent change from a five-year figure, take the fifth root of the expression $(1 + \text{five-year figure}/100)$, subtract 1, and multiply the result by 100.

That is, where f = five-year cumulative percent change, compound annual percent change $= 100 \times (\sqrt[5]{1 + f/100}) - 1)$. The five-year periods in question are the periods between identical points (year-end in most cases) of the years indicated in the column heading.

Average Annual Percent Change Figures   All figures cover a period of five years. Real growth of GDP and private consumption expenditure refer to the average of growth over each of the five years indicated. Population figures refer to imputed annual change in population at midyear over the period indicated. Wage growth figures refer to imputed annual change over the period indicated. Imports and exports growth figures refer to the annual change from year to year over the period indicated.

	Population				Gross Domestic Product			National Income	Average Hourly Wage	
	Total 1991 (millions)	Average Annual % Increase 1987–1991	Working Age 1991 (millions)	Average Annual % Increase 1987–1991	Total[1] 1991 (billions)	Average Annual Real % Increase 1986–1991	Per Capita 1991 ($)	Total[1] 1991 ($ billions)	1991[1] ($)	Average Annual % Increase 1986–1991
Western Europe										
EU										
Belgium	9.98	0.2	6.7	0.0	201.4	3.6	20,150	181.2	19.83	17.3
Denmark	5.15	0.1	3.5	0.4	130.3	1.8	25,298	112.9	18.26	17.6
France	57.05	0.5	37.7	0.4	1,194.2	3.4	20,933	1,038.5[10]	15.26	15.2
Germany	64.12	1.0	43.9	0.4	1,670.9	3.4	26,059	1,388.9	22.62	18.8
Greece	10.06	0.2	6.7	0.6	70.3	1.9	6,988	59.6[10]	6.82	13.3
Ireland	3.52	−0.1	2.2	0.8	43.6	5.4	12,384	34.8	12.07	15.8
Italy	57.05	−0.1	39.2	0.2	1,150.5	3.3	20,166	992.7	18.29	20.1
Luxembourg	0.38	0.5	0.3	−2.5	8.5	5.5	22,464	10.9[10]	17.65[10]	18.0[13]
Netherlands	15.06	0.5	10.4	0.7	290.9	3.3	19,313	257.4	18.42	15.6
Portugal	10.58	0.6	7.0	0.8	66.4	5.0	6,276	56.8[10]	4.15	22.1
Spain	39.02	0.2	26.0	0.8	527.1	5.0	13,509	464.3	12.20	20.6
United Kingdom	57.37	0.2	37.6	0.2	1,027.4	2.6	17,909	868.8[10]	13.76	17.3
Total EU[2]	**329.34**	**0.4**	**221.1**	**0.4**	**6,381.5**	**—**	**19,377**	**5,466.8**	**—**	**—**
EFTA										
Austria	7.82	0.7	5.3	0.7	165.4	3.7	21,150	143.7	17.39	19.1
Finland	5.03	2.0	3.4	0.0	124.5	2.2	24,760	112.0[10]	20.57	20.5
Iceland	0.26	0.9	0.2	−3.5	6.5	2.8	24,960	5.5	8.19[10]	—
Norway	4.26	0.3	2.8	0.4	105.9	2.0	24,870	87.7	21.63	15.3
Sweden	8.64	0.6	5.6	0.8	237.0	1.7	27,428	195.8[10]	22.15	18.1
Switzerland	6.79	0.7	4.6	0.6	232.0	2.8	34,169	217.7	21.69	17.6
Total EFTA[2]	**32.80**	**0.6**	**21.9**	**0.6**	**871.3**	**—**	**26,565**	**762.4**	**—**	**—**
Turkey	57.33	1.5	35.2	2.2	116.0	6.4	2,023	104.1[10]	2.20[10]	50.6[13]
Total Western Europe[2]	**419.47**	**0.5**	**278.1**	**0.6**	**7,368.8**	**—**	**17,567**	**6,333.3**	**—**	**—**
Eastern Europe										
Bulgaria	8.60	−0.8	5.8	−0.8	7.2*	−2.7	837	—	1.25[10]	−4.8[13]
CIS	290.10	0.6	188.3	0.3	180.0[14]	−1.8	650	—	2.09[10]	5.3[13]
Czechoslovakia	15.58	0.0	10.1	0.1	33.2	−1.9	2,129	—	2.09[10]	8.9[13]
Hungary	10.34	−0.5	6.9	−0.3	32.2	−2.1	3,114	—	1.40[10]	12.4[13]
Poland	38.24	0.3	24.8	0.1	75.5	−2.1	1,974	—	1.10[10]	5.0[13]
Romania	23.19	0.2	15.4	0.5	27.6	−4.9	1,190	—	0.83[10]	−4.3[13]
Yugoslavia	23.93	0.4	16.3	0.5	98.6[15]	−4.6	4,120	—	3.13[10]	35.3[13]
Total Eastern Europe[2]	**409.98**	**0.5**	**267.5**	**1.5**	**454.3**	**—**	**1,108**	**—**	**—**	**—**
Middle East										
Bahrain	0.52	2.9	0.3	3.3	3.5[9]	3.3[12]	7,000[9]	2.0[8]	—	—
Egypt	54.69	2.6	30.2	2.2	29.6	2.7	542	—	0.93[6]	—
Iran	57.73	4.7	30.5	4.3	47.0	1.4	814	155.7[5]	—	—
Iraq	19.58	3.5	10.0	3.8	14.5	−13.5	741	—	0.76[10]	—
Israel	4.97	2.8	3.0	3.1	59.1	4.2	11,897	23.6[6]	8.79	16.4
Jordan	4.14	2.5	2.1	2.7	4.1	−0.5	996	3.8[10]	0.55[10]	—
Kuwait	2.10	2.1	1.3	2.6	34.2[10]	−3.1[13]	11,259[9]	29.3[9]	—	—
Libya	4.71	4.7	2.4	4.9	33.1*	0.6[13]	7,023	—	—	—
Oman	1.56	3.9	0.8	3.4	10.2	3.6	6,557	—	—	—
Qatar	0.38	2.6	0.2	2.5	6.7	4.5	17,560	—	—	—
Saudi Arabia	14.69	4.1	7.6	3.6	106.4	4.2	7,243	98.0[4]	9.50[10]	—
Syria	12.99	3.6	6.4	3.7	27.2	2.4	2,096	—	0.64[10]	—
United Arab Emirates	1.63	3.3	0.9	0.0	33.7	2.1	20,656	17.4[6]	8.40[10]	—
Yemen	12.52	12.2	6.1	11.7	9.4	6.2	751	4.8[7]	—	—
Total Middle East	**192.21**	**4.1**	**101.9**	**3.7**	**418.8**	**—**	**2,001**	**—**	**—**	**—**
Africa										
Algeria	25.66	2.7	13.4	3.2	32.7*	0.2	1,274	—	1.15[10]	—
Angola	10.04	2.2	5.2	2.1	7.8[9]	8.6[11]	777	—	—	—
Burkina	9.24	5.3	4.9	5.3	3.0*	3.2	322	—	—	—
Cameroon	12.24	3.8	6.4	3.7	11.6[10]	−4.2	981[10]	6.8[4]	—	—
Congo	2.35	5.6	1.2	5.5	2.9*	−0.6	1,238	1.3[6]	—	—
Cote d'Ivoire	13.02	5.1	6.3	3.8	9.3*	−1.5	712	—	—	—
Ethiopia	53.38	3.6	27.5	3.2	6.2[10]	0.7[13]	116	—	—	—
Gabon	1.21	0.6	0.7	1.5	5.1*	−0.3	4,254	—	—	—
Ghana	15.51	2.0	8.0	2.5	6.5	5.0	421	5.8[10]	0.55[10]	—
Kenya	25.91	3.8	11.7	3.6	8.3	4.5	319	5.6[5]	0.53[10]	−7.6[13]
Madagascar	11.49	2.2	6.0	2.0	2.7*	1.4	233	—	—	—
Malawi	8.56	3.6	4.4	3.5	2.2	3.6	254	—	0.33[10]	—
Mauritius	1.07	0.0	0.7	0.8	2.7	6.7	2,517	1.4[6]	—	—
Morocco	25.70	2.7	14.3	3.0	27.7	4.2	1,076	22.6[8]	1.00[10]	—
Mozambique	16.08	2.7	8.5	2.0	1.1	2.8	66	3.3[5]	—	—
Nigeria	112.16	2.6	55.2	2.6	29.1	4.0	260	—	0.30[10]	—
Senegal	7.53	2.6	4.0	2.5	5.6	2.9	748	4.1[7]	—	—
Sierra Leone	4.26	2.9	2.2	1.8	0.5	1.5	120	1.2[5]	0.07[10]	—
South Africa	36.07	1.7	21.2	3.1	107.6	1.3	2,984	87.6	2.71[10]	13.4[13]
Tanzania	28.36	4.0	13.4	3.2	3.2	3.4	111	2.9	—	—
Tunisia	8.36	2.9	4.9	3.6	13.2	3.2	1,576	11.9	0.59[10]	—
Uganda	19.52	4.0	9.6	3.9	2.9	5.0	147	—	—	—
Zaire	36.67	3.5	18.8	3.2	0.9	−0.9	23	2.0[5]	—	—
Zambia	8.78	4.9	4.3	4.4	3.3	1.1	376	1.9[8]	0.12[10]	—
Zimbabwe	10.02	2.0	5.3	3.1	5.5	3.2	553	4.9[5]	1.96[10]	—
Total Africa[2]	**503.19**	**3.1**	**190.5**	**3.0**	**301.4**	**—**	**599**	**—**	**—**	**—**

[1]See text currency conversion; [2]Total available data. Totals may not agree due to rounding; [3]1983; [4]1984; [5]1985; [6]1986; [7]1987; [8]1988; [9]1989; [10]1990; [11]1984–1988; [12]1985–1989; [13]1985–1990; [14]NMP; [15]GSP. *EIU estimate.

Total Exports		Total Imports		Imports from U.S.		Imports from Japan		Imports from EU		
1991 f.o.b. (millions)	Average Annual % Increase 1986–1991	1991 c.i.f. (millions)	Average Annual % Increase 1986–1991	1991 c.i.f. (millions)	Average Annual % Increase 1986–1991	1991 c.i.f. (millions)	Average Annual % Increase 1986–1991	1991 c.i.f. (millions)	Average Annual % Increase 1986–1991	
										Western Europe
										EU
177,680	11.6	120,663	12.2	5,470	10.0	2,603	6.9	88,143	12.5	Belgium[2]
35,091	11.0	31,905	7.1	2,012	10.8	1,202	-0.4	16,876	7.6	Denmark
216,512	11.9	232,902	12.8	22,079	18.1	9,494	15.7	134,381	12.3	France
403,208	11.0	390,114	15.6	25,897	16.0	23,895	16.7	202,947	15.6	Germany
8,671	10.1	21,564	14.4	920	22.4	1,438	19.6	13,001	15.2	Greece
24,052	14.0	21,097	12.9	3,135	11.5	1,027	19.7	13,904	12.4	Ireland
169,594	11.9	182,697	13.1	10,196	12.5	4,463	16.9	105,507	14.1	Italy
—	—	—	—	—	—	—	—	—	—	Luxembourg[8]
133,076	10.8	135,482	10.9	9,814	10.6	4,575	13.4	80,634	11.0	Netherlands
16,245	18.1	26,078	23.2	884	6.0	751	20.2	18,759	27.9	Portugal
58,991	17.0	94,003	22.3	7,415	17.0	4,345	20.8	55,791	26.7	Spain
184,960	11.9	209,933	11.2	24,375	14.7	11,913	11.3	108,501	11.3	United Kingdom
1,368,080	**11.7**	**1,456,438**	**13.5**	**112,197**	**14.5**	**65,706**	**14.3**	**838,444**	**13.8**	**Total EU[3]**
										EFTA
40,511	13.0	51,347	14.2	1,859	17.0	2,403	16.0	35,315	14.8	Austria
23,079	7.8	21,809	8.5	1,492	17.2	1,317	8.0	9,998	10.1	Finland
1,543	7.4	1,721	10.4	178	21.4	126	19.5	902	10.3	Iceland
33,426	13.0	24,697	4.3	1,979	7.6	1,193	-2.8	11,827	3.8	Norway
55,004	8.4	49,652	9.7	4,237	11.7	2,551	9.2	27,297	8.8	Sweden
61,380	10.9	66,258	10.6	4,867	17.8	2,879	9.4	46,514	9.7	Switzerland
214,943	**10.5**	**215,484**	**10.0**	**14,612**	**13.8**	**10,469**	**7.7**	**131,853**	**10.0**	**Total EFTA[3]**
13,335	13.0	22,576	16.5	2,598	18.1	1,008	15.1	9,882	18.0	Turkey
1,596,358	**11.5**	**1,694,498**	**13.0**	**129,407**	**14.5**	**77,183**	**13.2**	**980,179**	**13.3**	**Total Western Europe[3]**
										Eastern Europe
2,159	-1.8	2,927	-7.1	156	18.4	40	-17.9	1,317	-3.3	Bulgaria
46,635	1.6	54,239	1.3	3,935	29.6	2,329	-6.7	19,437	13.7	CIS
10,921	-3.0	10,240	-4.1	184	39.6	121	22.2	3,287	0.6	Czechoslovakia[4]
10,514	2.9	11,312	4.2	282	9.0	247	13.0	4,737	20.0	Hungary
15,804	4.7	17,886	10.5	458	31.0	361	24.3	9,744	40.7	Poland[4]
4,193	-12.8	5,598	-5.0	127	6.9	47	-8.4	1,385	33.5	Romania[4]
16,235	9.5	17,653	9.1	553	-2.1	336	23.3	8,873	19.3	Yugoslavia
106,461	**1.2**	**119,855**	**1.4**	**5,695**	**17.2**	**3,481**	**-3.4**	**48,780**	**15.0**	**Total Eastern Europe[3]**
										Middle East
3,161	7 4	3,993	11.2	551	44.6	182	14.0	895	8.7	Bahrain
3,838	13.2	8,227	-0.1	1,324	1.1	335	5.1	2,267	7.8	Egypt
15,916	17.5	21,688	22.1	580	100.0	2,724	22.2	10,061	25.3	Iran
297	-11.1	284	-22.6	704[7]	16.0[7]	298[7]	19.0[7]	68*	-18.7*	Iraq
11,598	10.4	16,819	9.9	3,251	12.8	733	22.4	7,995	3.9	Israel
879	4.5	2,512	2.0	268	10.4	90	-12.1	752	5.3	Jordan
422	-14.4	3,882	-6.7	1,351	38.1	481	-17.3	962	-12.0	Kuwait
10,775	8.9	6,001	4.6	51[6]	—	152	10.6	3,712	2.2	Libya
7,236	25.1	3,310	6.7	224	9.0	674	17.2	1,040	11.1	Oman
3,198	5.1	1,862	11.5	162	26.5	230	4.7	823	12.1	Qatar
51,719	22.1	34,587	13.6	7,229	20.1	4,292	8.2	13,315	16.2	Saudi Arabia
3,700	30.6	2,857	2.4	240	16.6	125	21.9	1,108	5.1	Syria
24,261	9.4	16,049	20.6	1,601	22.6	2,374	16.0	5,016	12.6	United Arab Emirates
1,110	397.7	1,951	14.7	211	30.6	141	1.5	550	8.5	Yemen Arab Republic
138,110	**10.6**	**124,022**	**7.8**	**17,739**	**14.9**	**12,831**	**5.4**	**48,564**	**6.6**	**Total Middle East[3]**
										Africa
12,314	11.6	9,104	1.1	800	7.5	402	1.9	5,845	2.7	Algeria
3,091	16.7	1,971	13.4	207	19.4	153	94.1	1,283	8.0	Angola
197	17.8	552	6.6	26	23.4	21	8.0	251	2.4	Burkina
1,909	23.7	1,345	-1.1	79	3.1	72	-4.7	866	3.7	Cameroon
1,098	11.0	682	6.2	47	93.2	23	2.0	450	5.3	Congo
3,506	1.3	2,240	1.8	90	-7.1	74	-4.8	1,179	-1.6	Côte d'Ivoire
307	-6.0	1,114	1.0	231	19.1	61	0.5	405	-3.5	Ethiopia
2,573	16.9	962	1.7	93	35.0	66	12.7	627	2.2	Gabon
1,194	6.7	1,482	14.0	156	19.7	84	101.4	741	27.3	Ghana
1,324	3.2	2,229	6.8	101	8.2	227	6.8	1,008	6.2	Kenya
357	4.0	556	14.8	16	-7.0	27	14.8	224	14.8	Madagascar
443	16.0	545	17.8	60	60.2	44	20.7	163	-0.5	Malawi
1,120	12.1	1,445	18.2	17	186.9	86	19.0	490	4.1	Mauritius
5,149	26.0	7,458	13.9	443	3.2	140	19.3	4,897	12.8	Morocco
390	36.9	899	14.7	111	43.9	43	17.6	296	1.0	Mozambique
12,710	21.0	7,781	19.9	916	20.0	453	25.9	3,975	13.3	Nigeria
737	3.5	1,359	-1.4	84	18.2	29	9.5	753	2.2	Senegal
145	1.4	246	13.4	27	40.5	9	3.1	111	10.3	Sierra Leone
26,576	8.1	16,981	8.2	2,113	8.8	1,639	7.2	7,185	0.8	South Africa[4]
385	3.3	1,090	6.8	38	19.3	108	3.9	467	14.2	Tanzania
3,827	17.8	5,445	15.1	244	9.8	121	34.1	3,719	7.9	Tunisia
171	-15.7	464	6.4	15	59.7	43	29.3	185	-1.3	Uganda
1,572	9.5	992	5.3	68	-6.5	43	55.2	602	-0.4	Zaire
1,061	30.5	888	20.7	24	13.9	70	27.1	224	1.6	Zambia[4]
1,541	9.3	1,294	6.9	53	12.2	79	15.0	585	9.8	Zimbabwe[4]
83,697	**10.6**	**69,124**	**7.9**	**6,059**	**7.2**	**4,117**	**8.2**	**36,531**	**4.1**	**Total Africa[3]**

[1] See text on currency conversion; [2]Includes Luxembourg; [3]Total available data. Totals may not agree due to rounding; [4]Imports from United States, Japan, and the EU are fob; [5]U.S. imports date from 1986; [6]1986; [7]1990; [8]See Belgium. *EIU estimate.

	Population				Gross Domestic Product			National Income	Average Hourly Wage	
	Total 1991 (millions)	Average Annual % Increase 1987–1991	Working Age 1991 (millions)	Average Annual % Increase 1987–1991	Total[1] 1991 (billions)	Average Annual Real % Increase 1986–1991	Per Capita 1991 ($)	Total[1] 1991 ($ billions)	1991[1] ($)	Average Annual % Increase 1986–1991
North America										
Canada	27.0	1.0	18.3	0.7	593.2	2.1	21,978	500.3	17.18	14.8
United States	252.7	1.0	166.5	0.7	5,672.6	2.0	22,449	5,068.9	15.60	9.9
Total North America[2]	**279.7**	**1.0**	**184.8**	**0.7**	**6,265.8**	**—**	**22,403**	**5,569.2**	**—**	**—**
Latin America										
LAIA										
Argentina	32.7	1.1	20.0	0.9	184.9	1.7	5,653*	—	2.93[10]	22.2[12]
Bolivia*	7.6	3.1	4.0	2.4	6.1	2.0	797	4.5[6]	0.44[10]	—
Brazil	153.3	2.1	92.1	1.9	405.8*	1.9	2,647*	338.0[8]	2.79[10]	20.0[12]
Chile	13.4	1.7	8.5	1.3	31.3	6.2	2,338	21.1[9]	2.71[10]	—
Colombia*	33.6	2.8	20.1	2.6	41.7	4.2	1,240	37.3[8]	2.22[10]	—
Ecuador	10.9	2.4	6.0	2.2	11.6	2.4	1,070	9.1	1.09[10]	—
Mexico	87.8	1.6	51.8	2.8	282.5*	1.7	3,216*	145.4[8]	1.95	2.9[12]
Paraguay	4.4	3.0	2.5	2.9	5.7	3.7	1,294	5.8	0.69[10]	—
Peru*	22.0	1.7	12.6	1.6	48.2	-0.6	2,191	39.4[9]	0.25[10]	0.8[12]
Uruguay	3.1	0.5	1.9	0.4	9.5	3.0	3,048	7.8[9]	2.37[10]	22.8[12]
Venezuela*	20.2	2.6	11.7	2.4	53.4	4.4	2,642	48.8	2.27[10]	—
Ancom subtotal[2]*	94.3	2.5	54.5	2.3	161.0	—	1,707	139.0	—	—
Total LAIA[2]	**389.1**	**2.0**	**231.3**	**2.1**	**1,080.7**	**—**	**2,778**	**657.2**	**—**	**—**
CACM										
Costa Rica	3.1	2.8	1.8	2.3	5.5	4.2	1,801	5.3	1.20[10]	5.7[12]
El Salvador	5.4	2.1	2.8	-1.9	5.9	2.2	1,099	5.6	—	—
Guatemala	9.5	2.9	4.9	2.4	9.3	3.0	985	6.5[9]	0.75[10]	-3.4[12]
Honduras	5.3	3.1	2.7	3.2	3.0	3.5	567	2.6	1.00[10]	-3.9[12]
Nicaragua	4.0	3.4	2.1	3.0	1.8	-2.5	438	3.4[6]	—	—
Total CACM[2]	**27.2**	**2.9**	**14.3**	**1.7**	**25.5**	**—**	**938**	**23.3**	**—**	**—**
Caribbean										
Barbados	0.3	-0.2	0.2	0.3	1.5	1.3	5,802	—	2.25[10]	—
Cuba	10.8	1.3	7.6	2.4	23.6[15]	-4.5	2,177[15]	17.6[8]	1.05[10]	-2.0[12]
Dominican Republic	7.3	2.2	4.3	3.1	7.2	1.7	985	6.8	1.37[10]	—
Guyana	0.8	0.2	0.5	-3.5	0.3	-1.6	429	0.1[10]	0.88[10]	—
Haiti	6.6	2.0	3.8	0.5	1.6	0.1	242	2.4[10]	0.55[10]	—
Jamaica	2.4	0.2	1.4	0.5	3.5	3.7	1,473	3.2[9]	3.71[10]	—
Netherlands Antilles	0.2	0.9	—	—	1.4*	3.5	7,546	—	—	—
Panama	2.5	2.1	1.5	2.5	5.5	0.6	2,227	4.8	2.70[10]	8.2[12]
Puerto Rico	3.3	0.1	2.1	-1.1	22.7[16]	3.3	6,802[16]	18.2[8]	6.28[10]	3.9[12]
Trinidad and Tobago	1.3	0.8	0.8	0.7	5.3	-1.7	4,216	3.5[9]	2.63[10]	—
Total Caribbean[2]	**35.4**	**1.4**	**22.0**	**1.5**	**72.5**	**—**	**2,047**	**56.6**	**—**	**—**
Total Latin America[2]	**451.7**	**2.0**	**267.6**	**2.0**	**1,178.7**	**—**	**2,610**	**737.1**	**—**	**—**
Asia										
Afghanistan	16.4	1.5	9.1	2.4	—	-2.6[11]	—	—	—	—
Bangladesh	118.7	3.0	63.2	4.0	21.9*	4.0	185	—	0.21[10]	—
Cambodia	8.3	1.6	5.8	4.2	1.1*		132	—	—	—
China	1,160.0	1.4	788.8	2.8	371.2[16]	7.8	320	301.0	0.40[10]	21.9[12]
Hong Kong	5.7	0.3	3.9	1.0	82.5[17]	7.4	14,499		3.58	13.1[12]
India	849.6	1.7	501.3	2.0	268.0*	5.6	315	237.8	0.65[10]	11.3[12]
Indonesia	187.8	1.8	114.7	3.5	116.5	6.3	620	105.2	0.37[10]	—
Japan	123.9	0.3	86.5	1.0	3,346.4	4.5	27,005	2,675.4[9]	14.55[10]	11.3[12]
Korea, North	21.8	0.4	12.9	2.4						
Korea, South	43.3	0.8	28.3	1.4	283.0	10.0	6,540	253.4	4.39	23.5
Laos	4.3	2.6	2.3	3.7	0.9	3.0	209	—	—	—
Malaysia	18.3	2.4	11.0	3.7	46.6	7.1	2,542	—	0.47[10]	—
Myanmar[13]	42.6	2.0	25.0	2.7	28.1	-1.5	660	7.8[7]	0.10[10]	—
Nepal	19.6	2.6	10.7	3.3	2.8	4.5	144	2.3[5]		—
Pakistan	115.5	0.8	59.6	1.5	45.5	5.8	394	41.7	0.70[10]	—
Philippines	62.9	2.0	35.5	2.8	45.3	3.2	720	42.2	0.90[10]	19.2[12]
Singapore	2.8	1.1	2.0	1.9	40.0	7.8	14,497	21.1[8]	4.39	8.9[12]
Sri Lanka	17.2	0.8	10.7	1.9	9.1	3.9	526	—	0.31[10]	2.1[12]
Taiwan	20.6	0.9	13.5	—	175.7	8.5	8,529	149.5[10]	4.39	21.6[12]
Thailand	56.9	1.4	36.1	3.1	92.4	9.6	1,623	73.1[10]	1.05[10]	15.4[12]
Vietnam	67.7	1.5	38.2	2.4	37.1[10]	3.4[12]		37.1[10]		
Total Asia[2]	**2,964.0**	**1.5**	**1,859.2**	**2.6**	**4,977.0**	**—**	**1,679**	**3,947.5**	**—**	**—**
Oceania										
Australia	17.3	1.5	11.6	2.1	295.5	2.4	17,040	236.2	13.3	614.9
New Zealand	3.4	0.0	2.2	1.1	42.4	-0.2	12,547	36.6	8.3	69.8
Total Oceania[2]	**20.7**	**1.2**	**13.8**	**1.9**	**337.9**	**—**	**16,307**	**272.8**	**—**	**—**

[1] See text on currency conversion; [2] Total available data. Totals may not agree due to rounding; [3] GNP; [4] 1984; [5] 1985; [6] 1986; [7] 1987; [8] 1988; [9] 1989; [10] 1990; [11] 1985–1989; [12] 1985–1990; [13] Burma; [14] Produced National Income; [15] GSP; [16] GNP; [17] ADB Estimate; *EIU Estimate; •Andean Common Market member.

Total Exports		Total Imports		Imports from U.S.		Imports from Japan		Imports from EU		
1991 f.o.b. (millions)	Average Annual % Increase 1986–1991	1991 c.i.f. (millions)	Average Annual % Increase 1986–1991	1991 c.i.f. (millions)	Average Annual % Increase 1986–1991	1991 c.i.f. (millions)	Average Annual % Increase 1986–1991	1991 c.i.f. (millions)	Average Annual % Increase 1986–1991	
										North America
126,160	7.2	120,410	7.9	75,015	6.3	8,891	10.6	12,650	7.4	Canada[7]
421,755	14.4	509,300	5.7	—	—	95,010	2.2	89,433	2.5	United States
547,915	**12.5**	**629,710**	**6.1**	**75,025**	**6.0**	**103,901**	**2.8**	**102,083**	**3.0**	**Total North America**[2]
										Latin America
										LAIA
13,222	15.5	7,994	17.3	2,254	32.7	495	41.5	2,304	18.3	Argentina
652	2.9	878	7.2	209	8.3	55	-1.9	172	11.2	Bolivia*
32,424	8.4	23,420	8.9	5,536	10.2	1,336	6.9	5,128	8.5	Brazil
9,028	17.0	7,683	20.1	1,582	20.2	646	17.5	1,405	16.9	Chile
6,662	5.8	5,684	7.9	2,141	9.2	544	10.5	1,193	6.1	Colombia*
3,580	11.3	2,759	11.3	1,042	17.2	213	5.6	654	12.2	Ecuador*
38,868	20.2	47,033	33.7	33,276	36.8	2,822	45.7	5,935	30.7	Mexico[7]
737	32.6	1,335	26.1	195	28.9	161	52.6	174	19.8	Paraguay[7]
3,423	7.1	2,475	16.9	618	11.1	141	12.3	442	9.2	Peru[7]*
1,577	8.1	1,628	13.9	228	26.8	78	24.2	336	16.1	Uruguay
15,727	15.0	9,456	8.8	4,668	11.3	529	14.1	2,257	7.0	Venezuela[7]*
30,044	10.5	22,788	9.0	8,678	9.2	1,482	4.0	4,718	5.7	Ancom subtotal[2]*
125,900	**12.6**	**110,345**	**16.5**	**51,749**	**24.0**	**7,020**	**15.7**	**20,000**	**12.7**	**Total LAIA**[2]
										CACM
1,613	8.3	1,850	10.8	805	15.0	111	2.5	199	3.5	Costa Rica
723	0.6	1,498	10.8	587	10.5	68	20.0	235	20.2	El Salvador
1,202	3.0	1,851	15.1	784	14.1	122	20.7	229	12.5	Guatemala
780	0.9	880	4.2	357	9.3	79	2.2	133	5.3	Honduras
363	5.5	759	10.3	161	1,579.8	34	33.5	106	-7.1	Nicaragua
4,681	**3.6**	**6,838**	**10.1**	**2,694**	**13.2**	**414**	**7.9**	**902**	**5.1**	**Total CACM**[2]
										Caribbean
231	-0.3	625	2.0	208	-1.0	32	0.7	112	-1.0	Barbados
1,090	4.6	2,647	0.7	1	11.1	39	-26.2	858	5.8	Cuba
925	6.4	1,995	8.5	909	10.3	104	-7.5	283	13.0	Dominican Republic[7]
302	7.9	278	4.7	95	20.8	17	14.4	75	11.9	Guyana
317	13.8	663	16.2	431	22.8	23	0.1	67	13.0	Haiti
1,409	19.4	2,015	16.2	1,059	17.0	76	17.7	265	18.5	Jamaica
1,584	14.9	1,799	15.6	692	68.9	85	111.4	381	137.2	Netherlands Antilles
342	1.0	1,695	10.5	607	9.5	115	14.9	124	3.3	Panama
21,800	12.8	14,825	7.1	10,200	—	—	—	—	—	Puerto Rico
1,982	8.2	1,647	5.5	656	6.5	93	12.3	247	-1.0	Trinidad and Tobago
29,982	**11.3**	**28,189**	**6.4**	**14,858**	**51.1**	**584**	**7.4**	**2,412**	**8.2**	**Total Caribbean**[2]
160,563	**12.0**	**145,372**	**13.5**	**69,301**	**20.7**	**8,018**	**12.0**	**23,314**	**11.6**	**Total Latin America**[2]
										Asia
933	12.9	1,670	9.1	3	-15.6	127	1.5	72	2.5	Afghanistan
1,688	14.2	3,381	6.2	175	0.4	303	1.8	445	4.3	Bangladesh
40	94.6	44	25.0	—	—	7	79.0	9	67.0	Cambodia
71,986	18.2	63,957	8.9	8,003	12.7	10,079	-2.0	8,500	2.2	China
98,579	23.0	100,274	23.5	7,576	21.0	16,397	18.3	9,253	18.2	Hong Kong
20,492	17.6	21,687	7.9	2,234	10.9	1,634	-2.7	6,896	8.3	India
29,142	14.5	25,869	19.6	3,397	18.9	6,327	16.1	4,704	22.3	Indonesia
314,892	8.4	236,633	13.4	53,634	13.2	—	—	31,971	18.8	Japan
693	1.7	1,457	12.5	—	—	246	5.2	143	27.1	Korea, North[7]
69,489	15.7	81,114	20.8	19,183	24.7	21,334	14.6	12,298	30.6	Korea, South
84	254.8	150	52.9	1	50.3	23	55.7	14	28.6	Laos
34,405	19.8	36,749	27.8	5,626	22.7	9,582	34.1	5,001	26.5	Malaysia
588	24.5	1,073	52.5	26	11.9	91	-2.7	87	14.0	Myanmar[6]
256	15.8	455	9.6	7	113.3	108	12.5	49	7.9	Nepal
6,494	14.2	8,431	9.5	943	9.6	1,245	8.5	2,160	9.1	Pakistan
8,840	13.2	12,945	20.6	2,609	15.3	2,517	24.0	1,318	19.6	Philippines
59,188	21.7	66,257	21.4	10,501	23.0	14,115	23.3	7,978	22.4	Singapore
2,200	13.8	3,163	12.2	133	6.9	321	0.9	574	16.6	Sri Lanka
75,716	14.2	63,981	22.8	13,191	21.7	18,275	18.0	6,737	22.1	Taiwan
27,562	25.7	37,518	33.3	3,996	26.9	10,803	36.1	5,200	31.7	Thailand
1,598	37.3	1,620	23.7	4	-33.7	239	3.6	252	37.8	Vietnam
824,872	**13.8**	**768,428**	**17.1**	**131,242**	**16.8**	**113,773**	**15.1**	**103,661**	**17.2**	**Total Asia**[2]
										Oceania
42,044	13.5	41,501	10.5	9,455	13.1	6,799	6.1	8,054	5.6	Australia[7]
9,584	10.5	8,392	7.7	1,406	6.9	1,310	1.8	1,510	3.2	New Zealand
51,628	**12.9**	**49,893**	**9.9**	**10,861**	**12.1**	**8,109**	**5.1**	**9,564**	**5.0**	**Total Oceania**[2]

[1] Cumulative increase of total national energy consumption; [2] Total available data. Totals may not agree due to rounding; [3] 1991; [4] 1990; [5] 1988; [6] 1983–1988; [6] Burma; [7] Import figures from the United States, Japan, and the EU are fob. *Andean Common Market member.

	Private Consumption Expenditure					Passenger Cars		Trucks and Buses		Telephones
	Total 1991[1] ($ billions)	Average Annual Real % Increase 1987–1991	1990 % for Food	1990 % for Clothing	1990 % for Household	1991 (thousands)	Cumulative % Increase 1986–1991	1991 (thousands)	Cumulative % Increase 1986–1991	1991 (thousands)
Western Europe										
EU										
Belgium	126.7	3.0	22.8	7.7	13.2	4,013	14.9	419	14.5	5,691
Denmark	67.6	–0.1	20.9	5.4	6.3	1,591	6.0	302	13.1	5,000[10]
France	720.5	2.8	18.4	6.5	8.1	23,550	12.5	4,910	43.3	29,080
Germany	856.4	2.9	23.0	8.4	8.1	30,695	17.6	2,003	16.3	41,730[10]
Greece	49.6	2.2	31.8	12.5	7.8	1,730	36.9	793	27.7	4,980
Ireland	24.3	2.6	38.5	7.2	7.2	796	12.1	152	49.0	1,030
Italy	718.8	3.4	20.7	10.3	9.5	27,500	27.9	2,429	33.2	32,040[10]
Luxembourg	4.9[10]	—	20.9	6.3	8.7	—	—	—	—	—
Netherlands	172.9	2.8	18.3	6.6	8.7	5,509	12.4	582	36.0	10,500
Portugal	37.1[10]	5.1[15]	37.8	6.5	6.2	1,605	35.4	593	66.6	3,071
Spain	329.4	4.5	26.2	10.7	8.0	11,996	29.4	2,379	47.8	15,480[7]
United Kingdom	656.3	3.0	20.8	5.9	5.3	23,123	19.5	3,288	19.4	25,595
Total EU	**3,764.5**	**—**	**—**	**—**	**—**	**132,108**	**19.9**	**17,850**	**32.5**	**174,197**
EFTA										
Austria	90.8	3.1	22.3	10.1	8.1	2,991	18.2	295	14.3	4,732
Finland	68.6	2.2	22.5	5.3	6.7	1,926	24.6	271	34.8	3,800
Iceland	4.0	—	33.4	8.0	10.8	121	17.5	13	0.0	136
Norway	53.8	–0.7	25.2	7.6	7.0	1,613	6.5	330	32.0	2,198
Sweden	128.5	1.7	20.6	6.7	6.9	3,601	14.3	324	40.3	5,948
Switzerland	132.8	1.7	26.3	4.7	4.9	2,994	14.4	304	44.1	6,227
Total EFTA[2]	**478.5**	**—**	**—**	**—**	**—**	**13,246**	**15.6**	**1,537**	**32.0**	**23,041**
Turkey	69.6*	6.0	46.3	6.6	10.6	1,650	67.7	710	28.4	10,150
Total Western Europe[2]	**4,312.7**	**—**	**—**	**—**	**—**	**147,004**	**17.1**	**20,097**	**32.3**	**207,388**
Eastern Europe										
Bulgaria	—	—	43.2	10.0	14.1	1,234	19.8	169	12.7	2,515[9]
CIS	—	—	51.8	19.3	4.0	13,548	13.2	9,856	9.5	37,532[10]
Czechoslovakia	13.2	2.5	45.2	7.4	15.6	3,242	20.3	266	–37.4	4,432
Hungary	20.6[10]	–1.9[15]	26.8	4.9	5.4	1,944	35.4	289	29.6	1,956
Poland	34.4[10]	–4.7[15]	53.2	11.4	3.7	5,260	43.3	1,044	21.0	5,480
Romania	27.3[10]	0.0[15]	43.4	10.0	2.8	1,245	398.0	265	76.7	3,100
Yugoslavia	67.0[10]	–4.6[15]	48.6	8.9	4.4	3,526	23.8	913	205.4	4,550[9]
Total Eastern Europe[2]	**162.5**	**—**	**—**	**—**	**—**	**29,999**	**25.5**	**12,802**	**18.4**	**59,565***
Middle East										
Bahrain	1.4[8]	—	—	—	—	104	48.6	24	–7.7	163
Egypt	25.1	1.6	50.0[5]	11.0	3.0	1,168	174.8	380	55.7	2,500
Iran	38.3[10]	3.0[15]	46.9[7]	9.3	5.5	1,557	–2.0	553	2.6	2,270[10]
Iraq	—	—	—	—	—	672	160.5	368	34.8	886[5]
Israel	36.2	5.3	26.1	5.8	9.3	813	27.8	163	27.3	2,545
Jordan	3.8	–0.3	40.7[6]	5.6	4.9	162	19.1	86	34.4	350
Kuwait	7.5	–0.4	28.5[9]	8.4	12.6	499	–10.1	112	–45.1	362[8]
Libya	8.8[7]	—	—	—	—	448[10]	8.0[15]	322[10]	0.6[15]	500[7]
Oman	3.9	—	—	—	—	140	28.4	75	–54.8	263
Qatar	1.7[7]	—	—	—	—	115	47.4	47	–27.7	146
Saudi Arabia	38.7[9]	—	—	—	—	1,468	12.9	1,536	5.9	1,382[5]
Syria	21.2	1.8	—	—	—	112	17.9	131	–31.1	708
United Arab Emirates	14.0	–0.6	—	—	—	323	34.6	177	23.8	777
Yemen	4.7[8]	6.2[11]	—	—	—	145	367.7	219	259.0	136
Total Middle East[2]	**205.2***	**—**	**—**	**—**	**—**	**7,726**	**30.1**	**4,193**	**8.3**	**12,852**
Africa										
Algeria	25.2[9]	—	—	—	—	725	23.1	480	27.3	1,103[10]
Angola	4.3[8]	—	—	—	—	122	–3.2	41	–2.4	77[8]
Burkina	1.5[8]	—	—	—	—	11	0.0	13	0.0	18[8]
Cameroon	9.2[10]	–1.9[15]	24.0[5]	7.0	3.0	90	5.9	79	6.8	61[8]
Congo	1.2[10]	–0.5[15]	42.0[5]	6.0	4.0	26	0.0	20	0.0	26[9]
Côte d'Ivoire	6.4[10]	–1.3[15]	40.0[5]	10.0	3.0	155	–3.7	90	1.1	153[10]
Ethiopia	4.5	—	—	—	—	40	–2.4	18	–5.3	169
Gabon	2.0[10]	–7.5[15]	—	—	—	—	—	—	—	26[10]
Ghana	5.3[10]	2.8[15]	50.0[5]	13.0	3.0	82	39.0	42	–8.7	79[10]
Kenya	5.2	4.6	39.0[5]	7.0	6.0	136	7.9	158	18.8	383[10]
Madagascar	2.0[9]	—	—	—	—	47	–4.1	33	–25.0	60[10]
Malawi	1.7	6.3	—	—	—	15	0.0	17	13.3	55
Mauritius	1.8	—	—	—	—	47	51.6	9	–25.0	75[10]
Morocco	18.8	3.5	40.0[5]	11.0	5.0	664	48.9	282	41.7	561
Mozambique	1.1[9]	—	—	—	—	84	–3.4	25	4.2	69
Nigeria	12.9	–0.1	46.7	5.4	3.6	773	–1.7	606	–2.1	722[8]
Senegal	4.2[7]	2.8	50.0[5]	11.0	2.0	90	45.2	29	–21.6	48
Sierra Leone	0.4	—	—	—	—	36	89.5	12	20.0	35
South Africa	64.9	3.0	26.1	7.2	9.4	3,375	15.9	1,825	50.1	5,208
Tanzania	2.4	—	64.0[5]	10.0	3.0	44	4.8	54	5.9	140[10]
Tunisia	8.5	2.1	37.0[5]	10.0	5.0	320	82.9	174	–2.8	464
Uganda	2.6[9]	—	—	—	—	12	–62.5	15	15.4	59
Zaire	0.7	–1.0	55.0[5]	10.0	3.0	94	0.0	86	0.0	32[8]
Zambia	2.6[10]	6.8[15]	37.0[5]	10.0	1.0	96	–2.0	68	0.0	105
Zimbabwe	2.6[7]	1.9*	30.1[7]	10.3	12.9	173	–1.7	83	3.8	312
Total Africa[2]	**192.2**	**—**	**—**	**—**	**—**	**7,257**	**16.1**	**4,259**	**22.9**	**10,040**

[1] See text on currency conversion; [2] Total available data. Totals may not agree due to rounding; [3] 1983; [4] 1984; [5] 1985; [6] 1986; [7] 1987; [8] 1988; [9] 1989; [10] 1990; [11] 1984–1988; [12] 1985–1989; [13] 1980; [14] 1986–1989; [15] 1986–1990; *EIU estimate.

Televisions		Personal Computers	Steel Consumption		Cement Production		Electricity Production		Energy Consumption		
1992 (thousands)	Cumulative % Increase 1988–1992	1991 (thousands)	1991 (K MT)	Cumulative % Increase 1986–1991	1991 (K MT)	Cumulative % Increase 1986–1991	1991 (billion kwh)	Cumulative % Increase 1986–1991	1990 kg Oil Equivalent Per Capita	Cumulative[1] % Increase 1984–1990	
											Western Europe
											EU
4,200	32.3	995	3,693	-1.3	7,188	24.8	71.9	24.9	4,141	3.9	Belgium
2,500	-7.2	688	1,825	1.6	2,016	-0.6	24.4[3]	-16.1[6]	3,263	0.4	Denmark
29,300	33.4	8,008	16,588	14.2	25,020	15.9	427.7	24.6	2,776	2.3	France
30,500	-17.8	8,048	39,088	27.6	31,812	20.3	449.2[3]	10.4[6]	3,900	-1.6	Germany
2,300	31.1	—	2,386	21.8	11,808	-8.0	31.2	10.5	2,130	37.9	Greece
1,000	7.5	—	454	26.1	1,600[3]	9.8[6]	14.9	21.3	2,564	15.9	Ireland
17,000	-29.2	3,238	26,593	17.4	40,788[3]	9.5[6]	216.9[3]	19.0[6]	2,573	8.9	Italy
100	9.3	—	—	—	636[3]	86.4[6]	1.4	141.3	9,067	19.0	Luxembourg
6,000	-14.3	1,692	4,777	18.3	3,552	14.7	73.4	9.2	5,047	14.1	Netherlands
1,686	4.2	—	1,462	18.1	6,000[3]	13.7[6]	28.5[3]	50.0[6]	1,307	43.1	Portugal
17,000	14.3	2,405	11,170	26.6	27,576	25.3	163.6	26.7	1,768	18.5	Spain
20,000	-19.0	6,129	14,600	-1.5	14,736[3]	24.1[6]	319.9	7.3	3,492	8.4	United Kingdom
131,586	-5.9	31,203	122,636	17.3	172,732	14.7	1,823.0	15.2	3,014	6.5	**Total EU[9]**
											EFTA
2,706	-25.9	554	2,701	7.6	5,016	9.7	51.5	16.6	2,844	7.8	Austria
1,900	-20.8	572	1,454	-24.7	1,320	4.8	55.1	12.9	4,153	25.6	Finland
76	0.0	—	46[3]	6.1[6]	120	-0.9	4.6[3]	14.0[6]	4,379	20.4	Iceland
1,500	2.3	610	1,097	-29.8	1,260[3]	-6.2[6]	121.6[3]	17.8[6]	4,838	9.6	Norway
3,750	13.9	1,057	3,030	-14.5	2,360[3]	4.7[6]	142.5	3.2	3,315	-1.2	Sweden
2,200	-5.0	1,132	1,630	-33.1	5,206[3]	27.8[6]	54.1	-1.3	2,738	9.9	Switzerland
12,132	-8.1	3,925	9,958	17.3	15,282	8.3	429.3	-1.3	3,351	9.0	**Total EFTA[9]**
10,530	30.4	—	7,491	39.5	25,200	18.8	57.5[3]	69.8[6]	727	44.8	Turkey
154,248	-6.7	35,128	140,085	14.8	213,214	9.3	2,309.9	10.7	2,725	7.7	**Total Western Europe[9]**
											Eastern Europe
3,127	48.9	—	1,295	-57.1	4,716[3]	-11.6[6]	38.9	-6.9	3,013	-23.7	Bulgaria
95,000[10]	5.6[6]	934	131,865	-18.4	122,400	-8.5	1,726.0[3]	11.8[6]	4,684	15.8	CIS
5,720	30.4	182	7,062	-36.9	8,304	-19.3	83.4	-1.7	3,916	-9.7	Czechoslovakia
4,261	1.1	158	1,855	-47.0	2,532	-34.5	29.7	5.9	2,299	-13.4	Hungary
10,000	0.5	251	5,740	-64.1	12,024	-24.0	134.6	-4.1	2,603	-14.6	Poland
4,000	-0.1	—	5,930	-51.2	7,404	-43.3	56.2	-21.5	2,612	-14.2	Romania
1,642	-60.0	—	1,627	-72.8	6,000	-34.2	78.9	1.2	1,686	10.5	Yugoslavia
123,750	4.2	1,525	155,374	-27.2	163,380	-10.5	2,147.7	9.3	4,063	9.4	**Total Eastern Europe[9]**
											Middle East
270	54.3	—	44	-25.4	—	—	3.5[3]	63.8[6]	10,917	19.6	Bahrain
5,000	25.0	—	4,904	-12.3	14,111[3]	85.5[6]	39.6[3]	70.3[6]	515	13.4	Egypt
2,250	-10.0	—	8,440	94.3	12,520[3]	-4.6[6]	56.0[3]	50.1[6]	1,158	33.9	Iran
1,000	37.7	—	891[3]	1.5[6]	13,000[3]	62.7[6]	29.2[3]	55.4[6]	612	37.2	Iraq
1,500	66.7	—	1,061	57.0	2,868	86.7	20.7[3]	32.1[6]	2,234	28.0	Israel
250	-9.1	—	164	-59.9	1,780[3]	-1.1[6]	3.7[3]	49.2[6]	757	8.5	Jordan
800	30.5	—	49	-87.6	800[3]	-21.1[6]	20.6[3]	31.4[6]	4,906	-5.3	Kuwait
500	112.8	—	1,361	317.5	2,700[3]	30.0[6]	19.0[3]	132.6[6]	3,305	30.6	Libya
1,500	66.7	—	283	-0.4	—	—	5.3[3]	88.0[6]	2,768	-70.9	Oman
250	66.7	—	114	72.7	267[3]	-17.6[6]	4.6[3]	31.4[6]	16,584	9.6	Qatar
4,500	21.6	—	3,500	11.7	10,000[3]	8.3[6]	47.4[3]	46.3[6]	4,475	76.4	Saudi Arabia
700	16.7	—	180	-13.9	3,500[3]	-19.0[6]	10.6[3]	44.9[6]	745	-7.8	Syria
170	17.2	—	—	—	3,110[3]	24.9[6]	13.6[3]	17.2[6]	14,128	164.4	United Arab Emirates
100	-33.3	—	—	—	700[3]	0.3[6]	0.8[3]	67.0[6]	120	-9.8	Yemen
18,790	24.7	—	20,100	99.5	65,356	25.2	274.6[3]	51.2[6]	1,367	61.6	**Total Middle East[9]**
											Africa
2,000	29.0	—	1,964	-38.3	6,337[3]	-1.7[6]	16.0[3]	30.3[6]	1,038	94.0	Algeria
50	0.0	—	—	—	1,000[3]	156.4[6]	1.8[3]	2.8[6]	63	-25.0	Angola
45	9.8	—	—	—	—	—	0.2[3]	39.1[6]	20	-4.8	Burkina
15	200.0	—	—	—	586[5]	-2.0[8]	2.7[3]	21.1[6]	171	-46.7	Cameroon
8	60.0	—	—	—	58[3]	0.0[6]	0.4[3]	68.8[6]	261	307.8	Congo
810	29.6	—	—	—	500[3]	-35.5[6]	2.4[3]	32.8[6]	133	-7.6	Côte d'Ivoire
100	100.0	—	—	—	400[3]	48.1[6]	0.9[3]	9.5[6]	18	50.0	Ethiopia
40	8.1	—	—	—	115[3]	-45.5[6]	0.9[3]	70.4[6]	501	-40.1	Gabon
250	78.6	—	—	—	600[3]	174.0[6]	6.1	35.3	71	31.5	Ghana
260	92.6	—	224	29.5	1,512[3]	26.0[6]	3.2	25.8	78	21.9	Kenya
130	30.0	—	—	—	12	-62.5	0.6[3]	26.9[6]	28	0.0	Madagascar
—	—	—	—	—	101[3]	46.4[6]	0.7	40.9	24	-20.0	Malawi
138	25.5	—	—	—	—	—	0.7	39.0	347	71.8	Mauritius
1,210	0.3	—	567	9.7	5,381[3]	44.7[6]	9.6[3]	38.4[6]	257	12.2	Morocco
35	75.0	—	—	—	100[3]	37.0[6]	0.5[3]	-15.8[6]	22	-66.7	Mozambique
6,100	205.0	—	465	-6.6	3,500[3]	-3.4[6]	9.9[3]	10.4[6]	132	-19.5	Nigeria
61	-69.5	—	—	—	380[3]	2.2[6]	0.7[3]	-2.3[6]	99	-15.4	Senegal
25	-16.7	—	—	—	9[3]	800.0[7]	0.2[3]	-20.9[6]	52	10.6	Sierra Leone
3,445	14.8	680	5,013	-5.5	6,563[3]	5.0[6]	148.9	21.6	1,817	-15.1	South Africa
80	900.0	—	57	18.8	300[3]	-31.0[6]	0.9[3]	1.7[6]	25	-13.8	Tanzania
650	62.5	—	595	16.4	3,672	24.9	5.5[3]	30.3[6]	569	7.4	Tunisia
115	27.8	—	—	—	24	50.0	0.8	18.9	17	0.0	Uganda
22	46.7	—	34	54.5	460[4]	-13.9[7]	6.2[3]	33.3[6]	46	-6.1	Zaire
200	233.3	—	6	-78.6	432[3]	29.3[6]	7.8[3]	-23.0[6]	141	-40.0	Zambia
137	22.3	—	173	5.5	996[3]	53.7[6]	9.6[3]	119.9[6]	455	44.4	Zimbabwe
15,926	59.4	680	9,098	-12.9	33,038	12.6	237.1	20.1	301	11.6	**Total Africa[9]**

[1] Cumulative increase of total national energy consumption; [2] Includes Luxembourg; [3] 1990; [4] 1989; [5] 1988; [6] 1985–1990; [7] 1984–1989; [8] 1983–1988; [9] Total available data. Totals may not agree due to rounding; [10] 1991.

	Private Consumption Expenditure					Passenger Cars		Trucks and Buses		Telephones
	Total 1991[1] ($ billions)	Average Annual Real % Increase 1987-1991	1990 % for Food	1990 % for Clothing	1990 % for Household	1991 (thousands)	Cumulative % Increase 1986-1991	1991 (thousands)	Cumulative % Increase 1986-1991	1991 (thousands)
North America										
Canada	358.4	2.4	15.6	4.6	6.7	12,622	13.5	3,931	24.8	20,130[7]
United States	3,887.7	1.9	15.9	5.6	7.7	143,550	8.7	45,105	14.0	130,110
Total North America[2]	**4,246.1**	—	—	—	—	**156,172**	**9.0**	**49,036**	**14.8**	**150,240**
Latin America										
LAIA										
Argentina	45.0	1.2	39.6	4.5	5.1	4,186	9.2	1,494	4.7	4,622[10]
Bolivia*	4.3	1.3	—	—	—	261	690.9	561	19.1	198
Brazil	288.5	0.3	29.6[10]	5.0	5.0	9,527	-5.0	2,467	11.4	14,120[10]
Chile	20.9	5.8	29.6	5.0	5.0	707	42.5	260	7.9	1,146[10]
Colombia*	27.5	2.7	31.0[10]	6.1	6.0	715	21.0	665	11.0	3,795
Ecuador*	8.2	2.5	33.6[8]	10.1	5.4	85	10.4	165	-7.3	541
Mexico	205.5	4.7	33.7	10.0	11.6	6,819	32.2	3,063	35.9	10,838
Paraguay	4.6	3.5	30.0[5]	12.0	3.0	60	-1.6	33	10.0	133
Peru*	38.7	-3.7	41.0[7]	9.8	11.6	387	0.5	230	10.0	799
Uruguay	6.6	2.4	31.0[5]	7.0	5.0	167	0.6	81	-2.4	579[10]
Venezuela*	35.9	2.4	43.5	4.3	5.2	1,601	2.4	583	-36.4	1,794[10]
Ancom subtotal[2]*	114.6	—	—	—	—	3,049	15.1	1,699	-12.8	7,127
Total LAIA[2]	**685.7**	—	—	—	—	**24,515**	**9.5**	**9,097**	**11.0**	**38,565**
CACM										
Costa Rica	3.4	4.2	33.0[5]	8.0[5]	9.0[5]	144	82.3	113	71.2	452
El Salvador	5.2	2.5	33.0[5]	9.0[5]	7.0[5]	52	-1.9	65	0.0	260
Guatemala	8.0	3.1	36.0[5]	10.0[5]	5.0[5]	95	-2.1	93	-1.1	250[10]
Honduras	2.2	2.7	—	—	—	27	0.0	52	4.0	96
Nicaragua	1.5	-5.6	—	—	—	31	-3.1	43	53.6	50[4]
Total CACM[2]	**20.1**	—	—	—	—	**349**	**21.2**	**366**	**20.8**	**1,108**
Caribbean										
Barbados	1.1	—	—	—	—	39	11.4	10	42.9	109
Cuba	31.7[10]	—	—	—	—	19	—	33	—	611
Dominican Republic	6.1	0.4	46.0[5]	3.0[5]	8.0[5]	114	7.5	73	12.3	547
Guyana	0.2	—	—	—	—	24	-17.2	9	-25.0	33[6]
Haiti	1.5	—	—	—	—	32	0.0	21	23.5	50[8]
Jamaica	2.2[10]	1.7	—	—	—	95	-11.2	17	-43.3	192
Netherlands Antilles	—	—	—	—	—	73	10.6	17	21.4	65[3]
Panama	3.5	-1.7	38.0[5]	3.0[5]	6.0[5]	153	6.3	73	62.2	273
Puerto Rico	—	—	—	—	—	1,322	20.0	206	7.3	—
Trinidad and Tobago	2.5*	-3.9[10]	—	—	—	244	0.8	79	0.0	234
Total Caribbean[2]	**48.8**	—	—	—	—	**2,115**	**13.5**	**538**	**16.7**	**2,114**
Total Latin America[2]	**754.6**	—	—	—	—	**26,979**	**9.9**	**10,001**	**11.6**	**41,787**
Asia										
Afghanistan	—	—	—	—	—	31	-3.1	25	0.0	32[11]
Bangladesh	19.4[10]	3.2	—	—	—	33	-29.8	36	5.9	262
Cambodia	—	—	—	—	—	—	—	—	—	—
China	295.5	5.2	54.3	13.4	11.6	1,164	32.9	4,172	128.0	14,990
Hong Kong	46.2	6.4	17.8	19.3	11.2	216	16.1	172	97.7	3,455
India	171.2	4.7	46.4	9.8	2.6	2,481	119.9	1,491	25.4	6,021
Indonesia	64.2	5.6	53.4	4.5	8.0	1,294	34.1	1,478	42.1	1,505
Japan	1,895.5	4.1	25.4	7.4	4.0	34,924	25.4	22,773	24.4	66,636[5]
Korea, North	—	—	—	—	—	—	—	—	—	825[5]
Korea, South	149.2	9.7	32.0	8.3	5.7	2,075	272.5	1,320	137.0	17,697
Laos	—	—	—	—	—	—	—	—	—	7
Malaysia	25.8	11.3	41.6	7.0	11.0	1,811	61.1	616	90.1	2,023[10]
Myanmar[12]	9.9[8]	—	—	—	—	27	-3.6	42	-2.3	81[8]
Nepal	2.3	—	57.0[5]	12.0	2.0	—	—	—	—	67[9]
Pakistan	30.7	5.1	46.6	7.7	2.0	738	88.3	172	-36.3	1,295
Philippines	33.3	5.4	54.8	4.2	9.9	455	26.4	765	46.8	1,097
Singapore	17.4	8.4	23.7[9]	8.6	10.4	285	18.8	142	1.4	1,220[8]
Sri Lanka	7.0	3.6	43.1[8]	10.6	4.4	177	18.8	144	9.1	172
Taiwan	96.6	10.1	32.7[8]	4.9	5.1	1,837	100.5	613	42.9	6,000[10]
Thailand	53.1	9.3	33.1	14.2	2.0	827	70.5	1,987	183.0	1,000[6]
Vietnam	—	—	—	—	—	8	—	7	—	123[9]
Total Asia[2]	**2,917.4**	—	—	—	—	**48,383**	**39.0**	**35,955**	**40.3**	**124,508**
Oceania										
Australia	182.1	2.7	24.3	6.1	6.8	7,672	12.1	2,104	-1.5	8,727[5]
New Zealand	27.2	0.9	15.8	5.1	9.2	1,557	3.8	311	3.0	2,403[7]
Total Oceania[2]	**209.3**	—	—	—	—	**9,229**	**10.6**	**2,415**	**-1.0**	**11,130**

[1] See text on currency conversion; [2] Total available data. Totals may not agree due to rounding; [3] 1983; [4] 1984; [5] 1985; [6] 1986; [7] 1987; [8] 1988; [9] 1989; [10] 1990; [11] 1981; [12] Burma. *Andean Common Market member. *EIU Estimate.

Televisions 1992 (thousands)	Televisions Cumulative % Increase 1988–1992	Personal Computers 1991 (thousands)	Steel Consumption 1991 (K MT)	Steel Consumption Cumulative % Increase 1986–1991	Cement Production 1991 (K MT)	Cement Production Cumulative % Increase 1986–1991	Electricity Production 1991 (billion kwh)	Electricity Production Cumulative % Increase 1986–1991	Energy Consumption 1990 kg Oil Equivalent Per Capita	Energy Consumption Cumulative[1] % Increase 1984–1990	
											North America
17,400	10.8	3,933	10,670	-11.7	9,672	-6.8	489.9	4.6	7,179	10.0	Canada
215,000	9.8	58,325	93,325	-2.1	65,052	-8.5	3,079.1	18.5	6,970	9.7	United States
232,400	**9.9**	**62,358**	**103,995**	**-3.1**	**74,724**	**-8.3**	**3,569.0**	**16.3**	**6,971**	**9.7**	**Total North America**[2]
											Latin America
											LAIA
7,165	5.4	287	2,250	-10.4	5,280	-5.4	50.9[3]	12.4[8]	1,277	12.9	Argentina
500	-6.5	—	68	70.0	560[3]	132.4[8]	2.0[3]	15.9[8]	249	29.2	Bolivia*
30,000	7.1	648	9,874	-32.0	27,492	8.8	222.2[3]	15.2[8]	536	29.7	Brazil
2,000	-14.2	169	1,063	40.2	2,064	43.3	19.8	33.7	874	50.6	Chile
5,500	64.2	—	1,004	-15.9	6,384	7.9	36.0[3]	34.3[8]	540	10.9	Colombia*
900	9.1	—	259	-11.0	1,548[4]	-11.8[6]	6.3[3]	40.3[8]	508	26.7	Ecuador*
56,000	489.5	970	9,375	41.9	24,648	26.4	122.5[3]	31.1[8]	1,227	14.7	Mexico
350	0.0	—	99	147.5	468[3]	917.4[8]	2.4[3]	56.4[8]	159	17.1	Paraguay
2,000	25.0	—	553	-0.7	2,124	-3.8	13.8[3]	13.9[8]	343	0.2	Peru*
600	20.0	—	90	2.3	469	47.9[8]	7.4[3]	92.9[8]	522	20.7	Uruguay
3,700	34.1	249	3,094	18.4	5,996[3]	17.0[8]	61.0[3]	34.4[8]	1,988	0.7	Venezuela*
12,600	38.9	249	4,978	6.0	16,612	1.1	119.1	18.8	780	5.3	Ancom subtotal[2]*
108,715	**92.2**	**2,323**	**27,729**	**-5.1**	**77,033**	**12.1**	**544.3**	**16.2**	**829**	**16.6**	**Total LAIA**[2]
											CACM
340	-27.7	—	94	-16.1	315[4]	-32.8[6]	3.6[3]	27.8[8]	411	45.7	Costa Rica
500	17.6	—	43	-42.7	444[3]	-1.3[8]	2.3[3]	35.7[8]	173	34.6	El Salvador
475	46.2	—	28	-75.2	611[3]	6.4[8]	2.3[3]	31.1[8]	132	9.5	Guatemala
160	-51.5	—	48	-5.9	326[3]	-6.3[8]	1.1[3]	2.8[8]	119	-8.0	Honduras
210	-4.5	—	91	-6.2	225[4]	-19.6[6]	1.0[3]	-5.6[8]	182	4.5	Nicaragua
1,685	**-4.8**	**—**	**304**	**-32.1**	**1,921**	**-36.3**	**10.4**[3]	**23.8**[8]	**177**	**17.7**	**Total CACM**[2]
											Caribbean
69	4.5	—	—	—	216	5.9	0.5	35.4	1,161	29.8	Barbados
2,500	20.8	—	331	-72.1	3,696[3]	16.2[8]	16.2[3]	33.2[8]	1,012	7.6	Cuba
728	30.9	—	96	35.2	1,189[3]	18.8[8]	5.3[3]	32.1[8]	256	-12.2	Dominican Republic
15	-62.5	—	—	—	—	—	0.2[3]	-43.6[8]	264	-54.3	Guyana
25	0.0	—	—	—	226[3]	-14.4[8]	0.4	-1.4	36	-0.4	Haiti
484	79.3	—	—	—	396	65.0	2.7[3]	14.0[8]	582	-8.9	Jamaica
35	9.4	—	—	—	—	—	0.7[3]	—	6,814	-5.8	Netherlands Antilles
205	-46.2	—	39	-58.9	169[4]	-44.4[6]	2.7[3]	5.1[8]	429	3.3	Panama
830	0.0	—	—	—	1,272	24.7	15.7	22.2	2,104	11.3	Puerto Rico
250	-32.4	—	281	15.2	438[3]	35.2[8]	3.5[3]	14.7[8]	4,799	35.9	Trinidad and Tobago
5,141	**10.8**	**—**	**747**	**-53.2**	**7,602**	**14.3**	**48.1**	**19.3**	**871**	**8.9**	**Total Caribbean**[2]
115,541	**83.5**	**2,273**	**28,780**	**-8.0**	**86,556**	**10.5**	**602.7**	**16.5**	**793**	**15.9**	**Total Latin America**[2]
											Asia
100	-20.0	—	—	—	100[3]	-21.9[8]	1.1[3]	3.8[8]	154	163.9	Afghanistan
350	-25.5	—	322	-26.3	276	-4.2	8.4	64.1	51	64.0	Bangladesh
70	16.7	—	—	—	—	—	0.1[3]	-12.5[8]	19	10.1	Cambodia
126,000	0.0	490[3]	71,042	-8.4	244,656	51.3	671.0	49.3	569	37.2	China
1,749	28.9	243	1,143	-38.7	1,808[3]	-1.5[8]	28.4	32.4	1,240	18.1	Hong Kong
20,000	0.0	411	20,300	32.8	45,720[3]	22.4[8]	286.0[3]	51.7[8]	217	50.0	India
11,000	54.7	—	4,890	73.6	15,972[3]	60.7[8]	44.3[3]	243.1[8]	211	28.2	Indonesia
100,000	54.5	10,384	99,149	41.8	89,568	25.7	857.3[3]	27.3[8]	2,904	11.9	Japan
2,000	700.0	—	—	—	16,300[3]	103.8[8]	53.5[3]	11.5[8]	1,931	10.3	Korea, North
8,700	0.7	1,757	26,190	114.8	39,168	66.5	118.6	70.0	1,731	69.5	Korea, South
32	0.0	—	—	—	—	—	0.9[3]	-35.6[8]	25	23.8	Laos
2,000	27.8	222	3,583	129.1	7,452	134.3	28.3	75.9	1,055	84.2	Malaysia
1,000	1,381.5	—	—	—	444	0.0	2.6	18.5	42	-0.2	Myanmar
250	825.9	—	—	—	107[3]	11.5[8]	0.7[3]	81.1[8]	14	10.3	Nepal
2,080	37.8	—	1,880	10.1	7,488[3]	45.8[8]	41.4	60.6	194	51.2	Pakistan
7,000	14.8	—	2,100	105.9	6,360[3]	107.0[8]	22.5	0.8	210	32.4	Philippines
550	-42.1	186	3,631	74.7	1,848[3]	-7.2[8]	16.6	56.9	3,878	39.0	Singapore
700	32.1	—	—	—	566[3]	47.4[8]	3.4	27.1	91	10.9	Sri Lanka
7,000	27.3	1,280	18,850	140.6	18,044[4]	26.8[6]	74.4[3]	55.2[8]	—	—	Taiwan
3,300	-41.1	288	4,310	84.8	19,164	139.4	50.1	93.2	516	95.6	Thailand
2,500	13.6	—	—	—	2,534[3]	68.6[8]	8.7[3]	74.4[8]	99	43.0	Vietnam
296,381	**17.2**	**15,261**	**257,390**	**30.9**	**517,575**	**47.1**	**2,318.3**	**39.0**	**506**	**28.2**	**Total Asia**[2]
											Oceania
8,000	1.3	3,127	4,785	-19.2	6,108	1.6	154.6[3]	29.9[8]	5,271	28.3	Australia
1,100	-11.3	—	600	-7.0	576	-36.0	29.9	15.2	3,497	34.3	New Zealand
9,100	**-0.4**	**3,127**	**5,385**	**-18.0**	**6,684**	**-3.3**	**184.5**	**21.2**	**4,931**	**29.0**	**Total Oceania**[2]

[1] Cumulative increase of total national energy consumption; [2] Total available data. Totals may not agree due to rounding; [3] 1990; [4] 1989; [5] 1988; [6] 1984–1989; [8] 1985–1990; * Andean Common Market member.

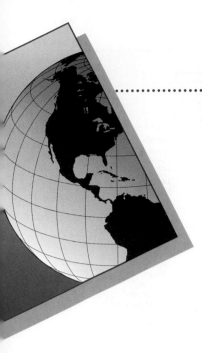

CHAPTER 4

The International Political and Legal Environment

THE INTERNATIONAL MARKETPLACE

Environmental Concern or the Politics of International Trade?

Increasingly, countries pass laws that create environmental standards. A recent German law regulates packaging, a U.S. law levies taxes on certain chemicals destined for toxic-waste dumps, a law in Denmark requires that drinks be sold in refillable bottles, and a Canadian regulation requires deposits on beer bottles.

On the surface, it appears that these laws are a necessary and appropriate response to growing world concerns about the environment. Yet these environmental standards may have been motivated at least in part by protectionist reasons. For example, a provision of Germany's packaging law requires that at most, 28 percent of all beer and soft-drink containers can be "one-trip" (disposable). Importers suspect the provision was designed to benefit small German brewers who will find it easier to collect and refill the empties. Packagers also dislike the law's insistence that companies collect their used packaging for recycling. The fact that this will be easier for local manufacturers may prejudice retailers in favor of domestically produced goods.

The General Agreement on Tariffs and Trade (GATT) insists that a country apply the same standards to imports and to domestic products. As long as such standards apply to all producers equally, they do not infringe on GATT rules. In 1989, GATT ruled that an American tax on certain chemicals, imposed to pay for cleaning up toxic-waste dumps, was legitimate because it was levied at the same rate on domestic and foreign producers. The panel ruled against an American tax on petroleum products, which was imposed at a higher rate on foreign producers.

However, sometimes environmental goals can interfere with free trade goals. Tensions are especially high in the EU because the building of the internal market requires that if a product meets standards set in its home market, it should generally be deemed to meet standards in other member states.

Trade problems can also emerge when countries try to ensure that their trading partners meet the same environmental constraints as their own producers. If companies in one country have to tighten pollution standards, they will likely want imports to meet the same rules. For example, American legislation bans imports of tuna from countries that kill 25 percent more dolphins than American fishermen do. Mexico claims that this law is designed to protect American tuna fishermen. The United States claims that the aim is to save dolphins.

Perhaps the most difficult and important issues concern global environmental problems such as ozone depletion. International efforts have been made to phase out chlorofluorocarbons (CFCs), which damage the ozone layer of the atmosphere. In these cases, the actions of one delinquent nation can have negative effects on the entire world. Increasing pressures to preserve the environment may compel nations to impose trade sanctions on those countries that do not comply with minimum environmental standards, especially when the effects reach beyond the offending country's borders.

Sources: "Free Trade's Green Hurdle," *The Economist,* June 15, 1991, 61–62, and "Should Trade Go Green?" *The Economist,* January 26, 1991, 13–14.

Much as most managers would like to ignore them, political and legal factors often play a critical role in international marketing activities. Even the best business plans can go awry as a result of unexpected political or legal influences, and the failure to anticipate these factors can be the undoing of an otherwise successful business venture.

Of course, a single international political and legal environment does not exist. The business executive must be aware of political and legal factors on a variety of levels. For example, although it is useful to understand the complexities of the host-country legal system, such knowledge does not protect against a home-country-imposed export embargo.

The study of the international political and legal environment must therefore be broken down into several subsegments. Many researchers do this by separating the legal from the political. This separation—although perhaps analytically useful—is somewhat artificial because laws generally are the result of political decisions. Here no attempt will be made to separate legal and political factors, except when such a separation is essential.

Instead, this chapter will examine the political-legal environment from the manager's point of view. In making decisions about his or her firm's international marketing activities, the manager will need to concentrate on three areas: the political and legal circumstances of the home country; those of the host country; and the bilateral and multilateral agreements, treaties, and laws governing the relations between host and home countries.

HOME-COUNTRY POLITICAL AND LEGAL ENVIRONMENT

No manager can afford to ignore the policies and regulations of the country from which he or she conducts international marketing transactions. Wherever a firm is located, it will be affected by government policies and the legal system.

Many of these laws and regulations may not be designed specifically to address international marketing issues, yet they can have a major impact on a firm's opportunities abroad, as The International Marketplace 4.1 shows. Minimum wage legislation, for example, affects the international competitiveness of a firm using production processes that are highly labor intensive. The cost of domestic safety regulations may significantly affect the pricing policies of firms in their international marketing efforts. For example, U.S. legislation that created the **Environmental Superfund** requires payment by chemical firms based on their production volume, regardless of whether the production is sold domestically or exported. As a result, these firms are at a disadvantage internationally when exporting their commodity-type products because they must compete against foreign firms that are not required to make such a payment in their home countries and therefore have a cost advantage.

Other legal and regulatory measures, however, are clearly aimed at international marketing activities. Some may be designed to help firms in their international efforts. The lack of enforcement of others may hurt the international marketer. For example, the U.S. government is quite concerned about lacking safeguards of **intellectual property rights** in China. Not only may counterfeiting result in inferior products and damage to the reputation of a company, but it also reduces the chances that an innovative firm can recoup its investment in research and development and spawn new products.

Violations of intellectual property rights can occur anywhere. As an example, in 1988, Anheuser-Busch agreed with Czechoslovak authorities to settle a trademark dispute with Budjovicki Budvar over the use of the name Budweiser. Anheuser-Busch agreed to give the Czech brewery a $15-million package, $10.3 million in brewing equipment and $4.7 million in cash, in return for which the two firms agreed to a division of the world into specified exclusive and shared markets. A later chapter will provide further in-depth discussions of intellectual property right problems and ways to protect a firm from infringements.

Another area in which governments may attempt to aid and protect the international marketing efforts of companies is that of **gray market** activities. Gray market goods are products that enter markets in ways not desired by their manufacturer. Companies may be hurt by their own products if they reach the consumer via uncontrolled distribution channels. Gray market activities will be discussed in detail later in the book.

Apart from specific areas that result in government involvement, the political environment in most countries tends to provide general support for the international marketing efforts of the country's firms. For example, a government may work to reduce trade barriers or to increase trade opportunities through bilateral and multilateral negotiations. Such actions will affect individual firms to the extent that they affect the international climate for free trade.

Often, however, governments also have specific rules and regulations restricting international marketing. Such regulations are frequently political in nature and are based on the fact that governments believe commerce to be only one objective among others, such as foreign policy and national security. Four main areas of governmental activities are of major concern to the international marketer here: embargoes or trade sanctions, export controls, import controls, and the regulation of international business behavior.

Embargoes and Sanctions

The terms **trade sanctions** and **embargoes** as used here refer to governmental actions that distort the free flow of trade in goods, services, or ideas for decidedly adversarial and political, rather than strictly economic, purposes. To understand them better, we need to examine the auspices and legal justifications under which they are imposed.

Trade sanctions have been used quite frequently and successfully in times of war or to address specific grievances. For example, in 1284, the Hansa, an association of north German merchants, felt that its members were suffering from several injustices by Norway. On learning that one of its ships had been attacked and pillaged by the Norwegians, the Hansa called an assembly of its members and resolved an economic blockade of Norway. The export of grain, flour, vegetables, and beer was prohibited on pain of fines and confiscation of the goods. The blockade was a complete success. Deprived of grain from Germany, the Norwegians were unable to obtain it from England or elsewhere. As a contemporary chronicler reports: "Then there broke out a famine so great that they were forced to make atonement." Norway was forced to pay indemnities for the financial losses that had been caused and to grant the Hansa extensive trade privileges.[1]

The League of Nations set a precedent for the international legal justification of economic sanctions by subscribing to a covenant that provided for penalties or sanctions for breaching its provisions. The members of the League of Nations did not intend to use military or economic measures separately, but the success of the blockades of World War I fostered the opinion that "the economic weapon, conceived not as an instrument of war but as a means of peaceful pressure, is the greatest discovery and most precious possession of the League."[2] The basic idea was that economic sanctions could force countries to behave peacefully in the international community.

The idea of the multilateral use of economic sanctions was again incorporated into international law under the charter of the United Nations, but greater emphasis was placed on the enforcement process. Once decided upon, sanctions are mandatory, even though each permanent member of the Security Council can veto efforts to impose sanctions. The charter also allows for sanctions as enforcement action by regional agencies such as the Organization of American States, the Arab League, and the Organization of African Unity, but only with the Security Council's authorization.

The apparent strength of the United Nations enforcement system was soon revealed to be flawed. Stalemates in the Security Council and vetoes by permanent members often led to a shift of emphasis to the General Assembly, where sanctions are not enforceable. Further, concepts such as "peace" and "breach of peace" are seldom perceived in the same way by all members, and thus no systematic sanctioning policy developed in the United Nations.[3]

Over the years, economic sanctions and embargoes have become an often-used foreign policy tool for many countries. Frequently, they have been imposed unilaterally in the hope of changing a country's government or at least changing its policies. Reasons for the impositions have varied, ranging from human rights to nuclear nonproliferation to antiterrorism.

The problem with sanctions is that frequently their unilateral imposition has not produced the desired result. Sanctions may make the obtaining of goods more difficult or expensive for the sanctioned country, yet achievement of the purported objective almost never occurs. In order to work, sanctions need to be imposed multilaterally, a goal that is clear, yet difficult to implement. Quite often, individual countries have different relationships with the country subject to the sanctions, and for one reason or another they cannot or do not wish to terminate trade relations.

In the recent past, however, the disappearance of the East-West confrontation has strengthened the sanction mechanism of the United Nations. For example, when Iraq

---

[1] Quoted in Philippe Dollinger, *The German Hansa* (Stanford, CA: Stanford University Press, 1970), 49.

[2] Robin Renwick, *Economic Sanctions* (Cambridge, MA: Harvard University Press, 1981), 11.

[3] Margaret P. Doxey, *Economic Sanctions and International Enforcement* (New York: Oxford University Press, 1980), 10.

4.2

THE INTERNATIONAL MARKETPLACE

Vietnam Embargo Ends, U.S. Firms Enter

One of the world's last relatively untapped opportunities for U.S. marketers was tapped with the stroke of a pen. The U.S. economic embargo against Vietnam that had been in place since 1975 was lifted by President Bill Clinton on February 3, 1994, and U.S. firms wasted no time moving into the market. Within two hours of the announcement, United Air Lines announced scheduled flights to Vietnam. At about the same time, Pepsi started its production line, which was fully operational within a week. Coke was not far behind, which started talk of the "new Vietnam war," Coke versus Pepsi. "There is a tremendous amount of euphoria about the prospects here," states the president of the American Chamber of Commerce in Hong Kong.

Why so much hoopla? Vietnam has a population of 71 million and has substantial natural resources, most importantly, oil. The economy is growing at more than 7 percent per year, inflation is under control, there is 88 percent literacy, and wages are low, making the country an ideal environment for investment. These conditions sound even better considering the host nation's plans to lure $20 billion in foreign investment by the end of the decade.

The bad news for U.S. marketers is that these opportunities have been available for some time and have been taken by practically all other interested nations. Non-U.S. investment in Vietnam has totaled $7.8 billion on 850 projects since 1987, with Taiwan and Hong Kong leading the way, followed closely by France and Australia. Many experts feel that Japan denied itself much of this ripe opportunity before the embargo was lifted in order to avoid problems with the United States. Now, however, it is expected that Japan will move forward at full speed and expand its control over strategic industries including oil and infrastructure development.

Despite the disadvantage of being a late arrival, U.S. firms are extremely optimistic: "It's going to be a scramble here; the country's so young in its economic development, there's room for everyone in every field," claims an American businessman living in Vietnam. Some of the key industries Americans expect to enter include oil exploration, construction, banking, and telecommunications. U.S. consumer goods are expected to do well because of pent-up Vietnamese demand. According to Eugene Matthews, an American private consultant in Vietnam, "particularly in consumer products and pharmaceuticals you will see the marketing muscle of American companies come into play."

"The best way to move trade is to have planes coming in and out," comments a Northwest Airlines official. Long forbidden in Vietnam, U.S. air carriers are positioning themselves to service the new market. All the major airlines are anxious to serve the expected flood of business travelers and the one million ethnic Vietnamese living in the United States. "Vietnam is one of the most promising countries in Asia" says a Continental Airlines executive.

Still to come are the resumption of full diplomatic relations, a bilateral trade pact, and debates about mutual tariff reductions. But even in this early stage, it can be expected that U.S. firms will eventually play a large role in Vietnam's future.

Sources: John Rogers, "Firms in Place Have Advantage; Newcomers Face Uphill Climb," *The Journal of Commerce*, February 7, 1994, 6A; Susan Carey and Laurence Zuckerman, "Many Want to Fly to Vietnam, but Only

Some May Land," *The Wall Street Journal,* February 7, 1994, B3; Peter Behr and Thomas Lippman, "New Market Means Prospects, Problems for American Firms," *The Washington Post,* February 4, 1994, A22; William Branigin, "Hanoi Hails Embargo End as Step to Better Ties," *The Washington Post,* February 4, 1994, A22; Urban Lehner, "U.S. Firms Head for Vietnam, but Find Asian, European Firms Already There," *The Wall Street Journal,* February 10, 1994, A14.

invaded Kuwait in August 1990, virtually all members of the United Nations condemned this hostile action and joined a trade embargo against Iraq. In this instance, both major and minor Iraqi trading partners—including many Arab nations—honored the United Nations trade sanctions and ceased trade with Iraq in an attempt to force it to withdraw its troops. With increased international collaboration, it may well be that sanctions will reemerge as a powerful and effective international political tool in the world. When one considers that sanctions may well be the middle ground between going to war or doing nothing, their effective functioning can represent a powerful arrow in the quiver of international policy measures.

Sanctions imposed by governments always raise the issue of compensation for the domestic firms that are affected. Obviously, a cutoff of trade with certain regions may result in significant losses of business, forcing selected firms to bear the brunt of governmental policy. Trying to impose sanctions slowly, in order to ease the burden on these firms, undercuts the ultimate chance that the sanctions will succeed. The international marketer is frequently caught in this political web and loses business as a result. All too often, innocent bystanders are hurt by sanctions. In many instances, the citizens of a country, rather than their government, are suffering from sanctions. Seeing that the targets of sanctions are often their own firms and nontargeted individuals, governments often modify their stance in order to define and target the sanctions better. As the International Marketplace 4.2 shows, sometimes sanctions are even lifted, an action that provides new market opportunities to firms.

Export Controls

Many nations have export control systems designed to deny the acquisition of strategically important goods to adversaries or at least to delay their acquisition. In the United States, the export control system is based on the Export Administration Act and the Munitions Control Act. These laws control all exports of goods, services, and ideas from the United States. The reasons for these controls are concerns about national security, foreign policy, short supply, or nuclear proliferation. In order for any export from the United States to take place, the exporter must obtain an export license from the Department of Commerce, which administers the Export Administration Act.[4] In consultation with other government agencies—particularly the Departments of State, Defense, and Energy—the Department of Commerce has drawn up a list of commodities whose export is considered particularly sensitive. In addition, a list of countries differentiates nations according to their political relationship with the United States. Finally, a list of individual firms that are considered to be unreliable trading partners because of past trade diversion activities exists for each country. Control determinants and the steps in the decision process are summarized in Figure 4.1.

This process may sound overly cumbersome, but it does not apply in equal measure to all exports. Many international marketing activities can be carried out with a **general**

[4] Robert M. Springer, Jr., "New Export Law and Aid to International Marketers," *Marketing News,* January 3, 1986, 10, 67.

FIGURE 4.1	U.S. Export Control System

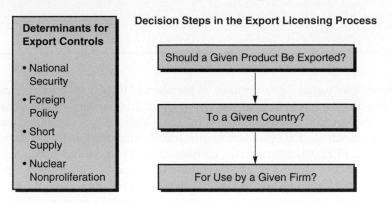

Determinants for Export Controls

- National Security
- Foreign Policy
- Short Supply
- Nuclear Nonproliferation

Decision Steps in the Export Licensing Process

Should a Given Product Be Exported?

To a Given Country?

For Use by a Given Firm?

license. Under such a license, which is not even in writing, the export can be freely shipped to most trading partners if neither the product nor the country is considered to be sensitive. The process becomes more complicated and cumbersome, however, when it involves products incorporating high-level technologies and countries not friendly to the United States. Corporations then need to apply for a **validated export license,** which consists of written authorization to send a product abroad.

The international marketing repercussions of export controls have become increasingly important. To design a control system that is effective and, in consideration of important national concerns, restricts some international business activities is one thing. It is quite another when controls lose their effectiveness and when, because of a control system, firms are placed at a competitive disadvantage with firms in other countries whose control system is less severe or nonexistent. Some complaints of U.S. firms are discussed in the International Marketplace 4.3.

Export controls are increasingly difficult to implement and enforce for several reasons. First, the number of countries that are able to manufacture products of strategic importance has increased. Industrializing nations, which only a decade ago were seen as poor imitators at best, are now at the forefront of cutting-edge technology. Their products can have a decidedly significant impact on a nation's capability for warfare. Second, products that are in need of control are developed and disseminated very quickly. Product life cycles have been shortened to such an extent that even temporary delays in distribution may result in a significant setback for a firm. Third, products that are in need of control are shrinking in size because of advancements in miniaturization. The smuggling and diversion of such products has become much easier because they are easier to conceal. Finally, quite apart from products, the transfer of technology and know-how has increasingly taken on major strategic significance. Yet such services are often invisible, are performed by individuals, and are highly personalized. They are easy to transship and therefore difficult to trace and control.

In order for export controls to result in a true denial of products and services, joint actions by the major producers are required. During the Cold War, the United States participated in COCOM, the Coordinating Committee for Export Controls, to achieve this goal. COCOM's member countries, which were mostly drawn from industrialized nations, attempted to formulate joint control policies that would be adhered to by all nations, that would be effective, and that would not allow firms to gain a competitive advantage from differing control regimes.

THE INTERNATIONAL MARKETPLACE

4.3

Export Controls Hurt U.S. Firms

The Japanese trade practices that exclude billions of dollars worth of U.S. exports are common knowledge. Not so visible are U.S. rules that forbid U.S. companies from selling abroad and block even more export sales.

Syracuse University economist J. David Richardson's comprehensive study of export disincentives estimates their cost to U.S. companies to be $21 to $27 billion a year. By comparison, a study done by the Institute for International Economics puts the annual loss of U.S. exports due to Japanese trade restraints at $9 to $18 billion. According to Richardson, the United States is the world's most aggressive controller of exports and Washington has been "unduly nonchalant" about the economic effect.

U.S. export controls target high-tech industries that are key to economic growth. Among those hit hardest are makers of computers, telecommunications equipment, machine tools, and civilian aircraft. Many of the firms affected are small companies that produce components.

Roughly 75 percent of denied exports fall under the category of "security controls." Such restrictions try to keep equipment for military use out of the hands of the world's present or potential bad actors. Many of the rules originated from Cold War measures meant to keep critical technology from the Soviet Union, China, and others. Newer rules focus on restricting the capabilities of nations such as Iran to build weapons of mass destruction.

American Telephone and Telegraph (AT&T) estimates that over the next five years, U.S. restrictions dating from the Cold War will cost it $500 million of foreign business. These are sales that probably will go to old competitors from Europe or Japan. AT&T Chairman Robert E. Allen complains to Congress, "It is unrealistic, perhaps bordering on arrogance, to think that any country would go without advanced information technology just because U.S. companies were forbidden to provide it." Many of the restrictions affecting AT&T will not disappear. According to Undersecretary of Defense John Deutsch, "Telecom is different; that may not be good news for AT&T, but that's the kind of balance that must be struck." Apparently, U.S. intelligence agencies block such exports so they can keep tapping older Russian and Chinese communications systems.

Westinghouse Electric Corporation can sell to China steam turbines for coal-fired plants but cannot sell identical equipment to those plants with nuclear reactors. "This has no logic" complains one company executive who currently has two orders but cannot get the rules changed. The United States is the only nation that will not permit companies to export to China any equipment destined for nuclear power plants—even if the products have nothing to do with the reactors.

Other export restrictions fall under the "foreign policy controls" category, which aims to symbolize America's official dislike of another nation's conduct. For example, Boeing Co. is not allowed to sell jetliners to Iran because the United States contends Tehran supports international terrorists. The planes have no relation to terrorism, and Iran can buy European jets as substitutes. Regardless, Washington sees the ban as a useful symbol of offical displeasure.

Source: Robert Keatley, "U.S. Rules Dating from the Cold War Block Billions of Dollars in Exports," *The Wall Street Journal*, October 15, 1993, A7.

A major shift in export controls occurred in the past few years. With the disintegration of the Soviet Union, many former enemies are no longer seen as strategic adversaries. As a result, there has been a substantial reduction in the number of controlled items. In addition, more favorable licensing requirements have been introduced for firms in the former Eastern, now Central, European countries.[5] At the same time, however, the focus of export controls has shifted. Away from an East-West orientation, the direction now seems to be a North-South one. From a national security perspective, the threat posed by regional conflicts has increased. Therefore, national security controls focus more on goods and services that could enhance the capability of countries that are part of such conflicts. In addition, the prominence of foreign policy controls is likely to increase. As it became more difficult for COCOM members to agree to what should be controlled and which countries should be considered adversaries, the organization was disbanded and many controls were eased in 1994. However, individual countries still formulate export control policies and negotiate with their major trading partners to achieve some kind of joint action. The United States, for example, will continue to control exports that would significantly and directly contribute to nuclear proliferation, terrorism, human rights abuses, or regional instability.

As a result of these changes, it appears that the international marketer is likely to experience much more freedom in conducting trade with former communist countries but may well be exposed to higher uncertainty as control policies quickly shift based on short-term regional developments.

Import Controls

Many nations exert substantial restraints on international marketers through import controls. This is particularly true of countries that suffer from major balance-of-trade deficits or major infrastructural problems. In these countries, either all imports or the imports of particular products are controlled through mechanisms such as tariffs, voluntary restraint agreements, or **quota systems.** On occasion, countries cut off imports of certain products entirely in order to stimulate the development of a domestic industry.

For the international marketer, such restrictions may mean that the most efficient sources of supply are not available because government regulations restrict importation from those sources. The result is either second-best products or higher costs for restricted supplies. This in turn means that the customer is served less well and often has to pay significantly higher prices and that the firm is less competitive when trying to market its products internationally.

Policymakers are faced with several problems when trying to administer import controls. First, most of the time such controls exact a huge price from domestic consumers. Even though the wide distribution of the burden among many consumers may result in a less obvious burden, the social cost of these controls may be damaging to the economy and subject to severe attack by individuals. However, these attacks are counteracted by pressures from protected groups that benefit from import restrictions. For example, although citizens of the European Union may be forced—because of import controls—to pay an elevated price for all agricultural products they consume, agricultural producers in the region benefit from higher levels of income. Achieving a proper trade-off is often difficult, if not impossible, for the policymaker.

---

[5] Thomas H. Stillman and Anne Q. Connaughton, "Export Controls in a Changing World," *Business America,* December 28, 1991.

A second major problem resulting from import controls is the downstream change in import composition that results from these controls. For example, if the import of copper ore is restricted, either through voluntary restraints or through quotas, producing countries may opt to shift their production systems and produce copper wire instead, which they then export. As a result, initially narrowly defined protectionist measures may have to snowball in order to protect one downstream industry after another.

A final major problem that confronts the policymaker is that of efficiency. Import controls that are frequently designed to provide breathing room to a domestic industry either to grow or to recapture its competitive position often turn out not to work. Rather than improve the productivity of an industry, such controls provide it with a level of safety and a cushion of increased income yet let overall technological advancement fall behind. Alternatively, supply may respond to artificial stimulation and grow totally out of proportion.

Regulation of International Business Behavior

Home countries may implement special laws and regulations to ensure that the international business behavior of their firms is conducted within the legal, moral, and ethical boundaries considered appropriate. The definition of appropriateness may vary from country to country and from government to government. Therefore, such regulations, their enforcement, and their impact on firms can differ substantially among nations.

Several major areas in which nations attempt to govern the international marketing activities of its firms are **boycotts,** antitrust measures, and corruption. Arab nations, for example, have developed a blacklist of companies that deal with Israel. Even though enforcement of the blacklisting has decreased, many Arab customers demand from their suppliers assurances that the source of the products purchased is not Israel and that the company does not do any business with Israel. The goal of these actions clearly is to impose a boycott on business with Israel. The U.S. government in turn, because of U.S. political ties to Israel, has adopted a variety of laws to prevent U.S. firms from complying with the Arab boycott. These laws include a provision to deny foreign income tax benefits to companies that comply with the boycott and also require notification of the U.S. government in case any boycott requests are received. U.S. firms that comply with the boycott are subject to heavy fines and denial of export privileges.

Boycott measures put firms in a difficult position. Caught in a web of governmental activity, they may be forced either to lose business or to pay fines. This is particularly the case if a firm's products are competitive yet not unique, so that the supplier can opt to purchase them elsewhere. Heightening of such conflict can sometimes force companies to withdraw operations entirely from a country.

The second area of regulatory activity affecting international marketing efforts of firms is **antitrust laws.** These can apply to the international operations of firms as well as to domestic business. In the United States, for example, the Justice Department watches closely when any U.S. firm buys an overseas company, engages in a joint venture with a foreign firm, or makes an agreement abroad with a competing firm. The department evaluates the effect these activities will have on competition and has the right to disapprove such transactions. However, given the increased globalization of national economies, some substantial rethinking is going on regarding the validity of current U.S. antitrust enforcement. One could question whether any country can still afford to define the competition only in a domestic sense or whether competition has to be seen on a worldwide scale. Similarly, one can wonder whether countries will accept the infringement on their sovereignty that results from the extraterritorial application of any nation's laws abroad. There are precedents for making special allowances for international marketers with regard to antitrust laws. For example, the Webb-Pomerene Act of 1918 excludes from antitrust prosecution those firms that are cooperating to develop foreign markets. This act was passed as part of an effort to aid U.S. export efforts in the face of strong foreign competition by oligopolies and monopolies. The exclusion of international marketing activity from antitrust regulation was further enhanced by the Export Trading Company Act of 1982, which does not expose cooperating firms to the threat of treble damages. It was specifically designed to assist small and medium-sized firms in their export efforts by permitting them to join forces in their international market development activities. Due to ongoing globalization of production, competition, and supply and demand, it would appear that over time the application of U.S. antitrust laws to international marketing activities will be revised to reflect global rather than national dimensions.

Other nations around the world have antitrust legislation as well. Yet not always is the legislation implemented to the degree that the law specifies. As the International Marketplace 4.4 shows, in spite of strong existing antitrust rules in Japan, there is a continuing strong collusion among firms that often results in the exclusion of foreign companies.

A third area in which some governments regulate international marketing actions concerns bribery and corruption. The United States has taken a lead on this issue. U.S. firms operating overseas are affected by U.S. laws against bribery and **corruption.** In many countries, payments or favors are a way of life, and "a greasing of the wheels" is expected in return for government services. In the past, many U.S. companies doing business internationally routinely paid bribes or did favors for foreign officials in order to gain contracts. In the 1970s, major national debate erupted over these business practices, led by arguments that U.S. firms should provide ethical and moral leadership, and that contracts won through bribes do not reflect competitive market activity. As a result, the Foreign Corrupt Practices Act was passed in 1977, making it a crime for U.S. firms to bribe a foreign official for business purposes.

A number of U.S. firms have complained about the act, arguing that it hinders their efforts to compete internationally against companies from countries that have no such antibribery laws. The problem is one of ethics versus practical needs and also, to some extent, of the amounts involved. For example, it may be difficult to draw the line between providing a generous tip and paying a bribe in order to speed up a business transaction. Many business managers argue that the United States should not apply its moral principles to other societies and cultures in which bribery and corruption are endemic. If they are to compete internationally, these managers argue, they must be free to use the most common methods of competition in the host country. Particularly in industries that face limited or even shrinking markets, such stiff competition forces firms to find any edge possible to obtain a contract. As the International Marketplace 4.5 shows, it can be easy to cross the border of legality.

On the other hand, applying different standards to management and firms, depending on whether they do business abroad or domestically, is difficult to envision. Also, bribes may open the way for shoddy performance and loose moral standards among managers and employees and may result in a spreading of generally unethical business practices. Unrestricted bribery could result in a concentration on how best to bribe rather than on how best to produce and market products.

The international manager must carefully distinguish between reasonable ways of doing business internationally—including compliance with foreign expectations—and outright bribery and corruption. To assist the manager in this task, revisions were made in the 1988 Trade Act to clarify the applicability of the Foreign Corrupt Practices legisla-

THE INTERNATIONAL MARKETPLACE   4.4

Construction Barriers in Japan

There may be something wrong when a particular industry has $250 billion worth of projects a year and, in spite of major efforts and capability, foreign competitors have less than 1 percent of the market. Yet, this is the case in Japan's construction industry, one of the more notorious in terms of restricting imports. There has traditionally existed what many call a "cozy network" among politicians, the industry, and regulators that, according to outsiders, ensures domestic collusion and excludes the entry of foreign competitors.

Many U.S. construction firms have tried to enter Japan's markets and failed. One Boise, Idaho, builder decided to make an attempt. "We thought U.S. contractors would be given a shot, but it just never sort of materialized; we felt it was a wasted effort," says Jim Ellis, the head of international operations. Michitaka Yamaguchi runs the Tokyo office for Baltimore-based RTKL International. He has stated, "There's some sense that the winners are already selected before the bid is announced." Yamaguchi claims that he read newspaper articles naming the Japanese companies that will be working on the 1998 Winter Olympics complex in Japan before official bidding had even begun.

In response to the complaints about restricting imports, Japan devised a "set-aside" program in 1988. In this affirmative action-type program, 17 major construction projects were designated as being particularly open to foreign competition, and restrictive government regulations, such as a requirement that a bidder must already have worked in Japan, were lifted. Since the program began, the number of American companies now licensed to do construction work in Japan jumped from 3 to 30. According to the Japanese government, Americans have won contracts totaling about $900 million.

Frustration still abounds, however, for U.S. construction firms in Japan. One builder said that when he inquires about projects not on the set-aside list, "We're told Americans don't need to be considered." Japanese officials contend that U.S. firms are not trying hard enough. Of 342 contracts that were bid on for the set-aside program, U.S. companies bid on only 87. U.S. firms counter by saying that there is really little point in trying. Hiring subcontractors and suppliers is a hassle because most are loyal to established Japanese companies. A Michigan glass maker says it cannot persuade Japanese glazers to install its windows in buildings, even with lower prices.

These obstacles are blamed on the so-called "cozy network" in the Japanese construction industry: The government provides very few details on upcoming projects; companies rely on the politicians and bureaucrats for the necessary inside information for which the politicians receive campaign cash; and the bureaucrats rely on the contractors to help shape the projects. Later on, these same bureaucrats will end up on the company payroll after retirement.

Source: Jacob Schlesinger, "Fenced Out: U.S. Contractors Find They Rarely Get Work on Projects in Japan," *The Wall Street Journal*, June 10, 1993, A1.

tion. These revisions clarify when a manager is expected to know about violation of the act, and a distinction is drawn between the facilitation of routine governmental actions and governmental policy decisions. Routine actions concern issues such as obtaining permits and licenses, processing governmental papers such as visas and work orders, providing mail and phone service, and loading and unloading cargo. Policy decisions

THE INTERNATIONAL MARKETPLACE

Buying Business Abroad

A problem meant to be resolved in the late 1970s through legislation has not only persisted, but is in fact growing. The problem is illicit payments made by U.S. defense contractors to land lucrative overseas projects. The issue is resurfacing due in large part to the end of the Cold War and the defense cuts that have followed.

The U.S. defense industry relies heavily on foreign orders to keep domestic plants running. Foreign business has become more important than ever in this highly competitive global arms market. To get such business, some companies have made payments that may violate the U.S. Foreign Corrupt Practices Act. According to an FBI official, as domestic orders dry up, "It's simply logical that there will be more of these foreign corruption cases." Agents are finding many more instances of kickbacks and suspicious payments outside the domestic market as desperate firms attempt to stay afloat.

It is often difficult to uncover illegal payments. Outside auditors see only what appear to be legitimate consulting agreements with no link to illegal activities. For Teledyne Industries, however, the link was found. The company pleaded guilty to hiding $3.2 million of illicit commissions from authorities for a span of four years. Teledyne had promised to pay a monthly retainer of up to $65,000 to a Taiwanese middleman, who was under no obligation to report or justify the fees.

Egypt and Taiwan have spent about $6.3 billion on U.S. weaponry since 1986 and are therefore natural targets for marketing campaigns by U.S. contractors. It is believed that many U.S. firms have gone to great lengths to gain entry to the military. A retired Egyptian air force general named Aly Mansour has stood out for his prestigious connections. In the past, he has boasted about recruiting a stable of recently retired generals to help General Electric, Loral, Lockheed Corp., Harris Corp., ITT Corp. and others land $1.5 billion of new contracts. When G.E. was considering hiring Mansour's firm, in-house memos stressed his "excellent relationships with the Minister of Defense and [key] ministry personnel." The Egyptian helped G.E. win an air-defense radar contract valued at $125 million; included in the dealings were a $5,000 clambake, an all-expenses-paid weekend in New York City, and a tour of Niagara Falls for Egyptian officers and paid for by G.E. These activities triggered a U.S. government investigation of possible illegal payments.

But not only industry giants are faced with such problems. Detroit Armor Corp., now called Darmor Corp., a small Illinois firm, paid an Egyptian middleman $92,000 in illegal commissions to land an indoor rifle-range contract. In the end, Darmor had to pay $700,000 in civil and criminal penalties.

Source: Andy Pasztor and Bruce Ingersoll, "Buying Business: Some Weapons Makers Are Said to Continue Illicit Foreign Outlays," *The Wall Street Journal*, November 5, 1993, A1.

refer mainly to situations in which obtaining or retaining contracts is at stake. Although the facilitation of routine actions is not prohibited, the illegal influencing of policy decisions can result in the imposition of severe fines and penalties.

A final, major issue that is critical for international marketers is that of general standards of behavior and ethics. Increasingly, public concerns are raised about such issues as global warming, pollution, and moral behavior. However, these issues are not of the same importance in every country. What may be frowned on or even illegal in one nation may be customary or at least acceptable in others. For example, cutting down the Brazilian rain forest may be acceptable to the government of Brazil, but scientists and concerned consumers may object vehemently because of the effect on global warming and other climatic changes. The export of U.S. tobacco products may be legal but results in accusations of exporting death to developing nations. China may use prison labor in producing products for export, but U.S. law prohibits the importation of such products. Mexico may permit the use of low safety standard for workers, but the buyers of Mexican products may object to the resulting dangers.

All of these issues of governmental regulation pose difficult and complex problems, for they place managers in the position of having to choose between home-country regulations and foreign business practices. This choice is made even more difficult because of diverging standards of behavior applied to businesses in different countries. The leaders of international firms must understand these conflicts and should assert leadership in implementing change. Not everything that is legally possible should be exploited for profit. Although companies need to return a profit on their investments, these issues must be seen in the context of time. By acting on existing, leading-edge knowledge and standards, firms will be able to benefit in the long term through consumer goodwill and the avoidance of later recriminations.

HOST-COUNTRY POLITICAL AND LEGAL ENVIRONMENT

The host-country environment, both political and legal, affects the international marketing operations of firms in a variety of ways. The good manager will understand the country in which the firm operates so that he or she is able to work within the existing parameters and can anticipate and plan for changes that may occur.

Political Action and Risk

Firms usually prefer to conduct business in a country with a stable and friendly government, but such governments are not always easy to find. Managers must therefore continually monitor the government, its policies, and its stability to determine the potential for political change that could adversely affect corporate operations.

There is **political risk** in every nation, but the range of risks varies widely from country to country. In general, political risk is lowest in countries that have a history of stability and consistency. Political risk tends to be highest in nations that do not have this sort of history. In a number of countries, however, consistency and stability that were apparent on the surface have been quickly swept away by major popular movements that drew on the bottled-up frustrations of the population. Three major types of political risk can be encountered: **ownership risk,** which exposes property and life; **operating risk,** which refers to interference with the ongoing operations of a firm; and **transfer risk,** which is mainly encountered when attempts are made to shift funds between countries. Political risk can be the result of government action, but it can also be outside the control of government. The type of actions and their effects are classified in Figure 4.2.

A major political risk in many countries involves conflict and violent change. A manager will want to think twice before conducting business in a country in which the likelihood of such change is high. To begin with, if conflict breaks out, violence directed

| FIGURE 4.2 | Exposure to Political Risk |

Loss May Be the Result of:

Contingencies May Include:	The actions of legitimate government authorities	Events caused by factors outside the control of government
The involuntary loss of control over specific assets without adequate compensation	• Total or partial expropriation • Forced divestiture • Confiscation • Cancellation or unfair calling of peformance bonds	• War • Revolution • Terrorism • Strikes • Extortion
A reduction in the value of a stream of benefits expected from the foreign-controlled affiliate	• Nonapplicability of "national treatment" • Restriction in access to financial, labor, or material markets • Controls on prices, outputs, or activities • Currency and remittance restrictions • Value-added and export performance requirements	• Nationalistic buyers or suppliers • Threats and disruption to operations by hostile groups • Externally induced financial constraints • Externally imposed limits on imports or exports

Source: José de la Torre and David H. Neckar, "Forecasting Political Risks for International Operations," in H. Vernon-Wortzel and L. Wortzel, *Global Strategic Management: The Essentials,* 2nd ed. (New York: John Wiley and Sons, 1990), 195. Copyright © 1990 John Wiley and Sons. Reprinted by permission of John Wiley and Sons, Inc.

toward the firm's property and employees is a strong possibility. Guerrilla warfare, civil disturbances, and terrorism often take an anti-industry bent, making companies and their employees potential targets. For example, in the spring of 1991, Detlev Rohwedder, chairman of the German Treuhand (the institution in charge of privatizing the state-owned firms of the former East Germany), was assassinated at his home in Germany by the Red Army Faction because of his "representation of capitalism."

International terrorists have frequently targeted U.S. corporate facilities, operations, and personnel abroad for attack in order to strike a blow against the United States and capitalism. U.S. firms are prominent symbols of the U.S. presence abroad, and by their nature they cannot have the elaborate security and restricted access of U.S. diplomatic offices and military bases. As a result, U.S. businesses are the primary target of terrorists worldwide and remain the most vulnerable targets in the future.[6] The methods used by terrorists against business facilities include bombing, arson, hijacking, and sabotage. To obtain funds, the terrorists resort to kidnapping, armed robbery, and extortion.[7] The locations and frequencies of such incidents against businesses around the world are shown in Figure 4.3.

In many countries, particularly in the developing world, coups d'etat can result in drastic changes in government. The new government may attack foreign multinational

[6] Michael G. Harvey, "A Survey of Corporate Programs for Managing Terrorist Threats," *Journal of International Business Studies* (Third Quarter 1993): 465–478

[7] Harvey J. Iglarsh, "Terrorism and Corporate Costs," *Terrorism* 10 (1987): 227–230.

Frequency of International Terrorist Incidents Over Time, 1968–1992 FIGURE 4.3a

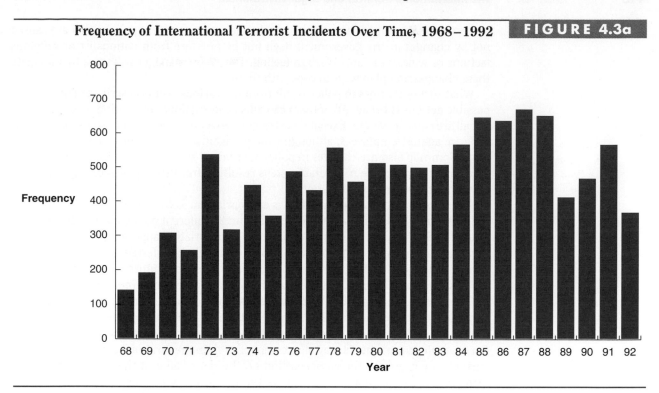

corporations as remnants of the Western-dominated colonial past, as has happened in Cuba, Nicaragua, and Iran. Even if such changes do not represent an immediate physical threat to firms and their employees, they can have drastic effects. The past few decades have seen such coups in the countries of Ghana, Ethiopia, and Iraq, to name a few. These coups have seriously impeded the conduct of international marketing.

Terrorist Incidents against Business FIGURE 4.3b

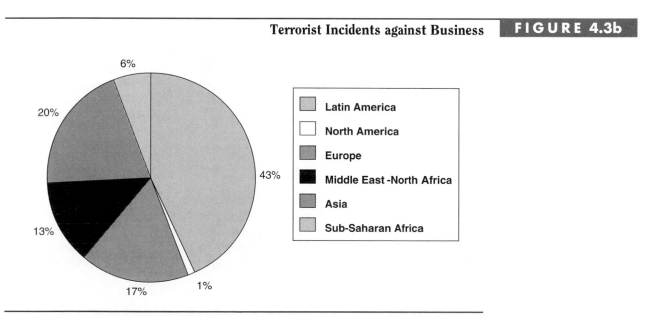

Source: U.S. Department of State, *Patterns of Global Terrorism*, 1992 (Washington, D.C., GPO, April 1993).

Less dramatic but still worrisome are changes in government policies that are caused not by changes in the government itself but by pressure from nationalist or religious factions or widespread anti-Western feeling. The aware manager will work to anticipate these changes and plan ways to cope with them.

What sort of changes in policy result from the various events described? The range of possible actions is broad. All of them can affect international marketing operations, but not all are equal in weight. Except for extreme cases, companies do not usually have to fear violence against employees, although violence against company property is quite common. Common also are changes in policy that take a strong nationalist and antiforeign investment stance. The most drastic steps resulting from such policy changes are usually confiscation and expropriation.

An important governmental action is **expropriation.** According to the World Bank, in the 1960s and 1970s, a total of 1,535 firms from 22 different countries have been expropriated in 511 separate actions by 76 nations.[8] Expropriation appealed to many countries because it demonstrated nationalism and immediately transferred a certain amount of wealth and resources from foreign companies to the host country. It did have costs to the host country, however, to the extent that it made other firms more hesitant to invest in the country. Expropriation does not relieve the host government of providing compensation to the former owners. However, these compensation negotiations are often protracted and result in settlements that are frequently unsatisfactory to the owners. For example, governments may offer compensation in the form of local, nontransferable currency or may base the compensation on the book value of the firm. Even though firms that are expropriated may deplore the low levels of payment obtained, they frequently accept them in the absence of better alternatives.

The use of expropriation as a policy tool has sharply decreased over time. In the mid-1970s, more than 83 expropriations took place in a single year. By the 1980s, the annual average had declined to fewer than three. Apparently, governments have come to recognize that the damage inflicted on themselves through expropriation exceeds the benefits.[9]

In that it results in a transfer of ownership from the foreign firm to the host country, **confiscation** is similar to expropriation. It differs, however, in that it does not involve compensation for the firm. Some industries are more vulnerable than others to confiscation and expropriation because of their importance to the host-country economy and their lack of ability to shift operations. For this reason, sectors such as mining, energy, public utilities, and banking have been targets of such government actions.

Confiscation and expropriation constitute major political risks for foreign investors. Other government actions, however, are nearly as damaging. Many countries are turning from confiscation and expropriation to more subtle forms of control, such as **domestication.** The goal of domestication is the same, to gain control over foreign investment, but the method is different. Through domestication, the government demands partial transfer of ownership and management responsibility and imposes regulations to ensure that a large share of the product is locally produced and a larger share of the profit is retained in the country.

Domestication can have profound effects on the international marketer for a number of reasons. First, if a firm is forced to hire nationals as managers, poor cooperation and communication can result. If the domestication is imposed within a very short time span, corporate operations overseas may have to be headed by poorly trained and inexperienced local managers. Further, domestic content requirements may force a firm to

---

[8] Joseph V. Miscallef, "Political Risk Assessment," *Columbia Journal of World Business* (January 1981): 47.

[9] Michael Minor, "LDCs, TNCs, and Expropriation in the 1980s," *CTC Reporter,* Spring 1988, 53.

purchase supplies and parts locally, which can result in increased costs, inefficiency, and lower-quality products, thus further damaging a firm's interest. Export requirements imposed on companies may also create havoc for the international distribution plan of a corporation and force it to change or even shut down operations in third countries. Finally, domestication will usually shield the industry within one country from foreign competition. As a result, inefficiencies will be allowed to grow due to a lack of market discipline. In the long run, this will affect the international competitiveness of an operation abroad and may become a major problem when, years later, the removal of domestication is considered by the government.

Most businesses operating abroad face a number of other risks that are less dangerous, but probably more common, than the drastic ones already described. Host governments that face a shortage of foreign currency sometimes will impose controls on the movement of capital in and out of the country. Such controls may make it difficult for a firm to remove its profits or investments from the host country. Sometimes, **exchange controls** are also levied selectively against certain products or companies in an effort to reduce the importation of goods that are considered to be a luxury or unnecessary. Such regulations are often difficult to deal with because they may affect the importation of parts, components, or supplies that are vital for production operations. Restrictions on such imports may force a firm either to alter its production program or, worse yet, to shut down its entire plant. Prolonged negotiations with government officials may be necessary in order to reach a compromise agreement on what constitutes a "valid" expenditure of foreign currency resources. Because the goals of government officials and corporate managers may often be quite different, such compromises, even when they can be reached, may result in substantial damage to the international marketing operations of a firm.

Countries may also raise the tax rates applied to foreign investors in an effort to control the firms and their capital. On occasion, different or stricter applications of the host country's tax codes are implemented for foreign investors. The rationale for such measures is often the seeming underpayment of taxes by such investors, when comparing their payments to those of long-established domestic competitors. Overlooked is the fact that new investors in foreign lands tend to "**overinvest**" by initially buying more land, space, and equipment than is needed immediately and by spending heavily so that facilities are state-of-the-art. This desire to accommodate future growth and to be highly competitive in the early investment stages will, in turn, produce lower profits and lower tax payments. Yet over time, these investment activities should be very successful, competitive, and job-creating. Such tax increases may result in much-needed revenue for the coffers of the host country, but they can severely damage the operations of the foreign investors. This damage, in turn, will frequently result in decreased income for the host country in the long run.

The international marketing manager must also worry about **price controls.** In many countries, domestic political pressures can force governments to control the prices of imported products or services, particularly in sectors that are considered to be highly sensitive from a political perspective, such as food or health care. If a foreign firm is involved in these areas, it is a vulnerable target of price controls because the government can play on its people's nationalistic tendencies to enforce the price controls. Particularly in countries that suffer from high inflation and frequent devaluations, the international marketer may be forced to choose between shutting down the operation or continuing production at a loss in the hope of recouping that loss once the government chooses to loosen or remove its price restrictions. How a firm can adjust to price controls is discussed in greater detail later in the book.

Managers face political and economic risk whenever they conduct business overseas, but there may be ways to lessen the risk. Obviously, if a new government that is dedicated to the removal of all foreign influences comes into power, a firm can do little. In less extreme cases, however, managers can take actions to reduce the risk if they understand the root causes of the host-country policies.

Adverse governmental actions are usually the result of a host country's nationalism, desire for independence, and opposition to colonial remnants. If a country's citizens feel exploited by foreign firms, government officials are more likely to take antiforeign action. To reduce the risk of government intervention, a firm needs to demonstrate that it is concerned with the host country's society and that it considers itself an integral part of the host country rather than simply an exploitative foreign corporation. Ways to do this include intensive local hiring and training practices, good pay, more charity, and more societally useful investment. In addition, a company can form joint ventures with local partners to demonstrate a willingness to share its benefits with nationals. Although such actions will not guarantee freedom from risk, they will certainly lessen the exposure.

Corporations can also protect against political risk by closely monitoring political developments. Increasingly, private-sector firms offer assistance in such monitoring activities, permitting the overseas corporation to discover potential trouble spots as early as possible and react quickly to prevent major losses. Figure 4.4 provides an example of such

FIGURE 4.4   **Assistance for Risk Management**

Source: Courtesy Palisade Corporation, Newfield, N.Y.

a service. Firms can also take out insurance to cover losses due to political risk. In the United States, for example, the Overseas Private Investment Corporation (OPIC) offers such insurance. Rates vary by country and industry, but for $100 of coverage per year for a manufacturing project, the base rate is $.60 for protection against inconvertibility, $.60 to protect against expropriation, and $1.05 to protect against political violence.[10]

Clearly, the international marketer must consider the likelihood of negative political factors in making decisions on conducting business overseas. On the other hand, host-country political and legal systems can have a positive impact on the conduct of international business. Many governments, for example, encourage foreign investments, especially if they believe that the investment will produce economic and political benefits domestically. Some governments have opened up their economy to foreign investors, placing only minimal constraints on them, in the hope that such policies will lead to rapid economic development. Others have provided for substantial subsidization of new investment activities in the hope that investments will generate additional employment. The international marketer, in his investment decision, can and should therefore also pay close attention to the extent and forms of incentives available from foreign governments. Although international marketing decisions should be driven by market forces, the basic economies of these decisions may change depending on incentives offered.

In this discussion of the political environment, laws have been mentioned only to the extent that they appear to be the direct result of political changes. However, each nation has laws regarding marketing, and the international manager must understand their effects on the firm's efforts.

Legal Differences and Restraints

Countries differ in their laws as well as in their use of these laws. For example, the United States has developed into an increasingly litigious society, in which institutions and individuals are quick to take a case to court. As a result, court battles are often protracted and costly, and simply the threat of a court case can reduce marketing opportunities. In contrast, Japan's legal tradition tends to minimize the role of the law and of lawyers. Some possible reasons include the relatively small number of courts and attorneys, the delays, the costs and the uncertainties associated with litigation, the limited doctrines of plaintiffs' standing and rights to bring class-action suits, the tendency of judges to encourage out-of-court settlements, and the easy availability of arbitration and mediation for dispute resolution.

Some estimates suggest that the number of lawyers in the United States is as much as 48 times higher than in Japan, based on the fact that Japan has only about 12,500 fully licensed lawyers. However, comparisons can be misleading because officially registered lawyers in Japan perform a small fraction of the duties performed by American lawyers. After accounting for the additional roles of American lawyers, the number of "lawyers" in Japan appears to be approximately one-fifth of those in the United States.[11] One effect of this smaller number of lawyers appears to be a different approach toward the settlement of conflicts, as shown in The International Marketplace 4.6.

Over the millennia of civilization, many different laws and legal systems emerged. King Hammurabi of Babylon codified a series of judges' decisions into a body of law. Hebrew law was the result of the dictates of God. Legal issues in many African tribes were settled through the verdicts of clansmen. A key legal perspective that survives today is

---

[10] *Investment Insurance Handbook* (Washington, D.C.: Overseas Private Investment Corporation, 1991).

[11] Stuart M. Chemtob, Glen S. Fukushima, and Richard H. Wohl, *Practice by Foreign Lawyers in Japan* (Chicago: American Bar Association, 1989), 9.

4.6

THE INTERNATIONAL MARKETPLACE

Two Air Disasters, Two Cultures, Two Remedies

When two jumbo jets crashed ten days apart in Dallas and in the mountains near Tokyo, Americans and Japanese shared a common bond of shock and grief. Soon, however, all parties in Japan—from the airline to the employers of victims—moved to put the tragedy behind them. In the United States, legal tremors will be felt for years.

Lawyers hustled to the scene of the Delta Air Lines accident at the Dallas–Fort Worth airport and set up shop at an airport hotel. Proclaimed San Francisco attorney Melvin Belli, "I'm not an ambulance chaser—I get there before the ambulance." "We always file the first suit," bragged Richard Brown, a Melvin Belli associate who flew to Dallas "to get to the bottom of this and to make ourselves available." He added: "We never solicited anyone directly. We were called to Texas by California residents who lost their loved ones." Within 72 hours, the first suit against Delta was filed. Insurance adjusters working for Delta quickly went to work as well.

Seven thousand miles away, Japan Air Lines President Yasumoto Takagi humbly bowed to families of the 520 victims and apologized "from the bottom of our hearts." He vowed to resign once the investigation was complete. Next of kin soon received "condolence payments" and negotiated settlements with the airline. Traditionally few, if any, lawsuits are filed following such accidents.

Behind these differences lie standards of behavior and corporate responsibility that are worlds apart. "There is a general Japanese inclination to try to settle any disputes through negotiations between the parties before going to court," said Koichiro Fujikura, a Tokyo University law professor. Added Carl Green, a Washington, D.C., attorney and specialist on Japanese law: "There is an assumption of responsibility. In our adversarial society, we don't admit responsibility. It would be admitting liability."

After a JAL jet crashed into Tokyo Bay in 1982, killing 24, JAL President Takagi visited victims' families, offered gifts, and knelt before funeral altars. JAL offered families about $2,000 each in condolence payments, then negotiated settlements reported to be worth between $166,000 and $450,000, depending on the age and earning power of each victim. Only one family sued.

Japanese legal experts expect settlements to be as high as 500 million yen—about $2.1 million—apiece. Negotiations may be prolonged. But if families believe that JAL is sincerely sorry,"I think their feelings will be soothed," predicted attorney Takeshi Odagi.

Japan's legal system encourages these traditions. "Lawyers don't descend in droves on accident scenes because they barely have enough time to handle the suits they have," said John Haley, a law professor at the University of Washington who has studied and worked in Japan. "There are fewer judges per capita than there were in 1890," Haley added. Only 500 lawyers are admitted to the bar each year.

Source: Clemens P. Work, Sarah Peterson, and Hidehiro Tanakadate, "Two Air Disasters, Two Cultures, Two Remedies," *U.S. News and World Report*, August 26, 1985, 25–26.

that of *theocracy.* For example, Islamic law, or the *sharia,* is the result of scripture, prophetic utterances and practices, and scholarly interpretations.[12] Together with He-brew law, these legal systems have faith and belief as their key focus and are a mix of so-cietal, legal, and spiritual guidelines.

While these legal systems are important to society from an international business perspective, two major legal systems exist worldwide: common law and code law. **Common law** is based on tradition and depends less on written statutes and codes than on precedent and custom. Common law originated in England and is the system of law found today in the United States.

On the other hand, **code law** is based on a comprehensive set of written statutes. Coun-tries with code law try to spell out all possible legal rules explicitly. Code law is based on Roman law and is found in the majority of the nations of the world. In general, countries with the code law system have much more rigid laws than those with the common law system. In the latter, courts adopt precedents and customs to fit the cases, allowing the marketer a better idea of the basic judgment likely to be rendered in new situations.

Although wide in theory, the differences between code law and common law, and their impact on the international marketer, are not always as broad in practice. For example, many common law countries, including the United States, have adopted commercial codes to govern the conduct of business.

Host countries may adopt a number of laws that affect a company's ability to market. To begin with, there can be laws affecting the entry of goods, such as tariffs and quotas. Also in this category are **antidumping laws,** which prohibit below-cost sales of products, and laws that require export and import licensing. In addition, many countries have health and safety standards that may, by design or by accident, restrict the entry of for-eign goods. Japan, for example, has particularly strict health standards that affect the import of pharmaceuticals. Rather than accepting test results from other nations, the Japanese government insists on conducting its own tests which are time consuming and costly. The claim is that these tests are necessary to take into account Japanese pecu-liarities. Yet some importers and their governments see these practices as thinly veiled protectionist barriers.

Other laws may be designed to protect domestic industries. Since 1990, the Chinese government has prohibited foreign investment for projects that are not in line with na-tional economic development and projects under the unified state plan. Barred project areas include developing and printing of color films; maintenance of household electric appliances; production of cigarettes, liquors, foods, and drinks targeted at the home market; and assembly lines of computers, refrigerators, washing machines, watches, and sewing machines.[13]

Very specific legislation may also exist to regulate, for example, where a firm can ad-vertise or what constitutes deceptive advertising. Many countries prohibit specific claims by marketers comparing their product to that of the competition and restrict the use of promotional devices. Even when no laws exist, the marketer may be hampered by regu-lations. For example, in many countries, governments require a firm to join the local chamber of commerce or become a member of the national trade association. These in-stitutions in turn may have internal regulations that set standards for the conduct of business and may be seen as quite confining to the international marketer.

---

[12] Surya Prakash Sinha, *What Is Law? The Differing Theories of Jurisprudence* (New York: Paragon House, 1989).

[13] *1991 National Trade Estimate Report on Foreign Trade Barriers* (Washington, D.C.: U.S. Government Printing Office, 1991), 50.

Finally, the enforcement of laws may have a different effect on national and on foreign marketers. For example, the simple requirement that an executive has to stay in a country until a business conflict is resolved may prove to be quite onerous on the international marketer.

The Influencing of Politics and Laws

To succeed in a market, the international marketer needs much more than business know-how. He or she must also deal with the intricacies of national politics and laws. Although to fully understand another country's legal and political system will rarely be possible, the good manager will be aware of the importance of this system and will work with people who do understand how to operate within the system.

Many areas of politics and law are not immutable. Viewpoints can be modified or even reversed, and new laws can supersede old ones. Therefore, existing political and legal restraints do not always need to be accepted. To achieve change, however, there must be some impetus for it, such as the clamors of a constituency. Otherwise, systemic inertia is likely to allow the status quo to prevail.

The international marketer has various options. One sometimes used is simply to ignore prevailing rules and expect to get away with it. Pursuing this option is a high-risk strategy because of the possibility of objection and even prosecution. A second, traditional option is to provide input to trade negotiators and expect any problem areas to be resolved in multilateral negotiations. The drawback to this option is, of course, the quite time-consuming process involved.

A third option involves the development of coalitions or constituencies that can motivate legislators and politicians to consider and ultimately implement change. This option can be pursued in various ways. First of all, direct linkages and their cost and benefit can be highlighted to legislators and politicians. For example, the manager can explain the employment and economic effects of certain laws and regulations and demonstrate the benefits of change. The picture can be enlarged by including indirect linkages. For example, suppliers, customers, and distributors can be asked to participate in delineating to decision makers the benefit of change.

Developing such coalitions is not an easy task. Companies often seek assistance in effectively influencing the government decision-making process. Such assistance usually is particularly beneficial when narrow economic objectives or single-issue campaigns are needed. Typical providers of this assistance are lobbyists. Usually, these are well-connected individuals and firms that can provide access to policymakers and legislators.

Foreign countries and companies have been particularly effective in their lobbying in the United States. For example, in 1975, only 35 U.S. firms had filed with the U.S. Department of Justice to state that they were lobbyists for foreign interests. By 1985, this number had grown to 105 U.S. firms retained under contract to represent foreign economic interests in the United States, beyond traditional diplomatic representation. Although estimates of the number of lobbyists on behalf of foreign entities in 1991 range into the thousands, only 745 have registered with the Justice Department.[14] As an example, Brazil has held on average nearly a dozen contracts per year with U.S. firms covering trade issues. Brazilian citrus exporters and computer manufacturers have hired U.S. legal and public relations firms to provide them with information on relevant U.S. legislative activity. The Banco do Brasil lobbied for the restructuring of Brazilian debt and favorable banking regulations. A key factor in successful lobbying, however, is the in-

---

[14] Gary Lee, "Hearings to Review Lobbyist Disclosure Law," *Washington Post,* June 10, 1991, A9.

THE INTERNATIONAL MARKETPLACE

4.7

Backbone of the New China Lobby: U.S. Firms

Every year, the U.S. government reviews whether China's Most Favored Nation (MFN) status should be extended. Since this status conveys the benefit of low tariffs on Chinese exports, one would expect the Chinese government to be the principal lobbyist in Washington. However, as the MFN debate of 1993 showed, it was U.S. corporations that played the leading role. Some companies possess potentially tremendous business interests—China is the fastest-growing major market for U.S. exports—and so they made sure to argue their case for keeping low tariffs for Chinese exports, which Beijing has demanded as a condition for buying American products.

Corporations involved in lobbying usually focus their efforts on the issue of U.S. jobs. According to one U.S. official involved, "We're dealing directly with CEOs, who are dealing with opportunities they can grasp. You're not talking about a theoretical China market—you're talking about jobs next year." CEOs from such giants as Boeing and Motorola met with the president on China's importance to their industries. Other Fortune 500 executives visited the Departments of Commerce and State, bringing with them estimates that exports to China create 157,000 U.S. jobs. Retail footwear lobbyists distributed results of a study showing that cheap imported shoes from China save U.S. consumers $16 billion a year; they then proceeded to flood the White House with letters from thousands of shoe store managers pleading for MFN's extension.

Since relations between the two countries were normalized in 1979, China has not had a strong lobbying presence in Washington. According to U.S. analysts, the real power of the China lobby comes from a strategy dating from imperial times: "Use barbarians to control barbarians." Beijing will open the trade door just enough to show the profitability of the Chinese market. It is then up to the profit-seekers to wield whatever political influence is needed to keep the door open.

Beijing certainly knows how to set business forces in motion. During the 1993 MFN debate, Chinese trade delegations in the United States went on a well-publicized, cross-country shopping spree. "China has been very effective in using its market opening to get maximum leverage over the American business community, motivating it to work their own government on MFN and other trade issues," says a former Bush assistant. Threats of cancellation of orders or a loss of future deals if MFN is not renewed are provided regularly by China, making it clear that it is in an enlightened American company's best interest to press the government to approve MFN without conditions.

Source: Michael Weisskopf, "Backbone of the New China Lobby: U.S. Firms," *The Washington Post*, June 14, 1993, A1.

volvement of U.S. citizens and companies. The International Marketplace 4.7 explains how a foreign country can gain their participation.

U.S. firms also have representation in Washington, D.C., as well as state capitals. Often, however, they are less adept at ensuring proper representation abroad. For example, a survey of U.S. international marketing executives found that knowledge and information about foreign trade and government officials was ranked lowest among critical international business information needs. This low ranking appears to reflect the fact that many U.S. firms are far less successful in their interaction with governments abroad and are far less intensive in their lobbying attempts than are foreign entities in the United States.[15]

Although representation of the firm's interests to government decision makers and legislators is entirely appropriate, the international marketer must also consider any potential side effects. Major questions can be raised if such representation becomes very strong. In such instances, short-term gains may be far outweighed by long-term negative repercussions if the international marketer is perceived as exerting too much political influence.

THE INTERNATIONAL ENVIRONMENT

In addition to the politics and laws of both the home and the host countries, the international marketer must consider the overall international political and legal environment. Relations between countries can have a profound impact on firms trying to do business internationally.

International Politics

The effect of politics on international marketing is determined by both the bilateral political relations between home and host countries and the multilateral agreements governing the relations among groups of countries.

The government-to-government relationship can have a profound effect, particularly if it becomes hostile. Numerous examples exist of the linkage between international politics and international marketing. The premier example is perhaps U.S.-Iranian relations following the 1979 Iranian revolution. Although the internal political and legal changes in the aftermath of that revolution would certainly have affected international marketing in Iran, the deterioration in U.S.-Iranian political relations that resulted from the revolution had a significant impact. U.S. firms were injured not only by physical damage caused by the violence but also by the anti-American feelings of the Iranian people and their government. The clashes between the two governments completely destroyed any business relationships, regardless of corporate feelings or agreements on either side.

International political relations do not always have harmful effects on international marketers. If bilateral political relations between countries improve, business can benefit. A good example is the thawing of relations between the United States and the former communist bloc. Political warming has opened up completely new frontiers for U.S. international marketers in Hungary, Poland, and Russia, just to name a few countries. Activities such as selling computers, which would have been considered treasonous only a few years ago, are now routine.

The good international marketer will be aware of political currents worldwide and will attempt to anticipate changes in the international political environment, good or bad, so that his or her firm can plan for them.

International Law

International law plays an important role in the conduct of international business. Although no enforceable body of international law exists, certain treaties and agreements

---

[15] Michael R. Czinkota, "International Information Needs for U.S. Competitiveness," *Business Horizons* 34 (November–December 1991): 86–91.

respected by a number of countries profoundly influence international business operations. As an example, the General Agreement on Tariffs and Trade (GATT) defines internationally acceptable economic practices for its member nations. Although it does not directly affect individual firms, it does influence them indirectly by providing a more stable and predictable international market environment.

A number of efforts have been made to simplify the legal aspects of business procedures. For example, firms wanting to patent their products in the past had to register them separately in each country in order to have protection. In response to the chaos and expense of such procedures, several multilateral simplification efforts have been undertaken. European countries have been at the forefront of such efforts with the European Patent Convention and the Community Patent Convention.

Similar efforts have been undertaken with regard to trademarks so that firms can benefit from various multilateral agreements. The two major international conventions on trademarks are the International Convention for the Protection of Industrial Property and the Madrid Arrangement for International Registration of Trademarks. Several regional conventions include the Inter-American Convention for Trademark Protection and a similar agreement in French West Africa.

In addition to multilateral agreements, firms are affected by bilateral treaties and conventions. The United States, for example, has signed bilateral treaties of friendship, commerce, and navigation (FCN) with a wide variety of countries. These agreements generally define the rights of U.S. firms doing business in the host country. They normally guarantee that the U.S. firms will be treated by the host country in the same manner in which domestic firms are treated. Although these treaties provide for some stability, they can be canceled when relationships worsen.

The international legal environment also affects the marketer to the extent that firms must concern themselves with jurisdictional disputes. Because no single body of international law exists, firms usually are restricted by both home- and host country laws. If a conflict occurs between contracting parties in two different countries, a question arises concerning which country's laws will be followed. Sometimes the contract will contain a jurisdictional clause, which settles the matter. If not, the parties to the dispute can follow either the laws of the country in which the agreement was made or those of the country in which the contract will have to be fulfilled. Deciding on the laws to be followed and the location to settle the dispute are two different decisions. As a result, a dispute between a U.S. exporter and a French importer could be resolved in Paris with the resolution based on New York State law.

If no satisfactory arrangement can be agreed on, the parties can choose either arbitration or litigation. Litigation is usually avoided for several reasons. It often involves extensive delays and is very costly. In addition, firms may fear discrimination in foreign countries. Companies therefore tend to prefer conciliation and arbitration because these processes result in much quicker decisions. Arbitration procedures are often spelled out in the original contract and usually provide for an intermediary who is judged to be impartial by both parties. Frequently, intermediaries will be representatives of chambers of commerce, trade associations, or third-country institutions.

SUMMARY

The political and legal environment in the home country, the environment in the host country, and the laws and agreements governing relationships among nations are all important to the international marketer. Compliance with them is mandatory in order to do business abroad successfully. To avoid the problems that can result from changes in the political and legal environment, the international marketer must anticipate changes and develop strategies for coping with them. Whenever possible, the manager must avoid being taken by surprise and thus not let events control business decisions.

On occasion, the international marketer may be caught between clashing home- and host-country laws. In such instances, the firm needs to conduct a dialogue with the governments in order to seek a compromise solution. Alternatively, managers can encourage their government to engage in government-to-government negotiations to settle the dispute. By demonstrating the business volume at stake and the employment that may be lost through such governmental disputes, government negotiators can often be motivated to press hard for a settlement of such intergovernmental difficulties. Finally, the firm can seek redress in court. Such international legal action, however, may be quite slow and, even if resulting in a favorable judgment for the firm, may not be adhered to by the government against which the judgment is rendered.

In the final analysis, a firm conducting business internationally is subject to the vagaries of political and legal changes and may lose business as a result. The best the manager can do is to be aware of political influences and laws and strive to adopt them as far as possible.

Questions for Discussion

1. Discuss this statement: "High political risk requires companies to seek a quick payback on their investments. Striving for such a quick payback, however, exposes firms to charges of exploitation and results in increased political risk."

2. How appropriate is it for governments to help drum up business for their companies abroad? Should commerce not be completely separate from politics?

3. Discuss this statement: "The national security that our export control laws seek to protect may be threatened by the resulting lack of international competitiveness of U.S. firms."

4. After you hand your passport to the immigration officer in country X, he misplaces it. A small "donation" would certainly help him find it again. Should you give him money? Is this a business expense to be charged to your company? Should it be tax deductible?

5. Discuss the advantages and disadvantages of common versus code law for the international marketer.

6. Research examples of multinational corporations that have remained untouched by waves of expropriation. What was the secret of their success?

7. The United States has been described as a "litigious" society. How does frequent litigation affect the international marketer, particularly in comparison with the situation in other countries?

8. What are your views on lobbying efforts by foreign firms?

Recommended Readings

Bertsch, G. K., and S. E. Gowen, eds. *Export Controls In Transition: Perspectives, Problems, and Prospects.* Durham, N.C.: Duke University Press, 1992.

Carter, Barry E. *International Economic Sanctions.* Cambridge: Cambridge University Press, 1988.

Choate, Pat. *Agents of Influence.* New York: Knopf, 1990.

Czinkota, Michael R., ed. *Export Controls.* New York: Praeger Publishers, 1984.

De la Torre, Jose, and David H. Neckar. "Forecasting Political Risks for International Operations." In *Global Strategic Management: The Essentials,* 2d ed., edited by H. Vernon-Wortzel and L. Wortzel. New York: John Wiley and Sons, 1990.

Export Controls: Multilateral Efforts to Improve Enforcement, Washington, D.C.: United States Accounting Office, GAO/NSIAD-92-167, 1992.

Finding Common Ground: U.S. Export Controls in a Changed Global Environment, Washington, D.C.: National Academy Press, 1991.

Gows, Joanne S. *Allies, Adversaries, and International Trade.* Princeton, N.J.: Princeton University Press, 1994.

Hufbauer, Gary Clyde, and Jeffrey J. Schott. *Economic Sanctions in Support of Foreign Policy Goals.* Washington, D.C.: Institute for International Economics, 1984.

Spar, Debora L. *The Cooperative Edge: The Internal Politics of International Cartels.* Ithaca, N.Y.: Cornell University Press, 1994.

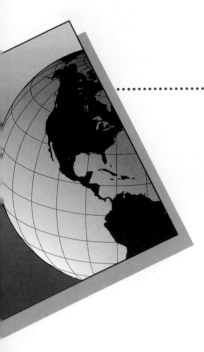

CHAPTER 5

The International Cultural Environment

THE INTERNATIONAL MARKETPLACE

Soup: Now It's Mmm-Mmm-Global

By the year 2000, Campbell Soup wants half of company revenues to come from outside domestic markets. It is an ambitious goal, since only 26 percent were from foreign sales in 1993. Adding to the challenge is the fact that prepared food may be one of the toughest products to sell overseas. It is not as universal or easily marketed as soap or soft drinks, given regional taste preferences. Italians, not surprisingly, shy away from canned pasta, and while an average Pole consumes five bowls of soup a week, 98 percent of Polish soups are homemade.

Campbell, however, has managed to overcome some cultural obstacles in selected countries. To shake the powdered soup domination in Argentina, it markets its Sopa de Campbell as "The Real Soup," stressing its list of fresh ingredients on the label. In Poland, Campbell advertises to working Polish mothers looking for convenience. Says Lee Andrews, Campbell's new-product manager in Warsaw, "We can't shove a can in their faces and replace Mom."

However, in many regions, Campbell is trying to cook more like mom. This means creating new products that appeal to distinctly regional tastes. The approach has been to use test kitchens and taste-testing with consumers. Results have included fiery cream of chile poblano soup in Mexico as well as watercress and duck gizzard soup for China.

In 1993, Asia accounted for only 2 percent of Campbell's worldwide sales, but the region—China in particular—is being targeted as the area with the strongest growth potential. New markets are entered gingerly. Campbell typically launches a basic meat or chicken broth, which consumers can doctor with meats, vegetables, and spices. Later, more sophisticated soups are brought on line. In China, the real competition comes from homemade soup, which comprises over 99 percent of all consumption. With this in mind, Campbell's prices have been kept attractive and its products promoted on convenience. While many of the products, such as corn and chicken soup, have been developed in the company's Hong Kong kitchens, some U.S. standbys, such as cream of mushroom, have been selling well, possibly to the segment of westernized Chinese.

Local ingredients may count, but Campbell draws the line on some Asian favorites. Dog soup is out, as is shark's fin, since most species are endangered. For most other options, an open mind is kept. This includes snake, for example.

Furthermore, Campbell is also finding that ethnic foods are growing in popularity around the world. With its emphasis on vegetables, Asian cuisine benefits from a healthy image in Europe and North America. This means that some new products currently being developed for the Asian consumer may become global favorites in no time.

Source: "Ethnic Food Whets Appetites in Europe, Enticing Producers to Add Foreign Fare," *The Wall Street Journal*, November 1, 1993, B5A; "Hmm. Could Use a Little More Snake," *Business Week*, March 15, 1993, 53; and "Canned and Delivered," *Business China*, November 16, 1992, 12.

Although the world has become smaller as a result of improvements in transportation and information systems, the behavioral patterns, values, and attitudes that govern human interaction remain relatively unchanged. Technological innovation is bringing about the internationalization of business, and employees at all levels are becoming involved in cross-cultural interaction. Firms expanding internationally acquire foreign clients as well as foreign personnel with whom regular communication is necessary, with the result that day-to-day operations require significant cross-cultural competence.

In the past, marketing managers who did not want to worry about the cultural challenge could simply decide not to do so and concentrate on domestic markets. In today's business environment, a company has no choice but to face international competition. In this new environment, believing that concern about culture and its elements is a waste of time often proves to be disastrous. An understanding allows marketers to determine when adaptation may be necessary and when commonalities allow for regional or global approaches, as seen in The International Marketplace 5.1.

Cultural differences often are the subject of anecdotes, and business blunders may provide a good laugh. Cultural incompetence, however, can easily jeopardize millions of dollars in wasted negotiations, potential purchases, sales and contracts, and customer relations. Furthermore, the internal efficiency of a firm may be weakened if managers, employees, and intermediaries are not "on the same wavelength."

The intent of this chapter is first to analyze the concept of culture and its various elements and then to provide suggestions for meeting the cultural challenge.

CULTURE DEFINED

Culture gives an individual an anchoring point—an identity—as well as codes of conduct. Of the more than 160 definitions of culture analyzed by Alfred Kroeber and Clyde Kluckhohn, some conceive of culture as separating humans from nonhumans, some define it as communicable knowledge, and some as the sum of historical achievements produced by man's social life.[1] All of the definitions have common elements: Culture is learned, shared, and transmitted from one generation to the next. Culture is primarily passed on from parents to their children but also by social organizations, special-interest groups, the government, the schools, and the church. Common ways of thinking and behaving that are developed are then reinforced through social pressure. Geert Hofstede calls this the "collective programming of the mind."[2] Culture is also multidimensional, consisting of a number of common elements that are interdependent. Changes occurring in one of the dimensions will affect the others as well.

For the purposes of this text, culture is defined as an integrated system of learned behavior patterns that are distinguishing characteristics of the members of any given society. It includes everything that a group thinks, says, does, and makes—its customs, language, material artifacts, and shared systems of attitudes and feelings.[3] The definition therefore encompasses a wide variety of elements, from the materialistic to the spiritual. Culture is inherently conservative, resisting change and fostering continuity. Every person is encultured into a particular culture, learning the "right way" of doing things. Problems may arise when a person encultured in one culture has to adjust to another one. The process of **acculturation**—adjusting and adapting to a specific culture other than one's own—is one of the keys to success in international operations.

Edward T. Hall, who has made some of the most valuable studies on the effects of culture on business, makes a distinction between high and low context cultures.[4] In **high context cultures,** such as Japan and Saudi Arabia, context is at least as important as what is actually said. The speaker and the listener rely on a common understanding of the context. In **low context cultures,** however, most of the information is contained explicitly in the words. North American cultures engage in low context communications. Unless one is aware of this basic difference, messages and intentions can easily be misunderstood. If performance appraisals of marketing personnel are to be centrally guided or conducted in a multinational corporation, those involved must be acutely aware of cultural nuances. One of the interesting differences is that the U.S. system emphasizes the individual's development, whereas the Japanese system focuses on the group within which the individual works. In the United States, criticism is more direct and recorded formally, whereas in Japan it is more subtle and verbal. What is not being said can carry more meaning than what is said.

Few cultures today are as homogeneous as those of Japan and Saudi Arabia. Elsewhere, intracultural differences based on nationality, religion, race, or geographic areas have resulted in the emergence of distinct subcultures. The international manager's task is to distinguish relevant cross-cultural and intracultural differences and then to isolate potential opportunities and problems. Good examples are the Hispanic subculture in the United States and the Flemish and the Walloons in Belgium. On the other hand, borrowing and interaction between national cultures may lead to narrowing gaps between cultures. Here the international business entity will act as a **change agent** by introducing new products or ideas and practices. Although this may consist of no more than shifting consumption from one product brand to another, it may lead to massive social change in the manner of consumption, the type of products consumed, and social

---

[1] Alfred Kroeber and Clyde Kluckhohn, *Culture: A Critical Review of Concepts and Definitions* (New York: Random House, 1985), 11.

[2] Geert Hofstede, "National Cultures Revisited," *Asia-Pacific Journal of Management* 1 (September 1984): 22–24.

[3] Robert L. Kohls, *Survival Kit for Overseas Living* (Chicago: Intercultural Press, 1979), 3.

[4] Edward T. Hall, *Beyond Culture* (Garden City, NY: Anchor Press, 1976), 15.

THE INTERNATIONAL MARKETPLACE

An American Park In Paris

EuroDisneyland, the world's biggest and splashiest theme park, opened April 12, 1992, some 20 miles east of Paris. According to Robert J. Fitzpatrick, the park's chairman, the park was supposed to "help change Europe's chemistry."

Not everyone was as excited about EuroDisneyland's prospects. Many critics in France, which is viewed as half of the theme park's market, have remained hostile. The criticisms have ranged from "not Europe's cup of tea" to a "cultural Chernobyl," a reference to the nuclear disaster in the Ukraine in 1986. Besides criticizing the cultural imperialism of the venture, many have doubted that Europeans would seek an entertainment experience in the suburbs of Paris given diversity in European tastes and the area's grim winter weather. The first year's results were not positive: Low attendance and penny-pinching guests due to Europe's recession resulted in a loss of $514 million.

Part of Disney's optimism about the park was a result of the success of Tokyo Disneyland. "Everything we imported that worked in the United States worked in Japan," says Ronald D. Pogue, managing director of Walt Disney Attractions Japan Ltd. The Europeans posed a totally different challenge, however.

European audiences tend to want more local content in their parks. While the Japanese are fond of American pop culture, Europeans are quite content with their own culture. To them, detail and craftsmanship in a theme park are more important than heart-stopping rides. While Disney's adaptation to European conditions was meticulous, some implementation issues were overlooked. "Everyone arrives at 9:30, leaves at 5:30, and wants lunch at 12:30," notes Michael Eisner, chairman of the Walt Disney Co. This resulted in huge crowds and surly patrons. The negative results in 1993 caused Disney officials to consider closing the $4 billion theme park, but a refinancing agreement saved the park.

Some are hopeful for a brighter future. The opening of the English Channel tunnel in May 1994 should bring a flood of British tourists. If forecasts for a European economic upturn become reality, the minimum attendance of 11 million for breakeven might easily be reached. At the moment, many others who had intended to develop parks in Europe are scared by the Disney experience.

Sources: "Is Disney Headed for the Euro-Trash Heap?" *Business Week,* January 24, 1994, 52; "Alarm Bells," *The Economist,* January 8, 1994, 5; David J. Jefferson, "Cheap Thrills," *The Wall Street Journal,* March 26, 1993, R11; Sara Khalili, "Is This Another Japanese 'Goofy' Investment?" *North American International Business,* February 1991, 74–75; and John Huey, "America's Hottest Export: Pop Culture," *Fortune,* December 31, 1990, 50–60.

organization. In markets such as Taiwan, the entry of McDonald's and other fast-food entities dramatically changed eating habits, especially of the younger generation.

In some cases, the international marketer may be accused of "cultural imperialism," especially if the changes brought about are dramatic or if culture-specific adaptations are not made in the marketing approach. This is highlighted in the experience of Disney in its expansion into Europe (The International Marketplace 5.2). Some countries, such as France, Canada, Brazil, and Indonesia, protect their "cultural industries" (e.g., music and movies) through restrictive rules and subsidies. The 1993 GATT agreement that will allow restrictions on exports of U.S. entertainment to Europe is justified by the Europeans as a cultural safety net intended to support a desire to preserve national and regional identities.[5]

THE ELEMENTS OF CULTURE

The study of culture has led to generalizations that may apply to all cultures. Such characteristics are called **cultural universals,** which are manifestations of the total way of life of any group of people. These include such elements as bodily adornments, courtship, etiquette, family, gestures, joking, mealtimes, music, personal names, status differentiation, and trade.[6] These activities occur across cultures, but their manifestation may be unique in a particular society, bringing about cultural diversity. Common denominators can indeed be found, but how they are actually accomplished may vary dramatically.[7] Observation of the major ones summarized in Table 5.1 suggests that the elements are both material (such as tools) and abstract (such as attitudes). The sensitivity and adaptation to these elements by an international firm depends on the firm's level of involvement in the market—for example, licensing versus direct investment—and the product or service marketed. Naturally, some products and services or management practices require very little adjustment, whereas others have to be adapted dramatically.

Language

Language has been described as the mirror of culture. Language itself is multidimensional by nature. This is true not only of the spoken word but also of what can be called the nonverbal language of international business. Messages are conveyed by the words used, by how the words are spoken (for example, tone of voice), and by nonverbal means such as gestures, body position, and eye contact.

Very often, mastery of the language is required before a person is accultured to a culture other than his or her own. Language mastery must go beyond technical competency because every language has words and phrases that can be readily understood only in context. Such phrases are carriers of culture; they represent special ways a culture has developed to view some aspect of human existence.

Language capability serves four distinct roles in international marketing.[8] Language is important in information gathering and evaluation efforts. Rather than rely completely on the opinions of others, the manager is able to see and hear personally what is going on. People are far more comfortable speaking their own language, and this should be treated as an advantage. The best intelligence is gathered on a market by becoming part of the market rather than observing it from the outside. For example, local managers of a multinational corporation should be the firm's primary source of political information to assess potential risk. Second, language provides access to local society. Although English may be widely spoken, and may even be the official company language, speaking the local language may make a dramatic difference. For example, firms that translate promotional materials and information are seen as being serious about doing

[5] Michael T. Malloy, "America, Go Home," *The Wall Street Journal,* March 26, 1993, R7.

[6] George P. Mundak, "The Common Denominator of Cultures," in *The Science of Man in the World,* ed. Ralph Linton (New York: Columbia University Press, 1945), 123–142.

[7] Philip R. Harris and Robert T. Moran, *Managing Cultural Differences* (Houston, TX: Gulf, 1987), 201.

[8] David A. Ricks, *Big Business Blunders* (Homewood, IL: Irwin, 1983), 4.

	Elements of Culture	**TABLE 5.1**

Language
  • Verbal
  • Nonverbal
Religion
Values and attitudes
Manners and customs
Material elements
Aesthetics
Education
Social institutions

business in the country. Third, language capability is increasingly important in company communications, whether within the corporate family or with channel members. Imagine the difficulties encountered by a country manager who must communicate with employees through an interpreter. Finally, language provides more than the ability to communicate. It extends beyond mechanics to the interpretation of contexts.

The manager's command of the national language(s) in a market must be greater than simple word recognition. Consider, for example, how dramatically different English terms can be when used in Australia, the United Kingdom, or the United States. In negotiations, U.S. delegates "tabling a proposal" mean that they want to delay a decision, whereas their British counterparts understand the expression to mean that immediate action is to be taken. If the British promise something "by the end of the day," this does not mean within 24 hours, but rather when they have completed the job. Additionally, they may say that negotiations "bombed," meaning that they were a success; to an American, this could convey exactly the opposite message. Similar challenges occur with other languages and markets. Swedish is spoken as a mother tongue by 8 percent of the population in Finland, where it has idioms that are not well understood by Swedes.

Difficulties with language usually arise through carelessness, which is manifested in a number of translation blunders. The old saying "If you want to kill a message, translate it," is true. A classic example involves GM and its "Body by Fisher" theme; when translated into Flemish, this became "Corpse by Fisher." There is also the danger of sound-alikes. For example, Chanel No. 5 would have fared poorly in Japan had it been called Chanel No. 4, because the Japanese word for four (shih) also sounds like the word for death. This is the reason that IBM's series 44 computers had a different number classification in Japan than in any other market in which they were introduced. The danger of using a translingual homonym also exists; that is, an innocent English word may have strong aural resemblance to a word not used in polite company in another country. Examples in French-speaking areas include Pet milk products and a toothpaste called Cue. A French firm trying to sell pâté to a Baltimore importer experienced a problem with the brand name Tartex, which sounded like shoe polish. Kellogg renamed Bran Buds in Sweden, where the brand name translated roughly to "burned farmer."

The two advertising campaigns presented in Figure 5.1 highlight the difficulties in transferring advertising campaigns between markets. Electrolux's theme in marketing its vacuum cleaners is interpreted in the United Kingdom literally, but in the United States, the slang implications would interfere with the intended message. In the Lucky Goldstar ad, adaptation into Arabic was carried out without considering that Arabic reads from right to left. As a result, the creative concept in this execution was destroyed.

Another consideration is the capability of language to convey different shades of

| FIGURE 5.1 | Ads May Not Always Transfer Easily |

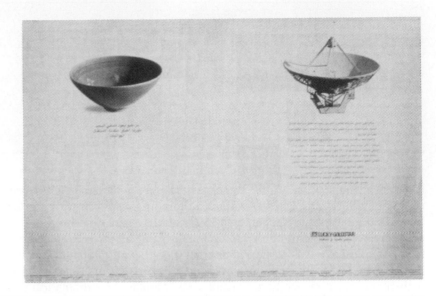

Source: "Viewpoint," *Advertising Age,* June 29, 1987, 20 and Mourad Boutros, "Lost in Translation," *M&M Europe* (September 1992): iv–v.

meaning. As an example, a one-word equivalent to "aftertaste" does not exist in many languages and in others is far-fetched at best. To communicate the idea may require a lengthy translation of "the taste that remains in your mouth after you have finished eating or drinking." If a brand name or an advertising theme is to be extended, care has to be taken to make sure of a comfortable fit. Kellogg's Rice Krispies snap, crackle, and pop in most markets; the Japanese, who have trouble pronouncing these words, watch the caricatures "patchy, pitchy, putchy" in their commercials.

The role of language extends beyond that of a communications medium. Linguistic diversity often is an indicator of other types of diversity. In Quebec, the French language has always been a major consideration of most francophone governments because it is one of the clear manifestations of the identity of the province vis-à-vis the English-speaking provinces. The Charter of the French Language states that the rights of the francophone collectivity are, among others, the right of consumers to be informed and served in French. The Bay, a major Quebec retailer, spends $8 million annually on its translation operations. It even changed its name to La Baie in appropriate areas.

Dealing with the language problem invariably requires the use of local assistance. A good local advertising agency and a good local market research firm can prevent many problems. When translation is required, as when communicating with suppliers or customers, care should be taken in selecting the translator. One of the simplest methods of control is **back-translation**—the translating of a foreign-language version back to the original language by a different person than the one who made the first translation. This approach may be able to detect only omissions and blunders, however. To assess the quality of the translation, a complete evaluation with testing of the message's impact is necessary.[9]

---

[9] Margareta Bowen, "Business Translation," *Jerome Quarterly* 8 (August–September 1993): 5–9.

Nonverbal Language

Managers must analyze and become familiar with the hidden language of foreign cultures.[10] Five key topics—time, space, material possessions, friendship patterns, and business agreements—offer a starting point from which managers can begin to acquire the understanding necessary to do business in foreign countries. In many parts of the world, time is flexible and not seen as a limited commodity; people come late to appointments or may not come at all. In Hong Kong, for example, it is futile to set exact meeting times, because getting from one place to another may take minutes or hours depending on the traffic. Showing indignation or impatience at such behavior would astonish an Arab, Latin American, or Asian.

In some countries, extended social acquaintance and the establishment of appropriate personal rapport are essential to conducting business. The feeling is that one should know one's business partner on a personal level before transactions can occur. Therefore, rushing straight to business will not be rewarded, because deals are made not only on the basis of the best product or price, but also on the entity or person deemed most trustworthy. Contracts may be bound on handshakes, not lengthy and complex agreements—a fact that makes some, especially Western, business people uneasy.

Individuals vary in the amount of space they want separating them from others. Arabs and Latin Americans like to stand close to people they are talking with. If an American, who may not be comfortable at such close range, backs away from an Arab, this might incorrectly be taken as a negative reaction. Also, Westerners are often taken aback by the more physical nature of affection between Slavs—for example, being kissed by a business partner, regardless of sex.

International body language must be included in the nonverbal language of international business. For example, an American manager may, after successful completion of negotiations, impulsively give a finger-and-thumb OK sign. In Southern France, the manager will have indicated that the sale is worthless, and in Japan that a little bribe has been asked for; the gesture is grossly insulting to Brazilians. An interesting exercise is to compare and contrast the conversation styles of different nationalities. Northern Europeans are quite reserved in using their hands and maintain a good amount of personal space, whereas Southern Europeans involve their bodies to a far greater degree in making a point.

Religion

Most cultures find in religion a reason for being. Religion can provide the basis for transcultural similarities under shared beliefs in Islam, Buddhism, or Christianity, for example.

An obvious example of the effect of religious beliefs on international marketing is the prohibition of pork products and alcoholic beverages in the Middle East. When beef or poultry is exported to a Muslim country, the animal must be killed in the "halal" method. Currently, 12 Islamic centers slaughter and certify meat for export. Recognition of religious restrictions can reveal opportunities as well as liabilities, as evidenced by the successful launch of several nonalcoholic beverages in some Middle Eastern countries. The impact of religion may vary from one country to another. For example, Islam requires extensive fasting during the holy month of Ramadan, the start and duration of

---

[10] Edward T. Hall, "The Silent Language of Overseas Business," *Harvard Business Review* 38 (May–June 1960): 87–96.

which varies because the lunar year is 11 to 12 days shorter than that based on the Gregorian calendar. Tunisia, however, has discouraged its people from too diligent observance of Ramadan to avoid marked drops in productivity. In Saudi Arabia, the pilgrimage to Mecca has forced the government to improve its transportation system. The primary responsibility for building a traffic system to Mecca was assumed by a Swedish firm, which found that non-Muslims are not allowed access to the sacred place. The solution was to use closed-circuit television to supervise the work.

Major holidays are often tied to religion. These holidays will be observed differently from one culture to the next, to the extent that the same holiday may have different connotations. Most Western cultures, because they are predominantly Christian, observe Christmas and exchange gifts either December 24 or December 25. However, the Dutch exchange gifts on St. Nicholas Day (December 6) and the Russians on Frost Man's Day (January 1). Tandy Corporation, in its first year in Holland, targeted its major advertising campaign for the third week of December with disastrous results. The international manager must see to it that local holidays are taken into account in the scheduling of events, ranging from fact-finding missions to marketing programs, and in preparing local work schedules.

The role of women in business is tied to religion, especially in the Middle East, where they are not able to function as they would in the West. This affects management in two ways: The firm may not be able to use women managers or personnel in certain countries, and women's role as consumers and influencers in the consumption process may be altogether different. Access to women in Islamic countries, for example, may be available only by using female sales personnel, direct marketing, and women's specialty shops.[11]

International marketing managers must be aware of religious divisions in the countries of operation. The impact of these divisions may range from hostilities, as in Sri Lanka, to below-the-surface suspicion—for example, in many European markets where Protestant and Catholic are the main religious divisions.

Values and Attitudes

Values are shared beliefs or group norms that have been internalized by individuals.[12] Attitudes are evaluations of alternatives based on these values. The Japanese culture raises an almost invisible—yet often unscalable—wall against all *gaijin*, foreigners. Many middle-aged bureaucrats and company officials, for example, feel that buying foreign products is unpatriotic. The resistance therefore is not so much against foreign products as those who produce and market them. Similarly, foreign-based corporations have had difficulty in hiring university graduates or mid-career personnel because of bias against foreign employers.

Even under these adverse conditions, the race can be run and won through tenacity, patience, and drive. As an example, Procter & Gamble has made impressive inroads with its products by adopting a long-term, Japanese-style view of profits. Since the mid-1970s, the company has gained some 20 percent of the detergent market and made Pampers a household word among Japanese mothers. The struggle toward such rewards can require foreign companies to take big losses for five years or more.

The more rooted values and attitudes are in central beliefs (such as religion), the more cautiously the international marketing manager has to move. Attitude toward

---

[11] Mushtaq Luqmani, Zahir A. Quraeshi, and Linda Delene, "Marketing in Islamic Countries: A Viewpoint," *MSU Business Topics* 23 (Summer 1980): 17–24.

[12] James F. Engel, Roger D. Blackwell, and Paul W. Miniard, *Consumer Behavior* (Hinsdale, IL: Dryden, 1986), 223.

change is basically positive in industrialized countries, whereas in more tradition-bound societies, change is viewed with great suspicion, especially when it comes from a foreign entity. These situations call for thorough research, most likely a localized approach, and a major commitment at the top level for a considerable period of time. For example, before launching Colac laxative in Japan, Richardson-Vicks studied the psychological dimensions of constipation. The reticent Japanese are willing to discuss such delicate subjects once they realize they are members of a group with a common problem, but not with Westerners present at the meetings. Research showed that the Japanese were dissatisfied with slow-acting herbal medicines but wary that a Western laxative might be too strong. Thus, Colac is presented as two little pink pills with natural qualities: "Three things to consider for stubborn constipation—salad, beauty exercise, and Colac before bedtime."

Cultural differences in themselves can be a selling point suggesting luxury, prestige, or status. Sometimes U.S. companies use domestic marketing approaches when selling abroad because they believe the American look will sell the product. In Japan, Borden sells Lady Borden ice cream and Borden cheese deliberately packaged and labeled in English, exactly as they are in the United States. Similarly, in France, General Foods sells a chewing gum called Hollywood with an accompanying Pepsi-generation type of ad campaign that pictures teenagers riding bicycles on the beach.

Occasionally, U.S. firms successfully use American themes abroad that would not succeed at home. In Japan, Levi Strauss promoted its popular jeans with a television campaign featuring James Dean and Marilyn Monroe, who represent the epitome of Japanese youths' fantasy of freedom from a staid, traditional society. The commercials helped to establish Levi's as *the* prestige jeans, and status-seeking Japanese youth willingly pay 40 percent more for them than for local brands. Their authentic Levi's, however, are designed and mostly made in Japan, where buyers like a tighter fit than do Americans.[13] At the same time, in the U.S. market, many companies have been quite successful in emphasizing a foreign, imported image.

Manners and Customs

Changes occurring in manners and customs must be carefully monitored, especially in cases that seem to indicate narrowing of cultural differences between peoples. Phenomena such as McDonald's and Coke have met with success around the world, but this does not mean that the world is becoming Westernized. Modernization and Westernization are not at all the same, as can be seen in Saudi Arabia, for example.

Understanding manners and customs is especially important in negotiations, because interpretations based on one's own frame of reference may lead to a totally incorrect conclusion. To negotiate effectively abroad, one needs to correctly read all types of communication. Americans often interpret inaction and silence as a negative sign, with the result that Japanese executives tend to expect by saying little to get Americans to lower prices or sweeten the deal. Even a simple agreement may take days to negotiate in the Middle East because the Arab party may want to talk about unrelated issues or do something else for a while. The abrasive style of Russian negotiators, and their usual last-minute change requests, may cause astonishment and concern on the part of ill-prepared negotiators. And consider the reaction of an American business person if a Finnish counterpart were to propose the continuing of negotiations in the sauna. Preparation is needed not only in the business sense but in a cultural sense as well, as shown

---

[13] "Learning How to Please the Baffling Japanese," *Fortune,* October 5, 1981, 122.

5.3

THE INTERNATIONAL MARKETPLACE

Business Is Business around The World, or Is It?

Mr. Smith, the head of a U.S. beverage firm, is involved in negotiations with a Japanese food company to export beer to Japan. Exploratory discussions have already been held with the U.S. representative for the Japanese company. Now Smith is flying to Japan to discuss details and, preferably, secure an agreement that can be drawn up for signature.

In the United States, he has usually concluded similar deals successfully in a day or two. His habit is to get down to business as soon as possible and not spend a lot of time on preliminaries. He would like to adopt the same approach in Tokyo, so he has allowed only three days for his stay. "Business is business," he says, and he has been briefed that his Japanese partners are just as interested in the planned cooperation as he is.

Once in Tokyo, Smith takes the opportunity to begin discussions on the main points of the projected transaction over dinner the first night of his stay. However, instead of definite statements, Smith hears nothing but friendly and noncommittal conversation. The following day, at his first meeting with the heads of the Japanese company, the situation remains unchanged. In spite of Smith's several attempts to begin discussions, his counterparts say nothing about the project but instead concentrate on talking about the history, traditions, and ethos of their company. Smith is also frustrated that only one member of the Japanese group speaks English.

Smith is irritated. After all, the principle that "time is money" surely must apply everywhere. He finally loses patience when he learns that the afternoon is not devoted to business discussions but has instead been reserved for sightseeing. In despair, he turns to the Japanese with a stern request that they get down to business. After a brief consultation among themselves, the Japanese finally agree to his request. However, contrary to his expectations, the negotiations do not progress as anticipated. They proceed without any definite statements, let alone promises, and no conclusions are reached. The fact that he puts forward specific proposals makes no difference. After three days of frustration and little progress, Smith flies home without having achieved, he feels, anything. He feels he was well prepared to discuss any aspect of the business deal and yet nothing happened.

Sources: Sergey Frank, "Global Negotiations: Vive Les Differences!" *Sales & Marketing Management* 144 (May 1992): 64–69; and Sergey Frank, "Avoiding the Pitfalls of Business Abroad," *Sales & Marketing Management* 144 (March 1992): 48–52.

in The International Marketplace 5.3. Some of the potential areas in which marketers may not be prepared include: (1) insufficient understanding of different ways of thinking; (2) insufficient attention to the necessity to save face; (3) insufficient knowledge and appreciation of the host country—history, culture, government, and image of foreigners; (4) insufficient recognition of the decision-making process and the role of personal relations and personalities; and (5) insufficient allocation of time for negotiations.[14]

---

[14] Sergey Frank, "Global Negations: Vive Les Differences!" *Sales & Marketing Management* 144 (May 1992): 64–69.

In many cultures, certain basic customs must be observed by the foreign business person. One of them concerns use of the right and left hands. In so-called right-hand societies, the left hand is the "toilet hand" and using it to eat, for example, is considered impolite.

Managers must be concerned with differences in the ways products are used. For example, General Foods' Tang is positioned as a breakfast drink in the United States; in France, where orange juice usually is not consumed at breakfast, Tang is positioned as a refreshment. The questions that the international manager must ask are, "What are we selling?" and "What are the use benefits we should be providing?"

Usage differences have to be translated into product form and promotional decisions. Maxwell House coffee is a worldwide brand name. It is used to sell coffee in both ground and instant form in the United States. In the United Kingdom, Maxwell House is available only in instant form. In France and Germany, it is sold in freeze-dried form only, whereas in the Scandinavian countries, Maxwell House is positioned as the top-of-the-line entry. As a matter of fact, Maxwell House is called simply Maxwell in France and Japan because "House" is confusing to consumers in those countries. In one South American market, a shampoo maker was concerned about poor sales of the entire product class. Research uncovered the fact that many women wash their hair with bars of soap and use shampoo only as a brief rinse or topper.

Many Western companies have stumbled in Japan because they did not learn enough about the distinctive habits of Japanese consumers. Purveyors of soup should know that the Japanese drink it mainly for breakfast. Johnson & Johnson had relatively little success selling baby powder in Japan until research was conducted on use conditions. In their small homes, mothers fear that powder will fly around and get into their spotlessly clean kitchens. The company now sells baby powder in flat boxes with powder puffs so that mothers can apply it sparingly. Adults will not use it at all. They wash and rinse themselves before soaking in hot baths; powder would make them feel dirty again. Another classic case involves General Mills' Betty Crocker cake mix. The company designed a mix to be prepared in electric rice cookers. After the product's costly flop, the company found that the Japanese take pride in the purity of their rice, which they thought would be contaminated by cake flavors. General Mills' mistake was comparable to asking an English housewife to make coffee in her teapot.

Package sizes and labels must be adapted in many countries to suit the needs of the particular culture. In Mexico, for example, Campbell's sells soup in cans large enough to serve four or five because families are generally large. In Britain, where consumers are more accustomed to ready-to-serve soups, Campbell's prints "one can makes two" on its condensed soup labels to ensure that shoppers understand how to use it.

In the United States, men buy diamond engagement rings for their fiancées. This custom is not global, however. In Germany, for example, young women tend to buy diamond rings for themselves. This precludes the use of global advertising campaigns by a company like De Beers.

Managers must be careful of myths and legends. One candy company was ready to launch a new peanut-packed chocolate bar in Japan, aimed at giving teenagers quick energy while they crammed for exams. The company then learned about a Japanese folk legend that eating chocolate with peanuts can cause nosebleed. The launch never took place.

Meticulous research plays a major role in avoiding these types of problems. Concept tests determine the potential acceptance and proper understanding of a proposed new product. **Focus groups,** each consisting of 8 to 12 consumers representative of the proposed target audience, can be interviewed and their responses used to check for disasters and to fine-tune research findings. The most sensitive types of products, such as consumer packaged goods, require consumer usage and attitude studies as well as retail distribution studies and audits to analyze the movement of the product to retailers and eventually to households.

Material Elements

Material culture results from technology and is directly related to how a society organizes its economic activity. It is manifested in the availability and adequacy of the basic economic, social, financial, and marketing **infrastructures.** The basic economic infrastructure consists of transportation, energy, and communications systems. Social infrastructure refers to housing, health, and educational systems. Financial and marketing infrastructures provide the facilitating agencies for the international firm's operation in a given market in terms of, for example, banks and research firms. In some parts of the world, the international firm may have to be an integral partner in developing the various infrastructures before it can operate, whereas in others, it may greatly benefit from their high level of sophistication.

The level of material culture can serve in segmentation efforts if the degree of industrialization is used as a basis. For companies selling industrial goods, such as General Electric, this can provide a convenient starting point. In developing countries, demand may be highest for basic energy-generating products. In fully developed markets, time-saving home appliances may be more in demand.

Technological advances have probably been the major cause of cultural change in many countries. For example, the increase in leisure time so characteristic in Western cultures has been a direct result of technological development. Workers in Germany are now pushing for a 35-hour work week. In Japan, consumers are seeking more diverse products—including convenience items—as a way of satisfying their demand for a higher quality of life and more leisure time. Marketers able to tailor and market their products to fit the new Japanese life-style stand to reap the benefits of this rich market. For example, the Japanese are showing greater acceptance of equipment for personal use, reflected in increased sales of mobile phones and small computers. With technological advancement also comes **cultural convergence.**[15] Black-and-white television sets extensively penetrated the U.S. market more than a decade before they reached similar levels in Europe and Japan. With color television, the lag was reduced to five years. With videocassette recorders, the difference was only three years, but this time the Europeans and the Japanese led the way while Americans concentrated on cable systems. With the compact disk, penetration rates were even after only one year. Today, with MTV available by satellite around the world, no lag exists at all.[16]

Material culture—mainly the degree to which it exists and how it is esteemed—will have an impact on marketing decisions. Many exporters do not understand the degree to which Americans are package-conscious; for example, cans must be shiny and beautiful. On the other hand, packaging problems may arise in other countries due to lack of certain materials, different specifications when the material is available, different line-fill machinery, and immense differences in quality and consistency of printing ink, especially in South America and the Third World. Even the ability of media to reach target audiences will be affected by ownership of television sets and radios.

[15] "The New Japanese Consumer: Affluent and Ready to Shop for the Right Products," *Business International,* January 27, 1992, 23.

[16] Kenichi Ohmae, "Managing in a Borderless World," *Harvard Business Review* 67 (May–June 1989): 152–161.

Aesthetics

Each culture makes a clear statement concerning good taste, as expressed in the arts and in the particular symbolism of colors, form, and music. What is and what is not acceptable may vary dramatically even in otherwise highly similar markets. Sex in advertising is an example. In an apparent attempt to preserve the purity of Japanese womanhood, Japanese advertisers frequently turn to blonde, blue-eyed foreign models to make the point. In the same vein, Commodore International, the U.S.-based personal computer manufacturer, showed a totally naked young man in ads that ran in the German version of *Cosmopolitan*. Approaches of this kind would not be possible in the United States because of regulations and opposition from consumer groups.

Color is often used as a mechanism for brand identification, feature reinforcement, and differentiation. In international markets, colors have more symbolic value than in domestic markets. Black, for instance, is considered the color of mourning in the United States and Europe, whereas white has the same symbolic value in Japan and most of the Far East. A British bank interested in expanding its operations to Singapore wanted to use blue and green as its identification colors. A consulting firm was quick to tell the client that green is associated with death there. Although the bank insisted on its original choice of colors, the green was changed to an acceptable shade.[17] Similarly, music used in broadcast advertisements is often adjusted to reflect regional differences.

International firms, such as McDonald's, have to take into consideration local tastes and concerns in designing their facilities. They may have a general policy of uniformity in building or office space design, but local tastes may often warrant modifications.

Education

Education, either formal or informal, plays a major role in the passing on and sharing of culture. Educational levels of a culture can be assessed using literacy rates and enrollment in secondary or higher education, information available from secondary data sources. International firms also need to know about the qualitative aspects of education, namely, varying emphases on particular skills, and the overall level of the education provided. Japan and the Republic of Korea, for example, emphasize the sciences, especially engineering, to a greater degree than do Western countries.

Educational levels will have an impact on various business functions. Training programs for a production facility will have to take the educational backgrounds of trainees into account. For example, a high level of illiteracy will suggest the use of visual aids rather than printed manuals. Local recruiting for sales jobs will be affected by the availability of suitably trained personnel. In some cases, international firms routinely send locally recruited personnel to headquarters for training.

The international marketing manager may also have to be prepared to fight obstacles in recruiting a suitable sales force or support personnel. For example, the Japanese culture places a premium on loyalty, and employees consider themselves to be members of the corporate family. If a foreign firm decides to leave Japan, employees may find themselves stranded in midcareer, unable to find a place in the Japanese business system. University graduates are therefore reluctant to join all but the largest and most well known of foreign firms.[18]

---

[17] Joe Agnew, "Cultural Differences Probed to Create Product Identity," *Marketing News,* October 24, 1986, 22.

[18] Joseph A. McKinney, "Joint Ventures of United States Firms in Japan: A Survey," *Venture Japan* 1, no. 2 (1988): 14–19.

If technology is marketed, the level of sophistication of the product will depend on the educational level of future users. Product-adaptation decisions are often influenced by the extent to which targeted customers are able to use the product or service properly.

Social Institutions

Social institutions affect the ways in which people relate to each other. The family unit, which in Western industrialized countries consists of parents and children, in a number of cultures is extended to include grandparents and other relatives. This will have an impact on consumption patterns and must be taken into account, for example, when conducting market research.

The concept of kinship, or blood relations between individuals, is defined in a very broad way in societies such as those in sub-Saharan Africa. Family relations and a strong obligation to family are important factors to be considered in human resource management in those regions. Understanding tribal politics in countries such as Nigeria may help the manager avoid unnecessary complications in executing business transactions.

The division of a particular population into classes is termed **social stratification.** Stratification ranges from the situation in Northern Europe, where most people are members of the middle class, to highly stratified societies in which the higher strata control most of the buying power and decision-making positions.

An important part of the socialization process of consumers worldwide is **reference groups.**[19] These groups provide the values and attitudes that become influential in shaping behavior. Primary reference groups include the family, coworkers, and other intimate groupings, whereas secondary groups are social organizations in which less-continuous interaction takes place, such as professional associations and trade organizations. Besides socialization, reference groups develop an individual's concept of self, which manifests itself, for example, through the use of products. Reference groups also provide a baseline for compliance with group norms through either conforming to or avoiding certain behaviors.

Social organization also determines the roles of managers and subordinates and how they relate to one another. In some cultures, managers and subordinates are separated explicitly and implicitly by various boundaries ranging from social class differences to separate office facilities. In others, cooperation is elicited through equality. For example, Nissan USA has no privileged parking spaces and no private dining rooms, everyone wears the same type of white coveralls, and the president sits in the same room with a hundred other white-collar workers.[20] The fitting of an organizational culture for internal marketing purposes to the larger context of a national culture has to be executed with care. Changes that are too dramatic may cause disruption of productivity or, at the minimum, suspicion.

SOURCES OF CULTURAL KNOWLEDGE

The concept of cultural knowledge is broad and multifaceted. Cultural knowledge can be defined by the way it is acquired. Objective or factual information is obtained from others through communication, research, and education. **Experiential knowledge,** on the other hand, can be acquired only by being involved in a culture other than one's own.[21]

[19] Engel, Blackwell, and Miniard, *Consumer Behavior,* 318–324.

[20] "The Difference That Japanese Management Makes," *Business Week,* July 14, 1986, 47–50.

[21] James H. Sood and Patrick Adams, "Model of Management Learning Styles as a Predictor of Export Behavior and Performance," *Journal of Business Research* 12 (June 1984): 169–182.

Types of International Information

TABLE 5.2

Source of Information	Type of Information	
	General	**Country-Specific**
Objective	Examples: • Impact of GNP • Regional integration	Examples: • Tariff barriers • Government regulations
Experiential	Example: • Corporate adjustment to internationalization	Examples: • Product acceptance • Program appropriateness

A summary of the types of knowledge needed by the international manager is provided in Table 5.2. Both factual and experiential information can be general or country-specific. In fact, the more a manager becomes involved in the international arena, the more he or she is able to develop a meta-knowledge, that is, ground rules that apply to a great extent whether in Kuala Lumpur, Malaysia, or Asunción, Paraguay. Market-specific knowledge does not necessarily travel well; the general variables on which the information is based do.

In a survey on how to acquire international expertise, managers ranked eight factors in terms of their importance, as shown in Table 5.3. These managers emphasized the experiential acquisition of knowledge. Written materials were indicated to play an important but supplementary role, very often providing general or country-specific information before operational decisions must be made. Interestingly, many of today's international managers have pre-career experience in government, the Peace Corps, the armed forces, or missionary service. Although the survey emphasized travel, a one-time trip to London with a stay at a large hotel and scheduled sightseeing tours does not contribute to cultural knowledge in a significant way. Travel that involves meetings with company personnel, intermediaries, facilitating agents, customers, and government officials, on the other hand, does contribute.[22]

Various sources and methods are available to the manager for extending his or her knowledge of specific cultures. Most of these sources deal with factual information that provides a necessary basis for market studies. Beyond the normal business literature and its anecdotal information, specific country studies are published by governments, private companies, and universities. The U.S. Department of Commerce's *Overseas Business Reports* cover more than 80 countries, while the Economist Intelligence Unit's *Country Reports* cover 180 countries. *Culturgrams,* which detail the customs of peoples of more than 100 countries, are published by the Center for International and Area Studies at Brigham Young University. Many facilitating agencies—such as accounting firms, advertising agencies, banks, and transportation companies—provide background information on the markets they serve for their clients. These range from the *International Business Guide* series published by Deloitte & Touche, which covers 107 countries and territories, to the *Business Profile Series* of the Hong Kong and Shanghai Banking Corporation's *Business Profile Series* for 20 countries in the Middle East and the Far East.

Blunders that could have been avoided with factual information about a foreign market are generally inexcusable. A manager who travels to Taipei without first obtaining

[22] Stephen J. Kobrin, *International Expertise in American Business* (New York: Institute of International Education, 1984), 36.

| TABLE 5.3 | Manager's Ranking of Factors Involved in Acquiring International Expertise |

Factor	Considered Critical	Considered Important
1. Business travel	60.8%	92.0%
2. Assignments overseas	48.8	71.2
3. Reading/television	16.0	63.2
4. Training programs	6.4	28.8
5. Precareer activities	4.0	16.0
6. Graduate course	2.4	15.2
7. Nonbusiness travel	0.8	12.8
8. Undergraduate courses	0.8	12.0

Source: Stephen J. Kobrin, *International Expertise in American Business* (New York: Institute of International Education, 1984), 38.

a visa and is therefore turned back has no one else to blame. Other oversights may lead to more costly mistakes. For example, Brazilians are several inches shorter than the average American, but this was not taken into account when Sears erected American-height shelves that block Brazilian shoppers' view of the rest of the store.

International business success requires not only comprehensive fact finding and preparation but also an ability to understand and appreciate fully the nuances of different cultural traits and patterns. Gaining this **interpretive knowledge** requires "getting one's feet wet" over a sufficient length of time.

CULTURAL ANALYSIS

To try to understand and explain differences among cultures and subsequently in cross-cultural behavior, the marketer can develop checklists and models showing pertinent variables and their interaction. An example of such a model is provided in Figure 5.2. This model is based on the premise that all international business activity should be viewed as innovation and as producing change processes.[23] After all, exporters and multinational corporations introduce, from one country to other cultures, marketing practices as well as products and services, which are then perceived to be new and different. Although many question the usefulness of such models, they do bring together, into one presentation, all or most of the relevant variables that have an impact on how consumers in different cultures may perceive, evaluate, and adopt new behaviors. However, any manager using such a tool should periodically cross-check its results with reality and experience.

The key variable of the model is propensity to change, which is a function of three constructs: (1) cultural life-style of individuals in terms of how deeply held their traditional beliefs and attitudes are, and also which elements of culture are dominant; (2) change agents (such as multinational corporations and their practices) and strategic opinion leaders (for example, social elites); and (3) communication about the innovation from commercial sources, neutral sources (such as government), and social sources, such as friends and relatives.

---

[23] Jagdish N. Sheth and S. Prakash Sethi, "A Theory of Cross-Cultural Buying Behavior," in *Consumer and Industrial Buying Behavior,* eds. Arch G. Woodside, Jagdish N. Sheth, and Peter D. Bennett (New York: Elsevier North-Holland, 1977), 369–386.

A Model of Cross-Cultural Behavior   **FIGURE 5.2**

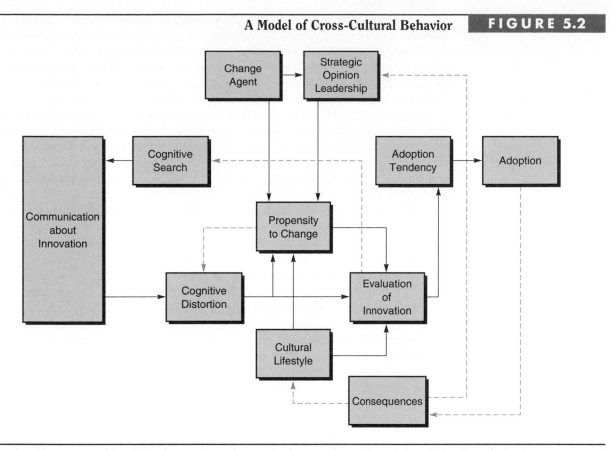

Source: Adapted by permission of the publisher from "A Theory of Cross-Cultural Buying Behavior," by Jagdish N. Sheth and S. Prakash Sethi, in *Consumer and Industrial Buying Behavior,* eds. Arch G. Woodside, Jagdish N. Sheth, and Peter D. Bennett, 1977, 373. Copyright 1977 by Elsevier Science Publishing Co., Inc.

It has been argued that differences in cultural life-style can be accounted for by four dimensions of culture.[24] These dimensions consist of (1) individualism (e.g., "I" consciousness versus "we" consciousness), (2) power distance (e.g., level of equality in a society), (3) uncertainty avoidance (e.g., need for formal rules and regulations), and (4) masculinity (e.g., attitudes toward achievement, roles of men and women). Knowledge of a target market's position on these dimensions will help the marketer design products and programs for optimum results. For example, since the United States highly regards individualism, promotional appeals should be relevant to the individual. Also, in order to incorporate the lower power distance within the market, copy should be informal and friendly.[25] Similarly, channel choice is affected by cultural factors. Firms in societies emphasizing individualism are more likely to choose channel partners based on objective criteria, whereas firms at the opposite end would prefer to deal with other firms whose representatives they consider to be friends.[26] When negotiating in Germany, one

[24] Geert Hofstede, *Culture's Consequences: International Differences in Work-Related Values* (Beverly Hills, CA: Sage Publications, 1984).

[25] Sudhir H. Kale, "Culture-Specific Marketing Communications: An Analytical Approach," *International Marketing Review* 8, no. 2 (1991): 18–30.

[26] Sudhir H. Kale, "Distribution Channel Relationships in Diverse Cultures," *International Marketing Review* 8, no. 3 (1991): 31–45.

can expect a counterpart who is thorough, systematic, very well prepared, but also rather dogmatic and therefore lacking in flexibility and compromise. Great emphasis is placed on efficiency. In Mexico, however, the counterpart may prefer to address problems on a personal and private basis rather than on a business level. This means more emphasis on socializing and conveying one's humanity, sincerity, loyalty, and friendship. Also, the differences in pace and business practices of the region have to be accepted.

Communication about the innovation takes place through the physical product itself (samples) or through a new policy in the company. If a new practice, such as quality circles or pan-regional planning, is in question, results may be communicated in reports or through word-of-mouth by the participating employees. Communication content depends on the following factors: the product's or policy's relative advantage over existing alternatives; compatibility with established behavioral patterns; complexity, or the degree to which the product or process is perceived as difficult to understand and use; trialability, or the degree to which it may be experimented with and not incur major risk; and observability, which is the extent to which the consequences of the innovation are visible.

Before the product or policy is evaluated, information about it will be compared with existing beliefs about the circumstances surrounding the situation. Distortion will occur as a result of selective attention, exposure, and retention. As examples, anything foreign may be seen in a negative light, another multinational company's efforts may have failed, or the government may implicitly discourage the proposed activity. Additional information may then be sought from any of the input sources or from opinion leaders in the market.

Adoption tendency refers to the likelihood that the product or process will be accepted. Examples of this are advertising in the People's Republic of China and equity joint ventures with Western participants in Russia, both unheard of a few years ago. If an innovation clears the hurdles, it may be adopted and slowly diffused into the entire market. An international manager has two basic choices: adapt company offerings and methods to those in the market or try to change market conditions to fit company programs. In Japan, a number of Western companies have run into obstructions in the Japanese distribution system, where great value is placed on established relationships; everything is done on the basis of favoring the familiar and fearing the unfamiliar. In most cases, this problem is solved by joint venturing with a major Japanese entity that has established contacts. On occasion, when the company's approach is compatible with the central beliefs of a culture, the company may be able to change existing customs rather than adjust to them. Initially, Procter & Gamble's traditional hard-selling style in television commercials jolted most Japanese viewers accustomed to more subtle approaches. Now the ads are being imitated by Japanese competitors.

Although models like the one in Figure 5.2 may aid in strategy planning by making sure that all variables and their linkages are considered, any analysis is incomplete without the basic recognition of cultural differences. Adjusting to differences requires putting one's own cultural values aside. James E. Lee proposes that the natural **self-reference criterion**—the unconscious reference to one's own cultural values—is the root of most international business problems.[27] However, recognizing and admitting this are often quite difficult. The following analytical approach is recommended to reduce the influence of one's own cultural values:

1. Define the problem or goal in terms of domestic cultural traits, habits, or norms.
2. Define the problem or goal in terms of foreign cultural traits, habits, or norms. Make no value judgments.

---

[27] James A. Lee, "Cultural Analysis in Overseas Operations," *Harvard Business Review* 44 (March–April 1966): 106–114.

3. Isolate the self-reference criterion influence in the problem and examine it carefully to see how it complicates the problem.
4. Redefine the problem without the self-reference criterion influence and solve for the optimal goal situation.

This approach can be applied to product introduction. If Kellogg's wants to introduce breakfast cereals into markets where breakfast is traditionally not eaten or where consumers drink very little milk, managers must consider very carefully how to instill this new habit. The traits, habits, and norms in terms of the importance of breakfast are quite different in the United States, France, and Brazil, and they have to be outlined before the product can be introduced. In France, Kellogg's commercials are aimed as much at providing nutrition lessons as they are at promoting the product. In Brazil, the company advertised on a soap opera to gain entry into the market because Brazilians often emulate the characters of these television shows.

Analytical procedures require constant monitoring of changes caused by outside events as well as the changes caused by the business entity itself. Controlling **ethnocentricism**—regarding one's own culture as superior to others—can be achieved only by acknowledging it and properly adjusting to its possible effects in managerial decision making. The international manager needs to be prepared and able to put that preparedness to effective use.[28]

THE TRAINING CHALLENGE

International managers face a dilemma in terms of international and intercultural competence. The lack of adequate foreign language and international business skills has cost U.S. firms lost contracts, weak negotiations, and ineffectual management. A UNESCO study of 10- and 14-year-old students in nine countries placed Americans next to last in their comprehension of foreign cultures. Even when cultural awareness is high, there is room for improvement. For example, a survey of European executives found that a shortage of international managers was considered the single most important constraint on expansion abroad.[29] The increase in overall international activity of firms has increased the need for cultural sensitivity training at all levels of the organization. Today's training must take into consideration not only outsiders to the firm but interaction within the corporate family as well. However inconsequential the degree of interaction may seem, it can still cause problems if proper understanding is lacking. Consider, for example, the date 11/12/94 on a telex; a European will interpret this as the eleventh of December, an American as the twelfth of November.

Some companies try to avoid the training problem by hiring only nationals or well-traveled Americans for their international operations. This makes sense for the management of overseas operations but will not solve the training need, especially if transfers are likely to a culture unfamiliar to the manager. International experience may not necessarily transfer from one market to another.

To foster cultural sensitivity and acceptance of new ways of doing things within the organization, management must institute internal education programs. These programs may include (1) culture-specific information (e.g., data covering other countries, such as videopacks and culturegrams), (2) cultural general information (e.g., values, practices,

[28] Peter D. Fitzpatrick and Alan S. Zimmerman, *Essentials of Export Marketing* (New York: American Management Organization, 1985), 16.

[29] "Expansion Abroad: The New Direction for European Firms," *International Management* 41 (November 1986): 20–26.

FIGURE 5.3   Cross-Cultural Training Methods

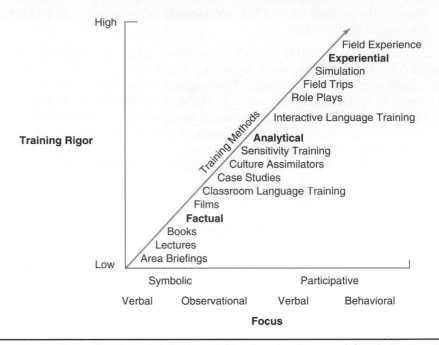

Source: J. Stewart Black and Mark Mendenhall, "A Practical but Theory-based Framework for Selecting Cross-Cultural Training Methods," in *International Human Resources Management,* eds. Mark Mendenhall and Gary Oddou (Boston: PWS-Kent, 1991), 188. © 1991 PWS-Kent.

and assumptions of countries other than one's own), and (3) self-specific information (e.g., identifying one's own cultural paradigm, including values, assumptions, and perceptions about others).[30] One study found that Japanese assigned to the United States receive mainly language training as preparation for the task. In addition, many companies use mentoring whereby an individual is assigned to someone who is expeienced and who will spend the required time squiring and explaining. Talks given by returnees and by visiting lecturers hired specifically for the task round out the formal part of training.[31]

The objective of formal training programs is to foster the four critical characteristics of preparedness, sensitivity, patience, and flexibility in managers and other personnel. These programs vary dramatically in terms of their rigor, involvement, and, of course, cost.[32] A summary of these programs is provided in Figure 5.3, and two Korean corporations' approaches are described in The International Marketplace 5.4.

Environmental briefings and cultural orientation programs are types of **area studies** programs. These programs provide factual preparation for a manager to operate in, or work with people from, a particular country. Area studies should be a basic prerequisite for other types of training programs. Alone, area studies serve little practical purpose because they do not really get the manager's feet wet. Other, more involved programs contribute the context in which to put facts so that they can be properly understood.

---

[30] W. Chan Kim and R. A. Mauborgne, "Cross-Cultural Strategies," *Journal of Business Strategy* 7 (Spring 1987): 28–37.

[31] Mauricio Lorence, "Assignment USA: The Japanese Solution," *Sales & Marketing Management* 144 (October 1992): 60–66.

[32] Rosalie Tung, "Selection and Training of Personnel for Overseas Assignments," *Columbia Journal of World Business* 16 (Spring 1981): 68–78.

THE INTERNATIONAL MARKETPLACE

Preparing For Global Markets

Samsung, Korea's largest conglomerate, has launched an internationalization campaign. The company wants to be culturally more sensitive, and not just to avoid gaffes. It believes that learning more about foreign countries can make its products more competitive. And it is not alone in these activities. A generation of Korean managers came of age thinking that if they built it, they could sell it. Today's international competitive environment requires more.

These programs have taken various forms. At Kumho Group, the chairman has ordered all airline and tire maker employees to spend an hour each morning learning a language or learning more about foreign cultures. Cards taped up in bathrooms teach a new phrase in English or Japanese each day. At Samsung, overseas-bound managers attend a month-long boot camp where they are awakened at 5:50 A.M. for a jog, meditation, and then lessons on issues such as table manners or avoiding sexual harassment. For example, students are taught not to ask female job applicants whether they are married, when they intend to marry, their age, or religion.

Samsung is sending 400 of its brightest junior employees overseas for a year. Their mission is not 100 percent business either: "International exposure is important, but you have to develop an appreciation of the foreign environment as well. You have to goof off at the mall, watch people, and develop international tastes," say Samsung officials. The program costs about $80,000 a year per person and takes key people out of circulation. But Samsung is convinced that cultural immersion will pay off in more astute judgments about what customers want. One concrete result is that the company is tailoring more products for specific overseas markets despite resistance of engineers in Seoul. "They want one model to sell to everyone. But they are accepting the concept now," state Samsung marketers. Much of that change has been attributed to people like Park Sang Jin who has been overseas for 15 years, mostly in the United States. "If we do not do this type of concept, we will never catch up with our competitors," he states.

Samsung employees coming back from overseas see much work to be done. After five years in Paris, Kim Jeong Kyu recognizes that time abroad has changed him. Now back in Seoul, he is trying to change Samsung—and having problems. "Even if I have a good idea, I will not suggest it too fast," Kim says. "They will say, 'He doesn't know the Korean situation. Maybe it will work in France, but not here.'"

Source: "Sensitivity Kick," *The Wall Street Journal*, December 30, 1992, 1, 4.

The **cultural assimilator** is a program in which trainees must respond to scenarios of specific situations in a particular country. These programs have been developed for the Arab countries, Iran, Thailand, Central America, and Greece.[33] The results of the trainees' assimilator experience are evaluated by a panel of judges. This type of program has been used in particular in cases of transfers abroad on short notice.

When more time is available, managers can be trained extensively in language. This may be required if an exotic language is involved. **Sensitivity training** focuses on

---

[33] Harris and Moran, *Managing Cultural Differences*, 267–295.

enhancing a manager's flexibility in situations that are quite different from those at home. The approach is based on the assumption that understanding and accepting oneself is critical to understanding a person from another culture. Finally, training may involve **field experience,** which exposes a manager to a different cultural environment for a limited amount of time. Although the expense of placing and maintaining an expatriate is high (and, therefore, the cost of failure is high), field experience is rarely used in training. One field experience technique that has been suggested when the training process needs to be rigorous is the host-family surrogate. This technique places a trainee (and possibly his or her family) in a domestically located family of the nationality to which they are assigned.[34]

Regardless of the degree of training, preparation, and positive personal characteristics, a manager will always remain foreign. A manager should never rely on his or her own judgment when local managers can be consulted. In many instances, a manager should have an interpreter present at negotiations, especially if the manager is not completely bilingual. Overconfidence in one's language capabilities can create problems.

SUMMARY

Culture is one of the most challenging elements of the international marketplace. This system of learned behavior patterns characteristic of the members of a given society is constantly shaped by a set of dynamic variables: language, religion, values and attitudes, manners and customs, aesthetics, technology, education, and social institutions. An international manager, to cope with this system, needs both factual and interpretive knowledge of culture. To some extent, the factual can be learned; the interpretation comes only through experience.

The most complicated problems in dealing with the cultural environment stem from the fact that one cannot learn culture—one has to live it. Two schools of thought exist in the business world on how to deal with cultural diversity. One is that business is business the world around, following the model of Pepsi and McDonald's. In some cases, globalization is a fact of life; however, cultural differences are still far from converging.

The other school proposes that companies must tailor business approaches to individual cultures. Setting up policies and procedures in each country has been compared to an organ transplant; the critical question centers on acceptance or rejection. The major challenge to the international manager is to make sure that rejection is not a result of cultural myopia or even blindness.

Fortune examined the international performance of a dozen large companies that earn 20 percent or more of their revenue overseas.[35] The internationally successful companies all share an important quality: patience. They have not rushed into situations but rather built their operations carefully by following the most basic business principles. These principles are to know your adversary, know your audience, and know your customer.

Questions for Discussion

1. Comment on the assumption, "If people are serious about doing business with you, they will speak English."

[34] Simcha Ronen, "Training the International Assignee," in *Training and Career Development,* ed. I. Goldstein (San Francisco: Jossey-Bass, 1989), 426–440.
[35] Kenneth Labich, "America's International Winners," *Fortune,* April 14, 1986, 34–46.

2. You are on your first business visit to Germany. You feel confident about your ability to speak the language (you studied German in school and have taken a refresher course), and you decide to use it. During introductions, you want to break the ice by asking "Wie geht's?" and insisting that everyone call you by your first name. Speculate as to the reaction.

3. What can a company do to culture-sensitize its staff?

4. What can be learned about a culture from reading and attending to factual materials? Given the tremendous increase in international marketing activities, where will companies in a relatively early stage of the internationalization process find the personnel to handle the new challenges?

5. Management at an American company trying to market tomato paste in the Middle East did not know that, translated into Arabic, tomato paste is "tomato glue." How could they have known in time to avoid problems?

6. Give examples of how the self-reference criterion might be manifested.

7. Is any international business entity *not* a cultural imperialist? How else could one explain the phenomenon of multinational corporations?

Recommended Readings

Axtell, Roger E. *Do's and Taboos around the World.* New York: John Wiley & Sons, 1993.

Bache, Ellyn. *Culture Clash.* Yarmouth, ME: Intercultural Press, 1990.

Bhagat, Ravi S., and Harry V. Triandis. *Management across Cultures.* Glenview, IL: Scott, Foresman and Company, 1984.

Brislin, R.W., W.J. Lonner, and R.M. Thorndike. *Cross-Cultural Research Methods.* New York: Wiley, 1973.

Copeland, Lennie, and L. Griggs. *Going International: How to Make Friends and Deal Effectively in the Global Marketplace.* New York: Random House, 1985.

Hall, Edward T., and Mildred Reed Hall. *Understanding Cultural Differences.* Yarmouth, ME: Intercultural Press, 1990.

Hofstede, Geert. *Culture's Consequences.* London: Sage Publications, 1981.

Segall, Marshall. *Cross-Cultural Psychology: Human Behavior in a Global Perspective.* Monterey, CA: Brooks/Cole, 1979.

Terpstra, Vern, and K. David. *The Cultural Environment of International Business.* Cincinnati, OH: Southwestern, 1991.

U.S. Department of Commerce. *International Business Practices.* Washington, D.C.: U.S. Government Printing Office, 1993.

Ward, T. *Living Abroad: The Book of Preparations.* New York: Free Press, 1984.

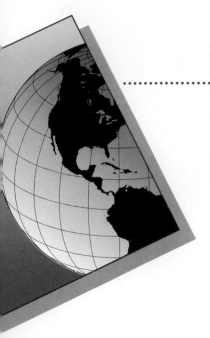

CHAPTER 6

The International Financial Environment

6.1

THE INTERNATIONAL MARKETPLACE

Easing the Credit Crunch

After years of feeling ignored by U.S. bankers, exporters and mid-size multinationals are being approached and actually getting their international trade transactions financed. "In 1992, bankers never called us to pitch their trade finance services," says Anthony R. Williams of Acclaim Entertainment Inc., a video game program designer for Nintendo that generates 25 percent of its sales from abroad. "Now we get calls from a half-dozen bankers a month promising flexible, cut-rate funding." This turnaround is dramatic after the bankers' aversion to foreign-country risk following the 1980s' Third World sovereign-debt crisis. According to estimates by the Export-Import Bank of the United States (Eximbank), only 25 commercial banks out of 11,328 (less than one-quarter of 1 percent) remained active providers of export loans to small and medium-sized exporters in the early 1990s.

The banks' change of heart has been prompted by a growing demand for trade loans and services from globally minded firms. Aided by the weaker dollar, these firms are emphasizing international expansion as a survival technique.

For their part, U.S. banks are eager to finance international trade because they have been able to shore up their capital and show the healthiest balance sheets in years. The level of problem assets is down, and in 1993 a total of 95 percent of U.S. banks were profitable. Banks have also been encouraged by the efforts of the Eximbank, the federal credit agency that guarantees and insures loans made by commercial banks. Over the past few years, Eximbank has made trade financing more attractive. It has increased its guarantee on export loans to 100 percent and has developed a program whereby banks can pool and scrutinize small trade loans and thus wipe the foreign-country risk off their books.

The banks expanding their scope range from small regionals to huge money-center institutions. For example, Silicon Valley Bank in San Jose finances fledgling technology exporters, while Capitol Bank in Los Angeles provides import and export financing to companies doing business in Taiwan or South Korea. Bank of America is expanding its product menu to meet its customers' global needs from pre-export financing to issuing import and export letters of credit to foreign exchange management to providing direct export loans backed by Eximbank. It plans to get involved in forfait financing, which involves the sale of discounted trade notes to institutions, international leasing, and local currency financing. And it will create an international database so customers can source goods as well as distributors and partners abroad.

As indicated by the activities of Bank of America, international marketers need more than just more advantageous financing. Because their needs are quite diverse, they have to rely on trade-finance banking relationships for advice on many issues.

Sources: Lori Ioannou, "When the Banks Chase Foreign Trade," *International Business*, October 1993, 58–62; and Gary Hector, "Coping with the Credit Quake," *International Business*, August 1993, 25–26.

In the extremely competitive international environment, a marketing entity cannot always expect to sell for its own currency with cash in advance, especially when large or long-term contracts are sought. Most companies will be required to go beyond their own working capital and banking lines of credit and expose themselves to new types of risk. The marketer can be sure that if he or she does not finance customers' international trade, the company's competitors or the competitors' governments probably will. Therefore, establishing relationships with sources of financing both in the private and public sectors are important, as seen in The International Marketplace 6.1.

This chapter will include a discussion of the financial concerns of the international marketer: How competitive is my total package? Am I going to be paid? What are the payment risks in executing the transaction? Who can I count on for support both in securing a contract, getting paid, and avoiding financial risk?

CREDIT POLICY

The international marketer cannot control the financial environment and thus needs to analyze it carefully and understand it in terms of the company's ability to operate within its demands. Effective financial arrangements can significantly support the marketing program if they are carefully formulated between the finance and marketing areas of the firm. Sales are often won or lost on the availability of favorable credit terms to the buyer. With large numbers of competent firms active in international markets, financing packages—often put together with the help of governments—have become more important. This is especially true in fields such as engineering and construction where superior technical capability and attractive cost may not be enough to secure a contract. Customers abroad may be prepared to accept higher prices if they can obtain attractive credit terms.[1]

---

[1] Llewellyn Clague and Rena Grossfield, "Export Pricing in a Floating Rate World," *Columbia Journal of World Business* 9 (Winter 1974): 17–22; Raj Aggarwal and Luc Soenen, "Managing Persistent Real Changes in Currency Values: The Role of Multinational Operating Strategies," *Columbia Journal of World Business* 24 (Fall 1989): 60–66.

The seller's primary concern is to be paid for the goods shipped. Before a particular order is received, the marketer has already formulated a policy on the acceptable degree of risk and preferable terms of international transactions. The extent of credit offered is determined by (1) firm-specific factors such as size, experience in international trade, and capacity for financing transactions; (2) market characteristics such as degree of economic development and availability of means of payment; and (3) factors relating to a particular transaction such as the amount of payment and the need for protection, terms offered by competitors, the relative strength and attractiveness of the trading partner,

---

FIGURE 6.1   **Financing Services of a Bank**

Source: Citicorp.

and the type of goods involved (for example, perishables or custom-made items). In some cases, the marketing and financial departments of the firm are at odds. Marketing may want to expand sales and move into new markets, whereas finance may want to minimize risks and, as a result, market selectively. Before finalizing any contract, the marketer must analyze the risks involved and decide how to manage them.[2]

The development of a credit policy requires teamwork between the company's marketing and finance departments and its commercial banks.[3] To get the best assistance, most companies need to access both regional banks, with which exporters maintain day-to-day relationships, and money-center banks, which typically provide more sophisticated services than regional banks can (for an example, see Figure 6.1). The larger banks provide a full range of finance, insurance, and advisory services. These are at the disposal of the exporter through the correspondent relationship that regional banks have with the large banks, although many large companies have direct relationships with money-center banks.

Both marketers and finance people need to properly understand the role of financing as a marketing tool. Export finance managers may not have time to listen to marketers and understand the kind of financing terms that are needed to make sales or to work on the more complicated financing solutions needed. This can be overcome by helping marketing personnel better understand financing options and by allowing marketers to communicate their needs directly to the banks. Action to accomplish this may include regular roundtable discussions between marketers and bankers and trips abroad by teams of marketers and finance people working together to understand the sale and financing package from start to finish. The goal is to seek and provide the kind of financing that wins business.

The credit policy, once developed, should (1) help the exporter determine the extent of risk he or she is willing to absorb, (2) allow the exporter to explore new ways of financing exports, and (3) prepare the exporter for a changing environment. Each of these elements will be discussed.

TYPES OF FINANCIAL RISK

Overseas political and commercial developments can destroy overnight even the most careful of credit judgments. In addition to macro-developments causing nonpayment, the buying entity may go out of business before paying the seller. The major types of financial risk are commercial risk, political risk, foreign exchange risk, and other risks such as those related to inflation.

The term **commercial risk** refers primarily to the insolvency of, or protracted payment default by, an overseas buyer. Commercial defaults, in turn, usually result from deterioration of conditions in the buyer's market, fluctuations in demand, unanticipated competition either domestically or internationally, or technological changes. The range of specific reasons may include:

1. Internal changes, such as the death or retirement of a key person. This is a likelihood because many importing entities are dependent on the owner-operator.
2. The buyer losing a key customer. This can occur when an importer buys raw materials or components to be used in production.

[2] U.S. Department of Commerce, *A Basic Guide to Exporting* (Washington, D.C.: Government Printing Office, 1989), 43.

[3] Christine Topoulos, "The Link between Export Sales and Financing," *Export Today* 4 (November–December 1988): 37–40.

3. Unexpected difficulty experienced by the buyer in meeting operating expenses. As an example, the importer's final product may fall under price controls while inputs may not be controlled, especially if this takes place in a high-inflation market.
4. Natural disasters, such as floods and industrial accidents. These can affect the ability of a buyer to operate in a market.
5. Slow payment by government buyers.

All of these risks can emerge in the domestic environment as well, but the geographic and psychological distances to international markets make the risks more severe and more difficult to anticipate.

Noncommercial, or **political risk,** is completely beyond the control of either the buyer or the seller. For example, the foreign buyer may be willing to pay, but the government may use every trick in the book to delay payment as far into the future as possible. In addition to exchange transfer delay, which has the most direct impact on a transaction, other political risks include war, revolution, or similar hostilities; unforeseen withdrawal or nonrenewal of a license to export or import; requisition, expropriation, confiscation, or intervention in the buyer's business by a government authority; transport or insurance charges caused by interruption or diversion of shipments; and certain other government acts that may prevent or unduly delay payment beyond the control of either the buyer or the seller.

The term **foreign exchange risk** refers to the effects of fluctuating exchange rates. The currency of quotation depends largely on the bargaining positions of the buyer and the seller as well as on accepted business practices in the industry. However, if the price quotation is not in the seller's currency, the seller firm must be prepared to protect itself against losses resulting from changes in the value of the currency transaction.

SOURCES OF FINANCING

Except in the case of larger companies that may have their own financing entities, most international marketers assist their customers abroad in securing appropriate financing. Export financing terms can significantly affect the final price paid by buyers. Consider, for example, two competitors for a $1 million sale. Exporter A offers an 8 percent interest rate over a ten-year payment period, while B offers 9 percent for the same term. Over the ten years, the difference in interest is $55,000. In some cases, buyers will award a contract to the provider of cheaper credit and overlook differences in quality and price.

Financing assistance is available from both the private and the public sectors. The international marketer should assess not only domestic programs but also those in other countries. For example, Japan, Taiwan, and Korea have import financing programs that provide U.S. exporters added potential in penetrating these significant markets.

Commercial Banks

Commercial banks the world over provide trade financing depending on their relationship with the exporter, the nature of the transaction, the country of the borrower, and the availability of export insurance. This usually means that financing assistance is provided only to first-rate credit risks, leaving many U.S. exporters to report major problems in enlisting assistance from U.S. commercial banks. This is best indicated by a 1988 survey of exporters in which 65 percent of respondents reported that competitive financing is generally not available from commercial lenders for exports even to markets where sales opportunities are promising and repayment would be likely.[4] Although the situa-

---

[4] Rosemary Mazon, "Where Have All the Banks Gone?" *Export Today* 4 (September–October 1988): 71–73.

tion has improved (as seen in the International Marketplace 6.1), exporters still continue to complain about lack of export financing as it pertains to developing countries, financing high technology, or lending against foreign receivables. Many exporters complain that banks will not deal with them without a guarantee from the Eximbank or rock-solid collateral.

This pullback in the 1980s was driven by debt problems of less-developed countries and by major changes in the U.S. banking system, notably the erosion of "relationship" banking.[5] Many banks have seen profits from international trade transactions as too small, too risky, and too time-consuming. In addition, investor pressures have led banks to minimize foreign credit risks. Earlier, banks—in return for interest-free corporate deposits—provided companies with loans on preferential terms and low-cost access to bank services, such as trade finance. With changes in the U.S. financial services industry, such financial ties have broken. The result is that exporters have to look abroad for such financing and that some sales are lost to other countries because of the lack of financing.

Forfaiting and Factoring

A trade financing technique that was developed in Europe has only in the past decade become widely known in the United States. **Forfaiting** was first used by European commercial banks in financing trade to the Eastern European countries and has since spread to banks throughout the world. Forfaiting provides the exporter with cash at the time of the shipment. In a typical forfait deal, the importer pays the exporter with bills of exchange or promissory notes guaranteed by a leading bank in the importer's country. The exporter can sell them to a third party (for example, Citicorp) at a discount from their face value for immediate cash. The sale is without recourse to the exporter, and the buyer of the notes assumes all of the risks. The discount rate takes into account the buyer's credit worthiness and country, the quality of the guaranteeing bank, and the interest cost over the term of the credit.[6]

The benefits to the exporter are the reduction of risk, simplicity of documentation (because the documents used are well known in the market), and 100 percent coverage, which official sources such as export-import banks do not provide. In addition, forfaiting does not involve either content or country restrictions, which many of the official trade financing sources may have.[7] The major complaints about forfaiting center on availability and cost. Forfaiting is not available where exporters need it most, that is, the high-risk countries. Furthermore, it is usually a little more expensive than using public sources of trade insurance.

Certain companies, known as **factoring** houses, may purchase an exporter's receivables for a discounted price (2 to 4 percent less than face value). Factors enable the exporter to receive payment for goods and provide relief of the administrative burden of collection. Arrangements are typically with recourse, leaving the exporter ultimately liable for repaying the factor in case of a default. Some factors accept export receivables without recourse but require a large discount.

Although the forfaiting and factoring methods appear similar, they differ in three significant ways: (1) factors usually want a large percentage of the exporter's business, while most forfaiters work on a one-shot basis; (2) forfaiters work with medium-term

[5] William F. Kolarik, "Financing American Exports: The Diminishing Role of U.S. Commercial Banks," in *Trade Finance,* ed. Michael R. Czinkota (Washington, D.C.: Government Printing Office, 1988), 76–85.

[6] Louis G. Guadagnoli, *Practical Guide to Export Financing and Risk Management* (Arlington, Va.: Government Information Services, 1989), III-33.

[7] "How U.S. Exporters Can Benefit from Forfait Financing," *Business International Money Report,* December 21, 1987, 418–420.

receivables (over 180 days to 5 years), while factors work with short-term receivables; and (3) factors usually do not have strong capabilities in the developing countries, but since forfaiters usually require a bank guarantee, most are willing to deal with receivables from these countries. Furthermore, forfaiters work with capital goods, factors typically with consumer goods.[8]

Official Trade Finance*

Official financing can take the form of either a loan or a guarantee, including credit insurance. In a loan, the government provides funds to finance the sale and charges interest on those funds at a stated fixed rate. The government lender accepts the risk of a possible default. In a guarantee, a private-sector lender provides the funds and sets the interest rate, with the government assuring that it will reimburse the lender if the loan is unpaid. The government is providing not funds but rather risk protection.[9] The programs provide assurance the governmental agency will pay for a major portion of the loss should the foreign buyer default on payment. The advantages are significant: (1) protection in the riskiest part of an exporter's business (foreign sales receivables), (2) protection against political and commercial risks over which the exporter does not have control, (3) encouragement to exporters to make competitive offers by extending terms of payment, (4) broadening of potential markets by minimizing exporter risks, and (5) the possibility of leveraging exporter accounts receivable.[10]

Because credit has emerged as an increasingly important component in export selling, governments of most industrialized countries have established entities that insure credit risks for exports. The international union of export credit and investment insurers, or the "Berne Union," was established in 1934 by the leading trading nations for the purpose of establishing a voluntary international understanding on export insurance terms by recommending the length of periods for which credit can be extended. Recommended periods range from 5 years for heavy capital goods to 18 months for consumer durable goods. The Agreement on Guidelines for Officially Supported Export Credits came into force in 1978 as a legally nonbinding agreement on the standardization of international financing.[11] Despite the agreement, some countries tend to circumvent the agreement by providing mixed credits—that is, a combination of commercial export financing funds and "soft" development aid funds. U.S. firms are estimated to lose from $400 million to $800 million yearly in export sales because of tied aid from other countries. International pressure has been directed at Japan, which typically reserves nearly half of its $11 billion in foreign aid for Japanese companies.[12]

The matrix of conditions in force in early 1994 is summarized in Table 6.1. Because of the increased elimination of subsidized trade, uniform rates for the relatively rich countries were done away with in 1988, and the rates for intermediate countries were eliminated in 1992. Rates are determined using Organization for Economic Cooperation and Development (OECD) Commercial Interest Reference Rates, which vary according to the main invoicing currency.

---

* The authors acknowledge the assistance of Robert J. Kaiser of the Export-Import Bank of the United States and Louis G. Guadagnoli in the preparation of this section.

---

[8] Mary Ann Ring, "Innovative Export Financing," *Business America,* January 11, 1993, 12–14.

[9] Office of Trade Finance, "Survey of Finance Topics of Current Interest," in *Trade Finance,* ed. Michael R. Czinkota (Washington, D.C.: Government Printing Office, 1988), 34–43.

[10] "EXIM-Bank Program Summary," in *Export-Import Bank of the United States* (Washington, D.C.: EXIM Bank, 1985), 1.

[11] Tuomas Larjavaara, *Export Credit Competition* (Helsinki, Finland: Helsinki School of Economics, 1988).

[12] "A Well-Hidden Pot of Gold," *Business International,* December 21, 1992, 2–3.

| | Interest Rates for Officially Supported Export Credits | | TABLE 6.1 |

| Borrower | Repayment Terms[a] | | |
	2 to 5 Years	5 to 8.5 Years	Over 8.5 Years
Relatively Rich (e.g., Finland)	—	—	—
Intermediate (e.g., Jordan)	—	—	—
Relatively Poor (e.g., Ethiopia)	5.54	6.15	6.48

[a]The minimum rates are reviewed each January and July. Rates quoted are from January 15, 1994.

The Export-Import Bank of the United States (Eximbank) was created in 1934 and established as an independent U.S. government agency in 1945. The purpose of the bank is "to aid in financing and facilitating exports." Since its inception, Eximbank has supported more than $250 billion in U.S. export sales, such as those described in The International Marketplace 6.2. In September 1992, Eximbank acquired its former insurance agent, the Foreign Credit Insurance Association (FCIA). The short-term insurance programs formerly offered by the FCIA are now offered as Eximbank insurance.

The data in Table 6.2 match products and services with the customary financing term and the appropriate Eximbank programs, although the applicability of a particular program depends on the details of the specific transaction.

Pre-export Support   One of the greatest impediments small businesses experience in attempting to fulfill export orders is a lack of adequate working capital to build the necessary inventory for the export order. In response to this need, Eximbank created a Working Capital Guarantee Program (WCG). It is the only pre-export program offered by Eximbank. All other Eximbank programs finance exports after shipment or performance.

Under this program, Eximbank guarantees the lender against default by the exporter. The guarantee is for 90 percent of the loan and interest up to 1 percent over the Treasury borrowing rate. The lender must retain 10 percent of the risk. Should the exporter default, only the commercial bank is covered. For example, if the foreign buyer of the U.S. goods defaults, only the exporter's outstanding loan to the commercial bank is covered under the WCG. For this reason, many exporters secure Eximbank insurance to protect themselves against failure of the foreign buyer to pay the obligation for either commercial or political reasons.

The WCG may be used for single sales or as a revolving facility. It may also be used for marketing and promotion purposes. However, most of the WCGs approved by Eximbank are for single-sale transactions. The exporter must put up collateral equal to 110 percent of the value of the loan. Eximbank takes a broad interpretation of acceptable collateral and will accept raw materials, fixed assets in certain cases, foreign receivables, or collateral. Frequently, the personal guarantee of the exporting company's officers is also required. The exporter may approach Eximbank directly for a WCG or go through its bank.

Export Credit Insurance   Any entity—including the U.S. exporter, a U.S. or foreign bank, or the foreign buyer—may apply to Eximbank for a premium quote, at no cost, to determine the availability and cost of export credit insurance.[13] Eximbank offers ten standard policies, which fall into two basic categories: multibuyer and single-buyer

---

[13] John A. Hanson, "The Government Can Help," *Export Today* 4 (July-August 1988): 62–63.

THE INTERNATIONAL MARKETPLACE

Inside the Export-Import Bank

The Company: Anadigics Anadigics, Inc., based in Warren, New Jersey, is a designer and manufacturer of RF, microwave, and high-speed digital Gallium Arsenide Integrated Circuits for wide-band communications applications. Anadigics was founded in 1985, and in 1989, the company's products began to penetrate key foreign markets, including Western Europe and the Far East. Today, international sales represent approximately 50 percent of its total revenue.
The Need: Analysts had determined that the technological revolution in the communications industry would result in new wide-band communications systems, with a projected market of $170 million by 1993. The performance and cost advantages to Anadigic's Gallium Arsenide Intergrated Circuit made the company ideally suited to meet the needs of the rapidly growing international market.

It was imperative, however, that Anadigics acquire more working capital if it was to participate in this growing market. Specifically, Anadigics needed working capital to support a $5.3 million contract from a European communications firm.
The Solution: After learning about the assistance available through the U.S. government, Anadigics applied for a $1.5 million working capital loan guarantee from Eximbank. Within two months, preliminary approval for the loan guarantee had been received. Anadigics then used the Eximbank preliminary commitment to obtain the working capital necessary to maintain and finance its European contract, as well as begin a concentrated international expansion effort.

The Company: Semiconductor Test Solutions Semiconductor Test Solutions Inc. (STS) of Santa Clara, California, designs, builds, markets, and supports value-engineered semiconductor test equipment. Established in 1978, STS offers test solutions that range from unique applications packages all the way to complete, high-performance automatic test-equipment systems. STS's business is based on providing the expanding worldwide semiconductor industry with the means to control both product quality and test cost. By mid-1989, 45 percent of STS's total sales were made to global clients.
The Need: Industry analysts are projecting $2.5 billion in worldwide capital investments in automatic testing equipment for the next three years. STS realized that to meet the demands of this rapidly expanding industry, it would need additional working capital. But the company had surpassed the legal lending limit of its current financial institution. To further expand international sales, STS needed to find alternative sources of financing for its export receivables, inventory, and marketing expenses.
The Solution: STS's financial needs were met with a $2-million loan from Eximbank's Working Capital Loan Guarantee Program, which provides U.S. exporters access to export-related working capital loans from private-sector financial institutions. STS export receivables and inventory were provided as collateral for the loan guarantee. The additional $2 million enabled STS to finance export receivables and to meet the growing inventory and marketing expenses needed to support its international export program.

Source: William A. Delphos, "Getting Help from Uncle Sam." Reprinted with permission of *Export Today* Magazine, Washington, D.C. (January–February 1990).

| Selection Chart for Eximbank | **TABLE 6.2** |

Exports	Appropriate Programs
Pre-export	
Any product or service when working capital is needed to fill an export order	Working capital loan guarantee
Short Term (up to 180 days)	
Consumables	Export credit insurance
Small manufactured items	
Spare parts	
Raw materials	
Services less than 1 year	
Short Term (up to 360 days)	
Consumer durables	Export credit insurance
Bulk agricultural commodities	
Medium Term (181 days to 5 years)	
Capital equipment	Export credit insurance
Mining and refining equipment	Intermediary credit
Construction equipment	Financial guarantees
Agricultural equipment	
General aviation aircraft	
Planning/feasibility studies	
Breeding livestock	
Long Term (5 years and longer)	
Power plants	Direct loans
LNG and gas-processing plants	Financial guarantees
Other major projects	PEFCO

types. These policies accommodate the special needs of various types of exporters and financing institutions, either of which can be an insured party. The insurance premiums charged are based on the buyer, the length of the repayment term, the country of importation, the experience of the insured, and the volume of business. The coverage offered under the policies may be comprehensive, meaning that both commercial and political risks of default are covered, or political only. A comprehensive policy is advisable because of the difficulty in predicting events. Also, devaluation is not covered as a political risk but, if it causes default, may be covered as a commercial risk. Eximbank does not offer commercial risk coverage alone. The policies have U.S. content requirements in order to fulfill the basic mission of supporting U.S. jobs. Products or services sold by small businesses with short-term repayment periods or products or projects sold by large U.S. exporters must have at least 85 percent U.S. content. No value may be added after shipment from the United States.

Multibuyer policies   These policies may cover short- or medium-term sales or a combination of both. They require that the insured pay premium on all, or a reasonable spread, of export credit sales. This requirement exists to prevent the insured from making an adverse selection of sales to be insured and increasing Eximbank's risk. Typically, it is used by an exporter for comprehensive coverage on worldwide short-term sales. Eximbank assigns an aggregate policy limit, which is the maximum dollar amount in claims that will be paid in a policy year. However, the insured must submit credit information to Eximbank and receive approval for each buyer whose receivables are to be insured. A discretionary credit limit may be granted to experienced insureds to relieve

TABLE 6.3

Example of Eximbank Insurance

(1) Contract value	$100,000
(2) Cash payment (15%)	15,000
(3) Financed portion (85%)	85,000
(4) Exporter commercial retention (10% of line 3)	8,500
(5) Eximbank commercial risks coverage (90% of line 3)	76,500
(6) Eximbank political risks (100% of line 3)	85,000

Source: Louis G. Guadagnoli.

them from obtaining preapproval for sales under a certain dollar amount, provided they maintain a credit file on the buyer. A first-loss deductible for commercial risk claims is typical. The minimum premium is usually $500 per year paid up front, and the insured pays premiums monthly, based on shipments. A typical example is provided in Table 6.3.

Single-buyer policies   This type of policy allows exporters to select the sales they desire to insure. There is no first-loss deductible. It may cover single or repetitive sales to one buyer.

The many standard Eximbank policies include several designed specifically for financing institutions such as banks. These include the Bank Letter of Credit Policy, which covers the obligation of a foreign bank to remit funds to a bank that has confirmed a letter of credit opened by that foreign bank for the purchase of U.S. goods. Also, the Financial Institution Buyer Credit Policy covers the short-term credit obligations of a foreign buyer of U.S. goods to its funding bank, and the Bank Supplier Credit Policy covers the short-term financing provided to a U.S. exporter by its bank related to export credit sales. Other policies, such as the Trade-Association Policy and Umbrella Policy, allow organizations experienced in export trade and financing to act as intermediaries between Eximbank and potential insureds. The administrators of these policies are not insured but assist the exporter in obtaining insurance, maintaining documentation, and filing claims. Eximbank offers insurance for leases as well as sales. The Operating Lease Policy covers a specific number of lease payments plus the depreciated value of the equipment if expropriation occurs. No down payment is required for this medium-term coverage. The Financing Lease Policy covers the total of the lease payments, but a 15 percent cash payment is required.

A combination of short- and medium-term insurance is available, used mainly to protect U.S. exporters who offer floor plans to overseas dealers and distributors. This option offers protection on parts and accessories sales on terms up to 180 days and capital equipment inventory financing for up to 270 days that can be converted to a medium-term receivable of up to 3 years.

To insure against risks from the date of signing the sales contract instead of from the date of shipment, Eximbank offers comprehensive preshipment coverage. This coverage is necessary when goods are specially manufactured or require a long factory lead time. Nonacceptance coverage against the arbitrary refusal of the buyer to accept products that conform to the contract of sale may be offered at no extra cost in addition to the normal coverage except when greater-than-normal risk exists, such as with perishable items. In addition, Eximbank will insure political risks for goods on consignment where payment is made to the exporter only after the goods have been sold. Should an exporter consummate a sale requiring payment in foreign currency rather than U.S. dollars, Eximbank will cover such transactions under all policies; however, coverage is limited to "freely transferable" currencies, and no exchange or transfer risk is insurable under this endorsement.

To encourage U.S. firms to expand their foreign business during a period when there is a strong overseas demand for services, Eximbank developed services coverage. Industries benefiting from this include management consultants, engineering service firms, transportation companies, and other firms offering the services of U.S.-based personnel to foreign buyers with repayment being made in U.S. dollars in the United States. The New-to-Export Policy is for companies without exporting experience or those that have had limited export sales in the past. The policy gives added commercial risk protection of 95 percent to further cushion any potential losses. These criteria have to be met by the applying company: average annual export credit sales of less than $2 million during the preceding two years, and prior direct coverage under any Eximbank insurance program.

The exporter who insures foreign accounts receivable is often able to obtain financing from banks and other lending institutions with Eximbank coverage. As a result, the exporter can extend credit on more favorable terms to overseas customers without tying up resources required for internal operations.

Claims may be submitted immediately upon default, or there may be a waiting period of up to eight months, depending on the provisions of the policy and the cause of the default. At the time of the claim, the exporter must submit certain documents, such as copies of bills of lading, the debt instrument, evidence of attempts to collect, and evidence of compliance with any special conditions imposed by Eximbank. The exporter must therefore retain all documents until the claim has been paid.

Guarantees   Eximbank guarantees to provide repayment protection for private-sector loans to creditworthy buyers of U.S. goods and services exports. Guarantees are available separately or with an intermediary loan and are backed in full by the U.S. government. Both medium- and long-term guarantees are available.

Medium-term guarantees   These are available for export transactions usually up to $10 million, with a maximum repayment term not to exceed seven years. Most typically, they are used by commercial banks that do not want exposure in a certain country or that have reached their internal "exposure limit" in a given country. The Eximbank guarantee overcomes these limitations. The medium-term guarantee provides the lender 100 percent political and commercial risk protection. Under this guarantee, the foreign buyer is required to make a 15 percent cash down payment, so the guarantee covers the "financed portion" of 85 percent.

Eximbank's fee schedule is determined by country risk and the repayment terms of the transaction. Rates vary from the highest-rated "A" country to the lowest-rated "E" country. By having a rate schedule based on perceived risk assumption, Eximbank is able to remain open for business longer in more countries because it is compensated for the risk it is being asked to take.

Long-term guarantees   These are used for transactions in excess of $10 million and repayment periods of eight or more years. The commercial and political risk cover is 100 percent. The fee structure is the same as under medium-term guarantees. One major difference in the long-term guarantee is that loans made under the long-term guarantee may be denominated in foreign currencies acceptable to Eximbank. This enables foreign buyers with access to foreign currency earnings to use this currency to repay loans. A good example of this would be a foreign airline with earnings, through its flight routes, in Japanese yen. The airline wishes to buy U.S.-made airplanes but wants to borrow in yen and use its yen earnings to service the debt. An Eximbank long-term guarantee could be utilized for such a transaction.

Eximbank, by statute, does not compete with commercial banks. It complements and supplements commercial bank support for exports by assuming risks unacceptable to the banks. As is well known, commercial banks will only rarely provide fixed interest rate loans for any type of commercial transaction. Yet today, in the highly competitive international marketplace, many foreign buyers can demand financial support as a precondition to their purchase of goods from abroad. These foreign buyers often require fixed-rate financing as a condition of their purchase.

Eximbank offers medium-term loans to commercial banks at a discount from the official OECD rates for the country of the purchaser. The commercial bank then on-lends to the foreign buyer at the full OECD rate. The discount the commercial bank receives (50 basis points) is based on the dollar amount of the medium-term credit. The maximum amount that a bank can borrow from Eximbank under this facility and still receive the discount is $10 million. Amounts in excess of $10 million do not receive a discount. The discount is available only to commercial banks. All other intermediary lenders, including the exporters themselves, may borrow from Eximbank at the official OECD rate and on-lend at the same OECD rate to the foreign buyer.

For fixed-rate loans in excess of $10 million and repayment periods of eight years or longer, Eximbank acts as a lender directly to the foreign buyer. This is because most commercial banks simply do not extend loans beyond seven-year repayment terms. Often, too, these transactions are large ones, in excess of $100 million, and commercial banks do not want such large exposure for long periods of time in one country or in that industrial sector. Such major projects, or large product purchases, are often let through international bids, and competition is keen to secure these major orders. Without Eximbank participation, American exporters would be unable to successfully compete. Under OECD regulations, a 15 percent cash down payment by the foreign buyer is required. Thus, the "financed portion" is 85 percent of the export value. Eximbank has eased its U.S. content requirements somewhat and is now prepared to finance up to a maximum of 15 percent foreign content in the export order. The rest of the export must be U.S.-produced goods and services. If the foreign content exceeds 15 percent of the shipment, then that foreign content will be excluded entirely from Eximbank support. Payment terms are normally determined by studying cash flow projections from the proposed project or the useful life of the product. In any case, repayment rarely exceeds a ten-year term. Normally, if a project is involved, repayment begins six months after the project commences commercial operations. For a product, such as a commercial jet aircraft, repayment begins six months after the plane goes into service.

An example of typical financing for a turnkey project is provided in Table 6.4. Eximbank funds or guarantees 85 percent of U.S. costs at a fixed rate, with the rate varying by country classification. The bank financing for infrastructure is a separate transaction. To be involved, Eximbank and commercial banks must be satisfied that the project is technically and financially feasible. For this they require extensive information, includ-

TABLE 6.4   **Typical Financing Plan for a Turnkey Project**

Costs (in millions)		Financing Plan (in millions)	
Hardware	$10.0	Eximbank credit/guarantee	$ 8.5
Infrastructure	5.0	U.S. banks—U.S. costs	1.5
Interest during construction	2.0	U.S. banks—infrastructure	5.0
Working capital requirements	2.0	Sponsor's equity	4.0
Total	$19.0	Total	$19.0

Source: Louis G. Guadagnoli.

ing a feasibility study. The balance of the financing requirements usually comes out of the project owner's resources.

Under its charter, Eximbank must have "reasonable assurance of repayment." Therefore, a careful analysis of the foreign buyer's creditworthiness and the project's viability is conducted. If necessary, government guarantees of the loan repayment, representing the full faith and credit of the host country of the foreign buyer, may be required. In other cases, guarantees of a commercial bank in the host country may also be satisfactory and necessary.

Annual competitiveness reports have assessed U.S. exporter ratings of official export credit facilities. Since the 1980s, Eximbank programs have been rated "basically competitive" or "uncompetitive." Where absolute improvement has been realized, other nations have matched these efforts.[14]

The export-import credit agencies of other countries should also be monitored to assess the structures, terms, and rates of import financing programs for U.S. goods and services. Included could be such entities as the Export-Import Bank of Japan or the Export Development Corporation of Canada.[15]

Other Public-Sector Financing Sources The Overseas Private Investment Corporation (OPIC) is a federal agency that offers investment guarantees, comparable to those offered by Eximbank, to U.S. manufacturers that wish to establish plants in less-developed countries, either by themselves or as a joint venture with local capital. OPIC finances and/or insures only foreign direct investment through (1) direct loans from $100,000 to $6 million per project with terms of 5 to 12 years, (2) loan guarantees to U.S. institutional lenders of up to $50 million per project, and (3) political risk insurance against currency inconvertibility, expropriation, or takeover, and physical damage resulting from political strife.[16] The importance of this activity is increasing rapidly because foreign direct investment enables firms to remain competitive in the world marketplace. It is difficult to maintain viable market share without presence as a producer, making trade more dependent on investment with time.[17]

The Agency for International Development (AID) administers most of the foreign economic assistance programs for the U.S. government. Because many AID agreements require that commodities be purchased from the United States, exporters should use this support mechanism. AID estimates that 70 percent of all U.S. aid comes back in purchases of goods and services from U.S. companies. In the long term, the agency's objective is to increase potential for increased exports by follow-up sales and by creating potential in the market for other purchases.[18] As a sister agency to AID, the U.S. Trade Development Program (TDP) uses foreign assistance funds to increase U.S. exports by financing the planning of projects and dispersing grants for feasibility studies of development projects.

In addition to these U.S. entities, the international marketer will find it worthwhile to monitor the activities of development banks such as the World Bank, regional development banks (such as the Inter-American Development Bank and the Asian Development

[14] Alfred C. Holden, "U.S. Official Export–Finance Support: Can American Exporters Expect a Competitive Eximbank to Emerge?" *Columbia Journal of World Business* 24 (Fall 1989): 33–46.

[15] Martin R. Brill, "The East Asian Edge," *Export Today* 4 (July-August 1988): 50–53.

[16] Craig A. Nalen, "Direct Investment: An Entree to Exporting," *Export Today* 4 (March–April 1988): 10–13.

[17] Peter Drucker, "From World Trade to World Investment," *The Wall Street Journal,* May 26, 1987, 33.

[18] "Foreign Assistance Funds: Marketing U.S. Exports through Economic Development," *Export Today* 4 (March–April 1988): 6–9.

THE INTERNATIONAL MARKETPLACE

Going for the Government Contracts

"There are major public-sector opportunities abroad," says Larry Mandell, senior vice president of the Keith Companies, a Costa Mesa, California–based group of environmental service companies. One of the most recent contracts received by the Keith Companies was for $1 million from the United States Agency for International Development (AID) to clean mud and ash off Mount Pinatubo. Also completed in 1993 was a $50,000 feasibility study for the Inter-American Development Bank in Costa Rica.

The Keith Companies is just one of many businesses benefiting from a new flow of funds being committed by multilateral banks to projects around the world. From 1988 to 1992, the World Bank Group and the African, Asian, European, and Inter-American Development Banks committed $162 billion in projects for agriculture, energy, industry and finance, transportation, and education. By the end of the century, they are committed to $410 billion to developing countries in these sectors. With such large amounts at stake, some international marketing managers believe that these funds are out of reach, too big, bureaucratic, or difficult to obtain. While some funds are subject to competitive international bidding, others, at the lower end of the scale, are accessible and available via different methods of procurement, including direct negotiation.

Government-funded counseling and information services for foreign trade make finding and securing multilateral bank contracts easier. For example, AID's goals are to counsel small to mid-size companies on doing business with developing countries. Another useful source is a United Nations publication, *Development Business*, which offers information on projects about to be launched in Africa, Asia, Latin America, and Eastern Europe. The publication is directly linked with the World Bank headquarters. This means that information on the global procurement market comes directly from the financial sources, enabling subscribers to monitor any development projects in the pipeline as well as bidding processes and contract awards.

Once a marketer has identified contracts on which to bid, Mandell advises not to pursue all available ones. "You must determine whether this is the market you want to be in. Select projects you are qualified for, and then team up with other companies." He recommends becoming involved with a project even before it is up for consideration by a multilateral bank. "Build relationships at the banks, make contacts in trade and commerce, and learn as much about specific countries as possible. Right now, Keith Companies is going after a $100-million contract in Brazil."

Sources: Adrian Feuchtwanger, "The Search for Eldorado," *World Trade*, November 1993, 116–118; and Nicholas H. Ludlow, "Tapping Development Bank Lines of Credit," *Export Today* 9 (October 1993): 26–30.

Bank), and many national development banks. These banks specialize in financing investment activities and can provide valuable leads for future business activity, as seen in The International Marketplace 6.3

The World Bank Group has, since its inception, provided more than $313 billion in financing for more than 5,800 projects. In 1993, loans totaled $23.6 billion for more than 200 new operations. Projects cover a wide spectrum, including agriculture, industry, transportation, telecommunications, and population planning. Loans are at variable rates, based on the cost of borrowing, and for 15- to 20-year terms. All loans must be guaranteed by the government of the borrowing country.[19] To get business from World Bank projects, international marketers have to closely monitor the entire process—from the identification of the project to the approval of the loan.

In April 1988, an affiliate of the World Bank began operation. The Multilateral Investment Guaranty Agency (MIGA) will encourage the flow of financial resources to its developing member countries. To accomplish this, MIGA is authorized to issue guarantees against noncommercial risks in host countries, so that investors may assess the benefits of projects on economic and financial grounds rather than political risk. In 1993, MIGA facilitated investments worth $1.9 billion in 27 projects.

Private-Sector Export-Credit Insurance

The Private Export Funding Corporation (PEFCO) is a private corporation founded in 1970 for the purpose of making fixed-rate U.S. dollar loans to foreign importers to finance purchases of goods and services of U.S. manufacture or origin. PEFCO's stockholders consist of 54 commercial banks, including most of the major U.S. banks involved in export financing, one investment banking firm, and seven manufacturing firms (Boeing, Cessna, Combustion Engineering, General American Transportation, General Electric, McDonnell Douglas Finance, and United Technologies). The Eximbank and PEFCO maintain an agreement whereby Eximbank guarantees the principal and interest on debt obligations that are issued by foreign purchasers of U.S. products and services by PEFCO. PEFCO thereby acquires a portfolio of Eximbank-guaranteed paper that can be used as the basis for raising funds in the private market. Because all of its loans are guaranteed, PEFCO itself does not evaluate credit risks, appraise economic conditions in foreign countries, or review other factors that might affect the collectibility of its loans.

The role of private export credit insurers has increased in the past few years.[20] For example, American International Underwriters, a division of American International Group, offers coverage of commercial credit and political risks similar to that offered by Eximbank. Other firms that offer limited forms of commercial and political risk coverage include Citicorp International Trade and American Credit Indemnity. Private underwriters offer political risk coverage for confiscation, expropriation, and nationalization risks—coverage that is similar to that provided by OPIC.

Proponents of the private insurers cite their faster processing time, lower rates because of selectivity, absence of U.S.-origin requirement, and ability to do business in countries embargoed by the U.S. government. The drawbacks, however, are that they require a minimum but substantial amount of business to be covered, they cater mainly to the large multinational corporations and are not as interested in smaller firms, and, the most important caveat, their insurance may not be as acceptable to commercial banks that will be providing the financing.

FINANCIAL RISK MANAGEMENT

After financial risks have been assessed, the international marketer needs to decide whether to do business in the particular environment. If the decision is to do so, risk needs to be minimized through actions by either the company itself or support systems. The

[19] Carol Stitt, "The World Bank and Project Finance," *Export Today* 5 (February 1989): 50–54.

[20] H. Allan Legge, Jr., "Private-Sector Export Insurance: Taking Care of Business," *Export Today* 4 (September–October 1988): 74–75.

TABLE 6.5	Sources of International Credit Information

Source	Response Time	Cost	Comments
1. Dun & Bradstreet	Same day to 50 days, depending on location	$122 to $495	Standard in the industry. Data are often sketchy, since subjects are reticent to respond to a credit inquiry.
2. World Traders Data Report	Variable; if known name, quick; otherwise, lengthy delays	$100	If prominent name, comprehensive. Tendency to be out of date.
3. Local Credit Agency Report	Long, start from scratch	$100 to $200	Quality varies. International market perspective lacking.
4. Bank Reports	Slow	None	Limited in scope.
5. FCIB-NACM Corporation	Same day to 5 weeks	Part of membership fee ($730)	Network of 18 agencies abroad.

decision must be an informed one, based on detailed and up-to-date information in international credit and country conditions. In many respects, the assessment of a buyer's creditworthiness requires the same attention to credit checking and financial analysis as that for domestic buyers; however, the assessment of a foreign private buyer is complicated by some of the following factors:

1. Credit reports may not be reliable.
2. Audited reports may not be available.
3. Financial reports may have been prepared according to a different format.
4. Many governments require that assets be annually revaluated upward, which can distort results.
5. Statements are in local currency.
6. The buyer may have the financial resources in local currency but may be precluded from converting to dollars because of exchange controls and other government actions.

More than one credit report should be obtained, and it should be determined how each credit agency obtains its reports. They may use the same correspondent agency. It does the exporter no good to obtain the same information from two sources and to pay for it twice. Table 6.5 provides a summary of the major sources of credit information. At least one of the credit reports solicited by the exporter should be the World Traders Data Report compiled by the U.S. Department of Commerce.

Beyond protecting oneself by establishing creditworthiness, an exporter can match payment terms to the customer. In the short term, an exporter may require payment terms that guarantee payment. In the long term, the best approach is to establish a relationship of mutual trust which will ensure payment even if complications arise during a transaction.[21] However, unless sales are secured by ironclad assurances, foreign cus-

---

[21] Michael S. Tomczyk, "How Do You Collect When Foreign Customers Don't Pay?" *Export Today* 9 (November–December 1993): 33–35.

THE INTERNATIONAL MARKETPLACE 6.4

Now for the Hard Part: Getting Paid for Exports

Smaller exporters often do not have the luxury that big corporations have to weigh risks of doing business abroad and to investigate the creditworthiness of foreign customers. The result may be a hard lesson about the global economy: Foreign sales do not help much when you cannot collect the bill.

More often than not, exporters will do less checking on an international account than they will on a domestic customer. For example, a U.S. fan blade manufacturer with less than $10 million in revenue was left with an overdue payment of $127,000 owed by an African customer. Before shipping the goods, the company had failed to call any of the customer's credit references. These turned out to be nonexistent—just like the company itself.

The simple guideline of selling only in countries where you are most likely to get paid may not be enough given that collection periods for some of the more attractive markets may be long (as shown in the table below). However, in many cases, basic information about the economic and political conditions in markets may be enough to warrant caution. Old World Industries Inc., a mid-sized maker of antifreeze fluid and other automotive products, found that out after selling 500,000 gallons of antifreeze to a customer in a newly emerging market. After two years, Old World is still waiting to be paid in full, because the foreign bank it is dealing with has trouble obtaining U.S. dollars despite the country's strengthening foreign reserve position.

Your Check Is In The Mail

Length of time required for American companies to collect on the average bill from concerns in selected foreign countries in the second quarter of 1992 as reported by the National Association of Credit Management (NACM).

Country	Number of Days
Iran	337
Kenya	129
Argentina	123
Brazil	119
Italy	90
India	80
Mexico	74
Taiwan	73
United Kingdom	70
Japan	58
Germany	54

Sources: "Congratulations, Exporter! Now About Getting Paid . . ." *Business Week,* January 17, 1994, 98; and "Small Firms Hit Foreign Obstacles in Billing Overseas," *The Wall Street Journal,* December 8, 1992, B2. Reprinted by permission of *The Wall Street Journal.* © 1992 Dow Jones and Company, Inc. All rights reserved worldwide.

tomers may be tardy or fall delinquent on payments, as seen in The International Marketplace 6.4.

Should a default situation occur in spite of the preparatory measures discussed above, the exporter's first recourse is with the customer. Communication with the customer may reveal a misunderstanding or error regarding the shipment. If the customer has financial or other concerns or objections, rescheduling the payment terms may be considered. Third-party intervention through a collection agency may be needed if the customer disputes the charges. Only when further amicable demands are unwarranted should an attorney be used.[22]

In many cases, financing requirements may go beyond export credits, and financial risk management gains added dimensions. In a hotly contested bid for its first two communications satellites, Brazil managed to bargain the price down to $150 million. In addition, it pressured the two consortia competing for the business, one French and one Canadian, to promise to buy shoes, coffee, and iron ore as partial payment. **Countertrade** provisions are making their way into many financing arrangements, especially when developing countries or centrally planned economies are involved. Because of the prominent position of countertrade in international trade (approximately 25 percent of the total), many firms not only have had to accept it but also have made major adjustments financially and organizationally to cope with it. Some U.S. construction companies are hoping to open new construction projects by devising ways to help debt-strapped developing countries with their financing problems. In Latin America, U.S. contractors, led by McDermott International, are experimenting with countertrade. McDermott is already grossing $700 million a year in countertrade in such commodities as steel, fertilizer, and chemicals. It also bought the international trading arm of Germany's Coutinho, Caro & Co. to help dispose of the items it takes in compensation for work performed abroad.[23]

A development related to the debt crisis is the emergence of debt/equity and debt/product swaps. Under a **debt/equity swap,** a firm wishing to invest in a country with debt problems arranges to swap the country's debt for an equity investment. For example, Chrysler purchased $110 million in Mexican debt for about 55 cents on the dollar. The debt was then converted into about $100 million in pesos and invested in the Mexican subsidiary.[24] Since suitable investments may not be available, **debt/product swaps** may be used as another vehicle for marketing debt. Peru has negotiated deals in which creditors have committed themselves to buying $3 worth of Peruvian products for every $1 of products paid by Peru against debt.[25]

Foreign Exchange Risk

When the international marketer is to receive payment in a currency other than that of his or her country, the risk exists of a decline (devaluation) in the foreign currency during the time between the signing of the contract and the receipt of the foreign currency. If the marketer takes no action to manage an exchange rate fluctuation, losses will be incurred. This is illustrated in Table 6.6, in which the British pound depreciates against the U.S. dollar. Protection against foreign exchange risk cannot be secured from the same sources as for commercial and political risk. It must emerge from sound management practices.

The Foreign Exchange Market

The foreign exchange market is the mechanism by which purchasing power between countries is transferred, credit is provided for international transactions, and exposure to the risks of exchange rate fluctuations can be minimized.[26] The participants in this

[22] David I. Herer, "Dealing with Default," *Export Today* 6 (January–February 1990): 52–54.

[23] "The Shrinking World of Engineering Contractors," *Business Week,* September 24, 1984, 84–90.

[24] "Debt-Business Boom in Latin America," *Euromoney,* September 1987, 81.

[25] "Drexel's Milken Is Trying to Find a Lode in Latin Debt," *The Wall Street Journal,* September 14, 1987, 6.

[26] David K. Eiteman, Arthur I. Stonehill, and Michael H. Moffett, *International Business Finance* (Reading, MA: Addison-Wesley, 1992), 78.

Example of Foreign Exchange Impact | **TABLE 6.6**

Monthly contract, £1,000
Cost of goods to marketer, $1,500

Date	Exchange rate	Revenue	Cost	Net Income
1/1	1£ = 1.55	$1,550	$1,500	$50
2/1	1£ = 1.50	1,500	1,500	0
4/1	1£ = 1.45	1,450	1,500	(50)

market include banks, governments, and speculators as well as individuals and firms conducting transactions.

The price of one currency in terms of another is called the **exchange rate.** Daily exchange rates such as those shown in Figure 6.2 are available from newspapers such as *The Wall Street Journal* and the *Financial Times*. The marketer, however, has to contact a particular bank's foreign exchange trader for a firm quote. Both spot and forward transactions are made in the market. The market for buying and selling on the current day is the **spot market.** The market for closing contracts on subsequent periods of 30,

Foreign Exchange Rates | **FIGURE 6.2**

EXCHANGE RATES

Monday, January 10, 1994

The New York foreign exchange selling rates below apply to trading among banks in amounts of $1 million and more, as quoted at 3 p.m. Eastern time by Bankers Trust Co., Telerate and other sources. Retail transactions provide fewer units of foreign currency per dollar.

Country	U.S. $ equiv. Mon.	U.S. $ equiv. Fri.	Currency per U.S. $ Mon.	Currency per U.S. $ Fri.
Argentina (Peso)	1.01	1.01	.99	.99
Australia (Dollar)	.6874	.6860	1.4548	1.4577
Austria (Schilling)	.08201	.08237	12.19	12.14
Bahrain (Dinar)	2.6518	2.6518	.3771	.3771
Belgium (Franc)	.02758	.02788	36.25	35.86
Brazil (Cruzeiro real)	.0029688	.0029688	336.83	336.83
Britain (Pound)	1.4935	1.4935	.6696	.6696
30-Day Forward	1.4904	1.4904	.6710	.6710
90-Day Forward	1.4855	1.4857	.6732	.6731
180-Day Forward	1.4793	1.4799	.6760	.6757
Canada (Dollar)	.7591	.7575	1.3173	1.3201
30-Day Forward	.7586	.7571	1.3182	1.3209
90-Day Forward	.7580	.7564	1.3192	1.3220
180-Day Forward	.7572	.7555	1.3206	1.3236
Czech. Rep. (Koruna)				
Commercial rate	.0338983	.0338983	29.5000	29.5000
Chile (Peso)	.002400	.002394	416.74	417.70
China (Renminbi)	.114965	.115075	8.6983	8.6900
Colombia (Peso)	.001437	.001445	696.01	692.08
Denmark (Krone)	.1485	.1488	6.7337	6.7182
Ecuador (Sucre)				
Floating rate	.000499	.000503	2004.01	1989.02
Finland (Markka)	.17378	.17446	5.7545	5.7318
France (Franc)	.16925	.16995	5.9085	5.8842
30-Day Forward	.16871	.16944	5.9275	5.9018
90-Day Forward	.16793	.16866	5.9549	5.9292
180-Day Forward	.16706	.16778	5.9860	5.9602
Germany (Mark)	.5765	.5789	1.7346	1.7275
30-Day Forward	.5749	.5774	1.7394	1.7320
90-Day Forward	.5727	.5751	1.7461	1.7388
180-Day Forward	.5701	.5725	1.7541	1.7468
Greece (Drachma)	.004006	.004027	249.60	248.35
Hong Kong (Dollar)	.12945	.12942	7.7250	7.7270
Hungary (Forint)	.0099810	.0099810	100.1900	100.1900
India (Rupee)	.03212	.03212	31.13	31.13
Indonesia (Rupiah)	.0004765	.0004734	2098.81	2112.51
Ireland (Punt)	1.4398	1.4356	.6945	.6966
Israel (Shekel)	.3422	.3423	2.9225	2.9210
Italy (Lira)	.0005851	.0005914	1709.02	1690.82

Country	U.S. $ equiv. Mon.	U.S. $ equiv. Fri.	Currency per U.S. $ Mon.	Currency per U.S. $ Fri.
Japan (Yen)	.008909	.008941	112.24	111.85
30-Day Forward	.008915	.008947	112.17	111.77
90-Day Forward	.008932	.008965	111.95	111.55
180-Day Forward	.008968	.009005	111.51	111.05
Jordan (Dinar)	1.4495	1.4495	.6899	.6899
Kuwait (Dinar)	3.3523	3.3501	.2983	.2985
Lebanon (Pound)	.000585	.000584	1709.50	1711.00
Malaysia (Ringgit)	.3753	.3805	2.6645	2.6284
Malta (Lira)	2.5478	2.5349	.3925	.3945
Mexico (Peso)				
Floating rate	.3270753	.3270753	3.0574	3.0574
Netherland (Guilder)	.5149	.5176	1.9420	1.9321
New Zealand (Dollar)	.5588	.5570	1.7895	1.7953
Norway (Krone)	.1335	.1341	7.4931	7.4576
Pakistan (Rupee)	.0333	.0334	30.05	29.98
Peru (New Sol)	.4726	.4759	2.12	2.10
Philippines (Peso)	.03683	.03704	27.15	27.00
Poland (Zloty)	.00004882	.00004866	20482.00	20551.00
Portugal (Escudo)	.005661	.005689	176.65	175.77
Saudi Arabia (Riyal)	.26702	.26667	3.7450	3.7499
Singapore (Dollar)	.6260	.6266	1.5974	1.5958
Slovak Rep. (Koruna)	.0299850	.0299850	33.3500	33.3500
South Africa (Rand)				
Commercial rate	.2944	.2940	3.3973	3.4010
Financial rate	.2336	.2341	4.2800	4.2720
South Korea (Won)	.0012293	.0012300	813.50	813.00
Spain (Peseta)	.006906	.006932	144.80	144.26
Sweden (Krona)	.1225	.1228	8.1613	8.1426
Switzerland (Franc)	.6793	.6821	1.4720	1.4660
30-Day Forward	.6787	.6815	1.4735	1.4674
90-Day Forward	.6781	.6809	1.4748	1.4686
180-Day Forward	.6776	.6806	1.4757	1.4692
Taiwan (Dollar)	.037760	.038066	26.48	26.27
Thailand (Baht)	.03917	.03915	25.53	25.54
Turkey (Lira)	.0000673	.0000674	14859.00	14834.00
United Arab (Dirham)	.2723	.2723	3.6725	3.6725
Uruguay (New Peso)				
Financial	.224719	.223214	4.45	4.48
Venezuela (Bolivar)				
Floating rate	.00951	.00951	105.20	105.12
SDR	1.37505	1.37136	.72725	.72920
ECU	1.11580	1.12170		

Special Drawing Rights (SDR) are based on exchange rates for the U.S., German, British, French and Japanese currencies. Source: International Monetary Fund.

European Currency Unit (ECU) is based on a basket of community currencies.

Source: "Currency Trading," *The Wall Street Journal*, January 11, 1994, C13.

60, or 90 days is called the **forward market.** For example, for the rates quoted for January 10, 1994, the forward quote for Britain is less than spot, and the pound is said to be selling at a discount to the dollar. When the foreign currency is more expensive in the forward market than in the spot market, the foreign currency is said to be selling at a premium. Forward contracts for lesser-known currencies are not readily available, and for unstable currencies, they are quite expensive.

Forward contracts provide a form of protection, or **hedge,** against exchange risks. When a forward exchange contract is signed, the forward quote (such as the 90-day quote for Germany) is the rate that applies, although no payment is generally made until the settlement date of the contract. The user pays the price of forgoing possible gains in order to ensure protection against possible losses.

Foreign exchange quotations are given either directly or indirectly. The quote $.16925/FF is a direct quote for the French franc because it is the home currency price of one unit of a foreign currency. The indirect quote, the amount of foreign currency for one unit of the domestic currency, in this case is FF5.9085/$.

The rate of exchange between two countries is the result of supply and demand as well as possible governmental policy. Changes in the supply and demand conditions will have an impact on the value of the currency if the currency is in a *free float*. For example, an increase in a country's exports or its interest rates would increase demand for its currency and thus lead to an increase in its currency value. In some cases, governments will establish an exchange rate for their currency and absorb and counter market pressures (and thus accept foreign currency losses) up to a point before allowing the exchange rate to change. Some currencies move in and out of various types of pegged exchange rate relationships; for example, in 1994, a total of 25 currencies were tied to the U.S. dollar. Occasionally, governments will coordinate their actions to rectify an imbalance in demand and supply conditions. In September 1985, for example, the United States, together with Great Britain, West Germany, Japan, and France, decided on a coordinated effort to bring the dollar down. Because market participants then expected the dollar to fall, they sold dollars, sparking a sharp decline in the value of the currency. A similar accord was reached in 1987 to stabilize the value of the dollar. The spot market exchange rate therefore reflects international trade flows, international capital flows, and governmental policy.

Forward markets exist for only a relatively small number of major currencies used in international transactions. The principal determinant for forward rates is the spot rate. Anything having an impact on the spot rate, such as balance-of-payments problems, will have the same impact on forward rates.

The Management of Foreign Exchange Risk

When an international marketer conducts transactions in foreign currencies, he or she runs the risk of suffering financial losses resulting from the change in the value of the currency used. Naturally, changes can also affect the marketer favorably. A firm is exposed to foreign exchange in three ways. **Transaction exposure** refers to the effect of outstanding contracts (for example, payables and receivables). Table 6.6 is an example of a loss to the U.S. exporter if it has chosen not to make any changes in policies or decided not to protect itself against such changes. If the contract had called for payment in U.S. dollars, however, the British buyer would have incurred the loss.

If the financial statements of the marketer are affected as a result of having to report consolidated worldwide results in home-country currency, the firm has **translation exposure.** If the exporter in the example maintained a British bank account with a balance of £100,000, it would initially be worth $155,000 (1/1). Three months later, the exporter would report, in its own books, the British bank balance to be worth $145,000. Translation

An Example of a Currency Options and Futures Provider **FIGURE 6.3**

Risk control for businesses that bruise easily.

When you ship $1.2 billion worth of bananas worldwide, a small flip in currency exchange rates could make a big difference in profits.

Chiquita, like many smart international companies, gets a good grip on those risks with currency options at the Chicago Mercantile Exchange. Hedging Deutschemarks, Pound Sterling and Yen, Chiquita has successfully guarded against financial bruising for years. And because 80% of all the exchange traded currency worldwide was traded on the CME's International Monetary Market, they've found it easy to slip in and out of currency options quickly.

"The IMM is where all information that impacts foreign exchange prices comes together," says David Groelinger, Chiquita VP and Treasurer. "That's where the most efficient pricing takes place."

Now, it will become even more efficient with the launch of GLOBEX—the computer network that expands futures and options trading around the world, around the clock.

If you're like the top bananas at Chiquita, and don't want your international earnings frittered away, the CME's currency futures and options should hold great appeal for you.

CHICAGO MERCANTILE EXCHANGE

The Exchange of Ideas

1-800-331-3332 (US) 01-920-0722 (Europe) 03-595-2251 (Pacific)

Source: Reprinted by permission of the Chicago Mercantile Exchange.

exposure for a U.S. firm is a function of the rules issued by the Financial Accounting Standards Board (FASB), in particular FASB 52 ("Foreign Currency Translation"), issued in 1981.[27] If the long-term health of a business entity is affected by foreign exchange beyond transaction and translation exposure, the entity has **economic exposure.**

[27] "Foreign Currency Translation," *FASB Statement No. 52* (December 1981), par. 15.

Response to economic exposure involves the application of long-term strategy by all of the functional units of the firm. Marketers can avoid unnecessary economic exposure by careful selection of target markets and prudent pricing and credit policies. Any firm with ongoing international marketing activities will have economic exposure.

Three types of devices to protect against currency-related risk have been proposed: (1) risk modifying, such as increasing prices and incurring local debt; (2) self-insuring, such as manipulating the leads and lags in terms of export and import payments in anticipation of either currency revaluations or devaluations; and (3) risk shifting, such as purchasing of options or futures.[28]

Options and futures are a relatively new development in the foreign exchange markets. An **option** gives the holder the right to buy or sell foreign currency at a prespecified price on or up to a prespecified date. The difference between the currency options market and the forward market is that the transaction in the options market gives the participant the *right* to buy or sell, whereas a transaction in the forward market entails a contractual *obligation* to buy or sell. The currency **futures** market is conceptually similar to the forward market; that is, to buy futures on the pound implies an obligation to buy in the future at a prespecified price. However, the minimum transaction sizes are considerably smaller on the futures market. Forward quotes apply to transactions of $1 million or more, whereas on the futures market, transactions will typically be well below $100,000. This market, therefore, allows relatively small firms engaged in international trade to lock in exchange rates and lower their risk. An example of an entity providing both such services for the international marketer is in Figure 6.3.

SUMMARY

The financing terms of a transaction are an important marketing tool. The basics of an international marketer's credit policy involve two major concerns: (1) getting paid and (2) avoiding unnecessary risk in the process. This requires a good understanding not only of the mechanisms of the foreign exchange market but also of the various types of financial assistance available to the international marketer.

To help the international marketer deal with financial risk, both the government and the private sector have established various programs. Support systems exist as well to provide information on international credit and country conditions.

Foreign exchange risk is present any time the international marketer is to receive payment in a currency different from his or her own. The marketer can be protected through the purchase of forward contracts, for example.

Use of the resources described in this chapter will allow the exporter to (1) offer competitive terms of payment to the buyer, (2) prudently penetrate foreign markets of higher risk, and (3) have greater financial liquidity and flexibility in administering the foreign receivables portfolio.

Questions for Discussion

1. Discuss the various types of financial risk in terms of their impact on an international marketing entity.

2. Eximbank does not finance export sales, yet it indirectly is quite involved. How?

---

[28] Richard D. Robinson, *Internationalization of Business: An Introduction* (Hinsdale, IL: Dryden Press, 1984), 200–207.

3. At times, subsidized export credit rates have been as low as half the rates at which national treasuries were borrowing. What is the rationale for this?

4. Should a government use its aid budget to promote the prosperity of its corporations?

5. Suggest possible reasons Eximbank does not cover 100 percent of commercial risk.

6. What accounts for the fact that export finance managers and export marketing managers have traditionally not worked together as closely as possible?

7. Comment on this statement: "Many commercial banks today have only two objections to financing international trade: one, it is international; two, it involves trade."

8. Suggest benefits and drawbacks of debt/equity swaps.

Recommended Readings

Chamber of Commerce of the United States. *Foreign Commerce Handbook*. Washington, D.C.: Chamber of Commerce, 1986.

Czinkota, Michael R., ed. *Trade Finance: Current Issues and Developments*. Washington, D.C.: Government Printing Office, 1988.

Exporter's Encyclopedia. 1993/94. New York: Dun and Bradstreet, 1994.

Foreign Credit Insurance Association. *Your Competitive Edge in Selling Overseas*. New York: FCIA, 1991.

Funabashi, Yoichi. *Managing the Dollar: From the Plaza to the Louvre*. Washington, D.C.: Institute for International Economics, 1989.

Guadagnoli, Louis G. *A Practical Guide to Export Financing and Risk Management*. Arlington, VA: Government Information Services, 1989.

Lanze, L.B. *Import/Export Can Make You Rich*. Englewood Cliffs, NJ: Prentice-Hall, 1988.

Shapiro, Alan C. *Multinational Financial Management*. Boston, MA: Allyn and Bacon, 1992.

Wamsley, Julian. *The Foreign Exchange Handbook*. New York: Wiley, 1983.

When "Fair Trade" Policies Backfire

In the summer of 1991, seven small American flat panel computer screen manufacturers persuaded the U.S. Department of Commerce to rule against Japanese manufacturers in an anti-dumping case. The American companies, calling themselves the Advanced Display Manufacturers of America, alleged that Japanese manufacturers were selling "active matrix" displays to U.S. computer manufacturers at unfairly low prices.

After investigating the allegations, the Commerce Department, in July 1991, found that foreign producers were dumping, that is, selling active matrix displays at a price far below market value in the United States. Commerce imposed a 63 percent tariff to crack down on the Japanese display makers. Although the tariff appeared to be a boon to the seven small American manufacturers hoping to compete with Japanese competitors, several large American computer manufacturers were upset because they believed prices for the displays would go up.

In August 1991, the U.S. International Trade Commission (I.T.C.) investigated the case to determine whether U.S. firms had been injured by the dumping. The I.T.C. ruled that U.S. industry had been materially injured by the low-priced Japanese imports. Excerpts from the hearings of the International Trade Commission appear at the end of this case.

ACTIVE MATRIX DISPLAYS

Active matrix liquid crystal displays provide sharper pictures and faster image changes than the passive liquid crystal displays that are more commonly used in laptop computers. Active displays use an electronic transistor to control each dot on the screen, whereas passive displays use a grid of wires. In the near future, the active matrix displays are destined to be crucial in aircraft cockpits, automobile dashboards, wall-sized "high-definition" television, advanced laptop computers, and potentially almost anywhere that information is electronically displayed.

Many industry experts see the new technology as a key to sustaining a healthy domestic electronics industry. "We have to do something," said Lewis Branscomb, director of the Harvard University technology policy program and the former chief scientist of IBM. "From a future trend point of view [the technology] is very important."

Considerable efforts are underway to improve and apply this emerging technology. IBM has formed a partnership with Toshiba Corp. to develop and make advanced displays in Japan. Many American universities as well as the military are also investing in the new technology. Eight major Japanese companies expect to spend about $2 billion over the next few years, in addition to participating in a cooperative research project that involves the Japanese government and 18 companies.

A U.S. Company, RCA Corp., invented the thin screen display in the 1960s using liquid crystals as an alternative to the bulky cathode ray tubes found in conventional dis-

Source: This case was written by Mitchell J. Peyser under the supervision of Michael R. Czinkota and is based on the following articles: T. R. Reid, "In Display-Screen Case, 'Fair Trade' Policy Does Americans a Disservice," *Washington Post,* June 24, 1991, WB 18; Andrew Pollack, "Duties Sought from Japan on Some Computer Screens," *New York Times,* July 9, 1991, D1; Evelyn Richards, "A Little Guy's Fight to Regain a U.S. Edge," *Washington Post,* August 4, 1991, H1; David E. Sanger, "I.B.M. Chief Issues Threat on U.S. Tariff," *New York Times,* November 8, 1991.

plays. But firms in the Far East honed the technologies and invested the large sums needed to mass produce the screens. Sharp Corp. and Hosiden Corp. have led the Japanese effort to refine active matrix technology.

U.S. PRODUCTION

As of July 1991, only one American firm, OIS Optical Imaging Systems, Inc., of Troy, Michigan, manufactured and sold the displays, mostly to the military. OIS pursued a major contract to make the displays for Apple Computer. In 1989, Apple awarded the contract to Hosiden Corporation, a Japanese supplier of the active matrix displays. OIS President, Zvi Yaniv, immediately suspected dumping. Yaniv banded together with six American firms that did not yet manufacture the displays on a commercial basis but were hoping to enter the market. The group, the Advanced Display Manufacturers of America, filed their claim with the Department of Commerce.

THE MANUFACTURER'S PERSPECTIVE

The Hosiden Corporation had been selling the active matrix screens in the United States at 63 percent below the production cost of domestic producers. Therefore, the Commerce Department imposed a 63 percent duty, which was designed to provide a substantial boost to domestic manufacturers capable of producing the displays. Such a boost was necessary to help the ailing domestic producers. For example, before the ruling, OIS had experienced yearly losses ranging from $2 to $9 million and had been struggling to stay in the business. The decline in U.S. military expenditures further threatened sales potential.

With the boost of the tariff, OIS hoped to make the difficult transition from the military market to the commercial market. The transition is a major one, since military orders are usually much smaller and offer higher prices than the commercial market. However, the commercial market offers a larger potential market. And with the duty to help keep prices up, other domestic firms plan to enter the market.

THE BUYER'S PERSPECTIVE

However, some major U.S. computer manufacturers were not so happy with the Commerce Department action. "We're deeply disappointed," said a spokesman for IBM. "It has the impact of increasing the cost of computers made in the U.S." The duty requires American computer companies such as IBM, Apple Computer Inc., Compaq Computer Corp., and Zenith Electronics Corp. to pay higher prices for the small computer display units they buy. Speaking in Tokyo on November 7, 1991, IBM Chairman John F. Akers said that the company might be forced to move production of some of its smallest machines out of the United States to avoid the tariff charges.

Apple Chairman John Sculley said, "The people who have lobbied Washington for protection have really misled the government people into believing they are a credible alternative. In a recession, the international market is the place computer companies are making their money. It's hard to compete if you're paying more than the other guy for displays." In fact, soon after the tariff was imposed, Apple Computer and the Toshiba Corporation had already begun to move their production of portable machines out of the United States. Computer systems that already contain the screens can be shipped to the United States without the tariff.

Excerpts from the meeting of the U.S. International Trade Commission, Washington, D.C., August 15, 1991

Commissioner Rohr: Ms. Baker, many of the U.S. companies manufacturing flat panel displays are in the so-called developmental stage. What kind of industry performance could one expect from companies at this stage?

Ms. Baker: When an industry or company is in the developmental stage, we should recognize the product is still being brought on stream. Therefore, when we are looking at industry indicators, such as production, shipments, and employment, it is to be expected that increases might be seen in those indicators, which was characteristic of this industry.

However, another industry performance, or industry indicator of performance, financial experience, was poor.

Commissioner Rohr: Can you characterize for me the overall performance of U.S. companies making flat panel displays, including your financial investigation of financial condition?

Ms. Baker: The overall condition shows expansions in production and shipments. However, the financial experience of companies is negative.

Mr. Stewart (office of investigations): The overall financial performance of the flat panel displays industry is poor. Sales are increasing. However, operating losses are very high. And these losses are compounded by the companies' difficulty in obtaining financing to start or increase production or to produce at a level to become profitable.

Commissioner Rohr: Thank you, very much. Ms. Baker, what has happened to U.S. imports of the subject merchandise during the period of investigation?

Ms. Baker: Commissioner Rohr, subject imports of active matrix LCDs and EL displays combined from Japan increased substantially in both 1989 and 1990. Market share of subject import also increased. Trends of subject imports, active matrix LCDs, and EL displays, separately, however, are confidential.

Commissioner Rohr: Thank you. Does the record show that price, that is, target prices, has a role in the decision to source from a particular supplier?

Ms. Baker: Yes, sir. The record does seem to indicate that price does have a role in the decision to source from specific suppliers. Although there are other considerations, most specifically the technical requirements of the end-user, prices also seem to have a role.

Commissioner Rohr: Thank you.

Mr. Workman, this is for you. What did our investigation discover concerning lost sales, underselling, price depression, and suppression?

Mr. Workman (office of investigations): Well, evaluation of price trends was made difficult by the fact that these are often very complex and individualized products. Nonetheless, we did get ten price series from various producers and importers. There were a couple of domestic series where the product seemed to be pretty consistent from one quarter to the next. And for the three-year period, from early 1988 on down through, it did show evidence of declining prices.

In the case of the other products, both domestic and Japanese, the series were very, very difficult to evaluate because of shifting product mix even within the category groupings that we had.

In the case of underselling, again, we had a problem in terms of our product groupings, not knowing exactly whether the products were the same or not. But in the one comparison we were able to make, it did show the Japanese—this was for the producers' and importers' questionnaire—it did show that the Japanese price was in fact lower. And there was some evidence from purchasers' questionnaires that similarly seemed to point to a somewhat lower price for imports. But this was not true in all cases.

In the lost sales, again, in discussions with purchasers, and evaluating lost sales, this was a very complex process because as has been described, the process of purchasing these flat panel displays is often driven by technology—very much so, in fact, perhaps redundantly. Yet, we did find one instance where the case of a sale lost because the import was priced lower than the domestic product.

And similarly, we found one instance of lost revenue, where the imports were available, and the purchaser was able to bid down the domestic price somewhat, as a result of these lower-priced imports.

Commissioner Lodwick: Mr. Bardos, does the statute authorize the International Trade Commission to consider U.S. consumer interests in making its less than fair value decisions? And if it does, how?

Mr. Bardos (office of the General Counsel): The statute does not direct the commission to consider U.S. consumer interests.

Chairman Brunsdale: Mr. Workman, can you summarize how major customers of active matrix flat panel displays responded to the lost sales and lost revenue allegations?

Mr. Workman: We found a couple of instances where there were lost sales or lost revenue allegations with respect to these active matrix displays. In one case, the purchaser didn't seem to feel at all that the domestic producer was capable of supplying what they needed. So, that transaction went absolutely nowhere. And in the second case, the domestic producer had actually made a prototype sale. Its price was very high, compared to the imports. But the purchaser indicated that they felt that the main problem here was that the domestic firm would not be able to supply the amount of active matrix displays that they would need for their use. And this seemed to drive their decision to switch to the imports much more than any price consideration.

Chairman Brunsdale: We are now ready for the vote in this case. Mr. Secretary, will you please call the roll in investigation 731-TA-469 (Final) involving HIC Flat Panel Displays from Japan?

Secretary Mason: Commissioner Newquist?

Commissioner Newquist: I vote in the affirmative.

Secretary Mason: Commissioner Brunsdale.

Chairman Brunsdale: I have a short statement to read in connection with my vote.

The commission has to decide in this case whether the domestic industry producing flat panel displays is materially injured, threatened with material injury, or materially retarded by reason of the dumped imports from Japan.

This case has attracted much attention and has also been discussed in the popular press as another area where Japanese firms are beating U.S. firms in a high-tech field and where competition from Japan may put U.S. firms out of business, unless the government steps in.

We at the commission cannot be swayed, and are not swayed, by the popular misconception that dumping laws are designed to bolster U.S. industries that face intense competition from abroad. An affirmative determination must be made on evidence that dumped imports cause material injury or material retardation. We cannot ask the question, would U.S. firms be better off if there were no Japanese flat panel display industry at all.

In this case, the evidence is overwhelming that the U.S. industry producing active matrix flat panel displays, used primarily in small portable computers, is not materially retarded by reason of dumped imports of flat panel displays from Japan. In the course of this investigation, major purchasers offered testimony and documentation indicating that they would not have purchased active matrix flat panel displays from U.S. producers for many reasons that had nothing to do with price.

In addition, given their relatively small market share and the low dumping margin found by the Department of Commerce, I find that the U.S. industry producing electro-luminescence flat panel displays, which are used primarily in medical and control equipment, is not materially injured by reason of the dumped imports.

I will, of course, provide a complete explanation of my decisions in my written opinion. Thank you.

Secretary Mason: Commissioner Rohr.

Commissioner Rohr: The staff and the commission have worked very hard and long to get to this critical day. We have studied hundreds of pages of submissions and testimony: we created a 300-page staff report which distills this information. We have examined under a microscope a small but critical high-technology industry and then tried to understand what relationship its situation has to dumping and to the dumping law.

After many hours of study and discussion, I have come to the conclusion that the U.S. flat panel display industry is injured and there is a relationship between the dumped imports of flat panel displays and that injury. My analysis of the dynamics of the flat panel display industry leads me to believe that, while there are differences between technologies, there are enough similarities to warrant a finding of one like product consisting of all flat panel displays and that, while price may not be the single most essential factor in the decision to purchase a particular flat panel display, it is nonetheless a very important one.

The industry is made up of small companies, a number of which are still in the developmental stage. In the presence of rapidly growing dumping imports, these companies have suffered substantial negative cash flows from operations and have found themselves unable to fund research and secure the necessary physical plant to become large-scale producers.

I have heard flat panel displays characterized as the invention that got away, meaning that U.S. firms failed to turn the technology into a marketable product. But there are a few of these firms still struggling to do just that. And as they are unable to meet Japanese prices, we have seen evidence of lost sales, price suppression and depression, and certainly the inability to sustain adequate profits even in the small market niches they now occupy.

Even should this industry achieve an affirmative commission finding, I must caution that no one should view this determination as a guarantee for success in the marketplace. A commission finding will not ensure appropriate capital backing, R&D success, product innovation, manufacturing capability, or long-term viability. The anti-dumping law has no place in that realm. Only business savvy, hard work, imagination, and good fortune will do that.

Some have said that this case represents a manipulation and abuse of the anti-dumping law. Nonsense. Utter nonsense. To some extent, every industry that comes before us attempts to mold the law to the facts of the case it is trying to make. We expect that. Clearly, dumping is not the major problem this industry faces. But that is not the determination the law asks us to make. Rather, we must determine whether the dumping already found by the Commerce Department is a cause of material injury to the domestic industry.

And I am compelled to determine that it is. Whether the domestic industry can change potential investors' strategies to their benefit, whether they can develop the breakthrough to achieve color, whether they can advance to produce products even beyond that is well beyond our ability to influence. The anti-dumping law can only attempt to mitigate the effects of injurious dumping—no more, no less.

I therefore make an affirmative determination.

Secretary Mason: Commissioner Lodwick.

Commissioner Lodwick: Today the International Trade Commission makes a final determination in investigation number 731-TA-469, High Information Content Flat Display Panels, and Subassemblies Thereof, from Japan.

The subject imports are active matrix liquid crystal and electroluminescent high information content flat panel displays and display glass. Therefore I find that there is one domestic product like these imports, namely high information content flat panel displays and display glass. I find that the U.S. industry has been materially injured by reason of the LTFV imports from Japan.

Factors that are important in my finding include (1) the ability of the United States HIC flat panel displays industry to raise capital and invest; (2) the existing production and development efforts of the domestic industry; and (3) the rapid increase in subject imports. My complete views will be available at the conclusion of this investigation.

Secretary Mason: Madam Chairman, by a vote of three to one, we have an affirmative determination.

Chairman Brunsdale: Thank you, Mr. Secretary. Thank you very much, staff, for your particularly fine efforts in this case.

Questions for Discussion

1. How can anti-dumping duties be used to protect domestic manufacturers?

2. How can anti-dumping laws hurt consumers?

3. Evaluate the decision by the International Trade Commission.

4. Did the United States intercede on behalf of seven small companies at the expense of computer makers and their employees?

5. How important is the role of domestic consumers for I.T.C. findings?

6. What does this case say about America's ability to compete?

One Afternoon at the United States International Trade Commission

....

Chairwoman Stern: We turn now to investigation TA-201-55 regarding nonrubber footwear. Staff has assembled. Are there any questions? Vice Chairman Liebeler has a question. Please proceed.

Vice Chairman Liebeler: My questions are for the Office of Economics, Mr. Benedick. Do foreign countries have a comparative advantage in producing footwear?

Mr. Benedick: Yes, foreign producers generally have a comparative advantage vis-à-vis the domestic producers in producing footwear. Footwear production generally involves labor-intensive processes which favor the low-wage countries such as Taiwan, Korea, and Brazil, which are the three largest foreign suppliers by volume. For instance, the hourly rate for foreign footwear workers in these countries ranges from about one-twelfth to one-fourth of the rate for U.S. footwear workers.

Vice Chairman Liebeler: Is it likely that this comparative advantage will shift in favor of the domestic industries over the next several years?

Mr. Benedick: It is not very likely. There seems to be little evidence that supports this. The domestic industry's generally poor productivity performance over the last several years, which includes the period 1977 to 1981, roughly corresponding to the period of OMAs (Orderly Marketing Arrangements) for Taiwan and Korea, suggests that U.S. producers must significantly increase their modernization efforts to reduce the competitive advantage of the imported footwear.

Vice Chairman Liebeler: Have you calculated the benefits and costs of import relief using various assumptions about the responsiveness of supply and demand to changes in price?

Mr. Benedick: Yes. On the benefit side, we estimated benefits of import restrictions to U.S. producers, which included both increased domestic production and higher domestic prices. We also estimated the terms of trade benefits resulting from import restrictions. These latter benefits result from an appreciation of the U.S. dollar as a result of the import restrictions.

On the cost side, we estimated cost to consumers of the increase in average prices on total footwear purchases under the import restrictions and the consumer costs associated with the drop in total consumption due to the higher prices.

Vice Chairman Liebeler: In your work, did you take into account any retaliation by our trading partners?

Mr. Benedick: No.

Vice Chairman Liebeler: What was the 1984 level of imports?

Mr. Benedick: In 1984, imports of nonrubber footwear were approximately 726 million pairs.

Vice Chairman Liebeler: If a six-hundred-million-pair quota were imposed, what would the effect on price of domestic and foreign shoes be, and what would the market share of imports be?

Mr. Benedick: At your request, the Office of Economics estimated the effects of the six-hundred-million-pair quota. We estimate that prices of domestic footwear would

---

Source: Excerpts from the *Official Transcript Proceedings before the U.S. International Trade Commission,* meeting of the commission, June 12, 1985, Washington, D.C.

increase by about 11 percent and prices of imported footwear would increase by about 19 percent.

The import share, however, would drop to about 59 percent of the market in the first year of the quota.

Vice Chairman Liebeler: What would aggregate cost to consumers be of that kind of quota?

Mr. Benedick: Total consumer cost would approach 1.3 billion dollars in each year of such a quota.

Vice Chairman Liebeler: What would be the benefit to the domestic industry of this quota?

Mr. Benedick: Domestic footwear production would increase from about 299 million pairs for 1984 to about 367 million pairs, or by about 23 percent. Domestic sales would increase from about $3.8 billion to about $5.2 billion, an increase of about 37 percent.

Vice Chairman Liebeler: How many jobs would be saved?

Mr. Benedick: As a result of this quota, domestic employment would rise by about 26,000 workers over the 1984 level.

Vice Chairman Liebeler: What is the average paid to those workers?

Mr. Benedick: Based on questionnaire responses, each worker would earn approximately $11,900 per year in wages and another $2,100 in fringe benefits, for a total of about $14,000 per year.

Vice Chairman Liebeler: So what then would be the cost to consumers of each of these $14,000-a-year jobs?

Mr. Benedick: It would cost consumers approximately $49,800 annually for each of these jobs.

Vice Chairman Liebeler: Thank you very much, Mr. Benedick.

Commissioner Eckes: I have a question for the General Counsel's Representative. I heard an interesting phrase a few moments ago, "comparative advantage." I don't recall seeing that phrase in Section 201. Could you tell me whether it is there and whether it is defined?

Ms. Jacobs: It is not.

Chairwoman Stern: I would like to ask about cost/benefit analysis. Perhaps the General Counsel's Office again might be the best place to direct this question. It is my understanding that the purpose of Section 201 is to determine whether a domestic industry is being injured, the requisite level for requisite reasons, imports being at least as important a cause of the serious injury as any other cause, and then to recommend a remedy which we are given kind of a short menu to select from to remedy the industry's serious injury.

Are we to take into account the impact on the consumer?

Are we to do a cost/benefit analysis when coming up with the remedy which best relieves the domestic industry's serious injury?

Ms. Jacobs: As the law currently stands, it is the responsibility of the commission to determine that relief which is a duty or import restriction which is necessary to prevent or remedy the injury that the commission has determined to exist. The president is to weigh such considerations as consumer impact, etc. The commission is not necessarily responsible for doing that. Of course, the commission may want to realize that, knowing the president is going to consider those factors, they might want to also consider them, but in fact, that is not the responsibility of the commission. It is the responsibility of the commission only to determine that relief which is necessary to remedy the injury they have found.

Chairwoman Stern: I can understand our reporting to the president other materials which aren't part of our consideration but nevertheless necessary for the president in his consideration, but having that information and providing it to the president is different from its being part of the commission's consideration in its recommendations.

Ms. Jacobs: That's right. Your roles are quite different in that respect.

Vice Chairman Liebeler: Nations will and should specialize in production of those commodities in which they have a comparative advantage. Fortunately, our country has a large capital stock which tends to provide labor with many productive employments. Our comparative advantage is in the production of goods that use a high ratio of capital to labor. Shoes, however, are produced with a low ratio of capital to labor.

Therefore, American footwear cannot be produced as cheaply as foreign footwear. The availability of inexpensive imports permits consumers to purchase less expensive shoes and it allows the valuable capital and labor used in this footwear industry to shift to more productive pursuits.

This situation is not unique to the footwear industry. The classic example is agriculture, where the share of the labor force engaged in farming declined from 50 percent to 3 percent over the last 100 years. This shift did not produce a 47 percent unemployment rate. It freed that labor to produce cars, housing, and computers.

The decline of the American footwear industry is part of this dynamic process. This process is sometimes very painful. Congress, by only providing for temporary relief, has recognized that our continued prosperity depends on our willingness to accept such adjustments.

The industry has sought this so-called temporary import relief before. The ITC has conducted approximately 170 investigations relating to this industry. This is the fourth footwear case under Section 201, and so far the industry has gotten relief twice. The 1975 petition resulted in adjustment assistance. The 1976 case resulted in orderly marketing agreements with Taiwan and Korea.

In spite of the efforts of the domestic industry to suppress imports, the industry has been shrinking. Between 1981 and 1984, 207 plants closed; 94 of these closings occurred just last year. The closing of unprofitable plants is a necessary adjustment. Import relief at this stage will retard this process and encourage entry into a dying industry.

Because there is no temporary trade restriction that would facilitate the industry's adjustment to foreign competition, I cannot recommend any import barrier.

Chairwoman Stern: The intent of the General Import Relief law is to allow a seriously injured industry to adjust to global competition. The commission must devise a remedy which corresponds to the industry and the market forces it must face.

No other manufacturing sector of our economy faces stiffer competition from abroad than the U.S. shoe industry. Imports have captured three-fourths of our market. No relief program can change the basic conditions of competition that this industry must ultimately face on its own. The best that we as a commission can do—and under Section 201 that the president can do—is to give the industry a short, predictable period of relief to allow both large and small firms to adjust, coexist, and hopefully prosper.

I am proposing to the president an overall quota on imports of 474 million pairs of shoes in the first year. Shoes with a customs value below $2.50 would not be subject to this quota. The relief would extend for a full five years.

Commissioner Lodwick: Section 201 is designed to afford the domestic industry a temporary respite in order to assist it making an orderly adjustment to import competition. The fact that the law limits import relief to an initial period of up to five years, to be phased down after three years to the extent feasible, indicates that Congress did not intend domestic producers to find permanent shelter from import competition under the statute.

Accordingly, I intend to recommend to the president a five-year quota plan which affords the domestic nonrubber footwear industry ample opportunity to implement feasible adjustment plans which will facilitate, as the case may be, either the orderly transfer of resources to alternative uses or adjustments to new conditions of competition.

Commissioner Rohr: In making my recommendation, I emphasize the two responsibilities which are placed on the commission by statute. First, it must provide a remedy which it believes will effectively remedy the injury which is found to exist.

Secondly, Congress has stated that we, as commissioners, should attempt, to the extent possible, to develop a remedy that can be recommended to the president by a majority of the commission. I have taken seriously my obligation to attempt to fashion a remedy with which at least a majority of my colleagues can agree. Such remedy is a compromise.

I am concurring in the remedy proposal which is being presented today by a majority of the commission. This majority recommendation provides for an overall limit on imports of 474 million pairs; an exclusion from such limitation of shoes entering the United States with a value of less than $2.50 per pair; a growth in such limitation over a five-year period of 0 percent, 3 percent, and 9 percent; and the sale of import licenses through an auctioning system.

Commissioner Eckes: It is my understanding that a majority of the commission has agreed on these points. I subscribe to that and will provide a complete description of my views in my report to the president.

Questions for Discussion

1. What are your views of the ITC recommendation?

2. Should the principle of comparative advantage always dictate trade flows?

3. Why are the consumer costs of quotas so often neglected?

4. Discuss alternative solutions to the job displacement problem.

5. How would you structure a "temporary relief program"?

Promoting U.S. Tobacco Exports:
A Conflict between Trade and Health

Tobacco and its related products have traditionally played an important role in the U.S. economy. Tobacco represents the sixth-largest cash crop in the United States. Twenty-one states and more than two million people are engaged in tobacco growing, manufacturing, and marketing.

On January 11, 1964, the *Surgeon General's Report* documented the adverse health effects of smoking. Since then, the Surgeon General and other medical experts have determined that smoking may cause lung cancer and low birth weights, as well as other health problems. Concurrent with these findings, U.S. cigarette consumption, as well as other forms of tobacco use, has been gradually decreasing. Although health considerations definitely played an important role in discouraging smoking, other factors such as higher cigarette prices, steeper federal and local taxes, and governmental restrictions on where smoking is permitted also contributed to the decline in U.S. cigarette consumption.

Although the use of tobacco products is no longer as socially acceptable as it used to be, tobacco use is still tolerated and even welcomed by the government as a source of tax revenues. Apart from the desire to discourage smoking, a major rationale behind raising taxes on tobacco products continues to be the positive revenue impact for the government. Even though many people have quit smoking, about 550 billion cigarettes were consumed in the United States in 1989. With a 16-cent federal excise tax per pack, the amount of taxes collected is very meaningful to a deficit-constrained budget process.

THE IMPORTANCE OF EXPORTS
FOR U.S. TOBACCO COMPANIES

In the face of higher domestic taxes, greater governmental restrictions on smoking in public places, and the growing unpopularity of tobacco use, U.S. tobacco companies are vigorously promoting cigarette exports overseas in order to compensate for their diminishing domestic market. Due to the high quality of American tobacco and the determination of U.S. tobacco companies to sell their products overseas, U.S. tobacco firms have been increasing their export shipments steadily since 1985.

The chief lobbyist for the tobacco industry, the United States Cigarette Export Association (USCEA), claims that the export of tobacco is beneficial to the U.S. economy. It contributes substantially to the lowering of the country's enormous trade deficit, and it generates hundreds of thousands of jobs for Americans. According to U.S. Department of Commerce statistics, U.S. net exports of unmanufactured tobacco in the first half of

Source: This case was written by Michael R. Czinkota with the assistance of Homer Teng, using the following background material: United States General Accounting Office, "Trade and Health Issues: Dichotomy between U.S. Tobacco Export Policy and Antismoking Initiatives," May 1990; Andrew Copenhaver, Statement on behalf of the United States Cigarette Export Association before the Subcommittee on Health and the Environment Committee on Energy and Commerce, United States House of Representatives, May 17, 1990.

1990 amounted to $362.9 million. During the same period, the trade surplus in cigarettes amounted to $2,021.3 million. More than 125,000 people were directly involved in tobacco exports in 1989, and many others were employed in the derivative areas of the tobacco industry.

U.S. TRADE POLICY

This recent boom in U.S. exports is the direct result of the opening of new overseas markets in Asia to American tobacco products. The opening was achieved due to the success of the United States Trade Representative (USTR) in negotiating the elimination of unfair trade barriers in Asia. The USTR is the governmental organization charged with the promotion of U.S. trade interests abroad. In the name of free trade, the USTR acts on behalf of U.S. companies in negotiating for the removal of unfair trade barriers and any discriminatory trade practices directed against U.S. products. Under Section 301 of the Trade Act of 1974, the United States Trade Representative is obligated to investigate cases of trade discrimination faced by U.S. companies abroad.

Throughout the 1980s, the USCEA filed several petitions under Section 301 of the Trade Act of 1974 aimed at removing unfair foreign trade barriers in Japan, South Korea, Taiwan, and Thailand, which restricted the export of American tobacco products. U.S. cigarette exporters had long been experiencing trade discrimination in these potentially lucrative Asian countries. In Thailand, for instance, over 60 percent of the adult male population smokes. According to figures from the mid-1980s, approximately 40 percent of the people of both Japan and South Korea smoke. The governments of these countries had restricted the sale of foreign tobacco products because tobacco production and manufacturing play a significant part in their national economies. For example, Japan and Taiwan are ranked 18th and 26th in terms of tobacco production, respectively, out of a total of 94 tobacco-growing countries worldwide. The estimated green-weight tobacco production figures are 71,000 tons for Japan and 20,100 tons for Taiwan.

Realizing the importance of tobacco to their agricultural sector and to their financial coffers, the governments of the aforementioned countries had set up monopolies to protect their tobacco industries from foreign competition. The following statement in the 1989 annual report of the Thailand Tobacco Monopoly (TTM) illustrates clearly the function of such a government-controlled monopoly:

> The outcome of operation of TTM not only creates income to the government to be used to develop the country, but also benefits many tobacco ranchers in the northern and northeastern regions whose major income is derived from tobacco plantations.

Japan, Taiwan, South Korea, and Thailand traditionally blocked the import of American cigarettes by imposing high import tariffs, discriminatory taxes, and unfair marketing and distribution restrictions. These trade practices caused outrage among the U.S. tobacco companies and led to the intervention of the USTR. The following are examples of USTR successes in opening the previously closed tobacco markets.

Following the discovery of evidence that Japan imposed high tariffs and severe restrictions on the import and manufacturing of foreign cigarettes, the president of the United States instructed the USTR to initiate a Section 301 action against the country on September 16, 1985. This led Japan to remove cigarette tariffs, as well as other discriminatory barriers directed against imported cigarettes. Similarly, on December 12, 1986, Taiwan lifted its restrictions on the distribution and sale of U.S. tobacco products following the threat of retaliatory measures from the United States. After prolonged negotiations with the USTR, the South Korean Monopoly Corporation, the government tobacco monopoly in that country, agreed to allow U.S. cigarettes to enter the Korean market without discrimination on February 16, 1988.

PROMOTION OF TOBACCO EXPORTS

Besides ensuring fair treatment for U.S. cigarettes overseas, the U.S. government actively supports the export of tobacco by funding three export promotion programs. These are the Department of Agriculture's Cooperator Market Development Program, the Targeted Export Assistance Program, and the Export Credit Guarantee programs.

The Department of Agriculture's cooperator program aims at expanding and seeking overseas markets for U.S. agricultural products through the efforts of private, nonprofit organizations. The Department of Agriculture allocates $150,000 to Tobacco Associates, the tobacco cooperator, to promote market development activities for U.S. tobacco products.

The Targeted Export Assistance Program's purpose is to counteract the adverse effects of subsidies, import quotas, or other unfair trade practices in foreign countries on U.S. agricultural products. Again, Tobacco Associates is the private organization entrusted to carry out this endeavor. In 1990, Tobacco Associates received $5 million in U.S. government funding to provide certain countries with the technical know-how, training, and equipment to manufacture cigarettes that use U.S. flue-cured and burley tobacco products.

Finally, the Department of Agriculture's Export Credit Guarantee programs, GSM 102 and 103, help U.S. farm export sales by stimulating U.S. bank financing of foreign purchases on credit terms. The GSM 102 program guarantees the repayment of loans extended up to three years, while the GSM 103 program guarantees loans of up to ten years. During the period between October 1985 and September 1989, 66 companies received GSM guarantee credits for the sale of 127 million pounds of tobacco, which had a market value of $214 million.

CONFLICTING OBJECTIVES

The involvement of the U.S. government in furthering the export of tobacco has generated controversy within the United States. This controversy centers on the dilemma of simultaneously pursuing policies that are obviously at odds with each other.

On one hand, the U.S. government, spearheaded by the Department of Health and Human Services, has been actively discouraging smoking on the domestic scene. Also, the United States is a strong supporter of the worldwide antismoking movement. The Department of Health and Human Services serves as a collaborating headquarters for the United Nations World Health Organization and maintains close relationships with other health organizations around the world in sharing information on the detrimental health effects of smoking. On the other hand, a different part of the government, the USTR, has been helping tobacco companies expand their export sales by opening up previously closed markets. In addition, the government is actively promoting tobacco exports overseas by funding three export market development programs. The U.S. trade policy that aims to boost the exports of tobacco products is clearly in conflict with the U.S. health policy aimed at reducing the use of tobacco.

THE CURRENT SITUATION

U.S. production of tobacco has risen in the last four years because of an increase in foreign demand for high-quality U.S. tobacco leaves. The Tobacco Merchants Association concluded in a 1989 report:

> As U.S. cigarette exports gain an even greater foothold in Asia, one would expect that the foreign monopoly demand for direct burley shipments, along with high-quality U.S. flue-cured, will grow as the monopolies compete head-to-head against U.S. cigarette blends.

These economic benefits, together with the fact that Asian countries such as Japan and Thailand are permitting tobacco advertisements, has led many members of Congress, such as Rep. Thomas J. Bliley of Virginia, to support U.S. tobacco exports. However, the health and moral questions surrounding tobacco exports continue to generate congressional and public opposition to tobacco exports. A vocal opponent of tobacco exports is Rep. Henry A. Waxman, who considers U.S. tobacco export policies morally offensive and comparable to the British exports of opium to China in the 19th century.

Questions for Discussion

1. Should U.S. exports of tobacco products be permitted in light of the domestic campaign against smoking?
2. Should the U.S. government get involved in tearing down foreign trade barriers to U.S. tobacco?
3. Should export promotion support be provided to U.S. tobacco producers?
4. To what degree should ethics influence government policy or corporate decision making in the case of tobacco exports?
5. Will your answers change if you differentiate between the short and the long term?

Sold But Not Delivered

Liquidity City had some outdated production equipment which Country Y wanted to purchase. Country Y told Liquidity City that the equipment would be used to advance its commercial communications. Under the terms of the contract, Liquidity City had the obligation to obtain the export license. Country Y was responsible for packing and shipping the equipment, with Country Y taking title of the equipment at Liquidity City's factory. Liquidity City was to be paid upon installation of the equipment in Country Y. Upon signing the contract, Liquidity City went to the Department of Commerce and formally applied for an export license, giving all the proper information concerning end-user and end use. The Commerce Department, after a 90-day review, returned the application without action, stating that the equipment involved was *General Destination*. (The U.S. Department of Commerce classifies commodities according to the levels of technical sophistication. *General Destination* is the lowest category available: i.e., items are not controlled except for proliferation concerns.)

Six months later, after Liquidity City had completed training of Country Y's personnel in the operation of the equipment, Country Y took title to the equipment, and had it packed and delivered to the dock for sea shipment the next day. That afternoon, Liquidity City received a telephone call from the Commerce Department advising that the Commerce Department, in accordance with the *Enhanced Proliferation Controls Initiative (EPCI)*, was providing Liquidity City with a *reason to know* letter. The *reason to know* letter stated that the U.S. government had reason to believe that the ultimate use of the equipment may be related to a nuclear, missile, biological, or chemical warfare program. Under such a situation, all exports require an individually validated license (IVL), even if the equipment involved does not normally require an export license for that destination. Liquidity City applied (again) for an export license. After multiple meetings with Commerce Department officials, that license was denied.

The equipment is sitting in a warehouse today. Title is held by Country Y. Liquidity City has not been paid for it. It is unlikely that another buyer for the equipment can be found. The contract between Liquidity City and Country Y calls for arbitration in a neutral third country to settle disputes. Country Y and Liquidity City would rather settle their disputes in a more amiable fashion.

Questions for Discussion

1. How would you settle this dispute?

2. Can a company protect itself against actions of government?

3. Should a government impose controls such as EPCI?

4. Why are international contracts often subject to arbitration?

5. If you were sitting on the arbitration panel, what would your decision be? (Bear in mind that the training and the technical know-how have already been effectively transferred.)

6. What changes would you have made in the sales agreement to provide for such a situation?

Source: This case was written by David W. Danjczek, vice president, Government and International Affairs, Western Atlas.

IKEA in the USA

IKEA, the world's largest home furnishings retail chain, was founded in Sweden in 1943 as a mail-order company and opened its first showroom ten years later. From its headquarters in Almhult, IKEA has since expanded to worldwide sales of $4 billion from 108 outlets in 24 countries (see Table 1). In fact, the second store that IKEA built was in Oslo, Norway. Today, IKEA operates large warehouse showrooms in Sweden, Norway, Denmark, Holland, France, Belgium, Germany, Switzerland, Austria, Canada, the United States, Saudi Arabia, and the United Kingdom. It has smaller stores in Kuwait, Australia, Hong Kong, Singapore, the Canary Islands, and Iceland. A store near Budapest, Hungary, opened in 1990, followed by outlets in Poland and the Czech Republic in 1991 and Slovakia in 1992. Stores are planned for Russia in the next few years.

The international expansion of IKEA has progressed in three phases, all of them continuing at the present time: Scandinavian expansion, begun in 1963; West European expansion, begun in 1973; and North American expansion, begun in 1976. Of the individual markets, Germany is the largest, accounting for 28.7 percent of company sales. The phases of expansion are detectable in the worldwide sales shares depicted in Figure 1. "We want to bring the IKEA concept to as many people as possible," IKEA officials have said. The company estimates that as many as 95 million people visited its showrooms in 1993.

THE IKEA CONCEPT

Ingvar Kamprad, the founder, formulated as IKEA's mission to "offer a wide variety of home furnishings of good design and function at prices so low that the majority of people can afford to buy them." The principal target market of IKEA, which is similar across countries and regions in which IKEA has a presence, is composed of people who are young, highly educated, liberal in their cultural values, white-collar workers, and not especially concerned with status symbols.

IKEA follows a standardized product strategy with an identical assortment around the world. Today, IKEA carries an assortment of thousands of different home furnishings that range from plants to pots, sofas to soup spoons, and wine glasses to wallpaper. The smaller items are carried to complement the bigger ones. IKEA does not have its own manufacturing facilities but designs all of its furniture. The network of subcontracted manufacturers numbers nearly 1,750 in 53 different countries.

Manufacturers are responsible for shipping the components to large warehouses, for example, to the central one in Almhult. These warehouses then supply the various stores, which are in effect mini-warehouses.

Source: This case, prepared by Ilkka A. Ronkainen, is based on "IKEA's No-Frills Strategy Extends to Management Style," *Business International,* May 18, 1992, 149–150; Bill Saporito, "IKEA's Got 'Em Lining Up," *Fortune,* March 11, 1991, 72; Rita Martenson, "Is Standardization of Marketing Feasible in Culture-Bound Industries? A European Case Study," *International Marketing Review* 4 (Autumn 1987): 7–17; Eleanor Johnson Tracy, "Shopping Swedish Style Comes to the U.S.," *Fortune,* January 27, 1986, 63–67; Mary Krienke, "IKEA—Simple Good Taste," *Stores,* April 1986, 58; Jennifer Lin, "IKEA's U.S. Translation," *Stores,* April 1986, 63; "Furniture Chain Has a Global View," *Advertising Age,* October 26, 1987, 58; Bill Kelley, "The New Wave from Europe," *Sales & Marketing Management,* November 1987, 46–48. Updated information provided directly by IKEA U.S., Inc.

TABLE 1   IKEA's International Expansion

Year	Outlets[a]	Countries[a]	Coworkers[b]	Catalog Circulation[c]	Turnover in Swedish Crowns[d]
1954	1	1	15	285,000	3,000,000
1964	2	2	250	1,200,000	79,000,000
1974	10	5	1,500	13,000,000	616,000,000
1984	66	17	8,300	45,000,000	6,770,000,000
1988	75	19	13,400	50,535,000	14,500,000,000
1990	95	23	16,850	n.a.	19,400,000,000
1992	119	24	23,200	n.a.	24,275,000,000

[a] Stores/countries being opened by July 1994.

[b] 23,200 coworkers are equivalent to 18,500 full-time workers.

[c] 13 languages, 29 editions; exact number no longer made available.

[d] Corresponding to net sales of the IKEA group of companies.

Source: IKEA U.S., Inc.

IKEA consumers have to become "prosumers"—half producers, half consumers—because most products have to be assembled. The final distribution is the customer's responsibility as well. Although IKEA expects its customers to be active participants in the buy-sell process, they are not rigid about it. There is a "moving boundary" between what consumers do for themselves and what IKEA employees will do for them. Consumers save the most by driving to the warehouses themselves, putting the boxes on the trolley, loading them into their cars, driving home, and assembling the furniture. Yet IKEA can arrange to provide these services at an extra charge. For example, IKEA coooperates with car rental companies to offer vans and small trucks at reasonable rates for customers needing delivery service.

Management believes that its designer-to-user relationship contributes to an unusual degree of adaptive fit. By not selling through dealers, the company hears directly from its customers.

FIGURE 1   IKEA's Worldwide Sales Expressed as Percentages of Turnover

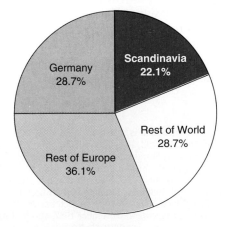

	The IKEA Concept	TABLE 2

Target market:	"Young people of all ages"
Product:	IKEA offers the same products worldwide. The countries of origin of these products are: Scandinavia (45 percent), Western Europe (30 percent), Eastern Europe (15 percent), and others (10 percent). Most items have to be assembled by the customer. The furniture design is modern and light. Textiles and pastels.
Distribution:	IKEA has built its own distribution network. Outlets are outside the city limits of major metropolitan areas. Products are not delivered, but IKEA cooperates with car rental companies that offer small trucks. IKEA offers mail order in Europe and Canada.
Pricing:	The IKEA concept is based on low price. The firm tries to keep its price-image constant.
Promotion:	IKEA's promotional efforts are mainly through its catalogs. IKEA has developed a prototype communications model that must be followed by all stores. Its advertising is attention-getting and provocative. Media choices vary by market.

Although IKEA has concentrated on company-owned, larger-scale outlets, franchising has been used in areas in which the market is relatively small or where uncertainty may exist as to the response to the IKEA concept. These markets include Hong Kong and the United Arab Emirates. IKEA uses mail order in Europe and Canada but has resisted expansion into it in the United States, mainly because of capacity constraints.

IKEA offers prices that are 30 to 50 percent lower than fully assembled competing products. This is a result of large-quantity purchasing, low-cost logistics, store location in suburban areas, and the do-it-yourself approach to marketing. IKEA's prices do vary from market to market, largely because of fluctuations in exchange rates and differences in taxation regimes, but price positioning is kept as standardized as possible.

IKEA's promotion is centered on the catalog. The IKEA catalog is printed in 13 languages and has a worldwide circulation of well over 50 million copies. The catalogs are uniform in layout except for minor regional differences. The company's advertising goal is to generate word-of-mouth publicity through innovative approaches. The IKEA concept is summarized in Table 2.

IKEA IN THE COMPETITIVE ENVIRONMENT

IKEA's strategic positioning is unique. As Figure 2 illustrates, few furniture retailers anywhere have engaged in long-term planning or achieved scale economies in production. European furniture retailers, especially those in Sweden, Switzerland, Germany, and Austria, are much smaller than IKEA. Even when companies have joined forces as buying groups, their heterogeneous operations have made it difficult for them to achieve the same degree of coordination and concentration as IKEA. Because customers are usually content to wait for the delivery of furniture, retailers have not been forced to take purchasing risks.

The value-added dimension differentiates IKEA from its competition. IKEA offers limited customer assistance but creates opportunities for consumers to choose (for example, through informational signage), transport, and assemble units of furniture. The

FIGURE 2   **Competition in Furniture Retailing**

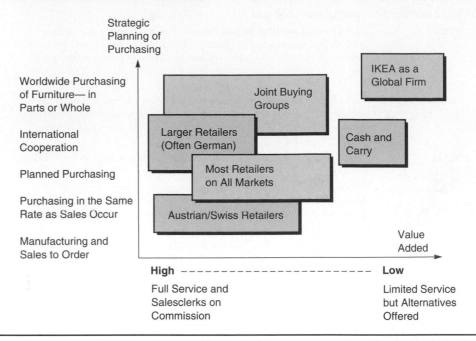

Source: Rita Martenson, "Is Standardization of Marketing Feasible in Culture-Bound Industries? A European Case Study," *International Marketing Review* 4 (Autumn 1987): 14.

best summary of the competitive situation was provided by a manager at another firm: "We can't do what IKEA does, and IKEA doesn't want to do what we do."

IKEA IN THE UNITED STATES

After careful study and assessment of its Canadian experience, IKEA decided to enter the U.S. market in 1985 by establishing outlets on the East Coast and, in 1990, one in Burbank, California. In 1992, a total of 12 stores (6 in the Northeast, 5 in California, and 1 in Texas) generated sales of $337 million. The stores employ 2,300 coworkers. The overwhelming level of success in 1987 led the company to invest in a warehousing facility near Philadelphia that receives goods from Sweden as well as directly from suppliers around the world. Plans call for two to three additional stores annually over the next 25 years, concentrating on the northeastern United States and California.

Questions for Discussion

1. What accounts for IKEA's success with a standardized product and strategy in a business that is usually described as having some of the strongest cultural influences? Consider, for example, that an American buying IKEA beds will also have to buy IKEA sheets because the beds are in European sizes.

2. Which features of the "young people of all ages" are universal and can be exploited by a global/regional strategy?

3. Is IKEA destined to succeed everywhere it cares to establish itself?

GLOBAL COMPARISON MAPS

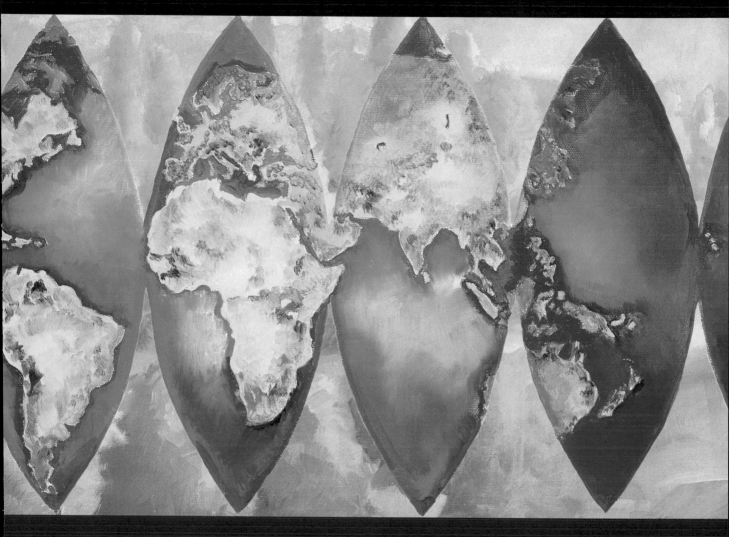

*Every business operation, from the large
multinational corporation to the small entrepreneurial firm,
is affected by the political, economic, and geographical
realities of the world as a whole. The maps in this special section
are intended to give readers a visual appreciation for those realities
as they pursue the study of international marketing.*

Economic Strength

Fifty Billion Dollar Economies

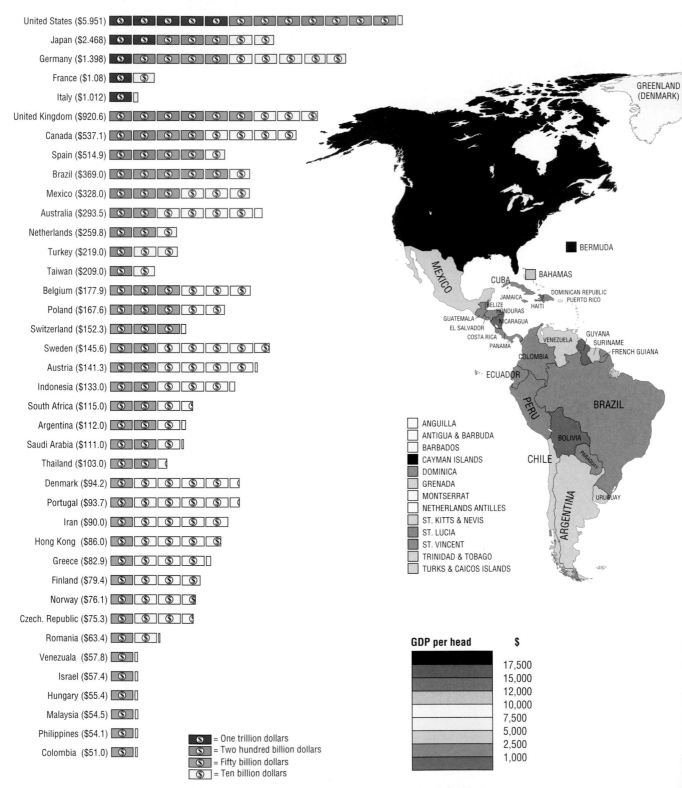

United States ($5.951)
Japan ($2.468)
Germany ($1.398)
France ($1.08)
Italy ($1.012)
United Kingdom ($920.6)
Canada ($537.1)
Spain ($514.9)
Brazil ($369.0)
Mexico ($328.0)
Australia ($293.5)
Netherlands ($259.8)
Turkey ($219.0)
Taiwan ($209.0)
Belgium ($177.9)
Poland ($167.6)
Switzerland ($152.3)
Sweden ($145.6)
Austria ($141.3)
Indonesia ($133.0)
South Africa ($115.0)
Argentina ($112.0)
Saudi Arabia ($111.0)
Thailand ($103.0)
Denmark ($94.2)
Portugal ($93.7)
Iran ($90.0)
Hong Kong ($86.0)
Greece ($82.9)
Finland ($79.4)
Norway ($76.1)
Czech. Republic ($75.3)
Romania ($63.4)
Venezuala ($57.8)
Israel ($57.4)
Hungary ($55.4)
Malaysia ($54.5)
Philippines ($54.1)
Colombia ($51.0)

= One trillion dollars
= Two hundred billion dollars
= Fifty billion dollars
= Ten billion dollars

GREENLAND (DENMARK)

BERMUDA

MEXICO
CUBA
BAHAMAS
JAMAICA
BELIZE
HONDURAS
HAITI
DOMINICAN REPUBLIC
PUERTO RICO
GUATEMALA
EL SALVADOR
NICARAGUA
COSTA RICA
PANAMA
VENEZUELA
GUYANA
SURINAME
FRENCH GUIANA
COLOMBIA
ECUADOR
PERU
BRAZIL
BOLIVIA
PARAGUAY
CHILE
URUGUAY
ARGENTINA

ANGUILLA
ANTIGUA & BARBUDA
BARBADOS
CAYMAN ISLANDS
DOMINICA
GRENADA
MONTSERRAT
NETHERLANDS ANTILLES
ST. KITTS & NEVIS
ST. LUCIA
ST. VINCENT
TRINIDAD & TOBAGO
TURKS & CAICOS ISLANDS

GDP per head	$
	17,500
	15,000
	12,000
	10,000
	7,500
	5,000
	2,500
	1,000

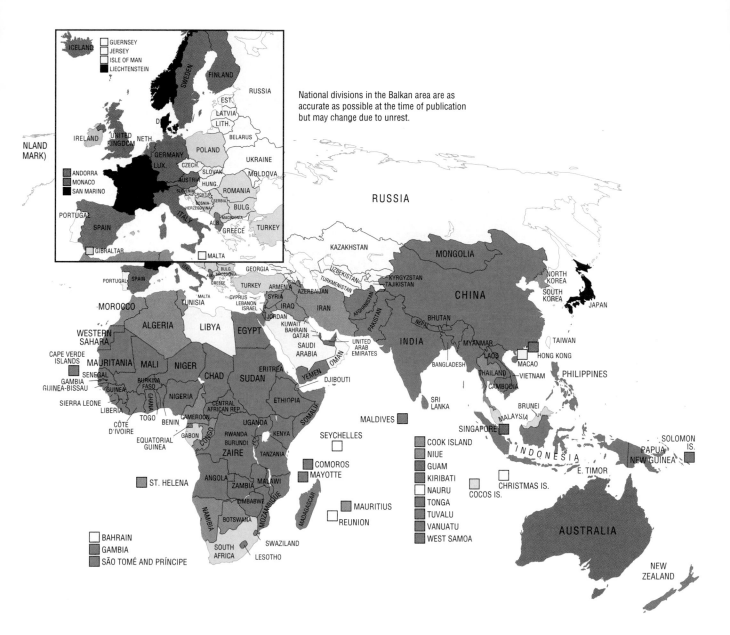

National divisions in the Balkan area are as accurate as possible at the time of publication but may change due to unrest.

Inset map legend:

GUERNSEY
JERSEY
ISLE OF MAN
LIECHTENSTEIN

ANDORRA
MONACO
SAN MARINO

GIBRALTAR
MALTA

Inset map labels:

ICELAND

SWEDEN
FINLAND
RUSSIA

EST.
LATVIA
LITH.
BELARUS

IRELAND
UNITED KINGDOM
NETH.
D

GERMANY
LUX.
POLAND
UKRAINE

CZECH.
SLOVAK.
MOLDOVA

AUSTRIA
HUNG.
ROMANIA

SLOVENIA
CROATIA
BOSNIA HERZEGOVINA
SERBIA
BULG.
MACEDONIA

ITALY
ALB.
GREECE
TURKEY

PORTUGAL
SPAIN

**NLAND
MARK)**

Main map labels:

RUSSIA

PORTUGAL SPAIN
BULG. MACEDONIA
GREECE
ALB.
ITALY
MALTA

MOROCCO
TUNISIA
GEORGIA
ARMENIA AZERBAIJAN
TURKEY
CYPRUS
LEBANON SYRIA
ISRAEL
JORDAN
IRAQ
IRAN

KAZAKHSTAN

UZBEKISTAN
TURKMENISTAN
KYRGYZSTAN
TAJIKISTAN

MONGOLIA

NORTH KOREA
SOUTH KOREA
JAPAN

CHINA

AFGHANISTAN
PAKISTAN
NEPAL
BHUTAN

TAIWAN

HONG KONG
MACAO

WESTERN SAHARA
ALGERIA
LIBYA
EGYPT
KUWAIT
BAHRAIN QATAR
SAUDI ARABIA
UNITED ARAB EMIRATES
OMAN

INDIA
MYANMAR
LAOS
THAILAND
VIETNAM
CAMBODIA
PHILIPPINES

CAPE VERDE ISLANDS
MAURITANIA
MALI
NIGER
CHAD
SUDAN
ERITREA
YEMEN
DJIBOUTI

SENEGAL
GAMBIA
GUINEA-BISSAU
GUINEA
BURKINA FASO
GHANA
NIGERIA
ETHIOPIA

SIERRA LEONE
LIBERIA
CÔTE D'IVOIRE
TOGO
BENIN
CAMEROON
CENTRAL AFRICAN REP.
UGANDA
SOMALIA

BANGLADESH
SRI LANKA

BRUNEI
MALAYSIA
SINGAPORE
INDONESIA
E. TIMOR

PAPUA NEW GUINEA
SOLOMON IS.

MALDIVES

EQUATORIAL GUINEA
GABON
CONGO
ZAIRE
RWANDA
BURUNDI
KENYA
TANZANIA

SEYCHELLES

COOK ISLAND
NIUE
GUAM
KIRIBATI
NAURU
TONGA
TUVALU
VANUATU
WEST SAMOA

ST. HELENA

COMOROS
MAYOTTE

ANGOLA
ZAMBIA
MALAWI
ZIMBABWE
MOZAMBIQUE
MADAGASCAR

MAURITIUS
REUNION

CHRISTMAS IS.
COCOS IS.

AUSTRALIA

NAMIBIA
BOTSWANA
SOUTH AFRICA
SWAZILAND
LESOTHO

BAHRAIN
GAMBIA
SÃO TOMÉ AND PRÍNCIPE

NEW ZEALAND

Source: *The World Factbook, 1993.*

The Balance of Visible Trade Based on Imports and Exports of Raw Materials and Manufactures

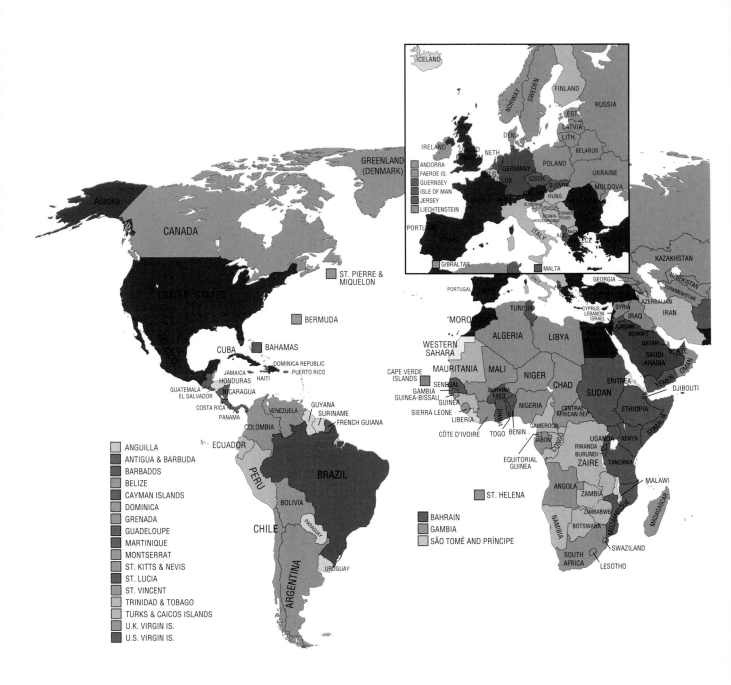

National divisions in the former Yugoslavia are as accurate as possible at the time of publication, but may change due to unrest.

Trade Balance $m

- 10,000 and greater
- 1,000 to 10,000
- 100 to 1,000
- 0 to 100
- 0 to -10
- -10 to -100
- -100 to -1,000
- -1,000 and greater

- No current data available

RUSSIA

KAZAKHSTAN

UZBEKISTAN

TURKMENISTAN

MONGOLIA

KYRGYZSTAN
TAJIKISTAN

AZERBAIJAN

IRAN

IRAQ

CHINA

NORTH KOREA

SOUTH KOREA

JAPAN

KUWAIT

QATAR

U.A.E.

SAUDI ARABIA

OMAN

YEMEN

DJIBOUTI

ETHIOPIA

SOMALIA

BHUTAN

INDIA

MYANMAR

LAOS

BANGLADESH

TAIWAN

HONG KONG

MACAO

VIETNAM

PHILIPPINES

CAMBODIA

SRI LANKA

BRUNEI

MALDIVES

SEYCHELLES

COMOROS
MAYOTTE

MADAGASCAR

MAURITIUS

REUNION

MALAYSIA

SINGAPORE

INDONESIA

PAPUA NEW GUINEA

SOLOMON IS.

AMERICAN SAMOA
COOK ISLAND
FIJI
FRENCH POLYNESIA
GUAM
KIRIBATI
NAURU
NIUE
NORFOLK ISLAND
TONGA
TUVALU
VANUATU
WALLACE & FUTUNA
WEST SAMOA

AUSTRALIA

NEW CALEDONIA

NEW ZEALAND

Source: *International Financial Statistics Yearbook*, 1992.

Top 50 Traders

($986.4)	USA
($732.5)	Germany
($572.4)	Japan
($443.0)	France
($398.0)	UK
($338.5)	Italy
($246.2)	Netherlands
($242.0)	Canada
($239.0)	Belgium
($238.0)	Hong Kong
($165.0)	China
($162.0)	Spain
($158.5)	South Korea
($130.7)	Switzerland
($127.9)	Singapore
($112.7)	Taiwan
($107.7)	Sweden
($94.2)	Austria
($79.5)	Australia
($78.9)	Malaysia
($75.6)	Mexico
($74.4)	Thailand
($74.3)	Saudi Arabia
($71.2)	Russia
($67.6)	Denmark
($62.1)	Norway
($55.0)	Brazil
($54.0)	Indonesia
($51.6)	Ireland
($45.3)	India
($45.2)	Finland
($42.3)	Portugal
($41.7)	South Africa
($38.2)	Iran
($36.6)	Puerto Rico
($35.1)	UAE
($34.8)	Turkey
($31.4)	Israel
($30.3)	Poland
($30.2)	Ukraine
($28.3)	Greece
($26.4)	Venezuela
($26.3)	Argentina
($24.3)	Philippines
($22.6)	Hungary
($20.5)	Nigeria
($19.8)	Algeria
($19.2)	Chile
($18.3)	Libya
($17.1)	Czech. Republic

= Twenty billion dollars

Source: *The World Factbook, 1993*.

International Groupings

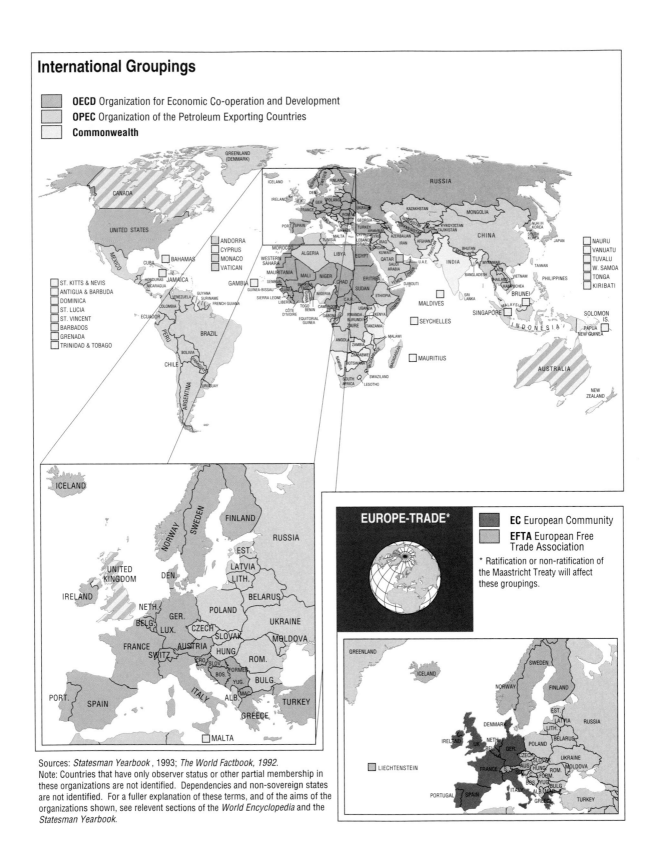

■ **OECD** Organization for Economic Co-operation and Development
■ **OPEC** Organization of the Petroleum Exporting Countries
□ **Commonwealth**

GREENLAND (DENMARK)

CANADA

UNITED STATES

MEXICO

CUBA
BAHAMAS
ST. KITTS & NEVIS
ANTIGUA & BARBUDA
DOMINICA
ST. LUCIA
ST. VINCENT
BARBADOS
GRENADA
TRINIDAD & TOBAGO

HONDURAS JAMAICA
NICARAGUA

VENEZUELA
GUYANA
COLOMBIA SURINAME FRENCH GUIANA
ECUADOR

PERU
BRAZIL
BOLIVIA
PARAGUAY
CHILE
ARGENTINA
URUGUAY

ANDORRA
CYPRUS
MONACO
VATICAN

GAMBIA

ICELAND
IRELAND
U.K.
DEN.
GER.
POLAND
FINLAND
FRANCE
PORT. SPAIN
GREECE
MALTA
TUNISIA
MOROCCO
WESTERN SAHARA
ALGERIA
LIBYA
EGYPT

MAURITANIA
MALI NIGER CHAD SUDAN ERITREA
SENEGAL
GUINEA-BISSAU BURKINA
SIERRA LEONE GUINEA
CÔTE D'IVOIRE LIBERIA
TOGO BENIN NIGERIA
C.A.R.
EQUITORIAL GUINEA GABON
ETHIOPIA DJIBOUTI
UGANDA SOMALIA
ZAIRE RWANDA KENYA
BURUNDI TANZANIA
ANGOLA
ZAMBIA MALAWI
NAMIBIA ZIMBABWE
BOTSWANA
SOUTH AFRICA SWAZILAND
LESOTHO
MADAGASCAR
MAURITIUS
SEYCHELLES
MALDIVES

RUSSIA
KAZAKHSTAN MONGOLIA
GEORGIA
TURKEY ARMENIA
AZERBAIJAN TURKMENISTAN UZBEKISTAN KYRGYZSTAN
CYPRUS SYRIA TAJIKISTAN CHINA
LEBANON IRAQ IRAN AFGHAN.
ISRAEL JORDAN KUWAIT PAKISTAN BHUTAN
QATAR SAUDI ARABIA U.A.E. INDIA MYANMAR
YEMEN OMAN BANGLADESH THAILAND VIETNAM
SRI LANKA KAMPUCHEA
NORTH KOREA
SOUTH KOREA
JAPAN
TAIWAN
PHILIPPINES
BRUNEI
MALAYSIA
SINGAPORE
INDONESIA
PAPUA NEW GUINEA

NAURU
VANUATU
TUVALU
W. SAMOA
TONGA
KIRIBATI

SOLOMON IS.

AUSTRALIA

NEW ZEALAND

(Europe inset)

ICELAND
NORWAY SWEDEN FINLAND
RUSSIA
EST.
LATVIA
LITH.
UNITED KINGDOM DEN.
BELARUS
IRELAND
NETH. POLAND
BELG. GER. UKRAINE
LUX. CZECH
FRANCE SLOVAK MOLDOVA
SWITZ. AUSTRIA HUNG. ROM.
CRO. SLOV. FORMER
BOS. YUG. BULG.
PORT. ITALY MAC.
SPAIN ALB. TURKEY
GREECE
MALTA

EUROPE-TRADE*

■ **EC** European Community
■ **EFTA** European Free Trade Association

* Ratification or non-ratification of the Maastricht Treaty will affect these groupings.

GREENLAND
ICELAND
SWEDEN
NORWAY FINLAND
DENMARK
EST.
LATVIA
LITH.
IRELAND UK NETH. POLAND
BEL. GER.
CZECH
FRANCE SLOVAK UKRAINE
AUS. HUNG. MOLDOVA
SWI. ROM.
BOS. YUG.
ITALY ALB. BULG.
PORTUGAL SPAIN GREECE
TURKEY
RUSSIA
BELARUS

□ LIECHTENSTEIN

Sources: *Statesman Yearbook*, 1993; *The World Factbook, 1992*.
Note: Countries that have only observer status or other partial membership in these organizations are not identified. Dependencies and non-sovereign states are not identified. For a fuller explanation of these terms, and of the aims of the organizations shown, see relevent sections of the *World Encyclopedia* and the *Statesman Yearbook*.

PACIFIC BASIN

☐ **ASEAN** Association of South East Asian Nations

MYANMAR
LAOS
THAILAND
CAM.
VIETNAM
PHILIPPINES
BRUNEI
MALAYSIA
SINGAPORE
INDONESIA
PAPUA NEW GUINEA

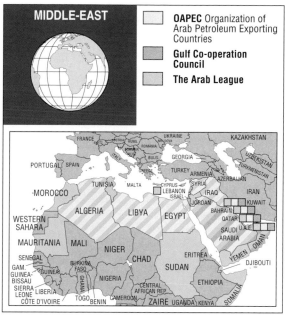

MIDDLE-EAST

☐ **OAPEC** Organization of Arab Petroleum Exporting Countries

☐ **Gulf Co-operation Council**

☐ **The Arab League**

FRANCE
UKRAINE
KAZAKHSTAN
AUSTRIA HUNG.
ROMANIA
MOLD.
BULG.
GEORGIA
UZBEKISTAN
PORTUGAL SPAIN
ITALY
GREECE
TURKEY
ARMENIA
AZERBAIJAN
TURKMENISTAN
CYPRUS
SYRIA
LEBANON
ISRAEL
IRAQ
IRAN
MOROCCO
TUNISIA
MALTA
JORDAN
KUWAIT
ALGERIA
LIBYA
EGYPT
BAHRAIN
QATAR
WESTERN SAHARA
U.A.E.
SAUDI ARABIA
OMAN
MAURITANIA
MALI
NIGER
CHAD
ERITREA
YEMEN
DJIBOUTI
SENEGAL
GAM.
GUINEA-BISSAU
GUINEA
BURKINA FASO
NIGERIA
SUDAN
ETHIOPIA
SIERRA LEONE
LIBERIA
GHANA
CENTRAL AFRICAN REP.
SOMALIA
CÔTE D'IVOIRE
TOGO
BENIN
CAMEROON
ZAIRE
UGANDA
KENYA

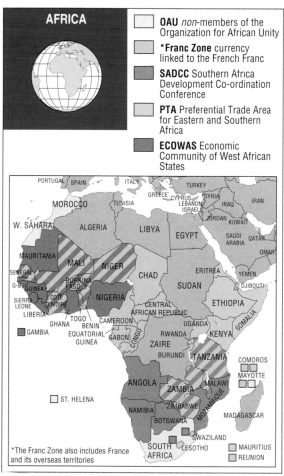

AFRICA

☐ **OAU** *non*-members of the Organization for African Unity

☐ ***Franc Zone*** currency linked to the French Franc

☐ **SADCC** Southern Africa Development Co-ordination Conference

☐ **PTA** Preferential Trade Area for Eastern and Southern Africa

☐ **ECOWAS** Economic Community of West African States

PORTUGAL SPAIN
ITALY
TURKEY
GREECE
CYPRUS
SYRIA
MOROCCO
TUNISIA
LEBANON
ISRAEL
IRAQ
IRAN
JORDAN
KUWAIT
W. SAHARA
ALGERIA
LIBYA
EGYPT
SAUDI ARABIA
QATAR
OMAR
MAURITANIA
MALI
NIGER
CHAD
ERITREA
YEMEN
SENEGAL
DJIBOUTI
G-B.
GUINEA
BURKINA FASO
NIGERIA
SUDAN
ETHIOPIA
SIERRA LEONE
CÔTE D'IVOIRE
CENTRAL AFRICAN REPUBLIC
LIBERIA
GHANA
TOGO
BENIN
CAMEROON
UGANDA
SOMALIA
☐ GAMBIA
EQUATORIAL GUINEA
GABON
CONGO
RWANDA
KENYA
ZAIRE
BURUNDI
TANZANIA
COMOROS
MAYOTTE
☐ ST. HELENA
ANGOLA
ZAMBIA
MALAWI
NAMIBIA
ZIMBABWE
MOZAMBIQUE
MADAGASCAR
BOTSWANA
SWAZILAND
☐ MAURITIUS
SOUTH AFRICA
LESOTHO
☐ REUNION

*The Franc Zone also includes France and its overseas territories

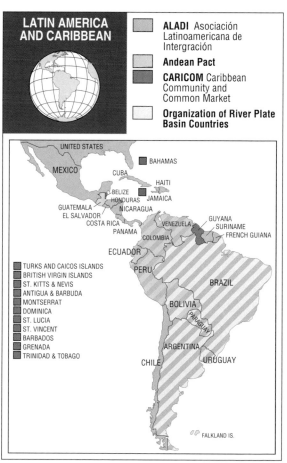

LATIN AMERICA AND CARIBBEAN

☐ **ALADI** Asociación Latinoamericana de Intergración

☐ **Andean Pact**

☐ **CARICOM** Caribbean Community and Common Market

☐ **Organization of River Plate Basin Countries**

UNITED STATES
MEXICO
CUBA
☐ BAHAMAS
HAITI
BELIZE
GUATEMALA
HONDURAS
JAMAICA
EL SALVADOR
NICARAGUA
COSTA RICA
GUYANA
PANAMA
VENEZUELA
SURINAME
COLOMBIA
FRENCH GUIANA
ECUADOR
PERU
BRAZIL
☐ TURKS AND CAICOS ISLANDS
☐ BRITISH VIRGIN ISLANDS
☐ ST. KITTS & NEVIS
☐ ANTIGUA & BARBUDA
☐ MONTSERRAT
☐ DOMINICA
☐ ST. LUCIA
☐ ST. VINCENT
☐ BARBADOS
☐ GRENADA
☐ TRINIDAD & TOBAGO
BOLIVIA
PARAGUAY
ARGENTINA
URUGUAY
CHILE
FALKLAND IS.

Population Density and Growth

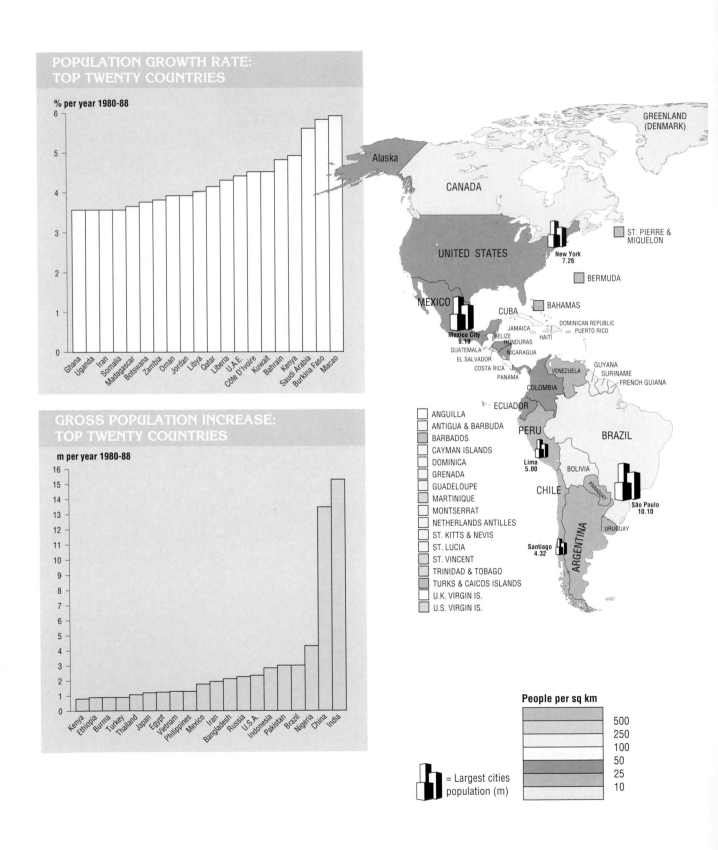

POPULATION GROWTH RATE: TOP TWENTY COUNTRIES

% per year 1980-88

Ghana, Uganda, Iran, Somalia, Madagascar, Botswana, Zambia, Oman, Jordan, Libya, Qatar, Liberia, U.A.E., Côte D'Ivoire, Kuwait, Bahrain, Kenya, Saudi Arabia, Burkina Faso, Macao

GROSS POPULATION INCREASE: TOP TWENTY COUNTRIES

m per year 1980-88

Kenya, Ethiopia, Burma, Turkey, Thailand, Japan, Egypt, Vietnam, Philippines, Mexico, Iran, Bangladesh, Russia, U.S.A., Indonesia, Pakistan, Brazil, Nigeria, China, India

GREENLAND (DENMARK)

Alaska

CANADA

ST. PIERRE & MIQUELON

UNITED STATES

New York 7.26

BERMUDA

MEXICO

BAHAMAS

CUBA

Mexico City 9.19

JAMAICA

DOMINICAN REPUBLIC
PUERTO RICO

BELIZE
GUATEMALA   HAITI
HONDURAS

EL SALVADOR   NICARAGUA

COSTA RICA

GUYANA

PANAMA

VENEZUELA

SURINAME

FRENCH GUIANA

COLOMBIA

ECUADOR

PERU

BRAZIL

Lima 5.00

BOLIVIA

São Paulo 10.10

CHILE

PARAGUAY

URUGUAY

Santiago 4.32

ARGENTINA

ANGUILLA
ANTIGUA & BARBUDA
BARBADOS
CAYMAN ISLANDS
DOMINICA
GRENADA
GUADELOUPE
MARTINIQUE
MONTSERRAT
NETHERLANDS ANTILLES
ST. KITTS & NEVIS
ST. LUCIA
ST. VINCENT
TRINIDAD & TOBAGO
TURKS & CAICOS ISLANDS
U.K. VIRGIN IS.
U.S. VIRGIN IS.

People per sq km

500
250
100
50
25
10

= Largest cities population (m)

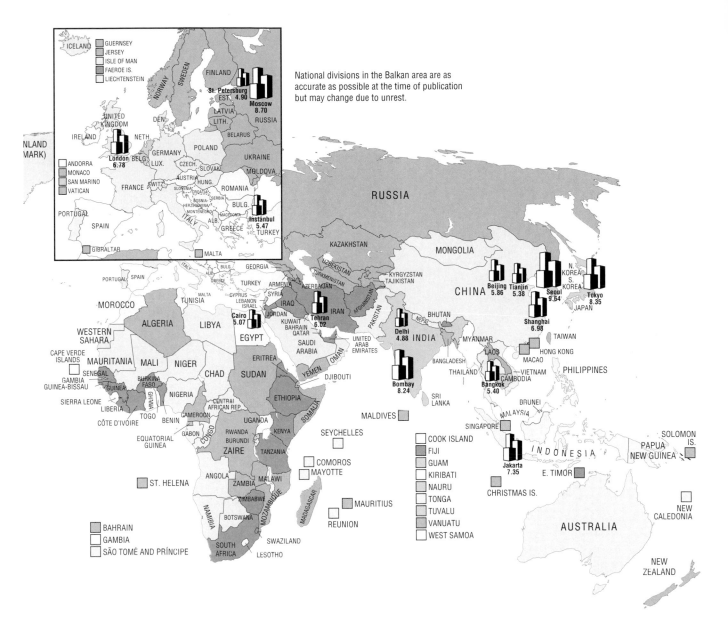

National divisions in the Balkan area are as accurate as possible at the time of publication but may change due to unrest.

Inset legend:

- GUERNSEY
- JERSEY
- ISLE OF MAN
- FAEROE IS.
- LIECHTENSTEIN

- ANDORRA
- MONACO
- SAN MARINO
- VATICAN

St. Petersburg EST. 4.90
Moscow 8.70
London 6.78
Istanbul 5.47

Beijing 5.86
Tianjin 5.38
Seoul 9.64
Tokyo 8.35
Shanghai 6.98
Cairo 5.07
Tehran 6.02
Delhi 4.88
Bombay 8.24
Bangkok 5.40
Jakarta 7.35

- BAHRAIN
- GAMBIA
- SÃO TOMÉ AND PRÍNCIPE

- COOK ISLAND
- FIJI
- GUAM
- KIRIBATI
- NAURU
- TONGA
- TUVALU
- VANUATU
- WEST SAMOA

Source: *The World Factbook, 1991; The Economist, 1992.*

The Global Environment: A Source of Conflict Between Developed and Less-Developed Nations

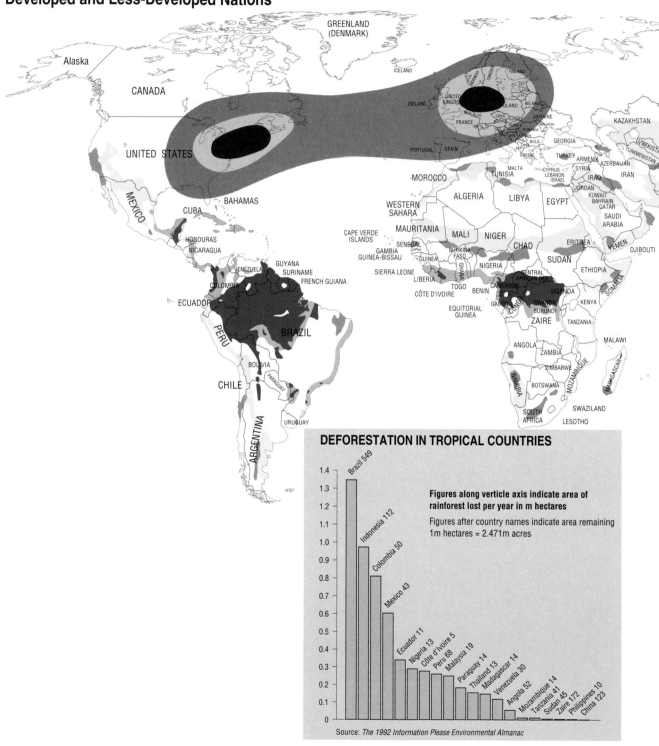

GREENLAND (DENMARK)

ICELAND

Alaska

CANADA

UNITED STATES

MEXICO

BAHAMAS

CUBA

HONDURAS

NICARAGUA

VENEZUELA

GUYANA

SURINAME

FRENCH GUIANA

COLOMBIA

ECUADOR

PERU

BRAZIL

BOLIVIA

PARAGUAY

CHILE

URUGUAY

ARGENTINA

IRELAND

UNITED KINGDOM

NORWAY

SWEDEN

FINLAND

EST

LATVIA

LITH

POLAND

BELARUS

FRANCE

BENELUX

GER

CZECH

UKRAINE

AUSTRIA

ROMANIA

MOLDOVA

PORTUGAL

SPAIN

GREECE

BULG

KAZAKHSTAN

UZBEKISTAN

TURKMENISTAN

GEORGIA

TURKEY

ARMENIA

AZERBAIJAN

MALTA

CYPRUS

LEBANON

ISRAEL

SYRIA

IRAQ

IRAN

MOROCCO

TUNISIA

ALGERIA

LIBYA

EGYPT

JORDAN

KUWAIT

BAHRAIN

QATAR

SAUDI ARABIA

WESTERN SAHARA

MAURITANIA

MALI

NIGER

CHAD

ERITREA

YEMEN

DJIBOUTI

CAPE VERDE ISLANDS

SENEGAL

GAMBIA

GUINEA-BISSAU

GUINEA

BURKINA FASO

NIGERIA

SUDAN

ETHIOPIA

SIERRA LEONE

LIBERIA

GHANA

TOGO

BENIN

CÔTE D'IVOIRE

CENTRAL AFRICAN REP.

CAMEROON

UGANDA

EQUITORIAL GUINEA

GABON

CONGO

RWANDA

BURUNDI

ZAIRE

KENYA

SOMALIA

TANZANIA

ANGOLA

ZAMBIA

MALAWI

MADAGASCAR

NAMIBIA

ZIMBABWE

MOZAMBIQUE

BOTSWANA

SOUTH AFRICA

SWAZILAND

LESOTHO

DEFORESTATION IN TROPICAL COUNTRIES

Figures along verticle axis indicate area of rainforest lost per year in m hectares

Figures after country names indicate area remaining

1m hectares = 2.471m acres

Brazil 549

Indonesia 112

Colombia 50

Mexico 43

Ecuador 11

Nigeria 13

Côte d'Ivoire 5

Peru 68

Malaysia 19

Paraguay 14

Thailand 13

Madagascar 13

Venezuela 30

Angola 52

Mozambique 14

Tanzania 45

Sudan 41

Zaire 172

Philippines 10

China 123

Source: *The 1992 Information Please Environmental Almanac*

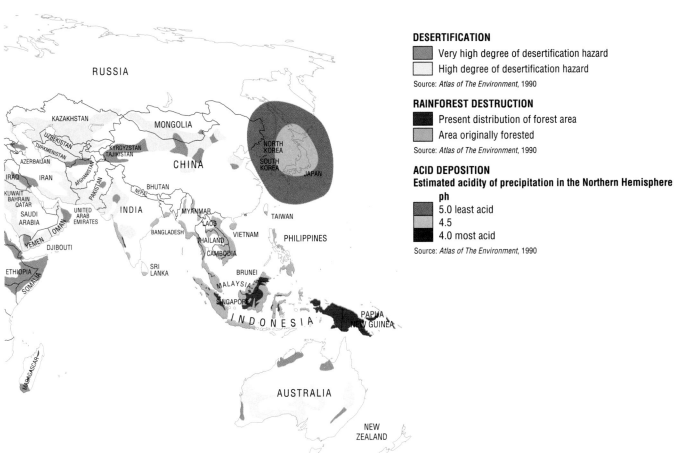

DESERTIFICATION
- Very high degree of desertification hazard
- High degree of desertification hazard

Source: *Atlas of The Environment*, 1990

RAINFOREST DESTRUCTION
- Present distribution of forest area
- Area originally forested

Source: *Atlas of The Environment*, 1990

ACID DEPOSITION
Estimated acidity of precipitation in the Northern Hemisphere

ph
- 5.0 least acid
- 4.5
- 4.0 most acid

Source: *Atlas of The Environment*, 1990

CARBON DIOXIDE

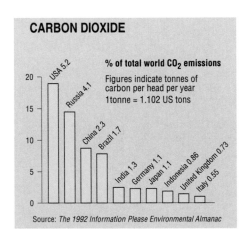

% of total world CO$_2$ emissions

Figures indicate tonnes of carbon per head per year
1 tonne = 1.102 US tons

USA 5.2
Russia 4.1
China 2.3
Brazil 1.7
India 1.3
Germany 1.1
Japan 1.1
Indonesia 0.86
United Kingdom 0.73
Italy 0.55

Source: *The 1992 Information Please Environmental Almanac*

GLOBAL WARMING

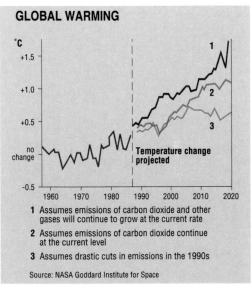

Temperature change projected

1 Assumes emissions of carbon dioxide and other gases will continue to grow at the current rate

2 Assumes emissions of carbon dioxide continue at the current level

3 Assumes drastic cuts in emissions in the 1990s

Source: NASA Goddard Institute for Space

Trade and Travel Networks

Civilization depends on trade for growth and travel makes this possible. Shipping is the most important method of world transport but economic progress and mobility are constantly being improved by the development of new routes and new methods of transport.

Road and Rail

Integrated road and rail networks are the basis of industrial society. Containerization and the extension of modern highway systems have increased flexibility and reduced the emphasis on railways transporting freight.

Roads

Bar length equals the total road network in log scale.
Number next to country name is the total road network in thousands of kilometers.

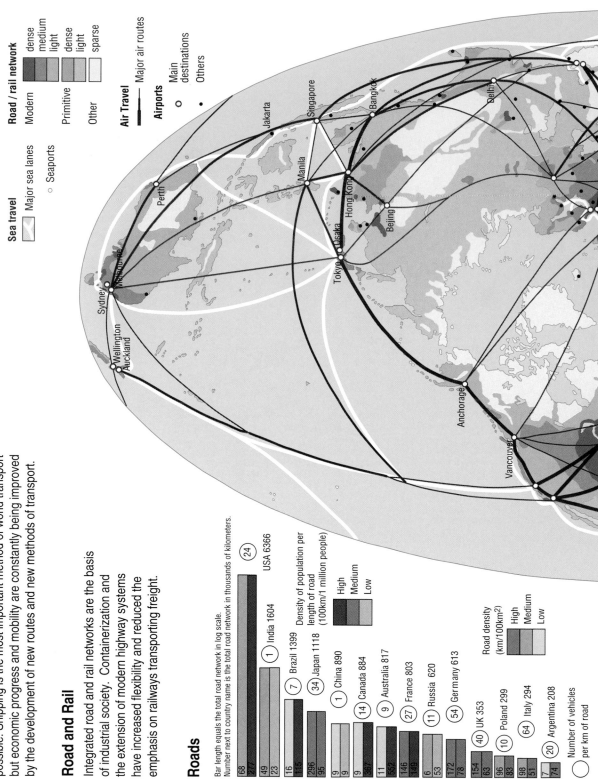

Sea travel
- Major sea lanes
- ○ Seaports

Road / rail network

Modern
- dense
- medium
- light

Primitive
- dense
- light

Other
- sparse

Air Travel
— Major air routes

Airports
- ○ Main destinations
- · Others

Density of population per length of road
(100km/1 million people)
- High
- Medium
- Low

Road density
(km/100km²)
- High
- Medium
- Low

○ Number of vehicles per km of road

(24)	68 / 277
	USA 6366 / 49 / 23
(1) India 1604	16
(7) Brazil 1399	115
(34) Japan 1118	296 / 95
(1) China 890	9 / 9
(14) Canada 884	9 / 367
(9) Australia 817	11 / 552
(27) France 803	146 / 149
(11) Russia 620	6 / 53
(54) Germany 613	172 / 78
(40) UK 353	154 / 63
(10) Poland 299	96 / 83
(64) Italy 294	98 / 51
(20) Argentina 208	7 / 74

Map labels: Perth, Jakarta, Singapore, Bangkok, Delhi, Manila, Hong Kong, Beijing, Osaka, Tokyo, Sydney, Melbourne, Wellington, Auckland, Anchorage, Vancouver

Railways

8 / 3	UK 18
7 / 4	Italy 20
8 / 7	Poland 24
7 / 2	Japan 26
0.4 / 3	Brazil 31
6 / 6	France 34
2 / 12	Argentina 35
0.5 / 27	Australia 40
3 / 5	Germany 41
0.5 / 1	China 50
2 / 1	India 61
7 / 26	Canada 68
0.5 / 6	Russia 86
3 / 14	USA 320

Density of population per
length of road
(100km/1 million people)

High
Medium
Low

Rail density
(km/100km^2)

High
Medium
Low

Bar length equals the total road network in log scale.
Number next to country name is the total road network in thousands of
kilometers.

Journey Time

The Suez Canal cuts 3600 nautical miles
off the London-Singapore route, while
the Concorde halves the London-New
York journey time.

Air and Sea Routes

A complex network of primary air routes
centered on the Northern Hemisphere provides
rapid transit across the world for mass travel,
mail, and urgent freight.

Ships also follow these principal routes,
plying the oceans between major ports and
transporting the commodities of world trade
in bulk.

| Sail (via Cape)
164 days | Steam (via Cape)
43 days | Steam (via Suez)
28 days | Supertanker (via Cape)
28 days | Diesel (via Suez)
15 days |
|---|---|---|---|---|

Singapore ⟷ London

| Concorde
3½ hours | Jet
7 hours | Propeller
12 hours | First Flight
4½ days |
|---|---|---|---|

London ⟶ New York

Source: Bartholomew, 1993

Telephones

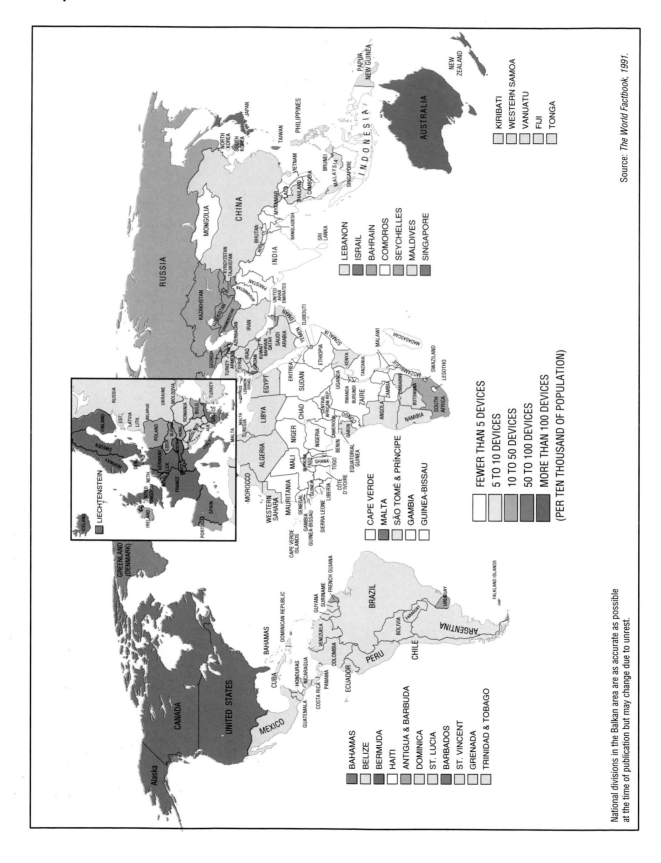

Source: *The World Factbook, 1991.*

National divisions in the Balkan area are as accurate as possible at the time of publication but may change due to unrest.

Data Transmission

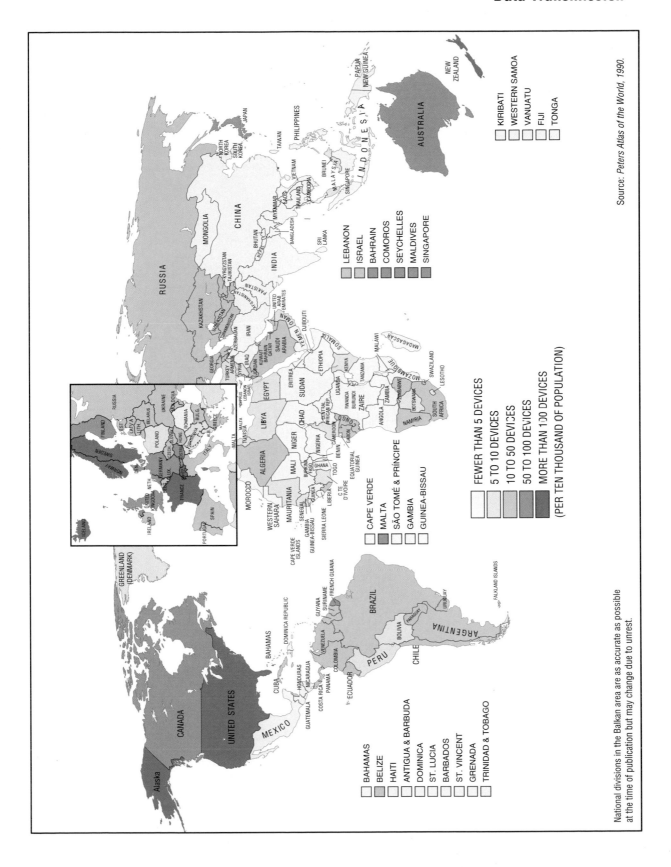

Source: *Peters Atlas of the World*, 1990.

National divisions in the Balkan area are as accurate as possible at the time of publication but may change due to unrest.

Legend (per ten thousand of population):
- FEWER THAN 5 DEVICES
- 5 TO 10 DEVICES
- 10 TO 50 DEVICES
- 50 TO 100 DEVICES
- MORE THAN 100 DEVICES

Caribbean/Americas inset:
- BAHAMAS
- BELIZE
- HAITI
- ANTIGUA & BARBUDA
- DOMINICA
- ST. LUCIA
- BARBADOS
- ST. VINCENT
- GRENADA
- TRINIDAD & TOBAGO

Africa inset:
- CAPE VERDE
- MALTA
- SÃO TOMÉ & PRÍNCIPE
- GAMBIA
- GUINEA-BISSAU

Middle East/Indian Ocean inset:
- LEBANON
- ISRAEL
- BAHRAIN
- COMOROS
- SEYCHELLES
- MALDIVES
- SINGAPORE

Pacific inset:
- KIRIBATI
- WESTERN SAMOA
- VANUATU
- FIJI
- TONGA

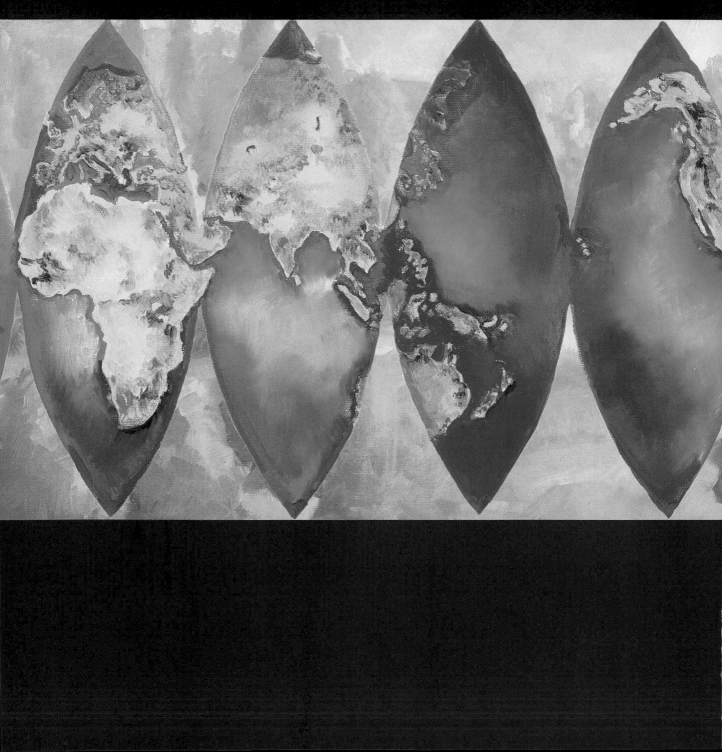

Hong Kong: The Market of the Future or No Future

The People's Republic of China (PRC) and the British Crown Colony of Hong Kong are inextricably linked. In fact, many will argue that Beijing never has fully recognized Hong Kong's separation from the mainland after the Opium War in 1840. As a result of long-standing economic and cultural relationships—primarily between southern China and Hong Kong—some view the reunification set for July 1, 1997, mainly as a symbolic flag-raising ceremony. What that symbolism will mean is debated. "Hong Kong will take over China, not the other way around," says a representative of the Hong Kong Trade Development Council, while an American businessman well-entrenched in China and its system warns: "Hong Kong is the scapegoat for what Chinese leaders perceive as Western injustice."

Although recent Eastern European history offers numerous examples of command economies giving way to market-oriented systems, it is difficult to predict what will happen when a command economy—the PRC—takes over an unbridled bastion of capitalism—Hong Kong. "There are bound to be, on both sides, uncertainties, and there are bound to be suspicions," said Sir David Wilson, governor of Hong Kong from 1987 to 1992. "This whole process is something which is unprecedented in terms of world history. There are no international historical blueprints to go by. We have to find our own way."

The 1984 Sino-British Joint Declaration and Basic Law that returns Hong Kong to Chinese sovereignty in 1997 makes it a Special Administrative Region (SAR) of China for at least 50 years, presumably enough time for the two political and economic systems to mesh. China has also pledged that when the British departed, Hong Kong would be run largely by its own people under the concept of "one country, two systems." This means continuing the system of an elected government, rule of law, independent courts, and wide personal freedoms. The SAR will be run by a chief executive selected among long-time Chinese residents of Hong Kong. Hong Kong will remain a free port and separate customs territory and will be able to decide on and conduct its own economic policies. This will be evident in practice through Hong Kong keeping its own currency and retaining its separate membership in the General Agreement on Tariffs and Trade (GATT).

HONG KONG AS A BUSINESS CENTER

Hong Kong is the world's tenth largest trading nation and the third largest financial center. In an area of just over 400 square miles, it has a population of 5.8 million. Its per-capita income is over $16,000, third in East Asia after Japan and Brunei. It's the world's largest free port and top-ranking manufacturer and exporter of textiles, clothing, and toys. No other business center in the Asia-Pacific is as friendly to business, offering free trade, free enterprise, a well-educated work force, a policy of "positive nonintervention" in trade matters, and low taxes. For a summary of Hong Kong economic facts, see Table 1.

The economy as a whole is externally oriented and its growth and well-being depend mainly on its trade performance. Apart from trade in goods, trade in services also

Source: This case study was written by Ilkka A. Ronkainen and funded in part by a grant from the Business and International Education Program of the U.S. Department of Education. The assistance of the U.S. Consulate in Hong Kong, Inchcape Pacific, the Customs and Excise Department of the Hong Kong Government, and the Hong Kong Trade Development Council is also appreciated.

TABLE 1	Hong Kong Essential Facts, 1992	
Population	5.8 million	
GDP	$95 billion	
GDP per Capita	$16,420	
Total Exports	$119 billion	
Domestic Exports	$30 billion	
Re-exports	$89 billion	
Imports	$122 billion	
U.S. Exports to Hong Kong	$7.9 billion	
U.S. Imports from Hong Kong	$8.3 billion	
Principal U.S. Exports	Electrical machinery, resins and plastic materials, transport equipment, office machines, tobacco manufactures	
Principal U.S. Imports	Garments, electronics, office machines, photographic apparatus, electrical machinery	
U.S. Investment in Hong Kong	$8 billion	
U.S. Expatriates in Hong Kong	23,500	
U.S. Firms with Offices/ Plants in Hong Kong	900	

contributes significantly to Hong Kong's growth. Given its strategic location and well-established infrastructure and business contacts, Hong Kong has developed into a center for trade, finance, communications, and business services for the entire Asia-Pacific region.

The Hong Kong government plays no favorites, putting foreign and locally owned companies on the same footing. While there are no special incentives offered to overseas business to relocate, formalities to setting up a business are kept to as few as possible. There are no regulations concerning the minimum capital requirement of a company, or any regulations concerning the relative degree of local/overseas participation in the ownership of the company. The Hong Kong government assists in finding suitable local partners for joint ventures. Likewise, there are no regulations concerning the relative proportion of local to overseas staff that may be employed. Typically, however, the high cost of living (i.e., mainly housing) discourages companies from using a large number of expatriates. There are no restrictions on foreign exchange or on transferring capital or profits in or out of the colony.

THE ECONOMIC INTERDEPENDENCE OF HONG KONG AND CHINA

Existing Hong Kong-PRC economic ties will set the pattern for future developments. The PRC is currently Hong Kong's largest trading partner and its main source of investment capital. Hong Kong has evolved as the "International Division of China Inc."—

both in managing China's exports and importing foreign goods for re-export to China. Approximately 70 percent of China's annual exports to the United States pass through Hong Kong in the form of re-exports. Hong Kong's established business and social connections with both China and the rest of the world, excellent telecommunications and transportation facilities, and financial sophistication make it uniquely suited to its role as facilitator. An important part of this facilitation is to serve as an intermediary in trade between China and Taiwan.

Since the PRC implemented an "open door" policy in the last decade, Hong Kong's and outsiders' economic importance to China has increased. There are now 84,000 foreign-funded enterprises in China, most of them in the South. These enterprises are estimated to account for 25 percent of all of China's foreign trade. The economic development of southern China—especially the Pearl River Delta in Guangdong Province and the coastal economic zones—has been the catalyst for China's economy to grow by almost 10 percent a year since 1978.

Guangdong Province itself has for the last ten years averaged real annual growth of a stunning 15 percent. Although the province has less than half a percent of China's land and a mere 16 million of its 1.2 billion people, it accounts for 5 percent of total industrial output and 10 percent of exports. Per-capita income in Guangdong Province is roughly $600, double that of China as a whole. The star of the province is Shenzhen, a city across the border from Hong Kong, set up as a special economic zone by Beijing in 1979. Shenzhen residents enjoy rapidly increasing per-capita incomes of $800, which is expected to increase to $2,800 by the year 2000. Figure 1 provides a summary of the major business centers of the Pearl River Delta.

The Fastest-Growing Economy on Earth   **FIGURE 1**

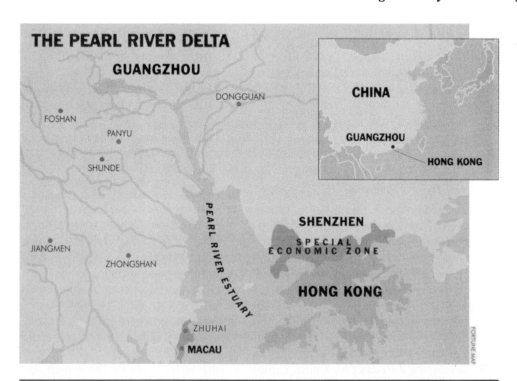

Source: Ford S. Worthy, "Where Capitalism Thrives in China," *Fortune*, March 9, 1992, 71. Copyright © Time, Inc. All rights reserved.

During its 15-year-old drive to attract foreign direct investment, $18.8 billion has been dispensed and commitments are up to $68.5 billion. About 60 percent is estimated to have come from or through Hong Kong. A full 80 percent of Hong Kong manufacturers have set up labor-intensive production facilities across the border. Hong Kong companies operating in Southern China now employ about 3 million people—more than four times the number of manufacturing-sector workers in Hong Kong itself. More than 60,000 Hong Kong managers, professionals, technicians, and supervisors are currently working in China. In addition, 20 percent of Hong Kong's currency circulation takes place in Guangdong Province.

At the same time, China is increasing its stake in Hong Kong. China is the biggest investor ($12–$13 billion) in the economy ahead of the United States and Japan, with major investments in the aviation sector (e.g., 22.5 percent of Cathay Pacific), telecommunications, and property. As a matter of fact, it is estimated that PRC buyers may control 20 percent of the Hong Kong property market by the time the takeover occurs. The Bank of China, which is the second largest banking group (after Hong Kong Bank) in Hong Kong, will start issuing in the colony's currency notes, fully backed by foreign exchange deposits with the Hong Kong government.

CHINA'S ECONOMIC AND CONSUMER BOOM

Economic growth in China has been rapid: GNP grew by 12.8 percent in 1992 (18 percent in Guangdong Province), and 1993 growth in the first half of the year was estimated at 14 percent. China's exports totaled $85 billion, imports $80.6 billion, resulting in a trade surplus of $4.4 billion.

Despite the austerity measures introduced in the summer of 1993 to cool down the economy, strong growth is still continuing. This growth is bringing affluence to many parts of China, not just the major cities, such as Guangzhou, Shanghai, and Beijing. Examples of the changes this growth is bringing include:

- Retail sales in China surged 10 percent in 1992 to approximately $200 billion. By the year 2000, annual retail sales are projected to have reached $600 billion.
- Department stores display a wide variety of consumer goods and are overflowing with eager consumers. Traffic through some of China's department stores is well over 100,000 people per day.
- For a working couple in Guandong Province, monthly household income may be 1,200 yuan ($210). Although Ferrero Rochet chocolates sell for 68 yuan, and a pack of Brand's Essence of Chicken is priced at 100 yuan, they sell very well to a broad range of customers.

While incomes in China are low by Western standards and by those in the developed economies of the Asia-Pacific, the proportion of disposable income is high as are savings. Living expenses take only 5 percent or less of family income in China, while the comparable figure in Hong Kong is 40 percent. There is tremendous pent-up demand for consumer goods among the population who have had nothing to spend their money on for many years. Private savings are high even by Asian standards and amount to one-third of an average worker's annual income.

Chinese consumers are quality-conscious. Joint-venture products (such as Head & Shoulders, Tang, and Pepsi-Cola) are perceived as quality items and often command double or triple the price of goods produced solely by Chinese companies.

In developing a strategy for China, companies such as Inchcape Pacific (which acts as a marketer and distributor for many companies including Cadbury's, SmithKline-

Beecham, and Kellogg's) consider approaching China as one big market a mistake. Inchcape's priority markets are Southern China (Pearl River Delta), Eastern China (Shanghai, Nanjing, and Hangzhou), and North China (Beijing, Tianjin, and Dalian). The rationale is that each is a very separate and different market from the others in terms of people, culture, dialect, way of life, climate, and diet. Most importantly, each is a huge consumer market in its own right. The sheer size and the logistics problems make national distribution in China an impossibility.

Taking advantage of this opportunity requires flexibility. Changes in the regulatory environment create both opportunities and challenges. Contacts have to be cultivated beyond the central government in Beijing. Provincial and municipal authorities enjoy autonomy and influence and tend to be quite entrepreneurial. The municipal government usually supports or has very close links with a few companies in its area. A potential entrant needs to develop good relations with these officials and the business leaders in the local companies.

HONG KONG-U.S. BUSINESS LINKS

The overall key to Asia is access—access to markets and market information. For many U.S. companies, Hong Kong's strategic location, developed infrastructure, and commercial expertise provide the best bang for the buck in Asia. Markets in Asia, China in particular, lack a solid legal framework for business and rely more on personal relationships. Leading Overseas Chinese entrepreneurs can be invaluable facilitators because they operate through a network of personal contacts. Procter & Gamble, for example, got into the Chinese market in 1988 by forming an alliance with Hong Kong businessman Li Ka-shing.

More than 900 U.S. companies had operations in Hong Kong in 1993, more than double the number of five years earlier. Virtually every Fortune 500 company that does business in the Asia-Pacific region maintains a presence in Hong Kong, usually a regional headquarters. A good example of this is Polaroid Far East Limited. A wholly owned subsidiary of Polaroid Corporation, Polaroid Far East Limited's Hong Kong office is headquarters for a region that covers South Korea, Singapore, Malaysia, Taiwan, China, Indonesia, Thailand, and India. The Hong Kong office, which opened in 1971 and now has 69 employees, controls finance, sales and marketing, and personnel.

Hong Kong is a major market for U.S.-made goods in its own right. As a matter of fact, Hong Kong imports more U.S. goods per capita than any country in the world—four times the level of Japan, five times that of Europe. Some of the major categories of traded goods can be found in Table 1.

Hong Kong also represents a convenient stepping-stone to China. Polaroid recently announced a manufacturing joint venture in Shanghai to produce consumer cameras for export. In addition to manufacturing cameras, Polaroid hopes to develop the Chinese domestic market for document photography. Hong Kong's role is to provide training for the new operation in China as well as sales and marketing support. C. C. Chan, sales and marketing manager for the Polaroid Far East China Trade Department, thinks most people in the PRC are still unfamiliar with free market Western-style business. "Hong Kong brings China closer to the world," says Chan.

Some of the other firms in the market are:

- Campbell Soup, which opened a $500,000 R&D center to spearhead its thrust into the Asia-Pacific. The new center will be developing a wide range of canned products for the Chinese palate. The operation is also intended as a springboard into China.

- Motorola, the world's fourth largest semiconductor manufacturer, opened a multi-million-dollar state-of-the-art chip-manufacturing plant in Hong Kong. The plant will supply the entire Pacific Rim, which is expected to be a $14 billion-market for semiconductors by 1995.
- Waste Management International has a 70 percent stake in a consortium that won a multimillion-dollar contract to build and operate Asia's first chemical waste treatment facility in Hong Kong.

THE OTHER SIDE OF THE COIN: MACRO AND MICRO CHALLENGES

Hong Kong's economy suffered badly as a result of the June 4, 1989, crackdown on student dissidents on Tiananmen Square. "The events reminded people of the uncertainty, risk, and lack of predictability in dealing with Beijing," says Robert Dorsee, vice president and managing director of Tyco (Hong Kong) Ltd., a division of American-owned Tyco Toys Inc.

Others are also considering changes as a result of growing concern over Hong Kong-China relations. In October 1992, the present governor of Hong Kong, Chris Patten, put forth proposals that would further democratic reform in Hong Kong by allowing more participation by the Hong Kong Chinese in the selection of members of the local legislature (the Legislative Council). The Chinese government has objected ferociously on the grounds that major changes are a violation of the Joint Declaration, and that the proposed reforms are in breach of the Basic Law. Rhetoric from Beijing has gone as far as to suggest that the treaty with Britain be "scattered to the wind," and even that China might grab control over the colony before 1997. Although discussions have been held to resolve the disagreement, the confidence of people both in Hong Kong and those interested in investing there has been shaken. For example, the Hong Kong Electronics Association, whose members do most of their manufacturing in the crown colony, has sponsored trips to the Philippines, Malaysia, and Thailand to study the climate for new investments in those Asian nations. One of their concerns is that export-control rules will cut their access to Western technology once China takes over. China's rough tactics may also endanger its already shaky most-favored-nation (MFN) status with the United States which was renewed after some controversy in June 1994.

The latter concern points out the fact that the greatest threat to Hong Kong may not come from China but from the United States. China's trade surplus with the United States reached $18.3 billion in 1992 (up from 12.7 billion the year before), a major irritant in the countries' trade relations. In October 1992, the two governments reached an agreement on market access (so-called 301 investigation), under which China pledged to liberalize its foreign trade regime. About 75 percent of the nontariff barriers will be eliminated by 1994, the rest by 1997. Tariffs will also be reduced. The agreement did not, however, clear the way for China to join GATT, as differences of opinion still remain between China and the United States.

If China loses its MFN status with the United States because of its human rights record or concerns over protectionism, military goods exports, and intellectual property, Hong Kong will suffer the most. This is why a special Hong Kong Business Mission has lobbied in Washington for the renewal of China's MFN status every time it has been up. U.S. exports would also suffer as China would undoubtedly retaliate with higher tariffs. When China lost its bid to host the 2000 Olympic Games, U.S. exporters worried about negative trade measures as a response to the opposition to the bid by the U.S. Congress.

| **Hong Kong's Possible Roles (before and after 1997)** | **TABLE 2** |

- Hong Kong will continue developing its entrepôt role—as the international marketing arm of China.
- Hong Kong is not just the world's gateway to China, it is also China's springboard to the world.
- Hong Kong has the knowledge and experience of international business; through Hong Kong, China can better understand how international business operates and what the expectations are.
- Hong Kong will continue acting as a broker for international firms looking to set up in China, often in three-way joint ventures.
- Hong Kong will continue to provide a secure base for capital.
- Hong Kong could also develop as China's own "Silicon Valley," providing R&D for China's expanding industrial sector. It can also train mainland staff in Hong Kong or provide on-the-job training in China.
- Hong Kong's role as the link between Taiwan and China will also continue in the foreseeable future.

Source: Stephen Clark, "Hong Kong's Role in the Development of Greater China," presentation given July 30, 1993, Chinese University of Hong Kong.

Although many Hong Kong-based U.S. executives are not planning to leave, their confidence is flagging. What is required for both the Chinese government and the Hong Kong government—still under British control—is to improve the investment climate. The Chinese government mainly has to confirm its commitment to living up to agreements in the eyes of U.S. and European firms.

Many hope that the statement by Lu Ping, director of China's Hong Kong and Macau Affairs office, holds true in the positive sense: "Hong Kong is bound up with its Motherland. It will serve as a bridge, channel, and window between China and the rest of the world, and play its unique and positive role in China's development in the next century."

Whatever happens, the colony will become Hong Kong Special Administrative Region of the People's Republic of China. Beijing will determine whether Hong Kong remains and grows as an open international business hub. It is already the unofficial commercial capital of the Overseas Chinese. For U.S. firms, Hong Kong will be the place to find appropriate partners and connections to enter the Chinese market. In many ways, Hong Kong's roles are, and continue to be, critical as seen in the summary provided in Table 2.

However, if Beijing reneges on its guarantee that Hong Kong can retain its position as China's capitalist gateway to the world, not only will Hong Kong become a backwater for global business, but China itself will be hurt in terms of attracting foreign direct investment and its most-favored-nation status with the United States.

Questions for Discussion

1. Would you agree or disagree with the following statement from the U.S. Information Agency in Hong Kong: "The reality, beyond the newspaper headlines, is that China is not going to kill the golden goose."
2. What are Hong Kong's benefits for a Western company that would make a move to the Philippines or Thailand undesirable or difficult?
3. Provide a possible strategy for a U.S. company operating in Hong Kong to leverage against political risk.
4. What are the benefits of using Hong Kong as a base for entering and marketing in the Chinese market?

References

Auerbach, Stuart. "Toy-Making Losing in China Some Appeal." *The Washington Post,* December 2, 1989, D11–13.

The Basic Law of the Hong Kong Special Administrative Region of the People's Republic of China. Hong Kong: The Consultative Committee for the Basic Law of the Hong Kong Special Administrative Region of the People's Republic of China, April 1990.

"Campbell Soup Targets Asia with New R&D Center." *Business International,* January 27, 1992.

Cheng, Paul M. F. "Gateway to Greater China." Sydney, Australia: Presentation made to the 36th CIES Annual Executive Congress, April 22–24, 1993.

"China at a Boiling Point." *The Economist,* July 10, 1993, 15.

Conley, Krista. "Hong Kong: Business Center of the Future." *Export Today* 7 (February 1991): 20–22.

Country Report: China, Mongolia, second quarter. The Economist Intelligence Unit, 1993.

Establishing an Office in Hong Kong. 6th ed. Hong Kong: The American Chamber of Commerce in Hong Kong, 1989.

Johnson, W. Todd. "Hong Kong Exporter's Gateway to China." *Export Today* 7 (June, 1991): 18–22.

Joint Declaration of the Government of the United Kingdom of Great Britain and Northern Ireland and the Government of the People's Republic of China on the Question of Hong Kong. Hong Kong: Hong Kong Government Information Services, December 1984.

Kraar, Louis. "Asia 2000." *Fortune,* October 5, 1992, 111–142.

———. "Storm over Hong Kong." *Fortune,* March 8, 1993, 98–105.

———. "Strategies that Win in Asia." *Fortune,* Fall 1991, 49–56.

Mutch, Andrew J. "Hong Kong: Tapping into the Dynamic Dragon." *Export Today* 9 (January/February 1993): 30–34.

Setting Up Business in Hong Kong. Hong Kong: Hong Kong General Chamber of Commerce, 1990.

Worthy, Ford S. "Where Capitalism Thrives in China." *Fortune,* March 9, 1992, 71–75.

The Tuna and the Dolphin

Marine scientists do not know why, but some kinds of dolphins swim above, or "associate with," schools of mature yellowfin, skipjack, and bigeye tuna. Thus, to catch quantities of tuna, fishermen look for the leaping dolphins and cast purse seines (nets pulled into a bag-like shape to enclose fish) around both tuna and dolphins. With this method, fishermen can efficiently and reliably catch a high number of good-sized tuna. The unfortunate side effect is that the dolphins also are caught. Because they are mammals, dolphins must surface to breathe oxygen. Entangled in the net or trapped below other dolphins, some are asphyxiated.

In the late 1960s and early 1970s, the "incidental" catch of various species of dolphins by tuna fishers in the eastern tropical Pacific (the "ETP" is a major tuna-fishing area) was in the hundreds of thousands. Because of society's growing and vociferous concern for these senseless deaths, new fishing techniques were developed to reduce dolphin mortality.

Perhaps the most important new technique is the "backdown operation." After "setting on dolphins" to catch tuna, that is, encircling both tuna and dolphins with the purse seine, the ship backs away, elongating the net, submerging the corkline in the back, and pulling the net out from under the dolphins. If the operation works correctly, and the captain and crew are willing to work with the by now sluggish and uncooperative dolphins, the tuna remain in the bottom of the net and the dolphins swim free. If, however, the operation is flawed, dolphins are injured or killed and discarded from the catch as waste.

Rather than relying on this imperfect correction of the purse seine method, some environmental groups think that entirely different methods of fishing for tuna should be employed. Alternatives could include using a pole and line or "setting" on tuna not associated with dolphins. However, according to marine scientists and fishermen, the alternative methods have serious drawbacks as well.

Some catch many sexually immature tuna, which for some reason don't associate with dolphins. Juvenile tuna often are too small to be marketed. If too many are caught, the sustainability of the population could be jeopardized. In addition, alternative methods frequently catch high numbers of other incidental species such as sharks, turtles, rays, mahi-mahi, and many kinds of noncommercial fish. Finally, all fishing methods expend energy. The practice of setting on dolphins uses the least amount of energy per volume of tuna caught.

According to many of the experts involved, including the Inter-American Tropical Tuna Commission, the U.S. National Marine Fisheries Service, and the scientific advisor to the American Tunaboat Association, the most efficient method for fishing tuna, in terms of operational cost, yield, and conservation of the tuna population, is to set on dolphins with a purse seine. From the point of view of the canning industry, only purse seine fishing provides the volume of catch necessary for growth of the industry.

Many experts also believe that with current technology, it is not possible to abandon the practice of setting on dolphins without falling into other, more grave, problems. While research to develop better techniques is now underway, positive results are not expected in the near future.

Source: This case was adapted from "The Tuna and Dolphin Controversy," by Saul Alvarez-Borrego, which was published in *UC Mexus News,* University of California Institute for Mexico and the United States 31 (Fall 1993): 8–13.

THE TRADE ASPECTS

This tuna-dolphin problem has engendered serious friction on the international level. The United States and Mexico, two countries sensitive to marine mammal protection and with solid laws in place for many years, have come head-to-head over the issue.

A U.S. trade embargo was imposed in February of 1991 on yellowfin tuna caught by Mexican fleets in the eastern tropical Pacific. This embargo resulted from violation of the Marine Mammal Act of 1972, which was amended in 1988 to prohibit the incidental kill of dolphins during commercial tuna fishing. The amendment requires the banning of tuna imports from any country that does not implement several specific measures to reduce dolphin mortality and achieve a kill-per-set rate (the number of dolphins killed in each casting of the fishing net of no more than 1.25 times the U.S. rate.

The dolphin kill rate of Mexican tuna fishers has changed dramatically over the years. Figure 1 shows that as recently as 1986, an average of 15 dolphins were killed per set by the Mexican fleet. By 1992, the Mexican fleet had achieved an average mortality of 1.85 dolphins per set, with further reductions expected. Although the dolphin populations have not regained original numbers, they continue to increase, thanks in large part to the backdown operation. Current scientific evidence indicates that the types of dolphins chiefly targeted in tuna fishing are neither rare nor in danger of extinction and, in fact, can withstand current fishing-related mortality.

Nevertheless, because Mexico did not meet the rate of comparison with the U.S. fleet specified in the Marine Mammal Protection Act, the embargo remains in effect. Mexico believes it has been penalized unfairly, since it has dramatically reduced the dolphin mortality caused by its fleet. Data show that the average kill-per-set rate for non-U.S. fishers in the affected areas dropped rapidly from 10.9 in 1989 to 3.1 in 1991. Mexico's rates dropped far more quickly. However, since the Mexican fleet's kill-per-set rate still is not within 125 percent of the U.S. rate, the embargo continues.

FIGURE 1   **Incidental Dolphin Mortality Rate, Mexican Tuna Fleet (sets on dolphins, 1986–1993)**

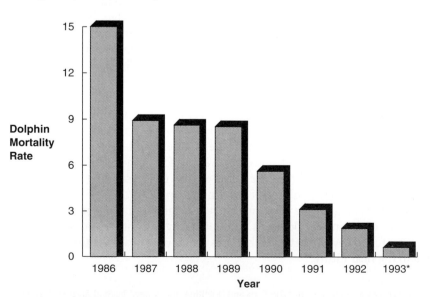

*Projected. Source: *UC Mexus News* (Fall 1993):12.

Some argue that it is unfair for the United States to unilaterally impose an embargo against tuna fishers only in the ETP and to disregard how tuna is fished in other oceans. The ETP hosts the best-known and best-managed tuna fishery in the world, employing scientific data to maintain a sustainable tuna yield and putting an observer on every ship to gather accurate statistics on the dolphin kill rate. It is contended that without observer programs in other oceans it is impossible to determine the number of dolphins killed in the pursuit of tuna not currently affected by the embargo.

In spite of the political tension, the Inter-American Tropical Tuna Commission has been working toward multilateral agreements on dolphin conservation. Commitments have been made by all governments represented in the ETP to adopt 100 percent observer coverage. Since 1993, a biologist is assigned to every ship to observe fishing methods and to record dolphin mortality. The participating governments also adopted a vessel quota system in which the overall yearly quota for dolphin mortality is equally divided among the boats fishing in the region. This way, each boat is individually held responsible for its dolphin kill. Otherwise, a few careless ships could destroy the entire fishery's attempts to meet lower mortality rates for the year. In addition to these measures, the governments agreed to support a stringent program to reduce annual dolphin mortality from 19,500 in 1993 to less than 5,000 in 1999.

Currently, the total yearly mortality for each dolphin species is under 1 percent of its population, an amount that can be sustained without reducing the total number; in fact, the populations are currently increasing. Thus, most scientists now view the mortality of dolphins incidental to tuna fishing not as an environmental problem but as one of avoiding unnecessary killing. In fact, a National Marine Fisheries Service scientist has stated that if Mexico has money for research, it would be better invested on behalf of the Vaquita, a species in real danger of extinction, than in the tuna-dolphin issue, since there is no danger to the dolphin population as a whole.

Strong opposition to current practices continues to be voiced by environmentalists. States David Phillips, executive director of the Earth Island Institute: "The goal is to eliminate the killing of dolphins entirely by prohibiting the technique of setting on them to catch tuna."

Questions for Discussion

1. Why is there such a concern about dolphins?

2. What is your view of using the technologically most advanced country's performance as a benchmark for evaluating other countries' activities?

3. Is the denial of market access an appropriate tool to enforce a country's environmental standards?

4. Is a zero-dolphin-death goal realistic?

North American Free Trade Agreement

The benefits of trade among nations are only available if countries are willing to relinquish some independence and autonomy. There are four basic levels of economic integration: the free-trade area, the customs union, the common market, and the economic union. This case, which looks at the trade pact developed between Canada, the United States, and Mexico, is an example of the first level of integration, the free-trade area.

Under a free-trade area, considered the least restrictive form of economic integration, all barriers to trade among members are removed. Goods and services are freely traded among members. The United States and Mexico began negotiating a free-trade agreement in late 1990. The pact, the North American Free Trade Agreement, also will include Canada. The Bush Administration began talks with Mexico on the belief that free trade with Mexico is crucial, and it pushed for quick approval by Congress. The fast-track approach means that when the negotiating on the agreement is done, Congress can vote the bill up or down, it cannot amend the agreement and cannot hold it up. When it came to a congressional vote the agreement faced formidable opposition in the United States.

One concern raised by opponents was whether Mexico's lower wages will make it an unfair competitor. The worry is that Mexican goods and services will be priced much lower than those of Canada and the United States because Mexico's costs are so much lower. Lower wages also are viewed as a threat to U.S. jobs.

"If you take the United States, an average manufacturing worker earns about $10.57 an hour, thereabouts," said U.S. Sen. Donald Riegle, D-Mich. "And down in Mexico it's a tiny fraction of that, about 57 cents an hour. So I think with those huge differentials, if you have a free trade agreement, what's going to happen is the manufacturing jobs are going to run out of the United States and go down to Mexico," he said. Ross Perot, a former presidential candidate, talked of "the giant sucking sound" created by the movement of U.S. jobs to Mexico.

Former U.S. Trade Representative Carla Hills disagrees. Jobs could have tumbled down south without a free-trade agreement, she counters. "What a free-trade agreement does is to reduce the barriers to our exports to Mexico."

Meanwhile, European countries are working to create economic integration through the European Union, designed to sweep away all trade barriers. Advocates of the North American Free Trade Agreement say its members, particularly the United States, need it to compete globally.

"It isn't the United States alone that's trying to produce," said U.S. Sen. John Chafee, R-R.I. "We're in a competitive position, whether we like it or not, with the European Union and with the Asian rim countries."

According to Hills, Japan has been enormously successful in developing collaborative arrangements with lower-wage countries in east Asia. Germany has created successful collaborations with Spain and Portugal, she said, "And I can't imagine why the United States would not want to have a close, collaborative arrangement with a neighbor with whom we share a 2,000-mile border."

In addition to the wage differential, treatment of the environment along the U.S.-Mexico border was another major concern of opponents. John O'Connor of the National

Source: This case was drawn from the Public Broadcasting System's television program "Adam Smith," which aired in 1991. Producer: Alvin H. Perlmutter, Inc.

Toxics Campaign said manufacturers are "turning the border into a 2,000-mile Love Canal, the largest toxic lagoon ever known to humankind."

Treasury Secretary Lloyd Bentsen of Texas, formerly a U.S. senator and chairman of the Senate Finance Committee, said he has seen enormous improvements in the way business is conducted along the border, especially with regard to environmental protection. "I was born and reared on that Mexican border, and I have never seen the kinds of changes that are happening there, such as the privatizing of industry and the lowering of tariffs," Bentsen said. "I've seen moves made on environmental improvement that I have not seen in any other developing country." But Bentsen, who led the fight on Capitol Hill for fast-track consideration of the free-trade agreement, concedes some environmental problems remain in that area.

"We've got a serious problem so far as the environment along the border," Bentsen said. "We've got a situation where in one of those towns they've been dumping 26 million gallons of raw sewage every day into the Rio Grande River. Well, that's a real problem. It creates problems of cholera and of water contamination generally. But now you're having a joint effort between the United States and Mexico to build the sewage plants, the treatment plants there. That's real progress."

Bentsen, the Democratic candidate for vice president in 1988, was asked what he says to labor unions, traditional supporters of the Democratic Party that typically oppose the free-trade accord. "I stated repeatedly during these debates for the fast track that it would depend on what came back, whether I supported it or not," Bentsen said. He would support an agreement that produces a net increase in jobs on both sides. "But if we don't get that, I'll fight it just as strongly as I worked to see that we got the fast track," he said.

In the fall of 1993, the U.S. Congress passed NAFTA by a narrow margin.

Questions for Discussion

1. Compare and contrast the other three levels of economic integration with that of NAFTA.

2. What are the central arguments for and against adopting NAFTA, as outlined in the case? Are there any noneconomic arguments for or against adopting NAFTA?

3. Should the United States have adopted NAFTA? Why or why not? Be prepared to explain your position.

4. How has NAFTA developed since this video was aired? Has former Sen. Bentsen's position changed since he has become Secretary of the Treasury?

Video Case: Lobbying in the United States

Success in the international marketplace often requires more than mere business know-how. A firm also must understand and deal with the intricacies of national politics and laws. In an era of increased business-government interaction, a firm's ability to anticipate, understand, and perhaps even shape government action may be critical for long-term market penetration. To become aware of government policies and to influence the government decision-making process, companies frequently use the assistance of lobbyists. Usually, these lobbyists are well-connected individuals and firms that can provide access to policymakers and legislators.

In the United States, firms have for a long time ensured that their voices are heard in Washington, D.C. Increasingly, foreign countries and companies have participated in this lobbying process as well. Since many government actions are likely to affect international business, numerous lobbyists have been hired to work for foreign firms.

Public attention has particularly focused on the "influence-buying" activities of Japan in the United States. Some believe that Japanese attempts at shaping or influencing U.S. trade policy are inappropriate. For example, Texas Congressman John Bryant claims that his bills, which seek more disclosure of Japanese investment activities in the United States, have repeatedly been rejected due to lobbying efforts by Japanese firms. He believes that as a result of these efforts, the U.S. government is less informed about foreign investment activities than it should be.

Another major concern to many is the fact that former U.S. policymakers often become key lobbyists for Japanese firms. Three former U.S. trade representatives, who were the heads of the government office that develops and executes U.S. international trade negotiations and policy, are now working for Japanese firms. For example, the law firm of Robert Strauss works for Fujitsu; William Brock represents Toyota; and William Eberle works for Nissan. Other examples are the former top Nixon aide Leonard Garment, who works for Toshiba, and the former national chairman of the Democratic party Charles Manatt, who now represents NEC. One Washington insider, Clyde Prestowitz, claims: "About 80 percent of former U.S. high-ranking government officials, and virtually every high-powered political lawyer in Washington, is retained in one way or another by Japanese interests. It is by far the biggest lobby in Washington, and the most well funded." States Pat Choate, author of the book *Agents of Influence:* "It is wrong, I believe, that so many Americans wind up on foreign payrolls, particularly after they have been in high positions in the U.S. government. Americans seem to be available so easily, so cheaply. This demeans us in the eyes of the world. It casts doubt in the minds of our own people about the integrity of our decision-making process."

Many believe that this easy availability of former U.S. trade negotiators to Japanese firms many undermine the U.S. policy process. It is claimed that these individuals may give away secret U.S. trade strategies or help Japanese companies find ways to circumvent existing trade legislation. Frequently cited is the case of a former U.S. negotiator in the automotive sector who applied for a position with Japanese firms while still holding his position in U.S. government.

Source: This case was written by Michael R. Czinkota and is based on *America for Sale: Japan's Buy-Out Binge,* Financial News Network, and William J. Holstein, "Japan's Clout in the U.S.," *Business Week,* July 7, 1988, 64–66.

Also of major concern are Japanese expenditures aimed at U.S. think tanks and universities. Critics argue that the funding of research projects or the endowment of chairs raises basic ethical questions. They say that Japan's wealth may tempt some of America's elite to accept Japanese funds at the expense of broader U.S. interests.

These views are vigorously disputed by others. For example, William Eberle, one of the former U.S. trade representatives mentioned earlier, maintains that his and other ex-trade officials' influence is greatly exaggerated. He states that he might be able to get the door open, but he doesn't think he has any more influence from the fact that he once held the job of U.S. trade representative. Others are more vocal. In their view, the Japanese funding provided to institutions such as the Reischauer Center of the Johns Hopkins University, or to think tanks like the Brookings Institution and the American Enterprise Institute, has no influence at all on the outcome of research projects. Scholars at these institutions are very upset at having their integrity questioned. States John Makin of the American Enterprise Institute, "This whole notion that anybody who talks about free trade is being paid off by the Japanese, which is what critics are essentially saying, is schlock."

Questions for Discussion

1. Should foreign firms be able to represent their interests in Washington, D.C.?

2. Should U.S. ex-policymakers be able to represent such foreign interests? How about domestic interests?

3. Should there be a cooling-off period before ex-policymakers can take on representation of foreign interests? If so, how long should such a period be? Is it fair to impose such an employment-restriction burden on former government officials?

4. Do you see the donation of funds by Japanese firms to U.S. think tanks as undermining U.S. interests?

PART TWO

Beginning International Marketing Activities

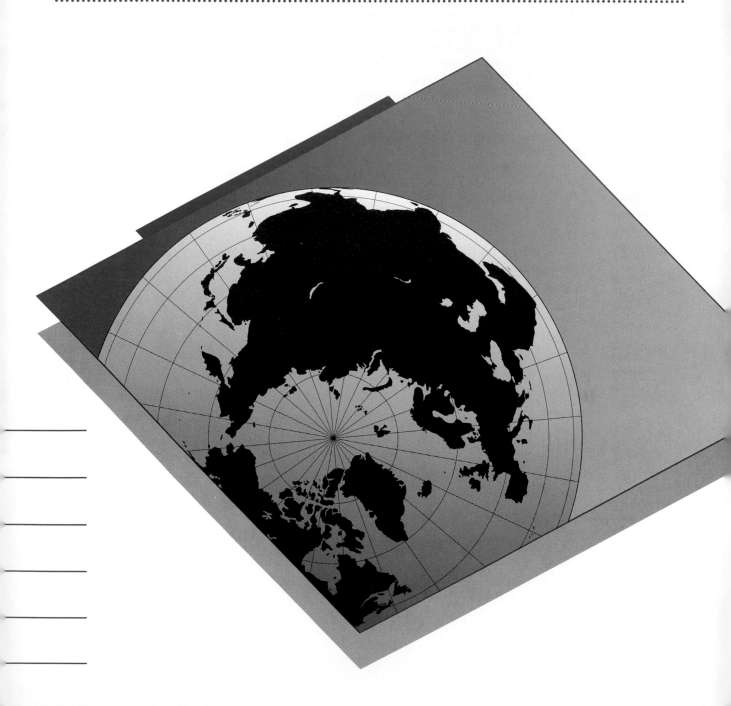

P art Two focuses on the company that is considering whether to fill an unsolicited export order, the manager who wants to find out how the current product line can be marketed abroad, or the firm searching for ways to expand its currently limited international activities. It concentrates on low-cost, low-risk international expansion, which permits a firm to enter the global market without an extraordinary commitment of human or financial resources. The reader will share the concerns of small and medium-sized firms—those that need international marketing assistance most and that supply the largest employment opportunities—before progressing to the advanced international marketing activities described in Part Three.

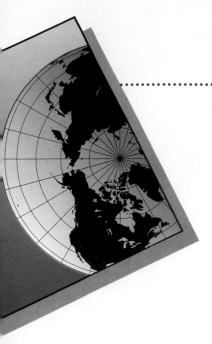

CHAPTER 7

The Export Process

THE INTERNATIONAL MARKETPLACE

Export or Perish?

Export or perish? This question faced the South Carolina–based Greenville Machinery Corporation (GMC) in 1980. A manufacturer of denim dyeing and finishing machines, the firm had exports previously accounting for only 20 percent of sales. However, as the 1970s drew to a close, GMC watched its primary customer base, U.S. textile mills, be forced out of business as a result of cheaper labor costs abroad. With no sign of the trend changing during the 1980s, an aggressive export campaign designed to find new customers abroad seemed the only way to stay in business.

Greenville CEO Wolf Stromberg led the export drive by emphasizing not only the firm's technological superiority but also its superior customer service and support. Since the machines are often tailored to the user's specific needs, a large part of Greenville's reputation is based on direct contact with textile manufacturers as well as the chemical companies who make the dye.

Accordingly, Stromberg paid particular attention to choosing the people to represent the company abroad. With a staff of only 130 people, there were significant budget and time constraints, so management decided to sell through carefully screened agents. Today, 30 of them represent diverse geographical regions. However, to keep the service reputation close to home, the agents do not get involved with the service aspect of the business. Machinery problems and repairs are handled exclusively by company staff members from South Carolina.

In addition to technological superiority and customer service, GMC also carefully researches each potential new market. Stromberg notes that to be successful in the foreign markets, "you have to have your homework done."

But you also must have patience. Up until 1987, GMC had not made a sale in China, despite repeated attempts. Then, as a result of a "healthy salesman and a lot of determination," GMC proceeded to sell three different million-dollar projects, lasting over two years. Similarly, in Turkey, after two long years of repeated sales pitches, GMC finally closed a deal. Venezuela and Mexico are similar success stories.

Today, GMC sells in 30 countries in Africa, Latin America, the Far East, and Asia. More than 60 percent of total sales are accounted for by exports, and this figure is expected to increase. Indeed, GMC has passed the hardest part of the process. As Stromberg notes: "You have the domino effect. If the machine runs well, people won't take a chance. They'll buy your machine."

Source: "Greenville Machinery Corp.," *Journal of Commerce*, September 6, 1991, 5A.

Participation in the international marketplace can be a very rewarding activity, as The International Marketplace 7.1 shows, and can be the key to survival. But most firms cannot simply jump into international marketing and expect to be successful. New activities in an unfamiliar environment also increase a firm's risk. Therefore, companies must prepare their activities and adjust to the needs and opportunities of international markets in order to become long-term participants. Because of the gradual globalization of the marketplace,[1] however, firms have less and less time to adjust to new market realities. In addition, many firms are so exposed to international competition that they must participate, whether they want to or not.[2]

Because most firms start their international involvement with exporting, this chapter will discuss the export process by addressing the activities that take place within the firm preparing to enter the international marketplace. It will focus on the basic stimuli for exporting and will discuss the change agents, both internal and external, that activate these stimuli. In addition, the concerns and preoccupations of firms as they begin their international marketing operations will be discussed. Finally, a model of the export development process and strategic issues within the firm will be presented.

Managers must understand what "sells" to owners and decision makers in the firm so that they can aid in the move toward internationalization. Current and prospective employees must be able to assess the strategic direction of the firm. An awareness of the inherent attributes that make firms international can aid students in selecting the best environment in which to become active in international marketing.

MOTIVATIONS TO INTERNATIONALIZE

Many researchers have worked on determining the reasons why firms go international. A key factor is apparently the type and quality of management. Some researchers have shown that dynamic management is important when firms take their first international

[1] Theodore Levitt, "The Globalization of Markets," *Harvard Business Review* 61 (May–June 1983): 92–102.
[2] Michael R. Czinkota and Ilkka A. Ronkainen, "The Globalization of the U.S. Economy: Consumer Market Implications," *Journal of International Consumer Marketing* 3 (1991): 51–68.

steps.[3] Over the long term, management commitment and management's perceptions and attitudes are also good predictors of export success.[4] Also, managers of exporting firms typically show a higher level of formal education and foreign language fluency than do managers of nonexporting firms.[5] Other researchers have differentiated between active and passive firms and shown linkages with internationalization efforts.[6] Similarly, firms have been segmented into aggressive and nonaggressive,[7] with aggressive firms typically found to be more long-term oriented and active in a larger number of markets.[8]

All of the differentiations point toward a conclusion that the international marketing behavior of firms is related to managerial aspirations, capabilities, and the level of commitment that management is willing to give to the international marketing effort. To a large extent, this conclusion has been formulated by reverse deduction: The managers of firms that are unsuccessful or inactive in the international marketplace usually exhibit a lack of determination or devotion to international marketing. Because international markets cannot be penetrated overnight—but rather require a vast amount of market-development activity, market research, and sensitivity to foreign market factors—the issue of managerial commitment is a crucial one. This commitment must be able to endure stagnation and sometimes even setbacks and failure. To obtain such a commitment, it is important to involve all levels of management early on in the export planning process and to impress on all players that the effort will only succeed with a commitment that is companywide.[9]

In addition to the broad commitment, it is also important to establish a specific export structure in which someone has the responsibility for exporting. Without some specified responsibility center, the focus that is necessary for success is lost. Just one person assigned part time to international marketing activities can begin exploring and entering international markets.

In most business activities, one factor alone rarely accounts for any given action. Usually a mixture of factors results in firms taking steps in a given direction. This is true of internationalization; motivation consists of a variety of factors both pushing and pulling firms along the international path.[10] Table 7.1 provides an overview of the major motivations to internationalize. They are differentiated into proactive and reactive motivations. Proactive motivations represent stimuli to attempt strategic change. Reactive motivations influence firms that are responsive to environmental changes and adjust to them by changing their activities over time.

---

[3] Warren J. Bilkey and George Tesar, "The Export Behavior of Smaller Sized Wisconsin Manufacturing Firms," *Journal of International Business Studies* 8 (Spring/Summer 1977): 93–98.

[4] Nils-Erik Aaby and Stanley F. Slater, "Management Influences on Export Performance: A Review of the Empirical Literature, 1978–1988," *International Marketing Review* 6 (1989): 7–26.

[5] F.N. Burton and B.B. Schlegelmilch, "Profile Analyses of Non-Exporters versus Exporters Grouped by Export Involvement," *Management International Review* 27 (First Quarter, 1987): 38–49.

[6] Finn Wiedersheim-Paul, H.C. Olson, and L.S. Welch, "Pre-Export Activity: The First Step in Internationalization," *Journal of International Business Studies* 9 (Spring/Summer 1978): 47–58.

[7] George Tesar and Jesse S. Tarleton, "Comparison of Wisconsin and Virginia Small and Medium-Sized Exporters: Aggressive and Passive Exporters," in *Export Management: An International Context,* eds. Michael R. Czinkota and George Tesar (New York: Praeger Publishers, 1982), 85–112.

[8] Angela de Rocha, Carl H. Christensen, and Carlos Eduardo da Cunha, "Aggressive and Passive Exporters: A Study in the Brazilian Furniture Industry," *International Marketing Review* 7 (1990): 6–15.

[9] S. Tamer Cavusgil, "Preparing for Export Marketing," *International Trade Forum* 2 (1993): 16–30.

[10] S. Tamer Cavusgil, "Global Dimensions of Marketing," in *Marketing,* eds. Patrick E. Murphy and Ben M. Enis (Glenview, IL: Scott, Foresman, 1985), 577–599.

Major Motivations to Internationalize Small and Medium-Sized Firms	TABLE 7.1

Proactive
- Profit advantage
- Unique products
- Technological advantage
- Exclusive information
- Managerial urge
- Tax benefit
- Economies of scale

Reactive
- Competitive pressures
- Overproduction
- Declining domestic sales
- Excess capacity
- Saturated domestic markets
- Proximity to customers and ports

Proactive Motivations

The most stimulating proactive motivation to become involved in international marketing is the profit advantage. Management may perceive international sales as a potential source of higher profit margins or of more added-on profits. Of course, the perceived profitability, when planning to enter into international markets, is often quite different from profitability actually attained. Recent research has indicated that initial profitability may be quite low, particularly in international start-up operations.[11] The gap between perception and reality may be particularly large when the firm has not previously engaged in international market activities. Despite thorough planning, imponderable influences often shift the profit picture substantially. For example, a sudden shift in exchange rates may drastically alter profit forecasts even though they were based on careful market evaluation.

A second major stimulus emanates either from unique products or from a technological advantage. A firm may produce goods or services that are not widely available from international competitors or may have made technological advances in a specialized field. Again, real and perceived advantages should be differentiated. Many firms believe that theirs are unique products or services, even though this may not be the case in the international market. If products or technology are unique, however, they can certainly provide a competitive edge and result in major business success abroad. One issue to consider is how long such a technological or product advantage will continue. Historically, a firm with a competitive edge could count on being the sole supplier to foreign markets for years to come. This type of advantage, however, has shrunk dramatically because of competing technologies and a frequent lack of international patent protection.

Exclusive market information is another proactive stimulus. This includes knowledge about foreign customers, marketplaces, or market situations that is not widely shared by other firms. Such special knowledge may result from particular insights based

---

[11] Masaaki Kotabe and Michael R. Czinkota, "State Government Promotion of Manufacturing Exports: A Gap Analysis," *Journal of International Business Studies,* Winter, 1992: 637–658.

on a firm's international research, special contacts a firm may have, or simply being in the right place at the right time (for example, recognizing a good business situation during a vacation trip). Although exclusivity can serve well as an initial stimulus for international marketing activities, it will rarely provide prolonged motivation because competitors—at least in the medium run—can be expected to catch up with the information advantage of the firm.

Managerial urge is a motivation that reflects the desire, drive, and enthusiasm of management toward international marketing activities. This enthusiasm can exist simply because managers like to be part of a firm that operates internationally. (It sounds impressive.) Further, it can often provide a good reason for international travel—for example, to call on a major customer in the Bahamas during a cold winter month. Often, however, the managerial urge to internationalize is simply the reflection of general entrepreneurial motivation—of a desire for continuous growth and market expansion.[12] The International Marketplace 7.2 provides an example of a firm that has been able to combine a passion for exporting with a unique product.

Tax benefits can also play a major motivating role. In the United States, a tax mechanism called the **Foreign Sales Corporation** (**FSC**) has been instituted to assist exporters. It is in conformity with international agreements and provides firms with certain tax deferrals, thus making international marketing activities potentially more profitable. Whether FSC tax benefits exceed the costs firms incur by having to comply with the regulations depends on the extent of international marketing activities. Among other things, the regulations require the formation of a foreign subsidiary and the holding of directors' meetings abroad. If realized, FSC tax benefits allow the firm either to offer its products at a lower cost in foreign markets or to accumulate a higher profit. This may therefore tie in closely with the profit motivation.

A final major proactive motivation is economies of scale. Becoming a participant in international marketing activities may enable the firm to increase its output and therefore climb more rapidly on the learning curve. Ever since the Boston Consulting Group showed that a doubling of output can reduce production costs up to 30 percent, this effect has been very much sought. Increased production for the international market can therefore also help in reducing the cost of production for domestic sales and make the firm more competitive domestically as well.[13] This effect often results in the seeking of market share as a primary objective of firms. At an initial level of internationalization this may mean an increased search for export markets; later on, it can result in the opening of foreign subsidiaries and foreign production facilities. These latter effects are discussed later in the book.

Reactive Motivations

A second type of motivations, primarily characterized as reactive, influences firms to respond to changes and pressures of the business environment rather than attempt to blaze trails.

A prime form of reactive motivation is reaction to competitive pressures. A firm may fear losing domestic market share to competing firms that have benefited from the effect

---

[12] Yoo S. Yang, Robert P. Leone, and Dana L. Alden, "A Market Expansion Ability Approach to Identify Potential Exporters," *Journal of Marketing* 56 (January 1992): 84–96.

[13] Michael L. Ursic and Michael R. Czinkota, "An Experience Curve Explanation of Export Expansion," in *International Marketing Strategy: Environmental Assessment and Entry Strategies* (Fort Worth, Dryden Press, 1994), 133–141.

THE INTERNATIONAL MARKETPLACE   7.2

A Passionate Commitment to Exporting

A unique product plus a zeal for exporting have equaled success for Mirus Industries Corporation of California. Mirus makes digital film recorders that "print" onto 35mm film, which then can be processed into slides for color presentations. In the United States, typical users are medical researchers, college professors, business executives, and government officials. However, "in all parts of the world there is the same need to communicate ideas in an efficient and effective way" explains Mirus President Bruce MacKay.

Mirus Industries needed no coaxing into the international field of play. It knew it had a product with universal appeal and was therefore on the ball from the beginning, before it even had a single customer. In the two years since exporting became the focus, Mirus has recruited ten distributors in the Middle East, Far East, and Europe and is now exporting 60 percent of its production.

A unique feature of this successful global company is that it has a mere 13 employees. When questioned about the ability of a 13-person firm to perform internationally the way Mirus does, MacKay replies, "The answer is that you must want to export and have the courage to do it. You must approach the export market with a passionate commitment, and you must have a well-thought-out plan."

Central to Mirus' plan is the relationship with the foreign distributors. For MacKay, locating suitable distributors abroad is a "very difficult task requiring diligence, patience, and often a little luck." The often-skeptical international distributors must be made to feel comfortable and trusting. They need to know that you will be around in six months, says MacKay. He goes on to conclude that "You cannot expect instant results—you must remain patient and consistent in your dealings with distributors."

Important to Mirus is the actual travel to the foreign markets to learn about market conditions firsthand. In 18 months, MacKay has traveled to Japan 4 times, to Southeast Asia 2 times, and to Europe 3 times. Mirus believes that communication, quality, and collaboration are the keys to success. "You must keep in mind that international distributors are very savvy people who know what is going on in this high-tech world. Fax machines, magazines, and fast travel keep everyone up-to-date. Your international distributors are your local partners, and they represent your reputation. Never forget that."

Source: "Exporting Pays Off," *Business America*, August 23, 1993, 20.

of the economies of scale gained by international marketing activities. Further, it may fear losing foreign markets permanently to domestic competitors that decide to focus on these markets. Observing that domestic competitors are beginning to internationalize, and knowing that market share is most easily retained by the firm that obtains it initially, firms frequently enter the international market head over heels. Quick entry may result in similarly quick withdrawal once the firm recognizes that its preparation has been insufficient.

Similarly, overproduction can serve as a major reactive motivation. Historically, during downturns in the domestic business cycle, foreign markets were initially unaffected because of time lags. They provided an ideal outlet for inventories that were significantly above desired levels. Frequently, however, international market expansion motivated by overproduction did not represent full commitment by management, but rather **safety-valve activity.** Rather than develop an international marketing perspective by adjusting the marketing mix to needs abroad, firms using this strategy typically are short-term oriented. Often, export sales are stimulated via short-term price cuts.[14] As soon as the domestic market demand returns to previous levels, international marketing activities are curtailed or even terminated. Firms that have used such a strategy may encounter difficulties when trying to employ it again because many foreign customers are not interested in temporary or sporadic business relationships. This reaction from abroad, together with the lessons learned in past recessions—which highlighted the danger of large inventories—and the fact that the major industrial economies appear to be increasingly synchronized, may well lead to a decrease in the importance of this motivation over time.

Stable or declining domestic sales, whether measured in sales volume or market share, have a similar motivating effect. Products marketed by the firm domestically may be at the declining stage of the product life cycle. Instead of attempting a push-back of the life cycle process domestically, or in addition to such an effort, firms may opt to prolong the product life cycle by expanding the market. In the past, such efforts often met with success because customers in many countries only gradually reached a level of need and sophistication already attained by customers in industrialized nations. Increasingly, however, if lag times exist at all in foreign markets, they are quite short. Nevertheless, this motivation is still a valid one, particularly in the context of developing nations, which often still have very good use for products for which the demand in the industrialized world is already on the decline. The International Marketplace 7.3 provides an example of such a product life cycle extension.

Excess capacity can also be a powerful motivation. If equipment for production is not fully utilized, firms may see expansion into the international market as an ideal possibility for achieving broader distribution of fixed costs. Alternately, if all fixed costs are assigned to domestic production, the firm can penetrate international markets with a pricing scheme that focuses mainly on variable costs. Although such a strategy may be useful in the short term, it may result in the offering of products abroad at a cost lower than at home, which in turn may trigger dumping charges. In the long run, fixed costs have to be recovered to ensure replacement of production equipment that growing international marketing activities may overtax. Market penetration strategy based on variable cost alone is therefore not feasible over the long term.

The reactive motivation of a saturated domestic market is similar in results to that of declining domestic sales. Again, firms in this situation can use the international market to prolong the life cycle of their product and of their organization.

A final major reactive motivation is proximity to customers and ports. Physical and psychological closeness to the international market can often play a major role in the export activities of a firm. For example, U.S. firms established near the Canadian border may not even perceive of their market activities in Canada as international marketing. Rather, they are simply an extension of domestic activities, without any particular attention being paid to the fact that some of the products go abroad. Except for some firms close to the Canadian or Mexican border, however, this factor is much less prevalent in the United States than in many other countries. Unlike European firms, most American

---

[14] C. P. Rao, M. Krishna Erramilli, and Gopala K. Ganesh, "Impact of Domestic Recession on Export Marketing Behaviour," *International Marketing Review* 7 (1990): 54–65.

THE INTERNATIONAL MARKETPLACE 7.3

Exports Permit Continued Growth

Sometimes a firm may find that its market has become "mature" and that future prospects for growth are dim. If the health of the enterprise is to be sustained, management will need to find a larger customer pool—often abroad.

This scenario is what drove Beral Inc. of Chatsworth, California, a manufacturer of medical laboratory products, into the global market. According to Ralph Garren, the president of Beral, "We faced strong competition in the United States, and with the recession, were no longer able to achieve the 20 percent growth that we once had. This growth level is important to the firm because it has high-volume, low-cost products."

Beral began its thrust toward the global market by sending press releases to international bio-tech and laboratory journals. The firm also placed advertisements in foreign professional publications. Another tactic was to advertise in the Commerce Department's catalog magazine *Commercial News USA.* Says Garren: "These ads opened up a dialog with potential overseas customers. They became aware of our products and our company."

As a next step, Beral decided to participate in crucial international trade fairs in Mexico, Germany, Spain, and Italy. Before attending the fairs, however, the firm made appointments with key decision makers from all around the world who were also attending the fairs.

Garren describes the results of these activities: "We are finding good, 'non mature' markets overseas. Some countries are 20 years behind the United States in the use of disposable laboratory products of the type we make."

Beral now has distributors in Europe and the Pacific Rim and negotiates with firms in Latin America. In the first year of exporting, foreign sales totaled 5 percent of total sales. Three years later, this figure has grown to almost 30 percent. Even though it took external forces and environmental change to push Beral into exporting, the 80-person company is now working hard and with dedication to attract global business.

Source: "Exporting Pays Off," *Business America,* May 31, 1993, 20.

firms are situated far away from foreign countries. Considering the radius of domestic activity of many U.S. firms, which may be 200 miles, and applying such a radius to a European scenario, most European firms automatically become international marketers simply because their neighbors are so close. As an example, a European company operating in Belgium need go only 50 miles to be in multiple foreign markets.

In this context, the concept of psychic or **psychological distance** needs to be understood.[15] Geographic closeness to foreign markets may not necessarily translate into real or perceived closeness to the foreign customer. Sometimes cultural variables, legal factors, and other societal norms make a foreign market that is geographically close seem psychologically distant. For example, research has shown that U.S. firms perceive Canada to be much closer psychologically than Mexico. Even England, mainly because of the

[15] Wiedersheim-Paul, Olson, and Welch, "Pre-Export Activity," 47–58.

similarity in language, is perceived by many U.S. firms to be much closer than Mexico or other Latin American countries, despite the geographic distances. However, in light of the reduction of trade barriers as a result of the North American Free Trade Agreement (NAFTA), this long-standing perception may well change rapidly.

An overall contemplation of these motivations should also consider the following factors. First, firms that are most successful in exporting are motivated by proactive—that is, firm-internal—factors. Second, the motivations of firms do not seem to shift dramatically over the short term but are rather stable. For the student who seeks involvement in international markets and searches for firms that provide the most adequate environment, an important strategic consideration is whether a firm is proactive or reactive.

The proactive firm is also more likely to be service oriented than are reactive firms. Further, it is frequently more marketing and strategy oriented than reactive firms, which have as their major concern operational issues. The clearest differentiation between the two types of firms can probably be made *ex post facto* by determining how they initially entered international markets. Proactive firms are more likely to solicit their first international marketing order, whereas reactive firms frequently begin international marketing activities after receiving an unsolicited order from abroad.

All of these considerations lead to the questions of how the activities of firms can be changed and, ideally, of how the student and future employee can be part of this change.

CHANGE AGENTS

For change to take place, someone or something within the firm must initiate it and shepherd it through to implementation. This intervening individual or variable is here called a **change agent.** Change agents in the internationalization process are shown in Table 7.2.

Internal Change Agents

A primary internal change agent is enlightened management. The current management of a firm discovers and understands the value of international markets and decides to pursue international marketing opportunities. Trigger factors frequently are foreign travel, during which new business opportunities are discovered, or the receipt of information that leads management to believe that such opportunities exist. Managers who have lived abroad, have learned foreign languages, or are particularly interested in for-

TABLE 7.2	**Change Agents in the Internationalization Process**

Firm Internal
- Enlightened management
- New management
- Significant internal event

Firm External
- Demand
- Other firms
- Distributors
- Banks
- Chambers of commerce
- Export agents
- Governmental activities

Key Managerial Characteristics Affecting Export Involvement	TABLE 7.3
Education International exposure Expertise International orientation Commitment	

Source: Michael R. Czinkota, "A National Export Development Strategy for New and Growing Businesses," Remarks Delivered to the National Economic Council, Washington D.C., August 6, 1993, 19.

eign cultures are likely, sooner rather than later, to investigate whether international marketing opportunities would be appropriate for their firm. Key managerial characteristics that have been shown to affect firms' export involvement are shown in Table 7.3.

A second set of major internal change agents consists of new management or new employees. Often, managers enter a firm having already had some international marketing experience in previous positions and try to use this experience to further the business activities of their new firm. Also, in developing their goals in the new job, managers frequently consider an entirely new set of options, one of which may be international marketing activities.

A significant internal event can be another major change agent. A new employee who firmly believes that the firm should undertake international marketing may find ways to motivate management. Overproduction or a reduction in domestic market size can serve as such an event, as can the receipt of new information about current product uses. As an example, a manufacturer of hospital beds learned that beds it was selling domestically were being resold in a foreign country. Further, the beds it sold for $600 each were resold overseas for approximately $1,300. This new piece of information served to trigger a strong interest on the part of the company's management in entering international markets.

Research has shown that in small and medium-sized firms, meaning firms with fewer than 250 employees, the initial decision to export usually is made by the president, with substantial input provided by the marketing department. The carrying out of the decision—that is, the initiation of actual international marketing activities and the implementation of these activities—is then primarily the responsibility of marketing personnel. Only in the final decision stage of evaluating international marketing activities does the major emphasis rest again with the president of the firm. In order to influence a firm internally, it therefore appears that the major emphasis should be placed first on convincing the president to enter the international marketplace and then on convincing the marketing department that international marketing is an important activity. Conversely, the marketing department is a good place to be if one wants to become active in international business.

External Change Agents

The primary outside influence on a firm's decision to become international is foreign demand. Expressions of such demand through, for example, inquiries from abroad have a powerful effect on initial interest in entering the international marketplace. Unsolicited orders from abroad are the one major factor that encourages firms to begin exporting—even though over the past decade, firms increasingly have come to recognize that they must take the initiative in getting started in exporting.[16]

---

[16] Anthony C. Koh and Robert A. Robicheaux, "Variation in Export Performance Due to Differences in Export Marketing Strategy: Implications for Industrial Marketers," *Journal of Business Research* 17 (November 1988): 249–258.

Another major outside influence is the statements and actions of other firms in the same industry. Information that an executive in a competing firm considers international markets to be valuable and worthwhile to develop easily captures the attention of management. Such statements not only have source credibility but also are viewed with a certain amount of fear because a too-successful competitor may eventually infringe on the firm's business. Formal and informal meetings among managers from different firms at trade-association meetings, conventions, or business roundtables therefore often serve as a major change agent.

A third, quite influential, change agent consists of distributors. Often, distributors of firms are engaged, through some of their other business activities, in international marketing. To increase their international distribution volume, they encourage purely domestic firms also to participate in the international market. This is true not only for exports but also for imports. For example, a major customer of a manufacturing firm may find that materials available from abroad, if used in the domestic production process, would make the product available at lower cost. In such instances, the customer may approach the supplier and strongly encourage foreign sourcing. Many firms, although they may not like the suggestion, are flexible when they face the loss or potential loss of a major account.

Banks and other service firms, such as accountants, can serve as major change agents by alerting domestic clients to international opportunities. Although these service providers historically follow their major multinational clients abroad, increasingly they are establishing a foreign presence. They frequently work with domestic clients on expanding their market reach in the hope that their services will be used for any international transactions that result.

Chambers of commerce and other business associations that interact with firms locally can frequently heighten international marketing interests. In most instances, these organizations function only as secondary intermediaries, because true change is brought about by the presence and encouragement of other managers.

Export agents are experienced in bringing about an international marketing orientation through two major kinds of activities. Some agents actively seek new international business activities. They visit firms and encourage them to penetrate international markets. In the past, firms often paid a basic fee to such agents and, subsequent to any sales, a commission on these sales. The incidence of such business transactions, however, is decreasing because fewer and fewer firms are willing to pay up-front fees. Increasingly, firms themselves seek out agents to market their products.[17]

In either case, several issues need to be considered. First, agents have limited expertise and usually are knowledgeable only in some markets or some product lines. Second, agents take on a product to generate a profit for themselves. Either they are quite selective in choosing customers and new products or they are not able to provide a substantial enough international marketing effort to be successful. In addition, agents charge directly or indirectly for all of the marketing functions they perform, which often may make international marketing efforts less profitable than originally expected.

Governmental efforts on the national or local level can also serve as a major change agent. In light of the contributions exports make to growth, employment, and tax revenue, governments increasingly are becoming active in encouraging and supporting exports. As was explained in a previous chapter, export promotion has become an integral part of most nations' trade policies. The International Marketplace 7.4 explains how Ghana goes about helping firms to export.

---

[17] John J. Brasch, "Using Export Specialists to Develop Overseas Sales," *Harvard Business Review* 59 (May–June 1981): 6–8.

THE INTERNATIONAL MARKETPLACE   7.4

The Ghana Export School

For developing nations, exporting is often a key element in the process of serious economic reform. One case in point is the West African nation of Ghana.

In an effort to diversify and promote exports, Ghana implemented a series of policy and institutional reforms. To expand the country's exports, a number of government goals were formulated: the need for increased knowledge of export opportunities, greater familiarity with export techniques, and a heightened export consciousness among current and potential export enterprises.

To meet these goals, a well-organized program of foreign trade training was called for, which could best be provided by a special school created for that purpose. A national survey showed that several existing training institutions were providing some programs in trade-related topics, but very few offered practical export marketing courses on a regular basis for business executives and trade promotion officials.

In April, 1989, the Ghana Export Promotion Council established the Ghana Export School (GES) with the following objectives:

- Generate export consciousness in the business sector, which had traditionally been import oriented;
- Create an awareness of the importance of exports in official circles to obtain positive responses from the government;
- Provide the business community with the necessary techniques for developing and managing export business efficiency;
- Spread the results of such training throughout the export community to as many companies as possible; and
- Provide a forum for discussing, evaluating, and finding solutions to export development problems in the country.

The Ghana Export School is a particularly innovative experiment, as it has no campus, training facilities, or a faculty of its own. It draws its speakers and course developers from business and government, uses the facilities of existing training institutions, and develops its own training materials based on local experience. By cooperating closely with the business sector and established training institutions, the school is able to provide a wide range of practical seminars and workshops in the foreign trade sector with minimum investment, tailored to the needs of the export community.

The GES offers approximately 20 training events annually. They cover a broad spectrum of subjects dealing with both techniques and products, reflecting exporters' training needs as well as the country's efforts to diversify its export product mix. The school holds workshops on mushroom production for export, packaging and labeling, the role of banks in export, export marketing for women entrepreneurs, and export production management for village enterprises.

The school has already trained nearly 1,600 government officials, export executives, and future exporters. It is expected that approximately 1,000 persons will be trained annually in the next several years. Besides serving as a means to upgrade export skills, the training programs have increased export consciousness in the country and have improved export performance. Through

continued

the training, exporters have been able to improve the quality and presentation of their products, which has resulted in a significant drop in the number of export goods rejected by both the Standards Institute in Ghana and importers in foreign markets.

Both the concept and the role of the Ghana Export School have been firmly accepted by the export community, academia, and trade-supporting institutions. A significant and sustainable contribution to the development of human resources in the foreign trade sector of Ghana has been achieved.

Source: Claude Cellich and Kwesi Ahwoi, "The Ghana Export School: Success with Minimum Investment," *International Trade Forum* (January–March 1992): 20–27.

In the United States, the Department of Commerce is particularly involved in encouraging exports. Its district offices are charged with increasing the international marketing activities of U.S. firms. Frequently, district officers, with the help of voluntary groups such as district export councils, visit firms and attempt to analyze their international marketing opportunities. Such activities raise questions about market and product specialization. Only rarely will Department of Commerce employees have expertise in all areas. However, they can draw on the vast resources of the department to provide more information to an interested firm. For a firm new to exporting, Department of Commerce activities can be quite useful. As firms acquire more expertise in international marketing, the assistance may decline in value.

Increasingly, other governmental entities are also actively encouraging firms to participate in the international market. This takes place primarily on the state and local level. Many states have formed economic development agencies that assist companies by providing information, displaying products abroad, and sometimes even helping with financing. Trade missions and similar activities are also being carried out by some of the larger cities. Although it is difficult to measure the effects of these efforts,[18] it appears that due to their closeness to firms, such state and local government authorities can become a major factor in influencing firms to go international.

INTERNATIONALIZATION STAGES

Normally, internationalization is a gradual process. Only rarely is a firm formed expressly to engage in international marketing activities, particularly in a market as large as the United States. In small markets, however, firms may very well be founded for the explicit purpose of marketing abroad because of the recogzized importance of international marketing and because the domestic economy may be too small to support their activities. Research conducted in Israel, for example, has shown that such **innate,** or start-up, **exporters** may have a distinct role to play in an economy's international trade involvement.[19] Nevertheless, in most instances, firms begin their operations in the domestic market. Over time, some of them become interested in the international market.

The development of this interest typically appears to proceed in several stages. In each one of these stages, firms are measurably different in their capabilities, problems,

---

[18] Thomas Singer and Michael R. Czinkota, "Factors Associated with Effective Use of Export Assistance," *Journal of International Marketing* 2 no. 1 (1994): 53–71.

[19] Joseph Ganitsky, "Strategies for Innate and Adoptive Exporters: Lessons from Israel's Case," *International Marketing Review* 6 (1989): 50–65.

and needs.[20] In looking at the internationalization process, one finds that initially the vast majority of firms are not at all interested in the international marketplace. Frequently, management will not even fill an unsolicited export order if one is received. Should unsolicited orders or other international market stimuli continue over time, however, a firm may gradually become a **partially interested exporter.** Management will then fill unsolicited export orders.

Prime candidates among firms to make this transition from unintereseted to partially interested are those companies that have a track record of domestic market expansion.[21] In the next stage, the firm gradually begins to explore international markets, and management is willing to consider the feasibility of exporting. After this **exploratory** stage, the firm becomes an **experimental exporter,** usually to psychologically close countries. However, management is still far from being committed to international marketing activities.

At the next stage, the firm evaluates the impact that exporting has had on its general activities. Here, of course, the possibility exists that a firm will be disappointed with its international market performance and will withdraw from these activities. On the other hand, frequently, it will continue to exist as an experienced small exporter. The final stage of this process is that of **export adaptation.** Here a firm is an experienced exporter to a particular country and adjusts exports to changing exchange rates, tariffs, and other variables. Management is ready to explore the feasibility of exporting to additional countries that are psychologically farther away. Frequently, this level of adaptation is reached once export transactions comprise 15 percent of sales volume. Just as parking ticket income, originally seen as surprise revenue, gradually became incorporated into city budgets, the income from export marketing may become incorporated into the budget and plans of the firm. In these instances, the firm can be considered a strategic participant in the international market.

INTERNATIONALIZATION CONCERNS

As can be expected, firms that enter the international marketplace are faced with a host of new problems. Table 7.4 lists main corporate concerns at the different internationalization stages. Uninterested firms are not included because the international marketplace appears too problematic and unrewarding to them to become active.

Firms at an export awareness stage—partially interested in the international market—are primarily concerned with operational matters such as information flow and the mechanics of carrying out international business transactions. They understand that a totally new body of knowledge and expertise is needed and try to acquire it. Companies that have already had some exposure to international markets begin to think about tactical marketing issues such as communication and sales effort. Finally, firms that have reached the export adaptation phase are mainly strategy and service oriented, which is to say that they worry about longer-range issues such as service delivery and regulatory changes. Utilizing the traditional marketing concept, one can therefore recognize that increased sophistication in international markets translates into increased application of marketing knowledge on the part of firms. The more they become active in international markets, the more firms recognize that a marketing orientation internationally is just as essential as it is in the domestic market.

---

[20] Masaaki Kotabe and Michael R. Czinkota, "State Government Promotion of Manufacturing Exports: A Gap Analysis," *Journal of International Business Studies* (Winter, 1992): 637–658.

[21] Yoo S. Yang, Robert P. Leone, and Dana L. Alden, "A Market Expansion Ability Approach to Identify Potential Exporters," *Journal of Marketing* 56 (January 1992): 84–96.

TABLE 7.4	Main Corporate Concerns in Each of the Internationalization Stages[a]				
Rank	2 Partially Interested Firm	3 Exploring Firm	4 Experimental Exporter	5 Experienced Small Exporter	6 Experienced Larger Exporter
1	Financing	Communication	Sales effort	Communication	Communication
2	Information on business practices	Sales effort	Obtaining financial information	Sales effort	Sales effort
3	Communication	Marketing information gathering	Physical product	Marketing information gathering	Marketing information gathering
4	Providing technical advice	Information on business practices	Marketing information gathering	Obtaining financial information	Providing repair service
5	Sales effort	Obtaining financial information	Information on business practices	Handling documentation	Information on business practices

[a]Firms in Stage 1 are uninterested in international activities.

Source: Michael R. Czinkota, *Export Development Strategies: U.S. Promotion Policy* (New York: Praeger Publishers, 1982), 101.

Linking the various decision components and characteristics discussed so far facilitates an understanding of the process that a firm must undergo in its internationalization efforts. Figure 7.1 presents a model of the internationalization process, with a particular focus on exporting. The model demonstrates the interaction between components and shows how a firm gradually grows into becoming a full participant in the global arena. With the help of this model, both management and the prospective employee can determine the firm's stage in the export development process and the changes needed to attain continued progress. To highlight the key implications of the different internationalization stages, the following profiles of companies delineate some of the more outstanding characteristics of firms in each one of these stages.

Stage 1: The Completely Uninterested Firm

Profile   Most firms at this stage have an annual sales volume of less than $5 million and fewer than 100 employees. The main decision maker is the president. The firm does not export and does not plan to do so in the future. Management is not exploring the possibility of exporting nor will unsolicited export orders be filled. Management tends to believe that exports will not contribute to the firm's profits or growth.

Assistance Requirements   Raise awareness level of exporting.

Implementation Strategies   Increase communication that expounds the value of exporting on an unsolicited basis. Through trade associations and miniconferences, communicate the tangible benefits of exporting. Use successful small exporters from a peer or reference group as role models, asking them to provide testimonials and case studies to firms not interested in exporting. Increase information dissemination showing the size and profitability of foreign markets. Increase international education in schools to foster awareness of the international marketplace. Expose management to export activity figures by industry, export profitability statistics, and data about the impact of specific export activities on the balance of trade.

A Model of the Export Development Process   **FIGURE 7.1**

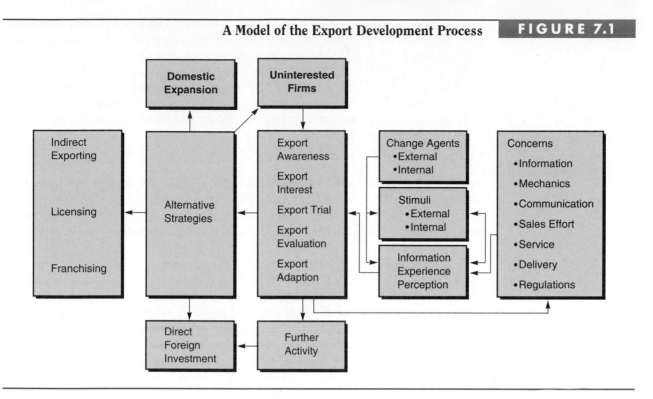

Stage 2: The Partially Interested Firm

Profile   Most firms have an annual sales volume below $5 million and fewer than 100 employees. The current average annual export volume is below $200,000, which is sold to fewer than ten customers. One-quarter of the firms have actively sought their first export order. Almost half of the firms started exporting to Canada, to which they currently ship half of their exports. The president of the firm has the most input in the export decision; the marketing manager is a close second. Management knows that the firm has exportable products and tries to fill export orders. Management tends to believe that exporting may be a desirable activity and undertakes some exploration of export possibilities. Management is uncertain whether the firm will export more in the future and whether exports will contribute to the firm's growth and profits. The main motivations for exporting are a unique product and profit advantage.

Areas that the firm tends to see as being to some degree a problem in the export effort are financing, information on business practices, communication, the providing of technical advice, and sales effort. Firms believe that outsiders can be of substantial help to their export effort by assisting with obtaining financial information, financing, documentation handling, communication, and funds transfer.

Assistance Requirements   Raise awareness levels of export benefits. Assist with information about the mechanics of exporting.

Implementation Strategies   Use case studies to demonstrate the benefits that can be derived from exporting. Increase communications to make firms more aware of existing services. Provide these services in an accurate and timely fashion. Respond to export financing requests from such firms through more active small-volume export financing by Eximbank or by establishing a facility that provides occasional exporters with small-sized credits (below $100,000) in a rapid fashion. Train employees to handle routine documentation problems and to have a general knowledge of the mechanics of the international transfer of funds. Institute a centralized task force within the Department of Commerce to provide rapid access for field officers with nonroutine problems. Encourage universities to include commercial aspects in their foreign language courses. Create university language banks that, for a small fee, aid firms in translating foreign documents.

Stage 3: The Exploring Firm

Profile   Most firms have an annual sales volume below $10 million and fewer than 100 employees. These firms export about $500,000 worth of merchandise to fewer than 20 customers. More than one-third of the firms have actively sought the first export order, which mainly originated from Canada. Currently, about one-third of their exports go to Canada.

In management, the president is the major export decision maker. The desirability of exporting is well known, as is the fact that the firm has exportable products. The firm is planning on exporting and is actively exploring export possibilities. The potential contribution of exporting to the firm's growth and profits is acknowledged, but past export profits have not met expectations. Having a unique product and obtaining a profit advantage are principal motivating factors for exporting. Important problems are encountered in the areas of communication, sales effort, marketing information gathering, information on business practices, and obtaining financial information.

Outside assistance is seen as valuable in the areas of obtaining financial information, information on business practices, marketing information gathering, documentation handling, and communication.

Assistance Requirements   Make exporting more profitable. Provide general information and practical assistance.

Implementation Strategies   To increase the profitability of exports, the use of a Foreign Sales Corporation (FSC) by such firms could be increased, resulting in a tax deferral. Tax legislation reducing the corporate tax rate on the first $200,000 of exports may also be a significant incentive. An increase in deductions for export losses may also help increase the profitability of exploring firms. The possibility of entering into risk- and profit-sharing agreements with a government agency for a specified amount of initial exports could also be considered. Books and brochures containing current general market data and a wide distribution of these publications can help satisfy the general information needs. Cooperation with universities, as mentioned for Stage 2, would also help.

Stage 4: The Experimental Exporter

Profile   Most firms have an annual sales volume of less than $5 million and have fewer than 100 employees. Average exports are about $750,000 and are shipped to about ten customers. One-third of the firms actively sought their first export order, which came mostly from Canada. Currently, one-third of the exports go to Canada.

The president is the major decision maker. Exporting is seen favorably, but little active exploration of export possibilities takes place. Principal motivating factors for exporting are a unique product, technological advantage, and profit advantage.

Important exporting problems are seen in the areas of sales effort, obtaining financial information, physical product adaptation, marketing information gathering, and information on business practices.

Outside assistance is seen as somewhat helpful in the areas of marketing information gathering, information on business practices, handling documentation, obtaining financial information, and communication.

Assistance Requirements   Encourage the active exploration of exporting. Provide general assistance and help with product adaptation.

Implementation Strategies   Provide management with foreign purchasing requests for products manufactured by these firms. Increase participation of these firms in foreign exhibitions. Search for contacts for these firms and carry out initial contacts for them. By functioning as an intermediary placing export orders with firms, an institution could clearly demonstrate the benefits of exporting without forcing firms to partake in the initial risk. Apart from the general assistance, increased information on foreign product standards should be communicated to these firms. Tax legislation that would permit increased deductions for costs incurred in product adaptations would help reduce the strength of this problem.

Stage 5: The Experienced Small Exporter

Profile   Average annual sales volume is below $10 million. Most firms employ fewer than 100 people. The export volume is slightly below $1.5 million and is shipped to an average of 40 customers. Four out of ten firms actively sought their first export order. One-third of the firms started their exporting to Canada, to which they currently ship one-fourth of their exports.

The president is the major decision maker, with strong input from the vice president for marketing. Exporting is seen in a very favorable light. Only the past profitability of export activities is called into question. Profit advantage, a unique product, managerial urge, and a technological advantage are the main factors motivating exporting. Problems encountered in exporting are important in the areas of communication, sales effort, marketing information gathering, obtaining financial information, and handling documentation. Outside assistance is seen as somewhat helpful in the areas of gathering information on business practices, marketing information gathering, obtaining financial information, communication, and financing.

Assistance Requirements   Make exporting more profitable. Provide general assistance. Help with financing.

Implementation Strategies   Encourage the use of FSC (Foreign Sales Corporation) for these groups. Financial assistance is now needed in greater size and for longer time periods than for firms in lower stages. Rapid responses to financing requests are not that important here. An increase in the cooperation with Eximbank will help satisfy this need. Training seminars on export financing would be of value to firms in this stage. Requests for financial information need to be addressed rapidly and accurately.

Stage 6: The Experienced Larger Exporter

Profile   Most firms have an average annual sales volume below $50 million and employ between 100 and 250 persons. Average annual export volume is about $6 million, shipped to about 140 customers. About one-half of the firms actively sought their first export order. One-fifth of the firms began their export activities with Canada, to which they now ship one-eighth of their exports.

The president and the marketing manager are the main export decision makers in the firm. Exporting is seen in a very favorable light, with the firm planning to be continuously active in the future. Main motivating factors for exporting are profit advantage, technological advantage, competitive pressures, FSC legislation, a unique product, and managerial urge. Important problems are encountered in the areas of communication, sales effort, marketing information gathering, the providing of repair service, and information on business practices. Outside assistance is seen as possibly helpful in the areas of marketing information gathering, information on business practices, obtaining financial information, financing, and funds transfer.

Assistance Requirements   Facilitate customer service. Provide general assistance.

Implementation Strategies   To facilitate customer service abroad, companies should be encouraged to train foreign personnel, enabling them to provide such services abroad. These training costs, jointly with the indirect cost of customer service, such as the translation of repair manuals, could receive preferential tax treatment through multiple deductions to allow firms export expansion without strong hindrance by customer-service cost consideration. The further granting of tax incentives to such firms should be reconsidered because they are currently satisfied with the profitability of the exporting efforts and sufficiently committed to the continuation of their international activities even without tax benefits.

CORPORATE STRATEGY AND EXPORTING

As a firm moves through the internationalization stages, unusual things can happen to both risk and profit. In light of the gradual development of expertise, the many concerns about engaging in a new activity, and a firm's uncertainty with the new environment it is about to enter, management's perception of risk exposure grows. Domestically, the firm has gradually learned about the market and therefore managed to decrease its risk. In the course of new international expansion, the firm now encounters new and unfamiliar factors, exposing it to increased risk. At the same time, because of the investment needs required by a serious export effort, immediate profit performance may slip. In the longer term, increasing familiarity with international markets and the benefits of serving diversified markets will decrease the firm's risk below the previous "domestic only" level and increase profitability as well. In the short term, however, managers may face an unusual, and perhaps unacceptable, situation: rising risk accompanied by decreasing profitability. In light of this reality, which is depicted in Figure 7.2, many executives are tempted to either not initiate export activities or to discontinue them.[22]

Understanding the internationalization stages together with the behavior of risk and profitability can help management overcome the seemingly prohibitive cost of going international and show that the negative developments are only short term. Yet, export success does require the firm to be a risk taker, and firms must realize that satisfactory export performance will take time.[23] This satisfactory performance can be achieved in three ways: export effectiveness, efficiency, and competitive strength. Effectiveness is characterized by the acquisition of market share abroad and by increased sales.

[22] Michael R. Czinkota, "A National Export Development Policy for New and Growing Businesses," *Journal of International Marketing* 2 no. 1 (1994): 91–101.

[23] Van Miller, Tom Becker, and Charles Crespy, "Contrasting Export Strategies: A Discriminant Analysis Study of Excellent Exporters," *The International Trade Journal* 7 no. 3 (1993): 321–340.

Profit and Risk During Export Initiation

FIGURE 7.2

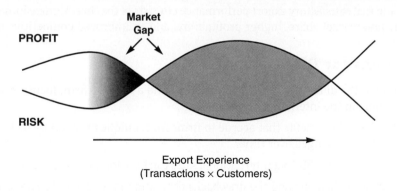

Source: Michael R. Czinkota, "A National Export Development Policy for New and Growing Businesses," *Journal of International Marketing* 2 no. 1 (1994): 95.

Efficiency is manifested later by rising profitability. Competitive strength refers then to the firm's position compared to other firms in the industry, and is, due to the benefits of international market experience, likely to grow. The international marketer must appreciate the time and performance dimensions associated with going abroad in order to overcome short-term setbacks for the sake of long-term success.

SUMMARY

Firms do not become experienced exporters overnight but rather progress gradually through an export development process. This process is the result of different motivations to internationalize different managerial and corporate characteristics of the firm, the efforts of change agents, and the capability of the firm to overcome internationalization barriers.

The motivations can be either proactive or reactive. Proactive motivations are initiated by the firm's management and can consist of a perceived profit advantage, technological advantage, product advantage, exclusive market information, or managerial urge. Reactive motivations are the responses of management to environmental changes and pressures. Typical are competitive pressures, overproduction, declining domestic sales, or excess capacity. Firms that are primarily stimulated by proactive motivations are more likely to enter international markets aggressively and successfully.

An international orientation can also be brought about by change agents both external and internal to the firm. Typically, these are individuals and institutions that, due to their activities or goals, highlight the benefits of international activities. They can be managers who have traveled abroad or have carried out successful international marketing ventures, foreign distributors who have inquired about the possibility of representing a firm, or organizations such as banks, government agencies, or trading consortia.

Over time, firms will progress through stages of international expertise and activity. In each one of these stages, firms are likely to have a distinct level of interest in the international market and require different types of information and help. Their outlook toward international markets is likely to progress gradually from purely operational concerns to a strategic international orientation. Only at that level will the firm have become a truly international marketer.

In spite of temporary unfavorable conditions for risk and profit, management must understand that export activities only develop gradually through the internationalization stages, and that satisfactory export performance consists of the three dimensions of growing sales and market share, higher profitability, and an improved competitive position.

Questions for Discussion

1. Discuss the difference between a proactive and a reactive firm, focusing your discussion on the international market.
2. How have the benefits that accrue to firms from unique products or technological advantages changed over time?
3. Explain the benefits that international sales can have for domestic market activities.
4. Discuss the benefits and the drawbacks of treating international market activities as a safety-valve mechanism.
5. What is meant by the concept of "psychological, or psychic, distance"?
6. Give some of the reasons why distributors would want to help a firm gain a stronger foothold in the international market.
7. To what well-known marketing concept does the export development process of the small or medium-sized firm relate?
8. How do the concerns of firms change as the firms progress in their internationalization efforts?

Recommended Readings

Cavusgil, S. Tamer, and Michael R. Czinkota, eds. *Trade Promotion and Assistance: International Perspectives.* Westport, CT: Quorum Books, 1990.

Czinkota, Michael R., and Ilkka A. Ronkainen. *International Marketing Strategy: Environmental Assessment and Entry Strategies.* Fort Worth: Dryden Press, 1994.

Czinkota, Michael R., and George Tesar, eds. *Export Management: An International Context.* New York: Praeger Publishers, 1982.

The Export Yellow Pages. Washington, D.C.: Venture Publishing Co., 1994.

Hibbert, Edgar P. *The Management of International Trade Promotion,* London: Routledge, Chapman, & Hall, Inc., 1990.

Joyner, Nelson, and Richard G. Lurie. *How to Build an Export Business.* Washington, D.C.: U.S. Department of Commerce, Office of Minority Business Enterprise, n.d.

Kaynak, Erdener, ed. *The Global Business: Four Key Marketing Strategies.* New York: International Business Press, 1993.

Luostarinen, Reijo, and Lawrence Welch. *International Business Operations,* Helsinki, Finland: Helsinki School of Economics, 1990.

Nothdurft, William E. *Going Global: How Europe Helps Small Firms Export.* Washington, D.C.: Brookings Institution, 1992.

Paliwoda, Stanley. *New Perspectives on International Marketing.* London: Routledge, Chapman, & Hall, Inc. 1991.

Root, Franklin R. *Entry Strategies for International Markets.* New York: Lexington Books, 1994.

Rosson, Philip J., and Stanley D. Reid. *Managing Export Entry and Expansion.* New York: Praeger Publishers, 1987.

Seringhaus, F. H. Rolf and Philip J. Rosson. *Export Development and Promotion: The Role of Public Organizations.* Boston: Kluwer Academic Publishers, 1991.

U.S. Department of Commerce. *A Basic Guide to Exporting.* Washington, D.C.: Government Printing Office, 1986.

CHAPTER 8

Secondary International Marketing Research

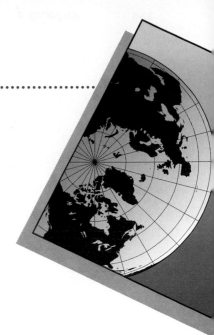

Even though most managers recognize the need for domestic marketing research, the single most important cause for failure in the international marketplace is insufficient preparation and information. When analyzing an international marketing failure, one often finds that major errors could have been avoided if only the firm and its managers had had an adequate understanding of the business environment.[1] This hindsight, however, does not lead to an automatic increase in international marketing research. Instead, failures continue to occur because firms either do not believe that international market research is worthwhile or face manpower and resource bottlenecks that impede research.

Two basic forms of research exist: primary research, where data are collected for specific research purposes, and secondary research, where use is made of data that have already been collected. The international marketing research issues discussed in this book are divided along these two lines. This chapter will focus on secondary research, which often is the only form of research a smaller firm carries out or can afford. The chapter will introduce ways of obtaining basic information quickly, ensuring that the information is reasonably accurate, and doing so with a commitment of limited corporate resources.

The field of primary research, which can answer more in-depth questions for the firm and is often crucial in carrying out a precise assessment of the market, is covered later in the text. Even though both smaller and larger firms can use such research, the larger ones are more likely to have the funding to carry out primary data collections or to develop an international marketing decision support system.

DEFINING THE ISSUE

To discuss international marketing research, we first need to clearly understand the meaning of marketing research. The definitions committee of the American Marketing Association (AMA) defines **marketing research** as "the systematic gathering, recording, and analyzing of data about problems relating to the marketing of goods and services."[2] This statement highlights several important aspects of marketing research. It emphasizes the need for systematic work, indicating that research should be the result of planned and organized activity rather than of coincidence. Second, it highlights the need to work with data rather than with judgment alone, therefore making information accumulation a necessary prerequisite for marketing research. Finally, it addresses the need for the data-gathering process to relate to specific problems. Marketing research cannot take place in a void; rather, it must have a business purpose.

A more recent definition states that marketing research is "a systematic and objective approach to the development and provision of information for the marketing management decision-making process."[3] This statement enriches the AMA's definition. It includes the term *objective,* which indicates that marketing research should strive to be unbiased and unemotional. In other words, research must apply the scientific method to marketing and be based on a common standard. The statement also uses the word *information* instead of *data,* highlighting management's need for data that are meaningful. Finally, it appropriately emphasizes the relationship between marketing research and the decision-making process. For marketing research carried out by the corporate world to be useful, it must obtain information that can be acted upon and that improves management's ability to guide the firm.

---

[1] David A. Ricks, *Blunders in International Business* (Cambridge, MA: Blackwell, 1993).

[2] *Report of the Definitions Committee of the American Marketing Association* (Chicago: American Marketing Association, 1961).

[3] Thomas C. Kinnear and James R. Taylor, *Marketing Research: An Applied Approach,* 3d ed. (New York: McGraw-Hill, 1987), 18.

LINKING RESEARCH TO THE DECISION-MAKING PROCESS

International marketing research should be linked to the decision-making process within the firm. The recognition that a situation requires action is the factor that initiates the decision-making process. The problem must then be defined. Often, symptoms are mistaken for causes; as a result, action determined by symptoms is oriented in the wrong direction. The research process begins here, because information must often be obtained to determine the precise nature of the problem.

Figure 8.1 provides an overview of the steps in the secondary research process. It begins with the recognition of the need for information. The value of research is then determined and research objectives are defined. Although this process appears simplistic,

Steps in the Secondary Research Process   FIGURE 8.1

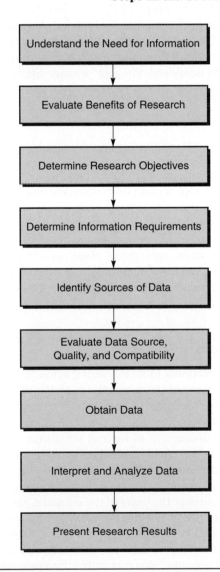

various groups within a firm often have different research objectives. These must be fully understood and integrated into one common research plan. The next steps in the research process are to determine information requirements and to identify possible sources of data. Time and financial constraints require the researcher to evaluate the quality of the data available and to assess how well the data fit with research objectives and information requirements. Next, the data are obtained and then interpreted and analyzed. Finally, the researcher presents the results to management, which can take appropriate action based on the research report.

DIFFERENTIATING INTERNATIONAL AND DOMESTIC RESEARCH

The tools and techniques of international marketing research are said by some to be exactly the same as those of domestic marketing research, and only the environment differs. However, the environment is precisely what determines how well the tools, techniques, and concepts apply to the international market. Although the objectives of marketing research may be the same, the execution of international research may differ substantially from the process of domestic research. As a result, entirely new tools and techniques may need to be developed. The four primary differences are new parameters, new environments, an increase in the number of factors involved, and the broader definition of competition.

New Parameters

In crossing national borders, a firm encounters parameters not found in domestic marketing. Examples include duties, foreign currencies and changes in their value, different modes of transportation, international documentation, and port facilities. A firm that has done business only domestically will have had little or no prior experience with these requirements and conditions. Information on each of them must be obtained in order for management to make appropriate business decisions. New parameters also emerge because of differing modes of operating internationally. For example, a firm can export, it can license its products, it can engage in a joint venture, or it can carry out foreign direct investment.

New Environments

When deciding to **go international** in its marketing activities, a firm exposes itself to an unfamiliar environment. Many of the assumptions on which the firm was founded and its domestic activities were based may not hold true internationally. Firms need to learn about the culture of the host country, understand its political systems, determine its stability, and appreciate the differences in societal structures and language. In addition, they must fully comprehend pertinent legal issues in the host country to avoid operating contrary to local legislation. They should also incorporate the technological level of the society in the marketing plan and understand the economic environment. In short, all the assumptions formulated over the years in the domestic market must be reevaluated. This crucial point has often been neglected because most managers are born into the environment of their domestic operations and have subconsciously learned to understand the constraints and opportunities of their business activities. The process is analogous to learning one's native language. Speakers with little knowledge of rules of grammar may nevertheless use the language correctly. Only in attempting to learn a foreign language will they begin to appreciate the complex structure of languages, the need for rules, and the existence of different patterns.

Number of Factors Involved

Going international often means entering into more than one market. As a result, the number of changing dimensions increases geometrically. Even if every dimension is understood, management must also appreciate the interaction between them. Because of the sheer number of factors, coordination of the interaction becomes increasingly difficult. The international marketing research process can help management with this undertaking.

Broader Definition of Competition

By entering the international market, the firm exposes itself to a much greater variety of competition than existed in the domestic market. For example, fishery products compete not only with other fishery products but also with meat or even vegetarian substitutes. Similarly, firms that offer labor-saving devices in the domestic marketplace may suddenly face competition from cheap manual labor. As a result, the firm must determine the breadth of the competition, track the competitive activities, and finally, evaluate the actual and potential impact on its own operations.

RECOGNIZING THE NEED FOR RESEARCH

To serve a market efficiently, firms must learn what customers want, why they want it, and how they go about filling their needs. To enter a market without conducting marketing research places firms, their assets, and their entire operation at risk. Even though most firms recognize the need for domestic marketing research, this need is not fully understood for international marketing activities. Most small or medium-sized firms conduct no international market research before they enter a foreign market. Often, decisions concerning entry and expansion in overseas markets and the selecting and appointing of distributors are made after a cursory subjective assessment of the situation. The research done is less rigorous, less formal, and less quantitative than for domestic marketing activities. Further, once a small or medium-sized firm has entered a foreign market, it is likely to discontinue the research of that market.[4,5] Many business executives therefore appear to view foreign market research as relatively unimportant.

A major reason that firms are reluctant to engage in international marketing activities is the lack of sensitivity to differences in consumer tastes and preferences. Managers often tend to assume that their methods are both best and acceptable to all others. This is fortunately not true. What a boring place the world would be if it were!

A second reason is a limited appreciation for the different marketing environments abroad. Often, firms are not prepared to accept that distribution systems, industrial applications and uses, the availability of media, or advertising regulations may be entirely

[4] Vinay Kothari, "Researching for Export Marketing" in *Export Promotion: The Public and Private Sector Interaction,* ed. M. Czinkota (New York: Praeger Publishers, 1983), 155.

[5] S. Tamer Cavusgil, "International Marketing Research: Insights into Company Practices," in *Research in Marketing,* vol. 7, ed. Jagdish N. Sheth (Greenwich, CT: JAI Press, 1984), 261–288.

THE INTERNATIONAL MARKETPLACE

Some First Steps in International Research

Most company executives know that they need to conduct careful research before they prepare to market abroad. But knowing what to do is not the same as knowing how to get it done. Because many small and medium-sized firms are looking at international markets for the first time these days, they frequently go charging off in the wrong direction or spend tremendous sums on research. In reality, a great deal of international research can be accomplished for very little money, if you know where to look.

When our firm is asked to help answer international research questions, we try very hard not to reinvent the wheel or redo research that is already available. One of the first things we do is check established sources of information. Typically, that involves several steps.

First, we check reference information on countries, products, markets, and competitors. We look at reference guides, country directories, and publications of industrial development organizations. We also use international sources, including the United Nations, the World Bank, and the Food and Agriculture Organization, where the right kind of digging can pay off with useful information. The same is true of U.S. government agencies.

Next, we conduct secondary research on-line and in the library. Here we check all secondary information that may help answer client questions regarding products, markets, opportunities, competitors, and the wisdom of alternative business strategies. Typically, we conduct on-line research through Dialog, Nexis, and other services. The trick here is knowing which of the hundreds of data bases to check for appropriate questions, key words, and subjects. After appropriate articles and published references have been identified, we spend time in the library reviewing abstracts and getting copies of pertinent articles and other references.

A third step then consists of identifying multiclient studies that have already been conducted that answer some of the questions we have. At this point, we know what is available. However, it is not cost efficient or wise to purchase every possible study, so some additional research is necessary. This involves contacting the publishers of the studies, requesting copies of the contents page and the prospectus for each study of interest.

Only after reviewing all the material obtained will we start developing a plan for proprietary primary research.

Source: Ian MacFarlane, "Do-It-Yourself Marketing Research," *Management Review*, May 1991, 34–37.

different from those in the home market. Barely aware of the differences, firms are unwilling to spend money to find out about them.

A third reason is the lack of familiarity with national and international data sources and the inability to use them if obtained. As a result, the cost of conducting international marketing research is seen as prohibitively high, and therefore not a worthwhile investment relative to the benefits to be gained.[6] Yet, as the International Marketplace 8.2 shows, much information can be gleaned from existing sources and may be relatively inexpensive.

[6] Susan P. Douglas and C. Samuel Craig, *International Marketing Research* (Englewood Cliffs, NJ: Prentice-Hall, 1983), 2.

Finally, firms often build up their international marketing activities gradually, frequently on the basis of unsolicited orders. Over time, actual business experience in a country or with a specific firm may then be used as a substitute for organized research.[7]

Yet, international marketing research is important. It permits management to identify and develop strategies for internationalization. This task includes the identification, evaluation, and comparison of potential foreign market opportunities and subsequent market selection. Second, research is necessary for the development of a marketing plan. In the initial internationalization process, the requirements for successful market entry and market penetration need to be determined. Subsequently, the research should define the appropriate marketing mix for each international market and should maintain a continuous feedback in order to fine-tune the various marketing elements. Finally, research can provide management with foreign market intelligence to help it anticipate events, take appropriate action, and adequately prepare for global changes.

EVALUATING BENEFITS OF RESEARCH

A primary constraint for international marketing research is resource allocation. To carry out international research, firms require resources in terms of both time and money. For the typical smaller firm, those two types of resources are its most precious and scarce commodities. To make a justifiable case for allocating resources to international marketing research, management must understand what the value of research will be. This is even more important for international market research than domestic market research because the cost tends to be higher.

The value of research can be assessed from two perspectives. One approach analyzes the benefits the firm receives from research. The other identifies the downside risk that the firm incurs if it does not carry out research.

The Benefits of Research

The value of research in making a particular decision may be determined by applying the following equation:

$$V(dr) - V(d) > C(r)$$

where

$V(dr)$ is the value of the decision with the benefit of research;
$V(d)$ is the value of the decision without the benefit of research;

and

$C(r)$ is the cost of research.

Obviously, the value of the decision with the benefit of research should be greater than the value of the decision without research by an amount exceeding the cost of the research. Otherwise, international marketing research would be a waste of resources. It may be difficult to quantify the individual values because often the risks and benefits are not easy to ascertain. Yet, the use of decision theory permits a comparison of alternative research strategies.[8] Using such a justification for research, however, may place the researcher at risk because once the research is carried out, the actual benefits are measurable and can be compared with the anticipated ones. If all the benefits do not materialize, the researcher may be charged with having inappropriately inflated his or her benefit expectation.

---

[7] Cavusgil, "International Marketing Research," 261–288.

[8] For an excellent exposition on measuring the value of research, see Gilbert A. Churchill, *Marketing Research,* 5th ed. (Hinsdale, IL: Dryden Press, 1991), 97–114.

The Risks of Inadequate Research

As an alternative to the benefit strategy, the researcher can point out in a "what if" fashion the risks that the company may incur by operating internationally without sufficient information. Such risks might include a loss of market penetration effectiveness, development of ill will abroad that precludes any further internationalization, and expropriation. In the long run, this justification is easier for the researcher to use than the benefit formula because he or she can point out that some of the worst-case scenarios have not materialized.

In any event, the researcher must demonstrate to management the need for information and therefore justify the allocation of scarce resources. This requirement suggests that international market research should aim at managerial rather than statistical significance. It should clearly aid management in improving its decision-making process in international marketing. At the same time, international market research should be recognized as a tool and not a substitute for judgment. Enough of the "right" information is never obtained within the time constraints to dictate the action or course to follow. However, research will aid in avoiding gross errors and compensate for inadequate experience or unreliable intuition.

DETERMINING RESEARCH OBJECTIVES

The researcher should take great care in determining research objectives. These objectives will vary from firm to firm because of the views of management, the corporate mission, and the marketing situation. In addition, as discussed earlier, the information needs of firms are closely linked with the level of existing international expertise.

Going International: Exporting

The most frequent objective of international market research is that of **foreign market opportunity analysis.** When a firm launches its international activities, information is needed to provide basic guidelines. The aim is not to conduct a painstaking and detailed analysis of the world on a market-by-market basis but instead to utilize a broad-brush approach. Accomplished quickly at low cost, this can narrow down the possibilities for international marketing activities.

Such an approach should begin with a cursory analysis of general market variables such as total and per-capita GNP, mortality rates, and population figures. Although these factors in themselves will not provide detailed market information, they will enable the researcher and management to determine whether the corporation's objectives might be met in those markets. For example, highly priced labor-saving consumer products may not be successful in the People's Republic of China because their price may be a significant proportion of the annual salary of a worker, and the benefit to the worker may be only minimal. Such cursory evaluation will help reduce the number of markets to be considered to a more manageable number—for example, from 181 to 25.

Next, the researcher will require information on each individual market for a preliminary evaluation. This information typically locates the fastest-growing markets, the largest markets for a particular product, market trends, and market restrictions. Although precise and detailed information for each product probably cannot be obtained, it is available for general product categories.

Both foreign markets and domestic restrictions relating to them must be considered. As an example, one can determine that Iraq represents a fast-growing market for computer hardware and software. However, an inspection of U.S. export licensing regulations will reveal that computer trade with Iraq is quite restricted. Again, this overview will be cursory but will serve to quickly evaluate markets and reduce the number for closer investigation.

A Sequential Process of Researching Foreign Market Potentials   `FIGURE 8.2`

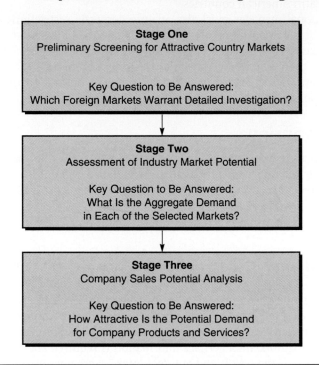

Source: S. Tamer Cavusgil, "Guidelines for Export Market Research," *Business Horizons* 28 (November–December 1985): 29. Copyright by the Foundation for the School of Business at Indiana University. Reprinted by permission.

At this stage, the researcher must select appropriate markets. The emphasis will shift to focus on market opportunities for a specific product or brand, including existing, latent, and incipient markets. Even though the aggregate industry data have already been obtained, general information is insufficient to make company-specific decisions. For example, the market demand for medical equipment should not be confused with the potential demand for a specific brand.[9] In addition, the research should identify demand-and-supply patterns and evaluate any regulations and standards. Finally, a competitive assessment needs to be made that matches markets with corporate strengths and provides an analysis of the best market potential for specific products. Figure 8.2 offers a summary of the various stages in the determination of market potential.

Going International: Importing

When importing, firms shift their major focus from supplying to sourcing. Management must identify markets that produce desired supplies or materials or that have the potential to do so. Foreign firms must be evaluated in terms of their capabilities and competitive standing.

Just as management would wish to have some details on a domestic supplier, the importer needs to know, for example, about the reliability of a foreign supplier, the consistency of his or her product or service quality, and the length of delivery time. Information obtained through the subsidiary office of a bank or through one's embassy can be very helpful.

In addition, foreign rules must be scrutinized as to whether exportation is possible. For example, India may set limits on the cobra handbags it allows to be exported, and

---

[9] S. Tamer Cavusgil, "Guidelines for Export Market Research," *Business Horizons* 28 (November–December 1985): 27–33.

laws protecting the cultural heritage may prevent the exportation of pre-Columbian artifacts from Latin American countries.

The international manager must also analyze domestic restrictions and legislation that may prohibit the importation of certain goods into the home country. Even though a market may exist in the United States for foreign umbrella handles, for example, quotas may restrict their importation in order to protect domestic industries. Similarly, even though domestic demand may exist for ivory, its importation may be illegal because of legislation enacted to protect wildlife worldwide.

Market Expansion

Research objectives may include obtaining detailed information for penetrating a market, for designing and fine-tuning the marketing mix, or for monitoring the political climate of a country so that the firm can expand its operation successfully. The better defined the research objective is, the better the researcher will be able to determine the information requirements and thus conserve time and financial resources of the firm.

DETERMINING INFORMATION REQUIREMENTS

Using the research objective as a guide, the researcher will be able to pinpoint the type of information needed. For example, if only general initial market information is required, perhaps macro data such as world population statistics will be sufficient. If research is to identify market restraints, then perhaps information is required about international accords, negotiations in the GATT, and any "voluntary" agreements. Alternatively, broad product category and production and trade figures may be desired in order to pinpoint general market activities. For the fine-tuning of a marketing mix, very specific detailed product data may be necessary to conduct a relevant analysis. Typically, management is likely to need both macro and micro data. Table 8.1 provides a listing of the type of information that, according to U.S. executives, is most crucial in international marketing.

In determining information requirements, the researcher should formulate appropriate research questions that he or she intends to answer. Table 8.2 provides samples of possible research questions on broad strategic issues, foreign market assessment and selection, and marketing mix determination.

TABLE 8.1   **Most Critical International Information for U.S. Firms**

Government Data
- Tariff information
- U.S. export/import data
- Nontariff measures
- Foreign export/import data
- Data on government trade policy

Corporate Data
- Local laws and regulations
- Size of market
- Local standards and specifications
- Distribution system
- Competitive activity

Source: Michael R. Czinkota, "International Information Needs for U.S. Competitiveness." Reprinted from *Business Horizons* (November–December 1991), p. 88. Copyright 1991 by the Foundation for the School of Business at Indiana University. Used with permission.

International Marketing Questions Determining Information Requirements TABLE 8.2

Broad Strategic Issues

What objectives should be pursued in the foreign market?

Which foreign market segments should the firm strive to satisfy?

Which are the best product, place-distribution, pricing, and promotion strategies for the foreign market?

What should be the product-market-company mix to take advantage of the available foreign marketing opportunities?

Foreign Market Assessment and Selection

Do opportunities exist in a foreign market for the firm's products and services?

What is the market potential abroad?

What new markets are likely to open up abroad?

What are the major economic, political, legal, social, technological, and other environmental facts and trends in a foreign country?

What impact do these environmental dimensions have on the specific foreign market for the firm's products and services?

Who are the firm's present and potential customers abroad?

What are their needs and desires?

What are their demographic and psychographic characteristics—disposable income, occupation, age, sex, opinions, interests, activities, tastes, values, etc.?

What is their life-style?

Who makes the purchase decisions?

Who influences the purchase decisions?

How are the purchase decisions made?

Where are the products purchased?

How are the products used?

What are the purchase and consumption patterns and behaviors?

What is the nature of competition in the foreign market?

Who are major direct and indirect competitors?

What are the major characteristics of the competitors?

What are the firm's competitive strengths and weaknesses in reference to such factors as product quality, product lines, warranties, services, brands, packaging, distribution, sales force, advertising, prices, experience, technology, capital and human resources, and market share?

What attitudes do different governments (domestic and foreign) have toward foreign trade?

Are there any foreign trade incentives and barriers?

Is there any prejudice against imports or exports?

What are different governments doing specifically to encourage or discourage international trade?

What specific requirements—for example, import or export licenses—have to be met to conduct international trade?

How difficult are certain government regulations for the firm?

How well developed are the foreign mass communication media?

Are the print and electronics media abroad efficient and effective?

Are there adequate transportation and storage or warehouse facilities in the foreign market?

Does the foreign market offer efficient channels of distribution for the firm's products?

What are the characteristics of the existing domestic and foreign distributors?

How effectively can the distributors perform specific marketing functions?

What is the state of the retailing institutions?

Marketing Mix Assessment and Selection

Product

Which product should the firm offer abroad?

What specific features—design, color, size, packaging, brand, warranty, etc.—should the product have?

What foreign needs does the product satisfy?

Should the firm adapt or modify its domestic market product and sell it abroad?

continued

TABLE 8.2   *Continued*

Should it develop a new product for the foreign market?
Should the firm make or buy the product for the foreign market?
How competitive is or will be the product abroad?
Is there a need to withdraw the product from the foreign market?
At which stage in its life cycle is the product in the foreign market?
What specific services are necessary abroad at the presale and postsale stages?
Are the firm's service and repair facilities adequate?
What is the firm's product and service image abroad?
What patents or trademarks does the firm have that can benefit it abroad?
   How much legal protection does the firm have concerning patents, trademarks, etc.?
What should be the firm's product mission philosophy in the foreign market?
Are the firm's products socially responsible?
Do the products create a good corporate image?
What effect does the product have on the environment?

Price
At what price should the firm sell its product in the foreign market?
Does the foreign price reflect the product quality?
Is the price competitive?
Should the firm pursue market penetration or market-skimming pricing objectives abroad?
What type of discounts (trade, cash, quantity) and allowances (advertising, trade-off) should the
   firm offer its foreign customers?
Should prices differ according to market segment?
What should the firm do about product line pricing?
What pricing options are available if costs increase or decrease?
Is the demand in the foreign market elastic or inelastic?
How are prices going to be viewed by the foreign government—reasonable, exploitative?
Can differentiated pricing lead to the emergence of a gray market?

Place-Distribution
Which channels of distribution should the firm use to market its products abroad?
Where should the firm produce its products, and how should it distribute them in the foreign
   market?
What types of agents, brokers, wholesalers, dealers, distributors, retailers, etc. should the
   firm use?
What are the characteristics and capabilities of the available intermediaries?
Should the assistance of EMCs (export management companies) be acquired?
What forms of transportation should the firm use?
Where should the product be stored?
What is the cost of distribution by channel?
What are the costs of physical distribution?
What type of incentives and assistance should the firm provide its intermediaries to achieve its
   foreign distribution objectives?
Which channels of distribution are used by the firm's competitors, and how effective are these
   channels?
Is there a need to develop a reverse distribution system, e.g., recycling?

Promotion—Nonpersonal (Advertising and Sales Promotion)
How should the firm promote its products in the foreign market? Should it advertise? Should it
   participate in international trade fairs and exhibits?
What are the communication needs of the foreign market?
What communication or promotion objectives should the firm pursue abroad?
What should be the total foreign promotion budget?
What advertising media are available to promote in the foreign market? What are their strengths
   and limitations? How effective are different domestic and foreign advertising media?
Should the firm use an advertising agency?
How should it be selected?
How effective and competitive are the firm's existing advertising and promotion programs con-
   cerning the foreign market?

What are the legal requirements?
Are there foreign laws against competitive advertising?

Promotion—Personal Selling
Is there a need for personal selling to promote the product abroad?
What assistance or services do foreign customers need from the sales force?
What should be the nature of personal selling abroad?
How many salespeople should the firm have?
How should the sales personnel be trained, motivated, compensated, assigned sales goals and
    quotas, and assigned foreign territories?
What should the nature of the foreign sales effort be?
How does the firm's sales force compare with its competitors?
What criteria should the firm use to evaluate sales performance?
How should the firm perform sales analysis?

Source: Adapted from Vinay Kothari, "Researching for Export Marketing," in *Export Promotion: The Public and Private Sector Interaction*, ed. M. Czinkota (New York: Praeger Publishers, 1983), 169–172. Reprinted with permission of Greenwood Publishing Group, Inc., Westport, CT. Copyright © 1993.

IDENTIFYING SOURCES OF DATA

Secondary data for international marketing research purposes are available from a wide variety of sources. The major ones are briefly reviewed here. In addition, Appendix A to this chapter lists more than 100 publications and organizations that monitor international issues.

U.S. Government

Of all data sources, the U.S. government has the greatest variety of data available. Most of them are collected by the Department of Commerce, the Department of Agriculture, the Department of State, the Department of the Treasury, and U.S. embassies abroad.

Typically, the information provided by the U.S. government addresses either macro or micro issues, or it offers specific data services. Macro information includes population trends, general trade flows between countries, and world agricultural production. Micro information includes materials on specific industries in a country, their growth prospects, and their foreign trade activities. Specific data services might provide custom-tailored information responding to the detailed needs of a firm. Alternatively, some data services may concentrate on a specific geographic region. An example of the wealth of information available, which is sometimes labeled "Washington's best-kept secret," is provided in The International Marketplace 8.3. More information on selected U.S. government publications and research services is presented in Appendix B to this chapter.

Other Governments

Even though many other governments do not collect as extensive data as does the United States, most countries have a wide array of national and international trade data available. Unfortunately, the data are often published only in the home countries and in the native languages. However, these information sources are often available at embassies and consulates, whose mission includes the enhancement of trade activities. The commercial counselor or commercial attaché can provide the information available from these sources.

8.3

THE INTERNATIONAL MARKETPLACE

Regional Data from the Commerce Department

Information and inquiries on market conditions are becoming a valued commodity as opportunities for commerce with Latin America grow. The U.S. government provides myriad resources for the researcher. Following is a sample of sources and data that potential exporters can tap for secondary marketing research on Latin America:

- **The Latin America/Caribbean Business Development Center.** Established by the Department of Commerce and the Agency for International Development, the center aims to help researchers understand and take advantage of the emerging commercial trends and opportunities in the region.
  —Business referrals. Consultations with the center's staff can help researchers identify available sources of assistance to address business concerns.
  —Matchmaking. The center draws upon U.S. and foreign contacts to match specific trading and investing objectives with those in the region.
  —Workshops/symposia/conferences. The center offers informative programs featuring experts on topics such as the regional commercial environment, U.S. government regulations and services, and how to conduct business abroad.
  —Business development missions. These are organized to provide support for businesses seeking to conclude trade or investment contracts.
  —Publications. Guidebooks are available for prospective traders as well as a *Business Bulletin* featuring regional news, business leads, and other opportunities.

- **The International Economic Policy Office of Latin America.** This office provides information regarding specific trade and investment options. Desk officers keep in frequent contact with commercial attachés at embassies and keep up-to-date with specific developments and business opportunities. It also
  —Services the exporter who needs specific country guidance;
  —Provides country information on trade policy issues; and
  —Provides country economic data and updates on significant political changes.

- **Flash Facts Mexico Information Hotline.** This automated information hotline is available to the business, nonprofit, and university communities 7 days a week, 24 hours a day. The hotline receives telephone inquiries and faxes printed material to the caller free of charge within an hour. Topics and issues include marketing, distribution, tariffs, company lists, customs procedures, trade statistics, economic data, and government services.

- **The Electronic Bulletin Board (EBB).** This personal computer-based electronic bulletin board is operated by the Commerce Department and can be accessed from most PCs with a modem and standard communications software. The EBB's menus help researchers locate and read press releases and data files, and optionally transfer them to their computers.

Source: U.S. Department of Commerce, Washington, D.C., 1994.

International Organizations

Some international organizations provide useful data for the researcher. The *Statistical Yearbook* produced by the United Nations contains international trade data on products and provides information on exports and imports by country. The *World Atlas* published by the World Bank provides useful general data on population, growth trends, and GNP figures. The Organization for Economic Cooperation and Development (OECD) also publishes quarterly and annual trade data on its member countries. Finally, organizations such as the International Monetary Fund (IMF) and the World Bank publish occasional staff papers that evaluate region- or country-specific issues in depth.

Service Organizations

A wide variety of service organizations that may provide information include banks, accounting firms, freight forwarders, airlines, and **international trade consultants.** Frequently, they are able to provide data on business practices, legislative or regulatory requirements, and political stability as well as basic trade data. However, although some of this information is available without charge, its basic intent is to serve as an "appetizer." Much of the initial information is quite general in nature; more detailed answers often require an appropriate fee.

Trade Associations

Associations such as world trade clubs and domestic and international chambers of commerce (for example, the American Chamber of Commerce abroad) can provide valuable information on local markets. Often, files are maintained on international trade flows and trends affecting international marketers. Useful information can also be obtained from industry associations. These groups, formed to represent entire industry segments, often collect from their members a wide variety of data that are then published in an aggregate form. Because most of these associations represent the viewpoints of their member firms to the federal government, they usually have one or more publicly listed representatives in Washington. The information provided is often quite general in nature because of the wide variety of clientele served. However, it can provide valuable initial insights into international markets.

Directories and Newsletters

A large number of industry directories are available on local, national, and international levels. These directories primarily serve to identify firms and to provide very general background information such as the name of the chief executive officer, the location, the address and telephone number, and some information on a firm's products. The quality of a directory depends, of course, on the quality of input and the frequency of updates. Some of the directories are becoming increasingly sophisticated and can provide quite detailed information to the researcher. Figure 8.3 shows an advertisement for one such directory.

Many newsletters are devoted to specific international issues such as international trade finance, international contracting, bartering, countertrade, international payment flows, and customs news. Published by banks or accounting firms in order to keep their clientele current on international developments, newsletters usually cater to narrow audiences but can provide important information to the firm interested in a specific area.

| FIGURE 8.3 | An Advertisement for a Trade Directory |

NOTHING HELPS IDENTIFY MORE PROMISING EXPORT MARKETS.

PIERS can show you the growth potential for your products in every country in the world. Plus, it reveals the names of competitors in each market, as well as how much and how often they export.

With PIERS, you can survey the market during active time periods, for an entire year or for the last 10 years.

No other source is as detailed, reliable or timely—because PIERS export information is gathered from the bills of lading for every ship calling at U.S. ports. Call PIERS today!

For details, call
Denise Simms at
212-837-7068
Two World Trade Center,
27th Floor
New York, NY 10048

Journal of Commerce, Inc.

A Knight-Ridder Business
Information Service

PIERS®
PORT IMPORT/EXPORT REPORTING SERVICE

Superior On Board Intelligence

Also ask about the Directory of U.S. Importers/Exporters in book form, PC diskettes, and CD-ROM.

Source: *The Wall Street Journal*, November 30, 1993, 15.

Data Bases

Increasingly, electronic data bases also provide international marketing information, ranging from the latest developments in product development to new writings in the academic and trade press and the latest updates in international trade statistics. Information services are provided through various media, including on-line interactive delivery, compact disc read-only memory, magnetic tape, floppy disk, interactive voice/audiotext, and on-line broadcast. The United States is the largest producer and consumer of electronic information services. In 1992, this $12 billion industry had more than 6,000 on-line services available, with a projected annual growth of 16 percent.[10]

Many of these information services are available for a subscription fee and often require payment on an as-used basis. As The International Marketplace 8.4 shows, in spite of their cost, data services are often well worth their price because of the rapid updates received, the convenience of access, and their frequently extensive search capabilities. With continuing improvements and progress in the area of telecommunications and computerization, the use of such data bases can be expected to increase in the future.

Other Firms

Often, firms can provide useful information for international marketing purposes. Firms appear to be more open about their international than about their domestic marketing activities. On some occasions, valuable information can also be obtained from foreign firms and distributors.

EVALUATING DATA SOURCE AND QUALITY

Before too much time and energy are spent obtaining the data, evaluations should be made of the quality of the data source, the quality of the actual data, and the compatibility of the data with information requirements.

Source Quality

In evaluating the quality of the data source, the researcher should determine who collected the data, the purpose of the original data collection, and how the data were collected. Ideally, the researcher would obtain the initial research specifications that were drawn up for the data collection. If these are not readily available, the organization that collected the data is occasionally willing to supply the specifications. In reviewing the specifications, the researcher can clearly determine the purpose and the method of the original data collection and therefore evaluate the data quality and fit.

Checking the quality of the source is important because there may be ulterior motives behind a specific form of data presentation, particularly for international statistics. As an example, some countries may wish to demonstrate that their economy is improving in order to attract foreign direct investment. As a result, some factors may be overstated. Other countries may wish to indicate a need for increased foreign aid and may therefore understate some statistics. Furthermore, many nations simply do not have sophisticated data-collection systems in place and therefore tend to supply data estimates that reflect wishes or goals rather than reality. Because the international organizations publishing these data serve only as information disseminators, all footnotes and introductory remarks that may clarify unusual methods of data collection should be carefully scrutinized.

---

[10] Mary C. Inoussa, "Information Services," *U.S. Industrial Outlook 1993,* (Washington, D.C.: U.S. Department of Commerce, 1993), 25-1–25-4.

On-line Decision Support

Did you know that American Express, Time Warner, and the National Basketball Association all are taking steps to protect their trademarks in Eastern Europe? That information is available on-line.

Did you know that KPMG Peat Marwick surveyed 700 U.S. CEOs and senior executives and found that 58 percent of their companies were planning to merge, acquire, or go into a joint venture with a European partner? That information is available on-line.

Did you know that Westinghouse is going to sell an $11 million air traffic control system to Poland? Or that Hungary and Czechoslovakia will decide soon on awarding new TV and radio frequencies? That information is available on-line, too.

Electronic information use among professional marketers is big and continues to grow. The industry spends $1.4 billion a year on electronic research, with more than $400 million devoted to on-line data bases. On-line services are driving an executive use trend by making data bases easier and more cost effective to use.

Continuing improvements in computer technology have contributed to the increased demand. More marketers than ever are using PCs, and as a result, electronic information systems are gaining in popularity. As these systems evolve, more efficient CD-ROM technology is replacing magnetic tape, and on-line data base services are introducing easier search protocols. In addition, recent software innovations have made research easier to accomplish and have diminished the need for training.

At present, marketers use the information most often to determine information about product movement, audience, demographics, and "competitive intelligence" (general corporate and business information), the fastest-growing area. The increasing need for competitive intelligence is driven by the quickening pace of technological change and intensified rivalries for market share.

The increasing availability of data has shortened the marketing life cycle. With more comprehensive data available more quickly from on-line sources that dramatically reduce research time, products and services are getting to market faster than ever. Speed is crucial, especially when you consider that a competitor halfway around the world may be looking at introducing a similar product or service in your market even as you sleep. The pressure to act quickly and make an informed marketing decision has never been greater.

Clearly, on-line information is making for more intelligent marketers and marketing decisions. No longer are marketing executives relying on past history or gut instinct to determine the marketability of products and services; they now have current, real-world data from a multitude of sources to support them.

And in the new, competitive global marketplace, that's one advantage not to be taken lightly.

Source: Keith Hawk, "More Marketers Are Going Online for Decision Support," *Marketing News*, November 12, 1990, 14.

Data Quality

The relevance of data to the researcher's information requirements plays a major role in assessing the quality of the data. The first test therefore is to determine whether the data provide responses to the firm's particular questions.

The accuracy and reliability of the data must be determined. Often, international data are approximated. Geographic or manpower limitations may render some countries unable, even if they are not unwilling, to be precise in their data collection. As a result, the margin of error of some international statistics can be as high as 25 percent.[11] Exploring the accuracy of the data, to the extent possible, can be carried out by investigating two dimensions. First, the researcher should determine the primacy of the data source. A primary source is the source that originated the data, whereas a secondary source has secured the data from an original source. The researcher should always attempt to obtain information from the primary source because this permits an evaluation of source credibility. Further, the primary source usually provides the most detail about data-collection methods. Second, the collection methods should be examined to determine whether proper research procedures were followed and whether definitions used are acceptable.

The recency of data can also be important. Few countries conduct data collection as often as does the United States, and even in the United States, international data are often found to be insufficient or outdated. In many nations, the most recent data available may be three to five years old. The effect of economic changes during these years on a firm's international business operations may be quite significant. Obtaining misleading information may lead to inappropriate decisions, a result that is contrary to the intent of marketing research.

Before a commitment is made to acquire data, both data sources and data quality must be carefully evaluated in terms of coverage, availability, accuracy, and timeliness.[12] This step is necessary not only to screen out data that may be expensive to obtain but also to minimize unnecessary cluttering of information. Even if data are free, working through them requires corporate resources that are usually scarce. The researcher therefore must ensure not only that data are acquired but that the right ones are obtained, using paucity as the key criterion. Otherwise, large data acquisitions are likely to lead to information overload within the firm, with the result that either the data are not used at all or their use becomes so time-consuming that the research is inefficient.

Data Compatibility

The compatibility and comparability of data need to be considered. Often in international marketing research, the researcher must compare different sets of data from different countries. Great care must therefore be taken to ensure that identical, or at least similar, units of measurement and definitional units are used.

OBTAINING THE DATA

The existence and the availability of international marketing data do not necessarily indicate that the data can be obtained. Obviously, to be useful for the corporation and the researcher, data need to be obtained in a timely manner and with relative ease. Furthermore, cost is a factor to consider.

---

[11] Kavil Ramachandran, "Data Collection for Management Research in Developing Countries," in *The Management Research Handbook,* eds. N. C. Smith and P. Dainty (London: Routledge, 1991), 300–309.

[12] Gillian Rice and Essam Mahmoud, "Forecasting and Data Bases in International Business," *Management International Review* 24 (Fourth Quarter 1984): 59–70.

The Department of Commerce will make U.S. government data available on request, charging only a modest user fee. However, several weeks may elapse before the data are finally received. This, of course, applies only to readily packaged information that has already been published and not to individual data runs, which may take even longer. Rather than wait for mail from Washington, researchers often can seek recourse from a local Department of Commerce district office that maintains substantial library holdings of department materials.

Many universities are designated as **official depositories** of U.S. government documents. Data can be rapidly reviewed in these libraries. Many public libraries maintain a holding of data from international organizations. If they are not available there, data can be ordered from the organizations directly.

A word of caution: The researcher must carefully scrutinize the data in advance to minimize the risk of having to discard data once the information is obtained. This is best done by precisely determining the information requirements, carefully matching the sources of data with these requirements, and selecting the data with the best fit.

Even though, or perhaps because, the capability to obtain data has increased dramatically, society has grown increasingly sensitive to the issue of **data privacy.** Readily accessible large-scale data bases may contain information valuable to marketers but considered privileged by the individuals who have provided the data. The international marketer must therefore also pay careful attention to the privacy laws in different nations and to possible consumer response to such data use before attempting to obtain personal data. Neglecting such concerns may result in a backfiring of research and a weakening of the corporate position.

INTERPRETING AND ANALYZING THE DATA

A critical task for the researcher begins after the data have been obtained. At this stage, the individual must use his or her research creativity to make good use of the data.

This often requires the combination and cross-tabulation of various sets of data or the use of proxy information in order to arrive at conclusions that address the research objectives. For example, the market penetration of television sets may be used as a **proxy variable** for the potential market demand for video recorders. Similarly, in an industrial setting, information about plans for new port facilities may be useful to determine future containerization requirements. Also, the beginning computerization of a society may highlight the future need for software.

The researcher must go beyond the scope of the data and use creative inferences to arrive at knowledge useful to the firm. However, such creativity brings risks. Once the interpretation and analysis have taken place, a consistency check must be conducted. The researcher should always cross-check the results with other possible sources of information or with experts.

In addition, the researcher should take another look at the research methods employed and, based on their usefulness, determine any necessary modifications for future projects. This will make possible the continuous improvement of international market research activities and enables the corporation to learn from experience.

PRESENTING RESEARCH RESULTS

Communicating the results to management is crucial to the success of the research. Care taken in preparing the research reports will reflect the desire of the researcher to communicate important knowledge to management.

Managers may not be aware of the many intricacies and subtleties of research, nor do they necessarily need to know about them. Management requires a palatable and useful presentation of the information. Although the temptation may be great to cart reams of computer printout into a meeting to demonstrate the vast data resources the researcher has used, such actions are inappropriate. Rather, the researcher's task is to distill the data into core components that will enable management to understand the course of action that is necessary.

The report to management therefore needs to be concise. Restricting the length of memos to one page, for example, is not an unreasonable measure. Rather, it acknowledges the value and scarcity of managerial time and the need to conserve it. Reports should be preceded by short and incisive abstracts. The researcher should then clearly define the major issues, highlight research information that will give management confidence in the results presented, and clearly demonstrate the conclusions. Detailed information that may or may not be necessary should be placed in appendixes. The data are then preserved but do not clutter the report.

The purpose of the presentation is effective communication—and a demonstration of both the utility of the results and the need for implementation. Because the report shapes the perception of the entire research, it is a crucial component in the research process. No matter how valuable the research, any report not understood or utilized by management results in a waste of resources.

SUMMARY

Constraints of time, resources, and expertise are the major inhibitors of international marketing research. Nevertheless, firms need to carry out planned and organized research in order to explore foreign market alternatives successfully. Such research needs to be closely linked to the decision-making process.

International market research differs from domestic research in that the environment, which determines how well tools, techniques, and concepts apply, is different abroad. In addition, the manager needs to deal with new parameters, such as duties, exchange rates, and international documentation, a greater number of interacting factors, and a much broader definition of the concept of competition.

The research process starts by recognizing the need for research, which is often not well understood. When the firm is uninformed about international differences in consumer tastes and preferences and about the foreign market environments, the need for international research is high. Yet an appropriate trade-off needs to be made between the costs and the benefits of research in order to spend resources wisely. The research objectives need to be determined, based on the corporate mission, the level of international expertise, and the marketing intent. These objectives will enable the researcher to identify the information requirements.

Given the scarcity of resources, companies beginning their international effort often need to use data that have already been collected, that is, secondary data. Such data are available from sources such as governments, international organizations, directories, trade associations, or data bases. Before using these data, however, the researcher needs to recognize that the quality, reliability, and usefulness of these data may be limited.

It is important to evaluate the quality of the data. This means exploring the purpose of the original data collection, the method underlying the data collection, the compatibility and comparability of the data, and their usefulness for the research task at hand.

Once the data are obtained, the researcher must creatively analyze them, resorting often to proxy variables to draw inferences useful to management. A presentation of research results in a concise and clear fashion will then aid the decision-making process with a contribution that can lead to the implementation of activities.

Questions for Discussion

1. What is the difference between domestic and international marketing research?

2. How does "going international" affect the environmental perspective of a firm?

3. What does international marketing research aim to achieve?

4. How would you justify the need for international marketing research?

5. You are employed by National Engineering Corporation, a U.S. firm that designs subways. Knowing that you had a course in international marketing, your boss asks you to explore international market entry possibilities and report within a week. How will you go about this task?

6. Discuss the possible shortcomings of secondary data.

7. Why would a firm use secondary data in spite of their shortcomings?

Recommended Readings

Churchill, Gilbert A. *Marketing Research: Methodological Foundations.* 6th ed. Hinsdale, IL: Dryden Press, 1994.

Delphos, William A. *Inside Washington: The International Business Executive's Guide to Government Resources.* Lanham, MD: Madison Books, 1988.

Delphos, William A., ed. *International Direct Marketing Guide: Regional Markets and Selected Countries.* Alexandria, VA: Braddock Communications, 1992.

Directory of Online Databases. Santa Monica, CA: Cuadra Associates, published annually.

Douglas, Susan P., and C. Samuel Craig. *International Marketing Research.* Englewood Cliffs, NJ: Prentice-Hall, 1983.

Interagency Task Force on Trade. *Exporter's Guide to Federal Resources for Small Business.* Washington, D.C.: Government Printing Office, 1988.

Predicasts Services. Cleveland, OH, published monthly.

Sheth, Jagdish N., and Abdolreza Eshghi. *Global Marketing Perspectives.* Cincinnati, OH: South-Western, 1989.

Smith, Craig N., and Paul Dainty. *The Management Research Handbook.* London: Routledge, 1991.

APPENDIX A

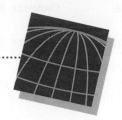

Monitors of International Issues

Selected Organizations

American Bankers Association
1120 Connecticut Avenue N.W.
Washington, D.C. 20036

American Bar Association
750 N. Lake Shore Drive
Chicago, IL 60611
and
1800 M Street N.W.
Washington, D.C. 20036

American Management Association
440 First Street N.W.
Washington, D.C. 20001

American Marketing Association
250 S. Wacker Drive Suite 200
Chicago, IL 60606

American Petroleum Institute
1220 L Street N.W.
Washington, D.C. 20005

Asian Development Bank
2330 Roxas Boulevard
Pasay City, Philippines

Chamber of Commerce of the
United States
1615 H Street N.W.
Washington, D.C. 20062

Commission of the European
Communities to the United States
2100 M Street N.W. Suite 707
Washington, D.C. 20037

Conference Board
845 Third Avenue
New York, NY 10022
and
1755 Massachusetts Avenue N.W.
Suite 312
Washington, D.C. 20036

Electronic Industries Association
2001 I Street N.W.
Washington, D.C. 20006

European Community Information
Service
200 Rue de la Loi
1049 Brussels, Belgium
and
2100 M Street N.W. 7th Floor
Washington, D.C. 20037

Export-Import Bank of the United
States
811 Vermont Avenue N.W.
Washington, D.C. 20571

Federal Reserve Bank of New York
33 Liberty Street
New York, NY 10045

Inter-American Development Bank
1300 New York Avenue N.W.
Washington, D.C. 20577

International Bank for
Reconstruction and Development
(World Bank)
1818 H Street N.W.
Washington, D.C. 20433

International Monetary Fund
700 19th Street N.W.
Washington, D.C. 20431

Marketing Research Society
111 E. Wacker Drive Suite 600
Chicago, IL 60601

National Association of
Manufacturers
1331 Pennsylvania Avenue
Suite 1500
Washington, D.C. 20004

National Federation of Independent
Business
600 Maryland Avenue S.W.
Suite 700
Washington, D.C. 20024

Organization for Economic
Cooperation and Development
2 rue Andre Pascal
75775 Paris Cedex Ko, France
and
2001 L Street N.W. Suite 700
Washington, D.C. 20036

Organization of American States
17th and Constitution
Avenue N.W.
Washington, D.C. 20006

Society for International
Development
1401 New York Avenue N.W.
Suite 1100
Washington, D.C. 20005

United Nations

Conference of Trade and
Development
Palais des Nations
1211 Geneva 10
Switzerland

Department of Economic and Social
Affairs
1 United Nations Plaza
New York, NY 10017

Industrial Development
Organization
1660 L Street N.W.
Washington, D.C. 20036
and   *(continued)*

United Nations (continued)

Post Office Box 300
Vienna International Center
A-1400 Vienna, Austria

Publications
Room 1194
1 United Nations Plaza
New York, NY 10017

Statistical Yearbook
1 United Nations Plaza
New York, NY 10017

U.S. Government

Agency for International
    Development
Office of Business Relations
Washington, D.C. 20523

Customs Service
1301 Constitution Avenue N.W.
Washington, D.C. 20229

Department of Agriculture
12th Street and Jefferson Drive S.W.
Washington, D.C. 20250

Department of Commerce
Herbert C. Hoover Building
14th Street and Constitution
    Avenue N.W.
Washington, D.C. 20230

Department of State
2201 C Street N.W.
Washington, D.C. 20520

Department of the Treasury
15th Street and Pennsylvania
    Avenue N.W.
Washington, D.C. 20220

Federal Trade Commission
6th Street and Pennsylvania
    Avenue N.W.
Washington, D.C. 20580

International Trade Commission
701 E Street N.W.
Washington, D.C. 20436

Small Business Administration
Imperial Building
1441 L Street N.W.
Washington, D.C. 20416

Trade Development Program
1621 North Kent Street
Rosslyn, VA 22209

World Trade Centers Association
1 World Trade Center Suite 7701
New York, NY 10048

Indexes to Literature

Business Periodical Index
H.W. Wilson Co.
950 University Avenue
Bronx, NY 10452

New York Times Index
University Microfilms International
300 N. Zeeb Road
Ann Arbor, MI 48106

Public Affairs Information Service
    Bulletin
11 W. 40th Street
New York, NY 10018

Readers' Guide to Periodical
    Literature
H.W. Wilson Co.
950 University Avenue
Bronx, NY 10452

Wall Street Journal Index
University Microfilms International
300 N. Zeeb Rd.
Ann Arbor, MI 48106

Periodic Reports, Newspapers, Magazines

Advertising Age
Crain Communications Inc.
740 N. Rush Street
Chicago, IL 60611

Advertising World
Directories International Inc.
150 Fifth Avenue Suite 610
New York, NY 10011

Arab Report and Record
84 Chancery Lane
London WC2A 1DL, England

Barron's
University Microfilms International
300 N. Zeeb Road
Ann Arbor, MI 48106

Business America
U.S. Department of Commerce
14th Street and Constitution
    Avenue N.W.
Washington, D.C. 20230

Business International
Business International Corp.
One Dag Hammarskjold Plaza
New York, NY 10017

Periodic Reports, Newspapers, Magazines (continued)

Business Week
McGraw-Hill Publications Co.
1221 Avenue of the Americas
New York, NY 10020

Commodity Trade Statistics
United Nations Publications
1 United Nations Plaza
Room DC2-853
New York, NY 10017

Conference Board Record
Conference Board Inc.
845 Third Avenue
New York, NY 10022

Customs Bulletin
U.S. Customs Service
1301 Constitution Avenue N.W.
Washington, D.C. 20229

Dun's Business Month
Goldhirsh Group
38 Commercial Wharf
Boston, MA 02109

The Economist
Economist Newspaper Ltd.
25 St. James Street
London SW1A 1HG, England

Europe Magazine
2100 M Street N.W. Suite 707
Washington, D.C. 20037

The Financial Times
Bracken House
10 Cannon Street
London EC4P 4BY, England

Forbes
Forbes, Inc.
60 Fifth Avenue
New York, NY 10011

Fortune
Time, Inc.
Time & Life Building
1271 Avenue of the Americas
New York, NY 10020

Global Trade
North American Publishing Co.
401 N. Broad Street
Philadelphia, PA 19108

Industrial Marketing
Crain Communications Inc.
740 N. Rush Street
Chicago, IL 60611

International Financial Statistics
International Monetary Fund
Publications Unit
700 19th Street N.W.
Washington, D.C. 20431

Investor's Daily
Box 25970
Los Angeles, CA 90025

Journal of Commerce
110 Wall Street
New York, NY 10005

Sales & Marketing Management
Bill Communications Inc.
633 Third Avenue
New York, NY 10017

Wall Street Journal
Dow Jones & Company
200 Liberty Street
New York, NY 10281

World Agriculture Situation
U.S. Department of Agriculture
Economics Management Staff
Information Division
1301 New York Avenue N.W.
Washington, D.C. 20005

World Development
Pergamon Press Inc.
Journals Division
Maxwell House
Fairview Park
Elmsford, NY 10523

World Trade Center Association
 (WTCA) Directory
World Trade Centers Association
1 World Trade Center
New York, NY 10048

Directories

American Register of Exporters and
  Importers
38 Park Row
New York, NY 10038

Arabian Year Book
Dar Al-Seuassam Est.Box 42480
Shuwakh, Kuwait

Directories of American Firms
  Operating in Foreign Countries
World Trade Academy Press
Uniworld Business Publications Inc.
50 E. 42nd Street
New York, NY 10017

Encyclopedia of Associations
Gale Research Co.
Book Tower
Detroit, MI 48226

Polk's World Bank Directory
R.C. Polk & Co.
2001 Elm Hill Pike
P.O. Box 1340
Nashville, TN 37202

Verified Directory of Manufacturers'
  Representatives
MacRae's Blue Book Inc.
817 Broadway
New York, NY 10003

World Guide to Trade Associations
K.G. Saur & Co.
175 Fifth Avenue
New York, NY 10010

Encyclopedias, Handbooks, and Miscellaneous

A Basic Guide to Exporting
U.S. Government Printing Office
Superintendent of Documents
Washington, D.C. 20402

Doing Business in . . . Series
Price Waterhouse
1251 Avenue of the Americas
New York, NY 10020

Economic Survey of Europe
The United Nations
United Nations Publication Division
1 United Nations Plaza
Room DC-0853
New York, NY 10017

Economic Survey of Latin America
United Nations
United Nations Publishing Division
1 United Nations Plaza
Room DC-0853
New York, NY 10017

Encyclopedia Americana,
    International Edition
Grolier Inc.
Danbury, CT 06816

Encyclopedia of Business
    Information Sources
Gale Research Co.
Book Tower
Detroit, MI 48226

Europa Year Book
Europa Publications Ltd.
18 Bedford Square
London WC1B 3JN, England

Export Administration Regulations
U.S. Government Printing Office
Superintendent of Documents
Washington, D.C. 20402

Export Shipping Manual
U.S. Government Printing Office
Superintendent of Documents
Washington, D.C. 20402

Exporters' Encyclopedia—World
    Marketing Guide
Dun's Marketing Services
49 Old Bloomfield Road
Mountain Lake, NJ 07046

Export-Import Bank of the United
    States Annual Report
U.S. Government Printing Office
Superintendent of Documents
Washington, D.C. 20402

Exporting for the Small Business
U.S. Government Printing Office
Superintendent of Documents
Washington, D.C. 20402

Exporting to the United States
U.S. Government Printing Office
Superintendent of Documents
Washington, D.C. 20402

Foreign Business Practices:
    Materials on Practical Aspects of
    Exporting, International
    Licensing, and Investing
U.S. Government Printing Office
Superintendent of Documents
Washington, D.C. 20402

A Guide to Financing Exports
U.S. Government Printing Office
Superintendent of Documents
Washington, D.C. 20402

Handbook of Marketing Research
McGraw-Hill Book Co.
1221 Avenue of the Americas
New York, NY 10020

International Encyclopedia of the
    Social Sciences
Macmillan and the Free Press
866 Third Avenue
New York, NY 10022

Market Share Reports
U.S. Government Printing Office
Superintendent of Documents
Washington, D.C. 20402

Marketing and Communications
    Media Dictionary
Media Horizons Inc.
50 W. 25th Street
New York, NY 10010

Media Guide International:
    Business/Professional
    Publications
Directories International Inc.
150 Fifth Avenue Suite 610
New York, NY 10011

Overseas Business Reports
U.S. Government Printing Office
Superintendent of Documents
Washington, D.C. 20402

Trade Finance Report
U.S. Department of Commerce
International Trade Administration
Washington, D.C. 20230

World Economic Conditions in
    Relation to Agricultural Trade
U.S. Government Printing Office
Superintendent of Documents
Washington, D.C. 20402

Yearbook of International Trade
    Statistics
United Nations
United Nations Publishing Division
1 United Nations Plaza
Room DC-0853
New York, NY 10017

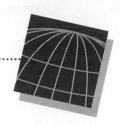

Description of Selected U.S. Government Publications and Services

Macro Data

World Population is issued by the U.S. Bureau of the Census, which collects and analyzes worldwide demographic data. Information is provided about total population, fertility, mortality, urban population, growth rate, and life expectancy. Also published are detailed demographic profiles, including an analysis of the labor force structure of individual countries.

Foreign Trade Highlights are annual reports published by the Department of Commerce. They provide basic data on U.S. merchandise trade with major trading partners and regions. They also contain brief analyses of recent U.S. trade developments.

Foreign Trade Report FT410 provides a monthly statistical record of shipments of all merchandise from the United States to foreign countries, including both the quantity and dollar value of exports to each country. It also contains cumulative export statistics from the first of the calendar year.

World Agriculture, a publication of the U.S. Department of Agriculture, provides production information, data, and analyses by country along with a review of recent economic conditions and changes in agricultural and trade policies. Frequent supplements provide an outlook of anticipated developments for the coming year.

Country Information

National Trade Data Bank, a key product of the U.S. Department of Commerce, provides monthly CD-ROM disks that contain overseas market research, trade statistics, contact information, and other reports that may assist U.S. exporters in their international marketing efforts.

Country Marketing Plan reports on commercial activities and climate in a country and is prepared by the Foreign Commercial Service staffs abroad. It also contains an action plan for the coming year, including a list of trade events and research to be conducted.

Industry SubSector Analyses are market research reports, ranging from 5 to 20 pages, on specific product categories, for example, electromedical equipment in one country.

Overseas Business Reports (OBR) present economic and commercial profiles on specific countries and provide background statistics. Selected information on the direction and the volume and nature of U.S. foreign trade is also provided.

Background Notes, prepared by the Department of State, present a survey of a country's people, geography, economy, government, and foreign policy. The reports also include important national economic and trade information.

Foreign Economic Trends presents recent business and economic developments and the latest economic indicators of more than 100 countries.

Product Information

Export Statistics Profiles analyze exports for a single industry, product by product, country by country, over a five-year period. Data are rank-ordered by dollar value for quick identification of the leading products and industries. Tables show the sales of each product to each country as well as competitive information, growth, and future trends. Each profile also contains a narrative analysis that highlights the industry's prospects, performance, and leading products.

U.S. Industrial Outlook, an annual publication of the U.S. Department of Commerce, provides an overview of the domestic and international performance of all major U.S. industries, complete with employment and shipment information and a forecast of future developments.

Export Information System Data Reports, available from the U.S. Small Business Administration, provide small businesses with a list of the 25 largest importing markets for their products and the 10 best markets for U.S. exporters of the products. Trends within those markets and the major sources of foreign competition are also discussed.

Services

Agent Distributor Service (ADS): The Foreign Commercial Service (FCS) provides a customized search for interested and qualified foreign representatives for a firm's product.

Aglink: Collaborative effort between the Foreign Agricultural Service and the Small Business Administration to match foreign buyers with U.S. agribusiness firms.

Catalog Exhibitions: The Department of Commerce organizes displays of product literature and videotape presentations overseas.

Comparison Shopping Service: The FCS provides a custom foreign market survey on a product's overall marketability, names of competitors, comparative prices, and customary business practices.

Economic Bulletin Board: The Department of Commerce provides access to the latest economic data releases, including trade opportunities, for on-line users.

Foreign Agricultural Service: Employees of the U.S. Department of Agriculture, stationed both abroad and in the United States with the mission to facilitate agricultural exports from the United States. Provides counseling, research, general market information, and market introduction services.

Foreign Buyer Program: The FCS brings foreign buyers to U.S. trade shows for industries with high export potential.

Going Global: A computerized, on-line information system which lists market opportunities, information on foreign countries and export intermediaries. Primarily focused on agricultural firms.

Matchmaker Events: The Department of Commerce introduces U.S. companies to new markets through short visits abroad to match the U.S. firm with a representative or prospective partner.

Seminar Missions: The Department of Commerce sponsors technical seminars abroad designed to promote sales of sophisticated products and technology.

Trade Missions: Groups of U.S. business executives, led by Commerce Department staff, meet with potential foreign buyers, agents, and distributors.

Trade Opportunity Program: The FCS daily collection of trade opportunities worldwide is published and electronically distributed to subscribers.

World Traders Data Reports: The FCS publishes background research conducted by FCS officers abroad on potential trading partners, such as agents, distributors, and licensees.

CHAPTER 9

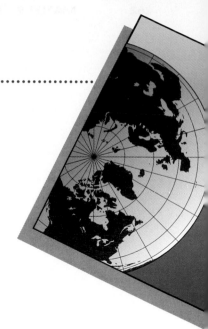

International
Product Adaptation

European Product Standards:
Headache or Headache Relief?

Murray Ohio Manufacturing has had to change the way it has made lawn-mowers for decades. Its riding and walking models are now quieter because of new noise standards imposed by the European Union (EU). "We had to slow down the fan blade to cut noise," says Ray Elmy, vice president for design engineering. "However, it will not exhaust and bag grass as well, and our costs have increased." In spite of increased production costs, the company made the changes because a significant portion of its $700 million in sales comes from European customers.

Murray's changes are not unique. For regulated products, that is, products covered by directive, the EU has developed single sets of requirements that must be met in order to sell products in the 12 member countries of the EU. With the European Economic Area (EEA) agreement in force January 1, 1994, the number of countries affected increased to 18. Many different categories of products are regulated—toys, construction products, pressure vessels, gas appliances, medical devices, telecommunications terminal equipment, and machinery, among others. Overall, approximately half of the annual $100 billion of U.S. goods exported to the EU falls within the regulated product category. The harmonization of technical standards focuses essentially on health and safety aspects of products, with minimum levels being established. Compliance with the standards means that goods may circulate freely throughout the EEA and bear the "CE" safety mark, if needed.

For unregulated products, that is, those not covered by Europewide directives, such as paper and furniture, mutual recognition of national standards applies. This means that a U.S. exporter can certify to U.S. standards, and if these standards are accepted by at least one member country, they will be accepted throughout the EEA. For example, a French charter airline was refused certification for a new-model Boeing 737 because no French standard for the model existed. The airline registered the aircraft in Ireland, and because the Irish Department of Transport had accepted U.S. requirements as an Irish standard, the airliner was then able to operate throughout Europe, including France.

The standards may sometimes force companies to make expensive changes that customers have not demanded. And the price of compliance may prove so stiff that some small exporters will stop doing business in Europe. However, the standards do come with these significant benefits:

- Companies that had to make as many as 18 versions of their products for Europe because of differing national standards, now are able to produce just one.
- Marketing should prove more efficient. Approval in one country will serve as an EEA passport permitting the sale throughout the market.
- U.S. manufacturers may be forced to improve the quality of all of their products, a benefit to American customers and U.S. competitiveness. To ensure that EU standards are not violated inadvertently through sloppy manufacturing, some product rules require adoption of an overall quality system approved by the International Standards Organization (ISO).

Sources: Phillippe Bruno, "EC Product Standards: Joint Standards Will Be Headache Relief," *Export Today* 9 (June 1993): 33–36; Patrick Oster, "Europe's Standards Blitz Has Firms Scrambling," *The Washington Post*, October 18, 1992, H1–H4; and Barbara H. Tucker and Michael G. Whyte, "Export Tactics Pending Harmonization," *Export Today* 6 (September 1990): 44.

This chapter is concerned with how the international marketer should adjust the firm's product offering to the international marketplace. An array of both external and internal variables, such as those in The International Marketplace 9.1, influences the degree to which the firm will cater to the unique needs of each of the markets it will enter. The decision is critical to all marketers, small and large, in their attempt to serve customers better, regardless of their geographic location, while maintaining overall profitability. The chapter will end with a discussion of how international marketers can defend themselves against foreign theft of ideas and innovations.

PRODUCT VARIABLES

The core of a firm's international operations is a product or service. This can be defined as the complex of tangible and intangible elements that distinguishes it from the other entities in the marketplace. The firm's success depends on how good its product or service is and on how well the firm is able to differentiate the product from the offerings of competitors. Theodore Levitt has stated that there is no such thing as a commodity; all goods and services are differentiable.[1] Products can be differentiated by their composition, by their country of origin, by their tangible features such as packaging or quality, or by their augmented features such as warranty. Further, the positioning of the product

---

[1] Theodore Levitt, "Marketing Success through Differentiation—of Anything," *Harvard Business Review* 58 (January–February 1980): 83–91.

Elements of a Product   FIGURE 9.1

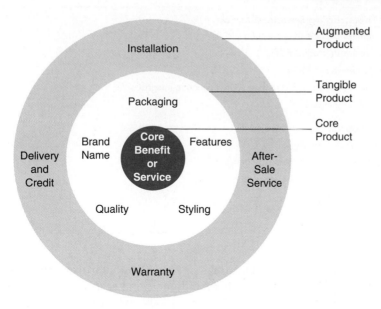

Source: Philip Kotler, *Principles of Marketing*, 3/e, © 1986, 297. Reprinted by permission of Prentice-Hall, Inc., Englewood Cliffs, New Jersey.

in consumers' minds (for example, Volvo's safety) will add to its perceived value. The **core product**—for example, the bios-ROM component of a personal computer or the recipe for a soup—may indeed be the same or highly similar to those of competitors, leaving the marketer with the other tangible and **augmented features** of the product to achieve differentiation. Very often, the accompanying service may be a good share of what the company is marketing; for example, Otis Elevator Company generates half of its worldwide revenues from the service contracts on its elevators. The elements of the product concept are summarized in Figure 9.1.

To the potential buyer, a product is a complete cluster of value satisfactions. A customer attaches value to a product in proportion to its perceived ability to help solve problems or meet needs. Therefore, IBM does not sell personal computers but rather help for problem solutions its customers are seeking. Charles Revson of Revlon summed it up best by stating that he manufactured cosmetics but sold hope. Within international markets, these psychological expectations may vary dramatically from one market to another without having a dramatic effect on the core product, yet warranting a careful assessment of choices to be made.

Standardization versus Adaptation

The first question after the internationalization decision has been made concerns the product modifications that are needed or warranted. A firm has four basic alternatives in approaching international markets: (1) selling the product as is in the international marketplace, (2) modifying products for different countries and/or regions, (3) designing new products for foreign markets, and (4) incorporating all the differences into one product design and introducing a global product. Firms may identify potential target markets and then choose products that can easily be marketed there with little or no modification.

TABLE 9.1	Standardization versus Adaptation

Factors Encouraging Standardization
- Economies of scale in production
- Economies in product R&D
- Economies in marketing
- "Shrinking" of the world marketplace/economic integration
- Global competition

Factors Encouraging Adaptation
- Differing use conditions
- Government and regulatory influences
- Differing consumer behavior patterns
- Local competition
- True to the marketing concept

The question of whether to standardize or to custom-tailor marketing programs in each country has continued to trouble practitioners and academics alike and has produced many and varied opinions. In the early 1960s, Robert Buzzell stated that it depends on the strengths of the barriers to standardization, such as national differences in consumer preferences and legal restrictions, and on the potential payoffs of standardizing marketing strategy.[2] Studies of how firms view standardization have found that arguments in favor of standardizing whenever possible fall into two categories: better marketing performance and lower marketing cost.[3] The general benefits and disadvantages of standardization versus adaptation are summarized in Table 9.1.

The benefits of standardization—that is, selling the same product worldwide—are cost savings in production and marketing. In addition to the economies of scale, many point to economic integration as a driving force to make markets more unified. As a response to integration efforts around the world, especially in Europe, many international marketers are indeed standardizing many of their marketing approaches, such as branding and packaging, across markets.[4] Similarly, having to face the same competitors in the major markets of the world will add to the pressure of a worldwide approach to international marketing. However, in most cases, demand and usage conditions vary sufficiently to require some changes in the product or service itself.

Coca-Cola, Levi's jeans, and Colgate toothpaste have been cited as evidence that universal product and marketing strategy can work.[5] Yet, the argument that the world is becoming more homogenized may actually be true for only a limited number of products that have universal brand recognition and minimal product knowledge requirements for use.[6] Although product standardization is generally increasing, there are still substantial differences in company practices depending on the products marketed and

[2] Robert Buzzell, "Can You Standardize Multinational Marketing?" *Harvard Business Review* 46 (November–December 1968): 98–104.

[3] Ralph Z. Sorenson and Ulrich E. Wiechmann, "How Multinationals View Marketing Standardization," *Harvard Business Review* 53 (May–June 1975): 38–56.

[4] Theodore Levitt, "The Globalization of Markets," *Harvard Business Review* 61 (May–June 1983): 92–101.

[5] W. Chan Kim and R. A. Mauborgne, "Cross-Cultural Strategies, " *Journal of Business Strategy* 7 (Spring 1987): 28–36.

[6] "Marketers Turn Sour on Global Sales Pitch Harvard Guru Makes," *The Wall Street Journal,* May 12, 1988, 1, 13.

Strategic Adaptation to Foreign Markets   FIGURE 9.2

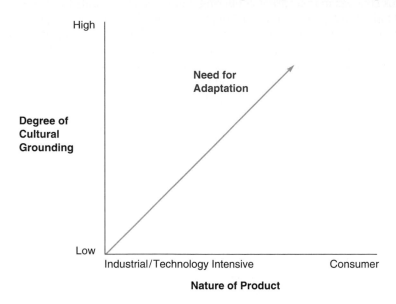

Sources: W. Chan Kim and R. A. Mauborgne, "Cross-Cultural Strategies," *The Journal of Business Strategy* 7 (Spring 1987): 31; and John A. Quelch and Edward J. Hoff, "Customizing Global Marketing," *Harvard Business Review* 64 (May–June 1986): 92–101.

where they are marketed.[7] As shown in Figure 9.2, industrial products, such as steel, chemicals, and agricultural equipment, tend to be less culturally grounded and warrant less adjustment than consumer goods. Similarly, marketers in technology-intensive industries, such as scientific instruments or medical equipment, find universal acceptability for their products.[8]

Adaptation needs in the industrial sector may exist even though the needs may not be overt. As an example, capacity performance is seen from different perspectives in different countries. Typically, the performance specifications of a German product are quite precise; for example, if a German product is said to have a lifting capacity of 1,000 kilograms, it will perform precisely up to that level. The U.S. counterpart, however, is likely to maintain a safety factor of 1.5 or even 2.0, resulting in a substantially higher payload capacity. Buyers of Japanese machine tools have also found that these tools will perform at the specified level, not beyond them, as would the U.S.-made counterparts.

Consumer goods generally require product adaptation because of their higher degree of cultural grounding. The degree of change introduced in consumer goods depends not only on cultural differences but also on economic conditions in the target market. Low incomes may cause pressure to simplify the product to make it affordable in the market.

Beyond the dichotomy of standardization and adaptation exist other approaches. The international marketer may design and introduce new products for foreign markets in addition to the firm's relatively standardized "flagship" products and brands. Some of these products developed specifically for foreign clients may later be introduced elsewhere, including in the domestic market.

---

[7] J. J. Boddewyn, Robin Soehl, and Jacques Picard, "Standardization in International Marketing: Is Ted Levitt in Fact Right?" *Business Horizons* 29 (November–December 1986): 69–75.

[8] S. Tamer Cavusgil and Shaoming Zou, "Marketing Strategy-Performance Relationship: An Investigation of the Empirical Link in Export Market Ventures," *Journal of Marketing* 58 (January 1994): 1–21.

Even companies that are noted for following the same methods worldwide have made numerous changes in their product offering. Some, like Coca-Cola Company's Hi-C Soy Milk in Hong Kong, may be restricted to markets for which they were specifically developed. Although Colgate toothpaste is available worldwide, the company also markets some products locally, such as a spicy toothpaste formulated especially for the Middle East. McDonald's serves abroad the same menu of hamburgers, soft drinks, and other foods that it does in the United States, and the restaurants look the same. But McDonald's has also tried to tailor its product to local styles; for example, in Japan, the chain's trademark character, known as Ronald McDonald in the United States, is called Donald McDonald because it is easier to pronounce that way.[9] Menu adjustments include beer in Germany and wine in France. Of course, marketers may have similar adaptation needs in their domestic operations; for example, menus of fast-food restaurants in the South carry iced tea, whereas those in the Northeast do not.

Increasingly, companies are attempting to develop global products by incorporating differences regionally or worldwide into one basic design. This is not pure standardization, however. To develop a standard in the United States, for example, and use it as a model for other markets is dramatically different from obtaining inputs from the intended markets and using the data to create a standard. What is important is that adaptability is built into the product around a standardized core. For example, IBM makes more than 20 different keyboards for its relatively standardized personal computers to adjust to language differences in Europe alone. The international marketer attempts to exploit the common denominators, but local needs are considered from product development to the eventual marketing of the product. Car manufacturers like Ford and Nissan may develop basic models for regional, or even global, use, but they allow for substantial discretion in adjusting the models to local preferences. Such an approach encourages "thinking globally, acting locally." Often this is best done in collaboration with a local joint venture partner or, in the case of large companies, in collaboration with the affected subsidiaries.

Factors Affecting Adaptation

In deciding the form in which the product is to be marketed abroad, the firm should consider three sets of factors: (1) the market(s) that have been targeted, (2) the product and its characteristics, and (3) company characteristics, such as resources and policy. In a survey of firms with products or services in the international marketplace, 40 percent said that the adaptation issue comes up frequently, whereas another 40 percent reported that the issue arises sometimes.[10] For most firms, the key question linked to adaptation is whether the effort is worth the cost involved—in adjusting production runs, stock control, or servicing, for example—and the investigative research involved in determining, for example, features that would be most appealing. For six out of ten firms surveyed, the expense of modifying products was moderate. This may mean, however, that the expense is moderate when modifications are considered and acted on, whereas modifications are considered but rejected when the projected cost is substantial.

A detailed examination of 174 consumer-packaged goods destined for the developing countries has shown that, on average, 4.1 changes per product were made in terms of brand name, packaging, measurement units, labeling, constituents, product features, and usage instructions.[11] Only one out of ten products was transferred without modification.

[9] "Why Some U.S. Companies Crack Japan's Market," *Business Week,* August 29, 1983, 33–34.

[10] V. Yorio, *Adapting Products for Export* (New York: Conference Board, 1983), 1.

[11] John S. Hill and Richard R. Still, "Adapting Products to LDC Tastes," *Harvard Business Review* 62 (March–April 1984): 92–101.

Factors Affecting Product-Adaptation Decisions   **FIGURE 9.3**

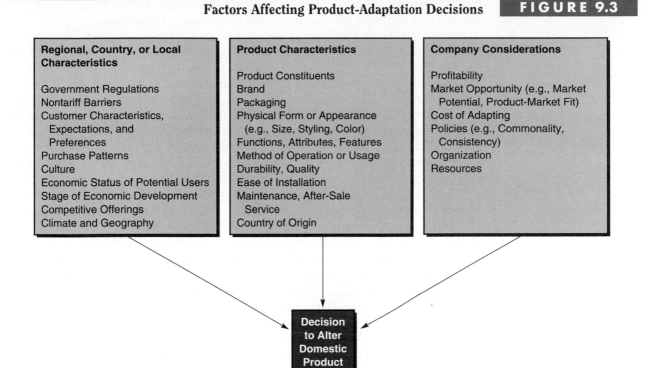

Regional, Country, or Local Characteristics

Government Regulations
Nontariff Barriers
Customer Characteristics,
   Expectations, and
   Preferences
Purchase Patterns
Culture
Economic Status of Potential Users
Stage of Economic Development
Competitive Offerings
Climate and Geography

Product Characteristics

Product Constituents
Brand
Packaging
Physical Form or Appearance
   (e.g., Size, Styling, Color)
Functions, Attributes, Features
Method of Operation or Usage
Durability, Quality
Ease of Installation
Maintenance, After-Sale
   Service
Country of Origin

Company Considerations

Profitability
Market Opportunity (e.g., Market
   Potential, Product-Market Fit)
Cost of Adapting
Policies (e.g., Commonality,
   Consistency)
Organization
Resources

Decision to Alter Domestic Product

Source: Adapted from V. Yorio, *Adapting Products for Export* (New York: Conference Board, 1983), 7. Reprinted with permission.

There is no panacea for resolving questions of adaptation. Many firms are formulating decision-support systems to aid in product adaptation, and some consider every situation independently. Figure 9.3 provides a summary of the factors that determine the need for either **mandatory** or **discretionary product adaptation.** All products have to conform to the prevailing environmental conditions, over which the marketer has no control. These relate to legal, economic, and climatic conditions in the market. Further adaptation decisions are made to enhance the exporter's competitiveness in the marketplace. This is achieved by matching competitive offers, catering to customer preferences, and meeting demands of local distribution systems.

THE MARKET ENVIRONMENT

Government Regulations

Government regulations often present the most stringent requirements. Some of the requirements may serve no purpose other than political (such as protection of domestic industry or response to political pressures). Because of the sovereignty of nations, individual firms need to comply but can influence the situation by lobbying, directly or through their industry associations, for the issue to be raised during trade negotiations. Government regulations may be spelled out, but firms need to be ever vigilant in terms of changes and exceptions. As an example, the metric standard applies to all commercial importation of distilled spirits to the United States. Bottle sizes must be 1.75 liters, 1.00 liters, and so on. Shipments that do not conform to these metric standards are denied entry by customs, except on written authorization by the Bureau of Alcohol, Tobacco, and Firearms, which is part of the U.S. Treasury Department.

Sweden was the first country in the world to enact legislation against most aerosol sprays on the grounds that they may harm the atmosphere. The ban, which went into effect January 1, 1979, covers thousands of hair sprays, deodorants, air fresheners, insecticides, paints, waxes, and assorted sprays that use Freon gases as propellants. It does not apply to certain medical sprays, especially those used by people who suffer from asthma. The Swedish government, which has one of the world's most active environmental-protection departments, was the first to take seriously warnings by scientists that continued release of these chemicals could eventually degrade the earth's ozone layer.

Although economic integration usually reduces discriminatory governmental regulation (as seen in The International Marketplace 9.1), some national environmental restrictions may stay in place. For example, a 1989 ruling by the European Court of Justice let stand Danish laws that require returnable containers for all beer and soft drinks. These laws seriously restrict foreign brewers, whose businesses are not on a scale large enough to justify the logistics system necessary to handle returnables.[12]

On occasion, it may be in the marketer's best interest to gain governmental approval for a product even though it may not be required. Testing by a governmental agency or an independent testing laboratory (equivalent to Underwriters Laboratory) may add to the product's acceptability in the foreign marketplace.

Government regulations are probably the single most important factor contributing to product adaptation and, because of bureaucratic red tape, often the most cumbersome and frustrating factor to deal with. In some cases, government regulations have been passed to serve as nontariff barriers to trade. To ease the situation, some industries are following agreed-upon international standards.

Nontariff Barriers

Nontariff barriers include product standards, testing or approval procedures, subsidies for local products, and bureaucratic red tape. The nontariff barriers affecting product adjustments usually concern elements outside the core product. For example, France requires the use of the French language in any offer, presentation, or advertisement whether written or spoken, in instructions for use, and in specification or guarantee terms for goods or services, as well as for invoices and receipts.

Because nontariff barriers are usually in place to keep foreign products out and/or to protect domestic producers, getting around them may be the toughest single problem for the international marketer. The expense of compliance with government regulations is high. As an example, Mack International has to pay $10,000 to $25,000 for a typical European engine certification. Brake system changes to conform with other countries' regulations run from $1,500 to $2,500 per vehicle. Wheel equipment changes will cost up to $1,000 per vehicle. Even with these outlays and the subsequent higher price, the company is still able to compete successfully in the international marketplace.

Small companies with limited resources may simply give up in the face of seemingly arbitrary harassment. For example, product testing and certification requirements have made the entry of many foreign companies into Japanese markets quite difficult, if not impossible.[13] Japan requires testing of all pharmaceutical products in Japanese laborato-

---

[12] Eric C. Friberg, "1992: Moves Europeans Are Making," *Harvard Business Review* 67 (May–June 1989): 85–89.

[13] Vernon R. Alden, "Who Says You Can't Crack Japanese Markets?" *Harvard Business Review* 64 (January–February 1986): 52–56.

ries, maintaining that these tests are needed because the Japanese may be physiologically different from Americans or Swiss. Similarly, foreign ski products were kept out because Japanese snow was somehow unique. Many exporters, rather than try to move mountains of red tape, have found ways to accommodate Japanese regulations. Famous Amos, for example, creates separate product batches to meet Japanese requirements and avoid problems with the Japanese Health and Welfare Agency.[14]

With a substantial decrease in tariff barriers, nontariff forms of protectionism have increased. On volume alone, agriculture dominates the list. In 1989, for example, the United States and the EU fought over beef produced with the aid of hormones. The hormones the Europeans banned in beef imports to the EU are almost undetectable and were declared safe by the U.N. health authorities in 1987.[15]

One way to keep a particular product or producer out of a market is to insist on particular standards. Since the EU chose ISO 9000 as a basis to harmonize varying technical norms of its member states, some of its trading partners have accused it of erecting a new trade barrier against outsiders.[16] ISO 9000, created by the International Organization for Standardization (ISO), is a set of technical standards designed to offer a uniform way of determining whether manufacturing plants and service organizations implement and document sound quality procedures. The ISO itself does not administer or regulate these standards; that job is left to the 95 countries worldwide that have voluntarily adopted them. The feeling that ISO registration is a trade barrier comes from the Europeans' earlier start and subsequent control of the program. While more than 20,000 companies in Europe have been registered, the respective number in the United States is only 700. As a matter of fact, a 1992 survey of senior executives found that 48 percent of them had not even heard of ISO 9000 standards.[17] There is no legal requirement to adopt the standards; however, many agree that these guidelines are already determining what may be sold to and within the EU.

Customer Characteristics, Expectations, and Preferences

The characteristics and behavior of intended customer groups are as important as governmental influences on the product adaptation decision. Even when the benefits sought are quite similar, the physical characteristics of customers may dictate product adaptation. For example, U.S.-based Erno Laszlo tried to market the same skin-care product to "fair-skinned Australians, swarthy Italians, and delicate Asian women" and failed in its effort.[18] The company also found that in Asia, skin-care customs vary widely from region to region. GE Medical Systems has designed a product specifically for Japan in addition to computerized tomography scanners produced for the U.S. market. The unit is smaller because Japanese hospitals are smaller than most U.S. facilities but also because of the smaller size of Japanese patients.[19]

Product decisions of consumer-product marketers are especially affected by local behavior, tastes, attitudes, and traditions—all reflecting the marketer's need to gain customers' approval. This group of variables is critical in that it is the most difficult to quantify but is nevertheless essential in making a go/no-go decision. The reason most

[14] Joel Kotkin, "Going through Customs," *Inc.*, December 1984, 180–184.

[15] Rahul Jacob, "Export Barriers the U.S. Hates Most," *Fortune*, February 27, 1989, 88–89.

[16] Amy Zuckerman, "Growing Concerns about ISO 9000," *Export Today* 9 (September 1993): 57–62.

[17] Cyndee Miller, "U.S. Firms Lag in Meeting Global Quality Standards," *Marketing News*, February 15, 1993, 1, 6.

[18] "Marketers Turn Sour," 1, 13.

[19] Kate Betrand, "Marketing to the Land of the Rising Yen," *Business Marketing* 12 (October 1986): 77–86.

9.2

THE INTERNATIONAL MARKETPLACE

Do Round-Toed Boots Contribute to the Trade Gap?

The sales of western footwear, especially cowboy boots, have been boosted dramatically in Europe since the mid-1980s by a fashion theme emphasizing the West and the outdoors. Estimates indicate that Germans, for example, buy up to 500,000 pairs of cowboy boots annually with sales growing at an 8 percent rate. U.S. companies, however, are not part of the evolving market. The boots may be as American as John Wayne, but most of those sold are European brands made in Spain. The main reason cited: The toes of U.S. boots are not pointy enough.

"American brands are not very popular because they are of a different style," says the owner of Dynamo, one of the largest shops specializing in boots in Germany. The U.S. style has a round toe, whereas Europeans prefer a pointed tip. An added problem is that American heels are perceived to be too wide as well. "They are practical, but not interesting."

Certainly, U.S. shoemakers have the technology to make pointy toes and narrow heels, which raises the question of why they do not do so. German buyers respond with two often-heard criticisms of U.S. manufacturers. First, U.S. companies do not export seriously, and second, they are unaware of foreign needs and tastes or are unwilling to adapt their products to foreign markets. The latter comment is highlighted by the market trend of another product born in the American West: jeans. Denim is popular in Europe, and traditional American brands are worn widely. But European brands have captured a large part of the market with vanguard designs.

Frank Scivetti, vice president for sales and marketing at Justin Boot Company in Fort Worth, Texas, said the higher prices of U.S. footwear, as well as import duties and other costs, give Spanish manufacturers an edge. "Germans are willing to settle for lower-priced products, while the French will pay higher prices for authentic boots made in the United States." German retailers agree that price is a consideration but argue that the difference of style is the main factor hurting the popularity of "authentic" western footwear.

Source: "Do Round-Toed Boots Contribute to Trade Gap?" *Journal of Commerce*, April 5, 1989, 1A, 12A.

Europeans who wear western boots buy those made in Spain may be that American footwear manufacturers are unaware of style-conscious Europeans' preference for pointed toes and narrow heels. They view American-made boots as "practical, but not interesting," as described in The International Marketplace 9.2.

Three groups of factors determine cultural and psychological specificity in relation to products and services: consumption patterns, psychosocial characteristics, and general cultural criteria.[20] The types of questions asked in Table 9.2 should be answered and systematically recorded for every product under consideration. Use of the list of questions will guide the international marketer through the analysis, ensuring that all of the necessary points are dealt with before a decision is made.

Because Brazilians are rarely breakfast eaters, Dunkin' Donuts is marketing doughnuts in Brazil as snacks, desserts, and for parties. To further appeal to Brazilians, the

---

[20] Steuart Henderson Britt, "Standardizing Marketing for the International Market," *Columbia Journal of World Business* 9 (Winter 1974): 32–40.

Cultural and Psychological Factors Affecting Product Adaptation

TABLE 9.2

I. Consumption Patterns
  A. Pattern of Purchase
    1. Is the product or service purchased by relatively the same consumer income group from one country to another?
    2. Do the same family members motivate the purchase in all target countries?
    3. Do the same family members dictate brand choice in all target countries?
    4. Do most consumers expect a product to have the same appearance?
    5. Is the purchase rate the same regardless of the country?
    6. Are most of the purchases made at the same kind of retail outlet?
    7. Do most consumers spend the same amount of time making the purchase?
  B. Pattern of Usage
    1. Do most consumers use the product or service for the same purpose or purposes?
    2. Is the product or service used in different amounts from one target area or country to another?
    3. Is the method of preparation the same in all target countries?
    4. Is the product or service used along with other products or services?

II. Psychosocial Characteristics
  A. Attitudes toward the Product or Service
    1. Are the basic psychological, social, and economic factors motivating the purchase and use of the product the same for all target countries?
    2. Are the advantages and disadvantages of the product or service in the minds of consumers basically the same from one country to another?
    3. Does the symbolic content of the product or service differ from one country to another?
    4. Is the psychic cost of purchasing or using the product or service the same, whatever the country?
    5. Does the appeal of the product or service for a cosmopolitan market differ from one market to another?
  B. Attitudes toward the Brand
    1. Is the brand name equally known and accepted in all target countries?
    2. Are customer attitudes toward the package basically the same?
    3. Are customer attitudes toward pricing basically the same?
    4. Is brand loyalty the same throughout target countries for the product or service under consideration?

III. Cultural Criteria
    1. Does society restrict the purchase and/or use of the product or service to a particular group?
    2. Is there a stigma attached to the product or service?
    3. Does the usage of the product or service interfere with tradition in one or more of the targeted markets?

Source: Steuart Henderson Britt, "Standardizing Marketing for the International Market," *Columbia Journal of World Business* 9 (Winter 1974): 32–40. Copyright 1974 Columbia Journal of World Business. Reprinted with permission.

company makes doughnuts with local fruit fillings like papaya and guava. Campbell Soup Company failed in Brazil with its offerings of vegetable and beef combinations mainly because Brazilians prefer the dehydrated products of competitors such as Knorr and Maggi; Brazilians could use these products as soup starter but still add their own flair and ingredients. The only way of solving this problem is through proper customer testing, which can be formidably expensive for a company interested only in exports.

Often, no concrete product changes are needed, only a change in the product's **positioning.** Positioning refers to consumers' perception of brand as compared with that of competitors' brands, that is, the mental image that a brand, or the company as a whole, evokes. For example, Gillette has a consistent image worldwide as a masculine, hardware, sports-oriented company. A brand's positioning, however, may have to change to reflect the differing life-styles of the targeted market. Coca-Cola Company took a risk in marketing Diet Coke in Japan, because trying to sell a diet drink is difficult in a nation

FIGURE 9.4	Diet Coke Marketed as Coke Light in Japan

Source: Used with permission of the Coca-Cola Company.

where "diet" is a dirty word and the population is not overweight by Western standards. The problem was addressed by changing the name of the drink to Coke Light and subtly shifting the promotional theme from "weight loss" to "figure maintenance." Japanese women do not like to admit that they are dieting by drinking something clearly labeled diet (see Figure 9.4).

Health- and beauty-care products often rely on careful positioning to attain a competitive advantage. Timotei shampoo, which is Unilever's brand leader in that category, has a natural-looking image with a focus on mildness and purity. Because people around the world have different hair, Timotei's formula varies, but it always has the same image. The selling of "life-style" brands is common for consumer goods for which differentiation may be more difficult. Life-styles may be more difficult for competitors to copy, but they are also more susceptible to changes in fashion.[21]

Culture

Cultural variables, as discussed earlier in the book, affect product decisions. Culture reflects the social, political, and religious heritage of the country, often presenting the hardest variable for any company to try to change. U.S. and European marketers have been accused of equating Japan's modernization with Westernization. More and more universal values certainly are seen, but these are interpreted differently in each country. A good example is symbols. Had the woman in Unilever's Surf detergent commercial in India not worn a "mangalsutra" necklace, many would have taken her white sari as a sign that she was a widow. Because "yellow" in Thai means "pus," Coca-Cola shortened the product name from Mello Yellow to simply Mello when the drink was introduced in Thailand. A correct interpretation of a culture in terms of language, religion, aesthetics, values and attitudes, and education requires help from people experienced in the particular market area.

Products that rely heavily on the written or spoken language have to be adapted for better penetration of the market. For example, SPSS Inc., the marketer of statistical software, localizes both DOS and Windows for German, English, Kanji, and Spanish. Producing software in the local language has also proven to be an excellent weapon in the fight against software piracy.

The influence of culture is especially of concern where society may restrict the purchase of the product or when the product or one of its features may be subject to a stigma. Uncle Ben's, Australia's foremost producer of pet foods, produces pork-free pet products for Muslim markets. A symbol in packaging may seem fully appropriate in one culture yet be an insult elsewhere. Dogs, for example, were alleged to have eaten one of Mohammed's regiments and therefore are considered signs of bad luck and uncleanliness in parts of North Africa. An American cologne manufacturer discovered this after launching a product featuring a man and his dog in a rural setting.

Another primary cultural consideration is the perception of numbers. In the West, 7 is considered lucky, whereas 13 is regarded as the opposite. In Japan, however, the ideogram for the number 4 can also be read as "death." Therefore, consumer goods shipped to Japan in packages of four have experienced limited sales. On the other hand, 3 and 5 are considered luckier numbers.[22]

Economic Development

Management must take into account the present stage of economic development of the overseas market. As a country's economy advances, buyers are in a better position to buy and to demand more sophisticated products and product versions. With broad country considerations in mind, the firm can determine potentials for selling certain kinds of products and services. In some cases, the situation in a developing market may require **backward innovation;** that is, the market may require a drastically simplified version of the firm's product due to lack of purchasing power or usage conditions.

Economic conditions will affect packaging in terms of size and units sold in a package. In developing markets, products such as cigarettes and razor blades are often sold

---

[21] "Better to Be on the Inside Looking Out," *Economist,* December 24, 1988, 96–98.
[22] Nancy Hollander, "Judging a Book by Its Cover," *Export Today* 4 (July–August 1988): 47–49.

by the piece so that consumers with limited incomes can afford them. Soft-drink companies have introduced four-can packs in Europe, where cans are sold singly, even in large stores. On the other hand, products oriented to families, such as food products, appear in larger sizes in developing markets. Pillsbury packages its products in six- and eight-serving sizes for developing countries whereas the most popular size in the North American market is for two.[23]

Competitive Offerings

The monitoring of competitors' product features, as well as determining what has to be done to meet and beat them, is critical. Competitive offerings may provide a baseline against which the firm's resources can be measured—for example, what it takes to reach a critical market share in a given competitive situation. An analysis of competitors' offerings may reveal holes in the market or suggest avoiding certain market segments. American Hospital Supply, a Chicago-based producer of medical equipment, adjusts its product in a preemptive way by making products that are hard to duplicate. As a result, the firm achieved increases of about 40 percent per year in sales and earnings in Japan over a ten-year period.[24] The products are so specialized that it would be hard for Japanese firms to duplicate them on a mass-production basis.

In many markets, the international marketer is competing with local manufacturers and must overcome traditional purchasing relationships and the certainty they provide. BBN, a marketer of highly interactive data-processing equipment and support services, is facing, with its $30 million in export sales, giants such as Siemens and Philips. BBN must prove not only that its products are competitive in price and quality but also that the company will honor its commitments and provide any necessary after-sales service. However, by concentrating on one area alone, and targeting carefully, BBN can invest far more resources and stay ahead of its competition.[25]

Climate and Geography

Climate and geography will usually have an effect on the total product offering: the core product, tangible elements, mainly packaging, and the augmented features. The international marketer must consider two sometimes contradictory aspects of packaging for the international market. On the one hand, the product itself has to be protected against longer transit times and possibly for longer shelf life; on the other hand, care has to be taken that no nonallowed preservatives are used. One firm experienced this problem when it tried to sell Colombian guava paste in the United States. Because the packaging could not withstand the longer distribution channels and the longer time required for distribution, the product arrived in stores in poor condition and was promptly taken off the shelves.

PRODUCT CHARACTERISTICS

Product characteristics are the inherent features of the product offering, whether actual or perceived. The inherent characteristics of products and the benefits they provide to consumers in the various markets make certain products good candidates for standard-

---

[23] John S. Hill and Richard R. Still, "Adapting Products to LDC Tastes," *Harvard Business Review* 62 (March–April 1984): 92–101.

[24] "Why Some U.S. Companies Crack Japan's Market," *Business Week,* August 29, 1983, 33–34.

[25] "Divide and Conquer," *Export Today* 5 (February 1989): 10.

ization, others not. Consumer nondurables, such as food products, generally show the highest amount of sensitivity toward differences in national tastes and habits. Consumer durables, such as cameras and home electronics, are subject to far more homogeneous demand and more predictable adjustment (for example, adjustment to a different technical system in television sets and videotape recorders). Industrial products tend to be more shielded from cultural influences. However, substantial modifications may sometimes be required—in the telecommunications industry, for example—as a result of government regulations and restraints.

The influence of the various market factors on product features varies dramatically by type and by impact.

Product Constituents

The international marketer must make sure products do not contain ingredients that might be in violation of legal requirements or religious or social customs. As an example, DEP Corporation, a Los Angeles manufacturer with $19 million annual sales of hair and skin products, takes particular pains to make sure that no Japan-bound products contain formaldehyde—an ingredient commonly used in the United States but illegal in Japan. To ensure the purity of the Japanese batches, the company repeatedly cleans and sterilizes the chemical vats, checks all ingredients for traces of formaldehyde, and checks the finished product before shipment.[26] When religion or custom determines consumption, ingredients may have to be replaced in order for the product to be acceptable. In Islamic countries, for example, animal fats have to be replaced by ingredients such as vegetable shortening.

Branding

Brand names convey the image of the product or service. The term brand refers to a name, term, symbol, sign, or design used by a firm to differentiate its offerings from those of its competitors. Brands are one of the most standardizable items in the product offering; they may allow further standardization of other marketing elements such as promotional items. The brand name is the vocalizable part of the brand, the brand mark the nonvocalizable part (for example, Camel's "camel"). The brand mark may become invaluable when the product itself cannot be promoted but the symbol can be used. As an example, Marlboro cannot be advertised in most European countries because of legal restrictions on cigarette advertising; however, Philip Morris features advertisements showing only the Marlboro cowboy, who is known throughout the world. Unfortunately, most brands do not have such recognition. The term *trademark* refers to the legally protected part of the brand, indicated by the symbol ®. Increasingly, international marketers have found their trademarks violated by counterfeiters who are illegally using or abusing the brand name of the marketer.

The international marketer has a number of options in choosing a branding strategy. The marketer may choose to be a contract manufacturer to a distributor (the generics approach) or to establish national, regional, or worldwide brands. The international diffusion of U.S. brands, for example, is quite limited. Except for certain **global brands,** the majority of U.S. brands achieve roughly four-fifths of their sales in the domestic market.[27] The use of standardization in branding is strongest in culturally similar markets; for example, for U.S. marketers this means Canada and the United Kingdom. Standardization

---

[26] Kotkin, "Going through Customs," 180–184.

[27] Barry N. Rosen, J. J. Boddewyn, and Ernst A. Louis, "U.S. Brands Abroad: An Empirical Study of Global Branding," *International Marketing Review* 6 (Spring 1989): 7–19.

of product and brand do not necessarily move hand in hand; a regional brand may well have local features, or a highly standardized product may have local brand names.[28]

The establishment of worldwide brands is difficult; how can a consumer marketer establish world brands when it sells 800 products in more than 200 countries, most of them under different names? This is Gillette's situation. A typical example is Silkience hair conditioner, which is sold as Soyance in France, Sientel in Italy, and Silkience in Germany. Gillette has announced, however, a massive standardization program of brand names, packaging, and advertising.[29] Standardizing names to reap promotional benefits can be difficult because a particular name may already be established in each market, and the action raises objections from local managers.

The psychological power of brands is enormous. Surveys of American consumer goods have shown the number-one brand in a product category to be earning a 20 percent return, the number-two brand around 5 percent, and the rest losing money.[30] Brand loyalty translates into profits despite the fact that favored brands may not be superior by any tangible measure. New brands may be very difficult and expensive to build, and as a result, the company may seek a tie-in with something that the customer feels positively toward. For instance, a small Hong Kong–based company markets a product line called American No. 1. This is because the market prefers U.S. products.

Brand names often do not travel well. Semantic variations can hinder a firm's product overseas. Even the company name or the trade name should be checked out. For instance, Mirabell, the manufacturer of the genuine Mozart Kugel (a chocolate ball of marzipan and nougat), initially translated the name of its products as "Mozart balls" but has since changed the name to the "Mozart round."[31] Most problems associated with brands are not as severe but require attention nevertheless. To avoid problems with brand names in foreign markets, NameLab, a California-based laboratory for name development and testing, suggests these approaches:

1. Translation. Little Pen Inc. would become La Petite Plume, S.A., for example.
2. Transliteration. This requires the testing of an existing brand name for connotative meaning in the language of the intended market. Flic Pen Corporation, for example, would be perceived in France as a manufacturer of writing instruments for the police because the slang term *flic* connotes something between "cop" and "pig."
3. Transparency. This can be used to develop a new, essentially meaningless brand name to minimize trademark complexities, transliteration problems, and translation complexities. (Sony is an example.)
4. Transculture. This would mean using a foreign language name for a brand.[32] Vodkas, regardless of where they originate, should have Russian-sounding names or at least Russian lettering, whereas perfumes should sound French.

Brands are powerful marketing tools; for example, the chemicals and natural ingredients in one popular perfume now retailing for $140 an ounce may be worth less than $3.[33]

Firms must also be aware of trademark registration requirements in foreign countries. Under U.S. law, based on English common law, rights to a trademark are created

[28] Boddewyn, Soehl, and Picard, "Standardization in International Marketing," 69–75.

[29] Dean M. Peebles, "Don't Write Off Global Advertising: A Commentary," *International Marketing Review* 6 (Spring 1989): 73–78.

[30] "The Year of the Brand," *Economist,* December 24, 1988, 95–96.

[31] "Mozart's Genius Extends to Selling Lederhosen in Japan," *The Wall Street Journal Europe,* January 6, 1992, Section 1, 1.

[32] "How Names Work," *NameLab* (San Francisco: NameLab, 1981), 3–4.

[33] "What Lies behind the Sweet Smell of Success," *Business Week,* February 27, 1984, 139–140.

and maintained through use; registration of the trademark is an added protection. In some other countries, such as in Europe, the law is based on the Roman civil code, and trademarks are generally awarded to the first one that registers. The trademark must be protected by registering it in any market where there is even a remote chance of using it. This calls for constant vigilance, which McDonald's found out in Latin America. McDonald's trademark was registered at the Venezuelan development ministry. The registration expired, and before anything could be done, a Mr. McDonald locked up the name in Valencia and Maracaibo, two of the country's largest cities, for his fast-food outlets featuring a plastic cup with drinking straws arched like the U.S. logo and an ad slogan that reads "Millions and millions will be served."[34]

In some markets, brand name changes are required by the government. In Korea, unnecessary foreign words are barred from use; for example, Sprite has been renamed Kin. The same situation has emerged in Mexico, where local branding is primarily used to control foreign companies in terms of the marketing leverage they would have with a universal brand.

Packaging

Packaging serves three major functions: protection, promotion, and user convenience. The major consideration for the international marketer is making sure the product reaches the ultimate user in the form intended. Packaging will vary as a function of transportation mode, transit conditions, and length of time in transit. Because of the longer time that products spend in channels of distribution, firms in the international marketplace, especially those exporting food products, have had to use more expensive packaging materials and/or more expensive transportation modes. The solution of food processors has been to utilize airtight, reclosable containers that reject moisture and other contaminants.

Pilferage is a problem in a number of markets and has forced companies to use only shipping codes on outside packaging.[35] With larger shipments, containerization has helped alleviate the theft problem. An exporter should anticipate inadequate, careless, or primitive loading methods. The labels and loading instructions should be not only in English but also in the market's language as well as in symbols.

The promotional aspect of packaging relates mostly to labeling. The major adjustments concern legally required bilinguality, as in the case of Canada (French and English), Belgium (French and Flemish), and Finland (Finnish and Swedish). Other governmental requirements include more informative labeling on products. Inadequate identification, failure to use the needed languages, or inadequate or incorrect descriptions printed on the labels may cause problems. If in doubt, a company should study foreign competitors' labels.

Package aesthetics must be a consideration in terms of the promotional role of packaging. This mainly involves the prudent choice of colors and package shapes. African nations, for example, often prefer bold colors, but flag colors may be alternately preferred or disallowed. Red is often associated with death or witchcraft. Color in packaging may be faddish. White is losing popularity in industrialized countries because name brands do not want to be confused with generic products. Black, on the other hand, is increasingly popular and is now used to suggest quality, excellence, and "class." Package shapes

---

[34] "Will the Real Big Mac Please Stand Up?" *Advertising Age,* August 22, 1983, 34.

[35] Barry M. Tarnef, "How to Protect Your Goods in Transit without Going Along for a Ride," *Export Today* 9 (May 1993): 55–57.

can be selected for promotional as well as handling and storage reasons, but marketers should also recognize reuse and waste as considerations.

Package size varies according to purchasing patterns and market conditions. For instance, a six-pack format for soft drinks may not be feasible in certain markets because of the lack of refrigeration capacity in households. Quite often, overseas consumers with modest or low discretionary purchasing power buy smaller sizes or even single units in order to stretch a limited budget. As a result, the smaller size or unit may sell for more per gram or ounce than the respective U.S. economy size, which has caused concern among supranational organizations and consumer groups monitoring the marketing activities of foreign firms.

Marketers are wise to monitor packaging technology developments in the world marketplace. One of the major innovations of the 1980s was in aseptic containers for fruit drinks and milk. Tetra Pak International, the $1.5-billion Swedish company, converted 40 percent of milk sales in western Europe to its aseptic packaging system, which keeps perishables fresh for five months without refrigeration. The company claimed 5 percent of the fruit juice packaging market and 20 percent of the fruit drink market in the United States.

Finally, the consumer mandate for marketers to make products more environmentally friendly also affects the packaging dimension, as can be seen in The International Marketplace 9.3.

Appearance

Adaptations in product styling, color, size, and other appearance features are more common in consumer marketing than in industrial marketing. Color plays an important role in how consumers perceive a product, and marketers must be aware of the signal being sent by the product's color.[36] Color can be used for brand identification—for example, the yellow of Hertz, red of Avis, and green of National. It can be used for feature reinforcement; for example, Honda adopted the color black to give its motorcycles a Darth Vader look, whereas Rolls Royce uses a dazzling silver paint that spells luxury. Colors communicate in a subtle way in developed societies; they have direct meaning in more traditional societies. For instance, in the late 1950s, when Pepsi Cola changed the color of its coolers and vending machines from deep regal blue to light ice blue, the result was catastrophic in Southeast Asia. Pepsi had a dominant market share, which it lost to Coca-Cola because light blue is associated with death and mourning in that part of the world. The only way companies can protect themselves against incidents of this kind is through thorough on-site testing.

Product Uses

The international marketer should be open to ideas for new uses for the product being offered. New uses may substantially expand the market potential of the product. For example, Turbo Tek Inc., which produces a hose attachment for washing cars, has found that foreign customers have expanded the product's functions. In Japan, Turbo-Wash is used for cleaning bamboo, and the Dutch use it to wash windows, plants, and the sidings of their houses.[37]

---

[36] Laurence Jacobs, Charles Keown, Reginald Worthley, and Kyung-Il Ghymn, "Cross-Cultural Colour Comparisons: Global Marketers Beware," *International Marketing Review* 8 (1991): 21–30.

[37] "Awash in Export Sales," *Export Today* 5 (February 1989): 11.

THE INTERNATIONAL MARKETPLACE

9.3

Thinking Green in Packaging

The European Union (EU) has launched a two-pronged attack on packaging waste. It wants to both decrease sharply the amount of packaging waste that is generated and to increase the level of recycling of necessary packaging. To accomplish these objectives, two key targets have been established. First, by 1998, 60 percent of packaging waste by weight has to be recoverable for recycling or other uses and by 2003, the percentage has to reach 90. The second target requires that no more than 10 percent by weight of the waste remains to be disposed of (e.g., in land fills).

The individual EU countries are free to determine on their own what methods they want to use to achieve these targets and how they will finance the necessary waste recovery infrastructure. Most countries will place the largest part of the burden on those manufacturing, using, or selling packaging. Marketers have been encouraged to adopt the four environmentally correct Rs: redesign, reduce, reuse, recycle.

Germany, which has been the front runner in this issue, requires producers, importers, distributors, wholesalers, and retailers to take packaging from their customers for use or recycling independently of the public waste disposal system. All packaging introduced on German territory must be reusable or recyclable, and packaging must be kept to the minimum needed for proper protection and marketing of the product. Transportation packaging (e.g., crates or sacks) must be taken back through the chain of distribution all the way to the economic operator that first introduced it in the German market.

Germany's consumer-goods marketers, retailers, and the packaging industry have banded together to form Dual System Deutschland to collect, sort, and recycle empty packaging throughout the country. The 600-member companies, including Procter & Gamble and Unilever, display green dot emblems on their products which will signal consumers to return the used packaging to the system's collection containers.

These criteria will directly affect U.S. and other exporters seeking markets in Europe. If packaging of exports does not meet the EU requirements, products may be denied entry. Exporters to the EU will seek out distributors with experience in dealing with waste management requirements. Distribution agreements will have to specify which party has to bear the cost of compliance with packaging requirements and/or participation in a private waste management system, as well as the cost of the green dot licensing fees in markets such as Germany. Because similar frameworks do not exist elsewhere (including the United States), exporters to Europe cannot and should not rely on their own domestic standards to meet European packaging requirements.

Sources: Phillippe Bruno and Bernd Graf, "The New EC Environmental Framework for Packaging," *Export Today* 9 (March 1993): 17–23; Dagmar Mussey and Juliana Koranteng, "Packaging Strict Green Rules," *Advertising Age*, December 2, 1991 (Reprinted with permission from the Dec. 2, 1991 issue of *Advertising Age*. Copyright, Crain Communication, 1991), S-4; and Alain Laufenburger, "The Greening of Western Europe," *Export Today* 7 (January 1991): 9.

Method of Operation

The product as it is offered in the domestic market may not be operable in the foreign market. One of the major differences faced by appliance manufacturers is electrical power systems. In some cases, variations may exist within a country, such as Brazil. An exporter can learn about these differences through local government representatives or various trade publications such as the U.S. Department of Commerce publication *Electric Current Abroad*. However, exporters should determine for themselves the adjustments that are required by observing competitive products or having their product tested by a local entity.

Many complicating factors may be eliminated in the future through standardization efforts by international organizations and by the conversion of most countries to the metric system. Some companies have adjusted their products to operate in different systems; for example, VCR equipment that will record and play back on different color systems.

The most blatant blunders in international marketing are usually the result of exporters' failure to adjust their products to local systems. But different operating systems and environments can also provide opportunities. When Canada adopted the metric system in 1977–1978, many U.S. companies were affected. Perfect Measuring Tape Company in Toledo, for example, had to convert to metric if it wanted to continue selling disposable paper measuring tape to textile firms in Canada. Once the conversion was made, the company found an entire world of untapped markets. It was soon shipping nearly 30 percent of its tape to overseas markets as disparate as Australia and Zimbabwe.[38]

An exporter may also have to adapt the product to the differing-use situations and conditions to which the product may be subject. MicroTouch Systems, which produces touch-activated computer screens for video poker machines and ATMs, makes a series of adjustments in this regard. Ticket vending machines for the French subway need to be waterproof, since they are hosed down. Similarly, for the Australian market, video poker screens are built to take a beating because gamblers there take losing more personally than anywhere else.[39]

Quality

Many Western exporters must emphasize quality in their strategies because they cannot compete on price alone. Many new exporters compete on value in the particular segments in which they have chosen to compete. In some cases, producers of cheaper Asian products have forced international marketers to reexamine their strategies, allowing them to win contracts on the basis of technical advantage. To maintain a position of product superiority, exporting firms must invest in research and development for new products as well as manufacturing methods. For example, Sargent and Burton, a small Australian producer of high-technology racing boats, invested in CAD/CAM technology to develop state-of-the-art racing boats that have proven successful in international competition against sophisticated overseas entries.[40]

---

[38] "Made in the U.S.A.," *Business Week,* February 29, 1988, 60–66.

[39] Carla Kruytbosch, "The Minds behind the Winners," *International Business,* January 1994, 56–70.

[40] Ian Wilkinson and Nigel Barrett, "In Search of Excellence in Exports: An Analysis of the 1986 Australian Export Award Winners," paper given at the Australian Export Award presentations, Sydney, November 28, 1986.

An important aspect of improving quality is an emphasis on design. Some countries, such as Singapore and Taiwan, provide financial assistance to help companies improve product design. Cash grants help defer design costs, and publicity-oriented programs increase overall design consciousness.[41]

Increasingly, many exporters realize that they have to meet ISO 9000 standards to compete for business abroad and to win contracts from multinational corporations. Foreign buyers, especially in Europe, are requiring compliance with international ISO 9000 quality standards. For example, German electronics giant Siemens requires ISO compliance in 50 percent of its supply contracts and is encouraging other suppliers to conform. This has helped eliminate the need to test parts, which saves time and money. DuPont began its ISO drive after losing a big European order for polyester films to an ISO-certified British firm.[42]

Service

When a product sold overseas requires repairs, parts, or service, the problem of obtaining, training, and holding a sophisticated engineering or repair staff is not easy. If the product breaks down, and the repair arrangements are not up to standard, the image of the product will suffer. In some cases, products abroad may not even be used for their intended purpose and may thus require modifications not only in product configuration but also in service frequency. For instance, snow plows exported from the United States are used to remove sand from driveways in Saudi Arabia. Closely related to servicing is the issue of product warranties. Warranties not only are instructions to customers about what to do if the product fails within a specified period of time but also are effective promotional tools.

Country-of-Origin Effects

The country of origin of a product, typically communicated by the phrase "made in (country)," has a considerable influence on the quality perceptions of a product. The manufacture of products in certain countries is affected by a built-in positive or negative stereotype of product quality, as seen in The International Marketplace 9.4. One study of machine-tool buyers found that the United States and West Germany were rated higher than Japan, with Brazil being rated below all three.[43] These types of findings indicate that steps must be taken by the international marketer to overcome, or at least neutralize, biases. This issue may be especially important to developing countries, which need to increase exports, and for importers, who source products from countries different from those where they are sold.[44] In some markets, however, there may be a tendency to reject domestic goods and embrace imports of all kinds.

Some products have fared well in the international marketplace despite negative country-of-origin perceptions. For example, Belarus tractors (manufactured both in

[41] John S. Blyth, "Other Countries Lead U.S. in Supporting Design Efforts," *Marketing News,* February 13, 1989, 14–15.

[42] "Want EC Business? You Have Two Choices," *Business Week,* October 19, 1992, 58–59.

[43] Phillip D. White and Edward W. Cundiff, "Assessing the Quality of Industrial Products," *Journal of Marketing* 42 (January 1978): 80–86.

[44] Warren J. Bilkey and Erik Nes, "Country-of-Origin Effects on Product Evaluations," *Journal of International Business Studies* 13 (Spring–Summer 1982): 88–99.

9.4

THE INTERNATIONAL MARKETPLACE

Not by Quality Alone

A 1991 survey by *Popular Mechanics* found that many U.S. car buyers say they would rather buy American than Japanese if the cars were similar. In his 1991 television commercials, Lee Iacocca stated that "our cars are every bit as good as the Japanese," with substantial evidence to back his claim. What happens when indeed the Japanese and American cars are not only similar but identical?

The Plymouth Laser and the Mitsubishi Eclipse are identical sports coupes built by Diamondstar Motors (a 50-50 partnership between Chyrsler and Mitsubishi). Whatever the nameplate, the car sold for $11,000 for a basic model, around $17,500 for a souped-up version, in 1991. Sales, however, were not the same. In 1990, Chrysler's 3,000 dealers sold 40,000 Lasers while Mitsubishi's 500 dealers sold 50,000 Eclipses. That astounding difference—100 cars per Mitsubishi dealer, 13 per Chrysler dealer—says a lot about the image problem facing American-made cars. "People perceive the Japanese car to be of better quality. It is a lot easier to sell than a Laser," says Ira Rosenberg, the owner of adjoining Plymouth and Mitsubishi dealerships in Crystal Lake, Illinois.

Chrysler is not the only one having problems with image. Hyundai, despite major marketing efforts to boost buyer confidence, has not been able to get over its image as a high-risk purchase. Hyundai's focus group research on its Elantra model shows good marks on styling and features, but when buyers are asked whether they would give the car any consideration, the answers were often negative. The overall perception is that Hyundai builds an inexpensive car that has very poor quality. Given that the United States accounts for more than 50 percent of the company's exports, it is necessary for the company to get U.S. buyers to even consider the product.

Sources: John Harris, "Advantage, Mitsubishi," Forbes, March 18, 1991, 100–104; "Hyundai May Be Running Out of American Road," *Business Week*, October 14, 1991, 25.

Belarus and Russia) have fared well in Europe and the United States not only because of their reasonable price tag but also because of their ruggedness. Only the lack of an effective network has hindered the company's ability to penetrate Western markets to a greater degree.[45]

Country-of-origin effects lessen as customers become more informed. Also, as more countries develop the necessary bases to manufacture products, the origin of the products becomes less important. This can already be seen with so-called hybrid products (for example, a U.S. multinational company manufacturing the product in Malaysia). The argument has been made that with the advent of more economic integration, national borders become less important.[46]

---

[45] Johny K. Johansson, Ilkka A. Ronkainen, and Michael R. Czinkota, "Negative Country-of-Origin Effects: The Case of the New Russia," *Journal of International Business Studies* 25 (first quarter 1994): 1–21.

[46] Johny K. Johansson, "Determinants and Effects of the Use of 'Made in' Labels," *International Marketing Review* 6 (1989): 47–58.

COMPANY CONSIDERATIONS

Before launching a product in the international marketplace, the marketer needs to consider organizational capabilities as well as the nature of the product and the level of adaptation needed to accommodate various market-related differences between domestic and international markets.

The issue of product adaptation most often climaxes in the question "Is it worth it?" The answer depends on the firm's ability to control costs, correctly estimate market potential, and finally, secure profitability, especially in the long term. However, the question that used to be posed as "Can we afford to do it?" should now be "Can we afford not to do it?"

The decision to adapt should be preceded by a thorough analysis of the market. Formal market research with primary data collection and/or testing is warranted. From the financial standpoint, some firms have specific return-on-investment levels to be satisfied before adaptation (for instance, 25 percent), whereas some let the requirement vary as a function of the market considered and also the time in the market—that is, profitability may be initially compromised for proper market entry.

Most companies aim for consistency in their marketing efforts. This translates into the requirement that all products fit in terms of quality, price, and user perceptions. An example of where consistency may be difficult to control is in the area of warranties. Warranties can be uniform only if the use conditions do not vary drastically and if the company is able to deliver equally on its promise anywhere it has a presence.

A critical element of the adaptation decision has to be human resources, that is, individuals to make the appropriate decisions. Individuals are needed who are willing to make risky decisions and who know about existing market conditions. A characteristic of the American export boom in the late 1980s was that foreigners and recent immigrants were often the first to see overseas opportunities. Foreign-born managers may look for goods that many native Americans overlook or consider too difficult for the international marketplace.[47]

PRODUCT COUNTERFEITING

Counterfeit goods are any goods bearing an unauthorized representation of a trademark, patented invention, or copyrighted work that is legally protected in the country where it is marketed. The International Trade Commission estimated that U.S. companies lose a total of $60 billion every year because of product counterfeiting and other infringement of intellectual property. Hardest hit are the most innovative, fastest-growing industries, such as computer software, pharmeceutical, and entertainment.[48]

The practice of product counterfeiting has spread to high-technology products and services from the traditionally counterfeited products: high-visibility, strong-brand-name consumer goods. In addition, previously the only concern was whether a company's product was being counterfeited; now, companies have to worry about whether the raw materials and components purchased for production are themselves real.[49]

---

[47] "The Little Guys Are Making It Big Overseas," *Business Week*, February 27, 1989, 94–96

[48] Faye Rice, "How Copycats Steal Billions," *Fortune,* April 22, 1991, 157–164.

[49] Ilkka A. Ronkainen, "Imitation as the Worst Kind of Flattery: Product Counterfeiting," *Trade Analyst* 2 (July–August 1986): 2.

The European Union estimates that trade in counterfeit goods now accounts for 2 percent of total world trade. The International Chamber of Commerce estimates the figure at close to 5 percent.[50]

Counterfeiting problems occur in three ways and, depending on the origin of the products and where they are marketed, require different courses of action. Approximately 75 percent of counterfeit goods are estimated to be manufactured outside the United States, and 25 percent are either made in this country or imported and then labeled here. Problems originating in the United States can be resolved through infringement actions brought up in federal courts. Counterfeit products that originate overseas and that are marketed in the United States should be stopped by the customs barrier. Enforcement has been problematic because of the lack of adequate personnel and the increasingly high-tech character of the products. When an infringement occurs overseas, action can be brought under the laws of the country in which it occurs. The sources of the largest number of counterfeit goods are Brazil, Taiwan, Korea, and India, which are a problem to the legitimate owners of intellectual property on two accounts: the size of these countries' own markets and their capability to export. Countries in Central America and the Middle East are not sources but major markets for counterfeit goods.

The first task in fighting intellectual property violation is to use patent application or registration of trademarks or mask works (for semiconductors). The rights granted by a patent, trademark, copyright, or mask work registration in the United States confer no protection in a foreign country. There is no such thing as an international patent, trademark, or copyright. Although there is no shortcut to worldwide protection, some advantages exist under treaties or other international agreements. These treaties include the Paris Convention for the Protection of Industrial Property, the Patent Cooperation Treaty, the Berne Convention for the Protection of Literary and Artistic Works, and the Universal Copyright Convention, as well as regional patent and trademark offices such as the European Patent Office. Applicants are typically granted international protection throughout the member countries of these organizations.[51]

After securing valuable intellectual property rights, the international marketer must act to enforce, and have enforced, these rights. Four types of action against counterfeiting are legislative action, bilateral and multilateral negotiations, joint private-sector action, and measures taken by individual companies.

In the legislative arena, the Omnibus Tariff and Trade Act of 1984 amended Section 301 of the Trade Act of 1974 to clarify that the violation of intellectual property rights is an unreasonable practice within the statute. The act also introduced a major carrot-and-stick policy: The adequacy of protection of intellectual property rights of U.S. manufacturers is a factor that will be considered in the designation of **Generalized System of Preferences (GSP)** benefits to countries. In 1988, the United States denied Thailand duty-free treatment on goods worth $165 million because of lax enforcement of intellectual property laws.

The Trademark Counterfeiting Act of 1984 made trading in goods and services using a counterfeit trademark a criminal rather than a civil offense, establishing stiff penalties for the practice. The Semiconductor Chip Protection Act of 1984 clarified the status and protection afforded to semiconductor masks, which determine the capabilities of the chip. Protection will be available to foreign-designed masks in the United States only if the home country of the manufacturer also maintains a viable system of mask protec-

[50] "MNCs Get New Ally in Their War against Counterfeiters," *Business International,* January 11, 1985, 11.
[51] "An Introductory Guide for U.S. Businesses on Protecting Intellectual Property Abroad," *Business America,* July 1, 1991, 2–7.

tion. The Intellectual Property Rights Improvement Act requires the U.S. Trade Representative to set country-specific negotiating objectives for reciprocity and consideration of retaliatory options to assure intellectual property protection. The United States imposed punitive tariffs on $39 million of Brazilian imports to retaliate against Brazil's refusal to protect American pharmaceutical patents.

The U.S. government is seeking to limit counterfeiting practices through bilateral and multilateral negotiations as well as education. A joint International Trade Administration and Patent and Trademark Office action seeks to assess the adequacy of foreign countries' intellectual property laws and practices, to offer educational programs and technical assistance to countries wishing to establish adequate systems of intellectual property protection, to offer educational services to the industry, and to review the adequacy of U.S. legislation in the area. Major legislative changes have occurred in the past few years in, for example, Taiwan and Singapore, where penalties for violations have been toughened. Since 1979, the United States and the EU have been urging the nations of GATT to adopt a counterfeiting code; however, it has been stalled by developing countries that believe the code would hinder their domestic industries. The GATT agreement reached in 1993 included new rules on intellectual property protection. Under them, trade-related intellectual property will enjoy 20 years of protection. More than 100 countries have indicated they will amend their laws and improve enforcement. Violators of intellectual property will face retaliation not only in this sector, but in others as well.[52]

A number of private-sector joint efforts have emerged in the battle against counterfeit goods. In 1978, the International Anti-counterfeiting Coalition was founded to lobby for stronger legal sanctions worldwide. The coalition consists of 375 members. The International Chamber of Commerce established the Counterfeit Intelligence and Investigating Bureau in London, which acts as a clearinghouse capable of synthesizing global data on counterfeiting.

In today's environment, companies are taking more aggressive steps to protect themselves, as can be seen in The International Marketplace 9.5. The victimized companies are losing not only sales but also goodwill in the longer term if customers believe they have the real product rather than a copy of inferior quality. In addition to the normal measures of registering trademarks and copyrights, companies are taking steps in product development to prevent knock-offs of trademarked goods. For example, new authentication materials in labeling are virtually impossible to duplicate.

Many companies maintain close contact with the government and the various agencies charged with helping them. Apple Computer, for example, loans testing equipment to customs officers at all major U.S. ports, and company attorneys regularly conduct seminars on how to detect pirated software and hardware.[53] Other companies retain outside investigators to monitor the market and stage raids with the help of law-enforcement officers. A series of raids in California by GM resulted in the confiscation of $360,000 worth of bogus parts.[54]

The issue of intellectual property protection will become more important for the United States and the EU in future years. Counterfeiting is changing its nature from a decade ago, when the principal victims were manufacturers of designer items. Today, the protection of intellectual property is crucial in high technology, one of the strongest

---

[52] "Intellectual Property . . . Is Theft," *The Economist,* January 22, 1993, 72–73.

[53] "What Apple Does to Catch and Convict High Tech Pirates," *Business International,* January 18, 1985, 17–18.

[54] "Companies Are Knocking Off the Knockoff Outfits," *Business Week,* September 26, 1988, 86–88.

Fighting Back against Counterfeiters

The American entertainment industry is enjoying a boom in Asia, but it has also suffered losses between $10 and $20 million each year in royalties because of counterfeiting. Walt Disney Productions has seen virtually all lines of the company's merchandise faked: fluffy Mickey Mouse dolls, videotapes of cartoon classics, children's clothing, books, pens, stationery, figurines, and watches. The extent of the problem reflects Disney's massive appeal among Asians. The retail value of Disney's consumer products, excluding videotapes, in Asia is estimated at more than $1 billion, and further growth is projected.

In China, for example, Disney discovered numerous counterfeiting operations, including a shoe factory in Zhejiang Province pirating Mickey Mouse and Donald Duck designs, and a factory in Guangdong producing imitation Disney character candy. Authorized manufacturers for Disney's U.S. licensees were found to be passing secrets to other factories. According to Disney's own estimates, the company may be losing as much as $15 to $20 million in forgone revenues each year due to intellectual property violation.

Disney follows a three-pronged strategy in combating intellectual property infringement. First, the company tries to bring the offender into the Disney family by converting it to a legitimate licensee. These local companies will then be a part of the fight against counterfeiters because their profits would be most affected by fakes.

If that fails, Disney stages raids in cooperation with the local authorities. Between April 1989 and October 1990, the company staged raids on 25 companies in Thailand, the country most problematic for Disney. Although the country affords copyright protection by law, it has become a haven for counterfeiters because of lax enforcement, low penalties, cheap labor, and vigorous entrepreneurial spirit. It has also become a big exporter of Disney fakes to the Middle East. The company did all the detective work through a private investigator and turned over the evidence to the police, which in turn confiscated $30,000 worth of merchandise. Disney also worked with a public relations firm to achieve the greatest public impact. The whole effort climaxed with public burnings of the confiscated goods at a city dump. "If you just go on a raid, you affect 20 people that work there; but by publicizing it, you reach 20 million people," say Disney officials. Similar efforts are undertaken in other markets such as Taiwan, South Korea, Malaysia, the Philippines, and Indonesia. One raid in Singapore resulted in a large out-of-court settlement and, more important to Disney, a series of full-page newspaper apologies paid for by the offender.

While counterfeiting problems drove Disney from the market in 1989, the signing of the Memorandum of Understanding on Intellectual Property Protection between the United States and China in 1992 contributed to Disney's decision to reenter. Disney signed a licensing agreement with Vigor International of Hong Kong to market a range of its products in China.

Disney goes to court as the last resort to protect its trademarks. As a proactive measure, the company works with the U.S. trade representative's office and with industry groups active in protecting intellectual property rights.

Sources: "Reviving the Disney Dream," *Business International,* November 2, 1992, 6–7; "Disney Is No Mouse with SE Asian Pirates," *Journal of Commerce,* International Edition, July 15, 1991, 1, 7; "Disney Attacks Asia Counterfeiters," *Honolulu Star-Bulletin,* June 26, 1989, C2, C4.

Which Is the Real Mickey?

Mickey Mouse doll on the left is counterfeit; the authentic Mickey is on the right.

© 1984 Walt Disney Productions.

Source: Eileen Hill, "Intellectual Property Rights," *Business America*, March 18, 1985, 3–9, a publication of the U.S. Department of Commerce.

areas of U.S. competitiveness in the world marketplace. The ease with which technology can be transferred and the lack of adequate protection of the developers' rights in certain markets make this a serious problem.[55]

SUMMARY

The international marketer must pay careful attention to variables that may call for an adaptation in the product offering. The target market will influence the adaptation decision through factors such as government regulation and customer preferences and expectations. The product itself may not be in a form ready for international market entry in terms of its brand name, its packaging, or its appearance. Some marketers make a conscious decision to offer only standardized products; some adjust their offerings by market.

Like the soft-drink and cigarette marketers that have led the way, the newest marketers of world brands are not producing necessarily identical products, but recognizable products. As an example, the success of McDonald's in the world marketplace has been based on variation, not on offering the same product worldwide.[56] Had it not been for the variations, McDonald's only customers overseas would have been American tourists.

Firms entering or participating in the international marketplace will certainly find it difficult to cope with the conflicting needs of the domestic and international markets.

---

[55] Michael G. Harvey and Ilkka A. Ronkainen, "International Counterfeiters: Marketing Success without the Cost and the Risk," *Columbia Journal of World Business* 20 (Fall 1985): 37–45.

[56] "Colleague [Philip Kotler] Says Levitt Wrong," *Advertising Age,* June 25, 1984, 50.

They will be certain to ask whether adjustments in their product offerings, if the marketplace requires them, are worthwhile. There are, unfortunately, no magic formulas for addressing the problem of product adaptation. The answer seems to lie in adopting formal procedures to assess products in terms of the markets' and the company's own needs.

The theft of intellectual property—ideas and innovations protected by copyrights, patents, and trademarks—is a critical problem for many industries and countries. Governments have long argued about intellectual property protection, but the lack of results in some parts of the world has forced companies themselves to take action on this front.

Questions for Discussion

1. Comment on the statement "It is our policy not to adapt products for export."
2. What are the major problems facing companies, especially smaller ones, in resolving product adaptation issues?
3. How do governments affect product-design decisions of firms?
4. Is the metric standard required by the U.S. government for imported distilled spirits actually a nontariff barrier?
5. Is any product ever the same everywhere it is sold?
6. Which of these groups of factors—product, market, or company—is the most important influence on product adaptation decisions?
7. Can a company make its products so that from the beginning they meet all of the regulations and other key requirements of any market, thus avoiding the discussion on adaptation altogether?
8. Propose ways in which intellectual property piracy could be stopped permanently.

Recommended Readings

Keegan, Warren J., and Charles S. Mayer. *Multinational Product Management.* Chicago: American Marketing Association, 1977.

Levitt, Theodore. *The Marketing Imagination.* New York: Free Press, 1986.

Lorenz, C. *The Design Dimension: Product Strategy and the Challenge of Global Markets.* New York: Basil Blackwell, 1986.

Papadopoulos, Nicolas, and Louise A. Heslop. *Product-Country Images.* Binghamton, NY: International Business Press, 1993.

Renner, Sandra L., and W. Gary Winget. *Fast-Track Exporting.* New York: AMACOM, 1991.

Ries, Al, and Jack Trout. *Positioning: A Battle for Your Mind.* New York: McGraw-Hill, 1981.

Rodkin, Henry. *The Ultimate Overseas Business Guide for Growing Companies.* Homewood, IL: Dow Jones-Irwin, 1990.

Urban, Glen L., and John Hauser. *Design and Marketing of New Products.* Englewood Cliffs, NJ: Prentice-Hall, 1980.

Webber, Robert. *The Marketer's Guide to Selling Products Abroad.* Westport, CT: Quorum Books, 1989.

CHAPTER 10

....

Export Pricing
Strategies

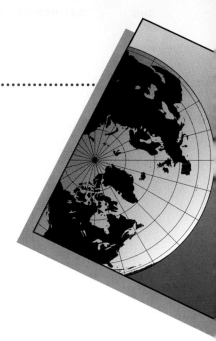

THE INTERNATIONAL MARKETPLACE

The Exporter's Pricing Dilemma

Setting the right price for a product can be the key to success or failure in the international marketplace. The complexity of export pricing as well as the importance placed on export operations cause companies to take different approaches to export pricing.

Dairy Equipment Co. produces milk machines, bulk coolers, and other high-quality equipment for the dairy industry. Although the company has exported continuously over the past decade, export earnings have been negligible. Gross profit has remained the company's primary export goal, but the rigid cost-plus strategy has not proved to be effective. The company has always sought equal profitability from foreign sales; however, fierce competition in some markets has forced it to consider lower profit margins. The company's export pricing policy remains a static element of the marketing mix.

Baughman, a division of Fuqua Industries, manufactures steel grain storage silos and related equipment. The company has traditionally exported approximately 30 percent of its sales. Baughman's products are of high quality, and pricing has not often been an active element of the marketing mix. The firm's export sales terms consist of an irrevocable confirmed letter of credit in U.S. dollars with no provisions for fluctuating exchange rates. Export and domestic prices are identical before exporting costs are added. However, Baughman will make concessions to this policy to secure strategically important sales.

Ray-O-Vac, a producer of batteries and other consumer goods, has been exporting successfully since the 1950s. Exports account for 20 percent of total business, and major markets include Europe, the Far East, and Japan. These markets are entered through wholly owned subsidiaries that are treated as cost or profit centers depending on market circumstances. Competitive pressures demand flexible pricing, and discounts are often granted to gain market share. Branch managers may adjust prices on a day-to-day basis to counter exchange rate fluctuations. Export pricing is a very active ingredient in the firm's marketing mix.

While many, especially new, exporters calculate their export price by the cost-plus method to counter the uncertainties of international business, market forces and internal goal setting may force them to reconsider their strategy.

Sources: "Price, Quotations, and Terms of Sale Are Key to Successful Exporting," *Business America*, October 4, 1993, 12–15; S. Tamer Cavusgil, "Unraveling the Mystique of Export Pricing," *Business Horizons*, 31 (May–June 1988): 54–63.

This chapter will focus on the pricing decision from the exporter's point of view: the setting of export price, terms of sale, and terms of payment. The setting of price is complicated by such factors as duties and intermediary margins. Two special considerations in export pricing—leasing and dumping—are discussed at the end of this chapter. Foreign-market pricing (by subsidiaries) and intracompany transfer pricing, that is, pricing for transactions between corporate entities, will be discussed in a later chapter.

PRICE DYNAMICS

Price is the only element of the marketing mix that is revenue generating; all of the others are costs. It should therefore be used as an active instrument of strategy in the major areas of marketing decision making, as seen in The International Marketplace 10.1. Price serves as a means of communication with the buyer by providing a basis for judging the attractiveness of the offer. Price is a major competitive tool in meeting and beating close rivals and substitutes. Competition will often force prices down, whereas intracompany financial considerations have an opposite effect. Prices, along with costs, will determine the long-term viability of the enterprise.

Price should not be determined in isolation from the other marketing mix elements. Price may be used effectively in positioning the product in the marketplace—for example, Perrier as a premium entry in the United States. It may be a major determinant in how the product is to be distributed. The feasibility range for price setting established by demand, competition, costs, and legal considerations may be narrow or wide in a given situation (for example, the pricing of a commodity versus an innovation). Regardless of how narrow the gap allowed by these factors, however, pricing should never be considered a static element.

A summary of international pricing situations is provided as a matrix in Figure 10.1. Pricing challenges—such as pricing for a new market entry, changing price either as an attack strategy or in response to competitive changes, and multiple-product coordination in cases of related demand—are technically the same as problems encountered in domestic markets. The scope of these pricing situations will vary according to the degree of foreign involvement and the type of market encountered.

In first-time pricing, the general alternatives are (1) skimming, (2) following the market price, and (3) penetration pricing. The objective of **skimming** is to achieve the

International Pricing Situations **FIGURE 10.1**

Pricing Situation	International Involvement		
	Exporting	Foreign-Market Pricing	Intracompany Pricing
First-Time Pricing			
Changing Pricing			
Multiple-Product Pricing			

Source: Adapted from Helmut Becker, "Pricing: An International Marketing Challenge," in *International Marketing Strategy,* eds. Hans Thorelli and Helmut Becker (New York: Pergamon Press, 1980), 207. Adapted with permission.

highest possible contribution in a short time period. For an exporter to use this approach, the product has to be unique, and some segments of the market must be willing to pay the high price. As more segments are targeted and more of the product is made available, the price is gradually lowered. The success of skimming depends on the ability and speed of competitive reaction.

If similar products already exist in the target market, **market pricing** can be used. The final customer price is determined based on competitive prices, and then both production and marketing must be adjusted to the price. This approach requires the exporter to have a thorough knowledge of product costs, as well as confidence that the product life cycle is long enough to warrant entry into the market. It is a reactive approach and may lead to problems if sales volumes never rise to sufficient levels to produce a satisfactory return. Although firms typically use pricing as a differentiation tool, the international marketing manager may have no choice but to accept the prevailing world-market price.

When **penetration pricing** is used, the product is offered at a low price intended to generate volume sales and achieve high market share, which would compensate for a lower per-unit return. This approach requires mass markets, price-sensitive customers, and decreasing production and marketing costs as sales volumes increase. The basic assumption of penetration pricing is that the lower price will increase sales, which may not always be the case.

Price changes are called for when a new product is launched, when a change occurs in overall market conditions (such as a change in the value of the billing currency), or when there is a change in the exporter's internal situation, such as costs of production. An exporter may elect not to change price even though the result may be lower profitability. However, if a decision is made to change prices, related changes must also be considered. For example, if an increase in price is required, it may at least initially be accompanied by increased promotional efforts. Price changes usually follow changes in the product's stage in the life cycle. As the product matures, more pressure will be put on the price to keep the product competitive despite increased competition and less possibility of differentiation.

With multiple-product pricing, the various items in the line may be differentiated by pricing them appropriately to indicate, for example, an economy version, a standard version, and the top-of-the-line version. One of the products in the line may be priced to protect against competitors or to gain market share from existing competitors. The other items in the line are then expected to make up for the lost contribution of such a "fighting brand."

Although foreign-market pricing and intracompany pricing are discussed later in conjunction with multinational pricing challenges, they do have an impact on the exporter as well. For example, distributors in a particular market may want to keep their profit margins up. This means that the exporter will have to lower prices to the distributor and take less profit to ensure sales and to remain competitive.[1] Similarly, the exporter, in providing products to its own sales offices abroad, may have to adjust its transfer prices according to foreign exchange fluctuations.

THE SETTING OF EXPORT PRICES

The setting of export price is influenced by both internal and external factors, as well as their interaction. Internal factors include the company's philosophy, goals, and objectives; the costs of developing, producing, and marketing the export product; and the nature of the exporter's product and industry. External factors relate to international markets in general or to a specific target market in particular and include such factors as customer, regulatory, competitive, and financial (mainly foreign exchange) characteristics. The interaction of these elements causes pricing opportunities and constraints in different markets. For example, company management may have decided to challenge its main foreign competitor in the competitor's home market. Regulation in that market requires expensive product adaptation, the cost of which has to be absorbed now for the product to remain competitive.

In setting the export price, a company can use a process such as the one summarized in Figure 10.2. As in all marketing decisions, the intended target market will establish the basic premise for pricing. Factors to be considered include the importance of price in customer decision making, the strength of the perceived price-quality relationship, and potential reactions to price manipulations by marketers. Customers' demands will also have to be considered in terms of support required by the intermediary. The marketing mix must be planned to match the characteristics of the target market. Pricing will be a major factor in determining the desired brand image as well as the distribution channels to be used and the level of promotional support required.

Pricing policies follow from the overall objectives of the firm for a particular target market and involve general principles or rules that a firm follows in making pricing decisions. Policies include profit maximization, market share, survival, percentage return on investment, and various competitive policies such as copying competitors' prices, following a particular competitor's prices, or pricing so as to discourage competitors from entering the market.[2] For example, an exporter entering a new market may allow wholesalers and retailers above-normal profit margins to encourage maximum sales volume, geographic distribution, and loyalty.

---

[1] "Sizing Up the Customers' Needs," *Export Today* 5 (February 1989): 32–35.

[2] Donald V. Harper and Jack L. Caldwell, "Pricing," in *Marketing Manager's Handbook,* eds. Steuart Henderson Britt and Norman Guess (Chicago: Dartnell, 1983), 723–736.

Stages in Setting of Prices   **FIGURE 10.2**

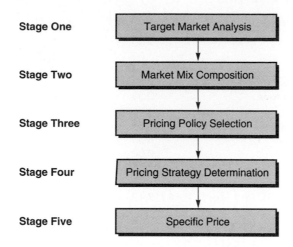

Stage One	Target Market Analysis
Stage Two	Market Mix Composition
Stage Three	Pricing Policy Selection
Stage Four	Pricing Strategy Determination
Stage Five	Specific Price

Source: Reprinted by permission of Harvard Business Review. An excerpt from Alfred R. Oxenfeldt, "Multistage Approach to Pricing," *Harvard Business Review* 38 (July–August 1960): 126. Copyright © by the President and Fellows of Harvard College; all rights reserved.

Export Pricing Strategy

Three general price-setting strategies in international marketing are a standard worldwide price; dual pricing, which differentiates between domestic and export prices; and market-differentiated pricing.[3] The first two methods are cost-oriented pricing methods that are relatively simple to establish and easy to understand. The third strategy is based on demand orientation and may thus be more consistent with the marketing concept. However, even the third approach has to acknowledge costs in the long term.

The **standard worldwide price** may be the same price regardless of the buyer (if foreign product or foreign marketing costs are negligible) or may be based on average unit costs of fixed, variable, and export-related costs.

In **dual pricing,** domestic and export prices are differentiated, and two approaches to pricing products for export are available: the **cost-plus method** and the **marginal cost method.** The cost-plus strategy is the true cost, fully allocating domestic and foreign costs to the product. Although this type of pricing ensures margins, the final price may be so high that the firm's competitiveness may be compromised. This may cause some exporters to consider a flexible cost-plus strategy, which allows for variations in special circumstances.[4] Discounts may be granted, depending on the customer, the size of the order, or the intensity of competition. Changes in prices may also be put into effect to counter exchange rate fluctuations. Although discounts are occasionally granted, profit is still a driving motive, and pricing is more static as an element of the marketing mix.

The marginal cost method considers the direct costs of producing and selling products for export as the floor beneath which prices cannot be set. Fixed costs for plants,

---

[3] Richard D. Robinson, *Internationalization of Business: An Introduction* (Hinsdale, IL: Dryden Press, 1984), 49–54.

[4] S. Tamer Cavusgil, "Unraveling the Mystique of Export Pricing," *Business Horizons* 31 (May–June 1988): 54–63.

| TABLE 10.1 | Export Pricing Alternatives |

Production Costs	Standard	Cost Plus	Marginal Cost
Materials	2.00	2.00	2.00
Fixed costs	1.00	1.00	0.00
Additional foreign product costs	0.00	0.10	0.10
Production overhead	0.50	0.50	0.00
Total production costs	3.50	3.60	2.10
U.S. marketing costs	1.50	0.00	0.00
General and administrative	0.75	0.75	0.00
Foreign marketing	0.00	1.00	1.00
Other foreign costs	0.00	1.25	1.25
Subtotal	5.75	6.60	4.35
Profit margin (25%)	1.44	1.65	1.09
Selling price	7.19	8.25	5.44

Source: Adapted from Lee Oster, "Accounting for Exporters," *Export Today* 7 (January 1991): 28–33.

R&D, and domestic overhead, as well as domestic marketing costs, are disregarded. An exporter can thus lower export prices to be competitive in markets that otherwise might have been beyond access. This may open a company to dumping charges, however, because determination of dumping may be based on average total costs, which are typically considerably higher.

A comparison of the cost-oriented methods is provided in Table 10.1. Notice how the rigid cost-plus strategy produces the highest selling price by full-cost allocation.

Market-differentiated pricing calls for export pricing according to the dynamic conditions of the marketplace. For these firms, the marginal-cost strategy provides a basis, and prices may change frequently due to changes in competition, exchange rate changes, or other environmental changes. The need for information and controls becomes crucial if this pricing alternative is to be attempted.

Export-Related Costs

In preparing a quotation, the exporter must be careful to take into account and, if possible, include unique export-related costs. These are in addition to the normal costs shared with the domestic side. They include the following:

1. The cost of modifying the product for foreign markets
2. Operational costs of the export operation: personnel, market research, additional shipping and insurance costs, communications costs with foreign customers, and overseas promotional costs
3. Costs incurred in entering the foreign markets: tariffs and taxes; risks associated with a buyer in a different market (mainly commercial credit risks and political risks); and risks from dealing in other than the exporter's domestic currency—that is, foreign exchange risk

The combined effect of both clear-cut and hidden costs results in export prices that far exceed domestic prices. The cause is termed **price escalation.**

Four different export scenarios are compared with a typical domestic situation in Table 10.2. The first case is relatively simple, adding only the CIF (cost, insurance,

International Marketing Channel Elements and Cost Factors	Domestic Wholesale-Retail Channel	Export Market Cases			
		Case 1 Same as Domestic with Direct Wholesale Import CIF/Tariff	Case 2 Same as 1 with Foreign Importer Added to Channel	Case 3 Same as 2 with VAT Added	Case 4 Same as 3 with Local Foreign Jobber Added to Channel
Manufacturer's net price	6.00	6.00	6.00	6.00	6.00
+ Insurance and shipping cost (CIF)	—	2.50	2.50	2.50	2.50
= Landed cost (CIF value)	—	8.50	8.50	8.50	8.50
+ Tariff (20% on CIF value)	—	1.70	1.70	1.70	1.70
= Importer's cost (CIF value + tariff)	—	10.20	10.20	10.20	10.20
+ Importer's margin (25% on cost)	—	—	2.55	2.55	2.55
+ VAT (16% on full cost plus margin)	—	—	—	2.04	2.04
= Wholesaler's cost (= importer's price)	6.00	10.20	12.75	14.79	14.79
+ Wholesaler's margin (33⅓% on cost)	2.00	3.40	4.25	4.93	4.93
+ VAT (16% on margin)	—	—	—	.79	.79
= Local foreign jobber's cost (= wholesale price)	—	—	—	—	20.51
+ Jobber's margin (33⅓% on cost)	—	—	—	—	6.84
+ VAT (16% on margin)	—	—	—	—	1.09
= Retailer's cost (= wholesale or jobber price)	8.00	13.60	17.00	20.51	28.44
+ Retailer's margin (50% on cost)	4.00	6.80	8.50	10.26	14.22
+ VAT (16% on margin)	—	—	—	1.64	2.28
= Retail price (what consumer pays)	12.00	20.40	25.50	32.41	44.94
Percentage price escalation over domestic		70%	113%	170%	275%
Percentage price escalation over Case 1			25%	59%	120%
Percentage price escalation over Case 2				27%	76%
Percentage price escalation over Case 3					39%

Export Price Escalation — TABLE 10.2

Source: Helmut Becker, "Pricing: An International Marketing Challenge," in *International Marketing Strategy*, eds. Hans Thorelli and Helmut Becker (New York: Pergamon Press, 1980), 215. Reprinted with permission.

freight) and tariff charges. The second adds a foreign importer and thus lengthens the foreign part of the distribution channel. In the third case, a **value-added tax (VAT)** is included in the calculations. This is imposed on the full export selling price, which represents the "value added" to or introduced into the country from abroad. In Italy, for example, where most food items are taxed at 2 percent, processed meat is taxed at 18 percent because the government wants to use the VAT to help reduce its trade deficit. The fourth case simulates a situation typically found in less-developed countries where distribution channels are longer. Lengthy channels can easily double the landed (CIF) price.

Price escalation can be combated through creative strategies such as reorganizing the channel of distribution. The example in Figure 10.3, based on import channels for spaghetti and macaroni in Japan, shows how the flow of merchandise through the various wholesaling levels has been reduced to comprise only a company internal wholesaler distribution center, resulting in savings of 25 percent and increasing the overall potential for imports. Other strategies to deal with price escalation include product modification either by eliminating costly product features or by bringing the product into the

| **FIGURE 10.3** | **Distribution Adjustment to Decrease Price Escalation** |

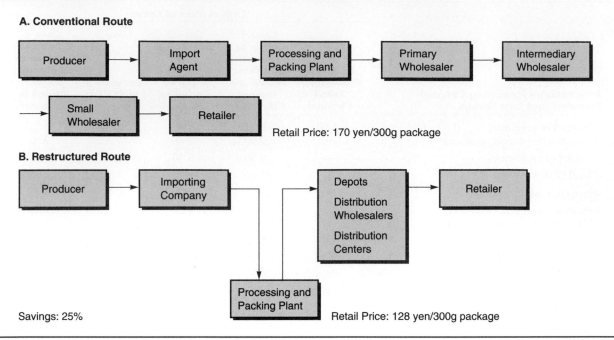

A. Conventional Route

Producer → Import Agent → Processing and Packing Plant → Primary Wholesaler → Intermediary Wholesaler

→ Small Wholesaler → Retailer

Retail Price: 170 yen/300g package

B. Restructured Route

Producer → Importing Company → Depots / Distribution Wholesalers / Distribution Centers → Retailer

Processing and Packing Plant

Savings: 25%

Retail Price: 128 yen/300g package

Source: Michael R. Czinkota, "Distribution of Consumer Products in Japan: An Overview," *International Marketing Review 2* (Autumn 1985): 39–51.

target country under a new, lower tariff classification. In the long term, the exporter may resort to overseas production or sourcing. Through foreign sourcing, the exporter may accrue an additional benefit to lower cost: **duty drawbacks.**[5] If a company imports components or raw materials for exports in a manufactured product, it can obtain a refund of the customs duty paid on the importation.

Appropriate export pricing requires the establishment of accounting procedures to assess export performance. Without such a process, hidden costs may bring surprises. For example, negotiations in the Middle Eastern countries or Russia may last three times longer than the average domestic negotiations, dramatically increasing the costs of doing business abroad. Furthermore, without accurate information, a company cannot combat phenomena such as price escalation.

TERMS OF SALE

The responsibilities of the buyer and the seller should be spelled out as they relate to what is and what is not included in the price quotation and when ownership of goods passes from seller to buyer. **Incoterms** are the internationally accepted standard definitions for terms of sale by the International Chamber of Commerce (ICC). The Incoterms 1990 went into effect on July 1, 1990, with significant revisions to better reflect chang-

---

[5] Al D'Amico, "Duty Drawback: An Overlooked Customs Refund Program," *Export Today* 9 (May 1993): 46–48.

ing transportation technologies and to facilitate electronic data interchange.[6] Although the same terms may be used in domestic transactions, they gain new meaning in the international arena. The most common of the Incoterms used in international marketing are summarized in Figure 10.4.

Prices quoted **ex-works** (**EXW**) apply only at the point of origin, and the seller agrees to place the goods at the disposal of the buyer at the specified place on the date or within the fixed period. All other charges are for the account of the buyer.

One of the new Incoterms is **free carrier** (**FCA**), which replaced a variety of FOB terms for all modes of transportation except vessel. FCA (named inland point) applies only at a designated inland shipping point. The seller is responsible for loading goods into the means of transportation; the buyer is responsible for all subsequent expenses. If a port of exportation is named, the costs of transporting the goods to the named port are included in the price.

Free alongside ship (**FAS**) at a named U.S. port of export means that the exporter quotes a price for the goods, including charges for delivery of the goods alongside a vessel at the port. The seller handles the cost of unloading and wharfage; loading, ocean transportation, and insurance are left to the buyer.

Free on board (**FOB**) applies only to vessel shipments. The seller quotes a price covering all expenses up to, and including, delivery of goods on an overseas vessel provided by or for the buyer.

Under **cost and freight** (**CFR**) to a named overseas port of import, the seller quotes a price for the goods, including the cost of transportation to the named port of debarkation. The cost of insurance and the choice of insurer are left to the buyer.

With cost, insurance, and freight (CIF) to a named overseas port of import, the seller quotes a price including insurance, all transportation, and miscellaneous charges to the point of debarkation from the vessel or aircraft. Items that may enter into the calculation of the CIF cost are (1) port charges: unloading, wharfage (terminal use) handling, storage, cartage, heavy lift, and demurrage; (2) documentation charges: certification of invoice, certificate of origin, weight certificate, and consular forms; and (3) other charges, such as fees of the freight forwarder and freight (inland and ocean) insurance premiums (marine, war, credit).

With **delivered duty paid** (**DDP**), the seller delivers the goods, with import duties paid, including inland transportation from import point to the buyer's premises. With **delivered duty unpaid** (**DDU**), only the destination customs duty and taxes are paid by the consignee. Ex-works signifies the maximum obligation for the buyer; delivered duty paid puts the maximum burden on the seller.

The careful determination and clear understanding of terms used and their acceptance by the parties involved are vital if subsequent misunderstandings and disputes are to be avoided.

These terms are also powerful competitive tools. The exporter should therefore learn what importers usually prefer in the particular market and what the specific transaction may require. An inexperienced importer may be discouraged from further action by a quote such as ex-plant Jessup, Maryland, whereas CIF Helsinki will enable the Finnish importer to handle the remaining costs because they are incurred in a familiar environment.

Increasingly, exporters are quoting more inclusive terms. The benefits of taking charge of the transportation either on a CIF or DDP basis include the following: (1) exporters

---

[6] Kevin Maloney, "Incoterms: Clarity at the Profit Margin," *Export Today* 6 (November–December 1990): 45–46.

FIGURE 10.4	Selected Trade Terms

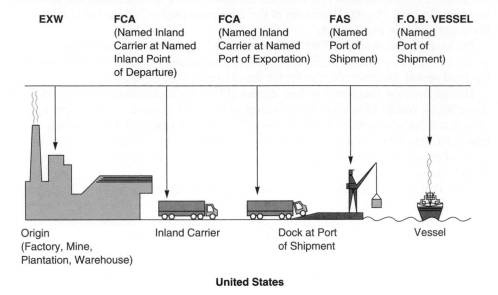

EXW	FCA (Named Inland Carrier at Named Inland Point of Departure)	FCA (Named Inland Carrier at Named Port of Exportation)	FAS (Named Port of Shipment)	F.O.B. VESSEL (Named Port of Shipment)

Origin (Factory, Mine, Plantation, Warehouse)   Inland Carrier   Dock at Port of Shipment   Vessel

United States

can offer foreign buyers an easy-to-understand "delivered cost" for the deal; (2) by getting discounts on volume purchases for transportation services, exporters cut shipping costs and can offer lower overall prices to prospective buyers; (3) control of product quality and service is extended to transport, enabling the exporter to ensure that goods arrive to the buyer in good condition; and (4) administrative procedures are cut for both the exporter and the buyer.[7] These benefits are highlighted in The International Marketplace 10.2.

When taking control of transportation costs, however, the exporter must know well in advance what impact the additional costs will have on the bottom line. If the approach is implemented incorrectly, exporters can be faced with volatile shipping rates, unexpected import duties, and restive customers. Most exporters do not want to go beyond the CIF quotation because of uncontrollables and unknowns in the destination country. Whatever terms are chosen, the program should be agreed to by the exporter and the buyer(s) rather than imposed solely by the exporter.

Freight forwarders are useful in determining costs, preparing quotations, and making sure that unexpected changes do not cause the exporter to lose money. Freight forwarders are useful to the exporter not only as facilitators and advisors but also in keeping down some of the export-related costs. Rates for freight and insurance provided to freight forwarders may be far more economical than to an individual exporter because of large-volume purchases, especially if export sales are infrequent.

TERMS OF PAYMENT

Export credit and terms add another dimension to the profitability of an export transaction. The exporter has in all likelihood already formulated a credit policy that deter-

---

[7] "How Exporters Efficiently Penetrate Foreign Markets," *International Business,* December 1993, 48.

Continued   FIGURE 10.4

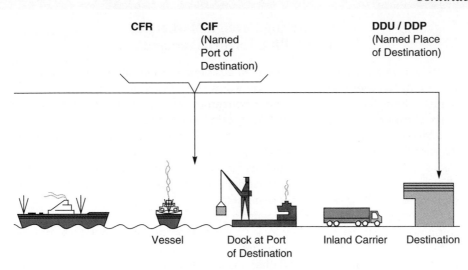

| CFR | CIF
(Named
Port of
Destination) | | DDU / DDP
(Named Place
of Destination) |

Vessel   Dock at Port   Inland Carrier   Destination
              of Destination

Country of Destination

mines the degree of risk the firm is willing to assume and the preferred selling terms. The main objective is to meet the importer's requirements without jeopardizing the firm's financial goals. The exporter will be concerned over being paid for the goods shipped and will therefore consider the following factors in negotiating terms of payment: (1) the amount of payment and the need for protection, (2) terms offered by competitors, (3) practices in the industry, (4) capacity for financing international transactions, and (5) relative strength of the parties involved.[8] If the exporter is well established in the market with a unique product and accompanying service, price and terms of trade can be set to fit the exporter's desires. If, on the other hand, the exporter is breaking into a new market or if competitive pressures call for action, pricing and selling terms should be used as major competitive tools.

The basic methods of payment for exports vary in terms of their attractiveness to the buyer and the seller, from cash in advance to open account or consignment selling. Neither of the extremes will be feasible for longer-term relationships, but they do have their use in certain situations. These methods are depicted in the risk triangle presented in Figure 10.5.

The most favorable term to the exporter is cash in advance because it relieves the exporter of all risk and allows for immediate use of the money. It is not widely used, however, except for smaller, first-time transactions or situations in which the exporter has reason to doubt the importer's ability to pay. Cash-in-advance terms are also found when orders are for custom-made products because the risk to the exporter is beyond that of a normal transaction. In some instances, the importer may not be able to buy on a cash-in-advance basis because of insufficient funds or government restrictions.

A **letter of credit** is an instrument issued by a bank, at the request of a buyer. The bank promises to pay a specified amount of money on presentation of documents stipulated in the letter of credit, usually the bill of lading, consular invoice, and a description

[8] Chase Manhattan Bank, *Dynamics of Trade Finance* (New York: Chase Manhattan Bank, 1984), 10–11.

10.2

THE INTERNATIONAL MARKETPLACE

Penetrating Foreign Markets by Controlling Export Transport

Companies that once sought short-term customers to smooth out recessions are searching for every means to get an edge over rivals in foreign markets. To achieve that, they are increasingly concerned about controlling quality and costs at every step, including the transportation process.

International transport costs are far higher than domestic shipping expenses. International ocean transport typically accounts for 4 to 20 percent of the product's delivered cost but can reach as high as 50 percent for commodity items. That makes transport a factor in situations where a single price disadvantage can cause a sale to be lost to a competitor.

Still, most U.S. companies continue to abdicate responsibility for export shipping—either because they lack sophistication or simply because they do not want to be bothered. Increasingly, however, companies like Deere & Co. are paying for, controlling, and often insuring transports from their factories either to foreign ports or to the purchasing companies' doorsteps.

Deere exports premium-quality farm and lawn equipment worldwide. For years, it has insisted on overseeing transportation because it boosts sales, cuts costs, and ensures quality. "We have a long-term relationship with our dealers. It is in our best interest to do the transport job," says Ann Salaber, an order control manager in the export order department.

One goal of Deere's approach to transportation is to ensure that equipment is delivered to customers in good condition—a factor that Deere considers central to its image as a quality producer. The goal is to avoid cases like the one in which an inexperienced customer insisted on shipping a tractor himself. The tractor was unwittingly put on a ship's deck during a long, stormy sea voyage and arrived in terrible shape.

The process also helps when Deere tractor windows are inadvertently broken during the transport. Because Deere closely monitors the tractors, it can quickly install new windows at the port and avoid the huge cost of flying replacements to a customer as far as Argentina.

Cost is an important consideration as well. Depending on where a $150,000 combine is shipped, transport costs can range between $7,500 and $30,000, or between 5 and 20 percent of delivered cost. Deere's ability to buy steamship space in volume enables it to reduce transport costs by 10 percent. That in turn enables it to cut the combine's delivered cost by between $750 and $3,000. "That adds up," says Salaber. Because of those savings, "you do not have to discount so much, and Deere gets more profit."

Source: Gregory L. Miles, "Exporters' New Bully Stick," *International Business*, December 1993, 46–49.

---

of the goods.[9] Letters of credit are one of the most-used methods of payment in international transactions. Figure 10.6 summarizes the process of obtaining a letter of credit and the relationship between the parties involved.

---

[9] David K. Eiteman, Arthur I. Stonehill, and Michael H. Moffett, *Multinational Business Finance* (Reading, MA: Addison-Wesley, 1992), 489–518.

Risk Triangle   **FIGURE 10.5**

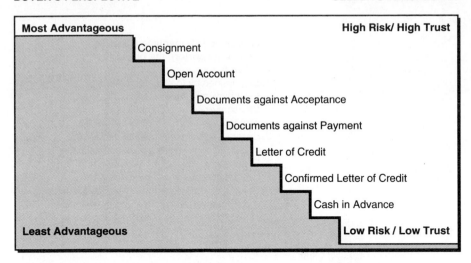

Source: Chase Manhattan Bank, *Dynamics of Trade Finance* (New York: Chase Manhattan Bank, 1984), 5.

Letters of credit can be classified along three dimensions:

1. **Irrevocable versus revocable.** An irrevocable letter of credit can neither be canceled nor modified without the consent of the beneficiary (exporter), thus guaranteeing payment. According to the new rules drawn by the International Chamber of Commerce, effective January 1, 1994, all letters of credit are considered irrevocable unless otherwise stated.[10]

2. **Confirmed versus unconfirmed.** In the case of a U.S. exporter, a U.S. bank might confirm the letter of credit and thus assume the risk, including the transaction (exchange) risk. The single best method of payment for the exporter in most cases is a confirmed, irrevocable letter of credit. Banks may also assume an advisory role but not assume the risk; the underlying assumption is that the bank and its correspondent(s) are better able to judge the credibility of the bank issuing the letter of credit than is the exporter.

3. **Revolving versus nonrevolving.** Most letters of credit are nonrevolving, that is, valid for the one transaction only. In case of established relationships, a revolving letter of credit may be issued.

Figure 10.7 provides an example of a letter of credit.

The letter of credit provides advantages to both the exporter and the importer, which explains its wide use. The approach substitutes the credit of the bank for the credit of the buyer and is as good as the issuing bank's access to dollars. In custom-made orders, an irrevocable letter of credit may help the exporter secure pre-export financing. The importer will not need to pay until the documents have arrived and been accepted by the bank, thus giving an additional float. The major caveat is that the exporter has to comply

---

[10] International Chamber of Commerce, *Uniform Customs and Practice for Documentary Credit/1993 Revision* (New York: ICC Publishing Corp., 1993).

| FIGURE 10.6 | Letter of Credit: Process and Parties |

A confirmed L/C involves 4 parties; the seller (exporter), the buyer, and two banks.

1. L/C opened by foreign customer at local bank and sent to U.S. bank.
2. L/C confirmed by U.S. bank and sent to exporter.
3. Exporter approves terms and conditions of L/C. Exporter ships goods against L/C.
4. Exporter sends shipping documents to U.S. bank and a draft for payment.
5. Bank examines documents for discrepancies.
6. If documents match terms and conditions of L/C, U.S. bank pays exporter for goods.

Source: Faren L. Foster and Lynn S. Hutchins, "Six Steps to Quicker Collection of Export Letters of Credit," *Export Today* 9 (November–December 1993): 26–30. Reprinted with permission from *Export Today* magazine.

with all of the terms of the letter of credit. For example, if the documents state that shipment is made in crates measuring $4 \times 4 \times 4$, and the goods are shipped in crates measuring $4 \times 3 \times 4$, the bank will not honor the letter of credit. If there are changes, the letter of credit can be amended to ensure payment. In some cases, the exporter must watch out for fraudulent letters of credit, especially in the case of less-developed countries. For example, exporters are advised to ship to Nigeria only on the basis of an irrevocable letter of credit, confirmed by their bank, even after the credentials of the Nigerian contact have been established.[11]

The letter of credit is a promise to pay but not a means of payment. Actual payment is accomplished by means of a **draft,** which is similar to a personal check. Like a check, it is an order by one party to pay another. Most drafts are documentary, which means that

[11] "Fraudulent Business Activity Is Growing in Nigeria, and Efforts are Often Made to Involve Foreign Firms," *Business America,* January 1992, 21–22.

Source: First American Bank, Washington, D.C.

the buyer must obtain possession of various shipping documents before obtaining possession of the goods involved in the transaction. Clean drafts—orders to pay without any other documents—are mainly used by multinational corporations in their dealings with their own subsidiaries and in well-established business relationships.

In **documentary collection** situations, the seller ships the goods, and the shipping documents and the draft demanding payment are presented to the importer through banks acting as the seller's agent. The draft, also known as the bill of exchange, may be

| FIGURE 10.8 | Drafts |

U.S. $20,000.00   December 10,   19XX

180 Days Sight of this First of Exchange (Second unpaid)   Pay to

the order of _____

_____ Twenty Thousand and ----------------------------------00/100 Dollars

"Drawn under Any Bank, N.A. Letter of Credit ID-000C"

Value received and charge the same to account of XYZ Imports, Inc.

To   Any Bank, N.A.
     123 15th Street, N.W.   Howard J. Homeyer
No. Washington, D.C. 20005   Howard J. Homeyer, President
                                       ABC Textiles, Ltd.

U.S. $20,000.00   December 10,   19XX

At Sight of this First of Exchange (Second unpaid)   Pay to

the order of _____

_____ Twenty Thousand and ----------------------------------00/100 Dollars

"Drawn under Letter of Credit ID-000C issued by Any Bank, N.A."

Value received and charge the same to account of XYZ Imports, Inc.

To   Any Bank, N.A.
     123 15th Street, N.W.   Howard J. Homeyer
No. Washington, D.C. 20005   Howard J. Homeyer, President
                                       ABC Textiles, Ltd.

Source: First American Bank, Washington, D.C.

either a sight draft or a time draft (see Figure 10.8). A sight draft documents against payment and is payable on presentation to the drawee, that is, the party to whom the draft is addressed. A time draft documents against acceptance and allows for a delay of 30, 60, or 90 days. When a time draft is drawn on and accepted by a bank, it becomes a banker's acceptance, which is sold in the short-term money market. Time drafts drawn on and accepted by a business firm become trader's acceptances, which are normally not marketable. A draft is presented to the drawee, who accepts it by writing or stamping a notice of acceptance on it. With both sight and time drafts, the buyer can effectively extend the period of credit by avoiding receipt of the goods. A date draft requires payment on a specified date, regardless of the date on which the goods and the draft are accepted by the buyer.

To illustrate, an exporter may have a time draft accepted by Citibank for $1 million to be paid in 90 days. Like many exporters who extend credit for competitive reasons, the firm may have immediate need for the funds. It could contact an acceptance dealer and sell the acceptance at a discount, with the rate depending on the market rate of interest. If the annual interest rate was 12 percent, for example, the acceptance could be sold for $970,873 ($1 million divided by 1.03). Interest rates for banker's acceptances of various maturities are listed daily in the *The Wall Street Journal*.

Even if the draft is not sold in the secondary market, the exporter may convert it into cash by **discounting.** To discount the draft simply means that the draft is sold to a bank at a discount from face value. If the discounting is with recourse, the exporter is liable for the payment to the bank if the importer defaults. If the discounting is without re-course, the exporter will not be liable even if the importer does not pay the bank. Dis-counting without recourse is known as factoring or, in the case of higher credit risk and longer-term receivables, forfaiting.

The normal manner of doing business in the domestic market is **open account** (open terms). The exporter selling on open account removes both real and psychological bar-riers to importing. However, no written evidence of the debt exists, and the exporter has to put full faith in the references contacted. Worst of all, there is no guarantee of pay-ment. If the debt turns bad, the problems of overseas litigation are considerable. Bad debts are normally easier to avoid than to rectify. The open-account arrangement is common in trade between European countries, and a European company that asked for a letter of credit would not be popular.[12] Trade practice does allow for letters of credit in certain industries or when goods are imported from countries more geographically re-moved, such as the United States, Japan, and Australia. In less-developed countries, im-porters will usually need proof of debt in the application to the central bank for hard currency, which will not allow them to deal on an open-account basis. Again, open ac-count is used by multinationals in their internal transactions and when there is implicit trust among the partners.

The most favorable term to the importer is **consignment selling,** which allows the importer to defer payment until the goods are actually sold. This approach places all of the burden on the exporter, and its use should be carefully weighed against the objec-tives of the transaction. If the exporter wants entry into a specific market through specific intermediaries, consignment selling may be the only method of gaining accep-tance by the middlemen. The arrangement will require clear understanding as to the parties' responsibilities—for example, which party is responsible for insurance until the goods have actually been sold.

ADJUSTING TO FOREIGN CURRENCY FLUCTUATIONS

Another important matter to be resolved in payment for exports is the currency in which to invoice. Unless currencies are closely linked, for example, between Germany and Aus-tria, exchange rate movements may harm one or the other of the parties. If the price is quoted in the exporter's currency, the exporter will get exactly the price it wants but may lose some sales as a result. The currency chosen will depend on the parties them-selves and the particular transaction. If the exporter needs the sale, the invoice may be in the importer's currency, and the exchange risk will be the burden of the exporter. Some exporters, if they are unable to secure payment in their own currency, try to minimize the risk by negotiating shorter terms of payment, such as 10 or 15 days. Ex-change risks may be a result of an appreciating or depreciating currency or result from a revaluation or devaluation of a currency by a central bank. Assume that a U.S. im-porter bought $250,000 or DM525,000 worth of goods from a German company, which agreed to accept U.S. dollars for payment within 90 days. At the time of the quota-tion, the exchange rate for $1 was DM2.10, whereas at the time of payment, the rate for $1 was DM2.00. This means that the German exporter, instead of eventually receiving DM525,000, received only DM500,000.

When invoicing in foreign currencies, an exporter cannot insulate itself from the problems of currency movements, but it can at least know how much it will eventually

---

[12] Paul Jermer, *Europe: An Exporter's Handbook* (New York: Facts on File, 1981), 145–147.

receive by using the mechanism of the **forward exchange market.** In essence, the exporter gets a bank to agree to a rate at which it will buy the foreign currency the exporter will receive when the importer makes payment. The rate is expressed as either a premium or a discount on the current spot rate. The risk still remains if the exchange rate does not move as anticipated, and the exporter may be worse off than if it had not bought forward.

The decline in the value of the dollar since the mid-1980s has substantially altered the competitive environment in various industries. Many non-U.S. companies have faced a serious pricing-versus-margin dilemma. Some of them have already left the international arena, unable to compete without major changes in their international marketing strategies. For U.S. exporters, the decision has been how to adjust their pricing to international customers in view of the more favorable dollar exchange rate.

For U.S. exporters, three alternatives are available. First, making no change in the dollar price could result in a more favorable price in foreign currencies and, likely, higher sales. Second, the export price could be increased in conjunction with decreases in the value of the dollar to maintain stable export prices in foreign currencies. This would result in improved margins if sales volume remained steady. The third alternative is to pass only a share of the savings to the customers, with the hope of increasing sales with improved margins.

The data in Table 10.3 show that on the average, foreign manufacturers absorbed about half of the decline in the trading value of the dollar between March 1985 and September 1987. If prices of nonfuel imports to the United States had fully reflected the dollars, they would have risen 34 percent on average; instead they rose only about 19 percent.

Meanwhile, U.S. exporters have in general lowered their foreign-currency-denominated prices to improve their competitive positions. For example, in 1988, the dollar price index for exports was up only 2.8 percent, while the foreign currency index was down 21.5 percent.[13] Some industries in the United States, such as the automobile industry, have been criticized for raising their domestic prices as the prices of Japanese imports have been forced up by the higher value of the yen. Instead of trying to capture market share, the automakers have gone for extra profits.[14]

Beyond **price manipulation,** other adjustment mechanisms exist. Table 10.4 summarizes the results of a survey of Japanese firms concerning their responses to the strong yen. Shift in production bases has been a predominant move. Matshushita Electric has adopted two strategies to combat the effect of the yen. First, it accelerated a shift in production from Japan to Southeast Asian nations, and second, it began to focus on products that are less sensitive to exchange rate changes. Komatsu launched a $1-billion joint venture with Texas-based Dresser Industries to build equipment in the United States.[15] When Japanese automakers began building cars in the United States, they relied heavily on parts imported from Japan. The strong yen has caused a steady increase in the domestic content of cars built in the United States.

Some exporters change the destination of their exports. With the lower value of the dollar making their cars more expensive in the United States, the German automakers Daimler-Benz and BMW have boosted their efforts in Japan. The German mark's value

---

[13] "How Dollar Weakness Affects Pricing Policies of U.S. and Non-U.S. Firms," *Business International,* December 7, 1988, 387.

[14] "Did U.S. Car Makers Err by Raising Prices When the Yen Rose?" *The Wall Street Journal,* April 18, 1988, 1, 14.

[15] "Japanese Firms Act to Lift Prices, Citing Dollar's Weakness against Yen," *The Wall Street Journal,* June 28, 1993, A2–6.

| | Effect of the Dollar's Fall on Trade Pricing | TABLE 10.3 |

Product Category	Imports to United States: Percent of Pass-through	Exports from United States: Percent of Pass-through
Beverages and Tobacco	23.5	89.9
Beverages	27.1	98.6
Tobacco	n.a.	89.1
Chemicals and Related Products	8.7	78.7
Pharmaceuticals	54.2	54.3
Essential oils and perfumes	46.1	66.8
Manufactured fertilizers	38.1	130.2
Artificial resins and plastics	20.4	42.1
Organic chemicals	n.a.	54.3
Miscellaneous chemical materials	21.3	106.8
Intermediate Manufactures	39.9	63.7
Paper and paperboard	69.9	29.4
Textiles	24.8	n.a.
Nonmetallic minerals	57.1	29.4
Iron and steel	17.2	58.5
Machinery	46.5	92.8
Specialized	59.0	95.9
Metalworking	75.6	65.7
General industrial	71.2	82.6
Office and data processing	37.1	113.0
Telecommunications and sound	11.4	78.1
Electric	38.8	92.4
Motor vehicles and parts	55.3	50.0
Power generating	n.a.	81.9
Miscellaneous Finished Manufactures	72.8	77.2
Plumbing, heating, light	44.8	n.a.
Furniture and parts	58.9	37.4
Apparel	89.7	n.a.
Footwear	43.8	n.a.
Scientific instruments	76.7	78.6
Photographic, watches, etc.	48.7	96.9

Note: The numbers indicate the percentage of foreign exchange loss U.S. exporters passed through to their overseas customers in the form of stable dollar prices, and the percentage of exchange gain non-U.S. exporters passed through to U.S. customers in the form of higher dollar prices, between March 1985 and September 1987.

Source: "How Dollar Weakness Affects Pricing Policies of U.S. and Non-U.S. Firms," *Business International*, December 7, 1988, 387. Reprinted with permission.

has changed very little against the yen since 1985, and the market, with increased affluence and fewer trade barriers, has become more attractive.

In some cases, even adverse developments in the currency market have not had an effect on some international markets or marketers. In the Far East, U.S. oil toolmakers and oil-field service companies were never hurt by the high value of the dollar because their expertise was in demand. Similarly, many U.S. firms, such as IBM, did not suffer because their exported products are both built and sold in other countries. In some

TABLE 10.4

Japanese Reaction to the High Value of the Yen

	All Industries	Manufac- turing	Nonmanu- facturing
Increase direct investment	30.9%	28.8%	34.1%
Change export destinations	1.1	1.9	—
Link with firms in same industry	3.4	4.3	2.2
Link with firms in other industries	5.1	3.4	8.0
Emphasize domestic market	50.4	52.9	45.6
Other	9.1	8.7	10.1
Total	100%	100%	100%

Source: "The Yen Strikes Home," *Far Eastern Economic Review,* Hong Kong; December 25, 1986, 61. Used with permission.

cases, imported goods may be in demand because no domestic production exists, which is the case in the United States with consumer goods such as electronics and cameras.

PRICE NEGOTIATIONS

The final export price is negotiated in person or electronically. Since pricing is the most sensitive issue in business negotiations, the exporter should be ready to discuss price as part of a comprehensive package and should avoid price concessions early on in the negotiations.[16]

An importer may reject an exporter's price at the outset in the hopes of gaining an upper hand or obtaining concessions later on. These concessions include discounts, an improved product, better terms of sales/payment, and other possibly costly demands. The exporter should prepare for this by obtaining relevant information on the target market and the customer, as well as by developing counterproposals for possible objections. For example, if the importer states that better offers are available, the exporter should ask for more details on such offers and try to convince the buyer that the exporter's total package is indeed superior.

During the actual negotiations, pricing decisions should be postponed until all of the major substantive issues have been agreed upon. Since quality and reliability of delivery are the critical dimensions of supplier choice (in addition to price), especially when long-term export contracts are in question, the exporter may want to reduce pressure on price by emphasizing these two areas and how they fit with the buyer's needs.

LEASING

Organizational customers frequently prefer to lease major equipment. About 30 percent of all capital goods are leased in the United States, with eight out of ten companies involved in leasing.[17] Although a major force in the United States, Japan, and Germany, leasing has grown significantly elsewhere as well; for example, one of the major international trade activities of Russia, in addition to shipping and oil, is equipment leasing.

---

[16] Claude Cellich, "Negotiating Strategies: The Question of Price," *International Trade Forum* 5 (April–June 1991): 10–13.

[17] "Leasing: A New Role," *Business Week,* May 15, 1989, 141–152.

The Russians view leasing not only as a potential source of hard currency but also as a way of attracting customers who would be reluctant to buy an unfamiliar product.[18]

Trade liberalization around the world is expected to benefit lessors both through expected growth in target economies and through the eradication of country laws and regulations hampering outside lessors. For example, the NAFTA agreement and the pent-up demand for machinery, aircraft, and heavy equipment for road building provide a promising opportunity for U.S. leasing companies in Mexico.[19]

For the industrial marketing manager who sells products such as printing presses, forklift trucks, and machine tools, leasing may allow penetration of markets that otherwise might not exist for the firm's products if the firm had to sell them outright. Balance-of-payment problems have forced some countries to prohibit the purchase and importation of equipment into their markets; an exception has been made if the import is to be leased.[20] In less-developed countries, the fact that leased products are serviced by the lessor may be a major benefit because of the shortage of trained personnel and availability of spare parts. The main benefit for the lessor is that total net income, after charging off pertinent repair and maintenance expenses, is often higher than it would be if the unit was sold.

In today's competitive business climate, traditional financial considerations are often only part of the asset-financing formula. Many leasing companies have become more than a source of capital, developing new value-added services that have taken them from asset financiers to asset managers or forming relationships with others who can provide these services. In some cases, lessors have even evolved into partners in business activities. Xerox Credit, for example, finances assets worth about $2 billion every year—$1 billion under captive leasing services from its parent, Xerox Corporation, and $1 billion as an equipment lessor competing in the open market. It has some copy equipment leases in which it provides both machinery and the personnel to operate the machinery.

DUMPING

Inexpensive imports often trigger accusations of dumping—that is, selling goods overseas for less than in the exporter's home market or at a price below the cost of production, or both. Charges of dumping range from those of Florida tomato growers, who said that Mexican vegetables were being dumped across the border, to those of the Canadian Anti-Dumping Tribunal, which ruled that U.S. firms were dumping radioactive diagnostic reagents in Canada.[21] Such disputes have become quite common, especially in highly competitive industries such as computer chips, ball bearings, and steel. In 1989, for example, AT&T, asserting that it had experienced "heavy and growing injury," asked the U.S. government to investigate its complaint that companies in Japan, Korea, and Taiwan were selling telephone equipment in the United States at unfair prices.[22] Similarly, in Europe, the European Union's Executive Commission investigated the imports from

---

[18] Herbert E. Meyer, "The Communist Internationale Has a Capitalist Accent," *Fortune,* February 1977, 134–142.

[19] Elnora M. Uzzelle, "American Equipment Leasing Companies Should Consider the International Arena," *Business America,* June 28, 1993, 11–12.

[20] David A. Ricks and Saeed Samiee, "Leasing: It May Be Right Abroad Even When It Is Not at Home," *Journal of International Business Studies* 5 (Fall 1974): 87–90.

[21] Steven Plaut, "Why Dumping Is Good for Us," *Fortune,* May 5, 1980, 11–22.

[22] "AT&T Files a Complaint on 'Dumping,'" *New York Times,* December 29, 1988, D1, D18.

10.3

THE INTERNATIONAL MARKETPLACE

Dumping in the United States

U.S. law prohibits dumping, but the federal government has been cautious in enforcing the law, especially in the case of allies. In the 1970s, Timken had to sue the U.S. government to force it to carry out its own dumping order against Japanese tapered roller bearings. Zenith labored for a decade to get U.S. dumping duties assessed against Japanese TV manufacturers, and then the governments of the two countries negotiated the penalty down to 10 cents on the dollar. Three times Hitachi was charged with dumping different types of semiconductors. But by the time the cases were resolved, Hitachi was dumping a whole new generation of chips. Between 1985 and 1988, the Japanese doubled their U.S. market share from 12 percent to 24 percent.

Timken, Smith Corona, Zenith, and the semiconductor industry claim that the way the United States calculates dumping margins—the difference between the home market price and the import price as a percentage of import price—makes it harder to prove dumping in the United States than in Europe. This is especially true when transactions include so-called related parties, such as manufacturers and their in-house distributors. In such cases, the United States, unlike most of its competitors, includes profits in its import price estimate (making the price higher) and excludes indirect selling costs in its calculation of the home market price (making that price lower). As a result, dumping margins can be lower in the United States than in Europe.

Importers counter that these companies are trying to use the dumping laws as protection against foreign competition. In October 1991, the U.S. Department of Commerce, after complaints from the U.S. paper industry, determined that Belgian, British, Finnish, French, and German producers had dumped lightweight coated magazine paper in the United States. The European companies vehemently denied any intentional dumping and referred to the substantial fluctuations in the value of the dollar as the main reason for lower prices. In December, the International Trade Commission exonerated the companies from having injured U.S. industry. Despite the favorable ruling, the Europeans had already suffered injury themselves. Sales had, in some companies' cases, dropped by half (due to U.S. customers' fears of price hikes caused by duties); furthermore, they had to pay substantial legal costs incurred during the defense.

Sources: "Hintojen Lasku Lamautti Kaupan Dumpingin Jalkeen," *Kauppalehti,* January 15, 1992, 4; Ann Reilly Dowd, "What to Do about Trade Policy," *Fortune,* May 8, 1989, 106–112.

Asia of audiocassette tapes that were allegedly being sold at below-market prices in the 12-nation trading bloc.[23]

Dumping ranges from predatory dumping to unintentional dumping. **Predatory dumping** refers to a tactic whereby a foreign firm intentionally sells at a loss in another country in order to increase its market share at the expense of domestic producers, which amounts to an international price war. **Unintentional dumping** is the result of time lags between the dates of sales transaction, shipment, and arrival. Prices, including exchange

[23] "Europe Inquiry on Asian Tapes," *New York Times,* January 16, 1989, D11.

rates, can change in such a way that the final sales price turns out to be below the cost of production or below the price prevailing in the exporter's home market.

In the United States, domestic producers may petition the government to impose antidumping duties on imports alleged to be dumped (see The International Marketplace 10.3). The duty is imposed if the Department of Commerce determines that sales have occurred at less than fair market value and if the U.S. International Trade Commission finds that domestic industry is being, or is threatened with being, materially injured by the imports. The remedy is an **antidumping duty** equal to the dumping margin. International agreements and U.S. law provide for **countervailing duties,** which may be imposed on imports that are found to be subsidized by foreign governments and which are designed to offset the advantages imports would otherwise receive from the subsidy. In one of these cases, the United States ruled that Israel was subsidizing exports of freshly cut flowers and ordered a countervailing duty of 1.55 percent, far below the 27 percent the industry requested.[24] Governmental action against dumping and subsidized exports violating GATT may result in hurting the very industries seeking relief. Action against European steel, for example, could result in retaliatory measures against U.S. steelmakers, who themselves export billions of dollars worth of steel products. European governments have also threatened to retaliate against U.S. exports of other products.

In some cases, dumping suits have strong competitive motivations, for example, to discourage an aggressive competitor by accusing it of selling at unfair prices. Antidumping and unfair-subsidy suits have led in some cases to formal agreements on voluntary restraints, whereby foreign producers agree that they will supply only a certain percentage of the U.S. market. One such arrangement is the semiconductor trade agreements signed by the United States and Japan in 1986 and 1991. The agreements required the Japanese to stop selling computer chips at below cost and called for the Japanese to try to increase sales of foreign-made computer chips in Japan.[25]

SUMMARY

The status of price has changed to that of a dynamic element of the marketing mix. This has resulted from both internal and external pressures on business firms. Management must analyze the interactive effect that pricing has on the other elements of the mix and how pricing can assist in meeting the overall goals of the marketing strategy.

The process of setting an export price must start with the determination of an appropriate cost baseline and should include variables such as export-related costs to avoid compromising the desired profit margin. The quotation needs to spell out the respective responsibilities of the buyer and the seller in getting the goods to the intended destination. The terms of sale indicate these responsibilities but may also be used as a competitive tool. The terms of payment have to be clarified to ensure that the exporter will indeed get paid for the products and services rendered. Facilitating agents such as freight forwarders and banks are often used to absorb some of the risk and uncertainty in preparing price quotations and establishing terms of payment.

Exporters also need to be ready to defend their pricing practices. Competitors may petition their own government to investigate the exporter's pricing to determine the degree to which it reflects costs and prices prevailing in the exporter's domestic market.

---

[24] "How Four Industries Are Hurt by Dumping," *U.S. News & World Report,* July 5, 1982, 45–46.
[25] "Chip Pact Falls Short of Goals," *New York Times,* August 2, 1988, D1.

Questions for Discussion

1. What are the implications of price escalation?
2. Discuss the use of the currency of quotation as a competitive tool.
3. Who is harmed and who is helped by dumping?
4. Why is there a tendency to underestimate the importance of price in developing a marketing mix?
5. Propose scenarios in which export prices are higher/lower than domestic prices.
6. Argue for the use of more inclusive shipping terms from the marketing point of view.
7. What are the possible exporter reactions to extreme foreign-exchange fluctuations?
8. Suggest different importer reactions to a price offer and how you, as an exporter, could respond to them.

Recommended Readings

Chase Manhattan Bank. *Dynamics of Trade Finance*. New York: Chase Manhattan Bank, 1984.

Lanze, L. B. *Import/Export Can Make You Rich*. Englewood Cliffs, NJ: Prentice-Hall, 1988.

Monroe, Kent B., and Albert DellaBitta. "Models for Pricing Decisions." *Journal of Marketing Research* 15 (August 1978): 413–428.

Oxenfeldt, Alfred R. "Multistage Approach to Pricing." *Harvard Business Review* 38 (July–August 1960): 125–133.

U.S. Department of Commerce. *A Basic Guide to Exporting*. Washington, D.C.: Government Printing Office, 1992.

Walmsley, James. *The Development of International Markets*. Hingham, MA: Graham and Trotman, 1990.

CHAPTER 11

··

International
Communications

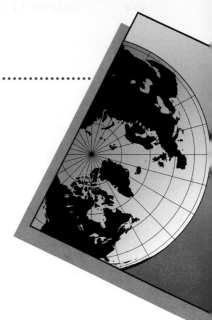

  **11.1**

Making Deals In Any Language

Effective communication as a cornerstone of marketing becomes even more important in the international arena. Whether it is a question of generating promotional campaigns or negotiating to set up a marketing system, the international marketer needs to understand what pleases or displeases the target audience.

One such interaction occurred between representatives of Atacs Products Inc.—a Seattle-based supplier of aircraft-repair systems—and Aviation Transactions Conseils, which stocks those supplies in Juilly, France, during the Goodwill Games International Trade Exhibition in Seattle.

Terry Cooney, Atacs' sales manager, established a mutual interest during a chance meeting with ATC's Pierre-Jean Back, president, and Patrick Naumann, sales manager. Cooney then arranged a more formal meeting, and they reconvened with Andrew Thibault, an interpreter.

Cooney began his presentation—speaking slowly and clearly, but without condescending—on technical fronts. During the product demonstration for a heat-sensitive device, Cooney took care to speak in terms of ambient temperature in Bordeaux instead of just saying "72 degrees." And Naumann understood English well enough to laugh at Cooney's references to misuse of the product causing "permanently curly hair."

Throughout the presentation, Thibault softly translated, primarily for Back's benefit. Occasionally, the demonstration slowed if either had a question.

After the demonstration, Cooney explained Atacs' stance on foreign distributors. "If you start losing business," he joked, "I'm in the Irish mafia."

He mentioned several sales techniques, whom to contact, and the latitude of offers ATC would be able to make to customers. Naumann and Back conferred

313

in French, and then Thibault presented Back's objection: What would prevent Atacs from ending its agreement once ATC had nurtured the territory?

Cooney said he didn't "know how to overcome" that objection. Then, force of personality began to transcend language. "I am soon to be the biggest (expletive) you ever met," Cooney said, "but I'm honest. I don't even cheat in tennis against my sons."

Cooney closed with two more appeals, posed vehemently yet calmly. One mentioned the amount of dollars it could cost ATC to not accept the arrangement. The other: "If you place an order, you still have 90 days for payment, unless the dollar drops against the franc. Then we'll give you 120 days."

They all laughed at that remark, but ATC's representatives still did not agree. Cooney said, "That's all I've got to say."

After the meeting, Back said in an interview, "I'm not suspicious of this gentlemen, in particular, but it's the general manner of doing business in the American way.

"In general, when working with Americans, when things are going fine, there's no problem. But when the market starts to go down, Americans tend to bail out.

"Good business relationships take time to develop. . . . You know that relations are really good when there are problems with money and they'll still allow you to operate.

"However, I would not trust a large American company. There's such a turnover rate in employees that from one day to another it changes completely, so it's really hard to have continuous relations.

"The best prospects for American businesses to operate in France is with small businesses because there's a more personal relationship."

Source: David Jacobson, "Marketers Swap More than Goodwill at Trade Show," *Business Marketing* 75 (September 1990): 48–51. Reprinted from *Business Marketing*, September 1990; © Crain Communications Inc.

Effective communication is particularly important in international marketing because of the geographic and psychological distances that separate a firm from its intermediaries and customers. By definition, communication is a process of establishing a "commonness" of thought between a sender and a receiver.[1] This process extends beyond the conveying of ideas to include persuasion and thus enables the marketing process to function more effectively and efficiently. Ideally, marketing communication is a dialogue that allows organizations and consumers to achieve mutually satisfying exchange agreements.[2] This definition emphasizes the two-way nature of the process, with listening and responsiveness as integral parts. The majority of communication is verbal, but nonverbal communication and the concept of silent languages must also be considered because they often create challenges for international marketers, as seen in The International Marketplace 11.1.

This chapter will include an overview of the principles of marketing communications in international markets. Because face-to-face, buyer-seller negotiations are possibly the most fundamental marketing process,[3] guidelines for international busi-

---

[1] Wilbur Schramm and Donald F. Roberts, *The Process and Effects of Mass Communications* (Urbana, IL: University of Illinois Press, 1971), 12–17.

[2] William G. Nickels, *Marketing Communication and Promotion* (Columbus, OH: Grid Publishing, 1980), 10.

[3] John L. Graham, Dong Ki Kim, Chi-Yuan Lin, and Michael Robinson, "Buyer-Seller Negotiations around the Pacific Rim: Differences in Fundamental Exchange Processes," *Journal of Consumer Research* 15 (June 1988): 48–54.

ness negotiations are first discussed. Second, the chapter will focus on the management of the international communications mix from the exporter's point of view. Because the exporter's alternatives may be limited by the entry mode and by resources available, the tools and the challenges are quite different from those of the multinational entity. The promotional approaches used by global marketers are discussed later in the book.

THE MARKETING COMMUNICATIONS PROCESS

As shown in the communications model presented in Figure 11.1, effective communication requires three elements—the sender, the message, and the receiver—to be connected by a message channel. The process may begin with an unsolicited inquiry from a potential customer or as a planned effort by the marketer. Whatever the reason for the communications process, the sender needs to study receiver characteristics before encoding the message to be sent in order to achieve maximum impact. **Encoding** the message simply means converting the message into symbolic form that is properly understood by the receiver. This is not a simple task, however. For example, a firm quoting an export price EXW may inadvertently convey to overseas clients that it is not overly interested in obtaining orders, because the more inclusive CIF is typically preferred by most importers. On occasion, the message in itself may be silence, allowing the receiver an opportunity to change an earlier position.

The message channel is the path through which the message moves from sender (source) to receiver. This link that ties the receiver to the sender ranges from sound waves conveying the human voice in personal selling to transceivers or intermediaries such as print and broadcast media. Although technological advances (for example, telex, fax, and video conferencing) may have made buyer-seller negotiations more efficient, the fundamental process and its purpose have remained unchanged. Face-to-face contact is still necessary for two basic reasons. The first is the need for detailed discussion and explanation, and the second is the need to establish the rapport that forms the basis of lasting business relationships.

The message channel applies also to mass communications. Complications in international marketing may arise if a particular medium is not available for commercial purposes, such as radio in some of the Northern European countries. Other examples of complications are the banning of advertising for certain product categories, such as cigarette advertising in most of Europe, and the fact that some marketing practices may not be allowed, such as door-to-door selling in France.

Once a sender has placed a message into a channel or a set of channels and directed them to the intended destination, the completion of the process is dependent on the receiver's **decoding**—that is, transforming the message symbols back into thought. If there is an adequate amount of overlap between sender characteristics and needs reflected in the encoded message and receiver characteristics and needs reflected in the decoded message, the communications process has worked.

A message moving through a channel is subject to the influence of extraneous and distracting stimuli, which interfere with the intended accurate reception of the message. This interference is referred to as **noise.** In the international marketing context, noise might be a bad telephone connection, failure to express a quotation in the inquirer's system of currency and measurement, or a highly cluttered medium such as Italian television, where all advertisements are aired in one half-hour period each night. A valid inquiry from overseas may not be considered seriously by an international marketer because of noise consisting of low-quality paper, grammatical errors, or a general appearance unlike domestic correspondence.

| FIGURE 11.1 | The Marketing Communications Process |

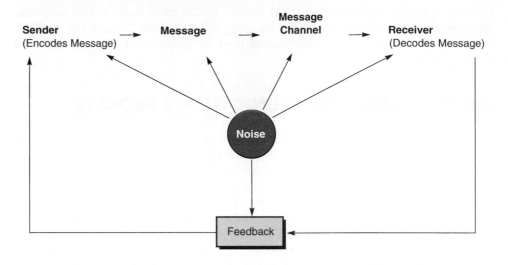

Source: Terence A. Shimp, *Promotion Management and Marketing Communications* (Hinsdale, IL: Dryden Press, 1990), 38. © 1990 by the Dryden Press.

The international marketer should be most alert to cultural noise. The lack of language skills may hinder successful negotiations, whereas translation errors may render a promotional campaign or brochure useless. Similarly, nonverbal language and its improper interpretation may cause problems. For example, in the United States, lack of eye contact is a signal that something is wrong. This is not necessarily so in Japan, where the cultural style of communication involves markedly less eye contact.[4]

Regardless of whether the situation calls for interpersonal or mass communications, the collection and observation of feedback is necessary to analyze the success of the communications effort. The initial sender-receiver relationship is transposed, and interpretative skills similar to those needed in developing messages are needed. To make effective and efficient use of the communications requires considerable strategic planning. Examples of concrete ways in which feedback can be collected are inquiry cards or toll-free numbers distributed at trade shows to gather additional information.

INTERNATIONAL NEGOTIATIONS

When international marketing managers travel abroad to do business, they are frequently shocked to discover the extent to which the many variables of foreign behavior and custom complicate their efforts.[5] One of these differences is negotiation. The process of negotiation in most countries differs from that typical in the United States. This means that international marketing managers have to adjust their approaches to establishing rapport, information exchange, persuasion, and concession making if they are to be successful in dealing with their clients and partners, such as intermediaries.[6] The

---

[4] John L. Graham, "A Hidden Cause of America's Trade Deficit with Japan," *Columbia Journal of World Business* 16 (Fall 1981): 5–15.

[5] Edward T. Hall, "The Silent Language of Overseas Business," *Harvard Business Review* 38 (May–June 1960): 87–96.

[6] John L. Graham, "Across the Negotiating Table from the Japanese," *International Marketing Review* 4 (Autumn 1986): 58–71.

negotiation process can be a short one, with the stages collapsing into one session, or a prolonged endeavor taking weeks.

Stages of the Negotiation Process

The process of international business negotiations can be divided into five stages: the offer, informal meetings, strategy formulation, negotiations, and implementation.[7]

The offer stage allows the two parties to assess each other's needs and degree of commitment. The initiation of the process and its progress are determined to a great extent by background factors of the parties (such as objectives) and the overall atmosphere (for example, a spirit of cooperativeness). As an example, many European buyers may be skittish about dealing with an American exporter, given the number of U.S. companies that "fold their tents and go away when an initial sale blitz fizzles" or when environmental factors turn sour.[8]

After the buyer has received the offer, the parties meet to discuss the terms and get acquainted. In many parts of the world (Asia, the Middle East, and Latin America), informal meetings may often make or break the deal. Foreign buyers may want to ascertain that they are doing business with someone who is sympathetic and whom they can trust. For example, U.S. exporters to Kuwait rank the strength of the business relationship ahead of price as the critical variable driving buying decisions.[9] In some cases, it may be necessary to utilize facilitators (such as consultants or agents) to establish the contact.

Both parties have to formulate strategies for formal negotiations. This means not only careful review and assessment of all of the factors affecting the deal to be negotiated but also preparation for the actual give-and-take of the negotiations. For example, research studies have found that U.S. and Canadian anglophone bargainers can be taken advantage of by competitive bargainers[10] and that they are more trusting than other cultural groups.[11] Thus, these managers should consciously and carefully consider competitive behaviors of clients and partners. Especially in the case of governmental buyers, it is imperative to realize that public-sector needs may not necessarily fit into a mold that the marketer would consider rational.

The actual face-to-face negotiations and the approach used in them will depend on the cultural background and business traditions prevailing in different countries.

How to Negotiate in Other Countries[12]

A combination of attitudes, expectations, and habitual behavior influences negotiation style. Although some of the following recommendations may go against the approach used at home, they may allow the negotiator to adjust to the style of the host-country negotiators.

---

[7] Pervez N. Ghauri, "Guidelines for International Business Negotiations," *International Marketing Review* 4 (Autumn 1986): 72–82.

[8] "Made in the U.S.A.," *Business Week,* February 29, 1988, 60–66.

[9] Virginia J. Rehberg, "Kuwait: Reality Sets In," *Export Today* 7 (December 1991): 56–58.

[10] Nancy J. Adler, John L. Graham, and Theodore Schwarz Gehrke, "Business Negotiations in Canada, Mexico, and the United States," *Journal of Business Research* 15 (1987): 411–429.

[11] D. L. Harnett and L. L. Cummings, *Bargaining Behavior: An International Study* (Houston, TX: Dame Publications, 1980), 231.

[12] John L. Graham and Roy A. Herberger, Jr., "Negotiators Abroad—Don't Shoot from the Hip," *Harvard Business Review* 61 (July–August 1983): 160–168.

1. *Team assistance.* Using specialists will strengthen the team substantially and allow for all points of view to be given proper attention. Further, observation of negotiations can be valuable training experience for less-experienced participants. Whereas Western teams may average two to four people, a Chinese negotiating team may consist of up to ten people.[13]

2. *Traditions and customs.* For newcomers, status relations and business procedures must be carefully considered with the help of consultants or local representatives. For example, in highly structured societies, such as Korea, great respect is paid to age and position.[14] What seem like simple rituals can cause problems. No first encounter in Asia is complete without an exchange of business cards. Both hands should be used to present and receive cards, and respect should be shown by reading them carefully.[15]

3. *Language capability.* Ideally, the international marketing manager should be able to speak the customer's language, but that is not always possible. The use of interpreters allows for longer response time and a more careful articulation of arguments (see The International Marketplace 11.2).

4. *Determination of authority limits.* The disadvantages of having full authority must be weighed against the expenses of communication with the home office. Announcing that the negotiators do not have the final authority to conclude the contract may be perceived negatively; however, if it is used as a tactic to probe the moves of the buyer, it can be quite effective.

5. *Patience.* In many countries, such as the People's Republic of China, business negotiations may take three times the amount of time that they do in the United States and Western Europe. Showing impatience in countries such as Brazil or Thailand may prolong negotiations rather than speed them up. Also, Americans tend to start relatively close to what they consider a fair price in their negotiations, whereas Chinese negotiators may start with "unreasonable" demands.

6. *Negotiation ethics.* Attitudes and values of foreign negotiators may be quite different from those that a U.S. marketing executive is accustomed to. Being tricky can be valued in some parts of the world, whereas it is frowned on elsewhere. For example, Western negotiators may be taken aback by last-minute changes or concession requests by Russian negotiators.[16]

7. *Silence.* To negotiate effectively abroad, a marketer needs to correctly read all types of communication. Americans often interpret inaction and silence as a negative sign. As a result, Japanese executives tend to expect that they can get Americans to lower prices or sweeten the deal.[17]

8. *Persistence.* Insisting on answers and an outcome may be seen as a threat by negotiating partners abroad. In some markets, negotiations are seen as a means of establishing long-term commercial relations, not as an event with winners and losers. Confrontations are to be avoided because minds cannot be changed at the negotiation table; this has to be done informally.

---

[13] Sally Stewart and Charles F. Keown, "Talking with the Dragon: Negotiating in the People's Republic of China," *Columbia Journal of World Business* 24 (Fall 1989): 68–72.

[14] Lennie Copeland and L. Griggs, *Going International: How to Make Friends and Deal Effectively in the Global Marketplace* (New York: Ballinger, 1985), 113.

[15] Frederick H. Katayama, "How to Act Once You Get There," *Fortune,* Fall 1989, 87–88.

[16] Ilkka A. Ronkainen, "Project Exports and the CMEA," in *International Marketing Management,* ed. Erdener Kaynak (New York: Praeger, 1984), 305–317.

[17] "Crossing Cultural Divides: Conducting Business Internationally," *T&E,* October 1985, 1.

THE INTERNATIONAL MARKETPLACE　　11.2

Interpreters as Part of the Marketing Team

An international marketing executive on a business trip abroad faces a risk seldom encountered at home: losing something in the translation—literally. Whether to take along an interpreter or have company materials translated into a foreign language is an early, key decision. To assume that English will be understood when speaking to businesses overseas, and then to discover that it is not, provides a rude shock.

Sarah Pilgrim, president of OmniLingua, Inc., has suggested: "You need to do some research and think about what you are doing. Are you going to sell your product? Or going for social reasons to develop contacts? Do the people you are meeting speak English—and with what level of competency? If you are making initial contacts, trying to find out about the market potential, you may not want to spend the money for an interpreter or translation of your literature. But if you are trying to sell something in a foreign country, it is important to have literature in the language of the target country. Although an interpreter costs $150 to $300 a day, it is wise to take one to important negotiations. If you bring your own interpreter, you can be sure that person is on your side. The interpreter should be well briefed ahead of time so he or she is familiar with the product and can act as a company representative."

An experienced and qualified individual can act as a consultant to help you avoid cross-cultural *faux pas,* tell you when to talk and when to listen, and become an integral part of the informal channel (to pick up casual conversations and communicate the nuances behind the official statements). The head of Osaka's $47-billion international airport project still tells a story of a U.S. construction company president who became indignant when he discovered that the project head could not speak English. As a matter of fact, according to one expert, "If you are with a Japanese who speaks fluent English, you may be dealing with the wrong person."

These eight rules should be followed when using interpreters: (1) plan to need more time for negotiation; (2) evaluate the interpreter's ability in terms of language skills, knowledge of technical terminology, and familiarity with appropriate dialects; (3) provide the interpreter with materials beforehand; (4) brief the interpreter on the purpose of the meeting; (5) avoid using slang; (6) ask questions that require short answers; (7) take breaks, and if negotiations are long, use multiple interpreters; and (8) make sure customs and traditions are followed (e.g., seating arrangements).

Some of the drawbacks of using interpreters are that (1) interpreters can slow down negotiations or inject their own point of view into the discussion; (2) they may diminish the spontaneity and negotiating strength of the presentation; (3) using an interpreter may offend a foreign business executive who thinks his or her English is good; and (4) interpreters are a risk in communicating confidential information.

Sources: "10 rules for Using an Interpreter," *Export Today* 9 (June 1993): 18; Takeru Ohe and George Koo, "How to Negotiate a Japanese Partnership," *Export Today* 7 (March–April 1991): 56–59; and Barbara Zigli, "Interpreter Can Be an Asset Abroad, *USA Today,* April 15, 1985, 15E.

9. *Holistic view.* Concessions should be avoided until all issues have been discussed so as to preclude the possibility of granting unnecessary benefits to the negotiation partners. Furthermore, in the Far East and elsewhere, concessions traditionally come at the end of bargaining.

10. *The meaning of agreements.* What constitutes an agreement will vary from one market to another. In many parts of the world, legal contracts are still not needed; as a matter of fact, reference to legal counsel may indicate that the relationship is in trouble.

When a verbal agreement is reached, it is critical that both parties leave with a clear understanding of what they have agreed to. This may entail only the relatively straightforward act of signing a distributor agreement, but in the case of large-scale projects, details must be explored and spelled out. For example, in contracts that call for cooperative efforts, the responsibilities of each partner must be clearly specified. Otherwise, obligations that were anticipated to be the duty of one contracting party may result in costs to another. For example, foreign principal contractors may be held responsible for delays that have been caused by the inability of local subcontractors (whose use might be a requisite of the client) to deliver on schedule.

MARKETING COMMUNICATIONS STRATEGY

The international marketing manager has the responsibility of formulating a communications strategy for the promotion of the company and its products and services. The basic steps of such a strategy are outlined in Figure 11.2.

Few, if any, firms can afford expenditures for promotion that is done as "art for art's sake" or only because major competitors do it. The first step in developing communications strategy is therefore assessing what company or product characteristics and benefits should be communicated to the export market. This requires constant monitoring of the various environments and target audience characteristics. For example, Volvo has used safety and quality as its primary themes in its worldwide promotional campaigns since the 1950s. This approach has provided continuity, repetition, and uniformity in positioning Volvo in relation to its primary competitors: Mercedes Benz (prestige) and BMW (sportiness).

Absolut, which is owned by the Swedish government, in 1979 started exporting its vodka into the United States with 45,000 cases and an introductory promotion effort. In 15 years, it has grown to number 10 in volume and number 3 in revenue in the U.S. spirits category. In addition to a strong marketing effort, Absolut benefited from changing American drinking habits. Vodkas are now the largest category in the distilled-spirits business, with Absolut ruling the high-class vodka crowd.[18] Certain rules of thumb can be followed in evaluating resources to be allocated for export communications efforts. A sufficient commitment is necessary, which means a relatively large amount of money. The exporter has to operate in foreign markets according to the rules of the marketplace, which in the United States, for example, means high promotional costs—perhaps 30 percent of exports or even more during the early stage of entry. For example, Absolut's annual promotional budget is approximately $20 million, a significant amount when compared with retail sales of $260 million.[19]

---

[18] "Neat Shot," *Marketing & Media Decisions* 24 (March 1989): 73–78.

[19] Ira Teinowitz, "Grand Met Thirsts or Absolut-Style Phenom," *Advertising Age,* January 10, 1994, 6.

Steps in Formulating Marketing Communications Strategy FIGURE 11.2

Step One	Assess Marketing Communications Opportunities
Step Two	Analyze Marketing Communications Resources
Step Three	Set Marketing Communications Objectives
Step Four	Develop/Evaluate Alternative Strategies
Step Five	Assign Specific Marketing Communications Tasks

Source: Wayne DeLozier, *The Marketing Communication Process* (New York: McGraw-Hill, 1976), 272.

Because of monetary constraints that most exporters face, promotional efforts should be concentrated on key markets. For example, European liquor marketers traditionally concentrate their promotional efforts on the United States, where volume consumption is greatest, and Great Britain, which is considered the world capital of the liquor trade. A specific objective might be to spend more than the closest competitors do in the U.S. market. In the United States, for example, this would require a new import brand, aimed at the lower-price segment, to spend at the minimum $10 million during the rollout year.[20] In some cases, an exporter will have to limit this to one country, even one area, at a time to achieve set goals with the available budget. International campaigns require patient investment; the market has to progress through awareness, knowledge, liking, preference, and favorable purchase intentions before payback begins. Payback periods of one or two years cannot be realistically expected. For many exporters, a critical factor is the support of the intermediary. Whether a distributor is willing to contribute a $3-million media budget or a few thousand dollars makes a big difference. In some cases, intermediaries take a leading role in the promotion of the product in a market. In the case of Absolut, for example, Carillon Importers has been credited with the creative advertising widely acknowledged as a primary reason for the brand's success. In most cases, however, the exporter should retain some control of the campaign rather than allow intermediaries or sales offices a free hand in the various markets operated. Although markets may be dissimilar, common themes and common objectives need to be incorporated into the individual campaigns. For example, Duracell, the world leader in alkaline batteries, provides graphics—such as logos and photos—to country operations. Although many exporters do not exert pressure to conform, overseas distributors take advantage of annual meetings to discuss promotional practices with their head office counterparts.

Alternative strategies are needed to spell out how the firm's resources can be combined and adapted to market opportunities. The tools that the international marketer

---

[20] Gary Levin, "Russian Vodka Plans U.S. Rollout," *Advertising Age*, November 11, 1991, 4.

has available to form a total communications program for use in the targeted markets are referred to as the **promotional mix.** They consist of the following:

1. Advertising: Any form of nonpersonal presentation of ideas, goods, or services by an identified sponsor, with predominant use made of the media of mass communication
2. Personal selling: The process of assisting and persuading a prospect to buy a good or service or to act on an idea through use of person-to-person communication
3. Publicity: Any form of nonpaid, commercially significant news or editorial comment about ideas, products, or institutions
4. Sales promotion: Direct inducements that provide extra product value or incentive to the sales force, distributors, or ultimate consumers[21]

In some cases, packaging serves a promotional role—for example, when it is distinctive and unique in its color or shape. The use of tools will vary by company and by situation. Although all Harley-Davidson motorcycles are on allocation in overseas markets, they are still promoted by advertising stressing postpurchase reinforcement. The company also sells "motor clothes," illustrated in catalogs. Copies are made to overseas dealers, who cannot afford to translate and reprint them, and they pass them on to their customers with notes that not all items are available or permissible in their markets.[22]

The choice of tools leads to either a push or a pull emphasis in marketing communications. **Push strategies** focus on the use of personal selling. Despite its higher cost per contact, personal selling is appropriate for the international marketing of industrial goods, which have shorter channels of distribution and smaller target populations than do consumer goods. Governmental clients are typically serviced through personal selling efforts. Some industries, such as pharmaceuticals, traditionally rely on personal selling to service the clientele.

On the other hand, **pull strategies** depend on mass communications tools, mainly advertising. Advertising is appropriate for consumer-oriented products with large target audiences and long channels of distribution. Of its promotional budget, Absolut spends 85 percent in print media in the United States, with the balance picked up by outdoor advertising, mainly billboards. The base of the advertising effort is formed by magazines such as *Sports Illustrated, Vanity Fair, Business Week, Rolling Stone, Esquire, Time,* and *Newsweek.*

No promotional tool should be used in isolation or without regard to the others. Use should be coordinated according to target market and product characteristics, the size of the promotional budget, the type and length of international involvement, and control considerations. As an example, industrial purchasing decisions typically involve 8 to 11 people. Because a salesperson may not reach all of them, the use of advertising may be necessary to influence the participants in the decision-making process.

Finally, specific marketing communications tasks must be assigned, which may involve deciding on a division of labor with foreign intermediaries or with other exporters for cooperative communications efforts.[23] For example, Koss, a Milwaukee-based company that is one of the most recognized names in stereophones, concentrates on in-store display through a cooperative program with its distributors.[24] More money is thus available for promotion, and its execution is carried out locally, with central control from Koss.

---

[21] Irving Shapiro, *Dictionary of Marketing Terms* (Totowa, NJ: Rowmen and Littlefield, 1981), 203.

[22] Mel Mandell, "Getting the Word Out," *World Trade,* November 1993, 30–34.

[23] Dean M. Peebles and John K. Ryans, *Management of International Advertising: A Marketing Approach* (Boston, MA: Allyn and Bacon, 1984), Chapter 8.

[24] "The Sound of America," *Export Today* 5 (February 1989): 33–34.

COMMUNICATIONS TOOLS

The main communications tools used by exporters to communicate with the foreign marketplace from their domestic base are business and trade journals, direct mail, trade fairs and missions, and personal selling. If the exporter's strategy calls for a major promotional effort in a market, it is advisable either to use a U.S.-based agency with extensive operations in the intended market or to use a local agency and work closely with the company's local representatives in media and message choices.

Because the promoter-agency relationship is a close one, it may be helpful if the exporter's domestic agency has an affiliate in the target foreign market. The management function and coordination can be performed by the agency at home, while the affiliate can execute the program as it sees appropriate in that market. An exporter, if it has a sufficient budget, may ask its domestic agency to set up a branch overseas. Some exporters, especially those that have a more significant presence overseas, leave the choice of the agency to local managers. If a local agency is to be chosen, the exporter must make sure that coordination and cooperation between the agency and the exporter's domestic agency can be achieved. Whatever the approach used, the key criterion must be the competence of the people who will be in charge of the creation and implementation of the promotional programs.

Business and Trade Journals

A wide range of business and trade publications is available to the exporter, as Figure 11.3 indicates. Many business publications, such as *Business Week, Fortune, The Economist, The Wall Street Journal,* and *Financial Times,* are standard information sources worldwide. An extension of these are their regional editions; for example, *The Asian Wall Street Journal* or *Business Week—Europe.* Trade publications can be classified as (1) horizontal, which cater to a particular job function cutting across industry lines, such as *Purchasing World,* and (2) vertical, which deal with a specific industry, such as *Chemical Engineering.* These journals are global, regional, or country-specific in their approaches. Many U.S.-based publications are available in national language editions, with some offering regional buys for specific export markets—for example, the Spanish edition of *Reader's Digest,* titled *Selecciones.*

The two main concerns when selecting media are effectiveness in reaching the appropriate target audience(s) and efficiency in minimizing the cost of doing so, measured in terms of cost per thousand. If the exporter is in a position to clearly define the target audience (for example, in terms of demographics or product-related variables), the choice of media will be easier. This is highlighted by the company example in The International Marketplace 11.3.

In deciding which publications to use, the exporter must apply the general principles of marketing communications strategy. Coverage and circulation information is available from **Standard Rate & Data Service.** SRDS provides a complete list of international publications in the International Section of the *Business Publication,* and audit information similar to that on the U.S. market is provided for the United Kingdom, Italy, France, Austria, Switzerland, Germany, Mexico, and Canada. Outside of these areas, the exporter has to rely on the assistance of publishers or local representatives. Actual choices are usually complicated by lack of sufficient funds and concern over the information gap. The simplest approach may be to use U.S. publishers, in which the exporter may have more confidence in terms of rates and circulation data. If a more localized approach is needed, a regional edition or national publications can be considered. Before

FIGURE 11.3   Examples of International Trade Publications

Source: Standard Rate & Data Service, *Business Publication Advertising Source*, Parts 1, 2, January 1994.

THE INTERNATIONAL MARKETPLACE   11.3

Crafting Image to Create Awareness

Conner Peripherals, Inc., a fast-track Silicon Valley disk-drive manufacturer, has based its worldwide success on two factors: cutting-edge products and customer relationships. Rather than creating a product and trying to sell it to computer makers, Conner works closely with OEMs (original equipment manufacturers) to get its drives designed into the products they are developing. To work with customers, Conner has established direct sales forces in its main markets. For example, its Japanese sales organization consists of 23 people, including "customer liaisons," service technicians, quality assurance reps, and administrators.

But no marketing toolbox is complete without advertising, as Conner Peripherals' ads in Japanese business and electronics magazines underscore.

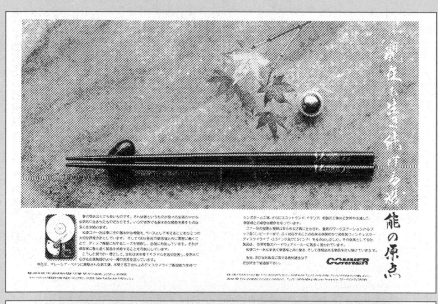

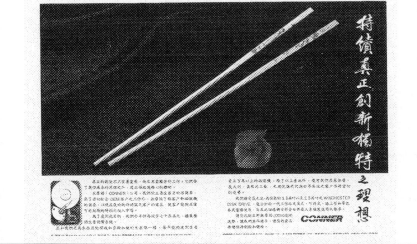

Courtesy Transphere International

continued

The company began advertising in Japan in mid-1990 with a spread designed specifically for that market. Headlined "Unique ideas are often the most enduring," the first ad featured a photograph of handmade chopsticks with a Japanese maple leaf.

A similar ad ran in other regions, including China and Southeast Asia. But the art direction was quite different in the non-Japanese spreads.

"When we did it for Southeast Asia, we used a whole different kind of chopstick, a different kind of scene, different coloration, different everything, to reflect obvious differences in culture," says Charles Schoenhoeft, president of Conner's ad agency, Transphere International. The San Francisco-based agency also works with Fujitsu, Panasonic Co., and other international advertisers.

The images in the Southeast Asian and Japanese versions of Conner's "Unique ideas" ad differed in subtle but important ways. For example, the Southeast Asian execution pictured bone Chinese chopsticks on a black cloth; the Japanese version showed enameled Japanese (pointed) chopsticks on a marble slab to appeal to a different aesthetic.

Visual and text messages in those ads, and another that followed in early 1991, held a softer sell than Conner's ads for Western markets.

In Japan, Schoenhoeft explains: "Subtle messages often work better. In the States we tend to hit each other on the head with a two-by-four. In Japan it's not that way. They feel you're bragging and wonder what's wrong with your product."

The ads have helped build awareness and preference for the drive maker among Japanese OEMs, according to Lynda Laszlo, manager of corporate communications with Conner.

She says the campaign's second ad, which pictures a Leonardo da Vinci-style rendering of a disk drive, received the highest readership score for ads in the September 1991 issue of *Nikkei Electronics.*

The campaign also is running in *Nikkei Business, Electronic Business Asia,* the Asian edition of *Electronic Design News,* and *Electronic World News,* a global publication.

Laszlo says Conner's total ad budget is $1.5 million to $2 million and estimates her company spends "more than 50%" of its Asian advertising budget to reach Japanese readers.

The company does not use direct mail or broadcast advertising but does supplement its print ads with trade shows, specifically Japan Data and Comdex. This year, for the first time, Conner had its own exhibit at Japan Data, a major electronics trade show held annually in Tokyo.

The company also participates peripherally in Comdex, the huge U.S. computer reseller exposition. It typically sets up suites at that show, instead of an exhibit, and hosts special events such as press conferences and golf tournaments.

According to Laszlo, Conner spends about 20 percent of its overall corporate communications budget on trade shows and special events.

Source: Kate Bertrand, "Conner's Japanese Success Drive," *Business Marketing,* December 1991, 18–20.

advertising is placed in an unfamiliar journal, its content and overall quality of presentation should be analyzed.

Direct Mail

Direct mail can be a highly personalized tool of communication if the target audience can be identified and defined narrowly. Ranging from notices to actual samples, it allows for flexibility in the amount of information conveyed and in its format. Direct mail is directly related in its effectiveness to the availability and quality of the mailing lists. Mailing lists may not be available around the world in the same degree that they are in, say, the United States. However, more and better lists are surfacing in Asia, Latin America, and the Middle East. In addition, reliable, economical, global postal service has become available. Magnavox CATV, which markets cable television equipment, has boosted its international mailings to support its broad schedule of trade shows, many of which are in developing regions.[25]

Even when mailing lists are available, they may not be up-to-date or as precise as the international marketer would desire. In the People's Republic of China, for example, lists are available to send literature directly to factories, ministries, professional societies, research institutes, and universities. However, such mailings can be extremely costly and produce few results. An effective and efficient direct-mail campaign requires extensive market-by-market planning of materials, format, and mode of mailing.

Catalogs are typically distributed to overseas customers through direct mail. Their function is to make the exporter's name known, generate requests for further information, stimulate orders, and serve as a reminder between transactions. Catalogs are particularly useful if a firm's products are in a highly specialized field of technology and if only the most highly qualified specialists are to be contacted. In many markets, especially the developing ones, people may be starving for technology information and will share any mailings they receive. Due to this unsatisfied demand, a very small investment can reach many potential end-users.

The growing mail-order segment is attracting an increasing number of foreign entrants to markets previously dominated by local firms. However, because consumers are wary of sending orders and money to an unknown company overseas, the key to market penetration is a local address. In Japan, L. L. Bean, the U.S. outdoor clothing merchandiser, works through McCann Direct, the specialized direct-marketing division of McCann-Erickson Hakuhodo Inc., Japan's largest foreign advertising agency. Bean places ads for its catalogs in Japanese media, orders for catalogs are sent to McCann Direct, and McCann Direct then forwards the addresses to Bean's headquarters in Maine, where all of the orders for catalogs or goods are filled.[26]

Trade Fairs and Missions

Marketing goods and services through trade fairs is a European tradition that dates back to 1240 A.D. After sales-force costs, trade shows are one of the most significant cost items in marketing budgets. Although trade fairs are usually associated with industrial firms, some consumer-products firms are represented as well. Typically, a trade show is an event at which manufacturers, distributors, and other vendors display their products or describe their services to current and prospective customers, suppliers, other business

---

[25] Kate Bertrand, "Warming Doorknobs Overseas," *Business Marketing,* November 1991, 56.

[26] "Direct Marketers in Japan Find Receptive Consumers But Practical Problems," *Business International,* September 14, 1992, 291.

associates, and the press. The International Automotive Services Industries Show and the International Coal Show, for example, run eight hours for three days, plus one or two preview days, and register 25,000 attendees. In the consumer-goods area, expositions are the most common type of show. Tickets are usually sold; typical expositions include home-garden, boat, auto, hi-fi, and antiques. Although a typical trade show or typical participant does not exist, an estimated $73,000 is allocated for each show, and the median manufacturer or distributor attends nine or ten shows annually.[27]

Whether an exporter should participate in a trade fair depends largely on the type of business relationship it wants to develop with a particular country. More than 8,000 trade shows create an annual worldwide amount of $25 billion in business.[28] A company looking only for one-time or short-term sales might find the expense prohibitive, but a firm looking for long-term involvement may find the investment worthwhile. Arguments in favor of participation include the following:

1. Some products, by their very nature, are difficult to market without providing the potential customer a chance to examine them or see them in action. Trade fairs provide an excellent opportunity to introduce, promote, and demonstrate new products.
2. An appearance produces goodwill and allows for periodic cultivation of contacts. Beyond the impact of displaying specific products, many firms place strong emphasis on "waving the company flag" against competition.[29] This facet also includes morale boosting of the firm's sales personnel and distributors.
3. Finding an intermediary may be one of the best reasons to attend a trade show. A show is a cost-effective way to solicit and screen candidates to represent the firm, especially in a new market.
4. Attendance is one of the best ways to contact government officials and decision makers, especially in the People's Republic of China. For example, participation in the Chinese Export Commodities Fair, which is held twice a year in Guangzhou, China, is "expected" by the host government.
5. Trade fairs provide an excellent chance for market research and collecting competitive intelligence. The exporter is able to view most rivals at the same time and to test comparative buyer reactions. Trade fairs provide one of the most inexpensive ways of obtaining evaluative data on the effectiveness of a promotional campaign.
6. Exporters are able to reach a sizable number of sales prospects in a brief time period at a reasonable cost per contact. More than 86 percent of all attendees represent buying influences (managers with direct responsibility for purchasing products and services). Of equal significance is the fact that trade show visitors are there because they have a specific interest in the exhibits.[30]

On the other hand, the following are among the reasons cited for nonparticipation in trade fairs:

1. High costs. These can be avoided by participating in events sponsored by the U.S. Department of Commerce or exhibiting at U.S. trade centers or export development offices. An exporter can also lower costs by sharing expenses with distributors or

---

[27] Thomas V. Bonoma, "Get More out of Your Trade Shows," *Harvard Business Review* 61 (January–February 1983): 137–145.

[28] Echo Montgomery Garrett, "Trade Shows," *World Trade,* December 1993, 88–89.

[29] Richard Barovick, "Exporters Fit Trade Fairs into Larger Marketing Strategy," *Business America,* December 10, 1984, 3–5.

[30] "Taking Advantage of Trade Fairs for Maximum Sales Impact," *Business International,* October 12, 1987, 321–323.

representatives. Further, the costs of closing a sale through trade shows are estimated to be much lower than for a sale closed through personal representation.

2. Difficulty in choosing the appropriate trade fairs for participation. This is a critical
decision. Because of scarce resources, many firms rely on suggestions from their
foreign distributors on which fairs to attend and what specifically to exhibit. Caterpillar, for example, usually allows its foreign dealers to make the selections for
themselves. In markets where conditions are more restricted for exporters, such
as the People's Republic of China, Caterpillar in effect serves as the dealer and thus
participates itself.

3. For larger exporters with multiple divisions, the problem of coordination. Several
divisions may be required to participate in the same fair under the company ban-
ner. Similarly, coordination is required with distributors and agents if joint participation is desired, which requires joint planning.

Trade show participation is too expensive to be limited to the exhibit alone. A clear
set of promotional objectives would include targeting accounts and attracting them to
the show with preshow promotion. Major customers and attractive prospects often
attend, and they should be acknowledged, for example, by arranging for a hospitality
suite.[31] Finally, a system is needed to evaluate postshow performance and to track qualified leads.

Exporters may participate in general or specialized trade fairs. Examples of general
trade fairs are the ones held in Hannover in Germany (See The International Marketplace 11.4) and Milan in Italy. An example of a specialized one is Retail Solutions, a four-
day trade show on store automation held in London.

Other promotional events that the exporter can use are trade missions, seminar
missions, solo exhibitions, and video/catalog exhibitions. **Trade missions** can be U.S.
specialized trade missions or industry-organized, government-approved (IOGA) trade
missions, both of which aim at expanding the sales of U.S. goods and services and the
establishment of agencies and representation abroad. The U.S. Department of Commerce
is actively involved in assistance of both types. **Seminar missions** are events in which
eight to ten firms are invited to participate in a one- to four-day forum, during which the
team members conduct generic discussions on technological issues—that is, follow a
soft-sell approach. This is followed up by individual meetings with end-users, government agencies, research institutions, and other potentially useful contacts. Individual
firms may introduce themselves to certain markets by proposing a technical seminar
there. Synopses of several alternative proposed lectures, together with company details
and the qualifications of the speakers, must be forwarded to the proper body, which will
circulate the proposals to likely interested bodies and coordinate all the arrangements.
The major drawback is the time required to arrange for such a seminar, which may be
as much as a year. **Solo exhibitions** are generally limited to one or, at the most, a few
product themes and are held only when market conditions warrant them. **Video/catalog
exhibitions** allow exporters to publicize their products at low cost. These programs
are organized by the Department of Commerce and related industry associations and
consist of 20 to 35 product presentations on videotapes, each lasting five to ten minutes.
They provide the advantage of actually showing the product in use to potential customers. All of the approaches require follow-up. An exporter may decide to follow up by
letter, by personal calls, by calling on embassies or foreign trade organizations (especially when centrally planned economies are concerned), or by combining any of these
methods.

---

[31] "Don't Just Exhibit—Do Something," *Business Marketing* 74 (May 1989): 78.

11.4

THE INTERNATIONAL MARKETPLACE

At the Fair

The Hannover Industrial Fair (Hannover Messe) is the Olympic Games of European industrial exposition. With more than 4,000,000 square feet of indoor exhibition space and 6,000 exhibitors, it is 10 times as large as most trade shows anywhere in the world. It is also superbly organized, with its own train station, post office, 35 restaurants, and 600 permanent staff. The show focuses on manufacturing equipment, technology, and such related subjects as materials, energy, and the environment.

The sheer magnitude of the Hannover Fair and the technology displayed there are impressive but are not the most significant aspects of this event. Rather, it is the opportunity it presents for people from everywhere in the world to view the technology and learn an incredible amount about their industries.

Most important, it provides the opportunity to meet hundreds of people who can be invaluable future resources, if not necessarily a direct source of future business. More than 500,000 people attend the event, and though only 25 percent are from outside Germany, almost all are from businesses rather than members of the general public.

Personal Selling

Personal selling is the most effective of the promotional tools available to the marketer; however, its costs per contact are high. The average cost of sales calls may vary from $200 to $1,100, depending on the industry and the product or service. Personal selling allows for immediate feedback on customer reaction as well as information on markets, as seen in The International Marketplace 11.5.

Personal selling may take place through intermediaries or as a direct effort. Intermediaries include manufacturers' representatives, selling agents, or distributors. Communication with intermediaries must ensure both that they are satisfied with the arrangement and that they are equipped to market and promote the exporter's product appropriately. Whatever the distribution arrangement, the exporter must provide basic selling aid communications, such as product specification and data literature, catalogs, the results of product testing, and demonstrated performance information—everything needed to present products to potential customers. In some cases, the exporter has to provide the intermediaries with incentives to engage in local advertising efforts. These may include special discounts, push money, or cooperative advertising. Cooperative advertising will give the exporter's product local flavor and increase the overall promotional budget for the product. However, the exporter needs to be concerned that the advertising is of sufficient quality and that the funds are spent as agreed.

A number of exporters employ sales representatives whose main function is to represent the firm abroad to existing and potential customers and to seek new leads. It is also important to sell with intermediaries, that is, by supporting and augmenting their efforts. This type of presence is essential at some stage of the firm's international involvement. Other promotional tools can facilitate foreign-market entry, but eventually some personal selling must take place.

Of the exhibits, 65 percent are German. The balance is mostly European, with France, Italy, Switzerland, Spain, Great Britain, Denmark, and the Netherlands accounting for an additional 25 percent. In 1993, U.S. firms accounted for only 56 (less than 1 percent) of the exhibits, excluding European subsidiaries of large U.S. multinationals.

The world's biggest industrial fair will soon take place in Hannover, Germany. If you don't go you could miss the boat.

Missed opportunities are bad for a company at the best of times. In the middle of a recession they could be fatal.

That's why a visit to the HANNOVER FAIR is essential. At the biggest industrial fair in the world, the opportunities to see the latest products and systems are unrivalled.

The breadth of the fair can help too in gaining an overview of the international market before making important investment decisions. It's a unique chance to assess the competition, meet the experts and make valuable new business contacts.

One visit to Hannover could save endless hours visiting lesser fairs trying to keep in touch.

Automation Technology	Power Transmission and Control
Electric Energy Technology	Energy and Environmental Technology
Installation Technology for Buildings	Lighting Technology
Plant Engineering and Industrial Materials	Tools and Factory Equipment
Subcontracting and Components	Research and Technology

The world's biggest industrial fair

HANNOVER MESSE '93
21st - 28th APRIL

Further information: Deutsche Messe AG, Messegelände, D-3000 Hannover 82, Tel.: (511) 89-0, Telex: 922728, Telefax: (511) 89-3 26 26

Source: Valerio Giannini, "The Hannover Messe," *Export Today*, 9 (July–August 1993): 29–32; advertisement from *The Economist*, March 6, 1993, 32.

The role of personal selling is greatest when the exporter sells directly to the end-user or to governmental agencies, such as foreign trade organizations. Firms selling products with high price tags (such as Boeing commercial aircraft) or companies selling to monopsonies (such as Seagrams liquor to certain Scandinavian countries, where all liquor sales are through state-controlled outlets) must rely heavily on person-to-person communication, oral presentations, and direct-marketing efforts. Many of these firms can expand their business only if their markets are knowledgeable about what they do. This

THE INTERNATIONAL MARKETPLACE

11.5

Automating the Salesforce

In the early 1990s, Dataram Corp. saw its sales shriveling and its distributor-based sales struggling to meet the needs of a rapidly changing market. To survive, Dataram executives decided the company had to go directly to its worldwide customers. However, with only a few in-house sales representatives and inadequate mechanisms to track leads and service customers, the Princeton, New Jersey-based supplier of storage and memory products for high-end computers faced an uphill battle against formidable odds.

The most critical decision in Dataram's change of approach was to automate its salesforce. The company's sales representatives and managers worldwide now are equipped with Dell notebook computers listing vital information about their clients and the company's products and services. The system is used to manage data-base marketing activity, such as lead generation and tracking, trade shows, telemarketing, advertising tracking, product support, and customer service. Management can also spot emerging trends, avert impending disasters, and forecast sales with the help of the system. "When a sales rep can answer a question in 15 minutes instead of three days, the company is perceived as a consultant as much as a vendor," say company officials. Recruiting salespeople may be easier when a company can offer state-of-the-art support. Furthermore, if turnover takes place, important customer information is not lost but preserved in the data base.

Salesforce automation, like anything else in marketing, is subject to the realities of the international environment: borders, time zones, languages, and cultures. Representatives in every country may want to do things slightly differently, which means that a system that can be localized is needed. This localization may be as comprehensive as complete language translations or as minor as changing address fields in the data base. Another issue to be considered is cost—hardware costs are higher in Europe, and telecommunications costs have to be factored in.

According to a recent study, automated companies have realized sales increases of 10 to 30 percent, and in some cases as much as 100 percent. In 1993, Dataram's sales team increased to 40, including representatives in Europe and Asia, and its sales topped $50 million per year.

Source: Eric J. Adams, "Power Tool," *World Trade*, November 1993, 42–44.

---

may require corporate advertising and publicity generation through extensive public-relations efforts.

Whatever the sales task, effectiveness is determined by a number of interrelated factors that are summarized in Figure 11.4. One of the keys to personal selling is the salesperson's ability to adapt to the customer and the selling situation.[32] This aspect of selling requires cultural knowledge and empathy; for example, in the Middle East, sales presentations may be broken up by long discussions of topics that have little or nothing to do with the transaction at hand. The characteristics of the buying task, whether rou-

---

[32] Alf H. Walle, "Conceptualizing Personal Selling for International Business: A Continuum of Exchange Perspective," *Journal of Personal Selling and Sales Management* 6 (November 1986): 9–17.

Determinants of Effectiveness in Personal Selling   FIGURE 11.4

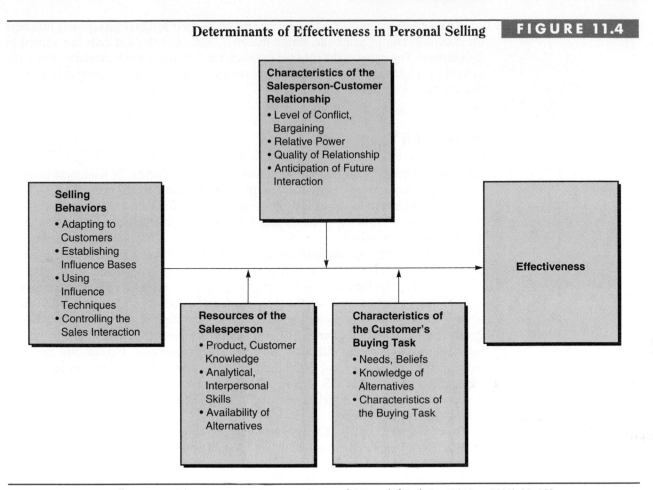

Characteristics of the Salesperson-Customer Relationship
- Level of Conflict, Bargaining
- Relative Power
- Quality of Relationship
- Anticipation of Future Interaction

Selling Behaviors
- Adapting to Customers
- Establishing Influence Bases
- Using Influence Techniques
- Controlling the Sales Interaction

Resources of the Salesperson
- Product, Customer Knowledge
- Analytical, Interpersonal Skills
- Availability of Alternatives

Characteristics of the Customer's Buying Task
- Needs, Beliefs
- Knowledge of Alternatives
- Characteristics of the Buying Task

Effectiveness

Source: Barton A. Weitz, "Effectiveness in Sales Interactions: A Contingency Framework," *Journal of Marketing* 45 (Winter 1981): 85–103.

tine or unique, have a bearing on the sales presentation. The exporter may be faced by a situation in which the idea of buying from a foreign entity is the biggest obstacle in terms of the risks perceived. If the exporter's product does not provide a clear-cut relative advantage over that of competitors, the analytical, interpersonal skills of the salesperson are needed to assist in the differentiation. A salesperson, regardless of the market, must have a thorough knowledge of the product or service. The more the salesperson is able to apply that knowledge to the particular situation, the more likely it is that he or she will obtain a positive result. The salesperson usually has front-line responsibility for the firm's customer relations, having to handle conflict situations such as the parent firm's bias for domestic markets and thus the possibility that shipments of goods to foreign clients receive low priority.

In the past, U.S. marketers thought that offices were almost essential to bring their companies closer to overseas customers. Now, international **telemarketing** is being promoted by Service 800 SA in Europe and AT&T in the United States. The main uses of the service are data transmission, service calls, customer inquiries, and even office-to-office communication. The quasi-toll-free service allows customers and prospects from 40 countries to contact a firm for little more than the cost of a local call. The service can handle both inbound and outbound calls. Many companies see this as a preliminary step to entering a foreign market with a branch office.

In Europe, companies using the service publicize their assigned local phone numbers on television and in print ads, direct mailings, and catalogs, and calls are routed to Switzerland. The name of the country in which the call originates is displayed above the switchboard so that it can be taken by an operator who speaks the language native to that country.[33]

SUMMARY

Effective communication is essential in negotiating agreements. To maximize the outcome of negotiations with clients and partners from other cultural backgrounds, international marketers must show adjustment capability to different standards and behaviors. Success depends on being prepared and remaining flexible, whatever the negotiation style in the host country.

Effective and efficient communication is needed for the dual purpose of (1) informing prospective customers about the availability of products or services and (2) persuading customers to opt for the marketer's offering over those of competitors. Within the framework of the company's opportunities, resources, and objectives, decisions must be made about whether to direct communications to present customers, potential customers, the general public, or intermediaries. Decisions must be made on how to reach each of the intended target audiences without wasting valuable resources. A decision also has to be made about who will control the communications effort: the exporter, an agency, or local representatives. The U.S. Department of Commerce is the single best source of export promotion support, which is essential in alleviating the environmental threats perceived by many exporters.

The exporting international marketer must also choose tools to use in the communications effort. Usually, two basic tools are used: (1) mass selling through business and trade journals, direct mail, trade fairs, and missions and (2) personal selling, which brings the international marketer face-to-face with the targeted customer.

Questions for Discussion

1. What is potentially harmful in going out of one's way to make clients feel comfortable by playing down status distinctions such as titles?
2. Discuss this statement: "Lack of foreign-language skills puts American negotiators at a disadvantage."
3. Compare and contrast the usefulness to a novice exporter of elements of the promotional mix.
4. Why do exporters usually choose U.S.-based publishers' services when placing advertisements to boost export sales specifically?
5. Some exporters report that they value above all the broad exposure afforded through exhibiting at a trade fair, regardless of whether they are able to sell directly at the event. Comment on this philosophy.
6. Discuss the benefits of horizontal versus vertical trade journals.

---

[33] Kevin T. Higgins, "Toll-Free Calling Offered to Global Marketers," *Marketing News,* November 22, 1985, 29, 34.

7. What specific advice would you give to an exporter who has used domestic direct mail extensively and wishes to continue the practice abroad?

8. Can an exporter be successful and yet not use local (national) media?

Recommended Readings

Baudot, Barbara. *International Advertising Handbook.* Lexington, MA: Lexington Books, 1990.

Contractor, Farok J., and Peter Lorange. *Cooperative Strategies in International Business.* Lexington, MA: Lexington Books, 1988.

Dunn, S. Watson, Arnold M. Barban, Dean M. Krugman, and Leonard N. Reid. *Advertising: Its Role in Modern Marketing,* 7th ed. Hinsdale, IL: Dryden Press, 1990.

Graham, John L., and Y. Sano. *Smart Bargaining: Doing Business with the Japanese.* Cambridge, MA: Ballinger, 1984.

Hendon, Donald, and Rebecca A. Hendon. "International Body Language and Effective Marketing." *Journal of International Consumer Marketing* 1 (Spring 1988): 51–74.

Kimball, Bob. *AMA Handbook for Successful Selling.* Chicago, IL: American Marketing Association, 1994.

Miller, Steve. *How to Get the Most Out of Trade Shows.* Lincolnwood, IL: NTC Business Books, 1993.

Shimp, Terence A. *Promotion Management and Marketing Communications,* 3rd ed. Hinsdale, IL: Dryden Press, 1993.

Webber, Robert. *The Marketer's Guide to Selling Products Abroad.* Westport, CT: Quorum Books, 1989.

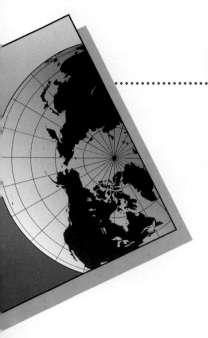

CHAPTER 12

International Channels
of Distribution

THE INTERNATIONAL MARKETPLACE

Choosing the Right System

The free market revolution sweeping South and Central America from Mexico to Chile, along with the emergence of trade pacts and falling tariff barriers, has led to a doubling of U.S. exports to the region's markets to about $60 billion in the last five years.

Boosting the attractiveness of the markets are changes occurring in distribution. Only a few years ago, the region's underdeveloped and monopolistic distributor networks gave exporters virtually no economical alternatives for marketing their goods. "When there was no outside competition, local distributors could afford to mismanage the relationship," says Julio Vitale, vice president of sales in Dow Chemical Company's Latin American unit. The main agent of change is competition. Today's exporters expect distributors to add value to what they do, either by carrying inventory, providing specialized packaging, or otherwise serving customers' needs. And if locals do not measure up, companies have been willing to put in their own people.

In the past, many U.S. exporters serviced the region out of Miami. From there, they passively waited for orders from intermediaries thousands of miles away in cities such as Rio De Janeiro or Santiago. These intermediaries often saw their prime roles as distributing sales literature, and when sales materialized, cutting through red tape. In the changed landscape U.S. firms are taking diverse distribution paths to the region. Most continue the practice of hiring local intermediaries, but some have them supervised by U.S. managers on the spot. Au Bon Pain Co., the Boston-based bakery and cafe chain, has company managers supervise every phase of supplying its Chilean food outlets. It has also hooked up with a local member of Chile's improving distributor base capable of offering the specialized frozen foods and food services required by the U.S. chain. Until the mid-1980s, distribution of Xerox products in Mexico was handled in-house. However, as part of an austerity program, Xerox decided to divest it. It offered the employees affected additional funds beyond severance if they formed independent distribution firms in the Xerox network. To service key accounts (such as the government and companies such as Copicenter), it retained in-house representation in the major cities. Distribution elsewhere is now independent. Other U.S. exporters move product through global U.S. distributors, such as Merisel, Inc., a $3 billion computer equipment distributor based in El Segundo, California. Merisel recently scooped up a large Mexican distributor and plans to set up shop in two more Latin American countries by 1995. Some companies, such as Ace Hardware Corp. ship directly to their dealers in South America. "Our only intermediary is the freight forwarder," says Michael Altendorf, international operations manager at Ace. Given the underdeveloped nature of the region's infrastructure, many exporters depend on transportation companies to play the ad hoc role distributor along some points of the distribution chain.

Despite the changes and improvements, exporters still need to do their homework. Experts warn that the region is not yet a single, borderless market like the European Union. Therefore exporters are recommended to restrict distributors to a single country, and perhaps even use several distributors within a national market due to political rivalries or remaining trade barriers.

Source: Joseph V. Barks, "Penetrating Latin America," *International Business,* February 1994, 76–80; and "Winning Approaches to Distribution in LA," *Business International,* January 13, 1992, 12–13.

Channels of distribution provide the essential linkages that connect producers and customers. The links are intracompany and extracompany entities that perform a number of functions. This chapter will focus on the ways an exporter can form an optimal distribution system in terms of design and choice of the individual **intermediaries.** More than a simple sequence of marketing institutions between producers and consumers, a channel of distribution should be a team working toward a common goal. The effort must be seen as a joint one by all of the participants in order to be successful in the long run.

The channel decision is the most long-term of the marketing mix decisions in that it cannot be readily changed. This makes the choice of channel structure crucial. Firm and market factors influence export task performance in various ways, as shown in The International Marketplace 12.1. An experienced exporter may decide that control is of utmost importance and choose to perform tasks itself and incur the information-collection and adaptation costs. An infrequent exporter, on the other hand, may be quite dependent on experienced intermediaries to get its product to markets. Whether export tasks are self-performed or assigned to export intermediaries, the distribution function should be planned so that the channel will function as one rather than as a collection of different or independent units. The decisions involved in the structuring and management of the export channel of distribution are discussed first. The chapter will end with a discussion of the steps needed in the preparation of an international shipment. Logistics issues will be discussed in detail in a later chapter.

CHANNEL STRUCTURE

A generalization of channel configurations for consumer and industrial products as well as services is provided in Figure 12.1. Channels can vary from direct, producer-to-consumer types to elaborate, multilevel channels employing many types of intermediaries,

| FIGURE 12.1 | Channel Configurations |

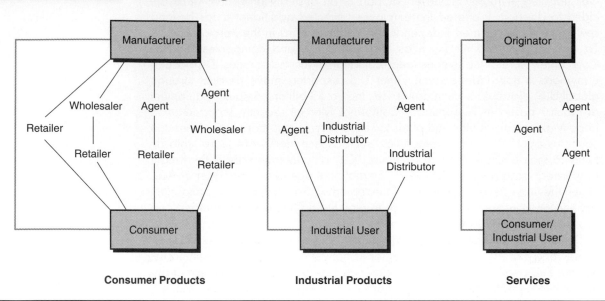

Consumer Products   **Industrial Products**   **Services**

each serving a particular purpose. For example, Amstrad, a British computer manufacturer, sells its products in Spain in more than 4,200 retail outlets. To have this reach, it sells through four types of channels: (1) large accounts, such as the country's largest department stores, (2) buyer groups, consisting of national and regional associations of consumer electronics retailers, (3) independent appliance retailers and informatics stores, and (4) wholesalers, who reach accounts that the other channel types cannot reach.[1]

Channel configurations will vary within industries, even within the same firm, for the same product because national markets quite often have their unique features. This may mean dramatic departures from accepted policy for a company. For example, IBM signed a deal in Britain to let Ferranti PLC sell PS/2s under its name to niche markets that are not often reached by IBM—the first time for IBM to use such an approach.[2] A firm's international market experience will also cause variation in distribution patterns. AMPAK, a manufacturer of packaging machinery, uses locally based distributors in markets where it is well established. Others are entered indirectly by using domestically based intermediaries: either by using the services of trading companies or through selling to larger companies, which then market the products alongside their own.[3]

The connections made by marketing institutions are not solely for the physical movement of goods. They also serve as transactional title flows and informational communications flows. Rather than unidirectional, downward from the producer, the flows are usually multidirectional, both vertical and horizontal. As an example, the manufacturer relies heavily on the retailer population for data on possible changes in demand. Communications from retailers may be needed to coordinate a cooperative advertising campaign instituted by a manufacturer. The three flows—physical, transactional, and infor-

---

[1] "How Amstrad Successfully Set Up a Distribution Channel in Spain," *Business International/Ideas in Action,* March 14, 1988, 4–6.

[2] "Mike Armstrong Is Improving IBM's Game in Europe," *Business Week,* June 20, 1988, 96–101.

[3] "Exporting Pays Off," *Business America,* October 7, 1991, 9.

mational—do not necessarily take place simultaneously or occur at every level of the channel. Agent intermediaries, for example, act only to facilitate the information flow; they do not take title and often do not physically handle the goods.

Because only a few products are sold directly to ultimate users, an international marketer has to decide on alternative ways to move products to chosen markets. The basic marketing functions of exchange, physical movement, and various facilitating activities must be performed, but the marketer may not be equipped to handle them. Intermediaries can therefore be used to gain quick, easy, and relatively low-cost entry to a targeted market.

CHANNEL DESIGN

The term *channel design* refers to the length and the width of the channel employed. Length is determined by the number of levels, or different types, of intermediaries. The most traditional is the producer-wholesaler-retailer-customer configuration. Channel width is determined by the number of institutions of each type in the channel. An industrial-goods marketer may grant exclusive distribution rights to a foreign entity, whereas a consumer-goods marketer may want to use as many intermediaries as possible to ensure intensive distribution.

Channel design is determined by factors that can be summarized as the 11 Cs, as listed in Table 12.1. These factors are integral to both the development of new marketing channels and the modification and management of existing ones. Their individual influences will vary from one market to another, and seldom, if ever, can one factor be considered without the interactive effects of the others. The marketer should use the 11 Cs checklist to determine the proper approach to reach intended target audiences before selecting channel members to fill the roles. The first three factors are givens, since the firm must adjust to the existing structures. The other eight are controllable to a certain extent by the international marketer.

Customer Characteristics

The demographic and psychographic characteristics of targeted customers will form the basis for channel design decisions. Answers to questions such as what customers need— as well as why, when, and how they buy—are used to determine ways in which the

Determinants of Channel Structure and Relationships	TABLE 12.1

External
    Customer characteristics
    Culture
    Competition

Internal
    Company objectives
    Character
    Capital
    Cost
    Coverage
    Control
    Continuity
    Communication

products should be made available to generate a competitive advantage. As an example, Anheuser-Busch entered Japan when Suntory, one of the country's largest liquor distillers, acquired the importing rights. Suntory's marketing plan stressed distribution of Budweiser in discos, pubs, and other night spots where Japan's affluent, well-traveled youth gather. Young people in Japan are influenced by American culture and adapt themselves more readily to new products than do older Japanese. Taking advantage of this fact, Suntory concentrated its efforts on one generation, and on-premise sales led to major off-premise (retail outlet) sales as well.

In the early stages of product introduction, the international marketer may concentrate efforts on only the most attractive markets and later, having attained a foothold, expand distribution. When Kronenbourg, the best-selling beer in Europe, entered the U.S. market, distribution was initiated in New York City and then extended to the metropolitan area. The reason was the area's prominence in both domestic and imported beer consumption. The national rollout took place five years later. In the industrial sector, certain industries cluster geographically, allowing the international marketer to take a more direct approach.

Customer characteristics may cause the same product to be distributed through two different types of channels. All sales of Caterpillar's earth-moving equipment are handled by 247 independent dealers, except that sales are direct to the U.S. government and the People's Republic of China. Furthermore, primary target audiences may change from one market to another. For example, in Japan, McDonald's did not follow the U.S. pattern of locating restaurants in the suburbs. The masses of young pedestrians that flood Japanese cities were more promising than affluent but tradition-minded car owners in the suburbs.[4]

Culture

In planning a distribution system, the marketer must analyze existing channel structures, or what might be called **distribution culture.** As an example, the manner in which Japanese channels of distribution are structured and managed presents one of the major reasons for the apparent failure of foreign firms to establish major market penetration in Japan.[5] The new firm must therefore be prepared to spend more time developing a working knowledge of the market for its products than is usually the case in other countries. The Japanese argue that channel patterns develop over time for a particular reason to "provide the most economical and efficient means of serving the market environment."[6] In any case, and in every country, international marketers must study distribution systems in general and the types of linkages between channel members for their specific type of product. Usually, the international marketer has to adjust to existing structures to gain distribution. For example, in Finland, 92 percent of all distribution of nondurable consumer goods is through four wholesale chains. Without their support, no significant penetration of the market is possible.

In addition to structure, functions performed by the various types of intermediaries have to be outlined. Retailers in Japan demand more from manufacturers and wholesalers than do American retailers; for example, they expect returns of merchandise to be

---

[4] Frederick H. Katayama, "Japan's Big Mac," *Fortune*, September 15, 1986, 114–120.

[5] Randolph Ross, "Understanding the Japanese Distribution System: An Explanatory Framework," *European Journal of Marketing* 17 (Winter 1983): 5–15.

[6] Yoshi Tsurumi, "Managing Consumer and Industrial Systems in Japan," *Sloan Management Review,* Fall 1982, 36–45.

	Channel Member	
Manufacturer	**Intermediary**	**Retail**
Production	Order taking	Selling
Advertising	Inventory maintenance	Organizing consumers
National sales promotion	Space control at the	In-store promotion
Dealer aids	retail level	
Education of dealers	Product assortment	
Financing	Dispatching of sales	
	support personnel	
	Area marketing	
	Financing	

TABLE 12.2

Examples of Function Performance in the Channel System for the Japanese Cosmetics Industry

Source: Michael R. Czinkota, "Distribution of Consumer Products in Japan: An Overview," *International Marketing Review* 2 (Autumn 1985): 39–51.

fully accepted even if there is no reason other than lack of sales. Retailers also expect significant amounts of financing and frequent delivery of products. Retailers, on their part, offer substantial services to their clientele and take great pains to build close relationships with their customers. As can be seen in Table 12.2, which lists channel members in the Japanese cosmetics industry, functions are—and should be—clearly delineated. Manufacturers concentrate mainly on production and promotional activities; intermediaries work on logistics activities, financing, and communication with manufacturers and retailers; retailers focus on sales and promotional activities.

Trying to change existing distribution systems may be quite difficult. Porsche tried to change the way it sold automobiles in the United States from traditional independent franchised dealers to a "dealerless system." Whereas dealers buy cars for resale, Porsche would have instituted agents who would order cars as they sold them and work on an 8 percent commission rather than the normal 16 to 18 percent margin. After an uproar, Porsche abandoned the plan.[7] Toys 'Я' Us, which opened its first outlet in Japan in 1992, is having a difficult time getting Japanese toy manufacturers to sell to it directly (as happens in the United States) rather than through multiple layers of distributors.

International marketers may benefit, however, from the internationalization of intermediaries and distribution formats. Breaking down traditional local ways of distribution may result in increased acceptance of their products and improved entry into new markets, as seen in The International Marketplace 12.2.

Additionally, an analysis is needed of the relationships between channel members—for example, the extent of vertical integration. The linkage can be based on ownership, contract, or the use of expert or referent power by one of the channel members. The Japanese distribution system often financially links producers, importers, distributors, and retailers, either directly or through a bank or a trading company. Interdependence in a number of southern European markets is forged through family relationships or is understood as an obligation.

Foreign legislation affecting distributors and agents is an essential part of the distribution culture of a market. For example, legislation may require that foreign firms be

[7] David B. Tinnin, "Porsche's Civil War with Its Dealers," *Fortune*, April 16, 1984, 63–68.

12.2

THE INTERNATIONAL MARKETPLACE

The Changing Landscape of Retailing

One of the strongest forces changing retailing in the 1990s will be the continuing internationalization of what has traditionally been only a domestic activity. Internationalization has taken two separate forms: the international expansion of retail formats and the internationalization of retail organizations.

Retailers in Asia are hoping that the surge of consumer demand in Asia is about to outpace the region's economies, many of which have grown 7 to 8 percent a year. This is because of a phenomenon retail analysts call "magic moments"—the point at which a large part of the population crosses an income level, thus allowing it to buy entirely new categories of goods. For example, in 1987, a mere 3 percent of the Taiwanese population bought groceries in a "modern" outlet, such as a supermarket. By 1993, that figure had risen to 50 percent.

In theory, a changing market should play to strengths of new entrants. Since consumers are now seeking new products and better prices, modern retailers, with their more efficient distribution systems and supply lines, should have a competitive advantage. Foreign department stores (e.g., Sogo, Yaohan, and Isetan from Japan) are trying to offer better service than their local rivals in Asia.

Foreign discounters are carrying the retail revolution one step further. They want to overturn the local distribution system by bypassing local intermediaries and squeezing local manufacturers on price. Wal-Mart and K-Mart from the United States are looking at expansion in China, Indonesia, Singapore, and Thailand. The trailblazer in discounting has been Dutch Makro, which sells in bulk mainly to small shopkeepers.

The retail revolution in Europe has also centered on discounting. Hard discounters like Germany's Aldi already account for a sizeable market share in Germany, Belgium, and Denmark, and are growing spectacularly fast in countries such as France. Staples, a U.S.-based discounter of office supplies, operates eight warehouse stores in Germany with a local partner called MAXI-Papier. Now, Europe's and the United States' biggest discount chains have set their sights on Britain. Price/Costco opened the first of its planned ten outlets in London November 30, 1993. Many see this as one of the first steps that will change Europe's retail culture, which has been dominated by high prices and limited selection.

Sources: "The New U.S. Push into Europe," *Fortune,* January 10, 1994, 73–74; "Teach Me Shopping," *The Economist,* December 18, 1993, 64–65; "Indigestion," *The Economist,* December 4, 1993, a survey of the food industry; "Europe's Discount Dogfight," *The Economist,* May 8, 1993, 69–70; Alan D. Treadgold, "The Developing Internationalisation of Retailing," *International Journal of Retail and Distribution Management* 18 no. 2 (1990): 4–11.

represented only by firms that are 100 percent locally owned. Some nations have totally prohibited the use of dealers in order to protect consumers from abuses attributed to intermediaries.

Competition

Channels used by competitors may be the only product distribution system that is accepted by both the trade and consumers. In this case, the international marketer's task is to use the structure effectively and efficiently. One challenge, even for a sizable entity such as IBM, may be to create a distribution system as extensive as that of an established competitor. IBM can send a sales team out of its Tokyo office or one of its 50 branch offices to sell a system to a large buyer, such as a bank or industrial company. Hitachi, on the other hand, has 10,000 exclusive retail dealers and a sales force already selling motors and other machinery to hundreds of commercial customers. To emulate the distribution approach of this major competitor, IBM enlisted the help of more than 60 outside dealers, such as Nissan Motor outlets, to sell small computers to their customers.

The alternative is to use a distribution approach totally different from that of the competition and hope to develop a competitive advantage. A new approach will have to be carefully analyzed and tested against the cultural, political, and legal environments in which it is to be introduced. For example, Black Box, a Pittsburgh-based manufacturer of computer-communications equipment, found that its independent foreign distributors often pushed only the most profitable lines regardless of who made them. Black Box's solution was to form jointly owned sales companies.[8] In some cases, the international marketer cannot manipulate the distribution variable. For example, in Sweden and Finland, all alcoholic beverages must be distributed through state monopoly-owned outlets. In Japan, the Japan Tobacco & Salt Public Corporation is a state monopoly that controls all tobacco imports and charges a 20 percent fee for distribution.

In some cases, all feasible channels may be blocked by domestic competitors either through contractual agreements or through other means. U.S. suppliers of soda ash, which is used in glass, steel, and chemical products, have not been able to penetrate the Japanese market even though they offer a price advantage. The reason is the cartel-like condition developed by the Japan Soda Industry Association, which allegedly sets import levels, specifies which local trading company is to deal with each U.S. supplier, and buys the imports at lower U.S. prices for resale by its members at higher Japanese prices. Efforts by U.S. producers to distribute directly or through smaller, unaffiliated traders have faced strong resistance. The end-users and traders fear alienating the domestic producers, on whom their business depends.

Company Objectives

A set of management considerations will have an effect on channel design.[9] No channel of distribution can be properly selected unless it meets the requirements set by overall company objectives for market share and profitability. Sometimes management may simply want to use a particular channel of distribution, and there may be no sound business basis for the decision.

Channels of distribution will have to change as the operations of the company expand. For example, Xerox set a goal of having noncopier sales account for 50 percent of the company's worldwide business in the 1990s. Before this decision, copiers, accounting for 95 percent of sales, were sold mainly through the company's own direct salesforce. In France, Xerox dramatically changed its distribution by setting up a chain of retail sales outlets, wholly owned and run by the company. To improve its coverage of rural areas and small towns, Xerox withdrew its direct salesforce and replaced it with independent distributors, called **concessionaires,** who work on an exclusive basis.[10]

Often, some management goals may have conflicting results. When investment in the restaurant business in Japan was liberalized, a number of U.S. fast-food chains rushed to capitalize on the development. Because they were unfamiliar with the features of the

---

[8] "Made in the U.S.A.," *Business Week,* February 29, 1988, 60–66.

[9] C. Glenn Walters and Blaise J. Bergiel, *Marketing Channels* (Glenview, IL: Scott, Foresman, 1982), 142–162.

[10] "Rank Xerox Reorganizes Distribution to Succeed in Europe," *Business International/Ideas in Action,* February 15, 1988, 2–5.

Japanese distribution system, most formed joint ventures with Japanese partners, partially adapting sales methods and American-type products to fit the market. The companies attempted to establish mass sales as soon as possible by opening numerous restaurants in the busiest sections of several Japanese cities. Unfortunately, control proved to be quite difficult because of the sheer number of openings over a relatively short period of time. The individual stores changed the product as they grew, ruining the major asset—standardization—that the U.S. companies offered.[11]

Character

The nature of the product, its character, will have an impact on the design of the channel. Generally, the more specialized, expensive, bulky, or perishable the product and the more after-sale service it may require, the more likely the channel is to be relatively short. Staple items, such as soap, tend to have longer channels.

The type of channel chosen must match the overall positioning of the product in the market. Changes in overall market conditions, such as currency fluctuations, may require changes in distribution as well. An increase in the value of the dollar may cause a repositioning of the marketed product as a luxury item, necessitating an appropriate channel (such as an upper-grade department store) for its distribution.

Rules of thumb aside, particular products may be distributed in a number of ways even to the same target audience. Figure 12.2 shows the variety of distribution alternatives for soap in Japan. Case 1 presents the most frequently used channel. Product deliveries are made from the manufacturer to a wholesaler, who in turn delivers to a retailer. Payment flows go from the retailer to the wholesaler, who in turn pays the manufacturer. In Case 2, the larger wholesaler acts as an agent, receiving a 5 percent commission on the sale from the manufacturer. Case 3 is an example of the channel structures necessary to ensure the most intensive type of distribution.

Capital

The term *capital* is used to describe the financial requirements in setting up a channel system. The international marketer's financial strength will determine the type of channel and the basis on which channel relationships will be built. The stronger the marketer's finances, the more able the firm is to establish channels it either owns or controls. Intermediaries' requirements for beginning inventories, selling on a consignment basis, preferential loans, and need for training all will have an impact on the type of approach chosen by the international marketer. For example, an industrial-goods manufacturer may find that potential distributors in a particular country lack the capability of servicing the product. The marketer then has two options: (1) set up an elaborate training program at headquarters or regionally or (2) institute company-owned service centers to help distributors. Either approach will require a significant investment.

Cost

Closely related to the capital dimension is cost—that is, the expenditure incurred in maintaining a channel once it is established. Costs will naturally vary over the life cycle of a relationship with a particular channel member as well as over the life cycle of the

[11] Robert H. Luke, "Successful Marketing in Japan: Guidelines and Recommendations," in *Contemporary Perspectives in International Business,* eds. Harold W. Berkman and Ivan R. Vernon (Chicago: Rand McNally, 1979), 307–315.

Variety of Distribution Alternatives: The Channels for Soap in Japan   FIGURE 12.2

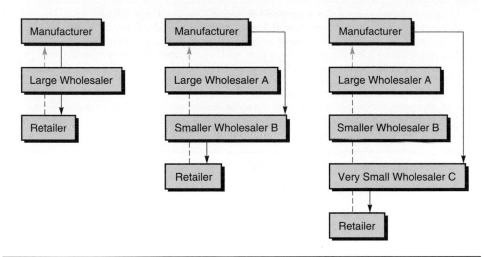

Source: Michael R. Czinkota, "Distribution of Consumer Products in Japan: An Overview," *International Marketing Review* 2 (Autumn 1985): 39–51.

products marketed. An example of the costs involved is promotional money spent by a distributor for the marketer's product. A cooperative advertising deal between the international marketer and the intermediary would typically split the costs of the promotional campaign executed in the local market.

Costs will vary in terms of the relative power of the manufacturer vis-à-vis its intermediaries. In the United Kingdom, for example, retail power is in the hands of giant multiple stores, such as Tesco, Sainsbury, and Asda. The centralized distribution systems being developed by these giants are eroding the marketing strength of manufacturers, which lay in their networks of distribution depots that delivered direct to stores. Now, retailers want delivery to their central distribution centers. In addition, they are pushing stockholding costs to manufacturers by demanding more frequent deliveries, in smaller, mixed loads, with shorter delivery time.[12]

Costs may also be incurred in protecting the company's distributors against adverse market conditions. A number of U.S. manufacturers helped their distributors maintain competitive prices through subsidies when the exchange rate for the U.S. dollar caused pricing problems. Extra financing aid has been extended to distributors that have been hit with competitive adversity. Such support, although often high in monetary cost, will pay back manyfold through a faultless manufacturer-distributor relationship.

Coverage

The term *coverage* is used to describe both the number of areas in which the marketer's products are represented and the quality of that representation. Coverage is therefore two-dimensional in that horizontal and vertical coverage need to be considered in channel design. The number of areas to be covered depends on the dispersion of demand in

---

[12] "How Dairy Crest Transformed Customer Service by Better Physical Distribution," *Business International/ Ideas in Action,* April 11, 1988, 8–11.

| TABLE 12.3 | Advantages of a Single Distributor |

> 1. One corporate presence eliminates confusion among buyers and local officials.
> 2. The volume of business that results when exports are consolidated will attract a larger distributor. The larger distributor will have greater influence in its local business community.
> 3. Communication is less plagued by noise. This will have a positive effect in many areas, from daily information flows to supervising and training.
> 4. More effective coordination of the sales and promotional effort can be achieved.
> 5. Logistics flows are more economical.
> 6. A stronger presence can be maintained in smaller markets or markets in which resources may dictate a holding mode, until more effective penetration can be undertaken.
> 7. Distributor morale and overall principal-intermediary relationship are better.

Source: Business International Corporation, *201 Checklists: Decision Making in International Operations* (New York: Business International Corporation, 1980), 26–27.

the market and also on the time elapsed since the product's introduction to the market. Three different approaches are available:

1. Intensive coverage, which calls for distributing the product through the largest number of different types of intermediaries and the largest number of individual intermediaries of each type
2. Selective coverage, which entails choosing a number of intermediaries for each area to be penetrated
3. Exclusive coverage, which involves only one entity in a market

Generally, intensive and selective coverage call for longer channels using different types of intermediaries, usually wholesalers and agents. Exclusive distribution is conducive to more direct sales. For some products, such as ethnic products, markets are concentrated geographically and allow for more intensive distribution with a more direct channel. A company typically enters a market with one local distributor, but as volume expands, the distribution base often has to be adjusted. The advantages of a single distributor are listed in Table 12.3.

Expanding distribution too quickly may cause problems. Benetton, one of Italy's major exporters of clothing, had planned to have 1,000 stores in the United States by 1990. The plan was abandoned because of concerns about oversaturation of certain urban areas and overprojection of retail sales. Rather, more emphasis is being put on customer service.[13] Similarly, expanding distribution from specialty outlets to mass distribution may have an impact on the product's image and the after-sales service associated with it.

Control

The use of intermediaries will automatically lead to loss of some control over the marketing of the firm's products. The looser the relationship is between the marketer and intermediaries, the less control the marketer can exert. The longer the channel, the more difficult it becomes for the marketer to have a final say in pricing, promotion, and the types of outlets in which the product will be made available.

The decision to use intermediaries or to distribute via a company-owned, or integrated, distribution channel requires a major trade-off between the desire to control export efforts and the desire to minimize resource commitment costs.[14] In the initial

---

[13] Curtis Pepper, "Fast Forward," *Business Month*, February 1989, 25–30.

[14] Erin Anderson and Hubert Gatignon, "Modes of Foreign Entry: A Transaction Cost Analysis and Propositions," *Journal of International Business Studies* 17 (Fall 1986): 1–26.

stages of internationalization or specific market entry, an intermediary's specialized knowledge and working relationships are needed, but as exporters' experience base and sales in the market increase, many opt to establish their own sales offices.

The issue of control correlates heavily with the type of product or service being marketed. In the case of industrial and high-technology products, control will be easier to institute because intermediaries are dependent on the marketer for new products and service. Where the firm's marketing strategy calls for a high level of service, integrated channels are used to ensure that the service does get performed.[15]

The marketer's ability and willingness to exercise any type of power—whether reward, coercive, legitimate, referent, or expert—determines the extent of control. The exercise of control causes more incidents of conflict in channels of distribution than any other activity in the relationship. This points to the need for careful communication with foreign intermediaries about the marketer's intentions and also the need for certain control measures. These might include the marketer's need to be the sole source of advertising copy or to be in charge of all product-modification activities. Generally, the more control the marketer wishes to have, the more cost is involved in securing that control.

Continuity

Channel design decisions are the most long-term of the marketing mix decisions. Utmost care must therefore be taken in choosing the right type of channel, given the types of intermediaries available and any environmental threats that may affect the channel design. Occasionally, however, unpredictable events may occur. As an example, Cockspur, the largest distiller of rum in Barbados, negotiated an arrangement with one of the largest distributors in the United States. Almost immediately, the distributor was acquired by a company which thought liquor distribution did not fit its mission and thus eliminated the products and reassigned the salespeople. Years later, Cockspur was still without substantial distribution in the United States.[16]

Nurturing continuity rests heavily on the marketer because foreign distributors may have a more short-term view of the relationship. For example, Japanese wholesalers believe that it is important for manufacturers to follow up initial success with continuous improvement of the product. If such improvements are not forthcoming, competitors are likely to enter the market with similar, lower-priced products, and the wholesalers of the imported product will turn to the Japanese suppliers.

The U.S. manufacturers of Odoreaters experienced such a development. After three years of costly market-development efforts together with a Japanese wholesaler, the firm had reached a sales level of 3.8 million pairs. However, six months after product introduction, 12 comparable Japanese products had already been introduced. Because Odoreaters was not able to improve its product substantially over time, its wholesaler made an exclusive agreement with a competing firm—Scholl Inc.—and terminated the relationship with Odoreaters. Even though Odoreaters managed to find a new distributor, its sales dropped significantly.[17]

Continuity is also expressed through visible market commitment. Industries abroad may be quite conservative; distributors will not generally support an outsider until they

---

[15] Erin Anderson and Anne T. Coughlan, "International Market Entry and Expansion via Independent or Integrated Channels of Distribution," *Journal of Marketing* 51 (January 1987): 71–82.

[16] We are indebted to Dr. James H. Sood of the American University for this example.

[17] Michael R. Czinkota, "Distribution of Consumer Products in Japan: An Overview," *International Marketing Review* 2 (Autumn 1985): 39–51.

are sure it is in the market to stay. Such commitments have included Kraft's listing on the Tokyo exchange[18] and some exporters' setting up wholly owned sales subsidiaries from the start in Europe—and staffing them with locals to help communicate that the company is there for the long term.[19]

Communication

Communication provides the exchange of information that is essential to the functioning of the channel. Communication is an important consideration in channel design, and it gains more emphasis in international distribution because of various types of distances that may cause problems. In the buyer-seller relationships in industrial markets, the distance that is perceived to exist between a buyer and a seller has five aspects:

1. Social distance: the extent to which each of the two entities in a relationship is familiar with the other's ways of operating
2. Cultural distance: the degree to which the norms, values, or working methods between the two entities differ because of their separate national characteristics
3. Technological distance: the differences between the product or process technologies of the two entities
4. Time distance: the time that must elapse between establishing contact or placing an order and the actual transfer of the product or service involved
5. Geographical distance: the physical distance between the locations of the two entities[20]

All of these dimensions must be considered when determining whether to use intermediaries and, if they are to be used, what types to use.

Communication, if properly utilized, will assist the international marketer in conveying the firm's goals to the distributors, in solving conflict situations, and in marketing the product overall. Communication is a two-way process that does not permit the marketer to dictate to intermediaries. Cases are well known in which the marketer is not able to make the firm's marketing program functional. Prices may not be competitive; promotional materials may be obsolete or inaccurate and not well received overall.[21] Solving these problems is important to the welfare of both parties. However, the marketer's attempts to solve them may have met with resentment because of the way the distributor was approached.

Channels of distribution, because of their sequential positioning of the entities involved, are not conducive to noiseless communication. The marketer must design a channel and choose intermediaries that guarantee good information flow. Proper communication involves not only the passage of information between channel members but also a better understanding of each party's needs and goals. This can be achieved through personal visits, exchange of personnel, or distribution advisory councils. Consisting of members from all channel participants, advisory councils meet regularly to discuss opportunities and problems that may have arisen.

---

[18] "Opening of Japan's Food Market Spells Opportunity for Foreign Corporations," *Business International,* November 21, 1988, 366.

[19] "Made in the U.S.A.," *Business Week,* February 29, 1988, 60–66.

[20] David Ford, "Buyer/Seller Relationships in International Industrial Markets," *Industrial Marketing Management* 13 (May 1984): 101–112.

[21] Philip J. Rosson, "Success Factors in Manufacturer-Overseas Distributor Relationships in International Marketing," in *International Marketing Management,* ed. Erdener Kaynak (New York: Praeger Publishing, 1984), 91–107.

SELECTION OF INTERMEDIARIES

Once the basic design of the channel has been determined, the international marketer must begin a search to fill the defined roles with the best-available candidates and must secure their cooperation.

Types of Intermediaries

Two basic decisions are involved in choosing the type of intermediaries to serve a particular market. First, the marketer must determine the type of relationship to have with intermediaries. The alternatives are distributorship and agency relationship. A **distributor** will purchase the product and will therefore exercise more independence than agencies. Distributors are typically organized along product lines and provide the international marketer with complete marketing services. **Agents** have less freedom of movement than distributors because they operate on a commission basis and do not usually physically handle the goods. In addition to the business implications, the choice of type will have legal implications in terms of what the intermediary can commit its principal to and the ease of termination of the agreement.

Second, the international marketer must decide whether to utilize indirect exporting, direct exporting, or integrated distribution in penetrating a foreign market.[22] **Indirect exporting** requires dealing with another U.S.-based firm that acts as a sales intermediary for the marketer, often taking over the international side of the marketer's operations. The benefits, especially in the short term, are that the exporter can use someone else's international channels without having to pay to set them up. But there may be long-term concerns in using this strategy if the marketer wants to actively and aggressively get into the markets itself. With **direct exporting,** the marketer takes direct responsibility for its products abroad by either selling directly to the foreign customer or finding a local representative to sell its products in the market. The third category of export marketing strategy, **integrated distribution,** requires the marketer to make an investment into the foreign market for the purpose of selling its products in that market or more broadly. This investment could be the opening, for example, of a German or EU sales office, a distribution hub, or even an assembly operation or manufacturing facility. Although the last set of strategies indicates longer-term commitment to a market, it is riskier than the first two because the marketer is making a major financial investment.

The major types of intermediaries are summarized in Table 12.4. Care should be taken to understand conceptual differences that might exist from one market to another. For example, a **commissionario** may sell in his or her own name (as a distributor would) but for an undisclosed principal (an agency concept). Similarly, a **del credere agent** guarantees the solvency of the customer and may therefore be responsible to the supplier for payment by the customer.[23]

The respective strengths and weaknesses of various export intermediary types are discussed in a later chapter.

---

[22] "Market Entry Strategy," *Business America,* March 25, 1991, 12–17; Frank Reynolds, "How to Capture the Flag," *Exporter* 3 (October 1991): 27–28.

[23] Peter B. Fitzpatrick and Alan S. Zimmerman, *Essentials of Export Marketing* (New York: American Management Association, 1985), 43.

| TABLE 12.4 | International Channel Intermediaries |

Agents

Foreign (Direct)	Domestic (Indirect)
Brokers	Brokers
Manufacturer's representatives	Export agents
Factors	EMCs
Managing agents	Webb-Pomere associations
Purchasing agents	Commission agents

Distributors

Distributors/dealers	Domestic wholesalers
Import jobbers	EMCs
Wholesalers/retailers	ETCs
	Complementary marketing

Sources: Peter B. Fitzpatrick and Alan S. Zimmerman, *Essentials of Export Marketing* (New York: American Management Association, 1985), 20; Bruce Seifert and John Ford, "Export Distribution Channels," *Columbia Journal of World Business* 24 (Summer 1989): 16.

Sources for Finding Intermediaries

Firms that have successful international distribution attest to the importance of finding top representatives. This undertaking should be held in the same regard as recruiting and hiring within the company because "an ineffective foreign distributor can set you back years; it is almost better to have no distributor than a bad one in a major market."[24]

The approach can be either passive or active. Foreign operations for a number of smaller firms start through an unsolicited order; the same can happen with foreign distribution. Distributors, wherever they are, are always on the lookout for product representation that can be profitable and status enhancing, as seen in the International Marketplace 12.3. The initial contact may result from an advertisement or from a trade show the marketer has participated in.

The marketer's best interest lies in taking an active role. The marketer should not simply use the first intermediary to show an interest in the firm. The choice should be a result of a careful planning process. The exporter should start by gaining an understanding of market conditions in order to define what is expected of an intermediary and what the exporter can offer in the relationship. At the same time, procedures need to be set for intermediary identification and evaluation.[25] The exporter does not have to do all of this independently; both governmental and private agencies can assist the marketer in locating intermediary candidates.

Governmental Agencies   The U.S. Department of Commerce has various services that can assist firms in identifying suitable representatives abroad. Some have been designed specifically for that purpose. The New Product Information Service (NPIS) provides worldwide publicity for new U.S. products available for export. This exposure enables foreign firms to identify and contact U.S. firms, thereby giving the U.S. company a direct indication of market interest. A firm can subscribe to the department's Trade Opportunities Program (TOP), which matches product interests of foreign buyers with

[24] "How to Evaluate Foreign Distributors: A BI Checklist," *Business International,* May 10, 1985, 145–149.
[25] "Finding a Distributor Takes Planning and Skill," *Business International,* March 8, 1985, 74–75.

THE INTERNATIONAL MARKETPLACE

12.3

Putting the Best Foot Forward

In the early 1980s, when most American exporters were getting out of foreign markets, Timberland Shoes decided to find a new market for its line of rugged, outdoor footgear. Initially, the firm had no idea it could be successful in international sales. "A tremendous amount of our decision was really luck. We were discovered by people in Europe who saw an opportunity for us to export at a time we did not believe we could. The good news is that once we realized there was an opportunity, we went after it," says the company's president.

Timberland's first choice—Italy—surprised many in the industry. Home to many of the world's best-known and high-priced brands of leather footwear, Italy had earned the reputation as the most sophisticated market in Europe. Today, Italy is one of the most profitable of Timberland's more than 50 export markets. The success gave Timberland the confidence to make exporting a major profit center for the company: exports have accounted for over 29 percent of net sales in the 1990s.

To find new markets, Timberland takes a somewhat unconventional approach. Instead of scouting for markets where management thinks it can get a foothold, the company responds especially to those distributors who approach it. "We have talented distributors who understand the market better than we ever could." Timberland looks at the line of footwear the distributor carries and how it is marketed. If the line is high quality and the distributor has a good success rate, then Timberland will go into the market.

Timberland also maintains close relationships with each distributor. Every year the company conducts two sales meetings in the United States and abroad for its foreign distributors. And despite a preference for coordinating international sales efforts from the United States, Timberland sends top officers from the company on periodic visits to each local market.

Source: "Sizing Up the Customers' Needs," *Export Today* 5 (February 1989): 32–33, updated by interview with Timberland, March/April 1994.

those indicated by the U.S. subscribers. The Commerce Department also collects data on foreign firms for the Foreign Traders Index (FTI). Covering 143 countries, the file contains information on more than 140,000 importing firms, agents, representatives, distributors, manufacturers, service organizations, retailers, and potential end-users.

Two services are specifically designed for locating foreign representatives. The Agent/Distributor Service (A/DS) locates foreign firms that are interested in export proposals submitted by U.S. firms and determines their willingness to correspond with the U.S. firm. Both U.S. and foreign commercial service posts abroad supply information on up to six representatives who meet these requirements. The World Traders Data Report (WTDR) is a valuable service, especially when the screening of potential candidates takes place. WTDRs provide a trade profile of specific foreign firms. They also provide a general narrative report on the reliability of the foreign firm. All of the services are available for relatively small fees; for example, the cost for an A/DS application is $250 per country.[26]

---

[26] U.S. Department of Commerce, *Commerce Export Assistance Programs* (Washington, D.C.: Department of Commerce, 1992).

FIGURE 12.3 **Sample Report from the World Traders Data Report**

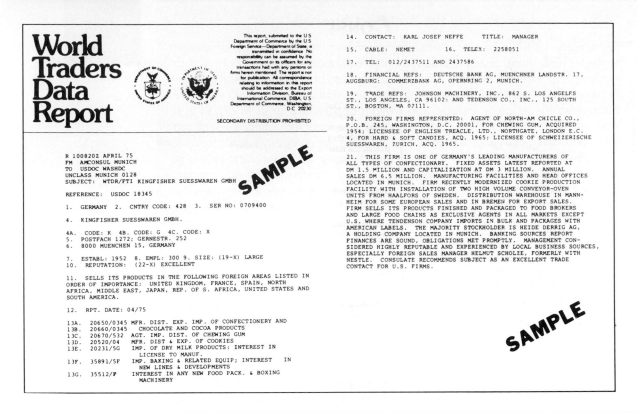

Source: U.S. Department of Commerce, *A Basic Guide to Exporting* (Washington, D.C.: Government Printing Office, 1989), 31–32.

An example of a WTDR is provided in Figure 12.3. Furthermore, individual state agencies provide similar services.

Private Sources   The easiest approach for the firm seeking intermediaries is to consult trade directories. Country and regional business directories such as Kompass (Europe), Bottin International (worldwide), Nordisk Handelskalendar (Scandinavia), and the Japan Trade Directory are good places to start. Company lists by country and line of business can be ordered from Dun & Bradstreet, Reuben H. Donnelly, Kelly's Directory, and Johnston Publishing. Telephone directories, especially the yellow-page sections or editions, can provide distributor lists. The Jaeger and Waldmann International Telex Directory can also be consulted. Although not detailed, these listings will give addresses and an indication of the products sold.

The firm can solicit the support of some of its facilitating agencies, such as banks, advertising agencies, shipping lines, and airlines. All of these have substantial international information networks and can put them to work for their clients. The services available will vary by agency, depending on the size of its foreign operations. Some of the major U.S. flagship carriers—for example, Northwest Airlines—have special staffs for this purpose within their cargo operations. Banks usually have the most extensive networks through their affiliates and correspondent banks.

The marketer can take an even more direct approach by buying space to solicit representation. Advertisements typically indicate the type of support the marketer will be able

Advertisement for an Intermediary   **FIGURE 12.4**

CONSUMER GOODS

Charcoal Briquets Light Instantly

"Just Light" instant-lighting charcoal briquets do not require lighter fluid, and take just 20 minutes to reach cooking temperature. Useable on any grill, the briquets allow food to be barbecued quickly and conveniently. This product is available with customized packaging in metric sizes and can use any client's label. This product's no-lighter-fluid characteristics will build charcoal sales volume and promote sales of other high profit barbeque cooking items, says the company. Agents and distributors are sought.

TARGET
Eastern Europe; Western Europe
Mexico, Central America, Caribbean; Canada
South America; Asia and Oceania
North Africa, Near East, South Asia
Africa (Sub-Sahara).

CONTACT
Gary Sigel, Vice Pres.,
Forest Products Charcoal Co., Dept. CN
845 Crossover Lane, Ste. 124
Memphis, Tennessee 38117 U.S.A.

TELEPHONE
901 – 761 – 4533

FAX
901 – 761 – 4543

BALLET SHOE MATERIAL CONFORMS TO FOOT

"ToeFlo Pointe Shoe Pads" are unique, self-adjusting pointe shoe pads that conform to the delicate irregularities of the foot. Unlike other types of padding, "FloLite," the flow material inside the pad acts hydraulically to evenly distribute pressure, thus relieving painful pressure points. This padding, already used in a wide variety of other applications, is now available to dancers to help alleviate the discomfort associated with dancing en pointe. Inquiries are sought from dancewear distributors only. Price: $7.50. **CONTACT:** Janet Kuennemann, Pres., DanzTech, Inc., Dept. CN, P.O. Box 1225, Salt Lake City, Utah 84110-1225 U.S.A. **TELEPHONE/FAX:** 801-363-5813.

FRAGRANCE COMES IN MANY FORMS

"Primrose Fragrance" can be used to brighten up any office, home, or hotel with its lovely colors and aroma. The fragrance comes in candle, sachet, potpourri, padded hanger, and spray form, each product packaged attractively in a stripe and floral design. Designed to capture the essence of a country garden, this complex floral fragrance uses the finest quality ingredients, says the firm. Other fragrances are available, and the company will custom-make any of its products. Price: $2-$3. Agents are wanted. **CONTACT:** Johan Hedberg, Div. of Intl. Mktg., Aromance Home Fragrance Products, Dept. CN, 4585 Simonton, Dallas, Texas 75244 U.S.A. **TELEPHONE:** 214-991-8094. **FAX:** 214-960-0219.

EASY-TO-APPLY VARNISH STOPS FIRE

"ClearCoat Varnish" protects wood against fire by making materials hard to ignite; if there is ignition, it keeps the materials burning slowly. Used by consumers, contractors, and woodworkers, this varnish is listed by Underwriters Laboratories as a Class A fire retardant. In addition to offering safety features, this varnish is water-based and uses special non-yellowing resins. It leaves a beautiful clear, satin finish. Price: $30/3.7 L. Agents are sought. **CONTACT:** Roni S. Lockhart, Mktg. Dir., Ocean Coatings, Dept. CN, 5364 Pan American NE., Albuquerque, New Mexico 87109 U.S.A. **TELEPHONE:** 505-883-8433. **FAX:** 505-888-9688.

Source: *Commercial News USA,* May 1992, 13.

to give to its distributor. An example of an advertisement for intermediaries placed in a government-sponsored medium is provided in Figure 12.4. Private-sector media vehicles are also used; for example, Medtech International, an exporter of surgical gloves advertises for intermediaries in magazines such as *International Hospital Supplies.* Trade

TABLE 12.5   Data Sources for Locating Foreign Intermediaries

1. Distributor inquiries
2. U.S. Department of Commerce
    New Product Information Service
    Trade Opportunities Program
    Foreign Traders Index
    Agent/Distributor Service
    World Traders Data Report
3. Trade sources
    Magazines, journals
    Directories
    Associations
    Banks, advertising agencies, carriers
4. Field sales organizations
5. Customers
6. Direct-mail solicitation/contact of previous applicants
7. Trade fairs
8. Independent consultants

fairs are an important forum to meet potential distributors and to get data on intermediaries in the industry. The marketer may also deal directly with contacts from previous applications, launch new mail solicitations, use its own sales organization for the search, or communicate with existing customers to find prospective distributors. The latter may happen after a number of initial (unsolicited) sales to a market, causing the firm to want to enter the market on a more formal basis. If resources permit, the international marketer can use outside service agencies or consultants to generate a list of prospective representatives.

The purpose of using the sources summarized in Table 12.5 is to generate as many prospective representatives as possible for the next step, screening.

Screening Intermediaries

In most firms, the evaluation of candidates involves both what to look for and where to go for the information. At this stage, the international marketer knows the type of distributor that is needed. The potential candidates must now be compared and contrasted against determining criteria. Although the criteria to be used vary by industry and by product, a good summary list is provided in Table 12.6. Especially when various criteria are being weighed, these lists must be updated to reflect changes in the environment and the marketer's own situation. Some criteria can be characterized as determinant, in that they form the core dimensions along which candidates must perform well, whereas some criteria, although important, may be used only in preliminary screening. This list should correspond closely to the exporter's own determinants of success—all the things that have to be done better to beat out competition.

Before signing a contract with a particular agent or a distributor, international marketers should satisfy themselves on certain key criteria. A number of these key criteria can be easily quantified, thereby providing a solid base for comparisons between candidates, whereas others are qualitative and require careful interpretation and confidence in the data sources providing the information.

Performance   The financial standing of the candidate is one of the most important criteria, as well as a good starting point. This figure will show whether the distributor is

	TABLE 12.6

Selection Criteria for Choosing an International Distributor

Characteristics	Weight	Rating
Goals and strategies		
Size of the firm		
Financial strength		
Reputation		
Trading areas covered		
Compatibility		
Experience		
Sales organization		
Physical facilities		
Willingness to carry inventories		
After-sales service capability		
Use of promotion		
Sales performance		
Relations with local government		
Communications		
Overall attitude		

Source: Franklin R. Root, *Foreign Market Entry Strategies* (New York: American Management Association, 1983), 74–75.

making money and is able to perform some of the necessary marketing functions such as extension of credit to customers and risk absorption. Financial reports are not always complete or reliable, or they may lend themselves to interpretation differences, pointing to a need for third-party opinion.

Sales are another excellent indicator. What the distributor is presently doing gives an indication of how he or she could perform if chosen to handle the international marketer's product. The distributor's sales strength can be determined by analyzing management ability and the adequacy and quality of the sales team.

The distributor's existing product lines should be analyzed along four dimensions: competitiveness, compatibility, complementary nature, and quality. Quite often, international marketers find that the most desirable distributors in a given market are already handling competitive products and are therefore unavailable. In that case, the marketer can look for an equally qualified distributor handling related products. The complementary nature of products may be of interest to both parties, especially in industrial markets, where ultimate customers may be in the market for complete systems or one-stop shopping. The quality match for products is important for product-positioning reasons; a high-quality product may suffer unduly from a questionable distributor reputation. The number of product lines handled gives the marketer an indication of the level of effort to expect from the distributor. Some distributors are interested in carrying as many products and product lines as possible to enhance their own standing, but they have the time and the willingness to actively sell only those that bring the best compensation. At this time, it is also important to check the candidate's physical facilities for handling the product. This is essential particularly for products that may be subject to quality changes, such as food products.

The distributor's market coverage must be determined. The analysis of coverage will include not only how much territory, or how many segments of the market, are covered but also how well the markets are served. Again, the characteristics of the sales force and the number of sales offices are good quantitative indicators. To study the quality of the distributor's market coverage, the marketer can check whether the sales force visits executives, engineers, and operating people or concentrates mainly on purchasing agents.

In some areas of the world, the marketer has to make sure that two distributors will not end up having territorial overlaps, which can lead to unnecessary conflict.

Professionalism The distributor's reputation must be checked. This rather abstract measure takes its value from a number of variables that all should help the marketer forecast effectiveness. The distributor's customers, suppliers, facilitating agencies, competitors, and other members of the local business community should be contacted for information on the business conduct of the distributor in such areas as buyer-seller relations and ethical behavior. This effort will shed light on variables that may be important only in certain parts of the world; for example, variables such as political clout, which is essential in certain developing countries.

The marketer must acknowledge the distributor as an independent entity with its own goals. The distributor's business strategy must therefore be determined, particularly what the distributor expects to get from the relationship and where the international marketer fits into those plans. Because a channel relationship is long term, the distributor's views on future expansion of the product line or its distribution should be clarified. This phase will also require a determination of the degree of help the distributor would need in terms of price, credit, delivery, sales training, communication, personal visits, product modification, warranty, advertising, warehousing, technical support, and after-sales service.[27] Leaving uncertainties in these areas will cause major problems later.

Finally, the marketer should determine the distributor's overall attitude in terms of cooperation and commitment to the marketer. An effective way of testing this, and weeding out the less-interested candidates, is to ask the distributor to assist in developing a local marketing plan or to develop one. This endeavor will bring out potential problem areas and will spell out which party is to perform the various marketing functions.

A criteria list is valuable only when good data are available on each and every criterion. Although the initial screening can take place at the firm's offices, the three to five finalists should be visited. No better method of assessing distributors exists than visiting them, inspecting their facilities, and interviewing their various constituents in the market. A number of other critical data sources are important for firms without the resources for on-site inspection. The distributor's suppliers or firms not in direct competition can provide in-depth information. A bona fide candidate will also provide information through a local bank. Credit reports are available through the National Association of Credit Management, Dun & Bradstreet, and local credit-reporting agencies. A list of the foreign sources of credit information is published by Trade Data Reports Inc.[28]

The Distributor Agreement

When the international marketer has found a suitable intermediary, a foreign sales agreement is drawn up. The agreement can be relatively simple, but given the numerous differences in the market environments, certain elements are essential. The checklist prepared by *Business International* (see Table 12.7) is the most comprehensive in stipulating the nature of the contract and the respective rights and responsibilities of the marketer and the distributor.

Contract duration is important, especially when an agreement is signed with a new distributor. In general, distribution agreements should be for a specified, relatively short

[27] "How to Evaluate Foreign Distributors," 145–149.
[28] "How to Check Credit Overseas," *Business International,* May 10, 1985, 149.

Elements of a Distributor Agreement   TABLE 12.7

A. Basic Components
    1. Parties to the agreement
    2. Statement that the contract supersedes all previous agreements
    3. Duration of the agreement (perhaps a three- or six-month trial period)
    4. Territory:
       a. Exclusive, nonexclusive, sole
       b. Manufacturer's right to sell direct at reduced or no commission to local government and old customers
    5. Products covered
    6. Expression of intent to comply with government regulations
    7. Clauses limiting sales forbidden by U.S. Export Controls or practices forbidden by the Foreign Corrupt Practices Act

B. Manufacturer's Rights
    1. Arbitration:
       a. If possible, in the manufacturer's country
       b. If not, before International Chamber of Commerce or American Arbitration Association, or using the London Court of Arbitration rules
       c. Definition of rules to be applied (e.g., in selecting the arbitration panel)
       d. Assurance that award will be binding in the distributor's country
    2. Jurisdiction that of the manufacturer's country (the signing completed at home); if not possible, a neutral site such as Sweden or Switzerland
    3. Termination conditions (e.g., no indemnification if due notice given)
    4. Clarification of tax liabilities
    5. Payment and discount terms
    6. Conditions for delivery of goods
    7. Nonliability for late delivery beyond manufacturer's reasonable control
    8. Limitation on manufacturer's responsibility to provide information
    9. Waiver of manufacturer's responsibility to keep lines manufactured outside the United States (e.g., licensees) outside of covered territory
   10. Right to change prices, terms, and conditions at any time
   11. Right of manufacturer or agent to visit territory and inspect books
   12. Right to repurchase stock
   13. Option to refuse or alter distributor's orders
   14. Training of distributor personnel in the United States subject to:
       a. Practicality
       b. Costs to be paid by the distributor
       c. Waiver of manufacturer's responsibility for U.S. immigration approval

C. Distributor's Limitations and Duties
    1. No disclosure of confidential information
    2. Limitation of distributor's right to assign contract
    3. Limitation of distributor's position as legal agent of manufacturer
    4. Penalty clause for late payment
    5. Limitation of right to handle competing lines
    6. Placement of responsibility for obtaining customs clearance
    7. Distributor to publicize designation as authorized representative in defined area
    8. Requirement to move all signs or evidence identifying distributor with manufacturer if relationship ends
    9. Acknowledgment by distributor of manufacturer's ownership of trademark, trade names, patents
   10. Information to be supplied by the distributor:
       a. Sales reports
       b. Names of active prospects
       c. Government regulations dealing with imports
       d. Competitive products and competitors' activities
       e. Price at which goods are sold
       f. Complete data on other lines carried (on request)
   11. Information to be supplied by distributor on purchasers

continued

| **TABLE 12.7** | *Continued* |

12. Accounting methods to be used by distributor
13. Requirement to display products appropriately
14. Duties concerning promotional efforts
15. Limitation of distributor's right to grant unapproved warranties, make excessive claims
16. Clarification of responsibility arising from claims and warranties
17. Responsibility of distributor to provide repair and other services
18. Responsibility to maintain suitable place of business
19. Responsibility to supply all prospective customers
20. Understanding that certain sales approaches and sales literature must be approved by manufacturer
21. Prohibition of manufacture or alteration of products
22. Requirement to maintain adequate stock, spare parts
23. Requirement that inventory be surrendered in event of a dispute that is pending in court
24. Prohibition of transshipments

Source: "Elements of a Distributor Agreement," *Business International,* March 29, 1963, 23–24. Reprinted with permission from Business International. Some of the sections have been changed to reflect the present situation.

period (one or two years). The initial contract with a new distributor should stipulate a trial period of either three or six months, possibly with minimum purchase requirements. Duration should be determined with an eye on the local laws and their stipulations on distributor agreements. These will be discussed later in conjunction with distributor termination.

Geographic boundaries for the distributor should be determined with care, especially by smaller firms. Future expansion of the product market might be complicated if a distributor claims rights to certain territories. The marketer should retain the right to distribute products independently, reserving the right to certain customers. For example, Parker Pen maintains a dual distribution system, dealing directly with certain large accounts. This type of arrangement should be explicitly stated in the agreement.

The payment section of the contract should stipulate the methods of payment as well as how the distributor or agent is to draw compensation. Distributors derive compensation from various discounts, such as the functional discount, whereas agents earn a specific commission percentage of net sales (such as 15 percent). Given the volatility of currency markets, the agreement should also state the currency to be used. The international marketer also needs to make sure that none of the compensation forwarded to the distributor is in violation of the Foreign Corrupt Practices Act. A violation occurs if a payment is made to influence a foreign official in exchange for business favors, depending on the nature of the action sought. So-called grease or **facilitating payments,** such as paying a small fee to expedite paperwork through customs, are not considered violations.[29]

Product and conditions of sale need to be agreed on. The products or product lines included should be stipulated, as well as the functions and responsibilities of the intermediary in terms of carrying the goods in inventory, providing service in conjunction with them, and promoting them. Conditions of sale determine which party is to be responsible for some of the expenses involved, which will in turn have an effect on the price to the distributor. These conditions include credit and shipment terms.

[29] Michael G. Harvey and Ilkka A. Ronkainen, "The Three Faces of the Foreign Corrupt Practices Act: Retain, Reform, or Repeal," in *1984 AMA Educators' Proceedings* (Chicago: American Marketing Association, 1984), 290–294.

Effective means of communication between the parties must be stipulated in the agreement if a marketer-distributor relationship is to succeed. The marketer should have access to all information concerning the marketing of his products in the distributor's territory, including past records, present situation assessments, and marketing research concerning the future. Communication channels should be formal for the distributor to voice formal grievances. The contract should state the confidentiality of the information provided by either party and protect the intellectual property rights (such as patents) involved.

CHANNEL MANAGEMENT

A channel relationship can be likened to a marriage in that it brings together two independent entities that have shared goals. For the relationship to work, each party must be open about its expectations and openly communicate changes perceived in the other's behavior that might be contrary to the agreement. The closer the relationship is to a distribution partnership, the more likely marketing success will materialize. Conflict will arise, ranging from small grievances (such as billing errors) to major ones (rivalry over channel duties), but it can be managed to enhance the overall channel relationship. In some cases, conflict may be caused by an outside entity, such as gray markets, in which unauthorized intermediaries compete for market share with legitimate importers and exclusive distributors. Nevertheless, the international marketer must solve the problem.

The relationship has to be managed for the long term. An exporter may in some countries have a seller's market situation that allows it to exert pressure on its intermediaries for concessions, for example. However, if environmental conditions change, the exporter may find that the channel support it needs to succeed is not there because of the manner in which it managed channel relationships in the past.[30]

Factors in Channel Management

An excellent framework for managing channel relationships is shown in Figure 12.5. The complicating factors that separate the two parties fall into three categories: ownership, geographic and cultural distance, and different rules of law. Rather than lament over their existence, both parties need to take strong action to remedy them. Often, the major step is acknowledgment that differences do indeed exist.

In international marketing, manufacturers and distributors are usually independent entities. Distributors typically carry the products of more than one manufacturer and judge products by their ability to generate revenue without added expense. The international marketer, in order to receive disproportionate attention for its concerns, may offer both monetary and psychological rewards.

Distance, whether it is geographic, psychological, or a combination of both, can be bridged through effective two-way communication. This should go beyond normal routine business communication to include innovative ways of sharing pertinent information. The international marketer may place one person in charge of distributor-related communications or put into effect an interpenetration strategy—that is, an exchange of personnel so that both organizations gain further insight into the workings of the

---

[30] Gary L. Frazier, James D. Gill, and Sudhir H. Kale, "Dealer Dependence Levels and Reciprocal Actions in a Channel of Distribution in a Developing Country," *Journal of Marketing* 53 (January 1989): 50–69.

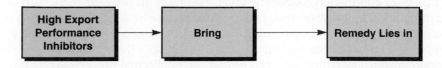

FIGURE 12.5   **Performance Problems and Remedies When Using Overseas Distributors**

High Export Performance Inhibitors	Bring	Remedy Lies in
Separate Ownership	• Divided Loyalties • Seller-Buyer Atmosphere • Unclear Future Intentions	Offering good incentives, helpful support schemes, discussing plan frankly, and interacting in a mutually beneficial way
Geographic and Cultural Separation	• Communication Blocks • Negative Attitudes toward Foreigners • Physical Distribution Strains	Making judicious use of two-way visits establishing a well-managed communication program
Different Rules of Law	• Vertical Trading Restrictions • Dismissal Difficulties	Full compliance with the law, drafting a strong distributor agreement

Source: Philip J. Rosson, "Success Factors in Manufacturer-Overseas Distributor Relationships in International Marketing," in *International Marketing Management,* ed. Erdener Kaynak, 1984 (New York: Praeger, 1984) 91–107.

other.[31] The existence of cross-cultural differences in people's belief systems and behavior patterns have to be acknowledged and acted on for effective channel management. For example, in markets where individualism is stressed, local channel partners may seek arrangements that foster their own self-interest and may expect their counterparts to watch out for themselves. Conflict is seen as a natural phenomenon. In societies of low individualism, however, a common purpose is fostered between the partners.[32]

Laws and regulations in many markets may restrict the manufacturer in terms of control. For example, in the European Union, the international marketer cannot prevent a distributor from reexporting products to customers in another member country, even though the marketer has another distributor in that market. The only remedy is to include the necessary stipulations in the distributor agreement, for example, a clause prohibiting transshipments.

Most of the criteria used in selecting intermediaries can be used to evaluate existing intermediaries as well. If not conducted properly and fairly, however, evaluation can be a source of conflict. In addition to being given the evaluation results in order to take appropriate action, the distributor should be informed of the evaluative criteria and should be a part of the overall assessment process. Again, the approach should be as a partnership, not buyer-seller.

A part of the management process is channel adjustment. This can take the form of channel shift (eliminating a particular type of channel), channel modification (changing

[31] Bert Rosenbloom, *Marketing Channels: A Management View,* 4th ed. (Hinsdale, IL: Dryden Press, 1991), 415.

[32] Sudhir H. Kale and Roger P. McIntyre, "Distribution Channel Relationships in Diverse Cultures," *International Marketing Review* 8 (1991): 31–45.

individual members while leaving channel structure intact), or role or relationship modification (changing functions performed or the reward structure) as a result of channel evaluation.[33] The need for channel change should be well established and not executed hastily because it will cause a major distraction in the operations of the firm. Some companies have instituted procedures that require executives to carefully consider all of the aspects and potential results of change before execution.

A Special Problem: Gray Markets

Gray markets, or **parallel importation,** refer to authentic and legitimately manufactured trademark items that are produced and purchased abroad but imported or diverted to the United States by bypassing designated channels.[34] The value of gray markets in the United States has been estimated at $6 to $10 billion at retail. Gray marketed products vary from inexpensive consumer goods (such as chewing gum) to expensive capital goods (such as excavation equipment). The phenomenon is not restricted to the United States; Japan, for example, is witnessing gray markets because of the high value of the yen and the subsidization of cheaper exports through high taxes. Japanese marketers often find it cheaper to go to Los Angeles to buy export versions of Japanese-made products.[35]

An example of the phenomenon is provided in Figure 12.6, which shows the flow of Seiko watches through authorized and unauthorized channels. Seiko is a good example of a typical gray market product in that it carries a well-known trademark. Unauthorized importers, such as Progress Trading Company in New York, and retailers, such as Montgomery Ward, buy Seiko watches around the world at advantageous prices and then sell them to consumers at substantial discounts over authorized Seiko dealers. Seiko has fought back, for example, by advertising warnings to consumers against buying gray market watches on the grounds that these products may be obsolete or worn-out models and that consumers might have problems with their warranties. Many gray marketers, however, provide their own warranty-related service and guarantee watches sold through them.

Various conditions allow unauthorized resellers to exist. The most important are price segmentation and exchange rate fluctuations. Competitive conditions may require the international marketer to sell essentially the same product at different prices in different markets or to different customers. Because many products are priced higher in, for example, the United States, a gray marketer can purchase them in Europe or the Far East and offer discounts between 10 and 40 percent below list price when reselling them in the U.S. market. Exchange rate fluctuations can cause price differentials and thus opportunities for gray marketers. For example, when the value of the dollar was high in 1984 and 1985, gray marketers imported Caterpillar excavators and loaders built in Scotland, Belgium, and Japan into the United States at prices 15 percent lower than those for the same equipment built in Caterpillar's domestic plants.[36] In some cases, gray markets emerge as a result of product shortages. For example, in 1988, many U.S. computer manufacturers had to turn to gray marketers to secure their supply of

---

[33] J. Taylor Sims, J. Robert Foster, and Arch G. Woodside, *Marketing Channels: Systems and Strategies,* 3d ed. (New York: Harper & Row, 1977).

[34] Ilkka A. Ronkainen and Linda van de Gucht, "Making a Case for Gray Markets," *Journal of Commerce,* January 6, 1987, 13A.

[35] Dan Koeppel, "'Gyakuyunyu' Takes Hold in Japan," *Adweek's Marketing Week,* March 20, 1989, 22.

[36] Frank V. Cespedes, E. Raymond Corey, and V. Kasturi Rangan, "Gray Markets: Causes and Cures," *Harvard Business Review* 66 (July–August 1988): 75–82.

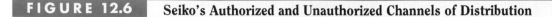

FIGURE 12.6   Seiko's Authorized and Unauthorized Channels of Distribution

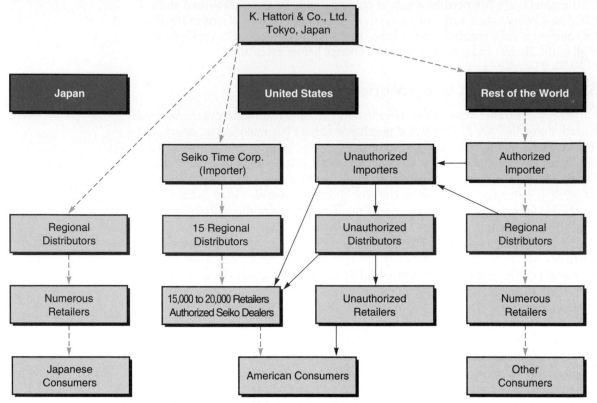

- - - ▶ Broken arrows denote the flow of Seiko watches through authorized channels of distribution.
——▶ Solid arrows denote the flow of Seiko watches through unauthorized channels of distribution.

Source: Jack Kaikati, "Parallel Importation: A Growing Conflict in International Channels of Distribution," Symposium on Export-Import Interrelationships, Georgetown University, November 14–15, 1985.

DRAMs or else watch their production lines grind to a halt.[37] However, in these cases, the gray market goods typically cost more than those usually available through authorized suppliers.

Opponents and supporters of the practice disagree on whether the central issue is price or trade rights. Detractors typically cite the following arguments: (1) the gray market unduly hurts the legitimate owners of trademarks; (2) without protection, trademark owners will have little incentive to invest in product development; (3) gray marketers will "free ride," or take unfair advantage of the trademark owners' marketing and promotional activities; and (4) parallel imports can deceive consumers by not meeting U.S. product standards or their normal expectations of after-sale service. The bottom line is that gray market goods can severely undercut local marketing plans, erode long-term brand images, eat up costly promotion funds, and sour manufacturer-intermediary relations.

Proponents of parallel importation approach the issue from an altogether different point of view. They argue for their right to "free trade" by pointing to manufacturers that are both overproducing and overpricing in some markets. The main beneficiaries are consumers, who benefit from lower prices, and discount distributors, with whom

[37] "How the Gray Marketeers Are Cashing In on DRAM Shortages," *Electronic Business*, June 1, 1988, 18–19.

THE INTERNATIONAL MARKETPLACE

12.4

No Black or White in Gray Market Cases

The battle over the proper treatment of gray market goods has raged for many years. On the one hand, authorized distributors insist that they should be able to block imports of merchandise intended for foreign markets because of quality differences of goods intended for their customers. Parallel importers say they should be able to roam the world for best buys, and that any product authorized to carry a brand name in even one country is a genuine article.

The U.S. Customs Service has been trying to steer a middle course. Under its policy, if an independent U.S. company buys the U.S. rights to sell a brand, it can block its sales by other companies. Similarly, if a U.S. manufacturer licenses an independent overseas company to use its trademark in its own country, the U.S. company can stop imports of that merchandise. But if the U.S. trademark owner and the foreign trademark owner are part of the same corporate family, there can be no bar to importation.

This has been official government policy since 1972, but in 1993, the U.S. Court of Appeals ruled that the policy is not correct. The ruling came in Lever Brothers' long battle to stop U.S. discounters from selling Sunlight brand dishwashing detergent produced for the British market. Because tap water is generally harder in Britain, formulation of the product there is different from Lever's U.S. version, which produces more lather. Lever says it received many complaints from customers who bought the British brand and were disappointed. In a similar situation with Shield deodorant soap, Lever reported losing $5 million in U.S. sales to the invading British version.

The ruling in *Lever Brothers v. U.S.* applies only to imports of goods that are substantially different from the U.S. version. But a ruling in another case in Boston found that Nestlé could use its right as exclusive importer of Perugina chocolates in the United States to keep out chocolates legally produced under that name in Venezuela. Even minor variations in quality-control procedures and in the recipes (the Italian version has 5 percent more milk fat than that made in Venezuela) are enough to mislead shoppers, the judges reasoned.

Source: "Brand Battles," *International Business*, April 1993, 83.

some of the manufacturers do not want to deal and who have now, because of gray markets, found a profitable market niche.

In response to the challenge, manufacturers have chosen various approaches. Despite the Supreme Court ruling in May 1988 to legitimize gray markets in the United States,[38] foreign manufacturers, U.S. companies manufacturing abroad, and authorized retailers have continued to fight the practice. In January 1991, the U.S. Customs Service enacted a new rule whereby trademarked goods that have been authorized for manufacture and sale abroad by U.S. trademark holders will no longer be allowed into the United States through parallel channels.[39] Those parallel importing goods of overseas manufacturers will not be affected. Recently, courts have taken an exception to cases that have shown evidence of consumer deception, as shown in The International Marketplace 12.4.

[38] "A Red-Letter Day for Gray Marketeers," *Business Week*, June 13, 1988, 30.

[39] Ellen Klein and J. D. Howard, "Strings Attached," *North American International Business* 6 (May 1991): 54–55.

The solution for the most part lies with the contractual relationships that tie businesses together. In almost all of the cases of gray marketing, someone in the authorized channel commits a diversion, thus violating the agreements signed. One of the standard responses is therefore disenfranchisement of such violators. This approach is a clear response to complaints from the authorized dealers who are being hurt by transshipments. Tracking down offenders is quite expensive and time-consuming, however. Some of the gray marketers can be added to the authorized dealer network if mutually acceptable terms can be reached, thereby increasing control of the channel of distribution.[40]

A one-price policy can eliminate one of the main reasons for gray markets. This means choosing the most efficient of the distribution channels through which to market the product, but it may also mean selling at the lowest price to all customers regardless of location and size. A meaningful one-price strategy must also include a way to reward the providers of other services, such as warranty repair, in the channel.

Other strategies have included producing different versions of products for different markets. For example, Minolta Camera Company markets an identical camera in the United States and Japan but gives it different names and warranties.[41] Some companies have introduced price incentives to consumers. Hasselblad, the Swedish camera manufacturer, offers rebates to purchasers of legally imported, serial-numbered camera bodies, lenses, and roll-fill magazines.[42]

Termination of the Channel Relationship

Many reasons exist for the termination of a channel relationship, but the most typical are changes in the international marketer's distribution approach (for example, establishing a sales office) or a (perceived) lack of performance by the intermediary.

If termination is a result of a structural change, the situation has to be handled carefully. The effect of termination on the intermediary has to be understood, and open communication is needed to make the transition smooth. For example, the intermediary can be compensated for investments made, and major customers can be visited jointly to assure them that service will be uninterrupted.

Termination conditions are one of the most important considerations in the distributor agreement because the just causes for termination vary and the penalties for the international marketer may be substantial. Just causes include fraud or deceit, damage to the other party's interest, or failure to comply with contract obligations concerning minimum inventory requirements or minimum sales levels. These must be spelled out carefully because local courts are often favorably disposed toward local businesses. In some countries, termination may not even be possible.[43] In the EU and Latin America, terminating an ineffective intermediary is time-consuming and expensive. One year's average commissions are typical for termination without justification. A notice of termination has to be given three to six months in advance. In Austria, termination without just cause and/or failure to give notice of termination may result in damages amounting to average commissions for between 1 and 15 years.[44]

[40] For a comprehensive discussion on remedies, see Robert E. Weigand, "Parallel Import Channels—Options for Preserving Territorial Integrity," *Columbia Journal of World Business* 26 (Spring 1991): 53–60, and S. Tamer Cavusgil and Ed Sikora, "How Multinationals Can Counter Gray Market Imports," *Columbia Journal of World Business* 23 (Winter 1988): 75–85.

[41] "Now, Japan Is Feeling the Heat from the Gray Market," *Business Week,* March 14, 1988, 50–51.

[42] Gay Jervey, "Gray Markets Hit Camera, Watch Sales," *Advertising Age,* August 15, 1983, 3, 62.

[43] Jack Kaikati, "The Marketing Environment in Saudi Arabia," *Akron Business and Economic Review* 7 (Summer 1976): 5–13.

[44] Ovidio M. Giberga, "Laws Restrain Agency Agreement Termination," in *Foreign Business Practices* (Washington, D.C.: Department of Commerce, 1981), 86–95.

The time to think about such issues is before the overseas distribution agreement is signed. It is especially prudent to find out what local laws say about termination and to check what type of experience other firms have had in the particular country. Careful preparation can allow the exporter to negotiate a termination without litigation.[45] If the distributor's performance is unsatisfactory, careful documentation and clearly defined performance measures may help show that the distributor has more to gain going quietly than by fighting.

THE INTERNATIONAL SHIPMENT

With a channel system in place, the next concern of the international marketer is getting the product to the distributor. In domestic operations, this typically involves only (1) the shipper, a carrier, and the receiver and (2) relatively simple paperwork. International shipments are more complicated on both dimensions.

International shipments usually involve not just one carrier but multiple types of carriers. The shipment must be routed to the port of export, where it is transferred to another mode of transportation—for example, from truck or rail to vessel. Documentation for international shipments is universally perceived as so complicated, especially by smaller firms, that it becomes a trade barrier. A Canadian study found that 46 person-hours were needed for the processing of one export shipment;[46] the U.S. Department of Transportation pegged the required time at 36 hours.[47] As the result of recent efforts toward standardization, most of the documents needed are now aligned through a system called the U.S. Standard Master for International Trade. Certain standard entries, such as export carrier and document number, are in the same position on all of the forms. As part of the 1992 program, the EU simplified its required documentation for shipments. Whereas drivers earlier needed two pounds of documents on a route, for example, from Amsterdam to Lisbon, they now need only a single piece of paper. The savings on the elimination of this red tape is significant.[48] Increasingly, electronic data transfer will be replacing paperwork.

Few international marketers, especially small or medium-sized firms and those new to exporting, are familiar with the many and varied details involved in transportation. These may include arranging for shipment from the factory, transfer from train to vessel, securing of rates and space on vessels, clearing U.S. Customs, stowing, delivery at the port of destination to docks, clearance through local customs, and finally, delivery to the buyer. Larger exporters have a separate department or staff to secure transportation services and proper documentation, whereas smaller firms rely on support agencies for this work.

Documentation

In the most simple form of exporting, the only documents needed are a **bill of lading** and an export declaration. Most exports fit under a general license, which is a generalized authorization consisting simply of a number to be shown on the documents. Certain goods

[45] "Foreign Distributors: How MNCs Can Avoid the Termination Minefield," *Business International,* July 12, 1985, 217–218.

[46] Wayne D. Mays, "Documentary Problems of International Transportation," *Journal of World Trade Law* 12 (November–December 1978): 506–518.

[47] Roy J. Sampson, Martin Farris, and David L. Shrock, *Domestic Transportation: Practice, Theory, and Policy* (Boston: Houghton Mifflin, 1985), 106.

[48] "Reshaping Europe: 1992 and Beyond," *Business Week,* December 12, 1988, 48–51

TABLE 12.8	Documentation for an International Shipment

A. Documents Required by the U.S. Government
  1. Shipper's export declaration
  2. Export license

B. Commercial Documents
  1. Commercial invoice
  2. Packing list
  3. Inland bill of lading
  4. Dock receipt
  5. Bill of lading or airway bill
  6. Insurance policies or certificates
  7. Shipper's declaration for dangerous goods

C. Import Documents
  1. Import license
  2. Foreign exchange license
  3. Certificate of origin
  4. Consular invoice
  5. Customs invoice

Source: Dun & Bradstreet, *Exporter's Encyclopedia* (New York: Dun & Bradstreet, 1985), and Marta Ortiz-Buonafina, *Profitable Export Marketing* (Englewood Cliffs, NJ: Prentice-Hall, 1984), 218–246.

and data require a special validated license for export, as discussed in a previous chapter. For importation, the basic documents are a bill of lading and an invoice. Table 12.8 provides a summary of the main documents used in international shipments.

The **bill of lading** (see Figure 12.7) is the most important document to the shipper, the carrier, and the buyer. It acknowledges receipt of the goods, represents the basic contract between the shipper and the carrier, and serves as evidence of title to the goods for collection by the purchaser. Various types of bills of lading exist. The inland bill of lading is a contract between the inland carrier and the shipper. Bills of lading may be negotiable instruments in that they may be endorsed to other parties (order bill) or may be nonnegotiable (straight). The **shipper's export declaration** (see Figure 12.8) states proper authorization for export and serves as a means for governmental data-collection efforts.

The packing list, if used, lists in some detail the contents, the gross and net weights, and dimensions of each package. Some shipments, such as corrosives, flammables, and poisons, require a **shipper's declaration for dangerous goods.** When the international marketer is responsible for moving the goods to the U.S. port of export, a dock receipt (for ocean freight) or a warehouse receipt (if the goods are stored) is issued before the issuance of the bill of lading. Collection documents must also be produced and always include a commercial invoice (a detailed description of the transaction), often a **consular invoice** (required by certain countries for data-collection purposes), and a **certificate of origin** (required by certain countries to ensure correct tariffs). Insurance documents are produced when stipulated by the transaction. In certain countries, especially in Latin America, two additional documents are needed. An **import license** may be required for certain types or amounts of particular goods, while a **foreign exchange license** allows the importer to secure the needed hard currency to pay for the shipment. The exporter has to provide the importer with the data needed to obtain these licenses from governmental authorities and should make sure, before the actual shipment, that the importer has indeed secured the documents. All commercial shipments to Germany, regardless of value or mode of transport, require a commercial invoice, bill of lading (or airway bill), certificate of origin, and any special documents required due to the type of goods being forwarded.

Bill of Lading **FIGURE 12.7**

ACL

BILL OF LADING

ACL

SHIPPER/EXPORTER	DOCUMENT NO. / BOOKING NO.
	EXPORT REFERENCES
	FORWARDER REF. NO.
	SHIPPER'S REF. NO.
CONSIGNEE	FORWARDING AGENT. F.M.C. NO.
	POINT AND COUNTRY OF ORIGIN / PLACE OF RECEIPT *
NOTIFY PARTY	DOMESTIC ROUTING/EXPORT INSTRUCTIONS
PIER	
EXPORTING CARRIER / PORT OF LOADING	PLACE OF DELIVERY *
PORT OF DISCHARGE / FOR TRANSSHIPMENT TO	

PARTICULARS FURNISHED BY SHIPPER

MARKS AND NUMBERS	NO. OF PKGS.	DESCRIPTION OF PACKAGES AND GOODS	GROSS WEIGHT	MEASUREMENT

*APPLICABLE ONLY WHEN USED AS THROUGH BILL OF LADING
AS PER CLAUSE 3 (III) ON REVERSE HEREOF.

PREPAID	COLLECT	FREIGHT AND CHARGES PAYABLE AT_____	ALL CHARGES EX SHIPS TACKLE FOR ACCOUNT OF CARGO

ACL
an affiliate of:
Cie Generale Maritime
The Cunard Steam-Ship Company Ltd.
Intercontinental Transport (ICT) BV
Swedish American Line
Swedish Transatlantic Line
Wallenius Line

RECEIVED by ACL for shipment by ocean vessel, between port of loading and port of discharge, and for arrangement or procurement of precarriage from place of receipt and on-carriage to place of delivery where stated above, the goods as specified above in apparent good order and condition unless otherwise stated. The goods to be delivered at the above mentioned port of discharge or place of delivery, whichever applicable. Subject always to the exceptions, limitations, conditions and liberties set out on the reverse side hereof, to which the Merchant agrees by accepting this B/L.

In Witness whereof three (3) original Bs/L have been signed, if not otherwise stated above, one of which being accomplished the other(s) to be void.

For **ACL**

B/L NUMBER	DATE

Source: Seaschott.

FIGURE 12.8 Shipper's Export Declaration

U.S. DEPARTMENT OF COMMERCE – BUREAU OF THE CENSUS – INTERNATIONAL TRADE ADMINISTRATION

FORM **7525-V** (1-1-88) **SHIPPER'S EXPORT DECLARATION** OMB No. 0607-0018

1a. EXPORTER *(Name and address including ZIP code)*

ZIP CODE

2. DATE OF EXPORTATION

3. BILL OF LADING/AIR WAYBILL NO.

b. EXPORTER'S EIN (IRS) NO.

c. PARTIES TO TRANSACTION ☐ Related ☐ Non-related

4a. ULTIMATE CONSIGNEE

b. INTERMEDIATE CONSIGNEE

5. FORWARDING AGENT

6. POINT (STATE) OF ORIGIN OR FTZ NO.

7. COUNTRY OF ULTIMATE DESTINATION

8. LOADING PIER *(Vessel only)*

9. MODE OF TRANSPORT *(Specify)*

10. EXPORTING CARRIER

11. PORT OF EXPORT

12. PORT OF UNLOADING *(Vessel and air only)*

13. CONTAINERIZED *(Vessel only)* ☐ Yes ☐ No

14. SCHEDULE B DESCRIPTION OF COMMODITIES,
15. MARKS, NOS., AND KINDS OF PACKAGES
(Use columns 17–19)

D/F (16)	SCHEDULE B NUMBER (17)	CHECK DIGIT	QUANTITY – SCHEDULE B UNIT(S) (18)	SHIPPING WEIGHT *(Kilos)* (19)	VALUE (U.S. dollars, omit cents) *(Selling price or cost if not sold)* (20)

21. VALIDATED LICENSE NO./GENERAL LICENSE SYMBOL

22. ECCN *(When required)*

23. Duly authorized officer or employee | The exporter authorizes the forwarder named above to act as forwarding agent for export control and customs purposes.

24. I certify that all statements made and all information contained herein are true and correct and that I have read and understand the instructions for preparation of this document, set forth in the "**Correct Way to Fill Out the Shipper's Export Declaration.**" I understand that civil and criminal penalties, including forfeiture and sale, may be imposed for making false or fraudulent statements herein, failing to provide the requested information or for violation of U.S. laws on exportation (13 U.S.C. Sec. 305; 22 U.S.C. Sec. 401; 18 U.S.C. Sec. 1001; 50 U.S.C. App. 2410).

Signature | **Confidential** - For use solely for official purposes authorized by the Secretary of Commerce (13 U.S.C. 301 (g))

Title | *Export shipments are subject to inspection by U.S. Customs Service and/or Office of Export Enforcement*

Date | 25. AUTHENTICATION *(When required)*

This form may be printed by private parties provided it conforms to the official form. For sale by the Superintendent of Documents, Government Printing Office, Washington, D.C. 20402, and local Customs District Directors. The "**Correct Way to Fill Out the Shipper's Export Declaration**" is available from the Bureau of the Census, Washington, D.C. 20233.

Source: Seaschott.

Two guidelines are critical in dealing with customs anywhere in the world: sufficient knowledge or experience in dealing with the customs service in question and sufficient preparation for the process.[49] Whatever the required documents, their proper preparation is of utmost importance. Improper or missing documents can easily lead to difficulties that will delay payment or even prevent it. Furthermore, improper documentation

[49] Philippe Bruno, "Getting Your Goods through EC Customs," *Export Today* 9 (January–February 1993): 17–23.

THE INTERNATIONAL MARKETPLACE   12.5

Dealing with Customs

The U.S. Customs Service is responsible for enforcing the rules and regulations of more than 40 government agencies. In 1993, Customs collected $21.6 billion in duties, taxes, and fees on goods. In its effort to fulfill its expanding tasks in an era of tightening budgets, the agency has centralized inspections, reassessed personnel needs, and deployed the Automated Commercial Service, a computer network for the management and processing of trade information. Because of automation, Customs handled a 100 percent increase in work load during the 1980s with only 7 percent more people.

The extent of its task and the volume of trade make the agency a target of criticism. It processes over seven million merchandise entries a year, and for the majority of importers, the main complaint is the delay in clearing their shipments. "You can get a shipment from the Orient in a matter of hours— and have it sit for 12 days in some cases," says Gordon Freund, chairman of the Textile and Apparel Group of the American Association of Exporters and Importers. Some shipments may be tied up longer if improprieties are alleged. Despite the automation, each shipment still requires an average of ten documents.

Customs officials reject the majority of such criticisms. A rising percentage of goods—about 80 percent in large ports like New York—is cleared without requiring any inspection beyond simple document checks. The most expensive checks for importers, such as those involving the emptying of entire shipping containers, rarely occur unless customs agents find discrepancies in documents or discover violations during cursory dockside inspections.

Customs violations run the gamut from innocent mistakes and simple negligence, such as improper labeling, to outright fraud by importers seeking to bring in counterfeit goods, dodge quotas, or avoid duties. Penalties for criminal fraud can be as severe as two years' imprisonment and a $5,000 fine for each violation. False labeling that results in underpayment of duty can lead to a penalty of eight times the amount of underpayment in the case of fraud or two times the value in the case of simple negligence.

Customs has the authority to seize goods, order them returned to their country of origin, damage them if necessary in its investigation, and order their return for further inspection if examination of samples raises questions. Disputes may last years if appealed to the federal courts.

Sources: "Modernizing U.S. Customs," *Journal of Commerce, International Edition* 42 (January 1992), 6; "Importers' 'Horror Stories,'" *New York Times*, April 21, 1987, D1; updated by interview January 1994.

may cause problems with customs, as shown in The International Marketplace 12.5. If a customs service seizes the merchandise, delays can be measured in weeks and may end up in a total financial loss for the particular shipment. However, with adherence to release procedures, a seizure case can usually be guided through without major loss to the international marketer.[50]

---

[50] David Serko and Barry Kaplan, "What to Do When Customs Seizes Your Merchandise," *Global Trade* 3 (October 1988): 15–16.

Support Agencies for International Shipments

Several types of support agencies provide services in the physical movement of goods. Since any delays in product delivery are likely to have an immediate adverse effect on future sales, one of the most crucial distribution decisions an exporter makes involves the selection of an international freight forwarder.[51] An **international freight forwarder** acts as an agent for the international marketer in moving cargo to the overseas destination. Independent freight forwarders are regulated and should be certified by the Federal Maritime Commission. The forwarder advises the marketer on shipping documentation and packing costs and will prepare and review the documents to ensure that they are in order. Forwarders will also book the necessary space aboard a carrier. They will make necessary arrangements to clear outbound goods with customs and, after clearance, forward the documents either to the customer or to the paying bank. A **customs broker** serves as an agent for an importer with authority to clear inbound goods through customs and ship them on to their destination. These functions are performed for a fee. Customs brokers are regulated by the U.S. Customs Service. Nonvessel-operating **common carriers** consolidate freight into containers and thus provide attractive rates to international marketers whose shipments are less than full containerloads.

SUMMARY

Channels of distribution consist of the marketing intermediaries that facilitate the movement of goods and services. Decisions that must be made to establish an international channel of distribution focus on channel design and the selection of intermediaries for the roles that the international marketer will not perform. The channel must be designed to meet the requirements of the intended customer base, coverage, long-term continuity of the channel once it is established, and the quality of coverage to be achieved. Having determined the basic design of the channel, the international marketer will then decide on the number of different types of intermediaries to use and how many of each type. The process is important because the majority of international sales involve distributors, and channel decisions are the most long-term of all marketing decisions. Once the channel is in place, shipping goods may require the help of additional support agencies. The more the channel operation resembles a team, rather than a collection of independent businesses, the more effective the overall marketing effort will be.

Questions for Discussion

1. Relate these two statements: "A channel of distribution can be compared to a marriage." "The number-one reason given for divorce is lack of communication."

2. Channels of distribution tend to vary according to the level of economic development of a market. The more developed the economy, the shorter the channels tend to be. Why?

3. If a small exporter lacks the resources for an on-site inspection, what measures would you propose for screening potential distributors?

4. The international marketer and the distributor will have different expectations concerning the relationship. Why should these expectations be spelled out and clarified in the contract?

---

[51] Ken Yokeum, "How to Select a Freight Fowarder," *Export Today* 6 (October 1990): 35–37.

5. What courses of action are open to an international marketer who finds all attractive intermediaries already under contract to competitors?

6. One method of screening candidates is to ask distributors for a simple marketing plan. What items would you want included in this plan?

7. What are the functions performed by an international freight forwarder?

8. Using the *Exporter's Encyclopedia* published by Dun & Bradstreet, outline the documentation needed for shipments to (a) France, (b) Senegal, (c) Argentina, (d) Papua New Guinea, (e) People's Republic of China, and (f) Canada.

Recommended Readings

Czinkota, Michael R., and Jon Woronoff. *Unlocking Japan's Market.* Rutland, VT: Tuttle Co., 1993.

Hutt, Michael D., and Thomas W. Speh. *Business Marketing Management.* Fort Worth, TX: Dryden Press, 1992.

International Chamber of Commerce. *Guide to Incoterms 1990.* New York: ICC Publishing Corp., 1991.

International Chamber of Commerce. *Model Agency Contracts for International Trade.* New York: ICC Publishing Corp., 1991.

U.S. Department of Commerce. *A Basic Guide to Exporting.* Washington, D.C.: Government Printing Office, 1992.

Rosenbloom, Bert. *Marketing Channels: A Management View.* Hinsdale, IL: Dryden Press, 1991.

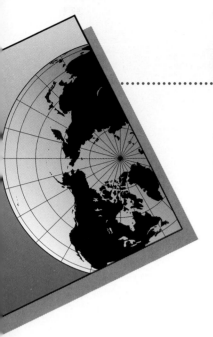

CHAPTER 13

Licensing, Franchising, and Export Intermediaries

13.1

THE INTERNATIONAL MARKETPLACE

Pizza Franchises Bring in the Dough

International franchising can be an extremely effective market-entry method. The phenomenal international expansion of Domino's Pizza illustrates the potential of franchising as a method of expanding into new markets while retaining the very elements of one's success: consistent products and services. Following this recipe, Domino's has made impressive strides exporting its marketing concept around the world. Throughout its expansion, Domino's found that, as is common with any international franchising program, the success of each franchise is dependent on foreign employees who uphold the standards of quality and service of the franchiser while accommodating cultural differences. Domino's Pizza in Japan is a good example of such a success.

When Ernest Higa, a Japanese-American, considered franchising Domino's, he found the history of pizza in Japan to be dismal. Faced with the research conclusion that pizza and Japan do not mix, Higa set out to prove otherwise. He believed that the key was to make suitable alterations appropriate for the market.

In Japan, the changes began with the size of the pizza. In Higa's words, "The Japanese aren't big eaters, big portions turn off consumers here, especially women." So he trimmed the product from 12 to 10 inches. Food delivery in Japan, "demae," is usually expected. Faced with such obstacles as crowded streets and very limited parking, Higa provided his employees with newly designed scooters to help them deliver the pizzas. Higa discovered that the Japanese consumer associates delivery businesses with small-scale, mom-and-pop operations and limited service capacity. Therefore, he upgraded the marketing materials provided by U.S. headquarters by producing four-color advertisements and handbills. And, of course, new pizza flavors were introduced, flavors so appetizing that taste-testers clamored for bowls of rice to go with them.

Today, Higa who now owns 98 franchises in Japan, runs the most successful Domino's operation abroad, and his franchises average more than double the volume of a typical American Domino's.

Adapted from Greg Matusky, "Going Global: Franchisors Crack New Overseas Markets," *Success*, April 1993, 59–63.

Quite frequently, firms recognize the value of marketing internationally, but either they lack sufficient capital or human resources for direct exporting or foreign direct investment, or they consider these strategies to be inappropriate. This chapter suggests alternatives for participation in the international marketplace. For the moving of services and expertise abroad, the chapter focuses primarily on licensing and franchising, an example of which is described in The International Marketplace 13.1. It describes how these arrangements function, the opportunities they provide, and their drawbacks. In addition, the use of market intermediaries is explained. These include, primarily, export management companies, Webb-Pomerene associations, and export trading companies.

Licensing, franchising, and the use of market intermediaries are alternatives open to and used by all types of firms, large and small. They offer flexibility in the foreign market approach, depending on the needs of the firm and the circumstances in the market. A small firm, for example, may choose to use licensing to benefit from a foreign business concept or to expand without much capital investment. A multinational corporation may use the same strategy to rapidly enter foreign markets in order to take advantage of new conditions and foreclose some opportunities to its competition. Similarly, a new-to-export firm may use intermediaries because of a lack of in-house expertise with exporting, whereas an experienced international firm may do the same to take advantage of specific country expertise. It is important to recognize licensing, franchising, and the use of export intermediaries as additional opportunities for market expansion. These options can be used both in lieu of or in addition to the trade strategies discussed previously. Another set of options—consisting of foreign direct investment, joint ventures, and management contracts—will be addressed later in the book.

LICENSING

Under a licensing agreement, one firm, the licensor, permits another to use its intellectual property in exchange for compensation designated as a royalty. The recipient firm is the licensee. The property might include patents, trademarks, copyrights, technology, technical know-how, or specific marketing skills. For example, a firm that has developed new packaging for liquids can permit other firms abroad to use the same process. Licensing therefore amounts to exporting and importing intangibles. As the International Marketplace 13.2 shows, licensing has great potential that may increase for a long time to come.

THE INTERNATIONAL MARKETPLACE

Technology Licensing Grows Rapidly

New-product development is regarded as crucial for a firm's competitiveness and success. As an alternative to firm-internal research and development, "technology licensing" is growing in popularity. Technology licensing is a contractual agreement by which a firm acquires the rights to product, process, or management technology from another firm for a lump-sum payment or royalties. In effect, the firm buys technology for product development.

Small firms are typically the licensee in such an arrangement. A firm's decision to engage in new-product technology licensing can be driven by any or all of the following reasons: to reduce risk and cost; to ensure speedy market entry; to fill product gaps; to overcome internal resource limitations such as lack of funds, product design skills, and time; and to ensure survival.

The international marketing implications of new-product technology licensing are important. Many industries and firms depend heavily on imported technology. The growing trends toward this form of licensing suggests that firms in the major technology source regions of North America, Europe, and Japan should promote the licensing of their technologies more. Many of them have impressive know-how that can give other firms improved technical skills and enhanced competitiveness—keys to global success. In addition, it has been suggested that the acquisition of foreign technology through licensing can serve as a viable tool for accomplishing renewal in small firms. With the increasing pace of technological change, market competition, and spiraling research and development costs, many see new-product technology licensing as the solution to a seemingly intractable problem of smaller-sized firms.

But potential licensors also need to calm the fears that many smaller firms may have of licensing arrangements. These include concerns about the complexity of the licensing process, the high cost of entry and exit, limitations on exports, and loss of control over strategic decisions such as pricing, production quantity, and quality control. Another concern is the effect technology licensing may have on the morale of firm-internal R&D staff. Licensors can help overcome such worries by simplifying the process and forming user-friendly arrangements with few restrictions.

Adapted from Kwaku Atuahene-Gima, "Buying Technology for Product Development in Smaller Firms," *Industrial Marketing Management* 22 (1993): 223–232.

Assessment of Licensing

Licensing has intuitive appeal to many potential international marketers. As an entry strategy, it may require neither capital investment nor knowledge and marketing strength in foreign markets. By earning royalty income, it provides an opportunity to obtain an additional return on research and development investments already incurred. After initial costs, the licensor can reap benefits until the end of the contract period. Licensing reduces risk of exposure to government intervention in that the licensee is typically a local company that can provide leverage against government action. Licensing will help to avoid host-country regulations that are more prevalent in equity ventures. Licensing may also serve as a stage in the internationalization of the firm by providing a means by which foreign markets can be tested without major involvement of capital or management time. Similarly, licensing can be used as a strategy to preempt a market before the entry of competition, especially if the licensor's resources permit full-scale involvement only in selected markets. A final reason why a licensor favors licensing is that intellectual property right protection in many countries is weak. In many instances, pirated technology, processes, and products are abundant, particularly in the developing world. In spite of the existence of legislation to protect intellectual property, the authorities' lack of attention to it results in billions of dollars of damages due to lost sales by the owners. Even though major progress has been achieved in the Uruguay round negotiations of the GATT, particularly in the area of strengthening of nations' obligations to provide effective enforcement for intellectual property rights and specific provisions on injunctions and damages,[1] it may take some time for such enforcement to become fully active. Therefore, a firm may still be better off receiving some licensing revenue rather than having its property stolen. In instances of high levels of piracy, a licensing agreement with a strong foreign partner may also add value because now the partner becomes a local force with a distinct interest in rooting out unlicensed activities.

Licensing has nevertheless come under criticism from supranational organizations, such as the United Nations Conference on Trade and Development (UNCTAD). It has been alleged that licensing provides a mechanism by which older technology is capitalized on by industrialized-country multinational corporations (MNCs). Licensees may often want labor-intensive techniques or machinery, however. Guinness Brewery, for example, in order to produce Guinness Stout in Nigeria, imported licensed equipment that had been used in Ireland at the turn of the century. Even though this equipment was obsolete by Western standards, it had additional economic life in Nigeria because it presented a good fit with Nigeria's needs.

Licensing offers a foreign entity the opportunity for immediate market entry with a proven concept. It therefore reduces the risk of R&D failures, the cost of designing around the licensor's patents, or the fear of patent infringement litigation. Furthermore, most licensing agreements provide for ongoing cooperation and support, thus enabling the licensee to benefit from new developments.

Licensing may enable the international marketer to enter a foreign market that is closed to either imports or direct foreign investments. In addition, licensing arrangements may enable the licensor to negotiate parallel contracts that are not related directly to the agreement but provide for foreign purchases of materials and components. The licensor can thereby expand participation in the particular market.

Licensing is not without disadvantages. To a large degree, it may leave the international marketing functions to the licensee. As a result, the licensor may not gain sufficient international marketing expertise to ready itself for subsequent world-market penetration. Moreover, the initial toehold in the foreign market may not be a foot in the door. Depending on the licensing arrangement, quite the opposite may take place. In exchange for the royalty, the licensor may create its own competitor not only in the markets for which the agreement was made but also in third markets. As a result, some companies are hesitant to enter licensing agreements. As an example, Japanese firms are delighted to sell goods to China but are unwilling to license the Chinese to produce the goods themselves. They fear that because of the low wage structure in China, such licenses could create a powerful future competitor in markets presently held by Japan.

Licensing agreements typically have time limits. Although terms may be extended one time after the start-up period, additional extensions are not readily permitted by a

---

[1] Letter from President Clinton to the Speaker of the House of Representatives, The White House, Washington D.C., December 15, 1993, 24.

number of foreign governments. If the licensee ties in with the licensor's global marketing network, quality control in terms of both production and marketing effort becomes a concern.

U.S. REGULATION OF LICENSING

The U.S. Department of Justice has nine specific patent license provisions (the nine no-nos of patent licensing) that it considers unlawful under the antitrust laws.[2] These provisions prohibit the licensor from controlling the licensee's distribution of a patented product. For example, it is illegal for the licensor to restrict a licensee's ability to resell a patented product, to restrict the licensee's ability to sell products that compete with the patented product (tie-out), or to require the licensee to adhere to a minimum price in the sale of the product. Other restrictions pertain to payments. It is illegal to require the licensee to purchase from the licensor products used with or in the patented product (tie-in), to offer to license only a group of patents rather than individual patents, or to base royalties on a measure other than one that corresponds to sales of products covered by the patent.

U.S. national security considerations must be kept in mind in terms of Export Administration regulations and U.S. jurisdiction over technology based on technical data originating in the United States. These regulations have to be considered especially in light of their match between national and regional policies, such as those of the EU.

The international marketer must also research national regulations concerning foreign involvement and foreign exchange restrictions that may have an impact on the payment of royalties by the licensee. In many countries, licensing regulations require government notification or approval of the licensing terms. Officials often have the right to question royalty and licensing fees and set payment ceilings.

PRINCIPAL ISSUES IN NEGOTIATING LICENSING AGREEMENTS

The key issues in negotiating licensing agreements include the scope of the rights conveyed, compensation, licensee compliance, dispute resolution, and the term and termination of the agreement.[3] The more clearly these are spelled out, the more trouble-free the association between the two parties can be.

The rights conveyed are product and/or patent rights. Defining their scope involves specifying the technology, know-how, or show-how to be included, the format, and guarantees. An example of format specification is an agreement on whether manuals will be translated into the licensee's language.

Compensation issues may be heavily disputed and argued. The costs the licensor wants to cover are (1) **transfer costs,** which are all variable costs incurred in transferring technology to a licensee and all ongoing costs of maintaining the agreement, (2) **R&D costs** incurred in developing the licensed technology, and (3) **opportunity**

---

[2] Roger B. Andewelt, "The Antitrust Division's Perspective on Intellectual Property Protection and Licensing—The Past, the Present, and the Future," paper presented at the annual meeting of the American Bar Association, London, England, 1985.

[3] Martin F. Connor, "International Technology Licensing," Seminars in International Trade, National Center for Export-Import Studies, Washington, D.C.

costs incurred in the foreclosure of other sources of profit, such as exports or direct investment. To cover these costs, the licensor wants a share of the profits generated from the use of the license.

Licensees usually do not want to include allowances for opportunity costs, and they often argue that R&D costs have already been covered by the licensor through the profit from previous sales. In theory, royalties can be seen as profit sharing; in practice, royalties are a function of both the licensor's minimum necessary return and the cost of the licensee's next-best alternative. In the past, U.S. marketers have been able to obtain licensing returns above their transfer costs as a result of the unique features of their technology and intellectual property, but changes in the marketplace may result in a different future.[4] These changes include maturing technologies, intensifying competition among suppliers, growing sophistication among licensees, and greater involvement by governments in arranging for the licensing agreements.

The methods of compensating the licensor can take the form of running royalties, such as 5 percent of the licensee sales, and/or up-front payments, service fees, and disclosure fees (for proprietary data). Sometimes, government regulations pose an obstacle to the collection of royalties or know-how payments. In such instances, the know-how transferred can be capitalized as part of a cooperative venture, where a specific value is attributed to the information. Payments are then received as profits or dividends.[5]

Licensee compliance on a number of dimensions must be stipulated in the agreement: (1) U.S. export administration regulations; (2) confidentiality of the intellectual property and technology provided; and (3) record keeping and provisions for licensor audits, which are done periodically, usually a minimum of once a year.

Dispute-resolution discussions center on the choice of law for contract interpretation and the choice of forum. Typically, the parties involved choose a third country's law to govern the agreement. Great care should be taken to determine the laws of the particular third country with respect to licensing. Swedish law, which is often used, stipulates on certain issues that the law of the licensee's country govern. When the parties cannot agree on an applicable legal system, an arbitration clause is warranted. This should be spelled out by using, for example, the International Chamber of Commerce model clause: "All disputes arising in connection with the present contract shall be finally settled under the Rules of Conciliation and Arbitration of the International Chamber of Commerce by one or more arbitrators appointed in accordance with the said rules." Also needed is a statement regarding the arbitrators' authority.[6]

Finally, the term, termination, and survival of rights must be specified. Government regulations in the licensee's market will have to be studied, and if the conditions are not favorable (for example, in terms of the maximum allowable duration), a waiver should be applied for.

Trademark Licensing

For companies that can trade on their names and characters, **trademark licensing** has become a substantial source of worldwide revenue. The total volume of trademark licensing in the United States reached $62 billion by 1990, with expected annual growth

---

[4] Franklin R. Root and Farok J. Contractor, "Negotiating Compensation in International Licensing Agreements," *Sloan Management Review* 22 (Summer 1981): 23–32.

[5] "International Licensing and Technology, Brazil," *Business International,* December 1987, 12.

[6] William W. Park, "Arbitration of International Contract Disputes," *Business Lawyer* 39 (August 1984): 83–99.

rates of 8.5 percent.[7] The names or logos of designers, literary characters, sports teams, and movie stars appear on clothing, games, foods and beverages, gifts and novelties, toys, and home furnishings. British designer Laura Ashley started the first major furniture program, licensing her name to Henredon Furniture Industries. Coca-Cola licensed its name to Murjani to be used on blue jeans, sweatshirts, and windbreakers. The licensors are likely to make millions of dollars with little effort, whereas the licensees can produce a branded product that consumers will recognize immediately. Licensing costs in such instances are typically an average fee of 5 percent of the wholesale price.

Both licensor and licensee may run into difficulty if the trademark is used for a product too far removed from the original success or if the licensed product casts a shadow on the reputation of the licensor. In licensing a trademark, consumer perceptions have to be researched to make sure the brand's positioning will not change. As an example, when Löwenbräu was exported to the United States, it was the number-one imported beer sold in the market. However, when the product name was licensed to Miller Brewing Company for domestic production, the beer's positioning (and subsequently its target audience) changed drastically in the minds of the consumers, resulting in a major decline in sales.

FRANCHISING

Franchising is a form of licensing in which a parent company (the franchiser) grants another, independent entity (the franchisee) the right to do business in a prescribed manner. This right can take the form of selling the franchiser's products, using its name, production and marketing techniques, or general business approach.[8] Usually, franchising involves a combination of many of these elements. The major forms of franchising are manufacturer-retailer systems (such as car dealerships), manufacturer-wholesaler systems (such as soft-drink companies), and service firm–retailer systems (such as lodging services and fast-food outlets). One can differentiate between product/trade franchising, where the major emphasis rests on the product or commodity to be sold, and business format franchising, where the focus is on ways of doing business. Even though many franchising firms are large, as the International Marketplace 13.3 shows, franchising can be a useful international market expansion method for any business operation needed abroad.

Although franchising is not a U.S. innovation (its origins are in Bavaria), it has been adopted by various types of businesses, mainly in the United States. Its U.S. market penetration has resulted in total 1992 franchising sales for goods and services of more than $803 billion, accounting for about 35 percent of all retail sales, with annual growth rates approximating 6 percent.[9] Concurrently, international franchising activities have grown spectacularly as well. In 1990, over 350 franchising companies in the United States operated more than 31,000 outlets in international markets.[10] Foreign franchisers are penetrating international markets as well. Examples include Holiday Rent-a-Car, of Canada,

---

[7] Kate Fitzgerald and Julie Liesse, "Jetsons Fly into Hot Licensing Year," *Advertising Age,* July 16, 1990, 43.

[8] Donald W. Hackett, "The International Expansion of U.S. Franchise Systems," in *Multinational Product Management,* eds. Warren J. Keegan and Charles S. Mayer (Chicago: American Marketing Association, 1979), 61–81.

[9] *Franchise Fact Sheet* (Washington, D.C.: International Franchise Association, 1993).

[10] Peng S. Chan and Robert T. Justis, "Franchise Management in East Asia," *Academy of Management Executives* 4 (1990): 75–85.

THE INTERNATIONAL MARKETPLACE   **13.3**

Looking for Leaks across the Globe

Large international companies are not the only ones franchising abroad. Quietly yet successfully, small companies have also entered the international arena. Five years ago, primarily large food franchisors were franchising overseas, but now even small chains are taking the plunge and going global. Expansion offers the best chance for companies to keep their growth curves moving upward in the face of increasing domestic competition and saturated U.S. markets. This is why many companies, both big and small, are taking advantage of international franchising as a means of growth.

One such example is that of American Leak Detection Inc. (ALD) of Palm Springs, California. ALD is in the business of finding leaks hidden in concrete and other inaccessible materials. President and founder Dick Rennick had expanded operations throughout the United States with 147 franchises. They have tracked down leaks in everything from the alligator pond at the Cleveland Metroparks Zoo to a water main buried deep under concrete at a Virginia power plant. However, the time had come for ALD to make the big leap overseas in order to expand the franchise even more.

When Rennick was considering where to expand the business abroad, he knew it had to be an English-speaking country that has a warm climate where water is precious and cannot be wasted in leaky pools, fountains, or spas. Australia fit the description. Its water is not only precious but it often has to be transported over long distances.

Rennick gathered statistics from the Australian Embassy on the population and number of pools. He was also able to obtain information on Australian building practices. "We wanted to make sure there was a lot of concrete slab construction because those are our bread-and-butter leaks, the kind you can't find easily," Rennick explains. In terms of competition, Rennick found a plumbing contractor in Sydney who kept two trucks on the road loaded with jackhammers and digging equipment used to break concrete to find leaks. This was good news because ADL's technology could do the same job much cheaper.

In terms of the actual franchise relationship, Rennick was able to get the word out by way of an article in a journal published by the Australian pool industry. John Myers, an Australian importer of Jacuzzi spas, read the article and later met with Rennick in the United States. Within two weeks of their meeting, Myers had paid $268,000 to buy American Leak Detection's franchise rights for Australia, New Zealand, Tasmania, and Papua New Guinea. ALD finally had its first international franchisee along with an agreement for 50 percent of the royalties collected by Myers from the sales of new franchises abroad.

Adapted from Greg Matusky, "Going Global: Franchisors Crack New Overseas Markets," *Success,* April 1993; 59–60.

and Descamps, a French firm selling linens and tablecloths. The principal types of U.S. international franchises and their locations around the world are shown in Figure 13.1.

The typical reasons for the international expansion of franchise systems are market potential, financial gain, and saturated domestic markets. U.S. franchisers expanded dramatically in Europe in the mid-1980s, taking advantage of the strong U.S. dollar. The

FIGURE 13.1   International Locations of U.S. Franchising Operations

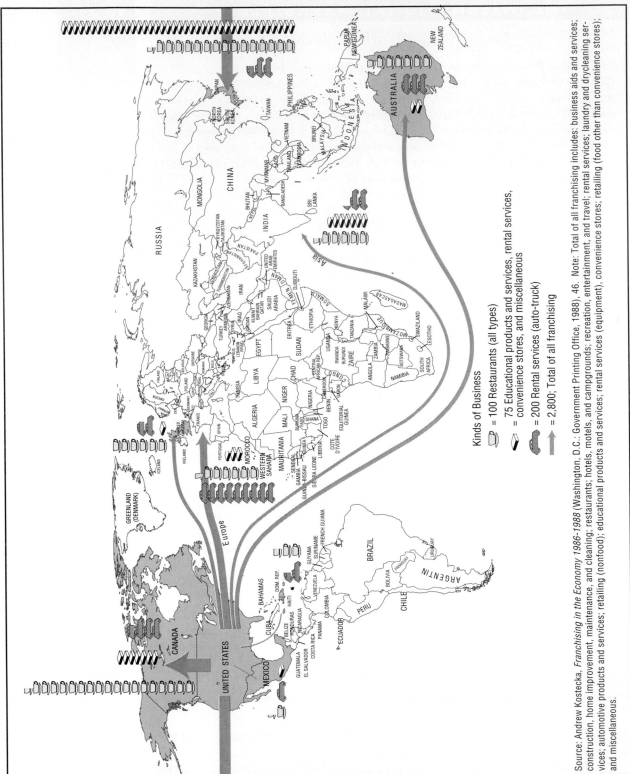

Source: Andrew Kostecka, *Franchising in the Economy 1986-1988* (Washington, D.C.: Government Printing Office, 1988), 46. Note: Total of all franchising includes: business aids and services; construction, home improvement, maintenance, and cleaning; restaurants; hotels, motels, and campgrounds; recreation, entertainment, and travel; rental services; laundry and drycleaning services; automotive products and services; retailing (nonfood); educational products and services; rental services (equipment); convenience stores; retailing (food other than convenience stores); and miscellaneous.

initial impetus for ComputerLand's expansion into the Asia/Pacific region was "Asian entrepreneurs coming knocking on our door asking for franchises."[11] In some cases, international expansion is a reaction to competitors' entry into foreign markets. In the 1980s, McDonald Corporation's biggest push was into France because France was the only major European country where McDonald's lagged behind Burger King.[12]

From a franchisee's perspective, the franchise is beneficial because it reduces risk by implementing a proven concept. In the United States, for example, between one-quarter and one-third of small businesses fail in their first year of operation. In contrast, only about 2.5 percent of franchise-owned outlets discontinue operations per year.[13]

Franchising agreements are usually also beneficial from a governmental perspective. From a source-country view, franchising does not replace exports or export jobs. From a recipient-country view, franchising requires little outflow of foreign exchange, and the bulk of the profit generated remains within the country.[14]

With all its benefits, franchising also encounters some problems. One key issue is the need for a great degree of standardization. Without such standardization, many of the benefits of the transferred know-how are lost. Typically, such standardization will include the use of a common business name, similar layout, and similar production or service processes. Apart from leading to efficient operations, all of these factors will also contribute to a high degree of international recognizability. At the same time, however, standardization does not mean 100 percent uniformity. Adjustments may be necessary in the final end product so that local market conditions can be taken into account. For example, fast-food outlets in Europe often need to serve beer and wine to be attractive to the local clientele. In order to enter the Indian market, McDonald's is developing non-beef burgers. Domino's Pizza in Japan serves seafood and eggplant pizza.[15] Key to success is the development of a franchising program that maintains a high degree of recognizability and efficiency benefits while being responsive to local cultural preferences.

Another key issue is the protection of the total business system that a franchise offers. Whereas it is possible to protect a name, the type of product or service and the general style of operation can be readily copied abroad.[16] As a result, franchise operations may meet head on with competition shortly after their introduction.

Government intervention can also represent major problems. For example, government restrictions on the type of services to be offered or on royalty remissions can prevent franchising arrangements or lead to a separation between a company and its franchisees.

Selection and training of franchisees present another potential problem area. McDonald's lag behind Burger King in France was a result of the company's suing to revoke the license of its largest franchise for failure to operate 14 stores according to McDonald's standards. Many franchise systems have run into difficulty by expanding too quickly and granting franchises to unqualified entities. Although the local franchisee knows the market best, the franchiser still needs to understand the market for product adaptation purposes and operational details. The franchiser should be the conductor of a

[11] "ComputerLand Debugs Its Franchising Program for Asia/Pacific Region," *Business International,* September 13, 1985, 294–295.

[12] "U.S. Fast-Food Giants Moving in on France," *Advertising Age,* October 22, 1984, 54.

[13] "Franchising Is Management for Success," *Small Business Reporter* 7 (1986).

[14] Nizamettin Aydin and Madhav Kacker, "International Outlook of US-based Franchisers," *International Marketing Review* 7 (1990): 43–53.

[15] Katherine Zapf, "Home Alone? Call the Pizza Lifeline," *City Life News Tokyo,* October 1993, 6.

[16] Lawrence S. Welch, "Diffusion of Franchise System Use in International Operations," *International Marketing Review* 6 (1989): 7–19.

TABLE 13.1	The Five Most Important Impediments to International Franchising
	Promotion
	Legal environment
	Corporate channel strategy
	Cost of securing franchises
	Incompetent middlemen

Source: Gordon Storholm and Sreedhar Kavil, "Impediments to International Franchising in the Business Format Sector," *Journal of Marketing Channels* 1 no. 4 (1992): 81–95.

coordinated effort by the individual franchisees—for example, in terms of sharing ideas and engaging in joint marketing efforts, such as cooperative advertising. However, even here difficulties can emerge consisting mostly of complications in selecting appropriate advertising media, effective copy testing, effective translation of the franchiser's message, and the use of appropriate sales promotion tools. Table 13.1 summarizes research findings regarding the challenges faced in international franchising.

To encourage better-organized and more successful growth, companies increasingly turn to the **master franchising system,** wherein foreign partners are selected and awarded the rights to a large territory in which they in turn can subfranchise. As a result, the franchiser gains market expertise and an effective screening mechanism for new franchises, without incurring costly mistakes.[17]

Franchising is often thought of as a strategy to be used for foreign-market entry only by large firms. Yet franchising may also be a viable alternative for small firms if the firm can offer a special business concept. Automation Papers Company, a New Jersey–based supplier of high-technology paper products, opted for franchising to gain exclusive representation by a highly motivated sales force in its target markets. The franchisees receive rights to the Automation Papers trademarks, intensive training for local staff members, and the benefit of the franchiser's experience, credit lines, and advertising budget.

FACILITATING INTERMEDIARIES

Firms with products or services that do not lend themselves to licensing or franchising, and firms that do not care to invest or export abroad, still can participate in international marketing by making use of facilitating international market intermediaries. One obvious possibility is the selling of merchandise to a domestic firm that in turn sells it abroad. For example, many products are sold to multinational corporations that use them as input for their foreign sales. Similarly, products sold to the U.S. Department of Defense may ultimately be shipped to military outposts abroad. An exporter may buy products domestically to round out an international product line. Table 13.2 provides more examples of "exporting in your own backyard."

More frequently, however, firms enter the international market with the help of market intermediaries who specialize in bringing firms or their products and services

---

[17] Agnes P. Olszewski, "International Marketing Strategies of U.S. Fast Food Franchises," in *Developments in Marketing Science,* eds. J. Hawes and J. Thanopoulos (Chicago: Academy of Marketing Science, 1989), 123–127.

Twelve Alternatives for Selling Abroad While Staying at Home	TABLE 13.2

1. Large U.S. companies purchasing U.S. goods for their own foreign affiliates
2. Large design and construction firms purchasing U.S. goods for foreign projects awarded to them
3. U.S. branches of gigantic foreign trading companies purchasing U.S. goods for their affiliates
4. Export merchants buying for their own account
5. Large foreign companies purchasing U.S. goods through their U.S. buying office or agents
6. U.S. military purchasing for use abroad
7. U.S. exporters seeking U.S. goods to round out their own lines
8. United Nations members purchasing for development projects
9. Foreign governments purchasing U.S. goods
10. Foreign department stores purchasing U.S. goods through U.S. buying offices
11. Foreign buyers on purchasing trips
12. AID-financed transactions requiring U.S. goods

Source: Nelson Joyner, Georgetown University, teaching notes, 1994.

to the global market. The International Marketplace 13.4 provides some examples of such intermediaries and their activities. These intermediaries can be crucial to success in international marketing because they can bridge performance gaps of firms with their specialized expertise. Table 13.3 shows those areas in which intermediaries have been found to be particularly helpful. This section will consider three such intermediaries: export management companies, Webb-Pomerene associations, and export trading companies.

Export Management Companies

Export Management Companies (EMCs) are domestic firms that specialize in performing international marketing services as commission representatives or as distributors for several other firms. Although few directories listing such firms are available, more than 1,000 of these firms are estimated to be actively operating in the United States. Most EMCs are quite small. They were frequently formed by one or two major principals with experience in international marketing or in a particular geographic area. Their expertise enables them to offer specialized services to domestic corporations.

EMCs have two primary forms of operation. They either take title to goods and operate internationally on their own account, or they perform services as agents. In the first instance, the EMC offers a conventional export channel in that it does not have any form of geographic exclusivity, and tends to negotiate price with suppliers on every transaction. As an agent, an EMC is likely to have either an informal or a formal contractual relationship, which specifies exclusivity agreements and, often, sales quotas. In addition, price arrangements and promotional support payments are agreed on, which simplifies ongoing transactions.[18] Because EMCs often serve a variety of clients, their mode of operation may vary from client to client and from transaction to transaction—that is, an EMC may act as an agent for one client, whereas for another client, or even for the same

[18] Daniel C. Bello and Nicholas C. Williamson, "Contractual Arrangement and Marketing Practices in the Indirect Export Channel," *Journal of International Business Studies* 16 (Summer 1985): 65–82.

THE INTERNATIONAL MARKETPLACE

13.4

A Sample of Export Intermediaries

Ultramedic International, New Hyde Park, New York, is a trading company that specializes in medical equipment and supplies. Orders are filled and sourcing is performed for customers in Latin America. In-country agents provide the necessary information to submit bids or pursue business and act as liaisons between the company and its customers. Ultramedic profits by buying products from a manufacturer at a 15 to 40 percent discount. All export activities are handled at a warehouse in New Jersey.

Brost International Trading Company, Chicago, is a demand-driven intermediary. First, products in demand abroad are identified as well as buyers who have purchasing capacity. Then U.S. suppliers are lined up. Brost buys and sells a variety of industrial products, such as building materials and agricultural equipment. Marketing of these products is done to government and private buyers overseas.

The Meridian Group of Companies, located in Los Angeles, is an export intermediary specializing in swimming pool equipment. Meridian has been exporting its products overseas for more than 40 years. Its products, including such items as filter systems and underwater lights, are supplied to foreign distributors and end-users. This intermediary works with several U.S. suppliers in each product group.

International Trade Marketing Corporation (ITM), a Washington, D.C.-based export management company, has exclusive agreements with ten U.S. suppliers of orthopedic equipment and materials. The firm's products are marketing on a worldwide basis, focusing on developing countries. ITM takes title to 90 percent of the goods it handles and profits by marking up prices for resale.

Overseas Operations Inc., Redondo Beach, California, manages the exports of several U.S. manufacturers' products, including builders' hardware, housing accessories, door closures and locks, as well as computer software and accessories. Overseas Operations represents these manufacturers on an exclusive basis and manages all aspects of every sale. The products are shipped directly from the manufacturer to the customer. Overseas Operations makes its profit by marking up the merchandise.

Adapted from Richard Barovick and Patricia Anderson, "EMCs/ETCs: What They Are, How They Work," *Business America* July 13, 1992, 2–3.

one on a different occasion, it may operate as a distributor. The International Marketplace 13.5 provides an example of such EMC activities.

The EMC as an Agent   When serving as an agent, the EMC is primarily in charge of developing foreign marketing and sales strategies and establishing contacts abroad. Because the EMC does not share in the profits from a sale, it depends heavily on a high sales volume, on which it charges commission. It may therefore be tempted to take on as many products and as many clients as possible in order to obtain a high sales volume. The risk in this is that the EMC will spread itself too thin and cannot adequately

How a Trade Intermediary Can Offer Assistance	TABLE 13.3

1. Knows foreign market competitive conditions
2. Has personal contacts with potential foreign buyers
3. Evaluates credit risk associated with foreign buyers
4. Has sales staff to call on current foreign customers in person
5. Assumes responsibility for physical delivery of product to foreign buyer

Source: Richard M. Castaldi, Alex F. De Noble, and Jeffrey Kantor, "The Intermediary Service Requirements of Canadian and American Exporters," *International Marketing Review* 9 no. 2 (1992): 21–40.

represent all the clients and products it carries. This risk is particularly great for small EMCs.

In addition to its international activities, this type of EMC must concentrate a substantial amount of effort on the development of domestic clients. These clients often are exactly the firms that are unwilling to commit major resources to international marketing efforts. They must be convinced that it is worthwhile to consider international marketing.

EMCs that have specific expertise in selecting markets because of language capabilities, previous exposure, or specialized contacts appear to be the ones most successful and useful in aiding client firms in their export marketing efforts. For example, they can cooperate with firms that are already successful in international marketing but have been unable to penetrate a specific region. By sticking to their expertise and representing only a limited number of clients, such agent services can be quite valuable.

The EMC as a Distributor   When operating as a distributor, the EMC purchases products from the domestic firm, takes the title, and assumes the trading risk. Selling in its own name offers the opportunity to reap greater profits than does acting as an agent. The potential for greater profitability is appropriate because the EMC has drastically reduced the risk for the domestic firm while increasing its own risk. The burden of the merchandise acquired provides a major motivation to complete an international sale successfully. The domestic firm selling to the EMC is in the comfortable position of having sold its merchandise and received its money without having to deal with the complexities of the international market. On the other hand, the firm is unlikely to gather much international marketing expertise and therefore relegates itself to some extent to remaining a purely domestic firm.

Compensation of EMCs   The mechanism of an EMC may be very useful to the domestic firm if such activities produce additional sales abroad that otherwise would not have occurred. However, certain services must be performed that demand resources for which someone must pay. As an example, to develop foreign markets, market development expenses must be incurred. At the very least, products must be shown abroad, visits must be arranged, or contacts must be established in order to enter the market. Even though it may often not be discussed, the funding for these activities must be found.

One possibility is a fee charged to the manufacturer by the EMC for market development, sometimes in the form of a retainer and often on an annual basis. These retainers vary and are dependent on the number of products represented and the difficulty of foreign market entry. Frequently, manufacturers are also expected to pay all or part of the direct expenses associated with foreign-market penetration. Some of these expenses may involve the production and translation of promotional brochures. Others may concern

13.5

THE INTERNATIONAL MARKETPLACE

Have Someone Manage Your Exports

Medical International Inc. of Spring Lake, NJ, an export management and trading company, believes its services are equally beneficial to U.S. manufacturers and to foreign buyers.

Carol Myers, the firm's export manager, says, "Small and medium-sized U.S. companies think it's great to have our expertise selling their products. Many of them wouldn't export at all on their own. Some get an unsolicited foreign order, and it sits on their desks for a long time and ends up in the trash can. The smaller companies don't know about such matters as letters of credit. They just don't feel comfortable with international marketing."

Medical International, which markets hospital and physician supplies and equipment, orthopedic appliances, rehabilitation equipment, home health-care products, X-ray equipment, dental supplies, and other products, will either (1) buy outright the products of the manufacturers it represents or (2) act as their export management agent on a commission basis. Ninety percent of the firm's business is in the first category, the remainder in the second.

The firm's export services include market research and consulting, establishment of overseas sales outlets, product promotion and advertising, international trade show representation, handling of all correspondence and inquiries, financing arrangements and payment risks, export documentation and letters of credit, and shipping and consolidation services.

What are the advantages for foreign customers in dealing with a trading company? Medical International claims that its chief selling point is the simplicity in ordering from just one purchasing point. The firm contends that this procedure saves foreign customers time and money by minimizing documentation and providing regular and routine shipments and efficient consolidation services. The firm publishes catalogs showing pictures of the various products of its 70 client manufacturers.

Medical International, which was formed in 1987, had a record-breaking year in 1990, when its gross sales exceeded $800,000 in Asia, the Middle East, South and Latin America, Europe, and Africa. It added ten new countries to its list of export destinations and increased its U.S. client base by 35 percent.

Source: "Exporting Pays Off," *Business America*, February 25, 1991, 35.

the rental for booth space at foreign trade shows, the provision of product samples, or trade advertising.[19]

Alternatively, the EMC may set the price for the product. Because it will take on many of the marketing activities for the manufacturer, the EMC wants the price discounted for these activities. Therefore, sales to EMCs may occur only at a reduced price.

In one way or another, the firm that uses an EMC must pay the EMC for the international marketing effort. This compensation can be in the form of fees and/or cost-sharing or in terms of lower prices and resulting higher profits for the EMC. Otherwise,

[19] John J. Brasch, "Export Management Companies," *Journal of International Business Studies* 9 (Spring–Summer 1978): 69.

despite promises, the EMC may simply add the firm and product in name only to its product offering and do nothing to achieve international market penetration. Manufacturers need to be aware of this cost and the fact that EMCs do not offer a free ride. Depending on the complexity of a product and the necessity to carry out developmental research, promotion, and service, manufacturers must be prepared to part with some portion of the potential international profitability to compensate the EMC for its efforts.

Power Conflicts between EMCs and Clients   The EMC in turn faces the continuous problem of retaining a client once foreign market entry is achieved. Many firms use an EMC's services mainly to test international markets, with the clear desire to become a direct exporter once successful operations have been established. Of course, this is particularly true if foreign demand turns out to be strong and profit levels are high. As a result there is a conflict between the EMC and its clients, with one side wanting to retain market power by not sharing too much international market information, and the other side wanting to obtain that power, which often results in short-term relationships and a lack of cooperation. Because international market development is based on long-term efforts, however, this conflict frequently precipitates unsuccessful international marketing efforts.

For the concept of an export management company to work, both parties must fully recognize the delegation of responsibilities; the costs associated with these activities; and the need for information sharing, cooperation, and mutual reliance. On the manufacturer's side, use of an EMC should be viewed as a domestic channel commitment. This requires a thorough investigation of the intermediary and the advisability of relying on its efforts, a willingness to cooperate on a prolonged basis, and a willingness to reward it properly for these efforts. The EMC in turn must adopt a flexible approach to managing the export relationship. It must continue to upgrade the level of services offered and highlight for the client the dimensions of post-sales service and of providing market information, which are its biggest sources of differential advantage.[20] By doing so, the EMC can clearly let the client know that the cost is worth the service.

Webb-Pomerene Associations

Legislation enacted in 1918 led to **Webb-Pomerene associations,** which permit firms, contrary to antitrust legislation, to cooperate in terms of sales allocation, financing, and pricing information regarding their international sales. The associations must take care not to engage in activities that would reduce competition within the United States. To more successfully penetrate international markets, however, they can use mechanisms such as market allocation, quota fixing, and selection of exclusive distributors or brokers.

In spite of this early effort to encourage joint activities by firms in the international market, the effectiveness of Webb-Pomerene associations has not been substantial. At their peak from 1930 to 1934, fifty Webb-Pomerene associations accounted for about 12 percent of U.S. exports. By 1991, only 22 associations were active and accounted for less than 2 percent of U.S. exports.[21] In addition, it appears that most of the members are not the small and medium-sized firms that the act was initially intended to assist but rather are the dominant firms in their respective industries.

[20] Daniel C. Bello, David J. Urban, and Bronislaw J. Verhage, "Evaluating Export Middlemen in Alternative Channel Structures," *International Marketing Review* 8 (1991): 49–64.

[21] Carl Hevener, Federal Trade Commission, Washington, D.C., 1992.

The limited success of this particular intermediary has mainly been ascribed to the fact that the antitrust exemption granted was not sufficiently iron-clad. Further, specialized export firms are thought to have more to offer a domestic firm than does an association, which may be particularly true if an association is dominated by one or two major competitors in an industry. This makes joining the association undesirable for smaller firms in that industry.

Trading Companies

A third major facilitating intermediary is the trading company. The concept was originated by the European trading houses such as the Fuggers and was soon formalized by the monarchs. Hoping to expand their imperial powers and wealth, kings chartered traders to form corporate bodies that enjoyed exclusive trading rights and protection by the naval forces in exchange for tax payments. Examples of such early trading companies are the East India Company of the Netherlands (Oost-Indische Compagnie), formed in 1602, followed shortly by the British East India Company and the French East India Company (La Compagnie des Indes).[22] Today, the most famous trading companies are the **sogoshosha** of Japan. Names like Sumitomo, Mitsubishi, Mitsui, and C. Itoh have become household words around the world. The nine trading company giants of Japan in 1991 acted as intermediaries for about half of the country's exports and two-thirds of its imports and accounted for 25 percent of Japan's gross national product.[23] These general trading companies play a unique role in world commerce by importing, exporting, countertrading, investing, and manufacturing. Because of their vast size, they can benefit from economies of scale and perform their operations at profit margins that are generally less than 1.5 percent.

Four major reasons have been given for the success of the Japanese sogoshosha. First, by concentrating on obtaining and disseminating information about market opportunities and by investing huge funds in the development of information systems, these firms now have the mechanisms and organizations in place to gather, evaluate, and translate market information into business opportunities. Second, economies of scale permit them to take advantage of their vast transaction volume to obtain preferential treatment by, for example, negotiating transportation rates or even opening up new transportation routes. Third, these firms serve large internal markets, not only in Japan but also around the world, and can benefit from opportunities for barter trade. Finally, sogoshosha have access to vast quantities of capital, both within Japan and in the international capital markets. They can therefore carry out many transactions that are larger and more risky than is palatable or feasible for other firms.[24] In the 1990s, as more Japanese firms set up their own global networks, the share of Japan's trade handled by the sogoshosha declined. However, these giants continued to succeed by shifting their strategy to expand their domestic activities in Japan, entering more newly developing markets, increasing their trading activities between third countries, and forming joint ventures with non-Japanese firms. Mitsui, for example, has more than 100 affiliated companies involved in joint ventures with local business groups in Thailand alone.[25]

---

[22] Dong-Sung Cho, *The General Trading Company: Concept and Strategy* (Lexington, MA: Lexington Books, 1987), 2.

[23] "Japanese Trading Companies," *The Economist*, August 8, 1992, 68.

[24] Yoshi Tsurumi, *Sogoshosha: Engines of Export Based Growth* (Montreal, Quebec: Institute for Research on Public Policy, 1980).

[25] Louise de Rosario, "Leaky Umbrellas," *Far Eastern Economic Review* 11 (February 1993): 48.

For many decades, the emergence of trading companies was commonly believed to be a Japan-specific phenomenon. Particularly, Japanese cultural factors were cited as the reason why such intermediaries could operate successfully only from that country. In 1975, however, trading companies were established by government declaration in Korea. The intent was to continue Korea's export-led growth in a more efficient fashion. With the new legislation, the Korean government tied access to financing and government contracts to the formation of trading companies. By 1981, the major trading companies of Korea (such as Hyundai, Samsung, and Daewoo) were handling 43 percent of Korea's total exports.[26] They were therefore considered to be a major success. Similarly, the Brazilian government stimulated the creation of trading companies by offering preferential financing arrangements. Within a short time, these Brazilian firms dramatically increased their activities and accounted for almost 20 percent of total Brazilian exports.[27] Also, the government of Turkey devised special incentives to develop export trading firms, which resulted within a few years in such trading companies accounting for 46 percent of Turkey's exports.[28]

Export trading company (ETC) legislation designed to improve the export performance of small and medium-sized firms has also been implemented in the United States. Bank participation in trading companies was permitted and the antitrust threat to joint export efforts was reduced through precertification of planned activities by the U.S. Department of Commerce. Businesses were encouraged to join together to export, or offer export services, by passage in 1982 of the Export Trading Company Act.

Permitting banks to participate in ETCs was intended to allow ETCs better access to capital and therefore to more trading transactions and easier receipt of title to goods. The relaxation of antitrust provisions in turn was to enable firms to form joint ventures more easily. The cost of developing and penetrating international markets would then be shared, with the proportional share being, for many small and medium-sized firms, much easier to bear. As an example, in case a warehouse is needed to secure foreign-market penetration, one firm alone does not have to bear all the costs. A consortium of firms can jointly rent a foreign warehouse. Similarly, each firm need not station a service technician abroad at substantial cost. Joint funding of a service center by several firms makes the cost less prohibitive for each one. The trading company concept also offers a one-stop shopping center for both the firm and its foreign customers. The firm can be assured that all international functions will be performed efficiently by the trading company, and at the same time, the foreign customer will have to deal with fewer individual firms.

The legislation permits a wide variety of possible structures for an ETC. General trading companies handle many commodities, perform import and export services, countertrade, and work closely with foreign distributors. Regional trading companies handle commodities produced in only one region, specializing in products in which this region possesses a comparative advantage. Product-oriented trading companies concentrate on a limited number of products and offer their market penetration services only for these products. Trading companies may also be geographically oriented, targeting one particular foreign region, or can be focused on certain types of projects, such as turnkey

---

[26] Chang-Kyun Shin, "Korean General Trading Companies: A Study of Their Development and Strategies," doctoral dissertation, George Washington University, Washington, D.C., 1984, 236.

[27] Umberto Costa Pinto, "Trading Companies: The Brazilian Experience," in *U.S. Latin American Trade Relations,* ed. M. Czinkota (New York: Praeger Publishers, 1983), 251.

[28] I. Atilla Dicle and Ulku Dicle, "Effects of Government Export Policies on Turkish Export Trading Companies," *International Marketing Review* 9 no. 3 (1992): 62–76.

operations and joint ventures with foreign investors. Finally, trading companies may develop an industry-oriented focus, handling only goods of specific industry groups, such as metals, chemicals, or pharmaceuticals.[29]

Independent of its form of operation, an ETC can deliver a wide variety of services. It can be active chiefly as an agent, or it can purchase products or act as a distributor abroad. It can provide information on distribution costs and even handle domestic and international distribution and transportation. This can range from identifying distribution costs to booking space on ocean or air carriers and handling shipping contracts.

Although ETCs seem to offer major benefits to many U.S. firms wishing to penetrate international markets, they have not been used very extensively. By 1994 only 143 individual ETCs had been certified by the U.S. Department of Commerce. Yet these certificates covered more than 5,000 firms, mainly because various trade associations had applied for certification for all of their members.[30] Perhaps the greatest potential of ETCs lies with trade associations. However, it may also be a worthwhile concept to consider by firms and banks.

Banks need to evaluate whether the mentalities of bankers and traders can be made compatible. Traders, for example, are known for seizing the opportune moment, whereas bankers often appear to move more slowly. A key challenge will be to find ways to successfully blend business entrepreneurship with banking regulations.

Banks also need to understand the benefits they can derive from working with small or medium-sized exporters. The first impression may be that an ETC offers only added risk and cost. Yet involvement with an ETC may provide the bank with a broader client base, profitable use of its extensive international information system and network of corresponding institutions, and a stepping-stone toward the internationalization of its own banking services. Because of the current international debt situation, many banks are hesitant to increase the volume of their international activities. This hesitation has been reinforced by the attitudes of shareholders. Research has shown that past announcements of ETC formation by U.S. banks caused significant negative stock price reactions. Apparently, the market believed that U.S. banks' involvement in ETCs would not be value-enhancing.[31] In the long run, however, an improved understanding of the type and profitability of transactions and the increasing pressures of a highly competitive deregulated home market may well lead again to more international involvement by U.S. banks.

Firms participating in trading companies by joining or forming them should be aware of the difference between product- and market-driven ETCs. Firms may have a strong tendency to use their trading company primarily to dispose of their merchandise. Foreign sales, however, depend primarily on the foreign demand and the foreign market. An ETC must therefore accomplish a balance between the demands of the market and the supply of the members in order to be successful.

The trading company itself must solicit continuous feedback on foreign-market demands and changes in these demands so that its members will be able to maintain a winning international product and service mix. Substantial attention must be paid to gathering information on the needs and wants of foreign customers and disseminating this

[29] *The Export Trading Company Act of 1982* (Washington, D.C.: Chamber of Commerce of the United States, 1983),4.

[30] Office of Export Trading Companies, U.S. Department of Commerce, Washington, D.C., January 6, 1994.

[31] Lawrence Kryzanowski and Nancy D. Ursel, "Market Reaction to the Formation of Export Trading Companies by American Banks," *Journal of International Business Studies* (Second Quarter 1993): 373–381.

Service Requirements for American Export Trading Companies   FIGURE 13.2

Suppliers Represented	Products Exported	
	Undifferentiated	**Differentiated**
Low Export Volume	Requires a Less-Than-Average Capability in Promotion, Market Contact, and Consolidation	Requires an Above-Average Capability in Promotion but an Average Capability in Market Contact and Consolidation
High Export Volume	Requires a Less-Than-Average Capability in Promotion but an Average Capability in Market Contact and Consolidation	Requires an Above-Average Capability in Promotion, Market Contact, and Consolidation

Source: Reprinted from Daniel C. Bello and Nicholas C. Williamson, "The American Export Trading Company: Designing a New International Marketing Institution," *Journal of Marketing* 49 (Fall 1985): 67, published by the American Marketing Association.

information to the participating U.S. firms. Otherwise, lack of responsiveness to foreign-market demands will result in a decline of the ETC's effectiveness.[32] The ETC also should determine the activities on which to concentrate, basing this determination on the types of suppliers represented and the types of products exported. Figure 13.2 provides one possible differentiation for such service requirements.

Depending on whether products are differentiated or undifferentiated, such as commodities, the ETC should place varying degrees of emphasis on developing its capability for international promotion. At the same time, undifferentiated products require greater price competitiveness, which may be precisely the chief advantage offered by an ETC as a result of economies of scale. For differentiated products, an ETC may be able to place emphasis on promotion and have greater flexibility in price determination.

The future success of U.S. export trading companies is still uncertain. Some believe that sufficient time has passed for the legislation to work and that businesses simply are not interested in joining forces to penetrate international markets.[33] On the other hand, the concepts of synergism and cooperation certainly make sense in terms of enhancing the international competitiveness of U.S. firms. Yet the focus of ETCs should perhaps not be pure exporting. Importing and countertrading may also generate substantial activity and profit. By carrying out a wide variety of export transactions, ETCs can obtain international market knowledge. This management and consulting expertise may in itself be a salable service.

---

[32] Michael R. Czinkota, "The Business Response to the Export Trading Company Act of 1982," *Columbia Journal of World Business* 19 (Fall 1984): 111.

[33] Donald G. Howard and James M. Maskulka, "Will American Export Trading Companies Replace Traditional Export Management Companies?" *International Marketing Review* 5 (Winter 1988): 41–50.

SUMMARY

In addition to direct exporting, other possibilities for international market entry or expansion are licensing, franchising, and the use of export intermediaries. The basic advantage of licensing is that it requires relatively less capital investment or knowledge of foreign markets than most other forms of international involvement. The major disadvantage is that licensing agreements typically have time limits, often prescribed by foreign governments, and may even result in creating a competitor. The principal issues in negotiating licensing agreements are the scope of the rights conveyed, compensation, license compliance, dispute resolution, and the term and termination of the agreement. Franchising is a form of licensing. Since 1970, the expansion of U.S. franchisers into foreign markets has been dramatic. The reasons for this international expansion are typically market potential, financial gain, and saturated domestic markets. Franchisers must strike a balance between the need to adapt to local environments and the need to standardize to maintain international recognizability.

Firms with products that do not lend themselves to licensing or franchising may use intermediaries in the existing infrastructure: EMCs, Webb-Pomerene associations, and trading companies. For international market entry mechanisms to be successful, various international marketing functions need to be performed. Export intermediaries can take on these functions. For them to do so viably, however, a proper form of compensation must exist. The major disadvantage to using such intermediaries is that they may take on more clients or more diverse functions than they are staffed to perform. Although the potential of the ETC mechanism is far from being fully utilized at this time, ETCs may yet become a useful and viable intermediary in the future.

Questions for Discussion

1. Comment on this statement: "Licensing is really not a form of international involvement because it requires no substantial additional effort on the part of the licensor."
2. Assume that the government of Thailand wants to start producing F-20 Tigershark fighter aircraft under license from Northrop. What types of concerns will enter into the negotiations?
3. Suggest reasons for the explosive international expansion of U.S.-based franchise systems.
4. What is the purpose of export intermediaries?
5. How can an export intermediary avoid circumvention by a client or customer?
6. What makes an export agent different from any other channel member?
7. Is there a need for export trading companies?
8. What makes a U.S. export trading company different from Japanese trading companies?
9. Why is it useful to have antitrust exemption for an export trading company?
10. Give examples of product-based and geographic ETCs.
11. How can the discrepancy between product-driven and market-driven orientations within export trading companies be resolved?
12. Why would a trade association want to form an ETC?

Recommended Readings

Cho, Dong-Sung. *The General Trading Company: Concept and Strategy.* Lexington, MA: Lexington Books, 1987.

Contractor, Farok J. *Licensing in International Strategy: A Guide for Planning and Negotiations.* Westport, CT: Quorum Books, 1985.

Directory of Leading U.S. EMCs, 3rd ed. Fairfield, CT: Bergano Book Co., 1990.

Egan, Mary Lou. "The Export Trading Company Act of 1982: An Analysis of Firms' Responses in Relation to the Goals of the Act." Doctoral dissertation, George Washington University, Washington, D.C., 1987.

Export Yellow Pages. Washington D.C.: Venture Publishing, 1994.

International Licensing Management. New York: Business International Corporation, 1988.

Justis, Robert, and Richard Judd. *Franchising.* Cincinnati, OH: South-Western, 1989.

Nye, William W. "An Economic Profile of Export Trading Companies." *The Antitrust Bulletin* (Summer 1993): 309–325.

Perry, Anne C. *The Evolution of U.S. Trade Intermediaries: The Changing International Environment.* Westport, CT: Quorum Books, 1992.

Tomas, Michael J. III, and Donald G. Howard. "The Export Trading Company Act: An Update." *Journal of Marketing Channels* 2 no. 1 (1993).

Trading Company Sourcebook. Bethesda, MD: National Federation of Export Associations, 1992.

Whitney, James D. "The Causes and Consequences of Webb-Pomerene Associations: A Reappraisal." *The Antitrust Bulletin* (Summer 1993): 395–418.

Yoshino, Michael Y., and Thomas B. Lifson. *The Invisible Link: Japan's Sogoshosha and the Organization of Trade.* Cambridge, MA: MIT Press, 1988.

Tollens N. V.—Holland
Surfstone

SURFSTONE

Peering out into the Amsterdam skyline, Kees van der Maas contemplates the result of the board meeting. Flat European sales have caused a great deal of concern for this Dutch maker of surfacing materials. Intense competition, difficulty of signing new distributors, and increasing cost of raw materials converged to create a somewhat pessimistic perspective for Surfstone in Europe. In order to maintain the healthy growth trend of the last eight years, a major shift in the strategic orientation of the company was required. Except for Mr. Rosier, the comptroller, the board in its majority concurred with this assessment. Part of the strategic change was to develop new markets for Surfstone. The most logical target, for its population size and per-capita income, is the United States. Kees, the idea champion, was given the charge of developing an entry strategy proposal for the United States. This was the first time the company would attempt to sell outside of Europe.

THE COMPANY

The company, Tollens N. V., was established in 1953 by its founder, master cabinet-maker Alex Tollens. Mr. Tollens saw a market for high-quality kitchen furnishings as the buying power of war-torn Holland increased. The company grew at a healthy pace throughout the 1950s and 1960s, expanding into neighboring Germany and Belgium.

During this period, the company expanded through the excellent reputation of its kitchen furnishings. The marketing effort was concentrated on creating and maintaining an excellent relationship with distributors based on commitment, honesty, and reliability. The company was not seen as an aggressive player in the industry; however, the loyalty of its distributor/fabricator organization was unbeatable in Northern Europe.

In the early 1970s, in reaction to the general economic contraction, the company engaged in an aggressive market expansion program. The results of these efforts became evident after 1977 when sales doubled 1971 revenues. In the period 1972 to 1977, Surfstone entered and developed a position in France, Switzerland, Italy, and the United Kingdom. Later expansions led to a broad coverage of Europe by 1990 (see Table 1). Also, at the urging of their distributors, Tollens expanded its product line to include furnishings for the bathroom.

Mr. Tollens died in 1982 and control of the company was passed to his three sons. After two months of indecision, the brothers decided to discard their father's strategy of relying solely upon their distributors to promote the product. They hired several experienced marketing managers to lead a Europe-wide marketing campaign; Kees van der

Source: This case was written by John M. Zerio, Ph.D., Associate Professor of Marketing, and Nittaya Wongtada, Ph.D., Assistant Professor of Marketing, Thunderbird-American Graduate School of International Management. This case was prepared as the basis for class discussion rather than to illustrate either effective or ineffective handling of an administrative situation. The assistance of Mr. Fred Rodkey (Thunderbird '90) is gratefully acknowledged.

Maas was one of these managers. The marketing effort increased sales by 90 percent over the next seven years. Competition in the industry began to stiffen during the late 1980s as new entrants from Europe and overseas challenged the established companies. One of Tollens's most successful products, the Surfstone line of solid surface material, had won 17 percent of the European market for solid surface materials.

Kees van der Maas was appointed director of sales in September of 1986. The boom of the 1980s gave him an opportunity to demonstrate his superb acumen for planning and managing of a complex web of salesmen, distributors, dealers, and fabricators. However, despite his skills, the increasing presence of foreign competitors in its major markets, coupled with a trend toward consolidation of distributors and fast growth of construction supply store chains, were rapidly compressing Tollens's margins. Even though Tollens's total sales in 1989 has risen to $435 million, margins had shrunk to 3.3 percent from a 1984 high of 4.2 percent. Indeed, were these trends to continue or accelerate, the attractiveness of the solid surface materials business would be highly questionable.

Tollens's expansion formula was based on a skillful association of its expertise in cabinet-making with the manufacturing of countertops. Recognizing the importance of local tastes and traditions, Tollens decided to concentrate its resources on the manufacturing of solid surface material sheets and develop a wide network of certified fabricators of countertops. Within five years, Tollens had trained personnel of over 350 fabricators. In addition, it strongly emphasized on-site training seminars for distributor's sales personnel. The importance of training in Tollens's success cannot be overemphasized.

At the heart of Tollens's competitive posture in Europe was the quality of its relationship with distributors. Trust and commitment were hallmarks of Tollens. Over 60 percent of Tollens's distributors had been with the company for ten years or more. Relationships were very personalized. Tollens's regional managers had built over the years strong personal links with distributors, fabricators, architects, and interior designers. Regional managers were indeed the glue and blood of Tollens's international distribution system. They were active in the recruiting, hiring, and training of fabricators, in recruiting and developing distributors, and were extensively involved in the continuous training of distributors' sales personnel.

They had become particularly valuable to the system for their ability to develop sales leads and opportunities which were quickly routed to distributors. Tollens's managers were very well positioned socially and professionally in the construction circles. They were particularly well connected with architects and interior designers associations. In a business environment where personal connections are essential, they excelled in the use of their network.

Sales Distribution—Surfstone, 1990

TABLE 1

Country	Sales Percentage	Number of Distributors	Number of Fabricators	Number of Warehouses
Holland	41	22	172	1
Belgium	19	12	102	2
Germany	14	13	33	2
Italy	7	1	78	1
U.K.	6	7	53	2
France	9	17	18	1
Spain	1	4	12	0
Others	3	12	23	1
Total	100	88	491	10

Training was an essential element of Tollens's differentiation strategy until 1986 when other competitors introduced their own massive certification programs. Training courses were offered on a regular basis in Amsterdam, and twice a year in every major European capital. A small team of highly trained instructors, former fabricators, or interior designers conducted the program. Tollens's distinctiveness in the eyes of major channel intermediaries became rapidly blurred. Although their image of top quality was not tarnished, the new competitive dynamics enormously raised end-users' price sensitivity.

Tollens's distinctive reputation was in great part based on its obsession with order fulfillment. Its ability to fill 92 percent of approved orders in five working days became a source of pride and an essential tool for maintaining an edge over competitors. Tollens maintained a number of warehouses strategically located near every major market (see Table 1) and a very efficient electronic order processing system. Each warehouse operated with a small fleet of medium-size trucks sufficient to serve a clientele within a 300-mile radius. In addition, a transportation agreement (piggy-back) was established with a large continental supplier of clay pipe and pipe connections for the servicing of clients outside of the warehouse radius. Only sporadically did Tollens have to hire the services of transportation companies.

THE PRODUCT

Solid surface materials are primarily used for countertops, although the product is becoming increasingly popular for molded items, for example, integrated countertop-sinks and integrated and separate lavatories. Although nearly three times more expensive, solid surface materials offer many advantages over laminated countertops. They are more durable than laminates and are easily repaired. Scratches may be removed by lightly sanding the damaged area. Chips and dents may be fixed by applying a repair compound and sanding after it has dried. The solid surface materials use a seamless installation technique which enhances the appearance of the product. In addition to the benefits of durability, the material may be finished using common woodworking tools. This significantly increases the attractiveness of the material, since installation and customizing do not require special tools or techniques. The solid surface material may also be used in powdered form for molding into desired shapes.

Surfstone is a polymer-based solid surface material. It is sold in several standard thicknesses and in 15 colors. Of these colors, eight are bright pastels and seven are granites. Surfstone offers standard sheets and a collection of molded parts, including a variety of integrated countertop-sinks and lavatories.

THE U.S. MARKET ENTRY

Kees had developed an affinity for the United States during a six-month college exchange student program, but he knew that marketing a product in the United States was a much greater challenge. Even though he relished the challenge of introducing the product in the American market, he was conscious of his limitations and of the need to obtain professional marketing assistance. Through a friend associated with the U.S. Kitchen and Bath Association, a consulting contract was negotiated with Jonathan Butler, a marketing consultant with over 20 years of experience in the industry. Mr. Butler's assignment comprised three major areas: the size and structure of the American market for solid surface materials; an analysis of the major end-users, their purchasing criteria, and their purchasing decision-making process; and a profile of the major solid surface manufacturers. Given this information, Kees felt he would be able to structure a comprehensive market-entry program for presentation to the board of directors. Six weeks later, a Federal Express courier delivered the following report to Mr. Kees, with a greeting card from Jonathan Butler and an invoice for $17,350.

APPENDIX

The American Solid Surface Materials Market

THE AMERICAN MARKET

In 1990, the American market for solid surface materials is estimated to be $600 million. Of this amount, approximately 33 percent, or $198 million, is used in the construction industry. This can be further broken down into 16 percent used by the hospital/laboratory industry and 17 percent used by a variety of sectors including restaurants and schools. The remaining 67 percent of the solid surface market is used by the residential home construction and renovation market. Kitchen renovation projects represent approximately 40 percent of the solid surface market, or $240 million.

THE MAJOR END-USERS

The Hospital Industry

According to Moody's, prospects for certain sectors of the medical facilities industry are positive, but the outlook for 1991 remains unfavorable. Inadequate reimbursement under Medicare and Medicaid programs, intensified competition, and rising operating costs all are contributing to the industry's troubles. The 1983 implementation of Medicare's prospective payment system (PPS) initiated a revolutionary change in the nation's health-care delivery system. PPS reimburses hospitals according to a fixed schedule of fees based on some 470 illness categories, or diagnostic related groups (DRGs). This more restrictive reimbursement environment had an immediate impact on the industry. Hospitals were forced to cut costs, curtail services, and otherwise increase efficiency to operate profitably with DRG constraints. As a result, admissions, average lengths of stay, occupancy rates, and other measures of inpatient utilization began a long, steady slide in 1984. Conversely, outpatient utilization has shown strong growth over the past five years, largely at the expense of inpatient business, and managed-care plans such as health maintenance organizations (HMOs) have gained in popularity. Finally, the more strenuous operating environment has led to a fair amount of consolidation and corporate restructuring, especially within the investor-owned segment of the business.

Prepared by Butler Consultants

New health-care-facility construction is expected to slow, but the renovation of existing facilities is expected to grow. The typical hospital now renovates every five years to keep up with technology and maintain the aesthetics of the facility. Solid surface materials are not widely used yet in hospitals because of the high cost. The areas of installation are generally in those with high public traffic, rest rooms for example, where durability and an aseptic appearance are prized.

The Laboratory Industry

The growth in the laboratory industry is expected to be slow but steady. Intense competition is causing the labs to become very cost-conscious. Most of the construction in the industry is expected to come from the renovation/replacement of existing facilities. Solid surfaces are very important to the laboratory industry: their nonpermeable surface discourages the growth of germs and mildew. The seamless construction of solid surface materials also increases the aseptic quality of the material. These are advantages which laminates cannot offer. The labs typically remodel every one to five years, depending upon their industrial sector. Most labs remodel due to technological improvements, state regulations, or for the maintenance of sterilization standards. As an example, public labs must change solid surfaces every year to comply with health and safety standards.

The Home Construction/Renovation Industry

According to Moody's Industry Surveys, the home-building industry is in the doldrums. Housing starts were down marginally. Estimates indicate housing starts for the full year 1991 at 1,410,000, down 5.7 percent from the 1989 level.

A major cause of these prospects resides in the negative demographics. The primary problem is the aging of the baby-boom generation and the arrival of the baby-bust generation. The transition quite simply means fewer household formations. In the 1970s, household formations averaged around 1.7 million per year. Not surprisingly, there were housing booms in several of those years. In the 1980s, the rate of formations slipped to about 1.5 million per year. In contrast, the demographics of the baby-bust generation point to housing formations of only about 1.2 million per year during the 1990s.

TABLE 2	Kitchen Colors and Material Often Used		
Kitchen Colors Most Frequently Requested	**Percentage**	**Kitchen Countertop Material Often Used**	**Percentage**
White	41	Laminate	63
Almond	25	Solid Surface	25
Wood Tones	19	Tile	5
Pastels	6	Granite	1
Gray	5	Marble	1
Other	3	Cult. Marble	1
		Other	4

Source: National Kitchen and Bath Association Survey.

Kitchen Countertop Material Used by Region TABLE 3

Region	Laminate (%)	SS (%)	Tile (%)	Granite (%)
Northeast	62	36	2	—
Mideast	80	18	2	—
Southeast	76	21	2	1
Midwest	70	22	8	—
Southwest	52	48	—	—
West	32	30	30	8

Source: National Kitchen and Bath Association Survey, 1989.

The lower numbers of household formations will affect two major markets, the market for first time homebuyers and the rental market for apartments. Small starter homes and apartments are generally where young individuals and couples enter the housing market.

There is one positive trend in the demographics of the 1990s: The aging of the baby-boom generation means that the market for larger homes should remain strong, as homeowners trade up to more spacious dwellings.

The renovation of existing homes is expected to continue its strong growth of the past several years. This growth in renovation is driven by do-it-yourselfers who are cutting costs and adding value to their properties. The primary areas of use for solid surface materials are in bathrooms and kitchens. There is also a strong trend toward more attractive, open, and brighter kitchens. Tables 2 and 3 and Figures 1 and 2 provide an overview of the kitchen color and countertop material preferences in the United States, and general information about the housing industry. Table 4 estimates the potential for solid surface sales in the kitchen industry.

Solid Surface Market Potential Estimate of Kitchen Industry TABLE 4

Kitchen jobs performed in 1990	5.5 Million
Estimated growth (conservative 7%)	10%
Kitchen jobs that install new countertops	60%
Kitchen jobs that use solid surface countertops	25%
Cost per kitchen job	$3,000–$4,000
Therefore the calculation	
Growth in kitchen jobs	5,500,000 × 1.07 5,885,000
Kitchen jobs with new countertops	5,885,000 × .60 3,531,000
Of these with solid surface countertops	3,531,000 × .25 882,800
Total industry	882,800 × $3,500 3,089,625,000
Total industry including labor	$3,089,625,000

Source: National Kitchen & Bath Association Survey, 1989.

FIGURE 1

Change in Total Households, Forecasted Change (%), 1987–1992

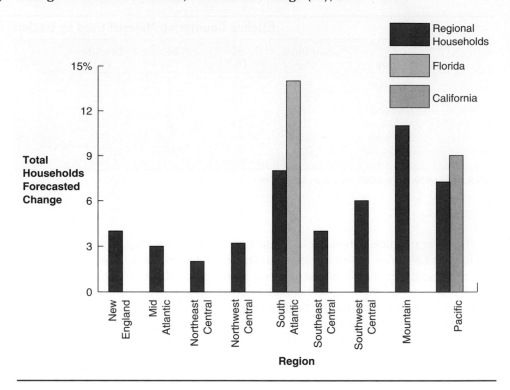

FIGURE 2

Total Households, 1992 Projections by Region

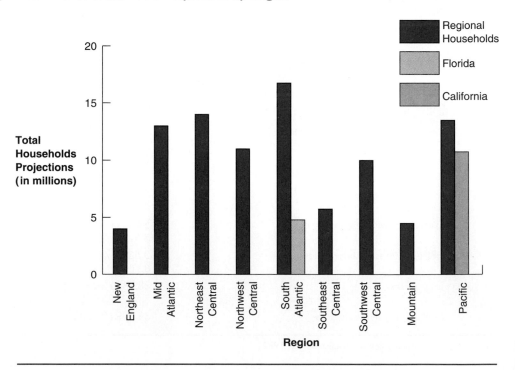

THE PURCHASE DECISION-MAKING PROCESS

Each of the above-mentioned industries has a particular decision process and specific participants with different roles and levels of influence.

The Hospital Industry

In the case of hospitals, architects make the decision to use solid surface materials. The subcontractor/fabricator may choose the brand if the architect has not specified one. The hospital administrators have final budgetary control. In times of tight budgets, the relatively expensive solid surface materials may be one of the first items to be slashed. In this purchasing process, price sensitivity is high since the solid surface materials are viewed as a luxury.

The Laboratory Industry

The laboratory industry may be broken down into four different subgroupings for further analysis of the purchasing decision process. These are the private labs, corporate labs, government labs, and academic labs.

Private labs are usually small and major construction material decisions are made by the owner/operator. The owner/operator usually makes the remodeling decisions. In the case of new construction, the architect decides upon the use of solid surface materials. The owner/operator may request a specific brand. If neither of these decision makers has specified a brand, the subcontractor/fabricator will decide. Since these labs are for-profit operations, cost is a major consideration.

Corporate labs use a centralized or a regional buying procedure. The local lab releases a request and specifications for a solid surface material. They may request a specific brand. The regional purchasing office solicits bids from suppliers and issues the purchase order. Depending upon the local lab/purchasing office relationship, the office may have veto rights over the local lab specification of a specific brand, especially if a large price disparity exists. Price and supplier location are the most important considerations.

Government labs utilize a complex purchasing process. If the cost of the work exceeds $500, the order must be placed through the local government purchasing office. The office matches the specifications of the request against the authorized list and solicits bids from the appropriate suppliers. The winning supplier must install the material. Cost is of the greatest importance, with warranty and supplier location being secondary.

Academic labs specify a purchase to their physical plant office. It is then the responsibility of the office to locate potential suppliers, solicit bids, order, and install the material. As in the case of the corporate lab, the lab director may specify the brand, depending upon his influence on the physical plant purchaser. Price, reputation, and location are of major importance to the physical plant purchasers.

Kitchen Renovation and Design

The purchasing decision-making process for this market is very complex, with many players involved. The distributors of solid surface materials are licensed by the manufacturer of the material and carry a line of brands. Certified Kitchen Designers (CKD) are often hired by homeowners to help make the decisions regarding kitchen renovation. The CKD may be following the materials choice of the customer, with budget being the only other factor, or the CKD may be acting as a "lifestyle counselor," given the charge of selecting the appropriate material for the customer's needs. In this case, the home-owner will approve the choice of certain colors/materials. The CKD may also play a role in the distribution chain, often being the licensed distributor/dealer for at least one solid surface material. Fabricators may serve an important role in the decision-making process and may be dealers themselves. They have "hands-on" experience and are looked upon by other decision makers for expert product advice. Fabricators are often certified by more than one solid surface company. A fabricator may be the licensed dealer and the distributor for the products it installs.

Residential Home Construction

The architect decides upon the specifications and passes these on to the builder. The purchasing agent solicits bids on a variety of materials available. The VP-Sales/Marketing reviews the available suppliers and determines the options to be offered. The kitchen countertop plan will offer a number of color and material options for the customer to choose from. Once the material has been selected, the subcontractor (who may also be the dealer and fabricator) will make the decision as to which material to use based upon financial constraints, ease of fabrication, and safety factors involved. These safety concerns arise from the dust and fumes created when working with the material. This is a major concern for the fabricators.

THE AMERICAN COMPETITION

Corian

The major competition in the United States comes from the giant Du Pont Co. concern and its Corian brand of solid surface materials. Corian was the original solid surface countertop, introduced in 1972. This material was unchallenged in the market for 13 years and now holds a commanding 85 percent of the market. The Corian product line includes sheets, integral and separate lavatories, and integral and separate kitchen and bar sinks. In addition, Corian offers prefabricated shower-surround and tub-surround kits. Ten colors are available. Sheets are offered in the standard $1/2''$ and $3/4''$ thicknesses, and are also available in a $1/4''$ sheet. These sheets come in a variety of lengths and widths. Du Pont offers a ten-year limited warranty against defects, which has become the industry standard. Du Pont also offers courses in the proper installation of Corian and certifies fabricators.

Du Pont's marketing strategy for Corian consists of a sophisticated network of elements which interact to produce brand awareness, and an image of Corian as the premium brand of solid surface materials. Du Pont uses print advertisement as a primary means of building brand awareness and recognition of the product's qualities and uses in various sectors of the distribution channel. Print ads appear in 19 trade publications which reach architects, interior designers, engineers, contractors, kitchen and bath designers, and end-users.

Other niche players have appeared over the last four years, three of which have captured approximately 3 percent of the market each.

Fountainhead

The manufacturer of Fountainhead is the Nevamar Corporation, Maryland, an experienced manufacturer of laminated countertops for 40 years. It has been producing the Fountainhead line of solid surface materials for two years. Fountainhead is a blend of polyester and acrylic in combination with an alumina trihydrate filler. This blend is considered superior to polyester in durability and workability. The Fountainhead line offers sheets and lavatory bowls available in nine colors. Like Corian, the sheets are offered in $1/4''$, $1/2''$, and $3/4''$ thicknesses, and in a variety of lengths and widths. A ten-year warranty covers the material against defects. Classes are held for the fabricators, although a formal certification is not given. There are approximately 80 Nevamar distributors scattered throughout the United States. Most of these distributors are wholly owned subsidiaries and can buy at cost from each other. In 1990, Nevamar had sales of $140 million.

Avonite

Avonite was the second entrant into the solid surface market, having entered four years ago. The product consists of a blend of polyester alloys and fillers. It has created a niche by offering a wide variety of color combinations and designs, positioning itself as the "Decorative Surface Material."

The sheets are available in 20 colors, including 13 granites and 7 agates (marble). The colors may be matched to any type of color for custom applications. They come in only one standard sheet size, available in $1/2''$ and $3/4''$ thicknesses. Custom sizes are available and a $1/8''$ thick sheet may be special-ordered. Avonite recently experienced an interruption in production due to the transfer of its manufacturing facilities from California to New Mexico, causing some damage to its market share. A new manufacturing facility will open in Vancouver which will produce shaped products. It plans to produce undermount and surface mount vanities, kitchen sinks, tubs, and pedestal vanities. It has just introduced a new product, Inlays, which is a sheet having two different colors in a Southwest pattern. Avonite, like the other manufacturers, carries a ten-year warranty, yet only if installed by a certified fabricator. The company conducts certification seminars.

Surrel/2000X

Manufactured by the well-known surfacing company Formica, Surrel complements a line of laminates and surface materials for walls and cabinets. Surrel is a fully densified polyester resin compound with fillers. It is available in sheets, vanity tops, shower walls, bath walls, tubs, and integral and separate lavatory bowls. Surrel is available in six colors, generally a pale pastel, although three granite colors will be available soon. The sheets come in $1/4''$, $1/2''$, and $3/4''$ thicknesses and in a variety of sizes. Expansion of its manufacturing capacity is expected soon. Surrel was the last of the above-mentioned to enter the market and owes much of its current success to its inclusion in the Formica line of products. Surrel carries the industry-standard warranty of ten years and provides a 32-page pictorial instruction book for the installers.

Until 1985, Formica was a division of Cyanamid. It was sold to its long-time top executives in a leveraged buyout for $200 million. In 1987, the company was taken public in an offering designed to lighten the company's debt load. Formica's management has taken harsh measures to make the company more competitive. In the United States, its market share (30 percent) is second to Ralph Wilson Plastics (35 percent). Formica sales in 1986 reached $378 million, 92 percent of which corresponded to sales of its high-pressure decorative laminates.

Other companies have entered the market with products which are not significantly different from the above products. One significant new entrant is the Gardsman Company with its Solidex brand. It is just arriving in the market and little data are available. The product has been successfully marketed in Canada. It is a polyester resin and is available in molded shapes in eight colors. Solidex is offered with a 12-year warranty, the only solid surface manufacturer offering this guarantee. The product is expected to be priced competitively.

PRICE

A manufacturer price comparison of $^1/_2''$ thick, $30'' \times 145''$, for these leading brands is used as an illustration. Prices vary with thickness, size, and color.

	New York	Los Angeles
Corian	$284	295
Fountainhead	$280	293
Avonite		
Standard	$387	375
Inlays	$514	487
Surrel	$332	332
Surfstone	$245*	266*

* DDP-delivered duties paid

Butler Consultants commissioned an independent laboratory test of Surfstone in comparison with the four main American competitors. The results showed that Surfstone was the least porous (therefore most hygienic) and proved the most resistant to chemicals. In addition, Surfstone produced the least amount of dust and fumes when cut.

Deciding a Strategy

Kees was very pleased with the report, but his presentation to the board is in just five days. He is expected to present an evaluation of the marketing opportunity presented by each market/industry and recommend a market for the initial introduction of Surfstone.

Undoubtedly, the board will be highly concerned with gaining a solid initial presence in the market, for it will surely determine the long-term prospects of the company. Kees is aware that the key to Tollens's success lies in a solid, yet aggressive, competitive positioning of company operations in the market. The ability to offer a high level of service, undoubtedly, is conditioned by the selection of market and type of entry strategy adopted. Should one of the European export models be transplanted to the United States, or would a nontraditional approach be more appropriate? In Italy, the strategy of exporting to a full-service master distributor has been very profitable. Equally attractive is the Belgian option of shipping directly to 12 regional distributors under the supervision of a Belgian sales manager. What is the best route to compete in the United States?

Even though other issues are highly critical, such as media selection, logistics, and pricing, they are not to be addressed at this stage.

Joemarin Oy

Finland's first customers in the sailboat business are generally believed to have been the Vikings. More recently, ships and boats were exported as part payment for World War II reparations. This long tradition in building sailboats is due, no doubt, to Finland's proximity to the sea, long coastline, and 60,000 lakes. Among luxury sailing yachts, the Swan boats of Nautor Oy and the Finnsailers of Fiskars Oy are internationally known and admired. There are, however, over 100 other boat builders in Finland that turn out 10,000 sailing yachts yearly.

Although most of the Finnish sailboat companies are situated on the coast, for obvious reasons, Joemarin Oy is located in the town of Joensuu, roughly 450 kilometers northeast of Helsinki. Joemarin was founded in the town that lends part of its name to the company because of the efforts of Kehitysaluerahasto, which is the Development Area Foundation of the Finnish government. Kehitysaluerahasto provided a loan of four million Finnish marks to Joemarin, a privately owned company, to start its operations in the Joensuu area because of the town's high rate of unemployment.

The present product line consists of three types of fiberglass sailboats. The Joemarin 17 is a coastal sailing yacht with a new design approach. (See Figure 1.) This approach is to provide a craft that enables a family to make weekend and holiday cruises in coastal waters and also offers exciting sailing. The sailboat is very fast. The Finnish Yacht Racing Association stated in its test in which the Joemarin 17 was judged to be the best in her class: "She is delicate, lively, spacious, and easy to steer. She is well balanced and has a high-quality interior. She is especially fast on the beat and lively to handle in a free wind."

The Joemarin 17, a small day cruiser with berths for two adults and two children, has a sail area of 130 square feet, weighs one-half ton, and has an overall length of a little over 17 feet. The hull is made of glass-reinforced plastic (GRP), and the mast and boom are made of aluminum. The boat has a drop keel that is useful when negotiating shallow anchorages or when lifting the boat on a trailer for transportation. The layout of the boat is shown in Figure 2.

The Joemarin 34 is a relatively large motor sailer that sleeps seven people in three separate compartments. The main saloon contains an adjustable dining table, a complete galley, and a navigator's compartment. The main saloon is separated from the fore cabin by a folding door. The aft cabin, which is entered by a separate companionway, contains a double berth, wardrobe, wash basin, and lockers. The toilet and shower are situated between the fore cabin and the main saloon. The boat has a sail area of 530 square feet, weighs about five tons, and has an overall length of 33 feet 9 inches. A significant feature of the craft is that she is equipped with a 47-horsepower diesel engine.

The Joemarin 34 has the same design approach as the 17. She is well appointed, with sufficient space for seven people to live comfortably. An important feature is that the three separate living compartments allow for considerable privacy. In addition, however, the modern hull is quite sleek, making her an excellent sailing yacht.

The Joemarin 36 was designed for a different purpose. Whereas the 17 and 34 are oriented toward a family approach to sailing—combining the features of safety and comfortable accommodations with good sailing ability—the 36 is first and foremost a sailing craft. It does have two berths, a small galley, and toilet facilities, but the emphasis is on

---

Source: This case was prepared by James H. Sood of the American University. Reprinted with permission.

FIGURE 1   Joemarin 17: Ideal for Family Cruising as Well as Exciting Racing

FIGURE 2   The Layout of the Joemarin 17

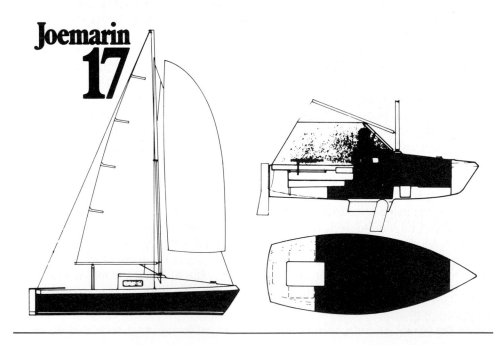

sailing and racing rather than comfort. The boat has a sail area of 420 square feet, weighs a little less than four tons, and has an overall length of 35 feet 10 inches. The boat is also equipped with a small (7-horsepower) diesel engine for emergency power situations. The Joemarin 36 is a traditional Swedish design and, therefore, is directed almost solely to the Swedish market.

The company was established in order to manufacture sailboats for export. The Finnish sailboat market is small because of the short sailing season. Nevertheless, the company has been successful in marketing the 17 in Finland, although this was difficult in the beginning because of the lack of boat dealers. To circumvent this problem, Joemarin persuaded a number of new car dealers throughout the country to handle the Joemarin 17 on an agency basis. This involved the company's providing one boat to each car dealer, who placed it in the showroom. The dealer then marketed the sailboats for a 15 percent sales commission.

Although many people scoffed at this idea, the system produced reasonable sales and also made the company known throughout Finland. This contributed to an arrangement with one of the largest cooperative wholesale-retail operations in Finland. Like most cooperatives, this organization began with agricultural products; however, the product range of the company now includes virtually every conceivable consumer product. The present contract states that the cooperative will purchase 80 Joemarin 17 boats per year for the next three years.

The Swedish market is served by a selling agent, although this representative has not been particularly effective. Because Sweden is also the home of many sailboat builders, the company has tried to market only the 36 in that country. In Denmark, France, Holland, Germany, and the United Kingdom, Joemarin has marketed the 34 through importers. These importers operate marinas in addition to new sailboat dealerships. They purchase the boats from Joemarin for their own accounts and mark up the price by about 20 percent. In return for exclusive marketing rights in their respective countries, they agree to purchase a minimum number (usually three or four) of the 34 design per year. None of these importers is interested in marketing the 17 or the 36; the shipping cost for the 17 is too high compared with the value of the boat, and there is little customer interest in the 36.

Joemarin is planning to introduce a new sailboat. Whereas the present products were designed by people in the company who were relatively unknown (to the customers), the hull of the new sailboat has been designed by an internationally known boat designer. The cost of these design services was a $10,000 initial fee plus a $1,200 royalty fee to be paid for each boat produced. The new sailboat, the Joemarin 29, has an interior quite similar to that of the Joemarin 34. This is not unexpected because the same Joemarin people designed the interiors and decks of both sailboats.

The new boat is a motor sailer that sleeps six people in three separate compartments, is 28 feet 9 inches long, weighs four tons, has a joined cabin space and a separate aft cabin, small galley, toilet and shower facilities, and a 12-horsepower diesel engine. Because of a new construction technique that greatly reduces the amount of fiberglass required, the variable costs to construct the boat are only 60 percent of the costs for the 34. With a preliminary selling price of 195,000 Finnish marks, the Joemarin 29 is receiving favorable attention, and the company is concerned that sales may have an adverse effect on sales of the 34.

The company categorizes the marketing expenses as fixed costs because allocating these expenses to specific products is difficult. The major element of the program is participation in international boat shows in London, Paris, Hamburg, Amsterdam, Copenhagen, and Helsinki. The initial purpose of participating in these shows was to locate

TABLE 1	Joemarin Sales

	Last Year			Present Year		
	No.	Average Price[a]	Revenue	No.	Average Price[a]	Revenue
J/M-17	200	27,000	5,400,000	240	29,700	7,128,000
J/M-29	—	—		—	—	
J/M-34	30	324,000	9,720,000	36	356,000	12,830,000
J/M-36	4	189,000	756,000	5	207,900	1,039,500
			15,876,000			20,997,900

[a]All prices are manufacturer's prices; prices and revenues are in Finnish marks: 1.00 Finnmark = U.S. $0.185.

suitable importers in the target markets; however, this effort is maintained in order to support the marketing programs of the importers. The importers are also supported by advertising in the leading yachting magazines in the national markets. Joemarin's personal selling effort consists primarily of servicing the importers and agents and staffing the exhibitions at the boat shows. Most of the sales promotion costs are the result of the elaborate sales brochures that the company has developed for each boat. These brochures are printed in four colors on three folded pages of high-quality paper. The costs are greatly increased, however, by having to print a relatively small number of each brochure in Finnish, French, English, German, and Swedish. The brochures are provided to the agents and importers and are used at the boat shows.

The company is in the process of preparing its production and marketing plan for the coming year in order to arrange financing. The president is strongly committed to the continued growth of the company, and the market indications suggest that there is a reasonably strong demand for the 17 in Finland and for the 34 in most of the other national markets. The sales results of the previous and present years are shown in Table 1; the profit statement for the present year is shown in Table 2.

The main problem in developing the plan for next year is determining the price for each sailboat in each market. In previous years, Joemarin had established its prices in

TABLE 2	Joemarin Profit Statement for Present Year

	In Finnmarks	As a Percentage of Sales
Sales revenue	20,790,000[a]	
Variable costs (direct labor and materials)	13,510,000	65.0%
Fixed costs:		
Production (building expenses, production management salaries)	945,000	4.5
Product design costs (salaries, prototypes, testing, consultants)	1,323,000	6.4
Administration costs (salaries, insurance, office expenses)	648,000	3.1
Marketing costs (salaries, advertising, boat shows, sales promotion, travel expenses)	2,284,000	11.0
Total fixed costs	5,200,000	25.0
Profit before taxes	2,080,000	10.0

[a]All prices are manufacturer's prices; prices and revenues are in Finnish marks; 1.00 Finnmark = U.S. $0.185.

**Retail Price in the European Market of
Sailing Yachts as a Function of Overall Length**

FIGURE 3

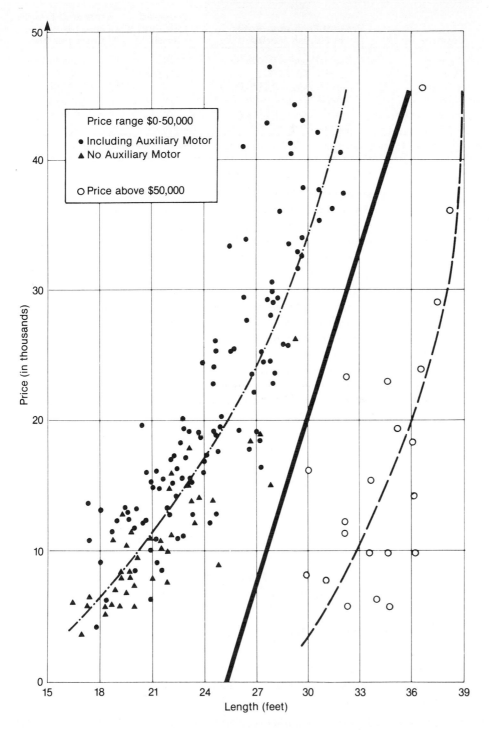

Note: All yachts to the right of the bold dividing line are priced above $50,000.

| TABLE 3 | Shipping Costs for Joemarin 36 to Sweden and Joemarin 29 and 34 to Other Countries |

Country	Present Exchange Rates in Finnish Marks	Expected Inflation Rates	Estimated Freight and Insurance Costs per Boat
Denmark	Danish Kroner = 0.628	12%	13,500 Fmks.
France	French Franc = 0.778	10%	19,000 Fmks.
Holland	Dutch Guilder = 2.015	9	17,000 Fmks.
Sweden	Swedish Kroner = 0.725	12	10,000 Fmks.
United Kingdom	English Pound = 8.308	14	22,000 Fmks.
Germany	German Mark = 2.204	7	17,000 Fmks.
Finland	—	12	—

Finnish marks, on an ex-factory basis. Management has become convinced, however, that it must change the terms of its prices in order to meet competition in the foreign markets. Thus, the company has decided to offer CIF prices to its foreign customers in the currency of the foreign country. The use of truck ferries between Finland and Sweden, Denmark, and Germany is expected to make this pricing approach more competitive.

Joemarin would also like to assure its agents and importers that the prices will remain in effect for the entire year, but the financial manager is concerned about the possible volatility of exchange rates because of the varying rates of inflation in the market countries. The present exchange rates, the expected inflation rates in the market countries, and the estimated costs to ship the Joemarin 36 to Stockholm and the Joemarin 29 and 34 to the other foreign marinas are shown in Table 3.

A second difficulty in pricing the product line of Joemarin is to establish a price for the 29 that will reflect the value of the boat but will not reduce the sales of the 34. There are three schools of thought concerning the pricing of motor sailers. The predominant theory is that price is a function of the overall length of the sailboat. A number of people, however, believe that the overall weight of the craft is a more accurate basis. The third opinion argues that price is a function of the special features and equipment. Figure 3, which was prepared by a Swiss market-research firm, shows the relationship between present retail prices and the length of new motor sailers in the West European market.

Questions for Discussion

1. Determine the optimal manufacturer's selling prices in the Finnish market for the four Joemarin sailboats for the coming year.

2. Determine the CIF prices for the Joemarin 36 to the final customer in Sweden for the coming year. The agent's commission is 15 percent of the final selling price, and the final selling price should be in Swedish kroner.

3. Recommend a course of action for the company to take in regard to the Joemarin 36.

4. Determine the CIF prices, in the foreign currencies, for the Joemarin 29 and 34 to the importers in Denmark, France, Holland, the United Kingdom, and Germany for the coming year.

5. Develop a production and marketing plan for Joemarin for the coming year. What steps can the company take to ensure that the plan is in line with the demand for its products in its foreign markets?

Sperry/MacLennan Architects and Planners

In August 1988, Mitch Brooks, a junior partner and director of Sperry/MacLennan (S/M), a Dartmouth, Nova Scotia, architectural practice specializing in recreational facilities, is in the process of developing a plan to export his company's services. He intends to present the plan to the other directors at their meeting the first week of October. The regional market for architectural services is showing some signs of slowing, and S/M realizes that it must seek new markets. As Sheila Sperry, the office manager and one of the directors, said at their last meeting: "You have to go wider than your own backyard. After all, you can only build so many pools in your own backyard."

ABOUT THE COMPANY

Drew Sperry, one of the two senior partners in Sperry/MacLennan, founded the company in 1972 as a one-man architectural practice. After graduating from the Nova Scotia Technical College (now the Technical University of Nova Scotia) in 1966, Sperry worked for six years for Robert J. Flinn before deciding that it was time to start his own company. By then he had cultivated a loyal clientele and a reputation as a good design architect and planner. In the first year, the business was supported part-time by a contract with the Province of Prince Edward Island Department of Tourism to undertake parks planning and the design of parks facilities, from park furniture to interpretive centers. At the end of its first year, the company was incorporated as H. Drew Sperry and Associates; by then Sperry had added three junior architects, a draftsman, and a secretary. One of those architects was John MacLennan, who would later become a senior partner in Sperry/MacLennan.

Throughout the 1970s, the practice grew rapidly as the local economy expanded, even though the market for architectural services was competitive. The architectural program at the Nova Scotia Technical College (TUNS) was graduating more architects wishing to stay in the Maritimes than could be readily absorbed. But that was not the only reason why competition was stiff; there was a perception among businesspeople and local government personnel that if you wanted the best, you had to get it from Toronto or New York. The company's greatest challenge throughout this period was persuading the local authorities that they did not have to go to Central Canada for first-class architectural expertise.

With the baby-boom generation entering the housing market, more than enough business came its way to enable Sperry to develop a thriving architectural practice, and by 1979 the company had grown to 15 employees and had established branch offices in Charlottetown and Fredericton. These branch offices had been established to provide a local market presence and meet licensing requirements during an aggressive growth period. The one in Charlottetown operated under the name of Allison & Sperry Associates, with Jim Allison as the partner, whereas in Fredericton, partner Peter Fellows was in charge.

Source: This case has been prepared by Dr. Mary R. Brooks, of Dalhousie University, as a basis for classroom discussion rather than to illustrate effective or ineffective handling of an administrative situation. The assistance of the Secretary of State, Canadian Studies Program, in developing the case is gratefully acknowledged. Copyright © 1990 Mary R. Brooks. Reprinted with permission.

But the growth could not last. The early 1980s was not an easy time for the industry, and many architectural firms found themselves unable to stay in business through a very slow period in 1981–1982. For Sperry/MacLennan, it meant a severe reduction in staff, and it also marked the end of the branch offices. Financially stretched and with work winding down on a multipurpose civic sports facility, the Dartmouth Sportsplex, the company was asked to enter a design competition for an aquatics center in Saint John, New Brunswick. They had to win or close their doors. The company laid off all but the three remaining partners, Drew, Sheila Sperry, and John MacLennan. However, one draftsman and the secretary refused to leave, working without pay for several months in the belief that the company would win; their faith in the firm is still appreciated today.

Their persistence and faith were rewarded. In 1983, Sperry won the competition for the aquatics facility for the Canada Games to be held in Saint John. The clients in Saint John wanted to build a new aquatic center that would house the Canada Games competition and provide a community facility that was self-supporting after the games were over. The facility needed to reflect a forward-thinking image to the world and act as a linchpin in the downtown revitalization plan. Therefore, it was paramount that the facility adhere to all technical competition requirements and that the design include renovation details for its conversion to a community facility sporting a new Sperry design element, the "indoor beach." The Saint John Canada Games Society decided to use Sperry for the contract and was very pleased with the building, the more so since the building won two design awards in 1985: the Facility of Merit Award for its "outstanding design" from *Athletics Business* and the Canadian Parks and Recreation Facility of Excellence Award. Sperry had gained national recognition for its sports facility expertise, and its reputation as a good design firm specializing in sports facilities was secured.

From the beginning, the company found recreational facilities work to be fun and exciting. To quote Sheila Sperry, this type of client "wants you to be innovative and new. It's a dream for an architect because it gives him an opportunity to use all the shapes and colors and natural light. It's a very exciting medium to work in." So they decided to focus their promotional efforts to get more of this type of work and consolidate their "pool designer" image by associating with Creative Aquatics on an exclusive basis in 1984. Creative Aquatics provided aquatics programming and technical operations expertise (materials, systems, water treatment, safety, and so on) to complement the design and planning skills at Sperry.

The construction industry rebounded in 1984; declining interest rates ushered in a mini building boom, which kept everyone busy for the 1984–1987 period. Jim Reardon joined the company in 1983 and quickly acquired the experience and knowledge that would ease the company through its inevitable expansion. John MacLennan, by then a senior shareholder in the firm, wanted to develop a base in the large Ontario market and establish an office in Toronto. Jim Reardon was able to take over John's activities with very little difficulty, since he had been working very closely with John in the recreational facilities aspect of the business. Reardon became a junior partner in 1986.

With John MacLennan's move to Toronto in 1985, the company changed its name to Sperry/MacLennan in hopes that the name could be used for both offices. But the Ontario Association of Architects ruled that the name could not include "Sperry" because Drew Sperry was not an Ontario resident, and the Toronto office was required to operate under the name of MacLennan Architects. The Ontario office gradually became self-supporting, and the company successfully entered a new growth phase.

Mitch Brooks joined the practice in 1987. He had graduated from TUNS in 1975 and had been one of the small number of his class to try and make a go of it in Halifax. The decision to add Brooks as a partner, albeit a junior one, stemmed from their compatibility. Brooks was a good production architect, and work under his supervision came in on budget and on time, a factor compatible with the Sperry/MacLennan emphasis on customer service. The company's fee revenue amounted to approximately $1.2 million in the 1987 fiscal year; however, salaries are a major business expense, and profits after taxes (but before employee bonuses) accounted for only 4.5 percent of revenue.

Now it is late August, and with the weather cooling, Mitch Brooks reflects on his newest task, planning for the coming winter's activities. The company's reputation in the Canadian sports facility market is secure. The company has completed or has in construction five sports complexes in the Maritimes and five in Ontario, and three more facilities are in design. The awards have followed, and just this morning, Drew was notified of their latest achievement—the company has won the $10,000 *Canadian Architect* Grand Award for the Grand River Aquatics and Community Center near Kitchener, Ontario. This award is a particularly prestigious one because it is given by fellow architects in recognition of design excellence. Last week, Sheila Sperry received word that the Amherst, N.S., YM-YWCA won the American National Swimming Pool and Spa Gold Medal for pool design against French and Mexican finalists, giving them international recognition. Mitch Brooks is looking forward to his task. The partners anticipate a slight slowdown in late 1988, and economists are predicting a recession for 1989. With 19 employees to keep busy and a competitor on the West Coast, they decided this morning that it is time to consider exporting their hard-won expertise.

THE ARCHITECTURE INDUSTRY

In order to practice architecture in Canada, an architect must graduate from an accredited school and serve a period of apprenticeship with a licensed architect, during which time he or she must experience all facets of the practice. At the end of this period, the would-be architect must pass an examination similar to that required of U.S. architects.

Architects are licensed provincially, and these licenses are not readily transferable from province to province. Various levels of reciprocity are in existence. For this reason, joint ventures are not that uncommon in the business. In order to "cross" provincial boundaries, architecture firms in one province often enter into a joint venture arrangement with a local company. For example, the well-known design firm of Arthur Erickson of Vancouver/Toronto often engages in joint ventures with local production architects, as was the case for its design of the new Sir James Dunn Law Library on the campus of Dalhousie University in Halifax.

In the United States, Canadian architects are well respected. The primary difficulty in working in the United States has been in immigration policies, which limit the movement of staff and provide difficulties in securing contracts. These policies will be eliminated with the Free Trade Agreement and the reciprocity accord signed between the American Institute of Architects and the Royal Architectural Institute of Canada, a voluntary group representing the provincial associations.

Because architects in Nova Scotia are ethically prohibited from advertising their services, an architect's best advertisement is a good project, well done and well received. The provincial association (Nova Scotia Association of Architects—NSAA) will supply potential clients with basic information about licensed firms, their area of specialization, and so on. NSAA guidelines limit marketing to announcements of new partners, presentations to targeted potential clients, advertisements of a business card size with "business card" information, and participation in media events.

The provincial association also provides a minimum schedule of fees, although many clients view this as the maximum they should pay. Although architects would like to think that the client chooses to do business with them because they like their past work, the price of the service is often the decision point. Some developers prefer to buy services on a basis other than the published fee schedule, such as a lump-sum amount or a per-square-foot price. Although fee cutting is not encouraged by the professional organization, it is a factor in winning business, particularly when interest rates are high and construction slow.

Because the "product" of an architecture firm is the service of designing a building, the marketing of the "product" centers on the architect's experience with a particular building type. Therefore, it is imperative that the architect convince the client that he or she has the necessary experience and capability to undertake the project and to complete it satisfactorily. S/M has found with its large projects that the amount of time spent meeting with the client requires some local presence, although the design need not be done locally.

The process of marketing architectural services is one of marketing ideas. Therefore, it is imperative that the architect and the client have the same objectives and ultimately the same vision. Although that vision may be constrained by the client's budget, part of the marketing process is one of communicating with the client to ensure these common objectives exist.

Architects get business in a number of ways. "Walk-in" business is negligible, and most of S/M's contracts are a result of one of the following five processes:

1. A satisfied client gives a referral.
2. A juried design competition is announced (S/M has found that these prestigious jobs, even though they offer "runners-up" partial compensation, are not worth entering except to win, since costs are too high and the compensation offered other entrants too low. Second place is the same as last place. The Dartmouth Sportsplex and the Saint John Aquatic Center were both design competition wins.)
3. A client publishes a "Call for Proposals" or a "Call for Expressions of Interest" as the start of a formal selection process. (S/M rates these opportunities; unless it has a 75 percent chance of winning the contract, it views the effort as not worth the risk.)
4. A potential client invites a limited number of architectural firms to submit their qualifications as the start of a formal selection process. (S/M has a prepared qualification package that it can customize for a particular client.)
5. S/M hears of a potential building and contacts the client, presenting its qualifications.

The fourth and fifth processes are most common in buildings done for institutions and large corporations. Since the primary buyers of sports facilities tend to be municipalities or educational institutions, this is the way S/M acquires a substantial share of its work. Although juried competitions are not that common, the publicity possible from success in landing this work is important to S/M. The company has found that its success in securing a contract is often dependent on the client's criteria and the current state of the local market, with no particular pattern evident for a specific building type.

After the architect signs the contract, there will be a number of meetings with the client as the concept evolves and the drawings and specifications develop. On a large sports facility project, the hours of contact can run into the hundreds. Depending on the type of project, client meetings may be held weekly or every two weeks; during the development of working drawings and specifications for a complex building, meetings may be as often as once a day. Therefore, continuing client contact is as much a part of the service sold as the drawings, specifications, and site supervision and, in fact, may be the key factor in repeat business.

Developers in Nova Scotia are often not loyal buyers, changing architects with every major project or two. Despite this, architects are inclined to think the buyer's loyalty is greater than it really is. Therefore, S/M scrutinizes buyers carefully, interested in those that can pay for a premium product. S/M's philosophy is to provide "quality products with quality service for quality clients" and thus produce facilities that will reflect well on the company.

THE OPPORTUNITY

In 1987, External Affairs and the Royal Architectural Institute of Canada commissioned a study of exporting opportunities for architects on the assumption that free trade in architectural services would be possible under the Free Trade Agreement. The report, entitled *Precision, Planning, and Perseverance: Exporting Architectural Services to the United States,* identified eight market niches for Canadian architects in the United States, one of which was educational facilities, in particular postsecondary institutions.

This niche, identified by Brooks as most likely to match S/M's capabilities, is controlled by state governments and private organizations. Universities are known not to be particularly loyal to local firms and so present a potential market to be developed. The study reported that "post-secondary institutions require design and management competence, whatever the source" (p. 39). Athletic facilities were identified as a possible niche for architects with mixed-use facility experience. Finally, the study concluded that "there is an enormous backlog of capital maintenance and new building requirements facing most higher education institutions" (p. 38).

In addition to the above factors, the study indicated others that Brooks felt were of importance:

1. The United States has 30 percent fewer architectural firms per capita than Canada.
2. The market shares many Canadian values and work practices.
3. The population shift away from the Northeast to the sunbelt is beginning to reverse.
4. Americans are demanding better buildings.

Although Brooks knows that Canadian firms have always had a good reputation internationally for the quality of their buildings, he is concerned that American firms are well ahead of Canadian ones in their use of CADD (computer-assisted design and drafting) for everything from conceptual design to facility management. S/M, in spite of best intentions, has been unable to get CADD off the ground but is in the process of applying to the Atlantic Canada Opportunities Agency for financial assistance in switching over to CADD.

Finally, the study cautions that "joint ventures with a U.S. architectural firm may be required but the facility managers network of the APPA [Association of Physical Plant Administrators of Universities and Colleges] should also be actively pursued" (p. 41).

Under free trade, architects will be able to freely engage in trade in services. Architects will be able to travel to the United States and set up an architectural practice without having to become qualified under the American Institute of Architects; as long as they are members of their respective provincial associations and have passed provincial licensing exams and apprenticeship requirements, they will be able to travel and work in the United States and import staff as required.

WHERE TO START?

In a meeting in Halifax in January 1988, the Department of External Affairs had indicated that trade to the United States in architectural services was going to be one positive benefit of the Free Trade Agreement to come into force in January 1989. As a response,

S/M has targeted New England for its expansion because of its geographical proximity to S/M's home base in the Halifax/Dartmouth area and also because of its population density and similar climatic conditions. However, with all the hype about free trade and the current focus on the United States, Brooks is quite concerned that the company might be overlooking some other very lucrative markets for his company's expertise. As part of his October presentation to the board, he wants to identify and evaluate other possible markets for S/M's services. Other parts of the United States, or the affluent countries of Europe where recreational facilities are regularly patronized and design is taken seriously, might provide a better export market, given S/M's string of design successes at home and the international recognition afforded by the Amherst facility design award. Brooks feels that designing two sports facilities a year in a new market would be an acceptable goal.

As part of searching for leads, Brooks notes that the APPA charges $575 for a membership, which provides access to its membership list once a year. But this is only one source of leads. And, of course, there is the U.S. Department of Commerce, Bureau of the Census, as another source of information for him to tap. He wonders what other sources are possible.

S/M looks to have a very good opportunity in the New England market with all of its small universities and colleges. After a decade of cutbacks on spending, corporate donations and alumni support for U.S. universities has never been so strong, and many campuses have sports facilities that are outdated and have been poorly maintained. But Mitch Brooks is not sure that the New England market is the best. After all, a seminar on exporting that he attended last week indicated that the most geographically close market, or even the most psychically close one, may not be the best choice for long-run profit maximization and/or market share.

Questions for Discussion

1. What types of information will Brooks need to collect before he can even begin to assess the New England market? Develop a series of questions you feel are critical to this assessment.

2. What selection criteria do you believe will be relevant to the assessment of any alternative markets? What preliminary market parameters are relevant to the evaluation of S/M's *global* options?

3. Assuming that S/M decides on the New England market, what information will be needed to implement an entry strategy?

Water from Iceland

Stan Otis was in a contemplative mood. He had just hung up the phone after talking with Roger Morey, vice president of Citicorp. Morey had made him a job offer in the investment banking sector of the firm. The interviews had gone well, and Citicorp management was impressed with Stan's credentials from a major northeastern private university. "I think you can do well here, Stan. Let us know within a week whether you accept the job," Morey had said.

The three-month search had paid off well, Stan thought. However, an alternative plan complicated the decision to accept the position.

Stan had returned several months before from an extended trip throughout Europe, a delayed graduation present from his parents. Among other places, he had visited Reykjavik, Iceland. Even though he could not communicate well, he found the island enchanting. What particularly fascinated him was the lack of industry and the purity of the natural landscape. In particular, he felt the water tasted extremely good. Returning home, he began to consider making this water available in the United States.

THE WATER MARKET IN THE UNITED STATES

In order to consider the possibilities of importing Icelandic water, Stan knew that he first had to learn more about the general water market in the United States. Fortunately, some former college friends were working in a market-research firm. Owing Stan some favors, these friends furnished him with a consulting report on the water market.

The Consulting Report

Primary types of water available for human consumption in the United States are treated or processed water, mineral water, sparkling or effervescent water, spring-well water, club soda, and tonic water.

Treated or processed water comes from a well stream or central reservoir supply. This water usually flows as tap water and has been purified and fluoridated.

Mineral water is spring water that contains a substantial amount of minerals, which may be injected or occur naturally. Natural mineral water is obtained from underground water strata or a natural spring. The composition of the water at its source is constant, and the source discharge and temperature remain stable. The natural content of the water at the source is not modified by an artificial process.

Sparkling or effervescent water is water with natural or artificial carbonation. Some mineral waters come to the surface naturally carbonated through underground gases but lose their fizz on the surface with normal pressure. Many of these waters are injected with carbon dioxide later on.

Club soda is obtained by adding artificial carbonation to distilled or regular tap water. Mineral content in this water depends on the water supply used and the purification process the water has undergone. Tonic water is derived from the same process as club soda, but has bitters added to it.

Source: This case was prepared by Michael R. Czinkota.

Minerals are important to the taste and quality of water. The type and variety of minerals present in the water can make it a very healthy and enjoyable drink. The combination of minerals present in the water determines its relative degree of acidity. The level of acidity is measured by the pH factor. A pH 7 rating indicates a neutral water. A higher rating indicates that the water contains more solids, such as manganese calcium, and is said to be "hard." Conversely, water with a lower rating is classified as "soft." Most tap water is soft, whereas the majority of commercially sold waters tend to be hard.

Water Consumption in the United States

Tap water has generally been inexpensive, relatively pure, and plentiful in the United States. Traditionally, bottled water has been consumed in the United States by the very wealthy. In the past several years, however, bottled water has begun to appeal to a wider market. The four reasons for this change are:

1. An increasing awareness among consumers of the impurity of city water supplies
2. Increasing dissatisfaction with the taste and odor of city tap water
3. Rising affluence in society
4. An increasing desire to avoid excess consumption of caffeine, sugar, and other substances present in coffee and soft drinks

Bottled water consumers are found chiefly in the states of California, Florida, Texas, New York, and Illinois. Combined, these states represent 88 percent of nationwide bottled water sales. California alone represents one-half of industry sales. Nationwide, bottled water is drunk by 1 out of every 2,000 persons. In California, however, one out of every six drinks bottled water.

Consumers differ in their reasons for drinking bottled water. In the Southwest, bottled water is regularly consumed in the home, the office, and restaurants. Consumers in this region are not as interested in the chic image of bottled water as they are its taste. In urban areas such as Chicago and New York City, bottled water is consumed as an alternative to alcoholic beverages, soft drinks, and coffee. Eighty-five percent of the consumers are women.

Before 1976, bottled water was considered primarily a gourmet specialty, an exotic demand of the rich. Since the entry of Perrier, an imported French water, however, U.S. bottled water consumption has shown exceptional growth. Bottled water sales rose from a level of 235 million gallons in 1971 to over 500 million gallons in 1983. Industry sales are expected to grow at a rate of 10 to 12 percent domestically. Imported water held a 5 percent share of the domestic market in terms of volume but held about a 26 percent share of total market in 1983 in terms of dollar sales.

The bottled water market in the United States was estimated to be approximately $480 million in terms of producers' prices. Domestically purified and processed water was thought to hold a 45 percent market share, with domestic mineral water holding 29 percent and imported mineral water holding 26 percent of market share. The leading exporting country is France, with a 91.7 percent share of imports in the United States. Other countries are Italy with 2.6 percent, Canada with 4 percent, and Germany with 1.7 percent of import share.

Among brands, Perrier is clearly the leader. Perrier is estimated to hold 5 percent of total unit volume of the bottled water market and 20 percent of the total dollar volume. Industry observers believe that the primary causes for Perrier's success are its heavy media budget, its national distribution network, and its focus on the soft drink market in general rather than on the bottled water market. As a result, Perrier is able to charge a premium price, with most of its product selling in supermarkets at an average price of four cents per ounce, compared with an average price of two cents per ounce for the rest of the industry.

Overall, a cursory analysis indicates good potential for success for a new importer of bottled water in the United States. This is especially true if the water is exceptionally pure and can be classified as mineral water.

ADDITIONAL RESEARCH

Further exploring his import idea, Stan Otis gathered information on various other marketing facets. One of his main concerns was government regulations.

Bottled Water Regulations in the United States

The bottled water industry in the United States is regulated and controlled at two levels—by the federal government and various state governments. The federal government code defines bottled water as "water that is treated and bottled or out of containers and intended for human consumption." Bottled water does not include mineral water or any food defined in other sections. Any bottled water that is moved in interstate commerce is subject to Food and Drug Administration regulations. Whereas the federal government has set quality and safety standards for bottled water that is consumed as a substitute for tap water, it has not defined and set such standards for mineral water. In cooperation with industry, and based mainly on the definition of mineral water in Europe, however, the federal government customarily sees mineral water as water that contains at least 500 parts per million of total dissolved solids (TDS) and that has not been artificially processed. If the water contains less than 500 parts TDS per million, it can still be labeled mineral water, but the TDS content must be shown on the label.

Some state regulatory officials hold that to be labeled as mineral water, water must contain a minimum amount of dissolved solids. California Code regulations require bottled water to contain at least 500 parts TDS per million to qualify as a mineral water. Michigan is considering legislation that will require mineral water to contain at least 1,000 parts TDS per million. In addition to state and federal regulation, the production and sale of bottled water can also be regulated by city and county agencies and public health authorities.

The Icelandic Scenario

Iceland is highly import-dependent. In terms of products exported, it has little diversity and is dangerously dependent on its fish crop and world fish prices. The government, troubled by high inflation rates and low financial reserves, is very interested in diversifying its export base. An Icelandic Export Board has been created and charged with developing new products for export and aggressively promoting them abroad.

The Ministry of Commerce, after consulting the Central Bank, has the ultimate responsibility in matters concerning import and export licensing. The Central Bank is responsible for the regulation of foreign exchange transactions and exchange controls, including capital controls. It is also responsible for ensuring that all foreign exchange due to residents is surrendered to authorized banks. All commercial exports require licenses. The shipping documents must be lodged with an authorized bank. Receipts exchanged for exports must be surrendered to the Central Bank.

All investments by nonresidents in Iceland are subject to individual approval. The participation of nonresidents in Icelandic joint venture companies may not exceed 49 percent. Nonresident-owned foreign capital entering in the form of foreign exchange must be surrendered.

Iceland is a member of the United Nations, the European Free Trade Association, and the General Agreement on Tariffs and Trade. Iceland enjoys "most favored nation" status with the United States. Under this designation, Iceland is subject to a tariff of 1.5 cents per gallon on imported water.

Questions for Discussion

1. Should water be bottled in Iceland for export or shipped in bulk and bottled in the United States?

2. Should the water from Iceland be marketed as natural, mineral, or sparkling water?

3. Which market segments would you recommend for an initial market-introduction effort?

4. Develop a marketing mix for Otis. Be sure to focus on distribution, pricing, and promotion.

5. Should Otis become an investment banker or implement his vision?

Damar International

Damar International, a fledgling firm importing handicrafts of chiefly Indonesian origin, was established in January 1984 in Burke, Virginia, a suburb of Washington, D.C. Organized as a general partnership, the firm is owned entirely by Dewi Soemantoro, its president, and Ronald I. Asche, its vice president. Their part-time unsalaried efforts, and those of Soemantoro's relatives in Indonesia, constitute the entire labor base of the firm. Outside financing has been limited to borrowing from friends and relatives of the partners in Indonesia and the United States.

Damar International imported its first shipment of handicrafts in April 1984 and estimates that its current annual sales revenues are between $20,000 and $30,000. Although the firm has yet to reach the break-even point, its sales revenues and customer base have expanded more rapidly than anticipated in Damar's original business plan. The partners are generally satisfied with results to date and plan to continue to broaden their operations.

Damar International was established to capitalize on Soemantoro's international experience and contacts. The daughter of an Indonesian Foreign Service officer, Soemantoro spent most of her youth and early adulthood in Western Europe and has for the past 18 years resided in the United States. Her immediate family, including her mother, now resides in Indonesia. In addition to English and Malay, Soemantoro speaks French, German, and Italian. Although she has spent the past four years working in information management in the D.C. area, first for MCI and currently for Records Management, Inc., her interest in importing derives from about six years she previously spent as a management consultant. In this capacity, she was frequently called on to advise clients about importing clothing, furniture, and decorative items from Indonesia. At the urging of family and friends, she decided to start her own business. While Soemantoro handles the purchasing and administrative aspects of the business, Asche is responsible for marketing and sales.

Damar International currently imports clothing, high-quality brassware, batik accessories, wood carvings, and furnishings from Indonesia. All of these items are handcrafted by village artisans working on a cottage-industry basis. Damar International estimates that 30 percent of its revenues from the sale of Indonesian imports are derived from clothing, 30 percent from batik accessories, 30 percent from wood carvings, with the remainder divided equally between brassware and furnishings. In addition, Damar markets in the eastern United States comparable Thai and Philippine handcrafted items imported by a small California firm. This firm in turn markets some of Damar's Indonesian imports on the West Coast.

Most of Damar's buyers are small shops and boutiques. Damar does not supply large department stores or retail chain outlets. By participating in gift shows, trade fairs, and handicraft exhibitions, the firm has expanded its customer base from the D.C. area to many locations in the eastern United States.

In supplying small retail outlets with handcrafted Indonesian artifacts, Damar is pursuing a niche strategy. Although numerous importers market similar mass-produced manufactured Indonesian items, chiefly to department stores and chain retailers, Damar knows of no competitors who supply handcrafted artifacts to boutiques. Small retailers

Source: This case was prepared by Michael R. Czinkota and Laura M. Gould.

find it difficult to purchase in sufficient volume to order directly from large-scale importers of mass-produced items. More important, it is difficult to organize Indonesian artisans to produce handcrafted goods in sufficient quantity to supply the needs of large retailers.

Damar's policy is to carry little if any inventory. Orders from buyers are transmitted by Soemantoro to her family members in Indonesia, who contract production to artisans in the rural villages of Java and Bali. Within broad parameters, buyers can specify modifications of traditional Indonesian wares. Frequently, Soemantoro cooperates with her mother in creating designs that adapt traditional products to American tastes and to the specifications of U.S. buyers. Soemantoro is in contact with her family in Indonesia at least once a week by telex or phone in order to report new orders and check on the progress of previous orders. In addition, Soemantoro makes an annual visit to Indonesia to coordinate policy with her family and maintain contacts with artisans.

Damar also fills orders placed by Soemantoro's family in Indonesia. The firm therefore in essence acts as both an importer and an exporter despite its extremely limited personnel base. In this, as well as in its source of financing, Damar is highly atypical. The firm's great strength, which allows it to fill a virtually vacant market niche with extremely limited capital and labor resources, is clearly the Soemantoro family's nexus of personal connections. Without the use of intermediaries, this single bicultural family is capable of linking U.S. retailers and Indonesian village artisans and supplying products that, though unique and nonstandardized, are specifically oriented to the U.S. market.

Damar's principal weakness is its financing structure. There are obvious limits to the amount of money that can be borrowed from family and friends for such an enterprise. Working capital is necessary because the Indonesian artisans must be paid before full payment is received from U.S. buyers. Although a 10 percent deposit is required from buyers when an order is placed, the remaining 90 percent is not due until 30 days from the date of shipment F.O.B. Washington, D.C. However, the simplicity of Damar's financing structure has advantages: To date, it has been able to operate without letters of credit and the concomitant paperwork burdens.

One major importing problem to date has been the paperwork and red tape involved in U.S. customs and quota regulations. Satisfying these regulations has occasionally delayed fulfillment of orders. Furthermore, because the Indonesian trade office in the United States is located in New York rather than D.C., assistance from the Indonesian government in expediting such problems has at times been difficult to obtain with Damar's limited personnel. For example, an order was once delayed in U.S. customs because of confusion between the U.S. Department of Commerce and Indonesian export authorities concerning import stamping and labeling. Several weeks were required to resolve this difficulty.

Although Damar received regulatory information directly from the U.S. Department of Commerce when it began importing, its routine contact with the government is minimal because regulatory paperwork is contracted to customs brokers.

One of the most important lessons that the firm has learned is the critical role of participating in gift shows, trade fairs, and craft exhibitions. Soemantoro believes that the firm's greatest mistake to date was not attending a trade show in New York. In connecting with potential buyers, both through trade shows and "walk-in scouting" of boutiques, Damar has benefited greatly from helpful references from existing customers. Buyers have been particularly helpful in identifying trade fairs that would be useful for Damar to attend. Here too, the importance of Damar's cultivation of personal contacts is apparent.

Similarly, personal contacts offer Damar the possibility of diversifying into new import lines. Through a contact established by a friend in France, Soemantoro is currently planning to import handmade French porcelain and silk blouses.

Damar is worried about sustained expansion of its Indonesian handicraft import business because the firm does not currently have the resources to organize large-scale cottage-industry production in Indonesia. Other major concerns are potential shipping delays and exchange rate fluctuations.

Questions for Discussion

1. Evaluate alternative expansion strategies for Damar International in the United States.

2. Discuss Damar's expansion alternatives in Indonesia and France and their implications for the U.S. market.

3. How can Damar protect itself against exchange rate fluctuations?

4. What are the likely effects of shipment delays on Damar? How can these effects be overcome?

Spectrum Color Systems Inc.

Anthony Cordera, executive vice president of Spectrum Color Systems, sighed as he hung up the phone. The conversation still raced through his mind as he surveyed the fall foliage outside his office window. Cordera went over every nuance of the telephone conversation he had just completed with Roberto Cortez, vice president of European operations at BASF International. BASF had been a good customer for Spectrum, but today Cortez spoke with disdain, accusing Spectrum of questionable practices in its dealings with BASF. Cordera hated to see such a profitable relationship sour, but he saw no solution. As he turned back toward his desk, he wondered whether Spectrum might soon face similar sentiment from other large multinational clients. At the same time, he wondered how to address this issue at the upcoming board meeting without alarming the company president and the board of directors.

HISTORY

Spectrum Color Systems is a medium-sized industrial firm with headquarters in the eastern United States. The firm was founded in 1952 when Daniel Clark, a government scientist working on techniques to measure aspects of color and appearance, was approached by Procter & Gamble (P&G).

Procter & Gamble recognized that customers held a perception of quality related to the color of its products. In order to offer consistency to its customers, and as part of its quality-control program, P&G sought a process to help it standardize the color and appearance of the products it manufactured. Clark balked at the request to work for P&G, building a machine that could quantify aspects of color, but as he recognized widespread commercial applications of such a machine, Clark went into business for himself. Spectrum Color Systems started with the simple philosophy of providing solutions to customers' problems relating to measurement and control of color and appearance attributes. The first machines were developed under contract with P&G. As the quality-control movement developed throughout the industrialized world, the demand for Spectrum's products grew.

Spectrum Color Systems remains privately held; majority ownership and controlling voting rights remain in the Clark family. In 1990, Daniel Clark passed away. His son Paul is CEO and president; he runs domestic sales, finance, and human resources. Anthony Cordera joined Spectrum in 1985. As executive vice president, he is responsible for manufacturing, engineering, international sales, shipping, and receiving. He reports directly to Paul Clark.

The Clark family retains approximately 55 percent of company stock, including all voting stock. The executive and associate staff participate in an employee stock ownership plan and together own the remaining 45 percent of shares.

Source: This case study was developed by Professor Michael R. Czinkota and MBA candidate Marc S. Gross. Funding support by the U.S. Department of Education is gratefully acknowledged. Some names have been disguised to protect proprietary interests.

PRODUCT LINE

Spectrum Color Systems manufactures and sells an extensive array of colorimeters and spectrophotometers. These machines quantify aspects of color and appearance. As Appendix A discusses, such measurements are important, but no easy task. A colorimeter is the most basic instrument, with some models starting at $2,000. Most large manufacturers choose spectrophotometers, which are more exacting in their measurement ability, providing better performance and more options. These are generally integrated systems that can cost as much as $150,000.

Spectrum offers both on-line products and lab products. On-line products are designed for use on a production line, where products run under the instrument, which continuously monitors the product's appearance. These systems are manufactured in batch operations and customized to meet customer specifications. Typically, custom features are oriented to specific user applications and include hardware components such as moving optical scanners that measure lateral color variance as well as software components designed to meet the needs of specific industries. The first instruments built in the 1950s provided users with numerical values via a primitive screen and tape printer system with a 15- to 30-second lag between measurement and numerical output. Today, all of Spectrum's products are driven by user-friendly software that monitors color trends throughout a production run with real-time output. Lab products are used when a customer takes a sample from a production line and brings it to the instrument for measurement.

Spectrum instruments are used in a wide variety of industries. Large food product companies measure the color of their products as well as packaging to ensure consistency. Paint companies purchase instruments to match colors and lease the machinery to paint stores. Automobile companies use Spectrum products to ensure that the color of interior cloth material, plastic molding, and exterior paint match. Some companies have forced suppliers to provide color-variance data sheets with all shipments. Spectrum recently supplied several instruments to a large bakery that produces buns for McDonald's. McDonald's had stipulated in its contract that buns be produced not only on time, but within certain color specifications. The bakery approached Spectrum to help meet these color standards.

A major manufacturer and supplier of denim uses Spectrum's "Color-Probe" spectrophotometer in its dye house to measure and grade the color of every strand of denim it produces. Color determines the value of the denim; it has tremendous impact when millions of yards of denim are produced and the price fluctuates significantly depending on color.

THE COMPETITION

The color- and appearance-measurement market is considered a niche market with approximately $130 million to $140 million in annual sales worldwide. Spectrum has averaged $20 million annually in both retail and wholesale sales revenue over the last three years, placing it second in terms of market share. The industry became concentrated in 1990 when Color Value, a Swiss company with $5 million to $10 million in annual sales revenue, decided to dominate the color business. Color Value International, owned by a large Swiss brewery, purchased two competitors: Color Systems (CS), based in the United States and representing $35 million in annual sales, and International Color, based in the United Kingdom and representing $20 million in annual sales. Two smaller

FIGURE 1   Color Industry Concentration

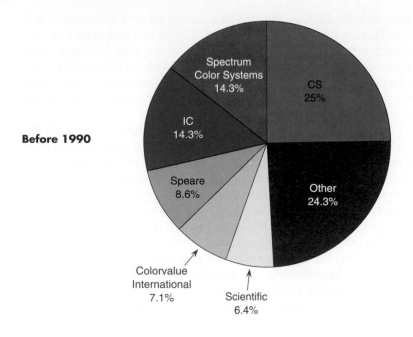

Before 1990

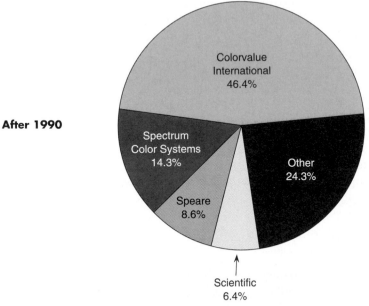

After 1990

companies occupy third and fourth market share position; Speare accounts for approximately $12 million a year in sales, and Scientific Color generates about $9 million a year in sales (see Figure 1).

Although Color Value International holds almost 50 percent of world market share, Cordera believes that Spectrum now has a unique window of opportunity. The confusion associated with integrating three companies and the loss of goodwill caused by changing CS's company name, a well-established and respected brand, to Color Value International gave Spectrum a sales advantage. In addition Spectrum entered the color matching and formulation market, one of Color Value's most profitable product lines. To gain market share in the United States, Spectrum's management decided to become the low-cost vendor and offered its new machines and color-matching software at prices of about one-half of the competition. Whereas the typical color-matching spectrophotometer by Color Value International was priced at $50,000, Spectrum offered a simpler $25,000 machine. In order to compete, Color Value International was forced to drastically reduce its prices to meet those of Spectrum, thus cutting deeply into profits.

INTERNATIONAL EXPANSION

In the 1950s and 1960s, Spectrum's management spent most of its time building the instruments and getting them out the door to meet the demand rather than developing a strategy to expand the company domestically and internationally. Spectrum's expansion into international markets succeeded despite its lack of strategic planning.

In the early days, Spectrum simply responded to requests from large companies such as Procter and Gamble to provide instruments to overseas subsidiaries. As the Clarks became more comfortable with this process, they decided to begin selling actively in Europe. By 1984 international sales comprised about one-fourth of total corporate sales. By 1992, the share had grown to more than one-third.

SALESFORCE

Spectrum Color Systems utilized independent sales agents domestically from its inception until 1986, when it developed an internal sales force. Cordera, drawing on his experience in marketing, set up the domestic sales force to provide more direct control over the marketing and sales strategies. After touring a number of agent offices, Cordera began to calculate the real cost of such a sales relationship. Working closely with Bob Holland, Spectrum's chief financial officer, Cordera tried to quantify some of the intangible and hidden costs of the agent relationship. Spectrum spent significant resources lobbying for agents' time and attention to sales of Spectrum products and provided all the technical support since few of the agents had technical expertise. Additionally, although Spectrum was responsible for billing customers and paid 15 percent of the sales price to the agent as commission, it had no access to lists of end-users and decision makers within the client's organization. Spectrum is an application-oriented company, thus access to decision makers and end-users within client organizations provides valuable information for product development and sales of transferable applications to current and future clients. A detailed financial analysis compared the true cost of using sales agents to the anticipated cost of an internal sales force. The analysis indicated that Spectrum could increase sales, reduce cost, and increase its control by developing its own sales force.

Internationally, Spectrum still relied mainly on independent distributors for its sales. Spectrum sold instruments outright to distributors at wholesale price. Spectrum billed the distributors 30-day net terms. Spectrum provided its distributors sales brochures and manuals in English. Distributors then translated these brochures as needed.

In the early days, distributors were selected largely through happenstance. Distributors of other products would hear about Spectrum and write a letter to the Clarks expressing interest in the distribution of their instruments. The Clarks would invite the distributor to the United States to see the products and get trained in their operation and thus become a Spectrum distributor. Spectrum now has distributors all over the world with extensive market penetration in Europe and the Far East. Although the company has encountered a steady international demand for its products, it continues to encounter problems with international distributors.

In 1984, Spectrum's sole French distributor, Gerard Bieux, abruptly closed his operation for medical reasons. Bieux had kept his sales operation close to his vest and thus maintained no customer lists or sales records. There was no one who could fill the void Bieux left, and Spectrum's management was forced to start over again building up its French distribution.

Cordera spent a great deal of time locating another French distributor and developing a profitable relationship. The relationship served Spectrum well until 1990, when a major competitor purchased the distributor. Again Cordera was left without a French representative for Spectrum instruments.

Cordera realized that the distributor-selection process was critical to Spectrum's international expansion and decided to become more proactive in selecting distributors. He worked closely with Holland to establish selection criteria for distributors based on financial stability, formal training programs, and financial goals. Additionally, Spectrum insisted that all distributors have service technicians trained at its U.S. facility. The distributor was responsible for paying the airfare for the technician, and Spectrum supplied food, lodging, and training. This strategy was not pursued so much for financial reasons, but to force the distributor to make both a financial and emotional investment in selling Spectrum products.

With the domestic direct salesforce up and running, Cordera decided that if he was going to put the effort into forging an international presence, Spectrum should move toward an international direct salesforce. In 1991, Spectrum opened its first European sales office in Paris. It opened an office in Germany in 1992.

DEVELOPMENT OF AN INTERNATIONAL DIRECT SALESFORCE

In spite of the detailed planning, financial budgeting, and strategy analysis that preceded the opening of both European offices, each showed a net loss in its first year of operation. Cordera consulted with large accounting firms in both France and Germany to gain insight into European business law and to develop first-year budget projections. In addition, Spectrum management solicited information from its state Department of Economic Development on issues of taxation, international shipping, work permits, and visa restrictions for U.S. nationals working abroad. Despite such efforts, the combination of operating costs, which exceeded Spectrum's estimates, and slow sales associated with the European recession resulted in first-year losses in both France and Germany.

Cultural differences contributed to rising costs. Unlike the U.S. salesforce where the majority of a sales representative's compensation consists of commission, European sales representatives are traditionally paid high salaries and relatively low commissions. In addition, employees are paid an annual salary bonus equivalent to one month's salary regardless of performance. Terminated employees can receive up to one year of severance pay based on the longevity of their relationship and position with the company. Middle managers and above expect to be provided with company cars, which was particularly difficult for Spectrum management to swallow since neither Cordera nor Clark was provided with a company car. Despite his uneasiness, Cordera agreed to provide these benefits since he felt it important to attract high-quality employees for the new offices. All of these benefits were stipulated in the long-term employment contracts required in Europe.

Difficulties soon became apparent with Spectrum's sales representative in Paris. In staffing the Paris office, Cordera, largely out of a desire to get someone out on the road in France, settled for an individual who, although the most qualified of the candidates, lacked the aggressiveness, sales orientation, and technical competence for the position. Cordera was disappointed by the sales representative's performance but found the process of terminating the employee a long and arduous one. Spectrum began working with an attorney in Paris, providing the employee with written documentation detailing the reasons for dissatisfaction, as well as sales goals that were to be met in order to retain the position. In the end, Spectrum was forced to negotiate an expensive severance package.

But now, the international activities seemed to be on track. Spectrum had two international offices abroad. The Paris office consists of the international sales director, one sales representative, one service technician, and two secretaries. From that office, Spectrum conducts marketing activities, sales, installation, and service for France. The German office employs two sales representatives, one secretary, and one service technician covering the German market.

To avoid future hiring difficulties, Cordera instituted a program that brings key individuals from European operations to its headquarters facility. The mission of this program is to integrate those individuals into Spectrum's corporate culture and create a team environment. On this point Cordera remarked, "The fax machine and telephone are great pieces of equipment, but nothing beats a face-to-face dinner or lunch where we can sit down and talk to each other."

COMMITMENT TO EUROPEAN CUSTOMERS

Spectrum management had historically marketed the same products throughout the world. Over time, Spectrum recognized that the European market and the U.S. market had different needs and preferences in both hardware and software. For example, Spectrum sales representatives frequently found their sales efforts focusing on the software that accompanies the instruments, since that is the part the customer sees, feels, and touches.

To achieve market success, Spectrum management felt it had to design products to meet the needs of European customers. There were two choices. The first was to translate existing software and then add the nuances the Europeans wanted. This proposition promised to be time consuming and very costly. The second option was to acquire a software company abroad.

In 1991, Cordera located a small software company in Switzerland that already had software written in German, French, Italian, and Spanish that was very applicable to the Spectrum system. Spectrum purchased the company for $275,000. Along with the company's assets and software copyrights, Spectrum also acquired the services of the company founder. This proved invaluable as he speaks five languages and can adapt Spectrum's software products to meet the needs of the European market.

Spectrum Color Systems paid for its acquisition out of the cash it had generated from operations. Spectrum management has historically taken a conservative view of financing. The focus is on cash management, trying to generate enough cash to finance any expansion. In fact, Spectrum would not have made the purchase unless it had the cash.

Spectrum does maintain a line of credit, but as yet it has not used loans to finance expansion. Occasionally, management borrows $500,000 on its credit line, invests in short-term CDs, and repays the loan early just to show activity on its account.

DECISION SITUATION

In all remaining international markets, Spectrum still uses distributors. Recently, this has resulted in significant problems. When BASF International in Germany purchased an instrument from Spectrum's German operation, it recommended that the BASF subsidiary in Spain buy the same instrument. When BASF received the invoice from Spectrum's Spanish distributor, the price was more than 50 percent higher than that paid in Germany. Cortez naturally felt that BASF was somehow being taken advantage of in Spain. However, there is little Spectrum can do about such disparities, since, pursuant to the distributor agreements, distributors purchase Spectrum products outright and determine the markup themselves. In addition, European Union antitrust regulations prevent Spectrum from setting a standardized price for its distributors.

This distributor arrangement is particularly advantageous in Italy and Spain. Given Spectrum's focus on cash management, the firm is leery about setting up direct operations in these countries. Cordera believes it is difficult to manage cash effectively in Italy and Spain, where vendors can wait six months to a year to receive payment from customers. There is an advantage to selling through distributors because Spectrum can collect cash on the sale in 30 or 45 days and the distributor has to wait for payment.

FUTURE STRATEGIES

By 1993, both European sales offices had become profitable. The emergence of the European Common Market could allow Spectrum to use its French and German operations as a base to expand into other countries without duplicating tasks. For example, the firm could place direct sales representatives throughout Europe with support provided by central office service technicians who would cross borders to perform installations and service. Yet Cordera still considered direct offices to be an expensive and somewhat risky proposition. His experience indicated that direct sales offices would not become self-sufficient for at least a year, and these types of financial losses caused friction with Spectrum's president and board of directors. Therefore, Cordera was not prepared for direct confrontation with distributors over markup. He dreaded the thought of being prematurely forced into opening other direct sales offices and repeating or even compounding the problems Spectrum had already endured.

In addition, recent changes in the exchange rates between the U.S. dollar and European currencies had tightened margins on export sales and decreased available cash. This pinch threatened to delay Cordera's planned expansion in the Far East.

Currently, Spectrum sells through distributors in the Pacific rim and China, but Cordera was in the process of negotiating a joint venture in China. Cordera thought that in order for Spectrum to continue its growth throughout the world and especially in the Pacific Rim, it should establish a joint operation. The cultural differences in the Pacific Rim seemed too great for Spectrum to overcome alone, so Cordera sought to marry Spectrum's technology and sales distribution with a company that has manufacturing capabilities similar to Spectrum's.

Questions for Discussion

1. Are current EU regulations beneficial or detrimental to Spectrum Color System's European operations in terms of distributor pricing and direct company sales?

2. How do fluctuations in the currency exchange rates affect Spectrum's revenues? Do you think Spectrum management would prefer to see a strong or weak dollar? Why?

3. How should Spectrum management respond to the BASF situation?

4. What has Spectrum done to meet the different needs of international customers? What more could be done to accommodate them?

APPENDIX A

THE BASICS OF COLOR AND APPEARANCE

What words would you use to describe a school bus? Yellow or slightly reddish yellow or perhaps orange? You might add the word shiny or maybe even glossy. But could the person on the other end of a telephone be expected to make a gallon of this paint for touch-up based on these words? Most likely not.

To further complicate matters, is your color vision the same as the person making the paint? What about the lighting under which you made the initial judgment of color? Have you ever noticed how some colors appear quite different under the lamps used in your home or office compared to the outdoors?

Appearance characteristics are difficult to communicate objectively. Certainly a sample of the product could be sent to another person, but what is "close enough" when deciding if a match exists?

THE LANGUAGE OF COLOR

Color is a three-dimensional characteristic of appearance consisting of a lightness attribute, often called "value," and two chromatic attributes, called "hue" and "chroma." Colors can be distinguished from one another by specifying these three visual attributes. Figure 2 shows a common arrangement of these three attributes often termed "color solid" or "color space."

Hue

Hue is often the first attribute of color that is mentioned. Consider the school bus. The most obvious thing about it is that it is a shade of yellow rather than blue or green. Hue is the attribute of color perception by which an object is judged to be red, yellow, green, blue, and so forth.

Chroma

A color specification requires more than just a designation of hue. How concentrated is the yellow? That is, how much color does there appear to be? Words such as depth, vividness, purity, and saturation have been used to convey how different the color is from gray. Chroma is the more accepted term and is used to specify the position of the color between gray and the pure hue.

Value

A third dimension is necessary to complete our specification. This is a luminous or lightness attribute, which distinguishes "light" colors from "dark" colors. Value is the term commonly used to express this attribute and is shown as the vertical axis in Figure 2.

FIGURE 2   **Three-Dimensional Color-Coordinate System**

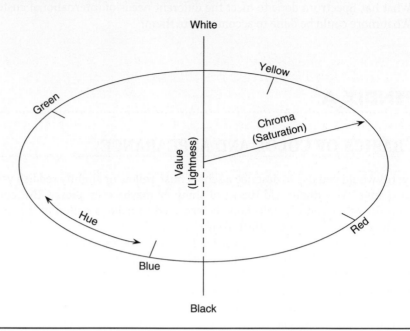

Video Case: Lakewood Forest Products

Since the 1970s, the United States has had a merchandise trade deficit with the rest of the world. Up to 1982, this deficit mattered little because it was relatively small. As of 1983, however, the trade deficit increased rapidly and became, due to its size and future implications, an issue of major national concern. Suddenly, trade moved to the forefront of national debate. Concurrently, a debate ensued on the issue of the international competitiveness of U.S. firms. The onerous question here was whether U.S. firms could and would achieve sufficient improvements in areas such as productivity, quality, and price to remain successful international marketing players in the long term.

The U.S.-Japanese trade relation took on particular significance because it was between those two countries that the largest bilateral trade deficit existed. In spite of trade negotiations, market-opening measures, trade legislation, and other governmental efforts, it was clear that the impetus for a reversal of the deficit through more U.S. exports to Japan had to come from the private sector. Therefore, the activities of any U.S. firm that appeared successful in penetrating the Japanese market were widely hailed. One company whose effort to market in Japan aroused particular interest was Lakewood Forest Products, in Hibbing, Minnesota.

COMPANY BACKGROUND

In 1983, Ian J. Ward was an export merchant in difficulty. Throughout the 1970s, his company, Ward, Bedas Canadian Ltd., had successfully sold Canadian lumber and salmon to countries in the Persian Gulf. Over time, the company had opened four offices worldwide. However, when the Iran-Iraq war erupted, most of Ward's long-term trading relationships disappeared within a matter of months. In addition, the international lumber market began to collapse. As a result, Ward, Bedas Canadian Ltd. went into a survivalist mode and sent employees all over the world to look for new markets and business opportunities. Late that year, the company received an interesting order. A firm in Korea urgently needed to purchase lumber for the production of chopsticks.

Learning about the Chopstick Market

In discussing the wood deal with the Koreans, Ward learned that in the production of good chopsticks, more than 60 percent of the wood fiber is wasted. Given the high transportation cost involved, the large degree of wasted materials, and his need for new business, Ward decided to explore the Korean and Japanese chopstick industry in more detail.

He quickly determined that chopstick making in the Far East is a fragmented industry, working with old technology and suffering from a lack of natural resources. In Asia, chopsticks are produced in very small quantities, often by family organizations. Even the largest of the 450 chopstick factories in Japan turns out only five million chopsticks a

Source: This case was written by Michael R. Czinkota based on the following sources: Mark Clayton, "Minnesota Chopstick Maker Finds Japanese Eager to Import His Quality Waribashi," *Christian Science Monitor*, October 16, 1987, 11; Roger Worthington, "Improbable Chopstick Capital of the World," *Chicago Tribune*, June 5, 1988, 39; Mark Gill, "The Great American Chopstick Master," *American Way*, August 1, 1987, 34, 78–79; "Perpich of Croatia," *Economist*, April 20, 1991, 27; interview with Ian J. Ward, president, Lakewood Forest Products.

month. This compares with an overall market size of 130 million pairs of disposable chopsticks a day. In addition, chopsticks represent a growing market. With increased wealth in Asia, people eat out more often and therefore have a greater demand for disposable chopsticks. The fear of communicable diseases has greatly reduced the utilization of reusable chopsticks. Renewable plastic chopsticks have been attacked by many groups as too newfangled and as causing future ecological problems.

From his research, Ward concluded that a competitive niche existed in the world chopstick market. He believed that if he could use low-cost raw materials and ensure that the labor-cost component would remain small, he could successfully compete in the world market.

The Founding of Lakewood Forest Products

In exploring opportunities afforded by the newly identified international marketing niche for chopsticks, Ward set four criteria for plant location:

1. Access to suitable raw materials
2. Proximity of other wood product users who could make use of the 60 percent waste for their production purposes
3. Proximity to a port that would facilitate shipment to the Far East
4. Availability of labor

In addition, Ward was aware of the importance of product quality. Because people use chopsticks on a daily basis and are accustomed to products that are visually inspected one by one, he would have to live up to high quality expectations in order to compete successfully. Chopsticks could not be bowed or misshapen, have blemishes in the wood, or splinter.

To implement his plan, Ward needed financing. Private lenders were skeptical and slow to provide funds. This skepticism resulted from the unusual direction of Ward's proposal. Far Eastern companies have generally held the cost advantage in a variety of industries, especially those as labor-intensive as chopstick manufacturing. U.S. companies rarely have an advantage in producing low-cost items. Further, only a very small domestic market exists for chopsticks.

However, Ward found that the state of Minnesota was willing to participate in his new venture. Since the decline of the mining industry, regional unemployment had been rising rapidly in the state. In 1983, unemployment in Minnesota's Iron Range peaked at 22 percent. Therefore, state and local officials were eager to attract new industries that would be independent of mining activities. Of particular help was the enthusiasm of Governor Rudy Perpich. The governor had been boosting Minnesota business on the international scene by traveling abroad and receiving many foreign visitors. He was excited about Ward's plans, which called for the creation of over 100 new jobs within a year.

Hibbing, Minnesota, turned out to be an ideal location for Ward's project. The area had an abundance of aspen wood, which, because it grows in clay soil, tends to be unmarred. The fact that Hibbing was the hometown of the governor also did not hurt. In addition, Hibbing boasted an excellent labor pool, and both the city and the state were willing to make loans totaling $500,000. Further, the Iron Range Resources Rehabilitation Board was willing to sell $3.4 million in industrial revenue bonds for the project. Together with jobs and training wage subsidies, enterprise zone credits, and tax increment financing benefits, the initial public support of the project added up to about 30 percent of its start-up costs. The potential benefit of the new venture to the region was quite clear. When Lakewood Forest Products advertised its first 30 jobs, more than 3,000 people showed up to apply.

THE PRODUCTION AND SALE OF CHOPSTICKS

Ward insisted that in order to truly penetrate the international market, he would need to keep his labor cost low. As a result, he decided to automate as much of the production as possible. However, no equipment was readily available to produce chopsticks because no one had automated the process before.

After much searching, Ward identified a European equipment manufacturer that produced machinery for making popsicle sticks. He purchased equipment from this Danish firm in order to better carry out the sorting and finishing processes. However, because aspen wood was quite different from the wood the machine was designed for, as was the final product, substantial design adjustments had to be made. Sophisticated equipment was also purchased to strip the bark from the wood and peel it into long, thin sheets. Finally, a computer vision system was acquired to detect defects in the chopsticks. This system rejected over 20 percent of the production, and yet some of the chopsticks that passed inspection were splintering. However, Ward firmly believed that further fine-tuning of the equipment and training of the new work force would gradually take care of the problem.

Given this fully automated process, Lakewood Forest Products was able to develop capacity for up to seven million chopsticks a day. With a unit manufacturing cost of $0.03 and an anticipated unit selling price of $0.057, Ward expected to earn a pretax profit of $4.7 million in 1988.

Due to intense marketing efforts in Japan and the fact that Japanese customers were struggling to obtain sufficient supplies of disposable chopsticks, Ward was able to presell the first five years of production quite quickly. By late 1987, Lakewood Forest Products was ready to enter the international market. With an ample supply of raw materials and an almost totally automated plant, Lakewood was positioned as the world's largest and least labor-intensive manufacturer of chopsticks. The first shipment of 6 containers with a load of 12 million pairs of chopsticks was sent to Japan in October 1987.

Questions for Discussion

1. What are the future implications of continuing large U.S. trade deficits?

2. What are the important variables for the international marketing success of chopsticks?

3. Rank the variables in Question 2 according to the priority you believe they have for foreign customers.

4. Why haven't Japanese firms thought of automating the chopstick production process?

5. How long will Lakewood Forest Products be able to maintain its competitive advantage?

PART THREE

Advanced International Marketing Activities

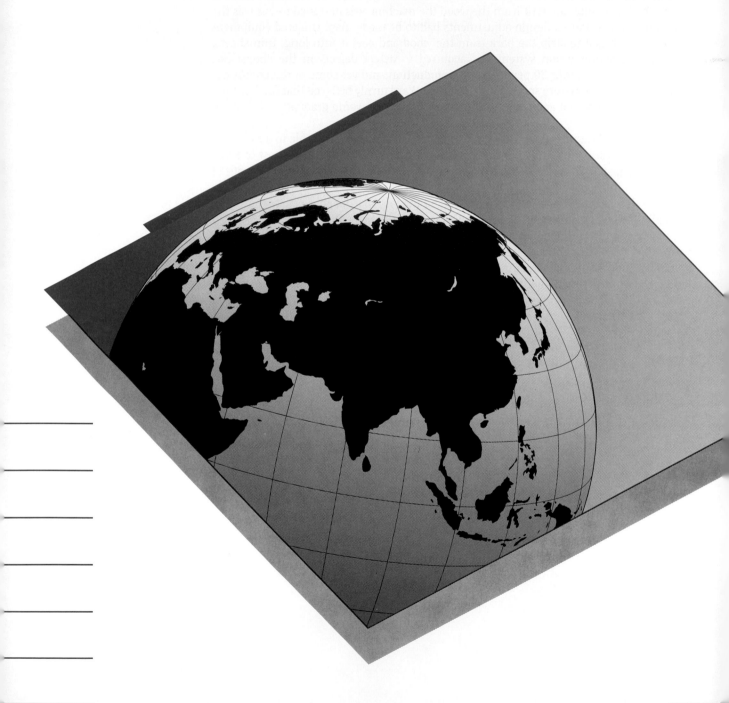

The core marketing concerns of the beginning internationalist and the multinational corporation are the same. Yet multinational firms face challenges and opportunities that are different from those encountered by smaller firms. These firms are able to expend more resources on international marketing efforts than are small and medium-sized firms. In addition, their perspective can be more globally oriented. Multinational corporations also have more impact on individuals, economies, and governments. Therefore, they are much more subject to public scrutiny and need to be more concerned about the repercussions of their activities. Yet their very size often enables them to be more influential in setting international marketing rules.

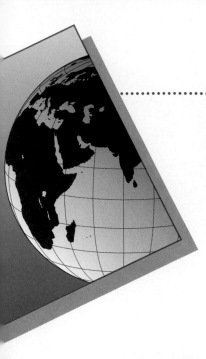

CHAPTER 14

Foreign Direct Investment and Management Contracts

THE INTERNATIONAL MARKETPLACE

Why Firms Invest Abroad

After decades as the leading source country for outward direct investment, by the mid-1980s the United States had become the world's number-one host country in total value of foreign-controlled business activity. As a consequence of the investment boom of the 1980s, foreign companies now play a prominent part in the daily lives of Americans. When an American consumer buys a new car, shops in a department store, or checks into a hotel, chances are good that the supplier of the good or service purchased will be the local subsidiary of a company based in Europe, Japan, or Canada.

To understand why foreign firms have been buying and building U.S. operations, it is helpful to look at direct investment as an integral part of a firm's overall strategy for global production and sales. The fact that successful firms expand operations overseas should not be surprising. Yet many firms sell abroad without undertaking direct investments. Investment abroad is not necessarily the most profitable avenue for increasing foreign sales—a foreign firm is almost always at some disadvantage when it operates away from its home base. Therefore, questions arise about a company's decision to invest in the United States; that is, why does a firm choose direct investment and how can it compete successfully with established U.S. companies?

Foreign direct investment in the United States can be a viable strategy only if the advantages outweigh the disadvantages vis-à-vis established U.S.-based competitors. Modern theories suggest that a firm will want to establish a U.S. subsidiary only if it enjoys a firm-specific **competitive advantage** over its rivals. For instance, R&D and advertising expenditures presumably create competitive advantages that allow firms to operate profitably in a foreign environment.

Empirical studies show that direct-investment activity in manufacturing is clustered in industries where R&D and advertising expenditures are important—electronics, chemicals, pharmaceuticals, processed foods, and autos are examples in the United States.

However, firms' competitive advantage can in many circumstances be better exploited by exporting from the home country. Therefore, an additional requirement for setting up U.S. operations is that it must offer some **locational advantage.** Without this advantage, the potential investor is likely to choose exporting over the more costly and risky option of direct investment. During the 1980s, increased protection and a decline in the relative cost of U.S. labor helped to tip the balance in favor of a U.S. location for Japanese auto producers. Previously, the same markets were served by exports.

The investing firm must also anticipate an **organizational advantage** from extending its managerial control across a national boundary. The underlying motives for foreign direct investment are essentially the same ones that promote expansion at home. But because of the added expense of international expansion, the anticipated benefit must be large enough to offset the higher cost. Otherwise, the firm will prefer an arm's-length alternative such as licensing.

Source: Rachel McCulloch, "Foreign Direct Investment in the United States" *Finance and Development,* March 1993; 13–15.

All types of firms, large or small, can carry out global market expansion through foreign direct investment or management contracts. As the International Marketplace 14.1 shows, key to the decision to invest abroad is the existence of specific advantages that outweigh the disadvantages and risk of operating so far from home. Since foreign direct investment often requires substantial capital and a firm's ability to absorb risk, the most visible players in the area are clearly multinational corporations. In this chapter, the section on foreign direct-investment strategies focuses on the rationale for such investment and on investment alternatives such as full ownership, joint ventures, and strategic alliances. The section on management contract activities focuses on the potential and the benefits and drawbacks of such arrangements.

FOREIGN DIRECT INVESTMENT

Foreign direct investment represents one component of the international investment flow. The other component is **portfolio investment,** which is the purchase of stocks and bonds internationally. Portfolio investment is a primary concern to the international financial community. The international marketer, on the other hand, makes foreign **direct investments** to create or expand a permanent interest in an enterprise. They imply a degree of control over the enterprise.[1]

---

[1] Frank G. Vukmanic, Michael R. Czinkota, and David A. Ricks, "National and International Data Problems and Solutions in the Empirical Analysis of Intraindustry Direct Foreign Investment," in *Multinationals as Mutual Invaders: Intraindustry Direct Foreign Investment,* ed. A. Erdilek (Beckenham, Kent, England: Croom Helm Ltd., 1985), 160–184.

This type of investment, although extremely important, has only recently received significant government attention. In 1974, for example, no comprehensive list was available of foreign firms investing in the United States, no one knew which firms were foreign-owned, and major shortcomings existed in the foreign direct-investment data that were available.[2] Because the U.S. data-gathering system is one of the more sophisticated ones internationally, very likely even less information about foreign direct investment is available in other countries.

Concerted data-gathering and estimation efforts by organizations such as the OECD and the International Monetary Fund (IMF) indicate that foreign direct investments have grown tremendously. The total global value of such investment, which in 1967 was estimated to be $105 billion, had climbed to an estimated $1,937 billion by the end of 1992.[3] Among foreign investors, U.S. firms are major players due to significant investments in the developed world and in some developing countries. In 1992, foreign direct investment abroad by U.S. firms amounted to $487 billion. Major foreign direct-investment activity has also been carried out by firms from other countries, many of which decided to invest in the United States. In 1982, direct investment by foreign firms in the United States totaled approximately $420 billion, up from $6.9 billion in 1960.[4] Foreign direct investment has clearly become a major avenue for foreign market entry and expansion.

MAJOR FOREIGN INVESTORS

Multinational corporations are defined by the United Nations as "enterprises which own or control production or service facilities outside the country in which they are based."[5] As a result of this definition, all foreign direct investors are multinational corporations. Today, there are more than 35,000 such corporations with 150,000 affiliates around the world and their global sales far exceed the value of global trade.[6] Yet large corporations are the key players. Table 14.1 lists the 25 largest industrial corporations around the world. They come from a wide variety of countries, depend heavily on their international sales, and in terms of sales are larger than many countries.

Many of the large multinationals operate in well over 100 countries. For some, their original home market accounts for only a fraction of their sales. For example, Philips' sales in Holland are only 4 percent, SKF's sales in Sweden are less than 4 percent, and Nestlé's sales in Switzerland are only 2 percent of total sales. In some firms, even the terms *domestic* and *foreign* have fallen into disuse. Others are working to consider issues only from a global perspective. For example, in management meetings of ABB Asea Brown Boveri, individuals get fined $100 every time the words *foreign* and *domestic* are used.

Through their investment, multinational corporations bring economic vitality and jobs to their host countries. For example, in the United States, foreign-owned firms pro-

[2] Jeffrey Arpan and David A. Ricks, "Foreign Direct Investments in the U.S. and Some Attendant Research Problems," *Journal of International Business Studies* 5 (Spring 1974): 1–7.

[3] Jeffrey Lins, U.S. Department of Commerce, Office of Trade and Economic Analysis, estimate based on data from national sources, IMF, and OECD, provided on February 9, 1994.

[4] U.S. Department of Commerce, Bureau of Economic Analysis, *Survey of Current Business,* August 1993.

[5] *Multinational Corporations in World Development* (New York: United Nations, 1973), 23.

[6] *World Investment Report: An Executive Summary* (New York: United Nations, 1993), 1.

		Sales (millions of dollars)	Foreign Revenue (as a percentage of total)	Foreign Profits (as a percentage of total)
	The 25 Largest Industrial Corporations Ranked by Sales, 1992			**TABLE 14.1**
1	General Motors/United States	123,780	31.8	P-D
2	Royal Dutch-Shell/U.K.-Holland	103,834	55.1*	37.6*
3	Exxon/United States	103,242	75.9	84.2
4	Ford Motor/United States	88,962	39.1	35.9
5	Toyota Motor/Japan	78,061	42.0	n.a.
6	IBM/United States	65,394	62.3	P-D
7	IRI/Italy	64,095	n.a.	n.a.
8	General Electric/United States	60,236	14.4	10.0
9	British Petroleum/U.K.	58,355	65.5	80.3
10	Daimler-Benz/Germany	57,321	61.0	n.a.
11	Mobil/United States	56,910	68.1	86.3
12	Hitachi/Japan	56,053	21.0	n.a.
13	Matsushita Electric/Japan	48,595	40.0	n.a.
14	Philip Morris/United States	48,109	27.4	25.4
15	Fiat/Italy	46,812	33.0	n.a.
16	Volkswagen/Germany	46,042	65.0	n.a.
17	Siemens/Germany	44,859	40.0	n.a.
18	Samsung Group/South Korea	43,701	n.a.	n.a.
19	Nissan Motor/Japan	42,905	n.a.	n.a.
20	Unilever/U.K.-Holland	41,262	42.0*	n.a.
21	ENI/Italy	41,047	19.0	n.a.
22	E.I. DuPont/United States	38,031	44.8	52.7
23	Texaco/United States	37,551	49.9	57.6
24	Chevron/United States	36,795	38.2	87.4
25	Elf Aquitane/France	36,315	38.0	n.a.

P-D Profit to deficit

* Non-European revenues and profits

Sources: "Everybody's Favourite Monsters," *The Economist,* March 27, 1993, S6–S7; "The Global 500," *Fortune,* July 27, 1993, 273; "U.S. Corporations with the Biggest Foreign Revenues," *Forbes,* July 20, 1993, 298–300; and various 1992 and 1993 corporate annual reports.

vide jobs for 4.7 million Americans and pay higher wages than do average U.S.-owned firms.[7] Since such contributions to employment are sometimes forgotten in the heat of political discussions, some investors take pains to point them out to the public. Figure 14.1 shows an advertisement by a Japanese investor in the United States that highlights the contribution made by the firm to the U.S. economy.

[7] *Foreign Direct Investment in the United States: An Update* (Washington D.C.: U.S. Department of Commerce, 1993).

FIGURE 14.1   Highlighting the Foreign Investment Contribution

AT TOYOTA we believe in the importance of investing in the economies where we do business. That's why we've invested over $5 billion in our operations here in America. That's why since 1988 we've increased our purchasing of U.S. made parts by 357% to over $4 billion per year. And that's why almost half the Toyota passenger cars sold in America are manufactured right here in Kentucky and California. *INVESTING IN THE THINGS WE ALL CARE ABOUT.* **TOYOTA**

For information on Toyota in America write Toyota Motor Corporate Services, 9 West 57th Street, Suite 4900, New York, NY 10019.

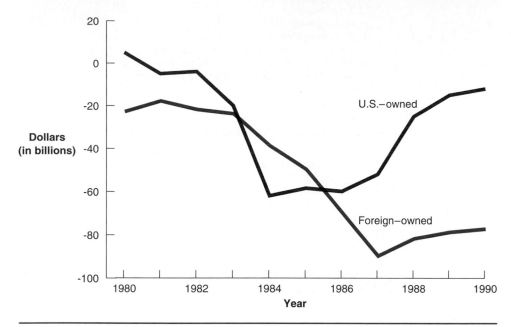

Merchandise Trade Balances: 1980–1990
(U.S.-owned and Foreign-owned U.S. Firms)

FIGURE 14.2

Source: Bureau of Economic Analysis, U.S. Department of Commerce, Washington D.C., 1993.

At the same time, however, trade follows investment. This means that foreign direct investors often bring with them imports on an ongoing basis. The flow of imports in turn may contribute to the weakening of a nation's international trade position. Figure 14.2 shows how foreign-owned firms in the United States import significantly more than do U.S.-owned firms.

Reasons for Foreign Direct Investment

Firms expand internationally for a wide variety of reasons. Table 14.2 provides an overview of the major determinants of foreign direct investment.

Marketing Factors   Marketing considerations and the corporate desire for growth are major causes for the increase in foreign direct investment. This is understandable in view of John Kenneth Galbraith's postulation that "growth means greater responsibilities and more pay for those who contribute to it."[8] Even the huge U.S. market presents limitations to growth. Some have argued that future competitive demands require firms to operate simultaneously in the "triad" of the United States, Western Europe, and Japan.[9] Corporations therefore need to seek wider market access in order to maintain and increase their sales. This objective can be achieved most quickly through the acquisition of

---

[8] John Kenneth Galbraith, *A Life in Our Times* (Boston: Houghton, Mifflin, 1981), 518.

[9] Kenichi I. Ohmae, *Triad Power: The Coming Shape of Global Competition* (New York: Free Press, 1985).

TABLE 14.2	Major Determinants of Direct Foreign Investment

A. Marketing Factors
  1. Size of market
  2. Market growth
  3. Desire to maintain share of market
  4. Desire to advance exports of parent company
  5. Need to maintain close customer contact
  6. Dissatisfaction with existing market arrangements
  7. Export base

B. Trade Restrictions
  1. Barriers to trade
  2. Preference of local customers for local products

C. Cost Factors
  1. Desire to be near source of supply
  2. Availability of labor
  3. Availability of raw materials
  4. Availability of capital/technology
  5. Lower labor costs
  6. Lower production costs other than labor
  7. Lower transport costs
  8. Financial (and other) inducements by government
  9. More favorable cost levels

D. Investment Climate
  1. General attitude toward foreign investment
  2. Political stability
  3. Limitation on ownership
  4. Currency exchange regulations
  5. Stability of foreign exchange
  6. Tax structure
  7. Familiarity with country

E. General
  1. Expected higher profits

Source: *International Investment and Multinational Enterprises* (Paris: Organization for Economic Cooperation and Development, 1983), 41.

foreign firms. Through such expansion, the corporation also gains ownership advantages consisting of political know-how and expertise. Examples are better intelligence about political actors and opportunities, readier access to political opinion makers and decision makers, and superior skills for influencing the latter.[10]

Another incentive is that foreign direct investment permits corporations to circumvent current barriers to trade and operate abroad as a domestic firm, unaffected by duties, tariffs, or other import restrictions.

In addition to government-erected barriers, restrictions may be imposed by customers through their insistence on domestic goods and services, either as a result of nationalistic tendencies or as a function of cultural differences. Further, local buyers may wish to buy from sources that they perceive to be reliable in their supply, which means buying from local producers. For some products, country-of-origin effects may

---

[10] Jean J. Boddewyn, "Political Aspects of MNE Theory," *Journal of International Business Studies* 19 (Fall 1988): 341–363.

force a firm to establish a plant in a country that has a built-in positive stereotype for production location and product quality.[11]

Still another incentive is the cost factor, with corporations attempting to obtain low-cost resources and ensure their sources of supply. Finally, once the decision is made to invest internationally, the investment climate plays a major role. Corporations will seek to invest in those geographic areas where their investment is most protected and has the best chance to flourish.

These determinants will have varying impact on the foreign direct-investment decision, depending on the characteristics of the firm and its management, on its objectives, and on external conditions. Firms have been categorized as resource seekers, market seekers, and efficiency seekers.[12] **Resource seekers** search for either natural resources or human resources. Natural resources typically are based on mineral, agricultural, or oceanographic advantages and result in firms locating in areas where these resources are available. The alternatives open to firms therefore depend on the availability of the natural resources sought. Companies seeking human resources are likely to base their location decision on the availability of low-cost labor that matches their needs in terms of output quality. Alternatively, companies may select an area because of the availability of highly skilled labor. If natural resources are not involved, the location decision can be altered over time if the labor advantage changes. When the differential between labor costs in different locales becomes substantial, a corporation, in continuing to seek to improve its human resource access, may relocate to take advantage of the "better" resources. A good example of such shifts was observed in Europe. In the 1980s, many non-European firms decided to gain their foothold in Europe by investing in the low-wage countries of Portugal, Spain, and Greece. In light of the major political changes of the 1990s, however, the investment interest has shifted and now focuses to a larger degree on Hungary, the former East Germany, and the Czech Republic. More recently, the implementation of the North American Free Trade Agreement (NAFTA) precipitated major investment flows from the United States into Mexico, led by firms seeking to obtain a key, low-cost Mexican factor endowment—labor.

Corporations primarily in search of better opportunities to enter and expand within markets are **market seekers.** Particularly when markets are closed or access is restricted, corporations have a major incentive to locate in them. **Efficiency seekers** attempt to obtain the most economic sources of production. They frequently have affiliates in multiple markets with highly specialized product lines or components and exchange their production in order to maximize the benefits to the corporation.

Derived Demand   A second major cause for the increase in foreign direct investment is the result of **derived demand.** As large multinational firms move abroad, they are quite interested in maintaining their established business relationships with other firms. Therefore, they frequently encourage their suppliers to follow them and continue to supply them from a foreign location. Many Japanese automakers have urged their suppliers in Japan to begin production in the United States in order for the new U.S. plants to have access to their products. The International Marketplace 14.2 shows how a few direct investments can gradually form an important investment preference for subsequent investment flows. The same phenomenon holds true for service

---

[11] Phillip D. White and Edward W. Cundiff, "Assessing the Quality of Industrial Products," *Journal of Marketing* 42 (January 1978): 80–86.

[12] Jack N. Behrman, "Transnational Corporations in the New International Economic Order," *Journal of International Business Studies* 12 (Spring–Summer 1981): 29–42.

THE INTERNATIONAL MARKETPLACE

Europe Loves Dixie

When German car maker BMW announced that it would build its first manufacturing plant in South Carolina, some people outside the area responded to the news with disbelief and derision. To them, the idea of a world-class corporation moving to this low-wage, southern state was surprising. However, those more familiar with what has been going on in South Carolina for the last 20 years were surprised only by the fact that BMW was considering any other state at all.

South Carolina is a state with an increasingly international economic base—mainly European. The Greenville-Spartanburg area, BMW's new plant site, is home to more than 60 European firms and boasts the highest density of European investment per capita in the United States. Due to the proliferation of German manufacturing operations along the area's connecting highway, the stretch has long been referred to as "the Autobahn." Some of the European firms include BASF Corp., Marzoli International Inc., Rieter Corp., and the Michelin Tire Corp., the next-largest employer after the state government. About 20 percent of the state's manufacturing workers are employed by European firms.

Over the past five years, the state has had more than $16 billion in new investment. One-third of this investment has been from abroad, mainly from Europe. This history of European firms setting up business and succeeding in South Carolina helped BMW calm its transatlantic jitters and trust the state's promises regarding the business climate.

To understand the region's successful pull, one needs to look back in time. By the mid twentieth century, the upstate region was almost completely an industrial economy, due mostly to a thriving textile industry. In the 1960s and 1970s, local textile mills began turning to foreign companies with greater technologies, to update their factories. As this trend grew, rather than shipping bulky machinery and servicing it from a European base, the companies decided to move next door to their customers. And this was the beginning of European interest in the region. "From there it sort of snowballed and diversified," says expert Doug Woodward. "[Europeans] saw this area as a good place to be; you were outside the major American manufacturing heartland and you could carve out your own niche. You were close to mountains and the ocean. From the European's perspective, it was like discovering America all over again."

The European presence, however, has gone beyond mere penetration of the economic scene; it is now an increasingly visible aspect of the local culture. Active Swiss and German clubs help organize everything from international festivals to church services held in their native tongue. Local businesses cater exclusively to native tastes, including grocery stores that carry otherwise rare European foods.

Another advantage for BMW and other German firms is the already existing German presence. Spartanburg County is home to an estimated 2,500 Germans. More than 1,100 live in homes where German is the primary language spoken. According to one group, "With so many Germans here, it helps [newcomers] with their families and just getting along here."

In the future, South Carolina may find itself working less and less to acquire more and more European business. Just in order to supply BMW, the state is expecting corporate relocations and expansions in the area to bring in 2,000 more jobs. As the state's reputation for foreign direct investment continues to grow, South Carolina hopes a domino effect of future investment inflow will be created.

Source: Matthew Davis, "Europe Loves Dixie," *Europe*, October 1992, 30–36.

firms. Advertising agencies often move abroad to service foreign affiliates of their domestic clients. Similarly, engineering firms, insurance companies, and law firms are often invited to provide their services abroad. Yet not all of these developments are the result of co-optation by client firms. Often, suppliers invest abroad out of fear that their clients might find good sources abroad and therefore begin to import the products or services they currently supply. Many firms therefore invest abroad in order to forestall such a potentially dangerous development. The International Marketplace 14.3 describes the international investment rationale for a U.S. firm that followed its clients abroad.

Government Incentives A third major cause for the increase in foreign direct investment is government incentives. Governments are increasingly under pressure to provide jobs for their citizens. Over time, many have come to recognize that foreign direct investment can serve as a major means to increase employment and income. Countries such as Ireland have been promoting government-incentive schemes for foreign direct investment for decades. Increasingly, state and local governments are also participating in investment-promotion activities. Some states are sending out investment missions on a regular basis, and others have opened offices abroad in order to inform local businesses about the beneficial investment climate at home.

Government incentives are mainly of three types: fiscal, financial, and nonfinancial. **Fiscal incentives** are specific tax measures designed to serve as an attraction to the foreign investor. They typically consist of special depreciation allowances, tax credits or rebates, special deductions for capital expenditures, tax holidays, and other reductions of the tax burden on the investor. **Financial incentives** offer special funding for the investor by providing land or buildings, loans, loan guarantees, or wage subsidies. Finally, **nonfinancial incentives** can consist of guaranteed government purchases; special protection from competition through tariffs, import quotas, and local content requirements; and investments in infrastructure facilities. Figure 14.2 provides an example of such state investment promotion offering several financial and fiscal incentives.

All of these incentives are designed primarily to attract more industry and therefore create more jobs. They may slightly alter the advantage of a region and therefore make it more palatable for the investor to choose to invest in that region. By themselves, they are unlikely to spur an investment decision if proper market conditions do not exist. Consequently, when individual states within the United States offer special incentives to foreign direct investors, they may be competing against each other for a limited pie rather than increasing the size of the pie. Further, a question exists about the extent to which new jobs are actually created by foreign direct investment. Because many foreign investors import equipment, parts, and even personnel, the expected benefits in terms of job creation may often be either less than initially envisioned or only temporary. One additional concern arises from the competitive position of domestic firms already in

14.3

THE INTERNATIONAL MARKETPLACE

R. R. Donnelley Invests Abroad

R. R. Donnelley & Sons Co. traditionally has been known as a printer of catalogs, phone books, and magazines. The firm is the world's largest printer of the Bible and was responsible for the famous Sears catalog before its demise. Until recently, Donnelley operated solely within the confines of the United States and was highly exposed to the slow-growth or recession-prone segments of its business.

In recent years, Donnelley has transformed itself into an international force in its field by investing in overseas markets. More than 30 of its 140 offices and sites are now outside the United States. In the past three years, the company has built plants in Singapore and Mexico, bought companies in Ireland, Britain, and the Netherlands, and has begun joint ventures in Thailand, Hong Kong, France, and Spain. Donnelley prints comic books in Bangkok, telephone books for Prague, IPO documents for Chinese companies, and childrens' books in Mexico. Such rapid internationalization is surprising, coming as it does from a company that not too long ago was grappling over whether or not to buy a printing press from an overseas supplier. At the time, the question had stumped the group because Donnelley had never dealt with issues such as foreign currency swings, international logistics, or tariffs.

The global moves undertaken by Donnelley are not entirely of its own creation. Chairman and chief executive John Walter explains: "We don't have some wild desire to be outside the borders of the United States, we go with our customers." Certain client groups, including computer hardware and software concerns, telecommunications companies, and financial houses, are moving into foreign markets and want their domestic service provider, Donnelley, to join them.

Computer hardware and software producers are increasingly turning to outside firms to translate, print, package, and distribute their product manuals. As these computer firms move overseas, along go such suppliers as Donnelley. Donnelley's computer documentation business in 1993 was expected to yield more than $500 million in revenue from 15 offices and plants around the world, compared to less than $50 million from one plant in Indiana in 1983.

Source: Susan Carey, "Donnelley Follows Its Customers around the World," *The Wall Street Journal*, July 1, 1993.

existence. Since their "old" investment typically does not benefit from incentives designed to attract new investment, established firms may encounter problems when competing against the newcomer.

A PERSPECTIVE ON FOREIGN DIRECT INVESTORS

All foreign direct investors, and particularly multinational corporations, are viewed with a mixture of awe and dismay. Governments and individuals praise them for bringing capital, economic activity, and employment, and investors are seen as key transferers of technology and managerial skills. Through these transfers, competition, market choice, and competitiveness are enhanced.

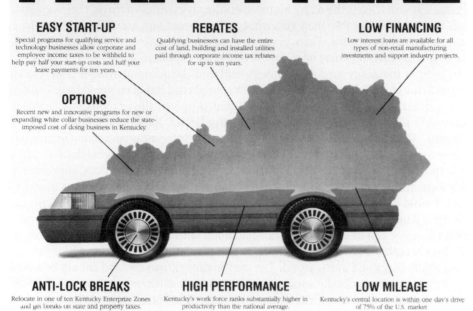

An Advertisement for Foreign Direct Investment   **FIGURE 14.3**

PARK IT HERE

EASY START-UP
Special programs for qualifying service and technology businesses allow corporate and employee income taxes to be withheld to help pay half your start-up costs and half your lease payments for ten years.

REBATES
Qualifying businesses can have the entire cost of land, building and installed utilities paid through corporate income tax rebates for up to ten years.

LOW FINANCING
Low interest loans are available for all types of non-retail manufacturing investments and support industry projects.

OPTIONS
Recent new and innovative programs for new or expanding white collar businesses reduce the state-imposed cost of doing business in Kentucky.

ANTI-LOCK BREAKS
Relocate in one of ten Kentucky Enterprize Zones and get breaks on state and property taxes.

HIGH PERFORMANCE
Kentucky's work force ranks substantially higher in productivity than the national average.

LOW MILEAGE
Kentucky's central location is within one day's drive of 75% of the U.S. market

Kentuckians built three of the top ten best selling vehicles in America last year, including the Ford Explorer, Ford Ranger and Toyota Camry.* That's just one impressive feature which makes Kentucky a smart move for manufacturing or white collar business. Locate your manufacturing or service business in Kentucky and drive down the road to success.

KENTUCKY
WE'RE SERIOUS ABOUT JOBS
1-800-626-2930

*Source: Automotive News

Source: *Site Selection and Industrial Development,* April, 1993. Courtesy of Kentucky Cabinet for Economic Development.

At the same time, the dependence on multinational corporations is seen negatively by many. Just as the establishment of a corporation can create all sorts of benefits, its disappearance can also take them away again. Very often, international direct investors are accused of actually draining resources from their host countries. By employing the best and the brightest, they are said to deprive other domestic firms of talent. By raising money locally, they are seen to starve smaller capital markets. By bringing in foreign technology, they are either viewed as discouraging local technology development or as perhaps transferring only outmoded knowledge. By increasing competition, they are declared the enemy of domestic firms. There are concerns about foreign investors' economic and political loyalty toward their host government and a fear that such investors will always protect only their own interests and those of their home governments. And, of course, their sheer size, which sometimes exceeds the financial assets that the government controls, makes foreign investors suspect.

Clearly, a love-hate relationship frequently exists between governments and the foreign direct investor. As the firm's size and investment volume grow, the benefits it brings to the economy increase. At the same time, the dependence of the economy on the firm increases as well. Given the many highly specialized activities of firms, their experts are often more knowledgeable than government employees and are therefore able to circumvent government rules. Particularly in developing countries, the knowledge advantage of foreign investors may offer opportunities for exploitation.

In light of the desire for foreign investment and the accompanying fear of it, a substantial array of guidelines for corporate behavior abroad has been publicized. Today, no set of normative corporate guidelines exists that is universally or globally accepted and observed.[13] Yet some organizations, such as the United Nations, the Organization for Economic Cooperation and Development, and the International Labor Organization, have recommended or proposed guidelines. Typically, these recommendations address the behavior of foreign investors in areas such as employment practices, consumer and environmental protection, political activity, and human rights. Corporations may not be legally bound by the guidelines but they should consider their implications for corporate activities. While the social acceptability of certain practices may vary among nations, the foreign investor can be expected to transfer, along with the best business practices, also such best acceptability across nations, therefore gradually increasing and improving the acceptability threshold in the world. The multinational firm can and should be a leader in improving economic and business practices and standards of living around the world. The true leaders will do so. Firms that do not accept national sovereignty or do not respect individuals will encounter growing hostility, resistance to their operations, and declining international success.

Types of Ownership

In carrying out its foreign direct investment, a corporation has a wide variety of ownership choices, ranging from 100 percent ownership to a minority interest. The different levels of ownership will result in varying degrees of flexibility for the corporation, a changing ability to control business plans and strategy, and differences in the level of risk assumed. Often, the ownership decision either is a strategic response to corporate capabilities and needs or is a necessary result of government regulations.

Full Ownership   For many firms, the foreign direct-investment decision is, initially at least, considered in the context of 100 percent ownership. Sometimes, this is the result of ethnocentric considerations, based on the belief that no outside entity should have an impact on corporation management. At other times, the issue is one of principle.

To make a rational decision about the extent of ownership, management must evaluate the extent to which total control is important for the success of its international marketing activities. Often, full ownership may be a desirable, but not a necessary, pre-

---

[13] William C. Frederick, "The Moral Authority of Transnational Corporate Codes," *Journal of Business Ethics* 10 no. 3 (1991): 165–177.

requisite for international success. At other times, it may be necessary, particularly when strong linkages exist within the corporation. Interdependencies between and among local operations and headquarters may be so strong that anything short of total coordination will result in a benefit to the firm as a whole that is less than acceptable. This may be the case if central product design, pricing, or advertising is needed, as the following example illustrates:

> The Crane Company manufactures plumbing fixtures, pumps and valves, and similar equipment which is used in oil refineries, paper mills, and many other types of installations. The firm sells to design engineers throughout the world; these engineers may not be actual buyers, but they design equipment into the plants they build, and so they at least recommend the equipment to be used. In advertising to this important segment of the international market, Crane recognizes that the design engineer in São Paolo reads engineering journals published in the United States, Great Britain, and perhaps Germany or France, as well as Latin America. So Crane wants its advertising in these journals to be consistent. Therefore, it does not let its foreign subsidiaries conduct their own advertising without advice and clearance from the New York headquarters. If Crane were to use joint ventures abroad, the partner would have to yield advertising authority to New York. This could conceivably lead to discontent on the part of the local partner. To avoid arguments on advertising policies, Crane insists on full ownership.[14]

As this example shows, corporations sometimes insist on full ownership for major strategic reasons. Even in such instances, however, it is important to determine whether these reasons are important enough to warrant such a policy or whether the needs of the firm can be accommodated with other ownership arrangements. Increasingly, the international environment is growing hostile to full ownership by multinational firms.

Many governments exert political pressure to obtain national control of foreign operations. Commercial activities under the control of foreigners are frequently believed to reflect the wishes, desires, and needs of headquarters abroad much more than those of the domestic economy. Governments fear that domestic economic policies may be counteracted by such firms, and employees are afraid that little local responsibility and empathy exist at headquarters. A major concern is the "fairness" of **profit repatriation,** or transfer of profits, and the extent to which firms operating abroad need to reinvest in their foreign operations. Governments often believe that transfer pricing mechanisms are used to amass profits in a place most advantageous for the firm and that, as a consequence, local operations often show very low levels of performance. By reducing the foreign control of firms, they hope to put an end to such practices.

Ownership options are limited either through outright legal restrictions or through measures designed to make foreign ownership less attractive—such as profit repatriation limitations. The international marketer is therefore frequently faced with the choice either of abiding by existing restraints and accepting a reduction in control or of losing the opportunity to operate in the country.

In addition to the pressure from host governments, general market instability can also serve as a major deterrent to full ownership of foreign direct investment. Instability may result from political upheavals or changes in regimes. More often, it results from threats of political action, complex and drawn-out bureaucratic procedures, and the prospect of arbitrary and unpredictable alterations in regulations after the investment decision has been made.[15]

[14] Richard H. Holton, "Making International Joint Ventures Work," presented at the seminar on the Management of Headquarters/Subsidiary Relationships in Transnational Corporations, Stockholm School of Economics, June 2–4, 1980, 4.

[15] Isaiah Frank, *Foreign Enterprise in Developing Countries* (Baltimore: Johns Hopkins University, 1980).

Joint Ventures   Joint ventures are a collaboration of two or more organizations for more than a transitory period.[16] In this collaboration, the participating partners share assets, risks, and profits. Equality of partners is not necessary. In some joint ventures, each partner holds an equal share; in others, one partner has the majority of shares. The partners' contributions to the joint venture can also vary widely. Contributions may consist of funds, technology, know-how, sales organizations, or plant and equipment. The International Marketplace 14.4 gives an example of one corporation's philosophy on joint ventures.

Advantages of Joint Ventures   The two major reasons for carrying out foreign direct investments in the form of joint ventures are environmental and commercial. Environmental reasons consist mainly of government pressures on firms either to form or accept joint ventures or to forgo participation in the local market. Such restrictions are designed to reduce the extent of control that foreign firms can exercise over local operations. As a basis for defining control, most countries have employed percentage levels of ownership. Over time, countries have shown an increasing tendency to adopt the thresholds of ownerships which define control. This tendency developed as it became apparent that even small, organized groups of stockholders may influence control of an enterprise, particularly if ownership is widely distributed.[17] At the same time, however, many countries are also recognizing the beneficial effects of foreign direct investment in terms of technological progress and international competitiveness and are permitting more control of local firms by foreign entities.

Another environmental reason may be the economic orientation of governments and a resulting requirement for joint venture collaboration. Joint ventures can help overcome existing market access restrictions and open up or maintain market opportunities that otherwise would not be available.

Equally important to the formation of joint ventures are commercial considerations. If a corporation can identify a partner with a common goal, and if the international activities are sufficiently independent from each other not to infringe on the autonomy of the individual partner, joint ventures may represent the most viable vehicle for international expansion. The following is an example of a nearly ideal joint venture:

> The Trailmobile Company of Cincinnati, Ohio, produces truck trailers. It now participates in 27 joint ventures abroad. Truck trailers do not move in international markets in significant numbers because transportation costs are high and, more importantly, because tariffs typically serve to insulate the markets from each other. Therefore, pricing can be decided at the level of the joint venture, because one joint venture cannot invade the market of another. Each joint venture serves its own local market, and these differ from each other in significant ways; hence, the marketing policy decisions are made at the local level. Only a modest part of the total cost of manufacturing the trailer is represented by components bought from Trailmobile. Thus, the interdependencies are limited, decision making can be delegated to the level of the joint venture, and conflicts can be minimized.[18]

Joint ventures are valuable when the pooling of resources results in a better outcome for each partner than if each attempted to carry out its activities individually. This is particularly the case when each partner has a specialized advantage in areas that benefit the joint venture. For example, a firm may have new technology available, yet lack sufficient capital to carry out foreign direct investment on its own. By joining forces with a partner, the technology can be used more quickly, and market penetration is easier. Similarly, one of the partners may have a distribution system already established or have better access

---

[16] W. G. Friedman and G. Kalmanoff, *Joint International Business Ventures* (New York: Columbia University Press, 1961).

[17] U.S. Department of Commerce, *Foreign Direct Investment in the United States*, vol. 1, April 1976, 5–6.

[18] Holton, "Making International Joint Ventures Work," 5.

THE INTERNATIONAL MARKETPLACE 14.4

Joint Ventures in Developing Countries: The Heinz Philosophy

Having determined to expand our business through new geography, we developed what we think are sensible and realistic guidelines for undertaking this expansion. The key to our strategy has been to use the joint venture as our entrée to a region. A joint venture offers the twin advantages of familiarity and facilities.

Obviously, an established business has greater familiarity with the political, economic, and social environment of its home market. The pioneering spirit can take an investment only so far. Rather than plant our flag and hope for the best, we believe it far more prudent to seek an experienced and knowledgeable partner in each region we enter. That partner may be a successful private business or it may be the host government.

The facilities of an existing enterprise offer us an important financial advantage in the early stage of an overseas venture. Because so many developing countries find their foreign currency in short supply, they may have difficulty importing material and equipment to build a plant. That bottleneck may be avoided by finding a factory with equipment and infrastructure in place.

Before we begin our courtship of a prospective partner, we ask ourselves how well it reflects the criteria we have devised to assess a project's desirability. Such criteria include:

- A company whose field is, or is closely related to, the food business
- A company staffed by nationals and not reliant on expatriates
- A company of sufficient size to serve as a continental base for expansion within the country and the region
- A company not heavily dependent on imported raw materials
- A company not dependent on exports and with ready markets for its products within its own country
- A company with good profit potential to justify the greater risk of investment in the Third World

Source: Anthony J. F. O'Reilly, "Establishing Successful Joint Ventures in Developing Nations: A CEO's Perspective," *Columbia Journal of World Business* 23 (Spring 1988): 66. Reprinted with permission.

to local suppliers, either of which permits a greater volume of sales in a shorter period of time.

Joint ventures also permit better relationships with local organizations—government, local authorities, or labor unions. Government-related reasons are the major rationale for joint ventures in less-developed countries, making them four times more frequent there than in industrialized nations.[19] Particularly if the local partner can bring political influence to the undertaking, the new venture may be eligible for tax incentives, grants, and government support and may be less vulnerable to political risk. Negotiations for certifications or licenses may be easier because authorities may not perceive themselves as dealing with a foreign firm. Relationships between the local partner and the local

---

[19] Paul W. Beamish, "The Characteristics of Joint Ventures in Developed and Developing Countries," *Columbia Journal of World Business* 20 (Fall 1985): 13–19.

financial establishment may enable the joint venture to tap local capital markets. The greater experience—and therefore greater familiarity—with the culture and environment of the local partner may enable the joint venture to be more aware of cultural sensitivities and to benefit from greater insights into changing market conditions and needs.

A final major commercial reason to participate in joint ventures is the desire to minimize the risk of exposing long-term investment capital while at the same time maximizing the leverage on the capital that is invested.[20] Economic and political conditions in many countries are volatile. At the same time, corporations tend to shorten their investment planning time span more and more. This financial rationale therefore takes on increasing importance.

Disadvantages of Joint Ventures Problem areas in joint ventures, as in all partnerships, involve implementing the concept and maintaining the relationship.

Many of the governments that require a joint venture formation are inexperienced in foreign direct investment. Therefore, joint venture legislation and the ensuing regulations are often subject to substantial interpretation and arbitrariness. Frequently, different levels of control are permitted depending on the type of product and the shipment destination. In some instances, only portions of joint venture legislation are made public. Other internal regulations are communicated only when necessary.[21] Such situations create uncertainty, which increases the risk for the joint venture participants.

Major problems can also arise in assuring the maintenance of the joint venture relationship. Seven out of ten joint ventures have been found to fall short of expectations and/or are disbanded.[22] The reasons typically relate to conflicts of interest, problems with disclosure of sensitive information, and disagreement over how profits are to be shared; in general, a lack of communication before, during, and after the formation of the venture. In some cases, managers are interested in launching the venture but are too little concerned about actually running the enterprise. Many of the problems stem from a lack of careful, advance consideration of how to manage the new endeavor. A partnership works on the basis of trust and commitment, or not at all.

Areas of possible disagreement include the whole range of business decisions covering strategy, management style, accounting and control, marketing policies and practices, production, research and development, and personnel.[23] The joint venture may, for example, identify a particular market as a profitable target, yet the headquarters of one of the partners may already have plans for serving this market, plans that would require competing against its own joint venture.

Similarly, the issue of profit accumulation and distribution may cause discontent. If one partner supplies the joint venture with a product, that partner will prefer that any profits accumulate at headquarters and accrue 100 percent to one firm rather than at the joint venture, where profits are partitioned according to equity participation. Such a decision may not be greeted with enthusiasm by the other partner. Further, once profits are accumulated, their distribution may lead to dispute. For example, one partner may insist on a high payout of dividends because of financial needs, whereas the other may prefer the reinvestment of profits into a growing operation.

Strategic Alliances One special form of joint ventures that is increasingly emerging is **strategic alliances,** or **partnerships.** The International Marketplace 14.5 discusses how a major alliance in the paper-producing industry can challenge the industry leader.

[20] Charles Oman, *New Forms of International Investment in Developing Countries* (Paris: Organization for Economic Cooperation and Development, 1984), 79.

[21] P. T. Bangsberg, "U.S. Lawyer Advises Companies on China," *Journal of Commerce,* August 22, 1985, 5A.

[22] Yankelovich, Skelly and White, Inc., *Collaborative Ventures: A Pragmatic Approach to Business Expansion in the Eighties* (New York: Coopers and Lybrand, 1984), 10.

[23] Holton, "Making International Joint Ventures Work," 7.

THE INTERNATIONAL MARKETPLACE 14.5

An Alliance Casts Its Net across Europe

The pan-European papermaking joint venture called Jamont is the second-largest paper producer in Europe. This venture is owned by James River Corporation from the United States, Oy Nokia Ab from Finland, and an Italian merchant bank Cragnotti & Partners Capital Investment. It got its start in 1987, when James River looked at the European markets and found them to be growing at twice the U.S. rate. It also saw a need to challenge its main worldwide competitor, Scott Paper Co., which in its 30 years in the European market had emerged as the largest paper producer there.

Papermaking then was highly fragmented, like every other industry in Europe. James River saw the chance to develop a pan-European manufacturing and marketing strategy. After acquiring 13 companies in 10 countries with its partners, efforts were combined into Jamont in 1990. By the end of 1994, Jamont plans to have finished its capital-investment program, overhauled manufacturing, developed consistent quality, and become the low-cost producer in each country in which it operates. Some efforts will be consolidated for cost savings. For example, before becoming part of Jamont, each company made its own deep-colored napkins (a complex process because dye changing takes a lot of time). Now, Jamont produces all such products at one plant in Finland.

The goal in the production of tissues is softness, strength, and absorbency at minimum cost. Although it sounds simple, getting ten cultures to cooperate makes it tough. To produce efficiently, Jamont needs to make napkins the same size throughout its operations. But some countries wanted to make them 30 cm by 30 cm and others 35 cm by 35 cm. Similar problems arose with computer systems and ways of measuring production efficiency. Finding the common ground that everyone respects proved to be difficult. On most issues, Jamont forms a committee to solve issues. This method is successful 80 percent of the time. When it is not, the CEO and his staff—four Frenchmen, two Americans, two Italians, a Finn, a Spaniard, and a Dutchman—take over. However, tension between decentralization and the drive to move in a common European direction will continue. And as tastes converge, so will the products Jamont sells.

The recent currency alignments are also a headache for Jamont. The company figured that since European currencies had been fixed for the last five years, such stability would continue. Then the United Kingdom and Italy pulled out of the Exchange Rate Mechanism, which raised costs to those markets by 10 to 15 percent. Not only will more time be spent hedging the balance sheet, but Jamont will also probably invest in new manufacturing facilities in the United Kingdom and Italy sooner than it would have otherwise.

Source: "A Joint-Venture Papermaker Casts Net Across Europe." *The Wall Street Journal*, December 7, 1992, B4.

Such ventures are central to the participant's future direction and means of achieving competitive advantages. The goals are to leverage critical capabilities, increase the flow of innovation, and improve flexibility in responding to market and technological changes.[24] A few years ago, it could be stated with impunity that "what the parent may

---

[24] Stanley J. Modic, "Strategic Alliances," *Industry Week*, October 3, 1988, 46–52.

get from a joint venture is money, but unlikely any substantial amount of new knowledge in technology, management, or the like."[25] However, given the growth of global competition, the large investment required for technological progress, and the resulting high risk of failure, corporations increasingly seek to join forces to spread the risk and to share capabilities.

A strategic alliance is an informal or formal arrangement between two or more companies with a common business objective. It is more than the traditional customer-vendor relationship, but less than an outright acquisition. These alliances can take forms ranging from information cooperation in the market development area to joint ownership of worldwide operations. For example, Texas Instruments has reported agreements with companies such as IBM, Hyundai, Fujitsu, Alcatel, and L. M. Ericsson using such terms as "joint development agreement," "cooperative technical effort," "joint program for development," "alternative sourcing agreement," and "design/exchange agreement for cooperative product development and exchange of technical data."

There are many reasons for the growth in such alliances. Market development is one common focus. Penetrating foreign markets is a primary objective of many companies. In Japan, Motorola is sharing chip designs and manufacturing facilities with Toshiba to gain greater access to the Japanese market. Some alliances are aimed at defending home markets. With no orders coming in for nuclear power plants, Bechtel Group has teamed up with Germany's Siemens to service existing U.S. plants.[26] Another focus is spreading the cost and risk inherent in production and development efforts. Texas Instruments and Hitachi have teamed up to develop the next generation of memory chips. The costs of developing new jet engines are so vast that they force aerospace companies into collaboration; one such consortium was formed by United Technologies' Pratt & Whitney division, Britain's Rolls Royce, Motoren-und-Turbinen Union from Germany, Fiat of Italy, and Japanese Aero Engines (made up of Ishikawajima Heavy Industries and Kawasaki Heavy Industries).[27] Finally, some alliances are formed to block and co-opt competitors.[28] For example, Caterpillar formed a heavy-equipment joint venture with Mitsubishi in Japan to strike back at its main global rival, Komatsu, in its home market.

However, such alliances are by no means confined to large multinational firms. As The International Marketplace 14.6 shows, small firms are taking advantage of the opportunities as well.

Of course, companies must carefully evaluate the effects of entering such a coalition. Depending on the objectives of the other partners, companies may wind up having their strategy partially driven by their competitors. Competitors may also gain strength through coalitions, unplanned transfers of technology might take place, and unexpected competitors might appear as a result.[29] Nevertheless, given continued increases in the complexity of competitiveness and the cost of technology, strategic alliances are likely to continue to grow in importance.

Recommendations The first requirement when forming a joint venture is to find the right partner. Partners should have a commonality of orientation and goals and should bring complementary and relevant benefits to the joint venture. The venture

[25] Lars Otterbeck, "Management of Joint Ventures," presented at the seminar on the Management of Headquarters/Subsidiary Relationships in Transnational Corporations, Stockholm School of Economics, June 2–4, 1980, 27.

[26] Louis Kraar, "Your Rivals Can Be Your Allies," *Fortune*, March 27, 1989, 66–76.

[27] "International Jet Bet," *Fortune*, November 28, 1983, 7.

[28] Jordan D. Lewis, *Partnerships for Profit: Structuring and Managing Strategic Alliances* (New York: Free Press, 1990), 85–87.

[29] Pedro Nueno and Jan Oosterveld, "Managing Technology Alliances," *Long Range Planning* (June 1988): 11–17.

THE INTERNATIONAL MARKETPLACE　14.6

Small Firms Use Alliances Too

When Michael Thiemann, vice president for new-product development at San Diego–based HCN Inc., went shopping in Japan, he was not looking for electronics or samurai swords. He wanted Japanese partners for his $14-million firm who could help in extending HNC's neural-network technology into new markets. After nine months, he had secured three agreements: one of them was with Sumitomo Heavy Industries, a major steelmaker, to apply HNC's image-processing system to apple sorting; a production agreement with another steelmaker served to develop a sophisticated chip; and a venture with a large Japanese leasing firm was designed to create a new credit-analysis program based on HNC's artificial intelligence capabilities.

HNC is one example of U.S. firms, mostly high-tech start-ups, seeking partnerships with Japanese companies. Such alliances can secure new markets, profits, and applications without loss of equity. To avoid the risks of investment, many firms are creating nonequity strategic alliances. These can include nonexclusive distribution or licensing deals. For example, Boston-based Avid Technology, a maker of video-editing systems, established a distribution agreement in 1990. One year later, sales in Japan accounted for almost a fifth of total sales. PeerLogic, a San Francisco–based firm specializing in advanced communications software, signed a licensing agreement with Chori Joho System Co. Says PeerLogic's Bob Scher of the match: "This is not just a licensing agreement, it's a relationship between our two companies. The better they do with our technology, the better we do."

Source: Peter Fuchs, "Strategic Alliances," *Business Tokyo*, April 1991, 22–27.

makes little sense if the expertise of both partners is in the same area—for example, if both have production experience but neither has distribution know-how. Similarly, bringing a good distribution system to the joint venture may be of little use if the established system is in the field of consumer products and the joint venture will produce industrial products.

Second, great care needs to be taken in negotiating the joint venture agreement. In these negotiations, extensive provisions must be made for contingencies. Questions such as profit accumulation and distribution and market orientation must be addressed in the initial agreement; otherwise, they may surface as points of contention over time. A joint venture agreement, although comparable to a marriage contract, should contain the elements of a divorce contract. In case the joint venture cannot be maintained to the satisfaction of the partners, plans must exist for the dissolution of the agreement and for the allocation of profits and cost.

Finally, joint ventures operate in dynamic business environments and therefore must be able to adjust to changing market conditions. The agreement therefore should provide for changes in the original concept so that the venture can grow and flourish.

Government Consortia　One newly emerging form of cooperation takes place at the industry level and is typically characterized by government support or even subsidization. Usually, it is the reflection of escalating cost and a governmental goal of developing or maintaining global leadership in a particular sector. A new drug can cost $200 million to develop and bring to market; a new mainframe computer or a telecommunications switch can require $1 billion. Some $7 billion will be needed to develop the next generation of computer chips.[30] To combat the high costs and risks of research and development, **research consortia** have emerged in the United States, Japan, and Europe. Since the passage of the **Joint Research and Development Act** of 1984 (which allows both domestic and foreign firms to participate in joint basic research efforts without the fear of antitrust action), well over 100 consortia have been registered in the United States. These consortia pool their resources for research into technologies ranging from artificial intelligence and electric car batteries to those needed to overtake the Japanese lead in semiconductor manufacturing. (The major consortia in the United States are the Battery Consortium and Sematech.) The Europeans have five mega-projects to develop new technologies registered under the names EUREKA, ESPRIT, BRITE, RACE, and COMET. Japanese consortia have worked on producing the world's highest-capacity memory chip and advanced computer technologies. On the manufacturing side, the formation of Airbus Industrie secured European production of commercial jets. The consortium, backed by France's Aerospatiale, Germany's Messerschmitt Bölkow Blohm, British Aerospace, and Spain's Construciones Aeronauticas, has become a prime global competitor.

MANAGEMENT CONTRACTS

One final major form of international market participation is the management contract. Firms have found this method to be a useful alternative or complement to other international options, since it permits the international use of corporate resources and can also be an acceptable response to government ownership restrictions. In a **management contract,** the supplier brings together a package of skills that will provide an integrated service to the client without incurring the risk and benefit of ownership. The activity is quite different from other contractual arrangements such as licensing because people actually move and directly implement the relevant skills and knowledge in the client organization.[31] Management contracts can be used by the international marketer in various ways. When equity participation, in the form of either full ownership or a joint venture, is not possible or must be relinquished, a management contract can serve to maintain participation in a venture. Depending on the extensiveness of the contract, it may even permit some measure of control. As an example, the manufacturing process might have to be relinquished to foreign firms, yet international distribution is needed for the product. A management contract could serve to maintain a strong hold on the operation by ensuring that all the distribution channels remain firmly controlled.

Yet management contracts should not be seen as a last line of defense. Whenever lack of expertise exists in a particular venture, management contracts can be a most useful tool to help overcome barriers to international marketing activities. This is particularly useful if an outside party has specialized knowledge that is crucial to international marketing success, whether in the area of distribution technology, marketing know-how, or worldwide contacts. Some companies in the service sector have independent entities

[30] "Can Europe Catch Up in the High-Tech Race?" *Business Week*, October 23, 1989, 142–154.
[31] Lawrence S. Welch and Anubis Pacifico, "Management Contracts: A Role in Internationalization?" *International Marketing Review* 7 (1990): 64–74.

that specialize in delivering management services. For example, the French airline UTA manages the operations of Air Zaire by handling the accounting system, setting salary and customer-service levels, and providing training programs.[32]

Often, a management contract is the critical element in the success of a project. A financial institution may gain confidence in a project because of the existence of a management contract and sometimes may even make it a condition of providing the funding.[33]

One specialized form of management contract is the **turnkey operation.** Here, the arrangement permits a client to acquire a complete operational system, together with the skills investment sufficient to allow unassisted maintenance and operation of the system following its completion.[34] The client need not search for individual contractors and subcontractors or deal with scheduling conflicts and difficulties in assigning responsibilities and blame. Instead, a package arrangement permits the accumulation of responsibility in one hand and greatly eases the negotiation and supervision requirements and subsequent accountability issues for the client.

Management contracts have clear benefits for the client. They can provide organizational skills that are not available locally, expertise that is immediately available rather than built up, and management assistance in the form of support services that would be difficult and costly to replicate locally. In addition, the outside involvement is clearly limited. When a turnkey project is on-line, the system will be totally owned, controlled, and operated by the customer. As a result, management contracts are seen by many governments as a useful alternative to foreign direct investment and the resulting control by nondomestic entities.

Similar advantages exist for the supplier. The risk of participating in an international venture is substantially lowered because no equity capital is at stake. At the same time, a significant amount of operational control can be exercised. Clearly, being on the inside represents a strategic advantage in influencing decisions in a number of areas that may be of long-term interest, such as design specifications or sourcing.[35] In addition, existing know-how that has been built up with significant investment can be commercialized. Frequently, the impact of fluctuations in business volume can be reduced by making use of experienced personnel who otherwise would have to be laid off. In industrialized countries like the United States, with economies that are increasingly service based, accumulated service knowledge and comparative advantage should be used internationally. Management contracts permit a firm to do so.

From the client's perspective, the main drawbacks to consider are the risks of overdependence and loss of control. For example, if the management contractor maintains all international relationships, little if any expertise may be passed on to the local operation. Instead of a gradual transfer of skills leading to increasing independence, the client may have to rely more and more on the performance of the contractor.

On the contractor's side, the major risks to consider are (1) the effects of the loss or termination of a contract and the resulting personnel problems and (2) a bid made without fully detailed insight into actual expenses. Winning a management contract could result in Pyrrhic victories, with the income not worth the expense.

---

[32] "Air Zaire Improving with Help from UTA," *Air Transport World* (June 1987): 170–173.

[33] Michael Z. Brooke, *Selling Management Services Contracts in International Business* (London: Holt, Rinehart & Winston, 1985), 7.

[34] Richard W. Wright and Colin Russel, "Joint Ventures in Developing Countries: Realities and Responses," *Columbia Journal of World Business* 10 (Spring 1975): 74–80.

[35] Lawrence S. Welch, "The International Marketing of Technology: An Interaction Perspective," *International Marketing Review* 2 (1985): 41–53.

SUMMARY

Foreign direct investment represents a major market-expansion alternative. Although such investment can be carried out by any type of firm, large or small, it typically occurs after some experience has been gathered with alternative forms of internationalization, such as exporting. The most visible and powerful players in the foreign direct-investment field are larger-sized firms and multinational corporations. Market factors, barriers to trade, cost factors, and investment climate are the major causes of foreign direct investment, with market factors usually playing the major role.

Different ownership levels of foreign investments are possible, ranging from wholly owned subsidiaries to joint ventures. Although many firms prefer full ownership in order to retain full control, such a posture is often not possible because of governmental regulations. It may not even be desirable. Depending on the global organization and strategic needs of the firm, joint ventures with only partial ownership may be a profitable alternative.

In a joint venture, the partners can complement each other by contributing the strengths and resources that each is best equipped to supply. Joint ventures offer significant benefits in terms of closeness to markets, better acceptance by the foreign environment, and a lessening of the risks involved, but they also pose new problems due to potential clashes of corporate cultures, business orientations, and marketing policies. It is therefore important to select the appropriate joint venture partner and to design an agreement that ensures the long-term approval of all participants.

Strategic alliances, or partnerships, are a special form of joint venture in which the participants, at either the industry or the corporate level, join forces in order to make major strategic progress toward technology development and competitiveness. Given the complexities and cost of technological progress, the number of these alliances, sometimes encouraged through government-sponsored consortia, is rapidly growing.

As countries increasingly develop a service-based economy, the usefulness of management contracts grows. Such contracts can enable the involvement of the international marketer in a project when equity participation is not possible or desirable. They also permit a client to acquire operational skills and turnkey systems without relinquishing ownership of a project. Because management assistance, service delivery, and project planning are increasingly important, international marketers can use management contracting to carve out a profitable market niche.

Questions for Discussion

1. How is an increase in protectionism likely to affect foreign direct-investment activities?
2. As a government official, would you prefer the foreign direct investment of a resource seeker, efficiency seeker, or market seeker?
3. Give some reasons why a multinational corporation might insist on 100 percent ownership abroad.
4. At what level of ownership would you consider a firm to be foreign controlled?
5. Do investment-promotion programs of state governments make sense from a national perspective?
6. Suggest a way of reducing the transfer pricing problem in joint ventures.
7. How can a management contractor have more control than the client? What can the client do under such circumstances?
8. Joining forces in strategic industry alliances may enhance technological progress, yet antitrust laws have prohibited such coalitions. Why? And why are they now possible?

9. Discuss the benefits and drawbacks of strategic partnerings at the corporate level.
10. What is the role of government consortia?

Recommended Readings

Bodaracoo, Joseph L. *The Knowledge Link: Competing through Strategic Alliances.* Boston: Harvard Business School Press, 1991.

Brooke, Michael Z. *Selling Management Services Contracts in International Business.* London: Holt, Rinehart & Winston, 1985.

Casson, Mark. *Multinational Corporations.* New York: Stockton Press, 1989.

Donaldson, Thomas. *The Ethics of International Business.* New York: Oxford University Press, 1989.

Dunning, John H. "Governments and Multinational Enterprises: From Confrontation to Co-operation?" *Discussion Papers in International Investment and Business Studies,* University of Reading, 1991.

Franko, Lawrence G. "Use of Minority and 50-50 Joint Ventures by United States Multinationals during the 1970's: The Interaction of Host Country Policies and Corporate Strategies." *Journal of International Business Studies* 20 (Spring 1989): 19–40.

Graham, Edward M., and Paul R. Krugman. *Foreign Direct Investment in the United States.* 2d. ed. Washington D.C.: Institute for International Economics, 1991.

International Direct Investment Statistics Yearbook. Paris: Organization for Economic Co-operation and Development, 1994.

James, Harvey S., and Murray Weidenbaum. *When Businesses Cross International Borders: Strategic Alliances and Their Alternatives.* Westport, CT: Praeger, 1993.

Lewis, Jordan D. *Partnerships for Profit: Structuring and Managing Strategic Alliances.* New York: Free Press, 1990.

United National Centre on Transnational Corporations. *The Determinants of Foreign Direct Investment: A Survey of the Evidence.* New York: United Nations, 1992.

Weiss, Stephen E. "Creating the GM-Toyota Joint Venture: A Case in Complex Negotiation." *Columbia Journal of World Business* 22 (Summer 1987): 23–37.

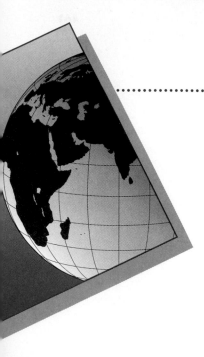

CHAPTER 15

Primary International Marketing Research and the Decision Support System

THE INTERNATIONAL MARKETPLACE

Adjusting Research to Market Conditions

Western businesses are on a mission to discover how Ivan shaves and what Olga uses to wash her hair. To find out, some marketers have hit the research trail in Eastern Europe, hoping to gain an upper hand on those waiting for the coast to clear of remaining uncertainties.

In order to carry out research, marketers need to think creatively and work around barriers. Surveying in the former Soviet Union calls for such measures. One U.S. researcher has developed an interesting system of dispersing questionnaires to interviewers distantly located. The routine is to find a willing traveler, perhaps a train conductor or Aeroflot stewardess, to deliver the package of questionnaires and then call ahead to the destination with a description of the ad hoc courier. Sometimes the plan works, other times it flops—like the time some filled-out questionnaires were stranded for weeks because of fighting in Armenia.

Eastman Kodak entered the Eastern Europe research scene in 1989 eager for valuable data. When he found very few data readily available, Kodak's research manager decided to join forces with other firms for a multiclient survey conducted by SRG International Ltd. that would include nine republics. Even this collaborative effort turned out problematic. The questionnaire had to be translated into nine languages. Kodak's usual practice of using pictures of cameras to determine which camera types people currently use had to be scrapped because researchers were unable to find usable pictures of Soviet cameras.

Special attention must be paid to training local interviewers and reviewing their work. One western researcher recalls a woman in Moscow being trained to be a focus group moderator. He described her as a drill sergeant while imitating her, "I just asked you a question and you have to respond." Another researcher's experience was with a local interviewer hired in the Ukraine. He left the questionnaires with the respondents instead of interviewing them and the whole process had to be redone.

Discussion groups can be a good method of finding important information on particular subjects. But unlike in the West, discussions have to be held on the same day as recruitment. Participants cannot be asked to come back in a couple of days because, one researcher comments, "They can't predict what they'll be doing in two days. They may have to stand in some line." Interpretation of data, once they have been collected, has its problems as well. Pepsi-Cola International received results from a survey in Hungary that said drugstores were an outlet for soft drinks. "But drugstores don't exist in Hungary," says the Pepsi marketing director. Apparently, the information obtained had been forced into categories developed in the West.

Some skeptics question the value of consumer studies in markets where the problem is often a lack of products, not the fickleness of the consumer. Since habits have been shaped by what is available, surveys are not a good indicator of how people would behave when Western brands are introduced, says one marketing consultant. However, many researchers plow full steam ahead, justifying their work by saying there is no alternative for getting around the scarcity of consumer information other than the first step they are taking. Besides, researchers are pleasantly surprised to find that the Eastern Europeans are not only willing to answer questions, but are flattered to be asked their opinion, which is a change from the past! A researcher from the Gallup organization recalls an old Hungarian woman who enthusiastically thanked her interviewer saying, "It was such a wonderful experience to have a chance to talk to you for so long. How much do I pay you?"

Source: Adapted from *The Wall Street Journal,* "Western Firms Poll Eastern Europeans to Discern Tastes of Nascent Consumers," April 27, 1992, B1.

This chapter focuses on the conduct of research abroad, the collection of primary data, and the minimization of research cost. The primary research process is explained by addressing the need for primary international research and the steps necessary for conducting it. Other issues covered are research administration, research technique, and research instruments.

In addition to specific international research projects, multinational corporations quite frequently desire to maintain continuous updates of changing market environments abroad and to obtain glimpses into the future in order to plan corporate strategy. The marketing decision support system necessary to achieve these goals is the topic of the second section of the chapter. Primary emphasis is on environmental scanning, the use of the Delphi research technique, and scenario building.

THE PRIMARY RESEARCH PROCESS

Primary research is conducted to fill specific information needs. The research may not actually be conducted by the firm with the need, but the work must be carried out for a specific research purpose. Primary research therefore goes beyond the activities of secondary data collection, which often cannot supply answers to the specific questions posed. Conducting primary research internationally can be complex due to different environments, attitudes, and market conditions. Yet it is precisely because of these differences that research is necessary. The International Marketplace 15.1 provides an example of such a situation.

The use of primary research internationally is much less widespread than it should be. Frequently, corporations are reluctant to engage in international research because of its cost. A basic cost-benefit evaluation would, for example, suggest that "management should simply fill a $10,000 order to an otherwise trustworthy distributor operating under a teetering Latin American junta rather than spend several thousand dollars on further research as well as divert managerial resources from elsewhere."[1] Also, doubts about the competence and reliability of foreign research companies and of international research agencies are often cause for hesitation.[2]

Yet corporations are increasingly recognizing the need for primary international research because of the large volume of their international business transactions and the growth in international risk. As the extent of a firm's international involvement increases, so does the importance and complexity of its international marketing research. Large companies are likely to engage in foreign marketing research more frequently and to use more rigorous techniques than are small or medium-sized firms. This difference results from the diversity of managerial talents and other resources in a larger firm and the increased dependence on profits from abroad.[3] Because the cost of research is often evaluated as a percentage of total business activity resulting from the research, the larger the intended or projected sales, the easier it becomes to justify primary research expenditures.

Understanding the Need for Primary Research

Figure 15.1 presents an overview of the steps necessary to plan and conduct primary research internationally and also outlines the subsequent research discussion of this chapter. As in secondary research, the first step consists of understanding the need for carrying out the research. Quite frequently, in a misguided effort to conserve funds, corporation management may insist on carrying out all research with secondary data. However, particularly for large-scale operations and pioneering activities, sooner or later very issue-specific questions must be answered. Secondary data only rarely provide sufficient information for such inquiries.

Primary research is essential for the formulation of strategic marketing plans. One particular area of research interest is that of international market segmentation. Historically, firms confined themselves to segment markets internationally based on macro variables such as income per capita or consumer spending on certain product categories. Increasingly, however, firms recognize that segmentation variables, such as life styles, attitudes, or personality, can play a major role in identifying similar consumer groups in different countries which can then be targeted across borders. One such group could consist, for example, of educationally elite readers who read *Scientific American, Time, Newsweek, The Financial Times,* and *The Economist.* Members in this group are likely to have more in common with each other rather than with their fellow

---

[1] S. Tamer Cavusgil, "International Marketing Research: Insights into Company Practices," in *Research in Marketing,* vol. 7, ed. J. N. Sheth (Greenwich, CT: JAI Press, 1984), 261–288.

[2] Susan P. Douglas and C. Samuel Craig, *International Marketing Research* (Englewood Cliffs, NJ: Prentice-Hall, 1983), 2.

[3] Cavusgil, "International Marketing Research," 261–288.

Steps in Primary International Research   FIGURE 15.1

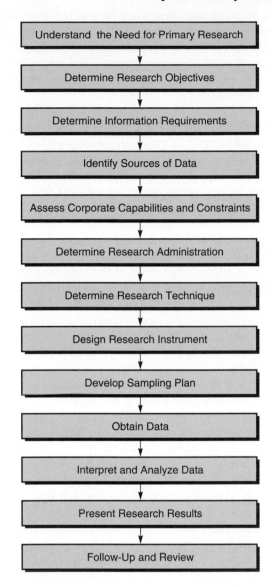

countrymen.[4] Alternatively, in marketing to women, it is important to understand the degree to which they have entered the work force in a country, what their life cycle stage is, and how different segments make or influence purchase decisions.[5] In order to identify these groups and to devise ways of meeting their needs, primary international market research is indispensable.

[4] Salah S. Hassan and A. Coskun Samli, "The New Frontiers of Intermarket Segmentation," in *Global Marketing: Perspectives and Cases,* eds. Salah S. Hassan and Roger D. Blackwell (Fort Worth: Dryden Press, 1994), 76–100.

[5] Rena Bartos, "Marketing to Women around the World," in *Global Marketing: Perspectives and Cases,* 119–146.

Determining Research Objectives

One of three possible research objectives must be selected: exploratory, descriptive, or causal. This differentiation is necessary because the objectives require varying commitments of time and funding. Further, the answers supplied will have varying utility to the corporation, ranging from purely tactical to strategic and long-term. Figure 15.2 depicts the changes in corporate usefulness of the three types of research. Each objective has merit, depending on corporate needs.

Exploratory Research   Exploratory research is most appropriate when the primary objective is to identify problems, to define problems more precisely, or to investigate the possibility of new alternative courses of action. Exploratory research can also aid in formulating hypotheses regarding potential problems or opportunities present in the decision situation.[6] Frequently, exploratory research is only the first step in further research activity. To some extent, it can be compared to a fishing expedition or to a charting of the waters for the uninitiated. Since international markets are often unfamiliar to management, such exploratory research can be very useful to gain initial insights into the new environment, its customers, and its suppliers.

Exploratory research is often characterized by the need for great flexibility and versatility. Because the researcher is not knowledgeable about the phenomenon under investigation, he or she needs to be able to quickly adapt to newly emerging situations in order to make the research worthwhile. The emphasis is on qualitative rather than quantitative data collection, and quick rather than slow answers are sought. This, of course, means that exploratory research is less subject to the rigors of more precise research and therefore is less reliable.

Exploratory research can be most useful in answering the basic question for the researcher: "What is the problem?" The defining and formulation of the problem is often far more essential than its solution, which may be merely a matter of mathematical or experimental skill. If the basic research objective is to define a problem or to gain "a feel" for a situation or to provide an overview, exploratory research may be the most appropriate activity from the standpoint of both time and money.

Descriptive Research   The aim of descriptive research is to provide a description of existing market phenomena. For example, market characteristics such as the socio-economic position of customers or their purchasing intent may be analyzed. Such research is often used to determine the frequency of occurrence of marketing events, such as the frequency of customers visiting a store, of machines needing to be replaced, or of lawyers being consulted. Descriptive research can also be used to determine, in a non-causal fashion, the degree to which marketing variables are associated with one another. Based on this determination, predictions can then be made regarding future occurrences in the market. In the international setting, the researcher typically uses descriptive work to look for similarities and differences between markets and consumer groups. Similarities can then be exploited through standardization, whereas differences can assist in formulating an adaptive business strategy.

Although several interviews may be sufficient for exploratory research, descriptive studies often require larger quantities of data because the requirements for accurately portraying the population under study are much more stringent. To carry out descriptive work, the researcher needs a substantial amount of information about the phenomenon under study. Hypotheses are customarily preformulated and subsequently tested

---

[6] Thomas C. Kinnear and James R. Taylor, *Marketing Research: An Applied Approach,* 3d ed. (New York: McGraw-Hill, 1987), 125.

FIGURE 15.2

Corporate Usefulness of Different Types of Research

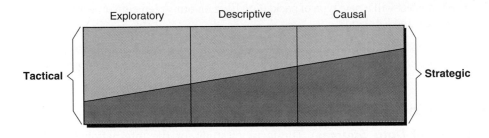

with the accumulated data. The research design needs to be carefully planned and structured. The intent of descriptive research is to maximize accuracy and to minimize systematic error. The researcher aims to increase reliability by keeping the measurement process as free from random error as possible.

Descriptive research does not provide any information about causal interrelationships, but this does not necessarily detract from its value. Quite often, firms have little interest in the underlying causes for interaction and are satisfied if linkages can be described. As an example, a firm may benefit from knowing that in January, soft drink sales will drop by 30 percent from December's levels. Whether this development results from lower temperatures or from decreased humidity may be much less useful information.

Causal Research The aim of causal research is to identify precise cause-and-effect relationships present in the market. The level of precision is higher than that for other types of research because reasonably unambiguous conclusions regarding causality must be presented. Therefore, causal research is often the most demanding type in terms of time and financial resources. It intends to present answers as to why things happen and to highlight details of the relationships among variables. To extract the causality from a variety of unrelated factors, investigators often need to resort to longitudinal and experimental measures. Longitudinal measures are required because after-the-fact measurement alone cannot fully explain the effect of causality. Similarly, experimentation is often necessary to introduce systematic variation of factors and then measure the effect of these variations. Obviously, causal research is useful only if the research objective is to identify these interrelationships and if this knowledge makes a contribution to the corporate decision process that justifies the investment.

Descriptive studies comprise the vast majority of international marketing research. Many times, exploratory research is seen as an insufficient basis for major corporate decisions, and causal research is seen as too time-consuming, too expensive, and too insufficient in benefit to be justified. Corporations are mostly satisfied when management believes that a thorough understanding of a market situation has been obtained and that reasonable predictability is possible. Since corporate research is usually measured by its bottom-line effect, descriptive studies often appear to be most desirable.

Determining Information Requirements

Specific research questions must be formulated to determine precisely the information that is required. The following are examples of such marketing questions:

- What is the market potential for our furniture in Indonesia?
- How much does the typical Nigerian consumer spend on soft drinks?

- What will happen to demand in Brazil if we raise our product price along monthly inflation levels?
- What effect will a new type of packaging have on our green consumers in Germany, France, and England?

Only when information requirements are determined as precisely as possible will the researcher be able to develop a research program that will deliver a useful product.

Identifying Data Sources

Location of Data Sources The focus of study for the international market researcher will customarily be a foreign market. However, primary data do not always have to be collected abroad. On some occasions, such data may be collected domestically. Interviews about foreign buyer behavior can, for example, be conducted with embassy personnel, foreign students, tourists, or domestic experts on the foreign market. Yet in spite of the ease of access, the researcher needs to be cautious in using these sources. Often they are not representative of typical consumers but rather reflect the thinking and behavior of a country's elite class. Frequently, these groups also know very little about specific industrial markets and products. Therefore, the likelihood of obtaining biased information from these data sources is extremely high. The researcher thus frequently needs to extend his or her efforts abroad. The specific country or region to be investigated must first be determined. Research in an entire country may not be necessary if only urban centers are to be penetrated. At other times, multiple regions of a country must be investigated if there is a lack of homogeneity between these regions as a result of different economic, geographic, or behavioral factors. For example, there are still large areas in Mexico where native Indian tribes speak languages other than Spanish. By conducting research only in Spanish, a large and important population group may be bypassed.[7] The researcher must, of course, have a clear concept of what the population under study should be and where it is located before deciding on the country or region to be investigated.

Industrial versus Consumer Research Whether to conduct research with consumers or with industrial users must also be decided. This decision will in part determine the size of the universe and respondent accessibility. For example, consumers are usually a very large group and can be reached through interviews at home or through intercept techniques. On the other hand, the total population of industrial users may be smaller and more difficult to reach. Further, cooperation by respondents may be quite different, ranging from very helpful to very limited. In the industrial setting, differentiating between users and decision makers may be much more important because their personality, their outlook, and their evaluative criteria may differ widely.

Assessing Corporate Capabilities and Constraints

The researcher must obtain input on what a corporation can and cannot do. Overoptimism may result in wrong decisions that can come back to haunt the researcher and the firm.

Corporations may estimate their internal strengths as greater than they are. As an example, a sales manager who is a native of Spain may not be the best person to entrust

---

[7] Jack Honomichl, "Research Cultures Are Different in Mexico, Canada," *Marketing News,* May 10, 1993, 12.

with research in that country. The individual may have outdated knowledge about the market, or the terminology used in Spain may differ substantially from what has been picked up in the United States. Friends who offer help may often not be qualified to provide such help professionally. Cost figures obtained may be totally out of date. Research skills that may have proven highly effective domestically may be inappropriate internationally. The research department possessing these domestic skills may therefore not be qualified to conduct international research.

Management should not reject out of hand the possibility of using its own staff to conduct international marketing research. However, a precise assessment is needed of corporate capabilities and strengths as well as possible weaknesses in an international marketing research effort. Estimates made of cost and time requirements should be increased generously in order to accurately reflect reality.

Determining Research Administration

The major issues in determining who will do the research are whether to use a centralized, coordinated, or decentralized approach and whether to engage an outside research service.

Degree of Research Centralization   The level of control that corporation headquarters exercises over international marketing research activities is a function of the overall organizational structure of the firm and the nature and importance of the decision to be made. The three major approaches to international research organization are the centralized, coordinated, and decentralized approaches.[8]

The centralized approach clearly affords the most control to headquarters. All **research specifications** such as focus, thrust, and design are directed by the home office and are forwarded to the local country operations for implementation. The subsequent analysis of gathered information again takes place at headquarters. Such an approach can be quite valuable when international marketing research is intended to influence corporate policies and strategy. It also ensures that all international market studies remain comparable to one another. On the other hand, some risks exist. For example, headquarters management may be insufficiently familiar with the local market situation to be able to adapt the research appropriately. Also, headquarter cultural bias may influence the research activities. Finally, headquarters staff may be too small or insufficiently prepared to provide proper guidance for multiple international marketing research studies.

A coordinated research approach uses an intermediary such as an outside research agency to bring headquarters and country operations together. This approach provides for more interaction and review of the international marketing research plan by both headquarters and the local operations and ensures more responsiveness to both strategic and local concerns. If the intermediary used is of high quality, the research capabilities of a corporation can be greatly enhanced through a coordinated approach.

The decentralized approach requires corporate headquarters to establish the broad thrust of research activities and then to delegate the further design and implementation to the local countries. The entire research is then carried out locally under the supervision of the local country operation, and only a final report is provided to headquarters. This approach has particular value if international markets differ significantly because

---

[8]   John W. Ewen, "Industrial Research in International Markets," presented at the American Marketing Association/Market Research Society Conference, New York, October 20, 1981.

it permits detailed adaptation to local circumstances. However, implementing research activities on a country-by-country basis may cause unnecessary duplication, lack of knowledge transference, and lack of comparability of results.

Local country operations may not be aware of research carried out by corporate units in other countries and may reinvent the wheel. This problem can be avoided if a proper intracorporate flow of information exists so that local units can check whether similar information has already been collected elsewhere within the firm. Corporate units that operate in markets similar to one another can then benefit from the exchange of research findings.

Local units may also develop their own research thrusts, tools, and analyses. A researcher in one country may, for example, develop a creative way of dealing with a non-response problem. This new technique could be valuable to company researchers who face similar difficulties in other countries. However, for the technique to become widely known, systems must be in place to circulate information to the firm as a whole.

Finally, if left to their own devices, researchers will develop different ways of collecting and tabulating data. As a result, findings in different markets may not be comparable, and potentially valuable information about major changes and trends may be lost to the corporation.

International marketing research activities will always be carried out subject to the organizational structure of a firm. Ideally, a middle ground between centralization and decentralization will be found, one that permits local flexibility together with an ongoing exchange of information within the corporation. The exchange of information is particularly important because global rather than local optimization is the major goal of the multinational corporation.

The Use of Outside Research Services   One major factor in deciding whether or not to use outside research services is, of course, the size of the international operations of a firm. No matter how large a firm is, however, it is unlikely to possess specialized expertise in international marketing research for every single market it currently serves or is planning to serve. Rather than overstretch the capabilities of its staff, or assert a degree of expertise that does not exist, a corporation may wish to delegate the research task to outside groups. This is particularly the case when corporate headquarters has little or no familiarity with the local research environment. Figure 15.3 provides an example of such a situation. The use of outside research agencies may be especially appropriate for large-scale international marketing research or if highly specialized research skills are required. Even though most U.S. market research firms still operate only domestically, a number of organizations provide international research. Table 15.1 provides a partial overview of such research firms.

The selection process for outside research providers should emphasize the quality of information rather than the cost. Low price is no substitute for lack in data pertinence or accuracy.

Before a decision is made, the capabilities of an outside organization should be carefully evaluated and compared with the capabilities available in-house and from competing firms. Although general technical capabilities are important, the prime selection criterion should be previous research experience in a particular country and a particular industry. Some experience is transferable from one industry or country to another; however, the better the corporation's research needs overlap an agency's past research accomplishment, the more likely it is that the research task will be carried out satisfactorily. Although the research may be more difficult to administer, multinational corporations should consider subcontracting each major international marketing research

THE INTERVIEWING IS EASY...
IF THIS MAN DOESN'T SHOOT YOU FIRST

TASK :

Interview Afghans who fled across the border into Pakistan to see if they're listening to the BBC. Problem: you have to get past the local warlords who control the area.

Hand this problem to any old research company claiming to do international research, and you're in trouble. The BBC turned to Research International.

KNOWING WHAT WORKS

In today's competitive world, companies are increasingly looking toward off-shore markets. And that means good information is essential, even in developed markets.

But international research isn't just a case of taking what you do here and transplanting it there.

A national probability sample in Brazil will have you climbing a palm tree. "I will buy" on a scale in Japan doesn't mean the same thing in Spain. In tax-shy Italy, quota sampling on the basis of income won't get you very far!

GLOBAL PERSPECTIVE
+ LOCAL INSIGHT

We have Research International offices on the ground in 38 of the world's most important markets, from France to Argentina, the USA to Russia, London to Singapore. All our companies are leaders in their markets.

Our professional staff know their markets because they live there—not through visits or by reading the statistics.

We have conducted more than 4,000 international projects. In the last two years alone, we've worked in over 100 countries.

We know what works. And what doesn't. We know what research should cost. We know how to insure comparable high quality standards worldwide.

RESEARCH INTERNATIONAL IN NORTH AMERICA

You may be surprised to know that Research International has 6 companies and 9 offices in this region. Whether it's large scale survey work, product testing, customer satisfaction research, qualitative or observational research, we can help.

We can put together an unrivaled team drawing on Research International resources in place in New York, Boston, San Francisco, Chicago, Toronto, Mexico City and in San Juan.

COMMITMENT TO
INNOVATION WORLDWIDE

Being on the ground all around the world also means that we have access to the best brains and the best thinking around the globe. Which means that we can offer our clients innovative, powerful techniques regardless of place of origin.

Our commitment to R. & D. runs very deep. Each year, we spend more of our own money on basic research than most of our competitors bring to the bottom line.

FREE OFFER

We've prepared a paper to help avoid some of the traps. Called "8 Common Pitfalls of International Research," it's free to marketers. Simply fax Daphne Chandler at—212-889-0487.

For specific help right now—call Daphne at 212-679-2500.

 **RESEARCH INTERNATIONAL**

Source: Reprinted by permission of Research International, The Leading Worldwide Research Company.

task to specialists, even if research within one country is carried out by various international marketing research agencies as a result. To have experts working on a problem is usually more efficient than to conserve corporate resources by centralizing all research activities with one service provider, who may be only marginally familiar with key aspects of the research.

| TABLE 15.1 | Top 50 U.S. Research Organizations | | | | | |

Rank 1992	Organization	Headquarters	Phone	Total Research Revenues* ($ millions)	Percent Revenues from outside United States (% of total)	Revenues from outside United States ($ millions)
1	Nielsen	Northbrook, IL	(708) 498-6300	$1,307.9	61.0%**	$795.0**
2	IMS International	Plymouth Meeting, PA	(215) 834-5000	586.0	65.0**	380.9**
3	Information Resources Inc.	Chicago, IL	(312) 726-1221	276.4	12.6	34.8
4	The Arbitron Co.	New York, NY	(212) 887-1300	178.0**		
5	Westat Inc.	Rockville, MD	(301) 251-1500	113.7		
6	Walsh/PMSI	Phoenix, AZ	(602) 381-9500	87.3	36.0	24.9
7	Maritz Marketing Research Inc.	St. Louis, MO	(314) 827-1610	69.7		
8	The NPD Group	Port Washington, NY	(516) 625-0700	57.1	23.0	13.1
9	The M/A/R/C Group	Las Colinas, TX	(214) 506-3400	53.9		
10	NFO Research Inc.	Greenwich, CT	(203) 629-8888	47.1		
11	Elrick & Lavidge Inc.	Atlanta, GA	(404) 885-8657	46.8		
12	Market Facts Inc.	Arlington Heights, IL	(708) 590-7000	40.7		
13	Walker Group	Indianapolis, IN	(317) 843-3939	38.7	1.5	.3
14	MRB Group	London, England	(44–81) 579-5500	34.1		
15	MAI Information Group	Livingston, NJ	(201) 716-0500	31.9		
16	Intersearch Corp.	Horsham, PA	(215) 657-6400	30.1		
17	The BASES Group	Covington, KY	(606) 655-6000	28.0	3.5	1.0
18	The National Research Group Inc.	Los Angeles, CA	(213) 856-4400	27.5	15.0	4.1
19	Abt Associates Inc.	Cambridge, MA	(617) 492-7100	27.2		
20	Millward Brown Inc.	Naperville, IL	(708) 505-0066	25.1		
21	Burke Marketing Research	Cincinnati, OH	(513) 241-5663	24.4		
22	Louis Harris and Associates Inc.	New York, NY	(212) 698-9600	24.1	70.0**	16.9**
23	Chilton Research Services	Radnor, PA	(215) 964-4660	23.8		
24	Research International USA	New York, NY	(212) 679-2500	22.9	26.0	5.0
25	Starch INRA Hooper Inc.	Mamaroneck, NY	(914) 698-0800	22.8	3.5	.8
26	J. D. Power & Associates	Agoura Hills, CA	(818) 889-6330	20.9		
27	Yankelovich Partners	Westport, CT	(203) 227-2700	19.9	7.5	1.5
28	Creative & Response Research Svcs.	Chicago, IL	(312) 828-9200	18.6		
29	ASI Market Research	New York, NY	(212) 807-9393	17.4		
30	Decision Research Corp.	Lexington, MA	(617) 861-7350	17.0		
31	Custom Research Inc.	Minneapolis, MN	(612) 542-0800	16.2		
32	M.O.R.-PACE	Farmington Hills, MI	(313) 737-5300	15.0	11.0	1.7
33	Data Development Corp.	New York, NY	(212) 633-1100	14.8		
34	The Wirthlin Group	McLean, VA	(703) 556-0001	13.6		
35	National Analysts	Philadelphia, PA	(215) 496-6800	13.2		
36	Lieberman Research West Inc.	Los Angeles, CA	(310) 553-0550	13.2	4.0	.5

Continued **TABLE 15.1**

Rank 1992	Organization	Headquarters	Phone	Total Research Revenues* ($ millions)	Percent and Revenues from outside United States (% of total) ($ millions)	
37	Total Research Corp.	Princeton, NJ	(609) 921-8100	$11.9	20.0%	$2.4
38	ICR Survey Research Group	Media, PA	(215) 565-9280	10.9		
39	MSW-McCollum Spielman Worldwide	Great Neck, NY	(516) 482-0310	10.6	5.0	.5
40	Strategic Research & Consulting	Maumee, OH	(419) 893-0029	10.5		
41	Market Strategies Inc.	Southfield, MI	(313) 350-3020	10.5		
42	Guideline Research Corp.	New York, NY	(212) 947-5140	10.4		
43	Research Data Analysis Inc.	Bloomfield Hills, MI	(313) 332-5000	10.3		
44	Response Analysis Corp.	Princeton, NJ	(609) 921-3333	10.3		
45	Conway/Milliken & Assocs.	Chicago, IL	(312) 787-4060	9.0		
46	Market Decisions	Cincinnati, OH	(513) 891-8000	8.9		
47	The Vanderveer Group	Fort Washington, PA	(215) 646-7200	7.7		
48	Shifrin Research Inc.	New York, NY	(212) 473-4050	7.6		
49	Newman-Stein Inc.	New York, NY	(212) 777-2700	7.4		
50	Gordon S. Black Corp.	Rochester, NY	(716) 272-8400	7.4		
			Subtotal, Top 50	$3,538.4	36.3%	$1,283.4
	All other (109 CASRO member companies not included in Top 50)***			337.6		
			Total (159 organizations)	$3,876.0		

*Total revenues that include nonresearch activities for some companies are significantly higher.

**Estimate.

***Total revenues of 109 survey research firms—beyond those listed in Top 50—that provide financial information, on a confidential basis, to the Council of American Survey Research Organizations (CASRO).

Source: *Marketing News*, June 7, 1993. Used with permission from the American Marketing Association.

Determining the Research Technique

Selection of the research technique depends on a variety of factors. First, the objectivity of the data sought must be determined. Standardized techniques are more useful in the collection of objective data than of subjective data. Also, the degree of structure sought in the data collection needs to be determined. Unstructured data will require more open-ended questions and more time than structured data. Since the willingness and ability of respondents to spend the time and provide a free-form response are heavily influenced by factors such as culture and education, the prevailing conditions in the country and segments to be studied need to be understood in making these decisions. Whether the data are to be collected in the real world or in a controlled environment also must be decided. Finally, a decision needs to be made as to whether the research technique is to collect historical facts or gather information about future developments. This is particularly important for consumer research because firms frequently desire to determine consumers' future intentions to purchase a certain product.

Cultural and individual preferences, which vary significantly among nations, play a major role in determining research techniques. U.S. managers frequently prefer to gather large quantities of data through surveys, which provide numbers that can be manipulated statistically, but managers in other countries appear to prefer the "soft" approach. For example, much of Japanese-style market research relies heavily on two kinds of information: **soft data** obtained from visits to dealers and other channel members and **hard data** about shipments, inventory levels, and retail sales. As the head of Matsushita's videocassette recorder division is reported to have said, "Why do Americans do so much marketing research? You can find out what you need by traveling around and visiting the retailers who carry your product."[9]

Once the structure of the type of data sought is determined, a choice must be made among the types of research instruments available. Each provides a different depth of information and has its unique strengths and weaknesses.

Interviews   Often, interviews with knowledgeable persons can be of great value to a corporation desiring international marketing information. Because bias from the individual may be part of the findings, the intent should be to obtain in-depth information rather than a wide variety of data. Particularly when specific answers are sought to very narrow questions, interviews can be most useful.

One government program that attempts to be responsive to such a need is a service of the U.S. Foreign and Commercial Service of the Department of Commerce. Called "The Comparison Shopping Service," it offers, for a set fee, the answers to nine company-specific questions. The questions are forwarded to the service in Washington, which in turn relays them to its foreign commercial outpost in the country under study. A Foreign Commercial Officer will then gather facts to provide the response.

Focus Groups   Focus groups are a useful research tool resulting in interactive interviews. A group of knowledgeable persons is gathered for a limited period of time (two to four hours). Usually, the ideal size for a focus group is seven to ten participants. A specific topic is introduced and thoroughly discussed by all group members. Because of the interaction, hidden issues are sometimes raised that would not have been addressed in an individual interview. The skill of the group leader in stimulating discussion is crucial to the success of a focus group. Discussions are often recorded on tape and subsequently analyzed in detail. Focus groups, like in-depth interviews, do not provide statistically significant information; however, they can be helpful in providing information about perceptions, emotions, and other nonovert factors. In addition, once individuals are gathered, focus groups are highly efficient in terms of rapidly accumulating a substantial amount of information. With the advances occurring in the communications field, focus groups can also be carried out internationally, with interaction between groups. The International Marketplace 15.2 provides an example.

When conducting international research via focus groups, the researcher must be aware of the importance of culture in the discussion process. Not all societies encourage frank and open exchange and disagreement among individuals. Status consciousness may result in situations in which the opinion of one is reflected by all other participants. Disagreement may be seen as impolite, or certain topics may be taboo.

Observation   Observation techniques require the researcher to play the role of a nonparticipating observer of activity and behavior. Observation can be personal or im-

---

[9] Johnny K. Johansson and Ikujiro Nonaka, "Market Research the Japanese Way," *Harvard Business Review* 65 (May–June 1987): 16–22.

THE INTERNATIONAL MARKETPLACE 15.2

Global Focus Groups

Now, companies can find out how consumers perceive their products in London and New York—at the same time. Thanks to video conferencing technology, market researchers can conduct focus groups in two different locations, with participants interacting with each other.

"It's a big opportunity, but people don't know it exists," says Thomas L. Greenbaum, executive vice president of Clarion Marketing and Communications, Greenwich, Connecticut. The technique allows marketers to compare regional perspectives without travel. Clarion set up a global focus group for a telecommunications company that sought representation from Europe and the United States. Focus groups were held in London and New York, with a moderator in each city.

FocusVision Network, Inc., of Newport Beach, California, plans to unveil an international network of focus facilities. The system, already in place in the United States, has the capability to broadcast live focus-group interviews from FocusVision facilities to a client's office. International expansion is a "logical and important application of video conferencing," says John J. Houlahan, president of FocusVision. "Instead of making the industry come to the technology, we're taking the technology to the industry."

Computer companies, telecommunications firms, and other high-tech companies will lead the way because their target audiences are "separated by the miles and different cultures but they inhabit similar worlds and have similar needs," says Hank Bernstein, senior vice president and director of consumer information services at DMB & B, Inc., New York. According to Bernstein, who participated in the London–New York focus group, once the participants got used to the technology, "they really did talk to each other across the continent."

Source: Cyndee Miller, "Anybody Ever Hear of Global Focus Groups?" *Marketing News,* May 27, 1991, 14.

personal—for example, mechanical. Observation can be obtrusive or inobtrusive, depending on whether the subject is aware or unaware of being observed. In international marketing research, observation can be extremely useful in shedding light on practices not previously encountered or understood. This aspect is particularly valuable for the researcher who is totally unfamiliar with a market or market situation and can be quickly achieved through, for example, participation in a trade mission. Observation can also help in understanding phenomena that would have been difficult to assess with other techniques. For example, Toyota sent a group of its engineers and designers to southern California to nonchalantly observe how women get into and operate their cars. They found that women with long fingernails have trouble opening the door and operating various knobs on the dashboard. Based on their observations, Toyota engineers and designers were able to "understand" the women's plight and redraw some of the automobile exterior and interior designs.[10]

Conducting observations can also have its pitfalls. For example, people may react differently to the discovery that their behavior has been observed. The degree to which the

---

[10] Michael R. Czinkota and Masaaki Kotabe, "Product Development in the Proper Context," *Product and Process Innovation,* November–December 1991, 33–37.

observer has to be familiarized or introduced to other participants may vary. The complexity of the task may differ due to the use of multiple languages. To conduct in-store research in Europe, for example, store checks, photo audits of shelves, and store interviews must be scheduled well in advance and need to be preceded by a full round of introductions of the researchers to store management and personnel. In some countries, such as Belgium, a researcher must remember that four different languages are spoken and their use may change from store to store.[11]

The research instruments discussed so far—interviews, focus groups, and observation—are useful primarily for gathering qualitative information. The intent is not to amass data, or to search for statistical significance, but rather to obtain a better understanding of given situations, behavioral patterns, or underlying dimensions. The researcher using these instruments must be cautioned that even frequent repetition of the measurements will not lead to a statistically valid result. However, statistical validity often is not the major focus of corporate international marketing research. Rather, it is the better understanding, description, and prediction of events that have an impact on marketing decision making. When quantitative data may also be desired, particularly when the research objectives are not exploratory but descriptive or causal, surveys and experimentation are appropriate types of research instruments.

Surveys   Survey research is useful in providing the opportunity to quantify concepts. In the social sciences, it is generally accepted that "the cross-cultural survey is scientifically the most powerful method of hypothesis testing."[12] Surveys are usually conducted via questionnaires that are administered personally, by mail, or by telephone. Use of the survey technique presupposes that the population under study is able to comprehend and respond to the questions posed. Also, particularly in the case of mail and telephone surveys, a major precondition is the feasibility of using the postal system or the widespread availability of telephones. Obviously, this is not a given in all countries. In many countries, only limited records are available about dwellings, their location, and their occupants. In Venezuela, for example, most houses are not numbered but rather are given individual names like "Casa Rosa" or "El Retiro." In some countries, street maps are not even available. As a result, it becomes virtually impossible to reach respondents by mail.

In other countries, obtaining a correct address may be easy, but the postal system may not function well. The Italian postal service, for example, repeatedly has suffered from scandals that exposed such practices as selling undelivered mail to paper mills for recycling.

Telephone surveys may also be inappropriate if telephone ownership is rare. In such instances, any information obtained would be highly biased even if the researcher randomizes the calls. In some instances, telephone networks and systems may also prevent the researcher from conducting surveys. Frequent line congestion or a lack of telephone directories are examples. There are also great variations between countries or regions of countries in terms of unlisted telephone numbers. For example, authors of comparative research have reported that only 2.1 percent of households with telephones in Kobe, Japan, have unlisted numbers, while the figure for Seattle's King County is estimated to be approximately 20 percent.[13]

---

[11] Cyndee Miller, "In-Store Research Catching on Quickly in Europe," *Marketing News,* September, 2, 1991, 1.

[12] Lothar G. Winter and Charles R. Prohaska, "Methodological Problems in the Comparative Analysis of International Marketing Systems," *Journal of the Academy of Marketing Science* 11 (Fall 1983): 421.

[13] Raymond A. Jussaume, Jr. and Yoshiharu Yamada, "A Comparison of the Viability of Mail Surveys in Japan and the United States," *Public Opinion Quarterly,* 54 (1990): 219–228.

Surveys can be hampered by social and cultural constraints. Recipients of letters may be illiterate or may be reluctant to respond in writing. In some nations, entire population segments—for example, women—may be totally inaccessible to interviewers. One must also assess the purpose of the survey in the context of the population surveyed. It has been argued, for example, that one should not rely on consumer surveys for new-product development information. Key reasons are the absence of responsibility—the consumer is sincere when spending but not when talking; conservative attitudes—ordinary consumers are conservative and tend to react negatively to a new product; vanity—it is human nature to exaggerate and put on a good appearance; and insufficient information—the research results depend on the product characteristics information that is given to survey participants and that may be incomplete or unabsorbed.[14]

In spite of all these difficulties, however, the survey technique remains a useful one because it allows the researcher to rapidly accumulate a large quantity of data amenable to statistical analysis. Even though quite difficult, **international comparative research** has been carried out very successfully between nations, particularly if the environments studied are sufficiently similar so that the impact of uncontrollable macrovariables is limited. However, even in environments that are quite dissimilar, in-depth comparative research can be carried out.[15] Doing so may require a country-by-country adjustment of details while preserving the similarity of research thrust. For example, researchers have reported good results in mail surveys conducted simultaneously in Japan and the United States after adjusting for the size of the cover letter, return envelope, outgoing envelope, address style, signature, and cover letter to meet specific societal expectations.[16] With constantly expanding technological capabilities, international marketers will be able to use the survey technique more frequently in the future.

Experimentation Experimental techniques are most useful in carrying out causal research. By determining the effect of an intervening variable, the researcher can establish precise cause-and-effect relationships. However, experimental techniques are difficult to implement in international marketing research. The researcher faces the task of designing an experiment in which most variables are held constant or are comparable across cultures. To do so represents a major challenge. For example, an experiment that intends to determine a causal effect within the distribution system of one country may be difficult to transfer to another country, where the distribution system is different. As a result, experimental techniques are only rarely used, even though their potential value to the international market researcher is recognized.

Designing the Research Instrument

The research instrument most appropriate to international marketing surveys is the questionnaire. It should contain questions that are clear and easy to comprehend by the

---

[14] R. Nishikawa, "New Product Planning at Hitachi," *Long Range Planning* 22 (1989): 20–24.

[15] For an excellent example, see Alan Dubinsky, Marvin Jolson, Masaaki Kotabe, and Chae Lim, "A Cross-National Investigation of Industrial Salespeople's Ethical Perceptions," *Journal of International Business Studies* 22 (1991): 651–670.

[16] Jussaume and Yamada, 222.

respondents, as well as easy for the data collector to administer. Much attention must therefore be paid to question format, content, and wording.

Question Format Questions can be structured or unstructured. Unstructured or open-ended questions permit the capture of more in-depth information, but they also increase the potential for interviewer bias. Even at the cost of potential bias, however, "the use of open-ended questions appears quite useful in cross-cultural surveys, because they may help identify the frame of reference of the respondents, or may even be designed to permit the respondent to set his own frame of reference."[17]

Another question format decision is the choice between direct and indirect questions. Societies have different degrees of sensitivity to certain questions. For example, questions related to the income or age of a respondent may be accepted differently in different countries. Also, the social desirability of answers may vary. As a result, the researcher must be sure that the questions are culturally acceptable. This may mean that questions that can be asked directly in some cultures will have to be asked indirectly in others. The researcher must also be sure to adapt the complexity of the question to the level of understanding of the respondent. For example, a multipoint scaling method, which may be effectively used in a developing country to discover the attitudes and attributes of company executives, may be a very poor instrument if used among rural entrepreneurs. It has been found that demonstration aids are useful in surveys among poorly educated people.[18]

The question format should also ensure data equivalence in international marketing research. This requires categories used in questionnaires to be comparatively structured. In a developed country, for example, a white-collar worker may be part of the middle class, whereas in a less-developed country, the same person would be part of the upper class. Before using categories in a questionnaire, the researcher must therefore determine their appropriateness in different environments. This is particularly important for questions that attempt to collect attitudinal, psychographic, or life-style data, since cultural variations are most pronounced in these areas.

Question Content When question content is planned, major consideration must be given to the ability and willingness of respondents to supply the answers. The knowledge and information available to respondents may vary substantially because of different educational levels and may affect their ability to answer questions. Further, societal demands and restrictions may influence the willingness of respondents to answer certain questions. For various reasons, respondents may also be motivated to supply incorrect answers. For example, in countries where the tax collection system is consistently eluded by taxpayers, questions regarding level of income may deliberately be answered inaccurately. Distrust in the researcher, and the fear that research results may be passed on to the government, may also lead individuals to consistently understate their assets. Because of government restrictions in Brazil, for example, individuals will rarely admit to owning an imported car. Nevertheless, when the streets of Rio de Janeiro are observed, a substantial number of foreign cars are seen. The international

---

[17] Sydney Verba, "Cross-National Survey Research: The Problem of Credibility," in *Comparative Methods in Sociology: Essays on Trends and Applications,* ed. I. Vallier (Berkeley: University of California Press, 1971), 322–323.

[18] Kavil Ramachandran, "Data Collection for Management Research in Developing Countries," in *The Management Research Handbook,* eds. N. Craig Smith and Paul Dainty (London: Routledge, 1991), 304.

market researcher is unlikely to change the societal context of a country. The objective of the content planning process should therefore be to adapt the questions to societal constraints.

Question Wording The impact of language and culture are of particular importance when wording questions. The goal for the international marketing researcher should be to ensure that the potential for misunderstandings and misinterpretations of spoken or written words is minimized. Both language and cultural differences make this issue an extremely sensitive one in the international marketing research process. As a result, attention must be paid to the translation equivalence of verbal and non-verbal questions that can change in the course of translation. In one frequently cited example, a translation from the Bible of "the spirit is willing but the flesh is weak" was retranslated into English as "the bourbon is good but the steak leaves a lot to be desired."

The key is to keep questions clear by using simple rather than complex words, by avoiding ambiguous words and questions, by omitting leading questions, and by asking questions in specific terms, thus avoiding generalizations and estimates.[19] To reduce problems of question wording, it is helpful to use a **translation-retranslation approach.** The researcher formulates the questions, has them translated into the language of the country under investigation, and subsequently has a second translator return the foreign text to the researcher's native language. Through the use of this method, the researcher can hope to detect possible blunders. An additional safeguard is the use of alternative wording. Here the researcher uses questions that address the same issue but are worded differently and that resurface at various points in the questionnaire in order to check for consistency in question interpretation by the respondents.

In spite of superb research planning, a poorly designed instrument will yield poor results. No matter how comfortable and experienced the researcher is in international research activities, an instrument should always be pretested. Ideally, such a pretest is carried out with a subset of the population under study. At least a pretest with knowledgeable experts and individuals should be conducted. Even though a pretest may mean time delays and additional cost, the downward risks of poor research are simply too great for this process to be omitted.

Developing the Sampling Plan

To obtain representative results, the researcher must reach representative members of the population under study. Many methods that have been developed in industrialized countries for this purpose are useless abroad. For example, address directories may simply not be available. Multiple families may live in one dwelling. Differences between population groups living, for example, in highlands and lowlands may make it imperative to differentiate these segments. Lack of basic demographic information may prevent the design of a sampling frame.

The international marketing researcher must keep in mind the complexities of the market under study and prepare his or her sampling plan accordingly. Often, samples need to be stratified to reflect different population groups, and innovative sampling

[19] Gilbert A. Churchill, Jr., *Marketing Research: Methodological Foundations,* 5th ed. (Fort Worth, TX: Dryden Press, 1991), 381–388.

15.3   THE INTERNATIONAL MARKETPLACE

Creative Primary Research

When American entrepreneur Peter Johns went to Mexico to do business, he couldn't buy what he needed most: information. So he dug it up himself. Johns wanted to distribute mail-order catalogs for upscale U.S. companies to consumers in Mexico. He thought that a large market was there just waiting to be tapped. However, when he tried to test his theory against hard data, he ran into a big blank.

Johns, who has spent 30 years in international marketing, couldn't find a useful marketing study for Mexico City. Government census reports weren't much help because they stop breaking down income levels at about $35,000, and they give ranges, rather than precise numbers, on family size.

So Johns embarked on some primary research. He went into the affluent neighborhoods and found just what he had suspected: satellite dishes, imported sports cars, and women carrying Louis Vuitton handbags. He reached his own conclusions about the target market for his catalogs. "There is no question there is a sense of consumer deprivation in the luxury market of Mexico City," says Johns.

After deciding to pursue his new enterprise, Johns reached another obstacle. His new enterprise, Choices Unlimited, had gotten rights from about 20 U.S. companies to distribute their catalogs in Mexico City. Now, he needed mailing lists—and he couldn't find them. Owners of mailing lists do not like to sell them because buyers tend to recycle the lists without authorization. Some of those that are available are expensive and may not include information like zip codes, important barometers of household wealth.

Johns asked his local investors for membership lists of the city's exclusive golf clubs. He also obtained directories of the parents of students at some of the city's exclusive private schools. Johns received these lists for free. "That's called grass-roots marketing intelligence," says Johns.

By 1993, Johns hopes to have a Mexican customer base of 7,500 families spending an average of $600 a year on his products. By then, he should have another product to sell: his customer list.

Source: Dianna Solis, "Grass-Roots Marketing Yields Clients in Mexico City," *The Wall Street Journal*, October 24, 1991, B2.

methods need to be devised in order to assure representative responses. The International Marketplace 15.3 provides an example of the creativity required.

Obtaining Data

When obtaining data, the international marketing researcher must check the quality of the data-collection process. In some foreign cultures, questionnaire administration is seen as useless by the local population. Instruments are administered primarily to humor the researcher. In such cases, interviewer cheating may be quite frequent. Spot checks on the administration procedures are vital to ensure reasonable data quality. A

realism check of data should also be used. For example, if marketing research in Italy reports that very little spaghetti is consumed, the researcher should perhaps consider whether individuals responded to their use of purchased spaghetti rather than home-made spaghetti. The collected data should therefore be compared with secondary information and with analogous information from a similar market in order to obtain a preliminary understanding of data quality.

Interpreting and Analyzing Data

Interpretation and analysis of accumulated information are required to answer the research questions that were posed initially. Analytical tools used in international marketing research are often quite shallow, and the sketchy evidence available suggests that analytical techniques, particularly quantitative ones, are not widely used by international marketing managers.[20] The researcher should, of course, use the best tools available and appropriate for analysis. The fact that a market may be in a less-developed country does not preclude the subjecting of good data to good analysis. On the other hand, international researchers should be cautioned against using overly sophisticated tools for unsophisticated data. Even the best of tools will not improve data quality. The quality of data must be matched with the quality of the research tools to achieve appropriately sophisticated analysis and yet not overstate the value of the data.

Presenting Research Results

The primary focus in the presentation of research results must be communication. In multinational marketing research, communication must take place not only with management at headquarters but also with managers in the local operations. Otherwise, little or no transference of research results will occur, and the synergistic benefits of a multinational operation are lost. To minimize time devoted to the reading of reports, the researcher must present results clearly and concisely. In the worldwide operations of a firm, particularly in the communication efforts, lengthy data and analytical demonstrations should be avoided. The availability of data and the techniques used should be mentioned, however, so that subsidiary operations can receive the information on request.

The researcher should also demonstrate in the presentation how research results relate to the original research objective and fit with overall corporate strategy. At least schematically, possibilities for analogous application should be highlighted. These possibilities should then also be communicated to local subsidiaries, perhaps through a short monthly newsletter. A newsletter format can be used regardless of whether the research process is centralized, coordinated, or decentralized. The only difference will be the person or group providing the input for the newsletter. It is important to maintain such communication in order for the entire organization to learn and to improve its international marketing research capabilities. As the International Marketplace 15.4 shows, there are still many areas in which global research faces challenges.

---

[20] Essam Mahmoud and Gillian Rice, "Use of Analytical Techniques in International Marketing," *International Marketing Review* 5 (Autumn 1988): 7–13.

15.4

THE INTERNATIONAL MARKETPLACE

Future Challenges for Global Research

Worldwide, the challenges of marketing research change as the industry matures. For those countries where research is still in its infancy, the basic issue is one of technique—finding and developing the methods to conduct research efficiently. Some of the main challenges of technique are:

- The search for better and more easily comparable sociodemographic data to support survey research and to provide intercountry comparisons
- The need to develop appropriate field work skills and networks, supported by executive training programs
- The development of more worldwide research supplier networks to provide speed plus local sensitivity without hassle
- A reduction in the costs of international research, especially in telephone and other technologically based techniques; a growth in the number of worldwide syndicated research projects

In those countries where the research industry's methods are established, the emphasis shifts from the issue of technique to that of application. This issue of application can be thought of as the broadening of the uses of marketing research across a range of industries that had not initially considered research to be of relevance and value. Some of the main challenges and opportunities of application are:

- The development of continentwide as well as worldwide surveys, regardless of national boundaries
- The development of niche marketing across national boundaries, for instance, the environmentally conscious and elderly
- The demise of the omnicompetent organization and the emergence of more of those that can specialize in particular products and services with appropriate expertise
- A rapid increase in the rate and spread of product innovation, with which research must keep pace; the end of slow-moving local or national test marketing results.

Source: Peter Bartram, "The Challenge of Research Internationally in the Decade of the 1990s," *Marketing and Research Today* 6 (1991): 101–106.

Follow Up and Review

Although the research process may be considered to be at an end here, from a managerial perspective, one more stage is important. Now that the research has been carried out, appropriate managerial decisions must be made based on the research, and the organization must absorb the research. For example, if it has been found that a product needs to have certain attributes to sell well in Latin America, the manager must determine whether the product development area is aware of this finding and the degree to which the knowledge is now incorporated into new-product projects. Without such follow-up, the role of research tends to become a mere "staff" function, increasingly isolated from corporate "line" activity and lacking major impact on corporate activity. If that is the case, research will diminish and even be disregarded—resulting in an organization at risk.

THE MARKETING DECISION SUPPORT SYSTEM

Many organizations have data needs going beyond specific international marketing research projects. Most of the time, daily decisions must be made for which there is neither time nor money for special research. An information system already in place is needed to provide the decision maker with basic data for most ongoing decisions. Information and data management for the international market are more complex than for the domestic market because of separation in time and space as well as wide differences in cultural and technological environments.[21] Yet these same factors highlight the increased need for an information system that assists in the decision-making process. Corporations have responded by developing marketing decision support systems such as the ones described in The International Marketplace 15.5. Defined as "an integrated system of data, statistical analysis, modeling, and display formats using computer hardware and software technology," such a system serves as a mechanism to coordinate the flow of information to corporate managers for decision-making purposes.[22]

To be useful to the decision maker, the system needs various attributes. First, the information must be *relevant*. The data gathered must have meaning for the manager's decision-making process. Only rarely can corporations afford to spend large amounts of money on information that is simply "nice to know." Second, the information must be *timely*. It is of little benefit to the manager if decision information help that is needed today does not become available until a month from now. To be of use to the international decision maker, the system must therefore feed from a variety of international sources and be updated frequently. For multinational corporations, this means a real-time linkage between international subsidiaries and a broad-based ongoing data input operation. Third, information must be *flexible*—that is, it must be available in the forms needed by management. A marketing decision support system must therefore permit manipulation of the format and combining of the data. Therefore, great effort must be expended to make diverse international data compatible with and comparable to each other. Fourth, information contained in the system must be *accurate*. This attribute is particularly relevant in the international field because information quickly becomes outdated as a result of major changes. Obviously, a system is of little value if it provides incorrect information that leads to poor decisions. Fifth, the system's information bank must be reasonably *exhaustive*. Because of the interrelationship between variables, factors that may influence a particular decision must be appropriately represented in the information system. This means that the marketing decision support system must be based on a broad variety of factors. Finally, to be useful to managers, the system must be *convenient,* both in use and accessibility. Systems that are cumbersome and time-consuming to reach and to use will not be used enough to justify corporate expenditures to build and maintain them.

---

[21] Sayeste Daser, "International Marketing Information Systems: A Neglected Prerequisite for Foreign Market Planning," in *International Marketing Management,* ed. E. Kaynak (New York: Praeger Publishers, 1984), 139–154.

[22] Kinnear and Taylor, *Marketing Research,* 146.

15.5

THE INTERNATIONAL MARKETPLACE

The Global Spyglass

Both Corning and Digital Equipment Corporation are strong believers in global computer networks for the gathering and dissemination of competitive intelligence.

Corning started its global system, called the Business Information Exchange Network, with a pilot program in early 1989. One key feature is a news-search service that lets users inform the system of topics that interest them. The system then automatically clips articles and places them in the user's electronic mailbox.

Digital Equipment launched its Competitive Information System (CIS) in 1984. Initially, it was mainly used to collect and distribute data on domestic competitors, but after four years, it became truly global. CIS contains product descriptions, announcements, internal and external competitive analyses, company strategies, policies and overviews, market analyses, and a direct feed from an external news wire. "Our data set serves both strategic and tactical needs," explains Laura J. B. Hunt, Digital's manager of information access services. Digital's competitive analysts use data from CIS for strategic decision making and planning. Its sales representatives use other pieces of CIS data to formulate sales tactics. The system now has more than 10,000 registered employee users and generates more than 100,000 log-ins worldwide.

Source: Kate Bertrand, "The Global Spyglass," in *Annual Editions: International Business*, ed. F. Maidment (Guilford, CT: 1992), 90–92.

There are various reasons why international marketing decision support systems are being developed successfully. As Table 15.2 shows, these are progress in computer technology in both hardware and software, environmental changes such as increased familiarity with technology, and the necessity of dealing with increasing shifts in market conditions. In addition, the advances made in utilizing vast quantities of information—through gains made in research on artificial intelligence and the development of expert systems—make it important for a firm, from a competitive viewpoint, to explore the use of decision support systems.[23]

To build a market decision support system, corporations use the internal data that are available from divisions such as accounting and finance and also from various subsidiaries. In addition, many organizations put mechanisms in place to enrich the basic data flow. Three such mechanisms are environmental scanning, Delphi studies, and scenario building.

Environmental Scanning

Any changes in the business environment, whether domestic or foreign, may have serious repercussions on the marketing activities of the firm. Corporations therefore understand the necessity for tracking new developments and obtaining continuous updates.

---

[23] Rowland T. Moriarty and Gordon S. Swartz, "Automation to Boost Sales and Marketing," *Harvard Business Review* 67 (January–February) 1989: 100–108.

Factors Contributing to the Success of Marketing Decision Support Systems

TABLE 15.2

Data Availability

More internal data captured
More external data available on a commercial basis
Data now captured of unique value for marketing analysis
Data available on an instantaneous basis

Information Technology

Automated data capture at point of creation
Point-of-sale systems
Telecommunications
Videotex
Integrated and flexible software and hardware
Increased computer accessibility

Refined Decision-Modeling Approaches

Manual decomposition techniques
Automated system-marketer decision analysis

Professional Sophistication

Familiarity with computer technology
Greater emphasis on decision methodology
Higher levels of education and training
Recognition of marketing function as necessary to success of the firm

Market Conditions

Increased corporate competition
Smaller margin for error
Faster decision feedback
Rapidly evolving marketplace
Increasingly volatile distribution channels and consumer demand

Source: Stephen W. Brown and Martin D. Goslar, "New Information Systems for Marketing Decision Making," *Business* 38 (July–August–September 1988): 23.

To carry out this task, some large multinational organizations have formed environmental scanning groups.

Environmental scanning activities are useful to continuously receive information on political, social, and economic affairs internationally; on changes of attitudes held by public institutions and private citizens; and on possible upcoming alterations in international markets. Environmental scanning models are used for a variety of purposes:

1. The provision of a mind-stretching or educational experience for management
2. The development of broad strategies and long-term policies
3. The development of action plans and operating programs
4. The development of a frame of reference for the annual budget[24]

Obviously, the precision required for environmental scanning varies with its purpose. Whether the information is to be used for mind stretching or for budgeting, for example, must be taken into account when constructing the framework and variables that will enter the scanning process. The more immediate and precise the exercise is to be in its

---

[24] Robert N. Anthony, John Dearden, and Richard F. Vancil, *Management Control Systems,* rev. ed. (Homewood, IL: Irwin, 1972), 471–472.

application within the corporation, the greater the need for detailed information. At the same time, such heightened precision may lessen the utility of environmental scanning for the strategic corporate purpose, which is more long-term in its orientation.

Environmental scanning can be performed in various ways. One method consists of obtaining factual input regarding many variables. For example, the International Data Base (IDB) of the U.S. Census Bureau collects, evaluates, and adjusts a wide variety of demographic, social, and economic characteristics of foreign countries. Estimates for all countries of the world are developed, particularly on economic variables, such as labor-force statistics, GNP, and income statistics, but also on health and nutrition variables. Similar factual information can be obtained from international organizations such as the World Bank or the United Nations.

Frequently, corporations believe that such factual data alone are insufficient for their information needs. Particularly for forecasting future developments, other methods are used to capture underlying dimensions of social change. One significant method is **content analysis.** This technique investigates the content of communication in a society and entails literally counting the number of times preselected words, themes, symbols, or pictures appear in a given medium. It can be used productively in international marketing to monitor the social, economic, cultural, and technological environment in which the marketing organization is operating. The use of content analysis is facilitated by the emergence of new tools such as optical scanners and new software packages. For example, today, personal computers can accommodate texts in Chinese, Japanese, Hebrew, Korean, and Arabic.[25]

Corporations can use content analysis to pinpoint upcoming changes in their line of business, and new opportunities, by attempting to identify trendsetting events. For example, the Alaska oil spill by the tanker *Valdez* resulted in entirely new international concern about environmental protection and safety, reaching far beyond the incident itself.

Environmental scanning is conducted by a variety of groups within and outside the corporation. Quite frequently, small corporate staffs are created at headquarters to coordinate the information flow. In addition, subsidiary staff can be used to provide occasional intelligence reports. Groups of volunteers are also formed to gather and analyze information worldwide and feed individual analyses back to corporate headquarters, where they can be used to form the "big picture." Increasingly, large corporations also offer services in environmental scanning to outsiders. In this way, profits can be made from an in-house activity that has to be conducted anyway. Figure 15.4 gives an example of such a service.

Typically, environmental scanning is designed primarily to aid the strategic planning process rather than the tactical activities of the corporation. A survey of corporate environmental scanning activities found that "the futurity of the scanning exercise ranges from the medium term (say about 5 years) to the truly long term (around 20 years) with the mode being about 10 years."[26] Environmental scanning, therefore, addresses itself mostly to the future in order to complement the continuous flow of factual data to the corporation.

Although environmental scanning is perceived by many corporations as quite valuable for the corporate planning process, there are dissenting voices. For example, it has

---

[25] David R. Wheeler, "Content Analysis: An Analytical Technique for International Marketing Research," *International Marketing Review* (Winter 1988): 34–40.

[26] Phillip S. Thomas, "Environmental Scanning—The State of the Art," *Long Range Planning* 13 (February 1980): 24.

An Advertisement Offering Environmental Scanning as a Service   FIGURE 15.4

World Information Services delivers:

- Data and guidance to enable you to operate more securely and efficiently in foreign markets

- A point of reference for management in dealing with financial and international business questions

- A tool to guide funding and financial management decisions

- A reliable database of quantitative information

- Authoritative global economic and strategic projections

- Access to a global intelligence network that is essential to informed policy debate and recommendations

- Practical working knowledge of the global economic and business environment

Country Outlooks	**$495 a year**
Country Data Forecasts	**$495 a year**
Country Risk Monitor	**$495 a year**
ALL THREE SERVICES	**$1290 a year**

Bank of America
World Information Services
Department 3015
555 California Street
San Francisco, California 94104

1-800-645-6667
From Outside the U.S. (415) 622-1446
Fax (415) 622-0909

BANK OF AMERICA NT&SA MEMBER FDIC
©1993 Bank of America

Source: Bank of America

been noted by researchers "that in those constructs and frameworks where the environment has been given primary consideration, there has been a tendency for the approach to become so global that studies tend to become shallow and diffuse, or impractical if pursued in sufficient depth."[27] Obviously, this presents one of the major continuous

---

[27] Winter and Prohaska, "Methodological Problems," 429.

challenges faced by corporations in their international environmental scanning. The trade-off between the breadth and the depth of information still exists. However, the continuous evolution of manipulative power through the ever-increasing capabilities of data processing may reduce at least the scope of the problem. However, the cost of data acquisition and the issue of actual data use will continue to be major restraints on the development of environmental scanning systems.

Delphi Studies

To enrich the information obtained from factual data, corporations frequently resort to the use of creative and highly qualitative data-gathering methods. One way is through Delphi studies. These studies are particularly useful in the international marketing environment because they are "a means for aggregating the judgments of a number of . . . experts . . . who cannot come together physically."[28] This type of research approach clearly aims at qualitative rather than quantitative measures by aggregating the information of a group of experts. It seeks to obtain answers from those who know instead of seeking the average responses of many with only limited knowledge.

Typically, Delphi studies are carried out with groups of about 30 well-chosen participants who possess particular in-depth expertise in an area of concern, such as future developments in the international trade environment. These participants are asked, most frequently via mail, to identify the major issues in the area of concern. They are also requested to rank their statements according to importance and explain the rationale behind the order. Next, the aggregated information is returned to all participants, who are encouraged to clearly state their agreements or disagreements with the various rank orders and comments. Statements can be challenged, and in another round, participants can respond to the challenges. After several rounds of challenge and response, a reasonably coherent consensus is developed.

The Delphi technique is particularly valuable because it uses the mail or facsimile method of communication to bridge large distances and therefore makes individuals quite accessible at a reasonable cost. It does not suffer from the drawback of ordinary mail investigations: lack of interaction among the participants. One drawback of the technique is that it requires several steps, and therefore months may elapse before the information is obtained. Also, substantial effort must be expended in selecting the appropriate participants and in motivating them to participate in this exercise with enthusiasm and continuity. When obtained on a regular basis, Delphi information can provide crucial augmentation to the factual data available for the marketing information system. For example, a large portion of the last chapter of this book was written based on an extensive Delphi study carried out by the authors. Since the study focused on the future of international marketing, and since we wanted to obtain interactive input from around the world, the Delphi method was one of the few possible research alternatives, and it produced insightful results.

Scenario Building

For information enrichment purposes, some companies use **scenario analysis.** The principal method here is to look at different configurations of key variables in the international market. For example, economic growth rates, import penetration, population growth, and political stability can be varied. By projecting such variations for medium-

---

[28] Andrel Delbecq, Andrew H. Van de Ven, and David H. Gustafson, *Group Techniques for Program Planning* (Glenview, IL: Scott, Foresman, 1975), 83.

THE INTERNATIONAL MARKETPLACE

15.6

Advice from Kissinger Associates

Kissinger Associates is a New York–based consulting firm established in 1982 by former Secretary of State Henry Kissinger, former Undersecretary of State Lawrence S. Eagleburger, and former National Security Advisor Brent Scowcroft. For its corporate clients, the firm offers broadbrush pictures of political and economic conditions in particular countries or regions along with analyses of political and economic trends. Because none of the founders is particularly known for his business or economic expertise, an investment banker and an economist were brought on board.

Some have argued that the pointing out of political trends is an insufficient base from which to make a living. Kissinger himself stated that to provide only abstract information on the political condition in a foreign country is not fair to the client. The firm considers its primary strength to be its sensitivity to the international political situation and its continued closeness to information sources. Although Kissinger Associates offers no voluminous country reports, the principals believe that by correctly assessing, for example, the political outlook in Greece for the next five years, they can help a client decide whether to make new investments there or preparations to leave in anticipation of a hostile socialist government. Similarly, the firm might help a U.S. oil company with limited Middle East experience in its first attempts to negotiate and work with a government in the region. Although this type of work does not deeply involve Kissinger Associates in specific business decisions, it does require a good understanding of clients' businesses and goals.

One practical reason for using high-powered consulting input was explained by a former member of Kissinger Associates: "These days, in case an investment goes sour, it is useful for (management) to be able to say, 'We got this expert advice and acted on that basis.' They have to show due diligence in exercising their fiduciary duties."

Even though client identities and fees are well-guarded secrets, congressional confirmation hearings for former employees of Kissinger Associates revealed that clients such as Union Carbide, Coca-Cola, Volvo, Fiat, and Daewoo pay between $150,000 and $400,000 per year for the firm's services.

Sources: Christopher Madison, "Kissinger Firm Hopes to Make Its Mark as Risk Advisors to Corporate Chiefs," *National Journal*, June 22, 1985, 1452–1456; and "The Out-of-Office Reign of Henry I," *U.S. News & World Report*, March 27, 1989, 10.

to long-term periods, companies can envision completely new environmental conditions. These conditions are then analyzed for their potential domestic and international impact on corporate strategy.

Of major importance in scenario building is the identification of crucial trend variables and the degree of their variation. Frequently, key experts are used to gain information about potential variations and the viability of certain scenarios. The International Marketplace 15.6 provides an example of input from such experts.

A wide variety of scenarios must be built to expose corporate executives to multiple potential occurrences. Ideally, even far-fetched variables deserve some consideration, if only to build worst-case scenarios. A scenario for Union Carbide Corporation, for example, could have included the possibility of a disaster such as occurred in Bhopal. Similarly, oil companies need to work with scenarios that factor in dramatic shifts in the supply situation, precipitated by, for example, regional conflict in the Middle East, and that consider major alterations in the demand picture, due to, say, technological developments or government policies.

Scenario builders also need to recognize the nonlinearity of factors. To simply extrapolate from currently existing situations is insufficient. Frequently, extraneous factors may enter the picture with a significant impact. Finally, in scenario building, the possibility of joint occurrences must be recognized because changes may not come about in an isolated fashion but may be spread over wide regions. An example of a joint occurrence is the indebtedness of Latin American nations. Although the inability of any one country to pay its debts would not have presented a major problem for the international banking community, large and simultaneous indebtedness posed a problem of major severity. Similarly, given large technological advances, the possibility of "wholesale" obsolescence of current technology must also be considered. For example, quantum leaps in computer development and new generations of computers may render obsolete the technological investment of a corporation or even a country.

For scenarios to be useful, management must analyze and respond to them by formulating contingency plans. Such planning will broaden horizons and may prepare management for unexpected situations. Familiarization in turn can result in shorter response times to actual occurrences by honing response capability. The difficulty, of course, is to devise scenarios that are unusual enough to trigger new thinking yet sufficiently realistic to be taken seriously by management.[29]

The development of a marketing decision support system is of major importance to the multinational corporation. It aids the ongoing decision process and becomes a vital corporate tool in carrying out the strategic planning task. Only by observing global trends and changes will the firm be able to maintain and increase its international competitive position. Many of the data available are quantitative in nature, but attention must also be paid to qualitative dimensions. Quantitative analysis will continue to improve, as the ability to collect, store, analyze, and retrieve data increases through the use of high-speed computers. Nevertheless, qualitative analysis will remain a major component of corporate research and strategic planning.

SUMMARY

To respond to specific information requirements, firms frequently need primary research. Depending on the research objective at hand, exploratory, descriptive, or causal research needs to be carried out.

In developing a research program, a company must take care to properly determine its information requirements. Subsequently, the data sources available and the type of data needed have to be investigated. The researcher then must critically assess corporate capabilities and constraints to determine where the research is to be carried out and whether the research program is to be centralized or decentralized. Although the latter decision may vary depending on the corporate orientation, research activities should always be coordinated across corporate functions in order to minimize overlap and to benefit from synergism.

The researcher then needs to select an appropriate research technique to collect the information needed. Sensitivity to different international environments and cultures

---

[29] David Rutenberg, "Playful Plans," Queen's University working paper, 1991.

will guide the researcher in deciding whether to use interviews, focus groups, observation, surveys, or experimentation as data-collection techniques. The same sensitivity applies to the design of the research instrument, where issues such as question format, content, and wording are decided. Also, the sampling plan needs to be appropriate for the local environment in order to ensure representative and useful responses.

Once the data are collected, care must be taken to use analytical tools appropriate for the quality of data collected so that management is not misled about the sophistication of the research. Finally, the research results must be presented in a concise and useful form so that management can benefit in its decision making, and implementation of the research needs to be tracked.

To provide ongoing information to management, a marketing decision support system is useful. Such a system will provide for the systematic and continuous gathering, analysis, and reporting of data for decision-making purposes. It uses a firm's internal information and gathers data via environmental scanning, Delphi studies, or scenario building, thus enabling management to prepare for the future and hone its decision-making skills.

Questions for Discussion

1. Why should a firm collect primary data in its international marketing research?

2. Should corporations conduct more causal international marketing research?

3. Discuss the trade-offs between centralized and decentralized international marketing research.

4. How is international market research affected by differences in language?

5. Compare the use of telephone surveys in the United States and in Egypt.

6. What are your thoughts on the characterization of international marketing research as unsophisticated and shallow?

7. Is highly priced personalized advice from an individual really worth the money?

8. What use do you see for an international marketing decision support system?

9. Does it make sense to spend money on 20-year forecasts?

10. What are some of the crucial variables you would track in a decision support system?

Recommended Readings

Barnard, Philip. "Conducting and Co-ordinating Multicountry Quantitative Studies across Europe." In *Global Marketing Perspectives,* edited by Jagdish Sheth and Abdolreza Eshghi, 56–73. Cincinnati, OH: South-Western, 1989.

Churchill, Gilbert A., Jr. *Marketing Research: Methodological Foundations.* 6th ed. Fort Worth, TX: Dryden Press, 1995.

Douglas, Susan P., and C. Samuel Craig. *International Marketing Research.* Englewood Cliffs, NJ: Prentice-Hall, 1983.

Hassan, Salah S., and Roger D. Blackwell. *Global Marketing: Perspectives and Cases.* Fort Worth, TX: Dryden Press, 1994.

Hassan, S., and E. Kaynak, eds. *Globalization of Consumer Markets: Structures and Strategies.* Binghamton, NY: The Haworth Press, 1993.

Malhotra, Naresh K. "A Methodology for Measuring Consumer Preferences in Developing Countries." *International Marketing Review* (Autumn 1988): 52–66.

Paliwoda, Stanley J. *New Perspectives on International Marketing.* London: Routledge, 1991.

Smith, N. Craig, and Paul Dainty, eds. *The Management Research Handbook.* London: Routledge, 1991.

Zikmund, William G. *Exploring Marketing Research.* 5th ed. Fort Worth, TX: Dryden Press, 1994.

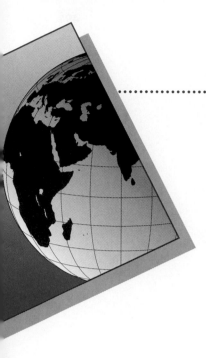

CHAPTER 16

Globalization

THE INTERNATIONAL MARKETPLACE

Appliance Makers on a Global Quest

The $11-billion home-appliance market is undergoing major consolidation and globalization. Many U.S.-based manufacturers are faced in their home markets with increased competition from foreign companies, such as the world's largest appliance maker, Electrolux. In addition, industry fundamentals in the United States are rather gloomy: stagnating sales, rising raw material prices, and price wars. On the other hand, the European market, for example, is growing quite fast, and the breakdown of trade barriers within the European Union makes establishing business there even more attractive. Market potential is significant as well: While 65 percent of U.S. homes have dryers, only 18 percent of Europeans have them.

As a move toward globalization, Maytag acquired Chicago Pacific Corporation, best known for the Hoover vacuum cleaners it markets in the United States and Europe. Chicago Pacific also makes washers, dryers, and other appliances carrying the Hoover name—and sells them exclusively in Europe and Australia. However, Hoover's position in Europe is tiny. It boasts a strong presence in the United Kingdom and Australia but is not a big player on the Continent. Thus, Maytag will essentially be introducing new products into new markets. Because Hoover appliances do have strong name recognition in the United Kingdom, Maytag will be able to exploit some synergies there. Similarly, in Australia, where Hoover has a notable presence, the product line can be expanded to include Maytag's washers and dryers. In that market, Maytag could be introduced as a premier line.

Other appliance manufacturers have formed strategic alliances and made acquisitions. General Electric entered into a joint venture with Britain's General Electric PLC, and in its strategic shift to move the company's "center of gravity" from the industrialized world to Asia and Latin America, joint ventures were established in India with Godrej and in Mexico with Mabe. Whirlpool bought the appliance business of Dutch giant N. V. Phillips, which made it the third largest in Europe with 12 percent of the market. Whirlpool's move gave it 10 plants on the European continent and some popular appliance lines, which is a major asset in a region characterized by fierce loyalty to domestic brands.

Product differences willl present global marketers with a considerable challenge. The British favor front-loading washing machines, while the French swear by top-loaders. The French prefer to cook their food at high temperatures, causing grease to splatter onto oven walls, which calls for self-cleaning ovens. This feature is in less demand in Germany, where lower temperatures are used. Manufacturers are hoping that European integration will bring about cost savings and product standardization. The danger to be avoided is the development of compromise products that in the end appeal to almost no one.

Although opportunities do exist, competition is keen. Margins have suffered as manufacturers (more than 300 in Europe alone) scrap for business. The major players have decided to compete in all the major markets of the world. "Becoming a global appliance player is clearly the best use of our management expertise and well-established brand line-up," Whirlpool executives have said.

Sources: "Whirlpool Hangs Its Rivals Out to Dry," *USA Today,* December 10, 1993, 3B; "GE's Brave New World," *Business Week,* November 8, 1993, 64–69; "Whirlpool Makes a Splash," *International Management* 23 (December 1991): 59–61; "Planning for Global Expansion at Whirlpool," *Business International,* April 15, 1991, 125–131; "Can Maytag Clean Up around the World?" *Business Week,* January 30, 1989, 86–87; "Whirlpool Plots the Invasion of Europe," *Business Week,* September 5, 1988, 70–72.

Many marketing managers have to face the same increasing globalization of markets and competition as described in The International Marketplace 16.1. The rules of survival have changed since the beginning of the 1980s when Theodore Levitt first coined the phrase *global marketing*.[1] Even the biggest companies in the biggest home markets cannot survive on their domestic markets if they are in global industries such as cars, banking, consumer electronics, entertainment, pharmaceuticals, publishing, travel services, or washing machines. They have to be in all major markets to survive the shake-outs expected to leave three to five actors per industry by the end of the 1990s.[2] The first part of this chapter will concentrate on developing a framework for the globalization of a marketer's efforts, with a concentration on product issues. Included will be the internal marketing efforts needed to ensure the appropriate implementation of global strategies.

Marketers are taking technologies and marketing concepts around the world with enormous speed, especially when compared with the 1980s. Sometime the approaches are identical; often they must be customized to local tastes. Critical to this effort is a product-development effort that is able to take into consideration the needs of major markets without forgetting the needs of smaller national or consumer markets.

Managing the resulting product portfolios will then have to consider the competitiveness of the company's product lines globally, regionally, and locally in terms of risks and returns. The second part of this chapter will therefore concentrate on the issues of product development and the management of the product portfolio.

---

[1] Theodore Levitt, *The Marketing Imagination* (New York: Free Press, 1983), 20–49.

[2] Jeremey Main, "How to Go Global—and Why," *Fortune,* August 28, 1989, 70–76.

GLOBALIZATION[3]

Globalization is a business initiative based on the belief that the world is becoming more homogeneous and that distinctions between national markets are not only fading but, for some products, will eventually disappear. As a result, companies need to globalize their international strategy by formulating it across markets to take advantage of underlying market, cost, environmental, and competitive factors.

As shown in Figure 16.1, globalization can be seen as a result of a process that culminates a process of international market entry and expansion. Before globalization, marketers utilize to a great extent a country-by-country **multidomestic strategy,** with each country organization operated as a profit center. Each national entity markets a range of different products and services targeted to different customer segments, utilizing different marketing strategies with little or no coordination of operations between countries.

However, with expanding operations, inefficiencies generated by the multidomestic approach, coupled with external forces integrating markets worldwide, start building pressure toward improved coordination across country markets.

Globalization Drivers

Both external and internal factors will create the favorable conditions for development of strategy and resource allocation on a global basis. These factors can be divided into market, cost, environmental, and competitive factors.

Market Factors   The world customer identified by Ernst Dichter more than 30 years ago has gained new meaning today.[4] For example, Kenichi Ohmae has identified a new group of consumers emerging in the **triad** of North America, Europe, and the Far East whom marketers can treat as a single market with the same spending habits.[5] Approximately 600 million in number, these consumers have similar educational backgrounds, income levels, life-styles, use of leisure time, and aspirations. One reason given for the similarities in their demand is a level of purchasing power (ten times greater than that of LDCs or NICs) that translates into higher diffusion rates for certain products. Another reason is that developed infrastructures—ownership of telephones and an abundance of paved roads—lead to attractive markets for other products. Products can be designed to meet similar demand conditions throughout the triad. These similarities also enhance the transferability of other marketing elements.

At the same time, channels of distribution are becoming more global; that is, a growing number of retailers are now showing great flexibility in their strategies for entering new geographic markets.[6] Some are already world powers (e.g., Benetton and McDonald's), whereas others are pursuing aggressive growth (e.g., Toys 'Я' Us and IKEA). Also noteworthy are cross-border retail alliances, which expand the presence of retailers to

[3] The section draws heavily from George S. Yip, "Global Strategy . . . In a World of Nations?" *Sloan Management Review* 31 (Fall 1989): 29–41; Susan P. Douglas and C. Samuel Craig, "Evolution of Global Marketing Strategy: Scale, Scope, and Synergy," *Columbia Journal of World Business* 24 (Fall 1989): 47–58; and George S. Yip, Pierre M. Loewe, and Michael Y. Yoshino, "How to Take Your Company to the Global Market," *Columbia Journal of World Business* 23 (Winter 1988): 28–40.

[4] Ernst Dichter, "The World Customer," *Harvard Business Review* 40 (July–August 1962): 113–122.

[5] Kenichi Ohmae, *Triad Power—The Coming Shape of Global Competition* (New York: Free Press, 1985): 22–27.

[6] Alan D. Treadgold, "The Developing Internationalisation of Retailing," *International Journal of Retail and Distribution Management* 18 (1990): 4–11.

Global Marketing Evolution FIGURE 16.1

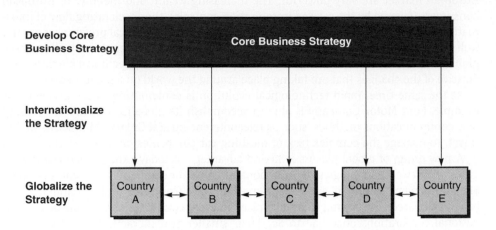

Source: Reprinted from "Global Strategy . . . In a World of Nations?" by George S. Yip, *Sloan Management Review* 31 (Fall 1989):30, by permission of the publisher. Copyright 1989 by the Sloan Management Review Association. All rights reserved.

new markets quite rapidly. The presence of global and regional channels makes it more necessary for the marketer to rationalize marketing efforts.

Cost Factors Avoiding cost inefficiencies and duplication of effort are two of the most powerful globalization drivers. A single-country approach may not be large enough for the local business to achieve all possible economies of scale and scope as well as synergies, especially given the dramatic changes in the marketplace. Take, for example, pharmaceuticals. In the 1970s, developing a new drug cost about $16 million and took four years to develop. The drug could be produced in Britain or the United States and eventually exported. Now, developing a drug costs from $250 to $500 million and takes as long as 12 years, with competitive efforts close behind. Only a global product for a global market can support that much risk.[7] Size has become a major asset, which partly explains the many mergers and acquisitions (Bristol Myers and Squibb as well as Smith Kline and Beecham) of the past few years.[8] In the heavily contested consumer-goods sectors, launching a new brand may cost as much as $100 million, meaning that companies, such as Unilever and Procter & Gamble, are not going to necessarily spend precious resources on one-country projects.

In many cases, expanded market participation and activity concentration can accelerate the accumulation of learning and experience. General Electric's philosophy is to be first or second in the world in a business or to get out. This can be seen, for example, in its global effort to develop premium computed tomography (CT), a diagnostic scanning system. In 1987, GE swapped its consumer electronics business with the French Thomson for Thomson's diagnostic imaging business. At the same time, GE established GE Medical Systems Asia in Tokyo, anchored on Yokogawa Medical Systems, which is 75 percent owned by GE.

Environmental Factors As shown earlier in this text, government barriers have fallen dramatically in the last years to further facilitate the globalization of markets and

---

[7] "Vital Statistic: Disputed Cost of Creating a Drug," *The Wall Street Journal,* November 9, 1993, B1.

[8] "The Stateless Corporation," *Business Week,* May 14, 1990, 98–106.

the activities of marketers within them. For example, the forces pushing toward a pan-European market are very powerful: The increasing wealth and mobility of European consumers (favored by the relaxed immigration controls), the accelerating flow of information across borders, the introduction of new products where local preferences are not well established, and the publicity surrounding the integration process itself all promote globalization.[9] Also, the resulting removal of physical, fiscal, and technical barriers is indicative of the changes that are taking place around the world on a greater scale.

At the same time, rapid technological evolution is contributing to the process. For example, Ford Motor Company is able to accomplish its globalization efforts by using new communications methods, such as teleconferencing and CAD/CAM links, as well as travel, to manage the complex task of meshing car companies on different continents.

A new group of global players is taking advantage of today's more open trading regions and newer technologies. "Mininationals," or newer companies with sales between $200 million and $1 billion, are able to serve the world from a handful of manufacturing bases, compared with having to build a plant in every country as the established multinational corporations once had to do. Their smaller bureaucracies have also allowed these mininationals to move swiftly to seize new markets and develop new products—a key to global success in the 1990s. For example, Symbol Technologies Inc. invented the field of handheld laser scanners and is number one in its niche in Europe and Cisco Systems Inc. claims 50 percent of the world market for gear that connects networks of computers.[10]

Competitive Factors   Many industries are already dominated by global competitors that are trying to take advantage of the three sets of factors mentioned earlier. To remain competitive, the marketer may have to be the first to do something or to be able to match or preempt competitors' moves. Products are now introduced, upgraded, and distributed at rates unimaginable a decade ago. Without a global network, a marketer may run the risk of seeing carefully researched ideas picked off by other global players. This is what Procter & Gamble and Unilever did to Kao's Attack concentrated detergent, which they mimicked and introduced into the United States and Europe before Kao could react.

With the triad markets often both flat in terms of growth and fiercely competitive, many global marketers are looking for new markets and for new-product categories for growth. Nestlé, for example, is setting its sights on consumer markets in fast-growing Asia, especially China, and is pursuing a takeover of the world's number-one cosmetics company, the French L'Oreal.[11]

Market presence may be necessary to execute global strategies and to prevent others from having undue advantage in unchallenged markets. Caterpillar faced mounting global competition from Komatsu but found out that strengthening its products and operations was not enough to meet the challenge. Although Japan was a small part of the world market, as a secure home base (no serious competitors), it generated 80 percent of Komatsu's cash flow. To put a check on its major global competitor's market share and cash flow, Caterpillar formed a heavy-equipment joint venture with Matsushita to serve the Japanese market.[12] Similarly, when Unilever tried to acquire Richardson-Vicks in the

[9] Gianluigi Guido, "Implementing a Pan European Marketing Strategy," *Long Range Planning* 24 (1991): 23–33.

[10] "Mininationals Are Making Maximum Impact," *Business Week,* September 1993, 66–69.

[11] "Nestlé: A Giant in a Hurry," *Business Week,* March 22, 1993, 50–54.

[12] Jordan D. Lewis, *Partnerships for Profit* (New York: Free Press, 1990): 86.

United States, Procter & Gamble saw this as a threat to its home market position and outbid its archrival for the company.

Globalization Dimensions

Decisions need to be made how to best utilize the conditions set by the four dimensions driving globalization. Decisions will have to be made in terms of five areas: market participation, product offering, marketing approach, location of value-added activities, and competitive moves.

Market Participation   The conventional wisdom of globalization requires a presence in all of the major triad markets of the world. In some cases, markets may not be attractive in their own right but may have some other significance, such as being the home market of the most demanding customers (thereby aiding in product development) or being the home market of a significant competitor (a preemptive rationale). In its challenge of IBM, Fujitsu has acquired a substantial presence both in North America (through AmdahlCorp., the $2.2-billion-a-year Silicon Valley maker of IBM-compatible mainframes) and in Europe (through International Computers Ltd., Britain's largest computer manufacturer at $2.7 billion in annual sales).[13]

Product Offering   Globalization is not equal to standardization except in the case of the core product or the technology used to produce the product. The components used in a personal computer may to a large extent be standard, with the localization needed only in terms of the peripherals; for example, IBM produces 20 different keyboards for Europe alone. Product standardization may result in significant cost savings upstream. For example, Stanley Works' compromise between French preferences for handsaws with plastic handles and "soft" teeth and British preferences for wooden handles and "hard teeth"—to produce a plastic-handled saw with "hard teeth"—allowed consolidation for production and resulted in substantial economies of scale. Local preferences may change the product somewhat; for example, CPC International Inc. sells 15 versions of minestrone soup in Europe.

Marketing Approach   Nowhere is the need for the local touch as critical as in the execution of the marketing program. Uniformity is sought especially in elements that are strategic (e.g., positioning) in nature, whereas care is taken to localize necessary tactical elements (e.g., distribution). This approach has been called **glocalization.** For example, Unilever achieved great success with a fabric softener that used a common positioning, advertising theme, and symbol (a teddy bear) but differing brand names (e.g., Snuggle, Cajoline, Kuschelweich, Mimosin, and Yumos) and bottle sizes. Gillette Co. scored a huge success with its Sensor shaver when it was rolled out in the United States, Europe, and Japan with a common approach based on the premise that men everywhere want the same thing in a shave. Although the language of its TV commercials varied, the theme ("the best a man can get") and most of the footage were the same. A comparison of the marketing mix elements of two global marketers is given in Table 16.1. Notice that adaptation is present even at Coca-Cola, which is acknowledged to be one of the world's most global marketers.

---

[13] Brenton A. Schlender, "How Fujitsu Will Tackle the Giants," *Fortune,* July 1, 1991, 78–82.

TABLE 16.1   Globalization of the Marketing Mix

Marketing Mix Elements	Adaptation		Standardization	
	Full	Partial	Partial	Full
Product design			N	C
Brand name			N	C
Product positioning		N		C
Packaging			C/N	
Advertising theme		N		C
Pricing		N	C	
Advertising copy	N			C
Distribution	N	C		
Sales promotion	N	C		
Customer service	N	C		

Key: C = Coca-Cola; N = Nestlé.

Source: John A. Quelch and Edward J. Hoff, "Customizing Global Marketing," *Harvard Business Review*, May–June 1986 (Boston: Harvard Business School Publishing Division), 61. Reprinted by permission of Harvard Business Review. Copyright © 1986 by the President and Fellows of Harvard College; all rights reserved.

Location of Value-Added Activities   Globalization strives at cost reductions by pooling production or other activities or exploiting factor costs or capabilities within a system. Rather than duplicating activities in multiple, or even all, country organizations, a firm concentrates its activities. For example, Texas Instruments has designated a single design center and manufacturing organization for each type of memory chip. To reduce high costs and to be close to markets, it placed two of its four new $250-million memory chip plants in Taiwan and Japan. To reduce high R&D costs, it has entered into a strategic alliance with Hitachi.

The quest for cost savings and improved transportation methods has allowed some marketers to concentrate customer-service activities rather than having them present in all country markets. For example, Sony used to have repair centers in all of the Scandinavian countries and Finland; today, all service and maintenance activities are actually performed in a regional center in Copenhagen, Denmark.

Competitive Moves   A company with regional or global presence will not have to respond to competitive moves only in the market where it is being attacked. A competitor may be attacked in its profit sanctuary to drain its resources, or its position in its home market may be challenged.[14] When Fuji began cutting into Kodak's market share in the United States in the mid-1980s, Kodak responded by drastically increasing its advertising in Japan and created a new subsidiary to deal strictly with that market.

Cross-subsidization, or the use of resources accumulated in one part of the world to fight a competitive battle in another, may be the competitive advantage needed for the long term.[15] One major market lost may mean losses in others, resulting in a domino effect. Jockeying for overall global leadership may result in competitive action in any part of the world, as can be seen in The International Marketplace 16.2. Given their multiple bases of operation, global marketers may defend against a competitive attack in one

[14] W. Chan Kim and R. A. Mauborgne, "Becoming an Effective Global Competitor," *Journal of Business Strategy* 8 (January–February 1988): 33–37.

[15] Gary Hamel and C. K. Prahalad, "Do You Really Have a Global Strategy?" *Harvard Business Review* 63 (July–August 1985): 75–82.

THE INTERNATIONAL MARKETPLACE

From the Cold War to the Cola Wars

There's plenty to be said for being first. By following American GIs overseas in World War II, Coca-Cola Co. built a powerful bottling system that 50 years later allows it to outsell Pepsi-Cola 6 to 1 in Western Europe. But Pepsi has its own first to boast about: It popped open the Soviet Union.

Pepsi's ties to Russia go back 33 years, to when Nikita Khrushchev tasted the bubbly stuff at an international trade fair. Don Kendall, Pepsi's CEO at the time, had called on his friend, Vice President Richard Nixon, to arrange a meeting. By 1973, Kendall had negotiated an exclusive agreement to sell cola in the Soviet Union, freezing out Coca-Cola until 1985. Thanks to those efforts, the former Soviet bloc is one of the few big markets where Pepsi enjoys a strong lead over Coke. Pepsi claims its current share of the Russian cola market is 92 percent. Coke prefers to describe it another way: While Pepsi holds 6 percent of the Russian soft-drinks market, Coke holds a strong 2 percent share. Coke sees itself as an aggressor against Pepsi's defensive position.

But now the cold war is being replaced by the cola wars. And as governments revert from communism to free-market economies, Coke isn't being shy about firing shots in Eastern Europe. It already has launched moves into eastern Germany, Romania, Poland, the Baltics, and Ukraine. And on January 16, 1992, Coke announced plans to build a syrup production plant in Moscow, which will allow it to set up 2,000 soda-fountain kiosks all around the city. "A feasible economic environment simply didn't exist before, so we didn't have an emphasis on Eastern Europe," says E. Neville Isdell, president of Coke's Northeast Europe/Africa division. "Now we do." The market potential in the region is enormous. Each of the 290 million citizens of the former Soviet Union consumes only 39 soft drinks a year on average, compared with the 770 servings each American guzzles.

Coke's main strength in the East is that it can tap the resources of a strong plant and distribution infrastructure in Western Europe as it expands. For instance, when Coke snapped up all five of the former East Germany's bottling plants—beating Pepsi to the punch—it imported managers from plants in Frankfurt and West Berlin to help refurbish them.

But Coke's presence still pales in comparison with Pepsi's. Pepsi's 85 joint bottling ventures scattered throughout the former Soviet Union and Eastern Europe give it critical mass. Pepsi also has strong countertrade agreements in the former Soviet Union. Because of the difficulties in converting rubles to dollars, it arranged in 1972 to exchange soft-drink concentrate for Stolichnaya Russian vodka. Coke has barter deals too, but it trades concentrate for products such as Russia's Lada autos, which are much less marketable than Stoli.

D. Wayne Calloway, Pepsi Co Inc.'s CEO, plays down the notion of a new cola war in Eastern Europe. "There's a big world out there," he says, "and there's more soft-drink business than either one of us can get going for a while." All the same, unless Calloway is willing to invest big and compete hard in the region, he could lose the edge his diplomatic predecessor negotiated so hard to achieve.

New battles are breaking out as well. The signing of the North American Free Trade Agreement signaled the beginning of cola wars in Mexico, which

Continued

boasts a per-capita consumption second only to the United States. The normalization of trade relations with Vietnam in 1994 allowed Coca-Cola to sign a joint venture pact for at least two bottling plants to serve a budding market of 70 million consumers.

Sources: "A Mexican War Heats Up for Cola Giants," *The Wall Street Journal,* April 20, 1993, B1; "CIS Is Next Battlefield of Cola Wars," *We/Mbl,* June 29–July12, 1992, 6; "Cola Wars: All Noisy on the Eastern Front," *Business Week,* January 27, 1992, 37; "Can Wayne Calloway Handle the Pepsi Challenge?" *Business Week,* January 27, 1992, 34–37.

country by countering in another country or, if the competitors operate in multiple businesses, countering in a different product category altogether.

The example of Nokia Mobile Phones, one of the leading manufacturers of cellular telephones in the world (with a market share of 10 percent, second only to Motorola's 22 percent) highlights globalization as a strategy. The company's focus is on cellular mobile telephones (manufactured in Finland, Germany, and South Korea). The objective is to be a volume manufacturer, that is, to provide products for all major systems through a presence in all major markets. A global product range with customized variation for different distribution channels assures local acceptance.[16]

Challenges of Globalization

Marketers who have tried the global concept have often run into problems with local differences. Especially in the 1980s, global marketing was seen as a standardized marketing effort dictated to the country organizations by headquarters. Procter & Gamble stumbled badly in the 1980s in Japan when customers there spurned its Pampers in favor of rival brands. P&G's diapers were made and sold according to a formula imposed by Cincinnati headquarters. Japanese consumers found the company's hard-sell techniques alienating.[17]

Pitfalls that handicap global marketing programs and contribute to their suboptimal performance include market-related reasons, such as insufficient research and a tendency to overstandardize, as well as internal reasons, such as inflexibility in planning and implementation.

Market Factors   Should a product be launched on a broader scale without formal research as to regional or local differences, the result may be failure. An example of this is Lego A/S, the Danish toy manufacturer, which decided to transfer sales promotional tactics successful in the U.S. market unaltered to other markets, such as Japan. This promotion included approaches such as "bonus packs" and gift promotions. However, Japanese consumers considered these promotions wasteful, expensive, and not very appealing.[18] Similarly, AT&T has had its problems abroad because its models are largely reworked U.S. models. Even after spending $100 million in adapting its most powerful switch for European markets, its success was limited because phone companies there prefer smaller switches.[19] Often, the necessary research is conducted only after a product or a program has failed.

[16] This example is courtesy of Jouko Hayrynen, vice president, exports, Nokia Mobile Phones Ltd.

[17] "Marketing Globally, Thinking Locally," *Business Week,* May 13, 1991, 20–24.

[18] Kamran Kashani, "Beware the Pitfalls of Global Marketing," *Harvard Business Review* 67 (September–October 1989): 91–98.

[19] "AT&T Slowly Gets Its Global Wires Uncrossed," *Business Week,* February 11, 1991, 82–83.

Internal Factors Globalization by design requires a balance between sensitivity to local needs and deployment of technologies and concepts globally. This means that neither headquarters nor independent country managers can alone call the shots. If country organizations are not part of the planning process, or if adoption is forced on them by headquarters, local resistance in the form of the **not-invented-here syndrome (NIH)** may lead to the demise of the global program or, worse still, to an overall decline in morale. Subsidiary resistance may stem from resistance to any idea originating from the outside or from valid concerns about the applicability of a concept to that particular market. Without local commitment, no global program will survive.

Localizing Global Marketing

The successful global marketers of the 1990s will be those who can achieve a balance between country managers and global product managers at headquarters. This balance may be achieved by a series of actions to improve a company's ability to develop and implement global strategy. These actions relate to management processes, organization structures, and overall corporate culture, all of which should ensure cross-fertilization within the firm.[20]

Management Processes In the multidomestic approach, country organizations had very little need to exchange ideas. Globalization, however, requires transfer of information between not only headquarters and country organizations but also between the country organizations themselves. By facilitating the flow of information, ideas are exchanged and organizational values strengthened. Information exchange can be achieved through periodic meetings of marketing managers or through worldwide conferences to allow employees to discuss their issues and local approaches to solving them. IBM, for example, has a Worldwide Opportunity Council which sponsors fellowships for employees to listen to business cases from around the world and develop global platforms or solutions. IBM has found that some country organizations find it easier to accept input of other country organizations than that coming directly from headquarters. The approach used at Levi Strauss & Co. is described in The International Marketplace 16.3.

Part of the preparation for becoming global has to be personnel interchange. Many companies encourage (or even require) midlevel managers to gain experience abroad during the early or middle stages of their careers. The more experience people have in working with others from different nationalities—getting to know other markets and surroundings—the better a company's global philosophy, strategy, and actions will be integrated locally.

The role of headquarters staff should be that of coordination and leveraging the resources of the corporation. For example, this may mean activities focused on combining good ideas that come from different parts of the company to be fed into global planning. Many global companies also employ world-class advertising and market research staffs whose role should be to consult subsidiaries by upgrading their technical skills and to focus their attention not only on local issues but also on those with global impact.

Globalization calls for the centralization of decision-making authority far beyond that of the multidomestic approach. Once a strategy has been jointly developed, headquarters may want to permit local managers to develop their own programs within specified parameters and subject to approval rather than forcing them to adhere strictly to the formulated strategy. For example, Colgate Palmolive allows local units to use their own ads, but only if they can prove they can beat the global "benchmark" version. With a

[20] John A. Quelch and Edward J. Hoff, "Customizing Global Marketing," *Harvard Business Review* 64 (May–June 1986): 59–68; Yip, Loewe, and Yoshino, "Take Your Company to the Global Market."

16.3

THE INTERNATIONAL MARKETPLACE

Finding the Fit Overseas

Twice a year, Levi Strauss & Co. calls together managers from its worldwide operations for a meeting of the minds. In sessions that could be described as a cross between the United Nations general assembly and MTV, the participants brainstorm and exchange ideas on what seems to work in their respective markets, regionally, or globally. If a marketing manager finds an advertising campaign appealing, he or she is encouraged to take it back home to sell more Levi's blue jeans.

All told, Levi's marketing approach epitomizes a slogan that is becoming popular among companies around the world: Think globally, act locally. Levi's has deftly capitalized on the Levi's name abroad by marketing it as an enshrined piece of Americana, and foreign consumers have responded by paying top dollar for the product. An Indonesian commercial shows Levi's-clad teenagers cruising around Dubuque, Iowa, in 1960s convertibles. In Japan, James Dean serves as a centerpiece in virtually all Levi's advertising. Overseas, Levi's products have been positioned upscale, which has meant highly satisfactory profit margins. To protect the image, Levi's has avoided the use of mass merchants and discounters in its distribution efforts.

Levi's success turns on its ability to fashion a global strategy that does not stifle local initiative. It is a delicate balancing act, one that often means giving foreign managers the freedom needed to adjust their tactics to meet the changing tastes of their home markets. In Brazil, Levi's prospers by letting local managers call the shots on distribution. For instance, Levi's penetrated the huge, fragmented Brazilian market by launching a chain of 400 Levi's Only stores, some of them in tiny, rural towns. Levi's is also sensitive to local tastes in Brazil, where it developed the Feminina line of jeans exclusively for women, who prefer ultratight jeans. What Levi's learns in one market can often be adopted in another. The Dockers line of chino pants and casual wear originated in the company's Argentine unit and was applied to loosely cut pants by Levi's Japanese subsidiary. The company's U.S. operation adopted both in 1986, and the line now generates $550 million in North American revenues.

Headquarters managers exercise control where necessary. To protect Levi's cherished brand identity and image of quality, the company has organized its foreign operations as subsidiaries rather than relying on a patchwork of licensees. "It is important for a brand like ours to have a single face," says Lee C. Smith, president of Levi Strauss International. "You cannot control that if you have 20 to 25 licensees around the world interpreting it in different ways." The company also keeps ahead of its competition by exporting its pioneering use of computers to track sales and manufacturing.

Ironically, it hasn't been that long since Levi's international marketing efforts were mired in errors. In 1984 and 1985, international operations lost money. A strong dollar adversely affected sales, and the designer-jeans craze made Levi's five-pocket model rather out of date. Furthermore, Levi's was losing its brand identity in jeans by getting into specialty apparel. Today, after a complete refocus on blue jeans, about 39 percent of the company's total revenues and 60 percent of its pretax profit before interest and corporate expenses come from abroad.

properly managed approval process, effective control can be exerted without unduly dampening a country manager's creativity.

Overall, the best approach against the emergence of the NIH syndrome is utilizing various motivational policies such as (1) ensuring that local managers participate in the development of marketing strategies and programs for global brands, (2) encouraging local managers to generate ideas for possible regional or global use, (3) maintaining a product portfolio that includes local as well as regional and global brands, and (4) allowing local managers control over their marketing budgets so that they can respond to local customer needs and counter global competition (rather than depleting budgets by forcing them to participate only in uniform campaigns).[21] Acknowledging this local potential, global marketers can pick up successful brands in one country and make them cross-border stars. Since Nestlé acquired British candy maker Rowntree Mackintosh, it has increased its exports by 60 percent and made formerly local brands, such as After Eight Dinner mints, pan-European hits. Similarly, when Procter & Gamble gets its hands on an innovation or a product with global potential, rolling it out quickly worldwide is important. As a result of global reach, the sales of Pantene shampoo increased from $50 million in 1985 to $700 million in 1993.

Organization Structures   Various organization structures have emerged to support the globalization effort. Some companies have established global or regional product managers and their support groups at headquarters. Their task is to develop long-term strategies for product categories on a worldwide basis and to act as the support system for the country organizations. This matrix structure focused on customers, which has replaced the traditional country-by-country approach, is considered more effective in today's global marketplace according to companies that have adopted it.

Whenever a product group has global potential, firms such as Procter & Gamble, 3M, and Henkel create strategic-planning units to work on the programs. These units, such as 3M's EMATs (European Marketing Action Teams) consist of members from the country organizations that market the products, managers from both global and regional headquarters, as well as technical specialists.

Corporate Culture   In truly global companies, very little decision making occurs that does not support the goal of treating the world as a single market. Planning for and execution of programs take place on a worldwide basis.

Examples of manifestations of the global commitment are a global identity that favors no specific country (especially the "home country" of the company). The management features several nationalities, and whenever teams are assembled, people from various country organizations get represented. The management development system has to be transparent, allowing nonnational executives an equal chance for the fast track to top management.[22]

[21] Quelch and Hoff, "Customizing Global Marketing."
[22] "Globalization Starts with Company's Own View of Itself," *Business International,* June 10, 1991, 197–198.

GLOBAL PRODUCT PLANNING AND DEVELOPMENT

Product development is at the heart of the global marketing process. New products should be developed, or old ones modified, to cater to new or changing customer needs on a global or regional basis. At the same time, corporate objectives of technical feasibility and financial profitability must be satisfied.

To illustrate, Black & Decker, manufacturer of power tools for do-it-yourself household repairs, has done some remodeling of its own. With total sales of $1.17 billion, the company in the early 1980s was the consummate customizer: The Italian subsidiary made tools for Italians, the British subsidiary for the British. At the same time, Japanese power-tool makers, such as Makita Electric Works Ltd., saw the world differently. Makita was Black & Decker's first competitor with a global strategy. Makita management did not care that Germans prefer high-powered, heavy-duty drills and that the Americans want everything lighter. They reasoned that a good drill at a low price will sell from Baden-Baden to Brooklyn. Using this strategy, Makita effectively cut into Black & Decker's market share. As a result, Black & Decker unveiled 50 new models—each standardized for world production.[23]

With increasing competition able to react quickly when new products are introduced, worldwide planning at the product level provides a number of tangible benefits. A firm that adopts a worldwide product management approach is better able to develop products with specifications compatible on a worldwide scale. A firm that leaves product development to independent units will incur greater difficulties in transfering its experience and technology.

In many multinational corporations, each product is developed for potential worldwide usage, and unique multinational market requirements are incorporated whenever technically feasible. Some design their products to meet the regulations and other key requirements in their major markets and then, if necessary, smaller markets' requirements are met on a country-by-country basis. For example, Nissan develops lead-country models that can, with minor changes, be made suitable for local sales in the majority of markets. For the remaining situations, the company also provides a range of additional models that can be adapted to the needs of local segments. Using this approach, Nissan has been able to reduce the number of basic models from 48 to 18.[24] This approach also means that the new product can be introduced concurrently into all of the firm's markets. Companies like 3M and Xerox develop most of their products with this objective in mind.

Some markets may require unique approaches to developing global products. At Gillette, timing is the only concession to local taste. Developing markets, such as Eastern Europe and China, are first weaned on older, cheaper products before they are sold up-to-date versions.[25] In a world economy where most of the growth is in developing markets, the traditional approach of introducing a global product may keep new products out of the hands of consumers rather than in them due to their premium price. As a result, Procter & Gamble figures out what consumers in various countries can afford and then develops products they can pay for. For example, in Brazil, the company introduced a diaper called Pampers Uni, a less-expensive version of its mainstream product. The strategy is to create price tiers, hooking customers early and then encouraging them to trade up as their incomes and desire for better products grow.[26]

[23] "Black & Decker's Gamble on 'Globalization,'" *Fortune,* May 14, 1984, 40–48.
[24] Kenichi Ohmae, "Managing in a Borderless World," *Harvard Business Review* 67 (May–June 1989): 152–161.
[25] "Blade-runner," *The Economist,* April 10, 1993, 68.
[26] Bill Saporito, "Behind the Tumult at P&G," *Fortune,* March 7, 1994, 74–82.

The main goal of the product-development process, therefore, is not to develop a standard product or product line but to build adaptability into products and product lines that are being developed to achieve worldwide appeal.

The Product-Development Process

The product-development process begins with idea generation. Ideas may come from within the company—from the research and development staff, sales personnel, or almost anyone who becomes involved in the company's efforts. Intermediaries may suggest ideas because they are closer to the changing, and often different, needs of international customers. Competitors are a major outside source of ideas. A competitive idea from abroad may be modified and improved to suit another market's characteristics. As an example, when the president of d-Con returned from a trip to Europe, he brought with him what would seem in the United States to be an unusual idea for packaging insecticides. In a market dominated by aerosols, the new idea called for offering consumers insect repellent in a "felt-tip pen." d-Con obtained U.S. rights for the product, which in Europe is marketed by Tamana, a subsidiary of Shell Oil.[27]

For a number of companies, especially those producing industrial goods, customers provide the best source of ideas for new products.[28] Of the 30 products with the highest world sales in 1990, 70 percent had their origins traced to manufacturing and marketing (rather than laboratories).[29] For some companies, procurement requisitions from governments and supranational organizations (for example, the United Nations) are a good source of new-product ideas.

Most companies develop hundreds of ideas every year; for example, 3M may have 1,000 new-product ideas competing for scarce development funds annually. Product ideas are screened on market, technical, and financial criteria: Is the market substantial and penetrable, can the product be mass produced, and if the answer to both of these questions is affirmative, can the company produce and market it profitably? For example, cereal producers may refrain from introducing their products to a market like Brazil, where breakfast is not normally eaten, because an expensive education process would be necessary.

A product idea that at some stage fails to earn a go-ahead is not necessarily scrapped. Most progressive companies maintain data banks of "miscellaneous opportunities." Often, data from these banks are used in the development of other products. One of the most famous examples concerns 3M. After developing a new woven fabric some 50 years ago, 3M's Commercial Office Supply Company did not know what to do with the technology. Among the applications rejected were seamless brassiere cups (too expensive) and disposable diapers. The fabric was finally used to make surgical and industrial masks.[30]

When a new-product idea earns a go-ahead, the first pilot models are built. This means a major commitment of funds, especially if the product requires separate facilities and special personnel. In the scale-up phase, which precedes full-scale commercialization, preliminary production units are tested on-site or in limited minilaunches.

All of the development phases—idea generation, screening, product and process development, scale-up, and commercialization—should be global in nature with inputs into the process from all affected markets. If this is possible, original product designs

---

[27] "D-Con Finds New Product Idea in Europe," *Advertising Age,* July 9, 1984, 58.

[28] Eric von Hippel, "Successful Industrial Products from Customer Ideas," *Journal of Marketing* 42 (January 1978): 39–49.

[29] "Could America Afford the Transistor Today?" *Business Week,* March 7, 1994, 80–84.

[30] "Herzog: New Products Mean New Opportunities," *International Ambassador,* March 23, 1979, 3.

can be adapted easily and inexpensively later on. The process has been greatly facilitated through the use of **computer-aided design (CAD).** Some companies are able to design their products so that they meet most standards and requirements around the world with minor modifications on a country-by-country basis. The product-development process can be initiated by any unit of the organization, in the parent country or abroad. If the initiating entity is a subsidiary that lacks technical and financial resources for implementation, another entity of the firm is assigned the responsibility. Most often this is the parent and its central R&D department. Larger multinational corporations naturally have development laboratories in multiple locations that can assume the task. Gillette, for example, maintains two toiletries laboratories, one in the United States and the other in the United Kingdom.[31] In these cases, coordination and information flow between the units are especially critical. Global companies may have an advantage in being able to utilize the resources from around the world. Otis Elevator Inc.'s latest product, the Elevonic, is a good example of this. The elevator was developed by six research centers in five countries. Otis' group in Farmington, Connecticut, handled the systems integration, Japan designed the special motor drives that make the elevators ride smoothly, France perfected the door systems, Germany handled the electronics, and Spain took care of the small-geared components. The international effort saved more than $10 million in design costs and cut the development cycle from four years to two.[32]

In some cases, the assignment of product-development responsibility may be based on a combination of special market and technical knowledge. When a major U.S. copier manufacturer was facing erosion of market share in the smaller copier segment in Europe because of Japanese incursions, its Japanese subsidiary was charged with developing an addition to the company's product line. This product, developed and produced outside the United States, has subsequently been marketed in the United States.

Even though the product-development activity may take place in the parent country, all of the affected units actively participate in development and market planning for a new product. For example, a subsidiary would communicate directly with the product division at the headquarters level and also with the international staff, who could support the subsidiary on the scene of the actual development activity. This often also involves the transfer of people from one location to another for such projects.

The activities of a typical global program are summarized in Figure 16.2. The managing unit has prime responsibility for accomplishing: (1) single-point worldwide technical development and design of a new product that conforms to the global design standard and global manufacturing and procurement standards as well as transmittal of the completed design to each affected unit; (2) all other activities necessary to plan, develop, manufacture, introduce, and support the product in the managing unit as well as direction and support to affected units to ensure that concurrent introductions are achieved; and (3) integration and coordination of all global program activities.

The affected units, on the other hand, have prime responsibility for achieving: (1) identification of unique requirements to be incorporated in the product goals and specifications as well as in the managing unit's technical effort; (2) all other activities necessary to plan, manufacture, introduce, and support products in affected units; and (3) identification of any nonconcurrence with the managing unit's plans and activities.

During the early stages of the product-development process, the global emphasis is on identifying and evaluating the requirements of both the managing unit and the affected units and incorporating them into the plan. During the later stages, the emphasis

[31] "How Gillette Keeps Research and Development Close to Local Markets," *Business International,* February 1, 1985, 33–34.
[32] "The Stateless Corporation," *Business Week,* May 14, 1990, 98–106.

Global Program Management **FIGURE 16.2**

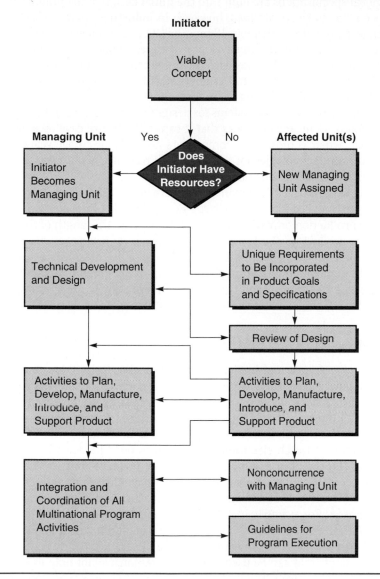

Source: Ilkka A. Ronkainen, "Product Development in the Multinational Firm," *International Marketing Review* 1 (Winter 1983): 24–30.

is on the efficient development and design of a global product with a minimum of configuration differences and on the development of supporting systems capabilities in each of the participating units. The result of the interaction and communication is product-development activity on a global basis as well as products developed primarily to serve world markets.

This approach effectively cuts through the standardized-versus-localized debate and offers a clear-cut way of determining and implementing effective programs in several markets simultaneously. It offers headquarters the opportunity to standardize certain aspects of the product while permitting maximum flexibility, whenever technically feasible, to differing market conditions. For instance, in terms of technical development, members of subsidiaries' staffs take an active part in the development processes to make sure that global specifications are built into the initial design of the product.[33]

The process has to be streamlined, however. In industries characterized by technological change, coming to market 9 to 12 months late can cost a new product half its potential revenues.[34] To cut down on development time, companies like NEC and Canon use multidisciplinary teams that stay with the project from start to finish, using a parallel approach toward product launch. Designers start to work before feasibility testing is over; manufacturing and marketing begin gearing up well before the design is finished. Such teams depend on computer systems for designing, simulating, and analyzing products. Toyota Motor Company estimates that it can in the future develop a new automobile in one year, whereas most of its competitors now take up to five years.[35] However, with new uncertain technologies for which market response is not clear, longer development cycles are still common and advisable.[36]

Firms using worldwide product management are better able to develop products that can be quickly introduced into any market.[37] Foreign market introduction can take the form of either production or marketing abroad. In general, the length of the lag will depend on (1) the product involved, with industrial products having shorter lags because of their more standardized general nature; (2) degree of newness; (3) customer characteristics—both demographics and psychographics; (4) geographic proximity; (5) firm-related variables—the number and type of foreign affiliations as well as overall experience in global marketing; and (6) degree of commitments of resources.

The Location of R&D Activities

The past tendency of most multinational corporations has been to locate most of their product-development operations within the parent corporation. Recently, however, a number of experts have called for companies to start using foreign-based resources to improve their ability to compete internationally. At Asea Brown Boveri, for example, 90 percent of its R&D is done in worldwide business units rather than in an isolated business laboratory.[38] Dutch electronics giant Philips once funded all of its R&D centrally, but now 70 percent of its funding comes from business units.[39] The benefits are accrued from acquiring international contacts and having R&D investments abroad as ways to add new items to the company's existing product line, thus increasing chances for global success.[40] For example, in 1988, W. R. Grace opened an $8-million R&D center in Japan. Although the costs are high and recruitment difficult, benefits are numerous as well. Japan provides the company heightened awareness of and access to technological developments that can be used to be more responsive not only to local markets but to global markets as well. The R&D center is part of Grace's triad approach involv-

---

[33] Ilkka A. Ronkainen, "Product Development in the Multinational Firm," *International Marketing Review* 1 (Winter 1983): 24–30.

[34] Bro Uttal, "Speeding New Ideas to Market," *Fortune,* March 2, 1987, 62–66.

[35] "Advantage for Toyota," *The Wall Street Journal,* August 5, 1988, 35.

[36] Edward G. Krubasik, "Customize Your Product Development," *Harvard Business Review* 66 (November–December 1988): 46–52.

[37] Georges LeRoy, *Multinational Product Strategies: A Typology for Analysis of Worldwide Product Innovation Diffusion* (New York: Praeger, 1976), 1–3.

[38] "In the Labs, the Fight to Spend Less, Get More," *Business Week,* June 28, 1993, 102–104.

[39] "For Best Results, Decentralize R&D," *Business Week,* June 28, 1993, 134.

[40] Alphonso O. Ogbuehi and Ralph A. Bellas, Jr., "Decentralized R&D for Global Product Development: Strategic Implications for the Multinational Corporation," *International Marketing Review* 9 no. 5 (1992): 60–70.

ing the three leading areas for diffusion of technology: the United States, Europe, and Japan.[41] A dozen other companies, including DuPont, Upjohn, Campbell, and Eastman Kodak, have launched similar centers.[42]

Investments for R&D abroad are made for four general reasons: (1) to aid technology transfer from parent to subsidiary, (2) to develop new and improved products expressly for foreign markets, (3) to develop new products and processes for simultaneous application in world markets of the firm, and (4) to generate new technology of a long-term exploratory nature. The commitment of the firm to international operations increases from the first type of investment to the third and fourth, in which there is no or little bias toward headquarters performing the job.[43]

A sample of 35 U.S.-based and 18 Europe-based multinational corporations was used in an attempt to determine the type of R&D being performed abroad, how the sites were selected, how they are managed, and relations with local entities as well as collaborative efforts.[44] In many cases, companies must be close to their markets to satisfy local styles and needs. This strategy or requirement is not limited to consumer-goods companies. Regulations in the pharmaceutical industry often require U.S. companies to have European formulation laboratories. In truly multinational companies, the location of R&D is determined by the existence of specific skills. For instance, all R&D concerning photography at 3M takes place in Italy at the Ferrania division, which was acquired by the company in the 1960s. At Ford Motor Company, development of a specific car or component will be allotted to whichever technical center has the greatest expertise, as seen in The International Marketplace 16.4. Placing R&D operations abroad may also ensure access to foreign scientific and technical personnel and information, either in industry or at leading universities. The local decision may also be driven by the unique features of the market. For example, most of the major car makers have design centers in California to allow for the monitoring of technical, social, and aesthetic values of the fifth-largest car market in the world. Furthermore, the many technological innovations and design trends that have originated there give it a trend-setting image. Many companies regionalize their R&D efforts; for example, U.S.-based multinational corporations often base their European R&D facilities in Belgium because of its central location and desirable market characteristics, which include serving as headquarters for the European Union and providing well-trained personnel. Regional centers may also be needed to adequately monitor customer trends around the world. Sharp, one of Japan's leading electronics companies, has set up centers in Hamburg, Germany, and Mahwah, New Jersey, in addition to its two centers at home.[45]

R&D centers are seen as highly desirable investments by host governments. Developing countries are increasingly demanding R&D facilities as a condition of investment or continued operation, to the extent that some companies have left countries where they saw no need for the added expense. Countries that have been known to have attempted to influence multinational corporations are Japan, India, Brazil, and France. Some governments, such as Canada, have offered financial rewards to multinational corporations

---

[41] "W. R. Grace Extends Global R&D to Japan," *Business International,* December 5, 1988, 377, 382.

[42] Susan Moffat, "Picking Japan's Research Brain," *Fortune,* March 25, 1991, 84–96.

[43] Robert Ronstadt, "International R&D: The Establishment and Evolution of Research and Development Abroad by U.S. Multinationals," *Journal of International Business Studies* 9 (Spring–Summer 1978): 7–24.

[44] Jack N. Behrman and William A. Fischer, "Transnational Corporations: Market Orientations and R&D Abroad," in *The Multinational Enterprise in Transition,* ed. Philip D. Grub et al. (Princeton, NJ: Darwin Press, 1984), 378–389.

[45] "Sharp Puts the Consumer on Its New-Product Team," *Business International,* December 14, 1992, 401–402.

16.4

THE INTERNATIONAL MARKETPLACE

Ford's Centers of Excellence

To carry its momentum in the 1990s, Ford is organizing design and engineering teams into centers of excellence. The approach has two goals: to avoid duplicating efforts, and to capitalize on the expertise of Ford's specialists.

Located in several countries, the centers will work on key components for cars. One will, for example, work on certain kinds of engines. Another will engineer and develop common platforms—the suspension and other undercarriage components—for similar-sized cars.

Designers in each market will then style exteriors and passenger compartments to appeal to local tastes. Each car will usually be built on the continent where it is to be sold. Ford of Europe introduced the Mondeo, which was designed to replace the aging ten-year-old Sierra line in Europe in 1993 and the Tempo/Topaz line in the United States in 1994. The one-year lag between the Europe and the United States introductions was to allow the same team of engineers to direct factory launches in both Genk, Belgium, and Kansas City, Missouri. The U.S. and European versions have 75 percent common parts, although the U.S. version will be slightly longer and have more chrome. Five Ford design studios had to compromise on design proposals that ranged from a soft, rounded body to a sharply angular one. Although European operations maintained the project leadership, key responsibilities were divided. The U.S. side took over automatic transmissions, with Europe handling the manual.

In the past, Ford's huge, autonomous European and North American auto operations designed and built completely different models, reflecting sharply divergent needs in the two markets. But now tastes are converging, and the company says it can no longer afford to duplicate efforts. "If we didn't do it this way the Americans and Europeans would have done their own vehicles," says Jacques Nasser, the chairman of Ford Europe. "What we have is a shortage of product-development resources, mainly engineering people, and this uses them more efficiently." In April, 1994, Ford announced a broad reorganization that will combine North American and European operations into a single division.

NORTH AMERICA
Dearborn, Mich.

FORD OF EUROPE
Brentwood, England

- Platform for cars to replace midsize Taurus, Sable, and Europe's Scorpio
- Six- and eight-cylinder engines
- Air-conditioning systems
- Automatic transmissions

- Platform for replacement of North American compacts Tempo and Topaz and Europe's Sierra
- Four-cylinder engines
- Manual transmissions

MAZDA (25% owned by Ford)
Hiroshima, Japan

- Platform for replacement of Escort subcompact, the best-selling car in the world
- Cars smaller than Escort

ASIA–PACIFIC
Melbourne, Australia

- Specialty sports cars, beginning with two-seater Capri

Sources: "Ford to Merge European, North American Car Units," *The Washington Post,* April 22, 1994, G1, G2; "Ford is Turning Heads with $6 Billion Cost to Design 'World Car,'" *The Wall Street Journal,* March 23, 1993, A1, A10; "Ford of Europe: Slimmer, But Maybe Not Luckier," *Business Week,* January 18, 1993, 44–46; "Can Ford Stay on Top?" reprinted from September 28, 1987, issue of *Business Week,* 78–86, by special permission, copyright © 1987 by McGraw-Hill, Inc.

to start or expand R&D efforts in the host markets. In addition to compliance with governmental regulation, local R&D efforts can provide positive publicity for the company involved. Internally, having local R&D may boost morale and elevate a subsidiary above the status of merely a manufacturing operation.[46]

In many multinational corporations that still employ multidomestic strategies, product-development efforts amount to product modifications—for example, making sure that a product satisfies local regulations. Local content requirements may necessitate major development input from the affected markets. In these cases, local technical people identify alternate, domestically available ingredients and prepare initial tests. More involved testing usually takes place at a regional laboratory or at headquarters.

The Organization of Global Product Development

The product-development activity is undertaken by specific teams, the task of which is to subject new products to tough scrutiny at specified points in the development cycle to eliminate weak ones before too much is invested in them and to guide promising prototypes from labs to the market.[47] Representatives of all of the affected functional areas are on each team to ensure the integrity of the project. A marketing team member is needed to assess the customer base for the new product, engineering to make sure that the product can be produced in the intended format, and finance to keep costs in control. An international team member should be assigned a permanent role in the product-development process and not simply called in when a need arises. In addition to international representation on each product-development team, some multinational corporations hold periodic meetings of purely international teams. A typical international team may consist of five members, each of whom also has a product responsibility (such as cable accessories) as well as a geographical responsibility (such as the Far East). Others

---

[46] S. Tamer Cavusgil, "Multinational Corporations and the Management of Technology Transfers," in *Technology Transfer,* ed. A. Coskun Samli (Westport, CT: Quorum Books, 1985), 217–229.

[47] "A Warm Feeling Inside," *Business Week,* December 2, 1991, 70.

may be from central R&D and domestic marketing planning. The function of international teams is to provide both support to subsidiaries and international input to overall planning efforts. A key input of international team members is the potential for universal features that can be used worldwide as well as unique features that may be required for individual markets.

Such multidisciplinary teams maximize the payoff from R&D by streamlining decision making; that is, they reduce the need for elaborate reporting mechanisms and layers of committee approvals.[48] With the need to slash development time, these teams can be useful. For example, in response to competition, Honeywell set up a multidisciplinary "tiger team" to build a thermostat in 12 months rather than the usual 4 years.[49]

Challenges to using teams or approaches that require cooperation between R&D centers are often language and cultural barriers. For example, pragmatic engineers in the United States may distrust their more theoretically thinking European counterparts. National rivalries may also inhibit the acceptance by others of solutions developed by one entity of the organization. Many companies have solved these problems with increased communication and exchange of personnel.

With the costs of basic research rising and product life cycles shortening, many companies have joined forces in R&D. The U.S. government and many U.S.-based multinational corporations have seen this approach as necessary to restore technological competitiveness. In 1984, the United States passed the National Cooperative Research Act, which allows companies to collaborate in long-term R&D projects without the threat of antitrust suits. Since then, more than 70 **R&D consortia** have been established to develop technologies ranging from artificial intelligence to those needed to overtake the Japanese lead in semiconductor manufacturing.[50] The major consortia in those fields are Microelectronics and Computer Technology Corporation and Sematech, both founded to match similar Japanese alliances. The consortium approach has also been used both by U.S. and European companies in the development of high-definition television (HDTV). Consortia exist in Europe as well, for example, the Joint European Submicron Silicon, which spends $1 billion a year on research.

These consortia can provide the benefits and face the challenges of any strategic alliance. Countering the benefits of sharing costs and risks are management woes from mixing corporate cultures as well as varying levels of enthusiasm by the participants.[51]

The Testing of New-Product Concepts

The final stages of the product-development process will involve testing the product in terms of both its performance and its projected market acceptance. Depending on the product, testing procedures range from reliability tests in the pilot plant to minilaunches, from which the product's performance in world markets will be estimated. Any testing will prolong full-scale commercialization and increase the possibility of competitive reaction. Further, the cost of test marketing is substantial—on the average, $1 to $1.5 million per market.

---

[48] "Companies Try New Approaches to Maximize Payoff from R&D," *Business International,* January 25, 1988, 17–21.

[49] "Manufacturers Strive to Slice Time Needed to Develop Products," *The Wall Street Journal,* February 23, 1988, 1, 24.

[50] "Why High-Tech Teams Just Aren't Enough," *Business Week,* January 30, 1989, 63.

[51] Lee Smith, "Can Consortiums Defeat Japan?" *Fortune,* June 5, 1989, 245–254.

Because of the high rate of new-product failure (estimated by the Conference Board at 67 percent in the United States[52]), usually attributed to market or marketing reasons, most companies want to be assured that their product will gain customer acceptance. They therefore engage in testing or a limited launch of the product. This may involve introducing the product in one country—for instance, Belgium—and basing the go-ahead decision for the rest of Europe on the performance of the product in that test market.

In many cases, companies rely too much on instinct and hunch in their marketing abroad, although in domestic markets they make extensive use of testing and research. Lack of testing has led to a number of major product disasters over the years.[53] The most serious blunder is to assume that other markets have the same priorities and life-styles as the domestic market. The failure of Coca-Cola, when first introduced in Germany in the 1920s, was attributed to German dislike of both the taste and the bottle design. Refrigeration was not commonly available, and this affected the taste. The result was the failure of a half-million-dollar ad campaign by J. Walter Thompson's Berlin branch. After a failure in introducing canned soups in Italy in the 1960s, Campbell Soup Company repeated the experience by introducing them in Brazil in 1979. Research conducted in Brazil after the failure revealed that women fulfill their roles as homemakers in part by such tasks as making soups from scratch. A similar finding had emerged in Italy more than 20 years earlier.[54]

Other reasons for product failure are a lack of product distinctiveness, unexpected technical problems, and mismatches between functions.[55] Mismatches between functions may occur not only between, for example, engineering and marketing, but within the marketing function as well. Engineering may design features in the product that established distribution channels or selling approaches cannot exploit. Advertising may promise the customer something that the other functions within marketing cannot deliver.

The trend is toward a complete testing of the marketing mix. All the components of the brand are tested, including formulation, packaging, advertising, and pricing. Test marketing is indispensable because prelaunch testing is an artificial situation; it tells the researcher what people say they will do, not what they will actually do. Test marketing carries major financial risks, which can be limited only if the testing can be conducted in a limited area. Ideally, this would utilize localized advertising media—that is, broadcast and print media to which only a limited region would be exposed. However, localized media are lacking even in developed markets such as Western Europe.

Because test marketing in Europe and elsewhere is risky or even impossible, researchers have developed three research methods to cope with the difficulty.[56] **Laboratory test markets** are the least realistic in terms of consumer behavior over time, but they will allow introduction of television exposure, which is impossible otherwise. **Microtest marketing** involves a continuous panel of consumers serviced by a retail grocery operated by the research agency. New products enter the market with high-quality, color-print ads, coupons, and free samples. Initial penetration and repeat buying are monitored. **Forced distribution tests** are based on a continuously reporting panel of

[52] David S. Hopkins, "Survey Finds 67% of New Products Fail," *Marketing News,* February 8, 1986, 1.

[53] David A. Ricks, *Big Business Blunders* (Homewood, IL: Dow Jones–Irwin, 1983), 23–35.

[54] "Campbell Soup Fails to Make It to the Table," *Business Week,* October 12, 1981, 66.

[55] Steven C. Wheelwright and W. Earl Sasser, Jr., "The New Product Development Map," *Harvard Business Review* 67 (May–June 1989): 112–125.

[56] B. C. Pymont, "Differences Make Europe Difficult Test Area," *Marketing News,* May 4, 1979, 12.

consumers, but they encounter new products in normal retail outlets. This is realistic, but competitors are immediately aware of the new product. An important criterion for successful testing is to gain the cooperation of key retailing organizations in the market. In Europe, retail trade is concentrated in a few companies, for example, in Finland by wholesaler cooperatives and in England by retail multiples. Mars Confectionery, which was testing a new chocolate malted-milk drink in England, could not get distribution in major supermarkets for test products. As a result, Mars changed its approach and focused its marketing on the home-delivery market.[57]

The Global Product Launch[58]

The impact of an effective global product launch can be great, but so can the cost of one that is poorly executed. High development costs as well as competitive pressures are forcing companies to rush products into as many markets as possible. But at the same time, a company can ill afford new products that are not effectively introduced, marketed, and supported in each market the company competes in.

A global product launch means introducing a product into countries in three or more regions within a narrow time frame. To achieve this, a company must undertake a number of measures. The country managers should be involved in the first stage of product strategy formulation to ensure that local and regional considerations are part of the overall corporate and product messages. A product launch team (consisting of product, marketing, manufacturing, sales, service, engineering, and communication representatives) can also approach problems from an industry standpoint, as opposed to a home-country perspective, enhancing product competitiveness in all markets.

Adequate consideration should be given to localization and translation requirements before the launch. This means that right messages are formulated and transmitted to key internal and external audiences. Support materials have to take into account both cultural and technical differences. The advantage of a simultaneous launch is that it boosts the overall momentum and attractiveness of the product by making it immediately available in key geographic markets.

Global product launches typically require more education and support of the sales channel than do domestic efforts or drawn-out efforts. This is due to the diversity of the distribution channels in terms of the support and education they may require before the launch.

A successful global launch by Apple Computer is described in The International Marketplace 16.5.

GLOBAL MANAGEMENT OF THE PRODUCT PORTFOLIO

As a result of development efforts, most marketers may have a considerable number of individual items in their product portfolios, consisting of different product lines—that is, groupings of products managed and marketed as a unit. Added to this, environmental differences will make the strategic planning process challenging. For global companies,

[57] Laurel Wentz, "Mars Widens Its Line in U.K.," *Advertising Age,* May 16, 1988, 37.

[58] Robert Michelet and Laura Elmore, "Launching Your Product Globally," *Export Today* 6 (September 1990): 13–15; Laura Elmore and Robert Michelet, "The Global Product Launch," *Export Today* 6 (November–December 1990): 49–52.

THE INTERNATIONAL MARKETPLACE 16.5

A Classic Global Launch

In the fall of 1990, in a major change of strategy, Apple Computer launched its Macintosh Classic, LC, and midrange IIsi computers simultaneously in 122 countries around the world. Like most companies, Apple had previously introduced products first in its home market and then sequentially in other countries. The new approach, however, enables the company to "maximize sales from the very beginning of the three products' life cycles," says Fred Forsyth, senior vice president of worldwide manufacturing. Coming on the heels of the firm's decision to expand market share by cutting prices and raising volume, the simultaneous launches represent a bold move to compete head-to-head with global competitors, particularly low-cost Asian producers.

The large, coordinated global launch offered Apple three immediate benefits. First, it permitted the company to showcase its latest technology in all major markets at the same time. Second, setting a single date for the launch functioned as a strict discipline and spur to productivity, forcing the entire organization to gear up quickly for a successful worldwide effort.

Perhaps most important, the multinational product introduction solved the traditional problem of having "lame duck" models on the shelves in some countries while new products were being offered elsewhere. This was a concern because two of the three new computers were replacing earlier models. "Given the rapid speed of modern communications, introducing new models in one country alerts dealers elsewhere that the old models will be discontinued," says Wayne Dyer, Macintosh product line manager. Once launched in the United States, the older computers in other countries could have been sold only with steep markdowns, if at all, adversely affecting revenues and profits.

Apple first contemplated a global launch as a way to combat the "ever-shortening life cycles of personal computers," according to Forsyth. Apple saw eliminating the lag between introduction in the United States and introduction abroad as a way to increase sales over the life cycles of its products. Moreover, since margins are highest at the beginning of a product's cycle, early introduction worldwide promised to boost profits—not only in the short term but over the full lifetime of each product. So far, the strategy has proven well founded; the Classic model, in particular, is experiencing robust demand.

Sources: "How Apple Introduced Three New Computers in Many Markets at Once," *Business International,* January 14, 1991, 15–19; Laura Elmore, "The Global Product Launch: Three Case Studies," *Export Today 7* (January 1991): 35–55.

planning on a country-by-country basis can result in spotty worldwide market performance. Planning processes that focus simultaneously across a broad range of markets provide global marketers with tools to help balance risks, resource requirements, competitive economies of scale, and profitability to gain stronger long-term positions.[59] For example, Mars has stayed out of the U.S. chocolate milk market, despite a product-

[59] Gilbert D. Harrell and Richard O. Kiefer, "Multinational Market Portfolios in Global Strategy Development," *International Marketing Review* 10 no. 1 (1993): 60–72.

company fit, because the market is dominated by Hershey and Nestlé. However, it has entered these particular markets elsewhere, such as in Europe.

Despite the challenge of the task, the multinational marketer needs to have a balanced product portfolio—a proper mix of new, growing, and mature products to provide a sustainable long-term competitive advantage for the firm.[60] Optimally, the portfolio will contain **cash cows,** which require little financing but generate cash flow, and **stars,** which are market leaders in growth markets.

Analyzing the Product Portfolio

Using the product portfolio approach to analyze international markets requires the inclusion of additional dimensions to the exercise.[61] These dimensions would include countries, modes of operation, product markets, target segments, and marketing strategies. The specific approach and variables used will vary by company according to corporate objectives and characteristics as well as the nature of the product market.

Various portfolio models have been developed as tools for the analysis. They typically involve two measures—internal strength and external attractiveness—and the international extension includes the development of either (a) a worldwide matrix in which the units classified are products by countries (for example, personal computers or mainframes in the United Kingdom, France, and so on) or (b) a separate classification matrix for each country.[62]

A product portfolio approach based on growth rates and market-share positions allows the analysis of business entities, product lines, or individual products. Figure 16.3 represents the product-market portfolio of Company A, which markets the same product line in several countries. The company is a leader in most of the markets in which it has operations, as indicated by its relative market shares. It has two cash cows (United States and Canada), four stars (Germany, Great Britain, France, and Spain), and one "problem child" (Brazil). In the mature U.S. market, Company A has its largest volume but only a small market share advantage compared with competition. Company A's dominance is more pronounced in Canada and in the EU countries.

At the same time, Company B, its main competitor, although not a threat in Company A's major markets, does have a commanding lead in two fast-growing markets: Japan and Brazil. As this illustration indicates, an analysis should be conducted not only of the firm's own portfolio but also of competitors' portfolios, along with a projection of the firm's and the competitors' future international products—market portfolios.[63] Building future scenarios based on industry estimates will allow Company A to take remedial long-term action to counter Company B's advances. In this case, Company A should direct resources to build market share in fast-growing markets such as Japan and Brazil.

In expanding markets, any company not growing rapidly risks falling behind for good. Growth may mean bringing out new items or lines or having to adjust existing products. Take, for example, the fastest-growing market in 1988 and 1989 for PCs: Europe.[64] Tandon of Moorpark, California, started selling PCs in Europe before entering

---

[60] George S. Day, "Diagnosing the Product Portfolio," *Journal of Marketing* 41 (April 1977): 8–19.

[61] Yoram Wind and Susan P. Douglas, "International Portfolio Analysis and Strategy: Challenge of the 80s," *Journal of International Business Studies* 12 (Fall 1981): 69–82.

[62] The models referred to are GE/McKinsey, Shell International, and A. D. Little product portfolio models.

[63] Jean-Claude Larréché, "The International Product-Market Portfolio," in 1978 *AMA Educators' Proceedings* (Chicago, IL: American Marketing Association, 1978), 276–281.

[64] Richard I. Kirkland, Jr., "Europe Goes Wild for Yankee PCs," *Fortune,* June 5, 1989, 257–260.

Example of a Product-Market Portfolio **FIGURE 16.3**

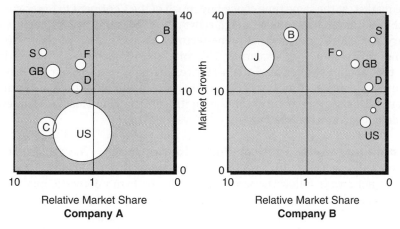

Company A

Company B

(B=Brazil, C=Canada, D=Germany, F=France, GB=Great Britain, J=Japan, S=Spain, US=United States)

Source: Jean-Claude Larréché, "The International Product-Market Portfolio," in *1978 AMA Educators' Proceedings* (Chicago, IL: American Marketing Association, 1978), 276.

the U.S. market. Olivetti lost market share when it took 18 months longer than Compaq to incorporate new technology into its PCs. For some, needed market share can be gained only through acquisitions, as with ICL's purchase of Nokia's data-processing operation.

Advantages of the Product Portfolio Approach   The major advantages provided by the product portfolio approach are as follows:

1. A global view of the international competitive structure, especially when longer-term considerations are included
2. A guide for the formulation of a global international marketing strategy based on the suggested allocation of scarce resources between product lines
3. A guide for the formulation of marketing objectives for specific international markets based on an outline of the role of each product line in each of the markets served—for example, to generate cash or to block the expansion of competition
4. A convenient visual communication goal, achieved by integrating a substantial amount of information in an appealingly simple format

Before making strategic choices based on such a portfolio, the international marketer should consider the risks related to variables such as entry mode and exchange rates; management preferences for idiosyncratic objectives, such as concentrating on countries with similar market characteristics; and marketing costs. For example, the cost of entry into one market may be less because the company already has a presence and the possibility exists that distribution networks may be shared.[65] Hoover Company, the U.S. industry leader for vacuum cleaners with approximately one-third of the market, long relied on the good performance of its European subsidiaries, mainly because of the stagnant market at home. In the early 1980s, after the European operations began running into problems, Hoover decided to diversify on a worldwide basis. Its three-pronged strategy for European operations included (1) cutting high British manufacturing costs and

---

[65] Wind and Douglas, "International Portfolio Analysis and Strategy."

shifting some production to France, (2) launching new lines of vacuum cleaners on the Continent, a market Hoover had neglected, and (3) concentrating on Britain's washing-machine market, at the same time conceding much of the Continent to lower-cost washing machines from Italian competitors. Meanwhile, Hoover Ltd., the company's British subsidiary, diversified on its own to home-security products, such as smoke detectors, fire extinguishers, and burglar alarms. This market in Europe is still in its infancy, whereas the vacuum cleaner markets in France, Germany, and Britain have shown no growth in unit volume. Also, competitors (AEG, Electrolux, Bosch-Siemens, and Vorwerk) have better name recognition on the Continent than does Hoover.[66] However, the Britons do not vacuum their homes, they "hoover" them.

Disadvantages of the Product Portfolio Approach   The application of the product portfolio approach has a number of limitations. International competitive behavior does not always follow the same rules as in the firm's domestic market; for example, the major local competitor may be a government-owned firm whose main objective is to maintain employment. The relationship between market share and profitability may be blurred by a number of factors in an international environment. Government regulations in every market will have an impact on the products a company can market. For instance, major U.S. tobacco manufacturers estimate they could capture 30 percent of Japan's cigarette market of $10 billion a year if it were not for restrictions that apply only to non-Japanese producers.

Product lines offered will also be affected by various local content laws—those stipulating that a prescribed percentage of the value of the final product must be manufactured locally. Market tastes have an important impact on product lines. These not only may alter the content of a product but also may require an addition in a given market that is not available elsewhere. The Coca-Cola Company has market leadership in a product category unique to Japan: coffee-flavored soft drinks. The market came into existence some 20 years ago and grew rapidly, accounting presently for 10 percent of soft drink sales. The beverage is packaged like any other soft drink and is available through vending machines, which dispense hot cans in the winter and cold servings during warm weather. Although Coca-Cola executives have considered introducing "Georgia" in the United States, they are skeptical about whether the product would succeed, mainly because of declining coffee consumption and the lack of a vending machine network. Also, adoption of the concept by Americans is doubtful.[67] Sunbeam, which generates 30 percent of its sales overseas, was the first to develop the ladies' electric shaver. "Success was substantial," said the Sunbeam chairman, "but when we introduced it in Italy, it failed." His explanation: Italian men like their women with hair on their legs.[68]

The fact that multinational firms produce the same products in different locations may have an impact on consumer perceptions of product risk and quality. If the product is produced in a developing country, for example, the international marketer has to determine whether a well-known brand name can compensate for the concern a customer might feel. The situation may be more complicated for retailers importing from independent producers in developing nations under the retailers' private labels. In general, country-of-origin effects on product perceptions are more difficult to determine since the introduction of hybrid products.

[66] "Hoover: Revamping in Europe to Stem an Earnings Drain at Home," *Business Week,* February 15, 1982, 144–146.

[67] "Coke in Japan Riding High with Georgia Coffee," *Advertising Age,* March 19, 1984, 48–52.

[68] Anne Helming, "Culture Shock," *Advertising Age,* May 17, 1982, M-8, M-9.

TABLE 16.2

Factors Affecting the Choice between
Concentration and Diversification Strategies

Factor	Diversification	Concentration
Market growth rate	Low	High
Sales stability	Low	High
Sales response function	Decreasing	Increasing
Competitive lead time	Short	Long
Spillover effects	High	Low
Need for product adaptation	Low	High
Need for communication adaptation	Low	High
Economies of scale in distribution	Low	High
Extent of constraints	Low	High
Program control requirements	Low	High

Source: Igal Ayal and Jehiel Zif, "Marketing Expansion Strategies in Multinational Marketing," *Journal of Marketing* 43 (Spring 1979): 89. Reprinted from *Journal of Marketing*, published by the American Marketing Association.

Concentration versus Diversification

The marketer will have to make specific product-line decisions in terms of country markets, optimal combinations of product lines and items, and market segments targeted.[69]

In choosing country markets, a company must make decisions beyond those relating to market attractiveness and company position. A market expansion policy will determine the allocation of resources among various markets. The basic alternatives are **concentration** on a small number of markets and **diversification,** which is characterized by growth in a relatively large number of markets. Expansion strategy is determined by market-, mix-, and company-related factors, listed in Table 16.2. Market-related factors determine the attractiveness of the market in the first place. With high and stable growth rates only in certain markets, the firm will likely opt for a concentration strategy, which is often the case for innovative products early in their life cycle. If demand is strong worldwide, as the case may be for consumer goods, diversification may be attractive. If markets respond to marketing efforts at increasing rates, concentration will occur; however, when the cost of market-share points becomes too high, marketers tend to begin looking for diversification opportunities. The uniqueness of the product offering with respect to competition is also a factor in expansion strategy. If lead time over competition is considerable, the decision to diversify may not seem urgent. Very few products, however, afford such a luxury. In many product categories, marketers will be affected by spillover effects. Consider, for example, the impact of satellite channels on advertising in Europe, where ads for a product now reach most of the West European market. The greater the degree to which marketing mix elements can be standardized, the more diversification is probable. Overall savings through economies of scale can then be utilized in marketing efforts. Finally, the objectives and policies of the company itself will guide the decision making on expansion. If extensive interaction is called for with intermediaries and clients, efforts are most likely to be concentrated because of resource constraints.

[69] Susan P. Douglas and C. Samuel Craig, *International Marketing Research* (Englewood Cliffs, NJ: Prentice-Hall, 1983), 298–303.

In determining the optimal combination of products and product lines to be marketed, a firm should consider choices for individual markets as well as transfer of products and brands from one region or market to another. This will often result in a particular country organization marketing product lines and products that are a combination of global, regional, and national brands.

Decisions on specific targeting may result in the choice of a narrowly defined segment in the countries chosen. This is a likely strategy for marketers of specialized products to clearly definable markets, for example, ocean-capable sailing boats. Catering to multiple segments in various markets is typical of consumer-oriented companies that have sufficient resources for broad coverage.

SUMMARY

Globalization has become one of the most important strategy issues for marketing managers in the 1990s. Many forces, both external and internal, are driving companies to globalize by expanding and coordinating their participation in foreign markets. The approach is not standardization, however. Marketers may indeed occasionally be able to take identical technical and marketing concepts around the world, but most often, concepts must be customized to local tastes. Internally, companies must make sure that country organizations around the world are ready to launch global products and programs as if they had been developed only for their markets.

In product development, multinational corporations are increasingly striving toward finding common denominators to rationalize worldwide production. This is achieved through careful coordination of the product-development process by worldwide or regional development teams. No longer is the parent company the only source of new products. New-product ideas emerge throughout the system and are developed by the entity most qualified to do so.

The global marketer's product line is not the same worldwide. The standard line items are augmented by local items or localized variations of products to better cater to the unique needs of individual markets. External variables such as competition and regulations often determine the final composition of the line and how broadly it is marketed.

Questions for Discussion

1. What is the danger in oversimplifying the globalization approach? Would you agree with the statement that "if something is working in a big way in one market, you better assume it will work in all markets"?

2. How can a company's product line reflect the maxim "think globally, act locally"?

3. What impact will the fact that products are now introduced, upgraded, and distributed at ever-increasing speeds have on a company's decision to globalize?

4. Will a globally oriented company have an advantage over a multidomestic, or even a domestic, company in the generation of new-product ideas?

5. What factors should be considered when deciding on the location of research and development facilities?

6. What factors make product testing more complicated in the international marketplace?

7. What are the benefits of a coordinated global product launch? What factors will have to be taken into consideration before the actual launch?

8. Assess the pros and cons of the product portfolio approach in making product-line decisions.

Recommended Readings

Davidson, William H. *Global Strategic Management.* New York: Wiley, 1982.

Bartos, Rena. *Marketing to Women around the World.* Cambridge, MA: Harvard Business Press, 1989.

The Economist Intelligence Unit. *151 Checklists for Global Management.* New York: The Economist Intelligence Unit, 1993.

Foster, Richard. *Innovation: The Attacker's Advantage.* New York: Summit Books, 1986.

Kaynak, Erdener, ed. *The Global Business.* Binghamton, NY: Haworth Press, 1992.

Kotabe, Masaaki. *Global Sourcing Strategy: R&D, Manufacturing, and Marketing Interfaces.* Greenwich, CT: Greenwood Publishing Group, 1992.

Makridakis, Spyros G. *Forecasting, Planning, and Strategy for the 21st Century.* New York: Free Press, 1990.

Marton, Katherin. *Multinationals, Technology, and Industrialization.* Lexington, MA: Lexington Books, 1986.

Prahalad, C. K., and Yves L. Doz. *The Multinational Mission: Balancing Local and Global Vision.* New York: Free Press, 1987.

Still, Richard R., and John S. Hill. "Multinational Product Planning: A Meta-Market Analysis." *International Marketing Review* 2 (Spring 1985): 54–64.

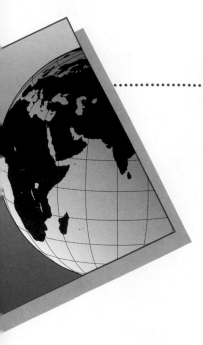

CHAPTER 17

The International Marketing of Services

THE INTERNATIONAL MARKETPLACE

U.S. Companies at Your Service

American companies that do not make a thing are turning the United States into an export powerhouse. They are doing it through something economists say is "invisible" because often it cannot be seen or touched. The "invisible" something is trade in services that, until recently, has been systematically under-reported. Even today's more accurate figures can be misleading. Unlike cars, VCRs, or airplanes, an engineering firm's exports or the money earned by a consultant abroad are not easily captured or quantified. Some services exports do not even seem like exports at all. For example, the money spent by foreign tourists in the United States generated almost $20 billion in 1992, and foreign enrollment in U.S. universities accounted for more than $5 billion.

A close look at the service trade figures shows an interesting picture. According to the Department of Commerce, the U.S. companies that sell services produced a trade surplus of more than $56 billion in 1992, up from only $6 billion in 1986. Allen Sinai, an economist with Lehman Brothers, predicts the surplus will grow to almost $200 billion by the year 2000.

Why is the United States such a force in services? Much of it has to do with the way U.S. services providers have been conditioned in their own domestic market. "In the U.S. we expect good service. That has forced U.S. companies to cater to it, and that is why we bring value," says Jan Neels, president of Pacific Telesis International. Many American companies dominate services markets abroad because they treat customers better than foreign rivals do.

Another advantage U.S. services companies have is their long experience with problems that other countries are just beginning to face. For example, U.S. environmental regulations have spawned a huge waste-handling industry that is nonexistent in most other parts of the world. Taking advantage of this situation, the U.S. giant Waste Management Inc. now operates in 20 foreign nations and has a 15-year contract with Hong Kong to process all of its industrial waste.

Experience with complicated legal and tax systems at home has provided a similar advantage to U.S. law and accounting firms abroad. The world's largest law firm, Chicago-based Baker and McKenzie, has over half of its 1,651 attorneys working overseas. While the firm started to go international in order to serve its U.S. clients wherever they operated, it now advises many foreign clients at home and abroad. The firm is now represented in all the major capitals of the world.

Source: Adapted from Ralph T. King, Jr., "U.S. Service Exports Are Growing Rapidly, but Almost Unnoticed," *The Wall Street Journal,* April 21, 1993, A1, A6.

The international marketing of services is becoming a major component of world business. As The International Marketplace 17.1 shows, all types of services are marketed globally. This chapter will highlight marketing dimensions that are specific to services, with particular attention given to their international aspects. A definition of services will be provided, followed by a discussion of the differences between the marketing of services and of products. The role of services in the U.S. economy and in the world economy will then be discussed. The chapter will explore the opportunities and new problems that have arisen from the increase in international services marketing, focusing particularly on the worldwide transformations of industries as a result of profound changes in the environment and in technology. The strategic responses to these transformations by both governments and firms will be described. Finally, the chapter will outline the initial steps that firms need to undertake in order to offer services internationally—and will look at the future of international services marketing.

DIFFERENCES BETWEEN SERVICES AND PRODUCTS

We rarely contemplate or analyze the precise role of services in our lives. Services often accompany products, but they are also, by themselves, an increasingly important part of our economy, domestically and internationally. One writer has contrasted services and products by stating that "a good is an object, a device, a thing; a service is a deed, a performance, an effort."[1] This definition, although quite general, captures the essence of the difference between products and services. Services tend to be more intangible, personalized, and custom-made than products. Services are also often marketed differently from products. While products are typically distributed to the customer, services can be transferred across borders or originated abroad, and the service provider can be transferred to the customer or the customer can be transferred to the service territory.

---

[1] Leonard L. Berry, "Services Marketing Is Different," in *Services Marketing,* ed. Christopher H. Lovelock (Englewood Cliffs, NJ: Prentice-Hall, 1984), 30.

Services are the fastest-growing sector of world trade, and U.S. service firms in particular have been consistently able to increase their world market share.[2] These major differences add dimensions to services that are not present in products and thus call for a major differentiation.

Linkage between Services and Products

Services may complement products; at other times, products may complement services. Offering products that are in need of substantial technological support and maintenance may be useless if no proper assurance for service can be provided. For this reason, the initial contract of sale often includes the service dimension. This practice is frequent in aircraft sales. When an aircraft is purchased, the buyer contracts not only for the physical product—namely, the plane—but often also for training of personnel, maintenance service, and the promise of continuous technological updates. Similarly, the sale of computer hardware is critically linked to the availability of proper servicing and software.

This linkage between products and services often makes international marketing efforts quite difficult. A foreign buyer, for example, may wish to purchase helicopters and contract for service support over a period of ten years. If the sale involves a U.S. firm, both the product and the service sale will require an export license. Such licenses, however, are issued only for an immediate sale. Therefore, over the ten years, the seller will have to apply for an export license each time service is to be provided. Because the issuance of a license is often dependent on the political climate, the buyer and the seller are haunted by uncertainty. As a result, sales may be lost to firms in countries that can unconditionally guarantee the long-term supply of product-supporting services.

Services can be just as dependent on products. For example, an airline that prides itself on providing an efficient reservation system and excellent linkups with rental cars and hotel reservations could not survive without its airplanes. As a result, many offerings in the marketplace consist of a combination of products and services. A graphic illustration of the tangible and intangible elements in the market offering of an airline is provided in Figure 17.1.

The simple knowledge that services and products interact, however, is not enough. Successful managers must recognize that different customer groups will frequently view the service/product combination differently. The type of use and usage conditions will also affect evaluations of the market offering. For example, the intangible dimension of "on-time arrival" by airlines may be valued differently by college students than by business executives. Similarly, a 20-minute delay will be judged differently by a passenger arriving at his or her final destination than by one who has just missed an overseas connection. As a result, adjustment possibilities in both the service and the product area can be used as a strategic tool to stimulate demand and increase profitability. As Figure 17.2 shows, service and product elements may vary substantially. The marketer must identify the role of each and adjust all of them to meet the desires of the target customer group. By rating the offerings on a scale ranging from dominant tangibility to dominant intangibility, the marketer can obtain a mechanism for comparison between offerings and also information for subsequent market positioning strategies.

---

[2] *Services: Statistics on International Transactions 1970–1989,* Organization for Economic Cooperation and Development, Paris, 1992.

Tangible and Intangible Offerings of Airlines   **FIGURE 17.1**

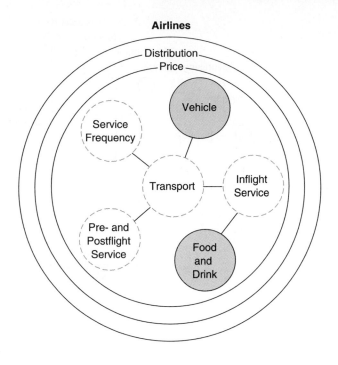

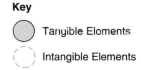

Source: G. Lynn Shostack, "Breaking Free from Product Marketing," in *Services Marketing*, ed. Christopher H. Lovelock (Englewood Cliffs, NJ: Prentice-Hall, 1984), 40.

Stand-Alone Services

Services do not always come in unison with products. Increasingly, they compete against products and become an alternative offering. For example, rather than buy an in-house computer, the business executive can contract computing work to a local or foreign service firm. Similarly, the purchase of a car (a product) can be converted into the purchase of a service by leasing the car from an agency.

Services may also compete against each other. As an example, a store may have the option of offering full service to consumers who purchase there or of converting to the self-service format. Only checkout services may be provided by the store, with consumers engaging in other activities such as selection, transportation, and sometimes even packaging and pricing.

Services differ from products most strongly in their **intangibility:** They are frequently consumed rather than possessed. Even though the intangibility of services is a primary differentiating criterion, it is not always present. For example, publishing services ultimately result in a tangible product, namely, a book or an article. Similarly,

| FIGURE 17.2 | Scale of Elemental Dominance |

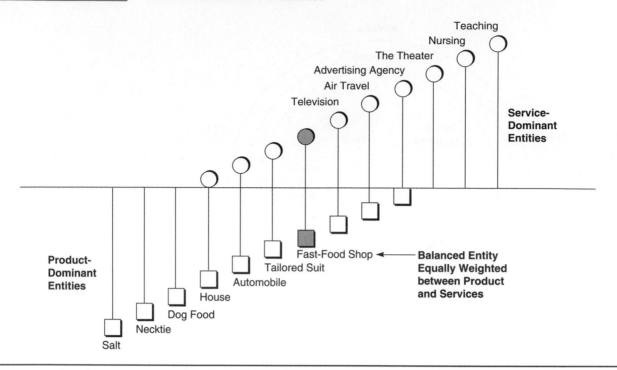

Source: G. Lynn Shostack, "How to Design a Service," in *Marketing of Services,* eds. J. Donnelly and W. George, 1981, p. 222, published by the American Marketing Association.

construction services eventually result in a building, a subway, or a bridge. Even in those instances, however, the intangible component that leads to the final product is of major concern to both the producer of the service and the recipient of the ultimate output because it brings with it major considerations that are nontraditional to products.

One major difference concerns the storing of services. Because of their nature, services are difficult to inventory. If they are not used, the "brown around the edges" syndrome tends to result in high services **perishability.** Unused capacity in the form of an empty seat on an airplane, for example, becomes nonsaleable quickly. Once the plane has taken off, selling an empty seat is virtually impossible—except for an in-flight upgrade from coach to first class—and the capacity cannot be stored for future usage. Similarly, the difficulty of inventorying services makes it troublesome to provide service backup for peak demand. To maintain **service capacity** constantly at levels necessary to satisfy peak demand would be very expensive. The marketer must therefore attempt to smooth out demand levels in order to optimize the use of capacity.

For many service offerings, the time of production is very close to or even simultaneous with the time of consumption. This fact points toward close **customer involvement** in the production of services. Customers frequently either service themselves or cooperate in the delivery of services. As a result, the service provider often needs to be physically present when the service is delivered. This physical presence creates both problems and opportunities, and it introduces a new constraint that is seldom present in the marketing of products. For example, close interaction with the customer requires a much

A Culturally Sensitive Telephone Number   FIGURE 17.3

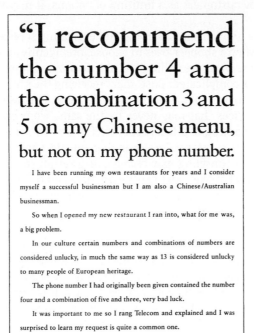

> **"I recommend the number 4 and the combination 3 and 5 on my Chinese menu, but not on my phone number.**
>
> I have been running my own restaurants for years and I consider myself a successful businessman but I am also a Chinese/Australian businessman.
>
> So when I opened my new restaurant I ran into, what for me was, a big problem.
>
> In our culture certain numbers and combinations of numbers are considered unlucky, in much the same way as 13 is considered unlucky to many people of European heritage.
>
> The phone number I had originally been given contained the number four and a combination of five and three, very bad luck.
>
> It was important to me so I rang Telecom and explained and I was surprised to learn my request is quite a common one.
>
> And they even helped me choose a new number which ends with a combination of lucky numbers, so I don't have to tell you how business is."
>
> So much better.   Telecom Australia

Source: *The Sydney Morning Herald,* June 16,1992.

greater understanding of and emphasis on the cultural dimension. A good service delivered in a culturally unacceptable fashion is doomed to failure. Sensitivity to culture, beliefs, and preferences is imperative in the services industry. In some instances, the need to be sensitive to diverse customer groups in domestic markets can assist a company greatly in preparing for international market expansion. Figure 17.3 provides an example of such a situation. A common pattern of internationalization for service businesses is therefore to develop stand-alone business systems in each country. At the same time, however, some services have become "delocalized" as advances in modern technology have made it possible for firms to delink production and service processes and switch labor-intensive service performance to countries where qualified, low-cost labor is plentiful.

The close interaction with customers also points toward the fact that services often are custom-made. This contradicts the desire of a firm to standardize its offering; yet at the same time, it offers the service provider an opportunity to differentiate the service from the competition. The concomitant problem is that in order to fulfill customer expectations, **service consistency** is required. As with anything offered on-line, however, consistency is difficult to maintain over the long run. The human element in the service offering therefore takes on a much greater role than in the product offering. Errors can enter the system, and nonpredictable individual influences can affect the outcome of the service delivery. The issue of quality control affects the provider as well as the recipient of services. In fact, efforts to increase such control through uniform service may sometimes be perceived by customers as a limiting of options. It may therefore have a negative market effect.[3]

Buyers have more problems in observing and evaluating services than products. This is particularly true when a shopper tries to choose intelligently among service providers. Even when sellers of services are willing and able to provide more **market transparency,** the buyer's problem is complicated: Customers receiving the same service may use it differently and service quality may vary for each delivery. This aspect of **service heterogeneity** results in services that may never be the same from one delivery to another. For example, the counseling of a teacher, even if it is provided on the same day by the same person, may vary substantially depending on the student. Over time, even for the same student, the counseling may change. As a result, service offerings are not directly comparable, which makes quality measurements quite challenging. Therefore, the reputation of the service provider plays an overwhelming role in the customer choice process.

Services often require entirely new forms of distribution. Traditional channels are often multitiered and long and therefore slow. They often cannot be used because of the perishability of services. A weather news service, for example, either reaches its audience quickly or rapidly loses its value. As a result, direct delivery and short distribution channels are often required. When they do not exist—which is often the case domestically and even more so internationally—service providers need to be distribution innovators in order to reach their market.

All these aspects of services exist in both international and domestic settings. However, their impact takes on greater importance for the international marketer. For example, because of the longer distances involved, service perishability that may be an obstacle in domestic business becomes a barrier internationally. Similarly, the issue of quality control for international services may be much more difficult to deal with due to different service uses, changing expectations, and varying national regulations.

Because services are delivered directly to the user, they are frequently much more sensitive to cultural factors than are products. Sometimes their influence on the individual may even be considered with hostility abroad. For example, the showing of U.S. films in cinemas or television abroad is often attacked as an imposition of U.S. culture. National leaders who place strong emphasis on national cultural identity frequently denounce foreign services and attempt to hinder their market penetration. Similarly, services are subject to many political vagaries occurring almost daily. Yet, as The International Marketplace 17.2 shows, coping with these changes can become the competitive advantage of the service provider.

THE ROLE OF SERVICES IN THE U.S. ECONOMY

Since the industrial revolution, the United States has seen itself as a primary international competitor in the area of production of goods. In the past few decades, however, the U.S. economy has increasingly become a service economy, as Figure 17.4 shows. The service sector now produces 68 percent of U.S. GNP and employs 79 percent of the work force.[4] The service sector accounts for most of the growth in total nonfarm employment:

---

[3] G. Lynn Shostack, "Service Positioning through Structural Change," *Journal of Marketing* 51 (January 1987): 38.

[4] "Summary of the Service Economy," *The Service Economy,* 7 no. 4, 1993, 15.

THE INTERNATIONAL MARKETPLACE   17.2

The Privilege of Membership Services

Membership has its privileges, even for hostages. As soon as Iraqi tanks invaded Kuwait in 1990, most bank card companies offering Visa and Mastercard immediately froze the accounts of all Kuwaitis. Those fortunate enough to have American Express cards or traveler's checks had no such problem. Even hostages inside Iraq and Kuwait could use their American Express cards or traveler's checks.

"We will probably lose a little money there, but it's worth it," said Richard Thoman, president of American Express International, reflecting on a philosophy that started well before Saddam Hussein's attack. American Express continued to provide service to customers during the aftermath of Mexico City's 1985 earthquake and during the U.S. invasion of Panama in 1989. During the 1989 student protests in Tiananmen Square, the local American Express office lost only one hour of service.

Ten million foreigners hold American Express cards—1 million in Japan, 5 million in Europe, and 4 million in Asia and Latin America. This represents 40 percent of the 25 million outstanding cards.

American Express Travel Related Services Group (TRS) offers charge cards and traveler's checks. Ten years ago, 90 percent of TRS International's profits came from U.S. citizens traveling abroad. Now, about 85 percent of its earnings comes from spending by foreigners using the services in their own countries.

Other international efforts include the $17-billion (in assets) American Express Bank, which services affluent customers from 83 offices in 39 countries. Consumer Financial Services, AmEx' newest overseas division, sells insurance, investment, and lending products.

Aggressive international marketing produced a 17 percent increase in American Express cardholders abroad, compared with only 9 percent domestically in 1990. These foreign growth rates are magnified in their effect on the bottom line. Foreign cardholders generally contribute more to company earnings because of lower delinquency rates.

Source: "Privileged Plastic," *Forbes*, January 7, 1991, 158.

Out of the approximately 19 million new workers added to the total U.S. employment payroll during the period from 1982 to 1989, for example, the service sector employed roughly 17.1 million, compared with approximately 1.9 million for the manufacturing sector.[5] Between 1959 and 1990, employment in the U.S. business and personal services sector almost tripled, while employment in the goods-producing industries increased only by 22 percent.[6] In excess of 45 percent of the average U.S. family's budget is spent on services.[7]

[5] Samuel D. Kahan, "The Service Economy—At Present, Employment Tells the Whole Story," *The Service Economy*, April 1990, 1.

[6] Jack E. Triplett, "Economic Concepts for Economic Classifications—Changes for the Future," *The Service Economy*, 7 no. 4, 1993, 1–6.

[7] Berry, "Services Marketing Is Different," 29.

FIGURE 17.4   **Employment in Industrial Sectors as a Percentage of the Total Labor Force**

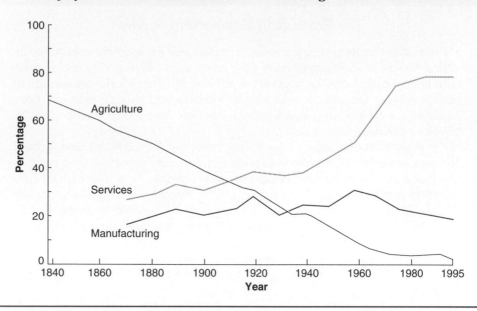

Source: J. B. Quinn, "The Impacts of Technology on the Services Sector," *Technology and Global Industry: Companies and Nations in the World Economy,* © 1987 by the National Academy of Sciences, Washington, D.C. Reprinted with permission.

Of course, only a limited segment of the total range of services is sold internationally. Federal, state, and local government employees, for example, sell few of their services to foreigners. U.S. laundries and restaurants only occasionally service foreign tourists. However, many service industries that do market abroad often have at their disposal large organizations, specialized technology, or advanced professional expertise. Strength in these characteristics has enabled the United States to become the world's largest exporter of services. Total U.S. services exported grew from $6 billion in 1958 to more than $158 billion in 1993,[8] with services exports nearly doubling in the five years from 1988 to 1993.[9] The contribution of services to the balance of payments is highlighted in Table 17.1. It shows that the U.S. services trade balance is producing a substantial surplus and makes up for a large part of the huge deficits in merchandise trade.

International service trade has had very beneficial results for many firms and industries. Citibank, for example, receives 65 percent of its total revenues from foreign operations; the top ten U.S. advertising agencies earn 51 percent of their total billings abroad. The ten largest management consulting firms derive a substantial volume of their revenue from international sources, as Table 17.2 shows. After many years of increasing activity by foreign insurance companies in the United States, U.S. firms are now aggressively beginning to enter the $1.4-trillion world insurance market. The International

[8] U.S. Department of Commerce, Bureau of Economic Analysis, *Survey of Current Business* (Washington, D.C.: U.S. Government Printing Office, March 1994): 15.

[9] U.S. Department of Commerce, *U.S. Industrial Outlook 1994* (Washington D.C.: U.S. Government Printing Office, 1994), 1.

U.S. Balances of Trade in Goods and Services, 1993 (in billions)

TABLE 17.1

Exports of Goods and Services		$596.4
Goods		438.2
As a percentage of total exports	73.5%	
Services		158.2
As a percentage of total exports	26.5	
Imports of Goods and Services		$675.7
Goods		572.3
As a percentage of total imports	84.7	
Services		103.3
As a percentage of total imports	15.3	
Balance on Goods Trade		−134.1
Balance on Services		+54.9
Balance on Goods and Services		−79.2

Source: U.S. Department of Commerce, Bureau of Economic Analysis, *Survey of Current Business,* March 1994: 15.

The Ten Largest Management Consulting Firms (by gross revenue, millions of dollars)

TABLE 17.2

Firm	Worldwide	U.S.
Andersen Consulting	2,720	1,250
McKinsey & Co.	1,200	480
Coopers & Co.	1,126	485
Ernst & Young	981	593
Mercer Consulting Group	908	581
KPMG Peat Marwick	829	324
Deloitte & Touche	825	502
Price Waterhouse	736	355
Towers Perrin	641	454
Booz-Allen & Hamilton	610	457

Source: *Consultants News,* Fitzwilliam, N.H., July 1993.

Marketplace 17.3 provides an example. Exports are a major component of 19 service industries, as shown in Table 17.3.

Large international growth, however, is not confined to U.S. service firms. The import of services into the United States is also increasing dramatically. In 1993, the United States imported more than $103 billion worth of services.[10] Competition in international services is rising rapidly at all levels. Hong Kong, Singapore, and Western Europe are increasingly active in service industries such as banking, insurance, and advertising. Years ago, U.S. construction firms could count on a virtual monopoly for large-scale construction projects. Today, firms from South Korea, Italy, and other countries are taking a major share of the international construction business. Partly due to this rising competition, Bechtel, a large U.S. construction firm, saw its annual

---

[10] U.S. Department of Commerce, *Survey of Current Business,* March 1994: 15.

17.3

THE INTERNATIONAL MARKETPLACE

Servicing the Chinese Market

American International Group Inc. (AIG) is the only foreign insurance company in China selling directly to Chinese citizens. The People's Republic of China, a communist nation with one-fifth of the world's population, has traditionally prohibited any such operations but is now beginning to make historic changes by opening up at least parts of the massive Chinese market to free enterprise. AIG's presence illustrates these changes. While foreign manufacturers have been active in China for some time, helping fuel recent growth, Beijing officials call AIG's presence an "experiment" to see whether service companies can also help China develop. If these policymakers are satisfied with AIG, its operating license will be extended to other high-potential areas outside Shanghai.

"We are optimistic about the potential for AIG in China," says Maurice R. Greenberg, the company's chairman. "In the long term, China will be reaching out for what is commonplace elsewhere. The people will want to buy life, education, and all other policies." So far, the service firm's results have agreed with the chairman. In just eight months, AIG has sold more than 12,000 policies. In one sale, the manager of a produce distributor bought policies for all 12 employees. The state system pays only five yuan a day toward hospital fees, half the cost, while the AIG plan pays 60, part of which is for lost compensation. In light of these figures, the manager decided he needed extra protection. AIG is enthusiastic to be inside the Chinese market. "There is so much business in China," says Ernest Stempel, vice chairman for life insurance. "It's a young population and so few are insured."

However AIG fares in the long run, the very fact that it has a shot is witness to China's reforms. In the not-to-too-distant past, it would have been preposterous to contend that foreign stockbrokers, merchant bankers, accountants, and insurance people could play a direct role in this all-important market. China was seen almost exclusively as a source of cheap toys and textiles. Accountants are hopeful that as Chinese industries enter global markets, improved accounting services will be on the top of their list. When Chinese companies raise capital, firms such as Merrill Lynch will want to underwrite the offerings and sell shares directly to Chinese investors. One U.S. freight-forwarding company is equally hopeful for the opportunity to operate a trucking line in China, if and when such operations are permitted.

Source: Robert Keatley, "AIG Sells Insurance in Shanghai, Testing Service Firm's Role, *The Wall Street Journal*, July 21, 1993, A1, A9.

revenues in the 1980s dwindle from over $14 billion to less than $6 billion.[11] Although the United States has long been recognized as the leader in software development, U.S. businesses are increasingly routing their software projects to India, China, and Eastern Europe.[12]

---

[11] Speech by Stephen D. Bechtel, Georgetown University, October 9, 1991.

[12] Richard Brandt, "Can the U.S. Stay Ahead in Software?" *Business Week*, March 11, 1991, 98–101.

	Major U.S. Exporters of Services, by Industry	**TABLE 17.3**

Accounting	Health care
Advertising	Hospital management
Architecture	Insurance
Banking and other financial services	Leasing
Communications	Legal
Computers	Lodging
Construction and engineering	Management and catering
Education and training	Management consulting
Equipment maintenance and repair	Publishing
Franchising	

THE ROLE OF INTERNATIONAL SERVICES IN THE WORLD ECONOMY

The rise of the service sector is a global phenomenon. Services contribute an average of more than 60 percent to the gross national product of all industrial nations. Even in low-income countries, services account for more than one-third of GNP.[13] In addition, world trade in services has grown much more rapidly than trade in merchandise. As a result, trade in services constitutes about 25 percent of overall world trade and, in some regions, accounts for well above 40 percent of merchandise trade. At the current time, services trade is taking place mainly between the developed countries, with the 13 member nations of the Organization for Economic Cooperation and Development (OECD) alone accounting for the largest portion of total trade. Within these countries, the names of such firms as American Express, McDonald's, Club Med, Thomas Cook, Mitsubishi, and Hilton have become widely familiar. The meteoric rise of these firms internationally, together with the increased service orientation of the developed world, has led to predictions that by the year 2000, more than half of all multinational enterprises will be service corporations.[14]

GLOBAL TRANSFORMATION IN THE SERVICES SECTOR

The rapid rise in international services marketing has been the result of major developments in the business environment and innovations in technology. One primary environmental change that has taken place in the past decade is the reduction of governmental regulation of services. This deregulation is most clearly seen within the United States. In the mid-1970s, a philosophical decision was made to reduce government interference in the marketplace, in the hope that this would enhance competitive activity. As a consequence, some service sectors have benefited, and others have suffered, from the withdrawal of government intervention. The primary deregulated industries in the United States have been transportation, banking, and telecommunications. As a result, new competitors participate in the marketplace. Regulatory changes were initially

---

[13] Valerie A. Zeithaml, A. Parasuraman, and Leonard L. Berry, "Problems and Strategies in Services Marketing," *Journal of Marketing* (Spring 1985): 33–48.

[14] J. J. Boddewyn, Marsha Baldwin Halbric, and A. C. Perry, "Service Multinationals: Conceptualization, Measurement, and Theory," paper presented at the annual meeting of the Academy of International Business, Cleveland, OH, October 1984, 1.

thought to have primarily domestic effects, but they have rapidly spread internationally. For example, the 1984 **deregulation** of AT&T has given rise to competition not only in the United States. Japan's telecommunication monopoly, NT&T, was deregulated in 1985. Partial European deregulation followed in the 1990s.

Similarly, deregulatory efforts in the transportation sector have had international repercussions. New air carriers have entered the market to compete against established trunk carriers and have done so successfully by pricing their services differently both nationally and internationally. In doing so, these airlines also affected the regulatory climate abroad. Obviously, a British airline can count only to a limited extent on government support to remain competitive with new low-priced fares offered by other carriers also serving the British market. As a result, the deregulatory movement has spread internationally, and fostered the emergence of new competition and new competitive practices. Because many of these changes resulted in lower prices, demand stimulation has taken place and has led to a rise in the volume of international services trade.

Another major change has been the decreased regulation of service industries by their industry groups. For example, business practices in fields such as health care, law, and accounting are increasingly becoming more competitive and aggressive. New economic realities require firms in these industries to search for new ways to attract market share. International markets are one frequently untapped possibility for market expansion and have therefore become a prime target for such service firms.

Technological advancement is another major factor in increasing service trade. Progress in technology offers new ways of doing business and permits businesses to expand their horizons internationally. Through computerization, for instance, service exchanges that previously would have been prohibitively expensive are now feasible. For example, Ford Motor Company uses one major computer system to carry out its new car designs in both the United States and Europe. This practice not only lowers expenditures on hardware but also permits better utilization of existing equipment and international design collaboration by allowing design groups in different time zones to use the equipment around the clock. However, this development could take place only after advances in data-transmission procedures.

In a similar fashion, more rapid transmission of data has permitted financial institutions to expand their service delivery through a worldwide network. Again, were it not for advances in technology, such expansion would rarely have been possible or cost efficient.

Another result of these developments is that service industry expansion has not been confined to the traditional services that are labor-intensive and could therefore have been performed better in areas of the world where labor possesses a comparative advantage because of lower prices. Rather, technology-intensive services are becoming the sunrise industries of the 1990s.

INTERNATIONAL TRADE PROBLEMS IN SERVICES

Together with the increase in the importance of service marketing, new problems have beset the service sector. Even though many of these problems have been characterized as affecting mainly the negotiations between nations, they are of sufficient importance to the firm in its international activities to merit a brief review.

Data-Collection Problems

The data collected on service trade are quite poor. Service transactions are often "invisible" statistically as well as physically. The fact that governments have precise data on the number of trucks exported, down to the last bolt, but little information on reinsurance flows reflects past governmental inattention to services.

Only recently has it been recognized that the income generated and the jobs created through the sale of services abroad are just as important as income and jobs resulting from the production and exportation of goods. As a result, many governments are beginning to develop improved measuring techniques for the services sector. For example, the U.S. government has improved its estimates of services by covering more business, professional, and technical services and incorporating improved measurement of telecommunications services and insurance services. New data are also developed on travel and passenger fares, foreign students' expenditures in the United States, repairs and alterations of equipment, and noninterest income of banks.[15]

It is easy to imagine how many data-collection problems are encountered in countries lacking elaborate systems and unwilling to allocate funds for such efforts. The gathering of information is, of course, made substantially more difficult because services are intangible and therefore more difficult to measure and to trace than products. The lack of service homogeneity does not make the task any easier. In an international setting, of course, an additional major headache is the lack of comparability between services categories as used by different national statistical systems.

Insufficient knowledge and information have led to a lack of transparency. As a result, governments have great difficulty gauging the effect of service transactions internationally or influencing service trade. Consequently, international services negotiations progress only slowly, and governmental regulations are often put into place without precise information as to their repercussions on actual trade performance.

U.S. Disincentives to International Services

In spite of its commitment to free trade, the United States has erected and maintained major barriers to international services. These disincentives affect both inbound and outbound services. Barriers to services destined for the U.S. market result mainly from regulatory practices. The fields of banking, insurance, and accounting provide some examples. These industries are regulated at both federal and state levels, and the regulations often pose a formidable barrier to potential entrants from abroad.

The chief complaint of foreign countries is not that the United States discriminates against foreign service providers but rather that the United States places more severe restrictions on them than do other countries. In addition, the entire U.S. regulatory process gives little weight to international policy issues and often operates in isolation from executive branch direction.[16] These barriers are, of course, a reflection of the decision-making process within the U.S. domestic economy and are unlikely to change in the near future. A coherent approach toward international commerce in services is hardly likely to emerge from the disparate decisions of agencies such as the Interstate Commerce Commission (ICC), the Federal Communications Commission (FCC), the Securities and Exchange Commission (SEC), and the many licensing agencies at the state level.

National Regulations of Services Abroad

Obstacles to service trade abroad can be categorized into two major types: barriers to entry and problems in performing services abroad. Governments often justify barriers to entry by reference to **national security** and economic security. For example, the impact of banking on domestic economic activity is given as a reason why banking should be

[15] U.S. Department of Commerce, *Survey of Current Business* (Washington, D.C.: Bureau of Economic Analysis, U.S. Government Printing Office, August 1991), 15.

[16] Gary C. Hufbauer, remarks, Seminar on Services in the World Economy, organized by the United States Council of the International Chamber of Commerce, New York, May 5, 1980, 3.

TABLE 17.4	Selected Barriers to the International Marketing of Services	
Type	**Example**	**Impact**
Tariff	Tax on imported advertising	Discriminates against foreign agencies
	Tax on computer service contracts	Prices international service providers higher than domestic providers which stand alone
	Higher fees for university students from outside the country	Decreases foreign student enrollment
Nontariff		
Buy national policies	U.S. government buying training services from only U.S. companies	Discriminates against foreign suppliers
Prohibit employment of foreigners	Canadian priority to citizens for available jobs	May prevent suppliers from going to buyers
Distance	International business education	May raise cost of bringing supplier to buyer, buyer to supplier
Direct government competition	Indonesian monopoly on telecommunications	Must market services to government
Scarce factors of production	Lack of trained medical workers in Biafra	Limits production of services
Restrictions on service buyers or sellers	North Korea limiting the number of tourists allowed to enter and exit the country	Limits the restricted industry

Source: Adapted from Lee D. Dahringer, "Marketing Services Internationally: Barriers and Management Strategies," *The Journal of Services Marketing,* 5 no. 3 (1991): 5–17.

carried out only by nationals or indeed be operated entirely under government control. Sometimes, the protection of service users is cited, particularly of bank depositors and insurance policyholders. Some countries hold that competition in societally important services is unnecessary, wasteful, and should be avoided. Another justification for barriers is the frequently used **infant industry** argument: "With sufficient time to develop on our own, we can compete in world markets." Often, however, this argument is used simply to prolong the ample licensing profits generated by restricted entry. Impediments to services consist of either tariff or nontariff barriers. Tariff barriers typically restrict or inhibit market entry for the service provider or consumer, while nontariff barriers tend to impede service performance. Table 17.4 shows selected tariff and nontariff barriers. Yet, defining a barrier to service marketing is not always easy. For example, Taiwan gives an extensive written examination to prospective accountants (as do most countries) to ensure that licensed accountants are qualified to practice. Naturally, the examination is given in Chinese. The fact that few U.S. accountants read and write Chinese, and hence are unable to pass the examination, does not necessarily constitute a barrier to trade in accountancy services.[17]

Even if barriers to entry are nonexistent or can be overcome, service companies have difficulty in performing effectively abroad once they have achieved access to the local market. One reason is that rules and regulations based on tradition may inhibit innovation. A more important reason is that governments aim to pursue social or cultural objectives through national regulations. Of primary importance here is the distinction between **discriminatory** and **nondiscriminatory regulations.** Regulations that

---

[17] Dorothy I. Riddle, *Key LDC's: Trade in Services* (Glendale, AZ: American Graduate School of International Studies, March 1987), 346–347.

impose larger operating costs on foreign service providers than on the local competitors, that provide subsidies to local firms only, or that deny competitive opportunities to foreign suppliers are a proper cause for international concern. The discrimination problem becomes even more acute when foreign firms face competition from government-owned or government-controlled enterprises, which are discussed in more detail in a later chapter. On the other hand, nondiscriminatory regulations may be inconvenient and may hamper business operations, but they offer less opportunity for international criticism.

All of these regulations make it difficult for the international service marketer to penetrate world markets. At the governmental level, services frequently are not recognized as a major facet of world trade or are viewed with suspicion because of a lack of understanding, and barriers to entry often result. To make progress in tearing them down, much educational work needs to be done.

GOVERNMENT RESPONSES TO PROBLEMS IN INTERNATIONAL SERVICES MARKETING

U.S. Developments

Greater experience and know-how give the United States a major comparative advantage in the international marketing of services. As a result, the United States has been the country most concerned with international problems in the providing of services. This concern originated in the private sector in the 1960s. International insurance companies began to organize into advisory committees, shortly to be joined by companies in the banking and transportation sectors.

A major boost to this effort occurred when the **Trade Act of 1974** pointedly expanded the definition of international trade to include trade in services, gave the president a mandate to negotiate reduced services barriers, and provided for presidential retaliation against countries that discriminate against U.S. service companies. In 1976, a White House study made a series of recommendations on services issues, including suggestions for international negotiations and government reorganization.[18] In 1978, the U.S. Chamber of Commerce founded its International Services Industry Committee to influence the formulation of policy.

The recommendation to reorganize resulted in 1978 in the creation of an international services division within the U.S. Department of Commerce. However, responsibility for services issues remained far-flung and dispersed across departments such as State, Treasury, and Transportation. The Trade Act of 1979 and trade reorganization plan assigned policy leadership in the area of services trade to the Office of the **United States Trade Representative** (USTR) and created a Services Policy Advisory Committee.

In its international efforts aimed at improving the climate for service trade, the United States has had some success with bilateral negotiations. For many decades, selected services had general coverage in bilateral treaties of Friendship, Commerce, and Navigation. Since 1980, however, specific services negotiations and agreements have been concluded with major trading partners. For example, bilateral negotiations resulted in Japan's lifting of restrictions on U.S. computer service sales. In 1983, the Korean insurance market began to open to foreign firms. In 1984, the banking sector in Japan was opened to foreign participation in offering financial services and syndicated loans. In 1987, U.S. lawyers were permitted to begin operations in Japan.

---

[18] "U.S. Service Industries in World Markets," in "Current Problems in Future Policy Development," White House Interagency Study, December 1976.

In addition, the United States has initiated various steps to strengthen its hand in future international negotiations. Most of these actions consist of threatening retaliation in the event that other nations refuse to liberalize services trade. **The International Banking Act of 1978,** for example, which established a comprehensive federal government role in the regulation of foreign bank participation, directed the government to submit a report to Congress on "the extent to which U.S. banks are denied, whether by law or practice, national treatment in conducting bank operations in foreign countries."[19] Congress has also added reciprocity provisions for services in various fields, with the general thrust that reciprocity should be a significant factor in determining whether and to what extent foreign firms would be able to participate in regulated industries in the United States. Usually this approach demands that for foreign firms to participate in the U.S. market, U.S. firms must have access to the foreign market.

International Developments

One of the early postwar multilateral efforts to liberalize international trade in services was the OECD code on invisible transactions, which in the 1950s removed some barriers to service trade. Within the GATT, the U.S. attempted in the late 1970s, near the end of the **Tokyo Round,** to add service issues to the agenda. However, this move was greeted with international suspicion. Because the United States has the largest service economy and the most service exports, other nations suspected that any liberalization would principally benefit the United States. Moreover, some of the negotiating partners had the same lack of knowledge about services trade that U.S. negotiators had had a few years before.

As a result, services were addressed only to a very limited extent in the Tokyo Round. Until recently, services therefore were covered only in the international trade framework by the **Government Procurement Code** and the **Subsidies and Countervailing Measures Code.** The former covers services only to the extent that they are ancillary to purchases of goods and do not exceed the goods in value. The latter is restricted to services that are ancillary to trade in goods.

In a major breakthrough in Punta del Este in 1986, the major GATT participants agreed to conduct services trade negotiations parallel with product negotiations in the Uruguay Round. These negotiations resulted in the forging of a **General Agreement on Trade in Services (GATS),** the first multilateral, legally enforceable agreement covering trade and investment in the services sector. Similar to earlier agreements in the product sector, GATS provides for most-favored-nation treatment, national treatment, transparency in rule making, and the free flow of payments and transfers. Market-access provisions restrict the ability of governments to limit competition and new-market entry. In addition, sectoral agreements were made for the movement of personnel, telecommunications, and aviation. However, in several sectors, such as financial services and entertainment, no agreement was obtained. In addition, many provisions, due to their newness, are very narrow. Therefore, future negotiations have been agreed upon, which, at five-year intervals, will attempt to improve free trade in services.[20]

The new GATS signifies major progress in recognizing the importance of trade in services. However, it can be expected that substantial improvements will still be necessary in order to allow services to be truly uninhibited internationally. The International Marketplace 17.4 discusses one conflict in services trade that remains unresolved.

---

[19] Geza Feketekuty, "International Trade in Banking Services: The Negotiation Agenda," draft, prepared for the International Law Institute Conference on the International Framework for Money and Banking in the 1980s, Washington, D.C., April 30–May 1, 1981, 8.

[20] Letter from President Clinton to Speaker of the House Tom Foley, Washington D.C., December 15, 1993.

THE INTERNATIONAL MARKETPLACE

17.4

When Entertainment Turns Serious

As the negotiations of the General Agreement on Tariffs and Trade drew to a close in early December of 1993, the hottest issue was not subsidies, dumping, or even agriculture. The focal point of disagreement was the entertainment industry.

The United States generates more than $4 billion annually in exports of films and television programs to Europe and commands two-thirds of its movie market. Some 40 percent of all U.S. film/TV/home video/pay TV revenues are gathered from international markets. Europeans view American programs five billion hours a year, while Americans spend only 180 million hours watching European fare. According to French officials, this American success is derived from U.S. producers exporting at cheap prices, having already made a profit in their home market. European negotiators painted a picture of being overrun by Hollywood productions and American culture. They therefore wanted to retain the right to subsidize film makers, already carried out at $500 million a year, and set quotas on the broadcast of foreign productions.

U.S. negotiators insisted on continued market access and wanted assurances in the GATT that as satellite, cable, and other communications technologies create new ways to deliver entertainment programming in Europe, American companies will not be frozen out by unworkable restrictions.

As the negotiations approached the critical end stage, the United States removed entertainment issues from the bargaining table, rather than risk all the other accomplishments of the GATT talks. President Clinton made the final decision one day before GATT's deadline. French Communications Minister Alain Carignon hailed the exclusion of entertainment issues as "a great and beautiful victory for Europe" and EU Trade Commissioner Leon Brittan declared a victory for Europe's "cultural pluralism." The United States proclaimed a loss for free speech and viewer choice and bemoaned the success of plain protectionism. The bottom line, however, was that the GATT talks were finally finished and the U.S. entertainment industry was left empty-handed.

Yet future trade relations may be somewhat bumpy between the two economic powers. By agreeing to disagree in Geneva, Hollywood gets nothing, but keeps its options open. The United States remains free to use its own trade laws to try to open European markets to U.S. films and television shows, including possible threats of sanctions. Sidney J. Sheinberg, president and chief operating officer at MCA Inc., says it might be appropriate for "us to solicit further counsel from the administration and possibly from Congress."

With the current levels of earnings and potential future profits from new technologies so high, this issue is far from over. The growing globalization of entertainment services is only going to fuel the unresolved problems.

Sources: Peter Behr, "U.S., Europe Reach Trade Agreement," *The Washington Post,* December 15, 1993, A1; Bob Davis and Lawrence Ingrassia, "After Years of Talks, GATT Is at Last Ready to Sign Off on a Pact," *The Wall Street Journal,* December 15, 1993, A1; Bob Davis and Lawrence Ingrassia, "Trade Pact Is Set by 117 Nations, Slashing Tariffs, Subsidies Globally," *The Wall Street Journal,* December 16, 1993, A3; Peter Behr, "Key Agreement Clears Way for Global Trade Pact," *The Washington Post,* December 13, 1993, A1; and David Lawday, "France Guns for Clint Eastwood," *U.S. News and World Report,* December 13, 1993, 72.

CORPORATE INVOLVEMENT IN INTERNATIONAL SERVICES MARKETING

Typical International Services

Although many firms are already active in the international service arena, others often do not perceive their existing competitive advantage. Numerous services have great potential for internationalization.

Financial institutions can offer some functions very competitively internationally in the field of banking services. U.S. banks possess advantages in fields such as mergers and acquisitions, securities sales, and asset management, as Figure 17.5 shows. Banks in Europe and Japan are boosting their leadership through large assets and capital bases, as seen in Table 17.5.

FIGURE 17.5   Financial Services Firm Positions Itself

EN ESPAÑA SOMOS ESPAÑOLES.

IN DEUTSCHLAND SIND WIR DEUTSCHE.

IN AUSTRALIA, WE ARE AUSTRALIAN.

日本では、日本人。

IN CANADA, WE ARE CANADIAN.

IN NEDERLAND ZIJN WE NEDERLANDS.

IN ENGLAND, WE ARE ENGLISH.

IN DER SCHWEIZ SIND WIR SCHWEIZER.

在香港我們是中國人。

IN AMERICA, WE ARE AMERICAN.

DI SINGAPURA KAMI IALAH ORANG SINGAPURA.

EN FRANCE, NOUS SOMMES FRANÇAIS.

AROUND THE WORLD WE ARE THE
CS FIRST BOSTON GROUP.

Announcing a worldwide investment banking firm that draws its strength from established investment banks in the world's financial capitals.

Operating as First Boston in the Americas, Credit Suisse First Boston in Europe and the Middle East, and CS First Boston Pacific in the Far East and Asia, the CS First Boston Group – together with Credit Suisse – offers unparalleled expertise in capital raising, mergers and acquisitions, securities sales, trading and research, asset management, and merchant banking.

So regardless of what language you speak, the words for powerful investment banking are the same all over the world – CS First Boston Group.

| **CS First Boston Group** | First Boston | Credit Suisse First Boston | CS First Boston Pacific |

Source: Courtesy First Boston Corporation.

			The World's 50 Largest Banks			**TABLE 17.5**

Rank 1992	Rank 1991	Company (Country)	Assets ($ millions)	Change from 1991	Capital ($ millions)	Net Income ($ millions)
1	1	Dai-Ichi Kangyo Bank (Japan)	$473,276	− 1.4%	$ 27,485	$ 669
2	3	Sumitomo Bank (Japan)	453,274	− 1.1	30,649	936
3	2	Sakura Bank (Japan)	446,448	− 2.6	28,556	647
4	5	Fuji Bank (Japan)	443,833	− 0.9	34,581	740
5	4	Sanwa Bank (Japan)	437,294	− 3.2	31,200	857
6	6	Mitsubishi Bank (Japan)	425,019	− 0.8	23,391	497
7	9	Credit Lyonnais (France)	350,870	22.1	34,461	− 335
8	11	Norinchukin Bank (Japan)	326,899	16.5	69,380	324
9	7	Industrial Bank (Japan)	321,188	− 1.2	206,378	470
10	10	Deutsche Bank (Germany)	305,002	10.4	42,587	1,108
11	8	Credit Agricole (France)	298,259	3.5	71,433	948
12	14	Banque Nationale de Paris (France)	283,361	9.5	26,974	392
13	12	Tokai Bank (Japan)	267,247	− 4.6	17,411	409
14	16	Mitsubishi Trust & Banking(Japan)*	266,996	− 1.0	8,458	281
15	23	Societe Generale (France)	257,024	16.8	24,499	592
16	15	HSBC Holdings (U.K.)	256,623	− 5.4	21,171	1,850
17	22	Long-Term Credit Bank (Japan)	255,291	6.0	162,722	505
18	20	ABN AMRO Holding (Netherlands)	253,054	10.9	31,985	926
19	13	Sumitomo Trust & Banking (Japan)*	249,978	0.8	8,874	258
20	27	Industrial & Commercial Bank(China)	245,484	28.3	13,691	2,765
21	21	Mitsui Trust & Banking (Japan)*	243,517	1.1	7,958	199
22	18	Bank of Toyko (Japan)	230,787	− 7.3	59,535	323
23	28	Bank of China (China)	227,883	29.7	14,743	2,128
24	17	Barclays (U.K.)	225,936	8.0	15,694	− 520
25	19	Asahi Bank (Japan)	225,406	− 8.3	15,181	303
26	24	National Westminster Bank (U.K.)	216,994	16.8	16,294	329
27	26	Citicorp (U.S.)	211,899	− 1.6	27,284	722
28	29	Compagnie Financiere de Paribas(France)	203,238	8.5	27,099	160
29	31	Dresdner Bank (Germany)	202,834	11.5	34,082	586
30	30	Daiwa Bank (Japan)	201,388	2.9	8,451	253
31	25	Yasuda Trust & Banking (Japan)*	193,822	− 2.2	6,801	186
32	33	Union Bank of Switzerland (Switzerland)	181,919	7.0	28,021	916
33	32	BankAmerica (U.S.)	179,203	− 5.7	31,883	1,492
34	35	Internationale Nederdanden (Netherlands)	177,980	8.7	14,274	921
35	40	Westdeutsche Landesbank (Germany)	168,680	19.2	35,275	141
36	37	Toyo Trust & Banking (Japan)*	163,190	2.0	5,908	145
37	34	Istituto Bancario San Paolo (Italy)	161,972	16.1	41,801	931
38	36	Cencep (France)	161,347	− 0.5	15,195	350
39	42	Bayerische Vereinsbank (Germany)	154,393	10.9	39,281	263
40	46	Agricultural Bank (China)	148,570	26.4	5,829	330
41	41	Commerzbank (Germany)	143,146	2.8	21,059	515
42	43	Nippon Credit Bank (Japan)	141,909	− 1.2	95,960	329

Continued

TABLE 17.5		*Continued*				

Rank		Company (Country)	Assets ($ millions)	Change from 1991	Capital ($ millions)	Net Income ($ millions)
1992	**1991**					
43	50	**Peoples Construction Bank** (China)	$139,790	21.9	$ 6,373	$ 269
44	44	**Chemical Banking** (U.S.)	138,263	0.5	16,225	1,086
45	39	**Swiss Bank** (Switzerland)	136,879	− 2.9	31,550	512
46	48	**Bayerische Hypo-Bank** (Germany)	134,576	13.5	34,510	226
47	52	**Bayerische Landesbank** (Germany)	131,129	15.0	25,209	270
48	47	**Rabobank** (Netherlands)	127,927	7.2	17,792	561
49	45	**DG Bank** (Germany)	126,746	0.4	23,779	29
50	51	**Bank Melli** (Iran)	124,789	25.5	693	125

Ranked by assets as determined by Worldscope; figures are based on each company's 1992 fiscal year results.

In millions of U.S. dollars at Dec. 31, 1992, exchange rates, percentage change based on home currency.

Note: For comparative purposes, assets are calculated without customer acceptance and loan-loss reserves. Capital includes long-term debt, nonequity reserves, minority interest, and shareholders' equity; and may include short-term debt where not able to separate.

*Assets

Source: "The World's 50 Largest Banks," *The Wall Street Journal,* September 24, 1993, R27. Reprinted by permission of The Wall Street Journal © 1993 Dow Jones and Company, Inc. All rights reserved worldwide.

Another area with great international potential is construction, design, and engineering services. Economies of scale can be effected not only for machinery and material but also for areas such as personnel management and the overall management of projects. Particularly for international projects that are large-scale and long-term, the experience advantage could weigh heavily in favor of U.S. firms. The economic significance of these services far exceeds their direct turnover because they encourage subsequent demand for capital goods. For example, having an engineering consultant of a certain nationality increases the chances that contracts for the supply of equipment, technology, and know-how will be won by an enterprise of the same nationality, given the advantages enjoyed in terms of information, language, and technical specification.[21]

Firms in the fields of legal and accounting services can aid their domestic clients abroad through support activities; they can also aid foreign firms and countries in improving business and governmental operations. In the field of computer and data services, international potential is rapidly growing. Knowledge of computer operations, data manipulations, data transmission, and data analysis are insufficiently exploited internationally by many small and medium-sized firms.

Similarly, communication services may encounter substantial future international market opportunities. For example, activities in the areas of video text, home banking, and home shopping may be valuable abroad, particularly where geographic obstacles make the establishment of retail outlets cumbersome and expensive. Figure 17.6 provides an example.

Many U.S. organizations have vast experience in the field of teaching services. Both the educational and the corporate sector, which largely have concentrated their work in the domestic market, have expertise in management motivation as well as the teaching

---

[21] "Engineering, Technical, and Other Services to Industry," Synthesis Report, Organization for Economic Cooperation and Development, Paris, 1988.

More International Marketing Requires More International Communication   **FIGURE 17.6**

The difference between international lines and international service.

If your business is crossing into foreign markets without AT&T, you might be working without a net. The fact is, nobody has more ways to help an international business.

We have the Export Hotline, which can help you discover and explore new markets for your products by providing you—free of charge—with insightful information on more than 50 industries throughout more than 75 countries. You pay only the transmission cost to your fax machine.

For more information call
1 800 222-0900

We have AT&T **Favorite Nation Option**,* a discount program that gives you savings on calls to the two countries you call the most each month—automatically.

We have AT&T **CustomNet**℠ **FAX** Option which offers some of the lowest prices in the industry for direct-dial international faxes under three minutes.

And if you're calling Japan, Hong Kong or the Philippines, there's AT&T **International Advanced FAX** Service, which offers access to special international digital phone lines which are constantly monitored to ensure higher quality and speed.

So if you want high-quality international phone service, call AT&T. Because your business is too important to leave hanging by a thread.

AT&T. Far and Away. The Best in the Business.℠

AT&T

Source: *The Wall Street Journal,* January 5, 1994, A7.

Education: A Prized Service in Trade

The former Soviet Union has the military capabilities and natural resources of a world power, yet its economy is little above that of the Third World. Bank checking is largely unknown, nearly all transactions are conducted in cash, and recently started electronic bank transfers take 30 days. With the official rejection of communism and its antimarket philosophy, and with the apparent move toward Western economic practices, Russia and other states are in desperate need of training that will bring them into the realm of market-oriented economics and late twentieth century financial know-how.

This business education is already under way, due in large part to U.S.-Russian partnerships. The U.S. Treasury Department is participating in an educational program in Moscow in which the focus is on banking, finance, and money management. In another partnership in eastern Russia, the University of Maryland is undertaking what officials believe to be the most ambitious educational effort an American university has ever attempted in this country—preparing managers for an evolving market system. These and other U.S. education providers are among the most capable and experienced in the world. With worldwide opportunities, these educators' services are extremely valuable.

A team of Treasury Department officials including Virginia Harter, who oversees 800 million government payments a year, is holding training sessions for nearly 100 Russians including representatives from the Finance Ministry, business owners, and executives from large industrial enterprises. The workshops encompass everything from elementary accounting procedures to reading financial statements to defining securities. One session was designed as a mock bank visit, during which the Russians filled out mortgage application forms, and the instructors, acting as loan officers, reviewed them.

When Treasury official Harter first arrived in Moscow, she could not believe the financial infrastructure: "It is 35 to 40 years behind ours, if not more; on one hand that was really surprising. . . on the other, it made us feel that we can really give them some knowledge that they need." Among other benefits, the educational effort should help Russians better manage the aid flowing from the West.

The University of Maryland is the only American college granting undergraduate degrees in Russia. At the program's two Russian universities, Maryland faculty are responsible for all instruction during the students' third and fourth years. Courses include information systems, office automation, organizational theory and behavior, and personnel management. At the end of the program, the students are awarded the same degree earned by other off-campus Maryland students.

Despite their dire economic straits, the Russians are willing to cover virtually all costs, with tuition ranging from $10,000 to $15,000 per student. This willingness to come up with scarce and highly prized dollars shows how desperately Russians want the skills that the Maryland program can teach. In nearly all cases, Russian businesses or regional governments pay tuition for students who are then expected to work two or three years for their sponsors after graduation. This strong support comes from the Russian private sector's "own enlightened self-interest," explains a program official. He adds, "They expect to get out of this employees who understand international economics and business and will be able to help them do international trade."

Sources: Arnold R. Isaacs, "Learning to Deal in Amerikanski," *The Washington Post Education Review,* August 1, 1993, 10, 12; Gary Lee, "Finance 101: Rubles and Sense," *The Washington Post,* July 6, 1993, A13.

of operational, managerial, and theoretical issues. As the International Marketplace 17.5 shows, existence of knowledge and the teaching of such knowledge can be in very high demand abroad.

In the same vein, management consulting services can be provided by firms to many foreign institutions and corporations. Of particular value could be management expertise in areas where U.S. firms maintain global leadership, such as the transportation and logistics sector. Such U.S.-based expertise can be provided by management consulting firms and also by U.S. corporations willing to sell their management experience abroad. Yet consulting services are particularly sensitive to the cultural environment, and their use varies significantly by country and field of consulting.

All service expenditures funded from abroad by foreign citizens also represent a service export. This makes tourism an increasingly important area of services trade. Every foreign visitor who spends foreign currency in the United States contributes to an improvement in the current account. With the value of the dollar declining, and given the vast natural resources and beauty offered by the United States, tourism services may well become a key U.S. export factor. For example, on a regional basis in the United States, tourism is the largest employer in 13 states. Table 17.6 provides an overview of the

Origin of and Spending by International Visitors to the United States, 1992–1995				**TABLE 17.6**

Origin of International Visitors to the United States, 1992–1995 (in thousands of visits)				
County or Region	**1992**	**1993**[1]	**1994**[2]	**1995**[2]
Canada	18,598	17,520	17,430	17,478
Mexico	8,258	9,249	10,239	11,293
Mexico[3]	1,344	1,493	1,618	1,750
Europe	8,262	8,922	9,749	10,669
France	795	826	862	896
Germany	1,692	1,947	2,268	2,650
Italy	590	595	620	644
Netherlands	342	365	393	422
Spain	344	349	369	385
United Kingdom	2,824	3,078	3,365	3,681
Asia and Middle East	5,470	5,388	5,729	6,117
Japan	3,653	3,325	3,425	3,551
South Korea	341	426	504	591
South America	1,770	2,089	2,381	2,704
Argentina	342	401	476	561
Brazil	475	575	634	688
Venezuela	372	454	538	640
Central America	481	557	626	687
Oceania	655	675	697	720
Australia	487	504	523	542
Africa	150	164	173	183
Caribbean	1,004	1,086	1,154	1,218
Total	44,648	45,648	48,177	51,067

[1]Estimate

[2]Forecast

[3]Airfare only

Continued

TABLE 17.6   *Continued*

	Spending by International Visitors in the United States, 1992–1995 (millions of dollars)			
	Expenditures			
County or Region	**1992**	**1993**[1]	**1994**[2]	**1995**[2]
Japan	9,169	8,647	9,216	9,995
Canada	7,975	7,776	8,015	8,387
Mexico	5,822	6,713	7,672	8,794
United Kingdom	5,478	6,152	6,943	7,899
Germany	3,371	3,991	4,792	5,805
France	1,560	1,672	1,804	1,954
Italy	1,218	1,269	1,368	1,480
Australia	1,180	1,261	1,353	1,461
Venezuela	888	1,112	1,358	1,674
Brazil	891	1,108	1,261	1,423
South Korea	654	838	1,020	1,242
Argentina	656	790	966	1,179
Netherlands	574	632	703	785
Spain	507	531	580	629

[1]Estimate

[2]Forecast

Note: Expenditures represent international visitor spending in the United States and payments to U.S. air carriers for international travel. Detail may not sum to total due to rounding.

Source: U.S. Department of Commerce: U.S. Travel and Tourism Administration (USTTA), Bureau of Economic Analysis; Statistics Canada; Mexico Secretariat of Tourism; Republic of China Tourism Bureau. Estimates and forecasts by USTTA.

countries of origin of international visitors to the United States and the contribution made by these visitors to U.S. service trade. Of sizable impact are also U.S. health services offered to citizens from abroad and U.S. education provided to foreign students. India is increasingly participating in the provision of international data services. Although some aspects of the data field are high-technology intensive, many operations still require skilled human service input. The coding and inputting of data often has to be performed manually because appropriate machine-readable forms may be unavailable or not usable. Because of lower wages, Indian companies can offer data-inputting services at a rate much lower than in more industrialized countries. As a result, data are transmitted in raw form to India, encoded on a proper medium there, and returned to the ultimate user. To some extent, this transformation can be equated to the value-added steps that take place in the transformation of a raw commodity into a finished product. Obviously, using its comparative advantage for this labor-intensive task, India can compete in the field of international services. However, many countries are also becoming providers of software for computer operations, thus moving up on the scale of value-added services.

A proper mix in international services might also be achieved by pairing the strengths of different partners. For example, U.S. information technology could be combined with the financial resources of individuals and countries abroad. The strengths of both partners can then be used to obtain maximum benefits.

Combining international advantages in services may ultimately result in the development of an even newer and more drastic comparative lead. For example, the United

States has an international head start in such areas as high technology, information gathering, information processing, and information analysis and teaching. Ultimately, the major thrust of U.S. international services might not rely on providing these service components individually but rather in ensuring that, based on all U.S. resources, better decisions are made. If better decision making is transferable to a wide variety of international situations, that in itself might become the overriding future comparative advantage of the United States in the international market.

Starting to Market Services Internationally

For services that are delivered mainly in the support of or in conjunction with products, the most sensible approach for the international novice is to follow the path of the product. For years, many large accounting and banking firms have done so by determining where their major multinational clients have set up new operations and then following them. Smaller service marketers who cooperate closely with manufacturing firms can determine where the manufacturing firms are operating internationally. Ideally, of course, it would be possible to follow clusters of manufacturers in order to obtain economies of scale internationally while, at the same time, looking for entirely new client groups abroad.

For service providers whose activities are independent from products, a different strategy is needed. These individuals and firms must search for market situations abroad that are similar to the domestic market. Such a search should concentrate in their area of expertise. For example, a design firm learning about construction projects abroad can investigate the possibility of rendering its design services. Similarly, a management consultant learning about the plans of a foreign country or firm to computerize operations can explore the possibility of overseeing a smooth transition from manual to computerized activities. What is required is the understanding that similar problems are likely to occur in similar situations.

Another opportunity consists of identifying and understanding points of transition abroad. Just as U.S. society has undergone change, foreign societies are subject to a changing domestic environment. If, for example, new transportation services are introduced, an expert in containerization may wish to consider whether to offer service to improve the efficiency of the new system.

Leads for international service opportunities can also be gained by keeping informed about international projects sponsored by domestic organizations such as the U.S. Agency for International Development, as well as international organizations such as the United Nations, the International Finance Corporation, or the World Bank. Very frequently, such projects are in need of support through services. Overall, the international service marketer needs to search for similar situations or similar problems requiring similar solutions in order to formulate an effective international expansion strategy.

Strategic Implications of International Services Marketing

To be successful in the international service offering, the marketer must first determine the nature and the aim of the services offering core—that is, whether the service will be aimed at people or at things and whether the service act in itself will result in tangible or intangible actions. Table 17.7 provides examples of such a classification that will help the marketer to better determine the position of the services effort.

During this determination, the marketer must consider other tactical variables that have an impact on the preparation of the service offering. In the field of research, the measurement of capacity and delivery efficiency often remains highly qualitative rather

| TABLE 17.7 | Understanding the Nature of the Service Act |

Nature of the Service Act	Direct Recipient of the Service	
	People	**Things**
Tangible Actions	Services directed at people's bodies:	Services directed at goods and other physical possessions:
	Health care	Freight transportation
	Passenger transportation	Industrial equipment repair and maintenance
	Beauty salons	Janitorial services
	Exercise clinics	Laundry and dry cleaning
	Restaurants	Landscaping/lawncare
	Haircutting	Veterinary care
Intangible Actions	Services directed at people's minds:	Services directed at intangible assets:
	Education	Banking
	Broadcasting	Legal services
	Information services	Accounting
	Theaters	Securities
	Museums	Insurance

Source: Christopher H. Lovelock, *Managing Services: Marketing, Operations, and Human Resources*, 1988, p. 47, Prentice-Hall, Inc., Englewood Cliffs, New Jersey.

than quantitative. In the field of communications, the intangibility of the service reduces the marketer's ability to provide samples. This makes communicating the service offer much more difficult than communicating a product offer. Brochures or catalogs explaining services often must show a "proxy" for the service in order to provide the prospective customer with tangible clues. A cleaning service, for instance, can show a picture of an individual removing trash or cleaning a window. However, the picture will not fully communicate the performance of the service. Because of the different needs and requirements of individual consumers, the marketer must pay very close attention to the two-way flow of communication. Mass communication must often be supported by intimate one-on-one follow-up.

The role of personnel deserves special consideration in the international marketing of services. Because the customer interface is intense, proper provisions need to be made for training personnel both domestically and internationally. Major emphasis must be placed on appearance. Most of the time, the person delivering the service—rather than the service itself—will communicate the spirit, value, and attitudes of the service corporation.

This close interaction with the consumer will also have organizational implications. Whereas tight control may be desired over personnel, the individual interaction that is required points toward the need for an international decentralization of service delivery. This, in turn, requires delegation of large amounts of responsibility to individuals and service "subsidiaries" and requires a great deal of trust in all organizational units. This trust, of course, can be greatly enhanced through proper methods of training and supervision. Sole ownership also helps strengthen this trust. Research has shown that service firms, in their international expansion, tend to greatly prefer the establishment of full-control ventures. Only when costs escalate and the company-specific advantage diminishes will service firms seek out shared-control ventures.[22]

The areas of pricing and financing require special attention. Because services cannot be stored, much greater responsiveness to demand fluctuation must exist, and, therefore, much greater pricing flexibility must be maintained. At the same time, flexibility is countered by the desire to provide transparency for both the seller and the buyer of services in order to foster an ongoing relationship. The intangibility of services also makes financing more difficult. Frequently, even financial institutions with large amounts of international experience are less willing to provide financial support for international services than for products. The reasons are that the value of services is more difficult to assess, service performance is more difficult to monitor, and services are difficult to repossess. Therefore, customer complaints and difficulties in receiving payments are much more troublesome for a lender to evaluate for services than for products.

Finally, the distribution implications of international services must be considered. Usually, short and direct channels are required. Within these channels, closeness to the customer is of overriding importance in order to understand what the customer really wants, to trace the use of the service, and to aid the consumer in obtaining a truly tailor-made service.

SUMMARY

Services are taking on an increasing importance in international marketing. They need to be considered separately from the marketing of goods because they no longer simply complement products. Often, products complement services or are in competition with them. Because of service attributes such as intangibility, perishability, custom-madeness, and cultural sensitivity, the international marketing of services is frequently more complex than that of goods.

Services play an increasing role in the economy of the United States and other industrialized nations. As a result, international growth and competition in this sector has begun to outstrip that of merchandise trade and is likely to intensify in the future. Even though services are unlikely to replace production, the sector will account for the shaping of new comparative advantages internationally.

The many service firms now operating domestically need to investigate the possibility of going global. The historical patterns in which service providers followed manufacturers abroad have become obsolete as stand-alone services have become more important to world trade. Management must therefore assess its vulnerability to service competition from abroad and explore opportunities to provide its services internationally.

Questions for Discussion

1. Discuss the major reasons for the growth of international services.
2. How does the international sale of services differ from the sale of goods?
3. What are some of the international marketing implications of service intangibility?
4. Discuss the effects of cultural sensitivity on international services.
5. What are some ways for a firm to expand its services internationally?

---

[22] M. Krishna Erramilli and C. P. Rao, "Service Firms' International Entry-Mode Choice: A Modified Transaction-Cost Analysis Approach," *Journal of Marketing* 57 (July 1993): 19–38.

6. Some predict that "the main future U.S. international service will be to offer better decisions." Do you agree? Why or why not?
7. How can a firm in a developing country participate in the international services boom?
8. Which services would be expected to migrate globally in the next decade? Why?

Recommended Readings

Bateson, John E. G. *Managing Services Marketing.* Hinsdale, IL: Dryden Press, 1992.

Berry, Leonard L., David R. Bennett, and Carter W. Brown. *Service Quality.* Homewood, IL: Dow Jones–Irwin, 1989.

Blum, Julius M. "World Trade in Services: Opportunities and Obstacles." In *1985 Proceedings of the Southwestern Marketing Association.* Denton, TX: Southwestern Marketing Association, 1985.

Delaunay, Jean-Claude. *Services in Economic Thought: Three Centuries of Debate.* Boston: Kluwer Publishers, 1992.

Feketekuty, Geza. *International Trade in Services.* Cambridge, MA: Ballinger, 1988.

Lovelock, Christopher H. *Services Marketing.* Englewood Cliffs, NJ: Prentice-Hall, 1991.

McKee, David L., and Don E. Garner. *Accounting Services, The International Economy and Third World Development.* New York: Praeger, 1992.

Paris OECD. *Trade Investment and Technology in the 90's.* Paris: OECD Publications and Information Centre, 1991.

Shames, Germaine W., and W. Gerald Glover. *World-Class Service.* Yarmouth, ME: Intercultural Press, 1989.

Smith, Roy C., and Ingo Walter. *Global Financial Services: Strategies for Building Competitive Strengths in International Commercial and Investment Banking.* New York: Harper Business, 1990.

U.S. Chamber of Commerce and the Bretton Woods Committee. *How U.S. Firms Can Boost Exports through Overseas Development Projects.* Washington, D.C.: Government Printing Office, 1986.

Weisman, Ethan. *Trade in Services and Imperfect Competition: Applications to International Aviation.* Boston: Kluwer Academic, 1990.

CHAPTER 18

Global Pricing Strategies

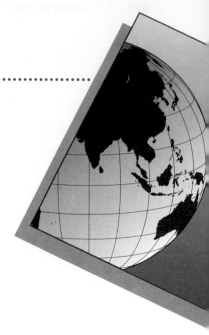

Tax Authorities to Have More Say over Transfer Pricing

The U.S. Internal Revenue Service has begun to look more closely at transfer pricing on sales of goods and services among subsidiaries or between subsidiaries and the parent company. It has filed claims against hundreds of companies in recent years, claiming that multinational companies too often manipulate intracompany pricing to minimize their worldwide tax bills. Experts calculate that foreign-based multinationals evade at least $20 billion in U.S. taxes. Other countries have also strengthened their review systems. Japan has created specific transfer pricing legislation that penalizes marketers for not providing information in time to meet deadlines set by the government. German tax authorities are carefully checking intracompany charges to deem their appropriateness.

In its biggest known victory, the IRS made its case that Japan's Toyota had been systematically overcharging its U.S. subsidiary for years on most of the cars, trucks, and parts sold in the United States. What would have been profits in the United States were now accrued in Japan. Toyota denied improprieties but agreed to a reported $1-billion settlement, paid in part with tax rebates from the government of Japan. At the same time, some U.S. multinationals are worrying about how Japan's National Tax Administration Agency will react. There is a possibility that the agency will begin to target sectors in which U.S. firms are doing well, such as pharmaceuticals, computers, and chemicals, for retaliatory tax investigations. Companies would also be questioned over intangibles, such as R&D and marketing costs, which are higher for U.S. firms.

Increasing communication among tax authorities is having a dramatic effect and will continue to accelerate, especially with the trend toward shifting profits. Historically, transfer pricing from the point of view of a U.S. company meant the shifting of income out of the United States, but with the corporate tax rate at 34 percent, many U.S. companies are now trying to use transfer pricing to shift profits into the country. Thus, U.S. multinationals must be prepared to justify transfer pricing policies on two or more fronts.

The entire tax equation has become more complicated because of changes in customs duties. In many countries, revenues from customs and indirect taxes are greater than revenue from corporate taxes. Authorities will jealously guard the income stream from customs taxes, and marketers could find gains on income taxes erased by losses on customs taxes.

Most multinationals are moving cautiously. Glen White, director of taxes at Dow Chemical, stresses this point. "I don't think anybody can afford to have a transfer-pricing system that cannot be revealed to all the relevant governments. If we were explaining to the Canadian tax auditor why we use our pricing system and our French tax inspector walked into the room, we would want to be able to invite him to sit down and then continue with the explanation."

Sources: "Pricing Yourself into a Market," *Business Asia,* December 21, 1992, 1; "The Corporate Shell Game," *Newsweek,* April 15, 1991, 48–49; "Worldwide Tax Authorities Promise Increased Scrutiny of Transfer Pricing," *Business International Money Report,* February 22, 1988, 72; "Smaller Bill Seen in Texaco Dispute," *New York Times,* January 19, 1988, D2.

Successful pricing is a key element in the marketing mix. A study of 202 U.S. and non-U.S. multinational corporations found pricing to rank second only to the product variable in importance among the concerns of marketing managers.[1] This chapter will focus on price setting by multinational corporations that have direct inventories in other countries. This involves the pricing of sales to members of the corporate family as well as pricing within the individual markets in which the company operates. With increased economic integration and globalization of markets, the coordination of pricing strategies between markets becomes more important.

TRANSFER PRICING

Transfer pricing, or intracorporate pricing, is the pricing of sales to members of the corporate family. It has to be managed in a world characterized by different tax rates, different foreign exchange rates, varying governmental regulations, and other economic and social challenges, as seen in International Marketplace 18.1. Allocation of resources among the various units of the multinational corporation requires the central management of the corporation to establish the appropriate transfer price to achieve these objectives:

1. Competitiveness in the international marketplace
2. Reduction of taxes and tariffs
3. Management of cash flows
4. Minimization of foreign exchange risks
5. Avoidance of conflicts with home and host governments
6. Internal concerns such as goal congruence and motivation of subsidiary managers[2]

[1] Saeed Samiee, "Elements of Marketing Strategy: A Comparative Study of U.S. and Non-U.S. Based Companies," *International Marketing Review* 1 (Summer 1982): 119–126.

[2] Wagdy M. Abdallah, "How to Motivate and Evaluate Managers with International Transfer Pricing Systems," *Management International Review* 29 (1989): 65–71.

| Influences on Transfer Pricing Decisions | **TABLE 18.1** |

1. Market conditions in the foreign country
2. Competition in the foreign country
3. Reasonable profit for the foreign affiliate
4. U.S. federal income taxes
5. Economic conditions in the foreign country
6. Import restrictions
7. Customs duties
8. Price controls
9. Taxation in the foreign country
10. Exchange controls

Source: Jane O. Burns, "Transfer Pricing Decisions in U.S. Multinational Corporations," *Journal of International Business Studies* 11 (Fall 1980): 23–39.

Intracorporate sales can so easily change the consolidated global results that they compose one of the most important ongoing decision areas in the company. Transfer prices are usually set by the major financial officer—normally the financial vice president or comptroller—and parent company executives are uniformly unwilling to allow much participation by other department or subsidiary executives.[3]

Transfer prices can be based on costs or on market prices. The cost approach uses an internally calculated cost with a percentage markup added. The market price approach is based on an established market selling price, and the products are usually sold at that price minus a discount to allow some margin of profit for the buying division. In general, cost-based prices are easier to manipulate[4] because the cost base itself may be any one of these three: full cost, variable cost, or marginal cost.

Factors that have a major influence on intracompany prices are listed in Table 18.1. Market conditions in general, and those relating to the competitive situation in particular, were mentioned as key variables by 210 senior financial officers of multinational corporations.[5] In some markets, especially in the Far East, competition may prevent the international marketer from pricing at will. Prices may have to be adjusted to meet local competition with lower labor costs. This practice may provide entry to the market and a reasonable profit to the affiliate. However, in the long term, it may also become a subsidy to an inefficient business. Further, tax and customs authorities may object because underpricing means that the seller is earning less income than it would otherwise receive in the country of origin and is paying duties on a lower base price on entry to the destination country.

Economic conditions in a market, especially the imposition of controls on movements of funds, may require the use of transfer pricing to allow the company to repatriate revenues. As an example, a U.S.-based multinational corporation with central procurement facilities required its subsidiaries to buy all raw materials from the parent; it began charging a standard 7 percent for its services, which include guaranteeing on-time delivery and appropriate quality. The company estimates that its revenue remittances

[3] J. Fremgen, "Measuring Profit of Part of a Firm," *Management Accounting* 47 (January 1966): 7–18; Jeffrey Arpan, "Multinational Firm Pricing in International Markets," *Sloan Management Review* 15 (Winter 1973): 1–9.

[4] Paul Cook, "New Techniques for Intracompany Pricing," *Harvard Business Review* 35 (July–August 1957): 37–44.

[5] Jane O. Burns, "Transfer Pricing Decisions in U.S. Multinational Corporations," *Journal of International Business Studies* 11 (Fall 1980): 23–39.

from a single Latin American country, which had placed restrictions on remittances from subsidiaries to parent companies, increased by $900,000 after the surcharge was put into effect.[6]

International transfer pricing objectives may lead to conflicting objectives, especially if the influencing factors vary dramatically from one market to another. For example, it may be quite difficult to perfectly match subsidiary goals with the global goals of the multinational corporation. Specific policies should therefore exist that would motivate subsidiary managers to avoid making decisions that would be in conflict with overall corporate goals. If transfer pricing policies lead to an inaccurate financial measure of the subsidiary's performance, this should be taken into account when a performance evaluation is made.

Use of Transfer Prices to Achieve Corporate Objectives

Three philosophies of transfer pricing have emerged over time: (1) cost based (direct cost or cost-plus), (2) market based (discounted "dealer" price derived from end-market prices), and (3) **arm's-length price,** or the price that unrelated parties would have reached on the same transaction. The rationale for transferring at cost is that it increases the profits of affiliates, and their profitability will eventually benefit the entire corporation. In most cases, cost-plus is used, requiring every affiliate to be a profit center. Deriving transfer prices from the market is the most marketing-oriented method because it takes local conditions into account. Arm's-length pricing is favored by many constituents, such as governments, to ensure proper intracompany pricing. However, the method becomes difficult when sales to outside parties do not occur in a product category. Additionally, it is often difficult to convince external authorities that true negotiation occurs between two entities controlled by the same parent. In a study of 32 U.S.-based multinational corporations operating in Latin America, a total of 57 percent stated that they use a strategy of arm's-length pricing for their shipments, while the others used negotiated prices, cost-plus, or some other method.[7]

The effect of environmental influences in overseas markets can be alleviated by manipulating transfer prices.[8] High transfer prices on goods shipped to a subsidiary and low ones on goods imported from it will result in minimizing the tax liability of a subsidiary operating in a country with a high income tax. For example, with the lowering in 1986 of the corporate tax rate in the United States to 34 percent, which is one of the lowest rates among industrialized nations, many multinational corporations now have an incentive to report higher profits in the United States and lower profits in other countries. On the other hand, a higher transfer price may have an effect on the import duty, especially if it is assessed on an ad valorem basis. Exceeding a certain threshold may boost the duty substantially when the product is considered a luxury and will have a negative impact on the subsidiary's competitive posture. Adjusting transfer prices for the opposite effects of taxes and duties is, therefore, a delicate balancing act.

Transfer prices may be adjusted to balance the effects of fluctuating currencies when one partner is operating in a low-inflation environment and the other in one of rampant inflation. Economic restrictions such as controls on dividend remittances and allowable deductions for expenses incurred can also be blunted. For example, if certain services

[6] "How to Free Blocked Funds via Supplier Surcharges," *Business International*, December 7, 1984, 387.

[7] Robert Grosse, "Financial Transfers in the MNE: The Latin American Case," *Management International Review* 26 (1986): 33–44.

[8] James Shulman, "When the Price Is Wrong—By Design," *Columbia Journal of World Business* 4 (May–June 1967): 69–76.

performed by corporate headquarters (such as product development or strategic planning assistance) cannot be charged to the subsidiaries, costs for these services can be recouped by increases in the transfer prices of other product components. A subsidiary's financial and competitive position can be manipulated by the use of lower transfer prices. Start-up costs can be lowered, a market niche carved more quickly, and long-term survival guaranteed.

With the increase of government regulation on foreign participation, transfer pricing becomes an important tool for recouping expenses from joint ventures, especially if there are restrictions on profit repatriation. A study of transfer price setting in Canada found that the impetus toward a high or low transfer price depends on the level of ownership in the subsidiary, the dividend payout ratios, the effective marginal tax rates in both parent and subsidiary countries, and the tariff on goods transferred.[9] A study of national differences in the use of transfer prices found that British companies set transfer prices at their best estimate of market prices, whereas the dominant feature of French companies is the use of transfer prices that are roughly equivalent to marginal cost.[10] Of two U.S. companies studied, one used a system of market prices, and the second used a system of marginal cost prices. Top management in the U.S. companies, however, was found to be more conscious than the British or the French of the importance and the difficulty of establishing transfer prices, and corporate headquarters played a far more active role in price setting.

Transfer pricing problems grow geometrically as all of the subsidiaries with differing environmental concerns are added to the planning exercise, calling for more detailed intracompany data for decision making. Further, fluctuating exchange rates make the planning even more challenging. However, to prevent double taxation and meet arm's-length requirements, it is essential that the corporation's pricing practices be uniform. Many have adopted a philosophy that calls for an obligation to maintain a good-citizen fiscal approach (that is, recognizing the liability to pay taxes and duties in every country of operation and to avoid artificial tax-avoidance schemes) and a belief that the primary goal of transfer pricing is to support and develop commercial activities.[11]

Transfer Pricing Challenges

Transfer pricing policies face two general types of challenges. The first is internal to the multinational corporation and concerns the motivation of those affected by the pricing policies of the corporation. The second, an external one, deals with relations between the corporation and tax authorities in both the home country and the host countries.

Performance Measurement Manipulating intracorporate prices complicates internal control measures and, without proper documentation, will cause major problems. If the firm operates on a profit-center basis, some consideration must be given to the effect of transfer pricing on the subsidiary's apparent profit performance and its actual performance. To judge a subsidiary's profit performance as not satisfactory when it was targeted to be a net source of funds can easily create morale problems. The situation may be further complicated by cultural differences in the subsidiary's management, especially if the need to subsidize less-efficient members of the corporate family is not

---

[9] D. J. Fowler, "Transfer Prices and Profit Maximization in Multinational Enterprise Operations," *Journal of International Business Studies* (Winter 1975): 9–26.

[10] David Granick, "National Differences in the Use of Internal Transfer Prices," *California Management Review* 17 (Summer 1975): 28–40.

[11] Michael P. Casey, "International Transfer Pricing," *Management Accounting* 66 (October 1985): 31–35.

made clear. An adjustment in the control mechanism is called for to give appropriate credit to divisions for their actual contributions. The method may range from dual bookkeeping to compensation in budgets and profit plans. Regardless of the method, proper organizational communication is necessary to avoid conflict between subsidiaries and headquarters.

Taxation   Transfer prices will by definition involve the tax and regulatory jurisdictions of the countries in which the company does business, as is pointed out in The International Marketplace 18.1. Sales and transfers of tangible properties and transfers of intangibles such as patent rights and manufacturing know-how are subject to close review and to determinations about the adequacy of compensation received. This quite often puts the multinational corporation in a difficult position. U.S. authorities may think the transfer price is too low, whereas it may be perceived as too high by the foreign entity, especially if a less-developed country is involved. **Section 482** of the Internal Revenue Code gives the Commissioner of the IRS vast authority to reallocate income between controlled foreign operations and U.S. parents and between U.S. operations of foreign corporations.

Before the early 1960s, the enforcement efforts under 482 were mostly domestic. However, since 1962, the U.S. government has attempted to stop U.S. companies from shifting U.S. income to their foreign subsidiaries in low- or no-tax jurisdictions and has affirmed the arm's-length standard as the principal basis for transfer pricing. Because unrelated parties normally sell products and services at a profit, an arm's-length price normally involves a profit to the seller.

A significant portion of Section 482 adjustments, including those resulting from the 1986 Tax Reform Act, have focused on licensing and other transfer of intangibles such as patents and trademarks. Historically, transfer pricing from a U.S. company's point of view has meant the shifting of income out of the United States. But with the lower corporate tax rate, the question now is how to use transfer pricing to shift profits into the United States.

According to Section 482, there are four methods of determining an arm's-length price, and they are to be used in the following order:

1. The comparable uncontrolled price method
2. The resale price method
3. The cost-plus method
4. Any other reasonable method

Beginning with the 1994 tax return, U.S. firms must disclose the pricing method they use so that the IRS can ascertain that the price was established using the arm's-length principle.[12] Guidelines of the Organization for Economic Cooperation and Development (OECD) to transfer pricing are similar to those used by U.S. authorities.[13]

The starting point for testing the appropriateness of transfer prices is a comparison with *comparable uncontrolled* transactions, involving unrelated parties. Uncontrolled prices exist when (1) sales are made by members of the multinational corporation to unrelated parties, (2) purchases are made by members of the multinational corporation from unrelated parties, and (3) sales are made between two unrelated parties, neither of which is a member of the multinational corporation. In some cases, marketers have created third-party trading where none existed before. Instead of selling 100 percent of the

---

[12] "Pricing Foreign Transactions," *Small Business Reports,* April 1993, 65–66.

[13] Organization for Economic Cooperation and Development, Paris, *1979 Report on Transfer Pricing,* 1979, para. 45.

product in a market to a related party, the seller can arrange a small number of direct transactions with unrelated parties to create a benchmark against which to measure related-party transactions.

If this method does not apply, the *resale* method can be used. This usually applies best to transfers to sales subsidiaries for ultimate distribution. The arm's-length approximation is arrived at by subtracting the subsidiary's profit from an uncontrolled selling price. The appropriateness of the amount is determined by comparison with a similar product being marketed by the multinational corporation.

The *cost-plus* approach is most applicable for transfers of components or unfinished goods to overseas subsidiaries. The arm's-length approximation is achieved by adding an appropriate markup for profit to the seller's total cost of the product.[14] The key is to apply such markups consistently over time and across markets.

Such comparisons, however, are not always possible even under the most favorable circumstances and may remain burdened with arbitrariness. Comparisons are impossible for products that are unique or when goods are traded only with related parties. Adjusting price comparisons for differences in the product mix, or for the inherently different facts and circumstances surrounding specific transactions between unrelated parties, undermines the reliance that can be placed on any such comparisons. The most accepted of the other *reasonable* methods is the functional analysis approach.[15] The functional analysis measures the profits of each of the related companies and compares it with the proportionate contribution to total income of the corporate group. It addresses the question of what profit would have been reported if the intercorporate transactions had involved unrelated parties. Understanding the functional interrelationships of the various parties (that is, which entity does what) is basic to determining each entity's economic contribution vis-à-vis total income of the corporate group.

Since 1991, the Internal Revenue Service has been signing "advanced pricing" agreements with foreign multinational corporations to stem the tide of unpaid U.S. income taxes by foreign companies. By early 1994, a total of 18 such agreements were completed and 75 were under negotiation.[16] Agreement on transfer pricing is set ahead of time, thus eliminating court challenges and costly audits. The main criticism of this approach is the exorbitant amounts of staff time that each agreement requires.[17] Some also argue that such agreements may result in worse transfer pricing systems, from the corporate point of view, because companies with effective intracompany bargaining processes may have to replace them with poorly designed ones to satisfy the tax authorities.[18]

The most difficult of cases are those involving intangibles, because comparables are absent in most cases. The IRS requires that the price or royalty rate for any cross-border transfer be commensurate with income; that is, it must result in a fair distribution of income between the units. This requires marketers to analyze and attach a value to each business function (R&D, manufacturing, assembly, marketing services, and distribution). Comparable transactions, when available—or, if absent, industry norms—should be used to calculate the rates of return for each function. Take, for example, a subsidiary that makes a $100 profit on the sale of a product manufactured with technology developed and licensed by the U.S. parent. If the firm identifies rates of return for manufacturing

[14] David P. Donnelly, "Eliminating Uncertainty in Dealing with Section 482," *International Tax Journal* 12 (Summer 1986): 213–227.

[15] Gunther Schindler, "Income Allocation under Revenue Code Section 482," *Trade Trends* 2 (September 1984): 3.

[16] Data provided by the Internal Revenue Service by inteview, March 1, 1994.

[17] Stephen Barlas, "Taxation of Foreign Companies," *Management Accounting* 74 (June 1993): 10.

[18] "Pricing Yourself into a Market," *Business Asia,* December 21, 1992, 1.

18.2

THE INTERNATIONAL MARKETPLACE

Taxing Mr. Smith's Brain

The U.S. Internal Revenue Service plans to extend its "commensurate with income" standard to include services provided by key employees. For example, a U.S. executive travels to the company's Argentine subsidiary to assist in the construction of a plant. The U.S. parent and the subsidiary agree to a $100 per diem fee as Mr. Smith's compensation. The subsidiary ultimately generates substantial income for many years from products manufactured at this plant. The IRS has suggested that the U.S. company may be required to quantify the value and contribution of Mr. Smith's knowledge and skills to reflect his actual benefit to the plant.

In many cases, multinationals are not told how the assessments of future impact are to be made. This is indeed a challenge, since errors in the estimates will cause the IRS to demand penalties.

Sources: "Tax Report," *The Wall Street Journal*, January 29, 1992, 1; "MNCs Face Tighter Net over Transfer Pricing Rules," *Business International*, October 31, 1988, 337–338.

and distribution of 30 percent and 10 percent, then $40 of the profit must be allocated to the subsidiary. The remaining $60 would be taxable income to the parent.[19] Needless to say, many of the analyses have to be quite subjective, especially in cases such as the one described in The International Marketplace 18.2, and may lead to controversies and disputes with tax authorities.

In the host environments, the concern of multinational corporations is to maintain the status of good corporate citizenship. Many corporations, in drafting multinational codes of conduct, have specified that their intracorporate pricing will follow arm's length.

PRICING WITHIN INDIVIDUAL MARKETS

Pricing within the individual markets in which the company operates is determined by (1) corporate objectives, (2) costs, (3) customer behavior and market conditions, (4) market structure, and (5) environmental constraints.[20] Because all of these factors vary among the countries in which the multinational corporation might have a presence, the pricing policy must vary as well. Despite the controversy over the desirability of uniform pricing in multinational markets, price discrimination is an essential characteristic of the pricing policies of firms conducting business in differing markets.[21] In a study of the price decision making for nondomestic markets of 42 U.S.-based multinational corporations, the major problem areas in international pricing were meeting

[19] "MNCs Face Tighter Net over Transfer Pricing Rules," *Business International*, October 31, 1988, 337–338.

[20] Helmut Becker, "Pricing: An International Marketing Challenge," in *International Marketing Strategy*, eds. Hans Thorelli and Helmut Becker (New York: Pergamon Press, 1980), 206–217.

[21] Peter R. Kressler, "Is Uniform Pricing Desirable in Multinational Markets?" *Akron Business and Economic Review* 2 (Winter 1971): 3–8.

competition, cost, lack of competitive information, distribution and channel factors, and government barriers.[22]

Although many global marketers, both U.S. based[23] and foreign based,[24] emphasize nonprice methods of competition, they rank pricing high as a marketing tool overseas, even though the nondomestic pricing decisions are made at middle management level in a majority of firms. Pricing decisions also tend to be made more at the local level, with coordination from headquarters in more strategic decision situations.[25]

Corporate Objectives

Global marketers must set and adjust their objectives based on the prevailing conditions in each of their markets. Pricing may well influence the overall strategic moves of the company as a whole. This is well illustrated by the decision of many foreign-based companies, automakers for example, to begin production in the United States rather than to continue exporting. To remain competitive in the market, many have had to increase the dollar component of their output. Apart from trade barriers, many have had their market shares erode because of higher wages in their home markets, increasing shipping costs, and unfavorable exchange rates. Market share very often plays a major role in pricing decisions in that marketers may be willing to sacrifice immediate earnings for market share gain or maintenance. This is especially true in highly competitive situations; for example, Fujitsu's one-year net income was only 5 percent of sales, compared with IBM's 12.7 percent worldwide and 7.6 percent in Japan.

Pricing decisions will also vary depending on the pricing situation. The basics of first-time pricing, price adjustment, and product-line pricing as discussed earlier apply to pricing within nondomestic situations as well. For example, companies such as Kodak and Xerox, which introduce all of their new products worldwide within a very short time period, have an option of either **skimming** or **penetration pricing.** If the product is an innovation, the marketer may decide to charge a premium for the product. If, however, competition is keen or expected to increase in the near future, lower prices may be used to make the product more attractive to buyers and the market less attractive to competition. The Korean general trading companies (such as Goldstar, Hyundai, and Samsung) were able to penetrate and capture the low end of many consumer-goods markets in both the United States and Europe based on price competitiveness over the past eight years (as shown in Table 18.2).

For the most part, the Korean general trading companies have competed in the world marketplace, especially against the Japanese, on price rather than product traits, with the major objective of capturing a foothold in various markets. For example, Samsung was able to gain access to U.S. markets when J. C. Penney was looking for lower-priced microwave ovens in the early 1980s. Samsung's ovens retailed for $299, whereas most models averaged between $350 and $400 at the time.[26]

---

[22] James C. Baker and John K. Ryans, "Some Aspects of International Pricing: A Neglected Area of Management Policy," *Management Decisions* (Summer 1973): 177–182.

[23] J. J. Boddewyn, Robin Soehl, and Jacques Picard, "Standardization in International Marketing: Is Ted Levitt in Fact Right?" *Business Horizons* 29 (November–December 1986): 69–75.

[24] Saeed Samiee, "Pricing in Marketing Strategies of U.S.- and Foreign-Based Companies," *Journal of Business Research* 15 (March 1987): 17–30.

[25] For an example of pricing processes by multinational marketers, see John U. Farley, James M. Hulbert, and David Weinstein, "Price Setting and Volume Planning by Two European Industrial Companies: A Study and Comparison of Decision Processes," *Journal of Marketing* 44 (Winter 1980): 46–54.

[26] Ira C. Magaziner and Mark Patinkin, "Fast Heat: How Korea Won the Microwave War," *Harvard Business Review* 67 (January–February 1989): 83–92

TABLE 18.2	South Korea's Price Edge over Japan					
	Korean Brand			Japanese Brand		
Product	1985	1989	1994	1985	1989	1994
Subcompact autos	Excel (Hyundai) $5,500–6,000	$5,999	$7,200	Sentra (Nissan) $7,600	$7,299	$9,400
Personal computers	Leading Edge (Daewoo) $1,495	$898	$899	Advanced-3 (NEC) $1,695	$998	$1,049
Videocassette recorders	Samsung $270	$189	$199	Toshiba $350	$299	$239
Compact refrigerators	Goldstar $149	$88	$99	Sanyo $265	$99	$109
13-inch color televisions	Samsung $148	$159	$159	Hitachi $189	$199	$219
Microwave ovens	Goldstar $149	$79	$120	Toshiba $180	$99	$130
Videocassettes	SKC (Sunkyong) $6	$6	$6	TDK $7	$7.50	$8

Source: L. Helm, "The Koreans Are Coming," *Business Week,* December 23, 1985, 46–52; direct manufacturer/retailer inquiries, June 1989 and March 1994. In the absence of information/availability, a similar make/model has been used.

Price changes may be frequent if the company's objective is to undersell a major competitor. A marketer may, for example, decide to maintain a price level 10 to 20 percent below that of a major competitor; price changes would be necessary whenever the competitor made significant changes in its prices. Price changes may also be required because of changes in foreign exchange rates. Many marketers were forced to increase prices in the United States on goods of non-U.S. origin when the dollar weakened during the late 1980s and early 1990s.

Product-line pricing occurs typically in conjunction with positioning decisions. The global marketer may have a premium line as well as a standard line and, in some cases, may sell directly to retailers for their private-label sales. Products facing mass markets have keener competition and smaller profit margins than premium products, which may well be priced more liberally because there is less competition. For example, for decades, Caterpillar's big-ticket items virtually sold themselves. But environmental factors, such as the U.S. budget deficit, the Gulf states oil crunch, and the Latin American debt crisis, resulted in fewer large-scale highway and construction projects. The company then focused on smaller equipment to remain competitive globally.[27]

Costs

Costs are frequently used as a basis for price determination largely because they are easily measured and provide a floor under which prices cannot go in the long term. These include procurement, manufacturing, logistics, and marketing costs, as well as overhead. Quality at an affordable price drives most procurement systems. The decision to turn to offshore suppliers may often be influenced by their lower prices, which enable

[27] Ronald Henkoff, "This Cat Is Acting Like a Tiger," *Fortune,* December 19, 1988, 69–76.

THE INTERNATIONAL MARKETPLACE 18.3

Coping with Inflation, Avon Style

Avon Products Inc., the multinational marketer of cosmetics and accessories, has developed a pricing tool to help local subsidiaries cope with extremely high inflation rates as well as major devaluations. The objective of the approach is to respond quickly to changes in the price level and thus preserve local-currency margins. This is crucial for the international marketers, who usually need longer lead times for creative marketing planning.

The first step of the approach requires local managers from the various functional areas to predict future replacement costs and adjust prices quickly in relation to both market conditions and inflation rate. Local vendors are instrumental in helping make these projections. After the projections are completed, the marketing department uses these costs to prepare sales campaigns as far as one year into the future—a long time in a country suffering hyperinflation. Regular meetings are scheduled to approve or revise prices before sales campaigns go into effect. Contingency plans must be ready to handle dramatic changes in the inflation rate. For example, in Argentina, inflation ranged from as high as 5,000 percent in 1989 to close to zero under price and wage controls a few years before.

Sources: "South America: Recovering from a Lost Decade," *Export Today* 6 (July–August 1990): 18–23; "Close-In Pricing System Protects Avon's Margins in Hyperinflationary Nations," *Business International,* February 3, 1986, 33–34; "Avon's Close-In Pricing: Four Steps toward Implementing the Strategy," *Business International,* February 10, 1986, 42–46.

the marketer to remain competitive.[28] Locating manufacturing facilities in different parts of the world may lower various costs, such as labor or distribution costs, although this may create new challenges. For example, during the 1980s, many multinational corporations established plants in the Far East in search of cheaper labor. Toward the end of the decade, however, labor costs rose dramatically (for example, the average industrial wage in South Korea has risen 110 percent since 1984), labor strife increased, and labor shortages developed. These challenges were compounded by strengthened local currencies, adding to the upward pressure on prices.[29] As a result, manufacturers looking to save on materials, labor, and general production costs have turned to other Asia Pacific countries, for example, Indonesia.[30]

Varying inflation rates will have a major impact on the administration of prices, especially because they are usually accompanied by government controls. The task of the parent company is to aid subsidiaries in their planning to ensure reaching margin targets despite unfavorable market conditions, as illustrated in The International Marketplace 18.3. Inflationary environments call for constant price adjustments; in markets with hyperinflation, pricing may be in a stable currency with daily translation into the local currency.

Internally, controversy may arise in determining which manufacturing and marketing costs to include. For example, controversy may arise over the amounts of research

---

[28] "The Why, How, and What of Overseas Purchasing," *Purchasing,* June 25, 1987, 54–55.

[29] "Is the Era of Cheap Asian Labor Over?" *Business Week,* May 15, 1989, 45–46.

[30] Carolyn B. Lamm, Kathryn Mack, and Robert Pothier, "Asia's Best-Kept Trade and Investment Secret," *Export Today* 7 (November–December 1991): 20–31.

and development to charge to subsidiaries or over how to divide the costs of a pan-regional advertising campaign when costs are incurred primarily on satellite channels and viewership varies dramatically from one market to the next.

Demand and Market Factors

Demand will set a price ceiling in a given market. Despite the difficulties in obtaining data on foreign markets and forecasting potential demand, the global marketer must make judgments concerning the quantities that can be sold at different prices in each foreign market. The global marketer must understand the **price elasticity of consumer demand** to determine appropriate price levels, especially if cost structures change. A status-conscious market that insists on products with established reputations will be in-elastic, allowing for far more pricing freedom than a market where price-consciousness drives demand. Many U.S. and European companies have regarded Japan as a place to sell premium products at premium prices. With the increased information and travel that globalization has brought about, status-consciousness is being replaced by a more practical consumerist sensibility: top quality at competitive prices.[31]

Care has to be taken that the price-quality perception of consumers does not turn against the global marketer. Competitively priced goods have made inroads against even well-entrenched competitors. One of the fastest-selling personal computers in the United States is the Leading Edge Model D, made by the Korean Daewoo Corporation, which sells for half the price of the comparable IBM model.[32] Another example is the Belorussian-made Belarus tractor, which fared quite well both in Western Europe and the United States mainly because of its highly attractive price. On the other hand, the marketer who wants to charge a premium price must make sure that customers are willing to pay the price; that is, positioning of the product and marketing communication become crucial.

Prices will have to be set keeping in mind not only the ultimate consumers but also the intermediaries involved. The success of a particular pricing strategy will depend on the willingness of both the manufacturer and the intermediary to cooperate. For example, if the marketer wants to undercut its competition, it has to make sure that retailers' margins remain adequate and competitive to ensure appropriate implementation. At the same time, there is enormous pressure on manufacturers' margins from the side of intermediaries who are growing in both size and global presence. These intermediaries, such as the French Carrefour and the British Marks & Spencer, demand low-cost, direct-supply contracts, which many manufacturers may not be willing or able to furnish.[33] The only other option may be to resort to alternate distribution modes, which may be impossible.

Market Structure and Competition

Competition helps set the price within the parameters of costs and demand. Depending on the marketer's objectives and competitive position, it may choose to compete directly on price or elect for nonprice measures.

[31] "The New Affluent Japanese Consumer: Affluent and Ready to Shop for the Right Products," *Business International,* January 27, 1992; Mike Van Horn, "Consumer Revolution in the Japanese Market," *Export Today* 7 (May 1991): 54–56.

[32] L. Helm, "The Koreans Are Coming," *Business Week,* December 23, 1985, 46–52.

[33] Alan D. Treadgold, "The Developing Internationalisation of Retailing," *International Journal of Retail and Distribution Management* 18 (1990): 4–11.

If a company's position is being eroded by competitors who focus on price, the marketer may have no choice but to respond. For example, IBM's operation in Japan lost market share in mainframes largely because competitors undersold the company. A Japanese mainframe was typically listed at 10 percent less than its IBM counterpart, and it frequently carried an additional 10 to 20 percent discount beyond that. This created an extremely competitive market. IBM's reaction was to respond in kind with aggressive promotion of its own, with the result that it began regaining its lost share.

In some cases, strategic realignment may be needed. To hold on to its eroding worldwide market share, Caterpillar has strived to shrink costs and move away from its old practice of competing only by building advanced, enduring machines and selling them at premium prices. Instead, the company has cut prices and has used strategic alliances overseas to produce competitive equipment.

Some marketers can fend off price competition by emphasizing other elements of the marketing mix, even if they are at an absolute disadvantage in price. Singer Sewing Machine Co., which has nearly half of its $500 million in non-U.S. sales coming from developing countries, emphasizes its established reputation, product quality, and liberal credit terms, as well as other services (such as sewing classes), rather than compete head-on with lower-cost producers.[34]

The pricing behavior of a global marketer may come under scrutiny in important market sectors, such as automobiles. If local companies lose significant market share to outsiders as a result of lower prices, they may ask for government interference against alleged dumping.

Environmental Constraints

Governments influence prices and pricing directly as well. In addition to the policy measures, such as tariffs and taxes, governments may also elect to directly control price levels. Once under **price controls,** the global marketer has to operate as it would in a regulated industry. Setting maximum prices has been defended primarily on political grounds: It stops inflation and an accelerating wage-price spiral, and consumers want it. Supporters also maintain that price controls raise the income of the poor. Operating in such circumstances is difficult. Achieving change in prices can be frustrating; for example, a company may wait 30 to 45 days for an acknowledgment of a price-increase petition.

To fight price controls, multinational corporations can demonstrate that they are getting an unacceptable return on investment and that, without an acceptable profit opportunity, future investments will not be made and production perhaps will be stopped.[35] Cadbury Schweppes sold its plant in Kenya in April 1982 because price control made its operation unprofitable. In 1983, Coca-Cola and PepsiCo withdrew their products from the shelves in Mexico until they received a price increase. Pakistani milk producers terminated their business when they could not raise prices, and Glaxo, a pharmaceutical manufacturer, canceled its expansion plans in Pakistan because of price controls.

In general, company representatives can cite these consequences in arguing against price controls: (1) the maximum price often becomes the minimum price if a sector is allowed a price increase, because all businesses in the sector will take it regardless of cost justification; (2) the wage-price spiral advances vigorously in anticipation of

---

[34] Louis Kraar, "How to Sell to Cashless Buyers," *Fortune,* November 7, 1988, 147–154.

[35] Victor H. Frank, "Living with Price Control Abroad," *Harvard Business Review* 63 (March–April 1984): 137–142.

controls; (3) labor often turns against restrictions because they are usually accompanied by an income policy or wage restrictions; (4) noninflationary wage increases are forestalled; (5) government control not only creates a costly regulatory body but also is difficult to enforce; (6) authorities raise less in taxes because less money is made; and (7) a government may have to bail out many companies with cheap loans or make grants to prevent bankruptcies and unemployment. Once price controls are invoked, management will have to devote much time to resolving the many difficulties that controls present. The best interest of multinational corporations is therefore served by working with governments, especially in the developing countries, to establish an economic policy centered on a relatively free market in order to ameliorate the problem of rapidly escalating prices without price controls.

PRICING COORDINATION

The issue of standard worldwide pricing is mostly a theoretical one because of the influence of the factors already discussed. However, coordination of the pricing function is necessary, especially in larger, regional markets such as the European Union. Standardization efforts usually involve price levels and the use of pricing as a positioning tool. For example, a particular product may be priced as a premium product in every market, regardless of the absolute price.

Of greatest importance to multinational corporations is the control and coordination of pricing. When currency exchange rate discrepancies widen, gray markets emerge. In this respect, many multinational marketers view economic integration with trepidation.[36] The concern is that when Europe is without trade barriers, goods sold in a country at a lower price can easily find their way into another country where the pricing structure for the same product is higher. Badedas shower gel, for example, is priced in the middle of the market in Germany by its marketer, Ligner & Fischer. In the United Kingdom, Beecham positions Badedas as a high-price product.[37] This discrepancy causes parallel imports to U.K. retailers from Germany. Though not illegal, such transshipments have been held at bay in Europe to some extent by complicated customs and shipping procedures. When the trade barriers fall, parallel imports by strong retail chains will start to flourish. Global marketers' only response, in addition to stricter distribution control, is a careful scrutiny of marketing policies. For example, the marketer could try to increase control of distribution channels in high-priced markets and then with the proceeds cross-subsidize aggressive pricing in others. Another approach could be to introduce visible low-cost brand names to discourage parallel importation.[38] These strategies are discussed further in The International Marketplace 18.4.

The need for pricing coordination is not limited to regions such as the European Union. With more global and regional brands in the global marketer's offering, control in pricing is increasingly important. Of course, this has to be balanced against the need for allowing subsidiaries latitude in pricing so that they may quickly react to specific market conditions.

Studies have shown that foreign-based multinational corporations allow their U.S. subsidiaries considerable freedom in pricing. This has been explained by the size and

---

[36] John A. Quelch, Robert D. Buzzell, and Eric R. Salama, *The Marketing Challenge of 1992* (Reading, MA: Addison-Wesley, 1990), 379.

[37] Kevin Cote, "1992: Europe Becomes One," *Advertising Age,* July 11, 1988, 46.

[38] John A. Quelch and Robert D. Buzzell, "Marketing Moves through EC Crossroads," *Sloan Management Review* 31 (1989): 63–74.

THE INTERNATIONAL MARKETPLACE

Coordinating Prices in Integrating Markets

Price differentials can survive across individual European Union markets only if marketers act decidedly. This calls for centralizing pricing authority and establishing "pricing corridors." Some marketers may have to pull out of low-margin markets where price increases cannot be sustained.

Future European price levels will be markedly lower than current ones, and firms must take quick action to avoid seeing prices fall to the lowest level prevailing in marginal markets. This is due to the large differentials that existed and continue to exist among EU member states. Prices in markets such as Greece, Portugal, and Spain are often significantly lower than those in northern Europe markets, where consumers can afford much larger margins and where costs are higher. The differentials can range from 30 percent for natural yogurt to as much as 200 percent for pharmaceuticals.

Parallel imports into affluent markets will force prices down as buyers simply go to the cheapest available source for their goods. If manufacturers leave it to market forces, prices may go down to the lowest level. For example, Portugal may influence prices in Germany through parallel imports and the centralization of buying power.

Manufacturers must take action now in order to avoid this situation. There has to be a compromise between the current policy of individually optimized prices and a uniform European price. Such a compromise will be possible because, even after 1993, Europe has not become a homogeneous market. Consumer habits will adjust gradually, allowing certain price differentials to be retained and defended.

Some experts recommend that manufacturers set up a European pricing corridor. In effect, this means converting present prices—dropping high ones somewhat and raising low ones—into a sustainable differential among markets in member states. The exact size of the corridor depends on the nature of the product; that is, it would be much narrower for easily transportable items such as photographic film than for heavy ones such as industrial machinery.

These changing market conditions imply a new focus on centralized price setting for Europe. The price corridor will be set by the head office, with local subsidiaries free to set prices within the corridor. This approach runs contrary to the prevailing corporate culture, which is based on decentralization and individual cost and profit centers.

Manufacturers ought to consider pulling out of poorer markets where price hikes cannot be sustained. It is better to lose a small percentage of sales rather than see turnover, margins, and profits plummet. So far, however, there appears to be little movement toward more centralized pricing. Some experts are concerned by the lack of urgency apparently felt by many European executives, who seem content to wait and see what happens.

Indeed, a number of European industrialists argue that large price differences can be maintained in Europe through product differentiation. Simpler products could be sold into less-prosperous markets, whereas more elaborate items might go to those markets that are able to afford them. Automobiles, for example, could be sold with different levels of options and accessory packages as a way of maintaining differentials.

Continued

But in at least one industry—pharmaceuticals—executives fear that neither pricing corridors nor product differences will prevent prices from falling to the lowest level. In markets such as France, Greece, Spain, and Portugal, prices for drugs are already very low because of national reimbursement schemes. In these countries, governments, not the manufacturers, effectively set prices.

"We are sandwiched between the European Commission, which is determined to eliminate all trade barriers at whatever cost, and some national governments that are keeping pharmaceutical products artificially low," comments an executive at a major European drug maker. "In practice, the Commission has absolutely no control over the prices set by national governments." Pharmaceutical firms, which have heavy research and development costs, say they need high margins if they are to continue investing and competing with Japanese and U.S. companies. But if countries such as France, which accounts for a substantial part of the European drug market, continue to keep prices low, customers from other countries will simply buy their supplies in those markets. Manufacturers may well find themselves locked in an untenable position in an industry in which specifications are standardized, products cannot be differentiated, and suppliers cannot withdraw from the market for ethical reasons.

Source: "Pricing in Post 1992 EC: Expert Urges Fast Action to Protect Margins," *Business International*," August 24, 1992, 267.

unique features of the market. Further, it has been argued that these subsidiaries often control the North American market (that is, a Canadian customer cannot get a better deal in the United States, and vice versa), and that distances create a natural barrier against arbitrage practices that would be more likely to emerge in Europe.[39] However, recent experience has shown that pricing coordination has to be worldwide because parallel imports will surface in any markets in which price discrepancies exist, regardless of distances.

SUMMARY

In a world of increasing competition, government regulation, accelerating inflation, and widely fluctuating exchange rates, global marketers must spend increasing amounts of time planning pricing strategy. Because pricing is the only revenue-generating element of the marketing mix, its role in meeting corporate objectives is enhanced. However, it comes under increasing governmental scrutiny as well, as evidenced by intracompany transfer pricing.

The three philosophies of transfer pricing that have emerged over time are cost based, market based, and arm's-length. Transfer pricing concerns are both internal and external to the company. Internally, manipulating transfer prices may complicate control procedures and documentation. Externally, problems arise from the tax and regulatory entities of the countries involved.

Pricing decisions are typically left to the local managers; however, planning assistance is provided by the parent company. Pricing in individual markets comes under the

[39] Samiee, "Pricing in Marketing Strategies of U.S.- and Foreign-Based Companies," 17–30.

influence of environmental variables, each market with its own unique set. This set consists of corporate objectives, costs, customer behavior and market conditions, market structure, and environmental constraints. The individual impact of these variables and the result of their interaction must be thoroughly understood by the global marketer, especially if regional, or even worldwide, coordination is attempted.

Questions for Discussion

1. Comment on the pricing philosophy, "Sometimes price should be wrong by design."

2. The standard worldwide base price is most likely looked on by management as full-cost pricing, including an allowance for manufacturing overhead, general overhead, and selling expenses. What factors are overlooked?

3. In combating price controls, multinational corporations will deal with agency administrators rather than policymakers. How can they convince administrators that price relief is fair to the company and also in the best interest of the host country?

4. Should there be governmental action against gray markets? Are gray markets not an expression of free trade?

5. Which elements of pricing can be standardized?

6. The approach of Avon Products, reported in The International Marketplace 18.3, is an example of headquarter's guidance in pricing. What are benefits of this approach?

7. If a price edge is based on cost advantages, such as those between Korea and most industrialized countries, what can the international marketer do to compete with a Korean marketer?

8. Describe the circumstances under which an international marketer can utilize a skimming strategy and charge what the market will bear.

Recommended Readings

Abdallah, Wagdy. *International Transfer Pricing Policy.* Westport, CT: Quorum Books, 1989.

Fuller, James P. *International Tax Aspects of the Transfer or Use of Intangibles.* Palo Alto, CA: Fenwick, Davis & West, 1985.

Harper, Donald V., and Jack L. Caldwell. "Pricing." In *Marketing Manager's Handbook,* eds. Steuart Henderson Britt and Norman F. Guess. Chicago: Dartnell Press, 1983.

Robinson, Richard D. *International Business Management.* Hinsdale, IL: Dryden Press, 1985.

Schuettinger, Robert, and Eamonn Butler. *Forty Centuries of Wage and Price Controls.* Washington, D.C.: Heritage Foundation, 1980.

"Setting Intercorporate Pricing Policies." *Business International.*

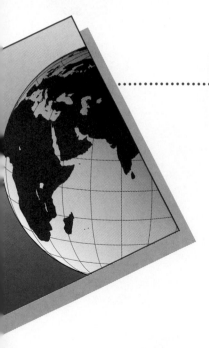

CHAPTER 19

International Logistics

19.1

A Meal from around the World

Picture this meal: The main course consists of shrimp (from Ecuador) sprinkled with ginger (from Fiji), lobster (from Nova Scotia), rice (from Thailand), and broccoli (from Mexico). During dinner, you sip a fine chablis (from Italy). For dessert, you have a fresh fruit salad made with bananas (from Honduras), grapes (from Chile), pineapple (from Hawaii), and kiwi (from New Zealand). Then you finish the meal with coffee (from Brazil) sweetened with sugar (from Guatemala). In a vase on the table are flowers (from Colombia).

For logistics managers to deliver these and other goods so far from their native lands, while at the same time clinging to cost-minimization, can be a daunting task. However, it can and is done every day through creative thinking and innovation.

The Challenge of Short Shelf Life   Chiquita (bananas) and Dole (pineapples) are experts at the logistics of international shipping. The success of their business depends on getting the product to the stores as quickly as possible, while the product is still ripe. Bananas, exported primarily from Latin American countries, are the most popular fruit consumed in the United States. Although Chiquita enjoys a high demand for its product, the firm faces significant logistics challenges. Specifically, Chiquita had to develop an international shipping system to ship the product fresh, keep the price low, and provide efficient and reliable delivery. With this in mind, a Chiquita researcher discovered that packing bananas in corrugated boxes and storing them at a temperature of 58 degrees Fahrenheit would greatly extend the ripening period. Although a 1950s advertisement featured a singing banana warning listeners that "bananas like the climate of the very, very tropical equator so you should never put bananas in the refrigerator," nearly all bananas shipped today are packed in carefully monitored refrigerated holds on ocean freighters.

But if ocean shipping is acceptable for bananas, Hawaiian pineapple growers have been increasingly turning toward airfreight. Discontented with the length of shipping time and the difficulty of getting fresh product to stores on the East Coast of the United States when shipping by ocean carrier, pineapple companies now fly their product. Although it was economically impossible to ship pineapples by air before the deregulation, the new and intense competition among airlines has significantly brought down shipping prices. Still, perishable low-margin products often cannot support independent airfreight services alone. Clever managers, like Sylvia Nam of Dole Fresh Fruit, solve the problem by identifying 747s with extra cargo space and now regularly use the commercial airlines for shipping fresh pineapples. Since these bookings take up otherwise unused space, the airlines often provide special rates. As long as the number of tourists to Hawaii continues to increase (tourism in Hawaii has grown 67 percent since 1979), Nam predicts that scheduling will get only easier.

Shipping the Highly Perishable Product   Lobster, perhaps one of the most sensitive and highly perishable of products, provides even more challenges for the international shipping manager. Lobster must arrive alive and in good health at the final destination, which for Ferguson's Lobster Pound, Ltd., based in Halifax, includes countries all over the world. The average length of time a lobster survives out of water is 30 to 40 hours. Shipping costs are too high to ship lobster in water containers. Managing the lobster shipping logistics, says Stewart Lamont, Ferguson's managing director, is "a 24-hour-a-day, 7 day-a-week business. It's unrelenting if you want to seriously serve the marketplace."

In response to the shipping challenges, Ferguson's has implemented several innovative programs. First, it formed an arrangement that would ensure regular delivery to European destinations. Before the arrangement, low-volume cargo—lobster included—moved on a space-available basis. As a result, last-minute changes in airline scheduling were fairly common. For Ferguson's, says Lamont, these changes "literally kill a marketplace. European buyers want 8 a.m. delivery so they can get it to the restaurants in time for lunch and dinner. If your flight doesn't get there until 4 p.m., that makes it real tough." Ferguson's solved the problem by working closely with Air Canada to quicken turnaround times at London's Heathrow airport, to establish state-of-the-art in-flight cooler facilities, and to ease the customs process. For lobster shipments to Japan, Air Canada flies the lobster to Los Angeles or San Francisco, where it is turned over to Japan Airlines for transport to Tokyo. Particularly for these trips from Halifax to Japan, which last about 30 hours, temperature control is critical. Rather than being wrapped in wet newspaper and packed in waxed corrugated boxes, as for European delivery, Japanese-bound lobsters travel in style: in an insulated container that has a separate compartment for dry ice and an attachment to a machine that periodically pumps in cool oxygen.

Continued

Although Ferguson's is happy with this arrangement so far, Lamont still spends seven days a week making arrangements. "Indeed," he says, "shipping perishables requires a different approach."

Sources: "Carriers, Ports Savor Growing Volumes," *Global Trade*, June 1992, 10; "Air Freight Makes Pineapples Fast Food," Special Report on Hawaii, *Journal of Commerce*, June 29, 1990, 11B; "Cargo Volume Climbs at Hawaiian Harbors," Special Report on Hawaii, *Journal of Commerce*, June 29, 1990, 9B; John Davies, "Ocean Carriers Fight for Lost Airline Business," Special Report on Refrigerated Transportation, *Journal of Commerce*, January 23, 1991, 2C; Jay Gordon, "The Logistics of Lobster," *Distribution*, October 1991, 38–40; Douglas C. Harper, "A Shipping Tale of Two Fruits," Special Report on Refrigerated Transportation, *Journal of Commerce*, January 23, 1991, 2C; Richard Malkin, "Shippers Shift Focus from Price to Service," *Distribution*, December 1990, 44.

For the international firm, customer locations and sourcing opportunities are widely dispersed. The physical distribution and logistics aspects of international marketing therefore have great importance, as is shown in The International Marketplace 19.1. To obtain and maintain favorable results from the complex international environment, the international logistics manager must coordinate activities globally, both within and outside of the firm. Neglect of logistics issues brings not only higher costs but also the risk of eventual noncompetitiveness due to diminished market share, more expensive supplies, or lower profits. In an era of new trade opportunities in regions such as Central Europe, which are suffering from major shortcomings in logistical infrastructure, competent logistics management is more important than ever before.

This chapter will focus on international logistics activities. Primary areas of concern are transportation, inventory, packaging, storage, and logistics management. The logistics problems and opportunities that are peculiar to international marketing will also be highlighted.

THE FIELD OF INTERNATIONAL LOGISTICS

The concept of business logistics is relatively new. Although some aspects were discussed as early as 1951, John F. Magee is generally credited with publishing the first article on logistics theory in 1960.[1] The theoretical development of international logistics is even more recent, probably originating in a 1966 article by Robert E. McGarrah on "Logistics for the International Manufacturer."[2]

A Definition of International Logistics

International logistics is defined as the designing and managing of a system that controls the flow of materials into, through, and out of the international corporation. It encompasses the total movement concept by covering the entire range of operations concerned with product movement, including the logistics relationships of the firm with suppliers and customers. An overview of the logistics function is provided in Figure 19.1. By taking a systems approach, the firm explicitly recognizes the linkages among the traditionally separate logistics components within the corporation. By recognizing the

---

[1] John F. Magee, "The Logistics of Distribution," *Harvard Business Review* 38 (July–August 1960).

[2] Robert E. McGarrah, "Logistics for the International Manufacturer," *Harvard Business Review* 44 (March–April 1966).

The Logistics Function **FIGURE 19.1**

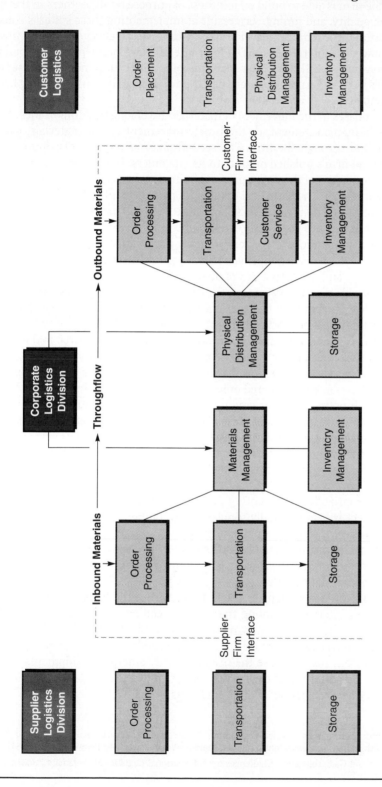

logistics interaction with outside organizations and individuals, such as suppliers and customers, the firm is able to build on jointness of purpose by all partners in the areas of performance, quality, and timing. As a result of implementing these systems considerations successfully, the firm can develop just-in-time (JIT) delivery for lower inventory cost, electronic data interchange (EDI) for more efficient order processing, and early supplier involvement (ESI) for better planning of product movement. The use of such strategic tools in the international arena can then assist the firm in developing key competitive advantages.

Two major phases in the movement of materials are of logistical importance. The first phase is materials management, or the timely movement of raw materials, parts, and supplies into and through the firm. The second phase is physical distribution, or the movement of the firm's finished product to its customers. In both phases, movement is seen within the context of the entire process. Stationary periods (storage and inventory) are therefore included. The basic goal of logistics management is the effective coordination of both phases and their various components to result in maximum cost-effectiveness while maintaining service goals and requirements. In the words of the director of international logistics operations of General Motors Corporation, the purpose of international logistics is "to plan cost-effective systems for future use, attempt to eliminate duplication of effort, and determine where distribution policy is lacking or inappropriate. Emphasis is placed on consolidating existing movements, planning new systems, identifying useful ideas, techniques, or experiences, and working with various divisions toward implementation of beneficial changes."[3]

The growth of logistics as a field has brought to the forefront three major new concepts: the systems concept, the total cost concept, and the trade-off concept. The systems concept is based on the notion that materials-flow activities are so extensive and complex that they can be considered only in the context of their interaction. Instead of each corporate function, supplier, and customer operating with the goal of individual optimization, the systems concept stipulates that collaboration and coordination will maximize the benefits of the system as a whole.

A logical outgrowth of the systems concept is the development of the total cost concept. To evaluate and optimize logistical activities, managers use cost as a basis for measurement. The purpose of the total cost concept is to minimize the firm's overall logistics cost by appropriately implementing the systems concept. Increasingly, however, the total cost concept is being partially supplanted by a total after-tax profit concept.[4] This takes into account the impact of national tax policies on the logistics function and has the objective of maximizing after-tax profits rather than minimizing total cost. Because tax variation in the international arena can often have major consequences, this focus appears quite appropriate.

The trade-off concept recognizes the linkages within the logistics systems, linkages that result in an interaction among the logistics components. For example, locating a warehouse near the customer may reduce the cost of transportation. However, additional costs are associated with new warehouses. Similarly, a reduction of inventories will save money but may increase the need for costly emergency shipments. Managers can maximize the performance of logistics systems only by formulating decisions based on the recognition and analysis of these trade-offs.

[3] Rex R. Williams, "International Physical Distribution Management," in *Contemporary Physical Distribution and Logistics,* 4th ed., eds. James C. Johnson and Donald F. Wood (Tulsa, OK: Penwell Books, 1981), 150.

[4] Paul T. Nelson and Gadi Toledano, "Challenges for International Logistics Management," *Journal of Business Logistics* 1 (1979): 7.

THE IMPACT OF INTERNATIONAL LOGISTICS

Logistics costs comprise between 10 and 25 percent of the total landed cost of an international order. International firms have already achieved many of the cost reductions that are possible in financing and production, and they are now beginning to look at international logistics as a competitive tool. Research shows that the environment facing logistics managers in the next ten years will be dynamic and explosive. Technological advances and progress in communication systems and information-processing capabilities will be particularly significant in designing and managing logistics systems.

For example, close collaboration with suppliers is required in order to develop a just-in-time inventory system, which in turn may be crucial to maintain manufacturing costs at a globally competitive level. Yet without electronic data interchange, such collaborations or alliances are severely handicapped. While most industrialized countries can offer the technological infrastructure for such computer-to-computer exchange of business information, the application of such a system in the global environment is often severely restricted. Often, it is not just the lack of technology that forms the key obstacle to modern logistics management, but rather the entire business infrastructure, ranging from ways of doing business in fields such as accounting and inventory tracking, to the willingness of businesses to collaborate with one another. A contrast between the United States and Russia is useful here.

In the United States it is expected that 40 percent of shipments made by 1995 will be under a just-in-time/quick response regime. For the U.S. economy, the total cost of distribution will be close to 11 percent of GNP. By contrast, Russia is only now beginning to learn about the rhythm of demand and the need to bring supply in line. The country is battling space constraints, poor lines of supply, nonexisting distribution and service centers, limited rolling stock, and insufficient transportation systems. Producers are uninformed about issues such as inventory carrying cost, store assortment efficiencies, and replenishment techniques. The need for information development and exchange systems for integrated supplier-distributor alliances and for efficient communication systems is only poorly understood. As a result, distribution cost remains at well above 30 percent of GNP, holding back the domestic economy and severely restricting its international competitiveness. Unless substantial improvements are made in the logistics area, major participation by Russian producers in world trade will be unlikely.[5]

It is fair to say that logistics may well become the key dimension by which firms distinguish themselves internationally. Given the speed of technological change and the efficiency demands placed on business, competitiveness, international sales growth, and international marketing success will increasingly depend on the logistics function.[6]

Differences between Domestic and International Logistics

In domestic operations, logistics decisions are guided by the experience of the manager, possible industry comparison, an intimate knowledge of trends, and discovered heuristics—or rules of thumb. The logistics manager in the international firm, on the other hand, frequently has to depend on educated guesses to determine the steps required to obtain a desired service level. Variations in locale mean variations in environment. Lack

[5] Michael R. Czinkota, "Global Neighbors, Poor Relations," *Marketing Management* 2 no. 4 (1994): 46–52.

[6] James H. Perry, "Emerging Economic and Technological Futures: Implications for Design and Management of Logistics Systems in the 1990s," *Journal of Business Logistics* 12 (1991): 1–16.

of familiarity with these variations leads to uncertainty in the decision-making process. By applying decision rules developed at home, the firm will be unable to adapt well to the new environment, and the result will be inadequate profit performance. The long-term survival of international activities depends on an understanding of the differences inherent in the international logistics field. These variations can be classified as basic differences and country-specific differences.[7]

Basic Differences   Basic differences in international logistics emerge because the corporation is active in more than one country. One example of a basic difference is distance. International marketing activities frequently require goods to be shipped farther to reach final customers. These distances in turn result in longer lead times, more opportunities for things to go wrong, more inventories—in short, greater complexity. Currency variation is a second basic difference in international logistics. The corporation must adjust its planning to incorporate the existence of different currencies and the changes in exchange rates. The border-crossing process brings with it the need for conformance with national regulations, an inspection at customs, and proper documentation. As a result, additional intermediaries participate in the international logistics process. They include freight forwarders, customs agents, customs brokers, banks, and other financial intermediaries. Finally, the **transportation modes** may also be different. Most domestic transportation is either by truck or by rail, whereas the multinational corporation quite frequently ships its products by air or by sea. Airfreight and ocean freight have their own stipulations and rules that require new knowledge and skills.

Country-Specific Differences   Within each country, the firm faces specific logistical attributes that may be quite different from those experienced at home. Transportation systems and intermediaries may vary. The reliability of carriers may be different. The computation of freight rates may be unfamiliar. Packaging and labeling requirements differ from country to country. Management must consider all of these factors in order to develop an efficient international logistics operation.

INTERNATIONAL TRANSPORTATION ISSUES

International transportation is of major concern to the international firm because transportation determines how and when goods will be received. The transportation issue can be divided into three components: infrastructure, the availability of modes, and the choice of modes.

Transportation Infrastructure

In the United States, firms can count on an established transportation network. Internationally, however, major infrastructural variations may be encountered. Some countries may have excellent inbound and outbound transportation systems but weak transportation links within the country. This is particularly true in former colonies, where the original transportation systems were designed to maximize the extractive potential of the countries. In such instances, shipping to the market may be easy, but distribution within the market may represent a very difficult and time-consuming task.

[7] Nelson and Toledano, "Challenges for International Logistics Management," 2.

The international marketer must therefore learn about existing and planned infrastructures abroad. In some countries, for example, railroads may be an excellent transportation mode, far surpassing the performance of trucking, whereas in others, the use of railroads for freight distribution may be a gamble at best. The future routing of pipelines must be determined before any major commitments are made to a particular location if the product is amenable to pipeline transportation. The transportation methods used to carry cargo to seaports or airports must also be investigated.

Extreme variations exist in the frequency of transportation services. For example, a particular port may not be visited by a ship for weeks or even months. Sometimes, only carriers with particular characteristics, such as small size, will serve a given location. All of these infrastructural concerns must be taken into account in the initial planning of the firm's transportation service.

Availability of Modes

Even though some goods are shipped abroad by rail or truck, international transportation frequently requires ocean or airfreight modes, which many corporations only rarely use domestically. In addition, combinations such as land bridges or sea bridges frequently permit the transfer of freight among various modes of transportation, resulting in intermodal movements. The international marketer must understand the specific properties of the different modes in order to use them intelligently.

Ocean Shipping   Water transportation is a key mode for international freight movements.[8] Three types of vessels operating in ocean shipping can be distinguished by their service: liner service, bulk service, and tramp or charter service. Liner service offers regularly scheduled passage on established routes. Bulk service mainly provides contractual services for individual voyages or for prolonged periods of time. Tramp service is available for irregular routes and is scheduled only on demand.

In addition to the services offered by ocean carriers, the type of cargo a vessel can carry is also important. Most common are conventional (break bulk) cargo vessels, container ships, and roll-on-roll-off vessels. Conventional cargo vessels are useful for oversized and unusual cargoes but may be less efficient in their port operations. Container ships carry standardized containers that greatly facilitate the loading and unloading of cargo and intermodal transfers. As a result, the time the ship has to spend in port is reduced. Roll-on-roll-off (RORO) vessels are essentially ocean-going ferries. Trucks can drive onto built-in ramps and roll off at the destination. Another vessel similar to the RORO vessel is the LASH (lighter aboard ship) vessel. LASH vessels consist of barges stored on the ship and lowered at the point of destination. These individual barges can then operate on inland waterways, a feature that is particularly useful in shallow water.

The availability of a certain type of vessel, however, does not automatically mean that it can be used. As The International Marketplace 19.2 shows, much depends on the local facilities and length of routing. The greatest constraint in international ocean shipping is the lack of ports and port services. For example, modern container ships cannot serve some ports because the local equipment is unable to handle the resulting traffic. This problem is often found in developing countries, where local authorities lack the funds to develop facilities. In some instances, nations purposely limit the development of ports to impede the inflow of imports. Increasingly, however, nations have begun to recognize

---

[8] Paul R. Murphy, Douglas R. Dalenberg, and James M. Daley, "Analyzing International Water Transportation: The Perspectives of Large U.S. Industrial Corporations," *Journal of Business Logistics* 12 (1991): 169–190.

19.2 THE INTERNATIONAL MARKETPLACE

Ro-Ro Your Boat

One may imagine the RORO technique of rolling bulky cargo right down a ramp and off the boat as the quick and easy way to ship goods. Yet a key problem arises from the fact that aboard the ship the wheeled trailers and their chassis cannot be stacked. As a result, a RORO vessel has only 30 percent of the capacity of a container ship and therefore generates much less revenue on a trip-by-trip basis. This is most relevant for long-distance shipments not only because of capacity inefficiency but also because the cost of expensive trailer equipment is tied up for a long time. As a result, alternatives such as the "stackable" container ship are becoming more popular for these routes as RORO service disappears.

But this is not the end for RORO shipping. RORO depends on the environment as does logistics. In Latin America and the Caribbean, such ramp service is actually expanding and increasing by leaps and bounds. Over the past three years alone, port locations in Venezuela and northern Central America have increased roll-on volume by 100 percent and 50 percent, respectively. Regional factors combined with the short distance of a U.S.-Latin route make RORO shipping competitive. In many cases, this region's ports will present obstacles such as primitive equipment, poor access, and traffic congestion. For these reasons, as Miami-based shipper Kenneth Coleman explains, "the idea is to get in quickly and get out quickly," and RORO "is just a faster method of moving cargo." Congestion can be simply bypassed because roll-on service allows a ramp to be dropped and unloaded right on the dock as opposed to waiting for special container cranes. The lack of availability and poor upkeep of container-related equipment can be ignored, particularly in many of the region's smaller ports that do not even have equipment for container ships. As a result, RORO definitely has a market niche, which in all likelihood will be there for a while.

Source: "Ro-Ro," Special Report, *Journal of Commerce*, July 21, 1993, 2c–4c.

the importance of appropriate port structures and are developing such facilities in spite of the heavy investments necessary. If such investments are accompanied by concurrent changes in the overall infrastructure, transportation efficiency should, in the long run, more than recoup the original investment.

Large investments in infrastructure are always necessary to produce results. Selective allocation of funds to transportation usually achieves only the shifting of bottlenecks to some other point in the infrastructure. If these bottlenecks are not removed, the consequences may be felt in the overall economic performance of the nation. A good example is provided by the Caribbean Basin Initiative. This initiative, designed to increase the exports of the Caribbean region to the United States, has still not taken full effect, mainly because of inadequate transportation links and an inadequate infrastructure. The Caribbean nations continue to be poorly served by ocean carriers, and products that could be exported from the region to the United States are at a disadvantage because they take a long time to reach the U.S. market. For many products, quick delivery is essential because of required high levels of industry responsiveness to orders.

International Air Freight, 1960–1992 | TABLE 19.1

Year	Tonne-Kilometers (billions)
1960	1.0
1965	2.6
1970	6.4
1975	11.7
1980	20.3
1983	24.9
1985	39.8
1990	46.4
1992	49.4

Note: Based on data supplied by member states of the International Civil Aviation Organization (ICAO). As the number of member states increased from 116 in 1970 to 150 in 1983, there is some upward bias in the data, particularly from 1970 on, when data for the U.S.S.R. were included for the first time.

Source: Civil Aviation Statistics of the World (Montreal: ICAO, 1993).

From a regional perspective, maintaining adequate facilities is therefore imperative in order to remain on the list of areas and ports served by international carriers.

Air Shipping Airfreight is available to and from most countries. This includes the developing world, where it is often a matter of national prestige to operate a national airline. The tremendous growth in international airfreight over past decades is shown in Table 19.1. However, the total volume of airfreight in relation to the total volume of shipping in international business remains quite small. It accounts for less than 1 percent of the total volume of international shipments, although it often represents more than 20 percent of the value shipped by industrialized countries.[9] Clearly, high-value items are more likely to be shipped by air, particularly if they have a high density, that is, a high weight-to-volume ratio.

Over the years, airlines have made major efforts to increase the volume of airfreight. Many of these activities have concentrated on developing better, more efficient ground facilities, introducing airfreight containers, and providing and marketing a wide variety of special services to shippers. In addition, some airfreight companies have specialized and become partners in the international logistics effort.

Changes have also taken place within the aircraft. As an example, 30 years ago, the holds of large propeller aircraft could take only about 10 tons of cargo. Today's jumbo jets can hold more than 30 tons and can therefore, as Figure 19.2 shows, transport bulky products. In addition, aircraft manufacturers have responded to industry demands by developing both jumbo cargo planes and combination passenger and cargo aircraft. The latter carry passengers in one section of the main deck and freight in another. These hybrids can be used by carriers on routes that would be uneconomical for passengers or freight alone.

From the shipper's perspective, the products involved must be amenable to air shipment in terms of their size. In addition, the market situation for any given product must

---

[9] Gunnar K. Sletmo and Jacques Picard, "International Distribution Policies and the Role of Air Freight," *Journal of Business Logistics* 6 (1984): 35–52.

FIGURE 19.2   Horses Are Loaded into an Air Container

Source: "Air Commerce" (Supplement of *Journal of Commerce*) Nov. 26, 1993: 12A.

be evaluated. For example, airfreight may be needed if a product is perishable or if, for other reasons, it requires a short transit time. The level of customer-service needs and expectations can also play a decisive role. For example, the shipment of an industrial product that is vital to the ongoing operations of a customer is usually much more urgent than the shipment of most consumer products.

Choice of Modes

The international marketer must make the appropriate selection from the available modes of transportation. This decision, of course, will be heavily influenced by the needs of the firm and its customers. The manager must consider the performance of each mode on four dimensions: transit time, predictability, cost, and noneconomic factors.

Transit Time   The period between departure and arrival of the carrier varies significantly between ocean freight and airfreight. For example, the 45-day transit time of an ocean shipment can be reduced to 24 hours if the firm chooses airfreight. The length of transit time will have a major impact on the overall logistical operations of the firm. As an example, a short transit time may reduce or even eliminate the need for an overseas depot. Also, inventories can be significantly reduced if they are replenished frequently. As a result, capital can be freed up and used to finance other corporate opportunities. Transit time can also play a major role in emergency situations. For example, if the shipper is about to miss an important delivery date because of production delays, a shipment normally made by ocean freight can be made by air.

Perishable products require shorter transit times. Rapid transportation prolongs the shelf life in the foreign market. As was seen in The International Marketplace 19.1, for products with a short life span, air delivery may be the only way to successfully enter foreign markets. For example, international sales of cut flowers have reached their current volume only as a result of airfreight, as Figure 19.3 shows.

This interaction between selling price, market distance, and form of transportation is not new. Centuries ago, Johann von Thünen, a noted German economist, developed

Advertisement for Cut Flowers   FIGURE 19.3

Source: Courtesy of Customer and Marketing Services Division, Aviation Department, Port Authority of New York and New Jersey.

models for the market reach of agricultural products and incorporated these factors. Yet given the forms of transportation available today, these factors no longer pose the rigid constraints postulated by von Thünen but rather offer new opportunities in international business.

Predictability   Providers of both ocean and airfreight service wrestle with the issue of **reliability.** Both modes are subject to the vagaries of nature, which may impose delays. Yet because reliability is a relative measure, the delay of one day for airfreight tends to be seen as much more severe and "unreliable" than the same delay for ocean freight. However, delays tend to be shorter in absolute time for air shipments. As a result, arrival time via air is more predictable. This attribute has a major influence on corporate strategy. For example, because of the higher predictability of airfreight, inventory safety stock can be kept at lower levels. Greater predictability can also serve as a useful sales tool for foreign distributors, who are able to make more precise delivery promises to their customers. If inadequate port facilities exist, airfreight may again be the better alternative. Unloading operations from ocean-going vessels are more cumbersome and time-consuming than for planes. Finally, merchandise shipped via air is likely to suffer less loss and damage from exposure of the cargo to movement. Therefore, once the merchandise arrives, it is more likely to be ready for immediate delivery—a facet that also enhances predictability.

Cost   A major consideration in choosing international transportation modes is the cost factor. International transportation services are usually priced on the basis of both cost of the service provided and value of the service to the shipper. Because of the high value of the products shipped by air, airfreight is often priced according to the value of the service. In this instance, of course, price becomes a function of market demand and the monopolistic power of the carrier.

The international marketer must decide whether the clearly higher cost of airfreight can be justified. In part, this will depend on the cargo's properties. For example, the physical density and the value of the cargo will affect the decision. Bulky products may be too expensive to ship by air, whereas very compact products may be more amenable to airfreight transportation. High-priced items can absorb transportation cost more easily than low-priced goods because the cost of transportation as a percentage of total product cost will be lower. As a result, sending diamonds by airfreight is easier to justify than sending coal by air. To keep cost down, a shipper can join groups such as shippers associations, which give the shipper more leverage in negotiations. Alternatively, a shipper can decide to mix modes of transportation in order to reduce overall cost and time delays. For example, part of the shipment route can be covered by air, while another portion can be covered by truck or ship. The International Marketplace 19.3 gives an example of such intermodal shipments.

Most important, however, are the overall logistical considerations of the firm. The manager must determine how important it is for merchandise to arrive on time. The need to reduce or increase international inventory must be carefully measured. Related to these considerations are the effect of transportation cost on price and the need for product availability abroad. For example, some firms may wish to use airfreight as a new tool for aggressive market expansion. Airfreight may also be considered a good way to begin operations in new markets without making sizable investments for warehouses and distribution centers.

Although costs are the major consideration in modal choice, the overall cost perspective must be explored. Simply comparing transportation modes on the basis of price

THE INTERNATIONAL MARKETPLACE

Sea-Air: The Best of Both Worlds

In a global economy, the need for timely and predictable transport of products and production materials is vital. Without a doubt, air transport is the quickest and most reliable mode. However, sea transport often qualifies as the cheapest mode. Customers love speedy delivery, yet the need to keep transportation costs low is equally vital. A real problem for the logistics manager, then, is the dilemma of one mode being absolutely too expensive and the other being absolutely too slow.

Ask shippers nowadays how they cope with the problem and they will give you a strange response: They use both! The method is called "sea-air" transport, whereby a ship and a plane are used together to avoid the two extremes of high cost and long shipping delays. For example, many Japanese shippers send Europe-bound cargo by ship to the U.S. West Coast. From there, the cargo is flown to its final destination in Europe. By combining the two modes of transport, the entire trip takes about two weeks, as opposed to four or five weeks with an all-water route, and the cost is about half of an all-air route. A growing practice among Japanese and European shippers sending goods to South America is to sail to U.S. ports and then fly south from there. Ocean carriers from Japan unload at the port of Los Angeles and either fly on from there or truck the cargo to Miami. From the growing sea-air port of Miami, the cargo proceeds by air to destinations such as Brazil. An all-water route from Japan to South America can take a month, while sea-air takes about 11 days. Certain types of cargo, such as perishables and bulky items, have to be shipped solely one way or the other, so sea-air is not for everyone. But for cargo that fits the bill, it can be the best of both worlds!

The key to the entire process is the transfer point. Specific capabilities are required at the port to justify sea-air activity. At this time, only three ports worldwide (Seattle, Singapore, and Dubai) have come close to perfecting the "switch." First of all, a short and easy commute is needed between the dock and the airport. The largest sea-air hub in the world, Seattle's ocean port, is just 13 miles from its airport. Second is the ability to quickly off-load from one mode, transport, and on-load to the second mode as smoothly as possible. A third vital feature is committed port authorities who can help minimize customs, paperwork, and other red tape that goes along with international transportation. Crucial to successful sea-air transport is also the willingness of local transportation providers to prioritize designated sea-air cargo. When all of these features are brought together, the utilization of sea and air can make for a happy ending.

Source: "Sea-Air: Cheap and Fast," *Global Trade*, February 1992, 16–18.

alone is insufficient. The manager must factor in all corporate activities that are affected by the modal choice and explore the total cost effects of each alternative.

Noneconomic Factors   Often, noneconomic dimensions will enter into the selection process for a proper form of transportation. The transportation sector, nationally and internationally, both benefits and suffers from heavy government involvement.

Carriers may be owned or heavily subsidized by governments. As a result, governmental pressure is exerted on shippers to use national carriers, even if more economical alternatives exist. Such preferential policies are most often enforced when government cargo is being transported. Restrictions are not limited to developing countries. For example, in the United States, all government cargo and all official government travelers must use national flag carriers when available.

For balance of payments reasons, international quota systems of transportation have been proposed. The United Nations Commission on International Trade and Development (UNCTAD), for example, has recommended a treaty whereby 40 percent of the traffic between two nations is allocated to vessels of the exporting country, 40 percent to vessels of the importing country, and 20 percent to third-country vessels. However, stiff international competition among carriers and the price sensitivity of customers frequently render such proposals ineffective, particularly for trade between industrialized countries.

Although many justifications are possible for such national policies, ranging from prestige to national security, they may distort the economic choices of the international corporation. These policies are a reflection of the international environment within which the firm must operate. The marketer must either accept these conditions or work creatively to adapt to them.

INTERNATIONAL INVENTORY ISSUES

Inventories tie up a major portion of corporate funds. As a result, capital used for inventory is not available for other corporate opportunities. Because annual **inventory carrying costs** (the expense of maintaining inventories) can easily comprise up to 25 percent or more of the value of the inventories themselves,[10] proper inventory policies should be of major concern to the international marketing manager. In addition, new just-in-time inventory policies are increasingly adopted by multinational manufacturers. These policies minimize the volume of inventory by making it available only when it is needed for the production process. Firms using such a policy will choose suppliers on the basis of their delivery and inventory performance. Proper inventory management may therefore become a determinant variable in obtaining a sale.

Although inventories are closely monitored domestically, this is often not the case internationally. This lack of preoccupation, however, does not reduce the importance of the issue. In its international inventory management, the multinational corporation is faced not only with new situations that affect inventories negatively but also with new opportunities and alternatives.

The purpose of establishing inventory—to maintain product movement in the delivery pipeline in order to satisfy demand—is the same for domestic and international inventory systems. The international environment, however, includes unique factors such as currency exchange rates, greater distances, and duties. At the same time, international operations provide the corporation with an opportunity to explore alternatives not available in a domestic setting, such as new sourcing or location alternatives. In international operations, the firm can make use of currency fluctuations by placing varying degrees of emphasis on inventory operations, depending on the stability of the currency of a specific country. Entire operations can be shifted to different nations to take advan-

---

[10] Bernard J. LaLonde and Paul H. Zinszer, *Customer Service: Meaning and Measurement* (Chicago: National Council of Physical Distribution Management, 1976).

tage of newly emerging opportunities. International inventory management can therefore be much more flexible in its response to environmental changes.

In deciding the level of inventory to be maintained, the international marketer must consider three factors: the order cycle time, desired customer-service levels, and use of inventories as a strategic tool.

Order Cycle Time   The total time that passes between the placement of an order and the receipt of the merchandise is referred to as order cycle time. Two dimensions are of major importance to inventory management: the length of the total order cycle and its consistency. In international marketing, the order cycle is frequently longer than in domestic business. It comprises the time involved in order transmission, order filling, packing and preparation for shipment, and transportation. Order transmission time varies greatly internationally depending on whether telex, telephone, fax, or mail is used in communicating. The order filling time may also be increased because lack of familiarity with a foreign market makes the anticipation of new orders more difficult. Packing and shipment preparation require more detailed attention. Finally, of course, transportation time increases with the distances involved. As a result, total order cycle time can frequently approach 100 days or more. Larger inventories may have to be maintained both domestically and internationally to bridge these time gaps.

Consistency, the second dimension of order cycle time, is also more difficult to maintain in international marketing. Depending on the choice of transportation mode, delivery times may vary considerably from shipment to shipment. This variation requires the maintenance of larger safety stocks in order to be able to fill demand in periods when delays occur.

The international marketer should attempt to reduce order cycle time and increase its consistency without an increase in total costs. This objective can be accomplished by altering methods of transportation, changing inventory locations, or improving any of the other components of the order cycle time, such as the way orders are transmitted. By shifting order placement from mail to telephone or to direct computer-order entry, for example, a firm can easily reduce the order cycle time by three to eight days. Yet because such a shift is likely to increase the cost of order transmittal, offsetting savings in other inventory areas must be achieved.

Customer Service Levels   The level of customer service denotes the responsiveness that inventory policies permit for any given situation. Customer service is therefore a management-determined constraint within the logistics system. A customer-service level of 100 percent could be defined as the ability to fill all orders within a set time—for example, three days. If within these three days only 70 percent of the orders can be filled, the customer service level is 70 percent. The choice of customer service level for the firm has a major impact on the inventories needed. In their domestic operations, U.S. companies frequently aim to achieve customer-service levels of 90 to 95 percent. Often, such "homegrown" rules of thumb are then used in international inventory operations as well.

Many managers do not realize that standards determined heuristically and based on competitive activity in the home market are often inappropriate abroad. Different locales have country-specific customer-service needs and requirements. Service levels should not be oriented primarily around cost or customary domestic standards. Rather, the level chosen for use internationally should be based on customer expectations encountered in each market. These expectations are dependent on past performance, product desirability, customer sophistication, the competitive status of the firm, and whether a buyers' or sellers' market exists.

Because high customer-service levels are costly, the goal should not be the highest customer-service level possible but rather an acceptable level. If, for example, foreign customers expect to receive their merchandise within 30 days, for the international corporation to promise delivery within 10 or 15 days does not make sense. Customers may not demand or expect such quick delivery. Indeed, such delivery may result in storage problems. In addition, the higher prices associated with higher customer-service levels may reduce the competitiveness of a firm's product.

Inventory as a Strategic Tool International inventories can be used by the international corporation as a strategic tool in dealing with currency valuation changes or hedging against inflation. By increasing inventories before an imminent devaluation of a currency, instead of holding cash, the corporation may reduce its exposure to devaluation losses. Similarly, in the case of high inflation, large inventories can provide an important inflation hedge. In such circumstances, the international inventory manager must balance the cost of maintaining high levels of inventories with the benefits accruing to the firm from hedging against inflation or devaluation. Many countries, for example, charge a property tax on stored goods. If the increase in tax payments outweighs the hedging benefits to the corporation, it would be unwise to increase inventories before a devaluation.

Despite the benefits of reducing the firm's financial risk, inventory management must still fall in line with the overall corporate market strategy. Only by recognizing the trade-offs, which may result in less-than-optimal inventory policies, can the corporation maximize the overall benefit.

INTERNATIONAL PACKAGING ISSUES

Packaging is of particular importance in international logistics because it is instrumental in getting the merchandise to the ultimate destination in a safe, maintainable, and presentable condition. Packaging that is adequate for domestic shipping may be inadequate for international transportation because the shipment will be subject to the motions of the vessel on which it is carried. Added stress in international shipping also arises from the transfer of goods among different modes of transportation. Figure 19.4 provides examples of some sources of stress that are most frequently found in international transportation.

The responsibility for appropriate packaging rests with the shipper of goods. The U.S. Carriage of Goods by Sea Act of 1936 states: "Neither the carrier nor the ship shall be responsible for loss or damage arising or resulting from insufficiency of packing." The shipper must therefore ensure that the goods are prepared appropriately for international shipping. This is important because it has been found that "the losses that occur as a result of breakage, pilferage, and theft exceed the losses caused by major maritime casualties, which include fires, sinkings, and collision of vessels. Thus, the largest of these losses is a preventable loss." [11]

Packaging decisions must also take into account differences in environmental conditions—for example, climate. When the ultimate destination is very humid or particularly cold, special provisions must be made to prevent damage to the product. The task

---

[11] Charles A. Taft, *Management of Physical Distribution and Transportation,* 7th ed. (Homewood, IL: Irwin, 1984), 324.

Stresses in Intermodal Movement   FIGURE 19.4

Acceleration	Acceleration	Acceleration	Acceleration	Heaving
Retardation	Retardation	Retardation	Dropping Impact	Pitching
Centrifugal Forces	Dropping Impact	Shunting Impact		Rolling
When Driving in		Centrifugal Forces		Centrifugal Forces
Curves		in Curves		Yawing
Vibrations		Vibrations		Swaying
				Vibrations

Note: Each transportation mode exerts a different set of stresses and strains on containerized cargoes. The most commonly overlooked are those associated with ocean transport.

Source: Reprinted with permission from *Handling and Shipping Management,* September 1980 issue, p. 47; David Greenfield, "Perfect Packing for Export." Copyright © 1980, Penton Publishing, Cleveland, OH.

becomes even more challenging when one considers that, in the course of long-distance transportation, dramatic changes in climate can take place.

Packaging issues also need to be closely linked to overall strategic plans. The individual responsible for international packaging should utilize transportation modes as efficiently as possible. This requires appropriate package design, which takes into account the storage properties of packaging.

The weight of packaging must also be considered, particularly when airfreight is used, since the cost of shipping is often based on weight. At the same time, packaging material must be sufficiently strong to permit stacking in international transportation. Another consideration is that, in some countries, duties are assessed according to the gross weight of shipments, which includes the weight of packaging. Obviously, the heavier the packaging, the higher the duties will be.

The shipper must pay sufficient attention to instructions provided by the customer for packaging. For example, requests by the customer that the weight of any one package should not exceed a certain limit, or that specific package dimensions should be adhered to, usually are made for a reason. Often they reflect limitations in transportation or handling facilities at the point of destination.

Although the packaging of a product is often used as a form of display abroad, international packaging can rarely serve the dual purpose of protection and display. Therefore, double packaging may be necessary. The display package is for future use at the point of destination; another package surrounds it for protective purposes.

One solution to the packaging problem in international logistics has been the development of intermodal containers—large metal boxes that fit on trucks, ships, railroad cars, and airplanes and ease the frequent transfer of goods in international shipments. In addition, containers offer greater safety from pilferage and damage, as the International Marketplace 19.4 shows. Of course, if merchandise from a containerized shipment is lost, frequently the entire container has been removed. Developed in different forms for both sea and air transportation, containers also offer better utilization of carrier space because of standardization of size. The shipper therefore may benefit from lower transportation rates.

Container traffic is heavily dependent on the existence of appropriate handling facilities, both domestically and internationally. In addition, the quality of inland

THE INTERNATIONAL MARKETPLACE

How to Ship Your Car

Automobiles are expensive. When a purchase is made, the consumer expects first-class quality and treatment in return for his or her business. Consumers do not expect such things as scratches and nicks in their new car before they have even driven it. Yet this is many times the case due to the grueling journey some cars make from the production site to the showroom.

Now there is a new method of automobile "packaging" on shipping routes. Its developers proclaim that within the next five years, "most of the major automobile manufacturers are going to start using it." The company is Greenbrier from Lake Oswego, Oregon, and its new alternative is known as "Autostack." At first, one may not think of automobile transport as involving much packaging. Autostack's containerization of cars, however, makes it clear that time devoted to packaging for just about any product can enhance the outcome.

As an alternative to the traditional ferry-like method of auto transport, Autostack mechanically inserts cars into a rack where they are nested. The loaded rack is then inserted into an enclosed container for the journey. Key to this packaging method is the enclosure, which will prevent vandalism, theft, paint chipping, ultraviolet damage, as well as water damage. Although cars can be, and sometimes are, driven into a container without the rack, Autostack proponents point out that if a driver does not dent the cars pulling them into the container, once inside its tight confines, the cars can receive damage from doors being opened.

And if this isn't enough for some auto shippers, six of the collapsible racks fit into one container for the return trip, freeing up the other five standardized containers for back-haul cargo revenue. Ford's use of Autostack from its Hermosilla, Mexico, plant enables it to use empty containers to ship auto parts back south.

Sea-Land, the largest U.S. shipper, is convinced that Autostack's packaging method can improve quality and provide better use of container and vessel space. Sea-Land currently transports 30,000 cars a year under the new method. Long-distance and potentially rough sea routes with predictable flows of back-haul cargo are the ideal conditions for this type of auto packaging. With the growth of international automobile shipments, Greenbrier is counting on a real boom with Autostack.

Source: "Auto Racks Sell Themselves, Thrall Says," *Journal of Commerce*, 2c; "Sea-Land to Use Autostack," *American Shipper*, July 1992, 59.

transportation must be considered. If transportation for containers is not available and the merchandise must be removed and reloaded, the expected cost reductions may not materialize.

In some countries, rules for the handling of containers may be designed to maintain employment. For example, U.S. union rules obligate shippers to withhold containers from firms that do not employ members of the International Longshoreman Association for loading or unloading containers within a 50-mile radius of Atlantic or Gulf ports. Such restrictions can result in an onerous cost burden.

Overall, close attention must be paid to international packaging. The customer who ordered and paid for the merchandise expects it to arrive on time and in good condition. Even with replacements and insurance, the customer will not be satisfied if there are delays. This dissatisfaction will usually translate directly into lost sales.

INTERNATIONAL STORAGE ISSUES

Although international logistics is discussed as a movement or flow of goods, a stationary period is involved when merchandise becomes inventory stored in warehouses. Heated arguments can arise within a firm over the need for and utility of warehousing internationally. On the one hand, customers expect quick responses to orders and rapid delivery. Accommodating the customer's expectation may require locating many distribution centers around the world. On the other hand, warehousing space is expensive. In addition, the larger volume of inventory increases the inventory carrying cost. The international marketer must consider the trade-offs between service and cost to determine the appropriate levels of warehousing. Other trade-offs also exist within the logistics function. As an example, fewer warehouses will allow for consolidation of transportation and therefore lower transportation rates to the warehouse. However, if the warehouses are located far from customers, the cost of outgoing transportation from the warehouse will increase.

Storage Facilities

The international marketer is faced with the location decision of how many distribution centers to have and where to locate them. The availability of facilities abroad will differ from the domestic situation. For example, whereas public storage is widely available in the United States, such facilities may be scarce or entirely lacking abroad. Also, the standards and quality of facilities abroad are often not comparable to those offered in the United States. As a result, the storage decision of the firm is often accompanied by the need for large-scale, long-term investments. Despite the high cost, international storage facilities should be established if they support the overall marketing effort. In many markets, adequate storage facilities are imperative in order to satisfy customer demands and to compete successfully.

Once the decision is made to utilize storage facilities abroad, the warehouses must be carefully analyzed. As an example, in some countries, warehouses have low ceilings. Packaging developed for the high stacking of products is therefore unnecessary. In other countries, automated warehousing is available. Proper bar-coding of products and the use of package dimensions acceptable to the warehousing system are basic requirements. In contrast, in warehouses still stocked manually, weight limitations will be of major concern.

To optimize the logistics system, the marketer should analyze international product sales and then rank products according to warehousing needs. Products that are most sensitive to delivery time may be classified as "A" products. "A" products would be stocked in all distribution centers, and safety stock levels would be kept high. Products for which immediate delivery is not urgent may be classified as "B" products. They would be stored only at selected distribution centers around the world. Finally, products for which short delivery time is not important, or for which there is little demand, would be stocked only at headquarters. Should an urgent need for delivery arise, airfreight could be considered for rapid shipment. Classifying products enables the international marketer to substantially reduce total international warehousing requirements and still maintain acceptable service levels.

Foreign Trade Zones

The existence of foreign trade zones can have a major effect on the international logistician, since production cost advantages may require a reconfiguration of storage, processing, and distribution strategies. Trade zones are considered, for purposes of tariff treatment, to be outside the customs territory of the country within which they are located. They are special areas and can be used for warehousing, packaging, inspection, labeling, exhibition, assembly, fabrication, or transshipment of imports without burdening the firm with duties.[12] Trade zones can be found at major ports of entry and also at inland locations near major production facilities. For example, Kansas City, Missouri, has one of the largest foreign trade zones in the United States. Figure 19.5 shows an advertisement by a trade zone.

Trade zones can be quite useful to the international firm. For example, in a particular country, the benefits derived from lower factor costs, such as labor, may be offset by high duties and tariffs. As a result, location of manufacturing and storage facilities in that country may prove uneconomical. Foreign trade zones are designed to exclude the impact of duties from the location decision. This is done by exempting merchandise in the foreign trade zone from duty payment. The international firm can therefore import merchandise; store it in the foreign trade zone; and process, alter, test, or demonstrate it—all without paying duties. If the merchandise is subsequently shipped abroad (that is, reexported), no duty payments are ever due. Duty payments become due only if and when the merchandise is shipped into the country from the foreign trade zone.

Firms can also make use of sharp differentials in factor endowments, such as labor costs, between adjoining countries by locating close to their border. For instance, the **maquiladora program** between the United States and Mexico permits firms to carry out their labor-intensive operations in Mexico while sourcing raw materials or component parts from the United States, free of Mexican tariffs. Subsequently, the semifinished or assembled products are shipped to the U.S. market and are assessed duties only for the foreign labor component. The benefits of the maquiladora program are available for any firm that chooses to locate close to the border and are therefore not restricted to U.S. companies alone. For example, many Japanese firms have made use of this program. Even though the eventual tariff reductions that will result from the signing of the North American Free Trade Agreement (NAFTA) will reduce some benefits of the maquiladora program, low Mexican labor cost will continue to attract labor-intensive industries.

One country that has used trade zones very successfully for its own economic development is China. Through the creation of *special economic zones* in which there are no tariffs, substantial tax incentives, and low prices for land and labor, the government has attracted many foreign investors bringing in billions of dollars. These investors have brought new equipment, technology, and managerial know-how and have therefore substantially increased the local economic prosperity. For example, the job-generation effect has been so strong that the central Chinese government has expressed concern about the overheating of the economy and the inequities between regions with and without trade zones.[13]

---

[12] Patriya S. Tansuhaj and George C. Jackson, "Foreign Trade Zones: A Comparative Analysis of Users and Non-Users," *Journal of Business Logistics* 10 (1989): 15–30.

[13] Li Rongxia, "Free Trade Zones in China," *Beijing Review,* August 2–8, 1993, 14–21.

An Advertisement by a Foreign Trade Zone   FIGURE 19.5

IT COMES WITH A FOREIGN TRADE ZONE AND ENDLESS POSSIBILITIES.

Come on, use your imagination. Think of what your company could do with a space like this. ⇌ *The Port of Tacoma will help you do all the planning. We have plenty of warehouse space and land available in and outside one of the largest Foreign Trade Zones in the United States. In fact, we moved $809 million through our Foreign Trade Zone in 1990. That's more than anyone else in the country.* ⇌ *Our system is streamlined to make your job easier. You'll have less paperwork and save money, too.* ⇌ *The Port of Tacoma, Washington is in the heart of a dynamic, growing market. Give us a call at 206-383-5841. Everything you need is here. It's up to you to take advantage of it.* ***The Port of Tacoma***

Source: *Journal of Commerce*, October 18, 1992, 10A. Jacobson Ray McLaughlin Fillips Advertising and Public Relations, Tacoma, Wash.

Both parties to the arrangement benefit from foreign trade zones. The government maintaining the trade zone achieves increased employment. The firm using the trade zone obtains a spearhead in or close to the foreign market without incurring all of the costs customarily associated with such an activity. As a result, goods can be reassembled and large shipments can be broken down into smaller units. Also, goods can be repackaged when packaging weight becomes part of the duty assessment. Finally, goods can be given domestic "made-in" status if assembled in the foreign trade zone. Thus, duties may be payable only on the imported materials and component parts rather than on the labor that is used to finish the product. Whenever use of a trade zone is examined, however, the marketer must keep the additional cost of storage, handling, and transportation in mind before making a decision.

MANAGEMENT OF INTERNATIONAL LOGISTICS

Because the very purpose of a multinational firm is to benefit from system synergism, a persuasive argument can be made for the coordination of international logistics at corporate headquarters. Without coordination, subsidiaries will tend to optimize their individual efficiency but jeopardize the overall performance of the firm.

Centralized Logistics Management

A significant characteristic of the centralized approach to international logistics is the existence of headquarters staff that retains decision-making power over logistics activities affecting international subsidiaries. Such an approach is particularly valuable in instances where corporations have become international by rapid growth and have lost the benefit of a cohesive strategy.

If headquarters exerts control, it must also take the primary responsibility for its decisions. Clearly, ill will may arise if local managers are appraised and rewarded on the basis of performance they do not control. This may be particularly problematic if headquarters staff suffers from a lack of information or expertise.

To avoid internal problems, both headquarters staff and local logistics management should report to one person. This person, whether the vice president for international logistics or the president of the firm, can then become the final arbiter to decide the firm's priorities. Of course, this individual should also be in charge of determining appropriate rewards for managers, both at headquarters and abroad, so that corporate decisions that alter a manager's performance level will not affect the manager's appraisal and evaluation. Further, this individual can contribute an objective view when inevitable conflicts arise in international logistics coordination. The internationally centralized decision-making process leads to an overall logistics management perspective that can dramatically improve profitability.

Decentralized Logistics Management

An alternative to the centralized international logistics system is the "decentralized full profit center model."[14] The main rationale for such decentralization is the fact that "when an organization attempts to deal with markets on a global scale, there are problems of coordination."[15] Particularly when the firm serves many international markets

[14] Jacques Picard, "Physical Distribution Organization in Multinationals: The Position of Authority," *International Journal of Physical Distribution and Materials Management* 13 (1983): 24.

[15] Philip B. Schary, *Logistics Decisions* (Hinsdale, IL: Dryden Press, 1984), 407.

that are diverse in nature, total centralization would leave the firm unresponsive to local adaptation needs.

If each subsidiary is made a profit center in itself, each one carries the full responsibility for its performance, which can lead to greater local management satisfaction and to better adaptation to local market conditions. Yet often such decentralization deprives the logistics function of the benefits of coordination. For example, whereas headquarters, referring to its large volume of total international shipments, may be able to extract bottom rates from transportation firms, individual subsidiaries by themselves may not have similar bargaining power.

Once products are within a specific market, however, increased input from local logistics operations should be expected and encouraged. At the very least, local managers should be able to provide input into the logistics decisions generated by headquarters. Ideally, within a frequent planning cycle, local managers can identify the logistics benefits and constraints existing in their particular market and communicate them to headquarters. Headquarters can then either adjust its international logistics strategy accordingly or can explain to the manager why system optimization requires actions different from the ones recommended. Such a justification process will greatly help in reducing the potential for animosity between local and headquarters operations.

Contract Logistics

While the choice is open to maintain either centralized or decentralized in-house logistical management, a growing preference among international firms is to employ outside logistical expertise. Often referred to as contract, or "third-party," logistics, it is a rapidly expanding industry with a third of the Fortune 500 companies as clientele. The main thrust behind the idea is that individual firms are experts in their industry and should therefore concentrate only on their operations. Third-party logistics providers, on the other hand, are experts solely at logistics, with the knowledge and means to perform efficient and innovative services for those companies in need. The goal is improved service at equal or lower cost. The International Marketplace 19.5 provides an example.

Logistics providers' services vary in scope. For instance, some may use their own assets in physical transportation, while others subcontract out portions of the job. Certain other providers are not involved as much with the actual transportation as they are with developing systems and data bases or consulting on administrative management services. The concept of improving service, cutting costs, and unloading the daily management onto willing experts is driving the momentum of contract logistics.

One of the greatest benefits of contracting out the logistics function in a foreign market is the ability to take advantage of an in-place network complete with resources and experience. The local expertise and image are crucial when a business is just starting up. The prospect of newly entering a region as confusing as Europe with different regulations, standards, and even languages can be frightening without access to a seasoned and familiar logistics provider.

One of the main arguments leveled against contract logistics is the loss of the firm's control in the supply chain. Yet contract logistics does not and should not require the handing over of control. Rather, it offers concentration on one's specialization—a division of labor. The control and responsibility toward the customer remain with the firm, even though operations may move to a highly trained outside organization.

19.5

THE INTERNATIONAL MARKETPLACE

Cutting Delivery from Two Weeks to Two Days

Today, information moves around the world in the blink of an eye, and semiconductors are instrumental in making this happen. Increasingly, producers of semiconductors recognize that their product itself needs to move from producer to customer nearly as fast.

One company that attempts to do just that is National Semiconductor Corporation (NSC) located in California. The firm realized that in order to allow greater speed of delivery, its global supply network needed an overhaul. The old logistical network of decentralized control was a tangle of unnecessary interchanges, propped up by 44 different international freight forwarders and 18 different air carriers. "The complexity of it all wasn't allowing consistent service," comments Kelvin Phillips, NSC director of worldwide logistics.

National Semiconductor wanted to change its 5- to 18-day delivery time and offer a 2-day delivery guarantee. The key factor in the strategy was the recruitment of a third-party logistics firm to provide valuable expertise as well as needed infrastructure. NSC turned to Federal Express's Business Logistics Services (BLS) as a partner. Explains Phillips, "Our company competes on technology; we cannot compete on logistics. Federal's core competency is delivery. It can do what we can't." BLS was able to provide National Semiconductor with a formidable logistics network by granting access to 420 aircraft; 1,869 worldwide facilities; more than 100,000 computer terminals; 31,211 surface vehicles; and an infrastructure with more than 90,000 employees. Phillips views NSC's partnership with Federal as "using the experts who spend billions on logistics."

Five Asian NSC plants produce 95 percent of its product. In the past, an unconsolidated system of distribution existed where each plant optimized its own business performance by individually holding an inventory, performing pick and pack, and directing shipments to the main distribution centers in Scotland and California. With the help of BLS, product pickups are now made at each of these plants and funneled to a centralized distribution center in Singapore. At this point, orders are consolidated for more cost-effective routing, and deliveries are made directly from Singapore within two business days. An additional advantage of using BLS is the availability of dedicated freighter capacity, something in short supply during certain seasons in this market.

NSC's overhaul was of no small scale, and as Phillips expresses, "When people have been doing things one way for 20 years, the switch is difficult." However, the cost of change is worth it in view of the savings gained from a more efficient and sensible global delivery system.

Source:"Macro Logistics for Microprocessors," *Distribution*, April 1993, 66–72.

LOGISTICS AND THE ENVIRONMENT

Apart from the structure of the logistics function, major changes are also occurring in the strategic orientation of the function. The logistician plays an increasingly important role in allowing the firm to operate in an environmentally conscious way. Environmental laws, expectations, and self-imposed goals set by firms are difficult to adhere to without a logis-

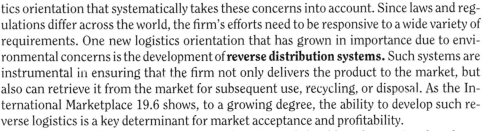

  19.6

Environmental Impact on Logistics

Increasingly, countries pass laws that create environmental standards. A recent German law regulates packaging, a U.S. law levies taxes on certain chemicals destined for toxic-waste dumps, a law in Denmark requires that drinks be sold in refillable bottles, and a Canadian regulation requires deposits on beer bottles.

On the surface, it appears that these laws are a necessary and appropriate response to growing world concerns about the environment. Yet these environmental standards may have been motivated at least in part by protectionistic reasons. For example, a provision of Germany's packaging law requires that at most, 28 percent of all beer and soft-drink containers can be "one-trip" (disposable). Importers suspect the provision was designed to benefit small German brewers who will find it easier to collect and refill the empties. Packagers also dislike the law's insistence that companies collect their used packaging for recycling. The fact that this will be easier for local manufacturers may prejudice retailers in favor of domestically produced goods.

Sources: "Free Trade's Green Hurdle," *The Economist*, June 15, 1991, 61–62; "Should Trade Go Green?" *The Economist*, January 26, 1991, 13–14.

tics orientation that systematically takes these concerns into account. Since laws and regulations differ across the world, the firm's efforts need to be responsive to a wide variety of requirements. One new logistics orientation that has grown in importance due to environmental concerns is the development of **reverse distribution systems.** Such systems are instrumental in ensuring that the firm not only delivers the product to the market, but also can retrieve it from the market for subsequent use, recycling, or disposal. As the International Marketplace 19.6 shows, to a growing degree, the ability to develop such reverse logistics is a key determinant for market acceptance and profitability.

Society is also beginning to recognize that retrieval should not be restricted to short-term consumer goods, such as bottles. Rather, it may be even more important to devise systems that enable the retrieval and disposal of long-term capital goods, such as cars, refrigerators, air conditioners, and industrial goods, with the least possible burden on the environment. The design of such long-term systems across the world may well be one of the key challenges and opportunities for the logistician and will require close collaboration with all other functions in the firm, such as design, production, and marketing.

On the transportation side, logistics managers will need to expand their involvement in carrier and routing selection. For example, for shippers of oil or other potentially hazardous materials, it will be increasingly expected to ensure that the carriers used have excellent safety records and use only double-hulled ships. Society may even expect corporate involvement in choosing the route that the shipment will travel, preferring routes that are far from ecologically important and sensitive zones.

In the packaging field, environmental concerns are also growing on the part of individuals and governments. Increasingly, it is expected that the amount of packaging materials used is minimized and that the materials used are more environmentally friendly. In response, corporations have begun to eliminate double packaging. For example, Isetan Co., Ltd., one of Japan's leading retail chains, has begun to use simplified wrapping for traditional mid-year and year-end gifts rather than the elaborate wrapping used earlier.[16]

---

[16] "Think Global, Act Local," *Jetro Monitor*, 6 (September 1991): 3.

The logistics function will also need to consider trade-offs between firm-specific performance and the resulting environmental burden. For example, even though a just-in-time inventory system may connote highly desirable inventory savings, the resulting cost of frequent delivery, additional highway congestion, and incremental air pollution also need to be factored into the planning horizon. Despite the difficulty, firms will need to assert leadership in such trade-off considerations in order to provide society with a better quality of life.

SUMMARY

The relevance of international logistics was not widely recognized in the past. As competitiveness is becoming increasingly dependent on cost-efficiency, however, the field is emerging as one of major importance because international distribution comprises between 10 and 25 percent of the total landed cost of an international order.

International logistics is concerned with the flow of materials into, through, and out of the international corporation and therefore includes materials management as well as physical distribution. The logistician must recognize the total systems demands of the firm in order to develop trade-offs between various logistics components.

International logistics differs from domestic activities in that it deals with greater distances, new variables, and greater complexity because of country-specific differences. One major factor to consider is transportation. The international marketer needs to understand transportation infrastructures in other countries and modes of transportation such as ocean shipping and airfreight. The choice among these modes will depend on the customer's demands and the firm's transit time, predictability, and cost requirements. In addition, noneconomic factors such as government regulations weigh heavily in this decision.

Inventory management is another major consideration. Inventories abroad are expensive to maintain yet often crucial for international success. The marketer must evaluate requirements for order cycle times and customer service levels in order to develop an international inventory policy that can also serve as a strategic management tool.

International packaging is important because it ensures arrival of the merchandise at the ultimate destination in safe condition. In developing packaging requirements, the marketer must consider environmental concerns as well as climate, freight, and handling conditions.

The marketer must also deal with international storage issues and determine where to locate inventories. International warehouse space will have to be leased or purchased and decisions made about utilizing foreign trade zones.

International logistics management is increasing in importance. Connecting the logistics function with overall corporate strategic concerns and with customers and suppliers alike will increasingly be a requirement for successful global competitiveness.

Questions for Discussion

1. Why do international firms pay so little attention to international logistics issues?
2. Contrast the use of ocean shipping to airfreight.
3. Explain the meaning and impact of transit time in international logistics.
4. How and why do governments interfere in "rational" freight carrier selection?
5. What is your view of the 40/40/20 freight allocation rule of the United Nations Commission on International Trade and Development?

6. How can an international firm reduce its order cycle time?

7. Why should customer-service levels differ internationally? Is it, for example, ethical to offer a lower customer-service level in developing countries than in industrialized countries?

8. How can an improved logistics infrastructure contribute to the economic development of Eastern Europe?

9. In which areas can contract logistics be most effective for the international marketer?

10. What steps can logisticians take to make their effort more environmentally friendly?

Recommended Readings

Ballou, Ronald H. *Basic Business Logistics.* 3d ed. Englewood Cliffs, NJ: Prentice-Hall, 1992.

Blanding, Warren. *Practical Handbook of Distribution/Customer Service.* Washington, D.C.: Traffic Service Corporation, 1988.

Bowersox, Donald J., Patricia J. Daugherty, Cornelia L. Droege, Richard N. Germain, and Dale S. Rogers. *Logistical Excellence.* Burlington, MA: Digital Press, 1992.

Christopher, Martin. *Logistics, The Strategic Issues.* New York: Chapman and Hall, 1992.

Johnson, James C., and Donald F. Wood. *Contemporary Logistics.* 5th ed. New York: Macmillan, 1993.

LaLonde, Bernard, and Martha Cooper. *Partnerships in Providing Customer Service: A Third Party Perspective.* Oakbrook, IL: Council of Logistics Management, 1989.

LaLonde, Bernard, Martha Cooper, and Thomas Noordewier. *Customer Service: A Management Perspective.* Oakbrook, IL: Council of Logistics Management, 1988.

Owen, Wilfried. *Transportation and World Development.* Baltimore, MD.: Johns Hopkins University Press, 1987.

United Nations Conference on Trade and Development (UNCTAD). Review conference on the United Nations Convention on a Code of Conduct for Liner Conferences, Geneva, July 11, 1991.

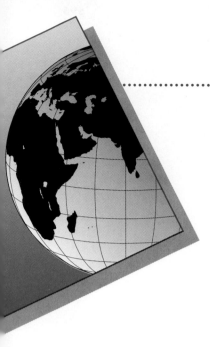

CHAPTER 20

Global Promotional Strategies

THE INTERNATIONAL MARKETPLACE

Communicating Globally, Executing Locally

Advertising as a key component of global marketing has undergone significant change in the recent past—and continues to be very much in a state of flux. Sweeping changes around the world are causing multinational marketers to rethink the way they promote and sell their products.

If current corporate practice in advertising proves anything, it is that there is no single right way to win customers in foreign markets. Finding the best strategy—or several—is the key challenge for executives. Uniformity in varying degrees seems to be the rule, however, as shown by the examples below.

- **American Express** launched a $100-million campaign in 1994 that will cover 30 nations and 60 ads focused on "places you want to go, people you want to be." All spots around the world follow the same formula: Merchants expound on their business philosophies, then talk about the card. Featured are, for example, British designer and retailer Sir Terence Conran, Italian fashion designer Ottavio Missoni, and Japanese innkeepers Koin and Emiko Horibe. The spots extend the series started in the United States in 1993 featuring people such as Toys 'Я' Us's Charles Lazarus. The mandate given to the company's advertising agency, Ogilvy & Mather, by Amex was: Do what it takes to create a series of ads that will give traveling cardholders the same campaign they see at home but will look like a domestic effort to locals.

- **Hewlett-Packard (HP)** is somewhat unusual in that it is a high-tech firm that does not formally centralize advertising strategy or implementation. On the contrary, HP delegates most product-related advertising decisions to its overseas activities. However, when designing local advertising strategies, business units are constrained by companywide identity and design standards and their budgets, which have been approved by headquarters. HP encourages general managers to be guided by local market personalities, business trends and cultural preferences in planning their advertising programs. The result is that advertisements for HP products in other countries usually bear little resemblance to those created in the United States, except where simultaneous worldwide campaigns are under way.

- **Nike,** the U.S. athletic shoe manufacturer, has created a worldwide advertising program at corporate headquarters, which it tailors to each overseas market where its shoes are sold. The basic advertisement is the "Bo Knows" commercial used until recently in Nike's U.S. campaign. Bo Jackson, a professional football and baseball player, is shown participating in such sports as tennis and basketball while wearing Nike shoes. A recognizable player from each of the sports exclaims that "Bo knows" his sport. For its international campaign, the company uses Jackson in similar advertisements with well-known foreign athletes, including cricket celebrity Ian Botham and soccer star Ian Rush. The advertisements run in local languages without subtitles.

- **Reebok,** Nike's chief competitor, has chosen the opposite advertising strategy—that is, it creates different, localized commercials for many country markets and sometimes even used different advertising themes. For the most part, Reebok's foreign advertisements feature actors and athletes famous in each country, who promote the company's shoes in campaigns devised locally. For instance, a typical UK advertisement depicts a British athlete praising the performance and reliability of Reebok's tennis or running shoes. Some country operations, however, have chosen to use Reebok's U.S. campaign. For example, the TV commercial featuring pop singer Paula Abdul singing about "The Reebok Lifestyle" is being shown in Japan, as well as in other Far Eastern markets.

- **Gillette** opted for a global advertising campaign to introduce its "Sensor Shaver" simultaneously in 19 countries throughout North America and Europe. Every commercial in every country uses the theme "Gillette, the best a man can get," which is accompanied by images of strong energetic men and a whisker-clipping diagram. Commercials are tailored to fit local circumstances by the corporate advertising staff in Boston and the company's advertising agency. Some of the required changes were quite subtle. For instance, to get the advertisement's theme across in French, the phrase "la perfection au masculin" was employed. Roughly translated, this phrase means "perfection, male-style." This particular locution was necessary because the word *perfection* in French takes the feminine article (*la*) and so could not be used by itself.

Sources: "Don't Leave Home Without It, Wherever You Live," *Business Week*, February 21, 1994, 76–77; "Global Marketing Strategies," *Business International*, July 9, 1990, 228.

The general requirements of effective marketing communications apply to the multinational corporation as well; however, the environments and the situations usually are more numerous and call for coordination of the promotional effort. Increasingly, marketers opt for varying degrees of pan-regional approaches to take advantage of similarities in markets they serve, as seen in The International Marketplace 20.1.

The technology is in place for global communication efforts, but difficult challenges still remain in the form of cultural, economic, ethnic, regulatory, and demographic differences in the various countries and regions. Standardization of any magnitude requires sound management systems and excellent communication to ensure uniform strategic and tactical thinking of all the professionals in the overseas marketing chain. One marketer has suggested the development of a worldwide visual language that would be understandable and that would not offend cultural sensitivities.[1]

This chapter will analyze the elements to be managed in promotional efforts in terms of environmental opportunities and constraints. A framework is provided for the planning of promotional campaigns. Although the discussion focuses mostly on advertising, other elements of the promotion mix, especially sales promotion and publicity, fit integrally into the planning model. Naturally, all of the mass selling methods have to be planned in conjunction with personal selling efforts. For example, personal selling often relies on updated direct mailing lists and promotional materials sent to prospects before the first sales call.

PLANNING PROMOTIONAL CAMPAIGNS

The planning for promotional campaigns consists of the following seven stages, which usually overlap or take place concurrently, especially after the basics of the campaign have been agreed on:

1. Determine the target audience
2. Determine specific campaign objectives
3. Determine the budget
4. Determine media strategy
5. Determine the message
6. Determine the campaign approach
7. Determine campaign effectiveness[2]

The actual content of these stages will change by type of campaign situation; compare, for example, a local campaign for which headquarters provides support versus a global corporate-image campaign.

The Target Audience

Global marketers face multiple audiences beyond customers. The expectations of these audiences have to be researched to ensure the appropriateness of the campaign decision making. Consider the following publics with whom communication is necessary: suppliers, intermediaries, government, the local community, bankers and creditors, media organizations, shareholders, and employees. Each can be reached with an appropriate mix of tools. A multinational corporation that wants to boost its image with the government and the local community may sponsor events. Exxon, for example, sponsored an exhibition of Colombian art in the United States. The acclaim this received created a better understanding of South American culture and led to the Colombian government's award-

---

[1] John Eger, "Globalancing Act Is Real," *Advertising Age,* January 30, 1984, 20, 24.

[2] Dean M. Peebles and John K. Ryans, *Management of International Advertising: A Marketing Approach* (Boston, MA: Allyn & Bacon, 1984), 72–73.

ing Exxon its highest decoration. This initiative helped Exxon to secure its market position as well as to create a favorable public image throughout South America.[3]

Some campaigns may be targeted at multiple audiences. For example, British Airways' "Manhattan Landing" campaign (in which Manhattan Island takes to the air and lands in London) was directed not only at international business travelers but also at employees, the travel industry, and potential stockholders (the campaign coincided with the privatization of the airline).[4]

As companies become more internationally involved, target audience characteristics change. In 1986, 70 percent of Quantas' passengers were from its home market, Australia; five years later, only 30 percent were from its home market.[5] Even American Airlines, which enjoys a huge domestic market, estimates that by the year 2000, foreign routes will generate 30 percent of revenue compared with virtually none in 1980.

An important aspect of research is to determine multimarket target audience similarities. If such exist, pan-regional or global campaigns can be attempted. Grey Advertising checks for commonalities in variables such as economic expectations, demographics, income, and education. Consumer needs and wants are assessed for common features. An example of such commonalities is provided in The International Marketplace 20.2. Often, however, problems may emerge. For example, Tang was marketed in the United States as an orange juice substitute, which did not succeed in testing abroad. In France, for example, Tang was repositioned as a refreshment because the French rarely drink orange juice at breakfast. In countries like the Philippines, Tang could be marketed as a premium drink, whereas in Brazil, it was a low-priced item.[6] Audience similarities are more easily found in business markets.[7]

Campaign Objectives

Nothing is more essential to the planning of international promotional campaigns than the establishment of clearly defined, measurable objectives. These objectives can be divided into overall global and regional objectives as well as local objectives. Compaq, for example, has declared that it intends to be number 1 in PC and workstation market share by 1996.[8] For Compaq to reach this goal, international sales will have to represent 50 percent of total sales. Such objectives offer the general guidelines and control needed for broad-based campaigns.

The objectives that are set at the local level are more specific and set measurable targets for individual markets. These objectives may be product- or service-related or related to the corporation itself. Typical goals are to increase awareness, enhance image, or improve market share in a particular market. Whatever the objective, it has to be measurable for control purposes.

Local objectives are typically developed as a combination of headquarters-country organization involvement. Basic guidelines are initiated by headquarters, whereas local organizations set the actual country-specific goals. These goals are subject to headquarters

[3] Edgar P. Hibbert, *Marketing Strategy in International Business* (London: McGraw-Hill, 1989), 76–77.

[4] "Berkeley Square Takes on Madison Avenue," *The Economist,* September 17, 1988, 25–28.

[5] Jeni Porter, "Worldwise Quantas," *Advertising Age,* October 21, 1991, 36.

[6] "Global Marketing Campaigns with a Local Touch," *Business International,* July 4, 1988, 205–210.

[7] Robert E. Hite and Cynthia Fraser, "International Advertising Strategies of Multinational Corporations," *Journal of Advertising Research* 28 (August–September 1988): 9–17.

[8] Stephanie Losee, "How Compaq Keeps the Magic Going," *Fortune,* February 21, 1994, 90–92.

20.2

THE INTERNATIONAL MARKETPLACE

The World Wants Its MTV!

MTV has emerged as a significant global medium, with more than 252 million households in 80 countries subscribing to its services. The reason for its success is simple—MTV offers consistent, high-quality programming that reflects the tastes and life-styles of young people.

Its balance of fashion, film, news, competitions, and comedy wrapped in the best music and strong visual identity has made it "the best bet to succeed as a pan-European thematic channel, with its aim to be in every household in Europe by the mid-1990s," according to *Music Week,* Britain's leading music trade paper. Given that 79 percent of the channel's viewers are in the elusive 16–34 age group, MTV is a force as an advertising medium for those who want to closely target their campaigns. MTV has proven to be the ultimate youth marketing vehicle for companies such as Wrangler, Wrigleys, Braun, Britvic, Pepsi, Pentax, and many others. Although many knock-offs have been started around the world, the enormous cost of building a worldwide music-video channel will most likely protect MTV.

MTV's global network consists of the following entities:

- **MTV USA** is seen 24 hours a day on cable television in 96 million U.S. television homes. Presented in stereo, MTV's overall on-air environment is unpredictable and irreverent, reflecting the cutting-edge spirit of rock 'n' roll that is the heart of its programming. Through its graphic look, VJs, music news, promotions, interviews, concert tour information, specials, and documentaries, as well as its original strip programming, MTV has become an international institution of pop culture and the leading authority on rock music since it launched on August 1, 1981.

- **MTV Europe** reaches 32 countries (58.7 million households), 24 hours a day in stereo, via satellite, cable, and terrestrial distribution. The station acquires its own video clips, drawing from the domestic markets in individual European countries to discover bands making an international sound. It has its own team of VJs presenting shows specially tailored for the European market. The channel's programming mix reflects its diverse audience, with coverage of music, style, news, movie information, comedy, and more. Launched August 1, 1987, MTV Europe is owned by Viacom.

- **MTV Asia** was launched September 15, 1991, and is tailored to the musical tastes, life-styles, and sensibilities of MTV's Asian audiences. MTV Asia reaches 41.5 million households in 30 countries on STAR TV, the first pan-Asian satellite television service. MTV Asia is based in Hong Kong and is an English-language network.

- **MTV Japan** is customized for the Japanese youth audience and features a mix of Japanese and English-language programming. MTV Japan was originally launched in October 1984, through a licensing agreement with Asahi Broadcasting Corporation; however, on December 24, 1992, a new licensing agreement between Viacom International and the Music Channel Co., Ltd. (which is a joint venture of Pioneer Electronic Corporation, TDK Corporation, and Tokyo Agency Inc.) was signed.

- **MTV Latino** is MTV's latest international network and it reaches 2.3 million households in 21 countries and territories. The network features a mix of American and Latin music, regional production, music and entertainment news, artist interviews, concert coverage, and specials.
- **MTV Internacional** is a one-hour weekly Spanish-language program. MTV Internacional is a mix of Spanish- and English-language videos, interviews, entertainment news, and on-location specials. Hosted by VJ Daisy Fuentes, the program is broadcast in the United States on the Telemundo Network and in various Latin American countries and is distributed by MTV Syndication Sales.
- **MTV Brasil** was launched in October 1990 following a licensing agreement with the Abril Group, Brazil's leading magazine publisher. The network, which is Portuguese-language, is broadcast via UHF in São Paulo and via VHF in Rio de Janeiro.

Sources: "Will MTV Have to Share the Stage?" *Business Week*, February 21, 1994, 38; Press releases from MTV, March 14, 1994.

approval, mainly to ensure consistency. Although some campaigns, especially global ones, may have more headquarters involvement than usual, local input is still quite important, especially to ensure appropriate implementation of the subsequent programs at the local level.

The Budget

The promotional budget links established objectives with media, message, and control decisions. Ideally, the budget would be set as a response to the objectives to be met, but resource constraints often preclude this approach. Many marketers use an objective-task method, as a recent survey of 484 advertising managers for consumer goods in 15 countries indicates (see Table 20.1); however, realities may force compromises between ideal choices and resources available.[9] As a matter of fact, available funds may dictate the basis from which the objective-task method can start.

Budgets can also be used as a control mechanism if headquarters retains final budget approval. In these cases, headquarters decision makers must have a clear understanding of cost and market differences to be able to make rational decisions.

In terms of worldwide ad spending, some of the leaders in 1991 were Procter & Gamble ($3.6 billion), Philip Morris ($2.6 billion), Unilever ($2.2 billion), Nestlé ($1.5 billion), Toyota ($1.1 billion), and Ford ($1.1 billion). Geographic differences exist in spending; for example, while Procter & Gamble spent 60 percent of its budget in the United States, Unilever's spending there was only 27 percent.[10]

---

[9] Nicolaos E. Synodinos, Charles F. Keown, and Laurence W. Jacobs, "Transnational Advertising Practices: A Survey of Leading Brand Advertisers in Fifteen Countries," *Journal of Advertising Research* 29 (April–May 1989): 43–50.

[10] "100 Leading Advertisers," *Advertising Age,* September 29, 1993, 60; "Unilever Leads with $1.6 Billion," *Advertising Age,* December 14, 1992, S-1.

| TABLE 20.1 | Budgeting Methods for Promotional Programs |

Budgeting Methods for Promotional Programs

Budgeting Method	Percentage of Respondents Using This Method*	Major Differences	
		Lowest Percentages	Highest Percentages
Objective and task	64	Sweden (36%) Argentina (44%)	Canada (87%) Singapore (86%)
Percentage of sales	48	Germany (31%)	Brazil (73%) Hong Kong (70%)
Executive judgment	33	Finland (8%) Germany (8%)	USA (64%) Denmark (51%) Brazil (46%) Great Britain (46%)
All-you-can-afford	12	Argentina (0%) Israel (0%)	Sweden (30%) Germany (25%) Great Britain (24%)
Matched competitors	12	Denmark (0%) Israel (0%)	Germany (33%) Sweden (33%) Great Britain (22%)
Same as last year plus a little more	9	Israel (0%)	
Same as last year	3		
Other	10	Finland (0%) Germany (0%) Israel (0%)	Canada (24%) Mexico (21%)

*Total exceeds 100 percent because respondents checked all budgeting methods that they used.

Source: Nicolaos E. Synodinos, Charles F. Keown, and Laurence W. Jacobs, "Transnational Advertising Practices," *Journal of Advertising Research* 29 (April–May 1989): 43–50.

Media Strategy

Target audience characteristics, campaign objectives, and the budget form the basis for the choice between media vehicles and the development of a media schedule. The major factors determining the choice of the media vehicles to be used are (1) the availability of the media in a given market, (2) the product or service itself, and (3) media habits of the intended audience.

Media Availability   Media spending varies dramatically around the world, as seen in Figure 20.1. In absolute terms, the United States spends more money on advertising than most of the other major advertising nations combined. Other major spenders are Japan, the United Kingdom, Germany, Canada, and France. The mature U.S. market anticipates slower growth in the future, but European integration and the development of the Pacific Rim's consumer markets are likely to fuel major growth.[11]

Naturally, this spending varies by market. Countries devoting the highest percentage to television were Peru (84 percent), Mexico (73 percent), and Venezuela (67 percent). In some countries, the percentage devoted to print is still high: Kuwait (91 percent), Norway

---

[11] Julie S. Hill, "Euro, Pacific Spending Spree," *Advertising Age,* April 10, 1989, 4, 55.

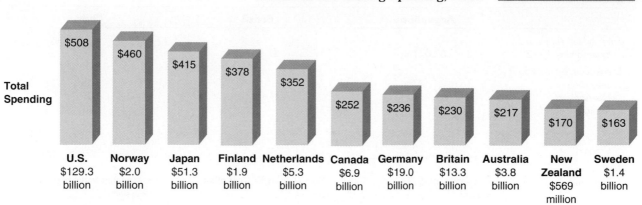

Worldwide Advertising Spending, 1992 — FIGURE 20.1

Country	Total Spending	Per capita(?)
U.S.	$508	$129.3 billion
Norway	$460	$2.0 billion
Japan	$415	$51.3 billion
Finland	$378	$1.9 billion
Netherlands	$352	$5.3 billion
Canada	$252	$6.9 billion
Germany	$236	$19.0 billion
Britain	$230	$13.3 billion
Australia	$217	$3.8 billion
New Zealand	$170	$569 million
Sweden	$163	$1.4 billion

Source: Adapted from "Where the Pitch Is the Loudest," copyright 1989, *U.S. News and Special Report,* reprinted with permission from the March 20, 1989 issue, 90.

(77 percent), and Sweden (77 percent). Radio accounts for more than 20 percent of total measured media in only a few countries, such as Trinidad and Tobago, Nepal, and Honduras. Outdoor/transit advertising accounted for 48 percent of Bolivia's media spending but only 3 percent in Germany.[12] Cinema advertising is important in countries such as India and Nigeria. Until a few years ago, the prevailing advertising technique used by the Chinese consisted of outdoor boards and posters found outside factories; today, more new TV and radio stations are coming on-air.

The media available to the international marketer in major Latin American countries are summarized in Table 20.2. The breakdown by media points to the enormous diversity in how media are used in a given market. These figures do not tell the whole story, however, which emphasizes the need for careful homework on the part of the international manager charged with media strategy. As an example, Brazil has five television networks, but one of them—Rede Globo TV—corners 70 percent of all television advertising spending. Throughout Latin America, the tendency is to allocate half or more of total advertising budgets to television, with the most-coveted spots on prime-time soap operas that attract viewers from Mexico to Brazil. In general, advertising in Latin America requires flexibility and creativity. Inflation rates have caused advertising rates to increase dramatically in countries like Argentina. In Mexico, advertisers can use the "French Plan," which protects participating advertisers from price increases during the year and additionally gives the advertiser two spots for the price of one. For these concessions, the advertiser must pay for the year's entire advertising schedule by October of the year before.

The major problems affecting global promotional efforts involve conflicting national regulations. Even within the EU there is no uniform legal standard. Conditions do vary from country to country, and ads must comply with national regulation. Most European countries either observe the Code of Advertising Practice of the International Chamber of Commerce or have their guidelines based on it.[13] J. Walter Thompson, one of the

---

[12] Compiled from Leo Burnett, *Worldwide Advertising and Media Fact Book* (Chicago: Triumph Books, 1994).

[13] Euromonitor, *European Advertising, Marketing, and Media Factbook 1992* (London: Euromonitor, 1992), section thirty-eight.

TABLE 20.2	Latin American Media Breakdown		
	Argentina*	**Brazil**	**Chile**
Total Advertising Expenditure, 1992	$1,071.4	$1,919.0	$344.4
Breakdown by Media			
Television	37%	59%	45%
Newspapers	34	24	35
Radio	8	5	11
Magazines	5	9	5
Outdoor	6	3	4
Cinema	2		
Media Facts			
Television	7 government, 5 private stations	Rede/Globo TV/and other private	Government and Chilean universities
Newspapers	384 national daily papers	Regional/local medium; no national newspapers	9 national and 43 regional dailies
Radio	247 AM and FM stations, all of which are commercial	1,519 AM and 1,127 FM stations, most of which are commercial	404 commercial stations
Media Buying	Handled by ad agencies. For TV, agencies combine clients' budgets for discounts	Done within the agency. Variation according to client, product, and ranking of media vehicle	Media and clients pay 15% commission

*1991 data

largest advertising agencies in the world, has estimated that advertising expenditures on Western European television would be $2.4 to $3.3 billion more should these regulations be eased.[14] Some of the regulations include limits on the amount of time available for advertisements; for example, in Italy, the state channels allow a maximum of 12 percent advertising per hour and 4 percent over a week, and commercial stations allow 18 percent per hour and 15 percent per week. Furthermore, the leading Italian stations do not guarantee audience delivery when spots are bought. Strict separation between programs and commercials is almost a universal requirement, preventing U.S.-style sponsored programs. Restrictions on items such as comparative claims and gender stereotypes are prevalent; for example, Germany prohibits the use of superlatives such as "best."

Until now, with few exceptions, most nations have been very successful in controlling advertising that enters their borders. When commercials were not allowed on the state-run stations, advertisers in Belgium had been accustomed to placing their ads on the Luxembourg station. Radio Luxembourg has traditionally been used to beam messages to the United Kingdom. By the end of the 1990s, however, approximately half of the homes in Europe will have access to additional television broadcasts through either cable or direct satellite, and television will no longer be restricted by national boundaries. The implications of this to global marketers are significant. The viewer's choice will be expanded, leading to competition among government-run public channels, com-

---

[14] D. Pridgen, "Satellite Television Advertising and the Regulatory Conflict in Western Europe," *Journal of Advertising* 14 (Winter 1985): 23–29.

Continued | **TABLE 20.2**

Colombia	Mexico	Peru	Venezuela
$775.3	$2,896.1	$237.1	$573.7
60%	73%	84%	67%
14%	8%	6%	25%
21%	11%	6%	2%
5%	4%	1%	3%
—	3%	1%	2%
—	1%	2%	1%
Government owned and operated	Televisia	One government, 6 private channels	Private (9) and government (2)
2 national dailies	6 national dailies	12 national, 15 regional	13 national dailies
545 commercial stations; 70% of inventory controlled by two large monopolies	923 commercial stations	Lima has 50 commercial stations; regional/local time are available	212 commercial stations
Agencies as well as clients negotiate with media; discounts prevalent	Payments in advance with bonuses up to 300%	Companies with large budgets negotiate directly. Intermediaries used in the interior of Peru	Only one media buying consortium exists for each group of agencies

Source: Compiled from Leo Burnett, *Worldwide Advertising and Media Fact Book* (Chicago: Triumph Books, 1994), 331–468.

peting state channels from neighboring countries, private channels, and pan-European channels.

This means that marketers need to make sure that advertising works not only within markets but across countries as well.[15] As a consequence, media buying will become more challenging.

Product Influences Marketers and advertising agencies are currently frustrated by wildly differing restrictions on how products can be advertised. Agencies often have to produce several separate versions to comply with various national regulations. Consumer protection in general has dominated the regulatory scene in the 1980s.[16] Changing and standardizing these regulations, even in an area like the EU, is a "long and difficult road." For example, after years of debate within Europe to prohibit tobacco advertising everywhere (except point-of-purchase ads in tobacco specialty shops), the EU decided that the final ratification of the Maastricht Treaty completed the single European market, and the mandate to come up with communitywide directives ended. The issue will now be handled by each member country separately.[17] While some

---

[15] John Clemens, "Television Advertising in Europe," *Columbia Journal of World Business* 22 (Fall 1987): 35–41.

[16] Jean J. Boddewyn, "Advertising Regulation in the 1980s," *Journal of Marketing* 46 (Winter 1982): 22–28.

[17] Amy Haight, "EC Ad Ban May Go up in Smoke," *Advertising Age,* January 17, 1994, I-8.

TABLE 20.3	Restrictions on Advertisements for Specific Products in Selected European Countries

Country	Cigarettes and Tobacco Products	Alcoholic Beverages	Pharmaceutical Products
France	Banned as of 1993	Banned (for products over 1.2% alcohol)	Prior authorization from appropriate government health authority required
Republic of Ireland	Banned in all media except magazines	Banned in broadcast; print allowed but regulated	Advertisements for certain products or treatments prohibited, others regulated
Italy	Banned	Restricted	Restricted; some products banned from TV
Netherlands	Banned in broadcast; must carry health warning elsewhere	Permitted in all media but regulated	Allowed but with restrictions in all media
United Kingdom	Banned in broadcast; approval needed for print	Banned in broadcast; other media carry voluntary restrictions	Prior opinion sought from Medical Advisory Board; advertisements for certain products or treatments prohibited

Sources: Euromonitor, *European Advertising, Marketing, and Media Factbook 1992* (London: Euromonitor, 1992), 751–767; D. Pridgen, "Satellite Television Advertising and the Regulatory Conflict in Western Europe," *Journal of Advertising* 14 (Winter 1985): 23–29.

countries have banned tobacco advertising altogether (e.g., France), some have voluntary restriction systems in place. For example, in the United Kingdom, tobacco advertising is not allowed in magazines aimed at very young women, but it is permitted in other women's magazines. A summary of product-related regulations found in Western Europe is provided in Table 20.3. Tobacco products and alcoholic beverages are the most heavily regulated products in terms of promotion.

However, the manufacturers of these products have not abandoned their promotional efforts. Philip Morris engages in corporate-image advertising using its cowboy-spokesperson. John Player sponsors sports events, especially Formula One car racing. Some European cigarette manufacturers have diversified into the entertainment business (restaurants, lounges, movie theaters) and named them after their cigarette brands. Tobacco and alcohol advertisers have also welcomed an innovation in advertising: in-flight ads. Brown & Williamson Tobacco Corporation, marketer of Kool cigarettes, sponsors the Kool Jazz Network, a music channel on American Airlines.

Certain products are subject to special rules. In the United Kingdom, for example, advertisers cannot show a real person applying an underarm deodorant; the way around this problem is to show an animated person applying the product. What is and is not allowable is very much a reflection of the country imposing the rules. Explicit advertisements of contraceptives are commonplace in Sweden, for example, but far less frequent in most parts of the world.

Audience Characteristics   A major objective of media strategy is to reach the intended target audience with a minimum of waste. As an example, Amoco Oil Company wanted to launch a corporate-image campaign in the People's Republic of China in the hope of receiving drilling contracts. Identifying the appropriate decision makers was not difficult because they all work for the government. The selection of appropriate media proved to be equally simple because most of the decision makers overseeing petroleum exploration were found to read the vertical trade publications: *International Industrial Review, Petroleum Production,* and *Offshore Petroleum.*

If conditions are ideal, and they seldom are in international markets, the media strategist would need data on (1) media distribution, that is, the number of copies of the print medium or the number of sets for broadcast; (2) media audiences; and (3) advertising exposure. For instance, an advertiser interested in using television in Brazil would like to know that the music show "Cassino do Chacrinha" averages a 25 rating and a 50 percent share of audience for the 4:00 P.M. to 6:00 P.M. time slot. In markets where more sophisticated market-research services are available, data on advertising perception and consumer response may be available.[18] In many cases, advertisers have found circulation figures to be unreliable or even fabricated.

Global Media   Media vehicles that have target audiences on at least three continents and for which the media buying takes place through a centralized office are considered to be **global media.** Global media have traditionally been publications that, in addition to the worldwide edition, have provided advertisers the option of using regional editions. For example, *Time* provides 133 editions, enabling advertisers to reach a particular country, continent, or the world. Other global publications include *International Herald Tribune, The Wall Street Journal,* and *National Geographic.*

Advertising in global media is dominated by major consumer-ad categories, particularly airlines, financial services, communications, automobiles, and tobacco. The aircraft industry represents business-market advertisers.[19] Companies spending in global media include AT&T, IBM, and General Motors. In choosing global media, media buyers consider the three most important media characteristics: targetability, client-compatible editorial, and editorial quality.[20] Some global publications have found that some parts of the globe are more appealing to advertisers than others; *International Management,* for example, had to eliminate its editions in Latin America, Africa, and Asia-Pacific because of lack of advertising.[21]

In broadcast media, pan-regional radio stations have been joined by television as a result of satellite technology. The pan-European satellite channels, such as Sky Channel and Super Channel, were conceived from the very beginning as advertising media. Many are skeptical about the potential of these channels, especially in the short term, because of the challenges of developing a cross-cultural following in Europe's still highly nationalistic markets.[22] Pan-European channels have had to cut back, whereas native-language satellite channels like Tele 5 in France and RTL Plus in Germany have increased their viewership. British Satellite Broadcasting, which will compete directly with U.K. networks ITV and the BBC, estimates that it alone will have 10 million viewers and ad revenues of $1.7 billion by the turn of the century.[23] The launch of Star TV (see Figure 20.2) has increased the use of regional advertising campaigns in Asia. While this medium is still

[18] Terence A. Shimp and M. Wayne DeLozier, *Promotion Management and Marketing Communications* (Hinsdale, IL: Dryden Press, 1986), 399–420.

[19] R. Craig Endicott, "International Print Builds Rates, Reach," *Advertising Age,* December 19, 1988, 21–22.

[20] David W. Stewart and Kevin J. McAuliffe, "Determinants of International Media Buying," *Journal of Advertising* 17 (Fall 1988): 22–26.

[21] Lawrence Wentz, "Why 'IM' Heads Away from Global," *Advertising Age,* December 2, 1985, 45, 58.

[22] Laurel Wentz, "Murdoch's Sky Takes a Fall," *Advertising Age,* October 3, 1988, 68.

[23] "European Satellite TV: Just So Much Pie in the Sky?" *Business Week,* October 24, 1988, 39–42.

FIGURE 20.2   Example of a Pan-Regional Medium

The brightest STAR in Asia is now in over 42,000,000 homes.

With unprecedented growth of **279%** in just one year, the STAR TV Network now brings together a total of almost **200 million** people in over **42 million*** households across Asia.

These households are home to the most affluent consumers in the region, which you can reach with one single, remarkably cost-effective, media buy.

STAR TV, the first and only pan-Asian satellite television network, provides 5 channels of non-stop entertainment. This makes the STAR TV Network Asia's most powerful advertising medium, broadcasting STAR Chinese Channel, STAR Plus, Prime Sports, MTV: Music Television and BBC World Service Television twenty four hours a day.

For more research data, programming information and advertising rates, please contact the STAR TV Network Sales Department at (852) 532 1888 or fax (852) 596 0469.

*Independent survey by Frank Small & Associates, November 1993.

STAR TV and ⭐ are trademarks of STAR Television Productions Limited and are used under licence. © STAR Television Productions Limited 1994.

Source: *The Economist,* January 22–28, 1994, 64.

regarded as a corporate advertising vehicle, it has nonetheless attracted the interest of consumer-goods manufacturers as well.[24] The alternative showing the most immediate promise is cable channels that cater to universal segments with converging tastes, such as MTV or The Children's Channel.

---

[24] "Remixing the Message," *Business Asia,* February 15, 1993, 4–5.

The Promotional Message

The creative people must have a clear idea of the characteristics of the audience expected to be exposed to the message. In this sense, the principles of creating effective advertising are the same as in the domestic marketplace. The marketer must determine what the consumer is really buying—that is, the customer's motivations. These will vary, depending on the following:

1. The diffusion of the product or service into the market. For example, to penetrate Third World markets with business computers is difficult when few potential customers know how to type.
2. The criteria on which the customer will evaluate the product. For example, in traditional societies, advertising the time-saving qualities of a product may not be the best approach, as Campbell Soup Company learned in Italy and Brazil, where women felt inadequate as homemakers if they did not make soups from scratch.
3. The product's positioning. For example, Parker Pen's upmarket image around the world may not be profitable enough in a market that is more or less a commodity business. The solution is to create an image for a commodity product and make the public pay for it—for example, the positioning of Perrier in the United States as a premium mineral water.

The ideal situation in developing message strategy is to have a world brand—a product that is manufactured, packaged, and positioned the same around the world. A good example of this type of situation is provided in The International Marketplace 20.3, which describes the promotional program developed by Xerox Corporation for the introduction of its new worldwide copier line. Companies that have been successful with the global approach have shown flexibility in the execution of the campaigns. The idea may be global, but overseas subsidiaries then tailor the message to suit local market conditions and regulations.

Executing an advertising campaign in multiple markets requires a balance between conveying the message and allowing for local nuances. The localization of global ideas can be achieved by various tactics, such as adopting a modular approach, localizing international symbols, and using international advertising agencies.[25]

Marketers may develop multiple broadcast and print ads from which country organizations can choose the most appropriate for their operations. This can provide local operations with cost savings and allow them to use their budgets on tactical campaigns (which may also be developed around the global idea). For example, the "Membership Has Its Privileges" campaign of American Express, which has run in 24 countries on TV and three more in print, was adjusted in some markets to make sure that "privileges" did not have a snob or elitist appeal, especially in countries with a strong caste or class system. Product-related regulations will affect advertising messages as well. When General Mills Toy Group's European subsidiary launched a product line related to G.I. Joe–type war toys and soldiers, it had to develop two television commercials, a general version for most European countries and another for countries that bar advertisements for products with military or violent themes. As a result, in the version running in Germany, Holland, and Belgium, jeeps replaced the toy tanks, and guns were removed from the hands of the toy soldiers. Other countries, such as the United Kingdom, do not allow children to appear in advertisements.

Marketers may also want to localize their international symbols. Some of the most effective global advertising campaigns have capitalized on the popularity of pop music worldwide and used well-known artists in the commercials, such as Pepsi's use of Tina Turner. In some versions, local stars have been included with the international stars to

25 "Global Marketing Campaigns with a Local Touch," *Business International,* July 4, 1988, 205–210.

20.3   THE INTERNATIONAL MARKETPLACE

Xerox Combats Worldwide Competition

When Xerox Corporation's leading position in photocopying started to decline in the mid-1970s, the company wanted to develop one comprehensive plan to combat competition, to stop the sales decline, and to restore its international leadership position.

A new line of products was developed by the various entities of the corporation. Fuji Xerox developed two copiers, the 1020 and the 1035, for the low-volume segment. Rank Xerox came up with an internationally developed entry, the 1045, for the middle-volume segment; and Xerox U.S. designed the Xerox 1075 for the high-volume market. With the product ready for global introduction, Xerox needed a comprehensive communications program. It wanted to promote the products with a single, powerful message instantly understood anywhere to convey the endurance of its products. The symbol chosen: the marathon.

The media program combined international with local media. An umbrella campaign in English-language print media (such as the international editions of *Time, Newsweek, Business Week,* and *Fortune,* and the European and Far Eastern editions of *The Wall Street Journal* and *Herald Tribune*) was supported by appropriate advertising in local languages. The ad on the left is part of the global campaign, whereas the ad on the right is an example of a local (Finnish) execution. Xerox also used two media aimed at business travelers: a

high-visibility poster program in major airports and a two-minute, editorial-style commercial shown before movies on international flights.

To reinforce the advertising program, Xerox sponsored marathon races around the world. World-class runners (such as Grete Waitz and Rob de Castella) agreed to appear in six races a year in Team Xerox uniforms.

The effort paid off in sales results. Although many factors contributed to the increase, the marathon campaign played a key role in generating speedy awareness of the new line of products.

Sources: "Why Planning at Xerox Means Consensus-Building," *Business International*, July 29, 1991, 253–254; William Wells, John Burnett, and Sandra Moriarty, *Advertising: Principles and Practice* (Englewood Cliffs, NJ: Prentice-Hall, 1989), 580–583.

localize the campaign. Aesthetics play a role in localizing campaigns. The global marketer does not want to chance the censoring of the company's ads or risk offending customers. For example, even though importers of perfumes into Saudi Arabia want to use the same campaigns as are used in Europe, they occasionally have to make adjustments dictated by moral standards, as illustrated in Figure 20.3. The European version shows a man's hand clutching a perfume bottle and a woman's hand seizing his bare forearm. In the Saudi Arabian version, the man's arm is clothed in a dark suit sleeve, and the woman's hand is merely brushing his hand.

The use of one agency—or only a few agencies—ensures consistency. The use of one agency allows for coordination, especially when the global marketer's operations are decentralized. It also makes the exchange of ideas easier and may therefore lead, for example, to wider application of a modification or a new idea. In May 1994 IBM concentrated its $500 million account to Ogilvy & Mather, from 40 different agencies in 144 countries.

Local Adjustment to Global Campaign   **FIGURE 20.3**

Source: Michael Field, "Fragrance Marketers Sniff Out Rich Aroma," *Advertising Age,* January 30, 1986, 10.

The environmental influences that call for these modifications, or in some cases totally unique approaches, are culture, economic development, and life-styles. Of the cultural variables, language is most apparent in its influence on promotional campaigns. The European Union alone has nine languages: English, French, German, Dutch, Danish, Italian, Greek, Spanish, and Portuguese. Advertisers in the Arab world have sometimes found that the voices in a TV commercial speak in the wrong Arabic dialect. The challenge of language is often most pronounced in translating themes. For example, Coca-Cola's worldwide theme "Can't Beat the Feeling" is the equivalent of "I Feel Coke" in Japan, "Unique Sensation" in Italy, and "The Feeling of Life" in Chile. In Germany, where no translation really worked, the original English-language theme was used. One way of getting around this is to have no copy or very little copy and to use innovative approaches, such as pantomime. Using any type of symbolism will naturally require adequate copy testing to determine how the target market perceives the message.

The stage of economic development—and therefore the potential demand for and degree of awareness of the product—may vary and differentiate the message from one market to another. Whereas developed markets may require persuasive messages (to combat other alternatives), a developing market may require a purely informative campaign. Campaigns may also have to be dramatically adjusted to cater to life-style differences in regions that are demographically quite similar. For example, N.W. Ayer's Bahamas tourism campaign for the European market emphasizes clean water, beaches, and air. The exceptions are in Germany, where it focuses on sports activities, and in the United Kingdom, where it features humor.

Unique market conditions may require localized approaches. Although IBM has utilized global campaigns (the Little Tramp campaign, for example), it has also used major local campaigns in Japan and Europe for specific purposes. In Japan, it used a popular television star in poster and door-board ads to tell viewers, "Friends, the time is ripe" (for buying an IBM 5550 personal computer). The campaign was designed to bolster the idea that the machine represents a class act from America. At the same time, IBM was trying to overcome a problem in Europe of being perceived as "too American." Stressing that IBM is actually a "European company," an advertising campaign told of IBM's large factories, research facilities, and tax-paying subsidiaries within the EU.

The Campaign Approach

Many multinational corporations are staffed and equipped to perform the full range of promotional activities. In most cases, however, they will rely on the outside expertise of advertising agencies and other promotions-related companies such as media-buying companies and specialty marketing firms. In the organization of promotional efforts, a company has two basic decisions to make: (1) what type of outside services to use and (2) how to establish decision-making authority for promotional efforts.

Outside Services   Of all the outside promotion-related services, advertising agencies are by far the most significant. A list of the world's top 50 agencies and agency groups is given in Table 20.4. Of the top 50 agencies, 21 are based in the United States, 15 in Japan, and the rest in the United Kingdom, France, Australia, South Korea, and Italy. Whereas the Japanese agencies tend to have few operations outside their home country, U.S. and European agencies are engaged in worldwide expansion. Size is measured in terms of gross income and billings. Billings are the cost of advertising time and space placed by the agency plus fees for certain extra services, which are converted by formula to correspond to media billings in terms of value of services performed. Agencies do not receive billings as income; in general, agency income is approximately 15 percent of billing.

		Top 50 Agencies Worldwide	**TABLE 20.4**

Rank	Agency	Worldwide gross income* 1993	Worldwide billings* 1993
1	WPP Group, London	$2,633.6	$18,485.3
2	Interpublic Group of Cos., New York	2,078.5	13,976.3
3	Omnicom Group, New York	1,876.0	13,839.1
4	Dentsu Inc., Tokyo	1,403.2	10,846.3
5	Saatchi & Saatchi Co., London/New York	1,355.1	10,809.6
6	Young & Rubicam, New York	1,008.9	7,559.0
7	Euro RSCG Worldwide, Neuilly, France	864.8	6,508.9
8	Grey Advertising, New York	765.7	5,171.8
9	Hakuhodo Inc., Tokyo	667.8	4,938.0
10	Foote, Cone & Belding Communications, Chicago	633.7	5,336.0
11	Leo Burnett Co., Chicago	622.4	4,223.5
12	Publicis Communication/Publicis-FCB, Paris	572.0	3,887.8
13	D'Arcy Masius Benton & Bowles, New York	553.6	4,770.1
14	BDDP Group, Boulogne, France	278.8	1,852.1
15	Bozell Worldwide, New York	269.9	2,135.0
16	Tokyu Agency, Tokyo	181.8	1,529.8
17	Daiko Advertising, Osaka, Japan	181.5	1,395.5
18	Asatsu Inc., Tokyo	171.3	1,308.8
19	Ketchum Communications, Pittsburgh	140.4	1,062.0
20	Dai-Ichi Kikaku, Tokyo	135.3	1,076.7
21	Dentsu, Y & R Partnerships, New York, Tokyo	124.5	937.3
22	Chiat/Day, Los Angeles	122.1	919.9
23	N W Ayer, New York	108.5	945.2
24	Yomiko Advertising, Tokyo	108.1	900.8
25	Cheil Communications, Seoul	106.6	397.1
26	I & S Corp., Tokyo	105.0	804.0
27	Gold Greenlees Trott, London	100.3	805.1
28	Ayer Europe, London	96.0	661.9
29	TMP Worldwide, New York	92.0	613.1
30	Asahi Advertising, Tokyo	91.6	592.8
31	Lopex, London	90.0	598.3
32	Man Nen Sha, Osaka, Japan	83.6	537.5
33	Ross Roy Communications, Bloomfield Hills, Mich.	81.0	540.0
34	Gage Marketing Group, Minneapolis	78.8	525.4
35	Oricom Co., Tokyo	73.6	497.2
36	DIMAC Direct, Bridgeton, Mo.	63.5	176.1
37	Clemenger/BBDO, Melbourne	61.7	369.0
38	Armando Testa International, Milan, Italy	61.1	477.6
39	Sogei Inc., Tokyo	59.2	376.9
40	Kyodo Advertising Co., Tokyo	54.5	389.3
41	Hal Riney & Partners, San Francisco	53.1	425.0
42	Earle Palmer Brown Cos., Bethesda, Md	53.1	409.6

Continued

| TABLE 20.4 | *Continued* |

Rank	Agency	Worldwide gross income* 1993	Worldwide billings* 1993
43	**Chuo Senko Advertising,** Tokyo	51.9	370.7
44	**Oricom Inc.,** Seoul	49.7	157.2
45	**W. B. Doner & Co.,** Southfield, Mich./ Baltimore	49.2	407.0
46	**Ally & Gargano,** New York	47.9	377.8
47	**Jordan, McGrath, Case & Taylor,** New York	46.5	420.0
48	**Bronner Slosberg Humphrey,** Boston	45.8	305.2
49	**Dualilbi Petit Zaragoza,** São Paulo, Brazil	43.6	N/A
50	**Springer & Jacoby,** Hamburg, Germany	43.2	N/A

*Gross income and billings are in millions of U.S. dollars.

Source: "World's Top 50 Advertising Organizations," *Advertising Age,* April 13, 1994, 12. Reprinted with permission. Copyright, Crain Communications, Inc., 1994.

Agencies form world groups for better coverage. The largest world "super" group, WPP Group, includes such entities as Ogilvy & Mather; J. Walter Thompson; Brouillard Communications; and Mendoza, Dillon & Asociados. Smaller advertising agencies have affiliated local agencies in foreign markets.

The choice of an agency will largely depend on the quality of coverage the agency will be able to give the multinational company. Global marketing requires global advertising, according to proponents of the globalization trend. The reason is not that significant cost savings can be realized through a single worldwide ad campaign but that such a global campaign is inseparable from the idea of global marketing. Saatchi & Saatchi Advertising Worldwide, which promotes itself as the leading world-brand agency, predicts that the whole industry will be concentrated into a few huge multinational agencies by the end of the decade.[26] Agencies with networks too small to compete have become prime takeover targets in the creation of worldwide mega-agencies. Many believe that local, midsized agencies can compete in the face of globalization by developing local solutions.[27]

Although the forecast that six large agencies will eventually place most international advertising may be exaggerated, global marketing is the new wave and is having a strong impact on advertising. In the 1980s, the major multinational agencies increased their share of the advertising market from 14 percent to over 20 percent.[28] Major realignments of client-agency relationships have occurred due to mergers and to clients' reassessment of their own strategies.

New markets are also emerging, and agencies are establishing their presence in them. For example, DDB Needham, which has been servicing its clients in the Chinese market from Hong Kong, formed a joint venture with the Chinese government in 1989.[29] In September 1988, Young & Rubicam signed a letter of intent to form a joint venture with the largest ad agency in the then Soviet Union, Vneshtorgreklama.[30]

Agency-client relations for the major multinational corporations and their international advertising agencies are shown in Table 20.5. According to a Grey Advertising

[26] Myron Magnet, "What Makes Saatchi & Saatchi Grow," *Fortune,* March 11, 1984, 46–56.

[27] "Ad Exec: Going Global Is Not Always the Best Choice an Agency Can Make," *Marketing News,* August 1, 1988, 15.

[28] Myron Magnet, "Saatchi & Saatchi Will Keep Gobbling," *Fortune,* June 23, 1986, 36–40.

[29] Nancy Giges, "DDB Needham to Enter China for Asian Growth," *Advertising Age,* May 1, 1989, 57–58.

[30] Charles Joseph, "Soviet Union," *Advertising Age,* November 9, 1988, 114.

	NW Ayer	BBDO	BDDP	Backer Spielvogel Bates Worldwide	Bozell, Jacobs, Kenyon & Eckhardt	Leo Burnett Co.	DDB Needham Worldwide	DMB&B	Foote, Cone & Belding	GGK	Grey Advertising	Hakuhodo Inc.	HDM	Ketchum Communications	Lintas Worldwide	Lowe International	McCann-Erickson Worldwide	Mojo	Ogilvy & Mather Worldwide	Publicis International	Roux, Seguela, Cayzac & Goudard	Saatchi & Saatchi Advertising	Scali, McCabe, Sloves	TBWA Advertising	J. Walter Thompson Co.	Univas	WCRS/Belier	Young & Rubicam
American Airlines					•		•																					
American Cynamid				•				•	•													•						
American Express																	•		•									
American Home Products								•									•											•
Anheuser-Busch							•	•																				
BAT				•							•				•				•								•	
Bayer		•					•	•			•				•		•		•		•						•	
Beecham											•							•	•			•						
Beiersdorf									•	•															•			
BMW				•															•								•	
Bristol-Myers							•	•			•								•								•	
BSN Gervais Danone			•										•									•		•			•	•
Cadbury-Schweppes								•											•			•						
Campbell Soup		•						•														•						
Cheesebrough-Pond's																	•								•			
Ciba Geigy				•													•		•									
Citicorp							•	•	•						•													
Coca-Cola Co.															•	•	•											
Colgate-Palmolive Co.								•					•															•
CPC International								•					•				•		•			•						
Dow Chemical Co.								•					•				•		•								•	
Du Pont	•	•											•						•									•
Duracell							•												•									
Eastman Kodak Co.																			•						•			•
Electrolux				•							•																	
General Foods								•			•								•									•
General Motors	•							•									•		•									
Gillette Co.	•	•							•										•			•						
Guinness								•											•			•						
H.J. Heinz						•	•	•																				•
Henkel		•						•		•			•				•		•					•				
Hewlett Packard						•							•															
Heublein																	•		•									
IBM																			•									

Continued

TABLE 20.5   *Continued*

	NW Ayer	BBDO	BDDP	Backer Spielvogel Bates Worldwide	Bozell, Jacobs, Kenyon & Eckhardt	Leo Burnett Co.	DDB Needham Worldwide	DMB&B	Foote, Cone & Belding	GGK	Grey Advertising	Hakuhodo Inc.	HDM	Ketchum Communications	Lintas Worldwide	Lowe International	McCann-Erickson Worldwide	Mojo	Ogilvy & Mather Worldwide	Publicis International	Roux, Seguela, Cayzac & Goudard	Saatchi & Saatchi Advertising	Scali, McCabe, Sloves	TBWA Advertising	J. Walter Thompson Co.	Univas	WCRS/Belier	Young & Rubicam
Jacobs Suchard													●								●				●			●
Johnson & Johnson		●					●				●				●		●		●			●						●
S.C. Johnson				●		●	●												●						●		●	
Kimberly-Clark							●	●											●									
Kraft						●			●								●								●			
Mars				●			●				●																	
Mars Petfood				●																								
Philip Morris						●																		●				
Nestlé		●							●						●		●		●	●		●			●		●	
L'Oreal														●			●			●						●		
Parker Pen																●												
PepsiCo		●			●	●													●			●			●			●
N.V. Philips		●					●				●				●				●	●					●			
Polaroid		●																	●									
Procter & Gamble						●		●			●														●			
Qantas																		●									●	
Quaker Oats Co.							●								●		●								●			
Reckitt & Colman											●				●		●	●				●			●			
Remy Martin															●												●	
Richardson-Vicks				●			●										●											
RJR Nabisco				●					●						●		●					●			●			
Rothmans	●	●									●																	
Rowntree-Macintosh		●													●				●									
Seagram						●													●								●	
Shell				●															●									
3M				●							●			●					●									
Unilever		●													●		●		●						●			
Volkswagen							●			●																		
Wm. Wrigley Jr. Co.		●							●		●								●									
Warner-Lambert Co.				●																					●			●
Xerox		●																	●								●	

Source: "International Agencies Report on Key Clients," *Advertising Age*, July 11, 1988, 56. Reprinted with permission from *Advertising Age*. Copyright 1988 Crain Communications, Inc. Updated from "World Brands," *Advertising Age*, September 2, 1991, 25–35.

survey of 50 multinational marketers, 76 percent believe the ideal situation is to use the same agency worldwide, with some local deviation as necessary. The same percentage believes an advertising agency should be centrally run, and 72 percent believe in using the same advertising strategy worldwide.[31] Most large companies typically use more than one agency, with the division of labor usually along product lines. For example, Matsushita Electric Industrial Company, an innovator in the consumer-electronics industry, uses two major agencies. Backer Spielvogel Bates Worldwide handles everything involving portables, audio, VHS, and television. Grey Advertising handles the hi-fi area, the Technics label, and telephone products. Panasonic, one of Matsushita's U.S. brands, has a small agency for primarily nonconsumer items.

The main concern arising from the use of mega-agencies is conflict. With only a few giant agencies to choose from, the global marketer may end up with the same agency as the main competitor. The mega-agencies believe they can meet any objections by structuring their companies as rigidly separate, watertight agency networks (such as the Interpublic Group) under the umbrella of a holding group. Following that logic, Procter & Gamble, a client of Saatchi & Saatchi Advertising Worldwide, and Colgate-Palmolive, a client of Ted Bates, should not worry about falling into the same network's client base. However, when the Saatchi & Saatchi network purchased Ted Bates, Colgate-Palmolive left the agency.

Despite the globalization trend, local agencies will survive as a result of governmental regulations. In Peru, for example, a law mandates that any commercial aired on Peruvian television must be 100 percent nationally produced. Local agencies also tend to forge ties with foreign agencies for better coverage and customer service and thus become part of the general globalization effort. A basic fear in the advertising industry is that accounts will be taken away from agencies that cannot handle world brands. An additional factor is contributing to the fear of losing accounts. In the past, many multinational corporations allowed local subsidiaries to make advertising decisions entirely on their own. Others gave subsidiaries an approved list of agencies and some guidance. Still others allowed local decisions subject only to headquarters' approval. Now the trend is toward centralization of all advertising decisions, including those concerning the creative product.

Decision-Making Authority The alternatives for allocating decision-making authority range from complete centralization to decentralization. With complete centralization, the headquarters level is perceived to have all the right answers and has adequate power to impose its suggestions on all of its operating units. Decentralization involves relaxing most of the controls over foreign affiliates and allowing them to pursue their own promotional approaches.

The Grey Advertising survey found that only 21 percent of multinational corporations surveyed were run centrally but that 41 percent were moving in that direction. However, multinational corporations are at various stages in their quest for centralization. Procter & Gamble and Gillette generally have an approved list of agencies, whereas Quaker Oats and Johnson & Johnson give autonomy to their local subsidiaries but will veto those decisions occasionally.

The important question is not who should make decisions but how advertising quality can be improved at the local level. Gaining approval in multinational corporations is an interactive approach using coordinated decentralization.[32] This six-step program,

[31] Dennis Chase, "Global Marketing: The New Wave," *Advertising Age,* June 25, 1984, 49, 74.

[32] Dean M. Peebles, John K. Ryans, and Ivan R. Vernon, "Coordinating International Advertising," *Journal of Marketing* 42 (January 1978): 28–34.

FIGURE 20.4   Coordinated Approach to International Advertising

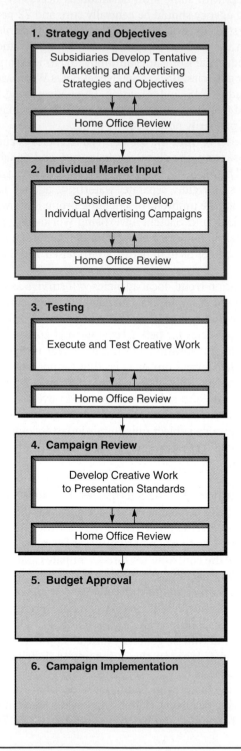

Source: Dean M. Peebles, John K. Ryans, and Ivan R. Vernon, "Coordinating International Advertising," *Journal of Marketing* 42 (January 1978): 30, published by the American Marketing Association.

which is summarized in Figure 20.4, strives for development of common strategy but flexible execution. The approach maintains strong central control but at the same time capitalizes on the greatest asset of the individual markets—market knowledge. Interaction between the central authority and the local levels takes place at every single stage of the planning process. The central authority is charged with finding the commonalities in the data provided by the individual market areas. This procedure will avoid one of the most common problems associated with acceptance of plans—the NIH syndrome (not invented here)—by allowing for local participation by the eventual implementers.

A good example of this approach was Eastman Kodak's launch of its Ektaprint copier-duplicator line in 11 separate markets in Europe. For economic and organizational reasons, Kodak did not want to deal with different campaigns or parameters. It wanted the same ad graphics in each country, accompanied by the theme "first name in photography, last word in copying." Translations varied slightly from country to country, but the campaign was identifiable from one country to another. A single agency directed the campaign, which was more economical than campaigns in each country would have been and was more unified and identifiable through Europe. The psychological benefit of association of the Kodak name with photography was not lost in the campaign.

Agencies are adjusting their operations to centrally run client operations. Many accounts are now handled by a lead agency, usually in the country where the client is based. More and more agencies are moving to a strong international supervisor for global accounts. This supervisor can overrule local agencies and make personnel changes. Specialty units have emerged as well. For example, McCann-Erickson has a global advertising unit of 25 professionals at headquarters in New York that specializes in developing global campaigns for its clients.[33]

Measurement of Advertising Effectiveness

John Wanamaker reportedly said, "I know half the money I spend on advertising is wasted. Now, if I only knew which half." Whether or not advertising effectiveness can be measured, most companies engage in the attempt. Measures of advertising effectiveness should range from pretesting of copy appeal and recognition, to posttesting of recognition, all the way to sales effects. The measures most used are sales, awareness, recall, executive judgment, intention to buy, profitability, and coupon return.[34]

The technical side of these measurement efforts does not differ from that in the domestic market, but the conditions are different. Very often, syndicated services, such as A.C. Nielsen, are not available to the global marketer. If available, their quality may not be at an acceptable level. Testing is also quite expensive and may not be undertaken for the smaller markets. Compared with costs in the U.S. market, the costs of research in the international market are higher in relation to the overall expenditure on advertising.[35] The biggest challenge to advertising research will come from the increase of global and regional campaigns. Comprehensive and reliable measures of campaigns for a mass European market, for example, are difficult because audience measurement techniques and analysis differ for each country. Advertisers are pushing for universally accepted parameters to compare audiences in one country to those in another.

---

[33] "International Approach of McCann," *New York Times,* February 27, 1989, 34.

[34] Nicolaos E. Synodinos, Charles F. Keown, and Laurence W. Jacobs, "Transnational Advertising Practices: A Survey of Leading Brand Advertisers in Fifteen Countries," *Journal of Advertising Research* 29 (April–May 1989): 43–50.

[35] Joseph T. Plummer, "The Role of Copy Research in Multinational Advertising," *Journal of Advertising Research* 26 (October–November 1986): 11–15.

OTHER PROMOTIONAL ELEMENTS

Personal Selling

Advertising is often equated with the promotional effort; however, a number of other efforts are used to support advertising. The marketing of industrial goods, especially of high-priced items, requires strong personal selling efforts. In some cases, personal selling may be truly international; for example, Boeing and Northrop salespeople engage in sales efforts around the world from their domestic bases. However, most personal selling is done by the subsidiaries, with varying degrees of headquarters' involvement. In cases where personal selling constitutes the primary thrust of the corporate promotional effort and where global customer groups can be identified, unified and coordinated sales practices may be called for. When distribution is intensive, channels are long, or markets have tradition-oriented distribution, headquarters' role should be less pronounced and should concentrate mostly on offering help and guidance.[36]

Eastman Kodak has developed a line-of-business approach to allow for standardized strategy throughout a region.[37] In Europe, one person is placed in charge of the entire copier-duplicator program in each country. That person is responsible for all sales and service teams within the country. Typically, each customer is served by three representatives, each with a different responsibility. Sales representatives maintain ultimate responsibility for the account; they conduct demonstrations, analyze customer requirements, determine the right type of equipment for each installation, and obtain the orders. Service representatives install and maintain the equipment and retrofit new-product improvements to existing equipment. Customer-service representatives are the liaison between sales and service. They provide operator training on a continuing basis and handle routine questions and complaints. Each team is positioned to respond to any European customer within four hours.

The training of the salesforce usually takes place in the national markets, but multinational corporations' headquarters will have a say in the techniques used. For instance, when Kodak introduced the Ektaprint line, sales team members were selected carefully. U.S. copier personnel could be recruited from other Kodak divisions, but most European marketing personnel had to be recruited from outside the company and given intensive training. Sales managers and a select group of sales trainers were sent to the Rochester, New York, headquarters for six weeks of training. They then returned to Europe to set up programs for individual countries so that future teams could be trained there. To ensure continuity, all the U.S. training materials were translated into the languages of the individual countries. To maintain a unified program and overcome language barriers, Kodak created a service language consisting of 1,200 words commonly found in technical information.

Foreign companies entering the Japanese market face challenges in establishing a salesforce. Recruitment poses the first major problem, since well-established, and usually local, entities have an advantage in attracting personnel. Many have, therefore, entered into joint ventures or distribution agreements to obtain a salesforce. Companies can also expect to invest more in training and organizational-culture-building activities than in the United States. These may bring long-term advantages in fostering loyalty to the company.[38]

---

[36] John S. Hill, Richard R. Still, and Unal O. Boya, "Managing the Multinational Sales Force," *International Marketing Review* 8 (1991): 19–31.

[37] Joseph A. Lawton, "Kodak Penetrates the European Copier Market with Customized Marketing Strategy and Product Changes," *Marketing News,* August 3, 1984, 1, 6.

[38] John L. Graham, Shigeru Ichikawa, and Yao Apasu, "Managing Your Sales Force in Japan," *Euro-Asia Business Review* 6 (January 1987): 37–40.

Sales Promotion

Sales promotion has been used as the catchall term for promotion that does not fall under advertising, personal selling, or publicity. Sales promotion directed at consumers involves such activities as couponing, sampling, premiums, consumer education and demonstration activities, cents-off packs, point-of-purchase materials, and direct mail. The use of sales promotions as alternatives and as support for advertising is increasing worldwide.[39] The appeal is related to several factors: cost and clutter of media advertising, simpler targeting of customers compared with advertising, and easier tracking of promotional effectiveness (for example, coupon returns provide a clear measure of effectiveness).

The success in Latin America of Tang, General Foods' presweetened powder juice substitute, is for the most part traceable to successful sales-promotion efforts. One promotion involved trading Tang pouches for free popsicles from Kibon, General Foods' Brazilian subsidiary. Kibon also placed coupons for free groceries in Tang pouches. In Puerto Rico, General Foods ran Tang sweepstakes. In Argentina, in-store sampling featured Tang pitchers and girls in orange Tang dresses. Decorative Tang pitchers were a hit throughout Latin America. Sales promotion directed at intermediaries, also known as trade promotion, includes activities such as trade shows and exhibits, trade discounts, and cooperative advertising.

For sales promotion to be effective, the campaigns planned by manufacturers, or their agencies, must gain the support of the local retailer population. Coupons from consumers, for example, have to be redeemed and sent to the manufacturer or to the company handling the promotion. A.C. Nielsen tried to introduce cents-off coupons in Chile and ran into trouble with the nation's supermarket union, which notified its members that it opposed the project and recommended that coupons not be accepted. The main complaint was that an intermediary, like Nielsen, would unnecessarily raise costs and thus the prices to be charged to consumers. Also, some critics felt that coupons would limit individual negotiations because Chileans often bargain for their purchases.

Tools of sales promotion fall under varying regulations, as can be seen from Table 20.6. A particular level of incentive may be permissible in one market but illegal in another. The Scandinavian countries present the greatest difficulties in this respect because every promotion has to be approved by a government body. In France, a gift cannot be worth more than 4 percent of the retail value of the product being promoted (subject to a maximum of 10 francs), whereas the maximum prize value in the Netherlands is 250 guilders, making certain promotions virtually impossible. Although competitions are allowed in most of Western Europe, to insist on receiving proofs of purchase as a condition of entry is not permitted in Germany.

Regulations such as these make truly global sales promotions rare and difficult to launch.[40] Although only a few multinational brands have been promoted on a multiterritory basis, the approach can work. In general, such multicountry promotions may be suitable for products such as soft drinks, liquor, airlines, credit cards, and jeans, which span cultural divides. Naturally, local laws and cultural differences have to be taken into account at the planning stage. Although many of the promotions may be funded centrally, they will be implemented differently in each market so that they can be tied with the local company's other promotional activities. For example, 7Up's multiterritory Music Machine promotion carries a common theme—youth-oriented rock music. The

[39] Jean J. Boddewyn, *Premiums, Gifts, and Competitions* (New York: International Advertising Association, 1986), Chap. 1.

[40] "An English Plan Abroad," *Sales Promotion*, April 25, 1985, 2–6.

TABLE 20.6   Regulations Regarding Premiums, Gifts, and Competitions in Selected Countries

Country	Category	No restrictions or Minor Ones	Authorized with Major Restrictions	General Ban with Important Exceptions	Almost Total Prohibition
Australia	Premiums	x			
	Gifts	x			
	Competitions		x		
Austria	Premiums				x
	Gifts		x		
	Competitions		x		
Canada	Premiums	x			
	Gifts	x			
	Competitions		x		
Denmark	Premiums			x	
	Gifts		x		
	Competitions			x	
France	Premiums	x			
	Gifts	x			
	Competitions	x			
Germany	Premiums				x
	Gifts		x		
	Competitions		x		
Hong Kong	Premiums	x			
	Gifts	x			
	Competitions	x			
Japan	Premiums		x		
	Gifts		x		
	Competitions		x		
Korea	Premiums		x		
	Gifts		x		
	Competitions		x		
United Kingdom	Premiums	x			
	Gifts	x			
	Competitions		x		
United States	Premiums	x			
	Gifts	x			
	Competitions	x			
Venezuela	Premiums		x		
	Gifts		x		
	Competitions		x		

Source: Jean J. Boddewyn, *Premiums, Gifts, and Competitions,* 1988, published by International Advertising Association, 342 Madison Avenue, Suite 2000, NYC, NY 10017. Reprinted with permission.

promotion involves sponsored radio shows, featuring specially recorded concerts by leading contemporary artists, and promotional gifts such as music videos and audiotapes.

In the province of Quebec in Canada, advertisers must pay a tax on the value of the prizes they offer in a contest, whether the prize is a trip, money, or a car. The amount of the tax depends on the geographical extent of the contest. If it is open only to residents of Quebec, the tax is 10 percent; if open to all of Canada, 3 percent; if worldwide, 1 percent. Subtle distinctions are drawn in the regulations between a premium and a prize. As an example, the Manic soccer team was involved with both McDonald's and Provigo Food stores. The team offered a dollar off the price of four tickets, and the stubs could be cashed for a special at McDonald's. Provigo was involved in a contest offering a year's supply of groceries. The Manic-McDonald's offer was a premium that involved no special tax; Provigo, however, was taxed because it was involved in a contest. According to the regulation, a premium is available to everyone, whereas a prize is available to a certain number of people among those who participate. In some cases, industries may self-regulate the use of promotional items.

Public Relations

Image—how a multinational corporation relates to and is perceived by its key constituents—is a bottom-line issue for management. Public relations is the marketing communications function charged with executing programs to earn public understanding and acceptance, which means both internal and external communication.

Especially in multinational corporations, internal communication is important to create an appropriate corporate culture. The Japanese have perfected this in achieving a **wa** (we) spirit. Everyone in an organization is, in one way or another, in marketing and will require additional targeted information on issues not necessarily related to his or her day-to-day functions. A basic part of most internal programs is the employee publication produced and edited typically by the company's public relations or advertising department. Some, such as the example in Figure 20.5 from Deere & Company, have

Internal Media: Deere & Company   FIGURE 20.5

Source: Deere & Company

foreign-language versions. More often, as at Mobil Corporation, each affiliate publishes its own employee publication. The better this vehicle can satisfy the information needs of employees, the less they will have to rely on others, especially informal sources such as the grapevine. Audiovisual media in the form of films, videotapes, slides, and in some firms, closed-circuit television are being used, especially for training and indoctrination purposes. Some of the materials that are used internally can be provided to other publics as well; for example, booklets, manuals, and handbooks are provided to employees, distributors, and visitors to the company.[41]

Externally, multinational companies are concerned about establishing global identities to increase sales, differentiate products and services, and attract employees. Non-U.S. marketers have been found to be far more active than U.S. firms in trying to boost their global identities.[42] These activities have been seen as necessary to compete against companies with strong local identities. External campaigns can be achieved through the use of corporate symbols, corporate advertising, customer relations programs, and publicity. For example, Black & Decker's corporate logo, which is in the shape and color of an orange hexagon, is used for all B&D products.[43] Some material is produced to assist specifically in personal selling efforts.

Publicity, in particular, is of interest to the multinational corporation. Publicity is the securing of editorial space (as opposed to paid advertising) to further marketing objectives. Because it is editorial in content, the consuming public perceives it as more trustworthy than advertising. A good example of how publicity can be used to aid in advertising efforts was the introduction by Princess Lines (known from the television show "Love Boat") of a new liner, The Royal Princess. Because of its innovative design and size, the Royal Princess was granted substantial press coverage, which was especially beneficial in the travel and leisure magazines. Such coverage does not come automatically but has to be coordinated and initiated by the public relations staff of the company. A significant part of public relations activity is portraying multinational corporations as good citizens of their host countries. Examples of initiatives taken by IBM to improve its corporate image abroad are summarized in The International Marketplace 20.4.

Public relations activity includes anticipating and countering criticism. The criticisms range from general ones against all multinational corporations to more specific ones. They may be based on a market; for example, doing business with prison factories in China. They may concern a product; for example, Nestlé's practices of advertising and promoting infant formula in developing countries where infant mortality is unacceptably high. They may center on conduct in a given situation; for example, Union Carbide's perceived lack of response in the Bhopal disaster. The key concern is that, if not addressed, these criticisms can lead to more significant problems, such as the internationally orchestrated boycott of Nestlé's products. The six-year boycott did not so much harm earnings as it harmed image and employee morale.

Crisis management is becoming more formalized in companies with specially assigned task forces ready to step in if problems arise. In general, companies must adopt policies that will allow them to effectively respond to pressure and criticism, which will continue to surface. Oliver Williams suggests that crisis-management policies have the following traits: (1) openness about corporate activities, with a focus on how these activities enhance social and economic performance; (2) preparedness to utilize the tremendous

---

[41] S. Watson Dunn, *Public Relations* (Homewood, IL: Irwin, 1986), 275–286.

[42] "Foreign Companies' Global Awareness Cited in Study," *Marketing News,* August 1, 1988, 14.

[43] "How Black & Decker Forged a Winning Brand Transfer Strategy," *Business International,* July 20, 1987, 225–227.

THE INTERNATIONAL MARKETPLACE

20.4

Expanding the Social Vision: Global Community Relations

At a time when many companies are making more money overseas than in their home countries, executives are realizing that they should devote substantial attention to community relations. This attention should not be developed only as a reaction to a crisis, nor should it be a fuzzy, piecemeal effort; instead corporations should have a social vision and a planned long-term social policy.

IBM's policy of good corporate citizenship means accepting responsibility as a participant in community and national affairs and striving to be among the most-admired companies in its host countries. In 1989, IBM introduced Worldwide Initiatives in Volunteerism, a $1-million-plus program to fund projects worldwide and promote employee volunteerism. In Thailand, for example, IBM provides equipment and personnel to universities and donates money to the nation's wildlife fund and environmental protection agency. In 1986, the firm became one of only two companies with a U.S.-based parent to win the Garuda Award, which recognizes significant contributions to Thailand's social and economic development. As part of its long-term strategy for growth in Latin America, IBM is investing millions of dollars in an initiative that brings the latest technology to local schools. IBM does not donate the computers (they are bought by governments, institutions, and other private firms), but it does provide the needed instruction and technological support. By 1993, some 800,000 children and 10,000 teachers had benefited from the program in ten countries. IBM Latin America's technology-in-education initiative is a creative combination of marketing, social responsibility, and long-term relationship-building that fits in with the company's goal of becoming a "national asset" in Latin American countries.

Increased privatization and government cutbacks in social services in many countries offer numerous opportunities for companies to make substantive contributions to solving various global, regional, and local problems. Conservative governments in Europe are welcoming private-sector programs to provide job training for inner-city youth, to meet the needs of immigrants, and to solve massive pollution problems. And in Eastern and Central Europe, where the lines between the private and public sectors are just now being drawn, corporations have a unique opportunity to take a leadership role in shaping new societies.

James Parkel, director of IBM's Office of Corporate Support Programs, summarizes the new expectations in the following way: "Employees don't want to work for companies that have no social conscience, customers don't want to do business with companies that pollute the environment or are notorious for shoddy products and practices, and communities don't welcome companies that aren't good corporate citizens. Many shareholder issues are socially driven."

Sources: "IBM Promotes Education," *Business Latin America*, May 24, 1993, 6–7; "Corporate Generosity Is Greatly Appreciated," *Business Week*, November 2, 1992, 118–120; "Achieving Success in Asia: IBM Sees 'Localization' as a Critical Element," *Business International*, November 11, 1991, 379–383; "Global Community Relations: Expanding the Social Vision," *Business International*, September 16, 1991, 313–314; "How Corporate Activism Can Spread Your Message," *Business International*, June 10, 1991, 199.

power of the multinational corporation in a responsible manner and, in the case of pressure, to counter criticisms swiftly; (3) integrity, which often means that the marketer must avoid not only actual wrongdoing but the mere appearance of it; and (4) clarity, which will help ameliorate hostility if a common language is used with those pressuring the corporation.[44] He proposes that the marketer's role is one of enlightened self-interest; reasonable critics understand that the marketer cannot compromise the bottom line.

Complicating the situation often is the fact that groups in one market criticize what the marketer is doing in another market. For example, the Interfaith Center on Corporate Responsibility urged Colgate-Palmolive to stop marketing Darkie toothpaste under that brand name in Asia because of the term's offensiveness elsewhere in the world. Darkie toothpaste was sold in Thailand, Hong Kong, Singapore, Malaysia, and Taiwan and was packaged in a box that featured a likeness of Al Jolson in blackface.[45] Colgate-Palmolive redid the package and changed the brand name to Darlie. Levi Strauss decided to withdraw from $40 million worth of production contracts in China after consultations with a variety of sources, including human rights organizations, experts on China, and representatives of the U.S. government, made it conclude that there was pervasive abuse of human rights.[46]

The public relations function can be handled in-house or with the assistance of an agency. Some multinational corporations maintain public relations staffs in their main offices around the world, while others use the services of firms such as Burson-Marsteller, Hill and Knowlton, and Grey & Company on specific projects.

SUMMARY

As multinational corporations manage the various elements of the promotions mix in differing environmental conditions, decisions must be made about channels to be used in the communication, the message, who is to execute or help execute the program, and how the success of the endeavor is to be measured. The trend is toward more harmonization of strategy, at the same time allowing for flexibility at the local level and early incorporation of local needs into the promotional plans.

The effective implementation of the promotional program is a key ingredient in the marketing success of the firm. The promotional tools must be used within the opportunities and constraints posed by the communications channels as well as by the laws and regulations governing marketing communications.

Advertising agencies are key facilitators in communicating with the firm's constituent groups. Many multinational corporations are realigning their accounts worldwide in an attempt to streamline their promotional efforts and achieve a global approach.

The use of other promotional tools, especially personal selling, tends to be more localized to fit the conditions of the individual markets. Decisions concerning recruitment, training, motivation, and evaluation must be made at the affiliate level, with general guidance from headquarters.

An area of increasing challenge to multinational corporations is public relations. Multinationals, by their very design, draw attention to their activities. The best interest of the marketer lies in anticipating problems with both internal and external constituencies and managing them, through communications, to the satisfaction of the parties.

[44] Oliver Williams, "Who Cast the First Stone?" *Harvard Business Review* 62 (September–October 1984): 151–160.

[45] "Church Group Gnashes Colgate-Palmolive," *Advertising Age,* March 24, 1986, 46.

[46] "Levi to Sever Link with China; Critics Contend It's Just a PR Move," *Marketing News,* June 7, 1993, 10.

Questions for Discussion

1. Comment on the opinion that "practically speaking, neither an entirely standardized nor an entirely localized advertising approach is necessarily best."

2. Discuss problems associated with measuring advertising effectiveness in foreign markets.

3. Should a company ever attempt perfect standardization of an advertising message? Is recognizability (by the consumer) enough for the general benefits of standardization to be achieved?

4. What type of adjustments must advertising agencies make as more companies want "one sight, one sound, one sell" campaigns?

5. What problems are created when an advertising message is extended to other markets through direct translation?

6. Assess the programmed management approach for coordinating international advertising efforts.

7. Is international personal selling a reality? Or is all personal selling national, regardless of who performs it?

8. How can the multinational corporation exert influence and strive for standardization in personal selling?

Recommended Readings

Dunn, S. Watson, Arnold M. Barban, Dean M. Krugman, and Leonard N. Reid. *Advertising: Its Role in Modern Marketing.* Hinsdale, IL: Dryden Press, 1990.

Kaynak, Erdener, ed. *The Management of International Advertising: A Handbook and Guide for Professionals.* Westport, CT: Quorum Books, 1989.

Kleinman, Philip. *Saatchi & Saatchi: The Inside Story.* Lincolnwood, IL: NTC Business Books, 1988.

Leo Burnett. *Worldwide Advertising and Media Fact Book.* Chicago, IL: Triumph Books, 1994.

Niefeld, Jaye S. *The Making of an Advertising Campaign: The Silk of China.* Englewood Cliffs, NJ: Prentice-Hall, 1989.

Nukhet, Vardar. *Global Advertising: Rhyme or Reason.* London: Paul Chapman Publishing Ltd., 1992.

Peebles, Dean M., and John K. Ryans. *Management of International Advertising: A Marketing Approach.* Boston, MA: Allyn & Bacon, 1984.

Roth, Robert F. *International Marketing Communications.* Chicago: Crain Books, 1982.

Starch INRA Hooper. *Twenty-fifth Survey of World Advertising Expenditures: A Survey of World Advertising Expenditures in 1990.* Mamaroneck, NY: Starch INRA Hooper, 1992.

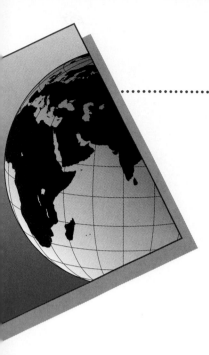

CHAPTER 21

International Marketing Organization and Control

THE INTERNATIONAL MARKETPLACE

Restructuring for NAFTA

A number of businesses are adopting strategic plans that take full advantage of the trilateral free trade pact of NAFTA. 3M's North American Operational Plan centers on organizational restructuring based on three concepts: simplification, linkage, and empowerment. The plan was fully implemented in the United States and Canada in 1992 with Mexico added in 1994.

"We always treated Mexico as a far-off, foreign country," says David Olsen, 3M's manager of customs and chairman of the company's task force on NAFTA. Now, the company intends to manage by area rather than by country. Key goals of the operational plan are:

- Eliminate the role of 3M International Operations in cross-border activities within North America. All business units in Canada and Mexico will deal directly with 3M's divisions in the United States.
- Redefine management functions. General sales and marketing managers in Canada and Mexico will have a new title—business manager—and will serve as the key link between local customers and the corresponding U.S. general managers. The business managers will also be members of 3M U.S.'s planning, pricing, and operating committees; participate in the early stages of the global business planning; and execute the global strategy in Canada and Mexico.
- Coordinate functions and share resources among the three countries, especially in marketing, advertising, and sales. New-product launches will be synchronized throughout North America, with standardized sizing and part numbers used wherever possible. Distribution strategies and agreements

will be coordinated. Sales literature, packaging, and labeling will be uniform, written in the appropriate local language.

- Establish North American tactical teams. Members from these groups, drawn from all three countries, will work on projects such as market research, new-product development, and competitor monitoring.
- Set up centers of excellence. To maximize efficiency and to avoid duplication of effort, each country will specialize in the function or process that it does best and eliminate those that can be performed elsewhere. These centers may be built around manufacturing of a product or product line, market niches, customer service, or technical skills.
- Modify performance-measurement criteria. North American performance will be gauged by North American—not U.S., Canadian, or Mexican—market share, earnings growth, and income.

At 3M Canada, major changes have taken place. Layers of management have been trimmed, communication and coordination have been greatly enhanced, and the requirement to go through the international division has been removed. Incorporating Mexico into the plan presents some unique challenges, however. For 3M U.S. headquarters, meeting or communicating electronically with Canadian counterparts is far easier than doing the same with Mexico. Language and cultural barriers also present potential challenges. Given that only products are free to cross borders—not people—sales personnel cannot solicit business across borders, and direct cross-border reporting may not be possible.

Source: "3M Restructuring for NAFTA," *Business Latin America*, July 19, 1993, 6–7.

As companies evolve from purely domestic entities to multinationals, their organizational structure and control systems must change to reflect new strategies. With growth comes diversity in terms of products and services, geographic markets, and personnel, leading to a set of challenges for the company. Two critical issues are basic to addressing these challenges: (1) the type of organization that provides the best framework for developing worldwide strategies and maintaining flexibility with respect to individual markets and operations and (2) the type and degree of control to be exercised from headquarters to maximize total effort. Organizational structures and control systems have to be adjusted as market conditions change, as seen in The International Marketplace 21.1.

This chapter will focus on the advantages and disadvantages of the organizational structures available as well as their appropriateness at various stages of internationalization. A determining factor is where decision-making authority within the organizational structures will be placed. Also, the roles of the different entities of the organization must be defined. The chapter will also outline the need for devising a control system to oversee the international operations of the company, emphasizing the control instruments needed in addition to those used in domestic business, as well as the control strategies of multinational corporations. The appropriateness and eventual cost of the various control approaches will vary as the firm expands its international operations. Overall, the objective of the chapter is to study intraorganizational relationships in the firm's attempt to optimize competitive response in areas most critical to its business.

ORGANIZATIONAL STRUCTURE

The basic functions of an organization are to provide (1) a route and locus of decision making and coordination and (2) a system for reporting and communications. Authority and communication networks are typically depicted in the organizational chart.

Organizational Designs

The basic configurations of international organizations correspond to those of purely domestic ones; the greater the degree of internationalization, the more complex the structures can become. The types of structures that companies use to manage foreign activities can be divided into three categories based on the degree of internationalization:

1. Little or no formal organizational recognition of international activities of the firm. This category ranges from domestic operations handling an occasional international transaction on an ad hoc basis to separate export departments.
2. International division. Firms in this category recognize the ever-growing importance of international involvement.
3. Global organizations. These can be structured by product, area, function, process, or customer.

Hybrid structures may exist as well, in which one market may be structured by product, another by areas. Matrix organizations have emerged in large multinational corporations to combine product, regional, and functional expertise. As worldwide competition has increased dramatically in many industries, the latest organizational response is networked global organizations in which heavy flows of technology, personnel, and communication take place between strategically interdependent units to establish greater global integration.

Little or No Formal Organization In the very early stages of international involvement, domestic operations assume responsibility for international marketing activities. The share of international operations in the sales and profits of the corporation is initially so minor that no organizational adjustment takes place. No consolidation of information or authority over international sales is undertaken or is necessary. Transactions are conducted on a case-by-case basis either by the resident expert or quite often with the help of facilitating agents, such as freight forwarders.

As demand from the international marketplace grows and interest within the firm expands, the organizational structure will reflect it. An export department appears as a separate entity. This may be an outside export management company—that is, an independent company that becomes the de facto export department of the firm. This is an indirect approach to international involvement in that very little experience is accumulated within the firm itself. Alternatively, a firm may establish its own export department, hiring a few seasoned individuals to take full responsibility for international activities. Organizationally, the department may be a subdepartment of marketing (alternative b in Figure 21.1) or may have equal ranking with the various functional departments (alternative a). This choice will depend on the importance assigned to overseas activities by the firm. Because the export department is the first real step for internationalizing the organizational structure, it should be a full-fledged marketing organization and not merely a sales organization.

Licensing is the international entry mode for some firms. Responsibility for licensing may be assigned to the R&D function despite its importance to the overall international strategy of the firm. A formal liaison among the export, marketing, production, and

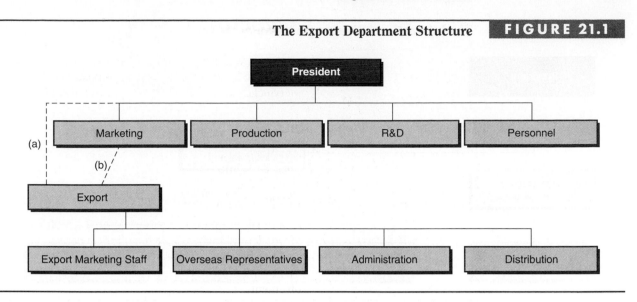

The Export Department Structure   FIGURE 21.1

R&D functions should be formed for the maximum utilization of licensing.[1] A separate manager should be appointed if licensing becomes a major activity for the firm.

As the firm becomes more involved in foreign markets, the export department structure will become obsolete. The firm may then undertake joint ventures or direct foreign investment, which require those involved to have functional experience. The firm therefore typically establishes an international division.

Some firms that acquire foreign production facilities pass through an additional stage in which foreign subsidiaries report directly to the president or to a manager specifically assigned this duty.[2] However, the amount of coordination and control that is required quickly establishes the need for a more formal international organization in the firm.

The International Division   The international division centralizes in one entity, with or without separate incorporation, all of the responsibility for international activities, as illustrated in Figure 21.2. The approach aims to eliminate a possible bias against international operations that may exist if domestic divisions are allowed to independently serve international customers. In some cases, international markets have been found to be treated as secondary to domestic markets. The international division concentrates international expertise, information flows concerning foreign-market opportunities, and authority over international activities. However, manufacturing and other related functions remain with the domestic divisions in order to take advantage of economies of scale.

To avoid situations in which the international division is at a disadvantage in competing for production, personnel, and corporate services, corporations need to coordinate between domestic and international operations. Coordination can be achieved through a joint staff or by requiring domestic and international divisions to interact in strategic

---

[1] Michael Z. Brooke, *International Management: A Review of Strategies and Operations* (London: Hutchinson, 1986), 173–174; and "Running a Licensing Department," *Business International*, June 13, 1988, 177–178.

[2] Stefan Robock and Kenneth Simmonds, *International Business and Multinational Enterprises* (Homewood, IL: Irwin, 1983), 414.

| FIGURE 21.2 | The International Division Structure |

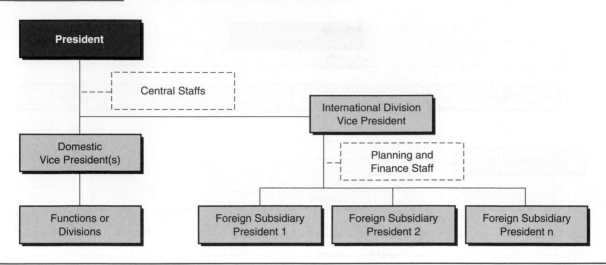

planning and to submit the plans to headquarters. Further, many corporations require and encourage frequent interaction between domestic and international personnel to discuss common challenges in areas such as product planning. At Loctite Corporation, for example, coordination is also important because domestic operations are typically organized along product or functional lines, whereas international divisions are geographically oriented.[3]

International divisions best serve firms with few products that do not vary significantly in terms of their environmental sensitivity, and when international sales and profits are still quite insignificant compared with those of the domestic divisions.[4] Companies may outgrow their international divisions as their international sales grow in significance, diversity, and complexity. This is especially true of European multinationals, which have typically outgrown the structure because of the relatively small size of their domestic markets. A number of U.S.-based companies in the 1970s shifted from a traditional organizational structure with an independent international division to entities built around worldwide or global structures with no differentiation between "domestic" and "international" operations.[5]

Size in itself is not a limitation to the use of the international division structure. Some of the world's largest corporations rely on international divisions.[6] The management of these companies believe that specialization is needed primarily in terms of the environment.

Global Organizational Structures   Global structures have grown out of competitive necessity. In many industries, competition is on a global basis, with the result that companies must have a high degree of reactive capability. European firms have tradi-

---

[3] "How Loctite Prospers with 3-Man Global HQ, Strong Country Managers," *Business International,* May 2, 1988, 129–130.

[4] Richard D. Robinson, *Internationalization of Business: An Introduction* (Hinsdale, IL: Dryden Press, 1984), 84.

[5] William H. Davidson, "Shaping a Global Product Organization," *Harvard Business Review* 59 (March–April 1982): 69–76.

[6] L. S. Walsh, *International Marketing* (Plymouth, England: MacDonald and Evans, 1981), 161.

The Global Product Structure   **FIGURE 21.3**

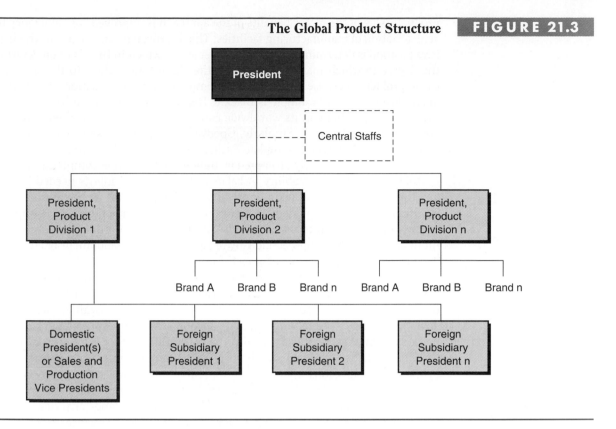

tionally had a global structure because of the relatively small size of their domestic markets. N. V. Philips, for example, could never have grown to its current prominence by relying on the Dutch market.

Five basic types of global structures are available:

1. Global product structure, in which product divisions are responsible for all manufacture and marketing worldwide
2. Global area structure, in which geographic divisions are responsible for all manufacture and marketing in their respective areas
3. Global functional structure, in which the functional areas (such as production, marketing, finance, and personnel) are responsible for the worldwide operations of their own functional areas
4. Global customer structure, in which operations are structured based on distinct worldwide customer groups
5. Mixed—or hybrid—structure, which may combine the other alternatives

Product Structure   The **product structure** is the one that is most used by multinational corporations.[7] This approach gives worldwide responsibility to strategic business units for the marketing of their product lines, as shown in Figure 21.3. Most consumer-product firms utilize some form of this approach, mainly because of the diversity of their

[7] See Joan P. Curhan, William H. Davidson, and Suri Rajan, *Tracing the Multinationals* (Cambridge, MA: Ballinger, 1977), 15; M. E. Wicks, *A Comparative Analysis of the Foreign Investment Evaluation Practices of U.S.-Based Multinational Corporations* (New York: McKinsey & Co., 1980), 3; and Lawrence G. Franko, "Organizational Structures and Multinational Strategies of Continental European Enterprises," in *European Research in International Business,* ed. Michel Ghertman and James Leontiades (Amsterdam, Holland: North Holland, 1977), 111–137.

products. One of the major benefits of the approach is improved cost-efficiency through centralization of manufacturing facilities. This is crucial in industries in which competitive position is determined by world market share, which in turn is often determined by the degree to which manufacturing is rationalized.[8] Adaptation to this approach may cause problems because it is usually accompanied by consolidation of operations and plant closings. A good example is Black & Decker, which in the mid-1980s rationalized many of its operations in its worldwide competitive effort against Makita, the Japanese power-tool manufacturer. Similarly, Goodyear reorganized itself in 1988 into a single global organization with a complete business team approach for tires and general products. The move was largely prompted by tightening worldwide competition.[9]

Another benefit is the ability to balance the functional inputs needed by a product and the ability to react quickly to product-specific problems in the marketplace. Even smaller brands receive individual attention. Product-specific attention is important because products vary in terms of the adaptation they need for different foreign markets. All in all, the product approach ideally brings about the development of a global strategic focus in response to global competition.

At the same time, this structure fragments international expertise within the firm because a central pool of international experience no longer exists. The structure assumes that managers will have adequate regional experience or advice to allow them to make balanced decisions. Coordination of activities among the various product groups operating in the same markets is crucial to avoid unnecessary duplication of basic tasks. For some of these tasks, such as market research, special staff functions may be created and then hired by the product divisions when needed. If product managers lack an appreciation for the international dimension, they may focus their attention on only the larger markets, often with emphasis on the domestic markets, and fail to take the long-term view.

Area Structure The approach adopted second most frequently is the **area structure,** illustrated in Figure 21.4. The firm is organized on the basis of geographical areas; for example, operations may be divided into those dealing with North America, the Far East, Latin America, and Europe. Regional aggregation may play a major role in this structuring; for example, many multinational corporations have located their European headquarters in Brussels, where the EU has its headquarters. The inevitability of a North American trading bloc led to the creation of Campbell Soup Co.'s North American division which replaced the U.S. operation as the power center of the company.[10] Today, Procter & Gamble's Latin American subsidiaries report to the Latin American headquarters located in Caracas, Venezuela, rather than Cincinnati where headquarters for Latin American operations used to exist.[11] Ideally, no special preference is given to the region in which the headquarters is located—for example, North America or Europe. Central staffs are responsible for providing coordination support for worldwide planning and control activities performed at headquarters.

The area approach follows the marketing concept most closely because individual areas and markets are given concentrated attention. If market conditions with respect to product acceptance and operating conditions vary dramatically, the area approach is the one to choose. Companies opting for this alternative typically have relatively narrow product lines with similar end uses and end-users. However, expertise is most needed in adapting the product and its marketing to local market conditions. Once again, to avoid

---

[8] William H. Davidson and Philippe Haspeslagh, "Shaping a Global Product Organization," *Harvard Business Review* 59 (March–April 1982): 69–76.

[9] "How Goodyear Sharpened Organization and Production for a Tough World Market," *Business International,* January 16, 1989, 11–14.

[10] Bill Saporito, "Campbell Soup Gets Piping Hot," *Fortune,* September 9, 1991, 94–98.

[11] Integration for Profit," *Business Latin America,* July 5, 1993, 6–7.

The Global Area Structure   FIGURE 21.4

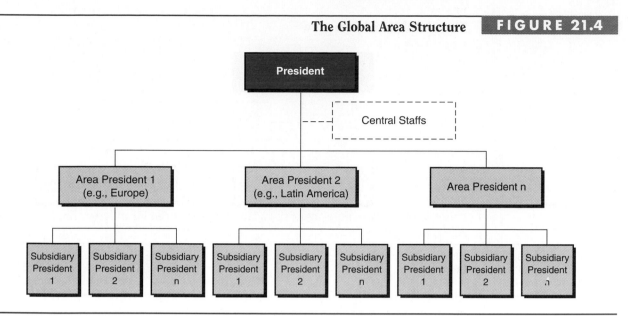

duplication of effort in product management and in functional areas, staff specialists—for product categories, for example—may be used.

Without appropriate coordination from the staff, essential information and experience may not be transfered from one regional entity to another. Also, if the company expands in terms of product lines, and if end markets begin to diversify, the area structure may become inappropriate.

Functional Structure   Of all the approaches, the **functional structure** is the most simple from the administrative viewpoint because it emphasizes the basic tasks of the firm—for example, manufacturing, sales, and research and development. This approach, illustrated in Figure 21.5, works best when both products and customers are relatively

The Global Functional Structure   FIGURE 21.5

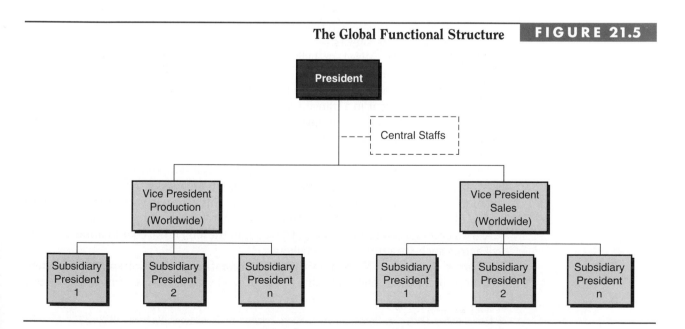

FIGURE 21.6   The Global Mixed Structure

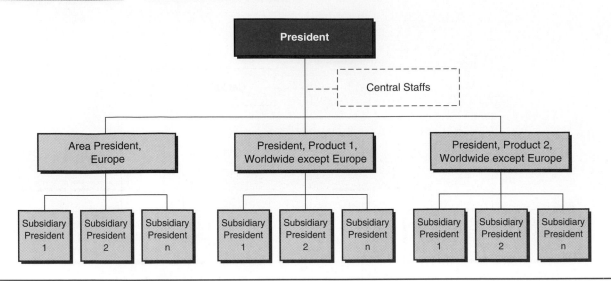

few and similar in nature. Because coordination is typically the key problem, staff functions have been created to interact between the functional areas. Otherwise, the company's marketing and regional expertise may not be exploited to the fullest extent.

A variation of this approach is one that uses processes as a basis for structure. The **process structure** is common in the energy and mining industries, where one corporate entity may be in charge of exploration worldwide and another may be responsible for the actual mining operation.

Customer Structure   Firms may also organize their operations using the **customer structure,** especially if the customer groups they serve are dramatically different—for example, consumers versus businesses versus governments. Catering to these diverse groups may require the concentrating of specialists in particular divisions. The product may be the same, but the buying processes of the various customer groups may differ. Governmental buying is characterized by bidding, in which price plays a larger role than when businesses are the buyers.

Mixed Structure   Mixed, or hybrid, organizations also exist. A **mixed structure,** such as the one in Figure 21.6, combines two or more organizational dimensions simultaneously. It permits attention to be focused on products, areas, or functions, as needed. This approach may occur in a transitionary period after a merger or an acquisition, or it may come about because of a unique customer group or product line (such as military hardware). It may also provide a useful structure before the implementation of the matrix structure.[12]

Organization structures are, of course, never as clear-cut and simple as they have been presented here. Whatever the basic format, inputs are needed for product, area, and function. One alternative, for example, might be an initial product structure that would eventually have regional groupings. Another alternative might be an initial area structure with eventual product groupings. However, in the long term, coordination and control across such structures become tedious.

Matrix Structure   Many multinational corporations—in an attempt to facilitate planning, organizing, and controlling interdependent businesses, critical resources,

---

[12] Daniel Robey, *Designing Organizations: A Macro Perspective* (Homewood, IL: Irwin, 1982), 327.

The Global Matrix Structure at N. V. Philips   FIGURE 21.7

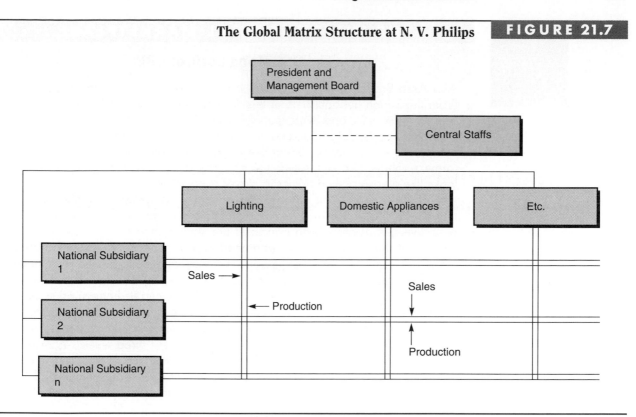

strategies, and geographic regions—have adopted the **matrix structure.**[13] Eastman Kodak shifted from a functional organization to a matrix system based on business units. Business is driven by a worldwide business unit (for example, photographic products or commercial and information systems) and implemented by a geographic unit (for example, Europe or Latin America). The geographical units, as well as their country subsidiaries, serve as the "glue" between autonomous product operations.[14]

Organizational matrices integrate the various approaches already discussed, as the N. V. Philips example in Figure 21.7 illustrates. The matrix structure manager has functional, product, and resource managers reporting to him or her. The approach is based on team building and multiple command, each team specializing in its own area of expertise. It provides a mechanism for cooperation between country managers, business managers, and functional managers on a worldwide basis through increased communication, control, and attention to balance in the organization.

The matrices used vary according to the number of dimensions needed. For example, Dow Chemical's matrix is three-dimensional, consisting of six geographic areas, three major functions (marketing, manufacturing, and research), and more than 70 products. The matrix approach helps cut through enormous organizational complexities by building in a provision for cooperation among business managers, functional managers, and strategy managers. However, the matrix requires sensitive, well-trained middle managers who can cope with problems that arise from reporting to two bosses—for example,

---

[13] Thomas H. Naylor, "International Strategy Matrix," *Columbia Journal of World Business* 20 (Summer 1985): 11–19.

[14] "Kodak's Matrix System Focuses on Product Business Units," *Business International,* July 18, 1988, 221–223.

21.2

THE INTERNATIONAL MARKETPLACE

The Organizing Logic of ABB

ABB Asea Brown Boveri is a global organization of staggering proportions. From the Zurich headquarters of this $25-billion electrical engineering giant, Swedish, German, and Swiss managers shuffle assets around the globe, keep the books in U.S. dollars, and conduct most of their business in English. Yet the companies that make up the far-flung operations tailor ABB's turbines, transformers, robots, and high-speed trains to local markets so successfully that ABB looks like an established domestic player everywhere.

To a large extent, this can be credited to the company's organization. Although ABB Asea Brown Boveri is a global organization of tremendous business diversity, its organizing principles are stark in their simplicity. Along one dimension, the company is a distributed global network. Executives around the world make decisions on product strategy and performance without regard for national borders. Along a second dimension, it is a collection of traditionally organized national companies, each serving its home market as effectively as possible. ABB's global matrix holds the two dimensions together.

At the top of the company sit CEO Percy Barnevik and 12 colleagues on the executive committee. The group, which meets every three weeks, is responsible for ABB's global strategy and performance. The executive committee consists of Swedes, Swiss, Germans, and Americans. Several members of the executive committee are based outside Zurich, and their meetings are held around the world.

Reporting to the executive committee are leaders of the 50 or so business areas (BAs), located worldwide, into which the company's products and services are divided. The BAs are grouped into eight business segments, for which different members of the executive committee are responsible. For example, the "industry" segment, which sells components, systems, and software to automate industrial processes, has five BAs, including metallurgy, drives, and process engineering. The BA leaders report to Gerhard Schulmeyer, a German member of the executive committee who works out of Stamford, Connecticut.

Each BA has a leader responsible for optimizing the business on a global basis. The BA leader devises and champions a global strategy, holds factories around the world to cost and quality standards, allocates export markets to each factory, and shares expertise by rotating people across borders, creating mixed-nationality teams to solve problems, and building a culture of trust and communication. The BA leader for power transformers, who is responsible for 25 factories in 16 countries, is a Swede who works out of Mannheim, Germany. The BA leader for instrumentation is British. The BA leader for electric metering is an American based in North Carolina.

Similarly, country organizations may be assigned as worldwide centers of excellence for a particular product category, for example, ABB Strömberg in Finland for electric drives, a category in which it is a recognized world leader.

Alongside the BA structure sits a country structure. ABB's operations in the developed world are organized as national enterprises with presidents, balance sheets, income statements, and career ladders. In Germany, for example, Asea Brown Boveri Aktiengesellschaft, ABB's national company, employs 36,000 people and generates annual revenues of more than $4 billion. The managing director of ABB Germany, Eberhard von Koerber, plays a role comparable to that of a traditional German CEO. He reports to a supervisory board whose members include German bank representatives and trade union officials. His company produces financial statements comparable to those from any other German company and participates fully in the German apprenticeship program.

The BA structure meets the national structure at the level of ABB's member companies. Percy Barnevik advocates strict decentralization. Wherever possible, ABB creates separate companies to do the work of the 50 business areas in different countries. For example, ABB does not merely sell industrial robots in Norway. Norway has an ABB robotics company charged with manufacturing robots, selling to and servicing domestic customers, and exporting to markets allocated by the BA leader.

There are 1,100 such local companies around the world. Their presidents report to two bosses—the BA leader, who is usually located outside the country, and the president of the national company of which the local company is a subsidiary. At this intersection, ABB's "glocal" structure becomes a reality.

Sources: "Percy Barnevik's Global Crusade," *Business Week*, Enterprise 1993, 204–211; "The Euro-Gospel According to Percy Barnevik," *Business Week*, July 23, 1990, 64–66; "The Stateless Corporation," *Business Week*, May 14, 1990, 98–106; William Taylor, "The Logic of Global Business," *Harvard Business Review* 68 (March-April 1990): 91–105.

a product-line manager and an area manager. At 3M, for example, every management unit has some sort of multidimensional reporting relationship, which may cross functional, regional, or operational lines. On a regional basis, group managers in Europe, for example, report administratively to a vice president of operations for Europe. But functionally, they report to group vice presidents at headquarters in Minneapolis–St. Paul.[15] The matrix at ABB is described in detail in The International Marketplace 21.2.

Many companies have found the matrix structure problematic.[16] The dual reporting channel easily causes conflict; complex issues are forced into a two-dimensional decision framework; and even minor issues may have to be resolved through committee discussion. Ideally, managers should solve problems themselves through formal and informal communication; however, physical and psychic distance often make that impossible. Especially when competitive conditions require quick reaction, the matrix, with its inherent complexity, may actually lower the reaction speed of the company.

Evolution of Organizational Structures   Companies develop new structures in stages as their product diversity develops and the share of foreign sales increases.[17] At the first stage are autonomous subsidiaries reporting directly to top management, followed by the establishment of an international division. With increases in product diversity and in the importance of the foreign marketplace, companies develop global structures to coordinate subsidiary operations and rationalize worldwide production. As

---

[15] "How 3M Develops Managers to Meet Global Strategic Objectives," *Business International*, March 21, 1988, 81–82.

[16] Thomas J. Peters, "Beyond the Matrix Organization," *Business Horizons* 22 (October 1979): 15–27.

[17] See John N. Stopford and Louis T. Wells, *Managing the Multinational Enterprise: Organization of the Firm and Ownership of the Subsidiary* (New York: Basic Books, 1972), 25; also A. D. Chandler, *Strategy and Structure* (Cambridge, MA: MIT Press, 1962), 3, and B. R. Scott, *Stages of Corporate Development* (Boston, MA: ICCH, 1971), 2.

| FIGURE 21.8 | Evolution of International Structures |

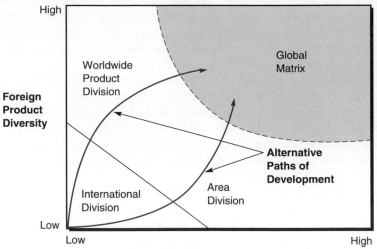

Source: From Christopher A. Bartlett, "Building and Managing the Transnational: The New Organizational Challenge," in Michael E. Porter, ed., *Competition in Global Industries*. Boston: Harvard Business School Press, 1986, p. 368. Reprinted by permission of Harvard Business School from *Competition in Global Industries*, Michael E. Porter, ed. Boston: 1986, p. 368. Copyright © by the President and Fellows of Harvard College.

multinational corporations have faced pressures to adapt to local market conditions while trying to rationalize production and globalize competitive reaction, many have opted for the matrix structure.[18] The matrix structure probably allows a corporation to best meet the challenges of global markets: to be global and local, big and small, decentralized with centralized reporting by allowing the optimizing of businesses globally and maximizing performance in every country of operation.[19] The evolutionary process is summarized in Figure 21.8.

Locus of Decision Making

Organizational structures themselves do not indicate where the authority for decision making and control rests within the organization. If subsidiaries are granted a high degree of autonomy, the result is termed **decentralization.** In decentralized systems, controls are relatively loose and simple, and the flows between headquarters and subsidiaries are mainly financial; that is, each subsidiary operates as a profit center. On the other hand, if controls are tight and if strategic decision making is concentrated at headquarters, the result is termed **centralization.** Firms are typically neither totally centralized nor totally decentralized. Some functions, such as finance, lend themselves to more centralized decision making, whereas other functions, such as promotional decisions, lend themselves to far less. Research and development is typically centralized in terms of both decision making and location, especially when basic research work is involved.

---

[18] Stanley M. Davis, "Trends in the Organization of Multinational Corporations," *Columbia Journal of World Business* 11 (Summer 1976): 59–71.

[19] Taylor, "The Logic of Global Business," 91–105.

Partly because of governmental pressures, some companies have added R&D functions on a regional or local basis. In many cases, however, variations in decision making are product and market based; for example, Corning Glass Works' television tube marketing strategy requires global decision making for pricing and local decisions for service and delivery.

Allowing maximum flexibility at the subsidiary level takes advantage of the fact that subsidiary management knows its market and can react to changes quickly. Problems of motivation and acceptance are avoided when decision makers are also the implementors of the strategy. On the other hand, many multinational companies faced with global competitive threats and opportunities have adopted global strategy formulation, which by definition requires some degree of centralization. What has emerged as a result can be called **coordinated decentralization.** This means that overall corporate strategy is provided from headquarters, but subsidiaries are free to implement it within the range established in consultation between headquarters and the subsidiaries.

Factors Affecting Structure and Decision Making

The organizational structure and locus of decision making in multinational corporations are determined by a number of factors. They include (1) the degree of involvement in international operations, (2) the business(es) in which the firm is engaged (in terms, for example, of products marketed), (3) the size and importance of the markets, and (4) the human resource capability of the firm.[20]

The effect of the degree of involvement on structure and decision making was discussed earlier in the chapter. With low degrees of involvement by the parent company, subsidiaries can enjoy high degrees of autonomy as long as they meet their profit targets. The same situation can occur in even the most globally involved companies, but within a different framework. As an example, consider North American Philips Corporation, a separate entity of the Dutch N. V. Philips. It enjoys an independent status in terms of local policy setting and managerial practices but is nevertheless within the parent company's planning and control system.

The firm's country of origin and the political history of the area can also affect organizational structure and decision making. For example, Swiss-based Nestlé, with only 3 to 4 percent of its sales in the small domestic market, has traditionally had a highly decentralized organization. Moreover, European history for the past 75 years, particularly the two World Wars, has often forced subsidiaries of European-based companies to act independently in order to survive.

The type and variety of products marketed will have an effect on organizational decisions. Companies that market consumer products typically have product organizations with high degrees of decentralization, allowing for maximum local flexibility. On the other hand, companies that market technologically sophisticated products, such as General Electric's turbines, display centralized organizations with worldwide product responsibilities. Even in matrix organizations, one of the dimensions may be granted more say in decisions; for example, at Dow Chemical, geographical managers have the strongest voice.

Going global has recently meant transferring world headquarters of important business units abroad. For example, Hyundai Electronics Industries moved its personal

[20] Rodman Drake and Lee M. Caudill, "Management of the Large Multinational: Trends and Future Challenges," *Business Horizons* 24 (May–June 1981): 83–91

computer division to San Jose, California, from Seoul, South Korea, to better compete in that industry's biggest market.[21]

Apart from situations that require the development of an area structure, the characteristics of certain markets or regions may require separate arrangements for the firm. For many Japanese and European companies, the North American market has been granted such attention with, for example, direct organizational links to top management at headquarters.

The human factor in any organization is critical. Managers both at headquarters and in the subsidiaries must bridge the physical and psychic distances separating them. If subsidiaries have competent managers who rarely need to consult headquarters about their problems, they may be granted high degrees of autonomy. In the case of global organizations, subsidiary management must understand the corporate culture because subsidiaries must sometimes make decisions that meet the long-term objectives of the firm as a whole but that are not optimal for the local market.

The Networked Global Organization

No international structure is ideal, and some have challenged the wisdom of even looking for an ideal one. They have called attention to new processes that would, in a given structure, develop new perspectives and attitudes to reflect and respond to complex demands of the opposite forces of global integration and local responsiveness.[22] Rather than a question of which structural alternative is best, the question is thus one of how best to take into account the different perspectives of various corporate entities when making decisions. In structural terms, nothing may change. As a matter of fact, N. V. Philips still has its basic matrix structure, yet major changes have occurred in internal relations.[23] The basic change was from a decentralized federation model to a networked global organization; the effects are depicted in Figure 21.9. The term **glocal** has been coined to describe the approach.[24]

Companies that have adopted the approach have incorporated the following three dimensions into their organizations: (1) the development and communication of a clear corporate vision, (2) the effective management of human resource tools to broaden individual perspectives and develop identification with corporate goals, and (3) the integration of individual thinking and activities into the broad corporate agenda.[25] The first dimension relates to a clear and consistent long-term corporate mission that guides individuals wherever they may work in the organization. Examples of this are Johnson & Johnson's corporate credo of customer focus and NEC's C&C (computers and communication). The second relates both to developing global managers who can find opportunities in spite of environmental challenges and to creating a global perspective among country managers. The last dimension refers to tackling the "not-

---

[21] "So Big," *Across the Board,* 30 (January–February 1993): 16–21.

[22] Christopher Bartlett, "MNCs: Get off the Reorganization Merry-Go-Round," *Harvard Business Review* 60 (March–April 1983): 138–146.

[23] Cheryll Barron, "Format Fears at Philips," *Management Today,* August 1978, 35–41, 101–102.

[24] Thomas Gross, Ernie Turner, and Lars Cederholm, "Building Teams for Global Operations," *Management Review,* June 1987, 32–36.

[25] Christopher A. Bartlett and Sumantra Ghoshal, "Matrix Management: Not a Structure, a Frame of Mind," *Harvard Business Review* 68 (July–August 1990): 138–145.

The Networked Global Organization   FIGURE 21.9

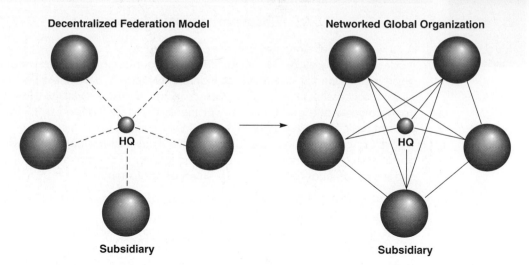

Source: Thomas Gross, Ernie Turner, and Lars Cederholm, "Building Teams for Global Operations," *Management Review*, June 1987, 34.

invented-here" syndrome to co-opt possibly isolated, even adversarial managers into the corporate agenda.

The network avoids the problems of duplication of effort, inefficiency, and resistance to ideas developed elsewhere by giving subsidiaries the latitude, encouragement, and tools to pursue local business development within the framework of the global strategy. Headquarters considers each unit as a source of ideas, skills, capabilities, and knowledge that can be utilized for the benefit of the entire organization. This means that the subsidiaries must be upgraded from the role of implementation and adaptation to that of contribution and partnership in the development and execution of worldwide strategies. Efficient plants may be converted into international production centers, innovative R&D units may become centers of excellence (and thus role models), and leading subsidiary groups may be given a leadership role in developing new strategy for the entire corporation.

One tool for implementing this approach is international teams of managers who meet regularly to develop strategy. Although final direction may come from headquarters, the input has included information on local conditions, and implementation of the strategy is enhanced because local managers were involved from the beginning. This approach has worked even in cases that, offhand, would seem impossible because of market differences. Both Procter & Gamble and Henkel have successfully introduced pan-European brands for which strategy was developed by European strategy teams. These teams consisted of local managers and staff personnel to smooth eventual implementation and to avoid unnecessarily long and disruptive discussions about the fit of a new product to individual markets.

As the discussion indicates, the networked approach is not a structural adaptation but a procedural one that requires a change in management mentality. Adjustment is primarily in the coordination and control functions of the firm. And while there is still considerable disagreement as to which of the approaches works, some measures have been shown to correlate with success, as seen in The International Marketplace 21.3.

21.3

THE INTERNATIONAL MARKETPLACE

Characteristics of Success

A survey of chief executive officers of 43 leading U.S. consumer companies, made by McKinsey & Co., sheds light on organizational features that distinguish internationally successful companies. Companies were classified as more or less successful compared to their specific industry average, using international sales and profit growth over the 1986–1991 period as the most important indicators of success.

The survey results indicate 11 distinctive traits that are correlated with high performance in international markets. The following are moves that companies can make to enhance prospects for international success:

- Take a different approach to international decision making
- Differentiate treatment of international subsidiaries
- Let product managers in subsidiaries report to the country general manager
- Have a worldwide management development program
- Make international experience a condition for promotion to top management
- Have a more multinational management group
- Support international managers with global electronic networking capabilities
- Manage cross-border acquisitions particularly well
- Have overseas R & D centers
- Focus on international
- Remain open to organizational change and continuous self-renewal

In general, successful companies coordinate their international decision making globally, with more central direction than less successful competitors, as seen in the following exhibit. This difference is most marked in brand positioning, package design, and price setting. The one notable exception is an increasing tendency to decentralize product development.

The Role of Country Organizations

Country organizations should be treated as a source of supply as much as they are considered a source of demand. Quite often, however, headquarters managers see their role as the coordinators of key decisions and controllers of resources and perceive subsidiaries as implementors and adapters of global strategy in their respective local markets. Furthermore, all country organizations may be seen as the same. This view severely limits the utilization of the firm's resources by not using country organizations as resources and by depriving country managers of possibilities of exercising their creativity.[26]

The role that a particular country organization can play depends naturally on that market's overall strategic importance as well as the competences of its organization. From these criteria, four different roles emerge (see Figure 21.10).

---

[26] Christopher A. Bartlett and Sumantra Ghoshal, "Tap Your Subsidiaries for Global Reach," *Harvard Business Review* 64 (November–December 1986): 87–94.

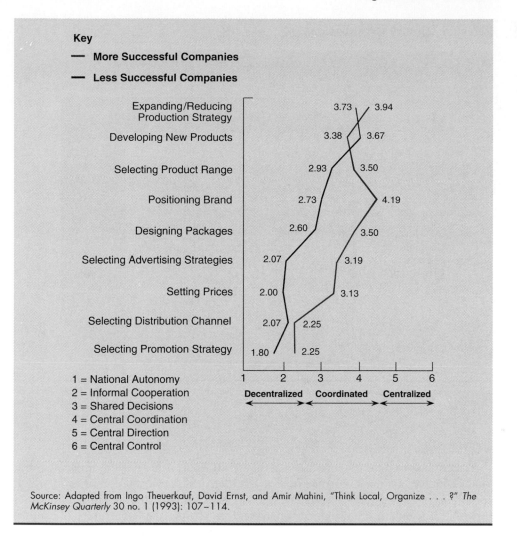

Key
— More Successful Companies
— Less Successful Companies

Expanding/Reducing Production Strategy — 3.73 / 3.94
Developing New Products — 3.38 / 3.67
Selecting Product Range — 2.93 / 3.50
Positioning Brand — 2.73 / 4.19
Designing Packages — 2.60 / 3.50
Selecting Advertising Strategies — 2.07 / 3.19
Setting Prices — 2.00 / 3.13
Selecting Distribution Channel — 2.07 / 2.25
Selecting Promotion Strategy — 1.80 / 2.25

1 = National Autonomy
2 = Informal Cooperation
3 = Shared Decisions
4 = Central Coordination
5 = Central Direction
6 = Central Control

Decentralized   Coordinated   Centralized

Source: Adapted from Ingo Theuerkauf, David Ernst, and Amir Mahini, "Think Local, Organize . . . ?" *The McKinsey Quarterly* 30 no. 1 (1993): 107–114.

The role of **strategic leader** can be played by a highly competent national subsidiary located in a strategically critical market. The country organization serves as a partner of headquarters in developing and implementing strategy. Procter & Gamble's Eurobrand teams, which analyze opportunities for greater product and marketing program standardization, are chaired by a brand manager from a "lead country."[27]

A **contributor** is a country organization with a distinctive competence, such as product development. Increasingly, country organizations are the source of new products. These range from IBM's recent breakthrough in superconductivity research, generated in its Zurich lab, to low-end innovations like Procter & Gamble's liquid Tide, made with a fabric-softening compound developed in Europe.[28]

[27] John A. Quelch and Edward J. Hoff, "Customizing Global Marketing," *Harvard Business Review* 64 (May–June 1986): 59–68.

[28] Richard I. Kirkland, "Entering a New Age of Boundless Competition," *Fortune,* March 14, 1988, 18–22.

FIGURE 21.10   Roles for Country Organizations

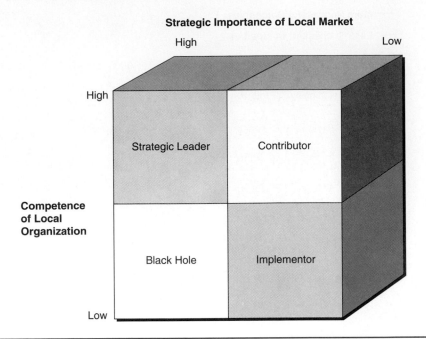

Source: Reprinted by permission of *Harvard Business Review.* An exhibit from "Tap Your Subsidiaries for Global Reach," by Christopher A. Bartlett and Sumantra Ghoshal, 64 (November/December 1986), p. 90. Copyright © 1986 by the President and Fellows of Harvard College; all rights reserved.

The critical mass for the international marketing effort is provided by **implementors.** These country organizations may exist in smaller, less-developed countries in which corporate commitment for market development is less. Although most entities are given this role, it should not be slighted: Implementors provide the opportunity to capture economies of scale and scope that are the basis of a global strategy.

The **black hole** is a situation that the international marketer has to work out of. As an example, in strategically important markets, such as the European Union, local presence is considered necessary for maintaining the company's overall global competitiveness and, in some cases, to anticipate competitive moves in other markets. One of the major ways of exiting this position is to enter into strategic alliances. AT&T, which had long restricted itself to its domestic market, needed to go global fast. Some of the alliances it formed were with Philips in telecommunications and Olivetti in computers and office automation.[29] In some cases, firms may use their presence in a major market as an observation post to keep up with developments before a major thrust for entry is executed.

Depending on the role, the relationship between headquarters and the country organization will vary from loose control based mostly on support to tighter control in making sure strategies are implemented appropriately. Yet in each of these cases, it is imperative that country organizations have enough operating independence to cater to local needs and to provide motivation to the country managers. For example, an implementor should provide input in the development of a regional or a global strategy or

---

[29] Louis Kraar, "Your Rivals Can Be Your Allies," *Fortune,* March 27, 1989, 66–76.

program. Strategy formulation should ensure that appropriate implementation can be achieved at the country level.

CONTROL

The function of the organizational structure is to provide a framework in which objectives can be met. A set of instruments and processes is needed, however, to influence the behavior and performance of organization members to meet the goals. Controls focus on actions to verify and correct actions that differ from established plans. Compliance needs to be secured from subordinates through various means of coordinating specialized and interdependent parts of the organization.[30] Within an organization, control serves as an integrating mechanism. Controls are designed to reduce uncertainty, increase predictability, and ensure that behaviors originating in separate parts of the organization are compatible and in support of common organizational goals despite physical, psychic, and temporal distances.[31] The critical issue is the same as with organizational structure: What is the ideal amount of control? On the one hand, headquarters needs information to ensure that international activities contribute maximum benefit to the overall organization. On the other hand, controls should not be construed as a code of law and allowed eventually to stifle local initiative.

Types of Controls

Most organizations display some administrative flexibility, as demonstrated by variations in the application of management directives, corporate objectives, or measurement systems. A distinction should be made, however, between variations that have emerged by design and those that are the result of autonomy. The one is the result of management decision, whereas the other has typically grown without central direction and is based on emerging practices. In both instances, some type of control will be exercised. Here, we are concerned only with controls that are the result of headquarters initiative rather than consequences of tolerated practices. Firms that wait for self-emerging controls often find that such an orientation may lead to rapid international growth but may eventually result in problems in areas of product-line performance, program coordination, and strategic planning.[32]

Not all control systems evolve in the way they were originally envisioned. For example, shifts may be triggered by changes over time in the relative importance of international activity. Hoover Corporation provides an example. Initially, Hoover's U.S. headquarters had strong control capability. As the European operations grew in importance, however, they assumed an increasing role in overall corporate planning and control.

In the design of the control system, a major decision concerns the object of control. Two major objects are typically identified: output and behavior.[33] Output controls consist of balance sheets, sales data, production data, product-line growth, or a performance

---

[30] Amitai Etzioni, *A Comparative Analysis of Complex Organizations* (Glencoe, England: Free Press, 1961), 8.

[31] William G. Egelhoff, "Patterns of Control in U.S., U.K., and European Multinational Corporations," *Journal of International Business Studies* 15 (Fall 1984): 73–83.

[32] William H. Davidson, "Administrative Orientation and International Performance," *Journal of International Business Studies* 15 (Fall 1984): 11–23.

[33] William G. Ouchi, "The Relationship between Organizational Structure and Organizational Control," *Administrative Science Quarterly* 22 (March 1977): 95–112.

TABLE 21.1   Comparison of Bureaucratic and Cultural Control Mechanisms

	Type of Control	
Object of Control	**Pure Bureaucratic/ Formalized Control**	**Pure Cultural Control**
Output	Formal performance reports	Shared norms of performance
Behavior	Company policies, manuals	Shared philosophy of management

Source: B. R. Baliga and Alfred M. Jaeger, "Multinational Corporations: Control Systems and Delegation Issues," *Journal of International Business Studies* 15 (Fall 1984): 28.

review of personnel. Measures of output are accumulated at regular intervals and forwarded from the foreign operation to headquarters, where they are evaluated and critiqued based on comparisons to the plan or budget. Behavioral controls require the exertion of influence over behavior after, or ideally before, it leads to action. This influence can be achieved, for example, by providing sales manuals to subsidiary personnel or by fitting new employees into the corporate culture.

To institute either of these measures, corporate officials must decide on instruments of control. The general alternatives are bureaucratic/formalized or cultural.[34] **Bureaucratic controls** consist of a limited and explicit set of regulations and rules that outline desired levels of performance. **Cultural controls,** on the other hand, are much less formal and are the result of shared beliefs and expectations among the members of an organization. A comparison of the two types of controls and their objectives is provided in Table 21.1.

Bureaucratic/Formalized Control   The elements of bureaucratic/formalized control are (1) an international budget and planning system, (2) the functional reporting system, and (3) policy manuals used to direct functional performance. **Budgets** are short-term guidelines in such areas as investment, cash, and personnel, whereas **plans** refer to formalized long-range programs with more than a one-year horizon. The budget and planning process is the major control instrument in headquarters-subsidiary relationships. Although systems and their execution vary, the objective is to achieve the best fit possible with the objectives and characteristics of the firm and its environment.

The budgetary period is typically one year because budgets are tied to the accounting systems of the company. The budget system is used for four main purposes: (1) allocation of funds among subsidiaries; (2) planning and coordination of global production capacity and supplies; (3) evaluation of subsidiary performance; and (4) communication and information exchange between subsidiaries, product organizations, and corporate headquarters.[35] Long-range plans, on the other hand, extend over periods of two years up to ten years, and their content is more qualitative and judgmental in nature than that of budgets. Shorter periods, such as two years, are the norm because of the uncertainty of diverse foreign environments.

Although firms strive for uniformity, this may be comparable to trying to design a suit to fit the average person. The budget and planning processes themselves are formalized in terms of the schedules to be followed.

Functional reports are another control instrument used by multinational corporations. The reports required by headquarters from subsidiaries vary in number, amount

---

[34] B. R. Baliga and Alfred M. Jaeger, "Multinational Corporations: Control Systems and Delegation Issues," *Journal of International Business Studies* 15 (Fall 1984): 25–40.

[35] Laurent Leksell, *Headquarters-Subsidiary Relationships in Multinational Corporations* (Stockholm, Sweden: Stockholm School of Economics, 1981), Chap. 5.

Type of Report	U.S. MNCs (33)	German MNCs (44)	Japanese MNCs (40)
Balance sheet	97	49	42
Profit and loss statement	91	49	42
Production output	94	50	47
Market share	70	48	31
Cash and credit statement	100	41	39
Inventory levels	88	46	38
Sales per product	88	37	44
Performance review of personnel	9	15	2
Report on local economic and political conditions	33	32	12

Types of Functional Reports in Multinational Corporations — TABLE 21.2

Source: Anant R. Negandhi and Martin Welge, *Beyond Theory Z* (Greenwich, CT: JAI Press, 1984), 18.

of detail, and frequency. Table 21.2 summarizes the various types of functional reports in a total of 117 multinational corporations in three countries—the United States, Germany, and Japan. The structure and elements of these reports are typically highly standardized to allow for consolidation at the headquarters level.

The frequency and types of reports to be furnished by subsidiaries are likely to increase because of the globalization trend. Managers in subsidiaries must therefore see the rationale for this often time-consuming task. When explaining the need for additional reports, two approaches used in tandem facilitate the process: participation and feedback. Involving the preparers of reports in their ultimate use serves to avoid the perception at subsidiary levels that reports are "art for art's sake." When this is not possible, feedback about results and consequences is an alternative. Through this process, communication is also enhanced.

Headquarters may want to guide the way in which subsidiaries make decisions and implement agreed-upon strategies. U.S.-based multinational companies, relying heavily on manuals for all major functions, tend to be far more formalized than their Japanese and European counterparts.[36] The manuals are for functions such as personnel policies for recruitment, training, motivation, and dismissal. The use of policy manuals as a control instrument correlates with the level of reports required from subsidiaries.

Cultural Control In countries other than the United States, less emphasis is placed on formal controls, which are viewed as rigid and too quantitatively oriented. Rather, the emphasis is on corporate values and culture, and evaluations are based on the extent to which an individual or entity fits in. Cultural controls require an extensive socialization process, and informal, personal interaction is central to the process. Substantial resources must be spent to train the individual to share the corporate culture, that is, "the way things are done at the company."[37] To build common vision and values, managers spend a substantial amount of their first months at Matsushita in what the company calls "cultural and spiritual training." They study the company credo, the "Seven Spirits of Matsushita," and the philosophy of the founder, Konosuke Matsushita. Then they learn how to translate these internalized lessons into daily behavior and operational decisions. Although more prevalent in Japanese organizations, many Western entities have

[36] Anant R. Negandhi and Martin Welge, *Beyond Theory Z* (Greenwich, CT: JAI Press, 1984), 16.

[37] Richard Pascale, "Fitting New Employees into the Company Culture," *Fortune*, May 28, 1984, 28–40.

similar programs, for example, Philips' "organization cohesion training" and Unilever's "indoctrination."[38]

The instruments of cultural control focus on the careful selection and training of corporate personnel and the institution of self-control. The choice of cultural controls rather than bureaucratic controls can be justified if the company enjoys a low turnover rate. Cultural controls are thus applied, for example, when companies offer lifetime or long-term employment, as many Japanese firms do.

In selecting home-country nationals and, to some extent, third-country nationals, multinational companies are exercising cultural control. They assume that these managers have already internalized the norms and values of the company. For example, only four of 3M's 53 managing directors of overseas subsidiaries are local nationals. The company's experience is that nonnationals tend to run a country operation with a more global view.[39] In some cases, the use of headquarters personnel to ensure uniformity in decision making may be advisable; for example, for the position of financial officer, Volvo uses a home-country national. Expatriates are used in subsidiaries not only for control purposes but also for initiating change, which has caused concern especially in Third World countries. Companies control the efforts of management specifically through compensation, promotion, and replacement policies.

When the expatriate corps is small, headquarters can exercise control through other means. Management training programs for overseas managers as well as visits to headquarters will indoctrinate individuals to the company's way of doing things. For instance, a Chinese executive selected to run Loctite's new operation in China spent two years at the company's headquarters before taking over in Beijing.[40] Similarly, visits to subsidiaries by headquarters teams will promote a sense of belonging. These may be on a formal basis, as for a strategy audit, or less formal—for example, to launch a new product.

Corporations rarely use one pure control mechanism. Rather, emphasis is placed on both quantitative and qualitative measures. Corporations are likely, however, to place different levels of emphasis on the types of performance measures and on the way the measures are taken.

Exercising Control

Within most corporations, different functional areas are subject to different guidelines. The reason is that each function is subject to different constraints and varying degrees of those constraints. For example, marketing as a function has traditionally been seen as incorporating many more behavioral dimensions than does manufacturing or finance. As a result, many multinational corporations employ control systems that are responsive to the needs of the function. Yet such differentiation is sometimes based less on appropriateness than on personality. One researcher hypothesized that manufacturing subsidiaries are controlled more intensively than sales subsidiaries because production more readily lends itself to centralized direction, and technicians and engineers adhere more firmly to standards and regulations than do salespeople.[41] This trend is causing a

[38] Bartlett and Ghoshal, "Matrix Management," 138–145.

[39] "How 3M Develops Managers," 81–82.

[40] Nathaniel Gilbert, "How Middle-Sized Corporations Manage Global Operations," *Management Review*, October 1988, 46–50.

[41] R. J. Alsegg, *Control Relationships between American Corporations and Their European Subsidiaries*, AMA Research Study No. 107 (New York: American Management Association, 1971), 7.

THE INTERNATIONAL MARKETPLACE   21.4

The Country Manager of the 1990s

Organizationally, the forces of globalization are changing the country manager's role significantly. With profit and loss responsibility, oversight of multiple functions, and the benefit of distance from headquarters, country managers enjoyed considerable decision-making autonomy as well as entrepreneurial initiative. Today, however, multinational companies have to emphasize the product dimension of the product-geography matrix, which means that power has to shift at least to some extent from country managers to worldwide strategic business unit and product-line managers. Many of the previously local decisions are now subordinated to global strategic moves.

The changing-task mix toward more implementation calls for action on the part of the multinational companies to retain the entrepreneurial drive needed at the country level. A sample of 50 country managers in Asian, European, and North American multinationals recommend the following skills and attitudes for future operations:

1. **External focus.** Country managers will have to spend less time on internal functions such as manufacturing and more time in the front office dealing with local customers, monitoring marketing initiatives by local and global competitors, and cultivating relations with trade, industry associations, and the government.

2. **Government relations.** Country managers will have to make sure that local governments see the subsidiary as a good corporate citizen of its host environment by contributing to the economy and to the local communities.

3. **Corporate perspective.** Country managers will be called to seek and identify similarities across national markets, encourage the export and import of good ideas among subsidiaries, and gather intelligence useful to others in the organization.

4. **Team player.** Country managers will have to derive satisfaction not only from enhancing the performance and capabilities of their subsidiaries, but also from influencing results beyond the boundaries of their own domains.

5. **Multiple roles.** For efficiency reasons, country managers may have to wear many hats. A country manager for Spain or Finland, for example, might also have to oversee a subregion such as Iberia or the Baltics, be the strategic director for a product line throughout southern or northern Europe, and oversee a function such as manufacturing on a pan-regional basis.

Source: John A. Quelch, "The New Country Managers," *The McKinsey Quarterly* 29 no. 4 (1992): 155–165.

significant change in the role of the country general manager, as seen in The International Marketplace 21.4. Despite increasing integration, country managers will retain an important role in staying close to local customers, competitors, and policymakers in host governments.

In their international operations, U.S.-based multinational corporations place major emphasis on obtaining quantitative data. Although this allows for good centralized comparisons against standards and benchmarks, or cross-comparisons between different corporate units, several drawbacks are associated with the undertaking. In the international environment, new dimensions—such as inflation, differing rates of taxation, and exchange rate fluctuations—may distort the performance evaluation of any given individual or organizational unit. For the global corporation, measurement of whether a business unit in a particular country is earning a superior return on investment relative to risk may be irrelevant to the contribution an investment may make worldwide or to the long-term results of the firm. In the short term, the return may even be negative.[42] Therefore, the control mechanism may quite inappropriately indicate reward or punishment. Standardizing the information received may be difficult if the environment fluctuates and requires frequent and major adaptations. Further complicating the issue is the fact that, although quantitative information may be collected monthly, or at least quarterly, environmental data may be acquired annually or "now and then," especially when crisis seems to loom on the horizon.

To design a control system that is acceptable not only to headquarters but also to the organization and individuals abroad, a firm must take great care to use only relevant data. Major concerns, therefore, are the data-collection process and the analysis and utilization of data. Evaluators need management information systems that provide for maximum comparability and equity in administering controls. The more behaviorally based and culture-oriented controls are, the more care that needs to be taken.[43]

In designing a control system, management must consider the costs of establishing and maintaining it and trade them off with benefits to be gained. Any control system will require investment in a management structure and in systems design. As an example, consider the costs associated with cultural controls: Personal interaction, use of expatriates, and training programs are all quite expensive. Yet these expenses may be justified in savings through lower employee turnover, an extensive worldwide information system, and a potentially improved control system.[44] Moreover, the impact goes beyond the administrative component. If controls are erroneous or too time-consuming, they can slow or misguide the strategy implementation process and thus the overall capability of the firm. The result will be lost opportunity or, worse, increased threats. In addition, time spent on reporting takes time away from other tasks. If reports are seen as marginally useful, the motivation to prepare them will be low. A parsimonious design is therefore imperative. The control system should collect all the information required and trigger all the intervention necessary but should not create a situation that resembles the pulling of strings by a puppeteer.

The impact of the environment must also be taken into account when designing controls. First, the control system should measure only dimensions over which the organization has control. Rewards or sanctions make little sense if they are based on dimensions that may be relevant for overall corporate performance but over which no influence can be exerted, for example, price controls. Neglecting the factor of individual performance capability would send wrong signals and severely impede the motivation of personnel. Second, control systems should harmonize with local regulations and cus-

[42] John J. Dyment, "Strategies and Management Controls for Global Corporations," *Journal of Business Strategy* 7 (Spring 1987): 20–26.

[43] Hans Schoellhammer, "Decision-Making and Intra-Organizational Conflicts in Multinational Companies," presented at the Symposium on Management of Headquarter-Subsidiary Relationships in Transnational Corporations, Stockholm School of Economics, June 2–4, 1980.

[44] Alfred M. Jaeger, "The Transfer of Organizational Culture Overseas: An Approach to Control in the Multinational Corporation," *Journal of International Business Studies* 14 (Fall 1983): 91–106.

toms. In some cases, however, corporate behavioral controls have to be exercised against local customs even though overall operations may be affected negatively. This type of situation occurs, for example, when a subsidiary operates in markets where unauthorized facilitating payments are a common business practice.

Corporations are faced with major challenges to appropriate and adequate control systems in today's business environment. With an increase in local (government) demands for a share in the control of companies established, controls can become tedious, especially if the multinational company is a minority partner. Even in a merger, such as the one between ASEA and Brown Boveri—or in a new entity formed by two companies as when Toyota and GM formed NUMMI—the backgrounds of the partners may be sufficiently different to cause problems in terms of the controls.

SUMMARY

The structures and control mechanisms needed to operate internationally define relationships between the firm's headquarters and subsidiaries and provide the channels through which these relationships develop.

International firms can choose from a variety of organizational structures, ranging from a domestic operation that handles ad hoc export orders to a full-fledged global organization. The choice will depend primarily on the degree of internationalization of the firm, the diversity of international activities, and the relative importance of product, area, function, and customer variables in the process. Another determining factor is the degree to which headquarters wants to decide important issues concerning the corporation as a whole or the subsidiaries individually. Organizations that function effectively still need to be reviewed periodically to ensure that they will remain responsive to changing environments. Some of the responses may not take the form of structural changes but rather are changes in internal relations. Of these, the primary one is the use of subsidiaries as resources, not merely as implementors of headquarters' strategy.

The control function is of increasing importance because of the high variability in performance that results from divergent local environments and the need to reconcile local objectives with the corporate goal of synergism. It is important to grant autonomy to country organizations so that they can be responsive to local market needs, but it is equally important to ensure close cooperation between units.

Control can be exercised through bureaucratic means, emphasizing formal reporting and evaluation of benchmark data. It can also be exercised through a cultural control process in which norms and values are understood by individuals and entities that compose the corporation. U.S. firms typically rely more on bureaucratic controls, whereas multinational corporations headquartered in other countries frequently control operations abroad through informal means and rely less on stringent measures.

The implementation of controls requires great sensitivity to behavioral dimensions and to the environment. The measurements used must be appropriate and must reflect actual performance rather than marketplace vagaries. Entities should be measured only on factors over which they have some degree of control.

A summary of organizational and control characteristics of nine of the world's most successful multinational corporations is provided in Table 21.3. As can be seen, the corporations display wide variation in their approaches, yet they all achieve an overall balance between control and attention to local conditions.

TABLE 21.3	Organizational and Control Characteristics of Selected Multinational Corporations

| Company | Parent Company Characteristics | |
	Dominant Organizational Concept	Planning and Control
American Cyanamid Company (U.S.)	Product divisions with global responsibility	Heavy reliance on strategic planning; under guidance of Corporate Planning and Development Department; plans prepared by designated business units; accompanied by annual profit plan; investment priority matrix to facilitate allocation of funds
Ciba-Geigy Limited (Switzerland)	Product divisions with global responsibility, but gradual strengthening of key regional organizations	Moderate reliance on strategic planning by global product divisions; gradual buildup of the role of key regional companies in the planning process; operational plans and capital budgets by country organizations and their product divisions, with the latter playing the more active role
The Dow Chemical Company (U.S.)	Decentralized geographically into five regional companies; central coordination through World Headquarters Group	Coordination of geographic regions through World Headquarters Group, particularly the Corporate Product Department; strategic planning at the corporate level on a product basis, and in the operating units on a regional basis; operational plans and capital budgets by geographic region; control function at the corporate level
General Electric Company (U.S.)	Product-oriented strategic business units on a worldwide basis	Heavy reliance on strategic planning; under guidance of Corporate Planning and Development Department; plans prepared by designated strategic business units; investment priority matrix to facilitate allocation of funds
Imperial Chemical Industries Limited (U.K.)	Product divisions with global responsibility, but gradual strengthening of regional organizations	Coordination of planning through Central Planning Department; strategic planning and operational planning at the divisional and regional levels; tight financial reporting and control by headquarters
Nestlé S.A. (Switzerland)	Decentralized regional and country organizations	Increasing emphasis on strategic planning, with recent formation of Central Planning and Information Services Department; annual plans (budgets) by each major company; tight financial reporting and control by headquarters
N. V. Philips (The Netherlands)	Product divisions with global responsibility, but gradual strengthening of geographic organizations; U.S. company financially and legally separate from parent	Moderate to heavy reliance on strategic planning by planning units in product divisions, selected national organizations, and Central Planning Department; operational plans by division and national organizations, with initiative from the former; monthly review of performance

Continued

TABLE 21.3

	Parent Company Characteristics	
Research and/or Product Development	**U.S. Companies: Handling of U.S. Business**	**European Companies: Handling of International Business**
Research and product development activities carried out by product divisions at five separate centers, each concentrating on a particular technology and/or market	Separate international operating divisions organized into two geographic areas; limited authority, serving primarily in staff capacity	(not applicable)
Research and product development activities carried out by domestic product divisions and certain product divisions in key geographic areas	(not applicable)	Dual reporting relationship, with U.S. company reporting directly to headquarters and its local divisions also reporting to their counterpart domestic divisions
Research and development activities heavily process oriented and usually associated with manufacturing facilities reporting to geographic regions; central coordination by World Headquarters Group	Highly decentralized organization of five geographic areas, each with almost complete authority over planning and operations	(not applicable)
Centralized research, with supportive product development activities at the operating level	International business sector, together with overseas activities in other sectors; nine country strategic business units, which prepare an international integration plan to coordinate activities with product SBUs	(not applicable)
Research and product development activities carried out by headquarters and selected regional organizations	(not applicable)	U.S. organization oversees ICI activities in the Americas and reports directly to headquarters; U.S. board has considerable authority regarding local decisions and activities
Highly centralized research, but local product development by regional and country organizations	(not applicable)	U.S. activities divided among three main companies, each with special reporting relationship to headquarters
Highly centralized research, but with product development by product divisions and large national organizations; other research centers located in four key countries	(not applicable)	No formal chain of command between headquarters and U.S. organization; latter operating under direction of U.S. Philips Trust

Continued

TABLE 21.3	*Continued*

| Company | Parent Company Characteristics | |
	Dominant Organizational Concept	Planning and Control
Rhône-Poulenc S.A. (France)	Product divisions with global responsibility, but major country organizations retain special status	Moderate reliance on strategic planning by Central Strategy and Planning Department; in addition, strategic planning at the operational level, primarily by product divisions; operational plans and capital budgets by divisions and country organizations; monthly review of performance
Solvay & Cie S.A. (Belgium)	Product divisions with global responsibility, but national and subsidiary organizations allowed to exercise a reasonable degree of autonomy	Increasing emphasis on strategic planning with the recent formation of Central Planning Department; operational plans and capital budget by country organizations

Source: Reprinted from *Business Horizons,* May–June 1981. Copyright 1981 by the Foundation for the School of Business at Indiana University. Used with permission. Updated by interview March 1990.

Questions for Discussion

1. Firms differ, often substantially, in their organizational structures even within the same industry. What accounts for these differences in their approaches?

2. Discuss the benefits gained in adopting a matrix approach in terms of organizational structure.

3. What changes in the firm and/or in the environment might cause a firm to abandon the functional approach?

4. Is there more to the "not-invented-here" syndrome than simply hurt feelings on the part of those who believe they are being dictated to by headquarters?

5. If the purposes of the budget are in conflict, as is sometimes argued, what can be done about it?

6. Performance reviews of subsidiary managers and personnel are required rarely, if at all, by headquarters. Why?

7. Why do European-based multinational corporations differ from U.S.-based corporations in the instruments they choose for exerting control?

8. One of the most efficient means of control is self-control. What type of program would you prepare for an incoming employee?

Recommended Readings

Bartlett, Christopher, and Sumantra Ghoshal. *Managing across Borders.* Cambridge, MA: Harvard Business School Press, 1989.

Davidson, William H., and Jose de la Torre. *Managing the Global Corporation.* New York: McGraw-Hill, 1989.

Deal, Terrence E., and Allen A. Kennedy. *Corporate Cultures: The Rights and Rituals of Corporate Life.* Boston: Addison-Wesley, 1982.

Goehle, Donna D. *Decision-Making in Multinational Corporations.* Ann Arbor, MI: UMI Research Press, 1980.

Hedlund, Gunar, and Per Aman. *Managing Relationships with Foreign Subsidiaries.* Stockholm, Sweden: Mekan, 1984.

Continued | **TABLE 21.3**

Parent Company Characteristics		
Research and/or Product Development	**U.S. Companies: Handling of U.S. Business**	**European Companies: Handling of International Business**
Research and product development activities carried out by product divisions; several large centers, each focusing on different specializations	(not applicable)	Special reporting relationship directly to headquarters; U.S. company coordinates activities with product divisions at headquarters
Centralized research and product development activities; major national organizations also carry out product development	(not applicable)	U.S. organization functions as legal entity, overseeing Solvay's activities in the United States; however, several of the U.S. businesses report independently to headquarters

Hulbert, James M., and William K. Brandt. *Managing the Multinational Subsidiary.* New York: Holt, Rinehart, and Winston, 1980.

Moran, Robert T., Philip R. Harris, and William G. Stripp. *Developing the Global Organization.* Houston, TX: Gulf Publishing Co., 1993.

Negandhi, Anant R., and Martin Welge. *Beyond Theory Z.* Greenwich, CT: JAI Press, 1984.

Otterbeck, Lars, ed. *The Management of Headquarters-Subsidiary Relationships in Multinational Corporations.* Aldershot, England: Gower Publishing Company, 1981.

Porter, Michael E., ed. *Competition in Global Industries.* Boston: Harvard Business School Press, 1986.

Stopford, John N., and Louis T. Wells. *Managing the Multinational Enterprise: Organization of the Firm and Ownership of the Subsidiary.* New York: Basic Books, 1972.

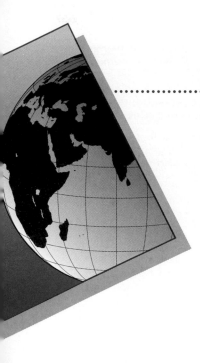

CHAPTER 22

Countertrade

THE INTERNATIONAL MARKETPLACE

Barter Deals Will Bring Trade Growth

Senator James Exon of Nebraska is a leading proponent of barter and authored legislation that created an Office of Barter and Countertrade in the U.S. Department of Commerce. He believes that "barter now constitutes about 20 percent of all international trade. If we want to deal with the republics of the former Soviet Union, we need to be creative and think of alternative ways to do business besides direct cash for goods. The capitalist system has a preoccupation with worshiping the almighty dollar. Unfortunately, the former Soviet Union doesn't have many dollars for us to worship. There are more possibilities for trade between our countries if we barter, especially in commodities in which we both have an abundance, such as oil for U.S. wheat. A barrel of oil purchased or bartered with the former Soviet Union could facilitate additional American sales of food and products, whereas a barrel of oil from a Persian Gulf nation would simply add to a bilateral trade deficit. In other words, oil from the former Soviet Union could equal new American exports."

In the senator's view, the federal government should undertake a much more active role in promoting barter. Otherwise, nations that are more agreeable to bartering will get ahead of the United States. He thinks that the federal role could include the establishment of a national data base of U.S. and CIS companies interested in barter opportunities, or a barter insurance program to guarantee some percentage of the barter arrangement. When confronted with arguments from U.S. Treasury Department officials, "Why barter when dealing in money is better?" he responds: "Well, one side doesn't have any money."

Source: Adapted from Bill Pietrucha, *WE/Mbl*, August 10–23, 1992, 7.

General Motors exchanged automobiles for a trainload of strawberries. Control Data swapped a computer for a package of Polish furniture, Hungarian carpet backing, and Soviet greeting cards. Ford traded cars for sheepskins from Uruguay, potatoes from Spain, toilet seats from Finland, cranes from Norway, and coffee from Colombia.[1] Pepsi has accepted, in exchange for soft-drink concentrate, products ranging from sesame seeds to sisal for making rope. Usbekistan, one of the new countries of the former Soviet Union, is offering crude venom of vipers, toads, scorpions, black widows, and tarantulas, as well as growth-controlling substances from snakes and lizards, in countertrade.[2]

All of these are examples of countertrade activities carried out around the world. This chapter will focus on the ancient, yet new, forms of barter and countertrade that are used in world trade. It will first explain the types of countertrade that currently exist and discuss why these types of transactions are reemerging. Policy issues associated with countertrade will be explored by examining the attitudes held toward countertrade by both national governments and international bodies such as the GATT, the OECD, and the UN. The countertrade situation of corporations will then be reviewed with an examination of what firms do and why they do it. Finally, information will be provided on how to organize for countertrade, what problems to look out for, and how countertrade can be used as an effective international marketing tool.

COUNTERTRADE DEFINED

Countertrade is a sale that encompasses more than an exchange of goods, services, or ideas for money. In the international market, countertrade transactions "are those transactions which have as a basic characteristic a linkage, legal or otherwise, between exports and imports of goods or services in addition to, or in place of, financial settlements."[3] Historically, countertrade was mainly conducted in the form of barter, which is a direct exchange, between parties, of goods of approximately equal value, with no money involved, as described in The International Marketplace 22.1. These transactions were the very essence of business at times when no money—that is, a common medium of exchange—existed or was available. Over time, money emerged as a convenient medium that unlinked transactions from individual parties and permitted greater flexibility in trading activities. Repeatedly, however, we can see returns to the barter system as a result of environmental circumstances. For example, because of tight financial constraints, Georgetown University, during its initial years of operation after 1789, charged its students part of the tuition in foodstuffs and required students to participate in the construction of university buildings. During periods of high inflation in Europe in the 1920s, goods such as bread, meat, and gold were seen as much more useful and secure than paper money, which decreased in real value by the minute. Even more recently, in the late 1940s, American cigarettes were an acceptable medium of exchange in most European countries, much more so than any currency except the dollar.

Countertrade transactions have therefore always arisen when economic circumstances made it more efficient to exchange goods directly than to use money as an intermediary. Conditions that encourage such business activities are lack of money, lack of value of money, lack of acceptability of money as an exchange medium, or greater ease of transaction by using goods.

[1] Raj Aggarwal, "International Business through Barter and Countertrade," *Long Range Planning* (June 1989): 75–81.

[2] *Trade Finance,* May 1992, 13

[3] "Current Activities of International Organizations in the Field of Barter and Barter-like Transactions," *Report of the Secretary General,* United Nations, General Assembly, 1984, 4.

These same reasons prevail in today's resurgence of countertrade activities. Beginning in the 1950s, countertrade and barter transactions were mainly carried out with countries from the then Socialist bloc. The currencies of these countries were not acceptable outside of the bloc because they were not freely convertible. At the same time, these countries did not possess sufficient foreign "hard" currency to make purchases of Western goods that were crucial for further economic development. To some extent, these countries solved their currency problem by depleting their gold reserves—which indirectly, because of the world market price for gold, was a financial transaction. Even so, these measures did not permit sufficient importation. Many of these countries therefore insisted in their dealings with Western nations that goods they produced be taken in exchange so as to reduce their need for foreign currencies.

In the 1980s, the use of countertrade steadily increased. In 1972, countertrade was used by only 15 countries. By 1983, the countries conducting countertrade transactions numbered 88, and by 1993 the number was 101. Figure 22.1 lists countries that are currently requesting countertrade transactions from their trading partners. Estimates as to the total volume of global countertrade vary widely. A consensus of expert opinions has put the percentage of world trade linked to countertrade transactions at between 20 and 25 percent.[4] Such an estimate conflicts with IMF figures, which attribute only a very small percentage of world trade to countertrade. Yet if all business transactions in which countertrade plays some kind of role are considered, the estimate of 20 to 25 percent could be reasonable.

Many countries are deciding that countertrade transactions are more beneficial to them than transactions based on financial exchange alone. A primary reason is that the world debt crisis has made ordinary trade financing very risky. Countries, particularly in the developing world, simply cannot obtain the trade credit or financial assistance necessary to afford desired imports. Heavily indebted nations, faced with the possibility of not being able to afford imports at all, resort to countertrade to maintain at least some trickle of product inflow.

A second reason is that many countries are again enamored by the notion of bilateralism. Thinking along the lines of "you scratch my back, and I'll scratch yours," they prefer to exchange goods with countries that are their major business partners.

Countertrade is also often viewed by firms and nations alike as an excellent mechanism to gain entry into new markets. When a producer feels that marketing is not its strong suit, particularly in product areas that face strong international competition, countertrade is seen as useful. The producer often hopes that the party receiving the goods will serve as a new distributor, opening up new international marketing channels and ultimately expanding the original market.

Conversely, because countertrade is highly sought after in many markets that have major demand for foreign products but only limited hard currency to pay for imports, markets such as China, Central Europe, South America, and the Third World, engaging in such transactions can provide major growth opportunities for Western firms.[5] In increasingly competitive world markets, countertrade can be a good way to attract new buyers. By providing marketing services, the seller is in effect differentiating his product from those of his competitors.[6]

---

[4] Sam Okoroafo, "Determinants of LDC Mandated Countertrade," *International Marketing Review,* Winter 1989, 16–24.

[5] Bill Neale, "Countertrade: Reactive or Proactive?" *Journal of Business Research* 16 (December 1988): 327–335.

[6] Jong H. Park, "Is Countertrade Merely a Passing Phenomenon? Some Public Policy Implications," in *Proceedings of the 1988 Conference,* ed. R. King (Charleston, SC: Academy of International Business, Southeast Region, 1988), 67–71.

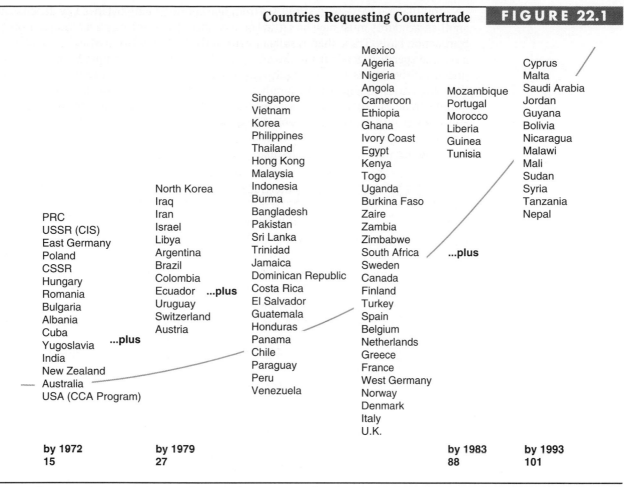

Countries Requesting Countertrade   FIGURE 22.1

by 1972	by 1979			by 1983	by 1993
PRC	North Korea	Singapore	Mexico	Mozambique	Cyprus
USSR (CIS)	Iraq	Vietnam	Algeria	Portugal	Malta
East Germany	Iran	Korea	Nigeria	Morocco	Saudi Arabia
Poland	Israel	Philippines	Angola	Liberia	Jordan
CSSR	Libya	Thailand	Cameroon	Guinea	Guyana
Hungary	Argentina	Hong Kong	Ethiopia	Tunisia	Bolivia
Romania	Brazil	Malaysia	Ghana		Nicaragua
Bulgaria	Colombia	Indonesia	Ivory Coast		Malawi
Albania	Ecuador ...plus	Burma	Egypt		Mali
Cuba	Uruguay	Bangladesh	Kenya		Sudan
Yugoslavia ...plus	Switzerland	Pakistan	Togo		Syria
India	Austria	Sri Lanka	Uganda		Tanzania
New Zealand		Trinidad	Burkina Faso		Nepal
Australia		Jamaica	Zaire		
USA (CCA Program)		Dominican Republic	Zambia		
		Costa Rica	Zimbabwe		
		El Salvador	South Africa ...plus		
		Guatemala	Sweden		
		Honduras	Canada		
		Panama	Finland		
		Chile	Turkey		
		Paraguay	Spain		
		Peru	Belgium		
		Venezuela	Netherlands		
			Greece		
			France		
			West Germany		
			Norway		
			Denmark		
			Italy		
			U.K.		

by 1972	by 1979		by 1983	by 1993
15	**27**		**88**	**101**

Sources: Willis A. Bussard. "Countertrade: A View from U.S. Industry." *Countertrade and Barter Quarterly,* May 1984, 54; and Pompiliu Verzariu, Office of Barter and Countertrade, U.S. Department of Commerce, October 1993.

Countertrade can also provide stability for long-term sales. For example, if a firm is tied to a countertrade agreement, it will need to source the product from a particular supplier, whether it wishes to do so or not. This stability is often valued highly because it eliminates, or at least reduces, vast swings in demand and thus allows for better planning.

Finally, under certain conditions, countertrade can ensure the quality of an international transaction. In instances where the seller of technology is paid in output produced by the technology delivered, the seller's revenue depends on the success of the technology transfer and maintenance services in production. Therefore, the seller is more likely to be dedicated in the provision of services, maintenance, and general technology transfer.[7]

In spite of all these apparent benefits of countertrade, there are strong economic arguments against this activity. These arguments are based mainly on efficiency grounds. As economist Paul Samuelson stated, "Instead of there being a double coincidence of wants, there is likely to be a want of coincidence; so that, unless a hungry tailor happens to find an undraped farmer, who has both food and a desire for a pair of pants, neither can make a trade."[8] Clearly, countertrade ensures that instead of balances being settled

[7] Rolf Mirus and Bernard Yeung, "Why Countertrade? An Economic Perspective," *The International Trade Journal* 7 no. 4 (1993): 409–433.

[8] Paul Samuelson, *Economics,* 11th ed. (New York: McGraw-Hill, 1980), 260

on a multilateral basis, with surpluses from one country being balanced by deficits with another, accounts must now be settled on a country-by-country or even transaction-by-transaction basis. Trade then results only from the ability of two parties or countries to purchase specified goods from one another rather than from competition. As a result, uncompetitive goods may be marketed. In consequence, the ability of countries and their industries to adjust structurally to more efficient production may be restricted. Countertrade can therefore be seen as eroding the quality and efficiency of production and as lowering world consumption. These economic arguments notwithstanding, however, countries and companies increasingly see countertrade as an alternative that may be flawed but worthwhile to undertake.

TYPES OF COUNTERTRADE

Under the traditional types of barter arrangements, goods are exchanged directly for other goods of approximately equal value. As Table 22.1 shows, such transactions can encompass the exchange of a wide variety of goods or services—for example, technical advice for cashmere or mango juice for a jet airplane. As Figure 22.2 shows, the items used for exchange both by industrialized and developing countries are almost limitless. However, straightforward barter transactions, which were quite frequent in the 1950s, are less often used today "because it is difficult to find two parties prepared to make a simultaneous or near-simultaneous exchange of goods of equivalent value."[9]

Increasingly, participants in countertrade have resorted to more sophisticated versions of exchanging goods that often also include some use of money. Figure 22.3 provides an overview of the different forms of countertrade that are in use today. One refinement of simple barter is the **counterpurchase,** or **parallel barter,** agreement. The participating parties sign two separate contracts that specify the goods and services to be exchanged. Frequently, the exchange is not of precisely equal value; therefore, some amount of cash will be involved. However, because an exchange of goods for goods does take place, the transaction can rightfully be called barter. A special case of parallel barter is that of reverse reciprocity, "whereby parallel contracts are signed, granting each party access to needed resources (for example, oil in exchange for nuclear power plants)."[10]

Another common form of countertrade is the **buy-back,** or compensation, arrangement. One party agrees to supply technology or equipment that enables the other party to produce goods with which the price of the supplied products or technology is repaid. These arrangements often "include larger amounts of time, money, and products than straight barter arrangements."[11] They originally evolved "in response to the reluctance of communist countries to permit ownership of productive resources by the private sector—especially by foreign private sectors."[12] One example of such a buy-back arrangement is an agreement entered into by Levi Strauss and Hungary. The company transferred the know-how and the Levi's trademark to Hungary. A Hungarian firm began producing Levi's products. Some of the output is sold domestically, and the rest is marketed in Western Europe by Levi Strauss, in compensation for the know-how. In the past decade, such buy-back arrangements have extended to encompass many developing and newly industrialized nations.

[9] "Current Activities of International Organizations," 4.

[10] Christopher M. Korth, "The Promotion of Exports with Barter," in *Export Promotion,* ed. M. Czinkota (New York: Praeger, 1983), 42.

[11] Donna U. Vogt, *U.S. Government International Barter,* Report No. 83–211 ENR (Washington, D.C.: Congressional Research Service, 1983), 65.

[12] Korth, "Promotion of Exports with Barter."

A Sample of Barter Agreements			**TABLE 22.1**

Country		Exported Commodity	
A	**B**	**A**	**B**
Hungary	Ukraine	• Food stuffs • Tinned foods • Pharmaceuticals	• Timber
Austria	Ukraine	• Power station emissions control equipment	• 800 megakilowatts/year for 15 years
U.S. (Chrysler)	Jamaica	• 200 pickup trucks	• Equivalent value in iron ore
Ukraine	Czech Republic	• Iron ore	• Mining equipment
U.S. (Pierre Cardin)	China	• Technical advice	• Silks and cashmeres
U.K. (Raleigh Bicycle)	CIS	• Training CIS scientists in mountain-bike production	• Titanium. Enough for 30,000 bike frames per year
Indonesia	Uzbekistan	• Indian tea • Vietnamese rice • Miscellaneous Indonesian products	• 50,000 tons of cotton/year for three years
China	Russia	• 212 railway trucks of mango juice	• Passenger jet

Sources: Aspy P. Palia and Oded Shenkar, "Countertrade Practices in China," *Industrial Marketing Management,* 1991, 58; Various Issues of *Trade Finance,* January, April, July, December 1992, June 1993.

A more refined form of barter, aimed at reducing the effect of the immediacy of the transaction, is called **clearing arrangements.** Here, clearing accounts are established to hold deposits and effect withdrawals for trades. These currencies merely represent purchasing power, however, and are not directly withdrawable in cash. As a result, each party can agree in a single contract to purchase goods or services of a specified value. Although the account may be out of balance on a transaction-by-transaction basis, the agreement stipulates that over the long term, a balance in the account will be restored. Frequently, the goods available for purchase with clearing account funds are tightly stipulated. In fact, funds have on occasion been labeled "apple clearing dollars" or "horseradish clearing funds." Sometimes, additional flexibility is given to the clearing account by permitting **switch-trading,** in which credits in the account can be sold or transferred to a third party. Doing so can provide creative intermediaries with opportunities for deal making by identifying clearing account relationships with major imbalances and structuring business transactions to reduce them.

Another major form of barter arrangement is called **offset.** These arrangements are most frequently found in the defense-related sector and in sales of large-scale, high-priced items such as aircraft. For example, when Saudi Arabia purchases military aircraft from a U.S. company, the contracts call for offsetting the cost through related investments. This arrangement, called the "Peace Shield" program, has sparked the investment in manufacturing plants and other defense-related industries on Saudi soil.[13] Such requirements are often a condition for the award of the contract and are frequently used as the determining attribute for contract decisions. Offset arrangements can take on many forms, such as coproduction, licensing, subcontracting, or joint ventures.

[13] Saudi Arabia Section, "Investing, Licensing, and Trading Conditions Abroad," *Business International,* May 1990, 5.

FIGURE 22.2   Preferred Items for Export in Countertrade Transactions

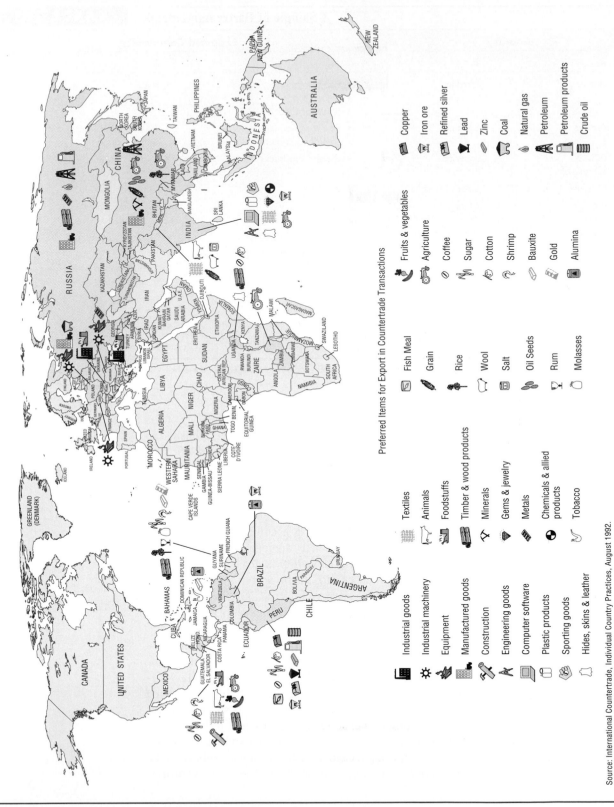

Source: International Countertrade, Individual Country Practices, August 1992.

Classification of Forms of Countertrade

FIGURE 22.3

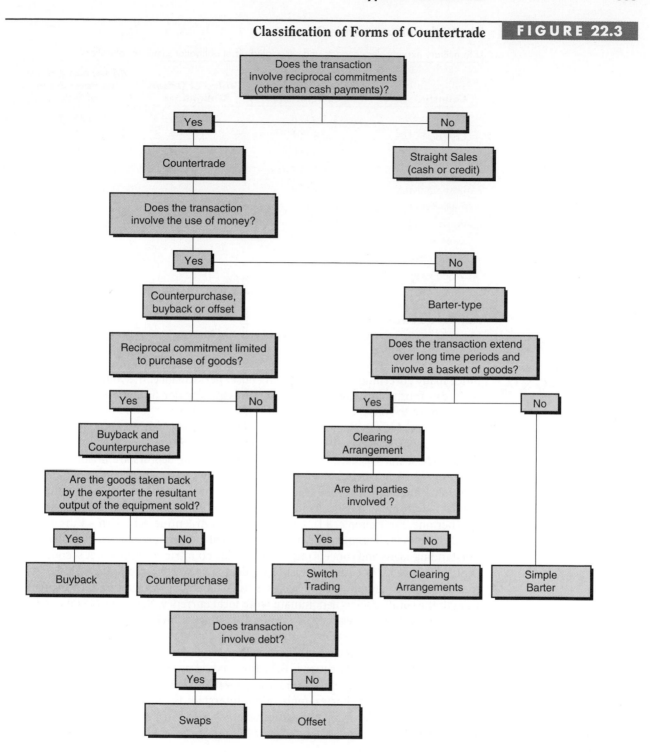

TABLE 22.2	The High Obligation from Offsets

U.S. military export sales contracts and associated offset obligations (millions of dollars)

Country	Value of Export Sales Contracts	Value of Offset Obligations	Offset Obligations as Percentage of Sales
Britain	$ 1,800.8	$ 1,896.5	105.3%
Canada	3,874.1	3,024.2	78.1
Egypt	383.0	87.8	22.9
Israel	6,083.7	1,384.2	22.8
NATO group	667.4	320.4	48.0
South Korea	1,055.8	488.0	46.2
Spain	2,151.3	2,851.1	132.5
Sweden	381.7	663.3	173.8
Switzerland	370.9	248.5	67.0
World total	$34,816.9	$19,929.1	57.2%

Note: Figures are for 1980–1987.

Basic data: U.S. Department of Defense.

Source: "Giving Away the Store," *U.S. News & World Report,* April 23, 1990, 53. Copyright 1990, U.S. News and World Report.

Since many governments are demanding offset performance, the volume of such obligations can mushroom quickly and may represent a major burden on firms. Table 22.2 lists some of the offset obligations incurred by U.S. firms.

A final, newly emerging form of countertrade consists of **debt swaps.** These swaps are carried out particularly with lesser-developed countries in which both government and the private sector face large debt burdens. Because the debtors are unable to repay the debt any time soon, debt holders have increasingly grown amenable to exchange of the debt for something else. Four types of swaps are most prevalent. One of them is a **debt-for-debt swap.** Here, the loan held by one creditor is simply exchanged for a loan held by another one. For example, a U.S. bank may swap Argentine debt with a European bank for Chilean debt. Through this mechanism, debt holders are able to consolidate their outstanding loans and concentrate on particular countries or regions. A second form of debt swap is **debt-for-equity swaps.** Here, debt is converted into foreign equity in a domestic firm. The swap therefore serves as the vehicle for foreign direct investment. Although the equity itself is denominated into local currency, the terms of conversion may allow the investor future access to foreign exchange for dividend remittances and capital repatriation.[14] In some countries, these debt-for-equity swaps have been very successful. For example, investments in Chile have so far retired about $13 billion of external debt.[15]

A third method of debt swaps is **debt-for-product swaps.** Here, debt is exchanged for products received. Usually, these transactions require that additional cash payment be made for the product. For example, First Interstate Bank of California concluded an arrangement with Peruvian authorities whereby a commitment was made to purchase $3 worth of Peruvian products for every $1 of products paid by Peru against debt.[16]

---

[14] Richard A. Debts, David L. Roberts, and Eli M. Remolona, *Finance for Developing Countries* (New York: Group of 30, 1987), 18.

[15] Pompiliu Verzariu, "An Overview of Nontraditional Finance Techniques in International Commerce," in *Trade Finance: Current Issues and Developments* (Washington, D.C.: Government Printing Office, 1988), 48, and Rudolph Mye, U.S. Department of Commerce, Chilean Desk, October 1991.

[16] Verzariu, "An Overview of Nontraditional Finance," 50.

THE INTERNATIONAL MARKETPLACE 22.2

Swapping Debt for Education

Struggling to finance a college education? If your debt grows large enough, a debt-for-education swap might be the answer. In 1990, Harvard University agreed to sponsor a program that converts Ecuadorian debt into a fund providing scholarships to Ecuadorian students and research grants for U.S. students and professors. There are four steps in the conversion process:

1. Harvard purchases $5 million of nonperforming Ecuadorian loans from banks at 15 percent of face value, or $750,000. The banks, faced with the possibility of having to swallow the defaulted loans, are happy to sell at the heavily discounted rate.
2. Harvard then presents the debt to Fundacion Capacitar, an educational foundation in Ecuador. The foundation sells the debt to the Ecuadorian government in exchange for bonds worth $2.5 million, or 50 percent of the original face value of the debt. The transaction reduces the government's outstanding debt by 50 percent.
3. Fundacion Capacitar then sells the bonds, which are valued in Ecuadorian currency, to local investors.
4. Income from the sale of the bonds is converted back into American dollars, invested in the United States, and used to set up a scholarship fund primarily for Ecuadorian students. Secondarily, the fund finances research grants to American students and professors.

The scholarship is expected to cover tuition and living expenses at Harvard for about 70 Ecuadorian students over the next 10 years. But who will actually receive the scholarship? Miguel Falconi, president of Fundacion Capacitar, claims that the fund "is mainly addressed to students without economic resources for studies." Critics of the program question whether the large landowners who dominate the countryside will support the program. They also question whether the rural student is equipped to handle life in Harvard yard.

Other American universities are actively negotiating similar agreements with the Ecuadorian government. Indeed, more than eight universities are expected to be involved in an exchange program that will provide study abroad financing to non-U.S. and U.S. students and teachers.

Source: Laurel Shaper Walters, "Debt Funds Scholars," *Christian Science Monitor*, July 30, 1990, 14.

The newest emerging form of debt swaps is that of swapping debt for social purposes. For example, environmental concerns can be addressed by applying debt to the preservation of nature. As repayment of debt becomes more and more difficult for a growing number of nations, these swaps of debt for social causes are likely to increase. In addition to the environmental field, these swaps can occur in many other areas of need. For example, **debt-for-education swaps** can be used to permit more students to study abroad, which could greatly contribute to international research, language training, and cultural sensitivity within educational systems.[17] The International Marketplace 22.2 describes an example of such a swap.

---

[17] Michael R. Czinkota and Martin J. Kohn, *A Report to the Secretary of Commerce: Improving U.S. Competitiveness—Swapping Debt for Education* (Washington, D.C.: Government Printing Office, 1988).

| FIGURE 22.4 | Countertrade Usage—By Types |

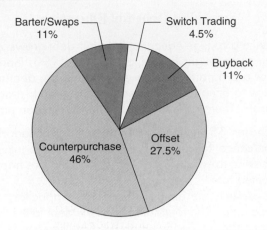

Source: Laura B. Forker, *Countertrade: Purchasing's Perceptions and Involvement* (Tempe: Center for Advanced Purchasing Studies, Arizona State University, 1991), 29.

With the increasing sophistication of countertrade, the original form of straight barter is less used today. Most frequently used is the counterpurchase agreement. Because of continued major military expenditures, offsets are also on the increase. Figure 22.4 presents the results of a survey of U.S. firms and shows the relatively low use of barter, a finding that has also been confirmed by other research.[18] Investigations of other countries have shown, however, that compensation or buy-back agreements are on the rise.[19]

OFFICIAL ATTITUDES TOWARD COUNTERTRADE

Official U.S. Policy

When trying to ascertain official U.S. government attitudes, the investigator must look at the different departments within the executive, the legislative, and judicial branches. On occasion, a coherent policy view can be identified. More often than not, discrepancies among the different groups will become visible because they have different outlooks and serve different constituencies. Such discrepancies are particularly obvious when looking at the issue of countertrade.

The foundation for the current U.S. position on countertrade is well presented in a report on U.S. competitiveness. The report briefly examines the incidence of counter-trade, its growth, and the incentives behind its practice. It concludes that "the transactions are purely bilateral in nature and are not competitive since they squeeze out competition from a third market or specify the export market. Trade is formulated on the basis of the willingness to countertrade and not on economic considerations."[20]

---

[18] Donald J. Lecraw, "The Management of Countertrade: Factors Influencing Success," *Journal of International Business Studies* 20 (Spring 1989): 41–59.

[19] Aspy P. Palia and Oded Shenkar, "Countertrade Practices in China," *Industrial Marketing Management* 20 (1991): 57–65.

[20] *Report of the President on U.S. Competitiveness,* transmitted to Congress, September 1980, V-45.

The Department of the Treasury tends to take a similarly dim view of countertrade. Treasury officials stated with regard to offsets and coproduction that they "suspect that offset and coproduction agreements mandated by governments (do not) promote . . . economic . . . efficiency. They may constitute implicit subsidies to the industry of the purchasing countries. They may result in diversion of business away from efficient U.S. producers . . . thus causing economic inefficiency and dislocations. . . . Since these practices appear to involve spillover effects on nondefense production and trade, they may have adverse effects on future U.S. production, trade, employment, and tax revenue."[21]

The Office of the U.S. Trade Representative, which is the chief U.S. trade negotiator, is somewhat more flexible. At a House of Representatives hearing, a negotiator testified that "our position is that countertrade is a second-best option for international trade transactions. It represents a distortion of international trade and is contrary to an open, free trading system. It is not in the long-run interest of the United States or the U.S. business community. Nevertheless, as a matter of policy, the U.S. government does not oppose U.S. companies participating in countertrade arrangements unless such actions could have a negative impact on national security. If a company believes a countertrade transaction is in its interest, the company is in a better position than we are to make that business decision."[22]

The Department of Defense is concerned with enhancing its principles of RSI, or rationalization, standardization, and interoperability. This means that the department strongly encourages other nations allied with the United States to use similar equipment, which can be interchanged in case of an armed conflict. For this reason, the Department of Defense tries to encourage foreign acquisitions of U.S. military hardware. Because such acquisition is likely to come about only through promises of offsets and coproduction, the department tends to display a policy of "positive neutrality" toward countertrade methods.

This attitude makes a lot of sense from the perspective of production cost. Given the economies of scale and the learning curve effects inherent in the manufacture of arms, more international sales result in longer production runs, which in turn permit weapons manufacturers to offer their products at a lower price. If the Department of Defense can encourage more international sales, it either can buy a given number of products for less money or can purchase more products with a given budget. From that perspective, one could argue that countertrade transactions contribute to the U.S. national security.

The Department of Commerce displays the most supportive view of countertrade in the policy community. Given its mandate to help U.S. firms compete internationally, the department has its own Office of Barter and Countertrade, which provides advice to firms interested in such transactions. However, the establishment of this office came about only after significant congressional pressure and passage of the 1988 Trade Act.

While all these different views exist within the departments of the administration, on the legislative side, Congress repeatedly has passed bills that permit or even encourage countertrade transactions. This legislation has primarily focused on barter possibilities

[21] John D. Lange, Jr., Director, Office of Trade Finance, U.S. Department of the Treasury, testimony before the House of Representatives, Economic Stabilization Subcommittee, Committee on Banking, Finance, and Urban Affairs, 97th Cong., 1st sess., September 24, 1981.

[22] Donald W. Eiss, Statement before the Subcommittee on Arms Control, International Security and Science and the Subcommittee on International Economic Policy and Trade, Committee on Foreign Affairs, U.S. House of Representatives, July 1, 1987, 4–5.

for U.S. agricultural commodities or for stockpiling purposes. As a result, the **Commodities Credit Corporation (CCC)** and the **General Services Administration (GSA)** have been carrying out countertrade transactions for years. An example was the swap of U.S. agricultural commodities for Jamaican bauxite. This large-scale transaction was designed to reduce the U.S. surplus of agricultural products in exchange for increasing national stockpiles of a strategic material.

On the judicial side, countertrade involvement stems mostly from the enforcement activities of the Internal Revenue Service. The IRS is, of course, primarily concerned with valuing countertrade transactions and with ensuring that proper tax payments are made. A proper assessment of taxes, however, usually requires a painstaking determination of all facets of the transaction. Difficulties are often encountered in ascertaining the exact value of the countertraded goods, the time when the income has been received, and the profitability of the entire transaction. As a result of these problems, tax authorities are not in favor of countertrade. Other judicial activities are mainly concerned with valuation issues for import purposes. One major issue is the threat of dumping, whereby goods obtained through countertrade transactions may be disposed of cheaply in the domestic market and therefore harm domestic competitors, who do not benefit from the sales end of a countertrade transaction.

One can conclude that as a nation, the United States is ambivalent toward countertrade. There are differing views within the administration and on the legislative and the judicial side. Countertrade is partially encouraged as long as no major negative effects on nonparticipants within the domestic economy are visible.

Other Government Views

Most industrialized countries, including Western Europe, Japan, New Zealand, and Australia, have actively participated in the growing countertrade phenomenon. Frequently, they are catalysts for countertrade transactions. The newly emerging market economies have largely continued to maintain a procountertrade stance, due to their ongoing inability to find hard currency for import purchases. Countries in the developing world have taken different positions. Indonesia, for example, cited two choices it faced as its export revenues declined dramatically: One was to drastically limit its imports; the other was to liberalize its trade with alternative measures such as countertrade. As a result, the government officially instituted a mandatory countertrade requirement for any transaction exceeding a value of $500,000.

Other developing countries have more subtle policies but are implementing and supporting countertrade nonetheless. Brazil, for example, keeps a low profile. Although the country "has issued no countertrade regulations and does not officially sanction its practice, CACEX, the foreign trade arm of the central bank, has made it quite clear that awards of import licenses and export performance are linked at the level of the firm."[23] This is a position taken more and more frequently by lesser-developed countries. Although officially abhorring the use of countertrade, unofficially they have made it clear that, in order to do business, countertrade transactions are mandatory.

---

[23] Steven M. Rubin, "Countertrade Controversies Stirring Global Economy," *Journal of Commerce,* September 24, 1984, 14.

Attitudes of International Organizations

International organizations almost uniformly condemn countertrade. Public statements by both the IMF and GATT indicate that their opposition "is based on broad considerations of macroeconomic efficiency." These authorities complain that instead of a rational system of exchange, based on product quality and price, countertrade introduces extraneous elements into the sales equation. Countertrade is viewed as being inconsistent with an open, free trading system and not in the best long-term interest of the contracting parties.[24] The GATT, for example, sees dangers to the principle of nondiscrimination and warns of the politicization of international trade.

Officials from the OECD (Organization for Economic Cooperation and Development) also deplore countertrade arrangements. They feel that such arrangements would lead to an increase in trade conflicts as competitive suppliers, unwilling to undertake countertrade arrangements, are displaced by less-competitive suppliers willing to undertake countertrade arrangements.[25]

The international organization most neutral toward countertrade is the United Nations. A report of the secretary general stated only that there appeared to be some economic and financial problems with countertrade transactions and that any global, uniform regulation of countertrade may be difficult to implement because of the complexity and variety of transactions. The report lacks any kind of general conclusion because such conclusions "may be somewhat hazardous in the absence of a sufficient volume of contracts that are easily available."[26]

This statement highlights one of the major problems faced by policymakers interested in countertrade. Corporation executives consider the subject of countertrade to be sensitive because public discussion of such practices could imply that a product line is difficult to sell or could indicate that the corporation is willing to conduct countertrade. Because such knowledge would result in a weakening of the corporation's international negotiation position, executives are usually tight-lipped about countertrade transactions.[27] At the same time, rumors about countertrade deals are often rampant, even though many of the transactions gossiped about may never materialize. To some extent, the public view of countertrade may resemble an inverted iceberg: There is much more on the surface than below. Policymakers are therefore uncertain about the precise volume and impact of countertrade, a fact that makes it all the more difficult to take proper policy actions.

Countertrade does appear to be on the increase. The main reason for that conclusion is the fact that countertrade may perhaps be the only practical solution to the fundamental difficulties in the world economy of which the proliferation of countertrade is a symptom. Access to industrialized markets for the lesser-developed countries has become increasingly limited. Balance-of-payment crises, debt problems, and other financial difficulties have hurt their ability to import needed products. In the face of limited trade opportunities, both lesser-developed countries and developed countries appear to regard countertrade as an alternative solution to no trade at all.[28]

---

[24] Patricia Daily and S. M. Ghazanfar, "Countertrade: Help or Hindrance to Less-Developed Countries," *The Journal of Social, Political and Economic Studies* 18 no. 1 (1993): 61–76.

[25] Jacques de Miramon, "Countertrade: A Modern Form of Barter," *OECD Observer,* January 1982, 12.

[26] "Current Activities of International Organizations," 4.

[27] Michael R. Czinkota, "New Challenges in U.S.-Soviet Trade," *Journal of the Academy of Marketing Science* 5 (Special Issue, Summer 1977): 17–20.

[28] Michael R. Czinkota and Anne Talbot, "Countertrade and GATT: Prospects for Regulation," *International Trade Journal* (Winter 1986): 155–174.

THE CORPORATE SITUATION

A few years ago, most executives claimed both in public and in private that countertrade is a hindrance to international marketing and is avoided by their firms. More recently, however, changes in corporate thought have taken place. Even though companies may not like countertrade transactions, a refusal to engage in them may cause the company to lose business to rival firms who are willing to participate in countertrade. Increasingly, companies are altering their perspective from a reactive to a proactive one. In the past, corporations frequently resorted to countertrade only because they were compelled to do so by local circumstance, usually government mandates. However, times have changed, as The International Marketplace 22.3 shows, and companies have now begun to use countertrade as a tool to improve their market position. Rockwell International Corporation, for example, uses its own internal barter capabilities through its trading subsidiary, which Rockwell created several years ago. As a result, Rockwell's products have a special appeal abroad because of the company's willingness to engage in countertrade.

Increasingly, companies are formulating market penetration strategies and are planning to acquire market share from their competition by instructing their staff to seek out countertrade opportunities that could lead to an expansion of their own product sales. These companies go beyond the traditional view that some sales, even those subject to countertrade, are better than no sales. They are using countertrade systematically as a marketing tool that brings with it favorable government consideration and a larger extent of pricing flexibility. The willingness to offer countertrade transactions may enhance the overall attractiveness of a firm to its customers and may even become a lever for continued business growth.

For longer-range countertrade transactions, executives may not be as risk averse as for shorter-range transactions. By the time the countertrade requirements fall due, which may be five to ten years in the future, they may not be around to take the blame if problems arise because they may have been promoted, have changed positions, or have retired. On the other hand, for these long-term risks, many companies make it clear that the preferred compensation is cash, preferably dollars, and that any kind of countertrade transaction is not acceptable. However, the number of stalwart defenders of strictly non-countertrade deals is decreasing.

Companies and countries imposing countertrade believe that there are more merits to these transactions than purely conserving foreign currency. For example, the countertrade partner can be used as a marketing arm to explore new markets. Long-term countertrade requirements can ensure markets for future output, which are particularly important to producers in industries highly sensitive to capacity utilization. Security and stability of purchasing and sales arrangements can also play a major role.

Sellers of countertraded products engage in countertrade for other reasons, such as to more effectively introduce new products, to enter new markets, and to expand a company's market share. Countertrade has been found to provide "outlets for integrative growth in addition to market penetration and development."[29] Finally, countertrade can provide markets and open up new trade channels for surplus products that could not be marketed otherwise.[30] Particularly when a world market glut exists for commodities

---

[29] Sandra M. Huszagh and Hiram C. Barksdale, "International Barter and Counter-trade: An Exploratory Study," *Journal of the Academy of Marketing Science* 14 (Spring 1986): 21–28.

[30] Lynn G. Reiling, "Countertrade Revives 'Dead Goods,'" *Marketing News,* August 29, 1986, 1, 22.

THE INTERNATIONAL MARKETPLACE   22.3

Countertrade at Bell Helicopters

The high-tech aerospace industry is just one more on the list of those embracing countertrade in a proactive and enthusiastic manner. Bell Helicopter Textron, a manufacturer of helicopters, has had an office of countertrade since 1986 that was in charge of handling offset requests from customers. Recently, however, the company has decided to change its stance. Bell now realizes that to remain competitive and successful in the industry, it must strategically pursue countertrade opportunities and take advantage of this form of trade as a valuable marketing tool.

Several reasons contributed to Bell's attitude adjustment toward countertrade. One is the liberalization of former centrally planned economies. While they were unable to make helicopter acquisitions in the past, these nations now comprise the prime markets for high-tech products such as Bell's. With few exceptions, these economies are also those with the most scant supply of hard currency. So the need for an acceptable exchange medium became the issue and, as one Bell official comments, "I certainly don't want to be the first in line to try to cash in my rubles." By actively pursuing countertrade, the opportunity developed for Bell to achieve greater export sales and expand market presence. As Bell rose to the challenge, a senior vice president commented, "All of the former Eastern Bloc countries have become terrific marketing opportunities."

Technology transfer has become another driving force behind the increased use of countertrade in Bell's industry. In the past, high-tech industries have usually crafted trade arrangements through some sort of joint production with trading partners. Today, the emphasis has shifted to providing assistance and training and establishing facilities in the foreign country. It is not only the cash-poor and developing nations that require countertrade activities in high-tech fields; today, nearly all international sales include elements of countertrade. For reasons such as employment and balancing trade, some use of nonmonetary transactions is almost inevitable for a high-tech industry such as helicopter production.

Bell Helicopters has become a convert to proactive countertrade by realizing that the old reactive attitudes no longer suffice. The company remains enthusiastic about the changes it has undertaken in its office of countertrade and is eyeing resource-rich Russia for future countertrade deals.

Source: "Bell Upgrades Barter Use to Expand Helicopter Sales," *Aviation Week & Space Technology*, October 26, 1992, 61–62.

that are in ample supply in some countries yet scarce in others, countertrade transactions may be an appealing trade mechanism.

For whatever reason firms engage in countertrade, it is important to develop a measuring system that permits the tracking of when the exchange takes place, what the value of the exchanged products is, and how the bottom line of the company is affected. While these requirements may sound simple, they prove to be very challenging to corporate accountants, as the International Marketplace 22.4 shows.

22.4   THE INTERNATIONAL MARKETPLACE

Countertrade Accountants in the Dark

For the exporter contemplating countertrade, there is more to the decision process than a simple yes or no. Key to a company's ability to perform countertrade in-house is its accounting capability. This facet of operations at first may seem of secondary consideration, but it is in fact a major problem spot for many countertraders. Along with such aspects as pricing and foreign regulations, accounting is a key consideration in developing an in-house system of countertrade. Countertrade poses unique and difficult situations for accountants due mainly to the partial or total absence of currency as a base for accounting practices. In addition, relevant guidelines for nonmonetary transactions are practically nonexistent. There is no mention of nonmonetary transactions in the Generally Accepted Accounting Principles. The one statement made by the Financial Accounting Standards Board concerning nonmonetary transactions was promulgated back when they were far more simple and uncomplicated. Today, countertrade arrangements can contain such complexities as multiyear contracts and the risk of noncompliance or substandard goods. Accountants responsible for dealing with these situations have very little to draw upon.

A whole array of problematic situations can confront accountants in a countertrading company. The first point of contention may very well be whether a sale or a purchase has occurred. In a goods-for-cash transaction, it is obvious whether you bought or you sold; the accountant has no problem making the correct entry. With countertrade, determining which action to record is a bit more nebulous. There are even those who believe that countertrade transactions should be viewed as both a purchase and a sale. An eighteenth-century textbook author once stated that "the exchange of goods for goods is nothing else but buying and selling blended together." The implications of not being able to distinguish between sales and purchases can only be imagined.

Problems also abound concerning the valuation of nontraditional goods, goods that will be received in the future, and goods that will be surrendered in the future, all under the agreed-to provisions. In many cases, the market value will fluctuate. Regardless, many accountants value those future obligations at current fair market value. Beyond this, questions exist as to when a transaction should be reported on a multiyear contract—now, because it is inevitable, or later, once it is realized?

Other uncertainties surround the timing and amounts for gains and losses, revenue recognition, countertrade fees and incidental expenses, and disclosure of increased risks. Until further pronouncements are made, accountants involved with countertrade will remain in the dark, and countertrade transactions will have to be scrutinized quite closely to determine their value.

Source: "Are We Ignoring Countertrade?" *Management Accounting*, December 1992, 43–47.

THE EMERGENCE OF NEW INTERMEDIARIES

The rise in countertrade transactions has resulted in the emergence of new specialists to handle such transactions. These intermediaries can be either in-house or outside the corporation. In many instances, firms will attempt to make use of the countertraded goods within the corporate structure, be that domestically or internationally. As Figure 22.5 shows, the majority of U.S. countertraded products will be used either back home or in foreign affiliates. Apart from the fact that such in-house use is likely to be seen as undesirable by a firm's current suppliers, the mere organization of an in-house unit can be quite difficult. For one, the tracking of opportunities is difficult, but the potential intraorganization conflicts should also not be neglected. The International Marketplace 22.5 describes the development of an in-house unit at a computer firm.

Many firms also seek recourse to outside intermediaries when confronted with countertrade situations. Some companies have been founded to facilitate countertrade transactions for other firms. By purchasing unwanted inventories at a steep discount, such companies can sometimes obtain very high profit margins. Other intermediaries that have benefited from the rise of countertrade are trading companies or trading houses that act frequently as third-party intermediaries. Figure 22.6 shows an advertisement by such a firm. Because of their widespread connections, these trading firms can dispose of unwanted countertraded goods more easily than individual corporations. They may also be more capable of evaluating the risks of such transactions and can benefit from both the discount and the markup portion of the exchange. Firms that deal with trading houses in order to receive assistance in their countertrade transactions need to be aware that the fees charged are often quite steep and may be cumulatively increasing. For example, there may be an initial consulting fee when the transaction is contemplated, a fee for the consummation of the acquisition, and a subsequent steep discount for the disposal of the acquired products. Also, these trading houses frequently

Use of Countertraded Goods   FIGURE 22.5

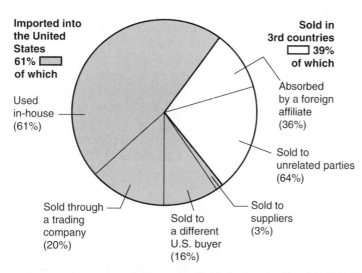

Source: Laura B. Forker, *Countertrade: Purchasing's Perceptions and Involvement* (Tempe: Center for Advanced Purchasing Studies, Arizona State University, 1991), 28–29.

22.5

THE INTERNATIONAL MARKETPLACE

Coping with Offsets

Many governments of countries that experience trade deficits view imports as a problem. As a result, they may limit imports through the use of tariffs, quotas, or other nontariff barriers. A small but growing number of governments restrict imports, and simultaneously encourage exports, by requiring firms to offset import sales with export spending. The rationale behind such actions is to restrict imports, increase exports, and create jobs.

One way governments "offset" a negative impact on the trade or current account is through offset purchasing. This means that a company that desires to import products must prove to the government that it is purchasing an agreed-upon percentage of these imports in local goods or services, which in turn are exported. The thought is that if the importer purchases local products for export, local companies will be strengthened, and export volume will grow.

The Business Development Group at a U.S. computer firm faces offset regulations every day. In its drive to open new markets around the globe, the firm is increasingly confronted with government demands to offset the trade balance effect of its computer imports. The Business Development Group works with the Procurement Group, third-party suppliers, and governments to comply with offset regulations. For example, the Business Development Group will attempt to source components that are required to build computers, printers, and peripherals from firms in those countries to which computers are exported. Often, the goals of the Business Development Group and the procurement organization within the firm tend to clash. Procurement favors those suppliers that offer the best combination of cost, quality, and delivery. Business Development, in turn, prefers sourcing from those suppliers that enable the company to fulfill offset requirements, since doing so will increase sales volume abroad. Unfortunately, these suppliers often do not offer lowest cost, highest quality, or fastest delivery. To reduce the intraorganizational conflict, Business Development has begun to work with foreign suppliers to give them the tools necessary to compete with other suppliers. As a result, technology transfer, training, and quality instructions are often provided abroad.

One concurrent problem faced by the Business Development Group is the fact that it is very difficult to count the dollar volume of purchases from countries. Today, international trade is so complex that it is difficult to tell from which country a good or service originated. Goods are often transshipped before arriving at their final destination. Distributors often do not know from where a certain shipment came. Goods and services often have component parts from a number of countries. In consequence, the Business Development Group is in the process of revamping the firm's entire sourcing system, in order to track country of origin more carefully.

Source: Scott Ciener, Georgetown University.

refuse to take countertraded goods on a nonrecourse basis, which means that the company that has obtained countertraded goods still shares some of the risks.

International banks have also begun to increase their countertrade capabilities to serve their clients better and to increase their own profitability. One pertinent development for the U.S. banking industry is the Export Trading Company Act of 1982. This

Advertisement Offering Countertrade Services   **FIGURE 22.6**

law stipulates that banks can participate in international trading activities, including countertrade transactions. U.S. banks can therefore be expected to become more active in this field in the future. Banks may be able to use their experience in international trade finance and apply it to the financial aspects of countertrade transactions. Banks may also have a comparative advantage over trading firms in having more knowledge and expertise in financial risk management and more information about and contacts with the global market.

Countertrade intermediaries need not be large in size. Smaller firms can successfully compete by pursuing a niche strategy. An entrepreneur who exploits specialized geographic or product knowledge and develops countertrade transactions that may be too small for a multinational firm can conduct trades with little capital yet receive sound profit margins.

Another type of intermediary is the countertrade information service provider. These firms are exemplified by Batis Ltd. in London and ACECO in France. They provide data bases on countertrade products and regulations in various countries for subscribers to tap into. They are beginning also to provide computerized matchmaking services between companies in debt to some country's counterpurchase system and those in credit, or those willing to buy counterpurchase items.[31] Table 22.3 provides a summary of the advantages and disadvantages of carrying out countertrade transactions within versus without.

---

[31] Kate Mortimer, "Countertrade in Western Europe," in *International Countertrade,* ed. Christopher M. Korth (Westport, CT: Quorum Books, 1987), 41.

TABLE 22.3	Organizing for Countertrade: In-House DIY versus Third Parties

Advantages	Disadvantages
In-House DIY	
• Lower costs	• Less expertise
• Customer contact	• Reselling problems
• More control	• Recruitment and training costs
• More flexibility	• Less objectivity
• More learning	• Problems coordinating interfunctional staff
Third Parties	
• Expert specialists	• May be costly
• Customer contacts	• Distanced from customer
• Reselling contacts	• Less flexibility
• Legal acumen	• Less confidentiality
• More objectivity	• Less learning

Source: Charles W. Neale, David D. Shipley, and J. Colin Dodds, "The Countertrading Experience of British and Canadian Firms," *Management International Review* 31 no. 1 (1991): 33.

PREPARING FOR COUNTERTRADE

Companies may wish to consider carrying out countertrade transactions in-house. If this can be done, the need for steep discounts may decrease, and the profitability of countertrade may improve. Developing an in-house capability for handling countertrade should be done with great caution.

First, from a strategic corporate perspective, the company should determine the import priorities of its products to the country or firm to which it is trying to sell. Goods that are highly desirable and/or necessary for a country mandating countertrade are less likely to be subject to countertrade requirements or are subject to less stringent requirements than imports of goods considered luxurious and unnecessary. As a next step, the company needs to identify which countertrade arrangements and regulations exist in the country to which it exports. An awareness of the alternatives available, and of the countertrade percentages demanded, will strengthen the company's bargaining position at the precontract stage. Obtaining this information is also important to incorporate possible countertrade cost into the pricing scheme. It is quite difficult to increase the price of goods once a "cash-deal" price has been quoted and a subsequent countertrade demand is presented.

At this stage, the most favored countertrade arrangement from the buyer's perspective should be identified. The company should find out why this particular arrangement is the most favored one and explore whether other forms of transactions would similarly meet the objectives of the countertrading partner. To do this, the company needs to determine the goals and objectives of the countertrading parties. As already discussed, these can consist of import substitution, a preservation of hard currency, export promotion, and so on.

The next step is to match the strengths of the firm with current and potential countertrade situations. This requires an assessment of corporate capabilities and resources. The company should explore whether any internal sourcing needs can be used to fulfill a countertrade contract. This may mean that raw materials or intermediate products currently sourced from other suppliers could now be obtained from the countertrade partner. However, this assessment should not be restricted to the internal corporate use of a countertraded product. The company should also determine whether it can use, for example, its distribution capabilities or its contacts with other customers and suppliers to help in its countertrade transactions. Moreover, an increase in the use of mandated countertrade by governments, combined with a more proactive approach toward such transactions by firms, may well result in companies expecting their suppliers to share in the burdensome effects of countertrade. Based on the notion that the supplier benefits from the export taking place due to the countertrade, it could very well be that main contractors will demand that major suppliers participate in disposing of the counter-traded goods. As a result, companies that do not see themselves as international marketers may suddenly be confronted with countertrade demands.

At this point, the company can decide whether it should engage in countertrade transactions. The accounting and taxation aspects of the countertrade transactions should be considered because they can often be quite different from current procedures. The use of an accounting or tax professional is essential to comply with difficult and obscure IRS regulations in this area.

Next, all of the risks involved in countertrade must be assessed. This means that the goods to be obtained need to be specified, that the delivery time for these goods needs to be determined, and that the reliability of the supplier and the quality and consistency of the goods need to be assessed. It is also useful to explore the impact of countertrade on the future prices, both for the price of the specific goods obtained and for the world market price of the category of goods. For example, a countertrade transaction may appear to be quite profitable at the time of agreement. Because several months or even years may pass before the transaction is actually consummated, however, a change in world market prices may severely affect the profitability. The effect of a countertrade transaction on the world market price should also be considered. In cases of large-volume transactions, the established price may be affected due to a glut of supply. Such a situation not only may affect the profitability of a transaction but also can result in possible legal actions by other suppliers of similar products.

In conjunction with the evaluation of the countertraded products, which should be specified in as much detail as possible rather than left open as a general requirement, the company must explore the market for these products. This includes a forecasting of future market developments, paying particular attention to competitive reaction and price fluctuations. It is also useful at this stage to determine the impact of the coun-tertraded products on the sales and profits of other complementary product lines currently marketed by the firm. What, if any, repercussions will come about from outside groups should also be investigated. Such repercussions may consist of antidumping actions brought about by competitors or reactions from totally unsuspected quarters. For example, McDonnell Douglas ran into strong opposition when it used bartered Yugoslavian ham in its employees' cafeteria and as Christmas gifts. The local meat-packers' union complained vociferously that McDonnell Douglas was threatening the jobs of its members. The International Marketplace 22.6 provides a detailed example of how countertrade transactions negotiated abroad can create difficulties for companies at home.

Using all of the information obtained, the company can finally evaluate the length of the intended relationship with the countertrading partner and the importance of this relationship for future plans and goals. These parameters will be decisive for the final action because they may form constraints overriding short-term economic effects. Overall, management needs to remember that, in most instances, a countertrade transaction should remain a means for successful international marketing and not become an end in itself.

22.6

THE INTERNATIONAL MARKETPLACE

A Countertrade Roadblock

The end of the Cold War is not good news to everyone. Consider the large defense contractors that for so many years engaged in big business and big profits with the U.S. government. Nowadays, with decreasing defense budgets, business is not as good for these contractors. Add in increasing foreign competition, and some contractors are downright scared.

This climate is driving industry giants to pursue countertrade deals. One such recent deal involved the production by Northrop and McDonnell Douglas of 64 fighter jets worth $3 billion to be sold to Finland. In return for Finland's business, the two coproducers would assist nondefense-related Finnish companies in landing $2.3 billion in U.S. sales. One of these assistance deals involved a $1.2-million offer by Northrop to help the Finnish company Valmet Corporation win a bid to sell a $50-million paper-producing machine, which it manufactures. As it worked out, Northrop had more to worry about than paying off Valmet.

When Harnischfeger Industries, a Wisconsin-based company in the same business as Valmet and competing for the same deal, caught wind of the offer, its U.S. senator was contacted and he in turn ordered an investigation by the U.S. General Accounting Office. The GAO's report satisfied the senator's suspicions, and the quiet little deal Northrop had hoped to accomplish came to the attention of the Secretary of Commerce who stated, "This issue is of great concern to me. We shall look into this case." Northrop's deal was then reviewed by the secretaries of state and defense and the attorney general.

In the end, the Wisconsin-based company won the bid to sell the paper-producing machine, yet the concern remains that such actions by defense contractors may unfairly cause other U.S. industries to lose business. In addition, calls have been made to properly review indirect offset deals in a similar fashion as direct offsets. One concern is that U.S. companies can include offset administrative charges on the bill to the foreign purchaser and are therefore not as inhibited in making such deals.

The outcome for Northrop shows that making the offset deal can be only half the story. Domestic risks are very real and can pose formidable barriers. For Northrop, these risks cost it a deal it needed to help complete its contract.

Source: Jeff Cole, "Pentagon Contractors Often Offer Cash to Help Foreign Firms Compete in U.S.," *The Wall Street Journal*, May 7, 1993, A4.

SUMMARY

Countertrades are business transactions in which the sale of goods is linked to other goods rather than to money only. Such transactions are emerging with increasing frequency due to hard-currency shortfalls in many nations around the world.

Concurrent with their increased use, countertrade transactions have also become more sophisticated. Rather than exchange goods for goods in a straight barter deal, companies and countries now structure counterpurchase, compensation, and offset agreements to aid in their industrial policies.

Governments and international organizations are concerned about the trend toward countertrade, yet in light of existing competition and the need to find creative ways of financing trade, very little interference with countertrade is exercised.

Corporations are increasingly using countertrade as a competitive tool to maintain or increase market share. The complexity of these transactions requires careful planning in order to avoid major corporate losses. Management must consider how the acquired merchandise will be disposed of, what the potential for market disruptions is, and to what extent countertraded goods fit with the corporate mission.

New intermediaries have emerged to facilitate countertrade transactions. Their services can be very expensive. However, they can enable firms without countertrade experience to participate in this growing business practice.

Questions for Discussion

1. What are some of the major causes for the resurgence of countertrade?

2. What forms of countertrade exist and how do they differ?

3. Discuss the advantages and drawbacks of countertrade.

4. How would you characterize the U.S. government's position toward countertrade?

5. How consistent is countertrade with the international trade framework?

6. Why would a firm take goods rather than cash?

7. Why would a buyer insist on countertrade transactions?

8. What particular benefits can an outside countertrade intermediary offer to a firm engaged in such transactions?

9. How would you prepare your firm for countertrade?

10. Discuss some of the possible accounting and taxation ramifications of countertrade.

11. Develop a corporate goals statement that uses countertrade as a proactive tool for international expansion.

12. Explain why countertrade may be encouraged by the increasing technology transfer taking place.

13. What are some of the dangers of using countertraded goods in-house?

14. What is your view of the future of countertrade?

Recommended Readings

Alexandrides, C. G., and B. L. Bowers. *Countertrade: Practices, Strategies, and Tactics.* New York: Wiley, 1987.

Caves, Richard E., and Dalia Marin. "Countertrade Transactions: Theory and Evidence." *The Economic Journal* 102 (1992): 1171–1183.

Countertrade and Barter. A magazine published by Metal Bulletin, New York, NY.

Forker, Laura B. *Countertrade: Purchasing's Perceptions and Involvement* (Tempe: Center for Advanced Purchasing Studies, Arizona State University, 1991).

Schaffer, Matt. *Winning the Countertrade War.* New York: Wiley, 1989.

Verzariu, Pompiliu. *International Countertrade, A Guide for Managers and Executives.* Washington, D.C.: U.S. Department of Commerce, 1992.

Verzariu, Pompiliu. *International Countertrade: Individual Country Practices.* Washington, D.C.: U.S. Department of Commerce, 1992.

Zurawicki, Leon, and Louis Suichmezian. *Global Countertrade: An Annotated Bibliography.* New York: Garland Publishers, 1991.

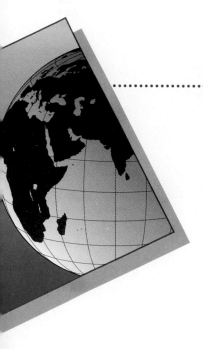

CHAPTER 23

Marketing in Transition

THE INTERNATIONAL MARKETPLACE

A Study of Two "Market" Strategies

Both China and Russia are transforming their economies, making them more market oriented. The adjustments under way could precipitate massive changes in the global economy and are therefore watched closely by the world.

Of particular interest are the differing approaches toward market orientation used by China and Russia. Both are moving away from centrally planned, socialist systems toward capitalist, profit-driven systems. China has adopted a policy of gradualism, implementing change step-by-step, a little at a time. In contrast, the economic changes in Russia have come quickly.

So how is each country performing? Chinese industrial production was growing at 29 percent at the end of 1993, while Russia's economic output shrank almost 15 percent for the year. Street vendors in Beijing can be seen hawking fresh grapes in winter at affordable prices, and nearby shops sell fancy mountain bikes. The leading businesses in Moscow appear to be prostitution and casino gambling. What does all of this mean for the question of which strategy works best in developing societies? Do economic reforms work best if they are introduced in a single 'Big Bang,' or should they measured out in tiny doses? From the evidence, it would appear that Chinese-style gradualism is the strategy to adopt. William Overholt, a Hong Kong–based investment banker, agrees: "The notion that one can have all good things—democracy and all forms of liberalization—instantly and simultaneously [is] a deeply held belief that has no grounding in practical historical experience." However, not everyone sees Russia's situation as definitive proof against quick and sudden change. Given the differences between the Russian and Chinese economies, some experts argue that meaningful comparisons are impossible. In a recent essay, the noted economists Jeffrey Sachs and Wing Thye Woo stated that those wanting Russia to follow China's gradualism "might as well advise Russia to solve its agricultural problems by shifting from wheat to rice."

The "gradualists," however, stick to their proposition: Shock therapy unleases chaos. Firms being privatized too quickly causes confusion about ownership, management responsibilities, product liability, and production strategy. Inflation is almost certain if prices are liberalized too quickly. If the central bank clamps down on the money supply to keep inflation low, unproductive enterprises will go bankrupt, workers will be stripped of their livelihoods, and social chaos will quickly follow. One Chinese leader has said that a socialist without a plan is like a bird without a cage—sure to fly away.

Once again, however, the differences between Russia's situation and China's are most important. During the early days of Chinese reform in the 1970s, 70 percent of labor was in agriculture, while less than 20 percent was in industry. The development solution was simple—do away with the agricultural collectives and turn the farmland over to the peasants. On the other hand, during Gorbachev's perestroika, more than half of Russia's labor was in industry and only 14 percent was in agriculture. The issue for Russia has therefore been how to transform a tangle of rusty, inefficient, defense-oriented, heavy industries supported by cheap credit from the state into lean, self-supporting producers of consumer goods—a task much different from and more complex than China's mission.

The difference that has arisen in China, according to many experts, is that the state concerns are tiny stones that are being submerged rapidly in the rising tide of the private sector. In Russia, however, such enterprises are hulking islands that cannot be washed away easily.

Source: Clay Chandler, "In Beijing and Moscow, Starkly Different Policies and Results," *The Washington Post,* January 30, 1994, H1, H5.

This chapter addresses major societal and ideological shifts that pose new challenges and opportunities to international marketers. The focus is on marketing activities in the newly emerging democracies of Central Europe and the new countries of the former Soviet Union and on the interface between marketing and state-owned enterprises. The former centrally planned nations are singled out due to the major political and economic changes that have occurred there. As a result of these shifts, marketing as a discipline is afforded a potentially pivotal role in accomplishing the transformation of these nations from planned into market economies. State-owned enterprises are discussed because, even though many of them exist in market economies, they reflect to a significant extent the desires of their governments. Even for those institutions, however, major changes are occurring as governments increasingly take the road toward privatization.

In both instances, marketing and the marketer are faced with transitions that have made the unexpected a reality. These changes result in the obligation of marketing to help restructure society and improve the standard of living of a large part of the world. At the same time, marketers must recognize the limits to change and the many societal constraints that result from decades of ideological pressures fundamentally opposed to the core aspects of marketing. As marketers, we are faced with new territory, both conceptually and pragmatically. But we should also be challenged by the potential to nourish the emergence of a new and better world order. It is here and now that marketing can become a true change agent for society. In spite of major difficulties, many countries may be ready for such change. But given the lack of experience with such massive transitions, there is little firm knowledge on which approach to use in order to best facilitate change. The International Marketplace 23.1 shows one example of conflicting approaches with vastly different outcomes. Therefore, in bringing about change, one must be cautious to contribute to the development of societal and economic structures that will make the quality of life a better one.

The chapter begins with a brief description of the historical economic structures in the newly emerging democracies (NEDs). Subsequently, the realities of economic change are discussed, and the alternatives facing the international marketer are highlighted.

MARKETING AND THE NEWLY EMERGING MARKET ECONOMIES

The newly emerging market economies are the independent states, which have succeeded the former Soviet Union, East Germany (now unified with West Germany), the Eastern and Central European nations (Albania, Bulgaria, the Czech and the Slovak Republic, Hungary, Poland, and Romania), and the People's Republic of China. As Table 23.1 shows, the populations and GDP of these nations are substantial and are likely to exert major influences on and offer significant opportunities for the international marketer.

It is often believed that business ties between the Western world and these nations are a new phenomenon. That is not the case. In the 1920s, for example, General Electric and RCA helped to develop the Soviet electrical and communications industries. Ford constructed a huge facility in Gorky to build Model A cars and buses. Du Pont introduced its technology to Russia's chemical industry. Conversely, Tungsram in Hungary conducted research and development for General Electric. However, by the mid-1930s, most American companies had withdrawn from the scene or had been forced to leave. Since then, former centrally planned economies and Western corporations engaged in international business have had rather limited contact.[1]

To a large extent, this limited contact was the result of an ideological wariness on both sides. Socialist countries often perceived international corporations as "aggressive business organizations developed to further the imperialistic aims of Western, especially American, capitalists the world over."[2] Furthermore, many aspects of capitalism, such as the private ownership of the means of production, were seen as exploitative and antithetical to communist ideology.[3] Western managers, in turn, often saw socialism as a threat to the Western world and the capitalistic system in general.

Over time, these rigid stances were modified on both sides. Decision makers in former centrally planned economies recognized the need to purchase products and technology that were unavailable domestically or that could be produced only at a substantial comparative disadvantage. They were determined to achieve economic growth and improve the very much neglected standard of living in their society, and decided that the potential benefits of cooperation in many instances outweighed the risks of decentralized economic power and reduced reliance on plans. As a result, government planners in former socialist economies began to include some market considerations in their activities and opened up their countries to Western businesses.

At the same time, the greater openness on the part of these governments resulted in more flexibility in Western government control of East-West trade. The drive toward

[1] Richard M. Hammer, "Dramatic Winds of Change," *Price Waterhouse Review* 33 (1989): 23–27.

[2] Peter G. Lauter and Paul M. Dickie, "Multinational Corporations in Eastern European Socialist Economies," *Journal of Marketing* 25 (Fall 1975): 40–46.

[3] Alan B. Sherr, "Joint Ventures in the USSR: Soviet and Western Interests with Considerations for Negotiations," *Columbia Journal of World Business* 23 (Summer 1988): 25–37.

Population and GDP of Emerging Market Economies			TABLE 23.1
	Population (millions)	**GDP (billions of $)**	**GDP per Capita**
Albania	3.3	$2.5	$760
Bulgaria	8.8	34.1	3,800
China	1,177.6	413.0*	350
Czech Republic	10.4	75.3	7,300
Hungary	10.3	55.4	5,380
Poland	38.5	167.6	4,350
Romania	23.2	63.4	2,730
Russia	149.3	n.a.	n.a.
Slovakia	5.4	32.1	6,100

Source: The World Factbook 1994 (Washington, D.C.: Central Intelligence Agency, 1994).

*1991 data

modernization of production and growing consumer demand greatly raised the attractiveness of doing business with the newly emerging democracies. Furthermore, many Western firms experienced a need to diversify their international business activities from traditional markets because of current trade imbalances and were searching for new opportunities. The large populations and pent-up demand of the NEDs offered them new markets.

A BRIEF HISTORICAL REVIEW

Due to differing politics and ideology, the trade history of socialist countries is quite different from that of the United States and the West. The former Soviet system of foreign trade dates back to a decree signed by Lenin on April 22, 1918. It established that the state would have a monopoly on foreign trade and that all foreign trade operations were to be concentrated in the hands of organizations specifically authorized by the state. These organizations served as the basis for all trade, economic, scientific, and technical transactions with foreign countries.[4] This system of a state-controlled monopoly was also adopted by the East European satellites of the Soviet Union and by the People's Republic of China.

In effect, this trade structure isolated the firms and consumers in socialist economies from the West and unlinked demand from supply. Any international transaction was cumbersomely reviewed by **foreign trade organizations (FTOs),** ministries, and a multitude of state committees. In addition, rigid state bureaucracies regulated the entire economy. Over time, domestic economic problems emerged. In spite of some top-down and bottom-up planning interaction, the lack of attention to market forces resulted in misallocated resources, and the lack of competition promoted inefficiency. Centralized allocation prevented the emergence of effective channels of distribution. Managers of plants were more concerned with producing the quantities stipulated by a rigid **central plan** (often five-year plans, one following another) than with producing the products and the quality desired. Overfulfillment of the plan was discouraged because it would result in a quota increase for the following year. Entrepreneurship was disdained, innovation

---

[4] Raymond J. Waldmann, *Managed Trade: The New Competition among Nations* (Cambridge, MA: Ballinger Press, 1986), 136.

risky. Consequently, socialist economies achieved only lackluster growth, and their citizens fell far behind the West in their standard of living.

In the early 1980s, the economic orientation of centrally planned economies began to shift. Hungary and Poland started to cautiously encourage their firms to develop an export-oriented strategy. Exporting itself was nothing new, because much trade took place between the countries belonging to the communist bloc. What was new was the fact that government policy emphasized trade with the West and increasingly exposed domestic enterprises to the pressure of international competition.[5] In addition, socialist countries began to import more equipment from the West and started to encourage direct investment by foreign firms.

In the mid-1980s, the Soviet Union developed two new political and economic programs: **perestroika** and **glasnost.** Perestroika was to fundamentally reform the Soviet economy by improving the overall technological and industrial base, as well as the quality of life for Soviet citizens, through increased availability of food, housing, and consumer goods. Glasnost was to complement these efforts by encouraging the free exchange of ideas and discussion of problems, pluralistic participation in decision making, and increased availability of information.[6]

These major domestic steps were followed shortly by legislative measures that thoroughly reformed the Soviet foreign-trade apparatus. In a major move away from previous trade centralization through the channels of the Ministry of Foreign Trade, organizations such as national agencies, large enterprises, and research institutes were authorized to handle their own foreign transactions directly. A 1987 decree asserted that it was essential to develop economic ties with the capitalist world in order to consistently move along the strategic course of using the advantages of the world division of labor, to strengthen the position of the USSR in international trade, and to introduce the achievements of world science and technology into the national economy.[7] By 1989, all Soviet enterprises that could compete in foreign markets were permitted to apply for independent trading rights.

Concurrent with the steps taken in the Soviet Union, other socialist countries also initiated significant reforms affecting international business. China began to launch major programs of modernization and developed multinational corporations of its own. Virtually all socialist countries began to invite foreign investors to form joint ventures in their countries to satisfy both domestic and international demand.

THE DEMISE OF THE SOCIALIST SYSTEM

By late 1989, all the individual small shifts resulted in the emergence of a new economic and geopolitical picture. With an unexpected suddenness, the Iron Curtain crumbled, and within two years, the communist empire disintegrated. Virtually overnight, Eastern Europe and the Soviet Union, with their total population of 400 million and a combined GNP of $3.5 trillion, shifted their political and economic orientation toward a market economy. The former socialist satellites shed their communist governments. Newly elected democratic governments decided to let market forces shape their economies. East Germany was unified with West Germany. On March 1, 1992, Hungary was admitted as an associate member of the EU. The Czech Republic and Poland announced their desire to achieve full convertibility of their currencies and to

[5] Mihaly Simai, "Problems, Conditions, and Possibilities for an Export-Oriented Economic Policy in Hungary," in *Export Policy: A Global Assessment,* ed. M. Czinkota and G. Tesar (New York: Praeger, 1982), 20–30.

[6] Eugene Theroux and Arthur L. George, *Joint Ventures in the Soviet Union: Law and Practice,* rev. ed. (Washington, D.C.: Baker & McKenzie, 1989), 1.

[7] Sherr, "Joint Ventures in the USSR," 27.

join the GATT system. The 12 republics of the CIS joined the IMF. By 1992, the entire Soviet Union had disappeared. Individual regions within the former Soviet Union reasserted their independence and autonomy, resulting in a host of newly emerging nations, often heavily dependent on one another but now separated by nationalistic feelings and political realities. Figure 23.1 provides an overview of the independent

The Commonwealth of Independent States **FIGURE 23.1**

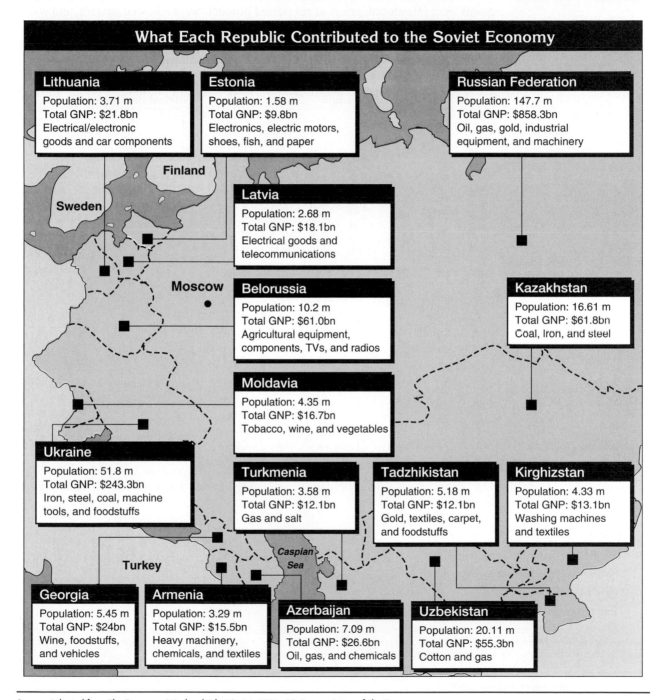

What Each Republic Contributed to the Soviet Economy

Lithuania
Population: 3.71 m
Total GNP: $21.8bn
Electrical/electronic
goods and car components

Estonia
Population: 1.58 m
Total GNP: $9.8bn
Electronics, electric motors,
shoes, fish, and paper

Russian Federation
Population: 147.7 m
Total GNP: $858.3bn
Oil, gas, gold, industrial
equipment, and machinery

Latvia
Population: 2.68 m
Total GNP: $18.1bn
Electrical goods and
telecommunications

Finland

Sweden

Belorussia
Population: 10.2 m
Total GNP: $61.0bn
Agricultural equipment,
components, TVs, and radios

Kazakhstan
Population: 16.61 m
Total GNP: $61.8bn
Coal, Iron, and steel

Moscow

Moldavia
Population: 4.35 m
Total GNP: $16.7bn
Tobacco, wine, and vegetables

Ukraine
Population: 51.8 m
Total GNP: $243.3bn
Iron, steel, coal, machine
tools, and foodstuffs

Turkmenia
Population: 3.58 m
Total GNP: $12.1bn
Gas and salt

Tadzhikistan
Population: 5.18 m
Total GNP: $12.1bn
Gold, textiles, carpet,
and foodstuffs

Kirghizstan
Population: 4.33 m
Total GNP: $13.1bn
Washing machines
and textiles

Caspian
Sea

Turkey

Georgia
Population: 5.45 m
Total GNP: $24bn
Wine, foodstuffs,
and vehicles

Armenia
Population: 3.29 m
Total GNP: $15.5bn
Heavy machinery,
chemicals, and textiles

Azerbaijan
Population: 7.09 m
Total GNP: $26.6bn
Oil, gas, and chemicals

Uzbekistan
Population: 20.11 m
Total GNP: $55.3bn
Cotton and gas

Source: Adapted from *The European*, Weekend July 12–14, 1991, 18. By permission of The European.

republics and shows the products that each of them has historically contributed to the former Soviet Union. Without the might of central planning, however, these established trade and supply relations are beginning to break down. Because of the split-up, the monolithic economy of the Soviet Union has been transformed into many smaller economic regions with varying levels of economic development and potential. Table 23.2 provides a perspective of these differences and shows the wide disparities in capabilities.

The political changes were accompanied by major economic actions. Austerity programs were introduced, prices of subsidized products were adjusted upward, and wages

TABLE 23.2	**Economic and Political Potential within the CIS**											
		Economic Criteria							**Political and Social Criteria**			
	Total Score All Criteria	Economic Base, Resource Potential	External Economic Position	Quality of Infrastructure	Industrial and Foreign Trade Structures	Quality of Economic Reforms	Efficiency of Economic Reforms	Total Score Economic Factors	Stability in Foreign Relations	Internal Stability	Social Structures	Mentality	Total Score Political and Social Factors
		1	2	3	4	5	6	1–6	7	8	9	10	7–10
Russia	60	9	6	5	7	6	4	37	4	6	7	6	23
Turkemenistan	55	7	4	6	5	4	6	32	7	8	4	4	23
Kazakhstan	50	6	4	4	6	4	5	29	6	6	5	4	21
Belorussia	48	4	2	7	4	2	2	21	7	8	7	5	27
Uzbekistan	46	6	3	4	4	4	6	27	5	6	4	4	19
Moldova	45	4	2	6	3	4	5	24	5	6	4	6	21
Ukraine	44	5	2	8	4	2	2	23	4	4	7	6	21
Kirghizstan	42	4	3	4	3	4	4	22	5	6	4	5	20
Georgia	39	3	2	6	3	3	3	20	2	1	7	9	19
Armenia	37	3	2	6	3	4	2	20	0	3	6	8	17
Azerbaijan	37	5	2	6	5	3	2	23	0	3	5	6	14
Tajikistan	26	4	2	3	2	2	2	15	5	0	3	3	11

10 Points = very good potential, low risk

5 Points = average potential, average risk

1 Point = weak potential, high risk

0 Points = no potential, extreme risk

Since each criterion rates different qualitites, the scores are not entirely comparable. Depending on the interests of the individual user (investor, exporter/importer, financial institution, politician etc), it may be advisable to give certain factors a higher weighting than others in an overall ranking. The total scores shown here are based on an equal weighting for all criteria.

Source: Deutsche Bank Research, Frankfurt, July 7, 1994

Effects of Economic Transformation   FIGURE 23.2

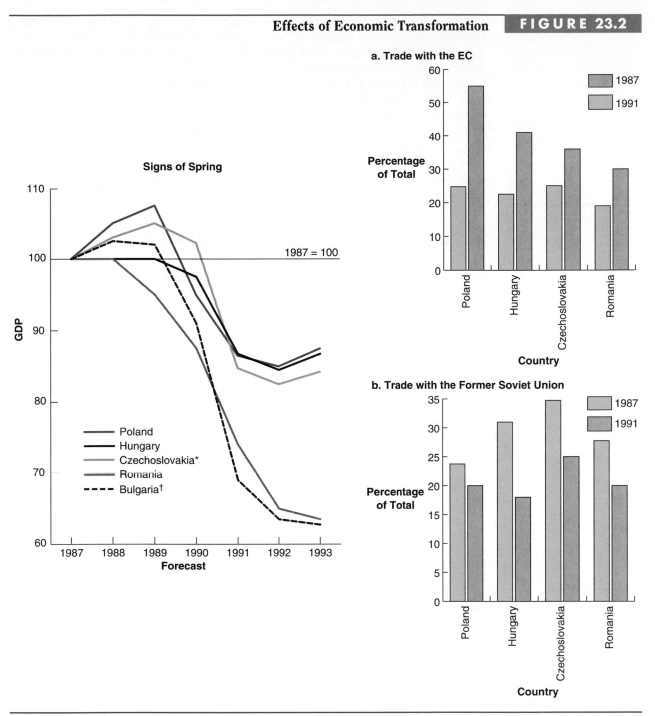

were kept in check to reduce inflation. Entire industries were either privatized or closed down. These steps led to a significant decrease in the standard of living of the population, as Figure 23.2 shows. Yet the support for internal economic transformation continued, demonstrating the great desire on the part of individuals and governments to participate in the world marketplace.

From a Western perspective, all these changes indicated the end of the cold war and a resultant significant decrease in the need to withhold economic benefits and technology from an entire world region. What had been a strictly guarded relationship between adversaries became an open market.

After the ebbing of the initial euphoria, it was also learned and understood on both sides that the shouts for democracy were, to a large degree, driven not only by political but also by economic desires. Freedom meant not only the right to free elections but also the expectation of an increased standard of living in the form of color televisions, cars, and the many benefits of a consumer society. To sustain the drive toward democracy, these economic desires had to appear attainable. Therefore, it was in the interest of the Western world as a whole to contribute to the democratization of the NEDs by searching for ways to bring them "the good life."

THE REALITIES OF ECONOMIC CHANGE

For Western firms, all these shifts resulted in the conversion of what had been a latent market into a market offering very real and vast opportunities. Yet these shifts are only the beginning of a process. The announcement of an intention to change does not automatically result in change itself. For example, the abolition of a centrally planned economy does not create a market economy. Laws permitting the emergence of private-sector entrepreneurs do not create entrepreneurship. The reduction of price controls does not immediately make goods available or affordable. Deeply ingrained systemic differences between the newly emerging democracies and Western firms continue. Highly prized fundamentals of the market economy—such as the reliance on competition, the support of the profit motive, and the willingness to live with risk on a corporate and personal level—are not yet fully accepted. It is therefore useful to review the major economic and structural dimensions of the newly emerging democracies to identify major shortcomings and opportunities for international marketers.

The elected democratic governments are a completely new phenomenon. Although full of good intentions, these governments are new to the tasks of governing and have either very limited experience or none at all. At the same time, they face major legal uncertainties and the existence of old, entrenched bureaucracies whose members are still deeply suspicious of any change and are less than helpful or forthcoming. Governments have precipitated the disappearance of the previous CMEA trading system but have yet to replace the old, imperfect set of trading relationships with a new one. Many old contracts are canceled, and few new ones are in sight. Major dislocations and long-standing dependencies, which have been eliminated or restructured overnight, sharply constrain the ability of governments to successfully shape the competitive environment of their nations.

Many of the NEDs also face major **infrastructure shortages.** Transportation systems, particularly those leading to the West, are either nonexistent or in disrepair. The housing stock is in need of total overhaul. Communication systems will take years to improve. Payments and funds-transfer systems are inadequate. Even though major efforts are under way to improve the infrastructure—evidenced, for example, by Russia's desire to obtain fiber-optic telephone lines or by Hungary's success in installing a cellular telephone system—infrastructure shortcomings will inhibit economic growth for years to come.

Capital shortages are also a major constraint. Catching up with the West in virtually all industrial areas will require significant capital infusions. In addition, a new environmental consciousness will require large investments in environmentally sound energy-generation and production facilities. Even though programs are being designed to attract hidden personal savings into the economies, NEDs have to rely to a large degree on attracting capital from abroad. Continued domestic uncertainties and high demand for capital around the world make this difficult.

Firms doing business with NEDs encounter very interesting demand conditions. Clearly, the pent-up demand from the past bodes well for sales. Yet buyers, in many instances, have never been exposed to the problem of decision making; their preferences are vague and undefined, and they are therefore poorly trained in making market choices.[8] As a result, buyers are unlikely to demand high levels of quality or service. Rather, their demand is driven much more by product availability than by product sophistication. Yet very limited accurate market information is available. For example, knowledge about pricing, advertising, research, and trading is virtually nonexistent, and few institutions are able to accurately assess demand and channel supply. As a result, corporate responsiveness to demand is quite difficult.

To the surprise of many investors, NEDs have substantial knowledge resources to offer. For example, it is claimed that Russia and Eastern Europe possess about 35 to 40 percent of all the researchers and engineers working in the world.[9] At the same time, however, NEDs suffer from the drawback imposed by a lack of management skills. In the past, management mainly consisted of skillful maneuvering within the allocation process. Central planning, for example, required firms to request tools seven years in advance; material requirements needed to be submitted two years in advance. Ordering was done haphazardly, since requested quantities were always reduced, and surplus allocations could always be traded with other firms. The driving mechanism for management was therefore not responsiveness to existing needs but rather plan fulfillment through the development of a finely honed **allocation mentality.**

Difficulties also exist concerning the commitment of managers and employees to hard work. By tradition, employees are still caught up in old work habits, which consisted of never having to work too much. The notion that "they pretend to pay us, and we pretend to work" is still very strong. The current dismantling of the past policy of the "Iron Rice Bowl," which made layoffs virtually impossible, is further reducing rather than increasing such commitment. Investors bringing with them new ways of doing business can introduce change only gradually. But progress is being made, as the International Marketplace 23.2 describes.

The new environment also complicates managerial decision making. Because of the total lack of prior market orientation, even simple reforms require an almost unimaginable array of decisions about business licenses, the setting of optimal tax rates, rules of business operation, definitions of business expense for taxation purposes, safety standards and rules concerning nondiscrimination, and consumer protection.[10]

To cope with all these new challenges, NEDs need trained managers. Since no large supply of such individuals exists, much of the training must be developed and offered. As The International Marketplace 23.3 shows, such training is becoming available and can make important contributions to the economic transformation of these societies.

---

[8] Johny K. Johansson, *Marketing, Free Choice, and the New International Order* (Washington, D.C.: Georgetown University, 1990), 10.

[9] Mihaly Simai, *East-West Cooperation at the End of the 1980s: Global Issues, Foreign Direct Investments, and Debts* (Budapest: Hungarian Scientific Council for World Economy, 1989), 21.

[10] Jerry F. Hough, *Opening Up the Soviet Economy* (Washington, D.C.: Brookings Institution, 1988), 46.

23.2

THE INTERNATIONAL MARKETPLACE

Kmart In the Czech Republic

Spending the summer working at Kmart may not sound like a very interesting time for a college student, but what if that Kmart was located in the Czech Republic or Slovakia? This is exactly what University of Florida at Gainesville business student Agnieszka Pjanka did. She was excited by "the idea of an American company trying to gain market share in Eastern Europe."

Polish-born and fluent in English, Polish, German, and Russian, Pjanka was selected by Kmart executives to participate in an internship at 2 of the 13 Kmarts in the former Czechoslovakia. The U.S. retail giant has acquired several stores in Eastern Europe and is now introducing Kmart's free market, discounter merchandising methods. Educating Czech and Slovak customers who are having a difficult time understanding the meaning of the term "discounter" will fall on the shoulders of the marketing department. One Kmart associate said, "It's difficult for them to grasp the idea of an attractive store selling sound products at prices that represent a value."

For Pjanka, it was a chance to try out some of her newly gained skills in business and marketing in a history-making setting. She says, "It was an experience I will never forget. Change is happening at such a rapid pace both at the Kmart store and in the city in general that I felt as though I could see progress almost every day."

One of the biggest challenges for Pjanka was imbuing Kmart's "customer-first" approach to Czech sales associates. There is much to learn when customer service is a totally new concept. For example, a middle-aged clerk did not hide her nostalgia for the good old times of communism. "It was easy before," she said. "We were just sitting behind the counter and customers came to us. Now we have to walk around and go to the customers. My feet hurt."

Despite some of the rough edges, Pjanka was proud to see a customer-service desk opened in the Prague store, the first of its kind in the Czech Republic. The desk is ready to offer information, exchanges, and refunds. Pjanka was able to feel at home with the Eastern European brand of Kmart, which displays a brightly lit selling floor and new coats of paint similar to Kmarts in the United States. "Everything is clean and bright [and] the shelves are packed full of merchandise," reports Pjanka.

Eastern Europeans are becoming more demanding shoppers with their new-found freedom. With the market becoming competitive, Pjanka believes people are looking for the best deal. Initially a bit uneasy about the way her temporary fellow employees might respond to her, Pjanka found them to be very warm and friendly. "They're hesitant about the changes that are happening all around them, yet they were more accepting of new things and ideas than I'd anticipated."

Sources: Susan Reda, "Aga's Maj Summer," *Stores*, November 1993, 28; Peter Maass, "Service with a Snarl," *The Washington Post*, August 17, 1993; D1, D10.

THE INTERNATIONAL MARKETPLACE   **23.3**

Education Is Key to Market Success

Five of the most influential business schools in the United States—Harvard, Wharton, Stanford, Northwestern, and MIT—try to make a difference in the management skills of Eastern European countries. The schools jointly launched a $3.5-million program designed to teach business basics to professors from universities and management in Central and Eastern Europe and to give them "an advanced management perspective on a market economy." The effort is concentrated on 120 of Eastern Europe's best professors of management, economics, and technology. While attending classes in the United States, the participants will be exposed to such unfamiliar fields as competitor analysis and marketing. The goal is to train them as multipliers so that they can lead the march to a market economy when they return home.

But Eastern Europe does not have to rely on the United States alone. France's INSEAD, the London Business School (LBS), and Switzerland's IMD also intend to educate Eastern professors in Western ways. LBS, INSEAD, and Spain's IESE have raised $4.4 million to help the former Soviet Union to bring its management education up to capitalist scratch. In addition, many schools are working with individual institutions. For example, Georgetown University is developing an executive-management program in the Czech Republic.

There is some concern that many East-West projects will fail if Western schools simply force-feed Eastern Europe with Western management theory. Says Bruno Dufour, of ESC in Lyon, France: "We have to remember that management is largely a cultural activity."

Adapted from "Educating Milos." *The Economist*, May 16, 1992, 86.

ADJUSTING TO RAPID CHANGE

Both institutions and individuals tend to display some resistance to change. The resistance grows if the speed of change increases. It does not necessarily indicate a preference for the earlier conditions but rather concern about the effects of adjustment and fear of the unknown. In light of the major shifts that have occurred both politically and economically in Central Europe and the former Soviet Union and the accompanying substantial dislocations, resistance should be expected. Deeply entrenched interests and traditions are not easily dislocated by the tender and shallow root of market-oriented thinking. The understanding of linkages and interactions cannot be expected to grow overnight. For example, greater financial latitude for firms also requires that inefficient firms be permitted to go into bankruptcy—a concept not cherished by many. The need for increased efficiency and productivity will result in sharp reductions in employment—a painful step for the workers affected. The growing ranks of unemployed are swelled by the members of the military that have been brought home or demobilized. Concurrently, wage reforms threaten to relegate blue-collar workers, who were traditionally favored by the socialist system, to second-class status while permitting the emergence of a new entrepreneurial class of the rich, an undesirable result for those not participating in the upswing. Retail price reforms may endanger the safety net of large

23.4

THE INTERNATIONAL MARKETPLACE

Is the West Ready for Change?

In spite of wholehearted Western support for Central European democracy and market adjustment, that support has limits, particularly when it comes to competition against domestic industries—as many Central Europeans are finding out.

Take the example of the Czech clothing company OP Prostejov. After losing its market in Russia, which used to buy half of the firm's output, the company found new customers in the United States, Germany, the Netherlands, Belgium, and Luxembourg. But when a ship loaded with woolen coats and suits arrived in New York, the company ran into import quotas designed to shield U.S. clothing makers from overseas competition. Or take the Russian MI-26 helicopters made by Mil Design Bureau. They are the behemoth of world helicopters and can lift 40,000 pounds, twice the capability of any U.S. heavy-lift chopper. When Mil Design tried to lease them to Alaskan loggers, the U.S. helicopter industry fought back. Roy Simmons, executive vice president of Columbia Helicopters, said the MI-26 would be dumped on the U.S. market. "They don't know what costing is, so they just give them away. How can we compete when we have banks and interest and principal and things like that?"

As Eastern European officials see it, the very industries that hold the best prospects for success correspond to politically powerful sectors in the West, which have enjoyed protection from imports. Conversely, they are finding Western trade policy is most generous in sectors that don't matter much. For example, the United States signed an agreement allowing U.S. imports of Czech small firearms. Czech officials view this concession as a drop in the Danube compared with what would be gained if the West opened up its textile and clothing markets.

Sources: Don Phillips, "Russian Helicopter Makers Seek Opening in U.S. Market," *The Washington Post*, March 20, 1992, A2; Tim Carrington, "East Looks West and Sees Trade Barriers," *The Wall Street Journal*, July 25, 1991, A5.

population segments, and wholesale price changes may introduce inflation. It is difficult to accept a system where there are winners and losers, particularly for those on the losing side. As a result, an increase in ambivalence and uncertainty may well produce rapid shifts in economic and political thinking, which in turn will produce another set of unexpected results.

But it is not just in the newly emerging democracies that major changes have come about. The shifts experienced there also have a major impact on the established market economies of the West. At an initial level, the immediate changes in the West were confined to the reduction of the threat of war and a redefinition of military and political strategy. Over time, however, Western governments are discovering that the formation of new linkages and dismantling of old ones will also cause major dislocations at home. For example, the change in military threat is likely to have an effect on military budgets, which for the United States alone was $300 billion annually. Budget changes in turn affect the production of military goods and the employment level in the defense sector. A declining size of armies will only reinforce the resulting employment needs.

Over the long term, major changes will also result from the reorientation of trade flows. With traditional and "forced" trade relationships vanishing, and the need for income from abroad increasing, most of the former socialist countries exert major efforts to become partners in global trade. They attempt to export much more of their domestic production. Many of these exports will be in product categories such as agriculture, basic manufacturing, steel, aluminum, and textiles, which are precisely the economic sectors in which the Western nations are already experiencing surpluses. As a result, the threat of displacement will be high for traditional producers in the West.

The immediate consequence of these shifts will likely be resistance to change. Typical of such resistance is government action that attempts to contain the effect of change abroad and limit its effect at home. The International Marketplace 23.4 provides examples of such actions.

Such governmental restrictions to trade flows from the newly emerging market economies are dangerous. Figure 23.3 provides various scenarios for Western economic relations with the newly emerging democracies. The two main dimensions guiding these scenarios are government restrictions to trade and the competitive gap between the two areas. In scenario 1, Western governments attempt to reduce the inflow of trade from these new regions. Concurrently, increases in economic integration in the West, combined with the significant competitive advantages of Western firms, will lead to a widening of the competitive gap between the two regions. In scenario 2, government restrictions remain high, but the competitive gap is diminishing—a result that would heavily depend on quick adjustment by the NEDs and sufficient resources to improve their competitive standing. Scenario 3 decreases government restrictions, but the competitive gap continues to increase. In scenario 4, government restrictions decrease together with a closing of the competitive gap.

An analysis of these four options shows that scenario 1 is likely to lead to major economic and political instability in the NEDs due to individual hardships and disappointed

**Scenarios for Western Economic Relations
with the Newly Emerging Democracies**

FIGURE 23.3

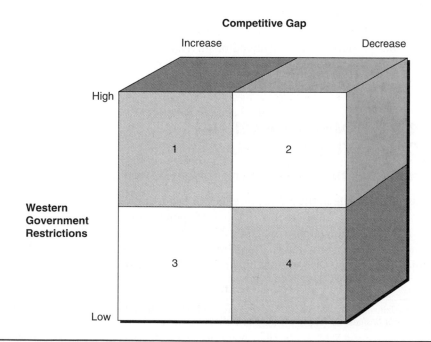

expectations. Scenario 2 is unlikely to materialize, since the investments required for a decrease in the competitive gap will not occur unless market opportunities for investment output exist in the West. Scenario 3 indicates that the lowering of government restrictions is a necessary but insufficient condition for the improvement of the competitive standing of the NEDs. Scenario 4 is the most desirable because it offers long-term change and economic improvement to the NEDs. Yet this scenario also will result in the highest internal adjustment needs by Western governments and firms and will require significant transfers of resources to close the competitive gap. This scenario will also depend on close collaboration between the public and the private sector. Private-sector investment will be required in order to transfer and generate the domestic resources necessary for economic competitiveness. Even with low government restrictions, private capital flows will need encouragement. Such encouragement will, to a large degree, depend on the domestic governmental actions of the NEDs. The providing of open markets and of governmental assistance on the part of the West, however, will also be instrumental. One could argue that governmental expenditures assisting the recovery of the economies of the NEDs should be minimized. This argument is substantially weakened if such expenditures are seen as investment or even as insurance. In light of the more than $500 billion in annual military expenses that the Western world imposed on itself during cold war days, protection against future instability may well be worth a small percentage of the armament expenditures of the past.

Disappointment and disenchantment in the NEDs bring with them the potential for social upheaval and chaos. One must recognize that economic borders can be just as divisive and perhaps even more painful than political ones.[11] Instability and confrontation result not only from tanks but also from poverty-driven countries' knowledge that the next-door neighbor lives in wealth and amplitude. To avoid conflict and increase opportunity, it is therefore in the long-term interest of Western governments and citizens to lower their restrictions to trade and assist in building up the competitive capabilities of the East. There is an urgent need to collaborate now to encourage the formulation of joint approaches and inhibit the advancement of disjointed, incompatible policies. Such collaboration will bring painful economic shifts in the West. Although governments and individuals may not be prepared for such pain, the burden must be borne in order to increase the likelihood of survival for market-oriented thinking and democracy in the NEDs and, in the longer term, to create new targets of opportunity abroad.

INTERNATIONAL MARKETING OPPORTUNITIES AND CHALLENGES

Marketing in the Newly Emerging Democracies

The pressure of change in the NEDs presents vast opportunities for the future expansion of international marketing activities. Their large populations offer potential consumer demand and production supply unmatched by any other region in the world. Furthermore, the knowledge of the international marketer may be particularly useful to these economies, where business skills are only rudimentary. These countries need assistance

---

[11] Michael R. Czinkota, "The EC '92 and Eastern Europe: Effects of Integration vs. Disintegration," *Columbia Journal of World Business* 26 (1991): 20–27.

and contacts to reshape their domestic economies and penetrate foreign markets. For example, Russia is asking for help in areas such as business and personnel training, marketing, banking, auditing, and compilation of statistics.[12]

One major challenge for the marketer is the lack of information about end-users. The entire marketing discipline is founded on the basic objective of satisfying the needs and wants of individuals and organizations. Unable to ascertain their desires directly, the international marketer must use secondary information such as hearsay, educated guesses, and the opinions of intermediaries.

Another major difficulty encountered in conducting business with these countries is the frequent unavailability of hard currency. Products, however necessary, often cannot be purchased by newly emerging market economies because no funds are available to pay for them. As a result, many of these countries resort to barter and countertrade. This places an additional burden on the international marketer, who not only must market products to the clients but also must market the products received in return to other consumers and institutions.

Of key concern to the international marketer, however, must be the degree to which the established Western marketing **focus, objectives,** and **techniques** fit with the newly emerging democracies. In light of the crumbled socialist system, the temptation is high to supplant failure with approaches that have been proven to work better. Since the United States is the cradle of marketing and since U.S. firms in particular have garnered competitive advantage by understanding, developing, and successfully implementing large-scale integrated marketing systems, one alternative might be to simply carry out a wholesale transfer of U.S. state-of-the-art marketing know-how. Alternatively, taking into account the lack of marketing infrastructure, one could try to take dated marketing knowledge and transfer that. Yet it may be wise to proceed only with caution. With regard to marketing focus, Western nations have traditionally placed the individual consumer on the pedestal. This focus contrasted markedly with socialist economies, where the group and society were of key concern. Today, at the same time that newly emerging democracies are bringing freedom to and displaying more concern about the individual, the traditional industrialized nations are discovering the pressing importance of issues such as global warming and pollution and are urging an increase in societal priorities. Rather than encouraging a simple replication of a consumption society in the NEDs, it may be wiser to help them achieve an improved standard of living while also passing on our own lessons learned and helping them to avoid some of the problems of such a consumption focus. The marketer can, for example, explore ways to reduce packaging and increase the environmental friendliness of products without waiting for society to grow concerned about such issues.

Similar questions can also be raised about marketing objectives. Key concerns in the West—such as highest levels of customer service, top-level product quality, timely delivery, or individual convenience—may at this time simply not be as relevant to a populace used to waiting 17 years to get a new car delivered. Perhaps the roles of time and place utilities, of appearance and design, and of durability and style are not the same in both regions.

In marketing techniques, key adaptation issues can also be identified. The interpretation of advertising pitches, the perspective of research, and the response to offers may

[12] Janet Porter, "Western Consultants Benefit as Soviets Restructure Business," *Journal of Commerce,* July 12, 1988, 1A, 3A.

23.5

THE INTERNATIONAL MARKETPLACE

Will Marketers Win the Battle for the Soul?

Five generations of Schmidts have lived in Hohewarte, a town in one of the new states of Germany. There are still only four telephones in this village of 900 people. But otherwise, much has changed.

In the bathroom of Peter and Undine Schmidt, the little shrine of empty Western cosmetic and perfume boxes that the family kept for years after receiving gifts from Western relatives is gone. Such things are commonplace now. They have a VCR and a ten-year-old Volkswagen Polo they bought for $2,200 after having waited 14 years, without success, for an East German Trabant. To make room to park the car, they had to give away the chickens they used to keep in the yard. The car has opened up the world. The Schmidts have been on family trips to Denmark and Hamburg. Peter smokes Marlboros now, and Undine has the cosmetics she had only dreamed about before.

A year ago, Undine's first visits to Western-style shops left her trembling. "They have different prices at different places for the same product," she said then. "It's very confusing. We have to rethink everything." Now they know the brands and can buy groceries in ten minutes—but now the groceries cost a lot. "You can get anything you want now, but you need the cash, and we don't have it. In former times, our money wasn't worth anything, but if there was something for sale, you could afford it," says Undine. "Oh give me a break," Peter says. "We got a car. We got a washing machine. A Fryer. A new color TV. We could never have gotten that." But then he adds, "Of course, that's not all there is in life."

But money is what's different about before and after. Every day, catalogues arrive in the mail, offering clothing, toys, kitchenware, shoes. Undine asked around and now understands how to order, but she is still mystified by how the catalogues get to her in the first place. And it took months for them to realize that no, just because the letter in the mail said the Schmidts had won a car in some sweepstakes, no one was going to deliver a new BMW to Hohewarte. "Oh, we got so excited in the beginning," Undine says. "The first time I won a car, I went running around town telling people. Now we just say, ach, another one."

Source: "The Schmidt Family," *The Washington Post*, October 5, 1991, D1, D4.

differ widely. A Backer Spielvogel Bates Worldwide Survey of consumers in the eastern states of Germany provided insightful findings: 59 percent of Easterners surveyed believed that advertising takes advantage of them; 87 percent believed that advertising makes them buy things they don't need; 64 percent believed that advertising gives a misleading impression of products; and 76 percent said that they were blitzed by too many product offers.[13] As The International Marketplace 23.5 shows, it may be more difficult than expected to achieve blanket acceptance of marketing in the NEDs.

---

[13] Joanne Lipman, "Eastern Germans Deeply Distrust Western World's Ad Campaigns," *The Wall Street Journal,* October 4, 1991.

All these concerns highlight that in order to be successful, the marketer must carefully scrutinize the societal dimension of the discipline as we know it and adapt it to the countries new to marketing. But since marketing has adaptation as one of its core postulates, the longer-term prospects should be bright.

Sourcing from the Newly Emerging Democracies

Apart from marketing to or within the NEDs, the marketer also needs to consider the possibility of obtaining products, services, or ideas from them. In this process, some special challenges have been encountered. Many firms have found that selling is not part of the economic culture in these countries. Descriptive materials often either are not available or are poorly written and devoid of useful information. Obtaining additional information and insights about a product may turn out to be difficult and time-consuming.

The quality of the products obtained can also be a major problem. In spite of their great desire to participate in the global marketplace, the NEDs still tend to place primary emphasis on product performance and, to a large extent, neglect style and product presentation. The result is "a willingness to leave equipment rough and unfinished when a lack of finishing does not significantly affect function."[14] Therefore, the international marketer needs to forge agreements that require the manufacturer to improve quality, provide for technical control, and ensure prompt delivery before sourcing products from newly emerging market economies.

Even when satisfactory products are obtained, the marketing of these products elsewhere can be a major problem. One study revealed negative attitudes toward products sourced from newly emerging market economies—particularly consumer products. International marketers may well "find a portion of the population [in the United States] hesitant to purchase [such] goods."[15]

Nevertheless, sufficient opportunities exist to make consideration of these international marketing activities worthwhile. Newly emerging market economies do have products that can be of use in free-market economies and that are often unique in performance. For example, a recent study showed that Russian tractors can be sold successfully in the United States. The study found that many of the previously held negative attitudes about imports from Eastern Europe have been modified by the improved political climate.[16] In addition, the newness factor may actually have a positive influence on the sales of products and services emanating from the region. Figure 23.4 shows advertisements for Russian products and services that attempt to focus on customers interested in the unusual.

Currently, most sourcing opportunities from Eastern Europe and the former Soviet Union are in the area of industrial products, which reflect the past orientation of research and development expenditures. Over time, however, consumer products may play a larger role. Lower labor costs and, in some instances, the greater availability of labor may enable newly emerging market economies to offer consumers in free-market

[14] John W. Kiser III, "Tapping Soviet Technology," in *Common Sense in U.S.-Soviet Trade,* eds. M. Chapman and C. Marcy (Washington, D.C.: American Committee on East-West Accord, 1983), 104.

[15] Robert D. Hisrich, Michael P. Peters, and Arnold K. Weinstein, "East-West Trade: The View from the United States," *Journal of International Business Studies* 12 (Winter 1981): 109–121.

[16] Johny K. Johansson, Ilkka A. Ronkainen, and Michael R. Czinkota, "Negative Country of Origin Effects: The Case of the New Russia," *Journal of International Business Studies* 25 no. 1 (1994): 157–176.

FIGURE 23.4	Advertising Unusual Products and Services from Russia

PROBABLY YOU HAVE SEEN THE SEVEN-SEAT LIMOUSINES WHICH WERE WIDELY USED BY SOVIET PARTY ELITE AND THE PRESIDENTS OF THE USSR.

These are unique hand-made automobiles. Now you have an opportunity
to purchase Gaz 1402 «Chaika» limousines which are no longer produced
and the price of which will only go up.
Cars are 1987-88 models.
Mileage between 14 and 95 thousand kilometers.
Cars run on high octane fuel AI-95 «extra». 220 horse power engines.
Cars in excellent condition.
Cars were used at Foros (Gorbachov's Dacha in Crimea) and the Kremlin.

«PROMINVEST»
Share holding
company

More information can be obtained by   *Fax in Minsk (0172) 27-63-31.*

Fly a *MiG*-29 at Mach 2.3 in Moscow*

MIGS *etc*., in conjunction with the Russian aerospace industry, has a
limited number of high-performance military flight packages available
for immediate booking. Flights on MiG-29, MiG-31, Su-27, and L-39
jets, among others, are offered. Custom flights and tours available.

You need not be a pilot. Accompanied by a top Russian test pilot, you
will take the controls of a legendary supersonic fighter with a flight
plan you help design.

Flight packages from $7,000.

MIGS

MIGS *etc*., Inc.
800 MIGS ETC [USA]
813 923-0607
813 923-8815 fax

*Yes, really

Sources: *The Washington Times,* August 16, 1993, A10; *The Washington Post,* February 6, 1994, A21.

economies a variety of products at a lower cost. Therefore, even if not interested in marketing to the NEDs, the international marketer should maintain relations with them in order not to lose a potentially valuable source of supply.

MARKETING WITH STATE-OWNED ENTERPRISES

One other area where the international marketer is confronted with a period of transition is that of state-owned enterprises. These firms, which are very active in many countries around the world, represent a formidable pool of international suppliers, customers, and competitors for the international marketing executive. At the same time, however, many of these firms are currently being converted into privately owned enterprises. This transition will also present new opportunities for the international marketer.

REASON FOR THE EXISTENCE OF STATE-OWNED ENTERPRISES

A variety of economic and noneconomic factors has contributed to the existence of state-owned enterprises. Two primary ones are national security and economic security. Many countries believe that, for national security purposes, certain industrial sectors must be under state control. Typically, these sectors include telecommunications, airline, banking, and energy.

Economic security reasons are primarily cited in countries that are heavily dependent on specific industries for their economic performance. This may be the case when countries are heavily commodity-dependent. For example, in 18 African countries, one commodity contributes more than half of export revenues.[17] Governments frequently believe that given such heavy national dependence on a particular industrial sector, government control is necessary to ensure national economic health.

Other reasons have also contributed to the development of state-owned enterprises. On occasion, the sizable investment required for the development of an industry is too large to come from the private sector. Therefore, governments close the gap between national needs and private-sector resources by developing industries themselves. In addition, governments often decide to rescue failing private enterprises by placing them in government ownership. In so doing, they fulfill important policy objectives such as the maintenance of jobs, the development of depressed areas, or the increase of exports.

Some governments have also maintained that state-owned firms may be better for the country than privately held companies because they may be more societally oriented and therefore contribute more to the greater good. This is particularly the case in areas such as telecommunications and transportation, where profit maximization, at least from a governmental perspective, may not always be the appropriate primary objective.

Over time, some governments that have controlled enterprises used this control for political purposes. Rather than focusing on the business aspects, these corporations became grazing grounds for political appointees or vote winners through job allocations.[18] As a result, many government-owned enterprises excelled in losing money.

[17] Martin C. Schnitzer, Marilyn L. Liebrenz, and Connard W. Kubin, *International Business* (Cincinnati: South-Western Publishing, 1985), 421.

[18] "European Privatization: Two Half Revolutions," *The Economist,* January 22, 1994, 55, 58.

RELEVANCE OF STATE-OWNED ENTERPRISES TO THE INTERNATIONAL MARKETER

Three types of activities in which the international marketer is likely to encounter state-owned enterprises are market entry, the sourcing or marketing process, and international competition. On occasion, the very existence of a state-owned enterprise may inhibit or prohibit foreign-market entry. For reasons of development and growth, governments frequently make market entry from the outside quite difficult so that the state-owned enterprise can perform. Even if market entry is permitted, the conditions under which a foreign firm can conduct business are often substantially less favorable than the conditions under which state-owned enterprises operate. Therefore, the international firm may be placed at a competitive disadvantage and may not be able to perform well, even though economic factors would indicate success.

The international marketer also faces a unique situation when sourcing from or marketing to state-owned enterprises. Even though the state-owned firm may appear to be simply another business partner, it is ultimately an extension of the government and its activities. Quite often, this may mean that a state-owned enterprise conducts its transactions according to the overall foreign policy of the country rather than according to economic rationale. For example, political considerations can play a decisive role in purchasing decisions. Contracts may be concluded for noneconomic reasons rather than based on product offering and performance. Contract conditions may depend on foreign-policy outlook, prices may be altered to reflect government displeasure, and delivery performance may change to "send a signal." Exports and imports may be delayed or encouraged depending on the current needs of a government. Even though an economic rationale appears to exist within a state-owned enterprise, the interests and concerns of the owners—the state—may lead it to be driven by politics.[19]

This also holds true when the international firm encounters international competition from state-owned enterprises. Very often, the concentration of these firms is not in areas of comparative advantage but rather in areas that at the time are most beneficial for the government owning the firm. Input costs often are much less important than policy objectives. Sometimes, state-owned enterprises may not even know the value of the products they buy and sell because prices in themselves have such a low priority. As a result, the international marketer may be confronted with competition that is very tough to beat.

THE STRATEGIC RESPONSE TO THE STATE-OWNED ENTERPRISE

Given the problems that state-owned enterprises can represent for the international firm and its management, various strategic alternatives for dealing with this challenge should be considered.

One alternative is to demonstrate the benefits of working through private-sector and free-market activities rather than government control. If results can show that the benefits gained from government control are far outweighed by its cost, foreign policymakers may reconsider the value of creating state-owned enterprises.

---

[19] Renato Mazzolini, "European Government-Controlled Enterprises: An Organizational Politics View," *Journal of International Business Studies* 11 (Spring–Summer 1980): 48–58.

A second response to the state-owned enterprise is international negotiation and government intervention to "level the playing field." Whenever discriminatory market conditions are encountered, complaints can be launched to the home government. These complaints in turn can be accumulated and aired at meetings of international trade negotiators, with the goal of eliminating the discrimination. Alternatively, particularly in the United States, lawsuits can be initiated against unfair competition from abroad. If the findings are favorable, penalties for subsidization or dumping are frequently imposed against foreign firms.

A third response lies in the antitrust area, particularly for firms or industries in which economies of scale play a major role. To provide relief for firms that are subject to pressures by large-scale, state-owned enterprises, governments can consider relaxing antitrust provisions. In the United States, for example, antitrust laws were originally written with domestic rather than global competition in mind. Their relaxation permits domestic firms to cooperate in domestic and international activities through measures such as joint research and development efforts.

The strategic responses described may be valuable in the medium and long term. For the short term, the international firm needs to persevere in the marketplace in spite of the existence of state-owned enterprises. This means that dealings with such enterprises are often necessary. In doing so, the international marketer must be wary of policy objectives and policy changes. Business proposals for either sourcing or selling must be structured with not only the economic rationale in mind but also the policy imperative under which the state-owned enterprise operates. Marketers may decide to license only older technology to state-owned enterprises. Moreover, to be at least partially insulated from sudden policy actions by state-owned enterprises, they must develop alternative sources of supply and contingency plans in case of rapid shifts in demand.

The international marketer can also seek opportunities that are created by the very existence of state-owned enterprises. For example, there may be room for joint ventures or cooperative agreements. Alternatively, the international firm may be able to provide services such as distribution agreements or management training.

State-owned enterprises often initiate very large projects. Because domestic supply is frequently insufficient for the needs of such projects, there may be room for the participation of foreign firms, particularly when new technology or sophisticated project-management techniques are required. Yet proper caution must be exercised so that the firm can be assured of participating in a successful venture.

In many instances, large-scale projects are cofinanced by international institutions such as the World Bank or by regional institutions such as the Interamerican Development Bank. Even though these organizations make allowances for the policy aims of the borrower, they also impose stringent requirements regarding the efficiency of the project. They may therefore permit a domestic sourcing preference but insist on limits to its extent. Cofinanced projects therefore offer interesting opportunities to the international firm, particularly because their contracting requirements are reasonably tightly defined and easily available internationally through the financing institutions.

PRIVATIZATION

Governments are increasingly recognizing that it is possible to reduce the cost of governing by changing their role and involvement in the economy. Through privatization, governments can cut their budget costs and still ensure that more efficient services— not fewer services—are provided to the people. In addition, the product or service may

23.6

THE INTERNATIONAL MARKETPLACE

Privatization Sweeps the Globe

After record privatization in Eastern Europe, Russia, Latin America, and Asia, privatization is now sweeping across Western Europe like a tidal wave. Italy is selling off giant industries that have been part of the government since the Mussolini era. State-owned industrial conglomerates have been turned into public-stock companies in fields such as oil, banking, food, power, and aerospace. France is cutting loose control over everything from computer companies to giant insurers. Even Germany is getting into the act by putting its national airline, Lufthansa, and Deutsche Bundespost Telekom on the block.

This is not an easy step to take. Says Daniel Gros of the Brussels-based Center for European Policy Studies: "Some diehards don't want to sell their state firms." They give the power to government to "give people hundreds of thousands of jobs. That's where they get their power from."

Why all the privatization? First of all, state enterprises were not very successful. Under state ownership, both managers and workers have strong incentives to "decapitalize" the enterprises that employ them by extracting as much wealth as they can for themselves. They have little or no incentive to increase the value of the firm through wise investments, increasing productivity, or restraining wages and employment, because they have little chance of sharing in the firm's future prosperity. But new rules in the European Union also helped. These rules have banned billions in state subsidies that uncompetitive state firms have relied on for decades to stay afloat. Finally, many countries see privatization as an opportunity to trim massive budget deficits and national debt.

Sources: Patrick Oster, "Europe Dashes to Jettison State-Owned Businesses." *The Washington Post,* July 23, 1992, D10, D14; "Owners Are the Only Answer," *The Economist,* September 21, 1991, 10.

also become more productive and more innovative and may expand choices for the private sector. Furthermore, in the process of disengaging government from enterprises, governments can raise large sums from investors that can be used for other pressing domestic needs.

In the mid-1970s, the United States took the lead in reducing government involvement with industry by deregulating domestic industries such as telephone service and airlines, which had been tightly controlled or regulated. Britain pioneered the concept of privatization in 1979 by converting 20 state firms into privately owned companies. After a slow start, privatization in the 1990s forms a key element of economic strategy around the world, from Asia to Africa and Latin America to Western Europe, as The International Marketplace 23.6 shows. The key challenge for privatization rests, of course, in Central Europe, where governments are attempting to convert thousands of enterprises to private ownership. The number of firms on the block in each country is in the thousands. For example, in only two years, Germany's Treuhandanstalt, placed in charge of disposing most of East Germany's state property, privatized more than 5,000 firms. Governments also enjoy the financial effects of their privatization activities which come in two forms. In times of tight budgets, income from the sale of government-owned assets can free up funds for many other projects, as Figure 23.5 shows. In addition, the

The Proceeds of Privatization   FIGURE 23.5

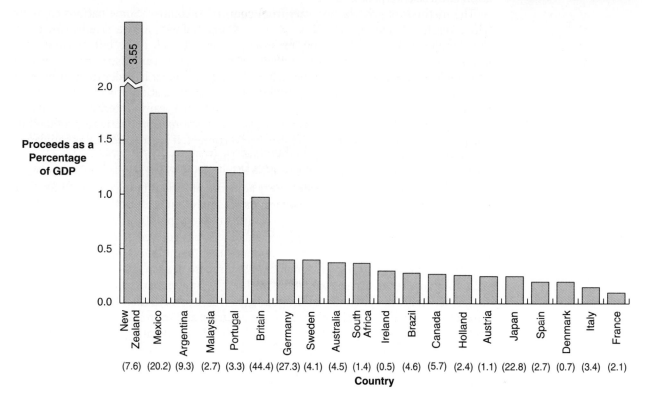

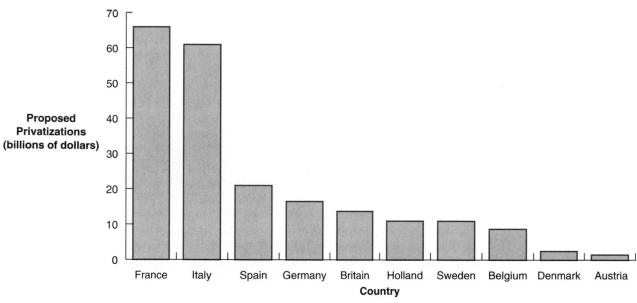

Numbers in parentheses indicate actual value in billions of dollars.

Sources: "Privatisation," *The Economist,* June 19, 1993, 112; "European Privatisation," *The Economist,* January 22, 1994, 58. Copyright © 1992, 1994 The Economist, Ltd. Distributed by The New York Times Special Features.

governments are also relieved of the obligation to make up deficits incurred in the operation of these enterprises.

The methods of privatization vary from country to country. Some nations come up with a master plan for privatization, whereas others deal with it on a case-by-case basis. The Treuhandanstalt of Germany, for example, aims to sell firms but maximize the number of jobs retained. In other countries, ownership shares are distributed to citizens and employees. Some nations simply sell to the highest bidder in order to maximize the proceeds. For example, Mexico has used most of its privatization proceeds to amortize its internal debt, resulting in savings of nearly $1 billion a year in interest payments.

The purpose of many privatization programs is to improve productivity, profitability, and product quality and to shrink the size of government. It is expected that as companies are exposed to market forces and competition, they will have to produce better goods at lower costs. In most instances, privatization also intends to attract new capital for these firms so that they can carry out necessary adjustments and improvements. Since local capital is often scarce, privatization efforts increasingly aim at attracting foreign capital.

The current trend toward privatization offers unique opportunities for international marketers. Existing firms, both large and small, can be acquired at low cost, often with governmental support through tax exemptions, investment grants, special depreciation allowances, and low interest rate credits. The purchase of such firms enables the international marketer to expand operations without having to start from scratch. In addition, since wages are often low in the countries where privatization takes place, there is a major opportunity to build low-cost manufacturing and sourcing bases. Furthermore, the international marketer can also act as a catalyst by accelerating the pace of transferring business skills and technology and by boosting trade prospects. In short, the very process of change offers new opportunities to the adept manager.

SUMMARY

Special concerns must be considered by the international marketer when dealing with newly emerging market economies or with state-owned enterprises. Although the former centrally planned economies offer vast opportunities for trade, business practices may be significantly different from those to which the marketer is accustomed.

In the NEDs, the key to marketing success will be an understanding of the fact that societies in transition require special adaptation of marketing skills. In the Western nations, marketers will need to recognize that the changes in the NEDs will also precipitate changes at home. An acceptance of these shifts will be crucial for the entrenchment of market-based economies worldwide.

Often, the international marketer is also faced with state-owned enterprises that have been formed for reasons of national or economic security. These firms may inhibit foreign-market entry, and they frequently reflect in their transactions the overall domestic and foreign policy of a country rather than any economic rationale.

The current trend toward privatization worldwide offers new opportunities to the international marketer either by participating in the transition through investments or by offering marketing knowledge and skills to assist in the success of privatization.

Questions for Discussion

1. Planning is necessary, yet central planning is inefficient. Why?
2. Discuss the observation that "Russian products do what they are supposed to do—but only that."

3. How can U.S. consumer acceptance of Central European products be improved?

4. Where do you see the greatest potential in future trade between newly emerging market economies and the West?

5. How can marketing adapt itself to the requirements of the NEDs?

6. What do you see as the role of marketing in making democracy succeed in the NEDs?

7. Under what circumstances would you be in favor of state-owned enterprises?

8. What are some of the dangers of dealing with a state-owned enterprise?

9. What are the benefits of privatization?

Recommended Readings

Boecker, Paul M., ed. *Latin America's Turnaround: The Paths to Privatization and Foreign Investment.* San Francisco: ICS Press, 1993.

Czinkota, Michael R. "The EC '92 and Eastern Europe: Effects of Integration vs. Disintegration." *Columbia Journal of World Business* 26 (1991): 20–27.

Gatti, Charles. "East-Central Europe: The Morning After." *Foreign Affairs* 69 (Winter 1990/1991): 5.

Goldman, Marshall. *What Went Wrong with Perestroika.* New York: W.W. Norton, 1992.

Hachette, Dominique, and Rolf Luders. *Privatization in Chile: An Economic Appraisal.* San Francisco: ICS Press, 1992.

Jones, Anthony, ed. *The Great Market Debate in Soviet Economics.* Armonk, NY: M.E. Sharpe, 1991.

Puffer, Sheila M., ed. *The Russian Management Revolution.* Armonk, NY: M.E. Sharpe, 1992.

Silverman, Bertram, Robert Vogt, and Murray Yanowitch, eds. *Labor and Democracy in the Transition to a Market System.* Armonk, NY: M.E. Sharpe, 1992.

CHAPTER 24

The Future

24.1

THE INTERNATIONAL MARKETPLACE

The Demise of the Global Firm?

Cyrus Freidheim, vice chairman of the consulting firm Booz, Allen & Hamilton, has a provocative perspective of the global firm. He predicts that current economic and political developments mean that global firms will be superseded by the "relationship-enterprise," a network of strategic alliances among big firms, spanning different industries and countries, but held together by common goals that encourage them to act almost as a single firm. He sees these enterprises to be corporate juggernauts, with total revenues approaching $1 trillion by early next century, larger than all but the world's six biggest economies.

He suggests that early in the 21st century, Boeing, British Airways, Siemens, TNT (an Australian parcel delivery firm), and SNECMA (a French aero-engine maker) might together win a deal to build ten new airports in China. As part of the deal, British Airways and TNT would receive preferential routes and landing slots, the Chinese government would buy all state aircraft from Boeing-SNECMA, and Siemens would provide the air-traffic control systems for all ten airports.

While this may sound far-fetched, consider that Boeing, members of the airbus consortium, McDonnell Douglas, Mitsubishi, Kawasaki, and Fuji are already talking about jointly developing a new super-jumbo jet. Mitsubishi and Daimler-Benz already share engineers. General Motors and Toyota are discussing the possibility of Toyota's building light trucks in a GM plant.

According to Freidheim, the conventional model of the global firm is flawed. Most so-called global companies are still perceived as having a home base. For example, in 1991, only 2 percent of the board members of big American companies were foreigners. In Japanese companies, foreign directors are as rare as British sumo wrestlers. Firms therefore have a natural home-country bias, with the big decisions kept firmly at home.

This bias, together with various other constraints, hinders companies' efforts to become truly global. For instance, when capital is limited, firms tend to protect their home market at the expense of developing untapped markets overseas. Second, antitrust laws limit the ability of global firms to expand through takeovers. But most important of all is the problem of nationalism. No country likes foreigners controlling its industries. By contrast, a relationship enterprise can sidestep these constraints. Such an alliance can draw on lots of money; it can dodge antitrust barriers; and with home bases in all the main markets, it has the political advantage of being a local firm almost everywhere.

Source: "The Global Firm: R.I.P." *The Economist*, February 6, 1993, 69.

International marketers are constantly faced with global change, as The International Marketplace 24.1 shows. This is not a new situation, nor one to be feared, because change provides the opportunity for the emergence of new market positions. Recognizing the importance of change and adapting creatively to new situations are the daily bread of marketing professionals.

Recently, however, changes are occurring more frequently and more rapidly and have a more severe impact. The past has lost much of its value as a predictor of the future. What occurs today may be not only altered in the future but completely overturned or reversed. For example, some countries can find that their major export industries, highly competitive for decades, can lose their international edge within a matter of months. A nation's political stability can be completely disrupted over the course of a few months. The world has witnessed how the might of the Soviet empire, benefiting from "stability" for more than 40 years, dissipated within less than 36 months. Countries that have been considered enemies, and to which no business executive would dream of selling, suddenly become close allies and offer a wealth of business opportunities. Just a short time later, these opportunities may shrink dramatically because of new government policies. In all, international marketers today face complex and rapidly changing economic and political conditions.

This chapter will discuss possible future developments in the international marketing environment, highlight the implications of these changes for international marketing management, and offer suggestions for a creative response. The chapter will also explore the meaning of strategic changes to the reader, with particular emphasis on career choice and career path alternatives in international marketing.

THE INTERNATIONAL MARKETING ENVIRONMENT

This section analyzes the international marketing environment by looking at political, financial, societal, and technological conditions of change and providing a glimpse of possible future developments as envisioned by a panel of experts.[1]

---

[1] This section draws heavily on research carried out by the coauthors of this book under the auspices of the American Marketing Association.

The Political Environment

The international political environment is undergoing a substantial transformation characterized by the reshaping of existing political blocs, the formation of new groupings, and the breakup of old coalitions.

The East-West Relationship   After 1945, the relationship between the dominant powers in the East and the West changed little. All interaction between the two superpowers and third countries were characterized by a key adversarial posture. Since the late 1980s, however, this relationship, and the global world order with it, have undergone a major transformation. Within only a few years, the Soviet empire crumbled and then disappeared. The former Eastern European satellite nations of the Soviet Union have reasserted their independence and are now much closer to Western Europe than to their former master. Both the collaborative military mechanism—the Warsaw Pact—and the key economic agreement of the communist bloc—the Council for Mutual Economic Assistance—have been disbanded.

These rapid transformations have resulted in major internal adjustments and economic dislocations, which in turn are likely to have political repercussions. It is likely that there will be a rapid rise of inflation in these nations, accompanied by deepening individual dissatisfaction due to unmet expectations of economic progress. Domestic markets and trade volumes shrink in the near and medium terms due to necessary adjustments in production capabilities based on market forces. The countries and the companies involved are likely to suffer from deteriorating liquidity positions and a growing number of insolvencies.

Both Eastern Europe, which increasingly sees itself as "Central Europe," and the independent states of the Commonwealth are likely to see some political benefit from the shedding of the communist system and embracing of market economics. For example, export controls to these destinations have been reduced, making the acquisition of more-sophisticated technology, particularly in the consumer sector, possible. The development of affiliate status with the European Union is likely to bring trade benefits and an increase in investment. A key question will be whether the "Western" economies will be capable and willing to transfer enough funds and know-how and also to sufficiently lower their own government trade barriers to permit these newly emerging democracies to catch up.

As a result of easing political tensions, firms will be presented with new opportunities. Demand—particularly for consumer products, which had been repressed in the past—can now be met with goods from the West. Yet due to very limited consumer choice skills and knowledge levels, firms entering these new markets need to develop demand from the ground up—a difficult task, as Figure 24.1 shows.

Concurrently, Central Europe is likely to emerge as a significant source of products and services destined for export. An increase in the formation of international joint ventures and cooperative alliances is also highly likely, particularly if current plans for privatization are implemented. Due to liquidity shortages, new trading and financing techniques will need to be developed in order to make business propositions viable.

Overall, many of these business activities will be subject to regional economic and political instability, increasing their riskiness for foreign business partners. It may well be that some of the emerging democracies will take a step back to the old days of planned economies and dictatorial government. Yet the attractiveness of large market potential, combined with the availability of a relatively cheap and well-trained labor

Developing Basic Awareness   FIGURE 24.1

Source: *Business in the USSR* 11 (April 1991): 37.

force and the expectation for the long-term success of market forces, may help sur-mount this risk.

The North-South Relationship   The distinction between developed and less-developed countries (LDCs) is unlikely to change. Some theoreticians argue that the economic gap between these two groups will diminish, whereas others hold that the gap will increase. Both arguments lead to the conclusion that a gap will endure for some time. The ongoing disparity between developed and developing nations is likely to be based, in part, on continuing debt burdens and problems with satisfying basic needs. As a result, political uncertainty may well result in increased polarization between the haves and the have-nots, with growing potential for political and economic conflict. De-mands for political solutions to economic and financial problems are likely to increase. Some countries may consider migration as a key solution to population growth problems, a policy that will be welcomed by firms—but only for highly skilled labor. In light of government barriers to such migration, some firms may also bring investment in labor- and skill-intensive manufacturing operations in order to circumvent such barriers.[2] Countries will also count on debt forgiveness on a broad scale and close collaboration with international financial institutions. In light of these scenarios, three possible alternatives emerge.

One alternative is continued international cooperation. The developed countries could relinquish part of their economic power to less-developed ones, thus actively contributing to their development through a sharing of resources and technology. Although such **cross-subsidization** will be useful and necessary for the development of LDCs, it may result in a declining rate of increase in the standard of living in the more-developed countries. It would, however, increase trade flows between North and South and precipitate the emergence of new international business opportunities.

A second alternative is confrontation. Because of an unwillingness to share resources and technology sufficiently (or excessively, depending on the point of view), the developing and the developed areas of the world may become increasingly hostile toward one another. As a result, the volume of international business, both by mandate of governments and by choice of the private sector, could be severely reduced.

A third alternative is isolation. Although there may be some cooperation between the two major blocs, both groups, in order to achieve their domestic and international goals, may choose to remain economically isolated. This alternative may be particularly attractive if the countries in each bloc believe that they face unique problems and therefore must seek their own solutions.

Emergence of New Political Blocs   Some foresee the realignment of global strategic power through the emergence of new political blocs. One such bloc would consist of a reshaped Europe, which would include political and economic membership of the 12 European Union nations, the EFTA countries, the Central European nations, and possibly even some of the Soviet republics. A second bloc would be led by Japan and would be mainly trade-based. Members here would come mostly from the Pacific Rim. A third bloc then could emerge in the Western Hemisphere, led by the United States and including Canada, Mexico, and several Central and South American nations. Such a bloc would be primarily trade-based but could eventually also incorporate many political dimensions.

These bloc formations could result in heightened business stability and cooperation within each arrangement. Yet a concurrent danger might be the emergence of bloc-based competition and protectionism. Such a development could force global firms to choose a "home bloc" and could introduce new inefficiencies into global trade relations. On the positive side, however, due to their relative equality of power, these blocs could also be the precursors of global cooperation, resulting in an even more open and free global business environment.

New Orientations   The people of some nations may possibly decide to reprioritize their values. The aim for financial progress and an improved quantitative standard of living may well give way to priorities based on religion, the environment, social relations, or other factors. Such a reorientation may result in complete reversals of currently held

---

[2] William B. Johnston, "Global Workforce 2000: The New World Labor Market," *Harvard Business Review* (March–April 1991): 115–127.

business values and the consumption orientation and may require a major readjustment of the activities of the international corporation in these countries. A continuous scanning of newly emerging national values thus becomes even more imperative for the international marketer.

The International Financial Environment

Even though the international debt problem of the developing world appears temporarily subdued, it will remain a major international trade and business issue throughout this century. Debt constraints and low commodity prices will continue to create slower growth prospects for many developing countries. They will be forced to reduce their levels of imports and to exert more pressure on industrialized nations to open up their markets. Even if these markets are opened, however, demand for most primary products will be far lower than supply. Ensuing competition for market share will therefore continue to depress prices.

A key issue in resolving the debt crisis will be how the indebted LDCs and newly industrialized countries can pursue necessary or imposed austerity policies and achieve reasonable development goals without seriously damaging the growth requirements and exports of other countries. Developed nations in turn will have a strong incentive to help the debtor nations. This incentive consists of the market opportunities that economically healthy developing countries can offer and of national security concerns. As a result, industrialized nations may very well be in a situation in which a funds transfer to debtor nations, accompanied by debt-relief measures such as debt forgiveness, is necessary to achieve economic stimulation at home.

The dollar will remain a major international currency, with little probability of gold returning to its former status in the near future. However, international transactions in both trade and finance are increasingly likely to be denominated in non-dollar terms, using regional currencies such as the European Currency Unit (ECU). The system of floating currencies will likely continue, with occasional attempts by nations to manage exchange rate relationships or at least reduce the volatility of swings in currency values. However, given the vast flows of financial resources across borders, it would appear that market forces rather than government action will be the key determinant of a currency's value. Factors such as investor trust, economic conditions, earnings perceptions, and political stability are therefore likely to have a much greater effect on the international value of currencies than domestic monetary and fiscal experimentation.

Given the close linkages between financial markets, shocks in one market will quickly translate into rapid shifts in others and easily overpower the financial resources of individual governments. Even if there should be decisions by governments to pursue closely coordinated fiscal and monetary policies, they are unlikely to be able to negate long-term market effects in response to changes in economic fundamentals.

A looming concern in the international financial environment will be the **international debt load** of the United States. Both domestically and internationally, the United States is incurring debt that would have been inconceivable only a decade ago. For example, in the 1970s, the accumulation of financial resources by the Arab nations was of major concern in the United States. Congressional hearings focused on whether Arab money was "buying out America." At that time, however, Arab holdings in the United States were $10 to $20 billion. Current rapid accumulation of dollars by foreigners in the United States is leading to much more significant shifts in foreign holdings.

In 1985, the United States became a net negative investor internationally. The United States entered the 1990s with an international debt burden of more than $800 billion, making it the largest debtor nation in the world, owing more to other nations than all the developing countries combined. Mitigating this burden are the facts that most of these debts are denominated in U.S. dollars and that, even at such a large debt volume, U.S. debt-service requirements are only a small portion of GNP. Yet this accumulation of foreign debt may very well introduce entirely new dimensions into the international relationships of individuals and nations. Once debt has reached a certain level, the creditor, as well as the debtor, is hostage to the loans.

Because foreign creditors expect a return on their investment, a substantial portion of future U.S. international trade activity will have to be devoted to generating sufficient funds for such repayment. For example, at an assumed interest rate or rate of return of 10 percent, the international U.S. debt level—without any growth—would require the annual payment of $80 billion, which amounts to about 13 percent of current U.S. exports. It thus seems highly likely that international marketing will become a greater priority than it is today and will serve as a source of major economic growth for firms in the United States.

To some degree, foreign holders of dollars may also choose to convert their financial holdings into real property and investments in the United States. This will result in an entirely new pluralism in U.S. society. It will become increasingly difficult and, perhaps, even unnecessary to distinguish between domestic and foreign products—as is already the case with Hondas made in Ohio. Senators and representatives, governors, municipalities, and unions will gradually be faced with conflicting concerns in trying to develop a national consensus on international trade and marketing. National security issues may also be raised as major industries become majority-owned by foreign firms.

At the same time, the U.S. international debt situation will, among other things, contribute to an increasingly tight money supply around the world. When combined with the financial needs of the emerging Eastern European market economies, the money required for the reconstruction of Kuwait and Iraq, the fund flows to the Commonwealth of Independent States, and the aid requirements of many developing nations, a more heated competition for capital is likely to emerge, with continuing scarcity leading to relatively high real interest rates worldwide. Industrialized countries are likely to attempt to narrow the domestic gap between savings and investments through fiscal policies. Without concurrent restrictions on international capital flows, such policies are likely to be of only limited success. Lending institutions can be expected to become more conservative in their financing, a move that may hit smaller firms and developing countries the hardest. Comparatively easier access to better financial resources will become a key competitive determinant and perhaps even be critical to the survival of many companies. At the same time, firms are likely to upgrade their currency-risk-management systems, review their asset-formation strategies, and formulate more flexible international sourcing and logistics strategies with a high degree of responsiveness to changing exchange rates.

The Societal Environment

The population discrepancy between less-developed nations and the industrialized countries will continue to increase. In the industrialized world, **population growth** will become a national priority, given the fact that in many countries, particularly in Western Europe, the population is shrinking rather than increasing. This shrinkage may lead to labor shortages and to major societal difficulties in providing for a growing elderly population.

In the developing world, the reduction of population growth will continue to be one of the major challenges of governmental policy. In spite of well-intentioned economic planning, continued rapid increases in population will make it more difficult to ensure that the pace of economic development exceeds population growth. If we determine the standard of living of a nation by dividing the GNP by its population, any increase in the denominator will require equal increases in the numerator to maintain the standard of living. Therefore, if the population's rate of growth continues at its current pace, even greater efforts must be made to increase the economic activity within these nations. With an annual increase in the world population of 100 million people, this task is daunting. It becomes even more complex when one considers that within countries with high population increases, large migration flows take place from rural to urban areas. As a result, by the end of this decade, most of the world's ten largest metropolitan areas will be in the developing world.[3]

Another problem of many less-developed countries is an **expectation-reality gap** felt by their population. Because the persistence of unfulfilled expectations fosters discontent, these countries must close the gap. This can be accomplished either by improving economic reality—that is, offering more goods at lower prices and increasing the general standard of living—or by reducing the expectations. Although nations will attempt to improve the living standards of their people, substantial efforts to reduce expectations also appear quite likely. The efforts to reduce expectations may increasingly require the use of de-marketing techniques on a national level. The goal would be the reduction of communication that fosters expectations—a quite difficult task, as explained below—and a conscientious restriction of the products and services offered or permitted.

The Technological Environment

The concept of the global village is commonly accepted today and indicates the importance of communication in the technological environment. It is already feasible to build satellite dishes out of easily obtainable components. The rapid growth of telefax machines, portable telephones, and computer communication devices points to the evolution of unrestricted communication flows. The importance of these technologies is driven home when one considers that since 1991, the fax traffic between the United States and Europe exceeded voice traffic.[4]

Concurrently, the availability of information to be communicated is increasing dramatically. Already more than 6,200 data bases are available worldwide.[5] Because all of this information includes details about life-styles, opportunities, and aspirations, international communication will be a great equalizer in the future.

Changes in other technologies will be equally rapid and will have a major effect on business in general. The appearance of superconductive materials and composite materials has made possible the development of new systems in fields such as transportation and electric power, pushing the frontiers of human activity into as yet unexplored areas such as outer space and the depths of the oceans. The development of biotechnology is

---

[3] *State of World Population,* United Nations Population Fund, London, 1993.

[4] John Naisbitt, *Global Paradox* (New York: Morrow and Co., 1994), 97.

[5] Mary C. Inoussa, "Electronic Database Services," *U.S. Industrial Outlook* (Washington, D.C.: U.S. Government Printing Office, 1992), 26–2.

already leading to revolutionary progress not only in agriculture, medicine, and chemistry but also in manufacturing systems within industry.[6]

High technology is expected to become one of the more volatile areas of economic activity. Order of magnitude changes in technology can totally wipe out private and public national investment in a high-technology sector. In the hard-hitting race toward technological primacy, some nations will inevitably fall behind, and others will be able to catch up only with extreme difficulty.

Even firms and countries that are at the leading edge of technology will find it increasingly difficult to marshal the funds necessary for further advancements. For example, investments in semiconductor technology are measured in billions rather than millions of dollars and do not bring any assurance of success. Not to engage in the race, however, will mean falling behind quickly in all areas of manufacturing when virtually every industrial and consumer product is "smart" due to its chip technology.

To spread the necessary financial commitments and to reduce the risk of permanent losses by participants in the race, firms will increasingly share technology provided that payment is made for shared information. In addition, cooperative agreements, joint ventures, and strategic partnerings will proliferate. Concurrently, governments will increase their spending on research and development and further techno-nationalism through the creation of more sources of technological innovation within their boundaries. Government-sponsored collaborative research ventures are likely to increase across industries and country groupings. However, difficulties may emerge when global firms threaten to rapidly internationalize any gains from such regionalized research ventures.

CHANGES IN TRADE RELATIONS

In spite of the Uruguay Round's conclusion, the international trade framework will remain under siege in the years to come. Key problems will be ongoing major imbalances in international trade flows and the need to incorporate newly industrialized and the former socialist countries into its structure.

A key question will be whether the World Trade Organization (WTO) will be sufficiently restructured to accommodate new challenges. **Multilateral trade negotiations** are essential to the survival of the multilateral trade system. Given the diverging interests of the participants in trade negotiations, however, widespread interest and support are difficult to generate. If trade relations cannot be continued on a multilateral basis, bilateral agreements and treaties will become more prevalent. As a result, protectionism would increase on a global scale as individual industrial policies are followed, and the volume of international trade would decline.

The international consensus in support of the WTO may also diminish in light of strengthened regional trading blocs. Disillusioned with the diversity of WTO members, some of the major trade players or blocs may form a new global trading system that will incorporate the largest portion of world trade volume. Smaller countries could then negotiate gradual access to such a new system. Such a scenario may still provide a bright outlook for international business in most developed nations, but it could cause major problems for firms in the developing world.

International trade relations will also be shaped by new participants bringing with them the potential to restructure the composition of trade. For example, new entrants with exceptionally large productive potential, such as the CIS and Central Europe, may

---

[6] Shinji Fukukawa, *The Future of U.S.-Japan Relationship and Its Contribution to New Globalism* (Tokyo: Ministry of International Trade and Industry, 1989), 10–11.

substantially alter world trade flows. The international firm may be required to change many trading practices as a result but may also benefit in terms of both market and sourcing opportunities.

Finally, the efforts of governments to achieve self-sufficiency in economic sectors, particularly in agriculture and heavy industries, have ensured the creation of long-term, worldwide oversupply of some commodities and products, many of which had historically been traded widely. As a result, after some period of intense market-share competition aided by subsidies and governmental support, a gradual and painful restructuring of these economic sectors will have to take place. This will be particularly true for agricultural cash crops such as wheat, corn, and dairy products and industrial products such as steel, chemicals, and automobiles. In light of the new trade potential emanating from the new market entrants discussed above, these adjustments will need to be made rapidly and thoroughly if a new and effective world order is to result.

GOVERNMENTAL POLICY

A clear worldwide trend exists toward increased management of trade by governments. International trade activity now affects domestic policy more than in the past. Governments, in their desire to structure their domestic economic activity, will be forced to intervene more and more in international markets. For example, trade flows can cause major structural shifts in employment. As a result of these shifts, other industries subsequently begin to undergo similar structural readjustments. Changes in automobile purchases will soon also affect the steel industry, and shifts in the sourcing of textiles will affect the cotton industry. As a result, changes in international trade will force many industries to restructure their activities and their employment because of productivity gains and competitive pressures. Yet such restructuring is not necessarily negative. Since the turn of the century, farm-sector employment in the United States dropped from more than 40 percent of the population to less than 3 percent. At the same time, the farm industry feeds 250 million people in the United States and produces large surpluses. A restructuring of industries can therefore greatly increase productivity and competitiveness and can provide the opportunity for resource allocation to newly emerging sectors of an economy.

Governments cannot be expected, for the sake of the theoretical ideal of "free trade," to sit back and watch the effects of de-industrialization on their countries. The most that can be expected is that they will permit an open-market orientation, subject to the needs of domestic policy. Even an open-market orientation is maintainable only if governments can provide reasonable assurances to their firms and citizens that this openness applies not only to their own markets but to foreign markets as well. Therefore, unfair trade practices, such as governmental subsidization, dumping, and industrial targeting, will be examined more closely, and retaliation for such activities will be increasingly swift and harsh.

Increasingly, governments will attempt to coordinate policies that affect the international marketing environment. The development of international indexes and trigger mechanisms, which precipitate government action at predetermined intervention points, will be a useful step in that direction. Yet for these to be effective, governments will need to muster the political fortitude to implement the policies necessary for successful cooperation. For example, international monetary cooperation will work, in the long term, only if domestic fiscal policies are responsive to the achievement of the coordinated goals.

At the same time as the need for collaboration among governments grows, it will become more difficult to achieve a consensus. In the Western world, the time from 1945 to 1990 was characterized by a commonality of purpose. The common defense against the communist enemy remanded trade relations to second place and provided a bond that encouraged collaboration. With the common threat gone, however, the bonds have also been diminished if not dissolved, and the priority of economic performance has increased. Unless a new key jointness of purpose can be found by governments, collaborative approaches will become increasingly difficult.[7]

Governmental policymakers must understand the international repercussions of domestic legislation. For example, the imposition of a special surcharge tax on the chemical industry designed to provide for the cleanup of toxic-waste products will need to be carefully considered in light of its repercussions on the international competitiveness of the chemical industry. Similarly, antitrust laws should be revised if these laws hinder the international competitiveness of domestic firms.

Policymakers also need a better understanding of the nature of the international trade issues confronting them. Most countries today face both short-term and long-term trade problems. Trade balance issues, for example, are short term in nature, whereas competitiveness issues are much more long term. All too often, however, short-term issues are attacked with long-term trade policy mechanisms, and vice versa. In the United States, for example, the desire to "level the international playing field" with mechanisms such as a strike force, vigorous implementation of import restrictions, or voluntary restraint agreements may serve long-term competitiveness well but does little to alleviate the publicly perceived problem of the trade deficit. Similarly, a further opening of Japan's market to foreign corporations will have only a minor immediate effect on that country's trade surplus or the U.S. trade deficit. Yet it is the expectation and hope of many in both the public and the private sectors that such immediate changes will occur. For the sake of the credibility of policymakers, it becomes therefore increasingly imperative to precisely identify the nature of the problem, to design and use policy measures that are appropriate for its resolution, and to communicate the hoped-for results.

Governments are likely to jawbone interindustry cooperation. For example, industries that benefit from the free-trade stance of their government currently reap those benefits without any quid pro quo. At the same time, firms that lose out in the free-trade environment are left to fend for themselves. Increasingly, it can be expected that governments will aim at a cross-fertilization between the industries benefiting and losing from free trade. This may mean that firms that are successful internationally will be asked to consider locating new plants or capacity expansion in those areas that suffer from high unemployment as a result of foreign competition. If quiet admonitions are not helpful in obtaining such objectives, governments may be substantially less enthusiastic in fighting for market access for their own industries abroad.

In the years to come, governments will be faced with an accelerating technological race and with emerging problems that seem insurmountable by individual firms alone, such as pollution of the environment and global warming. As a result, it seems likely that the concepts of administrative guidance and **government-corporate collaboration** will increasingly become part of the policy behavior of governments heretofore pledged to believe only in the invisible hand of the free market. Governments will be expected to assume a variety of supporting postures toward the international marketer, leading to more coordinated business-government marketing efforts.[8] The international marketer

[7] Michael R. Czinkota, "Rich Neighbors, Poor Relations," *Marketing Management,* Spring 1994, 46–52.

[8] William Lazer, "Changing Dimensions of International Marketing Management—The New Realities," *Journal of International Marketing* 1 no. 3 (1993): 93–103.

will in turn have to spend more time and effort dealing with governments and with macro rather than micro issues.

THE FUTURE OF INTERNATIONAL MARKETING MANAGEMENT

International change results in an increase in international risk. One shortsighted alternative for risk-averse managers would be the termination of international activities altogether. However, businesses will not achieve long-run success by engaging only in risk-free actions. Furthermore, other factors make the continuance of international marketing highly probable.

International markets continue to be a source of high profits, as a quick look at the list of Fortune 500 firms shows. International markets help cushion slack in domestic sales resulting from recessionary or adverse domestic market conditions. International markets also provide firms with foreign experience that helps them compete more successfully with foreign firms in the domestic market. Finally, international activities are necessary to compensate for foreign product and service inflows into the economy and to at least contribute to an equilibration of the balance of trade. As long as supply potential exceeds demand on an international level, an inherent economic motivation will exist for international marketing.

International Planning and Research

The focus on the customer will remain a major factor in marketing. The international marketer must continue to serve customers well. At the same time, governmental demands will increasingly intrude in the international marketing arena. This means that the international marketing manager will have to take general governmental concerns much more into account when planning a marketing strategy.

The diverging needs of foreign consumers will result in more available niches in which firms can create a distinct international competence. This points toward increased specialization and segmentation. Firms will attempt to fill very narrow and specific demands or to resolve very specific problems for their international customers. Identifying and filling these niches will be easier in the future because of the greater availability of international research tools and information.

The international marketer will also increasingly face problems of social responsibility. Governmental forces will demand that private marketing practices not increase public costs. Governments will expect marketers to serve their customers equally and nondiscriminately.[9] This concept runs directly counter to marketers' desire to serve first the markets that are most profitable and least costly. International marketers will therefore be torn in two directions, and in order to provide results that are acceptable both to customers and to the societies they serve, they must walk a fine line, balancing the public and the private good.

International Product Policy

The key issue affecting product planning will be environmental concern. Major growth in public attention paid to the rapid deterioration of the natural environment, environmental pollution, and global warming will provide many new-product opportunities and

---

[9] Robert Bartels, *Global Development and Marketing* (Columbus, OH: Grid Publishing, 1981), 111.

affect existing products to a large degree. Although many consumers will show a growing interest in truly "natural" products, even if they are less convenient, consumers in most industrialized nations will require products that are environmentally friendly but at the same time do not require too much compromise on performance and value. Management is likely to resist the additional business cost and taxes required for environmental protection, at least until investors and other constituent groups assure executives that environmental concern is acceptable even if it cuts into profit.

Two other trends are emerging in the product policies of multinational corporations. On one hand, automation and the search for increasing economies of scale demand that they serve more markets. Even large domestic markets such as the United States or Japan may be "too small to absorb the output of the world class automated plants needed for economies of scale in many product areas."[10] Europe, Japan, and the United States harbor the greatest buying power and demand concentration in the world for many products. These three regions account for nearly 85 percent of the world's demand for consumer-electronic goods; they consumed 85 percent of the computers and 70 percent of the machine tools produced in the world.[11] According to these facts, production should be concentrated in one of these regions and output widely distributed.

Although this trend would argue for greater exports and greater standardization of products, a counterargument holds that because of increasing protectionist policies and the desire of nations to obtain and develop their own technology, exports will be replaced by foreign direct investment.[12] If this is the case, marketing across international borders would be replaced in part by marketing abroad within foreign borders. As long as firms have the flexibility of choice of location, managers will have substantial leverage over domestic legislation and regulations that would affect their international marketing effort. Governments will run the risk of unemployment growth if domestic firms, because of an unsatisfactory **competitive platform,** move their operations abroad.

Regardless of which avenue firms take for marketing their products internationally, it appears certain that worldwide introduction of products will occur much more rapidly in the future. Already, **international product life cycles** have accelerated substantially. Whereas product introduction could previously be spread out over several years, firms now must prepare for product life cycles that can be measured in months or even weeks.[13] As a result, firms must design products and plan even their domestic marketing strategies with the length of the international product cycle in mind. Product introduction will grow more complex, more expensive, and more risky, yet the rewards to be reaped from a successful product will have to be accumulated more quickly.

Factor endowment advantages have a significant impact on the decisions of international marketers. Given the acceleration of product life cycles, nations with low production costs will be able to replicate products more quickly and cheaply. Countries such as India, Israel, and the Philippines offer large pools of skilled people at labor rates much lower than in Europe, Japan, or the United States. All this talent also results in a much wider dissemination of technological creativity, a factor that will affect the innovative capability of firms. For example, in 1993, nearly half of all the patents in the United States were granted to foreign entities. Table 24.1 provides an overview of the patents granted to foreign inventors.

---

[10] Kenichi Ohmae, "Only Triad Insiders Will Succeed," *New York Times,* November 2, 1984, 2f.

[11] Ibid.

[12] Bartels, *Global Development and Marketing,* 111.

[13] Michael R. Czinkota and Masaaki Kotabe, "Product Development the Japanese Way," in M. Czinkota and I. Roukainen, *International Marketing Strategy* (Fort Worth, TX: Dryden Press, 1994), 285–291.

U.S. Patents Granted to Foreign Inventors in 1993		**TABLE 24.1**	
Country	**Patents**	**Country**	**Patents**
Andorra	1	Jordan	0
Argentina	30	Kenya	3
Australia	433	Korea, Dem. Republic of	1
Austria	320	Korea, Republic of	789
Bahamas	4	Kuwait	2
Barbados	0	Lebanon	1
Belgium	351	Liechtenstein	14
Brazil	38	Luxembourg	37
British Virgin Islands	1	Malaysia	22
Bulgaria	5	Malta	2
Canada	2,198	Mauritius	1
Cayman Islands	0	Mexico	44
Chile	11	Monaco	6
China		Morocco	1
Mainland	58	Netherlands	961
Taiwan	1,423	Netherlands Antilles	0
Colombia	3	New Zealand	30
Costa Rica	3	Nicaragua	1
Cuba	1	Nigeria	0
Cyprus	1	Norway	120
Czechoslovakia	17	Oman	1
Denmark	288	Pakistan	0
Dominican Republic	0	Panama	1
Ecuador	1	Peru	2
Egypt	1	Philippines	6
Finland	328	Poland	7
France	3,165	Portugal	2
Germany	7,172	Romania	2
Greece	7	Russian Federation	2
Guatemala	1	Saudi Arabia	4
Guyana	0	Senegal	0
Honduras	1	Singapore	46
Hong Kong	174	Slovenia	1
Hungary	71	South Africa	89
Iceland	4	Soviet Union	68
India	21	Spain	160
Indonesia	7	Sri Lanka	3
Iran	1	Sweden	743
Ireland	63	Switzerland	1,193
Israel	350	Syria	0
Italy	1,452	Tanzania	1
Jamaica	0	Thailand	12
Japan	22,942	Trinidad and Tobago	0

Continued

TABLE 24.1	*Continued*			
Country	**Patents**			
Tunisia	0	Total patents issued in		
Turkey	0	U.S. 1993		107,332
United Arab Emirates	1	Total patents issued to		
United Kingdom	2,462	U.S. inventors		59,405
Uruguay	0	Total patents issued to		
Venezuela	28	foreign inventors		47,927
Yugoslavia	20	Foreign patents as a		
Zimbabwe	1	percentage of total		45%

Source: *Patent Counts by Country/State and Year, Design, Plant, and Reissue Patents,* Office of Information Systems, U.S. Patent and Trademark Office (Washington, D.C.: U.S. Government Printing Office, 1994).

This indicates that firms need to make such foreign know-how part of their production strategies, or they need to develop consistent comparative advantages in production technology in order to stay ahead of the game. Similarly, workers engaged in the productive process must attempt, through training and skill enhancement, to stay ahead of foreign workers who are willing to charge less for their time. However, this will be very difficult for a firm producing only in an industrialized country.

As a result, an increase will occur in the trend toward **strategic alliances,** or partnerings, permitting the formation of collaborative arrangements between firms. These alliances will enable firms to take risks that they could not afford to take alone, facilitate technological advancement, and ensure continued international market access. These partners do not need to be large in order to make a major contribution. Depending on the type of product, very small firms can serve as coordinating subcontractors and collaborate in product and service development, production, and distribution. For example, in the center of Europe, in Belgium, sits European Telecom, a company that allows customers to make international calls, by remote control by way of California, using American carriers. This saves customers one-third of the stiff European rates. European Telecom has only three employees and only $50,000 worth of equipment.[14]

International Communications

The advances made in international communications will have a profound impact on the international marketer. Entire industries are becoming more footloose in their operations; that is, they are less tied to their current location in their interaction with markets. For example, Best Western Hotels in the United States has channeled its entire reservation system through a toll-free number that is being serviced out of the prison system in Utah. Companies could as easily concentrate their communications activities in other countries. Communications for worldwide operations, for example, could be located in Africa or Asia and not impair international corporate activities.

[14] Naisbitt, *Global Paradox,* 18.

Staff in different countries not only can talk together but also can share pictures and data on their computer screens. Worldwide rapid product development therefore becomes technically feasible. Technology also makes it possible to merge the capabilities of computers, televisions, and telecommunications. Communication costs are likely to decrease significantly at the same time that the capabilities of communication tools increase. As a result, firms will have the opportunity for worldwide data exchange and will benefit from a virtually unlimited availability of detailed market and customer data. The challenge will then be to see who can best use and apply information technology.

Armed with all this information, marketers will be able to combine disparate data sources to create profiles down to the level of the individual consumer in order to respond to market requirements and exceed competitors' service.

Distribution Strategies

Worldwide distribution systems are beginning to emerge. Currently, only a few integrated systems, labeled sea bridges and land bridges, are operational. However, major trading routes that offer substantial distribution economies of scale are being developed. International marketers will experience relative ease in distribution as long as they stay within the established routes but will encounter difficulties when attempting to deviate from the routes. Customers who are on the routes will in turn benefit from the low cost of distribution and will see their choice of products widened. More distant customers may have their product choices reduced and pay increased prices for foreign products. Because of a lack of international competition, they will also have to live with high prices for domestic products.

The distribution systems will often become the deciding factor in whether markets can be served. Because communications advances will ensure that the customers in different markets are informed about product availability, distribution limitations will become even more painful.

More-sophisticated distribution systems will also offer new management opportunities to firms but, at the same time, introduce new uncertainties and fragilities into corporate planning. The development of just-in-time delivery systems will make firms more efficient yet, on an international basis, also expose them to more risk due to distribution interruptions. A strike in a faraway country may therefore be newly significant for a company depending on the timely delivery of supplies.

International Pricing

Many products, as they become distributed more widely throughout the world, will take on commodity characteristics, as semiconductors did in the 1980s. Therefore, price differentials of one cent per unit may become crucial in making international sales. However, because many new products and technologies will address completely new needs, firms will be forced to engage in forward pricing by distributing development cost over the anticipated volume of sales. This task will become increasingly difficult and controversial because demand levels for totally new products are impossible to predict accurately, with the result that firms will be open to charges of dumping.

Even for consumer products, price competition will be substantial. Because of the increased dissemination of technology, the country of origin of the manufacture will no longer be able to justify higher prices; domestically produced products of similar or equal quality will be quickly introduced. As a result, exchange rate movements may play more significant roles in maintaining the competitiveness of the international firm. Firms can be expected to prevail on their governments to manage the country's currency in order to produce a favorable exchange rate or to compensate them for the effects of adverse currency fluctuations.

Government management of trade will continue to influence international pricing in other ways. Through subsidization, targeting, and government contracts, nations will attempt to stimulate their international competitiveness. Because of the price sensitivity of many products, the international marketer will be forced to identify such unfair practices quickly, communicate them to his or her government, and insist on either similar benefits or government negotiation of an internationally level playing field.

Concurrently, however, international marketers will continue to differentiate themselves in the market on a nonprice basis. Major efforts will be undertaken to appeal to the market via services, quality, or other special aspects rather than on price alone. By accomplishing such an objective successfully, a firm can buy itself freedom from short-term fluctuations in its business relationships.

CAREERS IN INTERNATIONAL MARKETING

The student reader of this book, it is hoped, has learned about the intricacies, complexities, and thrills of international marketing. Of course, a career in international marketing does not consist only of jet travel between Rome, London, and Paris. It is hard work and requires knowledge and expertise. Globalites need to be well versed in the specific business functions and may wish to work at summer internships abroad, take language courses, and travel not simply for pleasure but to observe business operations abroad and to gain a greater understanding of different peoples and cultures. But as the International Marketplace 24.2 shows, there can also be great fulfillment in working abroad.

Further Training

One option for the student is to obtain further in-depth training by enrolling in graduate business school programs that specialize in international business education. Even though the international orientation of U.S. universities is relatively recent, a substantial number of schools have developed specific international programs. In addition, universities abroad specialize in developing international managers. INSEAD in France, the London Business School in England, the University of Western Ontario in Canada, IMEDE in Switzerland, and the Stockholm School of Economics are only a few examples of such universities.[15]

Many organizations are able to assist students interested in studying abroad or in gathering foreign work experience. Apart from individual universities and their programs for study abroad, various nonprofit institutions stand ready to help and to provide informative materials. Table 24.2 lists some of the programs and institutions that can be contacted.

---

[15] Donald A. Ball and Wendell H. McCulloch, Jr., "International Business Education Programs in American and Non-American Schools: How They Are Ranked by the Academy of International Business," *Journal of International Business Studies* 19 (Summer 1988): 295–299.

THE INTERNATIONAL MARKETPLACE   24.2

Women Excel in International Marketing

Women may do better managing abroad than they do at home according to research by Nancy Adler, management professor at McGill University in Montreal and author of a book on the subject. Despite expectations that the opposite would be true, in other countries, women are viewed first as foreigners and second as women. Because they are foreign, they are free of cultural expectations and can adopt the management style that suits them.

Of the 100 expatriate women managers studied by Adler, only 20 say being a woman is a disadvantage; almost half find it to be an advantage. One woman reports that in India and Pakistan, "I got in to see customers because they had never seen a female banker before." The biggest barriers, in fact, came from the home offices in the United States and Canada where executives are still reluctant to give women assignments abroad.

Nan Hunter, a field sales and operations director for Lancôme in Paris, feels freer bypassing cultural norms than she would in the United States. As an American in France, she can joke without it being perceived as a sexual advantage. She says, "You can crush people if you have to. They say, 'She's just an aggressive American woman.'"

Karla Barker is managing director of an AT&T Power Systems plant in Mexico. "They hadn't had a woman plant manager [before]. It still bothers some of the men. But then it does in the United States too," says Barker. Being a woman "doesn't hurt my position in the plant, and when I think there are important things I should be a part of, then I step in without being invited." And so far this has worked for her.

Only about 6 percent of expatriate North American managers are women, double the percentage in the mid-1980s according to Adler's research. Women managers tend to be clustered in a few companies such as AT&T Power Systems, but placements are increasing. Adler gives the following advice to women managers abroad: Be excellent at what you do and be "gently persistent." Assume your employer is naive about how you will be treated, and keep educating your employer about the advantages. In terms of advice for companies, do not assume that a promising woman candidate will not want to be uprooted. Adler found no difference between men and women in willingness to take foreign assignments; women may simply want a different package of benefits.

Source: Diana Kunde, "Management Opportunities for Women Brighten," *The Washington Post,* December 19, 1993, H2.

In addition, as the world becomes more global, an increasing number of scholarships and exchange programs become available and enable more people to gain international exposure. Table 24.3 lists some key exchange programs funded by the United States and the eligible participants.

For those ready to enter or rejoin the "real world," different employment opportunities need to be evaluated.

TABLE 24.2   Some Information Sources for Study and Travel Abroad

Where to Write

For information on year-off programs, contact youth groups, trade associations, embassies, travel and scientific groups, and educational foundations. Here are a few sources:

American Institute for Foreign Study
102 Greenwich Avenue
Greenwich, CT 06830
(203) 869-9090

British American Educational Foundation
351 East 74th Street
New York, NY 10021
(212) 772-3890

Center for Interim Programs
233 Mount Lucas Road
Princeton, NJ 08540
(609) 924-0441

Dynamy
57 Cedar Street
Worcester, MA 01609
(617) 755-2571

Earthwatch Expeditions Inc.
680 Mount Auburn Street
Box 403N
Watertown, MA 02272
(617) 926-8200

Foundation for Field Research
787 South Grade Road
Alpine, CA 92001
(619) 445-9264

Institute of International Education
809 United Nations Plaza
New York, NY 10017
(212) 883-8200

International Christian Youth Exchange
134 West 26th Street
New York, NY 10001
(212) 206-7307

Kibbutz Aliya Desk
27 West 20th Street, Ninth Floor
New York, NY 10011
(212) 255-1338

Open Door Student Exchange
250 Fulton Avenue, P.O. Box 71
Hempstead, NY 11551
(516) 486-7330

Up With People
3103 North Campbell Avenue
Tucson, AZ 85719
(602) 327-7351

Volunteers in Service to America
VISTA
Washington, D.C. 20525
(202) 634-9108
or contact your state ACTION office

What to Read

Academic Year Abroad, Institute of International Education, New York, NY, $16.95: Lists more than 1,100 study programs from eight weeks to a full year. IIE also publishes *Vacation Study Abroad,* $19.95, which lists more than 1,000 summer and short-term programs at all post-secondary-education levels.

Advisory List of International Educational Travel and Exchange Programs, Council on Standards for International Educational Travel, 1906 Association Drive, Reston, VA 22091, $5: Describes and evaluates 36 international organizations that run travel and study programs for high-school students and graduates.

Archaeological Fieldwork Opportunities Bulletin, Archaeological Institute of America, 675 Commonwealth Avenue, Boston, MA 02215: $6, published annually. Forty pages describing worldwide digs and their sponsors, sites, and costs.

International Workcamp Directory, VFP International Workcamps, Belmont, VT 05730, $10 (includes membership): Booklet that lists Volunteer for Peace member work camps worldwide.

The Teenager's Guide to Study, Travel, and Adventure Abroad, Council on International Educational Exchange, St. Martin's Press, New York, NY, $8.95: A how-to book that describes more than 150 programs, their sponsors and costs, and housing; interviews with participants and their parents.

Transitions Abroad, P.O. Box 344, Amherst, MA 01004, published five times a year, $15: Articles and listings cover overseas programs, seminars, publications, tips on travel, relocating, finding work, housing.

Volunteer Vacations, Chicago Review Press, 814 North Franklin Street, Chicago, IL 60610, (312) 337-0747, $11.95: Lists volunteer organizations that offer science and community-service projects.

The Young American's Scholarship Guide to Travel and Learning Abroad, Intravco Press, 211 East 43rd Street, Suite 1303, New York, NY 10017, by mail only, $14.95: Lists about 70 organizations with wide variety of interim programs and information about fees, scholarships, and locations.

Inventory of U.S.-Funded International Exchange and Training Programs   TABLE 24.3

Agency and Name of Program	Eligible Participants						
	Under-graduate Students	Graduate Students	Other Students	Teachers	Professors	Researchers	Post-doctorate Scholars
Agency for International Development							
Thomas Jefferson Fellowship Program	X	X		X	X	X	X
Participant Training Program Europe	X	X		X	X	X	X
Regional Human Resources Program	X	X		X			
Department of Agriculture							
Research and Scientific Exchange Program		X		X	X	X	X
Department of Commerce							
Exchange Visitor Program						X	
Special American Business Internship Training Program							
Department of Defense							
International Military Education and Training Program		X		X	X		
National Security Education Program	X	X					X
Navy Exchange Scientist Program							
Professional Military Education Exchanges							
U.S. Military Academies Exchanges	X						
Department of Education							
Foreign Language and Area Studies Fellowship Program		X					
Fulbright-Hays Group Projects Abroad	X	X		X	X		
Fulbright-Hays Doctoral Dissertation Research Abroad		X					
Fulbright-Hays Faculty Research Abroad					X	X	X
Fulbright-Hays Seminars Abroad				X	X		
Department of Health and Human Services							
International Research Fellowships						X	
Senior International Fellowships					X	X	
Scholars in Residence					X	X	
National Research Service Awards							
Visitor and Training Program							
Individual Health Scientist Exchanges and Biomedical Research Programs					X	X	
Visiting Program						X	
National Institutes of Health-French Postdoctoral Fellowship					X	X	

Continued

TABLE 24.3   *Continued*

Agency and Name of Program	Under-graduate Students	Graduate Students	Other Students	Teachers	Professors	Researchers	Post-doctorate Scholars
Inter-American Foundation							
Academic Fellowship Program		X					
Department of the Interior							
U.S.-Russia Environmental Agreement						X	
U.S.-China Nature Conservation Protocol						X	
Japan-U.S. Friendship Commission							
Japan-U.S. Friendship Commission Grants		X		X	X	X	X
Department of Labor							
International Visitors Labor Studies							
National Endowment for the Arts							
U.S. Artists at International Festivals and Exhibitions							
U.S.-Japan Artist Exchanges							
International Projects Initiative							
Travel Grants Program							
U.S.-Mexico Artist Residencies							
British America Arts Association Fellowships							
National Endowment for the Humanities							
Elementary and Secondary Education in the Humanities				X			
Higher Education in the Humanities					X		
NEH Teacher-Scholars				X	X		
Foreign Language Education				X	X		
Travel to Collections					X		X
Interpretive Research					X	X	X
Summer Seminars for School Teachers				X			
International Research							X
Summer Stipends				X	X		X
Humanities Projects in Museums and Historical Organizations						X	
Summer Seminars for College Teachers					X	X	X
Fellowship for College Teachers and Independent Scholars				X	X	X	X
Humanities Projects in Media					X	X	
Public Humanities Projects					X	X	
Centers for Advanced Study							X
Fellowship for University Teachers				X	X		X
Humanities Projects in Libraries and Archives						X	

Continued **TABLE 24.3**

Agency and Name of Program	Eligible Participants						
	Under-graduate Students	Graduate Students	Other Students	Teachers	Professors	Researchers	Post-doctorate Scholars
National Science Foundation							
Summer Institute in Japan		X					
U.S.-India Exchange of Scientists					X	X	X
Smithsonian Institution							
Bureau Appointments	X	X					X
Wildlife Conservation and Management Training	X	X		X	X	X	X
Department of State							
Russian, Eurasian, and Eastern European Studies Program		X			X	X	X
U.S. Information Agency							
Fulbright Academic Program	X	X		X	X	X	X
International Visitors Program					X		
Citizens Exchanges	X	X		X	X		
Hubert H. Humphrey Fellowship							
Youth Programs	X		X				
University Affiliations Program					X	X	X
Performing Arts Exchanges							
Study of the United States				X	X		
Academic Specialist Program					X		
U.S. Speakers					X	X	
Media Training Program							
Arts America Program							
Fulbright Teacher Exchange				X			
Library Fellows Program							
English Teaching Fellow				X			
American Cultural Specialists							
Artistic Ambassadors							
Arts America Speakers							

Source: U.S. General Accounting Office, *Exchange Programs: Inventory of International Educational, Cultural and Training Programs* (Washington, D.C., June 1993).

Employment with a Large Firm

One career alternative in international marketing is to work for a large multinational corporation. These firms constantly search for personnel to help them in their international operations. For example, a Procter & Gamble recruiting advertisement published in a university's student newspaper is reproduced in Figure 24.2.

Many multinational firms, while seeking specialized knowledge like languages, expect employees to be firmly grounded in the practice and management of business. Rarely, if ever, will a firm hire a new employee at the starting level and immediately place him or her in a position of international responsibility. Usually, a new employee is expected to become thoroughly familiar with the company's internal operations before being considered for an international position. The reason a manager is sent abroad is that the company expects him or her to reflect the corporate spirit, to be tightly wed to the corporate

Advertisement Recruiting New Graduates
for Employment in International Operations

EN BUSCA DE SU TALENTO

Procter & Gamble
División de Peru/Latino America

¤ Más de 40 productos de consumo en Latino America como Pampers, Ace, Ariel, Crest, Head & Shoulders, Camay y Vicks.

¤El area tiene el mayor volumen de ventas entre todas las divisiones Internacionales de P&G.

¤Oportunidades de desarrollar una carrera profesional en areas como Mercadeo, Finanzas, Computación, Ventas, etc.

Buscamos individuos con Talento, Empuje, Liderazgo, y continuo afán de superación para posiciones permanentes o practicas de verano en Peru, Puerto Rico, México, Colombia, Venezuela, Brazil, Chile, etc.

Es muy importante que envies tu RESUME pronto ya que estaremos visitando tu Universidad en la primera semana de Noviembre.

¿QUE DEBES HACER?
Envia tu resume tan pronto como sea posible a la atencion de Ms. Cynthia Huddleston (MBA Career Services) antes del 18 de Octubre.

Source: *The Hoya*, Georgetown University, October 6, 1989, 2.

The Price of an Expatriate

TABLE 24.4

An employer's typical first-year expenses of sending a U.S. executive to Britain, assuming a $100,000 salary and a family of four:

Direct Compensation Costs	
Base salary	$100,000
Foreign-service premium	15,000
Goods and services differential	21,000
Housing costs in London	39,000*
Transfer Costs	
Relocation allowance	$5,000
Airfare to London	2,000
Cost of moving household goods	25,000
Other Costs	
Company car	$15,000
Schooling (two children)	20,000
Annual home leave (four people)	4,000
U.K. personal income tax	56,000*
Total	$302,000

Note: Additional costs often incurred aren't listed above, including language and cross-cultural training for employee and family and costs of selling home and cars in the United States before moving.

*Figures take into account payments by employee to company based on hypothetical U.S. income tax and housing costs.

Source: Joann S. Lublin, "Companies Try to Cut Subsidies for Employees," *The Wall Street Journal*, December 11, 1989, B1; information provided by Organization Resource Counselors Inc.

culture, and to be able to communicate well with both local and corporate management personnel. In this liaison position, the manager will have to be exceptionally sensitive to both headquarters and local operations. As an intermediary, the expatriate must be empathetic, understanding, and yet fully prepared to implement the goals set by headquarters.

It is very expensive for companies to send an employee overseas. As Table 24.4 shows, the annual cost of maintaining a manager overseas is about three times the cost of hiring a local manager. Companies want to be sure that the expenditure is worth the benefit they will receive, even though certainty is never possible.

Even if a position opens up in international operations, there is some truth in the saying that the best place to be in international business is on the same floor as the chairman at headquarters. Employees of firms that have taken the international route often come back to headquarters to find only a few positions available for them. Such encounters lead, of course, to organizational difficulties, as well as to financial pressures and family problems, all of which may add up to significant executive stress during reentry.[16] Although many firms depend on their international operations for a substantial amount of sales volume and profits, less than 2 percent of U.S. companies have an overseas placement plan for rising young executives. Some claim that only a handful of major U.S. companies have effective international management development programs. Given the fact that management development programs are scarce, it is not surprising that reentry programs are even more scarce and are often viewed as an unnecessary expense. Yet, as the International Marketplace 24.3 shows, corporate attitudes are changing. As firms recognize the importance of international assignments and the benefits which the returning expatriate can bring to the home office, more effective reentry programs are put in place.

---

[16] Michael G. Harvey, "Repatriation of Corporate Executives: An Empirical Study," *Journal of International Business Studies* 20 (Spring 1989): 131–144.

24.3

THE INTERNATIONAL MARKETPLACE

Managing International Careers

Much is said about the strategic and competitive necessity of an effective global work force. Yet even today, American companies are terribly behind when it comes to managing international careers. Tales abound, from horror stories of not being properly prepared to go abroad to returning home and finding little has changed.

There are signs, however, that attitudes toward international assignments may be changing among companies. International assignments are moving to the forefront of management and organizational dynamics. Companies are realizing that well-managed foreign assignments are a key element in developing global corporate competencies. Such assignments are linked with executive and leadership development to create an experienced and effective global work force. Once regarded as a surefire way for employees to earn a lot of money but fall short of the top slot, international assignments are gradually regarded as logical and required steps in career paths.

A major problem viewed by many is the fact that very few companies aggressively reorient those returning from foreign assignments. Most corporations have been reluctant to take full advantage of their repatriated employees' knowledge. Finding ways to integrate and refine the information gained abroad by employees and to infuse that knowledge into operations will be a worthwhile challenge to U.S. businesses.

Changing attitudes toward foreign assignments must begin at the top. An important element is to include globalization issues in senior management performance evaluations, complete with specific goals. At Armstrong World Industries Inc., for example, three group vice presidents are each responsible for a portion of the company's international business as well as for managing global executive teams that meet three or four times a year to discuss strategies, exchange competencies, and solve problems.

Senior executives who remain at home in the domestic market cannot end up driving the corporation. Expatriate professionals agree that top executives must have at least one formal international assignment, for three to five years, during their career. A high percentage of the top 200 people at Ford Motor Co. have had a foreign assignment or are foreign nationals working in another country. "It is not unusual to be at a meeting in Dearborn and find seven or eight participants from other countries; we value people if they have served abroad; we do it almost routinely," explains W. R. Gromer, director of executive development, management, and organizational planning at Ford.

As those who make the corporate policies gain more international exposure, it is hoped that the benefits returning expatriates can bring to the company will be realized. These benefits include the expertise gained from the necessity of becoming familiar with all aspects of the job. An expatriate is often on his or her own—more so than an American in a comparable position in a U.S. division who can rely on others nearby for expertise. The expatriate often comes back with knowledge of trade rules and regulations, business practices, joint venture methodology, as well as fluency in the language and customs of the host country.

Monsanto Company recently undertook a detailed change of its repatriation policy to better utilize the knowledge which employees have gained abroad. Repatriation begins 6 to 18 months prior to the employees' return so that planned jobs are waiting for them, and an extensive debriefing program is in place for the employees and their families. At a debriefing with peers and managers, recommendations are expected about global developments. Peers are expected to discuss the differences and changes that occurred in the organization while the expatriate was abroad. Managers are encouraged to free up expatriates for committees, work groups, and demonstrations where their knowledge is needed, over and above the employee's normal job.

Capitalizing on the expertise and valuable experience of the expatriate is a step that companies need to take in order to be truly globally oriented.

Source: Barbara Ettorre, "A Brave New World: Managing International Careers," *Management Review* (April 1993): 10–15.

Employment with a Small or Medium-Sized Firm

A second alternative is to begin work in a small or medium-sized firm. Very often, these firms have only recently developed an international outlook, and the new employee will arrive on the "ground floor." Initial involvement will normally be in the export field—evaluating potential foreign customers, preparing quotes, and dealing with mundane activities such as shipping and transportation. With a very limited budget, the export manager will only occasionally visit foreign markets to discuss marketing strategy with foreign distributors. Most of the work will be done by mail, via telex, by fax, or by telephone. The hours are often long because of the need to reach contacts overseas, for example, during business hours in Hong Kong. Yet the possibilities for implementing creative business methods are virtually limitless, and the contribution made by the successful export manager will be visible in the firm's growing export volume.

Alternatively, international work in a small firm may involve importing—finding new, low-cost sources for domestically sourced products. Decisions often must be based on limited information, and the import manager is faced with many uncertainties. Often, things do not work out as planned. Shipments are delayed, letters of credit are canceled, and products almost never arrive in exactly the form and shape anticipated. Yet the problems are always new and offer an ongoing challenge.

As a training ground for international marketing activities, there is probably no better place than a smaller firm. Ideally, the person with some experience may find work with an export-trading or export-management company, resolving other people's problems and concentrating virtually exclusively on the international arena.

Self-Employment

A third alternative is to hang up a consultant's shingle or to establish a trading firm. Many companies are in dire need of help for their international marketing effort and are quite prepared to part with a portion of their profits to receive it. Yet in-depth knowledge and broad experience are required to make a major contribution to a company's international marketing effort or to successfully run a trading firm. Specialized services that might be offered by a consultant include international market research, international strategic planning, or, particularly desirable, beginning-to-end assistance in international market entry or international marketing negotiations.

The up-front costs in offering such a service are substantial and are not covered by turnover but rather have to be covered by profits. Yet the rewards are there. For an international marketing expert, the hourly billable rate typically is as high as $250 for

TABLE 24.5   Global Price Comparison

A monthly guide to the cost of selected goods and services around the world. Exchange rate current as of February 18, 1991.

	Exchange U.S. $ =	Business Lunch for Two	Aspirin 100 Tablets	Whiskey 750 ml	Man's Haircut	Tooth-paste 3.5 oz.	Hotel 3 star	Taxi Ride 2 km	Cab: Airport to City Center	State Dept. per Diem	ORC per Diem
Anchorage, Alaska	$1.00	$18.00	$5.72	$22.93	$21.75	$1.43	$158.22	$3.88	$12.00	$133.00	$243.00
Athens, Greece	159.00	26.72	3.21	16.57	19.81	1.86	164.72	1.89	12.09	131.00	280.27
Brisbane, Australia	1.27	18.12	5.46	24.18	16.23	1.25	185.97	2.51	17.73	137.00	286.05
Chicago	1.00	15.00	4.71	12.20	29.00	1.49	207.00	2.50	21.00	127.00	290.00
Copenhagen	5.71	27.89	8.16	45.76	39.44	4.46	227.87	6.13	16.48	181.00	346.19
Doha, Qatar	3.65	19.74	2.98	n.a.[1]	17.68	1.17	102.80	2.74	20.00	153.00	178.45
Geneva	1.28	32.21	15.37	38.04	26.71	2.00	214.45	7.07	15.71	199.00	359.78
Hamburg, Germany	1.49	22.22	11.95	19.56	21.08	2.25	170.37	5.49	16.84	157.00	263.97
Harare, Zimbabwe	2.69	8.49	1.77	6.48	7.36	1.62	143.50	0.82	7.00	123.00	152.73
Hong Kong	7.80	20.25	5.31	18.52	35.24	0.80	231.32	1.03	7.69	196.00	332.82
Kampala, Uganda	567.96	15.21	6.94	9.11	12.59	2.96	159.00	n.a.[2]	n.a.[2]	154.00	241.20
Karachi, Pakistan	22.21	9.68	1.98	26.27	6.08	1.96	95.23	0.54	5.00	92.00	135.76
Kinshasa, Zaire	2182.65	21.64	5.00	30.41	18.90	3.33	196.18	n.a.[2]	n.a.[2]	291.00	238.28
La Paz, Bolivia	3.47	6.59	2.97	10.56	8.16	2.63	87.50	1.48	8.50	87.00	127.95
Lusaka, Zambia	48.50	6.95	0.91	16.98	5.13	2.23	126.50	n.a.[2]	n.a.[2]	143.00	196.43
Lyon, France	5.05	25.74	8.27	22.05	30.56	2.39	158.35	3.43	49.50	163.00	276.92
Melbourne, Australia	1.27	18.91	5.52	23.36	16.40	1.27	205.67	2.54	24.00	192.00	311.27
Noumea, New Caledonia	89.29	26.88	14.35	27.15	30.80	2.83	144.48	6.72	55.99	186.00	270.31
Oslo	5.80	20.22	8.99	58.74	41.80	3.71	234.75	10.50	27.00	229.00	272.66
Paris	5.05	32.26	8.47	23.13	31.27	2.44	266.43	3.51	37.61	218.00	459.42
Quito, Ecuador	952.93	5.00	1.39	13.16	3.62	1.13	112.80	0.32	3.00	68.00	142.19
Seattle	1.00	17.00	5.42	20.07	28.75	1.34	148.00	4.40	24.00	103.00	245.00
Seoul, South Korea	724.13	27.76	10.36	23.71	30.38	0.91	203.93	1.10	7.00	153.00	313.55
Shannon, Ireland	0.56	25.18	4.64	20.54	15.27	1.83	97.12	5.43	47.50[3]	153.00	224.82
Singapore	1.72	20.36	6.53	34.50	17.60	1.27	197.21	1.28	7.50	163.00	350.11

n.a. = Not Available.

[1] Whiskey not available in Doha, Qatar, because of Islamic laws.

[2] Business visitors would not usually use local taxis, but arrangements for transport to and from airport would be made through other private services.

[3] Cab fare is to Limerick, the nearest major city.

The goods and services shown above represent average prices in U.S. dollars in the countries shown and include sales tax and value-added tax where appropriate.

The items shown are part of 11 goods and services categories gathered internationally by Organization Resources Counselors Inc. and include food at home, food away from home, alcohol, domestic service, medical care, personal care, and recreation.

All research is conducted by Organization Resources Counselors Inc., a New York City–based management consulting firm specializing in human resources.

Source: *North American International Business*, May 1991, 27. All research conducted by Organization Resource Counselors, Inc.

experienced principals and $100 for staff. Whenever international travel is required, overseas activities are often billed at the daily rate of $2,000 plus expenses. The latter can add up quickly to a substantial amount, as Table 24.5 shows. When trading on one's own, income and risk can be limitless. Even at these relatively high rates, solid groundwork must be completed before all the overhead is paid. The advantage is the opportunity to become a true international entrepreneur. Consultants and owners of trading firms will work at a higher degree of risk than employees, but with the opportunity for higher rewards.

SUMMARY

This chapter has provided an overview of the environmental changes facing international marketers and alternative managerial responses to these changes. International marketing is a complex and difficult activity, yet it affords many challenges and opportunities. "May you live in interesting times" is an ancient Chinese curse. For the international marketer, this curse is a call to action. Observing changes and analyzing how best to incorporate them in the international marketing mission are the bread and butter of the international marketer. If the international environment were constant, there would be no challenge. The frequent changes are precisely what make international marketing so fascinating to those who are active in the field. It must have been international marketers who were targeted by the old Indian proverb "When storms come about little birds seek shelter, while eagles soar." May you be an eagle!

Questions for Discussion

1. For many developing countries, debt repayment and trade are closely interlinked. What does protectionism mean to them?

2. Should we worry about the fact that the United States is a debtor nation?

3. What are some alternatives for governments in closing the expectation-reality gap of the populace?

4. With low wages prevalent abroad, how can U.S. workers expect to compete?

5. How can you advocate free trade when 200,000 workers in the U.S. textile industry are losing their jobs to foreign competition?

6. Is international marketing segmentation ethical if it deprives the poor of products?

7. How would our lives and our society change if imports were completely banned?

Recommended Readings

Behrman, Jack N. *The Rise of the Phoenix*. Boulder, CO: Westview Press, 1987.

Boddewyn, Jean J. "Comparative Marketing: The First Twenty-five Years." *Journal of International Business Studies* 12 (Spring–Summer 1981): 61–79.

Czinkota, Michael R., and Ilkka Ronkainen, "Global Marketing 2000," *Marketing Management,* Winter 1992, 36–45.

Naisbitt, John. *Global Paradox*. New York: Morrow and Co., 1994.

Smith, Allen E., James M. MacLachlan, William Lazer, and Priscilla LaBarbera. *Marketing 2000: Future Perspectives on Marketing*. Chicago: American Marketing Association, 1989.

Thurow, Lester. *Head to Head, The Coming Economic Battle among Japan, Europe and America*. New York: Morrow and Co., 1992.

United States General Accounting Office. *Exchange Programs: Inventory of International Educational, Cultural and Training Programs*. Washington D.C., June 1993.

CASES

PART THREE

Kaline

....

Kaline is a joint venture undertaken by a Swedish firm and a large U.S. company, each owning 50 percent. Both parent firms are known for their high technological standards, although they specialize in somewhat different product lines.

Kaline was formed in 1970. The president of the U.S. firm wanted to start a company with a new product line and sought out the Swedish partner because of its reputation. When the joint venture was formed, a detailed contract was signed by the partners. Products to be produced and marketed were specified, as were the conditions for technical support and other services, dividend policy, and profit distribution. Both parties clearly stated how they saw the new venture as a major part of their mission. Half of the board of directors was to be elected by each party, the chairman was to be elected from the U.S. board members, and the chairman of the shareholders meeting was to be elected by the Swedish partner. All major decisions specified in the agreement required a qualified majority (two-thirds) of the board members.

The agreement also contained a divorce clause, which specified that "either party can take the initiative to sell its shares at a price named in the notice. Such offer may be accepted by the noninitiating party or the noninitiating party may treat the offer as binding the initiating party to buy the noninitiating party's shares at the same price. Conversely, the initiating party may offer to buy the other party's shares at a price named in a notice. Such offer may be accepted by the noninitiating party or the noninitiating party may treat the offer as binding the initiating party to sell its shares at the same price. In any event, offers and acceptances must be for all the shares of the party."

In the initial year of formation, the Swedish partners were enthusiastic about the formation of Kaline. Prior to the joint venture, sales of Kaline's product line were flat. Because of new production technology brought to the table by the U.S. partner, however, Kaline was able to produce in the United States about 30 percent cheaper than in Sweden, including shipping costs and duties. The U.S. partner also had a ready and functioning sales organization. The joint venture therefore pursued a policy of entering the market and gaining market share and volume through price cutting.

Two years after the signing of the joint venture contract, Kaline had several hundred employees. Sales were high, but financial results were disastrous. Both parents were unwilling to invest new equity. The president of the U.S. firm took over also as president of Kaline. The initiator of the joint venture, he also had an excellent personal relationship with the president of the Swedish partner. He made several visits to Sweden to clear the air and succeeded in obtaining more updated technological knowledge and production rights.

Kaline's lack of profits during these years had severe effects on the quality of its personnel. Kaline as well as the U.S. partner had bonus-pay plans that were based on the profitability of the firm. Because no bonuses were paid at Kaline, an exodus of managers from Kaline back to the profitable parent firm resulted. Kaline became known as the dumping ground for managers.

In the fourth year of the joint venture, a young engineer in the U.S. parent company who had taken evening classes in marketing met with the president of Kaline. He had

Source: Lars Otterbeck, "Management of Joint Ventures," presented at the seminar on the Management of Headquarters/Subsidiary Relationships in Transnational Corporations, Stockholm School of Economics, June 2–4, 1980, 27–32.

found that in some segments, Kaline's product was one of the three market leaders. He suggested that the only possible cure for Kaline was to segment the market, emphasize the unique features of the product, differentiate it slightly, and raise prices. This suggestion was quite contrary to the previous high-volume philosophy. Only through personal intervention by the president of the U.S. partner directly with the president of the Swedish firm was the necessary technology transferred and the new policy cleared.

This process was by no means easy. Because of their culture, the Swedish engineers were totally against the idea. Sharing know-how and sharing it with a company that did not understand that volume was the oxygen of business was an alien thought.

One year later, the young engineer was president of Kaline, the company was a price-leader, its volume had gone up in the midst of a recession, and the company was making money. This success gave independence. The following exchange of communications regarding reporting routines illustrates the point.

The headquarters of the Swedish parent had sent a memo on corporate reporting to Kaline. Kaline's president responded by letter. "Your memo strikes us wrong. In essence it dictates a rigid policy of outside and inside auditing. Perhaps you do not recognize that Kaline is somewhat unique in your organization. The shares are not owned in a majority by you. We do realize that as a separate matter you do own 2 percent shares of our U.S. parent. This, however, does not give you control of us. The above is a statement of the relationship as we see it. I do propose that Kaline continue to be cooperative."

On the day the letter was received, the controller of the Swedish parent sent the following telex to Kaline: "The memo was sent to you by mistake. We are well aware of the uniqueness of Kaline. It is my intention to visit your company to discuss these questions. I think such a discussion will further improve our already good cooperation."

Two weeks later, Kaline's president wrote the Swedish parent: "Thank you for your telex, which clears the air completely. We would very much welcome your visit to Kaline in the near future."

This letter was filed at the Swedish headquarters together with a memo from the controller: "We should not demand more information from Kaline than they are prepared to give us. If we want the same information that is required from other subsidiaries, the matter must probably be dealt with by the presidents of the two parents. I have talked to the president of Kaline. He has nothing against giving information on Kaline to us. But he does not want to change his reporting routines."

Questions for Discussion

1. How would you have changed the initial joint venture agreement?
2. Would you characterize the relationship between Kaline and its parent companies as formal or informal?
3. How can a firm retain the profit incentive while making allowance for start-up costs?
4. Is it a sensible policy to structure controls as a function of profitability?
5. Discuss the current interaction between Kaline and its parent companies. How can the goal of corporate synergy accommodate the need for individualism?

Benetton

Benetton, the Italian manufacturer of sportswear, has been in the center of controversy ever since its "United Colors" campaigns were launched in 1985 to symbolize the marketer's "commitment to racial and multicultural harmony."

Benetton has 6,300 stores around the world and sales of $1.5 billion, with a total marketing budget of $78 million. It has been one of the most dynamic marketing entities of the last decade. But it has been the company's advertising that has cemented its reputation as an offbeat, socially conscious firm.

In the fall of 1991, Benetton launched a new series of ads, created in-house, which included a priest kissing a nun; a placenta-covered newborn baby with an umbilical cord still attached; and what the company calls an "angelic" white girl and a "dark and mysterious" black boy, replete with devilish horns. The campaign was intended for 92 countries to constitute the majority of countries' promotional efforts. For example, the $3.5-million U.S. magazine campaign represented half of Benetton's local budget. "It's fair to say that this is the most provocative campaign we have ever mounted," said Peter Fressola, director of communications for Benetton Services Corp., the company's U.S. marketing arm. "The images are more provocative, and there seem to be more of them."

Although previous campaigns showing black and white men handcuffed together and a black woman breast-feeding a white baby had generated publicity, the storm broke with the most recent series of ads.

After the effort was launched, various governmental and industry bodies in the United Kingdom, France, Germany, Italy, and Ireland asked Benetton to withdraw the campaign. For example, in the United Kingdom, the Advertising Standards Authority (ASA) formally asked Benetton to stop using outdoor boards showing the newborn.

In the United States, magazine publishers refused to run some or all of the campaign. *Self* and *YM* rejected the priest/nun combo; *Cosmopolitan, Elle,* and *Child* all passed on the newborn ad; and *Essence, YM,* and *Child* passed on the angel/devil ad. "We rejected the ads because being a book geared to the younger market, I think the spotlight is put on us a little more than the adult books," said Alex Mironovich, publisher of teen magazine *YM.* "I am Catholic and I was not offended by the priest kissing the nun, but I have to recognize that religion is very powerful in a lot of people's lives."

In the letter rejecting the newborn ad, Mary Anne Sommers, publisher of *Child,* wrote, "Birth is still an extremely private and personal subject for Americans . . . and there was a strong likelihood the ad would not be favorably received by a good portion of our readers." She also rejected the angel/devil ad, contending the image "will be perceived by our readers as reinforcing, rather than helping to eliminate, negative racial stereotypes." Benetton and its agency, J. Walter Thompson, offered two ads to each magazine but said if one or both were rejected, they would not be replaced by others.

At Benetton, the response was that of surprise. "We were very surprised by this general hysteria created by the new campaign," said Laura Pollini, Benetton's spokesperson in the United Kingdom. In the United States, Peter Fressola denied that there was any attempt to stir trouble. The creator of the ads, Oliviero Toscani, was astonished by the

Source: This case was prepared by Ilkka A. Ronkainen. It is largely based on "Benetton on Bosnia," *The Washington Post,* February 16, 1994, C3; "Benettonin Shokkimainosta Paheksutaan," *Iltasanomat,* February 4, 1992, A14; Eleana Bowes, "Benetton Forges Ahead," *Advertising Age,* September 9, 1991, 14; Gary Levin, "Benetton Gets the Kiss-Off," *Advertising Age,* July 22, 1991, 1, 40.

reaction to the campaign. The newborn ad is a documentary-style bit of "ultra-reality," he said, and there is "nothing sinful" about a priest and a nun kissing. "I tried to show the beauty of human relations that goes beyond the inhibitions of religion or race." Benetton expressed its confidence in Toscani and vowed not to interfere with his provocative style.

In 1992, Benetton used a picture of a man who had three minutes earlier died of AIDS in its newest worldwide campaign. The ASA recommended that publishers in the United Kingdom boycott the campaign. In early 1994, Bennetton made waves throughout the world with its new ad featuring the blood-soaked clothes of a soldier killed in Bosnia. The photo, which shows a white T-shirt pierced by a bullet hole, as well as a pair of combat trousers, is part of a $15-million campaign in newspapers and on billboards in 110 countries. Immediately, five publications in France, including *Le Monde* and *Le Figaro,* and Germany's *Frankfurter Allgemeine Zeitung* refused to publish the ad. The Vatican newspaper *L'Osservatore Romano* denounced the ad, calling it "a horrendous poster that has managed to make a mockery even of death." In the United States, many newspapers, such as *The Washington Post,* ran the ad. Benetton's reaction was as unique as expected. The company spokesperson was not optimistic about the campaign's ability to boost retail sales, saying, however, "if we were trying to sell T-shirts, there probably wouldn't be a worse way of doing it."

Questions for Discussion

1. Do shock and publicity value fit in with global advertising campaigns?

2. Is Benetton facing a crisis in various country markets, or will it benefit from the outcry?

3. Are there ways in which the social message of Benetton could be conveyed in a less-provocative manner?

Establishing an Overseas Law Office

Stuffim & Bacom is a 20-year-old, 125-member law firm based in St. Paul, Minnesota. Aside from its home office, the firm maintains offices in Washington, D.C.; Denver, Colorado; and Paris, France. As in any major firm, there are many areas of practice, but the firm's fastest-growing section is its international business department. This department is headed by the firm's principal rainmaker and senior Washington partner, Harley Hambone, assisted by an aggressive junior partner, Sylvester Soupspoon, also based in Washington.

Stuffim & Bacom has just begun to acquire business on the African continent. Their biggest client, Safari Air Lines (SAL), is an international airfreight company with corporate headquarters in Abidjan, Ivory Coast. Last year, SAL was the major airfreight carrier for all of East, Central, and West Africa. Recently, Hambone, an international finance expert and master salesman, persuaded SAL to drop the law firm of Bend, Spindell & Mutilate, an old-line New York City firm, as the company's U.S. counsel and transfer all of SAL's business to the Stuffim firm. SAL is now almost a $1-million-per-year account for Stuffim & Bacom, which includes work with airline regulatory agencies in the United States, as well as general advice regarding international aviation matters.

In addition, Soupspoon, a transportation attorney, recently brought in Livingstone Tours Inc., a small but burgeoning U.S.-based travel agency specializing in three-month African safaris, as a new client. Livingstone maintains its only overseas office in Nairobi, Kenya. Stuffim bills Livingstone less than $500,000 per year, mainly for preparing and negotiating agreements with international charter airlines and local tour operators serving East Africa.

Due to their already substantial client obligations, as well as the sudden, unexpected growth in their business on the African continent and the impracticality of handling this work out of their Washington, D.C., office, Hambone and Soupspoon have decided to propose that the firm open an office in Africa to cover its growing client needs in that part of the world. This would not only enable the firm to better serve SAL and Livingstone Tours, but it would also help the firm garner more African business.

SAL and Livingstone Tours are each pressing Stuffim & Bacom to set up an African office as soon as possible, preferably close to their respective African operations. This will require the firm to invest $250,000 to start up an office, as well as yearly expenditures (including related overhead) of $125,000 per U.S. attorney and $75,000 per local attorney to staff it with qualified lawyers.

Establishing a foreign office is nothing new to Stuffim & Bacom. For almost ten years the firm has maintained an office in Paris, France. As with many foreign branches of U.S. law firms, the Paris office generates very little profit and is regarded by the firm as something of a prestigious "foreign outpost." The firm continues to maintain the Paris office at a break-even level, mainly for the benefit of one major client, Ali Nord, an Arab- and French-owned freight forwarding company with extensive business in the United States, Central America, and the Middle East.

Source: This case was written by William E. Casselman II, a senior attorney and shareholder in the law firm of Popham, Haik, Schnobrich & Kaufman, Ltd. (Washington office). Reprinted with permission. It is intended only to describe fictional business situations, and any resemblance to real individuals or business organizations is purely coincidental. The various economic, legal, political, and cultural conditions described in the case are for illustration only and do not necessarily reflect the actual conditions prevailing within the regions or countries mentioned.

The Paris office's only attorney, Sylvia Souffle, a senior partner and member of the Colorado bar, is qualified under French law to advise clients, such as Ali Nord, on questions of foreign and international law but may not appear in French courts or advise clients regarding French law. After ten years of general corporate practice in France, she has recently indicated her desire to leave the Paris office and head the proposed office in the Ivory Coast, a former French colony in West Africa. Souffle has many contacts in the Ivory Coast, where French is the official language.

The firm has also opened two other offices abroad, neither of which succeeded. The first office was opened six years ago in Saudi Arabia to represent U.S. engineering and construction firms doing business there. This branch closed after one year due to a lack of business stemming from a decline in the price of oil and threats from Middle East terrorists, who were upset over Stuffim's representation of Ali Nord, which they wrongly believed to be a CIA front. More recently, a heretofore unknown terrorist group announced in the Middle East that it would "go to the ends of the earth" to wreak revenge upon Ali Nord and its "yellow running dog lackeys of Yankee imperialism," including the Stuffim firm.

The second office was opened three years ago in Bangkok, Thailand, to service Torch & Glow Industries, a Colorado corporation and major provider of fire-resistant tiling and roofing materials. Torch & Glow had experienced an unanticipated boom in business in Southeast Asia. Therefore, Stuffim & Bacom opened a regional office in Bangkok with special permission of the Thai government to represent Torch & Glow in Thailand, and then only on matters not requiring appearances in the courts of Thailand. Unfortunately, a massive class-action suit was brought against Torch & Glow in both the United States and Thailand for damages caused by the unexplained flammability of the company's products when used in tropical climates. As a result, Torch & Glow recently went out of business, as did Stuffim's office in Bangkok. Both of these failures cost the firm a great deal of money in lost start-up expense and attorney and employee severance payments, and the firm's partners swore never again to open another overseas office.

Undaunted by these past failures, Hambone and Soupspoon wish to pursue the concept of a Stuffim & Bacom office in Africa. They have several options, which include but are not limited to the following: First, they could send a contingent of at least three Stuffim lawyers, possibly led by Souffle, to establish an Abidjan office. Unfortunately, none of the firm's current attorneys, other than Souffle, speaks adequate French. Second, they could recruit a group of SAL's in-house Ivory Coast lawyers from its headquarters in Abidjan, make them special partners in the Stuffim firm, and have them run Stuffim's office. Third, they could send one or more lawyers to open an office in Kenya, an English-speaking nation and former British colony, to work principally on the Livingstone account and secondarily on the SAL account. Fourth, they could form a joint venture with a Kenyan law firm to staff and run the Nairobi office.

Soupspoon, aware that Livingstone already employs a local law firm, Amen & Hadafly, to handle some of its legal needs in Kenya, approached that firm about its willingness to form a joint venture with Stuffim to run the Nairobi office. However, Amen & Hadafly, although personal friends of Soupspoon, would agree only on the condition that they receive full partnership status, not just a share of the local office profits to which special partners are entitled. In view of this demand, as well as Amen & Hadafly's somewhat questionable reputation in the Kenyan legal community, Hambone was reluctant to accept this offer. On the other hand, because Amen & Hadafly is well connected to the local legal establishment, it is unlikely that any other local firm would agree to such a joint venture. There are no joint venture possibilities in the Ivory Coast, owing to SAL's having its own in-house attorneys and preferring to work only with the Stuffim firm because of its expertise in international transportation law.

In addition to the differences in legal systems and languages, Kenya and the Ivory Coast also have different infrastructure conditions. For example, Nairobi has good tele-communications but a shortage of available office space. Abidjan is known for its modern office buildings but lacks the more up-to-date communications facilities found in Nairobi. Both countries enjoy roughly the same political and economic stability and have a generally favorable attitude toward foreign investment.

Further complicating matters, the laws of both the Ivory Coast and Kenya place serious restrictions on foreign law firms establishing local offices with foreign lawyers, requiring any foreign law firm to employ a majority of local lawyers or to ensure that their local office is managed by a local lawyer. Moreover, any foreign lawyer wishing to practice before the courts of either country has to be certified by the local bar association as being competent to do so (and no Stuffim lawyers are so certified in either the Ivory Coast or Kenya). There is one exception—any lawyer qualified in a comparable legal system can practice without satisfying the formal requirements. The United States common law system has not been recognized in the Ivory Coast, but, because of the Ivory Coast's close ties to France, the French code system has. Conversely, the Kenyan bar recognizes the English and U.S. systems, but not the French system. Of course, it might be possible to persuade either government to create an exception for a single Stuffim & Bacom client, as was done in Thailand for Torch & Glow.

Even if Hambone and Soupspoon could persuade the governments involved to permit them to practice locally without meeting local requirements, they would still have to persuade the rest of Stuffim & Bacom's partners that an African office is a good idea. In light of the two recent overseas office failures, the remaining partners, most of whom are in the St. Paul office, are not expected to enthusiastically embrace Hambone and Soupspoon's idea for an office in Africa.

The time has come for Hambone and Soupspoon to lay their idea on the line. Hambone has arranged meetings with government officials in the Ivory Coast and Kenya to negotiate an office in one of the two countries. Soupspoon must convince the Stuffim & Bacom partners of the merits of establishing an African office in the country selected by Hambone. You have been asked by Hambone and Soupspoon to prepare them for these crucial meetings.

Questions for Discussion

1. Advise Hambone of the various business, legal, political, and cultural obstacles standing in the way of opening an office in each country and how he can best overcome them. Also make a recommendation as to where you think the office should be located and how (and by whom) it should be staffed and operated.

2. Advise Soupspoon as to how he can convince his fellow partners that an African office will be profitable for the firm, if not in the short term, then in the long term. This would include the type of representation arrangements that the Stuffim firm should make with its clients in Africa to minimize its financial risk.

3. How do you believe Stuffim & Bacom, as a growing international law firm, should respond to terrorist threats?

Toys 'Я' Us in Japan

Jumping out of his car in an empty parking lot 40 miles from Tokyo, Larry R. Bouts stands back and admires the white, spanking-new building before him. "Can you believe this?" he exclaims. "Pretty amazing." At Ibaraki, the store and 850-car parking lot are massive by Japanese standards. The colorful, English-language Toys 'Я' Us signs jump out at passers-by.

It is indeed amazing, given what it took to get there. Bouts is president of the international division of Toys 'Я' Us, and the real estate he admires is the company's inaugural store in Japan—the very first large U.S.-owned discount store there. When the store opened on December 20, 1991, it had gone through the swaps of Japanese bureaucracy, local vested interests, labyrinthine real estate practices, and heavy, often hostile, Japanese press coverage. But at the same time, it was a payoff of the U.S.-inspired Structural Impediments Initiative aimed at prying open new markets for U.S. companies in Japan. "We hope Toys 'Я' Us will be the first in a long line of stores to locate in Japan," commented U.S. Commerce Secretary Robert A. Mosbacher.

THE INTERNATIONALIZATION OF RETAILING

One of the most important forces of change shaping retailing in the 1990s will be the continuing internationalization of what has been historically only a domestic activity. The prevailing view that retail companies should confine their activities to only their local, home market is increasingly difficult to reconcile in a period when both political and perceptual barriers are being lowered, if not removed completely.

Although internationalization has happened for the most part within the three trading blocs of Europe, North America, and the Far East, a trading pressure in one bloc does not preclude the possibility of exploiting opportunities elsewhere. Consumers in these areas are familiar with department store formats, limited-line convenience stores, and shopping mall developments. Many of these stores are trading everywhere under the same name, such as Benetton and 7-Eleven. These and other retailers trading in developed markets are facing similar sets of problems and employing common solutions to these problems, including such approaches as the effective application of information technology to enhance business efficiency and to increase sophistication in market segmentation and consumer targeting. Indeed, the transfer between retailers in different countries of trading formats, ideas, and practices is at least as significant in the internationalization of retailing as the physical presence of the same retailer in a number of countries. Those retail companies that continue to trade only in their home markets will be participants, however passive, in the overall internationalization process of retailing.

Growing by developing activities outside of the home market seems to be many retailers' preferred strategy to seeking diversification in the home market, with the notable exception of U.S. retailers, some of which have actually divested some of their international interests (e.g., Sears and J. C. Penney).

Sources: This case was prepared by Ilkka A. Ronkainen. It is largely based on Emily Thornton, "Revolution in Japanese Retailing," *Fortune*, February 7, 1994, 143–146; "What? Everyday Bargains? This Can't Be Japan," *Business Week*, September 6, 1993, 41; "Guess Who's Selling Barbies in Japan Now," *Business Week*, December 9, 1991, 85–86; Alan D. Treadgold, "The Developing Internationalisation of Retailing," *International Journal of Retail & Distribution Management* 18 (1990): 4–11; T. M. Robinson and C. M. Clarke-Hill, "Directional Growth by European Retailers," *International Journal of Retail & Distribution Management* 18 (1990): 3–14.

FIGURE 1   A Typology of International Retailers

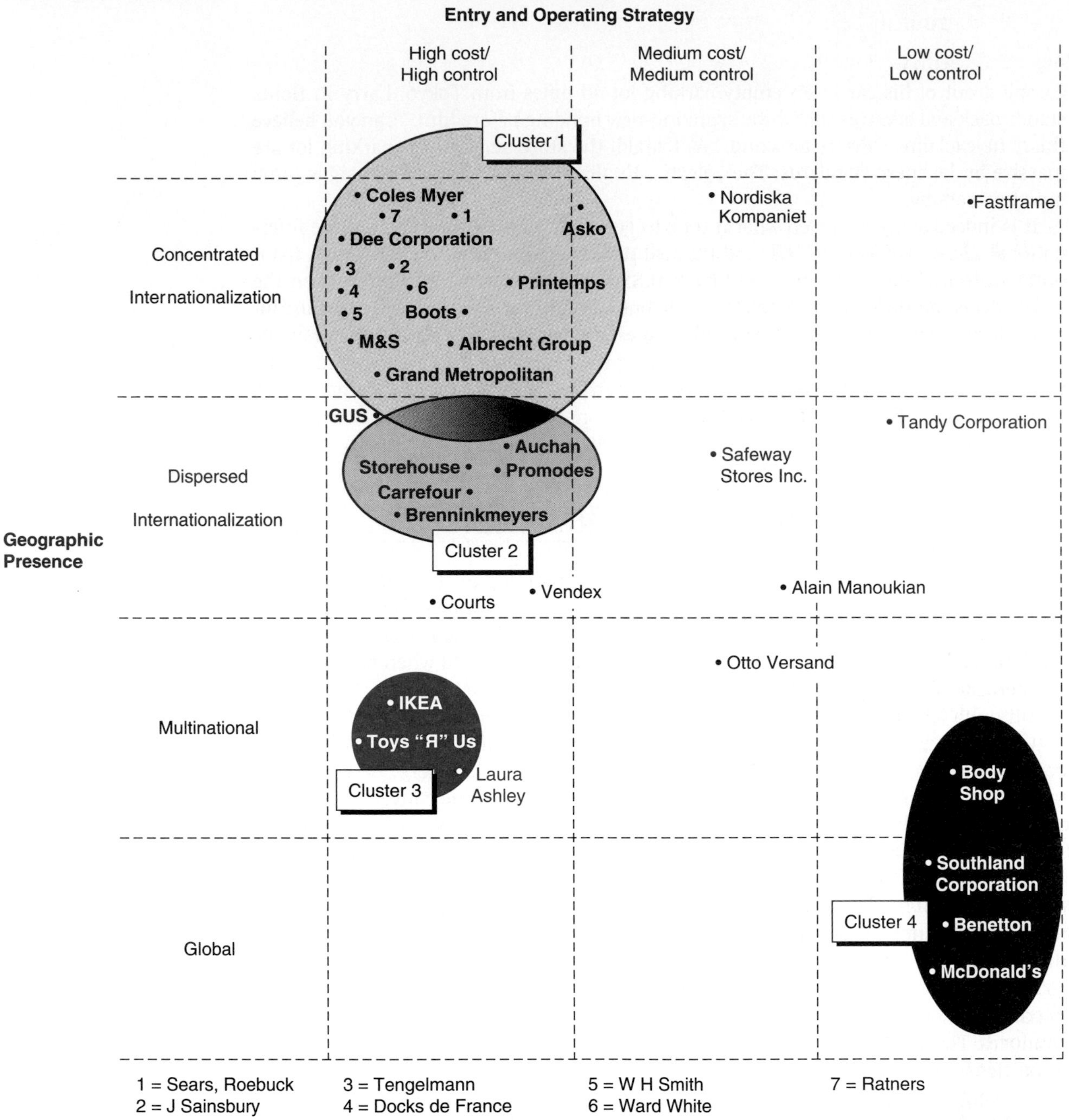

Note: Cluster 1—cautious internationalists; cluster 2—emboldened internationalists; cluster 3—aggressive internationalists; cluster 4—world powers.

Source: Alan D. Treadgold, "The Developing Internationalisation of Retailing," *International Journal of Retail & Distribution Management* 18 (1990): 10.

A classification of retailers trading internationally is provided in Figure 1. Companies have been assigned into clusters by the extent of their geographical trading presence (e.g., narrow versus broad) and by their preferred mode of entry (e.g., franchising versus company-controlled) into overseas markets. Although some are going to be quite aggressive in their moves, the majority are still cautious, implying moves to markets similar to the home market.

TOYS 'Я' US IN JAPAN

The Background

Toys 'Я' Us, with worldwide sales of $6.4 billion, is the world's largest toy retailer. Anticipating the day when it would saturate its domestic market, the company went international in 1984, first in Canada, then Europe, Hong Kong, and Singapore. Japan was always tempting in terms of the size of its toy markets (with more than $6 billion in annual sales, it is the world's second-largest toy market after the United States), but the country's laws and regulations stood in the way. The biggest barrier was the Large-Store Law, which is aimed at protecting the country's politically powerful small shopkeepers. Under the law, local communities and the Ministry of Trade and Industry (MITI) often managed to stall incursions by large retailers, even local ones.

The Japanese distribution system in itself is labyrinthine. The inefficiencies in the system developed for social and political reasons. For the last 50 years, a top priority of Japanese economic policy has been to protect the network of small neighborhood shops. Secondary and tertiary wholesalers evolved to supply them, often on a daily basis. The wholesalers in turn were linked through larger distributors to manufacturers or to Japan's trading companies. One out of every five Japanese workers is employed by distribution. To protect those jobs, retail regulations were developed. But, at the same time, the system created the world's most exorbitant prices.

But by late 1988, things started to change. Pressure was mounting from the United States, from big Japanese retailers (such as Daiei, Inc.), and from consumers looking for the lower prices that mass merchandisers could offer. By 1994, Japanese consumers, pinched by three years of recession and weary of subsidizing the low prices they see for Japanese goods elsewhere, were getting fed up.

Knowing the challenges of entering Japan, Toys 'Я' Us immediately began to look for a partner to assist them and found one in Den Fujita, president of McDonald's Co. (Japan). Since McDonald's serves a similar clientele—families with small kids—plans were made to build toy stores and restaurants on the same sites. McDonald's Japan quickly agreed to take a 20 percent stake in Toys 'Я' Us Japan.

By April 1990, MITI had agreed to shorten the big-store application process to no more than 18 months. Within weeks, the company had submitted building applications for several locations.

By early 1994, Toys 'Я' Us had 16 outlets in Japan. Plans call for the opening of 10 stores per year from 1993 through the end of the decade, with each to generate at least $15 million its first year. Annual sales would be at the minimum $1.5 billion by the year 2000, roughly half of which would be from toys made outside of Japan.

The typical small Japanese toy store stocks between 1,000 and 2,000 different items, whereas Toys 'Я' Us starts out with 8,000 and rises to 15,000 over time. If it can offer toys for 10 percent to 15 percent less than competitors, it could have a huge impact on Japanese toy retailing.

The Reaction

Based on the above facts, it is quite clear not everyone is as excited as Bouts and Fujita. Among the constituents to be dealt with included local communities, suppliers, and competitors.

Even after the Large-Store Law's amendment, local barriers still existed. In Samigahara, a Tokyo suburb of 520,000, the welcome was hardly warm. The site that Toys 'Я' Us had chosen did not fit the plans for development, and only after four meetings did the council (a MITI-inspired body of 18 consumers, merchants, professionals, and academics) give the green light in June 1991 for a store to open in December 1991. However, consultations over possible traffic problems and delays in construction forced the postponement of the site's opening until March 1992.

Toys 'Я' Us is also having a hard time winning low-cost, direct-supply contracts from local toy makers, who do not want to upset powerful wholesalers and longtime customers. Such arrangements are key to the ability of Toys 'Я' Us to discount. Initially, only one Japanese toy maker, Nintendo, had publicly stated it would sell directly to Toys 'Я' Us. However, hard times are giving discounters more clout with suppliers. Others have followed Nintendo's suit and others are reported to be reconsidering.

Local competitors have responded in various ways as well. Frightened toy-shop owners in the city of Niigata generated international headlines by clamoring against the application of Toys 'Я' Us to build a store there. They succeeded in delaying the opening until 1993. Others are already gearing up for competition. Katsuki Fuji, whose small Toy's House Joy is located quite close to the first Toys 'Я' Us outlet, plans to survive by finding a profitable niche. Many retailers also expect lower prices from wholesalers, and possibly financial support, if the competitive heat gets to be too much.

Questions for Discussion

1. Some argue that retailing concepts, strategies, and styles are firmly nationalistic and, as such, like cheap wine, do not travel well. The main argument is that the volume of such activity when measured against domestic turnover is still small. Present views for and against this opinion.

2. What are some of the critical lessons to be learned about international expansion and entry into Japanese markets from this case?

3. Toys 'Я' Us presents a departure from the existing distribution culture for both suppliers and customers. What factors may work for it in its quest for market share in Japan?

Agencia de Publicidad Aramburu S.A. (APA)

Mr. Aramburu was worried about the growing complexity of the operations of his advertising agency, from the point of view of both creativity and implementation of the advertising campaigns.

The agency not only created and implemented advertising campaigns for various Spanish products for the Spanish market but also had been creating and implementing since 1975—at least in part—the advertising campaigns for Semo semolina, manufactured by Invesa, in various East African countries, in Morocco, and in the Middle East; subsequently, since 1983, it had agreed to create advertising campaigns for African or Arab customers to be aired in their respective countries.

On the one hand, it seemed worthwhile to put to use the body of knowledge acquired over the last ten years on how to advertise in Africa and the Middle East. On the other hand, he wondered if these markets really offered any opportunities in the medium term or if the good results obtained so far owed more to having ridden on the crest of a wave of favorable circumstances.

PREVIOUS INTERNATIONAL EXPERIENCE

Agencia de Publicidad Aramburu S.A. (APA), had its origin in 1940 as the advertising department of a food conglomerate (Vascalisa) and gradually developed into Publicom S.A., a wholly owned subsidiary of Vascalisa. In 1985, APA was founded as the result of a management buy-out. The buy-out came about because Vascalisa was an industrial group with only limited interest in advertising activities. Even as a separate entity, APA continued to work with Vascalisa during a transitional period, on the basis of fees and other conditions stated in the purchasing contract.

EXPORTING ADVERTISING SERVICES

In 1975, Vascalisa set up an export department to sell semolina to countries in Africa and the Middle East. For this purpose, "Semo" was developed in 1977, a semolina which could be defined as a tropicalized durum formula Semolín. In the same year, the Vascalisa subsidiary Internacional Vasca Export S.A. (Invesa) was created as the company within the group that would manufacture and market Semo. Invesa soon began to open markets in Central and East Africa, especially in the countries that made up the Horn of Africa.

Vascalisa decided to rename its export semolina, calling it Semo—which locally sounds something like "semu"—which sounded better and was easier to pronounce than Semolín. The product itself was tropicalized too to make it more resistant in the environment of extreme climatic conditions, especially considering the length of time that passed between manufacture in Spain and consumption in countries such as Somalia, Tanzania, or Sudan. The product would be retailed in small individual bags, following local usage

Source: This case was prepared by Pere Gil, student 2° MED, under the supervision of Francesco Parés, Lecturer, and Professor Lluís G. Renart. It is intended to be used as a basis for class discussion rather than to illustrate either effective or ineffective handling of an administrative situation. Copyright © 1987, IESE, Barcelona, Spain. Reprinted with permission. No part of this publication may be reproduced without the permission of IESE.

and to increase rotation, instead of boxes containing several bags, which was the format used to sell Semolin in Spain.

Right from the start, Vascalisa turned to Publicom S.A. for help in designing its marketing strategy in Africa. The product's name, the adaptation of the product's quality to the markets it would enter, its presentation (without box) were all minutely analyzed. From the business point of view, Publicom S.A. treated Vascalisa just like any other company, providing full service within the legal restrictions imposed by each African country. Vascalisa paid Publicom S.A. in Spain, using pesetas for the services provided.

In 1979, both Vascalisa and Publicom S.A. began to feel the need to evolve toward a more aggressive sales strategy; by 1980, this feeling had become a determination to gradually progress from push marketing to pull marketing.

As Mr. Aramburu explained: "At first, we had to feel our way; it did not seem reasonable to us to invest in expensive advertising campaigns in markets whose possibilities we did not exactly know. Later on, we saw that the sales of Semo were growing, that we had a large potential market, and that it could be profitable to invest money in 'pulling' the product from the point of sale. We also understood that any campaign we made had to be aimed at promoting a specific demand, and not just a purely generic demand, as some Italian brands had already been around over there for much longer than us."

The first task was to decide *how to advertise*. It was obvious that the methods and ideas used in Spain could not be easily exported to the markets in East Africa. There was also the language problem: in Tanzania, for example, the only official language was Swahili,[1] a widely used native language that was written using the Latin alphabet, although English was fairly common at certain levels; there were also several major dialects that were spoken but not written. In view of the reduced level or even nonexistence of television and the low readership levels, especially among women, the medium that seemed to be the most suitable was radio; in any case, there were no audience surveys and it also had to be borne in mind that the radio stations were usually run by the respective governments, with very little room for maneuver, and centered on news. The same could be said about television in those countries where it existed, to the extent that there were no censuses of the number of television sets.

"Advertising," commented Mr. Aramburu, "is just one more cultural phenomenon. Each advertisement must stimulate the consumer's preference toward the brand, and the advertisement's message cannot be dissociated either from the product that sponsors it or from the idiosyncrasies of the potential consumer it is directed toward. We avoided 'advertising colonization' as much as possible because of our lack of knowledge concerning the region and because it seemed advisable to us from the point of view of working relationships with the government authorities. Thus, only an observant and open-minded person would realize that in those countries the housewife appearing in TV commercials would have to be a plump and well-fed woman; or that a dish must be tasted almost unavoidably with the fingers.

"In those countries where they existed, we reached agreements with local agencies. This was the case in Tanzania, Somalia, Ethiopia, and Kenya. In other countries where there were no established advertising agencies, we had to work directly with the advertising departments of the broadcasting stations."

---

[1] Swahili is a Bantu language spoken in Tanzania (including Zanzibar) and Kenya, where it is the official language; in Uganda, where it is the official language with English, and in some areas of the Congo River basin. It is the most widely spoken Black African language and has been considerably influenced by Arab and Persian. Although originally written in Arab characters, in the nineteenth century Latin characters were introduced. Swahili is widely used as a written language in magazines and newspapers.

Publicom S.A. tried to generate ideas in the meetings held with the staff of the local agencies. Normally, these were young people who had studied in Europe or occasionally an English expatriate who had started up on his own. All their ideas, collected in the field and processed in Bilbao, were expressed in a video, in a radio spot, in a jingle, in an image, that Publicom S.A. then showed in Madrid to a group of contacts from the country concerned—mostly students—to ensure that the message was appropriate.

"In Kenya, in 1983, we ran a campaign consisting of a truck with a film projector that toured through the jungle and when it arrived at a village, showed a promotional film; the driver-operator then handed out free samples of Semo to the audience. In 1984, we launched the multimedia campaign 'The Four Pleasures' in Tanzania, a country which has color television. It referred to the four pleasures of cooking: the purchase of the ingredients, the preparation of the dish by the housewife, the offering of the food to the head of the family (the father), without whose approval the meal cannot be served, and the tasting of the dish by him. The commercial was announced by a 'kotch-barma,' a mythical character, a king's witch doctor, a kind of oracle who—unlike other counselors who may indulge in intriguing—always tells the truth. This character combs his hair with two perpendicular partings so that it is divided into four parts, like a harlequin. In the commercial, the witch doctor shows his head with his hair dyed in the four colors of the Semo bags while he recommends its use for cooking to be able to enjoy the four pleasures it provides to the consumer. Before launching the message on the market, we wanted to be sure that the video would not be sacrilegious or scandalous and so we showed it to about a dozen Tanzanians we had contacted in Madrid who could read and write Swahili. This campaign was shown on television in two countries and broadcast on radio in a further five, produced in 14 different dialects, as well as Swahili, French, and English. At the time, it was the basic advertising communication in those markets.

"In 1984, we also launched a jingle on the radio in Uganda with such intensity that many thought that it was the national anthem and stood up every time they heard it. In each case, we tried to get maximum advertising benefit from the media available to us and for this we had to know the particular features of each region and the coverage of the various media. Thus, we discovered that in some villages it was the custom for families to get together in large groups to watch television. On other occasions, it was impossible for us to get around the pressure we were subjected to by associated agencies or the media themselves to advertise through certain media, such as newspapers, which seemed ineffective to us.

"We also launched two blind-test commercials; in these, people tasted two different soups, one of which was made with Semo. Everybody delightedly guessed which was Semo after successively dipping their fingers in each and licking them."

THE TRIPS TO AFRICA

In line with his philosophy of adapting the advertising and marketing to the particular idiosyncrasies of each national market, Mr. Aramburu went to Africa for the first time in 1982. The purpose of the trip was to "smell out" the market on the spot, to find out for himself what it was like. In Dar-es-Salaam, Carlos Aramburu had the opportunity to deal directly with the distributor of Semo, with some of his salesmen, and with retailers.

"One thing that stands out straight away is the vital importance of the point of sale for effectively marketing the product. In the markets of the large capitals, the stalls measure barely one meter square. They may be open-air or lightly covered and are usually attended by a mammy. [*Mammy* or, perhaps less frequently, *mummy* is used generically in Africa to refer to women who sell in the market.] These mammies are usually extraordinarily fat women who sit on a box and arrange the consumer products they sell on the ground in front of them. In the countryside, the retail outlets are shacks where no more than a dozen different brands are stacked.

"I have visited a large number of these bazaars and street markets, sticking stickers or offering posters showing the Semo squares, colors, and logo; this aspect of loyalty to an image is vital in those countries where the written transmission of slogans or even of the product's name is virtually useless. This direct contact with the mammies, with the salesmen, with the agents, even with the personnel of the media advertising departments, with the market, and with the country in general has been very useful. We have found out what the market is really like, it's given us ideas, it's enabled us to gain the channel's trust. In fact, I don't think that any other manufacturer has made so much effort to get close to the market. The fact is that we are gaining market share and I suppose the other manufacturers are getting pretty worried."

DIVERSIFICATION OF APA'S EXPORT BUSINESS AND ITS OPENING UP TO LOCAL ADVERTISERS

Little by little, on the basis of the reputation gained from the marketing of Semo, Publicom S.A. began to make a name for itself in some of the countries in which it operated. The distributors were pleasantly surprised by the success of Publicom S.A.'s campaigns; the personal contacts made during the visits helped to create an atmosphere of rapprochement and trust; the dinners held in the Carvajal family's house, to which the small but warm-hearted Spanish colony in Dar-es-Salaam was invited, were the scene of interminable conversations which gave Carlos Aramburu a clearer idea of life in those countries.

The importers and/or distributors of Semo were usually influential men of Indopakistani or Lebanese origin who had businesses in several industrial and commercial sectors. Mr. Aramburu spoke of them with a certain air of indecision. "In my opinion, it is vital to deal directly with people. I think that everyone likes being treated on an equal footing in a natural and respectful manner; I have always tried to establish a climate of polite deference and I think that it has opened a lot of doors for me. In any case, not all Europeans agree with me and there are some who have had undoubted success in the area in spite of—or perhaps thanks to—their rather arrogant and scornful attitude."

In the spring of 1983, the importer of Semo in Tanzania requested Publicom S.A. to design the advertising campaign for the umbrellas it manufactured and sold, bypassing Counterpoint, which was the local agency that Vascalisa, Publicom S.A., and the importer itself had worked with right from the first day Semo was marketed there. In another two countries, Publicom S.A. was also given direct assignments from the respective importers. The importer of Semo in Zanzibar also sold a line of Italian detergents and it placed Publicom S.A. in charge of the advertising campaign for these detergents.

The main problems facing Publicom S.A. at that time were basically twofold. First, the importers did not have or were simply not used to providing the type of information on the market, the channel, and the markups that was essential to organize a meaningful campaign. "Over there," said Mr. Aramburu, whose voice had recovered its forceful tone, "you've got to be prepared to listen. If you hand the potential client your BID,[2] the chances

---

[2] The BID—or Basic Information Document—was, in APA's terminology, what is usually known as a briefing or questionnaire often used by advertising agencies to gain information on the basic features of its client and the product to be marketed. This questionnaire is filled in by the potential client or by the agency itself after initial contact and will be used to draw the general lines of the advertising campaign.

are he won't be able to fill it in because to do so, certain basic knowledge is required not of marketing but of the market, of what you really want to achieve. Also, in addition to the problem of the lack of a qualified sales manager, you've also got the lack of statistics on media audiences and, worse still, the lack of awareness of advertising techniques."

There was also the problem of payment because until then Publicom S.A. had always been paid by Vascalisa in Spain, using pesetas. When it started to work directly for local companies, as the product that Publicom S.A. sold to its new companies was an intangible consisting of advertising ideas and action techniques, sometimes it was difficult to justify the origin of the dollars received in fees to the customs authorities at the airport when leaving the country.

BASIC FEATURES OF EXPORTING ADVERTISING SERVICES TO AFRICA

"In all these countries," said Mr. Aramburu, "the normal procedure is to start talking about money. When they decide to invest, it is because they feel it is advisable to do so but normally they don't know how much. It can even occur that they say to you, 'I've got so many million shillings. What can I do with them? Maybe I could put posters on buses, or print ads in the newspapers?' They are at that point where a country or company is starting to feel interested in advertising. It happened in Spain 30 years ago and it's happening to them now.

"The advertiser has no information on the market in his own country and neither do we. So somehow we have to complement the 'empirical' information available. Mr. Abdullah Bequer, for example, does not know for sure who is buying his products; he knows his customers are natives because he knows the points of sale. But he doesn't know their social class, their age, their background. Neither does he know to what extent his customers are loyal, that is, repeat buyers, or whether his sales are usually only occasional first purchases. You have to work a bit on trial and error to get an idea of the situation.

"Also, and as a result of the above, major changes may occur in the course of the campaign. For example, if it is seen that the campaign is successful, its budget may be considerably increased."

In Spain, on the other hand, the process was usually started on the advertiser's initiative, who nearly always had a certain idea of the market situation. The advertiser selected an agency, who proposed his fees and method. Advertiser-agency "marriages" were frequent, i.e., an advertiser may consistently use the same agency to advertise some or all its products. After preparing the briefing, the agency was in a position to be able to define the campaign's total cost. After that, it started to develop the creativity, the idea, or concept to communicate and the way to communicate it most effectively. The next steps were media definition, budget distribution, contracting the media chosen, and putting the campaign into action and monitoring it.

In other cases, it was the agency that took the initiative, seeking out a client with whom to reach an initial agreement for the presentation of a tentative campaign based on an overall budget. From that mutual loose commitment, the agency developed the creativity to present it to the advertiser. If the advertiser was satisfied with the agency's ideas, it implemented the ensuing steps of defining the media, distributing the budget, contracting the media, and executing the campaign. On the other hand, if the ideas created by the agency were not to the budding client's liking, it could cancel the contract on the spot.

Carlos Aramburu commented on the differences between the situation in Africa and the normal working methods used in Spain: "You cannot place all the local agencies under the same heading. For example, in Mogadishu, Vascalisa has its local agency, Oggi, which is very dependable. Oggi contracts the media and bills Vascalisa locally for them. Also, Oggi creates the idea, designs the storyboard, and films the commercial or records the spot or prepares the original graphics. Our function in this case is to closely supervise the operations and ensure that the standards desired by Vascalisa are met.

"In other cases, for example, the United Arab Emirates, APA does the complete creativity and the local agency buys the media, supervises the copy, determines the amount of posters to be printed, and gives information on local culture.

"Finally, in those countries where there are no local agencies, APA resorts to the managers of the advertising media for advice on local culture, review of the copy in the local language, hire actors and speakers."

CARLOS ARAMBURU'S CONCERNS IN SEPTEMBER 1986

Carlos Aramburu was aware of the prudence required to manage a company recently starting out on its own and with rather limited financial resources. He also liked to define himself as a businessman "like they used to be," concerned to get the most out of every peseta spent and unwilling to take on additional expenditure items if it was not clear that they were absolutely necessary.

As part of this line of thought, APA's prime goal was to consolidate a market in Spain. The image its team of professionals had created for themselves over the last 30 years, the successes achieved, and the enormous amount of creativity shown by campaigns as varied as those for a major Japanese photocopier manufacturer ("Japanese through a Tube"), a well-established Bilbao newspaper ("In Writing, Please"), a chain of supermarkets covering the entire Basque Country, Navarre, and Rioja ("We Sell Quality"), or a cookie manufacturer ("Heaps Better"), among many others, provided a major business asset which had to be capitalized upon.

Furthermore, the team of professionals in APA had been working in the sector for many years, knew everybody in Spain, and were in a position to present themselves as a group experienced in working together, that had been enriched after the purchase of Publicom S.A. with new human and technical resources and was able to offer each advertiser a dual response of creativity and service adapted to each client's particular situation.

However, the general manager of APA did not want to give up the idea of strengthening his markets abroad and he was well aware that a significant part of the agency's billing for creativity—excluding therefore the buying of media—came from Vascalisa and the overseas clients.

Carlos Aramburu realized the enormous prospects that were opening up to him in the East African and Arab countries. The multinational agencies had yet to establish any significant presence in these quasi-virgin territories, and Mr. Aramburu was afraid that, if he let time slip by, he would end up losing his lead to them. He had noticed that the sales office of an Italian agency in Mogadishu had been recently relaunched after years of inactivity. In this area, he considered that he had several possible alternatives: establish branches (wholly owned subsidiaries), continue as until now cooperating with the agencies existing in each country on the basis of agreed "contractual" collaborations, or form associations with the local agencies, buying some of their shares and providing basically technical assistance, such as training personnel in Spain or dealing with certain aspects of the creativity. In any case, it seemed clear that each country would require individual treatment.

APA, both in Spain and in the other nine countries it had worked in, had developed a know-how and an image that it should not let go to waste. They had been four years of work well done by Publicom S.A. and APA in Tanzania, Somalia, Kenya, Uganda, or Morocco, four years of traveling, learning, contacting markets, agencies, and media, of winning the company's first clients. To wait two years, which was the least time required to ensure continuity in Spain, for pushing strongly abroad, was not without risk.

Mr. Aramburu did not forget Vascalisa, the temporarily captive customer he had gained with the agency buy-out, which for the time being guaranteed a certain minimum billing for the agency. In any case, the terms were not particularly generous and Mr. Aramburu was considering renegotiating—updating—some of the clauses because, in his opinion, the quality of the service given by APA was improving day by day and in some cases was significantly higher than that given when the contract for the management buy-out of Publicom S.A. was written.

In Mr. Aramburu's opinion, the policy of exporting advertising services could be focused along two approaches: the European companies that exported to Africa and the Middle East and the local companies. APA had already made contacts with some Spanish companies that were looking for markets in those regions.

In addition to these general issues, Mr. Aramburu also pondered on a number of other more specific but no less important problems.

Among these was the question of the profitability of the foreign clients. Most of these were medium-sized companies and—especially in the case of the foreign clients—required traveling. This inevitably meant an increase in the cost of the service, should traveling expenses be charged direct to the clients, or a significant decrease in profitability, should APA include such costs as one more item in its income statement. Mr. Aramburu wondered to what extent, in the medium term, these charges could be borne by him or by his customers and, looking at the problem from another viewpoint, what should APA's fees be for it to be worthwhile for him and for his clients.

Mr. Aramburu was also aware that, in September 1986, APA had no export manager; there was the feeling in the agency that such a position would unnecessarily burden the overhead and the time for such a person was not yet ripe. As Mr. Aramburu explained: "There's no doubt that an export manager—or foreign accounts manager as we would call him—would significantly lighten my workload and enable me to give greater attention to the Spanish market. In November, for instance, I should be going to three countries and the way things are, it looks that I won't be able to go. A trip abroad, in addition to totally absorbing your attention for a few days, always leaves a few loose ends to be tied up because when you get back you have to send a leaflet or agenda to the inquisitive government officer who asked for them, send an answer to this or that client, review the conclusions of this or that matter, write a letter of intent, report to the board. But I think that it's best to wait a while because to fill this position would cost money and it's got to be done properly. We would need someone who would fit in with the company's corporate philosophy, who was familiar with the bureaucratic problems existing over there, who knew the methods of payment and the systems of credit, and who could feel at ease in those countries.

"Then there's what I call advertising 'colonization' and which we have consistently avoided: We sell creativity, not preconceived ideas tailored to the European markets; also, you've got to bear in mind our own limitations, our lack of in-depth knowledge of the reality and idiosyncrasies of each country, of the need to know how to work with people over there."

THE CONCEPTION OF A BUSINESS STRATEGY: STRENGTHS AND POSSIBILITIES

Deep down, what worried Mr. Aramburu most was the doubt he constantly had as to the suitability of the present business strategy. Sometimes, he caught himself muttering, "The idea of a medium-sized Basque agency going out and running campaigns in Africa is ridiculous! A thousand things could happen to convert it into instant disaster."

In any case, Carlos Aramburu tried to look at the situation from another viewpoint. He was aware that the agency he owned and managed had not yet had time to attain large volumes but he knew that he had a wide range of possibilities before him and the decision he took—which under no circumstances should endanger the company's continuity—could differentiate the advertising product he offered and speed up the company's growth path. In short, APA seemed to be facing the following strategic options:

1. Stop all exporting of advertising services—giving up also Vascalisa with a billing volume of 23 million pesetas and a margin of 12 million pesetas a year—in view of the risk that in the medium term, as local agencies appeared in the various countries, the local advertisers would leave APA, preferring to work with these native agencies. Mr. Aramburu could not quite get out of his mind the niggling sensation that all that had been achieved through Vascalisa was only a fly-by-night affair without any real substance.

2. Continue to let itself be carried along by Vascalisa without actively trying to gain new clients for campaigns outside Spain. This meant continuing to sell "without pushing," to carry on "waiting for them to come"; in any case, even if this option was chosen, it seemed advisable to define the time when such a strategy would no longer be sufficient and the company should launch itself with more determination in the conquest of new markets.

3. Continue to think how to make best use of the know-how acquired but to preferably direct efforts toward Spanish companies with sales activities in those countries. Mr. Aramburu could not wait to find out who was exporting to the countries that APA knew so well; Mr. Aramburu would initiate contacts—first by letter/pamphlet and then by personal visit to each of those exporters—to offer them APA's services, backed by the successes achieved with Vascalisa. This offer could be made in at least two ways:

   • Directly approach the exporting companies.
   • Approach these companies' advertising agencies. APA could act as a specialist consultant in those countries.

   Or, looking at things from another point of view:

   • Only approach those companies that were already exporting.
   • Try to find out (how? where?) which companies were potential exporters to the countries in the area and approach them.

4. Preferably, direct efforts at the native companies in each African country, which, to a certain extent, was the path followed so far under Vascalisa's wing. In any case, it seemed clear that the BID to be used for these local clients would have to be refocused.

Questions for Discussion

1. Which course of action do you recommend?
2. Who should implement the course of action?
3. Does APA supply the same services in Africa as it does in Spain?

The Audi 5000:
The Aftermath of Sudden Acceleration

In July 1989, Audi of America published multiple advertisements in business publications, newspapers, and journals across the United States declaring the "case closed" on the issue of sudden acceleration that had severely hampered its sales, stock values, and public relations during the preceding three years.

COMPANY BACKGROUND

Audi AG traces its history to 1909 when August Horch left his own company, A. Horch & Cie, to form a new firm called August Horch Automobilwerke GmbH. By 1914, the plant, in Ingolstadt, Germany, was manufacturing a range of models. In 1925, total production climbed to 1,116 vehicles. From 1912 through 1928, Audi was also involved in the production of military vehicles for the German army.

In 1932, because of the depression, Audi merged with Horch, Zschopauer Maschinenfabrik J. S. Rasmussen (DKW), and the car division of Wanderer Werke to form the Auto Union AG, with Daimler-Benz holding the majority of shares. Total production of the new company quickly rose to approximately 62,100 cars and 63,500 motorcycles.

Another year of transition was 1969, when Volkswagenwerk AG purchased Auto Union's stock from Daimler-Benz and merged the firm with the Neckarsulmer Strickmaschinenfabrik (NSU). This action brought together a conglomeration of expertise in the manufacturing of bicycles, motorcycles, typewriters, automobiles, aircraft, and submarine parts. The newly formed Audi NSU Auto Union AG experienced an explosive rate of expansion throughout the 1970s.

Throughout the history of the company, Audi cars were known for their performance, durability, and quality. Awards won by Audi cars include the U.S. Sports Car Club of America PRO Rally Manufacturers' Championship and the championships in the Pikes Peak Hill Climb.

ENTRY IN THE UNITED STATES

Auto Union GmbH had exported to the United States as early as 1940. From 1949 through 1960, Auto Union exported to the United States a total of 5,801 vehicles. Exports climbed slowly, and by the end of 1970, the newly formed Audi sold just under 7,700 cars through 138 dealers in the United States. A wholly owned subsidiary, Audi of America Inc., was established on September 1, 1985, and assumed from the American subsidiary of Volkswagen AG the functions of sales, service, advertising, merchandising, and public relations for Audi operations. By 1985, Audi of America's sales reached 74,061, capturing over 35 percent of Volkswagen of America's total sales in the United

Source: This case was written by Michael R. Czinkota and Bao-Nga Tran based on public sources such as *Automotive News* and *Automotive Litigation Reporter;* the videotape "Unintended Acceleration: The Myth and the Reality," Audi of America, Troy, Michigan, 1989; *History of Progress 1988,* Audi AG, Ingolstadt, West Germany, 1988; interviews with executives of Audi of America and Volkswagen of America.

States. Vice President Peter Fischer of Audi of America estimated in 1985 that Audi's "5000 series will be the 'backbone' of Audi's lineup and will represent 64 percent of Audi's U.S. sales in 1986."

ADVERSE MEDIA COVERAGE

In March 1986, the Center for Auto Safety submitted a petition to Audi of America, requesting the recall of all 1978 through 1986 Audi 5000 models because of repeated cases of dangerous malfunction. At the beginning of November 1986, New York's attorney general Robert Abrams publicly asked Audi of America to stop selling Audi 5000 automobiles with automatic transmissions. Both parties claimed that hundreds of accidents had been caused by the improper acceleration of Audi 5000s. Then, on the evening of November 23, 1986, CBS broadcast a "60 Minutes" episode with the Audi 5000 featured as one of its segments.

During this broadcast, Audi was accused before 65 million viewers of manufacturing and distributing the Audi 5000 series without warning the public of the possible danger of a phenomenon known as "sudden acceleration." Sudden acceleration was hypothesized to occur when "the driver starts the engine and moves the shift lever from 'park' into reverse or drive. The car [at times suddenly] hurtles forward or backward at great speed, with the driver unable to stop."

During the segment, CBS interviewed several drivers who claimed to have experienced the problem of unintended sudden acceleration. One man claimed he suffered shin splints because he pressed his foot too hard on the brake pedal. Another witness broke the car seat while fighting to brake her uncontrollable Audi. The most dramatic account of all came from Mrs. Brodosky, whose car killed her own son when it suddenly accelerated and pinned his body against the wall. These interviews quickly placed Audi on the defensive because the drivers were seen as helpless victims while operating a luxury automobile promised by Audi to be reliable and safe.

The "60 Minutes" broadcast included professional input from an automotive engineer and a representative of the American Standards Testing Bureau, who speculated on the cause of sudden acceleration. These professional opinions were both the same: "The idle stabilizer which keeps gas flowing to the engine may be fooled into sending too much. This transient malfunction would totally bypass the accelerator system, leaving the driver helpless, and would not leave any internal engine damage." To test this hypothesis, CBS had an engineer demonstrate how sudden acceleration could occur. The demonstrating driver shifted into drive with no foot on the brake or the accelerator pedals, and the car lurched forward.

AUDI'S RESPONSE

Following the CBS broadcast, Audi AG and Volkswagen of America denied the allegations, stating that sudden acceleration results from the negligence of the drivers. Through letters to Audi dealers and owners, both Audi and Volkswagen attempted "not only to counteract the ('60 Minutes') report, but really more to educate (consumers) as to the issue and assure them [they] are building safe cars." Audi, in addition, spent over $1 million in December 1986 placing ads in *The Wall Street Journal, USA Today,* and over 100 newspapers in 33 major cities, highlighting the fact that other manufacturers such as Nissan, Mercedes-Benz, and Volvo had received similar complaints.

By January 1987, Audi was forced to take more decisive action and recalled 25,000 of the 5000 series to install an idle stabilizer that required the driver to place a foot on the brake pedal before shifting gears. Further, Audi publicly denounced the CBS "60 Minutes" news team for news manipulation. In their opinion, CBS was unethical in not revealing to the public that the engineer interviewed on the program had to "dismantle three internal pressure relief valves, drill a hole into the transmission housing, and introduce artificial pressure from outside, pressure far greater than could ever occur in normal operation of the vehicle" in order to accelerate without pressing on the gas pedal. Audi executives believed that had this been revealed, the impact of the CBS theory would have been lessened.

THE MARKET RESPONSE

Within a year and a half following the CBS broadcast, Audi was beset with huge financial losses and faced hundreds of court cases from its customers and dealers.

In the four-year period from 1985 to 1988, the company's sales dropped from 74,061 to 22,943, as shown in Table 1. According to Audi AG Chairman Ferdinand Piech, the impact of falling sales resulted in a loss of $120 million in 1987 alone. In addition, Volkswagen's stocks, which closed on July 30, 1986, at 454.0, plummeted to a low of 248.5 by the close of July 29, 1988. A loss of public faith and interest is reflected in decreasing resale values of Audi 5000s in comparison to the Volvo 740 GLE and the BMW 325i 6, as highlighted in Table 2.

TABLE 1

Audi Sales in the United States, 1985–1988

Year	Number of Sales	Percent of Sales Total Import Sales	Loss in Sales since 1985
1985	74,061	2.61	—
1986	59,797	1.84	19.3%
1987	41,322	1.31	44.2
1988	22,943	0.75	69.0

TABLE 2

New versus Used Car Prices, 1985–1988

	1985	1986	1987	1988
New Prices				
Audi 5000	$18,160	$19,575	$20,460	$22,850
BMW 325i 6	21,105	20,455	22,850	25,150
Volvo 740 GLE	18,585	18,980	20,610	21,850
Used Car Wholesale Prices in 1989				
Audi 5000	$ 5,400	$ 7,650	$11,175	$14,550
BMW 325i 6	11,300	10,300	16,600	24,500
Volvo 740 GLE	10,325	11,000	13,100	15,850

Note: Figures effective for four-door sedans with automatic transmission.

Source: *Official Used Car Guide* (McLean, VA: National Auto Dealers Association, 1989).

Along with the financial losses, Audi of America and Volkswagen of America faced court suits for injuries suffered due to sudden acceleration and the loss of resale car value. For example, in the class-action suit of *Paul Perona et al.* v. *Audi AG et al.,* the plaintiffs list the following points of redress:[1]

- Breach of implied warranty of merchantability under the Uniform Commercial Code
- Violation of Consumer Fraud and Deceptive Trade Business Practice Act
- Breach of express warranties under the Uniform Commercial Code
- Breach of implied covenant of good faith and fair dealing
- Willful and wanton violation of Consumer Fraud and Deceptive Trade Business Practice Act
- Breach of contract

In addition, many owners filed independent suits against Audi and Volkswagen. By 1988, court fees alone were estimated to have cost Audi over $10 million. More than $4.6 million in payments have been awarded to injured parties throughout the United States, but Audi and Volkswagen continue to face a multitude of unsettled individual lawsuits involving sudden acceleration.

AUDI'S REPOSITIONING

With increasingly declining sales and bulging inventories, Audi once again was forced to take drastic action. In the spring of 1988, the firm began to offer $4,000 rebates to previous Audi owners toward the purchase of a new Audi 5000 model. In addition, to control costs, Audi of America reduced its work force by several hundred in response to the shutdown of an Audi assembly plant in Westmoreland, Pennsylvania. Concurrently, Audi's parent company, Volkswagen of America, executed four major shake-ups in Audi's top management.

Audi continued to run full one- and two-page advertisements directly addressing the issue of sudden acceleration. According to *Automotive News,* "ads captioned 'It's Time We Talked' . . . suggest that Audi erred at first when it decided to let the facts speak for themselves."[2] In February 1989, Audi kicked off the advertising year with the theme "The Alternate Route." Promotions during the year highlighted Audi's longer warranties and four-wheel-drive system as standard features of its newest lines. The new marketing approach was budgeted by Audi of America at approximately $60 million, almost twice the amount of previous years' promotional budgets.

In 1989, Audi discontinued the 5000 models and introduced a new 100/200 line to divorce itself from the issues that plagued the 5000 series. The new line represents "a major step in Audi's recovery program, as it refines, upgrades, and improves on the original 5000 series." With a better-built car and longer servicing warranties, Audi hopes its faithful clientele—as well as its own management—will encounter fewer complications and amend their relationship. To entice previous 5000 owners to accept their new offer, Audi provided a resale guarantee, limited to the first through fourth years of ownership, that would pay the customer the entire difference in retail trade-in values between the Audi 5000 and the comparable 260 E Mercedes-Benz, Volvo 740, and BMW 525.

---

[1] *American Litigation Reporter,* April 7, 1987, 8, 449–457.

[2] David Versical, "Audi Reports U.S. Loss, Beefs Up Ad Campaign," *Automotive News,* April 4, 1988, 3.

CASE CLOSED

A March 1989 National Highway Traffic Safety Administration study concluded that sudden acceleration may occur on a number of automobiles for a variety of reasons: "close lateral pedal placements, similarity of pedal force displacement, pedal travel and vertical offset, and vehicle acceleration capability that allows an error to occur before a driver has time to take corrective action." The study also explicitly stated that changes to the pedal design and placement in future models would only reduce the number of occurrences and not eliminate them altogether.

In July 1989, Audi of America took advantage of this conclusion and ran the "Case Closed" advertisement shown in Figure 1.

Audi Advertisement Announcing Final Decision of the National Highway Traffic Safety Administration

FIGURE 1

Case Closed.

Is there anyone who has not heard the rumors of "sudden acceleration" and Audi? We doubt it.

What you may not know, however, is that the final chapter has just been written.

Because on July 11, 1989, the National Highway Traffic Safety Administration officially completed its investigation and closed the file.

An investigation involving over 20 manufacturers, thousands of pages of test data and various other materials.

Their conclusion? No mechanical or electrical defect which would cause "sudden acceleration."

Their explanation? Pedal misapplication.

These findings coincide with similar investigations by the governments of Canada and Japan. As well as Audi's own analysis of the "sudden acceleration" incidents.

While there can be no happy ending to such a sad episode, the faith of our loyal owners and dealers has been justified.

Audi has been vindicated. Case closed.

© 1989 Audi of America

Source: *Washington Post,* July 1989.

TABLE 3	Audi Sales in the United States, 1989–1992

Year	Number of Sales	Percentage of Imports	Loss in Sales since 1998
1989	21,283	.77	7.2%
1990	21,106	.86	8.0%
1991	12,283	.58	46.5%
1992	14,756	.74	35.7%

Source: "1993 Market Databook," *Automotive News*, May 26, 1993, 28.

TABLE 4	Used Car Prices in 1993 (average trade-in, U.S. $)

	1989	1990	1991	1992	1993
Audi 100	7,125	10,225	13,200	17,900	20,700
BMW 325i	10,475	13,225	16,550	20,775	24,050
Volvo 740 GLE	10,350	12,425	15,925	17,950	18,500*

*940 model
Source: *Official Used Car Guide* (McLean, VA: National Auto Dealers Association, 1994).

In the following years, Audi continued to conduct major promotional campaigns. Even though major emphasis rested on the technology advantages of an Audi, rebates still played a major role. In addition, a new three-year, no-worry policy was offered to Audi buyers: The purchase price included all scheduled maintenance down to the windshield wipers. Maintaining an Audi therefore costs only the oil and gas needed to drive. Table 3 shows how sales developed over these years.

In spite of the major drop in sales, used car prices showed a gradual strengthening for the Audi. Table 4 shows these prices in comparison to similar models of BMW and Volvo.

Questions for Discussion

1. Would a U.S. automaker have responded differently to the CBS "60 Minutes" broadcast?

2. Evaluate the "re-marketing" efforts of Audi of America for 1986–1988 and 1989–1993.

3. Design an alternative response to maintain customer satisfaction.

4. Do you believe the case is closed on the Audi 5000?

Incident in Bhopal

On Sunday, December 3, 1984, the peaceful life of a U.S. corporate giant was joltingly disrupted. The Union Carbide plant at Bhopal, a city less than 400 miles from New Delhi, India, had leaked poisonous gas into the air. Within one week, over 2,000 people died, and more remained critically ill. Over 100,000 people were treated for nausea, blindness, and bronchial problems. It was one of history's worst industrial accidents.

Union Carbide is America's 37th-largest industrial corporation, with more than 100,000 employees and an annual sales volume of over $9 billion. The firm is active in petrochemicals, industrial gases, metals and carbon products, consumer products, and technology transfers.

Union Carbide operated 14 plants in India. Total Indian operations accounted for less than 2 percent of corporate sales. In spite of a policy by the Indian government to restrict foreign majority ownership of plants, Union Carbide owned 50.9 percent of the Bhopal plant. This special arrangement was granted by the government because the plant served as a major technology-transfer project. In order to achieve the goal of technology transfer, management of the plant was mostly carried out by Indian nationals. General corporate safety guidelines applied to the plant, but local regulatory agencies were charged with enforcing Indian environmental laws. Only three weeks before the accident, the plant had received an "environmental clearance certificate" from the Indian State Pollution Board.

The accident resulted in wide public awareness in the United States. A poll showed that 47 percent of those questioned linked Union Carbide's name to the Bhopal disaster. The direct impact of this awareness on Union Carbide's business remains uncertain. Most U.S. consumers do not connect the Union Carbide name to its line of consumer products, which consists of brands such as Energizer, Glad, and Presto. Industrial users, on the other hand, are highly aware of Union Carbide's products. One area that could be particularly affected is that of technology transfer, which in 1983 accounted for 24 percent of Union Carbide's revenues. The firm has concentrated increasingly on that sector, selling mainly its know-how in the fields of engineering, manufacturing, and personnel training.

THE PUBLIC REACTION

Internationally, the reaction was one of widespread consumer hostility. Environmentalists demonstrated at Union Carbide plants in West Germany and Australia. Some facilities were firebombed; most were spray painted. Plans for plants in Scotland had to be frozen. The operation of a plant in France was called into question by the French government.

Major financial repercussions occurred as well. Within a week of the accident, Union Carbide stock dropped by $10, a loss in market value of nearly $900 million. A $1.2-billion line of credit was frozen. Profits of Union Carbide India Ltd., which in 1984 had

Sources: This case study was written by Michael R. Czinkota by adapting secondary source materials from Alan Hall, "The Bhopal Tragedy Has Union Carbide Reeling," *Business Week*, December 17, 1984, 32; Clemens P. Work, "Inside Story of Union Carbide's India Nightmare," *U.S. News & World Report*, January 21, 1985, 51–52; Armin Rosencranz, "Bhopal, Transnational Corporations, and Hazardous Technologies," *Ambio* 17 (1988): 336–341; Sanjoy Hazarika, "Carbide Plant Closed by India Unrest," *New York Times*, Monday, May 13, 1991, D12; Scott McMurray, "India's High Court Upholds Settlement Paid by Carbide in Bhopal Gas Leak," *The Wall Street Journal*, October 4, 1991, B8.

been about 8.2 million rupees, or about $480,000, dropped by 1985 to 1.3 million rupees, or $78,000. By 1990, the company reported a loss of 132 million rupees, about $7.8 million.

In the ensuing debate of the Bhopal disaster, three basic issues were highlighted—responsible industrial planning, adequate industrial safety measures, and corporate accountability. In terms of industrial planning, both Union Carbide and the Indian government were said to have failed. The Indian subsidiary of Union Carbide did little to inform workers about the highly toxic methyl isocyanate (MIC) the plant was producing and the potential health threat to neighboring regions. When the accident occurred, the subsidiary's management team reportedly resisted the parent company's instructions to apply first aid to victims for fear of generating widespread panic within the corporation and the region. The Indian government, on the other hand, seemed to regard technology transfer as a higher priority than public safety. The local government approved construction of the plant with little medical and scientific investigation into its biological effects on the environment and on people.

The second issue was the absence of a "culture of safety" among Indian technicians, engineers, and management. From the very beginning, the project lacked a team of experienced maintenance personnel who would have recognized the need for higher safety measures and, more important, a different choice of technology. When the entire Indian government wholeheartedly approved the import of the most advanced chemical production facility in any developing country without qualified personnel to handle the material and without insight into appropriate precautionary measures in case of an accident, the seeds were sown for potential disaster.

The third area of interest in the Bhopal incident is that of corporate accountability. There are three general norms of international law concerning the jurisprudence of the home government over the foreign subsidiary:

1. Both state and nonstate entities are liable to pay compensation to the victims of environmental pollution and accidents.
2. The corporation is responsible for notifying and consulting the involved officials of actual and potential harm involved in the production and transport of hazardous technologies and materials.
3. The causer or originator of environmental damage is liable to pay compensation to the victims.

These and other developing norms of international law serve to make transnational corporations more responsible for their operation.

COMPENSATION TO VICTIMS

Five days after the incident, the first damage suit, asking for $15 billion, was filed in U.S. Federal District Court. Since then more than 130 suits have been filed in the United States and more than 2,700 in India. Union Carbide offered to pay $300 million over a period of 30 years to settle the cases before the courts in the United States and India. The Indian government rejected the offer, claiming that the amount was far below its original request of $615 million. By 1986, most U.S. lawsuits had been consolidated in the New York Federal Court. In May 1986, however, the judge presiding over the collective Bhopal cases ruled that all suits arising out of the accident should be heard in the Indian judicial system, claiming that "India is where the accident occurred, and where the victims, witnesses, and documents are located." Although this decision appeared to benefit Union Carbide because of lower damage awards in India, the judge explicitly stated that

(1) Union Carbide (USA) and its Indian affiliate must submit to the jurisdiction of the Indian court system, (2) Union Carbide must turn over all relevant documents to the plaintiffs' lawyers in India, as they would if in the United States, and (3) Union Carbide must agree to whatever judgment is rendered in India. This decision had a major effect on Union Carbide (USA) because (1) both Union Carbide (USA) and its Indian subsidiary now had to answer to the Indian court and (2) the entire company's assets had become involved.

In India, the class suit traveled from the Bhopal District Court to the Madhya Pradesh High Court and finally to the Indian Supreme Court. Although a settlement agreement was reached between Union Carbide and the Indian government, the descendents of the 2,000 victims were not satisfied. Several victims' consumer groups and public-interest lawyers filed petitions contesting the authority of the government to handle the lawsuit on behalf of the victims' descendents. The petitions claimed that the government had no right to represent the victims because governmental negligence had caused the accident in the first place and the government should be as much a target as Union Carbide in the suit itself. It was expected that if the Indian Supreme Court upheld this rationale, then the government would be unable to settle on the victims' behalf. In this case, the agreed-upon settlement amount would also be voided. As a result of the internal debate in India, the $421 million paid in settlement by Union Carbide was frozen. Instead, the Indian government itself disbursed 200 rupees, about $10, a month to all persons who lived in the neighborhoods affected by the gas leak.

On October 3, 1991, almost seven years after the incident, the Supreme Court of India rendered its decision. The total amount of $470 million, which had already been paid by Union Carbide, was upheld as settlement. Criminal charges against the Union Carbide corporation were reinstated, even though the court acknowledged that due to its lack of jurisdiction, it could not enforce any criminal fines in the United States.

Since the decision cannot be reviewed further, it freed up the frozen funds to be distributed to Bhopal victims and their families. Although many victims were delighted about that fact, Prashant Bhushan, a New Delhi attorney, had severe misgivings. He believed the upholding of the civil settlement to be a big blow to the development of law on the subject—particularly since he had argued that Carbide should be forced to pay "first-world" compensation rates to the victims rather than "third-world" rates.

The lessons learned? Several chemical companies have reduced the size of their storage tanks of toxic materials while others have cut their inventories by as much as 50 percent. Many have provided information to the communities in which they manufacture. Some have even invested in risk-assessment studies of their operations of hazardous materials.

Questions for Discussion

1. How could Union Carbide have planned for an event such as that in Bhopal?

2. How would such planning have improved corporate response to the disaster?

3. Does it make sense to base corporate strategy on worst-case scenarios?

4. Which other firms are exposed to similar risks?

5. What are the future implications for the management of Union Carbide?

6. What are the future implications for the government of India?

7. What are your views on the delay of compensation paid to the victims?

8. In general, should joint-venture partners absorb part of the blame and cost when accidents occur?

Nova Scotia

THE U.S. MARKET FOR CANADIAN TRAVEL SERVICES

The more than 12 million Americans who travel to Canada annually constitute 42 percent of all departures from the United States. The U.S. market is of crucial importance to the Canadian tourism industry because 95 percent of all tourists are Americans, who spend approximately $2.7 billion a year on these trips.

The 1980s witnessed a major escalation in campaigns that try to lure tourists to a particular state or foreign country. Tourism areas spent over $100 million in U.S. media annually in the 1980s, and the level is expected to grow considerably in the 1990s. Tourism Canada, the government tourist organization, in 1986 launched a campaign with the theme "Come to the world next door" as an umbrella campaign for Canada as a whole. The provinces conduct their own independent campaigns to segments they deem most attractive and profitable. For example, ads for Manitoba are mostly written for the outdoor vacationer.

The Canadian Government Office of Tourism (CGOT) sponsored a large-scale benefit-segmentation study of the American market for pleasure travel to Canada, the results of which are summarized in Table 1. Segmenting the market by benefits provides many advantages over other methods. Segmenting by attitude toward Canada or by geographic area would be feasible if substantial variation occurred. This is not the case, however. Segmenting by benefits reveals what consumers were and are seeking in their vacations. Knowing this is central to planning effective marketing programs.

A BENEFIT-MATCHING MODEL

Table 2 summarizes a strategic view for understanding tourism behavior and developing a marketing campaign. The model emphasizes the dominant need to define markets by benefits sought and the fact that separate markets seek unique benefits or activity packages. Membership in the segments will fluctuate from year to year; the same individuals may seek rest and relaxation one year and foreign adventure the next.

Identifying benefits is not enough, however. Competitors (that is, other countries or areas) may present the same type of benefits to the consumers. Because travelers seriously consider only a few destinations, a sharp focus is needed for promoting a destination. This also means that a destination should avoid trying to be "everything to everybody" by promoting too many benefits. Combining all of these concerns calls for positioning, that is, generating a unique, differentiated image in the mind of the consumer.

Three destinations are shown in Table 2. Each destination provides unique as well as similar benefits for travelers. Marketers have the opportunity to select one or two specific benefits from a set of benefits when developing a marketing program to attract visitors. The benefits selected for promotion can match or mismatch the benefits sought by specific market segments. The letters S, M, and N in the table express the degree of fit

Source: This case was written by Arch G. Woodside and Ilkka A. Ronkainen for discussion purposes and not to exemplify correct or incorrect decision making. The case is largely based on Arch G. Woodside, "Positioning a Province Using Travel Research," *Journal of Travel Research* 20 (Winter 1982): 2–6.

Benefit Segments of U.S. Travelers to Canada

TABLE 1

Segment I: Friends and relatives—nonactive visitor (29 percent). These vacationers seek familiar surroundings where they can visit friends and relatives. They are not very inclined to participate in any activity.

Segment II: Friends and relatives—active city visitor (12 percent). These vacationers also seek familiar surroundings where they can visit friends and relatives, but they are more inclined to participate in activities—especially sightseeing, shopping, and cultural and other entertainment.

Segment III: Family sightseers (6 percent). These vacationers are looking for a new vacation place that would be a treat for the children and an enriching experience.

Segment IV: Outdoor vacationer (19 percent). These vacationers seek clean air, rest and quiet, and beautiful scenery. Many are campers, and availability of recreation facilities is important. Children are also an important factor.

Segment V: Resort vacationer (19 percent). These vacationers are most interested in water sports (for example, swimming) and good weather. They prefer a popular place with a big-city atmosphere.

Segment VI: Foreign vacationer (26 percent). These vacationers look for a place they have never been before with a foreign atmosphere and beautiful scenery. Money is not of major concern but good accommodation and service are. They want an exciting, enriching experience.

Source: Shirley Young, Leland Ott, and Barbara Feigin, "Some Practical Considerations in Market Segmentation," *Journal of Marketing Research* 15 (August 1978): 405–412.

Benefit-Matching Model

TABLE 2

Markets	Benefits Sought	Benefit Match	Benefits Provided	Destinations
A →	A_s, B_s →	S ←	A_p, B_p ←	X
B →	B_s, C_s →	M ←	C_p, D_p ←	Y
C →	C_s, D_s →	N ←	E_p, F_p ←	Z

S = Supermatch, M = Match, N = Mismatch.

Source: Arch G. Woodside, "Positioning a Province Using Travel Research," *Journal of Travel Research* 20 (Winter 1982): 3.

between the benefits provided and those sought. For example, a mismatch is promoting the wrong benefit to the wrong market, such as promoting the scenic mountain beauty of North Carolina to Tennessee residents.

THE CASE OF NOVA SCOTIA

Canada has a rather vague and diffuse image among Americans. This is particularly true of the Atlantic provinces (see Figure 1). The majority of Nova Scotia's nonresident travelers reside in New England and the mid-Atlantic states of New York, Pennsylvania, and New Jersey. Most of these travelers include households with married couples having incomes substantially above the U.S. national average, that is, $50,000 and above. Such households represent a huge, accessible market—10 million households that are 1 to 2½ days' drive from Halifax, the capital. Most households in this market have not visited the Atlantic provinces and have no plans to do so. Thus, the market exhibits three of the four requirements necessary to be a very profitable customer base for the province: size, accessibility, and purchasing power. The market lacks the intention to visit for most of

FIGURE 1   Nova Scotia and Its Main Markets

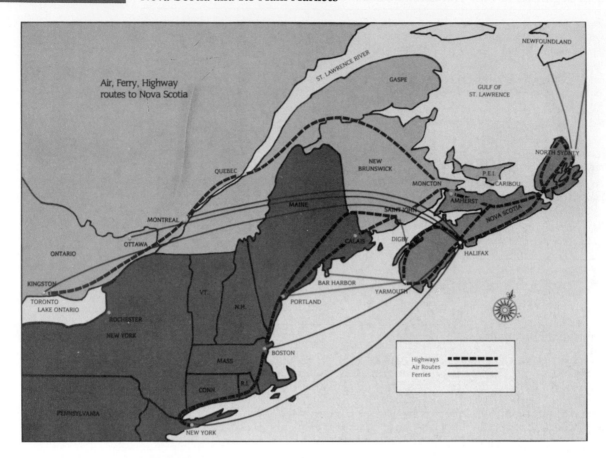

Source: "Nova Scotia," *Travel Agent,* February 27, 1986, 14.

the households described. Nova Scotia is not one of the destinations considered when the next vacation or pleasure trip is being planned. Worse still, Nova Scotia does not exist in the minds of its largest potential market.

In the past, Nova Scotia had a number of diverse marketing themes, such as "Good times are here," "International gathering of the clans," "The 375th anniversary of Acadia," "Seaside spectacular," and the most recent, "There's so much to sea" (see Figure 2). These almost annual changes in marketing strategy contributed to the present situation both by confusing the consumer as to what Nova Scotia is all about and by failing to create a focused image based on the relative strengths of the province. Some critics argue that Nova Scotia is not being promoted on its unique features but on benefits that other locations can provide as well or better.

EXAMPLES OF SUCCESSFUL POSITIONING

Most North Atlantic passengers flying to Europe used to have a vague impression of Belgium. This presented a problem to the tourism authorities, who wanted travelers to stay for longer periods. Part of the problem was a former "Gateway to Europe" campaign that had positioned Belgium as a country to pass through on the way to somewhere else.

Example of "There's So Much to Sea" Campaign   FIGURE 2

NOVA SCOTIA
Come for our natural treasures.

Atlantic salmon, the ultimate challenge.

Angling for Atlantic Salmon. The ultimate challenge. You'll find them in the Nova Scotian rivers where they were born. You can fish some of the finest salmon streams in North America and never work the same pool twice.

You'll get to know all our other treasures: brook, rainbow and brown trout, shad and the majestic treasure of the deep, the giant bluefin tuna. Savour the beauty and serenity of our crystal clear lakes and rivers.

Nova Scotians are a touch old-fashioned, so we care about our unspoiled wilderness. Join us for a real outdoor adventure. You'll treasure every moment of it. Your visit to Nova Scotia is an experience your family will treasure for a lifetime. That's what makes it such a great vacation value.

For more information write to: Tourism Nova Scotia, 129 Commercial Street, Portland, Me. 04101 ; or call toll free: 1-800-341-6096 (In Maine: 1-800-492-0643) FF2

NOVA SCOTIA
There's so much to sea

Honourable Bruce Cochran, Minister of Tourism

Source: "Nova Scotia Insert," *Travel Weekly,* April 15, 1986.

The idea for new positioning was found in the *Michelin Guides,* which rate cities as they do restaurants. The Benelux countries have six three-star cities (the highest ranking), of which five are in Belgium and only one (Amsterdam) is in the Netherlands. The theme generated was, "In Belgium, there are five Amsterdams." This strategy was correct in three different ways: (1) it related Belgium to a destination that was known to the traveler, Amsterdam; (2) the *Michelin Guides,* another entity already known to the traveler, gave the concept credibility; and (3) the "five cities to visit" made Belgium a bona fide destination.[1]

The state of Florida attracts far more eastern North American beach seekers than does South Carolina. Tourism officials in South Carolina had to find a way in which the state could be positioned against Florida.

The positioning theme generated was "You get two more days in the sun by coming to Myrtle Beach, South Carolina, instead of Florida." Florida's major beaches are a one-day drive beyond the Grand Strand of South Carolina—and one additional day back. Most travelers to Florida go in the May-to-October season when the weather is similar to that in South Carolina. Thus, more beach time and less driving time became the central benefit provided by the state.

POSITIONING NOVA SCOTIA

The benefits of Nova Scotia as a Canadian travel destination cover segments III to VI of U.S. travelers (see Table 1). Those providing input to the planning process point out water activities, seaside activities, camping, or scenic activities. The segment interested in foreign adventure could be lured by festivals and other related activities.

The planners' argument centers not so much on which benefits to promote but on which should be emphasized if differentiation is desired. The decision is important because of (1) the importance of the industry to the province and (2) the overall rise in competition for the travelers in Nova Scotia's market, especially competition by U.S. states.

Questions for Discussion

1. How would you position Nova Scotia to potential American travelers? Use the benefit-matching model to achieve your supermatch.

2. Constructively criticize past positioning attempts, such as "There's so much to sea."

3. What other variables, apart from positioning, will determine whether Americans will choose Nova Scotia as a destination?

---

[1] Al Ries and Jack Trout, *Positioning: The Battle for Your Mind* (New York: McGraw-Hill, 1980), 171–178.

Parker Pen Company

Parker Pen Company, the manufacturer of writing instruments based in Janesville, Wisconsin, is one of the world's best-known companies in its field. It sells its products in 154 countries and considers itself number one in "quality writing instruments," a market that consists of pens selling for $3 or more.

In early 1984, the company launched a global marketing campaign in which everything was to have "one look, one voice," and with all planning to take place at headquarters. Everything connected with the selling effort was to be standardized. This was a grand experiment of a widely debated concept. A number of international companies were eager to learn from Parker's experiences.

Results became evident quickly. In February 1985, the globalization experiment was ended, and most of the masterminds of the strategy either left the company or were fired. In January 1986, the writing division of Parker Pen was sold for $100 million to a group of Parker's international managers and a London venture-capital company. The U.S. division was given a year to fix its operation or close.

GLOBALIZATION

Globalization is a business initiative based on the conviction that the world is becoming more homogeneous and that distinctions between national markets are not only fading but, for some products, they will eventually disappear. Some products, such as Coca-Cola and Levi's, have already proven the existence of universal appeal. Coke's "one sight, one sound, one sell" approach is a legend in the world of global marketers. Other companies have some products that can be "world products," and some that cannot and should not be. For example, if cultural and competitive differences are less important than their similarities, a single advertising approach can exploit these similarities to stimulate sales everywhere, and at far lower cost than if campaigns were developed for each individual market.

Compared with the multidomestic approach, globalization differs in these three basic ways:

1. The global approach looks for similarities between markets. The multidomestic approach ignores similarities.
2. The global approach actively seeks homogeneity in products, image, marketing, and advertising message. The multidomestic approach produces unnecessary differences from market to market.
3. The global approach asks, "Should this product or process be for world consumption?" The multidomestic approach, relying solely on local autonomy, never asks the question.

Globalization requires many internal modifications as well. Changes in philosophy concerning local autonomy, concern for local operating results rather than corporate performance, and local strategies designed for local—rather than global—competitors

Source: This case was prepared by Ilkka A. Ronkainen for discussion purposes and not to exemplify correct or incorrect decision making. The case draws facts from Joseph M. Winski and Laurel Wentz, "Parker Pen: What Went Wrong?" *Advertising Age,* June 2, 1986, 1, 60–61, 71, and Lori Kesler, "Parker Rebuilds a Quality Image," *Advertising Age,* March 21, 1988, 49.

are all delicate issues to be solved. By design, globalization calls for centralized decision making; therefore, the "not-invented-here" syndrome becomes a problem. This can be solved by involving those having to implement the globalization strategy at every possible stage as well as keeping lines of communication open.[1]

GLOBALIZATION AT PARKER PEN COMPANY

In January 1982, James R. Peterson became the president and CEO of Parker Pen. At that time, the company was struggling, and global marketing was one of the key measures to be used to revive the company. While at R. J. Reynolds, Peterson had been impressed with the industry's success with globalization. He wanted for Parker Pen nothing less than the writing-instrument equivalent of the Marlboro man.

For most of the 1960s and 1970s, a weak dollar had lulled Parker Pen into a false sense of security. About 80 percent of the company's sales were abroad, which meant that when local-currency profits were translated into dollars, big profits were recorded.

The market was changing, however. The Japanese had started marketing inexpensive disposable pens with considerable success through mass marketers. Brands such as Paper Mate, Bic, Pilot, and Pentel each had greater sales, causing Parker's overall market share to plummet to 6 percent. Parker Pen, meanwhile, stayed with its previous strategy and continued marketing its top-of-the-line pens through department stores and stationery stores. Even in this segment, Parker Pen's market share was eroding because of the efforts of A. T. Cross Company and Montblanc of Germany.

Subsidiaries enjoyed a high degree of autonomy in marketing operations, which resulted in broad and diverse product lines and 40 different advertising agencies handling the Parker Pen account worldwide.

When the dollar's value skyrocketed in the 1980s, Parker's profits plunged and the loss of market share became painfully evident.

Peterson moved quickly upon his arrival. He trimmed the payroll, chopped the product line to 100 (from 500), consolidated manufacturing operations, and ordered an overhaul of the main plant to make it a state-of-the-art facility. Ogilvy & Mather was hired to take sole control of Parker Pen advertising worldwide. The logic behind going with one agency instead of the 40 formerly employed was cost savings and the ability to coordinate strategies on a worldwide basis. Among the many agencies terminated was Lowe Howard-Spink in London, which had produced some of the best advertising for Parker Pen's most profitable subsidiary. The immediate impact was a noticeable decline in employee morale and some expressed bitterness at the subsidiary being dictated to by a subsidiary that had been cross-subsidizing the American operations over the years.

A decision was also made to go aggressively after the low end of the market. The company would sell an upscale line called Premier, mainly as a positioning device. The biggest profits were to come from a roller-ball pen called Vector, selling for $2.98. Plans were drawn to sell an even cheaper pen called Itala—a disposable pen never thought possible at Parker.

Three new managers, to be known as Group Marketing, were brought in. All three had extensive marketing experience, most of it in international markets. Richard Swart, who became marketing vice president for writing instruments, had handled 3M's image advertising worldwide and taught company managers the ins and outs of marketing plan-

---

[1] Laurence Farley, "Going Global: Choices and Challenges," presented at the American Management Association Conference, June 10, 1985, Chicago, Illinois.

ning. Jack Marks became head of writing-instruments advertising. At Gillette, he had orchestrated the worldwide marketing of Silkience hair-care products. Carlos Del Nero, brought in to be Parker's manager of global marketing planning, had gained broad international experience at Fisher-Price. The concept of marketing by centralized direction was approved.

The idea of selling pens the same way everywhere did not sit well with many Parker subsidiaries and distributors. Pens were indeed the same, but markets, they believed, were different: France and Italy fancied expensive fountain pens; Scandinavia was a ballpoint market. In some markets, Parker could assume an above-the-fray stance; in others it had to get into the trenches and compete on price. Nonetheless, headquarters communicated to them all:

Advertising for Parker Pens (no matter model or mode) will be based on a common creative strategy and positioning. The worldwide advertising theme, "Make Your Mark With Parker," has been adopted. It will utilize similar graphic layout and photography. It will utilize an agreed-upon typeface. It will utilize the approved Parker logo/design. It will be adapted from centrally supplied materials.

Swart insisted that the directives were to be used only as "starting points" and that they allowed for ample local flexibility. The subsidiaries perceived them differently. The U.K. subsidiary, especially, fought the scheme all the way. Ogilvy & Mather London strongly opposed the "one world, one brand, one advertisement" dictum. Conflict arose, with Swart allegedly shouting at one of the meetings: "Yours is not to reason why; yours is to implement." Local flexibility in advertising was out of the question (see Figure 1).

The London-created "Make Your Mark" campaign was launched in October 1984. Except for language, it was essentially the same: long copy, horizontal layout, illustrations in precisely the same place, the Parker logo at the bottom, and the tag line or local equivalent in the lower right-hand corner. Swart once went to the extreme of suggesting that Parker ads avoid long copy and use just one big picture.

Problems arose on the manufacturing side. The new $15-million plant broke down repeatedly. Costs soared, and the factory turned out defective products in unacceptable numbers. In addition, the new marketing approach started causing problems as well. Although Parker never abandoned its high-end position in foreign markets, its concentration on low-priced, mass-distribution products in the United States caused dilution of its image and ultimately losses of $22 million in 1985. Conflict was evident internally, and the board of directors began to turn against the concept of globalization.

In January 1985, Peterson resigned. Del Nero left the company in April; Swart was fired in May, Marks in June. When Michael Fromstein became CEO of the company, he assembled the company's country managers in Janesville and announced: "Global marketing is dead. You are free again."

Questions for Discussion

1. Should the merits of global marketing be judged by what happened at Parker Pen Company?

2. Was the globalization strategy sound for writing instruments? If yes, what was wrong in the implementation? If not, why not?

3. What marketing miscalculations were made by the advocates of the globalization effort at Parker Pen?

4. The task is to "fix it or close it." What should be done?

FIGURE 1   Ads for Parker's Global Campaign

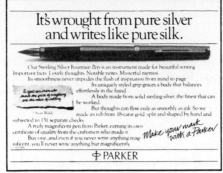

McDonnell Douglas: The F-18 Hornet Offset

In May of 1992, the Finnish government's selection of the F/A-18 Hornet over the Swedish JAS-39 Gripen, the French Mirage 2000-5, and fellow American F-16 to modernize the fighter fleet of its air force was a major boost to McDonnell Douglas (MDC) in an otherwise quiet market. The deal would involve the sale of 57 F/A-18 Cs and 7 F/A-18 Ds at a cost of FIM 9.5 billion (approximately $2 billion). Deliveries would take place between 1995 and 2000.

Winning the contract was critical since MDC had been on the losing side of two major aircraft competitions in the United States in 1991. In addition, one of its major projects with the U.S. Navy had been terminated (the A-12), and the government of the Republic of Korea had changed its mind to buy F-16 aircraft after it already had an agreement with MDC for F/A-18 Hornets.

However, the $2 billion will not be earned without strings attached. Contractually, McDonnell Douglas and its main subcontractors (Northrop, General Electric, and General Motors' subsidiary Hughes), the "F-18 Team," are obligated to facilitate an equivalent amount of business for Finnish industry over a ten-year period (1992–2002) using various offset arrangements.

OFFSETS

Offsets are various forms of industrial and business activities required as a condition of purchase. They are an obligation imposed on the seller in major (most often military hardware) purchases by or for foreign governments to minimize any trade imbalance or other adverse economic impact caused by the outflow of currency required to pay for such purchases. In wealthier countries, it is often used for establishing infrastructure. Two basic types of offset arrangements exist: direct and indirect (as seen in Figure 1). Although offsets have long been associated only with the defense sector, there are now increasing demands for offsets in commercial sales where the government is the purchaser or user.

Direct offset consists of product-related manufacturing or assembly either for the purposes of the project in question only or for a longer-term partnership. The purchase, therefore, enables the purchaser to be involved in the manufacturing process. Various Spanish companies produce dorsal covers, rudders, aft fuselage panels, and speed brakes for the F/A-18s designated for the Spanish Air Force. In addition to coproduction arrangements, licensed production is prominent. Examples include Egypt producing U.S. M1-A1 tanks, China producing MDC's MD-82 aircraft, and Korea assembling the F-16 fighter. An integral part of these arrangements is the training of the local employees. Training is not only for production/assembly purposes but also for maintenance and overhaul of the equipment in the longer term. Some offsets have buy-back provisions; that is, the seller is obligated to purchase output from the facility or operations it has set up or licensed. For example, Westland takes up an agreed level of parts and components

Source: This case study was written by Ilkka A. Ronkainen and funded in part by a grant from the Business and International Education Program of the U.S. Department of Education. The assistance of the various organizations cited in the case is appreciated. Special thanks to David Danjczek of Western Atlas, Inc.

FIGURE 1	The Offset Process

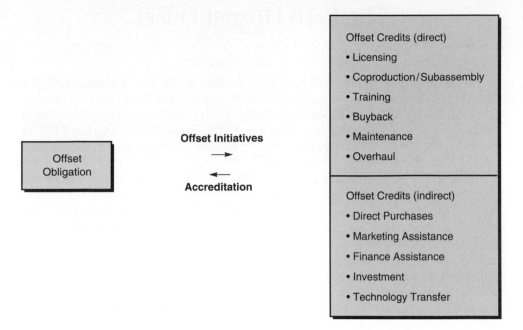

from the Korean plant that produces Lynx Helicopters under license. In practice, therefore, direct offsets amount to technology transfer.

Indirect offsets are deals that involve products, investments, and so forth which are not to be used in the original sales contract but that will satisfy part of the seller's "local" obligation. Direct purchases of raw materials, equipment, or supplies by the seller or its suppliers from the offset customer country present the clearest case of indirect offsets. These offset arrangements are analogous to counterpurchases and switch trading. Sellers faced with offset obligations work closely with their supplier base, some having goals of increasing supplier participation in excess of 50 percent. Teamwork does make the process more effective and efficient. There are various business activities taking place and procurement decisions being made by one of the sellers or its suppliers without offset needs that others may be able to use as offset credit to satisfy an indirect obligation.

Many governments see offsets as a mechanism to develop their indigenous business and industrial sectors. Training in management techniques may be attractive to both parties. The upgrading of humanware may be seen by the government as more critical for improving international competitiveness than efforts focused only on hardware. For the seller, training is relatively inexpensive, but it provides good credits because of its political benefit.

An important dimension of the developmental effort will relate to exports. This may involve the analysis of business sectors showing the greatest foreign-market potential, improving organizational and product readiness, conducting market research (e.g., estimating demand or assessing competition), identifying buyers or partners for foreign-market development, or assisting in the export process (e.g., company visits, support in negotiations and reaching a final agreement, facilitating trial/sample shipments, handling documentation needs).

Sales are often won or lost on the availability of financing and favorable credit terms to the buyer. Financing packages put together by one of the seller's entities, if it is critical in winning the bid, will earn offset credits.

Buyer nations focusing on industrial development and technology transfer have negotiated contracts that call for offsetting the cost of their purchases through investments. Saudi Arabian purchases of military technology have recently been tied to sellers' willingness to invest in manufacturing plants, defense-related industries, or special-interest projects in the country. British Aerospace, for example, has agreed to invest in factories for the production of farm feed and sanitary ware.

Most often, the final offset deal includes a combination of activities, both direct and indirect vis-à-vis the sale, and no two offset deals are alike. With increasing frequency, governments may require "pre-deal counterpurchases" as a sign of commitment and ability to deliver should they be awarded the contract. Some companies, such as United Technologies, argue that there is limited advantage in carrying out offset activities in advance of the contract, unless the buyer agrees to a firm commitment. While none of the bidders may like it, buyer's-market conditions give them very little choice to argue. Even if a bidder loses the deal, it can always attempt to sell its offset credits to the winner or use the credits in conjunction with other sales that one of its divisions may have. Some of the companies involved in the bidding in Finland maintain offset accounts with the Finnish government.

McDonnell's Deal with the Finnish Air Force

The F/A-18 Hornet is a twin-engine, twin-tail, multimission tactical aircraft that can be operated from aircraft carriers or from land bases (see Figure 2). It is both a fighter (air-to-air) and an attack (air-to-ground) aircraft. McDonnell Aircraft Company, a division of MDC, is the prime contractor for the F/A-18. Subcontractors include General Electric for the Hornet's smokeless F404 low-bypass turbofan engines, Hughes Aircraft Company for the APG-73 radar, and Northrop Corporation for the airframe. Approximately 1,100 F/A-18s have been delivered worldwide. Although it had been in use by the United States since 1983, it had been (and can continue to be) upgraded during its operational lifetime. Furthermore, it had proven its combat readiness in the Gulf War.

Only since June of 1990 has the F/A-18 been available to countries that are not members of the North Atlantic Treaty Organization (NATO). The change in U.S. government position resulted from the rapidly changed East-West political situation. The attractive deals available in neutral countries such as Switzerland and Finland helped push the government as well. When the Finnish Air Force initiated its program in 1986, MDC was not invited to (and would not have been able to) offer a bid because of U.S. government restrictions.

THE FINNISH GOVERNMENT POSITION

The Finnish government's role in the deal had two critical dimensions: one related to the choice of the aircraft, the other related to managing the offset agreement in a fashion to maximize the benefit to the country's industry for the long term.

Selecting the Fighter

In 1986, the Finnish Air Force (FAF) decided to replace its aging Swedish-made Drakens and Soviet-made MIG-21s, which made up three fighter squadrons. At that time, the remaining service life of these aircraft was estimated to be 15 years, calling for the new squadrons to be operational by the year 2000 and to be up-to-date even in 2025. Finland, due to its strategic geographic location, has always needed a reliable air-defense system.

FIGURE 2	**F/A-18 Hornet Strike Fighter**

Prime contractor	McDonnell Douglas
Principal subcontractor	Northrop Corporation
Type	Single- (C) and two-seat (D), twin-turbofan for fighter and attack missions
Powerplant	Two General Electric F404-GE-402 (enhanced performance engine)
Thrust	4800 kp each (approx.)
Afterburning thrust	8000 kp each (approx.)
Dimensions	
Length	17.07 m
Span	11.43 m
Wing area	37.16 m²
Height	4.66 m
Weights	
Empty	10 455 kg
Normal takeoff	16 650 kg
Maximum takeoff	22 328 kg
Wing loading	450 kg/m²
Fuel (internal)	6 435 litre (4925 kg)
Fuel (with external tanks)	7 687 litre
Armament	
Cannon	One General Electric M61A-1 Vulcan rotary-barrel 20-mm
Missiles	Six AIM-9 Sidewinder air-to-air
	Four AIM-7 Sparrow
	Six AIM-120 AMRAAM
Radar	AN/APG-73 multi-mode air-to-air and air-to-surface
Performance	
Takeoff distance	430 m
Landing distance	850 m
Fighter-mission radius	> 740 km
Maximum speed	1.8 Mach (1 915 km/h) at high altitude
	1.0 Mach at intermediate power
Service ceiling	15 240 m
Payload	7 710 kg
Used since	1983
Expected manufacturing lifetime	2000+
Users	USA, Australia, Canada, Spain, and Kuwait
Ordered quantity	1,168

The position of neutrality adopted by Finland had favored split procurement between Eastern and Western suppliers until the collapse of the Soviet Union in December of 1991 made it politically possible to purchase fighters from a single Western supplier.

The first significant contacts with potential bidders were made in 1988 and in February 1990, the FAF requested proposals from the French Dassault-Breguet, Sweden's Industrigruppen JAS, and General Dynamics in the United States for 40 fighters and trainer aircraft. In January 1991, the bid was amended to 60 fighters and 7 trainers. Three months later, MDC joined the bidding, and by July 1991, binding bids were received from all of the four manufacturers.

During the evaluative period, the four bidders tried to gain favor for their alternative. One approach was the provision of deals for Finnish companies as "pre-deal counterpurchases." For example, General Dynamics negotiated for Vaisala (a major Finnish electronics firm) to become a subcontractor of specialty sensors for the F-16. Before the final decision, the Swedish bidder had arranged for deals worth $250 million for Finnish companies, the French for over $100 million, and General Dynamics for $40 million. MDC, due to its later start, had none to speak of. Other tactics were used as well. The Swedes pointed out to long ties that the countries have had, and especially to the possibilities to develop them further on the economic front. As a matter of fact, offsets were the main appeal of the Swedish bid since the aircraft itself was facing development cost overruns and delays. The French reminded the Finnish government that choosing a European fighter might help in Finland's bid to join the European Union (EU) in 1995. Since the FAF prefers the U.S. AMRAAM missile system for its new fighters, the U.S. government cautioned that its availability depended on the choice of the fighter. The companies themselves also worked on making their bid sweeter: Just before the official announcement, General Dynamics improved its offer to include 67 aircraft for the budgeted sum and a guarantee of 125 percent offsets; that is, the amount of in-country participation would be 125 percent of the sale price paid by the Finnish government for the aircraft.

After extensive flight testing both in the producers' countries and in Finland (especially for winter conditions), the Hornet was chosen as the winner. Despite the high absolute cost of the aircraft (only 57 will be bought versus 60), the Hornet's cost-effectiveness relative to performance was high. The other alternatives were each perceived to have problems: The JAS-39 Gripen had the teething problems of a brand-new aircraft; the Mirage's model 2000-5 has not yet been produced; and the F-16 may be coming to the end of its product life cycle. The MIG-29 from the Soviet Union/Russia was never seriously in the running due to the political turmoil in that country. Some did propose purchasing the needed three squadrons from the stockpiles of the defunct East Germany (and they could have been had quite economically), but the uncertainties were too great for a strategically important product.

Working out the Offsets

Typically, a specific committee is set up by the government to evaluate which arrangements qualify as part of the offset. In Finland's case, the Finnish Offset Committee (FOC) consists of five members with Ministries of Defense, Foreign Affairs, as well as Industry and Trade represented. Its task is to provide recommendations as to which export contracts qualify and which do not. The Technical Working Group was set up to support its decision making, especially in cases concerning technology transfer. From 1977 to 1991, the procedures and final decisions were made by the Ministry of Defense; since then, the responsibility has been transferred to the Ministry of Trade and Industry (see Figure 3). The transfer was logical given the increased demands and expectations on the trade and technology fronts of the F/A-18 deal.

When the committee was established in 1977 in conjunction with a major military purchase, almost all contracts qualified until an export developmental role for offsets was outlined. The Finnish exporter is required to show that the offset agreement played a pivotal role in securing its particular contract.

Two different approaches are taken by the government to attain its developmental objective. First, the government will not make available (or give offset credit) for counter-purchasing goods that already have established market positions unless the counterpurchaser can show that the particular sale would not have materialized without its support (e.g., through distribution or financing). Second, the government will use compensation "multipliers" for the first time. While previous deals were executed on a one-on-one basis, the government now wants, through the use of multipliers, direct purchases to certain industries or types of companies. For example, in the case of small- or medium-sized companies, a multiplier of two may be used; that is, a purchase of $500,000 from

FIGURE 3   **Offset: Finnish Industry Input**

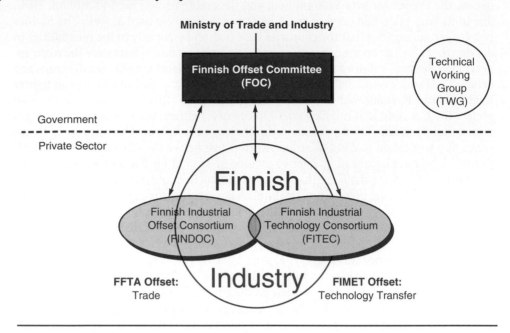

such a firm will satisfy a $1-million share of the counterpurchaser's requirement. Attractive multipliers also may be used which may generate long-term export opportunities or support Finland's indigenous arms or other targeted industry. Similarly, the seller may also insist on the use of multipliers. In the case of technology transfer, the seller may request a high multiplier because of the high initial cost of research and development that may have gone into the technology licensed or provided to the joint venture as well as its relative importance to the recipient country's economic development.

Finnish industry is working closely with the government on two fronts. The Finnish Industrial Offset Consortium (FINDOC) was established to collaborate with the Finnish Foreign Trade Association (a quasi-governmental organization) on trade development. FINDOC's 21 members represent 15 main business areas (e.g., aircraft, shipbuilding, pulp and paper machinery, and metal and engineering) and are among the main Finnish exporters. Their consortium was set up to take advantage of offset opportunities more efficiently and to provide a focal point for the F-18 Team's efforts. For example, MDC and FINDOC arranged for a familiarization trip to the United States for interested Finnish businesses in the fall of 1992. For those companies not in FINDOC, it is the task of the FFTA to provide information on possibilities to benefit from the deal. The Finnish Industrial Technology Consortium (FITEC) was established to facilitate technology transfer to and from the Finnish metal and engineering industries.

THE F-18 TEAM'S POSITION

The monies related to offset management and associated development are not generally allowed as a separate cost in the sales contract. Profit margins for aircraft sales are narrow, and any additional costs must be watched closely. Extraordinary demands by the buyer make bidding more challenging and time-consuming. For example, the customer may want extensive changes in the product without changes in the final price. Switzerland wanted major alterations made to the airframe and additional equipment which made its total cost per plan higher than the price in Finland. In the experience of high-tech firms, the add-on for direct offsets ranges from 3 to 8 percent, which has to be incorporated into the feasibility plans. Offsets have to make good business sense and, once agreed to, successfully executed.

Competing for the Deal

In accepting the offer to bid for the FAF deal, the F-18 Team believed it had only a 5 percent chance to win the deal but, given its size, decided to go ahead. From the time it received a request to bid from the FAF, MDC had three months to prepare its proposal. The only main negative factor from the short preparation time was MDC's inability to arrange for "prepurchase" deals and generate goodwill with the constituents.

After two fact-finding missions to Finland, MDC established an office in Helsinki in August 1991. The decision to have a full-time office in Finland (compared to the competitors whose representatives were in Helsinki two days a week on the average) was made based on the experiences from Korea and Switzerland. MDC's approach was to be ready and able to help the customer in terms of information and be involved with all the constituents of the process, such as the testing groups of the FAF, the Ministry of Defense (owners of the program), and the Parliament (supporters of the program).

Beyond the technical merits of the Hornet, MDC's capabilities in meeting the pending offset obligations were a critical factor in winning the deal. MDC had by 1992 a total of 100 offset programs in 25 countries with a value of $8 billion, and its track record in administering them was excellent. Another factor in MDC's favor was its long-term relation with Finnair, the national airline. Finnair's aircraft have predominantly come from MDC, starting with the DC-2 in 1941 to the MD-11 aircraft delivered in 1991.

Satisfying the Offset Obligation

Offset deals are not barter where the seller and the buyer swap products of equal value over a relatively short time period. The F-18 Team members have to complete the offset program by the year 2002 through a number of different elements including marketing assistance, export development, technology transfer, team purchases, and investment financing. One of the major beneficiaries of the offset arrangement is Valmet, the only major aircraft manufacturer in Finland. Valmet will assemble the 57 C-versions in Finland and is also counting on the F-18 Team's connections to open markets for its Redigo trainer aircraft. The F-18 Team works with Finnish companies to develop exports for their products and services by identifying potential buyers and introducing the two parties to each other. Purchases can come from within the contractor companies, suppliers to the F-18 contractors, and third parties. The motivation for completing offset projects is financial penalties for the prime team members if they do not meet contract deadlines.

However, no one in the F-18 Team or among its suppliers is obligated to engage in a given transaction just because Finland purchased fighters from McDonnell Douglas. The key point is that products must meet specifications, delivery dates, and price criteria to be successfully sold in any market. After an appropriate purchase has taken place, the F-18 Team receives offset credit based on the Finnish-manufactured content of the transaction value as approved by the Finnish Offset Committee. For example, when Finnyards won the bid to build a passenger ferry for the Danish Stena Line, Northrop received offset credits due to its role in financing Finnyard's bid.

The offset obligations are not limited to the United States. The Team has offset partners all over the world because the members operate worldwide. Furthermore, given the long time frame involved, there are no pressing time constraints on the members to earn offset credits.

Since 1992, the MDC office in Helsinki has had two officers: one in charge of the aircraft, the other focused on offsets. Due to the worse recession in recent Finnish history, the response to the offset program has been unprecedented, and the office has been inundated with requests for information.

ONE COMPANY'S EXPERIENCE

Hackman, one of Finland's leading exporters in the metal sector, started its cooperation with McDonnell Douglas by putting together a portfolio of Hackman products which offer the best offset potential. The proposal ended up covering a wide range of products ranging from tableware to turn-key cheese plants. Disinfecting machines and food processors created the most interest because of McDonnell Douglas' contracts in the hospital and construction sectors.

The first project identification came in July 1992 when word came from McDonnell Douglas that a $187-million hotel being planned for Denver, Colorado, was a potential offset target. The contractor was seeking export financing (e.g., through GE Finance) in exchange for sourcing products through offset from Finland for which offset credits could be used by MDC. Ideally, the contractor would get attractive financing, the F-18 Team would get offset credits, and Finnish participants would get a shot at a huge deal worth up to $40 million in total.

Questions for Discussion

1. Why would the members of the F-18 Team, McDonnell Douglas, Northrop, General Electric, and Hughes agree to such a deal rather than insist on a money-based transaction?
2. After the deal was signed, many Finnish companies expected that contracts and money would start rolling in by merely calling up McDonnell Douglas. What are the fundamental flaws in this thinking?
3. Why do Western governments typically take an unsupportive stance on countertrade arrangements?
4. Comment on this statement: "Offset arrangements involving overseas production that permits a foreign government or producer to acquire the technical information to manufacture all or part of a U.S.-origin article trade short-term sales for long-term loss of market position."

References

"Countertrade's Growth Continues." *BarterNews* 27 (1993): 54–55.

"Offsets in the Aerospace Industry." *BarterNews* 27 (1993): 56–57.

"Investing, Licensing, and Trading Conditions Abroad: Saudi Arabia." *Business International* May 15, 1990, 5.

Matthews, Ron. "Countering or Countenancing Countertrade." *Management Accounting* 53 (October 1991): 42–44.

Saastamoinen, Jukka. "Jaita Vastakauppiaan Hattuun." *Optio,* May 21, 1992, 26–28.

Silverang, Keith. "Behind the Myth of Offset." *Style & Steel* 2 (Spring 1992): 28–29.

Verzariu, Pompiliu, and Paula Mitchell. *International Countertrade: Individual Country Practices.* Washington, D.C.: U.S. Department of Commerce, Part 1, 1992.

Hathaway Electronics:
The Foreign Assignment

Charlie Dixon stared at the columns of figures on the page of the report in front of him without really seeing them. He took another gulp from his coffee mug and untangled a pile of paper clips on his desk, but he still couldn't concentrate on those numbers. He tried staring out the window of his fifth floor office, watched the small human figures strolling along the plaza-like area in front of the Hathaway Electronics Company building, and wondered why he felt uneasy. Things seemed to be going pretty well. He had started with Hathaway nine years ago, right out of college. His salary had increased satisfactorily each year. He'd had three different job assignments, starting in one of the branch plants as a cost analyst, then on to a departmental supervisory job here at headquarters, and now was an assistant controller with his name on the door, a rug on the floor, and his own secretary.

The phone interrupted his idle study of the patterns of the moving humanity below. It was his boss's secretary. "Mr. Wilbur would like to see you in his office at eleven." That was all. Charlie asked what the subject of the meeting was, who else was invited, what should he bring, but got zero answers. He swung around to the window again, staring at the people below. He chanced to gaze at a rather heavyset man, bustling toward the front entrance of the building. Even from his vantage point, Charles recognized the rumpled suit, vest unbuttoned, cigarette dangling from the lips, and the bulging, somewhat tattered briefcase under the arm. It was Frank Miller, the American who was the head of Hathaway's French subsidiary.

Hathaway Electronics generated about 20 percent of its sales overseas. The company sold its products through an export sales department which had eight sales offices located in major cities in Europe, South America, and the Far East. Overseas manufacturing activities were a more recent part of the company's strategy. First there was a joint venture with a Brazilian electrical firm. Then Hathaway formed a wholly owned subsidiary to manufacture components in Taiwan for shipment and ultimate incorporation into the products made in the U.S. plants. Encouraged by the success of these two foreign operations, the company looked for a way to establish a stronger position for its products in the larger market potential of Europe. The subsequent strategy was to buy majority control of an existing French company which made a few electronic components but less than half of the items in Hathaway's line. It was also believed by the Hathaway top management that their own products were technologically quite superior to French ones and that the French company's sales could be increased substantially by transfusions of the Hathaway "know-how" and research capabilities. Charlie didn't have very much responsibility for or contact with these foreign activities. However, one of his major tasks was to review requests for capital from all parts of the Hathaway organization.

That chance spotting of Frank Miller, striding across the elegant entranceway to the building, gave Charlie a jolt. Last week a very large request for capital had come to his desk from the French subsidiary. Charlie had given it careful study since it was for an amount well up into the board-approval category, and he had then written a strong

Source: This case is adapted from the book, *Hathaway Electronics* by Julian Allen and Gerald Parkhouse. For further information contact Gerald Parkhouse at Elmira College, Elmira, New York.

letter recommending rejection of the proposal. The request was for virtually a complete replacement of the French company's manufacturing equipment line. Charlie's recommendation faulted the absence of supporting data to justify the vastly increased sales projections. He had found arithmetic errors in the calculations of reduced costs. The French writer of the proposal had not handled depreciation costs as prescribed in the controller's procedures, and the savings claimed had overlooked taxes on the increased profits. Finally, the whole project had not been included in the subsidiary's capital budget for the year, and there was no explanation of changed circumstances to warrant this deviation from plan. In summary, it was one of the poorest requests Charlie had ever seen. He had sent out his expressive recommendations on Wednesday of last week, addressing his memo to the Controller, Bob Wilbur, the Financial Vice President, Frank Miller, and the Vice President of International Operations. Now, on Thursday, eight days later, he suddenly realized he had had absolutely no response to his written outburst. Now Charlie realized why he had been uneasy. The strange summons to an 11 a.m. meeting, and the sight of Frank Miller striding (angrily?) into the building, increased his anxiety. He went off to face the music.

The controller's secretary looked up and said, "Go right in. Mr. Wilbur is waiting for you."

Wilbur was standing, looking out of a window. He turned as Charlie came in. "Hi, Charlie. Close the door and have a chair."

"Did you want to discuss my recommendation on the French capital request?"

"No. I haven't read it yet."

A long pause followed. Wilbur resumed his study of the scene outside the window. Finally he said, "Have you ever been to France, Charlie?"

"No."

"Your personnel file says you're fluent in French."

"I had five years of it between high school and college. Tried it once outside the classroom on a visit to Quebec. Why?"

"International wants you to go to France."

Charlie frowned, "To check out that crazy capital request?"

"No. Transfer. To be the subsidiary's controller." He paused for about three seconds. "And vice president."

"Why me? Because I'm supposedly fluent in French? It's been ten years since I studied or used French. I don't think the French would consider me fluent."

Wilbur finally moved to his desk chair, leaned back, adjusted his shirt sleeves. "They've got a lot of problems over there. We've poured buckets of money into that outfit the last three years and sent over some top engineering talent, but we don't seem to get any results. They haven't gained market share, their costs have gone up, not down. Their financial statements don't come in on time. They don't seem to be able to explain the figures when we do get them. Last week Pierre Lanson, their controller, resigned. Miller told us he wanted an American this time. Someone who understood the figures and could explain them. Someone who understood what the top brass back here wanted, and someone who could speak French so he'd know what they're talking about."

Now Charlie was on the edge of his chair. Questions were flitting about in his mind faster than he could articulate them. Move to France? For how long? Where would they live? What would his wife think? What would the salary be? Should he take the eight-month-old car? School, my God, what about the kids' school? What kind of a guy would Miller be to work for? Suppose the whole subsidiary goes in the red, how long would the board hang on to it? What about his house, only 3 years into his 25-year mortgage?

Suddenly Charlie realized that Wilbur was still talking . . . "and you've probably got a lot of questions. Here's what I want you to do now. Frank Miller's in the next office waiting to meet with you. Now don't let him scare you. He's sort of gruff; he's personally sloppy—gets cigarette ashes all over his shirt all the time—and he gets very impatient with people he calls 'lousy bureaucrats.' But he's an absolute mechanical and electronic genius. Talk to Frank as long as you want, but don't give him an answer yet. I want you to also talk with two others. Go see Bill Bradshaw over in Personnel. He can answer a lot of the compensation questions that Miller can't. Then there's a man in the Marketing group on the second floor. I want you to see him. He'll be expecting you. His name is Ted Martin and he's rather new with us, but he lived in Europe for ten years working for two different American companies, and he can give you an unbiased rundown on what it's like to be an American working in a foreign country. Then, of course, talk it over at home."

"How soon does the company need my answer?"

"Well, Miller is going back on a Friday night flight, so we ought to know by tomorrow noon. If your answer is 'no,' Miller will have to stay over and talk with someone else. So on your way and I'll see you tomorrow."

Charlie's meeting with Frank Miller was not what he expected. First, Miller apologized for not being able to have lunch with Charlie, then spent only ten minutes with him before dashing off. Speaking very rapidly he outlined the job, indicating that in addition to the responsibilities the departing French controller had had, Miller wanted Charlie to take over all the "office functions" covering purchasing, production planning and scheduling, the treasury function and the Personnel Department (except for labor relations). His purpose in this reorganizing was to relieve himself (Miller) of all that "paper shoveling stuff" so he could concentrate all his time on engineering and manufacturing problems. In addition, he expected Charlie to handle most of the contacts with the U.S. headquarters. "Keep those guys out of my way. Handle it so there aren't any more memos like the one you just wrote about our expansion request. And design all the accounting and budget reports so both the French managers and the top management at home can use and understand the same figures. I gotta go. I'll see you tomorrow. Your salary will be increased 20% and there are some overseas fringe benefits which Bradshaw in Personnel will explain."

Frank Miller got up abruptly and left the office leaving a trail of cigarette ashes. Charlie sat still for a minute or two then decided to go back to his own office and try to reach Bradshaw. There he found Bradshaw reading *The Wall Street Journal,* sitting in Charlie's own chair, feet up on the desk. Seeing Charlie come in, he stood up, shook hands, and settled into another chair.

"I figured you'd be a bit late," Bradshaw explained, "so I've taken the liberty of having some sandwiches and coffee sent here so we can discuss your opportunity. Where shall we start?"

"He said you would explain the fringe benefits."

"That's the easy part. All the overseas benefits are based on your base salary. The new one, not your present salary. And all the overseas fringes apply only to the time you are actually overseas, and cease when you return to the U.S. First, there is an overseas salary premium—an extra amount theoretically based on the hardship of living in a foreign country. For France, it's 10%. Second, there's a housing allowance since living in the Paris area will cost more—whether you rent or buy—than in this area. It's not designed to cover your entire housing cost, but the assumed extra cost over what housing costs are—on the average—for someone in your salary grade living here. Of course, just as with a domestic transfer, the company will pay all your moving costs. Both ways, unless you should resign while over there."

"A subtle disincentive?"

"Sure. Next is a little complicated. While you're living in France, you'll have to pay some French taxes. There's a tax that is something like our Social Security tax which is deducted from your pay. It covers certain medical costs and provides, theoretically, for a retirement income. Since this is a payroll deduction some of your salary will be paid to you over there in France; the balance will be sent to your bank here in dollars. Since you are a U.S. citizen, you will still have deductions out of your check for Social Security and U.S. income taxes."

"How about French income taxes?"

"You'll owe those, too, but they don't have payroll withholding. Also, the U.S. in effect gives you credit for your French income taxes, so you don't pay twice on the same income. But you must file with both governments. The company will provide you with tax accounting to do this."

"What about schools?"

"Good question. You have two options, either send your kids to a French school or to the American School of Paris. It's a private school, K through 12th grade, standard American curriculum and activities. No football, though, nobody to play against. If you choose the American school, the company pays the tuition."

"Do they teach French?"

"I forgot to mention that. French classes are required at all grade levels."

Charlie sat reflecting on all this for a moment or two, then asked, "How long do you think the assignment would be?"

"There's no way to predict that. It could be a year, it could be ten years. I suppose in our history, the average overseas stint has been four to five years. Look, we do want you to talk to Ted Martin. He's on the third floor and he's expecting you."

Ted Martin was indeed expecting him. After appropriate self-introductions, Martin settled comfortably back in his chair and began what was essentially a monologue.

"I have some idea of what's going through your mind right now, so maybe I can help. You have the chance to take a new assignment which can either be the most exciting, challenging, and broadening experience in your life or it could be the most frustrating, discouraging, and seemingly unending assignment you've ever had. Probably the most important factor in determining which it will be both for you and your family is your own attitude about living in a foreign country. If you—or your family—approach the move as a rare chance to learn new things, meet new and different people, gain a new perspective on history (including the history of the U.S.), find that other cultures have different ways of looking at life, then you'll think it was the best thing that ever happened. But if you have what I call the 'peanut-butter syndrome,' you'll be miserable."

"What's the peanut-butter syndrome?"

"In many foreign countries you can't find peanut butter in the local markets. Or Post's 40% Raisin Bran Flakes or your particular brand of shampoo. If you miss these things, if you can't stand not watching Tom Brokaw every night or seeing three or four NFL games every weekend, you could be miserable. It's not the same as being a tourist, when you know that after seeing a certain number of cathedrals and museums and chateaux you'll be back in your own home. But if it's going to finally get to you to put up with door handles that don't work the way they do in the U.S. and tiny refrigerators and exasperating telephone service—then don't go. A tourist is only concerned about understanding the money and how good his hotel room is and what time the plane leaves for Rome. But an expatriate has a whole set of different problems. He has to get 'papers' from the government to have permission to live there, another set to have permission to work there. The whole business of home finding and the relationship between landlord and tenant is completely different from our practices."

"How do you find out things like that?"

"Generally the hard way—by doing it the wrong way first. Now all these things that are different lead many Americans to compare on a judgmental basis. The French way is better on this custom but the American way is better on that situation. The better or worse approach is self-defeating. Just think of it as different."

"I think I see your point," Charlie said. "Do you think it's possible for Americans and French to work together in the same organization?"

"Sure, but it's not easy. Imagine how you'd feel if a Japanese or a Saudi Arabian firm bought control of Hathaway and the new owners sent over their executives to take over Hathaway's top jobs. Then these new top people talked to each other in their own language, introduced different strategies for running the business, imposed a new and different accounting system, judged your performance in their home country's currency ignoring the differences in the accounting treatment of the two countries involved and also ignoring the fluctuations in the currency exchange rates."

"Wow! I see your point. Do we look that bad to the French?"

"Well, the phrase, 'The Ugly American' is more than just a book title. Working in the international arena of business does require a heightened degree of sensitivity to the other guy's viewpoint and some diplomatic skills as well. And mentioning the word diplomacy reminds me of another problem you might have to face. Sooner or later some issue will come up where the corporate made-in-the-U.S.A. policy or strategy will be in conflict with your host nation's policy. Another problem you might have to handle could come up where there is a conflict between the governmental policies of France and the United States."

"I'd expect that kind of problem would be handled by top management here."

"Sure, but you might be the one who identifies such a problem and presents it along with local French lawyers' opinions on the subject."

"Well, I'd just have to face those kinds of problems when and if they arise. But you can help me with a more immediate problem. Bradshaw told me our kids could go either to the French public schools or, at company expense, to the American school. Which would you advise?"

"Since I don't know your kids, I can't really advise you, but I can tell you about the experience of other Americans. The French schools are very good. Longer days, more hours per week, more homework. They have far more emphasis on languages, literature, history, philosophy—much less of the typical American emphasis on 'let's all learn to get along with each other!' If the child starts out in the French system at a very young age, he can do very well, mastering the new language in very short order. But the older child will find it far more difficult at first to learn both French and the material being taught at the same time. How old are your kids?"

"Five and eight."

"That's a tough call. Good luck. Any other questions?"

"I'll think of dozens as soon as I get home."

"OK. Give me a call at home tonight if I can help with anything else. If you take the job it will change your life and your family's lives to a far greater degree than any domestic move could. Most of those changes will be on the plus side. But there is one minus you should factor in. An overseas experience will increase your managerial ability significantly. You'll find ways to cope with problems that nobody here has ever experienced. You'll gain maturity and wisdom and perspective faster than if you remain on a U.S. assignment. But the fly in the ointment is that your career progress up the managerial ladder could be slower!"

"That doesn't make sense."

"It doesn't necessarily happen this way, but it does happen more often than it should. Let's say you stay in France for five years. You do a bang up job. You've achieved the goals set out for you. But except for the few people back here who have had international experience themselves, most of the top managers in the company have no appreciation of the magnitude of the problems you had to deal with or the progress you made in solving these problems. They will remember you the way you are today."

"Is there a solution to that problem?"

"Maybe not a solution, but a reduction of the possible magnitude of the problem. Undoubtedly your job in France will require your coming back here several times a year. These visits should be scheduled for long enough to allow time to get around and see everybody you can. Keep in touch with the changes going on here. Mend fences and so on. Don't let people forget who you are and what you're doing."

Charlie drifted through a meeting that had been scheduled for four o'clock. When it eventually ended he headed for the parking lot without his normal last check in at his own office. As he started his car for the 15-minute drive to his home, he grappled with the problem of how to introduce this unexpected turn of events to his family.

Questions for Discussion

1. Do you think the combination of Charlie Dixon with the current American general manager in France will be effective?

2. What should Charlie do if he suspects that he might suffer from the "peanut-butter syndrome"?

3. If you were Charlie, would you take the job?

German Luxury Cars: Made in the USA

Two southern U.S. states, South Carolina and Alabama, received what many view as just rewards for their hospitality, generosity, and pro-business environment. These rewards came in the form of multimillion-dollar investments for new automobile plants. The German luxury car legends BMW and Mercedes-Benz both chose to invest in new production sites in the southern United States. For BMW, the search ended in the summer of 1992, when management decided to locate its plant in the Greenville-Spartanburg area of South Carolina. Mercedes concluded its closely watched search in the fall of 1993, choosing tiny Vance, Alabama, as home for its new plant.

The German investments represent two key facets of a very competitive industry: the need to cut costs and easy access to target markets. U.S. wages are, on average, 60 percent lower than in Germany. Both German car makers are competing head-to-head with Japanese producers that are already well-ensconced on the U.S. production scene.

Both South Carolina and Alabama are celebrating the hard-fought battle that won them thousands of future jobs, potential financial returns in the billions, and the prestige of having landed such world-class companies. These developments are also expected to make other potential investors take a long, hard look at the two states as well.

Each investment decision was based on different details; however, the underlying case of trying to land a world-class investor at seemingly whatever means possible is present in both examples. A closer look at the two foreign direct investments provides the opportunity to view some of the different details and circumstances, as well as the similarities, that exist in luring desirable investment.

THE BMW DECISION

When BMW chose to locate in South Carolina, it was joining a group of European firms (BASF Corp., Rieter Corp., Marzoli International Inc., and Michelin Tire Corp.) that had already discovered the comparatively cheaper and competent work force as well as a hospitable, pro-business atmosphere. BMW plans to begin production in 1995 of a new, more affordable model that will be aimed at the American market, specifically, graying baby boomers. Over three years, the auto maker looked at 250 locations in 10 countries. When it was clear that BMW planned on producing this new model in the United States, a race ensued between competing states to win the cherished investment. In the end, the choice came down to Nebraska and South Carolina.

South Carolina Governor Carroll Campbell put up a strong recruiting effort, visiting BMW in Germany and making offers that were hard to refuse. In order to obtain the $640-million plant and the expected 6,000 new state jobs, a bit of Southern finesse was added. For instance, the site most desired by BMW had 134 separate landowners. In order to ease land acquisition problems, Gov. Campbell secured a $25-million appropriation

Source: This case was written by Michael R. Czinkota and Peter Fitzmaurice based on the following sources: "Why Mercedes Is Alabama Bound," *Business Week,* October 11, 1993, 138–139; "Alabama Steers Mercedes South," *ENR,* October 11, 1993, 6–7; "Mercedes-Benz Parks $300 Million Plant in Alabama," *Site Selection,* December 1993, 1292; "Europe Loves Dixie," *Europe,* October 1992, 30–36; "The Beemer Spotlight Falls on Spartanburg, USA," *Business Week,* July 6, 1992, 38; "The Boom Belt," *Business Week,* September 27, 1993, 98–104.

from the state legislature to buy the property. He personally telephoned reluctant sellers and within 14 weeks, the state and local governments had spent $36.6 million to buy every single property—including a home that one family had just finished building two weeks before they were approached. To sweeten the deal, new roads and site improvements were included, and the runway at the local airport was to be extended to accommodate BMW's cargo planes. The state also offered a $41-million property tax break to BMW. Furthermore, the local airport's free-trade-zone status was extended to include the 900-acre plant site, meaning BMW will not have to pay duties on parts imported from Germany or elsewhere until cars actually leave the plant for sale in the United States.

One of the big determinants for BMW was South Carolina's excellent technical school system. Under the investment agreement, the state customizes its training program for the company, even sending instructors to Munich to study the equipment that will be used. In all, the state has promised to spend $3 million to train workers for BMW alone, a considerable sum when one takes into account that in 1992 South Carolina spent $5.8 million on technical training for the entire state. In addition, local businesses offered to pay up to $3 million for additional training.

The constant stream of amenities and special treatment that South Carolina extended to BMW was especially critical to completing this deal, according to industry analysts, given the fact that BMW is considered to be a conservative corporation not prone to bold moves. The firm does not just want to be accepted, it wants to be welcomed. States Carl Flescher, a vice president with BMW North America: "I've only been down there for about 10 or 15 days and I am very impressed. The embracing of this whole thing is incredible. You go to the Holiday Inn and there is a sign that says 'Welcome BMW.' You pulled up to the Hertz rental car and they know who you are. People are genuinely friendly, open, and elated." Gov. Campbell sums up the whole mission best: "The name BMW is generally associated with excellence and quality and that by itself is a benefit. Other companies will say 'Well, wait a minute, BMW is rated as one of the best, and they chose South Carolina. So, they must be doing something right.'"

THE MERCEDES INVESTMENT

Mercedes offered the prospects of a $300-million plant and 1,500 new jobs. Initially, the firm's search included 170 sites in 30 states. Alabama knew that to win the investment, its offer to Mercedes would have to be outstanding. One state official recalls the message from a Mercedes consulting firm representative: "Everyone knows what South Carolina gave BMW. My client feels they are better than BMW!"

So the race was on and in the end, Alabama won the "industrial crown jewel," as Governor Jim Folsom, Jr. refers to it. The German company was impressed by the entrepreneurial, nonbureaucratic attitude of Alabama's state government. The firm also liked the access to interstate highways, railroads, and ports, adequate available labor, proximity to schools, quality of life, and, of course, a lucrative package of financial incentives. Here is a partial list of these incentives: $92.2 million to buy and develop the site, create a foreign trade zone, and build an employee training center; $77.5 million to extend water, gas, and sewer lines along with other infrastructure; $60 million in government funds to train Mercedes employees, suppliers, and workers in related industries, enriched by $15 million from the private sector; $8.7 million in tax breaks; in all, a total of more than $253 million.

The plant will make a sport utility vehicle costing between $20,000 and $30,000. About half of the annual output of 60,000 vehicles will be exported to Europe and other continents. Mercedes will ship engines and transmissions for the vehicle from Germany, but it expects to purchase most other parts from U.S. suppliers. Construction of the facility began in 1994, with production scheduled to start in 1997.

Alabama believes it invested wisely. One study found that the $253 million used to lure the German investment will yield shining returns of $365 million during the first year and $7.3 billion over the next 20 years.

But there are limits to the lure of state incentives. One state official commented: "Ultimately it comes down to the company's personal choice." Says Mercedes project leader Andreas Renschler: "Whether you get $10 million more or less in one state doesn't make any difference. We sensed a much higher dedication to our project."

A competing participant in the race to capture the Mercedes plant was North Carolina. The state's governor, Jim Hunt, criticized parts of Alabama's incentives package saying, "We do not need to risk the future of the franchise to recruit star players." In particular, Hunt pointed to what some refer to as the "Benz Bill," passed by the Alabama legislature during a special session. It allows 5 percent of corporate income tax from the plant and 5 percent of the plant's employees' taxes to be used to retire debt.

Critics are contending that states are "buying" industry at too steep a price. The financial incentives necessary to land the BMW plant—including a $1-a-year lease on the 900 acres—will cost South Carolina taxpayers $130 million over 30 years, although most of the incentives are in the first year.

North Carolina may be correct in denouncing certain types of tactics to lure investment. However, the attitude of not giving away "the franchise" is increasingly being seen as detrimental. A report by an international site-selection consultant, commissioned by North Carolina after losing the chance to land BMW, read that the state "is increasingly seen as a non-participant in incentive practices at a time when incentives are growing in importance." So the question, "How much is too much?" is complicated by the fact that growing expectations and necessities may warrant the types of grandiose offers that are portrayed in the Mercedes and BMW cases.

Questions for Discussion

1. Do you believe that states should encourage foreign direct investment? Why or why not?

2. Do incentives determine whether or not a company will invest in the United States?

3. How should a state government determine the upper limit of its investment support?

4. Do FDI incentives place local established firms at a disadvantage?

Video Case:
Poland's Dramatic Gamble:
From Marx to Markets

Over the last few years scholars, policymakers, and international business executives have studied the dramatic developments in Eastern Europe. Poland was one of the first countries to attempt a move from a planned, centrally run economy to a market economy. Many still ask: Can the Poles do it? What happens if they fail? And what's the impact on us?

Poland's troubles began at the end of World War II when the Russians liberated the country from the Germans. The communists implemented Stalinist Central Planning. Production was determined by state decree, not by markets. Huge state-run monopolies, such as Lenin Steel, dominated the economy. Prices and wages were set by the state. There was a saying in Poland, "We pretend to work, and the state pretends to pay us."

To achieve the communist goal of full employment, everyone was given a job, whether or not it was necessary. To employ so many people, wages had to be kept low. Therefore, subsidies were put in place for farmers and factories. This plan resulted in government budget deficits, a nonconvertible currency, low productivity, and shortages of almost everything.

According to one Polish citizen, "There was no food. We were lucky if we could find a kilogram of sausage . . . many times the last two kilograms of sausage were bought by the person in front of us in line."

By 1989, coping with continuing shortages and inflation running at more than 500 percent, the communists were forced to negotiate with Lech Walesa and the Solidarity Trade Union. The result was a Solidarity-led coalition government.

The new leaders did not choose a path of gradual reform. Instead, Finance Minister Leszek Balcerowicz, with the assistance of Western economists, came up with a radical plan of economic reform that would move Poland from central planning to free markets virtually overnight. The government reduced its budget deficit by slashing government subsidies. Enterprises had to show a profit, or face the possibility of bankruptcy. Many state-run enterprises were privatized, sold to investors. Prices were allowed to rise to whatever the market would bear, but wages were held in check. And the Polish currency, the zloty, was devalued as the first step toward making it compatible with Western currencies.

To eliminate long lines and shortages, the new plan allowed prices to rise so that producers would produce more. Prices went up for almost everything including gasoline. With gas prices and insurance so high, thousands of Poles stopped driving. Bread prices went up, electric bills quadrupled. Meanwhile, salaries only went up slightly, held in check to fight inflation. As a result of these events, the country was forced into recession. Fortunately, many enterprising Poles figured out ways to beat the old system. People sold goods from their cars and trucks, circumventing the state distribution system to lower prices on their products.

In the new free markets, farmers sell directly to customers. And industrious entrepreneurs have gone into business to bring products to market. One woman buys wheat from farmers, brings it to a mill to be ground, and sells the flour in Warsaw. Even stu-

---

Source: This case was drawn from the Public Broadcasting System's television program, "Adam Smith," which aired May 1, 1990. Producer: Alvin H. Perlmutter, Inc.

dents have gone into business for themselves. According to a Warsaw student, "It's great! We have a lot of customers, the business is growing. This is how it should be. This is a different market. And I'm sure, you know, in the United States it's the same. The market should be for the customer. If there is a demand, then we provide everything."

The profit motive is also one of the new laws at large state-run enterprises throughout Poland. Under the old communist system, factories sold as many products as the Central Committee told it to. Managers didn't actually know how much each product cost, and they didn't have control of costs. At the end of each fiscal year, managers would determine the loss, send it to the government, and the government would print the money to pay for it.

Under that system, line workers and managers had little or no incentive to be efficient in their work. There was little motivation for them to work harder because they were all paid the same wage. Employees who worked less got the same money as those who worked hard. Qualifications weren't important. It was more important to have a communist party card. Many party members were given jobs as directors at the factories. The general rule was that managers were "mediocre, but trustworthy."

Factories have been learning to operate under new rules. According to Jan Buczkowski, a production director, "now we have more problems than we had in the past. There are different troubles. We have to think about costs of our production. We have to think about the costs of spare parts. And we must think about our customers. It is a new market."

In the old days, workers didn't care if a line shut down for lack of parts, their jobs were guaranteed. Now if the factory doesn't turn a profit, it will be allowed to lay off workers, or worse, go bankrupt. In spite of personal hardship, many Poles seem to support the government's program.

According to Konstanty Gebert, a political analyst, the Polish people "reason in terms of a national emergency and are willing to accept sacrifices as long as they think that these sacrifices serve a general national cause. As long as they have trust and confidence in their leaders, who for the first time since the war they could democratically elect."

Privatization has been an important step on the road to reform. Laws for selling state enterprises to private investors were enacted. One of the first privatized firms was Omig, a maker of electronic components. As a private company, Omig operates more efficiently than it did before. According to Omig's Marek Ogradzki, "I think that the only way for Poland is privatization. In the future I think it will be 80 percent private sector and 20 percent state or government sector. Right now, it's the opposite way."

Privatization also includes ways of allowing workers and the public to buy shares in these companies, such as a stock exchange.

However, not all Poles are eager to buy into the reforms. Zbigniew Holdys is one of Poland's most famous rock stars. In the early 1980s his band, Perfect, filled stadiums until it was banned by the government. In spite of his position as a progressive artist, he is uneasy about life in the new Poland.

Holdys stated that, "In my generation—I am 38 years old right now—even people who are a little bit younger than me, I mean, about 30 years old feel that we are a loss for this country. I don't think anyone from our generation is ready to stand this situation. You have to learn to work in a different way, in a capitalist way."

According to Holdys, "there are hundreds, thousands, maybe even millions of people who were working in the old system. To take a man who worked in the Ministry of Culture and tell him that he must now be a manager—it's impossible. People are afraid. I don't think older generations are ready to change everything in a very short time. Probably this kind of Eden—this beautiful picture—will belong to my 2-year-old son when he is older."

Many Poles have not waited. They are learning the ways of capitalism and markets through another growth industry in Eastern Europe—entrepreneurship education. For example, young managers are attending courses at the International School of Management in Warsaw that are taught by visiting professors from the United States. The school teaches English and Western management skills, but the most important training is in developing an entrepreneurial mindset. Many institutions in Poland such as Solidarity have established links with universities in the United States to promote entrepreneurship and trade.

Poland needs Western management skills, modern Western technology, and, above all, Western capital to succeed with its dramatic transformation. Official U.S. investment has increased through U.S. congressional legislation called the S.E.E.D. Act. However, new private investment is the key to long-term development.

According to Dr. Jeffrey Sachs, a Harvard economist, "If the plan fails, I think there could be a terrible calamity, not only for the Poles, but for the West. There would be an explosion of political unrest and a loss of faith that moving toward a market economy is the right direction. It could lead to a rise in populism and an explosion of new hyperinflation in Poland and in the rest of the region. The crisis could become very deep and ugly, given all the ethnic and national tension in the region. And Eastern Europe and the former Soviet Union could be thrown into a cauldron of violence and nationalist conflict because they've lost a clear way out. I think their hope and belief—creating a market economy and integrating with Western Europe—is the direction for the future. If they lost heart in that strategy, what comes next? All sorts of terrible things could happen."

It's hard for Americans to comprehend a society in which you have to stand in line to buy everything, where the waiting time is 21 years for a telephone and 30 years for an apartment. In Poland, the lines are gone now, and so are the secret police and some of the communist apparatus. But it takes time to change the habits and the thinking of a people.

Poland's national anthem begins, "Poland has not yet perished." After surviving more than 50 years of oppression by Hitler, Stalin, and the Soviet Communist party, the Polish people clearly have the courage and commitment to rebuild and prosper. It may, however, take a generation to change the collective consciousness of the people. Do Polish people still have the patience to survive? Will the rest of the world invest for the long term?

Questions for Discussion

1. Explain the Polish expression, "We pretend to work and the state pretends to pay us." How have the Polish people adapted to market reforms and unemployment?

2. How did the old system of controlled management affect productivity and motivation in Poland's factories?

3. What have been the benefits of privatizing state-owned enterprises in Poland?

4. How has the Polish economy evolved since this program aired? Have the rapid reform programs succeeded in creating a free-market economy?

Video Case:
Music: America's Booming Export

International trade is imperative in today's world because the global nature of today's economy makes economic isolationism impossible. Failure to participate successfully in the global market will reduce a nation's economic influence and standard of living. Full participation can improve the quality of life.

While U.S. exports have not dropped in recent years, U.S. export growth has not kept pace with the total growth of world exports. Firms in economies torn by World War II have reestablished themselves and have obtained a share of the growing world trade for themselves.

Not all news about the U.S. trade position is bad news. An exception to the reduction in demand for American automobiles, steel, and television sets is the world's insatiable appetite for American entertainment. Some estimate that it is the country's second-largest export behind aircraft, but ahead of such staples as soybeans and coal.

Foreign sales account for two-thirds of the music market, and there is plenty of room for growth. Deregulation of broadcasting in Europe and around the world is expected to open up new outlets for music to air, and, presumably, young consumers will rush to the nearest record store with open wallets.

The industry is particularly interested in the former Soviet Union and China. Michael Jackson's album "Bad" sold half a million albums in China, a figure that looks very attractive to the music industry. The head of a major record company was asked why recorded American music sells so well. "If you had an on-street interview any place in the world, and you asked the kid or the 25-year-old to name the first 10 artists that come to mind, I think that at least 6 of those 10 are going to be artists that had their beginnings in the United States," said Robert Summer, president of CBS Records International.

This broad appeal is not just for consumption. It is also attracting foreign companies to purchase U.S. record companies. Bertelsmann, a giant German conglomerate, owns RCA Records. Sony paid $2 billion for CBS Records. Thorn-EMI, which owns Capital Records, is British, and so is Polygram. Only two of the six major record companies are U.S.-owned, MCA and Warner. And while the music industry searches out its next batch of superstars, some worry that those stars and the companies that earn money from them will be foreign. Entertainment executives were asked: Will the United States let this business slip offshore as so many other businesses have or is there something uniquely American about this product that will preclude limitations?

"I don't think the creative edge is going to be taken over until our cultural appeal worldwide is superseded," commented Sam Holdsworth, president of Billboard Entertainment Group.

Robert Huziak, president of RCA records, added, "I don't think that the United States will ever be without that creative motivation for the young people and hence we will always be able to continue to grow."

Joe Smith, president of Capital-EMI Music, was more pessimistic. He predicted a wave of Russian rock and roll to surface sometime before the end of this century. "Then

Source: This case was drawn from the Public Broadcasting System's television program, "Adam Smith," which aired on March 10, 1989. Producer: Alvin H. Purlmutter, Inc.

those guys that make these VCRs and the television sets are soon going to turn creative, and one day somebody in China is going to say 'let's rock 'n roll too.' I don't believe we can keep the edge unless we continue to develop our talent and do it," he said. "And that's my concern about the corporatization of rock and roll."

When asked whether the purchase of American record companies by Japanese and German firms will have an impact on the quality of the product, Smith said it depends on the dedication of the companies. "It won't have a great impact on our music unless they squeeze down on us and say, 'Well, don't sign so many new acts next year.' You only keep the edge by signing new talent, by mining what is the best in the country," said Smith. "In this country, a combination of blues and country and rock and roll got started here. We've still got the edge, but we can lose it because all that is very copyable."

"Somebody just with a headset and a CD can pick up every riff that Chuck Berry ever played or Joe Walsh, or Clapton," Smith said. "They can pick all that stuff up very quickly."

Questions for Discussion

1. How can the world demand for U.S.-produced entertainment, particularly in the music industry, have an effect on a macroeconomic level? On a microeconomic level? In your answer, define these two terms.

2. Explain the concept of "global linkages." Describe linkages that could be tied to the music industry on an international basis.

3. Should the United States be concerned about an increasing foreign presence within the American music industry? Why or why not? Will it affect the quality of the product? Explain.

4. What changes have occurred in the U.S. music industry since this PBS program was aired?

Video Case: A Taste of the West

In the mid-1980s, Mikhail Gorbachev introduced a new program called "perestroika" in the Soviet Union. Perestroika was to fundamentally reform the Soviet economy by improving the overall technological and industrial base as well as improving the quality of life for Soviet citizens through increased availability of food, housing, and consumer goods. It was hoped that this program would stimulate the entrepreneurial spirit of Soviet citizens and help the country and its government overcome crucial shortcomings. These shortcomings were the result of decades of communist orientation, which had led to significant capital and management shortages and inhibited the development of a market orientation and of consumer-oriented technology.

In subsequent years, a number of joint ventures between Western firms and Soviet institutions were either contemplated or even formed. However, many of these ventures, due to internal difficulties, met with only limited success. Nevertheless, the efforts of one firm, McDonald's—an icon of free enterprise—were hailed as a spectacular success.

The January 31, 1990, grand opening of McDonald's in the center of Moscow represented an important milestone for McDonald's Corporation and for the food-service industry in the Soviet Union. The state-of-the-art renovated building, formerly a cafe and a cultural gathering place, has indoor seating for over 700 people, has outside seating for 200, and is fully accessible to the handicapped. It currently employs over 1,000 people—the largest McDonald's crew in the world—and has served over 30,000 people per day. The original plans were to serve between 10,000 and 15,000 customers per day. The Soviet Union became the 52nd country to host the world's largest quick-service food restaurant company, and the Russian language is the 28th working language in which the company operates. McDonald's Corporation, based in Oak Brook, Illinois, serves over 22 million people daily in 11,000 restaurants in 52 countries. The Soviet population of over 291 million represented a major potential market of new customers for McDonald's.

THE NEGOTIATIONS

George A. Cohon, vice chairman of Moscow McDonald's and president and chief executive officer of McDonald's Restaurants of Canada, Limited, provided the leadership for the company's successful venture. His personal commitment and energy were irreplaceable during the long period of joint-venture discussions with the Soviet Union. Cohon's Canadian team spent over 12 years negotiating the agreement for McDonald's to enter into the Soviet market. In April 1988, agreement was reached on the largest joint venture ever made between a food company and the Soviet Union. This concluded the longest new-territory negotiations by the company since it was founded in 1955.

Sources: McDonald's corporate information, 1994; "A Month Later, Moscow McDonald's Is Still Drawing Long and Hungry Lines," *Houston Post,* March 1, 1990; background information from McDonald's Restaurants of Canada, Ltd.; Jeffrey A. Tannenbaum, "Franchisers See a Future in East Bloc," *The Wall Street Journal,* June 5, 1990, B1; Kevin Maney and Diane Rinehart, "McDonald's in Moscow Opens Today," *USA Today,* January 31, 1990, B1; "McDonald's on the Volga," *Employment Review* 3 (1990); Moscow McDonald's videotape produced for Dryden Press, 1990; Oliver Wates, "Crowds Still Gather at Lenin's Tomb, but Lineups Are Longer at McDonald's," *London Free Press,* June 9, 1990.

Cohon and his Canadian team had spent thousands of hours in Moscow making presentations to hundreds of senior trade officials, staff at various ministries, and countless other groups within the Soviet Union. Despite numerous setbacks and requests for endless submissions of and revisions to their proposals, Cohon persisted because many Soviets appeared to genuinely want to establish closer ties with the West. According to Cohon, McDonald's negotiations "outlived three Soviet premiers."

The historic joint-venture contract provided for an initial 20 McDonald's restaurants in Moscow and a state-of-the-art food production and distribution center to supply the restaurants. McDonald's accepts only rubles; future restaurants may accept hard currency. McDonald's Canada is managing the new venture in partnership with the Food Service Administration of the Moscow City Council in a 51 to 49 percent Soviet-Canadian partnership.

INTERNATIONAL TECHNOLOGY TRANSFER

Cohon stated that what ultimately sold the Soviets on McDonald's was the food technology it had to offer. In addition, the company's emphasis on quality, service, cleanliness, and value convinced the Moscow city officials that McDonald's could work in their city. Vladimir Malyshkov, chairman of the board of Moscow McDonald's, stated that McDonald's "created a restaurant experience like no other in the Soviet Union. It demonstrates what can be achieved when people work together."

Moscow McDonald's was clearly an international venture. McDonald's personnel from around the world helped prepare for the opening. Dutch agricultural consultants assisted in improving agricultural production. For example, they helped plant and harvest a variety of potato needed to make french fries that met McDonald's quality standards. Other international consultants assisted in negotiating contracts with farmers throughout the country to provide quality beef and other food supplies, including onions, lettuce, pickles, milk, flour, and butter. Once the Soviet farmers learned to trust the consultants, they became eager to learn about the new Western production technologies.

This technology transfer provided important long-term benefits to the Soviet citizenry. For example, through the transfer of agricultural technology and equipment, the Soviet potato farm Kishira increased its yield by 100 percent. According to the Kishira chairman, farmers from all over the Soviet Union requested technical training in production methods to increase their crop yields. Also, since the Soviet machinery lagged 15 to 20 years behind Western technology, new machinery from Holland was used to harvest the potatoes used to make french fries. However, according to a Dutch agricultural consultant, because of the McDonald's venture, it may not take the Soviets 20 years to catch up to Western production methods.

The development of a 10,000-square-meter food production and distribution center, located in the Moscow suburb of Solntsevo, was also an international effort involving equipment and furnishings from Austria, Canada, Denmark, Finland, Germany, Holland, Italy, Japan, Spain, Sweden, Switzerland, Taiwan, Turkey, the United Kingdom, the United States, and Yugoslavia. The center provides a state-of-the-art food-processing environment that meets McDonald's rigid standards.

At full capacity, the center employs over 250 workers. Also at full capacity, the meat line produces 10,000 patties per hour from locally acquired beef. Milk delivered in McDonald's refrigerated dairy trucks from a local farm is pasteurized and processed at the center. Flour, yeast, sugar, and shortening is used to produce over 14,000 buns per hour on the center's bakery line. Storage space at the center holds 3,000 tons of potatoes, and the pie line produces 5,000 apple pies per hour, made from fruit from local farmers.

MANAGEMENT TRAINING

Training for McDonald's crew and managers is essential to the customer service that the company provides. According to Bob Hissink, vice president of operations for Moscow McDonald's, hiring was just the beginning of assembling the largest McDonald's crew in the world. Over 25,000 applications were sorted, and 5,000 of the most qualified candidates were interviewed. Finally, the 630 new members of the first Moscow McDonald's team were selected. Initial training sessions were compressed into a four-week period with four or five shifts 12 hours a day. Seasoned McDonald's staff from around the world assisted the Soviet managers with crew training. The new crew of 353 women and 277 men was trained to work in several different capacities at the restaurant and had accumulated over 15,000 hours of skills development by opening day. During restaurant operating hours, about 200 crew members at a time are on duty.

The training requirements were more extensive for McDonald's managers. Four Soviets selected as managers of Moscow McDonald's spent more than nine months in North American training programs that must be completed by any McDonald's manager in the world. The Soviets graduated from the Canadian Institute of Hamburgerology after completing over 1,000 hours of training. Their studies included classroom instruction, equipment-maintenance techniques, and on-the-job restaurant management.

Their training also included a two-week, in-depth study program at Hamburger University, McDonald's international training center in Oak Brook, Illinois. With more than 200 other managers from around the world, they completed advanced restaurant operations studies in senior management techniques and operating procedures. The Soviet managers were thus qualified to manage any McDonald's restaurant in the world.

THE GRADUAL EXPANSION

Initially, McDonald's Corporation had expected a rather quick expansion of restaurants. However, political and economic difficulties slowed down progress. In 1991, the Soviet Union ceased to exist. From then on, the firm had to deal with the new Russian government. But at the original McDonald's on Pushkin Square, the 27 cash registers at the 70-foot service counter kept on ringing. In spite of all the political changes, by June 1993, over 50 million customers had been served at a rate of 40,000 to 50,000 a day. The original staff of 630 had grown to 1,500, and the initial 80 expatriates working in Moscow had dwindled to less than a dozen.

On June 1, 1993, the McDonald's office building opened in Moscow. The 12-story building had cost the equivalent of $50 million. It was the most modern office building in Moscow and had prestige tenants such as Coca-Cola, American Express, Mitsui, and the Upjohn Company. On its main floor was the second McDonald's restaurant, which was opened by Russian President Boris Yeltsin. Only one month later, the third McDonald's restaurant opened in Moscow's Arbat district. Like its predecessors, this restaurant too accepted only rubles. Ten thousand people waited in line for the opening to taste the food and see the restoration of the historic building in which the restaurant was located. By the end of the first day, this new restaurant had served 60,000 people. The day's receipts, an estimated 50 million rubles, were presented to Mrs. Yeltsin, in support of child health care.

THE LONG-TERM VISION

According to Cohon, "McDonald's is a business, but also is a responsible member of the communities it serves. The joint venture should help foster cooperation between nations and a better understanding among people. When individuals from around the world work shoulder-to-shoulder, they learn to communicate, to get along, and to be part of a team. That's what we call burger diplomacy." There is a Russian expression that says that you must eat many meals with a person before you come to know him. At 70,000 meals per day, it may not take long for the Russians to better understand the West through its corporate ambassador, McDonald's.

Questions for Discussion

1. Was Cohon's negotiation effort worth the success? Why or why not?
2. Discuss the extent of infrastructural investment necessary to start the first McDonald's restaurant in Moscow.
3. What is the effect of the "ruble only" policy?
4. How can McDonald's use the acquired rubles?

NAME INDEX

Aaby, Nils-Erik, 214
Abdallah, Wagdy M., 552, 567
Abdul, Paula, 597
Abrams, Robert, 756
Adams, Eric J., 332
Adams, Patrick, 142
Adler, Nancy J., 317, 725
Agarwal, Sanjeev, x
Aggarwal, Raj, 153, 659
Agnew, Joe, 141
Aho, C. Michael, 23
Ahwoi, Kwesi, 224
Akers, John F., 177
Alden, Dana L., 216, 225
Alden, Vernon R., 268
Alexandrides, C.G., 681
Allen, Julian, 781
Allen, Robert E., 107
Allison, Jim, 411
Alsegg, R.J., 650
Altendorf, Michael, 337
Alvarez-Borrego, Saul, 202
Aman, Per, 656
Amine, Lynn S., x, xi
Anderson, Erin, 346, 347
Anderson, Patricia, 384
Andewelt, Roger B., 376
Andrews, Lee, 128
Anthony, Robert N., 485
Arpan, Jeffrey, 440, 553
Asche, Ronald I., 421
Ashley, Laura, 378
Atuahene-Gima, Kwaku, 374
Auerbach, Stuart, 202
Axtell, Roger E., 151
Ayal, Igal, 519
Aydin, Nizamettin, 381

Bache, Ellyn, 151
Back, Pierre-Jean, 313, 314
Baker, James C., 559
Bailey, Jessica M., x
Balcerowicz, Leszek, 790
Baldassari, Mario, 49
Baliga, B.R., 648
Ball, Donald A., 724
Ballou, Ronald H., 595
Bangsberg, P.T., 454
Banks, Gary, 81
Barban, Arnold M., 335, 627
Barber, Edwin L., III, 25
Barker, Karla, 725
Barks, Joseph V., 337
Barksdale, Hiram C., 672
Barlas, Stephen, 557
Barnard, Philip, 491
Barnevik, Percy, 638, 639
Barovick, Richard, 328, 384
Barrett, Nigel, 280
Barron, Cheryll, 642
Bartels, Robert, 21, 719, 720

Bartlett, Christopher A., 640,
    642, 645, 646, 650, 656
Bartos, Rena, 465, 521
Bartram, Peter, 482
Bateson, John E.G., 550
Baudot, Barbara, 335
Beamish, Paul W., 453
Bechtel, Stephen D., 532
Becker, Helmut, 291, 295, 558
Becker, Tom, 230
Behr, Peter, 105, 539
Behrman, Jack N., 445, 509, 735
Bellas, Ralph A., Jr., 508
Belli, Melvin, 120
Bello, Daniel C., 383, 387, 391
Bennett, David R., 550
Bennett, Peter D., 144, 145
Bentsen, Lloyd, 206
Bequer, Abdullah, 751
Bergiel, Blaise J., 343
Berkman, Harold W., 344
Berliner, Diane T., 40
Bernstein, Hank, 475
Berry, Leonard L., 523, 529,
    533, 550
Bertrand, Kate, 269, 326, 327,
    484
Bertsch, G.K., 126
Bhagat, Ravi S., 151
Bhushan, Prashant, 763
Bickell, Alan, 33
Bilkey, Warren J., x, 214, 281
Black, J. Stewart, 148
Blackwell, Roger D., 57, 136,
    142, 465, 491
Blanding, Warren, 595
Bliley, Thomas J., 189
Blum, Julius M., 550
Blustein, Paul, 33, 35
Blyth, John S., 281
Bodaracoo, Joseph L., 461
Boddewyn, Jean J., 265, 275,
    276, 444, 533, 559, 605, 621,
    622, 735
Boecker, Paul M., 707
Bonoma, Thomas V., 328
Botham, Ian, 597
Boutros, Mourad, 134
Bouts, Larry R., 743
Bowen, Margareta, 134
Bowers, B.L., 681
Bowersox, Donald J., 595
Bowes, Eleana, 738
Bowman, Hank, 12
Boya, Unal O., 620
Bradshaw, Bill, 783
Brand, Joseph L., 75, 76
Brandt, Richard, 532
Brandt, William K., 657
Branigin, William, 105
Branscomb, Lewis, 176

Brasch, John J., 222, 386
Brill, Martin R., 165
Brislin, R.W., 151
Britt, Steuart Henderson, 270,
    271, 292, 567
Brittan, Leon, 539
Brock, William, 208
Brooke, Michael Z., 459, 461,
    631
Brooks, Mary R., 411
Brooks, Mitch, 411, 412, 413,
    415, 416
Brown, Carter W., 550
Brown, Richard, 120
Brown, Stephen W., 485
Bruno, Phillippe, 262, 279, 368
Bryant, John, 208
Burnett, John, 611
Burns, Jane O., 553
Burton, F.N., 214
Bussard, Willis A., 661
Butler, Eamonn, 567
Butler, Jonathan, 396, 397
Buzzell, Robert D., 85, 264, 564

Caldwell, Jack L., 292, 567
Calloway, D. Wayne, 499
Campbell, Carroll, 787, 788
Carey, Susan, 104, 448
Carignon, Alain, 539
Carlton, Jim, 81
Carrington, Tim, 694
Carter, Barry E., 126
Casey, Michael P., 555
Caspar, Christian, 84
Casselman, William E., II, 740
Casson, Mark, 461
Castaldi, Richard M., 385
Caudill, Lee M., 641
Caves, Richard E., 681
Cavusgil, S. Tamer, x, xi, 214,
    232, 237, 239, 241, 265, 290,
    293, 364, 464, 511
Cederholm, Lars, 643
Cellich, Claude, 224, 308
Cespedes, Frank V., 361
Chafee, John, 206
Chan, Alex, 33
Chan, C.C., 199
Chan, Peng S., 378
Chandler, A.D., 639
Chandler, Clay, 683
Chapman, M., 699
Chase, Dennis, 617
Chemtob, Stuart M., 119
Cheng, Paul M.F., 68, 202
Cho, Dong-Sung, 388, 393
Choate, Pat, 126, 208
Christensen, Carl H., 214
Christofedes, Alex, x
Christopher, Martin, 595

Churchill, Gilbert A., Jr., 239,
    254, 479, 491
Ciener, Scott, 676
Clague, Llewellyn, 153
Clark, Stephen, 201
Clarke-Hill, C.M., 743
Clayton, Mark, 433
Clemens, John, 605
Clinton, Bill, 31, 40, 104, 375,
    538, 539
Cohon, George A., 795, 796, 798
Cole, Jeff, 680
Coleman, Kenneth, 576
Conley, Krista, 202
Connaughton, Anne Q., 108
Conney, Terry, 313, 314
Connor, Martin F., 376
Conran, Terence, 596
Contractor, Farok J., 335, 377,
    393
Cook, Paul, 553
Cooper, Martha, 595
Copeland, Lennie, 318
Copenhaver, Andrew, 186
Corey, E. Raymond, 361
Cote, Kevin, 564
Coughlan, Anne T., 347
Craig, C. Samuel, 238, 254, 464,
    491, 494, 519
Crespy, Charles, 230
Crow, Ben, 74
Cummings, L.L., 317
Cundiff, Edward W., 281, 445
Curhan, Joan P., 633
Curran, John J., 73
Czinkota, Michael R., 32, 40, 41,
    47, 49, 83, 124, 126, 157,
    158, 175, 176, 186, 208, 213,
    214, 215, 216, 221, 224, 225,
    226, 230, 231, 232, 237, 242,
    245, 282, 296, 341, 345, 347,
    371, 389, 391, 417, 421, 424,
    433, 439, 475, 573, 662, 667,
    671, 686, 696, 699, 707, 718,
    720, 735, 755, 761, 787

Da Cunha, Carlos Eduardo, 214
Dahringer, Lee D., 536
Daily, Patricia, 671
Dainty, Paul, 251, 254, 478, 491
Dalenberg, Douglas R., 575
Daley, James M., 575
D'Amico, Al, 296
Danjczek, David W., 190, 773
Daser, Sayeste, 483
Daugherty, Patricia J., 595
David, K., 151
Davidson, William H., 521, 632,
    633, 634, 647, 656
Davies, John, 570
Davis, Bob, 539

799